T0368402

STATESMEN
and MISCHIEF MAKERS:

This book is dedicated to my grandfather,
Charles J. Mandel, my hero and the greatest man I ever knew.

STATESMEN

and MISCHIEF MAKERS:

VOLUME 1

*Officeholders Who Were Footnotes In The
Developments Of History From Kennedy To Reagan*

SCOTT CRASS

To order additional copies of this book, contact:
Xlibris
1-888-795-4274
www.Xlibris.com
Orders@Xlibris.com
626112

CONTENTS

Part II: A Few Wise Men – And Women: Profiles Of Tremendous National Influence

Part IV: The Kennedy/Johnson Connection

Part V: Key Watergate Figures

Part VI: Candidates Who Sought Their Party's Nomination and Runningmates

Cover:

Top Row: Senator Frank Church (D-Idaho); Senator Gale McGee (D-Wyoming); Senators Henry "Scoop" Jackson and Warren Magnuson (D-Washington); Congressman Wilbur Mills (D-Arkansas); Senator Margaret Chase Smith (R-Maine); Senator Stuart Symington (D-Missouri); Senator Gaylord Nelson (D-Wisconsin); Senator Frank Moss (D-Utah)

Second Row: Senator Lee Metcalf (D-Montana); Congressman Eddie Boland (D-Massachusetts); Governor George Romney (R-Michigan); Congressman Adam Clayton Powell (D-New York); Senator Ed Muskie (D-Maine); Congressman Morris K. Udall (D-Arizona); Congresswoman Bella Abzug (D-New York)

Third Row: Vice-President/Senator Hubert Humphrey (D-Minnesota); Speaker Thomas P. "Tip" O'Neill (D-Massachusetts)

Fourth Row: Speaker Sam Rayburn (D-Texas); Senator Everett Dirksen (R-Illinois); Senator Fred Harris (D-Oklahoma); Senator Mike Mansfield (D-Montana); Senator Barry Goldwater (R-Arizona); Senator George Aiken (R-Vermont); Senator Jacob Javits (R-New York); Congresswoman Barbara Jordan (D-Texas)

Bottom Row: Senator John Sherman Cooper (R-Kentucky); Senator Harold Hughes (D-Iowa); Senator Abe Ribicoff (D-Connecticut); Senator/Attorney General William Saxbe (R-Ohio); Senator Estes Kefauver (D-Tennessee); Senator Hugh Scott (R-Pennsylvania); Governor William "Bill" Scranton (R-Pennsylvania)

PROLOGUE

Alben Barkley once said, "A good story is like fine Kentucky bourbon. It improves with age and, if you don't use it too much, it will never hurt anyone."

I love a good story. But I also love the people who create them - in this case, politicians. That's where history comes in. History is "his story" - happenings that are out of the ordinary that pique the imagination. Sometimes, though, good stories are reality, and while it defies credulity to think that some of these tales are real life, stories and real life do go hand in hand.

America's 225-year history has produced some colorful characters. Some of these individuals do not require books or explanations about who they are. Their names speak for themselves and elicit many emotions, including feelings of pride. In this book, however, I am not necessarily talking about individuals whose names will forever be recognized at their mere mention. This publication is not about the Kennedys, the Johnsons, or the Reagans, but rather, the individuals who were part of them. Or who helped shape them, their policies and politics.

For instance, did you know that it was Abe Ribicoff, the durable Connecticut Governor and future Senator, who suggested to JFK that he make Bobby his Attorney General? Could you have guessed that the Harvard roommates of both JFK and Ted Kennedy would serve with them in Congress? What about the man Bobby Kennedy unseated to win a New York Senate seat, even though Bobby had no prior roots in the state? That man has a story also. So do the no less than seven officeholders to whom the Kennedy brothers dangled the Vice-Presidency - before Lyndon Johnson's name even entered the mix. Furthermore, who could imagine that those tales—inside baseball to all but the most extreme of political junkies—could offer powerful revelations about how history might have been different? One example: Missouri Senator Stu Symington was one of those who was highly sought out by Kennedy confidantes, but he hardly reciprocated. He wasn't interested. Yet, as Symington's son told this author, his dad would later feel guilty for not making his case - for, if he had, Kennedy "would never have gone to Dallas." Powerful!

This three-volume book reveals much, much more. Did you know that the interior West, where Democratic officeholders are all but extinct at the federal level, was once vibrant with elected officials within the party. Bet it didn't occur to you that there are many states that had a few venerable politicians who fought fiercely for their land and made their states what they are today, such as Washington's dynamic Senate duo, "Maggie and Scoop." And you think the scandals of Anthony Weiner and Mark Sanford are sensationalistic and extraordinary? That's nothing compared to pols such as Phil Burton and Wayne Hays.

That brings me to another category. Mention to Americans the names Barry Goldwater, Howard Baker, Margaret Chase Smith and Tip O'Neill, and you might find many who are familiar with them, but ask about specific accomplishments and more often than not, you'll get blank stares.

Goldwater was portrayed as an ideological extremist, but in later years, he made outspoken - and futile – attempts to get his party to moderate. Howard Baker gained a legacy for his "What did the President know and when did he know it," during the Watergate hearings. But it was a question that almost wasn't posed. Baker had run the line past his press secretary in a room outside where the hearings were being held. The aide approved but Baker, while not seeking publicity of any kind, didn't find the words "snappy" enough to get to the bottom of the matter. Still, he asked it because at the end of the day those words signified what Baker wanted to find out. Margaret Chase Smith is known for being a rare female Senator but most don't realize that her "Declaration of Conscience" speech helped turn the tide away from McCarthyism.

And O'Neill? Most can accurately identify him as a legendary Speaker of the House of Representatives but fail to recognize him as the man who for a time, made it okay to be civil to your political opponents - after 6 p.m. of course.

Others, like Kentucky's John Sherman Cooper and Montana's Lee Metcalf? Well, they're just special. However, both also played a significant role in the history books.

My book also reveals how even obscure – and in some cases fairly introverted members of Congress could have a link to celebrities in the most unexpected ways. Washington Senator Warren Magnuson would regularly gab with Elvis Presley. And the anything but introverted Adam Clayton Powell performed wedding nuptials for another legendary singer, Nat King Cole.

My subjects don't come without misconceptions. Public figures such as Sam Ervin and Bill Fulbright are revered for their roles in the Watergate hearings and foreign affairs, but they were actually members of the Southern Manifesto and the staunchest of segregationists. There are also figures I cover whom some may question the practicality of my singling out as footnotes of history.

Folks, this is only the tip of the iceberg. My book covers many individuals whose names will likely never grace a conversation, the History Channel, or even a book. But all have a story, an association with someone, or are part of an anomaly that makes for a good tidbit - and an even better thoughtful, well-told story. You will find these and much more in this book.

But for a few quips, Alben Barkley is not a part of this book. I chose to focus on folks who were in office by the start of 1960, the year John Fitzgerald Kennedy was elected our 35th President, or who served no later than 1988 as Ronald Reagan prepared to turn over the reins of power. And with the exception of overlaps among my subjects involving a particular theme (Morris K. Udall in my first chapter is one example), that chronology is my sole criteria for the entire book.

One caveat: I, by no means admire nor share the philosophy of every politician I have included; I am not hesitant about expressing my viewpoint that a few are outright disgraceful. However, their connections to, or impact on history makes them indelible nonetheless. In short, these are colorful stories that for too long have gone untold involving characters who, for better or for worse, were completely real. Some were statesmen, others were mischief makers, but all are important footnotes in history.

Now for some dedications. To the men and women of the Armed Forces whose sacrifices make it possible for us to elect these statesmen and mischief makers, this book is for you. To the crusaders who laid down their lives in pursuit of civil rights and human rights, this book is also for you. And to my mother Madeline, who gives me inspiration, you have my eternal love and gratefulness. On a lighter note, allow me to offer a shout-out to the many libraries (not to mention hotel business centers) I used to write this book, for it literally could not have been done without them. My debt and gratitude are everlasting. The same applies to my editor, Lauren Choplin, whose dedication and keen sense of accuracy was only exceeded by her love of animals.

Finally, to the politicians of the '60s, '70s, and '80s for providing me so much fodder, I hope I do you justice (or injustice as the case may be).

I hope you will have as much fun reading this book as I did writing it. There is a lot to learn. And most importantly, there is plenty to gain.

Enjoy!

Senator Mike Mansfield, Congressman Carl Albert, House Speaker Sam
Rayburn, Senate President Pro-Tem Carl Albert and House Majority Leader
John McCormack help ex-President Harry S. Truman celebrate his 74th
birthday in 1958. Each Conressional figure is portrayed in this volume
Photo taken by Ray Dockstader and used with the permission
of the Maureen and Mike Mansfield Foundation

LBJ and Lady Bird attended a barbecue with the large Senate class of '58.
Bottom Row (from left); Phil Hart (Michigan), Bob Bartlett
(Alaska), Stephen Young (Ohio), Vance Hartke (Indiana),
Ed Muskie (Maine), and Claire Engle (California)
Top Row: Harrison Williams (New Jersey); Frank Moss (Utah); Lady Bird
Johnson, Lyndon Johnson, Mrs. Gale McGee; Gale McGee (Wyoming);
and Ernest Gruening (Alaska-obscured). McGee, Moss and Cannon,
following tradition, hosted the barbecue for their colleagues. Each
Senator is portrayed in one of the first two volumes of this book.
Photo courtesy of the University of Alaska, Fairbanks

1958 produced a crop of young Democratic leaders which Look
Magazine profiled. They are Ed Muskie (Maine), Gale McGee
(Wyoming), Eugene McCarthy (Minnesota), Phillip Hart (Michigan),
and Frank Moss (Utah). All are profiled in the book.
Photo courtesy of Robert McGee

Martin Luther King, Jr, future Congressman John Lewis, and other civil
rights leaders confer with Dirksen during the March on Washington
Photo courtesy of the U.S. Senate Historical Office

Senators instrumental in the passage of the Civil Rights Act (Warren Magnuson
(D-Washington), Hubert Humphrey (D-Minnesota), Leverett Saltonstall
(R-Massachusetts), George Aiken (R-Vermont), Mike Mansfield (D-Montana),
and Everett Dirksen (R-Illinois). Each is portrayed prominently in this book.
Photo from Mike Mansfield Library

Hubert Humphrey (center) joins Ed Muskie, Bill Hathaway,
and other Maine Democrats at a local clam bake
Photo via the Edmund S. Muskie Archives and Special Collections Library

Tip O'Neill was a beloved figure on Capitol Hill, but no more so than with his Massachusetts colleagues of both parties. From left to right, Keith Hastings (R), Peggy Heckler (R), Phil Phibin (D), an unidentified man, O'Neill, James Burke (D) and Silvio Conte (R). Missing is his best friend and roommate Edward Boland (D) Photo courtesy of the Thomas P. O'Neill, Jr. Congressional Papers (Box 421, Folder 21), John J. Burns Library, Boston College

Democratic Senator Frank Church of Idaho a portrait of his one-time hero, Republican Senator William Borah of Idaho – who like Church would previously chair the Foreign Affairs Committee, to colleagues Bill Fulbright (Arkansas), Mike Mansfield (Montana) and Wayne Morse (Oregon) Photo via the Frank Church Papers, Special Collections and Archives, Boise State University.

Members of the House Watergate Committee. Chairman Peter Rodino is in the center of the podium. Many members of the committee are profiled in the book
Courtesy of the Peter W. Rodino Jr. Papers, Seton Hall University School of Law

Vice-Presidential nominee Tom Eagleton joins the Democratic candidates
who sought their party's nomination for President in 1972 after one
of them, George McGovern, delivered his acceptance speech.
From left to right: Eagleton, Hubert H. Humphrey, Shirley Chisholm,
McGovern, Henry "Scoop" Jackson, Ed Muskie, and Terry Sanford.
All are profiled in one of the three volumes of this book
Photo courtesy of Duke University

Mo Udall, Birch Bayh, Jimmy Carter and Fred Harris
during the 1976 Presidential campaign
Photo via Flickr

PART I

Setting The Tone: Heroes, Footnotes, and Statesmen
Who Epitomized Public Service At It's Best

CHAPTER ONE

White House Eluded Him But Humphrey Beloved By Political Friend and Foe Alike

Historic Quote: "He talks and talks and talks. I don't know about a politician but he'd make a hell of a wife." - Groucho Marx on Hubert Humphrey's propensity for over-loquaciousness.

Photo courtesy of the Library of Congress Prints and Photographs Division

On Capitol Hill, there was once a Senator from Minnesota. A staunch liberal and true champion of the underdog, a man whom many even in his own party disagreed with philosophically. The battles were often brutal. But this Senator transcended party politics. His genuineness as a person and statesmanlike dignity were second to none and in turn, he commanded the respect of friend and foe alike. In time, he became vice-president and at one point came nail-bitingly close to capturing the ultimate prize in the wake of very adverse circumstances. But for history's sake, Hubert Humphrey did achieve a victory more immortalizing than the White House: a reputation that still holds true today as being not only among the most influential figures in Congressional history, but also a truly wonderful human being who was among the most beloved individuals in the nation all-time.

Humphrey's story is as American as apple pie. His mission was to better America and, despite some failures, he succeeded with hands down.

Humphrey was the "Happy Warrior" who practiced the "Politics of Joy." He didn't always win, and often wasn't able to convert people to his point-of-view, but he enjoyed every minute of it. His ebullience was his personality and the manner by which he conducted himself was stand up. I am proud to call Humphrey, along with Harry Truman, my political hero.

Ex-Wisconsin Congressman Dave Obey reflected that Humphrey was "an incredibly decent person" and one who "loved politics and loved life." He recalled rooming with a guy named John Kennedy as a senior at the University of Wisconsin in 1960. Humphrey was seeking the Democratic Presidential nomination that year and was coming to the campus to speak. They created a group, "Kennedys for Humphrey." JFK won the primary.

Humphrey was a gentlemen and a gentle man, warm as can be. HHH, as he'd become known, was positive. He was not a screamer. His enthusiasm was infectious. When he lost Wisconsin, when he lost the down-to-the wire race for the White House, and when he was dying of cancer, Humphrey was lifting everyone else up. And most importantly, Humphrey was courageous, perhaps ahead of his time but not ahead of common sense. That may have come from his early years when he was a pharmacist, a customer-friendly profession that requires patience, an ability to communicate calmly, and a sunny disposition.

Considering his near-life long love affair was with the people of Minnesota, it may surprise some to learn that Humphrey actually grew up next door, in South Dakota. His introduction to Minnesota came when he attended college at the University. But his pharmacist father needed him during the Depression and he returned home to help him run the business. The younger Humphrey developed an affinity for the field and got his degree in Pharmaceuticals from the Capitol College of Pharmacy in Denver. It proved to be a lucky break that in many ways opened the door to the rest of his life. It was while in the store that he met Muriel Fay Buck. They married several years later and had four children and Muriel would emerge as Hubert's greatest asset in both politics and life.

With the exception of those early years when he practiced pharmacy, public service was Humphrey's mission throughout his life. It was after attaining his Masters from Louisiana State University that Humphrey would teach political science but he'd soon find employment with the Works Progress Administration (W.P.A).

Humphrey as the young Mayor of Minneapolis
Photos via the Minnesota Historical Society

In the 1940s, Humphrey, perhaps more than any individual in the Democratic Party set the stage for the ensuing struggle on civil rights. He was elected Mayor of Minneapolis at 34 and left no ambiguity about where he stood. In his inaugural address, Humphrey proclaimed, "government can no longer ignore displays of bigotry, violence, and discrimination." He proposed a fair housing ordinance only to see it rejected 3-2 by council. So he took the initiative on his own, establishing the Mayor's Committee on Human Relations.

Gradually, that initiative began yielding dividends. Five-hundred volunteers, known as the "Self Survey," would inspect the city for ongoing discrimination. As one biographer, Carl Solberg wrote, "Blacks and Jews walked side by side with Yankee housewives and Scandinavian farmers sons to check out discriminatory practices in specific areas - offices, factories, schools, etc." It was a mix of all races and given Humphrey's temperament, that was as appropriate as could be, for Humphrey was a man of all people.

The relationships he formed with Jewish groups in particular (while also being thought highly among Arabs) were legendary and would guide him for the rest of his life. When Israeli Prime Minister Golda Meir visited Humphrey in Washington shortly before his death, she told him, "I would have gone to Minnesota to see you." Solberg added, "Just as remarkable as the breadth of Humphrey's affiliations was his success in keeping them despite their obviously disparate interests . . . his circle of friends often included people who themselves were not on speaking terms."

Georgia Senator Herman Talmadge acknowledged that philosophically, he and Humphrey had little in common except party. But he would write in his autobiography, Talmadge that "it was impossible to be around Hubert for any like of time and not like him...even when he was telling you that you were dead wrong he had a twinkle in his eye."

At that time, it was becoming increasingly obvious that Humphrey's future was destined to extend well beyond Minnesota's borders. Alec Olson was a Congressman from Minnesota in the 1960's and the state's Lieutenant Governor in the 70's. He first saw Humphrey when he addressed his high school graduation in 1948, the year he was running for the Senate. Olson said his family wasn't very political but remembered telling his father just after Humphrey spoke that, "we'll hear again from this guy." Al Quie was also a member of Congress and later the Gopher State's GOP Governor. He said Humphrey had an unusual gift, one in which other politicians only dream of. That was an ability to "remember the names of people he had met in a totally different environment," in other words far removed from politics. He added that Humphrey "asserted himself in getting to know everybody."

By 1948, Humphrey was ready to take the message national.

Addressing the fractious Democratic Convention that year, he said, "To those who say, my friends, to those who say, that we are rushing this issue of civil rights, I say to them we are 172 years late! To those who say, this civil rights program is an infringement on states' rights, I say this: the time has arrived in America for the Democratic Party to get out of the shadow of states' rights and walk forthrightly into the bright sunshine of human rights!" Shortly before the speech got underway, Georgia Senator and leading segregationist Richard Russell asked, "Who the hell is that damned fool from Minneapolis who keeps talking about civil rights" and asked Sam Rayburn to cut him off, only to back off declaring, "If he wants to make a damned fool of himself, let him."

Later that year, Humphrey won a seat in the U.S. Senate. But while his maiden speech illustrated that he would not be bound by the slow pace of the Senate ("Sometimes I think we become so cozy-we feel so serene in our six year terms we forget that people want things done"), Senate leaders decided to teach him that patience was a virtue for moving ahead. They rejected his committee requests, granting him seats on Government Affairs and the Post Office Committees as opposed to Agriculture and Foreign Affairs. But just as he had demonstrated to future backers and detractors alike at the convention that there would be no turning back on civil rights, Humphrey would do the same in the Senate. Opposing a bill to cut spending by 10% across the board, Humphrey told colleagues, "To those who have been calling me the greatest spender, you haven't seen anything yet." The book, *Where Did The Party Go* quotes Humphrey as asserting proudly and without ambiguity, "I have always said that between the platforms of Santa Claus and Scrooge, I will stick with Jolly Santa. Anytime anyone wants to run on that platform, they can count me in." He'd show he meant it throughout his entire career.

Nearly all of the liberal legislation either prosed or enacted in the 1950s and 60s bears Humphrey's fingerprints – and with many, such as a worker safety program (finally enacted two decades later as OSHA), he was well ahead of his time.

The qualities that made Humphrey so endearing among colleagues also captured the hearts of voters. Norman Sherman was an assistant to Humphrey as a Senator and his press secretary when he was Vice-President. He recalls Humphrey as a man genuinely interested in his constituents. Two things in particular stood out.

On one occasion, Sherman recalls Humphrey "buzzing" him to his office and handing him a list of everyone who had won a prize at the Minnesota State Fair (Humphrey resisted the lead of other offices who were installing intercoms). He wanted each of the 600 winners to receive an official letter from Humphrey. These were the days before an electronic typewriter which meant Sherman would have to compose each letter by hand. But Humphrey's response was "there are a lot of people across Minnesota who don't get much mail and if they do something worthy," they should receive recognition.

Hubert and the love of his life, Muriel Humphrey
Photo courtesy of the Harry S. Truman Presidential Library and Museum

Another memorable episode was his response to a letter he had received from the sister of a man who had been serving time in Leavenworth, Kansas for a felony conviction. She had asked Humphrey to intervene so he could be closer to home and he ended up being transferred to Minnesota. Now his sentence was over and the woman was again seeking Humphrey's help finding him work. Humphrey assigned Sherman to the matter. Sherman had no idea how he could pull this off and put it in his back pile. But Humphrey persisted. Finally, Sherman used his contacts at the Governor's office to get him a truck driver's exam. He failed. A short time later, Humphrey brought the matter up again at which time he told him the man had failed. Humphrey's reply, "Get him another test." Sherman said Humphrey had to have known that this man could not have been registered to vote nor were any members of his family. But he was genuinely concerned about helping a man who needed it.

Despite different ideological differences with many colleagues, Humphrey nonetheless quickly became highly regarded in the chamber. But the tangles with Johnson that would sink him in 1968 started even in both men's early days. But in 1952, it was more out in the open. When Johnson was poised to become Minority Leader, Humphrey resisted. It wasn't simply that he had coveted the position himself (he quickly found obvious southern resistance) but many liberals were not enthralled by the prospect of two Texans as their chief spokesman (Sam Rayburn was untouchable in the House). As explained in Robert Caro's *Master of the Senate,* anti-Johnson liberals searched for other candidates before settling on Montana's 76-year-old James Murray, a "New Deal" era liberal whose age was showing. Humphrey was quick to add, "I do have a great respect for Lyndon Johnson."

Humphrey mesmerizing the 1948 Democratic
Convention with his call for civil rights
Photo courtesy of the Library of Congress Prints and Photographs Division

That may also have been his introduction to the future President's adroitness at maneuvering and counting votes. Just before the balloting, Johnson asked Humphrey how many votes he foresaw for Murray. Humphrey predicted between 13 and 17. Johnson replied, "First of all, you ought to be sure of your count," explaining that it was too divergent and that a number of the Senators Humphrey had expected were actually in his camp. So Humphrey went back to laboring for his causes, one of which was wilderness preservation. In the mid-1950s, Humphrey introduced the first bill on that issue though disputes with Native-American groups kept it from becoming law.

Occasionally, Humphrey could lend himself to minor embellishment. It was not uncommon for him to tell an audience in a small town that when he and Muriel retired, he could envision himself settling in that particular town. The problem is, he told that to audiences in multiple towns. And on occasion, he'd tell the press that he had recently finished talking with the president when in fact copies of the official White House schedule would have indicated that the president could not have been on hand at that time (luckily for him, the capabilities for conducting fact checking weren't widely available at that time).

1960 was an open Presidential race, and for the Democrats it was sure to produce a cornucopia of candidates. Humphrey was actually first out of the gate in declaring his candidacy and the first fight was in Wisconsin. With his familiarity to voters and the state's abundance of farmers, Humphrey may have found the best state aside from his own fertile ground in which to start off his candidacy (he was often called "our third Senator"). But a young Senator from Massachusetts had a similar idea and won a big victory, thereby dealing a major blow to Humphrey's chances. But Humphrey didn't sulk over his loss. He now had West Virginia on the brain and in characteristically positive fashion, he told the press, "I told you fellows politics could be fun, didn't I?"

But the battle that lay ahead wasn't fun. Due to a serious shortage of money, Humphrey would have to write personal checks to cover air time. He traveled in a bus labeled "Over the Hump with Humphrey" and guitarist Jimmy Wofford played at events, quipping, "He's your man and mine." Kennedy surprised the pundits once more by overcoming anti-Catholic sentiment by winning there as well, leaving Humphrey with just 39%. Kennedy even racked up large margins in the southern panels where his Catholicism seemed to generate more hostility. Humphrey immediately dropped out of the race and honored Minnesotans backing of Adlai Stevenson by voting for him at the Democratic National Convention. But he also made a solid push for Kennedy's election, critical in Minnesota no doubt, as Kennedy eked to victory in the "Gopher State" by 22,000 votes. And Humphrey landed on his feet. Very fast.

Image via the Minnesota Historical Society

That same day, Humphrey won a third Senate term and colleagues made him Majority Whip when Mike Mansfield moved up to the Leader's position after Lyndon Johnson became Vice-President. For a Senate that was still reeling from years of the Johnson treatment, Humphrey's style, even in a job that was to round up votes, was notably refreshing. "Sure you can browbeat people and threaten them and force them to do something. But that's manipulation, not leadership. I don't want artificial progress. I want people to understand what they are being asked to do. That's the only way a free people can be led."

Humphrey eloquently expanded his feelings about civility many times. "Men can disagree, argue, and debate without being personal," he said, "without being arrogant, without being insolent. I don't agree with all men. I just try to lead them into an area of agreement." But he was also steadfast in his belief that, "The right to be heard does not automatically include the right to be taken seriously."

In the early part of the decade, winning support for the Nuclear Test Ban Treaty was high on Humphrey's plate. He was genuinely concerned about the risk of nuclear war before nearly anyone else of Congressional prominence and in 1955, gave himself a perch by which to pursue that? How? By creating a subcommittee on Foreign Affairs that he'd chair. This required the approval of the Majority Leader, who happened to be Johnson and as Robert Wagman, author of *Hubert Humphrey: The Man and His Dream* explained how "Johnson insisted that the subcommittee be a composite one," which meant "Humphrey had to accept colleagues from the Pentagon-minded Armed Services Committees as well as a couple from Foreign Relations." He did. The following year, he was a member of the U.S. delegation to New York and in 1957, he took to the Senate floor for four hours and delivered a 70 page speech urging, among other things, an end to sneak attacks by nations and troop withdrawal from Russia. His remarks were derided by *The Daily News*. But his efforts were fulfilled within six years when President

Kennedy signed the Treaty about a month before his assassination. He presented Humphrey the pen he used for the occasion saying, "Hubert, I hope this works."

Humphrey's role in passage of the Civil Rights Act was among the most prominent of his accomplishments. Johnson tapped Humphrey as Democratic floor leader and by naming "captains" to assist him, he could ensure himself an ability to always have allies on the floor when he was away plotting strategy. This would ensure that a Southern parliamentary maneuver to kill the bill would not succeed. On occasion, Humphrey did find himself in the awkward position of opposing his fellow liberal lion, Ted Kennedy. Abolishing the poll tax was one issue, as Humphrey and Mansfield worried that inclusion might jeopardize the constitutionality of the whole bill. Humphrey also faced accusations from civil rights leaders of being a "sell-out" for negotiating with Everett Dirksen but that was a necessity to overcome the recalcitrance of the Southerners from his own party.

Nevertheless, the bill passed and Humphrey's efforts gained him a major reward: selection as LBJ's running-mate in 1964. His campaign plane was called, "the Happy Warrior Express." The duo won a smashing victory and by becoming vice-president, Humphrey would frustrate adversaries again (chief among them Dick Russell, whom he had stared down and won on civil rights.

The mayhem at the 1968 Democratic Convention proved costly to Humphrey
Photo via Jo Freeman

When LBJ announced his surprise departure from the race, Humphrey was waiting at the gate. Not all allies, including then-Senator Walter Mondale, felt he should get in, thinking Kennedy would be tough to beat. But Humphrey was in and he was determined to overcome any and all obstacles that lay in his way.

Ultimately, it was LBJ who may have been Humphrey's biggest adversary. He was said to have consulted little with Humphrey, but expected him to be his loyal soldier, even if he disagreed. Vietnam was a major issue, and Humphrey, while privately having reservations as the conflict dragged on, could do little publicly but tow the company line. Many think Vietnam was his ultimate downfall with a Presidency that was so closely in reach that he later said he "could reach out and touch it."

Humphrey won the Democratic nomination in Chicago. The nation was torn apart by the war, and Bobby Kennedy's assassination. Kennedy had of course been seeking the Democratic nod when he was killed. Some think Kennedy would have gone all the way though others believe Humphrey would have ultimately ended up winning the nomination. Either way, his death left disenchantment among the young and the core Democratic activists who were already angry at Humphrey for his proximity to the Johnson administration. And that came to a head at the Democratic Convention.

While few could have predicted the violence at the Democratic convention, the timing was actually LBJ's. As titular head of the party, he could set the date for the convention and chose late August in order to minimize the time between the convention and general election. Little did anyone – likely including LBJ know that he would be opting out of a re-election campaign.

**With singer Frank Sinatra and on the stump during the 1968 campaign
Left photo via pophistorydig.com and right photo
courtesy of the Kheel Center, Cornell University**

In his acceptance speech, Humphrey told delegates to "take heart" . . . and make this moment of crisis . . . a moment of creation." But he left Chicago well behind in cash, a place he'd stay for almost the entire campaign. At that point, he was nearly 15% down to Richard Nixon. What was once "Over the Hump" now became "Dump the Hump."

Images via ronwadebuttons.com and the Minnesota Historical Society

That invited yet another dilemma. Humphrey knew he had to excavate himself from Johnson but there was no easy way to do it. On the one hand he'd look like an opportunist. On the other hand, he'd threaten a revolt from Johnson loyalists, including Texas Governor John Connally. Finally, he convinced Johnson to let him go his own way on Vietnam, or did he tell Johnson he didn't have a choice in the matter? When he met with LBJ, he reacted by saying, "Hubert, you're not asking for my advice, I gather. You're just informing me." I said, "Mr. President, I guess that's about right." This enabled him to close the gap significantly as the campaign neared its final stages.

LBJ hampered Humphrey's ability to carve out his own niche on the Vietnam War
Photo courtesy of the Lyndon B. Johnson Presidential Library

Whatever the case, Humphrey, as despondent as he was about his chances, was determined to go full speed ahead. Calling himself the "Lonesome Ranger," he hit the trail with energy and gusto and pulled no punches with the rhetoric. *Newsweek* noted that Humphrey portrayed Nixon as "Richard the Chicken Hearted" for refusing to debate as well as the "Fearless Fosdick" for sending mixed signals on law and order. And the magazine picked up on standard Humphrey lines. "Any person who'd trust Mr. Nixon with Medicare is going to have a lifetime of illness" and "if the Republicans get in, you're in for another recession."

By Election Day, Humphrey had hoped that if he couldn't win the Electoral College outright, he could at least keep Nixon below 270. With George Wallace in the race, that seemed entirely possible. But Humphrey made at least some progress winning back the Wallace Democrats, which may have helped move Michigan from a "toss-up" and Pennsylvania from "Lean Nixon" to states Humphrey won. At this point, he had completely erased Nixon's California lead and now trailed his rival there by one percentage point.

Photo via Ebay

Counting went on all night and at one point, Humphrey had surged to a 600,000 vote lead in the popular vote. But by 1 a.m., Bergman noted that New Jersey, which Humphrey had been counting on, had slipped into the Nixon camp. Humphrey called Governor Dick Hughes and asked, "Are sure everything is in and there aren't any errors in the computers?" Moments later, Hughes called back and told them, "That's it." And when Wisconsin was reporting neck and neck, only to slip into the Nixon column, Humphrey exclaimed that a single visit could have put him over.

And by the early morning hours, a handful of key states were up for grabs. Humphrey emerged with only Texas. By 7 a.m., it became clear that Humphrey had fallen short (Illinois, which Nixon felt had been infamously snatched from him in 1960, put him over the top). The popular vote was 43-42% (600,000 votes), but electorally, Humphrey had garnered just 191 to Nixon's 303 (Wallace ended up with 45).

In his concession, Humphrey acknowledged the "tough year for the American people" but mostly spoke wistfully. We "couldn't possibly be any happier than in the knowledge that we had done the right thing. We have said what we believed, we have spoken the hard facts of our country as we saw them. We have offered what we thought were the alternatives and the solutions. We placed our case before the American people. We did it in a short period of time against tremendous odds, and all I can say tonight to the American people is they have been mighty good to us. They have given us a great vote of confidence in this popular vote." He closed by saying, "I have done my best. I have lost, Mr. Nixon has won. The democratic process has worked its will."

Again, Humphrey refused to appear downcast and his positive nature was on display even in the hours after he had lost. Prior to his concession, he ordered breakfast which Sherman recalls was taking an awfully long time to arrive. When it did, the waiter was forced to admit that he had dropped the entire tray and had to return to the kitchen to have it made again. Humphrey quipped, "that's what happens when you lose."

He told the assembled press, many of whom had been with him for months to, "go have some fun." But the true Humphrey may have come as he was making his way from Minneapolis' Leamington Hotel ballroom following his concession and encountered an obviously pained volunteer. "You look so sad," Humphrey asked Petra Kelly as he squeezed her hand. "What's the matter?" "I don't know what to do anymore," she replied to which Humphrey told her "you have to have cheer." Humphrey did not know it but she was a German immigrant and he had sponsored her citizenship.

But privately, Humphrey was not always full of cheer, telling one confidante he "know(s) how Adlai Stevenson felt. But damnit, I did worse – at least Adlai lost to Eisenhower. Imagine Nixon, the President of the United States – no warmth, no spirit, no heart. I guess I've let everybody – a whole nation down." And at midnight on New Year's Eve, Humphrey simply flushed the toilet, his way of signaling a desire to forget a bitter year.

In his book, *Man of the House,* Tip O'Neill, who said he "idolized the man," writes that LBJ should have let him off the hook earlier. Humphrey may have realized that. Humphrey may have realized that. Years later, he'd confide to friends, "I should never have let him do it to me." Obey said he spoke with Humphrey in '68 when Johnson was running. Obey was still backing Johnson but told Humphrey that unless his Vietnam policy changed, it could cause him to lose the Wisconsin primary. Obey gave Humphrey a letter signed by a number of folks, which Humphrey said he'd give to Johnson. Obey warned against it, but the next time he encountered the vice-president, he told him that he had indeed given it to LBJ. O'Neill also singled out Gene McCarthy, who had galvanized the anti-war crowds during primary season. McCarthy, he said, should have endorsed him sooner (ironically, it was McCarthy who submitted Humphrey's name President before the Democratic Convention in 1952 (it was an honorary nomination) and he called him someone who "by birth, by rearing, by education and by tradition is a true Democrat."

Humphrey resumed teaching at the University of Minnesota and Macalester College but got an opportunity to return to the Senate in 1970 after McCarthy retired (it would have been near impossible to have won re-election). Calling the opportunity, "a resurrection," Humphrey jumped at the chance with characteristic enthusiasm ("I'm as high as a kite! I'm on the run! I'll win in a walk"). But his reputation as a crowd pleaser came about again when a White House recruited candidate, a Minnesota Congressman named Clark MacGregor, made an ill-advised remark that while, "Hubert's a nice guy, he can't say no. If he was a woman, he'd be pregnant all the time." Humphrey won 58-42%. He made another bid for the Presidency in 1972 and, despite support from organized later and a few primary wins, he lost to McGovern in the crucial state of California.

And Humphrey's identity with liberal causes had not been extinguished by a long-shot. He was hardly back in the saddle when he introduced a universal school lunch program. "We have compulsory education...We have compulsory military service. We don't say if your daddy has money buy your own uniform and food." Humphrey acknowledged that it "would cost considerably more than what we are doing now, but it is a wise investment." He told Congressional Quarterly in 1972 the program would "improve nutrition, health and school attendance."

By this time, Nearly a quarter of a century had passed since his "human rights" speech at the convention but now, he found himself at least partially in favor of another measure to combat at least one racial inequity; busing. At a speech in Florida, Humphrey called busing "the emotional issue that grabs the headlines . . . But the needs of the American people go far beyond the school bus. Busing is not the total answer but is one of the tools needed to provide quality education until all schools are upgraded."

For all of his numerous accomplishments, the name Hubert Humphrey might forever be synonymous with warmth - as a person and as a boss. Sherman recalls several examples, the first of which took place when Humphrey was vice-president and Sherman was preparing to get married. The mother of Sherman's bride was very conservative and had vowed to not attend the ceremony if Humphrey was in attendance. As the wedding approached, Humphrey asked Sherman why the wedding wasn't on his schedule, noting his commitments were increasing by the minute. Sherman painstakingly replied, "Mr. President, you're not invited." Humphrey, evidently doubting his seriousness, went about his business. Days later, he asked Sherman again and got the same response. And yet one more time until Sherman got testy with the boss ("when I say you're not invited, I mean you're not invited"). The awkward predicament went away when the mother-in-law relented and allowed Humphrey to be present. Sherman told him and he replied, "Tell my secretary to clear my schedule."

Sherman also recalls Humphrey's kindness when it came to his kids. When he heard they were going back to Minnesota from Washington D.C., he told

Sherman they could fly with him on Air Force Two where he was going to be making a brief stop at the Harry S. Truman Presidential Library where Johnson was going to sign Medicare into law. After, he'd be returning to Minnesota as well. Sherman noted in awe that his kids got to witness a historic ceremony, the fly with him back home.

Photo via the Minnesota Historical Society

Dr. Edgar Berman, Humphrey's biographer, said he never held a grudge against anyone, even the people who did him wrong. He often ended up doing favors for people who hadn't exactly given him due respect at earlier times. No ill will toward Johnson was ever expressed. No more was Humphrey's penchant of forgiveness more evident than with Gene McCarthy. Many viewed his 11th hour '68 endorsement of Humphrey as too little, too late and wouldn't give McCarthy the time of day but not Humphrey. Even though Sherman said Humphrey "resented" McCarthy for not getting behind him sooner in '68, not only would he regularly meet his former colleague/rival for drinks but one month before he died, he wistfully waxed poetic about another joint public appearance. "You could give the philosophy and the jokes," Humphrey told McCarthy, "and I could give the issues and the pep talk. The guest speaker would not even want to come on, and everybody there would be happy." Days before his death, Humphrey called Nixon to wish him a happy 65th birthday.

Humphrey's warmth had even partisan adversaries mesmerized. Jesse Helms, who was as conservative as Humphrey was liberal, recalled his last Senate appearance when the once tireless leader was now gravely ill. Humphrey said to Helms, "I love you." Helms kept a picture of Humphrey in his office. Milton Young, a North Dakota conservative, vowed to campaign against any Democrat except for Humphrey because "he comes over to my desk and asks about my migraines." Young said no one else does that. And Barry Goldwater, who was on the receiving end of a brutal '64 campaign, grew extremely close to his ticket rival (both shared mutual dislike for LBJ).

But perhaps most evocative of Humphrey's wide-spread respect came during the heat of battle. It was the 1968 campaign and vice-presidential nominee Spiro Agnew had attacked Humphrey for being soft on communism. Gerald Ford, then the party's Republican leader in the House, asked him to stop. Humphrey returned the favor during Ford's losing '76 campaign. He privately told the President he'd "be getting some votes from the Humphrey family."

Ford and nearly everyone else Humphrey encountered got a taste of his penchant for talking. One day in 1976 during his scorched earth battle with Ronald Reagan for the GOP Presidential nomination, Ford conducted an imaginary call with Humphrey at a Gridiron event. In his book, A Time To Heal, Ford recalls saying, "Hello Hubert,' only to say from then on "Uh-huh, uh-huh, uh-huh. I put the receiver down on the lectern, picked up my pipe and stuffed it with tobacco. Then I lit the pipe. That took thirty more seconds. I picked up the receiver again and pressed it close to my ear. 'Uh-huh, uh-huh, uh-huh.' Thirty more seconds elapsed. 'Goodbye Hubert,' I said. Goodbye, Hubert . . . Goodbye, Hubert.'" After the "conversation" ended, Ford recounts telling his visitors, "That was Hubert. He just wanted to say hello." Incidentally, Humphrey's speech making could even earn him a gentle ribbing from his own wife who once told him, "Hubert, a speech doesn't have to be eternal to be immoral."

On another occasion, as Humphrey was preparing to speak at a banquet that Mo Udall, another Democratic legend in his own time was emceeing, Udall, well aware of Humphrey's reputation for being overly loquacious, told him that he only had three minutes at the podium. Exasperated, he turned to Udall and said, "Mo, I can't even clear my throat in three minutes let alone give a speech."

Another quality that defined Humphrey was his energy and that would be notable his entire life. During his freshman year in high school, a teacher told him, "Hubert, if you don't throttle down you'll be dead before you're a senior." One day, then Secretary of Agriculture and future New Mexico Senator Clinton Anderson, appearing on a radio show with Humphrey, was astonished. "He gave more force and coherence to the idea of democracy and the needs for famine relief than I ever could – and I was a cabinet member."

Humphrey explained it thus. "It is the duty of a leader to get just a bit ahead of the people on an issue. And then it is in his duty to educate the people. He can't get too far ahead, or he'll be alone and he can't lecture to them or talk over their heads. I try to be a leader by staying just a bit ahead of prevailing public opinion at any time. And I try to get the people interested and involved in an issue, so they will educate themselves."

Above all, Humphrey was so zealously committed to his ideological dogma that he required neither pain nor prodding when it came to defending it. "Compassion," he said, "is not weakness, and concern for the unfortunate is not Socialism. Liberalism, above all, means emancipation - emancipation from one's fears, his inadequacies, from prejudice, from discrimination, from poverty." He was even less tentative in shooting down equations with his advocacy that government could lend a helping hand and socialism. "Compassion is not weakness, and concern for the unfortunate is not socialism."

The true impact Humphrey had on his colleagues may have been evident in his final speech to Capitol Hill when he addressed a joint session of Congress. As it was being arranged, O'Neill had been asked if there was a House rule that prohibited Senators from addressing the chamber and he replied that he didn't know of one. After, the press followed Humphrey back to his office where he would end up and consoling everyone else. Humphrey would lose his battle in January of 1978 and his body would lie in state.

As a testament to the respect Humphrey enjoyed, over 35,000 people filed past his casket within nine hours of his lying in state at the U.S. Capitol. His funeral was attended by many, including Nixon, who as a fitting display of how Humphrey could bring friends and foes together, made his first trip back to Washington since he had resigned nearly four years earlier. And in the ultimate tribute, Minnesota's Governor enabled Muriel Humphrey to continue her husband's legacy by appointing her to fill his seat. She declined to run in the special election that November but during her 11 months in Washington worked on advancing the Equal Rights Amendment (ERA) and addressing mental disabilities. It was a far cry from the life she had imagined when she married that gregarious young pharmacist from South Dakota four decades before. Even before becoming a Senator, Mrs. Humphrey had said, "If someone had told me what would be happening to me today, well, it would have been an awful thing to have thought of. I just wanted to be a wife" (she once shook noticeably and uncontrollably at an early speaking engagement for her husband before a group of attorneys in San Francisco during the '60 campaign, until as the Washington Post wrote, "her Midwestern charm and unassuming directness won over the crowd, and the lawyers gave her a standing ovation." But her impact was large from start to finish. On her death at age 86 in 1998, former Vice-President and fellow Minnesotan Walter Mondale said, "half of what we credit Hubert for we should credit Muriel [for], because they were a team from beginning to end."

The Senator's son, Hubert "Skip" Humphrey III, who later embarked on a political career of his own (he served two-terms as Minnesota's Attorney General) said, "One of the things I most appreciate about my father was his willingness to persist, often with patience, to see goals achieved. He also was very willing to work with and share leadership on key issues, policies and legislative accomplishments with colleagues. For him, achieving the changes that better our society and enhance our peace was paramount."

One of Humphrey's most famous statements among many was uttered near the end of his life. It went, "The moral test of a government is how it treats those who are at the dawn of life, the children; those who are in the twilight of life, the aged; and those who are in the shadow of life, the sick, the needy, and the handicapped." If true, Humphrey passed that test in all aspects of life with flying colors. And the nation has so much to show for it.

The crowd lined up to pay final respects to Humphrey was extraordinary
Photo via the Minnesota Historic Society

Beneath Udall's Wit And Determination Was A Decency Recognized Across Partisan Divide

Historic Quote: "I have learned the difference between a cactus and a caucus is that with a caucus, the pricks are on the inside." - Ex-Arizona Congressman Mo Udall

Photo courtesy of Keith Wessel

My previous chapter covered Hubert Humphrey, a gentle soul whose beloved stature crossed the partisan divide. Congress once had another longtime member whose temperament was different but whose reputation across the ideological spectrum was equally stellar. He was garrulous, wily, and had a wit that could leave all under the table with laughter. But he was also a man of solid accomplishments whose skill was recognized by all. And had a handful of votes in key primaries gone his way, he may well have received the prize as well.

If Humphrey was all about forgiveness and looking the other way when it came to foes, Morris "Mo" Udall was the opposite. In fact, he had no problems suffering fools gladly, aided by a biting, jaw-dropping sense of humor that charmed friends and left opponents speechless. But even his opponents saw his good heart.

John McCain called him one of "the loveliest men" and Barry Goldwater singled out Udall as among one of four folks on the Hill (the others being Ted Kennedy, Jay Rhodes, and Paul Laxalt) who were special friends.

A fair number of Udall's his closest friends on the Hill were Republicans – Bob Dole, Alan Simpson and New York Congressman Barber Conable. James said the latter would often visit Udall's office when Mo acquired a new Coconino (Native-American art). Goldwater was another. Roughly once a month, Udall and Wright would often walk across the Capitol and sit down with Goldwater to talk about "what can we do that's in the best interest of Arizona" (Goldwater's dad had bailed out Udall's grandpa in the 1880s when he was charged with perjury (erroneously, it turned down) on a land-deal that involved the grandfather of George Romney). And House Speaker Tip O'Neill, even though the pair were often on opposite sides of House leadership elections, would often call the office and ask Wright, "How's my buddy Mo doing. Can I talk to him?"

Even with an abundance of indelible legislative accomplishments, Udall's eternal reputation may be cemented by his love of humor. Obey called him "the best there was about bringing humor to everyone," adding that he was able to enlighten any situation with humor. His book, *Too Funny To Be President*, which he and a chief aide, Bob Neumann wrote, is among the most widely recognized memoirs for pols.

Among the highlights of his jocularity:

"The difference between a cactus and a caucus is that in a caucus, the pricks are on the inside."

"The people have spoken — the bastards" (following a string of primary losses).

"If you can find something everyone agrees on, they're wrong."

"Let's turn inflation over to the post office. That'll slow it down."

"Lord, give us the wisdom to utter words that are gentle and tender, for tomorrow, we may have to eat those words."

"Everything that needs to be said has been said but not everyone's said it."

When you're not sure of a Congressman's name, simply address him as, "Mr. Chairman." Because so many members of the majority caucus hold a committee or subcommittee gavel, doing so will turn nearly every head.

Udall also came up with a creative way for staffers and some members of Congress to get around forgetting names. With so many Congressmen in the majority party chairing a full committee or subcommittee, Udall's remedy was to call everyone "Mr. Chairman." That way, he figured, all heads would turn.

Udall loved to tell the story about the men at the barbershop he met during his campaign in New Hampshire. He proceeded to introduce himself and tell them he was running for President. One of the men replied, "Yep, we were just laughing about that yesterday."

Udall could even be creative on the baseball field. As a member of the Congressional Softball team, Udall created the "Goodell play." Charlie Goodell was a Republican who had succeeded RFK in the Senate but had gradually moved left on Vietnam. Udall instructed his team to move left when someone called out "Goodell." Basketball was not left out either. "One day, he called a particular ball movement, "the détente dribble. It only goes one way."

Mark James began working for Udall at the age of 23 and said his sense of humor was "always there" and he noted his boss's exuberance for his own lines, saying "every time he used one, he'd get a kick out of it." Many of the lines Udall used were genuinely his and he'd come up with them on the fly." One day, a staffer for Arizona Senator Dennis DeConcini came to the office to make a presentation. Her name was Irene Hamburger. When the presentation was over, Udall looked up and said, "Well done, hamburger." Still, Udall didn't have a patent on all of the lines he used and James said his rule was that you "use it three times and give someone the credit" before adopting it as your own.

That's not to say humor was always prevalent. Bruce Wright was his former Chief of Staff and said that while it always played a role in the office, "on a one-on-one basis, Mo was a pretty serious guy when focused on his work." Another staffer, Donna Taylor echoed that. Wright said Udall "had a knack for knowing when to use (the humor) and it was more in a social setting."

As his career progressed and Udall's one-lines piled up, he could not possibly store them in his head – or his index cards where he kept his "famous" political lines in a locked-up box. That's where James came in. In 1983, he was among the first members of Udall's staff to have a computer and Udall asked him one day if he could devise a system where a line could be easily located in the system. James and several interns typed the jokes into the computer and came up with three different ways to cross-reference them. For example, if Udall was looking for a joke about Abraham Lincoln, James said it could be easily found.

Wright said that even in the midst of "a hostile town-meeting in Southwestern Arizona, Udall could "use humor to get (constituents) to listen to what he came to talk about." North Carolina Democratic Congressman David Price who served in the House with Udall recalls how he addressed a North Carolina Democratic dinner one year. His father, a Republican attended. Price said his dad thought "Mo Udall was the funniest man he had seen or heard anywhere, almost enough to make a Democrat out of him."

Jimmy Carter was a rare politician for whom Udall didn't have a lot of love. James called the relationship between the two "stormy." A natural tension was initially inevitable they had been rivals (during the campaign, Udall had labeled the Georgia Governor's position on the jobs bill he was proposing as "fudge, fudge, fudge"). One day, shortly after Carter took office, he invited Udall to a basketball game. Udall, thinking the game could be a start to a strong working relationship, eagerly accepted. He met Carter at the White House and the two took a helicopter to the Capital Center where the game was taking place. A reporter snapped their picture but, the duo was only together about 15 minutes. James said Udall's theory was that the trip was more window dressing, saying it was more about Carter wanting to show the nation he was "mending fences with Mo" but doing little else to offer legislative or personal outreach going forward. In fact, in his memoir, *True Compass*, Ted Kennedy (another close Udall friend) cited a conversation with Carter in which he was urging the President to name famed Watergate prosecutor Archibald Cox to a federal judgeship. Carter balked because Cox had supported Udall in '76, to which Kennedy had to remind Carter that not only had he won, Cox was supporting Udall for Udall, not acting in disdain for Carter (it was to no avail. Cox didn't get the post).

Ronald Reagan was a different story. The two were polar opposites for sure but a genial working relationship was formed when Reagan reached out to Udall and sent a legislative liaison to "build a relationship." That relationship, Wright said, was "positive and warm even though on many issues they disagreed." Still, it wasn't all sunshine and lollipops. Udall was often exasperated with the secretary of Interior in the Reagan administration, James Watt but, how did he diffuse tensions when sparring with him on an issue or two (the National Park and Wilderness Area, for one. You guessed it. With humor. Wright said Mo "would always turn a meeting around by starting with humor."

Udall's Arizona heritage began with his great-grandfathers who had led the first Mormons into Arizona from Utah. Recalling his birthplace of St. Johns, Arizona near the New Mexico border, Udall joked it "wasn't until fifth grade that he learned the town's name was not, 'Resume Speed.'"

Mo's father, Levi Udall, who served on the Arizona Supreme Court, encouraged his boys to heed the calling of public service. He credits his leadership of an all-black squadron as having "really shaped my life. I fought their fights with them. We had some battles over local discrimination." But Udall got an early taste of bigotry on a personal level. It was while stationed at Lake Charles, Louisiana and in his book, *Too Funny To Be President*, Udall recalls introducing himself to the major and getting the response, "Morris? What kind of name is that?" He writes that when the major "saw a referral letter from Judge Levi Udall . . . for six long months, he treated me as he did his Jewish officers – badly. It proved a painful but eye opening experience."

**Mo Udall with his two boys, Randy (left) and Mark, a future U.S. Senator
Photo courtesy of Senator Mark Udall**

In college, the 6'5 Udall would played for the Arizona Wildcats and, after "one of those games you dream about" when he made every shot, a reporter accused him of not truly having a "glass eye." That may have been any critics' first exposure to Mo Udall for he "plucked the slippery orb" out of its socket and handed it to him saying, 'Mister, I haven't been able to see much out of this one, you try it.'" Apparently, few others needed convincing because Udall was soon picked up by the Denver Nuggets. There was no pretending the team was a good one. He wrote, "The 1948/49 Denver Nuggets rank among the worst basketball teams ever. Our performance on the court was abysmal and we set a record for consecutive losses."

Now it was time to settle down and Udall and his older brother Stewart launched a law firm, Udall and Udall. In his book, Mo recalls one of his first cases. His client had been fined for drunk driving and Udall writes that "he brought five of his drinking buddies to court to attest to his sobriety."

"Mo" was actually the younger Udall brother and initially, the lesser known. Stewart was JFK's Secretary of the Interior but prior to holding this position had been a Congressman from Arizona's second Congressional district. "Mo" succeeded him when JFK made the appointment and immediately gained recognition from his colleagues for being a strong leader.

It did not translate into automatic success in leadership contests, however. He challenged John McCormack for Speaker in 1969 and made the unusual promise of moving to re-opening the nomination if he emerged on top "so that other candidates can be considered with me on the final balloting." For Udall saw his challenge to McCormack as more than holding the gavel. It was due to "an overriding need for new direction and new leadership." McCormack prevailed 178-58 but handed reform Democrats a victory of sorts; the Speaker became amenable to monthly caucus meetings.

As an early promoter of institutional reform, Udall failed at his attempts to take on the seniority system by having the caucus choose among the top three members of a committee for a chairmanship. In particular, Udall had trouble wooing his Southern counterparts. "Southerners are the best politicians around here," explained one. "They want a man they can deal with in their own way. That's not Udall. They don't feel they can come in and see him." Udall may also have been hurt by having voted against the repeal of a portion of the Taft/Hartley law in 1965. That was one reason his challenge to Hale Boggs for Majority Leader failed in 1971.

Udall's record was almost solidly liberal. On the Post Office and Civil Services Committee, he fought to increase benefits for civil service employees. He was also a genuine advocate of good government and without question practiced what he preached. He was among the first members to disclose his finances and income taxes. And he led efforts to remove embattled Education and Labor Chair Adam Clayton Powell from office though he did not go along with those who felt the duly elected member should be stripped of his seat in Congress. In fact, when the effort began to do just that, it was Udall who proposed letting a committee take up the matter prior to carrying out that action. And his record included some pretty big accomplishments, the crown jewel of which was a campaign finance law. But Udall was less successful with his advocacy of public financing of campaigns.

Commitment to wildlife was long a passion. In 1971, Udall proposed a five year moratorium on the killing of ocean mammals. He said, "We know next to nothing about the marine mammals of the world. The moratorium would allow us a minimal period during which we could get to really know these strange and fascinating aquatic neighbors and head off the irrepairable tragedy of extinction – a tragedy some believe would be the inevitable result of present policies."

Banning the advertising of cigarettes during televised sport events was another cause that went nowhere. A biography on Udall by Donald Carson notes that he "had it in for the Marlboro Man almost from the day he stepped onto the House floor." Udall was one of seven members of Congress (Bobby Kennedy was another) who signed a letter to President Johnson urging him to veto cigarette warning labels because he felt they didn't go far enough. "Instead of protecting the health of the American people," the letter read, "(the label) protects only the cigarette industry."

But if many were aware that Udall had political legs, James Perry in an article, "This Fella From Arizona," said that changed when he stated his epiphany on the Vietnam War at a 1967 speech before the Sunday Evening Forum, a business group that featured many conservatives who were in full support of the mission. But he told awed attendees that he had, "come here tonight to say as plainly and as simply as I can that I was wrong two years ago, and I firmly believe President Johnson's advisers are wrong today. Unless the nation changed direction, he warned, "I predict we will have 750,000 troops committed to Vietnam within the next eighteen months. There will be more bombing, more civilian deaths in South and North Vietnam, more American casualties…We are on a mistaken and dangerous road…I propose," he said, "that the United States halt all further escalation and Americanization of this war and that it discontinue sending any more Americans to do a job that ought to be done and can only be done by Vietnamese." Perry said the address, "made headlines across the land, from the *Nogales Herald* to the front page of *The New York Times*."

**Stu Udall and Mo (far right) with their Uncle Jesse Udall, a
former Chief Justice of the Arizona Supreme Court
Photo via downwithtyranny.org**

By early 1975, a group of Democratic House members, recognizing the wide-open field for the Presidential nomination, wanted one of their own to move forward. Obey and his Wisconsin colleague, Henry Reuss, several members from south Florida, and eventually, Tip O'Neill, also chose Udall. The latter had his mind set on the Speakership and perhaps wanted to eliminate a potential rival. This was the post-Watergate era and many new Democratic Congressmen had just been elected. Many were very liberal. That kind of made him an elder statesman of sorts and, with at least some name recognition and what the *New York Times* called a "tall, (6 foot 5) witty, a strong campaigner with a good reputation on ecology issues," he seemed a natural. But as "a one-eyed Mormon Democrat from conservative Arizona," he was also aware of the hurdles he'd face, noting, "You can't have a higher handicap than that."

And Udall's energy was second-to-none. One day, he was engaged in non-stop handshaking at the Boston Airport. After shaking one hand, he heard a voice on the other hand tell me, "I'm Birch Bayh. You're my second choice" (Bayh of course was the Indiana Senator who was also seeking the Democratic nomination that year.

Beneath his extroverted wit, Udall was a man of deep principle and he spoke openly and angrily about not only refusing to share a ticket with George Wallace or, as *Congressional Quarterly's* Candidate's '76 noted, "deal with Wallace to win the nomination for himself." He even denounced the Governor in his home state of Alabama. That might have been one reason Udall was able to penetrate support from at least one prominent officeholder in Carter's backyard. State Senator Julian Bond, perhaps leery of Carter's early record on civil rights, backed Udall. So did another southerner, then-Arkansas Governor David Pryor.

Udall vowed that, "The first priority of a Udall administration will be jobs. We need a frontal attack on unemployment and a legislative mandate to create the machinery that will fulfill the goal of full unemployment set 30 years ago. This is not an impossible dream." During a visit to the Milwaukee Police Training Center, Udall told his audience that, "The best way we can reduce crime in Milwaukee and the nation is to give people jobs. People who have jobs are not the muggers, burglars and hold-up men who are causing the national crime statistics to rise."

Udall enjoyed much support from the influential Miami-Dade area Democratic delegation and his early inclination was to "let Wallace and Jackson fight for Tallahassee. I'll take Dade County." But he ultimately failed to compete in Florida, with Carter having gained momentum through the early primaries, including in New Hampshire where Udall finished a strong second. After Massachusetts, where he was edged out by "Scoop" Jackson (just 23%-18%), he declared that "Mo Udall has clearly been established as the candidate of the progressive wing. There just isn't any other horse to ride."

Mo Udall during his 1976 Presidential bid
Photo courtesy of the University of Arizona Library

Udall mounted it all on Wisconsin where he was not expecting a win. But toward the end of the race, including for a few hours on primary night, he appeared to have broken through. A number of state networks and ABC projected Udall the winner, and he gave a victory speech against the advice of Obey. The 10:00 news wanted to get Udall on TV but Obey urged him not to declare. They thought he'd be best to say "we've done a lot better than we expected . . . this rejuvenates the campaign." But the rural areas in Wisconsin reported late, and Carter showed unexpected strength. When it was over, Carter had taken the state by 8,000 votes, 36-35%. The next day, Udall reversed his declaration by telling reporters, "You know all the times I said 'win' last night? Well, I want you to insert the word 'lose.'"

Campaigning in Massachusetts and a standard Udall image
Left photo via barnesandnobleblogspot.com;
Image via ronwadebuttons.com

The Michigan primary was eerily similar and when the voting stopped, Udall had finished a mere 1,800 votes behind Carter. Udall also finished strongly in South Dakota, but at that late date, a state that small wouldn't have made a difference. All told, he had finished second in six states. But he ended his bid with characteristic humor and grace. So frequent were Udall's close shaves that he soon acquired the nickname, "Second Place Mo."

When he finally did withdraw, Udall wouldn't have been Udall without a few memorable lines. "Well, I suppose I've had more kicks in the ass, more practice at coming in second, and been the subject of more political obituaries than any other candidates in modern times, but that has just taught me the wisdom of what Will Rogers once said: "Live your life so when you lose, you are ahead." He then paid effusive homage to his team.

Udall returned to the House with his stature enhanced but not necessarily with increased popularity in his home district. He won re-election in 1976 with 60%, of the vote, then was held to just 54% against a low-spending opponent in 1978. By 1980, conservatives had put a target on his back. But he turned it back easily as many equally liberal and more senior Democratic colleagues were taking a bloodbath at the polls.

Photo courtesy of the University of Arizona Library

For the duration of his career, Udall focused on Arizona and land issues, helped by his Chairmanship of the House Interior Committee. The National Wildlife

Federation had named him its legislator of the year in 1973. He continued to champion their interests.

A key example of his passion and success was the expansion of Redwood National Park in California. Opponents contended that provisions calling for preservation of the trees in the park would harm the local economy but Udall questioned this logic: "What kind of country is it if we can't protect these tall trees that were here at the time of the birth of Christ?" He led efforts to curb strip mining, which President Ford vetoed. But it was Udall's love of the outdoors and opposition to drilling in Alaska and shepherding an Alaska land bill into law that galvanized his Congressional accomplishments and earned him the enmity of the folks in that state.

Indeed, Obey couldn't "think of anyone who disliked (Udall) except for the folks in Alaska," where his efforts to preserve public land were not accepted. One day, while visiting Juneau, he was asked if he wanted to run a fishing line. At first, Udall resisted, but did ultimately take them up on their offer. After some time, officials asked to see Udall's fishing license, anticipating that he wouldn't have one. But he was prepared and pulled it out. Obey said Udall had outsmarted them. Yet as a sign of how politics could be separated from the personal, James said that even Alaska's junior Senator, Republican Frank Murkowski, enjoyed a genial relationship (he notes the state's legendary senior Senator, Ted Stevens, could "always be a little prickly").

As James Perry wrote, when Udall stepped off the plane and looked at the magnificent, cavernous Alaskan canyons around him, he reportedly exclaimed, "I want it all." Pursuing his wants, Udall on the opening day of the 95th Congress introduced what would become the iconic Alaskan land bill. AK History notes "the bill was named H.R. 39, and would become famous in Alaska by that name." The Congress dragged on but Udall seemed likely to conquer his "wants" at its close in October 1978 when all sides – including the gruff and fiercely parochial Stevens, had reached an accord and Udall urged everyone to go home so the staff could amalgamate the details into a final document. But Alaska's junior Senator, Mike Gravel, a Democrat, presented Udall with "a few things I want." They proved to be anything but and the compromise fell apart.

With success so close, Udall entered the next Congress very optimistic about passage. Illinois Republican John Anderson was the prime-sponsor which added even more credibility. But hope proved premature as Udall found himself thwarted in his own committee when language that he advocated was rejected in favor of a substantially watered down proposal by fellow Democrat, Jerry Huckaby of Louisiana (Huckaby's Bayou State colleague, John Breaux got similar language to clear the Merchant Marine Committee over a Udall-backed proposal by Gerry Studds of Massachusetts). The mighty John Dingell of Michigan was also on the alternative measure.

While Carter strongly supported Udall, the renegade bill had the backing of the NRA which led Udall to quip that under the confines of their park, someone could "shoot a caribou every hour on the hour, and in one corner there would be a pizza parlor and a concession for a shoe factory." The temporary defeat was reversed on the House floor by a surprisingly lopsided margin and while Udall credited the "oil boys" as "fabled for their operation," he ruefully noted, "they were outfoxed by the tremendous sophisticated grassroots lobby of the Alaska coalition." But the bill again stalled in the Senate.

Time was ticking again as the 1980 saw the election of a new Republican president and Senate. But fruition ultimately came together during "lame-duck" as Udall abandoned hopes for a stronger measure (instead urging House members to adopt the Senate product that bore Ted Stevens' fingerprints) and President Carter signed into law the Alaska National Interest Land Conservation Act (ANILICA) that December. The result was protection of 104 million acres of land. Udall lavished praise on Carter, contending that, "No president, with the possible exception of Theodore Roosevelt, has ever done more for conservation, and no one can ever take that away from you, Mr. President." But the truth was that Udall's persistence made a dream a reality.

Udall's zeal for legislating also centered around encouraging increased citizen participation. In 1978, he authored an op/ed entitled, "Your Right to Write," which explained how citizens could most effectively get a responsive government.

Despite failing to attain the Presidency, Udall took heart in the signing of the Alaska Wilderness Act Photo courtesy of the University of Arizona Library

In Udall's obituary, *The New York Times* quoted McCain as saying that Udall "helped me in 50 different ways . . . There's no way Mo could have been more wonderful. And there was no reason for him to be that way." Whenever he takes the Senate floor on behalf of American Indians or argues that the Republican Party should support environmentalism, the Senator said, he "remembers his debt to Mo Udall."

Upon his death, columnist David Broder wrote that "the legacy (Udall) left is imposing and enduring . . . For a whole generation of congressmen, Udall became a mentor and a model – and they will miss him as much as the press galleries do." And that's inspiring to Mark, Tom, and a whole generation of Udalls and Americans who aspire to do best by public service.

By 1990, Udall announced that his re-election would be his last. But Parkinson's was taking effect and he resigned a little early, in May of 1991. But he saw the humor even in that. He compared the disease to lobbyist Paula Parkinson, who had been rumored to be having affairs with several members of Congress. To that, Udall would quip that they "both cause you to lose sleep. And they both give you the shakes."

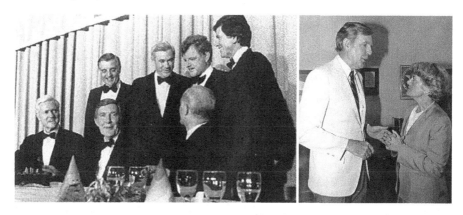

**Udall at a birthday roast on his 61ˢᵗ birthday and with
Vice-Presidential nominee Geraldine Ferraro
Photos courtesy of the University of Arizonal Library**

Udall died in December 1998 at 76 but lived just long enough to see his son Mark (and nephew Tom) win election to the House.

Image via Wikipedia

CHAPTER THREE

When Class Trumps All:
The Character of Tip O'Neill

Historic Quote: "Tip felt he could ignore Gingrich like a mosquito but after a period of time, people began to tell him that he better be careful because the mosquito was carrying malaria." - Geraldine Ferraro.

A past Speaker and a future Speaker
Photo courtesy of the Collection of the U.S. House of Representatives

With malice toward none.

Those are the words most often associated with Abraham Lincoln. But for Tip O'Neill, they are equally fitting. The longtime House Speaker was strong-minded, had little patience for those who tried to mess with his ideals, and ruled the House with an iron fist. But nothing was personal. Except when foes made it so.

And how else can I tell the story of Tip O'Neill?

He was Boston, he was Irish, he was the machine, he was power, he was capable, he was plain-spoken, he was human, he was civil, he was all about family, and he was as lovable as can be. Not a single person this author spoken to about this chapter could express anything other than the greatest affection for O'Neill, and it was not unusual for some, without prompting to say, "I loved Tip."

Speaker Carl Albert, in presenting O'Neill to the House at the beginning of the new Congress in 1973, caricatured the man who would become his successor beautifully. O'Neill, he said, is "a big man wth a heart and a mind and a sense of compassion equal to his size. He is a man of immense dedication and intense loyalty." He called him "destined to become one of the great leaders of the House of Representatives." How right he was.

Indeed, O'Neill was beloved by nearly everyone including those on the right. The few times that he'd curse in front of women, he'd immediately apologize, thus cementing his true gentlemanlyness. Judy Lemons, assistant to Phil Burton said "Tip was always a gentleman. Phil wasn't always a gentleman." One colleague upon O'Neill's death called him a "jolly-good fellow." Memoirs of leading political figures from all generations illustrate the respect O'Neill commanded. Pat Schroeder called him "a wonderful human being with the heart of a washtub." Paul Simon said he "liked him a lot." And Charlie Rangel spoke of the ultimate O'Neill gift; not only having "so many stories" but "always telling them in the right place at the right time."

The rare exceptions were a small group of very conservative Republicans, though, in at least a few instances, O'Neill may have inadvertently provided fuel for the fire.

There are things about O'Neill that everyone knows. The "All Politics Is Local" adage. The story of his neighbor Mrs. O'Brien, who told him she would vote for him in his first race despite the fact that he mowed her lawn and picked up her groceries because "Tom, people like to be asked." And the legend of O'Neill battling the daylights out of foes during the day and loving every minute of it only to be friends again after 6. But aside from the Kennedys, he may be the most famous Irish pol in history and that made him as proud as punch.

A true and proud son of North Cambridge, Massachusetts, O'Neill's background was working class and Irish. So embedded were his Irish roots that O'Neill declared late in life, "I knew I was Irish even before I knew I was an American." The neighborhood where he grew up was called "Old Dublin" and his father was a bricklayer who also served a stint on the Cambridge Council before thriving for thirty-five years as superintendent of sewers (neighborhood folks called him "The Governor"). But O'Neill suffered a tragedy almost at birth. His mother died of tuberculosis when he was nine months old, leaving he and his two siblings (a brother Bill and a sister Mary) to be looked after by a housekeeper. His father, Thomas P. O'Neill, Sr., remarried when O'Neill was eight.

The nickname "Tip," forever enduring, came about from a St. Louis Brown's baseball player, James Edward O'Neill who tipped off fouls. It stuck, though not with the old-timers. Only a few local folks would continue to call O'Neill "Tom" but most were acquaintances from boyhood. To everyone else, he was "Tip."

And Tip O'Neill arguably had better luck in sports than his namesake. As a student at St. John's High School, he excelled at basketball and was captain of the team. He excelled at friendships, often hanging out at "Barry's Corner" on Sheridan Avenue. And he excelled at finding his life's partner.

It was during his senior year, Tip became acquainted with arguably the one person who, along with the five children they'd raise, would mean more to him than the House of Representatives; Mildred Miller (she was a junior). How is that certain? Because O'Neill said so himself. In his autobiography, *Man of the House*, O'Neill referred to "Millie" as "The Speaker of My House; A loving wife, mother and my partner through so many triumphs and trials." As you'll see later in the chapter, O'Neill wasn't always without critics but Millie was his constant rock who provided a daily lift for his spirits every morning when he'd leave for work.

O'Neill (top row, center) was Captain of the Basketball team at St. Joseph High School; Photo courtesy of the Thomas P. O'Neill, Jr. Congressional Papers, (Box 463, Folder 1), John J. Burns Library, Boston College; Right, O'Neill's Boston College yearbook photo Courtesy of the University Archives

To their many friends and to the American public, Millie was known as a person of intellect, empowerment and human kindness and together they were quite a couple. In fact, with O'Neill's Speakership encompassing the unpopularity of Carter and much of a time when Reagan's family differences were known and popularity was so-so, the O'Neills, with an aunt and avuncular style and closeness as a family could easily have been considered America's first family.

Tip and Millie would date for 11 years (during the Depression years, it was not uncommon for folks deeply in love to put off marriage) but all around them knew they were destined for each other almost immediately. When Tip did propose at a Boston College Hockey game ("I don't know—I just brought it up, I guess,") she accepted. He could regularly be seen singing "Apple Blossom Time" to her and would often call her "mom" in conversation.

Another trait evident about O'Neill in those early years was his ability to rally people. One of his teachers, Sister Clarita recalls, "Tom was never much of a student. But he was always popular and a leader even then. He led the boys' debating team and always won. Tom could talk you deaf, dumb and blind." A *People Magazine* profile in 1980 noted O'Neill leading a rally in protest of a $25 tuition hike at Boston College. A friend remembers, "The priest came out on the lawn and said, 'Boys, you've already missed two classes, and if you're not in your seats for the next class, you'll be tossed out of school." We marched back in. We couldn't afford another school."

The future Speaker became acquainted with the political bug early. He got practice launching get-out-the-vote efforts for Al Smith, when not yet 15, then ran for office himself, for the Cambridge council. O'Neill lost by 156 votes, the only electoral defeat he'd ever know.

It was during that campaign that the two most famous O'Neill legends came about. One of course was the Mrs. O'Brien story which O'Neill adhered to from then on. He would even ask Millie for her vote and she'd reply, "Tom, I'll give you every consideration." And it was when his father who impressed on him the "All politics is local" mantra after that close loss.

In any case, O'Neill rebounded and won a seat in the Massachusetts House 1936. He would stay there 16 years and serve as both Minority Leader and Speaker (the latter resulting from a major push by O'Neill – encouraged by Massachusetts Congressman and future U.S. House Speaker John McCormack) which produced a 122-118 majority). He was the first Irish-American Catholic Speaker.

Tip and Mildred O'Neill on their wedding day in 1941
Photo courtesy of Rosemary O'Neill

Despite the Democrats narrow margin in the House (the State Senate was tied and in fact would rotate between partisan control over the next two years), the party had something fairly close to a mandate. Paul Dever had won the Governorship by the largest margin in state history and had set forth a sweeping agenda that would reach virtually every facet of the Commonwealth's oversight. O'Neill vowed to serve as Dever's loyal foot soldier and delivered.

Road construction was at the top of the lot. This included modernizing the highway system, constructing Rt. 128 (the Yankee Division Highway), a "mid-Cape highway" and establishing the Massachusetts Turnpike Authority. Thus, O'Neill's role was such that he could arguably be considered a founding father of the Mass. Turnpike.

Other Dever initiatives were repairing aged buildings and, partially due to O'Neill's prodding, addressing mental health issues, in particular state facilities. O'Neill had called conditions at mental health facilities "barbaric" and vowed "this legislature is going to do more for mental health services than has been done in the state for the last 20 years." And O'Neill opposed a bill requiring teachers to take a loyalty oath, angering the American Legion but fulfilling his conscience.

It was also during this period that O'Neill's notoriety for fairness passed its first test. As Farrell explains, the issue was over construction of a "Charles River Speedway" and resistance stemmed from previous fatalities on what had been known as Storrow Drive. O'Neill sought to end the long debate by locking down the chamber, twice adjourning the House and immediately gaveling it back into session (thus getting around a three day rule requirement). A Republican legislator raised an angry question of parliamentary but O'Neill gained the backing of the House Republican leader.

In 1952, O'Neill won the Congressional seat being vacated by a Senator-elect named John F. Kennedy. While relinquishing the power he had accumulated on Beacon Hill required adjusting, history would prove the move as a testament to O'Neill's sound mind. For starters, the Speaker of the House was from Massachusetts. His name was Joe Martin and he told O'Neill and his staff after his election to "feel free to ask" if there was any help he could provide. While, it's not clear that O'Neill ever took him up on his entreaties, he said it "was like having a friendly hand on your shoulder."

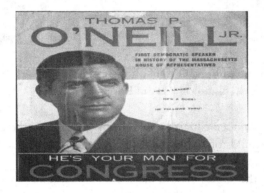

Photo courtesy of the Thomas P. O'Neill, Jr. Congressional Papers, (Box 4, Folder 1), John J. Burns Library, Boston College

O'Neill was such an influence on early Cambridge politics that, politically speaking, he knew where the bodies were buried - for he helped to do it. In 1947, he had campaigned against Donnelly for a council seat. By 1978, Donnelly's nephew Brian made it to Congress with little help from the then-Speaker. O'Neill had actively backed his rival in the primary. Donnelly won, and upon his arrival in Congress, O'Neill apologized for "what I did to your uncle." Donnelly replied, "Yeah, and thanks for trying to keep me from getting here." The two became close and Donnelly went to bat for O'Neill against fellow Democrats who plotted to take aim at the Speaker in the mid-80s. But other ideological rivals, particularly young Republican Congressmen, kept it personal and that ushered in an era that brought down the comity that O'Neill put so much effort into fostering.

Many of those Congressmen took advantage of a new Congressional tool, C-Span by addressing the House under special orders that is, after the regular session has concluded but where members of Congress are still permitted to make speeches on the floor. By this point, the chamber is almost totally deserted. O'Neill had instructed the cameras to focus on the GOP Congressman addressing the near empty chamber. When they were alerted, they attacked it as an indication of the way the House was being run.

That led to another incident. In one of those speeches, Georgia Congressman Newt Gingrich had attacked the actions of a number of members during the Vietnam War, including Eddie Boland. Boland had long been O'Neill's roommate and O'Neill would not let that stand. He said, "You attacked him when he wasn't there to defend himself. That's the lowest thing I've seen in my 32 years in Congress." Republicans demanded that O'Neill's words be stricken from the record. The presiding chair - an O'Neill contemporary (from Massachusetts no less) - named Joe Moakley, had to call him out of order." Incidentally, the next day, O'Neill, then presiding over the House, tried futilely to give Gingrich a chance to explain himself but he declined.

O'Neill said in *Man of the House* that "he's always enjoyed good personal relationships with the Republican members, no matter how conservative." But he noted that some individuals changed that. First, he said, "it wasn't just their politics that were vicious, but their personal attitudes." A Long Island freshman Republican named John LeBoutillier illustrated that. He called the federal deficit "big, fat, and out of control — just like Tip O'Neill." Republicans ran ads that linked their challengers to O'Neill, showing a gray-haired man driving a car and running out of gas.

It's easy to see how O'Neill would have been easy to caricature. A big, avuncular, gray-haired man with a booming voice, a cigar drawling from his mouth, and a deep, plain-spoken Boston accent, O'Neill was as genuine as they come. One reason was because he embodied the proverbial saying, "never forget where you come from." Indeed, Cambridge was his home. He'd return there on weekends, get his hair cut at the local barbershop, attend annual "Barry's Corner" reunions and ultimately, retire and die there. As the book, *How the Good Guys Won* by Jimmy Breslin observes, O'Neill's Russell Street residence "three houses away from the two-family house in which he was born," was "the part of Cambridge where people do not go to Harvard." Another reason was that he was an average guy, symbolized by his penchant for playing cards: "Some fellas like women," he'd say. "Other fellas like booze. Other fellas like cards. Cards kept you out of trouble." One of his boyhood pals, Frank "Red" McGrail, once summed it up: "He never forgets a face or a name . . . In Washington, the cabdrivers, the guys who are raking the lawn at the capital, they all love him."

O'Neill with his volunteers (Box 437, Volume 2) and casting his vote on Election Day, 1952 (Box 437, Volume 2) Photos courtesy of the Thomas P. O'Neill, Jr. Congressional Papers, John J. Burns Library, Boston College

In his book, *Man of the House*, O'Neill wrote that he had never considered himself a figure of much influence until LBJ demanded to see him in the Oval Office first thing the next morning (Johnson's staff had been camped out at this house waiting for him to come home the night before). Johnson had been alerted to O'Neill's comments on the Vietnam War and, "as the first member of the Democratic establishment to oppose me on this thing," worried about its impact. He asked O'Neill to promise to "give me time on this. Don't go running to the press or telling everybody your views on the war." O'Neill agreed but later wrote, "In retrospect, I'm sorry I went along."

O'Neill may have been one of the few who, on occasion, demonstrated a willingness to resist the "LBJ treatment." As John A. Farrell portrayed it in his book, *Tip O'Neill and the Democratic Century*, it was mere weeks after the new President had taken office that Johnson announced that he was going to close the Boston Navy Yard, which O'Neill did not take kindly to. Ultimately, Johnson and Defense Secretary Bob McNamara decided to postpone a decision until after the '64 election but another administration misstep gave O'Neill more ammunition.

Photo courtesy of Rosemary O'Neill

O'Neill had invited Johnson to address Boston College's Commencement but the President chose to speak at Holy Cross instead - without informing O'Neill. That prompted an O'Neill-style scolding to White House aide Jack Valenti who, detailing it to other White House aides, made clear that "I am relating this to you in a far more milder form than it was given to me." How did O'Neill respond? By rounding up enough votes in the Rules Committee to defeat Johnson's transportation bill. Presidential aide Larry O'Brien relayed to LBJ that "O'Neill did a pretty good job on us today." Thus, O'Neill displayed himself as a force to be reckoned with and was not yet even in leadership.

O'Neill's first leadership position was deputy Majority Whip, and had it not been for the prodding of Millie, O'Neill may not have won it at all. Until the day the leadership had to make its choice, O'Neill believed that New Yorker Hugh Carey would be awarded the position. When his wife called to check how it was going, O'Neill gave her the news and said he wasn't going to make his case to leadership. Millie admonished him, saying after all these years of telling that Mrs. O'Brien story, "You're not going to ask." He did and he received (it was said that a number of prominent New Yorkers had lobbied against Carey because he had a tendency to take credit for their projects).

O'Neill took on another role which enabled him to expand his "all politics is local" axiom to the benefit of marginal members. In the late 1960s, O'Neill was tapped to replace Michael Kirwan as head of the Democratic Congressional Campaign Committee amid concerns by younger members that the octogenarian Kirwan lacked knowledge of modern campaign techniques. O'Neill undertook the job with rigor. "That job really propelled me into the political lives of the members. It required that I have a detailed knowledge of every congressional district in America to decide how much money we would put into each race. I had to know the makeup of our candidate and of the opposition."

O'Neill became Majority Leader when Hale Boggs was killed in an Alaska plane crash (he checked with Boggs' widow before launching his campaign), fending off Florida's Sam Gibbons, who wisely withdrew before the voting. He told O'Neill, "Tip, you don't have a single enemy."

Berkley Bedell's evolving relationship with O'Neill was evidence of that. Bedell was a very junior Congressman from Iowa when O'Neill was set to become speaker. Bedell and at least one colleague had reservations. When word reached O'Neill, he asked to meet with Berkley and quarried him about the resistance. Bedell told him some folks, "think you will keep a list of your friends and enemies, and reward your friends and punish your enemies." O'Neill vowed to not do that and earned Bedell's support. Two years later, Bedell asked O'Neill help at securing a vacancy on the Foreign Affairs Committee and the Speaker delivered. Beyond that, he asked Bedell's son to deliver a prayer at the opening of a House session. The enduring friendship the two men would forge was unmistakable.

As *The New York Times* said in its obituary of O'Neill, he "was an old-style politician and proud of it, a House Speaker comfortable with his liberalism who clung to his brand of liberalism long after it ceased to be fashionable, even among his fellow Democrats." O'Neill's Speakership began in 1977, just as the Carter Presidency came into fruition. It's hard to tell whether O'Neill was more frustrated during the Carter years or the Reagan.

Photo courtesy of the Thomas P. O'Neill, Jr. Congressional Papers, (Box 458, Folder 21), John J. Burns Library, Boston College

Under Carter, O'Neill - even as Speaker - found himself as a back-bencher, as he felt it was his duty to let the White House set the agenda and for O'Neill to cobble together the votes to pass it. He recalled that in their first meeting, Carter had said "he told me how he handled the Georgia Legislature by going over their heads directly to the people." Jim Wright, who was at that meeting, said O'Neill looked like he had been handed "strychnine on the rocks."

O'Neill biographer James Farrell writes that "Carter put O'Neill and the others like him in the same category, with the corrupt Georgia courthouse pols that he had been fighting for much of his life . . . and that he supposedly was elected to change." He added: "Tip came from Massachusetts, where the ethnic wars over the years had been between the happy-go-lucky Irish, and the very rich, pious Protestants. He tended to lump Jimmy Carter in with his lifelong political enemies, who were the Brahmins of Massachusetts with their great rectitude and their great piety."

This meant stylistic differences as well, which would prove detrimental when it came to governing. As Carter came up with initiative after initiative that he wanted passed, he urged Carter, through Vice-President Mondale and Jody Powell, to "whittle it down" to four. They obliged but Carter put it back to 12. One was a water project. Carter wanted to cut it, which drew an angry barrage from members. The House refused to take it out and O'Neill told him he'd hate for him to veto it. Carter capitulated, though later regretted it, for he showed his malleable card early in his Presidency.

O'Neill on his first day as Speaker
Photo courtesy of the Thomas P. O'Neill, Jr., Congressional Papers,
(Box 428, Folder Three), John J. Burns Library, Boston College

But when it came to Carter's energy policy, O'Neill was there every step of the way. O'Neill wanted to head off the schisms within the party. In a maneuver that was the essence of his deftness, O'Neill appointed a committee, to be chaired by amiable Ohioan "Lud" Ashley. Because energy was not at the forefront of Ashley's legislative interests, O'Neill thought he'd have credibility with everyone. But he also admonished his team to seize the moment, for there were twice as many other applicants he could have easily selected. "I selected you," he said. My reputation, our party's reputation, and the House's reputation are tied up with this legislation."

O'Neill rarely hesitated to carry Carter's water. But privately, he seethed at the way Carter handled matters even as late as Election Night. His early concession cost west coast House members their seats, which prompted O'Neill, who had warned Carter aide Jody Powell to hold off, to tell him "you came in as pricks and you're going out as pricks." He referred to Hamilton Jordan as "Hannibal Jerkin."

After the election, one of O'Neill's aides wrote to him: "Until such time as we nominate a new presidential candidate, you are the leader of the Democratic Party as well as the highest official of that party." O'Neill was giving Reagan a lesson on Congress and Reagan initially adopted the California mentality. He viewed Reagan as a "pretty smart politician who attracted a very good team." His daughter Rosemary recalled the start of the Presidential inauguration where O'Neill brought Reagan to a holding room filled with Democratic staff. When they entered the room, Reagan was greeted with applause. He seemed surprised and genuinely moved.

Certainly, O'Neill's influence was at its peak under Reagan. During O'Neill's tutorial for the newly-elected President at the Capitol, Reagan likened it to his Governorship, when he had a Democratic Assembly. O'Neill, ever the sports buff, said that the Governorship was "the minor-leagues. These are the big leagues." But it was partly out of frustration. One of the reasons was because now that the American people had changed the guard, O'Neill knew he had to guard the change and protect what had been implemented over the past 40 years.

At first, he did not succeed. The Gramm/Latta bill passed with a number of "Boll Weevil" Democrats joining them. But O'Neill, ever the old-school politician, phoned Reagan to congratulate him. "No hard feelings, ol pal. It's a great two-party system we have. We gave it our best and you outdid us." That was classic O'Neill. One day, when Reagan and Congressional leaders were in a holding room prior to the President's delivery of the State of the Union, O'Neill turned to Reagan to "welcome (him) to the room where we plot against you." Reagan replied, "oh no, not after 6."

O'Neill's daughter Rosemary makes clear that the relationship was "very confrontational, but not behind each other's backs. It was in the open." She cites an example of a "fairly contentious" meeting on Reagan's policy toward Central

America which O'Neill opposed. This came just before the President was to leave for a summit with Soviet Premier Mikhail Gorbachev. But upon leaving, the Speaker turned to Reagan and wished him well. He wanted Gorbachev to know that the whole country was behind the President. Rosemary said the key to maintain such a productive relationship was that "neither one were haters. They had firm beliefs. They didn't hate people."

But that comity could only go so far. Reagan, O'Neill would say, was "Herbert Hoover with a smile" and "a cheerleader for selfishness." After Reagan's re-election, O'Neill was futilely lobbying Reagan about the unemployed when he snapped. "Don't give me this crap. The guy in Youngstown, Ohio who's been laid off at the steel mill and has to make mortgage payments — don't tell me he doesn't want to work. I thought you would have grown in the five years you've been in office but you're still repeating those same simplistic explanations." Rosemary said her father felt Reagan, who grew up "lower middle class," changed with Hollywood. There, she said, he "got hooked up with the crowd that was on the high-end of life and lost sight of working class people. That made dad very angry."

But Reagan was also Irish and much of their time together was spent exchanging St. Patrick's Day stories. In fact, the duo inaugurated the bi-partisan St. Patrick's Day Luncheon, an event held annually to this day. But even that could go so far. When Reagan got wind that O'Neill's dream was to become Ambassador to Ireland, O'Neill joked, "What? And have your picture on the wall of my office? No way." In December of 1988, President-elect George H.W. Bush did offer O'Neill the job. Sensing hesitation, Bush urged O'Neill to take his dream job, "if only for six months," but he decided against it.

Whether it was St. Patrick's Day (left) or just an ordinary White House visit (right), Reagan and O'Neill knew how to put differences aside "after 6" and maintain colleiality Photos courtesy of the Thomas P. O'Neill, Jr. Congressional Papers, (Box 461, Folder 2), John J. Burns Library, Boston College

O'Neill knew he had an image problem of sorts – that the caricature opponents could paint had the potential to get in the way of the message, and the agenda. And so it was that a future television news star named Chris Matthews came aboard. Matthews acknowledged O'Neill's sensitivity "about his appearance," saying that aside from his weight, "he used to talk about his cabbage ears and big nose." To compound O'Neill's inferiority complex, "Reagan, on the other hand had the charm and the good looks of Hollywood and the great - Tip would always talk about his (Reagan's) physique, he was an athlete who had made his name in the movies by playing a football star, and he did worry about the camera. And he also would say things to me like Reagan's voice, that cowboy voice of his is just unbeatable. He thought Reagan's looks weren't quite as important as that wonderful voice of his that in the old days of the drive-in movie theater, like Dean Martin, he had one of those voices that just crackled through the speaker into your car."

A young Chris Matthews on right
Photo courtesy of the Cambridge Public Library Archives and Special Collections

But in O'Neill, what Matthews saw was a distinguished gentleman. "He was a big guy with white hair. He had great hair . . . He was 6'3", strong guy, strong arms . . . I thought the older he got, the more he looked great. By the way, what's Tip O'Neill supposed to look like? He looked like Tip O'Neill." So Matthews vow was to fight fire with fire. Against the advice of other O'Neill folks, he decided to make use of the television. And it worked in a way that not only Democrats to hold their own, but make more conservative elements of the party comfortable around O'Neill.

Another person quite instrumental in helping Tip through his difficulties was Millie. Solicited or not, she was not gun-shy about giving him advice. Rosemary said she "could see a fake a mile away." In turn, he respected her judgement immensely. Rosemary recalled how during the Reagan administration, "everybody deserted my dad." One day, she asked how he was getting through it. Tip's response, "Your mother. Every day," he explained, "when I'm leaving the house she'd ask, 'Do you believe what your doing is right?'" When he'd answer "yes," she'd order him to "go to it."

Millie protected him in other ways. Every day, she would screen the mail at their home and remove the really hateful material (unbeknownst to O'Neill, Leo Diehl would be doing the same at the office). She was also a major force behind making the House a more family friendly institution. She persuaded O'Neill to adjourn the House at a reasonable hour so members could spend time with their families.

O'Neill wasn't against conservative Democrats. He just didn't want them opposing him on rudimentary matters such as procedural votes or approving the day's journals, which are mere formalities in an otherwise arcane government. One day, when they sided against a ruling of the chair, O'Neill had written them a letter saying that future revulsion could result in the loss of committee assignments and lead to other "disciplinary measures." His ability to connect with the average Joe put him in an uncanny position to preach the necessity of doing so to his members. "I don't know how you are going to get yourself out of this," he told a caucus after Gramm/Latta to watch their backs, because "the opinion of the man in street changes faster than anything in this world."

Republicans were another matter. When O'Neill campaigned for Barney Frank despite labeling Marge Heckler a friend, reporters asked how that could be so. O'Neill verified that she was a friend but also cited her Republicanism. "I'd campaign against my own brother if he was a Republican." But Bob Michel, whose tenure as Majority Leader overlapped with much of O'Neill's time as Speaker, said his word was always good. O'Neill's familiarity with the minority party may have had to do with the fact that, while in the Massachusetts House, he had been the Minority Leader.

That said, it's highly unlikely that O'Neill's proclivity for getting along with and cultivating the other side case from his days in the Massachusetts House. With Republicans having controlled the body for more than a hundred years, the bipartisanship there was almost non-existent (strict discipline existed for Democrats even entering the Speaker's office). Rosemary said, "Dad had to learn how to cooperate."

O'Neill's introduction to Washington seemed to be little different. Again, he was part of the minority party. He and his best friend Eddie Boland were two rare Democratic freshman who had won their seats in the Eisenhower landslide, a year that also enabled Republicans to take control of the House. But Sam Rayburn met with the freshmen and famously gave them the advice that "you have to go along to get along." It helped that the new Speaker, Joe Martin was from Massachusetts. And in later years, Silvio Conte of western Massachusetts, elected in 1958, would share with him some of the Republicans concerns.

**Millie, O'Neill's wife of 53 years, was the love of his life and major confidante
Photo courtesy of the Thomas P. O'Neill, Jr. Congressional
Papers, (Box 467), John J. Burns Library, Boston College**

The nature of relationships were different as well. The city of Daytona Beach, Florida would typically open its doors to members and families of both parties would take the bus provided. Rosemary recalls Tip instructing her to "be nice" to the Republicans (Jerry Ford and his family took part in at least one of those trips). Once there, the kids would go swimming and the parents would socialize.

O'Neill's early setbacks led many to think he might lose the Speakership. But by 1982, Reagan's popularity had tanked and Democrats gained 26 House seats. With O'Neill seemingly safe for as long as he'd want, he himself began contemplating retirement during the 1984 election cycle. He told one person, "if (Walter) Mondale loses, I'll leave in two years. If he wins, I'll stay til the end of the (Presidential) term." Mondale did lose of course and O'Neill made good on his vow, stepping down in 1986.

One reason O'Neill may have been so beloved was because he treated members young and old like part of the family. In the 1980s, four increasingly prominent but very junior members – George Miller, Leon Panetta, Marty Russo and Charles Schumer roomed together in what has become a legendary fraternity house. One night, O'Neill popped by to tell their children stories and answer their questions. He once called the lawmakers around midnight and jokingly asked, "What kind of mischief are you guys going to cause me tomorrow."

O'Neill sits in a replica of the Speaker's Office
Photo courtesy of the John J. Burns Library, Boston College

When O'Neill did retire, he had been in office well over 50% of his life and he had been returned to one House or the other (Massachusetts or the U.S. Congress) resoundingly every two years. His approval rating was now 63%. In his farewell speech before a hushed House of Representatives, O'Neill vowed he "would always be a man of the House."

O'Neill stayed active on the political circuit. He briefly battled cancer but returned stronger than ever and was among the few prominent politicians who defended Bush when early in his Presidency, he proposed a pay-raise for members of Congress, arguing, "They work hard." And though he spent part of the year in Florida, he never felt comfortable going far from his roots. *The Harvard Crimson* noted that even while Speaker, he used the same cobbler, John Gimigliano, who opened his shop when Tip was in high school. And when he'd go next door to the Frank Manelli's barber shop, Manelli would say, "He waits for his turn just like anybody else." *The Crimson* noted that O'Neill was once an hour later for an interview on his way back from the Cape but called his office to say, "I'm going to Frank's for a haircut." All the locals called him, if not "Tip," than, "Tom." Never, "Mr. Speaker."

O'Neill died on the table of his doctor's office in January of 1994 at age 81. At the end of the year, the Republicans took control of the House for the first time in 40 years. Seeing that would have broken his heart.

Though it's not particularly well-known, Millie was a force in her own right in the nation's capital. She was chairwoman of Ford's Theater and raised $4 million for a capital improvement project. She was also involved with the Board of the March of Dimes and the International Club. And in a case of not forgetting your roots, she helped with St. Johns Rebuilding Fund. Millie died a true and proud Bostonian. One day in the fall of 2003, she decided to take a nap so she'd be well-rested enough to watch the Boston Red Sox play that evening. She died in her sleep at age 89. Congressman Ed Markey called the O'Neills "one of the greatest couples of the greatest generation."

Congressman Barney Frank may have best captured the prevailing sentiment when, on Millie's death said, "Whenever you were with the two of them, everybody was happy. They were like some couple out of the movies. The sense of warmth that existed between the two of them was just extraordinary."

The bottom line is that Tip O'Neill was gifted with an unusual set of qualities, starting with his own values and decency that, whether operating on his side or against, made him beloved in all quarters. And as a result, the American people were gifted too.

O'Neill's colorful story was subject to a play, "According To Tip."
Dick Flavin, drawn by Paul Szep, portrayed the Speaker
Caricature courtesy of Paul Szep

CHAPTER FOUR

Men of the House:
O'Neill's Roommate, JFK's Roommate, and Speaker McCormack

Historic Tidbit: In JFK's 1946 race for Massachusetts Eighth Congressional District, Tip O'Neill and Leo Diehl, his dear-friend and later trusted aide, backed ex-Massachusetts House Speaker and Cambridge Mayor Mike Neville in the primary. O'Neill recognized that Joe Kennedy was convincing numerous folks to change their mind to Kennedy and as a result, implored --- to not mortgage his house, for he felt he'd lose ("you have no idea the reach of these people"). The Kennedy's came calling on O'Neill and Diehl as well and asked them to support JFK. They stuck with Neville who predictably lost. The morning after, Kennedy called O'Neill and told him that every other person "we" approached, for whatever reason, switched except for you and Diehl. "You're the kind of friends I want in the future."

**Left; Two Massachusetts Speakers – one outgoing and one future, 1970;
Right; O'Neill, Boland, and the other members of the Massachusetts
delegation saluting retiring Congressman Jimmy Burke
Photo courtesy of the Thomas P. O'Neill, Jr. Congressional Papers, (Box 422,
Folder 16 and Box 421, Folder 16), John J. Burns Library, Boston College**

We've all heard the expression "six degrees of separation." In John F. Kennedy's and Tip O'Neill's day, in Massachusetts politics it was more like "three and a half." And that meant colorful stories and great historical connections.

O'Neill roomed in Washington with colleague Eddie Boland; JFK's Harvard roommate Torbert MacDonald eventually made it to the House (see next chapter); and a long history ensued between the first Bostonian of the era to become Speaker, John McCormack, and the man who would become future President - often brokered by the next Bostonian area person to become Speaker, Tip O'Neill.

O'Neill's roommate was Boland, who became famous for anti-Contra aid legislation. Save the first two years of Boland's tenure in the Legislature and his last two in Congress, his career is almost perfectly intertwined with O'Neill's (though there was a gap when he went to the war). Boland's proud roots were on the other end of the state. He was born the youngest of four to an Irish family on Essex Street in Springfield. He lived in the Hungry Hill section, attended the local schools and won a seat in the Legislature at 23.

Boland made it to Washington the same year, 1952 and was in the chamber when Puerto Rican nationalists wounded five Congressmen (he helped put one on a stretcher). Boland and O'Neill roomed together for a quarter of a century in Washington before O'Neill became Speaker. Boland for much of that time was a bachelor, before tying the knot for the first time at age 62 to a Springfield Council President who was 30 years younger. The couple went on to have four kids.

It was Boland at one point who appeared to be proceeding to run for Majority Whip, at which time O'Neill, who didn't realize he was interested, naturally said he wouldn't challenge his roommate - before he withdrew and threw his support to Hale Boggs. As O'Neill would note, "people used to say that we were the original "Odd Couple" and there's a lot of truth to that." *The Boston Globe* noted the differences between the pair, as well, calling Boland "neat, trim, and reserved, O'Neill just the opposite." But Boland insisted that their relationship was harmonious. They'd play cards and go to countless games together. We never had "an argument and we never had a meal." O'Neill noted that the only four things in the refrigerator "were orange juice, diet soda beer, and cigars." He joked that we "didn't even realize we had an oven."

O'Neill had a reputation for spending money so he'd have to keep extra money around. It was Boland who was with O'Neill when he became Speaker — of the Massachusetts House in 1948. O'Neill asked Boland to accompany him to the Speaker's office, where Democrats had been forbidden, and it was there that O'Neill was handed the key.

No one could rival O'Neill's position of power and it's not clear that Boland even desired to do so. In contrast to the ubiquitous and effervescent O'Neill, Boland would rarely speak on the House floor and often got other colleagues to put their name on legislation so he wouldn't have to sponsor it. The only press he'd grant interviews to would be those in his district. Jim McGovern, who served as the aide to another gentleman from Massachusetts, Joe Moakley, before becoming a Congressman himself, said that "there was nothing flashy about Eddie Boland.

He had a job to do and he did it." His successor, Richard Neal recalled "Boland had one fund-raiser, and really was upset that he had to go to it. He thought that the only allegiance he owed to anyone was to those people back in the Second District of Massachusetts." But he was endeared to his colleagues, in part because as a gym rat, he chaired the committee that had oversight over the facilities and expanded the equipment.

**Boland with Kennedy on a trip to Springfield the
day before he'd be elected President
Photo courtesy of The Republican Company. Reprinted with Permission**

Boland was a solid liberal. During debate on the Nedzi/Whalen amendment that would prohibit any monetary aid to southeast Asia post-1971, Boland noted the horrific toll of the war: "The United States has already paid dearly for what the State Department likes to call our 'commitment' to South Vietnam – more than 50,000 soldiers killed and more than $250 billion squandered draining our resources and dividing our people. This war is now little more than an exercise in futility." But he was an avid proponent of progress and staunchly in favor of NASA. Noting that he chaired the Appropriations subcommittee that allocated funding for the space programs, Boland called the deploying of the Hubble telescope "almost as exciting as seeing a child graduate from college afer the trials and tribulations of infancy and adolescence."

By 1980, many liberals hoped to draft Boland as Chairman of the Appropriations Committee but he refused to challenge the far more conservative but fairly mainstream Mississippian Jamie Whitten. Boland attained a great deal of notoriety in his own right.

O'Neill appointed him to chair the House Intelligence Committee, and the amendment that bore his name, the Boland Amendment, which Reagan actually signed, prohibited funding from going to the Nicaraguan contras. That didn't exactly turn out as planned. A second amendment cut off funding at $24 million.

Eventually, that led to Oliver North's indictment. But Boland dismissed criticism, saying that "we were complimented for the way in which we handled highly sensitive, top secret information, and I am not aware of any leaks that came out of that committee. And one of the reasons for it is because the committee acted in a very non-partisan and bipartisan manner."

Ed Boland was O'Neill's roommate and dearest friend in Congress
Photos courtesy of the Thomas P. O'Neill, Jr. Congressional Papers, (Box 421,
Folder 9 and Box 421, Folder 7), John J. Burns Library, Boston College

When Boland donated his papers to Boston College, he made clear he "was most proud of those laws, not because they provoked a confrontation with a powerful and popular President but because they prevented, in my judgement, the use of American troops to secure by force what the Nicaraguan people were able to secure for themselves by the free exercise of the ballot (Violetta Chamarro upset President Daniel Ortega).

O'Neill was not the only Massachusetts pol that Boland was close to. Kennedy called him "my man in Congress." In fact, he was invited by the President to travel to Dallas but declined. On other matters, Boland was as solid a liberal as they come. For example, he marched with Martin Luther King, Jr. in Selma in 1965.

Boland hailed from the opposite end of the state as O'Neill. He was a proud Springfield son, and second district voters were happy to have him. They sent him to Washington for 36 years.

He announced his retirement in 1988, two years after O'Neill, saying he wanted to spend more time with his kids, though age - he was 77 - undoubtedly played a role in his decision. Ed Markey, who served with Boland for 12 years, said that "on his last day in Congress, he still had the energy of a teenager coupled with the wisdom of a grandfather." He outlived O'Neill by seven years, dying in 2001 at age 90.

As O'Neill tells it in his autobiography, *Man of the House*, Kennedy and McCormack were never close. O'Neill writes that Kennedy had been the only New Englander to not sign McCormack's petition pardoning James Michael Curley and that irritated him. When O'Neill got JFK's seat, he admonished O'Neill to "not make the mistake I did" and get on McCormack's bad side.

Early in their tenure, he and O'Neill were not exactly best friends either, as the pair were on opposite sides of a slate dispute for delegates at the 1948 convention. The slate that McCormack was backing won, but only after accusations of vote fraud which they were persuaded not to contest. O'Neill knew McCormack was not involved, and at their first meeting McCormack urged O'Neill to strive for the impossible: attaining a majority in the Massachusetts House. O'Neill laughed but they went at it, ultimately winning 38 of the 40 contested districts.

**Boland in 1998 with winners from the Edward Boland Scholarship
program and his widow at the dedication of his statue, 2003
Photos courtesy of The Republican Company, Reprinted with Permission**

The Almanac of American Politics noted that "venerability for McCormack in Boston was so high that shopkeepers had pictures of him in their windows." *The Almanac* also speaks of his dignified delivery. For most of his early political career, McCormack and O'Neill weren't even on the same team. McCormack helped JFK in the '52 Senate race. But the relationship between the future President and Speaker soon went south and never completely recovered.

Kennedy had taken on McCormack during his reorganization of the Massachusetts Democratic State Committee. Specifically, Kennedy privately at least had a low opinion of the current state chair, William H. "Onions" Burke. McCormack on the other hand faulted Kennedy for doing little to help Foster Furcolo unseat Republican Senator Leverett Saltonstall and defended his chair by saying, "Mr. Burke, as I did, vigorously supported the party's nominees for 1954. It is through no fault of Burke or myself that Foster Furcolo was not elected United States Senator in 1954." Meanwhile, Kennedy forces were backing Pat Lynch for chairman and he dethroned Burke 47 to 31.

By 1956, McCormack wasn't fully on board with Kennedy's nearly successful bid to capture the Vice-Presidential nomination. But in doing so, he might have had the last laugh. As the proceedings were at a deadlock between Kennedy and Tennessee Senator Estes Kefauver, McCormack could be heard pleading, "Sam, Sam." He was standing with the Missouri delegation and wanted Rayburn, who controlled the floor, to recognize that delegation. Rayburn was opposed to Kefauver getting the nod and by recognizing Missouri at McCormack's insistence, assumed that he had persuaded the "Show-Me" delegation to cast its lot for Kefauver. He was wrong. Missouri not only went for Kefauver but put him over the top. McCormack called the dispute "completely exaggerated" but *Time* opined that McCormack "had settled a score."

McCormack with President Kennedy, his sometimes nemesis
Photo courtesy of the John F. Kennedy Presidential Library and Museum

That said, history suggests that the celebrated Boston-Austin connection may well have begun with McCormack. He backed Sam Rayburn for Speaker in 1936 and Rayburn reciprocated. By 1940, McCormack was Majority Leader and well before McCarthy, co-chaired the Un-American Activities Committee. It was the 1930s and the goal was to stamp out Nazi propaganda. He was one of only three siblings out of 12 to live to maturity. McCormack graduated from law school at 21, and became a legislator at 26, winning a Massachusetts House seat in 1917. By the time he retired in 1970, he had held office for 53 years. He was called "Rabbi John" for his strong relations with Boston's Jewish community but mostly "Old Jawn" with heavy emphasis on the accent.

McCormack became Speaker at the end of same year Kennedy took the oath as President (Sam Rayburn died that November). O'Neill wrote in *Man of the House* that despite being devout Catholics, they "couldn't have been more different." McCormack was devoted to the church. As for Jack, "Let's just say that during his years in the House, he showed considerably more interest in his social life than legislation." To him, Kennedy was a "playboy" whose presence in Washington, as noted in *JFK: The Man and the Myth* was dependent on "the weather in Palm Beach."

But O'Neill would write that "whatever problems had existed between them in the past, it was clear that the President needed his full help and cooperation to get his legislation passed." But that was tested one more time. The Speaker's nephew, Eddie, wanted to win JFK's seat in the Senate; so did the President's brother Ted. The latter would of course win but not before a somewhat bitter primary.

Eddie was the Attorney General of the Bay State while Teddy at age 30 had just barely met the Constitutional age requirement to serve. According to *Man of the House*, Kennedy asked O'Neill to serve as intermediary. He was unsuccessful in getting McCormack out, and of course he uttered that famous line in the debate, "if you're name were Edward Moore and not Edward Moore Kennedy, your candidacy would be a joke." Kennedy won.

Still, McCormack played a good soldier. Despite his age, (he was 70 when he assumed the Speakership), McCormack *was* the 1960's legislatively. He shepherded civil rights and the Great Society into passage. And he never hesitated to cater to rural interests, such as getting farm legislation through the House despite the fact that there aren't "more than five flower pots in my whole district."

Speaker John McCormack
Photo courtesy of the Lyndon B. Johnson Presidential Library

Gerald Ford, in his autobiography, *A Time To Heal*, called McCormack's lifestyle "one of Spartan simplicity . . . he was married to a wonderful woman whom he idolized and I've been told they had dinner together every evening for a period of some 35 years." Ford recalls the fairness McCormack granted him even as leader of the opposition party. "Now Jerry," he'd say when Ford asked him for help, "If I can do it I will." Ford wrote, "He always kept his word." But he did back Vietnam and that brought about strains within his caucus following the 1968 elections.

A number of liberals, notably New York's Benjamin Rosenthal, while acknowledging McCormack's "very kind and genteel statesman who has served long and well," nevertheless suggested he not run again for the post. When McCormack indicated he had no plans to step aside, he was challenged by Mo Udall. McCormack handily put it down but still faced discontent. One such example was the equivalent of a "no-confidence" vote in early 1970. McCormack beat that back as well and agreed to compromise with the liberals who advocated directly challenging the seniority system for chairs. McCormack agreed to the idea of a committee that would study the seniority system ("The times have changed and we have to change with them").

In the meantime, McCormack was forced to deny rumors that he was indeed considering retirement. But a few months later, he reversed himself ("It is consistent with theology to deny certain things"). McCormack was now 79 and his wife was ill. He lived another ten years. To this day, after 42 years of service, he remains the longest serving member from the Massachusetts House delegation.

According to McCormack's obituary, everyday he'd go into the office in the building that bore his and eat each night at Jimmy's Harborside seafood restaurant in Boston. On his death, O'Neill said he "lost a friend and a mentor of 40 years." And Ted Kennedy, in a sign of time healing old wounds, remembered that despite beating his nephew he "will remember his many kindnesses to me when I first came to Congress and thereafter."

Other Massachusetts notables of the Kennedy/O'Neill circle: Harold Donohue, a Worcester Congresssman who would often plop himself down on the House floor even when votes were not actually ongoing, sometimes sleeping, other times swapping Irish stories. A bachelor, he looked the part of an old-style pol, yet more a small-town one. His life had a true up-by-the-bootstraps feel.

After graduating from St. John's School, Donohue worked his way through Northeastern University School of Law at night, supporting himself by working during the day as a clerk for the Worcester Street Railway Co. A few years later, he won a seat on the town's Common Council, then advanced to the Board of Alderman. *The Worcester Telegram* notes he "spent his last two years as President and was the first Democrat to serve in that position in the board's history." But in 1942 it was off to war as Donohue enlisted in the Navy and was discharged as a lieutenant commander.

Donohue actually assumed his House seat with Kennedy in 1946, upsetting incumbent Pehr G. Holme, and putting the seat in Democratic hands for the first time since 1910. Moreover, Donohue was only one of two Democrats to unseat a GOP incumbent that year. His 1948 opponent tried to link Donohue with Henry Wallace (Donohue called the allegations laughable, contending he has long articulated anti-communism). In 1950, he faced the grandson of a popular ex-Mayor of Worcester and won handily.

Donohue left no ambiguity on where he stood on issues of social progress in his earliest days. His staunch liberalism on social issues and his fierce commitment to international progress would be a hallmark throughout his career. On the issue of refuges following World War II, he said, "In world leadership we can speak more convincingly for freedom everywhere when we have done our fair share to bring real freedom to those who have suffered most." In 1950, after just four years in office, he was given the Americanism Medal from the Jewish War Veterans.

Donohue was considered a pleasant jovial man who loved sports. The Telegram credits his favorites as being baseball, basketball, fishing, golf and hockey.

A humorous anecdote is associated with Donohue from his early years. One day, he was late for a Congressional speech being given by President Harry S. Truman. He was late for the speech and "one of the doormen who knew me told me there was only one seat empty. And that was the chaplain's, who was away so I took it." It might have given Donohue more publicity than he was used to. That week, *The Saturday Evening Post* ran a cover painting of the President addressing Congress as Donohue sat in the chaplain's seat.

Donohue was not someone who sought the limelight, instead preferring to focus on the needs of his district. He once said, "If political popularity is based upon services rendered to individuals, family units, veterans and small businessmen and those in distress, then I want to plead guilty to that charge." And he did. On Saturdays, he would host constituents in his law office, a press release on his death calling the problems he was trying to solve "sometimes large, sometimes small." Even when Donohue deserved recognition, he shunned it. One day, he rescued a drowning man in "roaring surf," at Narragansett Pier. His response: "There was nothing spectacular about it." The man would likely beg to differ.

Congressman Harold Donohue takes students to a White House tour
Photo courtesy of the John F. Kennedy Presidential Library and Museum

Worcester Congressman Harold Donohue was prominent in the Kennedy/O'Neill/
McCormack circle, as was Worcester Congressman Harold Donohue (right)
Photo courtesy of the Thomas P. O'Neill, Jr. Congressional
Papers, John J. Burns Library, Boston College

It wasn't until his final year in office when Donohue would enjoy his fifteen minutes of fame. It was during Watergate and Donohue ranked second on the House Judiciary Committee to the more junior Peter Rodino. But Donohue would often get to hold the gavel during committee hearings when Rodino would step out of the room. Yet he was by no means a back player when it came to Watergate.

Two articles of impeachment bore his name. The first said Nixon, whom Donohue had met 30 years earlier at an Ottumwa, Iowa Naval Air Station, "prevented, obstructed and impeded the administration of justice," while a second said he "abused the powers vested in him as President . . . either directly or through his subordinates or agents." Nixon, he said, "by his conduct warrants impeachment and trial and removal from office." In order to keep the coalition assembled, Donohue's resolution was substituted by Maryland Democrat Paul Sarbanes who offered a more toned down Article designed to attract on-the-fence Republicans. But the point was made. Incidentally, Donohue's administrative assistant was a war buddy whom he also met at the Iowa naval base.

**Kennedy's signing of the Cape Cod National Seashore Act drew
the attendance of Boland, Donahue, Philbin, Burke and a
number of other pols from Massachusetts and the nation
Photo courtesy of the John F. Kennedy Presidential Library and Museum**

Donohue also recognized the test of history the hearings would pose. He told constituents at one forum that it must be carried out "in an absolutely thorough and impartial manner, because it is a blemish upon the face of our own country that all of us must try to remove."

At the end of the year, Donohue returned to Worcester and died a decade later. A press release called him "a product of the times. A war veteran. A man with fierce national pride. A man who exemplified the representative system – a servant of the people of Washington." That was the legacy of Harold Donohue.

Phillip Philbin was another member who, with Donohue and Burke, would often make the drive from Boston to Washington with O'Neill (he drove the Lark, Burke the Cadillac). He was one of those members of a bygone era, a World War 1 Navy seaman and one who like Donohue, as John Farrell notes in *Tip O'Neill and the Democratic Century* notes, "would slump in the soft leather chairs of the House chamber each afternoon like aged hotel detectives, whiling away the hours with gossip and the occasional rousing snore." Philbin was a Harvard educated/ Columbia Law school grad who worked for Massachusetts' first Irish Senator, David Walsh. His acquired name, "Fighting Phil Philbin," came from his Harvard days when, as a center on the Harvard football team in 1919, he was instrumental in aiding the team to victory in the Rose Bowl over Oregon.

Philbin's specialty was labor law and he served as a referee for the U.S. Department of Labor while slowly becoming active in Democratic politics in the town of Clinton. After his 700 vote win over incumbent Republican Alfred Woolacott in 1942, Philbin never struggled until 1968. That year, he beat a multiple field of candidates with under 50% in the primary and took roughly the same showing in the general, where an Independent actually outpolled the Republican nominee.

By that point in his tenure, Phibin was the second ranking Democrat on the House Armed Services Committee but was being criticized as a backbencher. In normal times, he might have been able to rely on his longevity to sustain him but these were not normal times. The Vietnam War was raging and Philbin was considered a supporter Vietnam War. Father Robert Drinan attacked him as "an unthinkable rubber-stamp." Philbin refused to debate, contending he didn't have time but did continue making the rounds in the district Drinan started out with a big deficit in the polls and was forced to contend with the reticence of many voters of sending a Priest to Congress. But the anti-war movement won the day and Drinan beat the incumbent. As it happened, Philbin wouldn't have lived to serve his next term. He died in 1972 at age 74.

Philbin's most lasting contribution was his bill sponsoring the Cape Cod National Seashore Park, a gift to countless Americans of all generations who travel hours to enjoy the Cape. To listen to Philbin commemorating its enactment nearly a decade later, that's exactly what Philbin had in mind. He said he was "prompted to Introduce this bill, numbered H.R. 6720, largely as the result of the special National Park Service study, 'Our Vanishing Shoreline,' which showed that out of the 3,700 miles of Atlantic and gulf coasts shoreline only 240 miles were held by the State or Federal Governments for public recreational use."

Congressman Phillip Philbin
Photo courtesy of the Collection of the U.S. House of Representatives

Finally, there was Jimmy Burke. He had served as Assistant Floor Leader in the House alongside O'Neill's Speakership and made it to Washington in 1958 (he and O'Neill would drive from Boston to Washington together). He was also storied in Boston politics. He began his career as the city's Registar of Vital Statistics and was vice-president of the Massachusetts Democratic Party. He was a special agent for counter-intelligence during World War II.

Congressman Jimmy Burke and his wife. Tip used to
ride back to Washington in Burke's Cadillac
Photo courtesy of the Thomas P. O'Neill, Jr. Congressional Papers
(Box 421, Folder 15), John J. Burns Library, Boston College

During his House tenure, Burke served on the Ways and Means Committee and, through his chairmanship of the subcommittee on Social Security, took steps to make sure it remained safe and sound. He held complex hearings and wrote numerous bills that would keep the disability insurance program solvent – and not always to the pleasure of interests of both parties. On a local note, Burke pushed through the restoration of the home of John Quincy Adams who also happened to be one of his predecessors.

Toward the end of his career, Burke's judgments weren't always the greatest, as the Ways and Means vet backed Wilbur Mills for President. A 1976 primary challenger fired 43% of the vote at Burke, surprising many and leading him to conclude that it was time to retire in '78, a realization that came after he had declared "They are not going to put me out to pastures."

Silvio Conte was the lone Republican in the group not because O'Neill didn't befriend many Republicans but a reminder that even in those days, GOP Congressmen were few and far between in the "Bay State." In fact, after Margaret Heckler lost her seat in a 1982 redistricting matchup with Barney Frank, Conte would be the only Republican in the delegation until his death in 1991.

In an extraordinary compliment even in an age where the partisan divide was limited, Conte called O'Neill "my mentor, my friend and my conscience across the aisle . . . Few people have a greater impact on my life." So close were O'Neill and Conte that the former Speaker watched the Super Bowl at his house just two weeks before Conte died.

It's easy to see why Conte was so beloved – by O'Neill and everyone else. The website *Mass Memories* said Conte "projected the image of 'a regular guy who would happily sit at your kitchen table and have a plate of spaghetti and a glass of wine.'" Indeed, Conte, the son of Italian immigrants, was known to many of his colleagues as the "quintessential Italian man." But his gift was his ability to reach out to anybody. On St. Patrick's Day, he would call himself, Silvie O'Conte and march in parades with a shillelagh (near the end of his, hampered by bad knees, life he would ride). Conte was a master of retail politicking to the point that *Mass Memories* says a proud boast among schoolboys boys would be, "My old man knows Conte. 'The problem was that everyone knew Conte.'"

Keeping in touch, beyond regular events, was done through questionnaires. He would regularly pop by newspaper offices to chat. At a memorial service following his death, Cokie Roberts noted how, "we could commit to editors and producers of the most improbable stories if we promised them that it would have a good Sil Conte bite in there".

It was those characteristics that made Conte exceedingly popular in an area that, outside of Boston and Cambridge was actually among the most Democratic in the state (his daughter and son-in-law actually volunteered for George McGovern in his 1972 campaign for President). In fact, after bucking the anti-Republican climate to win his seat with 55% in 1958 by beating future Roosevelt biographer James MacGregor Burns, then inching up to 60% two years later, Conte would fall below 70% only once in his subsequent 15 re-elections; in 1976 when he took 64%. In an extraordinary measure of the depth of his support, when Conte faced a spirited challenge in 1986, many local Democrats came to his rescue. He secured his last term with 78%.

Photo courtesy of the Conte Family

Conte and O'Neill were as close as close could be. When they met, Conte says, "We just hit it off." When O'Neill didn't drive back to Washington with some of the other Boston area members, he would take the train. Nora Devlin, a John Burns Library Research Assistant would write, Conte would often join him and be his card partner, as "sometimes long into the night." O'Neill would often attend cookouts at Conte's house, writing in *Man of the House* how "Sil's a great cook." Both shared a love for cigars. In the halls of Congress, it would not be unusual for Conte to emerge from the Republican cloakroom and share some of the concerns his party was having with O'Neill.

Boland was also among the Conte confidantes. The two overlapped districts for three decades and upon Conte's death said, "I don't think two members of Congress from different parties were closer than Representative Conte and I." Conte himself said "I think people feel we're part of a family - Democrat, Republican or whatever."

Conte's commitment to his people and his country were laudable. He was born to Italian immigrants and lived in the town of Pittsfield his entire life, working as a machinist at the Pittsfield General Electric Plant and a pressman for *The Berkshire Evening Eagle*. Eventually, it was off to the Navy where during World War II, he was a Seabee in the South Pacific. It was while recovering from injuries that he fell in love with the nurse treating him, Corrine. From there, it was on to Boston College and Boston College Law. Conte took a seat in the Massachusetts Senate in 1950 when his most famous colleague was already serving as Speaker of the other body. In those days, it was the Republicans that presided over the chamber and each year, Conte and O'Neill would take the train to New York to attend an insurance convention. Conte's recollection of partying was slightly better than O'Neill's. They would stay at the Lexington Hotel and have late-night card games and alcohol ("we were young," he said).

On the Hill, Conte's sports fanaticism was legendary. For years, he was the Republican captain of the Congressional Baseball team (he called baseball "the glue that could hold the most politically polarized group of people together"). He had the honor of witnessing Boston College's basketball arena named for him. During Congressional breaks, he would travel to Alaska for a fishing expedition and upon returning, cook the fish for his friends. His home in Pittsfield was near a lake and often, Conte would turn these into weekend events there. His car was a legend in itself. It was a Pontiac GTO convertible that he called, "The Judge." It was bright red with yellow flames on the side. His daughter, Michelle Conte Webb says "he drove it like a race car and with the top down often smoking his cigars." One harrowing experience occurred in 1987 when he was in an accident in the car going to work on the Rock Creek Parkway. The engine caught on fire. He was pulled out of the car by someone driving by. Conte's son John now owns it. And he was legenday for his love of wine – California or Italian (Barberesco).

In Congress, Conte was called "an Italian in an Irish milieu, a Republican in a Democratic House, and a liberal in a conservative party." But that hardly limited his effectiveness. Conte worked with O'Neill to protect the home heating program that serves New England residents. He fought for training of healthcare workers and put in among the earliest appropriation for AIDS research. He was unafraid to take on Presidents of his own party. After Reagan's 1986 State of the Union, Conte said, "There is no way that we can meet our deficit targets, increase defense spending and meet our domestic needs without an increase in revenues. That is a trick that even the great Houdini couldn't do if he came back today."

When Reagan was elected, Conte's initial proclivity was to give him the benefit on major issues and in 1981, cast a crucial vote to aid to El Salvador. But eventually, he moved away from that, opposing the MX missile and aid to the Nicaraguan contras. Any potential rifts this could cause with Republican leaders were overtaken by Conte's personality. House Minority Leader Robert Michel said during his eulogy, "He had no fancy airs. He was not a pretentious man. He really didn't bother to spruce himself up all that much either. He was something like a comfortable old shoe . . . we all loved him."

**Conte's role as captain of the Republican softball
team probably gave him the most pleasure
Photo courtesy of the Conte Family**

While Conte often found himself at opposite ends of his party near the end of his career, he found himself frequently backing a President of the opposite party early in his career. Often, he would urge backing for President Kennedy's proposals. That led his brother Ted to say years later, "Sil risked his own career when he voted against his party leadership to expand the House Rules Committee and end its resistance to my brother's proposals My brother never forgot what Sil had done." In 1964, Conte took on the futile task of seeking to moderate Barry Goldwater's arch conservative platform.

Conte was a career-long member of the Appropriations Committee and by 1979, despite the consternation of a number of more conservative Republicans, he attained the top GOP slot. One thing he had in common with that wing was a mutual dislike of unnecessary spending. He once wore pig snouts and ears on the House floor to signify this, complete with oinks ("They had their schnozzles right in the trough"). He opposed acid rain, many farm subsidies, and backed Jimmy Carter's much maligned water projects veto. But he always saw that Massachusetts got its fair share. In particular, he steered education grants to the University of Massachusetts. He brought a major Army contract to Pittsfield's General Electric Plant. Preserving Amtrak service was a must. *The Union News* wrote how on one occasion, "he showed up on the steps of the Capitol in an exterminator's uniform, complete with 'roach-buster' cap and spray can, to bring national attention to a West Springfield company's involvement in fighting cockroaches." And just before he died Conte was able to see a project to fruition that brought salmon back to the Connecticut River.

Aside from being pro-life, Conte was almost as liberal as most Democrats. His Americans for Democratic Action score in 1988 was 90% and his American Conservative Union Score was just 8%. He cast one of three Republican votes against the Persian Gulf War. One reason was that he had backed the Gulf of Tonkin resolution a quarter of a century earlier and had nearly instantly regretted it. He said the Vietnam War led to "tragedy and needless loss of lives, and I pray this one will not." But once the mission had been authorized, he expressed full support. In willing to make his distaste for the Vietnam War known, Conte chose the forum of a veterans group. After the Gulf War was authorized, Conte called for a windfall tax, expressing "fear that oil companies will take the opportunity to rake consumers over the coals."

Conte was known for taking people under his wing and making them staffers. When Conte's office announced his passing following a recurrence of cancer at age 69, a portion of the statement read that "staff simply wishes to express our love for a great man." O'Neill gave one of the eulogies for Conte "I don't know how many places we went around the world together, but Sil could ask the leader of a nation the most pertinent question that would have taken a diplomat two years to ask. He could get to the point." He also told her, "If the Founding Fathers came back and picked from our 200-year history one member of Congress to show how they intended the Congress to work," O'Neill is said to have told the lawmaker's widow, Corinne, "they would have selected Silvio Conte."

When Millie O'Neill died in 2003, Mary Boland and Corrine Conte were present at her funeral.

Photo courtesy of the Conte Family

A word also needs to be said about Leo Diehl. He was not an officeholder – at least not a member of the U.S. Congress. But he along with Boland was O'Neill's most trusted advisor – and lifelong friend. They were elected to the House together in 1936 from neighboring Cambridge districts when Democrats were actually the minority and Diehl was the body's youngest member. Diehl had become acquainted with O'Neill about a year before while watching him play football ("This was no Kennedy touch football. It was no pads and he was a big, tough guy").

After his House days, Diehl became chair of the Massachusetts Tax Commission. Little known about Diehl was that he was a paraplegic, having been afflicted with polio at the age of six. But Diehl would never use that as a barrier. After undergoing rehabilitation at the Massachusetts Hospital School and earned his degree in accounting from Bentley College. Diehl was a man who loved sports and would not let his disability dictate what he could or could not do. He was determined to walk and did so on crutches. More remarkably, not only did he play goalie in a hockey game but at 14, pitched in a 27 inning baseball game while sitting down.

Leo Diehl was Tip O'Neill's most trusted advisor
Photo courtesy of Nancy DiGiovanni

It was after the 1970 elections, after Tip had been elected Whip, that he called his old friend and asked him to run his office. Diehl was not only taken aback but hesitant asking, "What the hell do I know about running the Whip office of the U.S. Congress?" O'Neill replied, "Well, what the hell do I know about it. I was never a Whip. Let's do it together." And Diehl felt, "How could I say no?" His adroitness, capabilities and gift at understanding not only the needs of the Democratic members but also his boss easily made him O'Neill's Sancho Panza. And the partnership, friendship and trust of the O'Neill/Diehl relationship made it the most powerful alliances ever on Capitol Hill. As evidence: after O'Neill's passing, Diehl was among the first people Millie called. That same year, the annual charity golf tournament that took place as part of the Leo Diehl Foundation was renamed the O'Neill-Diehl Charity Golf Tournament.

Diehl died at 92, twelve years after his most famous pal and was eulogized on the House floor.

Images courtesy of Nancy DiGiovanni

And of course, there was the man who went the furthest. JFK maintained ties to all of these men, nobody more so than O'Neill. While they were not exceptionally close, Tip truly liked Jack and the feeling was mutual (Bobby, he felt was underhanded and disrespectful while Teddy was the best legislator whom he was very fond of). O'Neill believes his last conversation with the President came after an official event when Kennedy called him to the Portico and began asking him about ordinary Bostonians both men knew from the days of yore. Some doubted the veracity of that story but Rosemary says it's all true. She also recalls that when Kennedy died and her dad saw the *Boston Herald* headline at the airport when picking her up at school, he broke down. It was, she said, one of two times she had seen him cry.

Fittingly, a chapter in the book, *Tip O'Neill and the Democratic Century* by John Farrell is entitled, "My Beloved Jack."

CHAPTER FIVE

JFK's Roomate Became A Very Influential Congressman In From – You Guessed It, Massachusetts

Historic Tidbit: As he geared up for his 1960 White House bid, Richard Nixon approached Tip O'Neill. Though he was still a junior member of Congress, Nixon knew O'Neill was a man of great influence. As O'Neill tells it in his book, *Man of the House*, Nixon was sure Lyndon Johnson would be his opponent and felt he could make a play for Massachusetts. He asked O'Neill to give him a few names that might be able to aid him. O'Neill assured him Kennedy would be getting the nomination but, not wanting to be rude, gave Nixon a few names. One was Bradford Morse, about to be elected to Congress. The other was "a smart guy" named Chuck Colson a man who would eventually become Nixon's self-described hatchet man and go to prison for his role in Watergate. Everything starts somewhere.

The famous "wedding photo" with Torby Macdonald standing to the far-right of the newly married couple. Teddy Kennedy is directly behind them
Photo courtesy of the John F. Kennedy Presidential Library and Museum

Torbert Macdonald won a House seat in 1954 when his Harvard roomie who would eventually win the White House was already serving in the Senate.

But it would be understating the relationship to simply call Macdonald Kennedy's roommate. He enjoyed a proximity to the 35th President few have, was there for his children, went on secret missions at his request and can even be at least partially credited with nursing him back to health at a crucial time in young JFK's life when he aspired to become an athlete and before going to war.

Even in the world of overachievers from Harvard, Torbert Macdonald stood out. His son, Torbert Macdonald, Jr., revealed an interesting anecdote about JFK during his college years. At Harvard, he was unknown as "Macdonald's roommate because my father was captain of the football team and Kennedy was just the son of another rich guy." But Kennedy had hoped to become a world-class athlete as well and when influenza threatened that, Macdonald was there to guide him. "I'd sneak into the infirmary with some food for him . . . As soon as he'd eaten, we'd slip out the back door, and I'd drive him to the indoor athletic building, where's he'd doggedly practice his backstroke. Then I'd drive him back to the hospital."

After college, the duo roomed at the Winthrop House with two other football players. MacDonald often hosted parties with Bobby Kennedy during the time when JFK faced a primary challenge in his first run for Congress in 1946 and managed his campaign headquarters. He was an usher at his wedding and served as an honorary pallbearer at his funeral. In turn, JFK was the godfather of the Macdonald's first born son who would routinely be the recipient of Christmas presents from President and in the year immediate following his death, Jacqueline. Days after the 1960 election, Macdonald was with Kennedy at the LBJ Ranch and a week before the assassination, he accompanied the President to his Palm Beach estate, La Guerida. The family would often spend leisure time with the First Family at the White House, time that included sailing, afternoon swims and watching a movie on the weekend of the Bay of Pigs.

The best friends during wartime
Photo via the John F. Kennedy Presidential Library and Museum

Macdonald was born to a working class family in Everett though the place he would call his home from boyhood to death was Malden. But his blue-collar roots belied the fact that in many ways, Macdonald's life was almost as storied as the Kennedy's. Captain of the Harvard football team and a major league baseball player, Macdonald married actress Phyllis Brooks, who starred in such hits as *Little Miss Broadway* and *In Old Chicago*. He also served on a PT boat in the Pacific during World War II. While Kennedy was forced to perform rescue missions, Macdonald took on a major combat mission singularly and voluntarily. Macdonald's unit encountered five Japanese boats and while, they succeeded in taking out four of them, the fifth was on the verge of making a get-away. But Macdonald went after it and succeeded in "torpedoing" it. His legs sustained serious injury when a shell exploded and he was awarded the Purple Heart and Silver Star.

**Torbert MacDonald was captain of the football team.
Photo via MySpace**

But Macdonald's athletic abilities were such that he was a legend in his time at Harvard. His abilities on the football team was credited in part with a smashing 1938 season - an obituary notes the team beat Princeton and Yale, and he was chosen as captain the next season. Even in seasons when the team wasn't beating Yale, Macdonald's presence was still commanding. An obituary notes "he scored his team's only touchdown in the waning minutes of a 20-to-7 defeat." Years later, Macdonald would be among the first to be named to the Harvard Football Hall of Fame.

Aside from his football accolades, Macdonald excelled in track and baseball. The former was noted at Harvard nearly for nearly 40 years after Macdonald graduated as he held the record for the 220-yard dash. The latter could have seen big national dividends had war not intervened as he was signed by the New York

Yankees and spent the summer of 1940 playing on one of their minor league teams. He was an outfielder.

Kennedy and Macdonald spent much social time together. Torbert Macdonald, Jr., called them "twin souls. They were ebullient, fun-loving, witty, charismatic, handsome, with a strong interest in sports and women. They were all-American boys. Anyone who was ever around them tried not to cry from laughing." Macdonald would visit Hyannis Port and Kennedy would often trek up to York Beach, Maine where Macdonald's parents ran a bathhouse. The duo traveled to Germany in 1939 and in a diary entry two years later as Macdonald was about to get married, JFK writes about driving to Boston to visit him. Kennedy recounts: "I then drove back down here (HyannisPort) and as I couldn't get my top up I froze my ba--s off and have been in bed ever since." And, John H. Davis writes in *The Kennedys: Dynasty and Disaster* that he and MacDonald went to Europe together before his marriage to Jacqueline, leaving her to "manage the wedding plans."

In the close-knit Kennedy circle, Macdonald's family path even crossed with Kennedy's aides. His father Jack and Cleo, the dad of JFK's famed press secretary Kenny O'Donnell were roommates at Holy Cross College.

Macdonald's trusted friendship would be evident when both were comfortably ensconced in their final offices. The Bay of Pigs led Kennedy to not trust the CIA to the point that he would confine himself to a small circle. One was Macdonald. In fact, in the fall of 1963, the President sent Macdonald on a mission to Saigon to warn South Vietnamese President Diem about a plot to assassinate him. He urged Diem to seek refuge at the American embassy but Diem refused ("he just won't do it. He's too stubborn," MacDonald told Kennedy on his return). The mission was a secret (a biography by James Douglass notes that Macdonald flew in on civilian, not military aircraft) and that Macdonald told virtually no one of this in the years that followed (his son and administrative aides were two exceptions). One reason could conceivably have been his devastation by his friend's death. But another is that he simply was not willing to capitalize on his association with Kennedy. Kennedy biographer Seymour Hersh called him "trusted, a trust that he validated after Kennedy's assassination." Hersh notes that even the unsealing of his papers revealed little in the way of sensitive information.

Macdonald claimed his Congressional seat by beating Republican incumbent Angler Goodwin 53% in 1954 but, after increasing that a notch to 55% two years later, never again fell below 62% in subsequent re-elections, and it wasn't unusual for him to top 70%).

Historically, Torbert Macdonald's name may not stand out but legislatively, he surely should. For his accomplishments were world-changing. Michael Dukakis, who was Governor of Massachusetts on Macdonald' praised him for his willingness to defy the naysayers when it consumer reform. "During the 1960s, when not too many people were paying attention to consumer protection on the national scene, Torby Macdonald was an inspiration to those of us at the State House who were concerned . . . His was one of the few voices to be heard nationally on the issue."

When folks watch PBS or listen to NPR, they're not out-of-line for owing a debt of gratitude to Macdonald, as many of his colleagues referred to him as the "Father of Public Broadcasting" for his sponsorship of the Corporate Public Broadcasting funding, which Ford signed into law in 1975. He shepherded the Emergency Petroleum Allocation Act into law to help Americans receive their fair share of oil. He also used his position on the House Commerce Committee (he chaired Commerce's Communication's subcommittee) to push through "blackout" games for sold-out sporting events.

Macdonald was also well ahead of his time pressing campaign spending measures. In 1969, he introduced legislation allowing Congressional candidates to purchase advertising at 20 to 30 percent of regular rates. Advertising rates had jumped an astounding 40 percent from 1956 to 1968 on Presidential campaigns but were also trickling down to the Congressional level. Macdonald acknowledged that the measure would not be a panacea for the skyrocketing costs of running campaigns but said "the success of a limited measure such as (what) we propose would go far toward encouraging the search for other campaign spending reform . . ." He was correct though he lived to see very few enacted.

Prior to chairing the Communication panel, Macdonald held the gavel of Interstate and Foreign Commerce's Subcommittee on Communications and Power. In 1969, he held hearings on the Electric Power Coordination Act of 1969. He cited the New York City area blackout and a 1967 power failure that impacted ten million people in four mid-Atlantic states as a reason to ensure adequate power was available. After that crisis, he introduced President Lyndon Johnson's measure to give the Federal Power Commission the authority to license extra voltages.

Macdonald's long-time Massachusetts colleague Jimmy Burke said he was always "into things that affected New England people in an economic way" and as befitting of a Congressman from a state with cold temperatures, Macdonald pushed hard for his constituents to get their fair share of energy relief. Lower electric rates were always a legislative priority. During the 1973 Arab embargo, he fought for increased oil supply. He got through the House his Emergency Petroleum Allocation Act directing the President to promote regulations. While the law would not touch "imported," oil, it set up regulations for "old" and "new" oil, the objective being "independent" and "branded" gas stations had to take an equal hit in supplies. Some gas would even be in the control of respective state Governors.

The bill was extended by President Ford in 1975 but phased out by the Reagan administration six years later. Macdonald also proposed requiring the President to notify Congress when he impounded funds. Macdonald's interest on energy led him to fiercely defend his turf when in 1971, Congressman Richard

Fulton of Tennessee proposed a select committee to investigate much of what was on Macdonald's plate. As the Rules Committee debated the proposal, Macdonald told a supporter of the new committee, Richard Andersen, he "would like to know from the gentleman why he thinks another committee is necessary to do a job that we are currently doing.' While Anderson contended it would simply be "valuable assistance,' members sided with Macdonald and defeated the new committee by a vote of 128-218.

Macdonald drew the line, however, when it came to gas deregulation. Though he did not live to see that occur, he was leery of doing so. He wanted to make sure enough gas would be available to consumers, not just companies with high windfall profits.

Holding energy companies feet to the fire was not the only utility company Macdonald took on. When AT&T proposed a rate increase in 1975, Macdonald held a hearing. In particular, he focused on the lack of latitude of the FCC to oversee the matter. "It is apparent to me that the FCC has not been adequately equipped by the Congress for dealing with rate increases such as the filing made earlier this month by AT&T for (a) $717 million increase in its long distance telephone charges."

The same went with the herculean effort to establish corporate public broadcasting. It was actually a nearly five year effort that initially resulted in President Nixon's veto of the first piece of legislation in 1973, after his administration gave assurances that he'd sign it. Even after Macdonald shepherded the bill to fruition (The Public Broadcasting Finance Act was signed into law by President Ford on New Year's Eve, 1975), he continued to take great interest its development. At one hearing, he scolded Corporate Public Broadcasting Chair Robert Benjamin for lack of progress on minority needs, telling him, "I am not being sarcastic and I hope you don't take my remarks unkindly but, it reminds me of the musical, 'Promises, Promises,' You have not taken much action, even on the hiring item."

Photo courtesy of the U.S. Government Printing Office

Early bills Macdonald sponsored included a 1957 measure increasing annuity payments from the civil service and disability fund and a proposal the following year amending the Outer Continental Shelf Lands Act to guarantee the revenue generated would go toward educational opportunities.

Macdonald, who was called "The Needle" for his sharp sense of humor and for his integrity, was respected enough by his colleagues to be chosen New England Regional Whip. O'Neill relates that Markey succeeded him and continued his quest to work on complex telecommunications issues through the Commerce committee."

Macdonald was known for his deep integrity. Harley Staggers, Sr. said "he would give you his word and stick to it, even if it hurt him politically." His longtime Massachusetts colleague Burke called him "a hard worker and a highly principled fellow."

Macdonald developed cancer in 1975 and despite the fact that he declared himself to be "cured," he announced his retirement from Congress in 1976. Recovery, he said, was anticipated but only if "I am able to remove as many pressures as possible." But that May, he suffered a setback and requested no further life-saving treatment be given. His daughter Laurie asked if he realized that meant he might not survive and Macdonald responded, "yes." He was only 58.

Ted Kennedy delivered the eulogy for Macdonald speaking of the "special bond of friendship with President Kennedy (that was) shared and treasured by all the members of my family." Residents of the town of Malden lined the streets during Macdonald's funeral procession. A stone monument outside Malden's City Hall and the Macdonald Park in Medford are two lasting tributes to the Congressman.

CHAPTER SIX

A Tennessean Named Estes:
Courage Above All

Historic Tidbit: When Ron Dellums an African-American and Pat Schroeder, a woman, were appointed to the Armed Services Committee in 1973, Chairman Ed Hebert only provided one chair. Rather than make a fuss, they decided to share it. They joked they sat "cheek-to-cheek." Barney Frank would later call it "the only half-assed thing Ron and Pat ever did."

Photo via Getty Images

Last August 10th marked 50 years since the death of Tennessee Senator Estes Kefauver. Later that month, America observed the 50th anniversary of the "March on Washington," which culminated with Martin Luther King, Jr.'s exhilarating "I Have a Dream" speech.

While Kefauver's life came to an untimely end at age 60, it perhaps seems fitting that the two events came in such close proximity for Kefauver was arguably the one Southern politician of his day who openly favored civil rights. And at a time when support for civil rights was not only unpopular but highly dangerous, he managed to use his political capital and skills to stare down political opponents who tried to make hay of the issue and win.

If JFK were alive today and wrote a modern version of *Profiles in Courage*, I suspect the number one recipient would be Kefauver. Among vice-presidential nominees who never quite made it, Kefauver is the most underrated as far as talents and character. But his stature among Presidential wannabees is also high as Theodore H. White called him, "the best man never to become President."

It is especially appropriate for Kefauver to have hailed from the "Volunteer State" because someone from the South had to have a hand in the civil rights battle - for credibility's sake and for history's.

He'd come to be known as "the Keef," and as *the Evening Independent* observed, he was "a big friendly man with a wide campaign grin and reached out to shake any hand in sight." And he was an imposing man. Kefauver was 6 foot 3 and weighed 200 pounds. Kefauver was not a great speaker but his relations with the common folk were extraordinary. And the coonskin cap, which as the *Independent* noted he turned into "a personal campaign symbol that would be recognized throughout the nation," made him unstoppable.

A young Kefauver
Photo courtesy of the Ray Hill Collection

Kefauver was a Yale man, attending law school there. Yet having grown up in the "Great Smokies," he was most comfortable in Tennessee, and that's where he returned. His family had stature but Kefauver proved most comfortable among the ordinary folks he'd make a career of fighting so hard for.

Kefauver got the Presidential bug at an early age. He'd never come close to being President but did win a place on the national ticket. By good fortune and a rare decision by the standard bearer, Kefauver became the vice-presidential standard bearer on the Democratic ticket. He was far from the favorite and had to beat, among others, Kennedy and Al Gore, Sr., his fellow Tennessean, to get it.

Kefauver first won a Congressional seat in a 1939 special election and became a reliable backer of the "New Deal" and TVA. He opposed the "poll tax" to the end of his life (backing the 24th Amendment which would do so) and "lynching laws" and refused to back the "Southern Manifesto." Somewhat courageously, Kefauver sponsored with Senator Joe O'Mahoney of Wyoming and Frank Church of Idaho a pivotal jury trial amendment that many saw as necessary to salvaging the bill. But rather than present it in the form of progress for blacks, Kefauver spoke of it under the guise of helping unions. The bill, he said, "clearly distinguishes between civil and criminal contempt.... (It) represents a great advance of civil liberties because...it covers all actions for contempt. It again will assure labor unions of their day in court before a jury of their peers...."

The Evening Independent said that these positions would "win him no political friends among the southern bloc." And it would also mean trouble back home, which came in the form of a primary challenge in 1960.

Kefauver was called "too liberal for Tennessee" and was expected to have a battle that was nip'n'tuck. But he put it down with 64%. *The Nashville Banner* called that outcome "one of the most surprising votes in Tennessee's political history."

In their column, Brown and Allen wrote that "on election eve, nobody could be found who "intended to vote for Kefauver and that on the day after the election, nobody could be found who would admit having voted for him."

Kefauver's career was about taking on the bosses and winning, and at least one of them thought he was too high and mighty for him for his tastes. This moment came when Kefauver decided to give up his safe House seat and enter the 1948 Senate primary. Many, including his own father, had urged him to abandon the risky venture but Kefauver would have none of it ("I'm going to the Senate or I'm going back to practicing law").

Ed Crump ruled Memphis with an iron fist and Kefauver, from the other end of the state, had to get past him and the candidate he was backing, Judge John Mitchell. Inadvertently but ironically, it was an ill-fated Crump maneuver that allowed Kefauver to sneak past Mitchell in the primary. The current U.S. Senator was A. Tom Stewart, a two-termer who not only had a long-standing affiliation with Crump but also the state's very senior Senator, Kenneth McKellar (he was called McKellar's "me-too man"). Kefauver had first considered seeking McKellar's seat two years earlier but concluded he could not unseat the aging but venerable Senator. But he did himself no favors. McKellar told Crump that Kefauver was "as stupid as they make them," reciting a story that Kefauver believed Thomas Jefferson had actually been born in Tennessee.

Left memorabilia courtesy of Peggy Dillard (Tennrebgirl.com); right via Ebay.com

But after Stewart nearly lost his seat in the 1942 primary (it came down to Shelby County to save him), Crump began slowly backing away from him. He had tried to get Stewart to retire in '48 but he was in no mood to do so. But Crump decided to back Mitchell. Because Mitchell and Stewart hailed from the same region, a vote split would certainly work for to Kefauver's benefit, a fact Crump realized late in the campaign (his calls to urge Mitchell to bow out went nowhere).

Well aware that his chances of stopping Kefauver were slipping away, Crump began to try a different tack. That meant linking him with "pinkos and communists." He called him a raccoon and a "pet coon," tying his voting record to an open Communist-sympathizing Congressman from New York named Vito Marcantonio. The "Keef"' replied, "I may be a pet coon but I'm not Boss Crump's pet coon." It was then that he donned the coon and began wearing it from stop-to-stop. He said, "A coon may have rings around his tail but this coon will never have rings around his nose."

The result was what many had anticipated. Kefauver won the primary but with well below a majority. But his 42% outdistanced Stewart's 31% and Mitchell's 24% (Stewart was relegated to literally a couple thousand votes in Shelby). Crump wouldn't lift a finger for Kefauver in the general. He was backing Strom Thurmond for President and would "rather vote for Marcantonio" than Kefauver. It mattered little. Republicans were non-entities in those days and Kefauver won the general election against ex-East Tennessee Congressman and Republican National Committee chair Carroll Reece with two thirds of the vote.

Theodore Brown, Jr., and Robert Allen said in a piece that Kefauver "hated elitist politics . . . was never afraid to share his insight and vision with his constituents and never shirked his responsibility to lead public opinion on complex and controversial issues. Indeed, he Kefauver was the only member of the Senate to vote against making membership of the Communist Party a crime. This was all the more notable in the days before McCarthy's status tanked.

The famous "Coonskin Cap,"
Photo courtesy of the National Portrait Gallery

Enter organized crime, which gave way to the "Kefauver Hearings," Concerned with the growing problem of the criminal underworld, Kefauver in 1950 introduced a Senate resolution to establish a committee to investigate labor racketeering in interstate commerce. Guess who got to chair it? Kefauver? He'd get a budget of $150,000, much of which was used to conduct hearings in cities across the nation.

Pop History Dig observed that "it was through the Kefauver Hearings that Americans came to learn of the Mafia. The committee would travel from city to city, often tangling with local law enforcement who sought to limit media."

As described in *Smithsonian's The Senator and the Gamblers*, Kefauver "brought a parade of gamblers, hoodlums, crooked sheriffs and organized-crime figures out from the shadows to sit and testify before the white-hot lights and television cameras. Housewives were glued to their sets day after day, while in barrooms and cafeterias, men gathered on their lunch breaks to witness the proceedings." Local movies houses showed it. As Pop History Dig put it, the Kefauver hearings had "the advantage of being the best show in town."

Life Magazine wrote that "never before had the attention of the nation been riveted so completely on a single matter," adding that "the week of March 12, 1951, will occupy a special place in history."

And the "deliberate-speaking, endlessly polite Southern senator in horn-rimmed glasses named Estes T. Kefauver," as Smithsonian put it, "not yet halfway through his first term, became an overnight sensation. He was even asked to have a cameo in Humphrey Bogart's *The Enforcer*.

Senate leaders were not pleased about Kefauver's hearings. In particular, they tried to talk him out of holding one in Cook County, Illinois where Senate Majority Leader Scott Lucas was up for re-election. Kefauver refused to entertain pleas to hold them elsewhere and Lucas lost re-election to Everett Dirksen. That made Kefauver a pariah of sorts in the Senate who believed Kefauver was all about

Kefauver. Hill notes he was "loathed by many members of the Senate as a result." The state's junior Senator, Al Gore, Sr., put it more succinctly.

In an oral history project in 1976, Gore recalled having to intervene with leadership on his colleague's behalf several times. He explained that, "Senator Kefauver was not the usual type of legislator. Senator Kefauver was in many respects a public relations senator. He was a national figure; he personalized or epitomized many popular causes. And because of the renown he achieved and also because he seemed to eschew the daily give-and-take of legislation, he was never particularly popular with his colleagues in the Senate. To put it in common parlance, he was never exactly a member of the Senate club." This was particularly true among the Southern caucus. Senate Secretary Bobby Baker called Kefauver "despised among all the Southern Democrats. Not a one of them liked him." Baker credits much of this to an anti-discrimination Fair Employment Housing bill that he sponsored during his first Senate term. Georgia Democrat Herman Talmadge, a staunch segregationist, called Kefauver "a Democrat from the South but not a Southern Democrat." Yet another Senator may have best captured the sentiment on Kefauver. "It isn't that we don't like Estes but he isn't around for the infighting. He skims off the cream of the headlines and he's off. He doesn't stick to the job and he doesn't cooperate." (Baker did say Kefauver was beloved by his staff).

Photo courtesy of the Ray Hill Collection

Arguably, the hearings accomplished little as far as revelations were concerned as "ambiguous answers and flat-out denials were the norm." But they did change the culture, particularly as far as how the FBI treated organized crime.

For instance, in Vegas, Kefauver suggested a 10% tax on gaming. That couldn't possibly happen but within five years, casino licensing was created. A state gaming board was later enacted. The final *Kefauver Report* was 11,000 pages.

Kefauver tried to convert his fame into Presidential success. Harry Truman was unpopular but had not yet announced he would forego re-election. Sidney Hart noted that "with no professional organization and little money," Kefauver had stunned Truman in the New Hampshire primary - by 4,000 votes out of 34,000 cast. That would land him on the cover of *Time Magazine* and help him go on to win 12 of the 15 contests in all, including racking up an amazing 57% in Minnesota where the party's two rising stars, Hubert Humphrey and Orville Freeman, had been furiously stumping for Stevenson.

Senior historian Sidney Hart observed that "reporters noted that voters were disarmed by (Kefauver's) earnest demeanor as he shook their hands and introduced himself, a plainspoken man of strong facial features, with thin lips that broke easily into a wide time." Declaring, "We love him because of the enemies he's made," Tennessee Governor Gordon Browning placed Kefauver's name in nomination. He urged delegates to "climb aboard the Chattanooga Choo-Choo, a fearless man with a touch of nobility." But delegate strength was what mattered in those days and Adlai Stevenson gradually overtook him to gain the nomination.

Kefauver returned to the Senate and attacked the Eisenhower administration for putting many defense contracts "into one or two companies," particularly singling out General Motors. But by 1956, he was ready to try once more. And again, it would start with New Hampshire, where, the *Concord Monitor* remarked, he "had become the unofficial leader of the state's Democrats, since the entire congressional delegation was Republican."

Kefauver carried many of the northern states, including New Jersey, Wisconsin, Minnesota, Indiana, and Montana. He lost Florida 52-48% and California 63-37% and withdrew soon after. But when Stevenson shocked the convention by instructing them to choose the vice-presidential nominee, Kefauver saw a chance. Others recognized it as well and for one reason or another set out to stop him. The ultimate winner was not important. Stopping Kefauver was the only thing that mattered. This was the case for a variety of reasons. Some northern delegations were fearful of his crusades against organized crime while Southerners were angered by his "betrayal" on civil rights. Senator George Smathers of Florida noted, "The South is always more apt to go for a Northerner who doesn't know any better than for a Southerner who should know better but doesn't."

To get the nomination, Kefauver had to battle at least one fellow Tennessean and an ambitious Massachusetts Senator. In fact, on the first ballot, Kennedy came within 39 votes of winning the nomination outright (another irony is that he was 39-years-old).

Image from the collection of Ernie Wentrcek

But then the maneuvering really began. According to a biography of JFK, "within minutes, no delegate could buy his own drink and no elderly lady could cross a Chicago street without help from an eager delegate." As W.H. Lawrence described it in the *New York Times* the day after, "The Keef" had Ohio and Michigan as well as most of the rest of the Midwest down pat from the start. Eventually, he gained backing from Pennsylvania. But not in the South, including Tennessee. Delegates there were for either Al Gore, Sr., (his junior colleague in the Senate) or Governor Frank Clement.

Illinois mostly favored Kennedy and New York for Mayor Wagner. Kentucky gained a laugh by casting its vote "unpredictable." Eventually, Humphrey and Freeman (now Governor) found themselves, at Kefauver's urging, compensating for their mistake in '52. Humphrey had been pursuing the vice-presidency as well but had now realized it was a lost cause. When Kefauver begged him for help (both men were literally in tears), Humphrey vowed to talk to Freeman who told him to "go out on the floor and switch our delegates to Kefauver."

At that point Gore, who had finished third on the first ballot, withdrew and endorsed Kefauver (when Gore told Clement, he exclaimed, "oh no, not Estes"). Florida switched to him as well. But it still seemed that Kennedy had irreversible momentum. But when Gore bowed out, Oklahoma balked at switching to him, primarily because of farm issues. Kefauver emerged as their man. Indiana did the same (it was said that had ex-Congressman Andy Jacobs, Sr. been willing to back Kennedy, his delegation would have followed and the game would have been over). But ironically, it was Missouri - where Harry Truman had so hoped to influence the convention but had been pronouncing "The Keef's" name as "Cowfever" - whose 33 votes put him over the top.

Kefauver signing autographs and with his Tennessee colleague, Al Gore Sr
Photo courtesy of the Ray Hill Collection

The final tally was 755 1/2 for Kefauver and 589 for Kennedy, who moved that the nomination be given by acclamation. Upon asking for the convention to ratify that, Speaker Sam Rayburn joked, "no "noes." It would be JFK's only political defeat.

Calling Kefauver an "old friend and able leader," Stevenson said "what has occurred this afternoon is clear evidence of the great vitality and virility of the Democratic Party. I am happy that Senator Estes Kefauver is to be my running mate. I know how formidable a candidate he will be, because I ran against him in several primaries."

But the civil rights issue loomed hard in the South with Mississippi Gov. James P. Coleman saying it "leaves the situation (there) in grave doubt." In the fall, Stevenson/Kefauver lost 41 states, including Tennessee (by 6,000 votes), and garnered just 43% of the national vote.

Meanwhile, despite the rivalry with Kennedy, Kefauver's daughter Diane said he and the future President "were friendly enough," in the Senate though adds that "Kennedy did not treat him very well, especially on his work on drug investigations and medical legislation." With Johnson, things were even less cordial. The Majority Leader wanted to deny Kefauver a seat on Foreign Affairs so badly that he maneuvered to keep him off. He encouraged New Mexico's Clinton Anderson to seek the position as well. Because both men had entered the Senate at the same time, Johnson had latitude over whom to appoint. He chose a more junior John F. Kennedy.

Kefauver did have laws enacted. The Kefauver/Harris Drug Control Act required that drugs be proven safe before use. His best friend in the Senate was Paul Douglas, an Illinois Democrat who, like Kefauver, who pressed harder than many colleagues would have liked on important issues but who was also ahead of his time. Hubert Humphrey was another confidante. But Kefauver was also close with the other Senator from Illinois, Everett Dirksen. Despite the fact that they rarely agreed on issues, Diane Kefauver says the pair "still went out and had a drink at the end of the day."

On a lighter note, Diane says that in his free time, her father "liked to play with his children," adding that there were "lots of pets, bikes, sleds. He loved building things with us and taking us on little adventures." And Kefauver loved

Tennessee. Most weekends were spent either stumping the state and meeting with constituents or visiting his elderly father.

At the end of the day, it can be said that Kefauver literally died fighting for Tennessee. He and Gore were on the Senate floor trying to stop the Communications Satellite Organization, which he felt would give the communications industry too many breaks at the expense of the public. It was attached to a NASA bill, and Kefauver wanted them reimbursed by the company. During debate, he suffered a mild heart attack, later revealed to be an aortic aneurism. He died later that night, hours before a scheduled operation to correct it. It was thought that Kefauver's problem with alcohol, legendary on the Hill, contributed to his ailment.

The *Ellenberg Daily Record,* in an editorial after Kefauver's death, wrote, "We call some men opportunists, bombastic, publicity seekers, but many such men are deeply in earnest and their messages have a warning for us, the common people, if we will only stop and pay attention."

Each November 15, the Mob Museum, The National Museum of Organized Crime and Law Enforcement in Las Vegas hosts "Kefauver Day." His daughter Diane was on hand in 2012. Just three when the hearings began, she nonetheless has vague recollections of the atmosphere. "My family watched the hearings. I remember touching my father's face on the TV screen because we weren't seeing him much at home during this time. Although the hearings were taking place over the country, and I recall hearing talk about various threats against our family and having security around our house, my mother was ferociously protective of us. She tried to give us as normal of a life as possible during this time and beyond."

Photo courtesy of the Mob Museum, Las Vegas, Nevada

Mike Mansfield: the 20th-Century's Winningest Senator and a Calm and Wondrous Man

Historic Tidbit: This is nothing short of amazing. John Tyler, our nation's 10th President, was born in 1790. Married twice, he fathered 15 children, the most of any President. His youngest child, a daughter, was born in 1860. And amazingly, two of his grandchildren, both in their 80s, survive today.

"And so she took a ring from her finger and placed it in his hands." Those were the words of Montana Senator Mike Mansfield as he eulogized the 35th President of the United States, John F. Kennedy. It was a line he closed with each of his first four sentences of the remarks, and it illustrated the originality and sincerity for which the longest-serving Senate Majority Leader in history is so well-known.

If Don Shula is known as America's "winningest coach," Mansfield may be the "winningest Senator." While often surpassed in the history books by the Johnsons, Humphreys, Ted Kennedys, and Dirksens, Mansfield's leadership was responsible for the passing of the most dramatic and fundamental legislation that shaped the second half of the 20th-century and would have lasting impact for generations to come. He was also a greatly humble man, of decency, and one deeply adored by his colleagues on all ideological spectrums. That makes Mansfield, in my opinion, the most important Senator of the 20th-century.

The Economist described Mansfield as "neither witty nor eloquent, Mansfield could be monosyllabic in public." But he was viewed by ordinary Montanans and colleagues alike as a wonderful human being, a compassionate man with deep sincerity, with a zest for service and a feeling that, whether it be a junior colleague or a young reporter looking for a tip, he was above no one.

By his final years in the Senate, Mike Mansfield was not a household name, nor did he need to be one. But on countless issues (civil rights, the Great Society, 18-year-olds being given the right to vote, and Vietnam), he was as big a player as any President whose tenure as Leader would span longer than anyone before or since. Without that, his eulogy of John F. Kennedy at his official funeral would make him one for the books.

Mansfield was a Brooklynite but he moved to Montana to live with family after his mother died. Service came to Mansfield naturally and with passion. At the age of 14, he lied about his age and joined the Navy. He also served in the

Air Force and Marines. Upon returning, he worked as a "mucker" in Montana's copper mine. But he would get homesick whenever away from Montana and with his future bride's help, he eventually graduated from the University of Montana and began teaching.

Mansfield with the love of his life, Maureen. They were married 67 years
Photo via the Mike and Maureen Mansfield Library at the University of Montana

It was in 1940 that Mansfield embarked on a run for Congress but lost a close primary to Representative Jerry O'Connell. By 1942, Jeannette Rankin faced anger over her opposition to the U.S. entry into World War II and decided not to stand for re-election. Mansfield ran to succeed her and won. It would be the beginning of a 34 year tenure in Washington that would be surpassed only by Max Baucus in 2009.

A solid liberal with internationalist views representing a constituency that didn't share it, Mansfield insisted that Montanans call him "Mike." He was re-elected by large margins. In 1952, he took on freshman incumbent Zales Ecton who attracted a visit from none other than Joseph McCarthy. Mansfield squeaked into the seat 51-49%, even as Eisenhower was handily carrying the state. In the Senate, McCarthy asked Mansfield how things were going in Montana, to which he replied, "better since you've left, sir." But he was developing a beautiful relationship with a future President. He and JFK served together in both Houses of Congress and Mansfield opined early in his Senate tenure that "Kennedy was a charmed person and would be President someday."

**Mansfield stood behind President Kennedy both politically and on the
mound ("Scoop" Jackson bats during a Senate baseball game)
Photo courtesy of the Mike and Maureen Mansfield Foundation**

Mansfield's service in Asia gave him much zest for foreign affairs and with
LBJ's help, he was placed on Foreign Relations. This was unusual for a freshman,
which prompted his assistant, Jim Rowe, to pen LBJ a note. "I don't know how
it was done but I know who did it. So does Mike."

LBJ had other things in line for Mansfield. At a time when the position was
filled by the Leader, Johnson made Mansfield his Whip. He was not the future
President's first choice for the job; that was Florida Senator George Smathers. But
Smathers wasn't shy about telling Johnson that his style was off-putting and for
that reason, he suggested Mansfield for the job. "Lyndon," he said, "the only guy
that could probably put up with you is that angel, Mansfield. Mansfield's nature
is such that he could probably stand it."

In that regard, Mansfield dutifully served as the yin to LBJ's yang. And when
Johnson became Vice-President, Mansfield again proved his reticence for moving
up just for the sake of doing so as he had to be persuaded to take the position of
Majority Leader.

Mansfield's rise to both the Leader and Whip position arguably came from
maneuvering and views of future Presidents and a vice-president who warily eyed
one another. Johnson was prepared to make a deal with Hubert Humphrey to
deliver the liberal colleagues. He said if Humphrey didn't, he'd make Mansfield
Whip. Humphrey refused.

And JFK was reported to tell skeptical confidants the reason he picked LBJ
was to have a Senate Majority Leader he could work with. "Did it occur to you
that if Lyndon becomes the vice president, I'll have Mike Mansfield as the leader
in the Senate, somebody I can trust and depend on?"

**Mansfield on the Capitol steps and visiting the troops in his early days in Congress
Photo via the Mike and Maureen Mansfield Library at the University of Montana**

The Washington Post observed that "instead of Johnson's browbeating tactics, Mansfield led by setting an example of humility and accommodation." Smathers himself said he was "just totally the opposite. He was a thoughtful, kind, sweet, nice guy, hardly ever raised his voice." Arkansas Senator William Fulbright called Mansfield, "perfectly willing to explain a bill but he would very rarely ask, 'Say, would you please vote for a certain bill?'" *The Almanac of American Politics* writes that "his regard for the rights of his opponents are matched only by an unflagging determination to make is own point." Joe Biden even managed to fit his name into his vice-presidential debate with Sarah Palin. He recalled getting angry at Jesse Helms early in his first year, only to have Mansfield admonish him to "never question another Senator's motives." Indeed, his rigidity for decorum in the chamber was so well-known that one day, when a colleague was not speaking well another, Mansfield took him aside and admonished him by saying, "Senator, we just don't use that kind of language on the floor of the Senate."

The New York Times, in Mansfield's obituary, observed that "in Congress, where bombast and pomposity are common, Mr. Mansfield was unusually modest and self-effacing." Ex-Montana Governor Ted Schwinden said he couldn't remember Mike saying "a mean word about anyone." And Gene McCarthy, not one known to lavish gratuitous praise on his fellow man, said of Mansfield's effectiveness and quiet demeanor, "A man of gentle nature can be framed in steel."

Mansfield's many accomplishments belied a very shaky early start. Johnson had just been elected Vice-President but, with his trusted aide Bobby Baker, he devised a way to stay involve in Senate affairs - by attending and presiding over Democratic lunches. Mansfield readily approved the deal but almost his entire caucus rebelled in the name of separation of powers. Mansfield told his caucus he had "no intention of sharing his responsibilities or authority" but vowed to not accept the post of leader unless the caucus certified Johnson's inclusion. The then very junior Robert Byrd said the move may have reflected Mansfield's "quiet and unassuming manner but it was a mistake."

**Mansfield addressing the press with other Democratic
Congressional leaders during the Kennedy Presidency
Photo courtesy of the John F. Kennedy Presidential Library and Museum**

Those were traits the whole nation would see in his eulogy for Kennedy. "There was a sound of laughter; in a moment, it was no more. And so she took a ring from her finger and placed it in his hands. There was a wit in a man neither young nor old, but a wit full of an old man's wisdom and a child's wisdom, and then in a moment, it was no more. And so she took a ring from her husband's finger and placed it in her hands."

Mansfield's laid-back style was sometimes to the consternation of fellow Democrats, and it begs the question as to whether a man who, as Randall Woods in *Vietnam and the American Tradition* observed, was "not a compulsive seeker of power and not all-consumed with politics," could succeed today as a senator, much less as a leader. When he assumed the Presidency, this irritated Johnson as well. When Johnson told Mansfield he'd like more loyalty, Mansfield replied, "Mr. President, I'm not yours. I'm the Senate's" (still, Mansfield was said to have been LBJ's second choice to Hubert Humphrey for the vice-presidency in 1964.

But what he lacked with rhetoric, Mansfield compensated for with an abundance for his members behind the scenes, which would have an indelible change on the institution. He wanted junior members, rather than the committee chairs, to have say, and accountability. His Senate biography says Mansfield "quietly abolished most patronage positions to establish a professional staff, assigned office space by seniority rather than as favors, and refrained from handing out committee assignments in return for senators' support." Ross Baker of Rutgers writes that these moves "allowed the modern Senate of equals to emerge." As for him, he didn't have a press secretary and responded personally to many letters.

That was Mansfield's institutional impact. Then there was the legislative. And boy were there many!

Photo via the Mike and Maureen Mansfield Library at the University of Montana

When one thinks of household names instrumental in the passage of civil rights legislation, Mansfield's name doesn't come up. That usually turns to the Kennedys, LBJ, and Hubert Humphrey. But excluding him is a colossal mistake.

In early 1964, when prospects for passage of a civil rights bill were still well up in the air, Mansfield vowed to keep the Senate in session all year to ensure passage. It was Mansfield's intuitiveness at re-instituting "second reading" on the bill in February that managed to remove it from the Senate Judiciary Committee, where it would languish to a certain death.

Ultimately, Mansfield, along with Senate Minority Leader Everett Dirksen, helped forge the famous compromise, and, following a 54-day filibuster, had the legislative wisdom to know when it was time to move the bill to a vote. During the debate, Mansfield dramatically read a letter from a Montana woman who thanked God her "kids were born white." It worked. The filibuster was broken 73-27 and the most meaningful domestic legislation of the 20th-century was passed.

The legislation associated with "Great Society" also sailed through with Mansfield as leader of the helm, which caused one of his aides to remark, "I had not seen so much activity in my life around here. We were passing major bills every week."

Aside from civil rights, Mansfield's biggest legacy was likely his sponsorship of the amendment giving 18-year-olds the right to vote. Addressing the Flatbed High School graduation he declared, "young people under twenty-one are regarded as old enough and wise enough to marry, to enter into contracts, to be treated as adults in the courts, to pay taxes, and to risk their lives in war . . . They are mature enough to participate in the selection of their representatives in government." It was ratified a year later.

In 1968, when opponents of Abe Fortas' nomination to be Chief Justice of the Supreme Court began filibustering the matter, Mansfield said that if it were successful, it would be "at the expense of the Constitutional structure of the federal government." Earlier he had said "the Senate ought to have to face up to the President's request and I think the President is entitled to the courtesy of an up-and-down vote." Not all of his words about Fortas were praiseworthy. He called the Justice's acceptance of a $15,000 fee for a training session at American university "unfortunate."

Around that time, Mansfield began using his means to shape an end to Vietnam. He had long been frustrated by the Vietnam War. His foresight came fast. He had warned Kennedy as early as 1962 that South Vietnamese leader Ngo Din Diem wasn't using U.S aid wisely. History.org credited him with being the "first American official to refuse to make an optimistic public comment on the progress of the war." Yet Mansfield later told Johnson to his face that escalation was a mistake and though initially supporting the war, he called it "a grotesque mistake." Yet he also tried being a realist in the matter. When Wayne Morse, one of two opponents of the authorization in '64, sought to overturn as the Senate debated a supplemental in March of 1966, Mansfield successfully launched a move to table it. His reasoning: overturning it is "inappropriate and inadvisable in connection with this bill at this time . . . we are in too deep now. The situation is one of the utmost delicacy and the risk of misinterpretation is very great."

Photo via the Mike and Maureen Mansfield Library at the University of Montana

But the future would be another story. In seeking to avoid it from happening again, he was a major force behind the "War Powers Act."

Nolan Franti, in a piece on Mansfield, said that the Senator outlined his desire to shape the war's conclusion legislatively in a letter to Michael Lopach, a young student despondent over the forthcoming end of his draft deferments. "Admittedly, it is an awkward way to proceed" in ending U.S. involvement, he added. "I know of no other way of responding to the urges of conscience and what I believe to be the overriding sentiments of the people of our state." In a touch of the compassion he displayed that made him so endearing to Montana and the nation, Mansfield enclosed an addendum to the letter that read, "Mike - I am indeed sorry that I can't be more encouraging. I hope you will understand my difficulty. Mike M."

But in the ensuing years, Mansfield lived up to his promise to try to bring the war to a close. The Mansfield Amendment, enacted in 1970, would bar the Defense Department from "to carry out any research project or study unless such project or study has a direct and apparent relationship to a specific military function." He put together a compromise of Cooper/Church which Nixon signed, and McGovern/Hatfield, which the Senate didn't pass. And he got the Senate to reject the Foreign Authorization Act when language limiting U.S. involvement in Vietnam was stripped.

Mansfield's simplicity was useful in ongoing debates. One was school prayer which his counterpart, Dirksen, was moving to allow by virtue of amending the Constitution. Citing the confusion that could result in allowing school districts to select a prayer, Mansfield called the issue "too personal, too sacred, too private to be influenced by the pressures for change each time a new school board is elected to office."

Mansfield's style as a boss resulted in tremendous loyalty. Ray Dockstader was Mansfield's chief aide for his entire 24 year Senate tenure. Many others have remained active members of his cause – in particular taking part in the Mike and Maureen Mansfield Foundation in Washington D.C.

Photo via the Great Falls Tribune

Watergate occupied much of Mansfield's later tenure as he organized the Select Committee. His decision to name North Carolina Senator Sam Ervin chair of the Senate Committee was not unanimously hailed as a fair number of liberals were bothered by Ervin's segregationist views. And when the House Judiciary Committee passed an impeachment resolution, Mansfield said that the "line of demarcation has been reached" and began consulting with Republican leader Hugh Scott for Senate preparations. That wouldn't become necessary as Nixon resigned.

At home, Mansfield was unassailable but his position of head Democratic spokesman in the Senate did not come without risks. He supported gun control and faced a sporting good salesman and gun-lover in 1970. The Gun Control Act of 1968 came immediately following the murders of Robert Kennedy and Martin Luther King, Jr., in 1968 and Mansfield at first resisted restrictions. But a Montana Marine, Thaddeus Lesnick, had also lost his life to gun violence and Mansfield felt compelled to act. Lesnick's mother wrote to Mansfield and he responded by saying, "frankly, that I do not expect that it [gun control] is any sort of cure-all of the problem. Nevertheless, I have taken this course in the hope and belief that there can be some mitigation in the rising level of the violence of the gun which has come to plague our land . . . If I ever had any doubts as to the course which I have chosen, your deeply moving letter has dispelled them."

Citizens for Montana ran an ad calling Mansfield's vote "a slap-in-the-face to every Montana sportsman and citizen . . . Help us in our fight to keep YOUR right as granted in the Constitution! DEFEAT MANSFIELD IN 1970! WHEN THEY VOTE AGAINST YOU—YOU VOTE AGAINST THEM.'" But Montanan's relished his leadership and he won with 61%, down only slightly from the 65% he had taken in 1964, a year that Everett Dirksen said, referring to campaigning for Republican Senate contenders that he'd go anywhere in the nation to stump, "even to the moon, but please, not Montana."

Mansfield fought hard for Montana. He favored installing the first Minuteman Missile in his state. He refused to allow the elimination of Amtrak service in Montana and helped build an airport terminal in Great Falls and the Hungry Horse Dam. As a reflection of the kind of mild-mannered person he was, Mansfield late in his tenure authored a bill calling for "Good Neighbor Day."

Mansfield's simple style was typified by his simple answers ("yup" or "nope") to questions. After his Senate term ended, Mansfield was appointed Ambassador to Japan by President Jimmy Carter. That is far from unusual among Congressional leaders past and present. But what is unusual is the fact that Mansfield was kept on by President Reagan of the opposite party.

Mansfield Ambassadorship commenced amid a period of huge problems and disputes, particularly in the area of automobiles. William Breer, a senior foreign service officer who served as political minister under Mansfield during much of his time in Japan, said he dealt with the issues "deftly." While "he probably didn't completely satisfy the trade hawks in D.C.," he was able to negotiate a fair amount of what was possible under the Japanese." Calling Mansfield, a "consummate politician and statesmen in the good sense," Breer said "he had all the skills and the personality to deal with political and diplomatic problems." And Mansfield was able to use those same skills that served him so well in the Senate. Breer adds that he "dealt with people with a great deal of humility. He always got the point across but was never demanding. He always had respect for the Japanese."

Mansfield served as Ambassador Japan under President Jimmy Carter, a Democrat and Ronald Reagan, a Republican Photo courtesy of the Mike and Maureen Mansfield Foundation

Philosophically, Mansfield believed "The U.S.-Japan relationship is the most important bilateral relationship in the world, bar none," This ultimately became one of his most famous statements. Mansfield seemed to reflect on that progress upon bidding farewell, when on his 1988 retirement he credited Japan for having "grown in its relationship with the United States from a nephew . . . into one of a brother. The Japanese have come to where they are on the world scene because of their ability to rise like a phoenix from the ashes and to make something of their country, which has no natural resources except for its great people."

On a lighter note, Breer says Mansfield was "friendly and knew everyone's name," noting, "he could entertain 300 people at a reception and say goodbye to nearly everyone by name." He took a particular liking to greeting people at the door as they entered. In his office, he surprised virtually every visitor with Nescafe coffee which he brewed himself. Maureen made quite the impression as well. Breer describes her as "good to embassy staff whereas historically, that wasn't always the case (among spouses)," adding "she took an interest in what they did."

Mansfield had open heart surgery in 1987 but despite his advancing age, that hardly slowed him down. He retired in 1988 at age 85, having come to be known in Japan as "omono taishi," or big-name ambassador.

But the quiet Mansfield would have one more brush with fame. In March 1998, he delivered the speech he had intended to give on the Senate floor the day Kennedy was assassinated (it was inserted into the record). Colleagues of both sides filled the Old Senate chamber. Afterwards, Mansfield was seen shaking hands with the late President's brother Ted. Kay Bailey Hutchison, noting Mansfield's regular attendance at the Senate prayer breakfasts with bacon in hand, noted it's nice to see "a guy being a guy."

After leaving Japan, Mansfield became employed at the Goldman Sachs group and showed up until just before he went into the hospital in his final days. He died in 2001 at age 98, just a year after his wife of 67 years, whom he absolutely adored, has passed away. As a sign of his simplistic nature, his gravestone made no mention of his long political career. It simply reads, "Michael J. Mansfield, PVT U.S. Marine Corps." That is similar to Thomas Jefferson whose own gravestone makes no mention of the fact that he served as President. How is that ironic. Because Ted Kennedy once compared Mansfield to the Founding Fathers saying that if he had to choose two of the numerous colleagues he served with to send to the Continental Congress, it would be Daniel Patrick Moynihan of New York and Mansfield.

There have been many biographies of Mansfield. One should be called "Mr. Decency." And the results of his decency will be seen from generation to generation.

Left photo; Mansfield, 95, addressing a Senate breakfast in 1998; Right photo, The Mike and Maureen statue at the Montana state capitol Left photo courtesy of the U.S. Senate Historical Office: Right photo courtesy of the Mike and Maureen Mansfield Foundation

CHAPTER EIGHT

Maggie and Scoop Partnership Meant
The Best For Washington State

Historic Tidbit: "I don't even know if I'm a liberal anymore but at least I can call myself one." – Washington Senator "Scoop" Jackson to Daniel Patrick Moynihan. Jackson was unhappy that his Democratic opponent during the 1976 primary season, Jimmy Carter, was trying to position himself as more moderate.

Property of University of Washington Libraries, Special Collections Division

**The effectiveness of Warren "Maggie" Magnuson and Henry "Scoop"
Jackson was the envy of every delegation in Washington D.C.
Photo Courtesy of the University of Washington
Libraries, Special Collections Divisions**

In the Senate, many states have had colleagues who have served together for decades. In fact, in a chamber where age 75 is considered young, it's almost assured. But perhaps the most wondrous and legendary pair, as well as the couple that delivered the best of good government, were two Washingtonians. From the other Washington that is.

"Maggie and Scoop" (Warren Magnuson and Henry Jackson) were Senate colleagues for 28 years, longer than all but five delegation mates – and their longevity was such that their service in Congress overlapped with all five (one pair, Iowa's Charles Grassley and Tom Harkin, were in the House during Magnuson and Jackson's Senate days). Others included Strom Thurmond/Ernest "Fritz" Hollings of South Carolina (36 years), Jim Eastland/John Stennis of Mississippi (32 years) and John McClellan/Bill Fulbright of Arkansas, who clocked in at 30.

According to a *Seattle Times* article, "The Twin Towers of Power," the duo's "names seem inseparable, as familiar and comfortable together as other famous pairs of the 1960's, like Huntley and Brinkley, or even Batman and Robin." But their durability exceeded both. Combined, they had nearly 87 years in Congress. But to paraphrase the poem "What about the Dash," it's not the dates that matter, it's what they did with their shared time in government. And for "Maggie and Scoop," friend and foe alike (the latter of which there were few) could have come up with a single word to describe their working relationship: indelible.

For America, the National Institutes of Health, the National Environmental Policy Act, the Federal Lands for Parks and Recreation Act, and other laws that today are simple household terms were all acts of which either Magnuson, Jackson, or in some cases both. They were not just Founding Fathers, but the leading creators. Regionally, their footprints on dams, facilities and land have had a lasting effect on the economy. Both pushed The National Health Services Corps, an act which allowed military doctors to fulfill a requirement in poor or rural areas. And when Hanford was threatened with cutbacks many times, "Maggie and Scoop's" heft not only left it untouched, but usually led to increased production.

Magnuson and Jackson's partnership was so productive in part because of their friendship. Their similarities were many, but often they complimented each other, even in terms of personal qualities. Jackson was one of few people who could simply walk into Magnuson's personal office unannounced. He would often ask Dr. Art Bergen, a prominent doctor and advisor, if he could "get Maggie to lose some weight?" Magnuson in turn would always say "when Scoop asks me to do something, I do it."

Other characteristics while similar in nature invited deep contrasts. Both were bachelors until the 1960s (though Magnuson had been married 30 years earlier), and as such were prominent on the social circuit. Maggie was a man about town who embraced the nightlife. Jackson would often be seen out as well but, as a non-smoker and seldom drinker, would "hold a cup of wine at parties to not feel awkward." Maggie bemoaned the headlines; Scoop ran for President twice. And while Maggie was notorious for fluffing up names and phrases (he once called LBJ's advisor Joe Califano "Joe Cauliflower"), Jackson, though not a compelling speaker, presented a statesmanlike stature.

The pair's roots and practices were also similar. Both grew up Scandinavian and poor. Both were retail politicians and neither were publicity seekers, with both loathe to wear their many accomplishments on their sleeves. Each had been their respective county prosecutors in the mid-1930s (Magnuson in King County, Jackson in Snohomish County). And they were longtime powerhouses. Maggie chaired the Commerce Committee in the Senate and in his last two years, Appropriations, while Jackson held the gavel at Interior, along with a high ranking post on Armed Services. It was on those panels that the duo made their marks and their legacies - for themselves and for Washington.

Stylistically, the pair could be different at times. One person who knew them both recalled, "Scoop would act like a schoolteacher. Maggie would open his cigar, mumble, and respond, 'Yeah, that's right.'" Future Vice-President Walter Mondale delineated the difference between the pair, observing, "Maggie never directly asks for a vote for fear of embarrassing a colleague; Scoop warns that if he doesn't get the Senator's vote, there'll be fewer national parks in his home state."

Often, they compensated for one another. On one occasion "Scoop" was lobbying for the 1974 World's Fair to take place in Spokane. To do so, it had to go through Arkansas Senator Bill Fulbright, who often had a testy relationship with Jackson. As Magnuson's assistant and future Congressman Norm Dicks recalled, "Fulbright wasn't going to give Washington State anything. So Maggie went to Fulbright and requested a hearing on the authorization of Spokane for a world's fair." It passed.

Because their personal characteristics were different, Gerry Johnson, a Chief of Staff to Magnuson late in his tenure said "it's not like they didn't have their spats." But more often, it was their staffs that took on more of the rivalry, if not outright animosity. Still, Johnson said the pair "worked so well and supported each other" that at the end of the day, they "leveraged their two positions for a state that was much smaller than we are now." That sums up the two in a nutshell as the combined leadership of Maggie and Scoop proved transformative, the likes of which no other state will see any time soon.

Warren Magnuson

For those who consider Lyndon Johnson the best-known wheeler and dealer, Magnuson must be considered a respectable second. And he liked it that way. It was he who spoke of "show horses and workhorses. Workhorses usually return," he added. "The show horses run into trouble." The Associated Press upon Magnuson's death noted that he "built a reputation as a potent yet genial wheeler-dealer who preferred to remain little-known, except by the voters back home who called him "Maggie."' He'd sit behind a wooden desk with two French chairs on the other side and a Congressional aide said, "you'd almost have to perch to him" during those meetings.

**Photo Courtesy of the University of Washington
Libraries, Special Collections Divisions**

But shunning the limelight didn't mean Magnuson wasn't content to surround himself with public figures. Today, there is often such antagonism between Presidents and Congressional appropriators that strong relationships might be unheard of. But Magnuson thrived on them. Known to set aside poker nights, he often played with both FDR and Truman. Jack Kennedy came to Seattle for Magnuson's 25th anniversary in office, and LBJ not only hosted a wedding reception for him at the White House but can reasonably claim to have encouraged the wedding (he told Magnuson that he had been a bachelor long enough, though he had actually been married briefly to a "Miss Seattle" three decades earlier). Indeed, Magnuson and Johnson were so close that the Senator never addressed the chief executive as "Mr. President.

For a person who would become one half of Washington State's greatest public servants, Magnuson did not set foot in its land until well into his college years. Born in Moorhead, Minnesota, he was adopted at birth. As a student, he acquired wide popularity, becoming a quarterback on the high school football team. That's where he earned his enduring nickname, "Maggie." The Washington Secretary of State's History Link project says that while Magnuson "recognized it as a badge of popularity, (he) never particularly liked the nickname. His family and close friends called him Warren."

Magnuson actually enrolled in college in North Dakota but ultimately found his way to Washington. He graduated in 1929 and was immediately hired by the Seattle Municipal League which enabled him to develop business and labor contacts important in Democratic circles. But Magnuson had already been toying in party politics. A year earlier, he had campaigned for Al Smith and Scott Bullitt, the party's nominee for Governor. But he was now ready to exert his own leadership. That meant helping to found the Young Democrats of Washington and eventually going for the prize himself.

Magnuson captured a State House seat in 1932 and the History Link project notes that "in his single term in the state legislature, he demonstrated the legislative skill he later used in the U.S. Senate. He supervised passage of a bill creating a $10 million bond issue to hire unemployed workers on public works projects - one of the nation's first unemployment relief acts."

Two years later, Magnuson was King County Prosecutor, a post that arguably gave him even more critical visibility as he prepared to embark on a higher political endeavor back East; Congress. In fitting with his character, he was not flashy about seeking it. But the Congressman from the First Congressional district, Marion Zioncheck, died suddenly in 1936 and Democratic leaders tapped Magnuson to fill the slot. He won with 63% and after just eight months in office, had major legislation signed into law; the National Cancer Institute Act. He was re-elected four times by similar margins and served his country in the Pacific aboard a ship during World War II. But when President Roosevelt ordered the return of all members of Congress, Magnson obliged. He made it to the Senate later that year – 1944, as the President was winning his 4th term. From then on, his record was his own. And it would be big.

The History Makers Project lists a number of Magnuson's accomplishments. The Commerce Committee portion reads like a what's what of consumer protection laws, and the Appropriations encompass most of what modern-day Washington is known for throughout the rest of the nation – and world.

For those who have utilized the National Institutes of Health (NIH), Magnuson is your Senator. If you or a family member have had to utilize the world-renowned cancer institute in Seattle, Magnuson made that happen. If you fly on Northwest Airlines, Magnuson helped make Seattle a prominent hub. For the Safe Drinking Water Act, Fair Credit Advertising Act, Door to Door Sales Act, country of orgin labeling, food ingredient labeling, think Magnuson. For those who see or heed anti-smoking labels, Magnuson again. Laws making sleepwear flame resistant, regulation of automobile safety, manufactures warranty enforcements, and safety standards for children's toys, it's all Maggie. Those are just some laws Magnuson is credited with steering to passage.

A Magnuson poster (left) and a visit by JFK to Seattle (right) marking his 25 years in Congress. 3,000 people paid $100 to attend the event Left image courtesy of the Washington Secretary of State; Right image courtesy of the University of Washington Libraries, Special Collections Divisions

Magnuson's commitment to natural resources also defined his legacy. The Marine Mammal Protection Act was enacted in 1972 and the Magnuson-Stevens Fishery Conservation and Management Act (Ted Stevens of Alaska was another legendary Northwest Appropriator) governs waterways within a 200 mile radius of U.S. coastline. It was enacted in 1976.

JFK once joked that Magnuson "sends messages to the rostrum, and when he is asked, 'What is it?' he replies, 'It's nothing important.' And Grand Coulee Dam is built." Development of the Columbia River Dams were part of Magnuson's legacy, and according to one biography, in his first ten years of the Senate, eight dams on the river were subsidized. Ditto with the development of the Hanford Nuclear Facility. He used his influence to save the B-52 but, as one who was near told it, "Maggie never blew his horn."

In terms of dollars, Magnuson was able to lure two World Fairs to Washington State, secure money for hatcheries and the tourist friendly Pike's Peak, and in his last year in office, pushed through $1.2 billion in emergency disaster relief following the eruption of Mount St. Helen's. The Lower Snake (River) Conservation Program is his, as is the Puget Sound Naval Shipyard.

In some cases, Magnuson gave Washingtonians more than they wanted. Federal funds for various Seattle transit projects were rejected by Seattle voters. But that was an exception. Usually the dollars were going toward a necessary cause. One meeting in his office was aimed at saving the Bremerton, Washington headquarters of the Trident submarine, one of two that the Defense Department had in its site to promote efficiency. Magnuson asked the officials how much they needed. The folks initially resisted but eventually obliged, at which time he ended the meeting by saying, "I guess I've solved your problem."

Magnuson did his work on social issues as well. During debate on civil rights legislation, he worked closely with Hubert Humphrey and Ted Kennedy to fend off poison amendments by opponents.

Magnuson arguably learned the art of the deal from another master. As a House member, he attended Speaker Sam Rayburn's exclusive "Board of Education" meetings which Texas Senator Lloyd Bentsen in saluting Magnuson four decades later would call "no better or more effective on-the-job training for public service."

LBJ and Magnuson - the two ultimate wheelers and dealers
Photo courtesy of Tom Keefe

By Magnuson's last term, he was in a position to trade in the Commerce gavel for Appropriations which a top aide, Gerry Johnson said "was not a hard choice for him." Enriching his state was his top priority. And boy did he deliver! Walter Mondale said he divided the loot "50-50. Half went to Washington State and half went to everyone else." He was only partially joking. It was said that one of every six dollars went to Washington State. That was not unlike the legacy of more nationally known chairs who succeeded him, Robert Byrd and Ted Stevens who also took care of their home states. Yet Magnuson also described himself as a taxpayer's friend.

When it came to the environment, Magnuson made the most of his Appropriations Chair as well. He amended The Marine Mammal Protection

Act to prohibit federal permit for crude oil in the Sound unless it is necessary for Washington State. In his speech before the Senate, Magnuson called the sound "a fragile and important asset," adding, "The waters of Puget Sound, and the attendant resources, are indeed a major national environmental treasure. Puget Sound ought to be strictly protected; its resources ought not to be threatened. Since tanker accidents are directly related to the amount of tanker traffic, there should not be an expansion of traffic over what now presently exists." In a sign of his leverage, the Senate and House cleared the bill within 24 hours. But there was one detractor who couldn't be ignored.

Washington Governor Dixy Lee Ray, a fellow Democrat but one whose lifelong advocacy was for atomic energy, was against the move. She in turn called Magnuson a "dictator" (and on another occasion told an aide that he wasn't "Jesus Christ") and sought to find a primary challenger in his upcoming re-election campaign. That failed and in an ironic twist, Ray lost her own primary, in large part due to her unabashed support of atomic energy. Meanwhile, Magnuson's fight to preserve Puget Sound continued and he would soon push through language limiting the size of tankers in the Sound.

It would seem that all of this activity might get under someone's skin, but Senate Majority Leader Mike Mansfield said Magnuson didn't "have an enemy on either side of the aisle," a fact reflected by the fact that colleagues elected him President Pro-Tem in 1978. What made him so popular? For starters, in the words of Gerry Johnson, he was "not a mean person." He gave all of his colleagues – Democrats and Republicans the utmost respect. Johnson paraphrased his boss's philosophy by saying your "enemy should be a high priority for converting to a friend." He gave the Republicans a fair share of the Appropriations and was especially close with New Hampshire's Norris Cotton and Milton Young, a North Dakotan with whom he entered the Senate the same year (Young had arrived two months later). Their cooperation was in the mutual interest of both states as the price of wheat impacted the Port of Seattle. Indeed, Magnuson was quite convivial – he loved telling stories.

Even as one of the biggest fishes in a heavily Democratic chamber, Magnuson treated the tiniest with due respect. Commerce aide Tom Keefe recalls being with Magnuson on the Senate floor managing the Interstate Horse Racing Act when it came time to vote. Cliff Hansen, a relatively junior Senator from Wyoming and a Republican approached and asked him what the vote was. Magnuson told him but addressed him as "Governor." That prompted Keefe to ask him why he called Hansen "Governor," to which Magnuson told him he once had been one. "But he's a Senator now," Keefe replied. But Magnuson explained that the title of Governor is higher than Senator and he wanted to address him with due respect.

**In his office and with his nemesis, Washington State Governor Dixy Lee Ray
Left photo courtesy of Tom Keefe; Right photo courtesy of the
University of Washington Libraries, Special Collections Divisions**

On another occasion, Magnuson was on the receiving end of a tirade from a first-term Senator, Wendell Ford of Kentucky over an appointment to the Federal Trade Commission who happened to be a former Magnuson staffer. Ford was resisting and warned Magnuson that as head of the Democratic Senatorial Campaign Committee, he was "trying like hell to re-elect guys like you." So Keefe, who had to arrange the meeting, said Ford was shocked into silence when Magnuson calmly replied, "Wendell, I don't take this stuff personally." Indeed, while it may be unheard of for a powerful baron to be strong-armed by a freshman, Magnuson didn't show it. Keefe says, he "never carried grudges or never tried to get even with people. Every day was a new day."

That led to another surprise about Magnuson. Given Magnuson's power and gift as a wheeler and dealer, he was not flamboyant. In fact, Keefe calls him "kind of shy on a personal level. He didn't have a ton of ego. He liked being a legislator. He liked getting things done."

For the most part, Magnuson's manners were second-to-none as a boss. Johnson recalls he had a big staff and being such an "active legislator . . . always hired really smart people." Yet he naturally had "high expectations for his staff." Johnson, calling his service to Magnuson "real work, hard work and complicated work," said "it wasn't summer camp," explaining that while he was "a very nice man and genuinely good-hearted person, he had high standards." Still, his appreciation for his staff was evident and the office camaraderie was good.

For a man who shunned the spotlight, Magnuson sure kept celebrated
company. After the divorce of his first marriage, he dated a covergirl, June
Millarde and an actress, Carol Parker. Early in his tenure, he decided to purchase
property in Palm Springs, California where he'd travel for seclusion on weekends
when he didn't have to be in Washington State. He got to know many celebrities
and even dated one actress, Toni Seven.

Keefe learned of Magnuson's link to the famous years after Magnuson had
left office while on a business matter. Barbara Sinatra, the famous entertainer's
wife, was seeking a grant for a center to combat child abuse and Keefe was in a
position to help. He flew to California and had dinner at the couple's home. "Ol
Blue Eyes" had been performing in Vegas but as the dinner was winding down,
Barbara asked Keefe to stick around. Sinatra had just left Las Vegas in his plane
and would be back in Palm Springs shortly. Though tired and curious as to why
Sinatra would want to meet him, he obliged. When Sinatra came in, Keefe told
him of his relationship with Magnuson at which time Sinatra said, 'Oh yeah,
Maggie. Jimmy Van Heusen's old buddy. He (Maggie) used to live up the canyon
next to Elvis. They were "chewing the fat."

Keefe was flabbergasted. What he would have given, he thought to see Elvis
and Magnuson "chewing the fat." Keefe immediately asked Magnuson's widow
about this and she confirmed it was true. When he pressed her as to why he had
never mentioned it, she replied "Maggie never bragged about who his friends
were."

Incidentally, the Keefe family's durability to Magnuson could easily have
been a microcosm of his tenure – not to mention the growth of the state. Keefe
called himself a third-generation Magnusonian. His aunt worked for him and his
grandmother was what Magnuson would call, "an FDR political boss who could
deliver Western Washington with a single phone call."

For years, the respect that Magnuson enjoyed from all also seemed to be
the case at home. His campaigns were effortless and he was usually assured
of getting in the mid-60s. But by 1980, things were changing. Diabetes gave
Magnuson a slower gait and his hearing wasn't great. His refusal to debate was
more fodder for Republicans. But in perhaps the most clever political ad of all
time, he said, "so I don't walk as fast as I used to. The meeting can't start until
I get there anyway."

Photo Courtesy of the University of Washington
Libraries, Special Collections Divisions

In almost any other year, it may've been enough. But 1980 was Reagan's year, and it helped Attorney General Slade Gorton, who contrasted the age by jogging from Seattle to Olympia to file his Senate papers, unseated Magnuson 54-46%. As returns from the rest of the nation showed Democratic casualties piling up prior to the polls closing in Washington, Magnuson said, "If this is a title wave, I don't want to survive it." When it became clear he had lost, Keefe recalls Magnuson surveying the room and fixing his eyes on one man in particular and saying, "Mitch, you're the only guy in the room who knows how I feel right now." He was talking to Hugh Mitchell, a former U.S. Senator who had taken his seat along Magnuson in 1945 only to lose it two years later in a landslide of similar proportions. But Magnuson's biographer, Shelby Scates, notes, "Tears fell. Magnuson was as composed as anyone" and Keefe, whose job it was to telephone Senate Majority Leader Robert Byrd with the news, was amazed than in defeat, he was composed enough to think back to the 1940s. He told close friends, "There is a time to come and a time to go and I guess after 48 years they decided to turn me out to pasture." But he proceeded to deliver a very gracious concession.

One half of the Maggie-Scoop legacy was gone. Magnuson died in 1989.

But the other half was alive and continued to thrive, and the love affair between Scoop Jackson and Evergreen State voters never diminished.

**Photo courtesy of the University of Washington
Libraries, Special Collections Divisions**

Henry "Scoop" Jackson (1912-1983)

Jackson may've been the original "New Democrat" before Bill Clinton made it cool. He advocated a muscular defense that previous Democratic Presidents had championed and was unmistakably a believer that America should lead from the world stage. On his death, *The Seattle Times* called him, "The Senate's most steadfast cold-warrior for three decades." But on domestic issues, no one could accuse Jackson of being anything other than a card-carrying member of the Democratic wing of the Democratic Party. So strong were his connections to Democratic interest groups – primarily labor that many believe, had it not been for his support of the Vietnam War, he may have succeeded in capturing the Democratic nomination for President in 1972.

Jackson's identity from cradle to grave was Everett, Washington. His parents would arrive there from Norway in 1898 and Jackson himself would expire in the town 85 years later.

As a boy, Jackson delivered newspapers and did it so well that the book, *Outstanding Environmentalists of Congress* said he was "reported to have set a local record by delivering 74,880 papers without a single complaint for non-delivery." But that's not how he acquired his enduring nickname. "Scoop" had been a comic-strip character who routinely succeeded in having others do his chores and, despite the fact that Jackson's work ethic was sterling, his sister felt it applied to him.

Jackson discovered his political aspirations early in life. Very early. In fact, he had told his teacher as early as the third grade that he wanted to be President. Harry Waddington, a *Herald* employee, recalled on his death that "while other delivery boys spent free time playing softball, Jackson always talked politics." At the time, that might have been an afterthought. But a bout with tonsillitis at twelve years old might have made that a reality. John Salter was hospitalized for the same ailment and he became skilled in running campaigns. Salter went to the other Washington with Jackson and served as his right-hand man for three of his four decades in Congress.

First, however, Jackson would attend law school at the University of Washington, become situated in the local welfare office, then be plucked up by a law firm. Before long, he was the Pierce County Prosecutor and in that office, acquired an easily explainable nickname: "Soda-pop Scoop" for never indulging in alcohol.

Jackson's first campaign slogan for Congress was, "Vote for a Man Who Has the Courage of his Convictions." It may have governed his principles throughout his entire career.

Jackson's election to the House at age 28 made him its youngest member (upon his death, only he, Claude Pepper of Florida, and Mississippi's Jamie Whitten, and West Virginia's Jennings Randolph had sat in the chamber as members of Congress when FDR gave his Pearl Harbor speech). Randolph joined Jackson in the Senate and at age 81, was still serving when Jackson died. He recalled how "Young Henry had a way of providing constructive leadership that was essential to the passage of legislation." One was the expansion of the Olympic National Park, which the book, *Outstanding Environmentalists of Congress* describes as "a mountain wilderness containing remnants of the Pacific Northwest rain forest, active glaciers, and rare elk."

If any year proved transformative to Jackson's philosophy, it was likely 1945. His visit to the Nuremberg concentration camp led him to see the horrors of genocide. Later in the year, as President Harry S. Truman's U.S. delegate to the International Labor Organization Meeting in Norway, Jackson saw, as his biographer, Robert Gordon Kaufman wrote, "the fears the Norwegians expressed about their Soviet neighbors," which "opened his eyes" (it was a near death recovery from a fever that kept him there so long). That year, House Speaker Sam Rayburn offered him the chance to chair the House Un-American Committee but, having voted against funding numerous times, he opted not to serve.

For a very junior Congressman, Jackson endeared himself to Truman. As early as 1948, the President wanted to name Jackson Undersecretary of the Interior but he declined. Beyond that, he supported nearly every aspect of the President's agenda, including his ambitious health care proposals and his North Korea policy. His rise in the House was taking shape as well as he won a seat on the Appropriations Committee as he entered his third term. That same year, he took a seat on the Joint Committee on Atomic Energy where he sided with pro-defense advocates by coming out in favor of the hydrogen bomb.

In those early years, Jackson lived in the same apartment building as John F. Kennedy near the Supreme Court and the pair would often walk to the Capitol together. Then-Congressman Estes Kefauver of Tennessee was another early and close friend and they would often spend Congressional breaks together until the Tennessean died suddenly in 1963 (ironically of the same heart ailment that would take Jackson's life two decades later nearly to the day).

Jackson's first Senate win in 1952 actually countered a nationwide Republican sweep but his opponent was a low-thought-of incumbent who brought Joseph McCarthy to Seattle to stump for him. But he never had to rely on his opponents' weaknesses again. His six re-elections were routinely won by more than 2/3 of the vote, and in 1970, it exceeded 80%. One-time Washington GOP Chair Mort Frayne, acknowledging "the well runs dry for us when Scoop runs," called him "the personification of a straight guy," adding that he "gets most of the Republican money when he runs." Legislative assistants in 1973 rated him "the single most effective Senator." At home and in the other Washington, that meant influence galore. Nationally, however, that could prove a menace.

For Jackson, being a hawk was nothing new. He advocated for major increases on atomic weaponry at the start of the Cold War, concerned about a "Communist menace" but also with an eye on jobs at Hanford. He was critical of the Eisenhower administration for not spending more on defense. After Sputnik, he accused them of underestimating the Russians. Jackson was suspicious until the end of the Soviet Union. He backed the first SALT Treaty only with modifications but refused to support the second. He endorsed Nixon's China policy. Like Magnuson, Jackson sponsored landmark legislation too. Jackson-Vanik prohibited "Most Favored Nation" status to nations that discriminate.

While Jackson's strong defense stands naturally won him many allies among the Senate's more conservative members (John Tower), it did not inhibit his respect with the body's liberals – Eugene McCarthy actually campaigned for Jackson's 1970 primary opponent on the Vietnam War issue. Jackson was exceedingly well-respected. For he was socially liberal and personal friendships transcended minor disputes on issues. In the fall of 1980, he spent numerous time in South Dakota stumping for George McGovern who ultimately lost his re-election bid. He did the same for Frank Church in Idaho. Peter Jackson, the Senator's son said Church "was always doing things that drove dad nuts (such as meeting with Castro) but, he loved Frank Church." And the respect was mutual. Peter says the only colleague Jackson "detested" was Bill Fulbright, not because they were opposites but because he was "a snob." He was the only fellow Senator Jackson ever said anything mean about.

Peter Jackson said Vietnam "challenged his (dad's) thinking in a way he didn't expect. Describing him as "a classic old war liberal - you fight them in a way you fight companies that try to take advantage of its workers." Still, it did not please some anti-war folks back home as Peter notes that protesters shouted obscenities at him during Earth Day celebrations back home.

Jackson's impact on domestic affairs was not limited. His Interior sub-committee chairmanship gave him a major role in shepherding Alaska and Hawaii to statehood. But his advocacy for those young states didn't end. By 1963, he was chair of the Interior and Insular Affairs Committee – a post he would hold longer than any other member and was in a position to ardently advocate for Indian reservations. This helped produce the Alaska Native Claims Settlement Act of 1971.

Jackson's crown legislative achievement may have been his sponsorship of the National Environmental Policy Act. This led to the creation of the Environmental Protection Agency, which Richard Nixon established by Executive Order. In a tribute to Jackson on the 100th anniversary of his birth, Washington Democratic Congressman Norm Dicks noted the Act "has been emulated by more than 80 countries." Dicks pointed out that "Scoop Jackson sponsored or co-sponsored the 1964 National Wilderness Act, the 1965 Land and Water Conservation Fund Act, the Redwoods National Park Act of 1968, the North Cascades National Park Act of 1968, and the Wild and Scenic Rivers Act of 1968," adding, "that was in just the first few years of his chairmanship." Dicks also cited the Alpine Lakes Wilderness Act of 1976 and ANILCA - the Alaska National Interest Lands and Conservation Act of 1980.

Photos courtesy of the University of Washington
Libraries, Special Collections Division

But it was Jackson's support of Washington-based Boeing's super-sonic transport, which ultimately failed, that earned him the moniker, "the Senator from Boeing," a nickname actually given to him by local Democrats who organized a challenge to him in the 1958 Senate primary because of his advocacy of a military buildup. Jackson had been a supporter of keeping the company in Seattle since his House days, when it had previously come under attack. Boeing meant jobs which is why Jackson was a staunch defender.

While Magnuson was a consummate deal-maker among his colleagues, Jackson had a gift for weaving together surprising solutions that would ultimately make for sound public policy. The Federal Lands for Parks and Recreation Act and the ABM (anti-ballistic missile system) would seem to have nothing in common, but one is actually a by-product of the other. The Parks legislation actually resulted from dismay by Seattle residents over Jackson's proposal to house an ABM facility at an area of Fort Lawton, a military base in the Puget Sound. Many residents opposed it and wanted to see the site used for a park. Jackson convinced officials to move ABM (by then faltering with his Senate colleagues) to a lightly populated area, and make the leftover military space part of a park. For the nation, the icing on the cake was that the Act would make funds available for many other cities to do the same.

Though a bachelor for his first 49 years, Jackson's wife Helen Hardin and his children, Anna Marie and Peter, became an integral part of his life
Photos courtesy of the Washington Secretary of State and the
University of Washington Libraries, Special Collections Division

His efforts were similar on Hanford. He backed a Columbia Valley Authority which would mirror the TVA. He backed a dual-purpose nuclear reactor at Hanford and passed the Northwest Power Planning and Conservation Act of 1980. Rights for Native-Americans made the priority list for Jackson as well. In

1970, he led to Senate passage complicated legislation that would give federal land to the Natives along with monetary payments by the federal government. While the House never took up the measure, Jackson's efforts set the stage for passage in the next Congress. Nationally, Jackson became known for his genuine interest in defense matters. After the Soviets successfully launched a rocket into space – Sputnik, Jackson called it "a devastating blow to the prestige of the U.S. as the best in the scientific and technical world."

Hempleman believes that one Jackson characteristic that earned him universal respect of his Senate colleagues was that "he wanted to know the facts and he wanted to make sure he had the facts right. When he wanted to see legislation passed, he was a master because he would compromise. When he compromised, he didn't lose. He saw that as a win. He was always willing to engage the (Republicans) and cross the aisle." Peter Jackson credits that as a major reason liberals, despite a few high-profile differences, held him in such high esteem. His longevity was such that, "he had worked with every member on one subject or another."

Jackson's influence even in his early Senate years was such that he was on JFK's short-list for VP in 1960, with Bobby Kennedy even telling the Washington State delegation that "Scoop" is my personal choice, and Jack likes Scoop," adding, "You've got to give us some pegs to hang our hats on. Go, go, go!" But he also indicated that balance issues might ultimately force JFK to go elsewhere and they surely did. Jackson loyalists recognized this as well. Washington State had nine electoral votes in at the time and Lyndon Johnson's presence on the ticket was needed to barely push Texas over the top.

Instead, Jackson gave the nominating speech for Johnson, whom he assured delegates would be Kennedy's "strong right arm."

Photo courtesy of Florida Memory

Jackson's responsibilities in national politics were already high. He was Democratic National Committee Chair that year and spent numerous time campaigning in the South. His aim was to convince voters hesitant about supporting Kennedy because of his Catholicism that if elected, he would not be taking orders from the Pope. The Kennedy campaign might have surmised that Jackson had credibility as a Lutheran and he would tell them, "I'm one of you." His appearances on "Meet the Press" and other national shows had impact. One person who especially felt it was Norman Vincent Peale, a rabidly anti-Catholic nationally known minister who ironically had authored the book, The Power of Positive Thinking. Jackson taking him on over the religious issue led to his career being temporarily derailed (Peale would later officiate at the wedding of Richard Nixon's daughter Julie to Dwight Eisenhower's grandson David).

Jackson hosted a big gathering for faithful Democrats during the long, tense Election Night that ended with Kennedy's election. Jackson had predicted a landslide and admitted himself stunned at the closeness of the race. Addressing reporters at around 2 a.m., one woman yelled out the question of why Nixon hadn't yet conceded. Jackson quipped he might be waiting for Lodge to do so for him (Nixon's running-mate had come under fire during the campaign for publicly suggesting cabinet appointments).

Remarkably, when Nixon did win the White House eight years later, he reportedly asked him to be Secretary of Defense. There was a reason for that. One quality that endeared Jackson to nearly everyone – from President's to foreign leaders and colleagues "The Kennedy's trusted him," Hempleman said. "JFK trusted Jackson. Bobby trusted Jackson (Teddy was a close personal friend). They knew where he was on every issue. They knew he had done his homework."

Hempleman recalls one call in the middle of the night. The angry voice on the other end said, "This is Lyndon. I want to talk to Scoop. Wake him up!" When Hempleman asked if he could tell him what it was about, Johnson snapped, "God dammit! The Russians have invaded Czechoslovakia!" (Jackson counseled patience). He had less use for Carter as the duo often tangled over his energy strategy. Conversely, Reagan was on the other side of the aisle but his respect for Jackson was equally strong (he may have hearkened back to memories of Jackson from the 1950s when Scoop was already a Senator but the 40th President was still a Democrat – both were anti-communist). Jackson prevailed on Reagan to appoint a Central American Commission and appointed members Jackson recommended (which New York Republican Congressman Jack Kemp suggested renaming as the Jackson Commission).

But that comity only went so far. During Jackson's 1982 re-election, he bashed Reagan's economic policies. "The President reminds me of a softball coach whose team is behind 35-0 in the middle of the second half. He's called the same play 15 times and he's gained a total of six yards. And believe it or not, he doesn't want to change the game plan. Well, were going to change the game plan for him in November."

Jackson sought the White House twice, in 1972 and 1976, and one of his failings on the Presidential front was Vietnam, where he stood to the right of every major Democratic candidate.

**Stumping during the 1972 campaign
Photo Courtesy of the University of Washington
Libraries, Special Collections Divisions**

In a column about Jackson written years later, Bergen compared campaigning for him in Madison, Wisconsin in 1972 to "campaigning for Benjamin Netanyahu in present day Cairo." Jackson was dependably pro-civil rights (though anti-busing) and pro-labor, even opposing Boeing's quest to become a "Right to Work" company. He boasted of enormous support from the Jewish community for his support of Israel and Soviet Jewry, and of Native-Americans. But Bergen also noted impediments.

In 1972, his campaign collapsed after Florida, an early primary state. Many saw the entrance of Hubert Humphrey as a prime factor since they had many of the same support bases. But Jackson had expectations that 1976 would be different.

Jackson had a superb campaign organization and led the pack in both money raised and personal contributions. He excelled at one-on-one campaigning. But that was no longer practical. Bergen said "adjusting his words to fit a sound bite was an alien concept," also noting his failure "to claim credit for measures he was largely responsible for." Nor did Jackson set the world on fire with his speeches. The joke was when Scoop Jackson gives a Fireside chat, the fire falls asleep." Jackson did have a sense of humor. One day, as he was campaigning, the floor caved in. Jackson quipped that he was "standing on one of the planks of the Republican platform." But his opportunities to use that were few and far between.

Photo Courtesy of the Henry M. Jackson Foundation

Disdain from the hard-core left was evident. One former McGovern backer expressed a common sentiment: "When Goldwater lost in 1964, he retained a veto over the 1968 candidate. That's one of the reasons Nelson Rockefeller couldn't make it. We're going to have that veto in 1976 and we're going to use it against Jackson."

But perhaps more fatal to Jackson's chances was his decision to skip Iowa and New Hampshire, a mistake he would be far from the last to make. Post-Watergate, voters were looking for a fresh face, and while Jackson did win Massachusetts in New York, Carter finished him off in Pennsylvania. The experience he would've provided would've been stellar. And even in victory, the Carter administration never fully recognized the value of Jackson's knowledge. On one occasion, Hamilton Jordan told Tom Foley it wasn't necessary to reach out to Jackson because "we whipped his ass in the Pennsylvania primary." For an administration that saw a number of foreign policy debacles, that was probably a mistake.

Images courtesy of ronwadebuttons.com

For all his power, Jackson's biggest give to Evergreeners was just being a regular guy. Dr. Abe Bergman describes his "shock" when during a routine visit to the other Washington, they received a note at their hotel saying Jackson wanted to meet them for lunch in the Senate dining room. He later learned that Jackson was a constituent connoisseur. That's what he did. Bergman, who later became an advisor, says Jackson "did not meet every voter in Washington State, but he sure made the attempt." Scoop's daughter, Anna Marie Laurence, notes that trait also extended to their homelife. She recalls her dad would grill her dates, sometimes for as long as a half-hour and that he would spend as long as it took (in one case 2 ½ hours) on the phone helping her with homework. She recalls he flew home once just to take her to debutante. Beyond that, however, when their mom would be cooking and ask him to run to the grocery store to buy milk, he would stop to talk to grocers. In restaurant, it would not be unusual for him to go into the kitchen and chat with the help.

On a personal level, Jackson displayed tremendous loyalty and compassion for his staff members and their families. John Hempleman worked for Jackson from 1960 through 1972, and again on his Presidential campaign four years later. He calls him "like my second father." It didn't matter that Hempleman was a freshman at Georgetown. "He gave me challenging tasks and convinced me I could do them. Whenever I had doubts, he'd tell me I could do it."

As a measure of Jackson's insistence that staffers follow their conscience, Hempleman recounts telling him during his Congressional campaign (which Jackson prodded him into undertaking) that he felt it was time for U.S. operations in Southeast Asia to wind down. Hempleman wanted to make that point on the campaign trail but told Jackson he didn't "want to embarrass you." Jackson's reply: "You've done your homework and you've made your decision." But Jackson's next words were something he wasn't prepared for and they would impact him ever since. Jackson told him, "You've got your head screwed on straight." From Scoop Jackson, that proved the highest compliment possible. Incidentally, Jackson also persuaded another staffer, Tom Foley, to file for an unwinnable House seat an hour before the deadline. Foley won.

At Jackson's insistence, Hempleman often stayed with him when his wife and young family returned home to Everett, Washington. He jokes Jackson drove him to work (which sometimes proved a harrowing experience) and always loved to talk during the ride.

How far did Jackson go to embrace his staff? Far enough to marry one of them.

Jackson, who once upon a time had been viewed as Washington's most eligible bachelor, exchanged vows with his secretary, Helen Hardin, in 1961, whom he had met in an elevator on her first day of working in the nation's capitol as a staffer for New Mexico Democratic Senator Clinton Anderson. He was 49 and she 28 (he continued residing in an apartment with his two sisters). At one point years earlier, Jackson, when confronted with rumors that he had tied the knot, issued an emphatic and unambiguous denial: He was "not now married, never have been married and has no plans to be married."

Helen joked after their two-week honeymoon in Hawaii that "half the State of Washington appeared to be in Hawaii," and Jackson did indeed interrupt their honeymoon at least once to attend a briefing. During his Presidential campaigns, The Seattle Times called Helen his "ever-cheerful sidekick." They would have two children and Peter would call his mom "the linchpin to Scoop's success.... She breathed life into his unfinished work." Helen established a legacy of her own, taking on a major role in the release of Jewish migration from the Soviet Union, which led to her founding and co-chairing the Congressional Wives for Soviet Jewry in the 1970s. An ally and close friend in that endeavor was Mrs. Natan Sharansky.

When he died, Helen used his left-over campaign funds not for herself, but to establish the Henry M. Jackson Foundation. The mission statement is to "assist public officials, diplomats, and journalists in addressing international problems and funds scholarships, visiting faculty, and other programs at the University of Washington's Jackson School of International Studies.

After the Presidential bid, Jackson returned to the Senate and was literally active until the last possible moment. He never forgot about Everett. The fall before he died, he attended his high school reunion.

In September 1983, having just won a seventh sixth-year term with 70% of the vote, Jackson was giving a press conference following the Soviet shooting down of a plane that killed 250 people. Jackson called that "a dastardly, barbaric act against humanity." But he was noticeably tired and that evening, an aortic aneurism killed him.

Outpourings were near universal. President Reagan called the Jackson home that evening, vowing to rename the new U.S.S. Rhode Island The U.S.S. Scoop Jackson (Helen christened it the following year). 60 Senate colleagues attended the funeral. Three Senate colleagues - Kennedy, Daniel Patrick Moynihan and of course Magnuson, delivered eulogies. And on that sad occasion that marked his funeral, Magnuson's poignancy unmistakably signaled the end of an era: "We served together in the House and Senate nearly half a century," he said. "We worked as a team shoulder-to-shoulder. Now that team is dissolved."

Photo via Argenta Images

And while the Democratic Party of today may not be in sync with Jackson's philosophy, a prominent, albeit vanishing breed are proud to call themselves "Scoop Jackson Democrats." Three decades after Jackson's death, it's a term that still endures.

The Legacy

Maggie and Scoop are no longer with us but arguably, two like-minded individuals have moved into their seats. Patty Murray and Maria Cantwell have represented the Evergreen State together for more than a decade - like Magnuson and Jackson, they came to the chamber eight years apart, and with each being 42 upon taking office, only a few years older than both Maggie and Scoop, they have the prospect of serving just as long. Murray may one day chair Appropriations while Cantwell, like Jackson, concentrates more on Resources issues. Whatever the case, both have great role models. And the state will be forever grateful for their work.

CHAPTER NINE

When the Interior West Was Won By Democrats: Church, Moss, and McGee

Historic Tidbit: Did the war terms "hawk" and "dove" originate in a CBS television news debate? It was March of 1965, a month after the Johnson administration had launched a series of counter-attacks in retaliation for an attack on American soldiers at Pleiku. Democratic Senators George McGovern and Gale McGee appeared on a CBS Reports debate moderated by Charles Collingwood entitled, "Vietnam: Hawks and the Doves." McGovern was solidly anti-war even at that early date while McGee was giving the benefit to the administration. McGovern said later he believed this to be the first time the terms had been used in the war context. Meanwhile, McGovern and McGee, close friends, continued their debate of sorts throughout the nation, often debating at college campuses on McGovern's "Vietnam Teach-ins."

In 1961, when Senators Church, McGee, and Moss traveled to Africa, President Kennedy asked them to let his brother Teddy, then 28 and not yet a Senator, tag along to get foreign policy experience for what would be an inevitable political career.
Photo courtesy of Robert McGee

D id you hear about the man who asked Billy Joel if he could play the piano with him at a concert? Joel stunned everyone in attendance by saying yes. How about the high school student who asked Kate Upton to the prom? She too said she'd check her schedule. When one contemplates the idea of electing Democrats to federal office from Idaho, Utah, and Wyoming, it seems likely that the struggle they face may illicit similar feelings. A mentality of, you'd have to get really lucky or something. But it wasn't always like that. In fact, once upon a time, the Democratic Party in these three states, while not dominant, was quite competitive. In fact, three men—Frank Church, Frank Moss, and Gale McGee held U.S. Senate seats in these states for more than a couple of years.

Church, Moss, and McGee gave their respective states one Democratic Senator from the mid-1950s through their defeats in the mid-1970s, and the latter two were basically as surprised as everyone else by their losses on election night in 1976. Church's loss four years later was less unexpected. As recently as 1960, the Republican bent of the states was barely more than a lean. Kennedy hit 45% in Utah and Wyoming and hit 46% in Idaho.

For a time, Wyoming may have actually been the most Democrat-friendly states and Idaho was perhaps the most Republican. In the latter, Goldwater was just 5,000 votes behind LBJ in 1964, making it the closest of the 44 states he lost. Conversely, he took just 46% in Utah and 43% in Wyoming. But by 1968, the Democratic flirtation was over. Humphrey was eviscerated in all three states and no Democrat has exceeded 40% in any of the three states since. A more typical ceiling is the low 30s, which in some cases doesn't even happen. In Utah, Republican presidential candidates have exceeded 70% five times since 1972.

Even after these losses locally, Democrats had no problem holding their own—for a time anyway. Though Senate seats would prove elusive in Idaho and Utah (John Evans almost won back Church's seat for his party in 1986), both states elected two Democratic members of Congress simultaneously as recently as the 1990s.

Oddly enough, it's Wyoming that's had the longest federal drought, as the last Democrat to win a federal race was Teno Roncalio in 1976. When he retired two years later, he was succeeded by Dick Cheney. But the state came so very close on two separate occasions to changing that.

In 1988, incumbent Malcolm Wallop, who was 20 points ahead in the summer, came within 1,300 votes of being upset by a populist saloon owner named John Vinich. And Barbara Cubin survived her 2006 re-election bid, conducted with much clumsiness, by about 1,000 votes. She wisely retired two years later and while her opponent, Gary Traunertried again, he fell way short, losing to a new Republican nominee without flaws in a state that gave McCain a big margin.

Statewide can be different, but barely. And lately, rare. Neither Idaho nor Wyoming had a Republican Governor from 1970 through 1994. Utah had two Democratic chiefs from 1964 through 1984. Wyoming elected another Democrat, Dave Freudenthal, in 2002, revealing voters who said they had no problem with him but were not about to elect a Democrat federally. But even that has proven to be the exception rather than the rule. Idaho has not been governed by a Democrat since 1994; and Utah, ten years before that. Moreover, not only does the GOP control every statewide office in those states but its control of the legislature in each chamber well exceeds a two-thirds super-majority.

Kennedy at the White House with Senator's Church and Moss (photo courtesy of the John F. Kennedy Presidential Library and Museum) and with Senator Gale McGee during a visit to Wyoming two months before his assassination (photo courtesy of Robert McGee)

One Democrat, Jim Matheson, has managed to hold his House seat since 2000, including in 2012 by the narrowest of margins (768 votes), but the Matheson name is holy in Utah—his father Scott was one of the Democratic Governors I cited. Republicans have tried to redistrict him out of office so ferociously over two separate decades that he is well known even well outside his Salt Lake City base.

For history's sake, Moss, McGee, and Church are some of the most underrated Senators in a variety of areas – Moss on health care related issues, McGee on foreign affairs, and Church on the building his state. All were men with large families who possessed unquestioned integrity, a deep sense of what was right, and a following guided by their infectious personalities. More importantly, the careers of each embarked on pursuing causes far larger than their own careers. But electorally, much of their appeal in Republican leaning states had to do with their youth and outsider status, which enabled all to oust GOP incumbents who assumed they were in the same mistakenly secure position.

Church meeting with constituents (left) and with Bethine, the love of his life who strived to continue his legacy long after his untimely death
Photos via the Frank Church Papers, Special Collections and Archives, Boise State University

McGee's birth continued an uncanny tradition to the Irish-Scotish family. It was on St. Patrick's Day. His father and grandfather had been born the very same day. Though McGee was born in Lincoln, Nebraska, he grew up in the smaller town of Norfolk and came of age during the Depression. Politics might not have been the first thing on his mind. His mother wanted him to become a minister because, as McGee's son Robert would recall, "her other two sons were a doctor and an undertaker and she wanted to have her bases covered." Instead, one could say he split the difference as politics would provide him a pulpit of sorts and help people at the same time.

That said, the thought of public service didn't come entirely out of thin air. Taking first place in a competition as a boy brought him to Washington D.C., and, observing the Senate in session, convinced him that he wanted to become a U.S. Senator.

First came education and marriage.

It was while earning his teaching certificate at Wayne State that he met his bride, Loraine, the daughter of a country doctor in Iowa. They married shortly after graduation and would raise two sons and two daughters. Loraine became McGee's true partner in politics and in life. Though her advice was only informal, she did regularly write a column for Wyomingites about the happenings of Washington. It was called, "A Line From Loraine." She also traveled with him on every trip. Why? McGee was a diabetic who at one time wasn't expected to live past 40 and as Bob notes, "she learned to recognize his symptoms of insulin reaction almost before he did."

From Wayne, it was on to the University of Colorado to earn a Masters. Then it was on to the world of academia. McGee received his Ph.D. in history from the University of Chicago after writing his dissertation, "The Founding Fathers and Entangling Alliances."

McGee and his handsome family on a Christmas card
Courtesy of Robert McGee

Eventually, he settled as a professor at the University of Wyoming where he taught, among others, future U.S. Senator Alan Simpson. He also headed the Institute of International Affairs, a center that would see its prestige skyrocket under McGee's tenure. Harry Truman would address students. So would Henry Morgenthau. Eleanor Roosevelt visited the campus as well and the McGee's hosted her for lunch at their home. Academia also led to an acquaintanship with another well-known colleague with whom he'd serve, George McGovern who would be teaching in South Dakota during that time.

Though McGee had held no office prior to his Senate run, he had strong connections as a staffer to the legendary Wyoming Senator Joseph O'Mahoney, taking a leave from the University to go on his payroll. O'Mahoney may have recognized his star-potential because he asked McGee to work out of the Washington D.C. office to learn the ways of the Senate. Local Democrats spotted it as well. They tried to get him to seek elective office as early as 1950. McGee demurred, preferring to wait until the climate for Democrats had improved. His timing proved awesome in 1958 as President Dwight Eisenhower was facing the second mid-term of his Presidency, a term known today as the "six year-itch."

McGee became a Senate candidate that year and attacked the Republican incumbent he was challenging, Frank Barrett, for "a 19ᵗʰ century outlook who did not get good appointments for Wyoming citizens." He attacked the administration for "bankrupt leadership and faltering economy." Eisenhower had been giving Democrats ammunition through a series of scandals that forced the resignation of his Chief of Staff, Sherman Adams. But Barrett was hurt by the Soviet launch of the Sputnik rocket and his inability to articulate a strategy that would calm American fears about an increasingly inevitable "Cold War." All of this was critical in enabling McGee to unseat Barrett by 2,000 votes.

While McGee acknowledged that his "victory can be attributed in part, but not entirely to the Democratic trend," he also surmised that "frank liberalism must also have had some appeal too." But he may have been selling his personal attributes short and that was his immense popularity as a professor. He excelled at public speaking, a trait that would separate him from most of his colleagues even in a chamber referred to as "the most deliberative body" (*Esquire* in 1967 called him one of the best speakers in the Senate). But that attribute also helped make McGee literally among the most beloved professors on campus to the point that Robert noted that students "would be practically hanging by the rafters for a chance to enter his class." That gave him a faithful base among current and former students, many of whom had returned to their home-towns and eagerly hit the trail for McGee.

Still, when he announced his candidacy, McGee was seen as enough of a long-shot that the University did not want him to a leave to mount his campaign. So Robert recalls he'd "get in a station wagon" at the end of a school-day and would be back the next morning for his class. He used his connections to get Mrs. Roosevelt, who had accepted a McGee invitation years earlier to deliver a lecture at the University, to raise money for him. Harry Truman came to Cheyenne to stump for him. A young Massachusetts Senator named John F. Kennedy did the same, flying into Laramie on his plane, "the Caroline." And Senate Majority Leader Lyndon Johnson, who grew to admire McGee's capabilities as an O'Mahoney staffer, lent his presence as well. Johnson had been hoping to bolster the near parity between the two parties in the upper-chamber and told voters he would place McGee on the Appropriations Committee, an appointment that Robert called "unprecedented" for a freshman. He delivered and it would give him an opportunity to do wonders for a small and relatively young state.

As late returns pushed McGee into the lead, he and his wife held up a photograph of the McGee's taking part in a Truman style pose of the early edition of the *Rocky Mountain Daily News*. The headline said, "GOP Win Seen in Wyoming." He would win two more elections fairly comfortably. And as a counter to the axiom that "no one is indispensable," the Institute of International Affairs, which McGee had labored hard to turn into a nationally known mecca on that subject, disbanded shortly after.

**McGee and his wife in a Truman style pose the morning after his
Senate election. Later, meeting with the former President himself
Photos courtesy of Robert McGee**

McGee provided two major footnotes to history. One had national ramifications while the other was internal. Nationally, it was standing on a chair begging his delegation for four votes to put Kennedy over the top at the 1960 convention (a year earlier he said Johnson would make "a honey of a president," likely a reciprocation of Johnson's promise). But to his Senate colleagues before and after, McGee has an unsung legacy as well. The August recess is now as common as apple pie but, that wasn't always the case. McGee's rationale was, "It is time to stop kidding ourselves. It's time to face the facts of legislative life." At first, many senior members of the body were resistant to the idea but slowly, it picked up steam. A test-run was tried in 1969 and was enacted into law the following year as per the Legislative Reorganization Act.

Moss had sought office before - Utah's Governorship - but didn't win it. A native of Holaday, Utah, Moss was born to a man who would gradually attain hero-like status throughout the state. Jimmie Moss was a high school teacher in Utah who rose to become, "the father of high school athletics." But his personality was infectious and the elder Moss became beloved by Utahans of all generations. It is quite likely that Moss was a chip off the old block. In the ultimate compliment all politicians dream of, Val Halamandaris, a longtime Moss staffer, would say of his boss, "to those who monitor the Washington scene, he became known as one of the three or four most powerful men in the nation; he was a role model, teacher, inspiration, and friend."

First came the background. A stellar student at the University of Utah, Moss went east to attain his law degree from George Washington. But he couldn't let go of a woman from the University with whom he had also been acquainted in high school. Her name was Phyllis Hart. So Moss proposed a solution to that problem – literally. He gave a wedding ring to a college buddy and asked her to present it to her in his stead. She readily accepted and after the ceremony, she joined him back east. The Moss's were married 69 years and had three sons and a daughter.

Moss's first job was in the General Counsel's Office of the Securities and Exchange Commission. Following World War II where he served in the Air Corps, he became Salt Lake County Attorney.

Moss, Photo via the Frank Moss Collection

Launching his Senate run, Moss had the good fortune to put his name up in 1958 on the advice of his father and office-staff. But he was even more fortunate to have been around amid the divisions of McCarthyism. Two-term Republican incumbent Art Watkins had chaired the committee that ultimately decided to censure Joe McCarthy, which brought an angry third-party challenge from ex-Utah Governor Bracken Lee. On top of a far-right philosophy, Lee was known for refusing to pay his income tax.

Moss told Utahans their Senator could be more effective as a member of the majority and said Lyndon Johnson as Majority Leader had promised him a key committee assignment.

The result was that Moss squeaked into the seat with 39%. He told *U.S. News and World Report* after that, "My opponents preferred to campaign on personalities. The voters expressed their resentment at this." But Moss's dynamism worked to his advantage as well. Halamandaris, one of the many students Moss mentored and hired, recalled Moss being "such a great campaigner that anyone who met with him could see that he was as honest as the day was long. If there was a quintessential Mormon, he was it. Honest, hard-working. He was an Eagle Scout." The latter was true in the literal sense, for Moss was an Eagle Scout. Additionally, the statewide network that his dad had amassed worked like magic for Ted as many voters backed him as a testimonial to his dad. Be that as it may, those same attributes led Moss to easy wins in his first two subsequent re-elections, in 1964 and 1970.

Halamandaris used two words to describe Moss: "joyous and judicious." He remembers him as "someone who was always happy, fun to be around. People loved being around him. He had a magnetic personality. I don't ever remember seeing him glum." Moss, he said, "always saw the glass full. (He) believed we as a country could do anything and we as human beings, working together, could do anything." Apparently, his colleagues recognized that as well. Moss was known by fellow Senators as "Mr. Integrity," and Halamandaris said that by putting his name on a bill, he "could get half the Senate or more."

Moss had a soft-spot for both the environment and staffers. More national parks became a reality as a result of his legislation than any Senator in history – a record that holds true today, including the Canyonlands National Park, the Golden Spike Historic Site and Capital Reef National Park to name a few.

He would amass almost the same reputation on healthcare. He shepherded more health care legislation into law than virtually any other colleague. In fact, on the latter, his expertise was so strong that Claude Pepper, a Florida Congressman who was generally viewed as the father of senior issues, deferred to Moss. His philosophy was, "It is hell to be old in this country. It is a simple truth for most of our elderly." And he would go to almost any length to change the system.

Moss was a high-ranking member of the Senate Committee on Aging who held nearly 40 hearings on quality-of-life issues all across the nations. But it didn't stop there. Committee staff often posed as Medicaid patients and uncovered illegal billing practices. Not wanting to be outdone, Moss himself got in on the action. As Halamandaris pointed out in a chapter on Moss for *Profiles in Caring: Advocates for the Elderly*, Moss one day put on old clothes, let his whiskers grow," and "was taken to the roughest areas of New York – East Harlem, Fort Apache in the Bronx, and into the den of drug dealers on the Lower East Side." These were known as "Medicaid Mills" and the result was exposing mind-boggling Medicaid fraud and legislation that produced top stories on evening news programs and the network news. Tangibly, it led to the creation of the Office of Inspector General in the Department of Health and Human Services.

Moss's imprint on the policy aspect of health issues was endemic as well. He was an original sponsor of Medicare and Medicaid and was key to expanding dental and eyeglass coverage. Among the other sweeping health related legislation he pushed through: eliminating mandatory retirement, increasing the income limits for working Americans on Social Security, and home health care. On the latter, he was more influential than any other Senator. He once said, "You only have to ask yourself which you would prefer. To be uprooted and placed in a nursing home or to remain at home with nursing and other medical needs, therapeutic and social services delivered to your door." Moss also proposed early hospice legislation. His work in that area continued even after he left office. In 1977, Moss and Halamandaris authored a book, *Too Old, Too Sick, Too Bad* designed to shed light on the inequities in the world of healthcare for the elderly.

Moss (second from left)
Official White House Photograph

Regarding staffers, Halamandaris called Moss "the kind of man for whom everyone would love to work." One person who did get lucky in that regard was Chris Matthews who in those days was struggling as a police officer (when Matthews tried his own hand at politics, losing a Congressional primary in his native Pennsylvania, Moss helped him land back on his feet by getting him a job with his good friend and colleague, Maine Senator Ed Muskie whom Moss had helped establish the Senate Budget Committee). Matthews spared nothing when it came to praise for Moss. Calling him "a western progressive," Matthews said, "He protected Utah's natural beauty. He believed in the positive role of the American government. He was a man of great personal character and a wonderfully kind boss."

Halamandaris, a fellow Utahan just coming off the presidency of Boys State, was another Moss hire. He was evocative of a common Moss trait – befriending students and taking them under his wing. For Halimandaris, it was convincing him to go to his alma mater for law school, George Washington University. He did but soon enough landed a job with Moss. He stayed with him for 15 years, eventually rising to Chief of Staff.

One person Moss did not have a soft-spot for was his Senate leader, Lyndon Johnson and that started before Moss even made it to Washington. Johnson had promised Moss badly needed money - $5,000, for a price. That Moss would never vote against the oil industry, particularly a repeal of the oil depletion allowance. Moss didn't see the soundness in that proposition and, according to Halamandaris, told him to go to hell. When this author asked if those were the words he used, he replied that it was "pretty close." Moss complained and was given $2,000. But for Johnson, the line of demarcation had been past.

The repercussions came on the so-called committee pledge for unlike with McGee, his colleague to the North, Johnson did not deliver. In fact, Moss did not land any of his top three choices. Instead, he landed on what Halamandaris described as "the dregs of committee assignments, the Senate Interior and Public Works Committees."

For his part, Halamandaris said Johnson personally liked Moss, "but liked him better when he did what he wanted." But that was Moss in a nutshell. "Too honest." In other words, "not always adept at playing the political game." But it wasn't just Johnson for whom Moss refused to play the game. In 1963, Moss was seeking a seat on the Senate Appropriations Committee. The panel's chairman, Richard Russell of Georgia, agreed to give him a seat, but only if Moss would agree to oppose any attempt to weaken the filibuster, a key tool for southerners to continue blocking civil rights legislation. Moss refused and was denied the post.

Moss in 1965 spoke in favor of legislation put forth by his Alaska colleague, Ernest Gruening, that would authorize the conducting of population studies and dispense information on family planning (i.e., birth control). "To postpone action in this vital area of human procreation," Moss said, "is to invite, indeed even to push, disaster onto the shoulders of those who follow us. Inaction of this generation might well force future generations to live and respond as animals caught in a labyrinth of too many numbers in too little space with too few resources to sustain life with dignity."

Church at age 32 was the biggest Cinderella story. In fact, more than two decades later as he prepared to leave office, one colleague, Democrat Abe Ribicoff of Connecticut, noted how few childhood dreams come true but Church, having made it to the Senate, proved the exception. A look back signifies he was taking steps to prepare even as a youth. Friends and relatives would joke about his studious nature. His cousin Harmon recalled later, "My mother used to say that the problem was that I was reading comic books and Frank was reading *The Atlantic Monthly*." At age 14, Church had a letter to the newspaper published arguing that that United States should stay out of war. Church won a four year college scholarship to Stanford (which he selected) by topping 108,000 entrants to win the American Legion National Oratorical Contest. His speech was called, "The American Way of Life." Though his education was interrupted by the war (where he served as a military intelligence officer in the Chinese-Burma theater), Church got his degree and stayed at Stanford and received his law degree in 1950.

The remarkable thing about Church becoming a loyal Democrat was that his parents were stern Republicans. Church's hero in fact was longtime Idaho Senator William Borah, an isolationist and chair of the Senate Foreign Relations Committee.

Like Moss, Church had made a single attempt at office once before and lost (the Idaho Legislature), and his run for the Senate in 1956 was initially thought to be a similarly uphill quest. But after a cancer diagnosis in which he was given months to live (a last-minute persuasion by a physician to try an x-ray treatment ultimately cured him), he learned to adopt the creed that "life itself is such a chancy proposition that the only way to live is by taking great chances." At first, he practiced law and taught public speaking at the local junior college. Then came the Senate race.

Forget the general election: when Church entered the Senate race he wasn't even favored to win the primary. His opponent was a familiar name to Idahoans - former Senator Glen Hearst Taylor, who had been Henry Wallace's running-mate in 1948. This made Taylor sour to many Democrats. But Church traversed the state and played up his support of the Hells Canyon Dam which Taylor opposed. He edged Taylor by 200 votes but didn't receive a concession. Instead, Taylor charged irregularities.

**Church's assets included a handsome young family
and a magnetic presence on the stump
Photos via Frank Church Papers, Special Collections
and Archives, Boise State University**

Church was certified the winner but again, was not favored in the general. But incumbent Herman Welker was so closely identified with Joe McCarthy that he was called "Little Joe from Idaho" (curiously, both were dead less than a year later). In an awesome display of ticket splitting, Church won big even as Eisenhower was waltzing in the Gem State. Church was a master of defying expectations. A proud son of Boise, Idaho, he won a $4,000 American legion prize in high school for his speaking ability (no small potatoes in those days). He used the money to attend Stanford.

Church was the youngest Senator at that time. In fact, he looked so youthful that he was often mistaken for a page. One day, a woman approached him and said, "I understand one of you page boys often gets mistaken for Senator Frank Church," to which Church replied, "Yes, ma'am. One of us often does." But there was no mistaking the fact that Church was a Senator and with the office came a sporadic rise. It meant playing a serious role in a major part of the first Civil Rights Act to clear Congress; giving the 1960 keynote speech to the Democratic National Convention; a serious, albeit late-starting Presidential campaign; and winning three more terms. No other Democratic Senator from Idaho had even won a second.

Hells Canyon was so important that Church made it the topic of his maiden speech in the Senate floor. He was also among six Senators who voted with the

South to house the Civil Rights bill in the Judiciary Committee rather than on the Senate floor in exchange for passage of Hells Canyon. And in 1962, Church went to the mat for another dam project—the $186-million Bruce's Eddy. "If they strike out Bruce's Eddy," he said, "I shall hold the Senate floor for as long as GOD gives me the strength to stand."

Bethine Church became nearly the force in Idaho politics as her husband, often being referred to as the Gem state's "third Senator" Photo via Frank Church Papers, Special Collections and Archives, Boise State University

The three Democrats from Idaho, Utah, and Wyoming thrived by staying with their party on social issues (the Equal Rights Amendment) but at the same time giving a local flavor to their service. The trio stayed with their roots by hewing closely to their states' local needs. All opposed gun control and championed water issues. They worked closely together and usually had a powerful ally in their interior neighbor, Majority Leader Mike Mansfield of Montana. McGee and Moss would regularly host one another in their respective states and McGee and Church would occasionally carve out weekend family time in Fenwick Island, Delaware (Ed Muskie would do the same on occasion). And in an anecdote that would prove more than a footnote for public service, the three men were part of a delegation to Africa in 1961. This was just after JFK had taken office and, upon learning of the trip, he called McGee (who was leading the delegation) and asked him to bring Teddy (then 28 and not a senator) along. The idea was to groom the younger Kennedy to gain international exposure for a political career that was obvious would be beginning sooner rather than later. Garry Wenske, a top Church aide who now serves as the Executive Director at the Frank Church Institute at Boise State, says the men, fairly new colleagues, truly bonded and also took a tremendous liking to Teddy. A Congressional report was issued on the trip.

But the trio was also binded by another tie: automobiles. McGee was among the first Senator to buy a yellow Mustang convertible. Within a few months, Moss and Church followed and Robert McGee recalls the base of the Senate steps (where members were allowed to park in those days) being illuminated by the three cars.

Church and Moss sponsored the first legislation to expand Medicare to provide hospice care. It didn't pass in their time but did become law in 1982. Church followed Moss as Chair of Aging and pushed through a Social Security cost-of-living adjustment (including a 20% increase in 1972 and 11% in '74) as well as a capital gains exclusion for sale of residences. Wenske credits his work on behalf of senior citizens as "another key to his election success." Even in retirement, the bond continued. After leaving office, Moss, McGee and ex-Oklahoma Republican Senator Henry Bellmon founded a consulting firm, Moss, McGee, and Bellmon.

Abandoning their party on high-profile issues was rare but far from harmful because on at least some occasions, their constituents and home-state GOP colleagues took similar stands. Moss's colleague for most of his tenure was Wallace Bennett, whose son Robert later held his father's seat for three terms. Bennett backed the Civil Rights Act. McGee's service overlapped for a brief time with Milward Simpson, the father of Al. He had opposed the Civil Rights Act (on the grounds that he had signed a measure into law as Wyoming's Governor) but did back the Voting Rights Act. None of these Republicans voted for many elements of the "Great Society," but voters even in these let-government-do-less states didn't seem particularly concerned.

Moss near the end of his tenure
Photo courtesy of the Deseret News

Moss, meanwhile, was not content to rest with having delivered monumental changes on two major areas. He would also become a zealous consumer watchdog. As chair of the Commerce Committee's Consumer Safety Program, Moss was the second prime Senate sponsor on a bill with Washington's Warren Magnuson to regulate warranty enforcement (ironically, California Congressman John Moss, a relative who was also part of the class of '58 was the chief House sponsor), which also played a role in the establishment of the Consumer Product Safety Commission. Along with Magnuson, he was responsible for cigarette warning labels and taking ads off television. He sponsored the Poison Prevention and Toy Safety Act, nutritional labeling, and, according to Halamandaris in *Profiles in Caring: Advocates for the Elderly*, took the lead role in establishing "standardized warranties so that no manufacturer could avoid the responsibility of standing behind a product." He gave increased latitude to the Federal Trade Commission. He also pushed through legislation creating the Office of Coal Research as well as minimum safety standards for mines.

Locally, he immersed himself in water and environmental issues, writing a book, *The Water Crisis* to inform Americans of air pollution and water management. Internationally, he was known for his advocacy of nuclear disarmament. And for bettering people's lives, he was simply daring. He took an unusually early stand against apartheid which as Halamandaris notes was nearly a quarter of a century before the rest of the world began to take notice.

Later in his career, Moss had finally made up for lost time in terms of stature. After the 1970 election, which he won with 56%, his colleagues elevated him chairman of the Steering Committee, the third ranking elected position in the Senate. And he finally attained the chairmanship of the Aeronautics and Space Committee. From that post, Moss championed a robust space program that would accentuate the necessity of researching findings from outer-space, and the cracking down on government waste.

McGee made a name for himself in the middle of his first year when he answered the call of Clinton Anderson, his New Mexico colleague who was leading the fight to kill the nomination of Lewis Strauss, President Eisenhower's pick to lead the Commerce Department. Anderson was not a member of the Senate Commerce Committee and needed to enlist a colleague who was. McGee took up the fight. But he also made the fight very much his own. His staff worked long hours investigating leads and interviewing witnesses. Joined by O'Mahoney and Oregon's Wayne Morse, the nomination was defeated.

While paling in comparison to Strauss, McGee also joined other colleagues that year in expressing regret over the confirmation of another nomination: Clare Booth Luce to be Ambassador to Brazil. McGee, along with all but 11 colleagues, voted in favor of Luce. But when he heard of her remarks taking aim at Morse – who led the fight to stop her, McGee and several others said they were sorry for having done so. He called it potentially harmful to have a diplomat "who might make the sort of intemperate statements Mrs. Luce just made."

McGee backed his party on social matters but took more of a middle ground on Vietnam not because he was enamored with the war, as his son said, but because he "wanted to make sure we had a good exit." He didn't want to "turn his back on the President and go with the flow." On Korea, he urged caution, even after the seizing of the USS Pueblo and the capture of 86 crewmen. He delivered a speech on the Senate floor which Robert Byrd included in his *History of the Senate* book. He called it one of the 100 best speeches ever given in the Senate.

While often overshadowed by other Senators, McGee's expertise on foreign affairs was extraordinary. In his third year in the Senate, he became chair of the Appropriations African Affairs sub-committee. Unlike Moss, McGee's relationship with LBJ was first-rate. Johnson offered him the position of Ambassador to the U.N. when Arthur Goldberg resigned and in a phone call, even dangled the prospect of Secretary of State before him. It remains how serious the latter offer was as it was suspected that the President was using his famous "Johnson treatment" to gain a concession on another matter. Either way, McGee was content to remain in the Senate and Johnson soon left office. But even then, he wasn't finished with McGee. Shortly after his Presidency ended, Johnson asked McGee and his wife to stay at the LBJ Ranch and help him sort out the Vietnam War for his memoirs. The two stayed up most of the night (LBJ reportedly asked McGee to run his Presidential Library but his interest was non-existent).

McGee enjoyed a close relationship with Johnson
Left photo courtesy of the Chuck Morrison Collection, Western
History Center, right photo courtesy of Robert McGee

McGee's outsized influence extended to the Nixon Presidency. The President named him to a Congressional delegation led by Warren Magnuson that was the first to visit China following Nixon's first-of-a-kind visit by a President. Remarkably, Nixon directed Spiro Agnew to stay out of Wyoming during the 1976 election cycle (McGee was seeking his fourth term) and Henry Kissinger honored McGee's request to speak at the University of Wyoming on foreign policy. Because Kissinger was the Secretary of State at the time, this could not be billed as a political trip but it still signified the deep bipartisan respect of McGee.

At no time did McGee make clear he understood the complexities of foreign affairs when he opposed an amendment by Kennedy to cut aid to Chile until the nation approved its record of human rights. "All of us," he said, "seem to be playing secretary of state on the floor of the Senate at a moment when these questions are deeply involved in diplomacy." Kennedy's amendment was adopted 47-41.

With all of McGee's gravitas in the area of foreign affairs, why wasn't his name more of a household word with the likes of Bill Fulbright and Wayne Morse. Because, to hear his son tell it, he never cared about who received the credit – on any political endeavor he undertook.

Another little known fact about McGee is that for much of his tenure, he was the number one target of the extreme-right John Birch Society. Much of it had to do with his tenure at the University of Wyoming when, as chair of the Institute of International Affairs, he invited the tempestuous Alexander Kerensky. But McGee also never hesitated to speak his mind (including very strongly against censorship of textbooks, etc), and that often caused him problems with the board at UW. Beyond that, McGee never gave the staunch anti-communist folks any ammunition to believe he remotely supported their views but he did lead the first delegation of UW students to the Soviet Union and visited a number of churches in Moscow, including one that was hidden in a warehouse (his son jokes some people were actually practicing religion). Upon his return, he shared his experiences with Wyomingites.

This was just as the McCarthy era was taking shape and it made him the recipient of hate-mail. Some of the mail was quite vituperative but McGee actually joked about it. As if to prove the saying that if one says something enough, folks will believe it, McGee's wife later told her boys that not only did some residents of their hometown (Laramie, Wyoming) not want to associate with them, but the children were not permitted to play with the McGee kids. Later, *Parade Magazine* ran a piece on hate-mail in which McGee was featured.

Though McGee was not one who sought the limelight, his dress did gain him recognition in the most flattering way. Edward Brooke, a Massachusetts Republican known foir his dapper attire, said he joined McGee and Oregon Republican Mark Hatfield as being "sartorial dandies."

Locally, McGee opposed federal strip mining and clear cutting, which were particularly important issues in his community. The National Committee on Food Marketing was his. But McGee's crown jewel was the Postal Service

Reorganization Act, which demanded that the pay of postal workers be in line with other federal workers. Ultimately, it privatized the post office rather than serving at the hands of the President.

But he didn't need any luck in holding the seat for two subsequent elections. Wyoming State GOP Committee Chair John Wold was McGee's general election opponent in both 1964 and 1970, garnering 46% and 44% respectively (for the second race, Wold was a freshman House member). He acknowledged fifty years later that Nixon did little to help him, saying, "We weren't at the top of the list for him." As for his direct opponent, he said, "Gale is a guy that I always had a high regard towards. I didn't agree with him politically but he was sincere."

By the time of McGee's final re-election campaign, Republicans used his chairmanship of the Post Office and Civil Service Committee to make an issue out of postal service satisfaction. But the chairmanship gave McGee foresight on other issues. It was he who introduced the Voter Registration Act of 1973 which would allow potential voters to register with post office credentials. Bill Clinton signed a descendant of the bill into law in 1993 (with the place of registration becoming motor vehicle agencies) and McGee's wife Loraine was present. The Senator had died a year earlier.

Before it became clear how seriously Watergate had inhibited Nixon's ability to govern, McGee took a middle ground. In June of 1973, he associated himself with a column by Washington Post columnist Joseph Kraft stating "the President can continue to govern while the Watergate investigation goes forward," while adding, "there is no need to sprint through the hearings as is now argued by those who used to favor a total cover-up." McGee asked that it be placed into the *Congressional Record.*

McGee's experience following the Saturday Night Massacre was evocative of the fast-moving developments that consumed the whole affair. He was traveling from Laramie, Wyoming to Dallas, Texas to address a United Nations event. When he deplaned, he was met by 'an assemblage of reporters." Spiro Agnew had resigned the previous weekend and McGee thought they were asking for his reaction to that. When McGee made his remarks on the Senate floor a few days later, he joked that he had his press secretary research the number of times he had "summoned the media to make statements about developments in the Watergate case." He figured that "six times he made the mistake of being inexact." He added, "that shows what can happen when one gets on an airplane. It is a kind of shattering experience to think that one can ride on a plane for a couple of hours and not learn that tumultuous events are happening on the ground."

McGee's respect in the area of foreign policy cut across partisan lines. Above, he can be seen with Secretaries of State Henry Kissinger and Dean Rusk and with Chinese Premier Zhou Enlai. McGee was among the first Congressional delegation to China following Nixon's 1972 visit Photos courtesy of Robert McGee

And even while championing local issues, McGee didn't hesitate to go against the majority of Wyomingites when he felt the causes he advocated for were in the national interest. During the oil embargo, for example, McGee ignored pleas from his constituents not to lower the speed limit to 55.

Another trait that made McGee so popular as a Democrat in a Republican state was his notes to constituents on special occasions (birthdays, graduations, etc). This was not unique among members of Congress, as it was a strong tool for putting their names before voters. But the fact was that the Senator and his wife authored these notes themselves, and that was a true rarity.

Wallop's campaign skills did not set the world on fire but he was out and about while McGee stayed in Washington. Regulation was an issue. T.A. Larson, author of *The History of Wyoming*, credits the National Taxpayers Union for effectively branding McGee as the "taxpayer's best friend" for championing benefit increases for federal workers. Another issue was the diminished impact of labor; as the *The Washington Post* noted, the race "brought unions and right-to-work in direct battle with each other." Wallop was also seen as an environmental moderate based on a previous campaign for Governor.

On Election Day, Ford was winning the state big and Wallop took 55%. Robert McGee recalled having "the unenviable task" of watching the returns in Washington with McGee's staff, some of whom were former students who had served him for his full 18 years (McGee was a very generous boss and treated them like family). He acknowledged that his dad began the campaign so heavily favored that his "campaign apparatus" was not as strenuous as it should have been. Still, as a symbol of respect McGee had built up, the first prominent person to telephone McGee after his defeat was Richard Nixon. Though no longer President, Nixon relied on White House telephone operators to find McGee at the Holiday Inn in Laramie. When he returned to Washington to complete his term, the first person to visit him was George H.W. Bush, then head of the CIA, with whom a friendship had gone back to 1971 when McGee was named the congressional member on the UN delegation during the Fall General Assembly meeting.

McGee post-Senate, as Ambassador to the Organization of
American States with Secretary of State Cyrus Vance
Photo courtesy of Robert McGee

McGee's gestures as a former Senator made it easy to see why he was so respected across partisan lines. Shortly leaving office, President Carter had named him Ambassador to Organization of American States. McGee invited Wallop to the swearing-in. He wasn't about to let an old rivalry get in the way of his learning to make the appropriate contacts to help Wyoming. Ex-Secretaries of State William Rogers and Kissinger attended as well. In his new role, McGee lobbied hard for passage of the Panama Canal Treaty. He served for the entire Carter Presidency and into the first year of Reagan's.

McGee's fidelity to Wyoming was so strong that on a rare occasion that it was questioned, he fought back. Six years after he left the Senate, a new county clerk didn't want to reissue his Albany County-5 Wyoming license plate because his primary residence was Maryland. McGee turned to a local attorney, Rodger McDaniel for help and McDaniel was able to reinstate the license. He is now writing a separate biography of the Senator. When he died in 1992 at 77, Nixon wrote Loraine a note. He told her Gale always put his country before politics.

The shift in Wyoming from liberal to conservative was a storyline that has played out many times in the interior west many times since then, including four years later with Church in Idaho.

The thing that was so remarkable about Church taking a front row on the 1957 Civil Rights Act was that he had initially told his wife, "I've got a lot on my platter. It's not something I'm going to get involved over my head with" (Idaho had few African-Americans). But he soon sensed history was calling. "This is my fight too," his wife, Bethine, recalls him saying. "I'm A United States Senator and this is the only right way for the country." Robert Caro in *Master of the Senate* recalls him "drafting, often at home on a legal pad," his thoughts on the jury trial amendment which he thought could be made more feasible eventually if mixed juries were required. Therefore, his contribution was that the words, "any citizen" competent enough to serve could be invited to do so (Robert Caro in Master of the Senate noted that it would exclude illiterates, mental incompetents and convicted criminals"). "Bethine, who served as his counsel throughout, agreed. She later said Church knew, "it was a tremendous challenge, and Frank never loved anything as much as a challenge."

Church had introduced the amendment with his Wyoming colleague, Democrat Joe O'Mahoney and Estes Kefauver of Tennessee. On the Senate floor, Church said it was "designed to eliminate whatever basis there may be for the charge that the efficacy of trial by jury in the Federal courts is weakened by the fact that, in some areas, colored citizens, because of the operation of State laws, are prevented from serving as jurors. We believe the amendment constitutes a great step forward in the field of civil rights. We believe also that it can contribute significantly in forwarding the cause to which most of us are dedicated— the cause of enacting a civil rights bill in this session of the Congress…We need not impair the right to jury trial…to better protect the right to vote.…The accused may still be fined or imprisoned, and his punishment may even be more onerous than in the case of criminal contempt, but here he holds the key to his own cell.… This amendment re-establishes, through the whole fabric of the Federal law, equal treatment for those who stand accused of violating injunctions issued by Federal courts. Under the present law, a citizen charged with criminal contempt is generally entitled to trial by jury, unless the action is brought in the name of the United States. Why a man accused by any other party of criminal contempt should have the question of his guilt or innocence determined by a jury, while the same man, if accused by the Government of having committed the same act, should be deprived of his right to a jury trial has neither been explained nor justified.…"

The amendment passed 51-42 and in an oral history project in 1981, Church recalls" that John Kennedy was leaving the Senate through the revolving doors on the first floor or the Senate wing, and my wife was coming through at the same time. And he said through the door as they passed one another, 'Frank did a great thing today. He enabled me to, he made it possible for me to vote for the jury trial.'"

In the Senate, Church became one of the most important 20th-century figures on foreign policy. His speech-making ability was remarkable, and his early and aggressive outspokenness against Vietnam led LBJ to call him Frank "Sunday School" Church. There was a reason for that. As a junior Senator, Church had tangled with LBJ once before in his first months in the Senate, and the Majority Leader retaliated by keeping him out of his circle for six months. But soon all was well and the pair grew close. Still, Church labored hard against Vietnam. While he voted for initial appropriations, he did have serious misgivings by 1966 that he cited on the Senate floor. "No nation," he said, "not even our own, possesses an arsenal so large, or a treasury so rich, as to damp down the fires of smoldering revolution throughout the whole and awakening world."

This stance would again pit Church against the President. And unlike LBJ's method of roughing up other Senators, with Church things appeared to be personal. One day, after Church opposed the administration on a bill, Johnson summoned Church to the White House to explain himself. Church explained that noted journalist Walter Lippman opposed the bill and that he was quite respected by Idahoans. Johnson's reply: "Frank, next time you want a dam in Idaho, you call Walter Lippmann and let him put it through."

By 1970, Johnson was no longer in the White House but Church's misgivings about Vietnam continued. Church-Cooper was a bi-partisan amendment designed to cut off funds for operations in Cambodia and Laos. Church viewed as nonsense critics charge that the amendment would tie the President's hand. "By enacting the amendment, we would be strengthening the President's hand, helping him overcome foot-dragging by his own bureaucracy and foreign-allies." The amendment passed the Senate 58-37 though a weaker version was ultimately signed into law by President Nixon. Beyond Vietnam, Church chaired the Subcommittee on Multi-National corporations that investigated companies like ITT in Chile and Lockheed in Japan (the Japanese Prime Minister was forced to resign as a result). The Church Committee investigated covert operations by the CIA and FBI during the war. One would be hard-pressed to name any other committee with higher esteem during and since.

In 1974, in the wake of high gasoline prices, Church proposed an amendment to cut off aid to the 13 member-nation OPEC. His rationale: it "makes no more sense to me that...we should continue to allocate over a quarter of a billion dollars in our money to these countries than it would make for one to be caught by the throat by an assailant and stuff money in his pocket while being choked to death." The amendment, which allowed for aid to resume to any individual nations who made a "good-faith" effort to address the high prices was tabled.

Church had a scholarly theory on Watergate which he delineated to a Delaware audience. "The Vietnam War," he said, "had begat Watergate. The war itself had been a grotesque creation of a foreign policy based on secrecy, deception, and an arrogant refusal to let Congress play its rightful role. Under the Nixon administration," he continued, "we have come full circle. If dirty tricks were acceptable in foreign policy, why...were they any less so in domestic affairs?" His opinion was that "Watergate could not have happened but for the moral and political perversion generated by Vietnam."

Unlike McGee who shunned the limelight, Church eagerly sought it. But as biographers LeRoy Ashby and Rod Gramer pointed out, "it was not a mere reflection of vanity...he recognized the press as a shaper and mirror of public opinion." On a personal level, Wenske, who worked for Church for ten years, notes having served a number of members of Congress but that "Frank Church was the best." He calls him "the most high-quality guy, the most honest, and most caring." Church, he adds, was "brilliant," to the point that he could be so deep into policy that he was "often in his own world," to the point that staff would drive him. While he was "often in dreamland, humming to himself," Wenske notes that was just a result of his deep thought.

In 1976, Church decided to throw his hat into the wide open field for President. But he got a very late start. Primary season was already underway but, so was the Church Committee, which led press aide Bill Hall to acknowledge not wanting "to blow his biggest assignment yet in the Senate." Still, Church gave it his all, speaking of a current "leadership and fear." His first priority, he said, would be "the restoration of the federal government in the eyes of the people" and he cited his "twenty years of experience" for making that happen. From the time he announced, Church vowed to use his late entry to his advantage saying it was "never too late – nor are the odds too great – to try. In that spirit the West was one and in that spirit I now declare my candidacy." While Church did win like-minded states (his own, Montana, Nebraska, and Oregon), Carter was ultimately too far ahead to catch. Church was interviewed for the number-two slot but it went to Mondale at which time Church told reporters that he had known he wouldn't be the pick because lightening had just stricken his Bethesda, Maryland home. And lightening, he said, "never strikes twice."

On environmental issues, for a time all three Senators found themselves caught between their personal views and their state's industrial interests, which came to a head during consideration of a wilderness bill. Moss backed a committee amendment by Colorado Republican Gordon Allott to require Congressional approval of any wilderness designation, a defeat for committee chair Clinton Anderson. He took Moss aside and said, "If you want to support your enemies go ahead but it doesn't make a lick of sense." Moss said, "I have tried to help the wilderness bill all the way through. I don't believe that the cattle and mining crowd helped me at any time and I have not done so badly without them."

**During his 1976 Presidential campaign
Photos via Frank Church Papers, Special Collections
and Archives, Boise State University**

But Church gradually found himself leading on environmental matters. In 1961, Interior Chair Clinton Anderson had asked him to become the Senate floor manager of a controversial wilderness bill. Church hesitated because he was coming up for re-election and was fearful of angering the lumber and miners. But Church ultimately agreed, leading Anderson to write, "Frank had the character and guts and he accepted the challenge that I thrust on him." It hardly stopped there. Other major wilderness legislation he passed: the Sawtooth National Recreation Area, the Craters of the Moon National Monument, the Owyhee Canyonlands and the Boulder White Clouds, though it took more than three decades for protections of the latter two to be fully codified by law).

As impressive as the trio's survival was, even their talent could not last in perpetuity. Moss fell to Utah's Orrin Hatch, who portrayed himself as a fresh face and latched on strongly to Ronald Reagan. In doing so, Hatch found a way to turn Moss's greatest asset, his seniority, against him. He asked the voters, "What do you call a Senator who has been in office for 18 years? You call him home." At the same time, *U.S. News &World Report* identified Moss as among the Senators least likely to lose. Moss was unseated by an almost identical margin to McGee's. But Halamandaris made clear that in no way did that impact his sunny disposition. Describing him as "very philosophical," Moss said he'd "figure out another way to serve." That, he did.

Frank Church
is the man who
has the knowledge
the abiding sense
of ethics the anger
and the wisdom to
lead this nation out
of its difficulties.

until you've heard
Frank Church

Images via ronwadebuttons.com

After his defeat, Moss alternated between practicing law in Salt Lake City and in Washington, D.C. In 1980 he joined another Mountain area Senator who had been ousted over ideology - Colorado's Floyd Haskell - in backing Independent John Anderson for President. But it was charity that consumed a good portion of his time. One endeavor was chairing the Museum of National Art at the Smithsonian. But perhaps worthwhile was founding, along with Halamandaris, Caring Incorporated, a non-profit organization whose mission is "to honor and promote the values of caring, integrity, and public service." Who inspired them to do so? Mother Theresa. Her motto was "If you use the power of caring, that's one word that runs through all religions."

Moss's son Brian tried to unseat Hatch in 1988 but by then the Senator was so entrenched that he prevailed with two-thirds of the vote. McGee lost by a nearly identical margin to Malcolm Wallop, which set the stage for successful "New Right" challenges that brought even bigger names and allowed the GOP to take control of the Senate in 1980. Church was one of those casualties.

Church had the kitchen sink thrown at him yet remarkably came darned close to winning. The battle began as early as January 1979 as Church was one of five Senators targeted by the National Conservative Political Action Committee, which also successfully took aim at Birch Bayh and George McGovern (Tom Eagleton narrowly survived and Alan Cranston's race wasn't even close). It was called the "Sagebrush Rebellion."

More than one factor accounted for what Church was up against. For one, he was ardently pro-choice. More detrimentally, he shepherded the Panama Canal Treaty which was heavily opposed by Idahoans. Though not yet chair of Foreign Relations, 78 year old John Sparkman of Alabama was not in a position to undertake such a vigorous task. So prescient was Church's mind that when Senate Majority/Minority Leader's Robert Byrd and Howard Baker would approach the White House with compromise amendments to the Treaty, in many cases it was based on Church's language or ideas. Church's closing argument on the Senate floor was, "A vote against this treaty represents a vein attempt to preserve the past. It represents a futile effort to perpetrate an American colony in Panama against the wishes of the Panamanian people." Wenske said Church knew that the Treaty was deeply unpopular in Idaho (the estimation was that 25,000 Idahoans voted for Symms because of it), but he thought it was the right thing to do. It was not unlike his earlier opposition to the Vietnam War, also an unpopular position in Idaho, but he had time to educate his constituents about that (Oregon Senator Mark Hatfield once validated this by calling Church "so far ahead of his constituency that anything he did on this subject was an act of courage."

Ironically, another thing that hampered Church's ability to earn votes was that he was performing his dream job in Washington. When Church finally ascended to the chairmanship of the Foreign Affairs Committee, the amount of time required to devote to it kept him in the nation's capital rather than campaigning. Wenske cited the many hours spent on hearings on the SALT agreement (Vice-President Walter Mondale called him "the most important man in America" on that issue. There was the Taiwan Relations Act, which had the goal of protecting Taiwan after Carter recognized Beijing. And in 1979, over the opposition of conservatives and some Democrats, including Washington's Scoop Jackson, Church traveled to Cuba in 1979 where he succeeded in releasing 60-80 political prisoners. Incidentally, disagreements with Jackson in no way impeded their friendship. Representing neighboring states, the pair worked long and hard together on many natural resources issues and Jackson stumped hard for his colleague in 1980 because, as the Senator's son, Peter Jackson said, "he loved Frank Church."

Church did try to maintain his appeal by opposing gun control and supporting local water rights, both of which were of critical importance to Idahoans.

The interesting thing is, with the exception of the Kennedy administration, Church's Presidential support scores, even when a Democrat held the White House, were not particularly high. In 1964, when the Democratic Party's popularity was at its peak, Church supported Lyndon B. Johnson 63% of the time. By 1968, it had diminished to 29%, just a point higher than his support of the Nixon Administration in 1972 and 1973. Meanwhile, Steve Symms was an apple farmer who was serving his 4th term in the House. His ad urged voters to "take a bite out of government." Symms had some personal vulnerabilities, which may have kept the vote close. In the end, the margin between the two was just 50-49% as Symms prevailed by 4,000 votes among 233,000 cast.

In any other year, Church would've held his seat. But as one of Church's sons said, "Once Reagan hit 70% [he actually took 66%] his odds of survival were too long." Having realized that fellow liberals Bayh, McGovern, Gaylord Nelson and Warren Magnuson, to name only a few, had also gone down, Church remarked that he would at least be going out in "good company." It's not that any one issue doomed the Senators but conservatives were more vocal in framing the battles as ideological and one of more government versus less. In the years since, Democrats have seen openings, only to be stymied by the times. All involved land to some degree, as the federal government owns large portions in these states, where suspicion of the federal government runs deep to which attempts at gun control undoubtedly contributes. Other issues are case-by-case. In Wyoming, for example, the increase in federal grazing fees led some to declare an initiation of a "War on the West," which hurt Democrats even in years that were more favorable to Democrats nationally. In Idaho, monuments were an issue. As for Utah, *The Almanac of American Politics* theorizes that the growing influence of the Mormon Church, big families, and a feeling that a 1950s lifestyle is still possible may doom a bigger-government culture. Guns also no doubt play a role.

Sadly, Church's retirement did not last long. The cancer he had beaten three decades earlier returned, and claimed Church before his 60th birthday in 1984. Ted Kennedy and George McGovern visited his bedside. His biggest monument in Idaho may be the Frank Church River-of-No-Return Wilderness, the largest in the lower 48 states. Wenske says that "had he lived longer, he would no doubt have played a major foreign policy role in a future Democratic Administration."

At several recent Democratic National Conventions, Bethine Church, the late Senator's wife, announced her state's delegate choices during the roll call that officially nominates Presidential standard bearers, Before announcing the total, she ended one with the statement "we will come back." It's hard to imagine this happening any time soon.

McGee died at 77 in 1992. Moss, the oldest of the trio, spoke at his funeral. He would live another decade, to age 91. Matthews was on hand to deliver a testimonial.

Unlike the mid-20th century, the GOP lean of Idaho, Utah, and Wyoming is clearly incredibly imposing. Should Democrats give up? No. That's not what democracy is about. But they may have to wait—a long, long time. Or hope that lightening strikes. For it may take a Todd Akin-like scandal to send votes their way and even this would lack a guarantee. Alternatively, they could get comfortable with a good Smokey Robinson set. Because winning is "Gonna Take A Miracle."

Chairing the esteemed Church Committee (left) and meeting Sadat.
To Church's left is a young Delaware Senator named Joe Biden
Photo courtesy of the U.S. Senate Historic Collections

CHAPTER TEN

Ribicoff: Most Distinguished Nutmegger and Heir To Many Footnotes in History

Historic Quote: "It's not the Pope I'm afraid of, it's the Pop." - Harry Truman as JFK was about to be nominated for President in 1960.

Image via ronwadebuttons.com

Were I ever to name a "Nutmegger of the Century," Abe Ribicoff would undoubtedly be the man. More than any other individual from Connecticut, Ribicoff impacted the tone and progress of the state. As a Senator, Governor, and Congressman (not to mention cabinet Secretary), Ribicoff served Connecticut for 38 years and presided through some of the state's era-shaping times. But besides his honesty, leadership abilities, and solid progressive accomplishments, he had many at the time personal quests that made him, though he couldn't know it at the time, a major footnote to history.

One was his Kennedy connection. The two had served in the House together from neighboring states (Ribicoff's election came in 1948, two years after the future President's). And Ribicoff spotted the potential in his colleague in no time. Ribicoff himself explained it. "In 1950, I said that Kennedy would be the first Catholic president of the United States. In Worcester, at the Massachusetts Democratic Convention of 1956, I proposed Jack for vice president. I nominated him in Chicago." In that speech, he asserted Kennedy "would have wide appeal because he is a middle-of-the-roader." He added "Southerners would like his position on most matters."

And, get this! Upon turning down JFK's offer to be Attorney General, it was Ribicoff who suggested he consider Bobby. As Ribicoff told it, JFK replied, "You're crazy, Abe. I don't think the people would stand for it to appoint my brother." Ribicoff replied that "whenever you've got a problem, you automatically turn to Bobby for his advice. You have to put him in a prominent position where people take it for granted that when you have a problem you're going to consult with him, because his judgment means a lot to you."

That alone merits Ribicoff a true place in history. But it doesn't come close to ending there.

Ribicoff's next major brush with national fame came via putting another national aspirant's name in contention. For political watchers, Ribicoff may have bellowed among the most famous utterances in 20th-century history. As the infamous violence ensued at the 1968 Democratic National Convention in Chicago, Ribicoff, who was placing George McGovern's name in nomination, angrily glared down at Mayor Richard Daley and bellowed, "If George McGovern were President, we wouldn't have Gestapo tactics in the streets of Chicago." The line was replayed over and over and still stands out as a highlight of Election '68. As members of the Illinois delegation yelled for Ribicoff to "get down, get down," Ribicoff replied, "How hard it is . . . how hard it is to accept the truth." But the vituperativeness continued as Daley let loose, hurling words which allegedly were, "F—k you, you Jew son-of-a-bitch."

Ribicoff helped sell Kennedy's candidacy to political figures who harbored major doubts, including ex-President Harry S. Truman
Photo courtesy of Jane Ribicoff-Silk

The ruckus didn't win Ribicoff unanimous backing from his home delegation either. Norwalk Congressman Donald Irwin who lent Ribicoff his badge to get onto the podium, had angry words for his Senator the next morning which ended with, "I hope they mace you." Future Congresswoman Barbara Kennelly, whose father John Bailey was the Democratic National Chairman, was on hand and joked, "I suppose, being the national chairman, he might have wished he was a Senator from another state." But Ribicoff's Senate colleague, Joe Tydings of Maryland, who ended up seconding McGovern's nomination, called it "a very important public confrontation on the convention floor."

Years later, Ribicoff said he didn't regret a thing. "It was something that had to be said, and it was something that was important to be said. And, I would do it all over again because I thought that what was going on was absolutely the wrong thing to happen." His daughter, Jane Silk, echoed that but added that he believed it had impact. "He felt that he had gotten the best of Daily's brutal suppression of dissent during the convention - which ultimately tarnished the city's image."

The Chicago episode may not have helped Ribicoff, who was facing re-election in Connecticut in '68, and he surely had fences to mend. But he did and held his seat with 54%. When McGovern did win the nomination four years later, he offered Ribicoff the number two slot but was turned down. "I didn't lust for that type of office. I didn't want to run all over the country doing the chicken circuit and making political speeches, and I liked the Senate," he told TheHartford Courant. His daughter Jane had a different take. Even with close friends, her dad, she said, "never liked being second-best. He enjoyed being his own man. That is why he left" his position of Secretary even when his close friend Jack Kennedy was President. But 36 years later in a *New York Times* op/ed, McGovern would cite another reason for Ribicoff saying no. He was about to get married and, "I just can't cancel a honeymoon and take on a national campaign."

Ribicoff standing beside Kennedy at opening day
Photo courtesy of the John F. Kennedy Presidential Library and Museum

But Ribicoff would provide yet one more major footnote. In the late 1970s, President Carter wanted to send American warplanes to Egypt and Saudi Arabia. Many were against it, particularly those who, like Ribicoff, were strongly pro-Israel.

The Senator took the view that the Middle East peace process, then in its infancy, required working together. As such, he asked Sadat if he would be willing to take part in "a full discussion on how to achieve a real peace without preconditions."

Sadat said yes and the sale was approved, leading Jimmy Carter to give Ribicoff the credit for both the sale and the historic handshake. "We would never have induced President Sadat to come to Camp David had it not been for that vote," Carter said.

Ribicoff had served Connecticut for four decades. He won a seat in the Connecticut House in 1938. After his stint in the U.S. House, he put his odds on a Senate seat. But it was 1952, Eisenhower was taking Connecticut big, and Ribicoff lost to Prescott Bush, the future President's father. The margin was just 3,000 votes.

Ribicoff rebounded by winning the Governorship two years later, beating incumbent John David Lodge. Many attribute the 3,200-vote margin to an Election Eve appearance in which Ribicoff sought to address anti-Semitism which many felt he could fall victim to. "In this great country of ours, anybody, even a poor kid from immigrant parents in New Britain, could achieve any office he sought, or any position in private or public life, irrespective of race, color, creed or religion."

An anti-speeding crusade was among Ribicoff's shining successes. It mandated 30-day license suspensions for drivers convicted of speeding. Traffic fatalities via speeding were at a high, and 10,346 licenses were suspended for speeding. In 1955, it had been just 372. Ribicoff chaired the Governors' Conference Committee on Highway Safety which produced a report that, among other things, ordered each state to "make a survey of its deficiencies," "plan an assault on all phases of the problem and establish priorities for action best fitting its needs." Other directives included the extension of driver training, standards for licenses, and a look for "glaring weaknesses." The mission took a toll on Ribicoff's popularity but he was undeterred. "Unless public officials have the guts to see it through, nothing will work," he said. "We need tough, hard measures if we are to save lives."

That Kennedy and Ribicoff would become natural allies during their early careers might seem a misnomer to some. Colleagues and New England neighbors they were but at first glance, they had little in common stylistically or in terms of personality. Ribicoff was born to Polish Jewish parents (his father was a factory worker) while JFK grew up in privilege. Ribicoff worked at the G. E. Prentiss Company in order to earn money for NYU (a Prentiss promotion would later take him to the University of Chicago) while the Kennedys were often vacationing abroad. And Ribicoff would settle down with a bride at 21 while the future President at that age was already cementing a reputation as a "playboy." But the two hit it off and Ribicoff, always a strong judge of character, immediately saw potential in his younger colleague. And of all of his footnotes, that would prove yet his biggest contribution to history.

In his '56 convention speech that placed his New England neighbor's name in nomination for the vice-presidency, Ribicoff literally inserted John F. Kennedy's name into every sentence. His speech went, "John Kennedy of Massachusetts is a great Democrat. John Kennedy of Massachusetts is a seasoned campaigner and a successful candidate every time he has run for public office. John Kennedy is something new. John Kennedy brings the vigor and youth and fresh breeze that blows through this great nation of ours. John Kennedy has a voice and personality that appeals to independent voters. John Kennedy has a personality that will appeal to many Democrats and his record shows that he is universally successful in making converts in the Republican ranks, too."

When Kennedy did reach the White House four years later, he unambiguously expressed his appreciation to Ribicoff. He would be the new Secretary of Health and Human Services, where his most notable accomplishment was the elimination of a requirement that folks receiving Aid to Dependent Children have one child rather than two. By 1962, Bush was retiring. Ribicoff was considered the odds-on favorite to succeed him. In fact, the election was supposed to be such a runaway that, as the saying goes, they could have called it off. But Republican Congressman Horace Seely-Brown used Ribicoff's national stature against him, attacking him not so much on where he's been but where he might be going, posing the question, "What does he really want – Governor, the Supreme Court, the Senate, or what . . . Does he want the people to support him forever."

Seely-Brown also benefitted from his own appeal with blue-collar workers to his advantage, and he accompanied it with his own catchy gimmick. Rather than hand out standard campaign literature, Seely-Brown would offer potential voters, many of whom he greeted in factories during a shift-change with potholders bearing his name. "People throw campaign cards and buttons away," he said. "They keep potholders in their kitchens."

Ribicoff addressed his prestige head-on. "Yes, I had it made," he told voters. "I was the President's buddy. I attended large receptions at the White House with the President and his wife while little Caroline played in the next room. I had a Cadillac and a chauffeur and much prestige. This was pretty good stuff, pretty heady stuff for a kid who was born in a slum." But he made clear that his heart was firmly in Connecticut. Voters agreed. Barely.

On Election Day, Ribicoff won a mere 27,000 votes ahead of Seely-Brown, enough for only a 51-49% victory. Still, Ribicoff was off to the Senate and he would make the most of it.

In the Senate, Ribicoff was concerned about a number of firms winning bids to conduct the Vietnam War and launched an investigation. One such firm was Halliburton. He sponsored an amendment to an Appropriations bill that would pump an extra $1 billion into school districts for desegregation purposes. He helped create the Department of Education and Head-Start. And he authored one of seven major healthcare proposals but one that had been seen as the most serious, for the other name on the bill was a powerful, and rather conservative Democrat, Louisiana's Russell Long. It was called the Catastrophic

Health Insurance and Medical Assistance Reform Act and called for providing coverage to families exceeding 60 days in the hospital and $2,000 in medical bills. President Nixon had labeled healthcare a priority for the year but Watergate likely doomed any chances of its inception for decades to come.

The battle over busing gave Ribicoff a chance to prove that his liberalism was altruistic. He proposed an amendment to fiscal years 1974 and '75 allocating $1 million each for school districts and requiring "by 1985 the desegregation of all metropolitan-area schools in the nation."

Ribicoff's desire to present the public with the truth led him to take on "the rush of politicians stumbling over each other to oppose busing . . . The arguments we rejected for years, . . . are now embraced by liberals . . ."We have an obligation to confront the problem of segregation squarely and develop solutions . . . "To that end, he was not impressed by colleagues seeking middle ground. "Some are talking now of compromises on the question of busing, perhaps resulting in an amendment introduced by liberals that would appear to be against busing without really ending it . . . This may be fine for our conscience . . . but it hardly qualifies as constructive leadership." His courage did not translate into votes as just 29 colleagues voted to go along.

Ribicoff's busiest period in the chamber might have been the 94th Congress. This was the new Congress immediately following Nixon's resignation and members were concerned with bringing a new level of trust to the people. Ribicoff chaired the Government Affairs Committee and he undertook that responsibility. He sponsored the Watergate Reorganization and Reform Act. And he sponsored major lobbying disclosure legislation, saying, "The business of seeking to influence Congress is now big business."

While Ribicoff conceded that the bill before the committee was not a panacea, he contended "it does turn the healthy light of disclosure on lobbying and so discourage any lobbying practices which cannot withstand the light of day . . . Disclosure will help insure public confidence in the integrity of the government." Lobbying has an important role in the legislative process but it must be brought into the open so that the voice of the few, and the money of the few, do not make it impossible to hear the voice of the many." While the bill did clear both Houses of Congress, differences between the two versions had to be worked out. By the time this happened, Congress was on its way out of town and Ribicoff was unable to secure the unanimous consent necessary to fast track it.

Ribicoff was also underrated when it came to expressing his view of what he felt was right. Maryland Senator "Mac" Mathias, a Republican from Maryland, recalled a trip he took with Ribicoff and other members of Congress to the Soviet Union. Mathias recalled how in Lenigrad, the Soviet host rose to make the "customary Soviet toast to 'peace and freedom.'" Ribicoff, he said, "rose to respond and delivered extemporaneously the most eloquent and moving exhortation to peace that I have ever heard. When Abe finished, the room fell silent." Mathias continued that "although we had among us some of the Senate's most famous orators, including the mellifluous Hubert Horatio Humphrey, no one moved to speak . . . There was nothing left to say."

After 1968, the seat was Ribicoff's as long as he wanted it. The only other time after the Chicago melee his name appeared on the ballot was 1974, when his re-election wasn't even in doubt. During that period, Ribicoff, now a widower, remarried. During the courtship, his future wife Lois, hoping to throw the press off, identified herself as "Dr. Casey" (modeled after the television series "Ben Casey") while leaving messages at his offices.

Turning 70 in 1980, Ribicoff decided to retire, stating "There is a time to stay and a time to go." But Ribicoff wouldn't have been Ribicoff had it not been for one last influence of history. During the lame-duck period of 1980 when President Carter had lost re-election and Republicans had gained the Senate, one of the few Judicial nominations the Senate was considering was Stephen Breyer. A number of Democrats were upset that Breyer was being taken up while others were not. Ribicoff met with Breyer and convinced enough of his colleagues that he ought be confirmed. Had he not, he likely never would have come into contention for the Supreme Court opening more than a decade later.

In retirement, Ribicoff signed up with a law firm but continued the traits for which he had long been known: wisdom, kindness, and dressing dapper. *The New York Times* noted "Into his 80's he was still a model of sartorial elegance, able to fit into the Saville Row suits he had bought 25 years earlier." By the end of his life, Ribicoff had become a respected public statesman. And with integrity above all. He said he'd do it all again.

Ribicoff died at age 87 in 1998, and Joe Lieberman said, "the extraordinary life he led is a testament to the American dream." And he lent his service to providing that dream to many "Nutmeggers" and Americans.

Photo courtesy of Jane Ribicoff Silk

CHAPTER ELEVEN

Was Phil Burton Capitol Hills Genius
Or Madman? Probably Both

John Farrell, author of *Tip O'Neill and the Democratic Century* tells a story
of Phil Burton taking House Speaker Carl Albert to his hometown, San
Francisco. Despite their very different backgrounds and personalities, Albert
liked Burton, even though he was "far out in left field" and "the buddy of
the homos and all that stuff." Albert recalled Burton taking him to a club
that had "(this) topless and bottomless stuff" where Burton introduced the
Speaker to a well-renowned stripper named Carol Doda. The 5'4 Albert was
under the mistaken impression that Doda was Jewish and began telling her
how much he liked Golda Meir. Perplexed, Doda eventually asked Burton,
"Who is this little man and why is he talking to me about Golda Meir?"

Photo courtesy of the U.S. National Park Service

Save for House Speakers and Senate leaders, California Democrat Phil Burton
may rank as among the most legendary political figures on Capitol Hill in
the last half of the 20thcentury – and his proud-as-punch progressivism has little
to do with it. Rather, Burton's pugnacious streak, penchant for wine, women and
song several times over loom large. But it was Burton's gift at uniting disparate

factions, embracing friends and threatening to extinguish foes that made him in many ways king-of-the-hill.

Most remarkable about this reputation was that Burton was more than once on the losing end of attempts to secure a leadership post, including that famous 1976 cliffhanger vote for Majority Leader which ended with a single-vote loss to Jim Wright of Fort Worth. But his legislative accomplishments in spite, or perhaps because, were among the most significant in history for the poor, working-class, disabled and the environment. They include the enactment of OSHA, ERISA, SSI for the poor (complete with cost-of-living increases) and a massive "park-barrel" bill that created 100 national parks, more than any at a single time.

Procedurally, Burton's convincing of Ways and Means Chair Wilbur Mills to let a tax bill to advance to the House floor under an "open rule" meant that many amendments heretofore could be proposed by folks who wanted to either strengthen or weaken the legislation. This was the first time since the 1920s that this had been allowed, which enabled David Frum to write that Burton in large part "created the modern Congress." He called an aggressive Democratic redistricting plan he engineered, "My contribution to modern art." And given a little more time, he just may have ushered through a major campaign finance reform measure that many believed could have changed the culture of Washington.

Yes, Phil Burton accentuated a caricature of both the positives and the negatives of a politician. Strong beliefs but a wheeler and dealer, complete with the alcohol, Casanova mentality (and Chesterfield cigarettes) that could bring people together. A keen mind but with a temper that likely proved his undoing at least with aspirations for a leadership post, Burton, in the words of *Congressional Quarterly* on his death, possessed "a vocabulary that would make a sailor blush."

To some he was a political "nymphomaniac." Judy Lemons, who served as Burton's personal assistant, describes him as "eccentric, crazy, just a maniac but you knew you were watching a genius at work. You knew what he believed and what he was trying to do." So strong a force was he that fellow Californian Henry Waxman recalled one of the first things his daughter learned to say was "Phil Burton's on the phone." And his wife Sala and, for a time, brother John, were part of his fiefdom.

Burton unabashedly portrayed himself as "a fighting liberal" and that became clear from the moment he burst onto the political scene at 30, the youngest member in the California Assembly at the time. When he made it to Congress in a 1964 special election, Burton immediately made an impact. He was one of just three members to oppose a $700 million Appropriation for the Vietnam War.

As the cost escalated, Burton started "The Group," composing of like-minded members throughout the country. But the impression he made was so strong that colleagues elected him to chair the Democratic Study Group, a role which saw him aid first-time candidates like Charlie Rose and Pat Schroeder in 1972 with novel techniques that helped them to victory. The Almanac of American Politics said Burton's helmsmanship at the DSG made the group "a real power – perhaps the only power of the House" and even upon passing the baton to others continued as "the real driving force behind the organization." Even foes took notice. David Cohen of Common Cause noted how "In the old days, the DSG was viewed as a band of Young Turks." "Now," he said, "its leaders are matured legislators with a sense of how power relationships work."

Burton's first crack at the leadership came following that election cycle and it seemed poised to be a success. Majority Leader Hale Boggs had perished in a plane crash over Alaska and current Majority Whip Tip O'Neill was moving up to his position. Burton went for Whip and expected to attain that post by a rule change he was pushing which would allow the caucus to elect their Whip rather than the Majority Leader filling it. In an initial vote, the change appeared to be codified by a vote of 115-110. But O'Neill opposed it and during a lunch recess, made his case to a number of other members. When the caucus reconvened, he took the unusual step of asking to speak. Shortly after, the vote occurred and the rules change was defeated. O'Neill gave the position to John McFall, the much older and more senior but dull and politically impotent Congressman from California.

Photo courtesy of Judy Lemons

But another opportunity was soon forthcoming. By 1976, O'Neill was poised to move up yet again with the retirement of Speaker Carl Albert, Burton was seen as the man to beat for Majority Leader. In fact, so sure were many, including Burton himself of victory that when asked what he'd do if he lost, he replied "the thought hasn't crossed my mind for even a fraction of a second."

With four candidates in the race, no one was able to secure a majority on the first ballot. But Burton's 106 votes was well ahead of Bolling's 81 and Wright's 77. The second ballot was a cliffhanger – for the all critical second place. Burton wanted to face Wright and he got his wish, as he beat Bolling 95-93 (several Burton allies purposely voted for Wright, believing him to be the easier man to beat). Burton still appeared headed for a victory in the third round but the vote was tied with 3 of the 4 ballot boxes counted. When the fourth box was opened, Wright had prevailed by a single vote of 148-147. While Ohio's "Lud" Ashley scribbled out his initial vote for Burton at the insistence of Dan Rostenkowski, it was known that at least one Californian – Leo Ryan, voted for Wright. But Lemons, the Executive Assistant, notes he "always thought (San Jose Democrat Norm) Mineta betrayed him," noting her boss was too meticulous a vote-counter to have slipped up on his math.

An additional factor that tarred Burton was his ties to another certified mischief maker, Wayne Hays of Ohio. At first glimpse, even by Capitol Hill standards, the alliance was bizarre. But Lemons offered an explanation for the alliance: power. "Phil knew where the power was. In those days, being chairman of House Administration was a really big deal. Phil ended up with extra offices. No one knew how many offices he had." More importantly, "he knew Hays could eventually help him become Speaker and help him with conservative firebrands."

A test-run of that scenario was conducted following the '74 elections. Hays was prepared to endorse Burton for Caucus Chair in exchange for Burton's backing of Hays retaining his powerful committee post. This was the post-Watergate election and many newly-elected freshman wanted entrenched, autocratic chairs voted out. Several were. But Hays hung on. Still, when he got into trouble, Burton approached O'Neill who interpreted Burton of wanting to protect Hays, though Burton denied it (he cited guidance for handling the matter as caucus chair as reason for approaching O'Neill). The Ohioan was past the point of return and many wanted him out.

Photo courtesy of the National Park Service

Burton was hurt by his defeat but swung back in the legislative process. Mo Udall, who backed Burton, said he decided after the vote "he was going to go somewhere. The vehicle he chose was parks" and besides the "park-barrel," which impacted parks in 44 states, he helped Udall enact the Alaska Wilderness Protection legislation. In 1981, Burton traded his Interior panel for a chairmanship of the Labor-Management Relations subcommittee on Education and Labor. *Congressional Quarterly* said he hoped to "protect unions from what he saw as a hostile Reagan administration."

Campaign finance was a passion he pursued even before it became a popular cause among colleagues. A package he unveiled in 1975 called for a $25,000 campaign finance limit, matching funds and a spending ceiling of $150,000 for candidates who would accept matching funds."

Burton left his grip on much other territory. He had urged abolition of the House Un-American Activities Committee in 1962 as early as his State Assembly days which garnered the attention of then-Gubernatorial candidate Richard Nixon. He persisted until the final nail in the coffin was administered to that committee a dozen years later. He united southern Democrats with liberals by linking more welfare money to increased farm subsidies. And he won voting-rights for American Samoa and championed the interests of all the U.S. territories. And in his final years, Burton was one of the first lawmakers to recognize the AIDS epidemic. That was among his major legislative initiatives when he died.

Of Burton, Mo Udall once said, "He has the personality of a Brillo-Pad but he's effective" (and Udall was an ally). Wisconsin Democrat Dave Obey said "he could alternatively delight you and drive you up the wall." Biographer John Jacobs in an appropriately titled biography, *A Rage For Justice: The Passion and Politics of Phillip Burton*, called him "animated by a sometimes frightening drive for power—his only modern counterpart is Lyndon Johnson."

Much of this was carried out in a smoke-filled room where he'd be armed with three packs of Chesterfield cigarettes. Or Stoly (Stolychnaya) Russian Vodka. Or just simple conversations via Burton-style business. A key example was importuning Coal Consolidated President John Corcoran to accept legislation benefitting black lung disease. "If you don't accept this, we'll f----n" socialize your industry."

Another legendary tale about Burton was his unmitigated energy for women. *A Rage For Justice* portrays escapades that included numerous travel and women. A classic example was a trip to Europe that included two days of non-stop womanizing. Jacobs writes he left one pub with a "prostitute on each arm." He dragooned an aide into joining him with women of his own. When he asked the aide if he wanted to continue, he demurred, citing exhaustion and turned in for the evening. But Burton didn't stop. He was called a "blast furnace."

Lemons concedes Burton was "a womanizer," but adds that, "given the context of the times, that's part of the definition of 'Old Bull.' They could have whatever they wanted. They were like rock-stars," adding that women "would clamor over them." It was not uncommon for office-staff to report to the office in the morning and find a pretty lady in their midst. When they'd ask who she was, she'd reply, "Phil hired me last night." Most weren't exactly Elizabeth "I can't type, Wayne," Ray's but Lemons adds, "we were stuck with her." He could fire people on Constitution Avenue at midnight in a drunken-rage, then question where that person was the next morning (the staff would have to tell him there had been a problem).

Eventually, Burton would learn that his behavior had consequences. John Farrell in his O'Neill biography portrayed the Speaker's recollection of being at a club with Burton in San Francisco for a fundraiser. Despite repeated admonition by O'Neill to stop, Burton kept using the "f" word. Women were present and O'Neill noted that if his kids used that word, his wife would wash their mouths out. Burton continued. It had historical consequences. Years later, Burton's wife Sala asked O'Neill if his behavior that night was a factor in O'Neill picking McFall to which he acknowledged it was. Lemons said, "Tip was a gentleman. Phil wasn't always a gentleman."

It wasn't just this episode that Burton was on Tip's bad side. Burton was so ambitious that he often had to fend off rumors, well before a vacancy even occurred that he would challenge O'Neill for the Speakership. Burton denied the rumors but couldn't completely escape them. And O'Neill found himself constantly looking over his shoulders when it came to a Burton challenge but Lemons doesn't think Burton "was nipping at his heels." That's not to say that "if there had been an opening or Tip had been going down the wrong path," Burton wouldn't have tried but there was never an, "I'm taking him down moment."

Phil and Sala Burton
Photo courtesy of Judy Lemons

Whatever his personal faults, Lemons is very clear that "when it came to ethics, Phil was a straight arrow . . . clean as a whistle." One example was the birthday cakes that Sears-Roebucks would give members. She notes his instructions were that "we were to stand at the door and refuse it." If he cut a deal, it was to help what was usually considered the longer or common-good."

Much of Burton's propensity for scrupulousness came when he took over the Government Affairs subcommittee from Frank Thompson, a time when it was discovered "there were a lot of dead bodies" (ghost employees, etc). Burton could not retain all of them and in fact was forced to let 14 people go. But rather than dismiss each one willy-nilly, he met with each person and asked about their financial obligations, children, etc., and took that into consideration.

Burton came to San Francisco via Cincinnati by way of Wisconsin, the son of a doctor. He served in World War II and Korea and graduated from Golden Gate Law School. He was elected to the California Assembly at 30 and immediately began going to work for the little people. It started by passing pension legislation. By 1959, just two years into his tenure, Burton was chairing the Social Welfare Committee when well-known labor leader Dolores Huerta approached him about passing the bill. Even the liberal lion however needed convincing. Initially, he maintained that existing laws should do the trick. But by the time he finished, Burton was advocating it nearly as loudly as Huerta. Upon introducing it, he called it "the most important piece of Social Welfare Legislation before us this session."

Burton would protect his colleagues at the ballot box. In 1982, he engineered a redistricting plan that was overwhelmingly favorable to California Democrats and would ultimately award them 28 seats to 17 for the Republicans. Republicans winced with GOP assembly Caucus Chair Robert Naylor "congratulat(ing) Congressman Burton on what certainly is a masterpiece, a diabolical masterpiece." There was some sign of backlash. *The San Francisco Chronicle* praised Burton's political skills but opined "this time, he has gone too far." At least some voters agreed. That fall, Burton won re-election with a paltry 58% against a respected State Senator. But it helped ensure Democratic dominance in the delegation and the House for the next decade.

Sala and John Burton
Left Photo courtesy of the Collection of the U.S. House of Representatives;
right photo courtesy of the U.S. Government Printing Office

For all of his monumental accomplishments, Burton couldn't keep his drinking, or his temper in check. Often, if he got wind that Sala was near, he would throw his Stoli's in his left desk drawer (they lived in the Capitol Club just off the Hill – Sala didn't like to cook). Lemons says some "didn't like to be around Phil if he was drunk. Especially if Sala wasn't on the trip, you knew he was going to be out of control." One day following the 1982 elections, Burton was at a bar where he encountered newly elected John Bryant, then challenging a Burton mentee, Howard Berman for a seat on the Steering and Policy Committee. Burton threatened to "pulverize" Bryant and "make your life miserable," adding that, "When I'm through with you, you'll be no better than a used condom." This went on for 20 minutes before an aide removed him. The heavily favored Berman prevailed by the slimmest of margins.

Lemons calls Burton a "one-man walking computer" who "didn't need any staff" or "didn't need any advice . . . Anyone who says they were Phil Burton's right hand man is totally mistaken."

But that doesn't mean he loved solitary time. He never liked to be alone. After hours, he'd get someone (often a very junior, thirty-something Congressman named George Miller) to stay by his side. At 6 p.m. in Washington it was 3 P.M. in California and he could make his calls. A day would not go by that he didn't speak with Michael Berman, Howard's brother who was a master strategist in California politics.

Lemons also cites Burton's propensity for having "his hands on everything." That extended to even vacations. She recalls he and Sala were once on a beach in Puerto Rico. A native family was nearby. At one point, the family left their chairs to go for a swim and what did Phil do? He rearranged their chairs." The same went for staff. "He expected you to be at every official event."

For Burton, Berman's win may have been among the final legislative hurrahs. In April of 1983, he suffered an aneurysm and died. He was only 56. The left-draw in his office was full of Stoly Straight Russian Vodka's which he'd hide from Sala when she was approaching. But she succeeded him and served two terms before her own untimely death from cancer four years later at 61.

Sala was extraordinary in her own right. Under the threat of Jewish persecution, she and her family left Poland in 1939 when Sala was a young girl, just before the Nazis were taking over. They settled in San Francisco. That would shape her whole worldview. As she explained it years later, "I saw and felt what happened in Eastern Europe when the Nazis were moving. You learn that politics is everybody's business." At 23, Sala became associate director of the California Public Affairs Institute. It was there that she met Phil. And even being married to someone as brash and irreverent as Phil, when he'd speak to her – at least in front of others, he'd call her "heart."

Though Sala was quiet, she was not removed from the Washington circle scene. In the early 1970s, she was President of the Democratic Wives of both Houses of Congress. But when she made it to Congress, California colleague Don Edwards recalled "she astounded everybody . . . When she got on Rules, she was among the very strongest members for national Democratic Party policies. She was an advocate for poor people, education, the environment, and arms reduction. She was a pillar of strength. She didn't give an inch."

Sala was a solid liberal. One such program that bore Sala's name was a child-care program for "latchkey kids." She backed provisions of the Higher Education Act for child care to enable poor women to attend school, co-sponsored ERA, and in 1986 sought to ease federal restrictions on the elderly seeking public housing. She pressed the case for releasing more Soviet dissidents and worked on protecting historic ships in San Francisco Bay, an addendum to the Golden Gate National Recreation Area her husband had shepherded to creation.

In 1986, Sala was diagnosed with colon-cancer. Her deterioration was gradual but only Lemons had known how severely. By early '87, she was seriously ill, so sick that she was unable to take the oath of office in the House chamber as she began her third term (she did show up for work that morning but found herself too weak to go to the House floor). The House unanimously voted to allow her to take the oath from her home which enabled Edwards, the Dean of the California delegation to administer. He recalls, "she took the oath, signed all the papers, and gave me a bottle of champagne." As she lay dying, she summoned a

47 year old mother to talk about succeeding her. That person agreed and narrowly won the primary. It was future House Speaker Nancy Pelosi. Tom Lantos whose Congressional district encompassed the other portion of San Francisco called her "a Congresswoman of the highest caliber."

John Burton may have been a Phil mini-me with differing results. Few doubted his capabilities to the point that he'd get under folk's skin even deeper than Phil. But he got distracted easily and was not as task oriented as Phil. These problems, coupled with the onset of a cocaine addiction late in his tenure, found him temporarily sidelined and nearly ruined.

Burton was in many ways his brother's keeper and that made him a known entity before he even held office. In fact, when Phil was getting ready to vacate his Assembly seat to go to Congress, someone noted that his erstwhile foe, Assembly Speaker Jess Unruh seemed unhappy. Unruh replied, "He'll be replaced by Johnny who'd be worse." John did indeed win the election and went on to chair the powerful Rules Committee. His one attempt at higher office failed when he challenged Marks for a Senate seat but he lost by 6,000 votes.

In many ways, Burton showed his legislative acumen quickly. After the '76 elections, he became Chair of the Government Affairs Committee on Transportation. Lemons said John was not a regular in Phil's office. "He'd pop in but was doing his own thing." But his interests were second-to-none.

But Burton's worsening problem vastly limited what the committee was able to accomplish. Phil's attempt to draw a safe district for his brother invited much of the criticism in his own race. In March, 1982, just two days before the filing deadline, Burton announced his retirement. He was succeeded by Barbara Boxer. But he didn't inform his brother that he was dropping out and Sala never forgave him.

But Burton did get a second act so rare in politics. He returned to the Assembly and resumed his chairmanship of Rules. He since became Chair of the California Democratic Party, a position he still holds. His state-of-mind has been restored but his devotion to liberal causes hasn't changed a bit.

In closing, what of the legacy of Phil? *The LA Times* years after his death described Burton thus: "He had a gargantuan appetite for work and success, matched only by his appetite for vodka and steak. His behavior, with friends and enemies alike, was usually obnoxious and sometimes downright disgusting. And, surprisingly, given his other traits, he was seemingly incorruptible, both financially and in his devotion to the common man."

Lemons clearly captured a microcosm of her former boss. Burton, she said, was "amazing, eccentric, (and) one-of-a-kind." But a statue of Burton, unveiled in the Great Meadow of Fort Mason overlooking the Golden Gate Bridge, may have best captured the sentiment. In the pocket, there is an inscription. It reads, "When you deal with exploiters, terrorize the bastards."

The statue of Phil Burton was dedicated in 1991 by Assembly Speaker Willie
Brown and Sala Burton's successor and future House Speaker Nancy Pelosi
Photo courtesy of the National Park Service

CHAPTER TWELVE

When Conscience Trumps Party:
John Sherman-Cooper

Historic Quote: "When the end of the world comes, I want to be in Kentucky because it is 20 years behind the rest of the world." Mark Twain

Photo courtesy of the John Sherman Cooper Collections,
University of Kentucky Special Collections

Early in his Senate career, Senate Majority Leader Robert Taft presented his fellow Republican from Kentucky, John Sherman Cooper, with a question: "Are you a Republican," Taft asked, "or a Democrat? When are you going to start voting with us?" Cooper's reply was for the books. "If you'll pardon me. I was sent here to represent my constituents, and I intend to vote as I think best."

And that's what we need. In this hyper-partisan age, a statesman or two would be nice. Politicians who neither posture, nor worry about offending colleagues by straying from the line. Folks who don't read polls or strain for public opinion. Simply doing right by country. And conscience. Cooper was a mid-20th-century public servant who lived by that idea—and the result from his colleagues was not detachment, but respect. When Nixon asked Mike Mansfield whom he should name as a replacement for Vice-President Agnew, Cooper was the first name Mansfield suggested (Carl Albert suggested Ford who obviously carried the day).

It may've mattered little that Cooper was a man of fortune. Not all who have been blessed with such good fortune have had a "to hell with popular opinion" approach. But that's what made him so remarkable.

Cooper was first and foremost, to quote the title of the 1989 documentary, the "Gentleman from Kentucky." With that characterization came a reputation for being a stubborn advocate for independence. His party unity score was just 51%—almost unimaginable today—and if not a maverick, he had an independent streak that was noted by colleagues early on.

Early in his career, the Senator from Somerset, Kentucky opposed his party's plan to reduce funding for the Marshall Plan and GOP attempts to override Truman's tax cuts, and he sponsored legislation increasing highway and education funding. He turned on Joseph McCarthy before it was common and was a fierce advocate of Civil Rights, even fighting Jim Crow Laws. The issue on which he tangled with Taft was war bonds. However, the latter, who in name and deed was "Mr. Republican," learned quickly that to know Cooper was to work productively with him, and he and Taft wound up sponsoring the first federal education bill enacted into law.

In Washington, the company he kept was a mixture of journalists and politicians, a group referred to as the "Georgetown Set." Cooper, whose friendship with President Kennedy was well-known, also proved his mettle as a sponsor of Medicare, becoming one of four Republicans (along with New York Republicans Javits and Keating and Kuchel of California) to back the original version that failed in 1962; he had a herculean task convincing many of his own supporters that he was not off the reservation. Cooper told Robert Schulman, author of *The Global Kentuckian*, of the "thousands" of letters he had received from physicians urging him to oppose the bill, but he waxed poetic on his Pulaski County days and added that "I noticed that the old country doctors and county officials, people who had been out in the country and had seen the plight of the people who live in the hollows and down in the dirt roads—they were for it . . . no one would help (the poor) but these country doctors. You just can't let people go hungry. You can't ignore the sick and let them die."

Photo courtesy of the Library of Congress

Earlier, Cooper had worked with Montana Democrat James Murray on a massive education aid package which the Eisenhower administration opposed. And during the ideological struggles between the Goldwater and Rockefeller wings at the platform committee at the 1964 GOP convention, Cooper was the only member of the Kentucky delegation to rise during a vote on condemning groups such as the John Birch Society. That may have been predictable.

The website osi-speaks.blogspot notes how, just weeks earlier, a 22-year-old Cooper intern asked him how he so sternly supported the Civil Rights Act over the opposition of so many Kentuckians. Cooper's reply: "I not only represent Kentucky, I represent the nation, and there are times when you follow, and times when you lead." But well before that, Cooper's independence was one thing for Kentucky voters but quite another for the colleagues who wanted a more partisan man at the helm.

After the 1958 elections, he squared off against Everett Dirksen for the position of Senate Minority Leader. Cooper's bid offered a three-pronged platform. The first was working together as Republicans with the goal of "achieving better results." Second, Cooper advocated "a more positive, constructive legislative program to the Congress and to the country." Finally, there would be "greater influence to members at conference committees." His bid was championed by a prominent group of centrist colleagues (George Aiken, Tom Kuchel, Jacob Javits, Ken Keating, and Cliff Case) but Dirksen still beat him 20-14.

When Kennedy was murdered, C. David Heymann wrote that "of all his many friends and admirers, none was more anguished by his death than John Sherman Cooper." It's not hard to see why. During a visit to Louisville to support Democratic Congressional candidates, Kennedy was effusive in his praise of Cooper, telling voters, "You have a great Republican . . . who represents the best of his party, and who votes with us when he thinks we're right" (Cooper was not up for re-election that year). But the ties made him a natural for LBJ when he needed to fill the Senate Republican spot on the Warren Committee. When he told Jackie Kennedy of its conclusions, she replied, "What difference does it make? Knowing who killed him won't bring Jack back." He concurred that indeed it wouldn't, but "it's important for this nation that we bring the true murderers to justice."

Photo courtesy of the John Sherman Cooper Collections, University of Kentucky Special Collections

Cooper's independence was to the consternation of both Democratic and Republican Presidents, particularly on judicial matters. Cooper opposed the nominations of both Abe Fortas and Haynesworth, though he backed Nixon's second nominee to the court, Harrold Carswell. In reaching his conclusion on Carswell, Cooper said, "I consider that the absence of such claims against Judge Carswell and his experience as a trial and appeals judge are positive factors supporting his confirmation." Because Cooper commanded so much respect, the Nixon White House hailed him. But it wasn't enough.

Late in his career, Cooper became known for his opposition to U.S. involvement in Vietnam, which came in spite of his having backed the Gulf of Tonkin. As such, he authored an amendment with Democratic Senator Frank Church to end U.S. military involvement in Cambodia and Laos. It garnered the support of Democratic Leader Mike Mansfield but President Nixon threatened to veto it. Ultimately, the amendment was stricken from the final bill.

While not especially known as a man-about-town, Cooper nonetheless gained a reputation for being the master of enviable social gatherings. Massachusetts Republican Senator Edward Brooke said John and Lorraine "entertained luxuriously in their home in Georgetown where I spent many a pleasant evening."

With Constituents
Photo courtesy of the John Sherman Cooper Collections,
University of Kentucky Special Collections

Politically, Cooper may be an example of, if at first you don't succeed, try, try, again. He was first appointed to the Senate to fill the vacancy of another legendary Kentuckian, "Happy" Chandler, who had given up his seat to become the second Baseball Commissioner. He was defeated in his bid for a full term but not before his fellow Kentucky Senator Alben Barkley, a Democrat, basically said Cooper deserved more than two years to continue his work. The fact that Barkley was his party's Vice-Presidential nominee made his statement more remarkable.

In 1952, another vacancy arose and Cooper won it. The comeback was short-lived, however, as Cooper again lost, to Barkley, who, no longer the Veep, was seeking a comeback at age 77. But Barkley died a year and a half later and Cooper, though reluctant, heeded Eisenhower's entreaties to regain the seat. He won and credited three factors. "One, a gain from Negro voters (in Louisville in particular). Two, from labor, and three, from general approval of the President." And he resumed his go-his-own-way approach. Kentuckians responded with a roar of approval. Cooper's final two re-election margins were the largest margin for a Senator in state history, not to be broken until Mitch McConnell exceeded it in 2002. Labor gave him much aid.

Cooper had attended Yale University and Harvard Law School and was chauffeured to work each day, but had a personable, empathetic disposition. He called himself a "truly terrible speaker." But that mattered little, for he was one of the most respected statesmen in the Senate and out. After the close of World War II, he was appointed to lead Bavaria. Even after his first short Senate span, Cooper had made such an impression on Harry Truman that the Democrat appointed Cooper a delegate to the United Nations. Kennedy asked him to head a fact-finding mission to Moscow and New Delhi. Following Kennedy's assassination, he was the Senate Republican whom President Johnson selected to serve on the Warren Commission, and after his retirement, he was appointed by Ford to be Ambassador to East Germany.

With his junior colleague, Marlow Cook during Cooper's last days in the Senate and with President Gerald Ford in 1974 Photo via the Kenton County Public Library

Cooper served until his retirement in 1972, and, save his brief stint as an Ambassador, spent his remaining days in Kentucky. He died at age 89 in 1991.

There were a few other Senators famously known for abiding by their convictions. Barry Goldwater was notorious, once instructing a staffer to "do what you feel is right even if it goes against me." Wisconsin's Bill Proxmire's staunch oversight had him always offending someone and found him often casting lone votes on bills. Paul Wellstone has been called a more modern-day "conscience of the Senate." But in an era when it wasn't demanded, Cooper stands out most.

The website The Northumbrian Countdown wrote: "Cooper is the sort of man who just isn't well remembered today, and that is a great shame." For in an age when personal convictions outweighing offending friendships are few and far between, they are true models. Let's hope the states send more our way who will do them—and the country they serve—proud.

**Cooper (far right) at the unveiling of the statue in his name. Ex-Kentucky
Governor and Baseball Commissioner "Happy" Chandler is at left
Photo courtesy of the John Sherman Cooper Collections,
University of Kentucky Special Collections**

CHAPTER THIRTEEN

CHAPTER THIRTEEN

Montana's Metcalf Sponsored Medicare Bill; Right In Foxhole With Colleague Mansfield; Maneuvers Ended Civil Rights Filibuster

Historic Tidbit: In 1865, there was a Michigan Congressman who voted for 13th Amendment named Charles Upson, who represented Kalamazoo. One of his successors has an eerily similarly sounding name: Fred Upton. He holds a descendant of the Upson seat that also encompasses Kalamazoo. Of course, Michigan had just six House seats in the 1860s. But my guess is Fred Upton's bigger boast is that *Sports Illustrated* supermodel Kate Upton is his niece. Too good to pass up.

Lee Metcalf
Photo courtesy of the U.S. Senate Historical Office

There was once a very special Senator from the state of Montana. His name will never have the familiarity of Mike Mansfield's and, having not been leader of the chamber, could not possibly get the exposure that Mansfield did. But as Mansfield pushed the measures through, Lee Metcalf was deep in the foxhole with him, often steering the ship, and ahead of many of his colleagues. He was as genuine as they come. And when it came to Montana, his love was second to none.

Consider this. Metcalf introduced the Medicare bill as far back as ten years before it was actually signed into law. Known as "Mr. Education," Metcalf sponsored the Elementary and Secondary Education Act, which was a hallmark of the "Great Society" and took a lead role in passage of the Peace Corps and the Wilderness Act. When Allard Lowenstein had approached George McGovern about challenging LBJ in the '68 primaries (Bobby Kennedy had already turned him down before eventually reconsidering), McGovern had suggested he seek out Metcalf. He called it "ridiculous" (four years later, Metcalf did not return the favor as he became the first Senator to endorse Ed Muskie over McGovern for the Democratic nomination). And he advocated pesticide control for fish and wild animals. But passage of the Civil Rights bill, while his name may not appear to be among the major players, may not have come had it not been for Metcalf.

It was Metcalf who, through his Mansfield appointed role as acting President Pro-Tem, was presiding in the chair during debate on the Civil Rights Act, and he and Hubert Humphrey pensively anticipated opponents to block it with procedural wrenches. Metcalf blocked every one of those attempts, leading one southerner to affirm that "Metcalf has stripped us of any parliamentary weapon. That man was the civil rights bill's secret weapon."

Republican El Cederberg, a freshman Republican who took his seat alongside Metcalf called him "a go-getter" with "contagious" energy. Ed Muskie called him "the Senate's lawyer" and another colleague said he possessed "one of the greatest legal minds I've ever seen." Those skills immediately enabled Metcalf to get results almost upon arrival. Fellow Montana Congressman Wesley D'Ewart had introduced the Uniform Federal Grazing Land Act but Metcalf mobilized efforts to kill it. Matthew Peek of Montana History Blog Spot inserted Metcalf's statement of opposition during committee consideration. It went, "In the light of industrial development and expansion we should continue to be alert to protect our water...and to follow the leadership of enlightened local community leaders who know the problems and are familiar with local conditions. A balanced constructive legislative program is needed." He succeeded. Ditto with the Ellsworth Timber Exchange Bill that same year.

Along with colleagues Gene McCarthy and Frank Thompson, he organized meetings that would form the Democratic Study Group. The goal was to enunciate a liberal agenda for the party and the "Liberal Manifesto" was the document that governed it (civil rights, health care, education, etc). They would meet in someone's office or the Longworth House Office Building Cafeteria. The London Economist called the group, "The Ginger Caucus." The DSG actively supported like-minded candidates throughout the nation and as Democratic ranks swelled following the election of 1958, the 80 members selected Metcalf to chair it. The group truly became a force to be reckoned with. Perhaps its greatest contribution to history was the advancement of a "discharge petition," which required legislation to be voted on if 218 members were willing to sign it.

Metcalf as a Congressman always had a jovial disposition
Photo courtesy of the Montana Historical Society

When Metcalf made anti-Vietnam war comments to a reporter he was asked if he would tell the same thing to the President. Metcalf replied, "You're Goddamned right I would. If I were going to the White House every Tuesday, I'd tell Nixon every Tuesday that we've got to get the hell out of Vietnam. I would say it every day to the President, if I could go to the White House every day." By no colleague was Metcalf more viewed highly than his own. Mike Mansfield seriously raised Metcalf's name to succeed Abe Fortas on the Supreme Court.

But while Metcalf apparently had no taste for a seat on the high-court himself, he had no qualms about rejecting Richard Nixon's choices. On his vote against Haynsworth, Metcalf said, "In the light of (his) record, it is plain that… the highest qualification for a seat on the Supreme Court is complete ideological identification with the reactionary tenets of the administration's southern strategy."

Metcalf had a gift on local matters as well. It was called persistence. A 1971 Interior Committee hearing examined clear-cutting practices by the timber industry and many Montanans had trekked across the country to testify on its ill-effects. John Morrison and Catherine Wright note in *Mavericks: The Lives and Battles of Montana's Political Legends* that "as the hearings drew to a close, timber industry advocates had dominated the proceedings while many citizen witnesses had not been given a chance to testify. Metcalf raised his voice and brought down his fist."

The book notes journalist John Burke's take on what happened next. "The committee recessed to a back room and seemed poised to adjourn when, "from behind the closed oak doors, a voice boomed loud enough to be heard in the committee room: 'No dammit, we can't quit now. I can't go back in there and tell my people to go home. They haven't even had a chance to present their case."

If Metcalf was in the spotlight in an area, it was probably his fastidiousness on the environment and that gained him another title: "Mr. Wilderness." He was an original sponsor of the 1964 Wilderness Act and ten years later, introduced one specifically for Montana. This was called the Wilderness Study Act and its prime purpose was to emulate what he had done with the Spanish Peaks in '64; preserving them as wilderness until Congress legislated otherwise. In '74, Metcalf had proposed ten areas be designated in the study and it cleared Congress just before he died.

Everyone interviewed for this book all noted how Metcalf was dogged by one thing throughout nearly his entire tenure. Mansfield was Senate Majority Leader so Metcalf naturally toiled in his shadows. This might have bothered many politicians but apparently, not Metcalf. Ex-Senator John Melcher, who actually became the junior Senator under Metcalf when Mansfield retired, noted "Mike helped him out a lot," but said he was not a headline seeker. Teddy Roe, his Legislative Director, said that like Mansfield, he "hid his lights under a bushel." His temper on other matters was a different story.

Metcalf overlooking his beloved Montana
Photo courtesy of The Billings Gazette

Pat Williams, who would win the House seat Metcalf held the year the senator died, wrote on the 30th anniversary of Metcalf's death that he "changed both Washington DC and us; doing it in an incredibly quiet but effective manner."

When Mansfield won his Senate seat in 1952, Metcalf rebutted the Eisenhower landslide and kept his House seat in Democratic hands, 50.3-49.7% and his respect was such that he was selected by his colleagues to chair the Democratic Study Group. But Metcalf's career reads like a what's what of offices in Montana. He served in the Montana Legislature, assistant Attorney General, and as a Justice on the state Supreme Court before winning his House seat. That made Metcalf, as Williams noted, "the most experienced Montana ever to be elected to the U.S. Congress."

And while Mansfield came to Montana by way of New York City, Metcalf was born there, in the small town of Stevensville.

As a member of the Army during World War II, Metcalf was in both the Battle of the Bulge and Normandy. He helped displaced Jews in Germany take part in elections.

And there were the votes Metcalf took that of course couldn't please everyone. He backed busing, higher taxes on the wealthy, cast the deciding vote for the Lockheed loans, the Equal Rights Amendment, and was a solid backer of labor. His scores often topped 100%. Locally, Evan Barrett points out that he opposed "corporate statism," borne out by his forcing the Anaconda Copper Company to pay miners for the time they spent in the mines, not just when they reported to work. He worked on consumer, library, small business, and work safety issues.

But Metcalf's focus was on energy issues, and when it came to the power companies, he saw to it that his state got a square deal, as Williams said he "threw the bright light of public scrutiny" on them. Yet he was protective of Montana and used his seat on Interior Affairs to protect its interests.

With early Montana colleagues Mansfield and James Murray (left) and with later Montana colleagues Mansfield, Baucus, and Melcher
Photo via makeitmissoula.com

Perhaps the biggest reward was Metcalf's ability to keep getting re-elected. While his margins were never as large as Mansfield's, he nonetheless turned back two serious challenges in Republican years. In 1966, Metcalf beat a former Governor 53-47%. And in '72, he edged ahead of a State Senator 52-48% as

Nixon was getting 60%. Montanans evidently noticed Metcalf's genuineness and were willing to give him a pass for being perhaps slightly to their left.

Metcalf's staff respected him too. At least three top members were with him from his early days as a Senator, with several having served him even longer. One, Vic Reinemer, said, "There are two kinds of public officials. The consensual who wait for the majority support before they move and, to coin a word, the inconsensual, the few trailblazers who light the way of the herd behind. Lee Metcalf was one of those rare point men out front."

Metcalf chaired the Joint Committee on Government Operations. His role as acting President Pro-Tem was intended for when Carl Hayden, 86, was unavailable to fulfill his duties. But Metcalf kept the title long after Hayden retired (Mansfield remained leader and certainly wouldn't strip his home-state colleague of it), and held the post until he died in January of 1978, a record in the Senate.

At that time, Metcalf, 66, was in failing health and had decided early on that he would not seek re-election that year. But though he did suffer from heart ailments, death in his sleep was nonetheless unexpected.

Wyoming Congressman Teno Roncalio said Metcalf "has done a great deal to assist us in becoming better legislators." Indiana Congressman John Brademas called him "gifted with a first-class mind and characterized by unimpeachable integrity." And New York Senator Jacob Javits labeled Metcalf "one of the most extraordinarily fine, high-level characters that ever served in this body. I know of nothing Lee ever did that he did not really have his heart in. In his case, what had to be done politically I don't think existed at all."

His ashes are scattered in his beloved Montana, a land that he did so much to preserve.

Five years after Metcalf died, the Lee Metcalf Wilderness area was designated for him. But he needn't know it. Roe, reflecting on his nonchalant style, said he'd "be spinning in his grave."

PART II

A Few Wise Men – And Women: Profiles
Of Tremendous National Influence

CHAPTER FOURTEEN

Ed Muskie:
The Best Man Who Never Became Vice-President

Historic Tidbit: Shortly before ending his 1972 Presidential bid, Ed Muskie told a story of "this fellow who got his car stuck in the mud. When asked by a farmer if he was really stuck, the man replied, 'You could say I was stuck if I was going anywhere.'"

The 1968 ticket-Humphrey and Muskie
Photo via the Edmund S. Muskie Archives and Special Collections Library

On a personal and political level, Hubert Humphrey was my hero. Had he managed to prevail in his 1968 race for President, a race he would lose by a hair despite daunting odds, Edmund Sixtus Muskie would have been vice-president. And from there, who knows? And so America was deprived of a man whose capabilities, judgement, and skill were second-to-none.

Muskie's story was authentic, up-by-the-bootstraps American. The Muskies (then named Marciszew-ski) had moved from Poland to Rumford, Maine before Ed was born, and he would often experience taunts about his heritage. But he would be the only one of his six siblings to go to college.

Muskie's abilities were also recognized by his classmates at Stephen's High. Under his senior picture in the yearbook, *The Broadcast* it was written, "there is

183

probably heaps more to tell of the honorable deeds of this mastermind but the boy is modest and modest people don't relish being held up as an example. However, when you see a head and shoulders towering above those of the common heard in the halls of Stephens you should know that your eyes are feasting on a future President of the United States."

As a student at Bates, 1932
Photo via the Edmund S. Muskie Archives and Special Collections Library

Next, it was on to Bates College where Muskie would excel at sports and debating. *The Making of the President, 1972* notes that Muskie was "singled out" by the President of Bates College as to whether he was indeed a Democrat. Muskie had no choice but to acknowledge its truth (remember, this was 1936, the year GOP Presidential candidate Alf Landon could carry only Maine and Vermont). But the "New Deal" helped Muskie.

Muskie served in the Navy during World War II after which was asked by Maine Democrats to stand for the legislature because the party wanted veterans. Against the odds, he won. To say the party could caucus in a phone booth would be an understatement. Of the 151 House members, just 24 were Democrats. In the Senate, there were a mere two.

By 1954, Muskie was the state Democratic chair and was actively seeking Democrats to challenge incumbent Republican Governor Burton Cross. One Mainer prominent on the political scene recalls Muskie "calling people up all over the state and asking them to run and they all turned him down because no one wanted to be the sacrificial goat." Finally, he was told that if he was so devoted to seeing a Democrat elected, he would have to take the plunge himself. He was far from favored. But Cross was tainted by a liquor scandal and found himself on the defensive.

Still, Cross was so confident he resisted Muskie's call to debate saying, "I'm happy to talk to Ed any time after the election." The Friday before the election, he predicted he'd win by 45,000 votes. Conversely, at 11:00 p.m. on Election Night, Muskie didn't even believe it. He was just starting to take the lead having lost most of the early reporting sea-coast towns when a waitress asked for his autograph. "Tomorrow," she said, "you may be Governor." Indeed, by the time the counting was done, Muskie had pulled off a solid 8.5% victory, becoming the first Democratic occupant of the "Blaine House" since 1932.

As Governor, Muskie reinvigorated the Democratic Party of Maine
Photo via the Edmund S. Muskie Archives and Special Collections Library

Like so many Governors of his era, Muskie set Maine on a path to progress. His National Governor's Association Bio credits him with the creation of the Maine Industrial Building Authority and the Department of Development of Commerce and Industry. Aid to schools and hospitals were increased and a $29 million highway bond issue was created. Much of these improvements were financed by a 1% increase in the sales tax.

But Muskie's advocacy of clean air defined his legacy as he would doggedly promote it throughout his entire national career.

Stan Tupper, a Republican who had served under Muskie as Governor and who in the 1960s was a colleague in Congress (Tupper was in the House and Muskie the Senate), cited Maine's polluted waters as the impetus for his commitment to clean air in an oral history project. "The Kennebec River was yellow, Brunswick, you'd go through there and the water stunk to high heaven and it was yellow and green and fish wouldn't live in the rivers. And the air was so bad that it would take the paint off from houses.... That was what Ed Muskie saw and that was why Ed Muskie was adamant about the need to clean up the air."

Tupper also cited another Muskie strength: his one of us personality. Mainers, he said, "don't want someone to appear in a stiff collared shirt and, you know, looking very severe. I think he identified on a one to one very well, and he could, he had such a quick mind that Ed could quick study, he could learn, if he didn't know something about something, within a half hour of briefing he could talk to people." On a personal note, he adds, that Muskie, "allowed the commissioners pretty good latitude."

By 1958, Muskie decided to stand for the Senate, and despite challenging an incumbent, prevailed with a solid 61%. Maine held its general elections in September (that changed in 1960) so Muskie's win truly fueled Democratic optimism for November. And in this case, it proved that "As Maine Goes, So Goes the Nation."

Shortly after, Muskie met with Lyndon Johnson, then the Majority Leader. He told Muskie that it wouldn't be unusual for him to not decide how to vote on a matter "until they call the "M's." Shortly after, Democrats were holding their caucus and Johnson informed members he was considering changing Rule 22 which dealt with the use of the filibuster. After a while, he noticed Muskie was being relatively quiet. The junior Senator replied, "Well, Lyndon, we haven't gotten to the 'Ms' yet."

It was perhaps always facing a GOP legislature in Maine that made Muskie aware of the need to reach out, and early on, he gained recognition for his bipartisan proclivities that led to landmark accomplishments. And that applied to non-politicians, too. Muskie would often invite protesters onto the stage with him.

In his early years, Muskie made his biggest mark on environmental matters. Three major water and air quality acts that became law were his bills, including legislation that would reduce emissions in cars. He helped shepherd creation of the Environmental Protection Agency and worked on major oil-spill legislation, the final product of which he thought made too many concessions to the corporations.

But his drive wasn't limited to the environment. The Department of Housing and Urban Development in 1965 and the Model Cities Act of 1966 were both Muskie bills (curious for a Senator from Maine). The Truth-in-Government Act, which created an independent board authorized to make available to the public government documents available to the public was his as well, as was the 1970 Securities Investor Protection Act, which insured investors if brokerage houses failed.

When it came to civil rights, Muskie had little patience for those who were thwarting progress. Shortly after the devastating Hurricane Camille hit the gulf region in 1970, Muskie and Indiana Senator Birch Bayh wrote to Public Works Committee Chair Jennings Randolph (D-West Virginia) to ask him to hold hearings on Mississippi's slow response toward providing relief to African-American areas. Randolph obliged and Muskie held Governor John Bell Williams' feet to the fire. Later, he read the report, "In the Wake of Hurricane Camille: An Analysis of the Federal Response" on the Senate floor. The report stated that Mississippi administrators "have been oblivious to the needs of the poor in the Gulf Coast area" in the area of disaster relief. But federal officials were not left out of the criticism. The report faulted the Department of Housing and Urban Development for not using it's "authority to make all emergency housing rent-free. Instead, the report continued, it "requires the poor to pay up to 25 percent of their monthly income for rent."

Exploring the Maine coast with Stewart Udall on the Maine coast
Photo via the Edmund S. Muskie Archives and Special Collections Library

On social matters, Muskie was a solid liberal, though he did oppose banning mail-sale rifles, which even his Republican colleague, Margaret Chase Smith, supported.

Then, he went national.

Humphrey spotted Muskie's potential early and was said by biographer Edgar Bergen to have brought up his name after a memorial service for Bobby Kennedy when he invited Muskie and his wife Jane to lunch. Bergman said Humphrey mentioned Muskie's positive attributes, his "stability, his executive experience as Governor, and his interest in budgetary matters." Humphrey, Bergen said, kidded that he's also "a Pole, a Catholic, and looks enough like Abe Lincoln." Even as early as 1968, some anti-war backers, not wanting Humphrey but believing Gene McCarthy could not win the White House following the death of Bobby Kennedy, tried to draft Muskie to seek the Democratic nomination but he was uninterested.

Muskie became the pick and was a capable running mate. He had a saying that was in part perhaps directed at the widely mocked Spiro Agnew, "In Maine, we have a saying that you don't say anything that doesn't improve on silence."

Muskie brought a number of traits to the race, one of which was demonstrated at a college appearance in Pennsylvania when Muskie's speech was interrupted by students chanting, "Stop the war." Muskie's response amazed the crowd. "I will suggest something right now to you gentleman," he said. "You pick one of your best numbers to come up right here right now, and I'll give him ten minutes of uninterrupted attention. There is another side of this bargain . . . and you listen to this part of the bargain: you give me your uninterrupted attention." The students agreed on Rick Brody whom Muskie's biography describes as "almost straight out of central casting . . .21 years old; he had long hair and dirty jeans." Brody, acknowledging, "this is a chance we usually don't get," explained the nature of the Democrats problem that year. "No one listened to us in Chicago when Senator McCarthy showed through the primaries that seventy percent of the American public was dissatisfied with President Lyndon Baines Johnson's stand on Vietnam and domestic issues."

Early on Election Night, 1968
Photo via the Edmund S. Muskie Archives and Special Collections Library

After that speech, Muskie was greeted by roaring applauses which caused many to question whether the Democrats had developed a formula for dealing with apathy among their base. And by Election Day, the ticket rallied but ultimately lost in a squeaker that lasted through the wee hours of the morning.

When Humphrey lost, Muskie immediately became the odds-on favorite to capture the Democratic nomination in 1972. It was almost fait accompli, like Mitt Romney was always the man to beat following 2008. Muskie had endorsements, fame, and a style that suited many. Furthermore, his closing message for his party on Election Eve in the 1970 mid-terms was said to have been a riveting call that awed the party faithful.

It wasn't until January of 1972 that Muskie formally announced his long anticipated candidacy for the presidency. He charged Muskie charging that "an administration that has so failed us in the past cannot take us to the future," As the primaries approached, he seemed unstoppable. The Nixon White House recognized this also. And they wanted to stop him.

It was widely believed that the Nixon White House was most fearful of a Muskie candidacy. A fake letter circulated that said someone had told him had told him that "Canncks" were the "blacks of New Hampshire" and that Muskie laughed. "Cannuck" is a derogatory for French Canadians, who in those days encompassed the vote of a large portion of its neighbor to the south's vote. The episode made its way to the cameras. Further, William Loeb, the publisher of *The Manchester Union Leader* and the unsung hero of conservative causes, reported that Jane Muskie was often seen in public drunk and telling dirty jokes ("unladylike"). Later, it was determined that the memo was forged by Nixon staffers.

Muskie gave all he had to his 1972 Presidential campaign
Left image via ronwadebuttons.com;
Right photo via the Edmund S. Muskie Archives and Special Collections Library

Muskie defended his wife on the flatbed of a truck outside *The Union Leader's* headquarters. He called Loeb a "gutless coward" whose "fortune was that he is not standing on this stage."

David Broder said Muskie had "tears streaming down his face," But it was snowing that day and even Broder said it could have been snowflakes. Stephen Muskie, the Senator's son, was on the platform with his father that day. He told me he didn't appear to be crying but acknowledged he was "exhausted" and that on the campaign plane the day before, he "spoke bitterly with his aides about Loeb's treatment of my mother in *The Union Leader*." Stephen said he was speaking "extemporaneously," which, combined with the extreme fatigue, likely produced sentiments that should've come out differently. Watching the video, snowflakes were evident but there appeared to be at least some mist from Muskie.

Today, it's not uncommon at all to see the most battle-tested male politicians wiping away tears, particularly when defending wives. But in 1972, it was more of a novelty, and that apparently weakened the Quincy-like stability that Muskie possessed. He acknowledged that "it changed people's minds about me. They were looking for a strong, steady man, and here I was weak." McGovern years later would say he didn't believe the purported crying "diminished him in the least . . . it was an indication of his humanity and his essential decency."

That incident aside, the snowflake incident wasn't the first where the weakness factor came out. Someone once observed that Muskie doesn't "shoot for the jugular. He aims for the capillaries."

Snowflake or not, one striking irony in Muskie being forced to defend his wife in New Hampshire was that, she had been such an asset to him with audiences there. At one rally, she told the crowd, "Oh, I think I'm going to faint. But before I do, I'd like to say a few words about my husband." The audience roared.

Muskie received 46%, but McGovern was comparatively and unexpectedly close with 37%

McGovern won handily in the academic towns and Muskie prevailed in "working class towns." But an expected large number in Manchester turned into just a 600-vote plurality.

In actuality, Muskie's poor showing had occurred a week earlier, which should have foreshadowed New Hampshire, or at least raised concern. For a time, he soldiered on. But by Wisconsin, it became clear that he could do so no more and he dropped out.

Muskie had been perhaps hampered by facing a wide open-field of candidates, including Humphrey and Gene McCarthy. *The Almanac of American Politics 1974* observed that Muskie seemed to lack the drive to be President. With lack of seared ambition comes the ability to go off message. Could his Presidential bid have been salvaged if Muskie's team had those qualities? Maybe. Maybe not. But its combination was fatal.

The irony was that in the Senate, Muskie was a decisive and impetuous man. Weakness was a word few would equate with him. So was Muskie's ability to articulate his reasons for running. It wasn't quite a Ted Kennedy-Roger Mudd moment. But *The Making of the President 1972* described him as an "administered managerial candidate" which may have been enough in a smooth progression, but not when a crisis hit. Muskie himself said of the press he "never could find a way to turn them off with a humorous answer."

Could Muskie have defeated Nixon if he had captured his party's nomination? It's not likely. He surely would have exceeded McGovern's 39%, perhaps getting as high as 45%. Nixon's large margin was aided in fact by many Democrats who felt McGovern was too far to the left. The blue-collar Muskie undoubtedly would have attracted many.

Back in the Senate, Muskie was now a figure of national prominence but Tupper said it "never went to his head… he was as accessible…he'd write the same friendly notes, he'd insist on scribbling something on a note if he didn't write it. I would think he was exactly the same person. Busier perhaps."

Ed and Jane Muskie, whose honor he went down defending
Photo via the Edmund S. Muskie Archives and Special Collections Library

One attribute about Muskie nobody could deny was his temper. David Nevin in *Muskie of Maine* detailed a strategy session by one of his opponents in a race early in his career just prior to a debate. Their goal was to come up with ways "to get Ed mad. You know, get him to blow up on TV and look bad." Nevin called it "an old saw in Washington . . . I asked Muskie about his temper - and he lost his temper." Stephen said his father many times would lose his temper out of passion but that it also wasn't unusual to do so over "trivial" matters. He added his staff often "bore the brunt" of the yelling. Alice Rivlin was Muskie's candidate to lead the newly created Congressional Budget Office (she prevailed over a contender favored by House members) and she joked that she was always careful to never, "get on the bad side of him."

Muskie displayed his pugnacious side to a fellow Democrat in 1977 when the Senate debated capping honoraria at 15% of a Senator's salary. Muskie vehemently opposed the proposal and offered two amendments aimed at thwarting it. He accused sponsor, Wisconsin Democrat Gaylord Nelson of "putting a cap on my income and he has not given a damn from what I can see as to what the consequences on my personal financial life or that of my family may be." Nelson, he said, Nelson "has not asked me, for example, whether the choice will be to send my son to a first rate law school or to a third rate . . ." He called the speaking limitations meaningless and said, "What is created is a sort of lynch mob environment in which people will just vote for anything in the name of ethics." Instead, he argued that full disclosure was the best remedy for cracking down on excessive influence by groups that pay a Senator to speak but it lost 35-62.

After the primaries, Muskie immersed himself in his Senate duties where he was instrumental in the creation of the Budget Committee. Mainers still loved him. His 60% was slightly lower than his previous two elections, but still mighty comfortable. But Muskie never shied from speaking his mind. Paul Simon, in his autobiography, *P.S.*, recalls he and Muskie were once attendees at a White House meeting on the economic situation and when the meeting degenerated to a number of topics, Muskie essentially told President Carter to take control of the situation. Simon observed that a number of participants – among them Rosalyn Carter, cringed.

But it was Carter who awarded Muskie his biggest prize, tapping him to be his Secretary of State in 1980. Muskie was able to keep his enthusiasm in cheek. "It's funny," he said. "Of all the jobs I've been ambitious for, this is one that never crossed my mind." At any rate, he accepted and that would mean saying goodbye to the Senate and hello to Foggy Bottom. With Carter's defeat that fall, the stint would be short, and the Iranian hostage drama occupied most of his time.

Muskie would return to practicing law and served on the Iran Contra investigation commission where he, like other members of the Commission were "appalled by the absence of the kind of alertness and vigilance to (Ronald Reagan's) job and to these policies that one expects of a President." On Reagan not remembering seemingly key events, Muskie said on "Face the Nation", "Of course that worries us. I mean, to have the President not focusing and not recalling what he did on these significant occasions is worrisome."

Muskie died two days before his 82nd birthday in 1996, having nothing to be ashamed of.

Muskie as a Senator
Photo courtesy of the United States Senate Historical Office

CHAPTER FIFTEEN

Papa-Bear
Conservative Goldwater Scorned Party's Social Stances

Historic Quote: To serve in the military, "you don't have to be straight; you just have to shoot straight." - Barry Goldwater.

**Goldwater found southern hospitality in his futile quest to unseat Johnson
Photo courtesy of the Senator Barry M. Goldwater Papers, Arizona
Historical Foundation, Collection, Arizona State Libraries**

May it please thy court that the man who is considered at least one of two founders of modern- day conservatism (Barry Goldwater is considered second to only Ronald Reagan) would castigate his party in later years because of their concentration on social issues. And with his characteristic bluntness and perhaps unintended humor, one can't help but think that, even if they weren't in total agreement, this would have been the most common-sense expression they'd ever heard. Which inevitably would cause many to ask, could this be the same Barry Goldwater? Indeed, it was.

The most famous example of his perhaps surprising position on was on social issues had to do with gays in the military. Goldwater, who had served in the war, once said, "Everyone knows that gays have served honorably in the military since at least the time of Julius Caesar." He added, "You don't have to be straight, you just have to shoot straight." Concerning Watergate, everyone remembers his words: "The best thing Nixon could do for the country is to get the hell out of the White House." Concerning Reagan and Iran Contra, it was "the god-damned stupidest foreign policy blunder this country's ever made!'" Concerning John Tower's embattled nomination, he said, "If everybody in this town connected with politics had to leave town because of chasing women and drinking, you would have no government." And in response to Jerry Falwell saying "every good Christian should be concerned." about abortion, Goldwater retorted, "every good Christian should line up and kick Jerry Falwell's." There is even a story that when Goldwater tried to play golf at a club that denied admittance to Jews, he replied, "I'm half Jewish. Can I play nine holes."

In the early days of his career, there was nothing ambiguous about Goldwater's commitment to the most hard core of conservatism. His best known phrase of course came in his acceptance speech for the Presidency in 1964, when, having wrested control from the moderate wing of the party, he said, "I would remind you that extremism in the defense of liberty is no vice! And let me remind you also that moderation in the pursuit of justice is no virtue!" It was quite possibly the most famous, and most mocked, lines ever uttered by a losing Presidential nominee, although in recent years, the statement, "I voted for it before I voted against it" gives it a run for its money. Goldwater called welfare "socialism," and opposed the Civil Rights Act of 1964, in response to which, he contended that the issue wasn't segregation or integration but "freedom." He said he encouraged integration in Phoenix and was taking the same position for clubs that barred Jews (Goldwater was half-Jewish).

And the ironic thing about Reagan was that he considered Goldwater a mentor. He of course gained fame from a highly regarded commercial on Goldwater's behalf near the election that was credited with thrusting his career.

Unlike members of the "Neanderthal" (southern) caucus," no one who knew Goldwater ever thought he had a bigoted bone in his body. As historian Tim Stanley writes, Goldwater had backed past legislation and encouraged desegregation in Arizona. In 1987, after Republican Governor Evan Mecham vetoed a bill making Martin Luther King, Jr.'s, Birthday a holiday, Goldwater called on him to resign (ultimately he was impeached). He said he was concerned about the violation of the Constitution.

If folks ever wondered what a Michele Bachmann or Steve King general election campaign would look like, Goldwater in 1964 should offer clues.

His slogan was "In your heart you know he's right," to which the LBJ camp responded, "In your gut you know he's nuts," or, to more aptly illustrate the point, "In your heart you know he might." The latter not so subtly was a question to voters about whether they'd want Goldwater's hands on "the button." How did these questions come about? Throughout the campaign, Goldwater had openly spoken about "conventional nuclear weapons" and Democrats were only too happy to brand that in with other views that were thought to be extreme.

Goldwater genuinely liked Kennedy and was devastated by his assassination
Photo via the Library of Congress Prints and Photographs Division

That inspired the famed ten-second "mushroom cloud" ad which, prior to Willie Horton, may have been the single most devastating ad for a Presidential candidate in the age of modern television. It was aired only once but that was enough. *NBC's Monday Night at the Movies* had a huge audience and the Johnson camp shrewdly picked that time to choose to run it.

Goldwater's opinion of Johnson was not high. The President, he said, "used every dirty trick in the book." At one point during the heat of the commercials, Goldwater was so incensed that he called Johnson and asked him to stop airing some of them. If not, he told the President to expect legal action. Johnson did cease. But that was far from his only frustration. Goldwater was also annoyed by Johnson's refusal to debate. On Election Day, before the polls were closed, Goldwater told advisors, "If Jack had been here we would have had a good campaign." Later, with characteristic Goldwater humor, he joked that if half the things they said about Barry Goldwater were true, "I would have voted against the son-of-a-bitch myself."

Goldwater was also hampered by residual damage with moderates from the Republican Convention. After a scorched-earth battle for the Republican platform, moderates were not happy. That forced Goldwater into a series of meetings. The first was in Hershey, Pennsylvania with Eisenhower, Nixon, William Miller, Scranton, Romney, and Rockefeller where he promised to "seek the support of no extremists of the left or the right . . . character assassins, vigilantes, Communists, and any group such as the KKK which seeks to impose its views through terror, threat, or violence." He pledged to back the "proven Eisenhower-Dulles (foreign) policy."

Goldwater did hope to capitalize on the Walter Jenkins sex scandal that surfaced less than three days before Election Day. But while the matter did generate media coverage and prove distracting to the President, he responded by continuing to hammer his rival.

The result was the most infamous electoral disaster for a modern party in history. Goldwater lost to Johnson by an unambiguous 22%, clearly costing his party big in Congress. He took just five Southern states and managed to eke out a mere 5,000 vote victory in his home state where, despite a very close call in 1980, he was never rejected by the voters.

So what happened? Well, it's difficult to attribute the later Goldwater to maturity. After all, in 1964, he was already 55-years-old. For starters, it's possible that he realized that he had been a little too explicit in his desire to end government.

Goldwater's Campaign Button
Photo via tumblr.com

In his memoir, *Goldwater*, he acknowledged that his decision "to discuss the selling of the Tennessee Valley Authority in Knoxville and Social Security's financial crunch in Florida" may not have been wise. Ben Bradlee of *The Washington Post*, which had been hard on Goldwater during the campaign, later admitted "Barry Goldwater is not a zealot. He has never been a zealot. He's a traditional person, a traditional Jeffersonian, not a single issue person." His son, Congressman Barry Goldwater, Jr., went further, declaring it was all in the message. "I wouldn't consider my father a terrific politician," he said. "I think he was more of a statesman who didn't blush about letting people know about (his views)." He added that the examples used (the TVA, social Security, etc.), "may have overshadowed the point."

And team Johnson's response
Photo via tumblr.com

As the years went by, it's not so much that Goldwater relaxed his opposition to conservative ideas, but rather that he took each issue as it came. And he evidently came to the conclusion that a right-leaning philosophy and liberal positions on social issues were not mutually exclusive.

For Goldwater's personal integrity was never questioned. He once instructed a staffer not to go against her personal principles "even if you disagree with me."

Goldwater's generosity also extended to strangers. One woman from New Jersey spoke of a flight to Arizona with her two year- old-son. The Goldwater's were sitting in the front of the plane and when they learned the child was on board, they asked to see him. The mother recounts that the couple had the boy on their laps for an hour, entertaining him and looking out the window. What was most remarkable: the mother and child were strangers.

Concerning abortion, Goldwater in his book maintained that he was personally pro-life but as a matter of policy seemed to think it was a personal matter. His wife may have influenced that way of thinking, and quite possibly, a long-ago incident involving his daughter. Goldwater in 1955 had paid for her to obtain an illegal abortion. But by the 1990's, he had come full circle.

How did Goldwater respond to charges that he was abandoning conservatism? "Today's so-called 'conservatives' don't even know what the word means," he said. "They think I've turned liberal because I believe a woman has a right to an abortion. That's a decision that's up to the pregnant woman, not up to the pope or some do-gooders or the Religious Right. It's not a conservative issue at all."

He spoke against Arizona's Proposition 101, which would severely restrict abortions in the state. In a 1992 Congressional race, Goldwater dissed Republican Doug Wead, backing Democrat Karan English instead. Goldwater explained that English had lived in the state over 20 years and Wead just two. "Karan has lived in the state," he said, "long enough to know its problems." Some Republicans advocated removing Goldwater's name from the state Republican headquarters.

Many could be forgiven for wondering if this was the same person. But this boldness of opinion began even earlier. Goldwater refused to join conservatives opposing busing and prayer in the schools and was not particularly vehement in his opposition to the Panama Canal Treaty. His conservatism was common-sense, which as far as civil liberties were concerned may have been one and the same.

But as Goldwater explained it, "We began walking separate roads when the New Right began pushing special social agendas involving legitimate legal, religious, and other differences. I support much of what they say but not at the risk of compromising constitutional rights." Barry Jr., believes his father's believes his father's mantra was "always believing these things as a libertarian. You cannot talk about limited government and having government out of your life and turn around and talk about abortion and gay rights." Yet this was also around the time Ronald Reagan nominated Sandra Day O'Connor to the Supreme Court and Falwell and his allies opposed her because she was not sufficiently conservative. O'Connor was an Arizonan who had known Goldwater for years and when Falwell turned on her, his son described it as a "Where the hell did this come from" like occurrence.

In later years, Goldwater became deeply close to Hubert Humphrey, Johnson's ticket-mate as well as Jacob Javits, with whom he had tangled over civil rights and who spoke warmly of him.

Watergate brought about more characteristic Goldwater bluntness. Goldwater and Nixon had tangled before, in 1964, when it was unclear whether Goldwater would win the nomination. Nixon had sent word that Rockefeller should be his choice. That was a continuation of bitterness between the three men from 1960.

That year, Nixon, then about to become his party's official nominee for President, established a "compact" with Rockefeller in a meeting at the latter's Fifth Avenue apartment, even offering him the vice-presidency. It became known as the "Fifth Avenue compact." Goldwater was furious, calling the arrangement the "Munich of the Republican Party." And Nixon was "a two-fisted, four square liar."

From cactus to cameras, Goldwater wanted to show the world his Arizona roots
Photo courtesy of the Senator Barry M. Goldwater Papers, Arizona
Historical Foundation, Collection, Arizona State Libraries

Goldwater, who thus far had resisted efforts by conservatives to place his name in nomination, suddenly decided to allow it to go forward. In addressing supporters, however, he urged them to take the high road and support Nixon. "This country is too important for anyone's feelings," he said. "This country in its majesty is too great for any man . . . to stay home and work just because he doesn't agree. Let's grow up, conservatives."

Fast forward to Watergate.

In his memoirs, Goldwater recounts that, when Al Haig telephoned Goldwater to gauge Republican opinion on Nixon, Goldwater suspected he was on the other line listening in. He told Haig he "lied to me for the last time." On August 7, it fell to Goldwater who along with Hugh Scott and John Rhodes, had gone to the Oval Office to give Nixon the bottom line - that his Presidency could not be saved. He told the President: "Things are bad . . . ten (votes) at most. Maybe less . . . You have four firm votes. The others are really undecided. I'm one of them."

Nixon announced his resignation the next day. Later, when Ford pardoned Nixon, Goldwater questioned his authority to do so. He would call Nixon "the most dishonest individual I have ever met in my life."

Nor would Goldwater's old acquaintances with Rockefeller be forgotten. When Gerald Ford selected the now ex-New York Governor to be the new vice-president, Goldwater was dismayed. "I prophesy that within six months to a year the country will hear more of Rockefeller than of Ford and Ford will gradually fade into the background as Rockefeller moves in with all of his power accumulated over the years." Goldwater voted "no" on the Senate floor.

Goldwater married Margaret Johnson in 1934 and would have four children one of whom, Barry, Jr., would serve in Congress from California for nearly 14 years. Affectionately known as "Peggy," the couple's lives together was a storybook romance that lasted 51 years. She would accompany her husband to Washington for Congressional sessions. But the rhetoric of the campaign could take its toll. Daughter JoAnn Goldwater calls her "a kind and gentle person but also quite shy." She adds that "she was very supportive when he ran for President but secretly wished he'd come home," adding, "I'm sure the comments made about dad hurt her more than him. He had a pretty tough skin. Peggy says her mom's chief hobby was painting.

Goldwater was a proponent of fellow Arizonan Sandra Day
O'Connor's nomination to the Supreme Court
Photo courtesy of the Senator Barry M. Goldwater Papers, Arizona
Historical Foundation, Collection, Arizona State Libraries

Goldwater committed the unfathomable when he ousted Senate Majority Leader Ernest McFarland (one of the "Fathers of the GI Bills) 51-49%. He had initially eyed the 1950 Arizona Governor's race but yielded when Howard Pyle jumped in. He agreed to become Pyle's campaign manager and by taking advantage of radio, he helped him eke out a 3,000-vote win over longtime State Auditor Ana Frohmiller.

He recounts in his memoir *Goldwater* that Everett Dirksen was visiting Phoenix in 1951 and first spoke to him about taking on McFarland. But Arizona was a one-party state in those days and as Goldwater later wrote, "My friends said if I ever opposed him, he'd saw me in half." But Goldwater labeled McFarland "the darling of the Truman gang" (the departing President was widely unpopular by then). He got mileage out of McFarland calling Korea a "cheap war," to which

Goldwater responded "find anywhere within the borders of these United States a single mother or father who counts their casualties as cheap." *The Arizona Republic* piled on as well. Calling McFarland an "administration mouthpiece," the paper endorsed Goldwater. And Goldwater composed a jingle:

"Mac is for Harry.
Harry's all though.
You be for Barry
'Cause Barry's for you."

Goldwater was a pilot in the war
Photo courtesy of the Senator Barry M. Goldwater Papers, Arizona Historical Foundation, Collection, Arizona State Libraries

After '52, Goldwater's elections were easy. In fact, Democrats' failure to unseat him in the tsunami of 1958 proved to be virtually their only failure. While he had to surrender his seat to run for President, he won Arizona's other seat over respected opposition with 57%. In the Watergate election of 1974, he took 58% with one prominent Arizona politico asserting, "Christ couldn't beat Goldwater." But by 1980, he was in the fight of his life.

At the beginning of the year, Goldwater had just turned 71 and wasn't even certain he'd be running again. He was tired but also plagued by minor health problems which became major when he had to have hip surgery. Further, about 400,000 Arizonans had moved to the state since he last appeared on the ballot and many were relatively young.

Goldwater's ads weren't setting the world on fire either. He writes in his book that the ads of his opponent, businessman Bill Schultz, were among the "slickest ads any of us had seen," and that many thought Goldwater "looked like Rip Van Winkle." He also admitted that he didn't take his race as seriously as he should have. Many of his loyal Arizona friends were running the campaign, just like '64.

But this was a race he could win. With the presidential race, Goldwater knew even before he got in that he'd lose to Johnson.

Goldwater asked his former pollster Dick Wirthlin to conduct a poll. Wirthlin came back with the words, "Barry, you're in trouble." It found Schultz leading Goldwater 46-44%. Goldwater writes in his book we "revamped our campaign in a big way with three weeks to go." Schultz outspent him 2 to 1 and on Election Eve, it seemed as though that might be enough.

It seemed unfathomable for the man who gave way to modern conservatism to lose his seat in his home state when conservatism was, for the moment anyway, about to be validated in a big way. Yet it almost happened. Goldwater trailed for almost the entire evening. It was only in the morning, after some 400,000 absentees were counted that he learned he had escaped defeat by fewer than 9,000 votes. Ronald Reagan's favor for Goldwater 16 years earlier had come full circle. His coattails brought him to victory.

Goldwater returned to Washington with Republicans in control and the chairmanship of the Senate Intelligence Committee. He had long made clear that he was in his final Senate term and would happily devote his remaining years to Peggy. But she died in late-1985, a year before the term would end. Barry Jr., said "it broke his heart."

After his retirement, Goldwater remarried and lived until 1998, when he succumbed to Alzheimer's at age 89. His kind-heartedness and generosity were Goldwater traits on display throughout his career. On his departure from the Senate, he treated his personal and committee staff to dinner and presented them with momentoes. They did the same.

In early 1996, Goldwater gained unwanted attention by claiming that the only way he'd vote for Bob Dole would be if "he were unopposed." Goldwater later said he was joking and even joked upon endorsing Dole in 1996 that the two were "liberals." Nobody would dare go that far. But for a man no one would dare try to have out-conservative in 1964, his metamorphosis was notable.

Still, for those who wonder how Goldwater's turn toward moderation may have been possible for a man who displayed such hard-lined views, Ted Kennedy, speaking to a friend, may have captured it best: "I think my brother Jack liked Barry Goldwater so much because Barry was good at poking fun at himself. I believe just about everybody in Washington likes Barry today because he came out of his 1964 loss with grace and humor. He started over."

Goldwater's relationship with his Senate staff was legendary
Photo courtesy of the Senator Barry M. Goldwater Papers, Arizona
Historical Foundation, Collection, Arizona State Libraries

Photo courtesy of the Senator Barry M. Goldwater Papers,
Arizona Historical Foundation, Collection, Arizona
State Libraries

CHAPTER SIXTEEN

McGovern's Presidential Bids Went Nowhere But His Devotion Among Liberals and Students A Legend Of Our Time

**Historic Quote: "I wanted to run for President in the worst way - and did."
– George McGovern on his 1972 Presidential campaign.**

H istorically, the term "McGovernism" is equated with a staunch, anti-Vietnam liberalism that inspired a young generation, including many college students. Ask many young people what sparked their political interest, and the answer will invariably be McGovern. So great was their allegiance, commitment, and idealism that the defeated candidate, in the midst of his concession, paid homage to the "greatest outpouring of energy and love that any political effort has ever inspired at least in my lifetime."

The term McGovernism also suggests conservative derision for a candidate of who was associated – by virtue of his supporters and opponents alike, as the candidate of abortion and acid, which partially resulted in a lopsided 49-state loss to incumbent President Richard Nixon. But there is plenty more to the man; despite his dovishness, he was actually a decorated war pilot in the Second World War. Beyond that, his gentle soul and passion for eliminating hunger made him a prototype of the "Greatest Generation."

McGovern was born in the 600-person town of Avon to the son of a preacher, a Methodist minister who could have had a baseball career. That was unappealing, however, because of "too many gamblers, prostitutes and drinkers associated with traveling baseball teams." McGovern grew up in the town of Mitchell where the Great Depression impacted his family directly but even more so indirectly insofar as they witnessed the hardships it brought to others. McGovern did his part to help his family through the Depression; Robert San Anson, in a biography of McGovern, cites "afternoons of grass-cutting . . . and nights of babysitting for his sisters." Ultimately, he thrived. He was a terrific student and a champion debater who was rewarded with a scholarship to Dakota Wesleyan University.

The McGoverns were a Republican family, but George was moved by the aura of FDR and his passion for helping people. Consequently he Democrats officially captured his allegiance in 1945, with McGovern proclaiming the "party was more on the side of average Americans." At Dakota Wesleyan, where

McGovern was in the top ten percent of his class, McGovern found another success: his bride. They met at the Mitchell Rolling Rink where Eleanor was with her sister Ila. George initially asked Ila to be his skating partner and date. She said yes to the former but no to the latter, for she was involved with someone else. He then asked Eleanor.

McGovern's enlistment in the Army came after Pearl Harbor. He flew 35 missions on the plane he named "The Dakota Queen." On the last mission, he was forced to land his plane and won the Distinguished Service Cross. During the '72 campaign, many advisors begged him to talk about his military service. He demurred, believing it would be "bragging."

Upon the war's conclusion, McGovern took advantage of the GI Bill and returned to Dakota Wesleyan; then it was on to Garrett Theological Seminary on the campus of Northwestern where he pursued the ministry. But that lifestyle didn't appeal to him, and he switched to history and pursued his M.A. Meanwhile, Dakota Wesleyan was glad to have him back as a professor. And as a history teacher and debate coach, he was quite beloved—so much so that some students dedicated their yearbook to him. In that time, McGovern began broadening his political views outside the classroom.

Photo courtesy of the Senator George McGovern Collection, Dakota Wesleyan University Archives, Dakota Wesleyan University, Mitchell, South Dakota

1952 was a Presidential election year; during this time, McGovern wrote stories for *The Daily Republic* about the strengths of Democratic nominee Adlai Stevenson. These stories gave him visibility with local Democrats who sought him out and offered him the position of Executive Director of the state's Democratic Party - to the point that a party even existed. Republicans outnumbered Democrats in the legislature 108-2; it was an uphill climb, which, along with family demands and his own increasing academic success, led him to consider declining the offer. McGovern was also pursuing his Doctorate: in 1953, he presented his thesis, a 450-page account of the Colorado Coal Strike, 1913–1914. However, he did ultimately accept the local Democrats' offer and upon doing so would not be deterred. For example, he drove around the state in a beaten-up car trying to get to voters, which made some impact. In the '54 cycle, Democrats increased their margin to 24 seats. McGovern then decided to aim high.

Though freshman Republican Senator Karl Mundt was never in serious jeopardy of losing his seat, McGovern recruited a serious challenger, Kenneth Holum, to oppose him. McGovern linked Mundt to the McCarthy hearings - not a stretch considering Mundt was chairing the committee. He also took advantage of the unpopular policies of controversial Agriculture Secretary Ezra Taft Benson, which went over very well in the state's rural areas. Holum took 43% (two years later, Holum challenged the state's other Senator, Francis Case, and in a very Republican year came within a tantalizing 1% of unseating him).

Meanwhile, *The Daily Republic*, in a profile on McGovern, in part revealed the secret to his success. "When he met someone new, he wrote notes about the person on a 3x5 note card. He filed the cards in a shoe box, with tabs for counties and cities. When he made a repeat visit somewhere, he reviewed the cards for that place so he could call people by name and inquire about things they discussed previously. He continued the practice throughout his political career, eventually accumulating thousands of cards and switching from a shoebox to metal file cases."

In 1956, McGovern decided to run for office himself. His target very much seemed elusive. Harold Orrin Lovre had served eight years, Eisenhower was headed for a landslide sweep, and McGovern was forced to respond to Lovre's contention that he was soft on Communism by virtue of the fact that he favored admitting China to the United Nations. McGovern responded that he "always despised communism and every other ruthless tyranny over the mind and spirit of man." Lovre had other problems. The Farmers Union and the National Farmers Association, angered by Benson, were firmly behind McGovern. When the dust had settled, McGovern had ousted the incumbent by a solid 53-47% margin. The South Dakotans Washington neighbors would be his geographical neighbors: Hubert and Muriel Humphrey of Minnesota.

George and Eleanor McGovern
Photo courtesy of the Senator George McGovern Collection, Dakota Wesleyan
University Archives, Dakota Wesleyan University, Mitchell, South Dakota

Anson wrote that, "within months of taking office, he established a reputation in his home state as 'the man you write to when you want something done.'" Chief among these were congratulatory letters, etc. Meanwhile, McGovern had developed his niche on an issue: alleviating hunger—an aspiration that was not only humane but could also had the potential to beneficial to his many constituents in the Farm Belt. Area redevelopment and moving excess food from the jurisdiction of the Department of Agriculture to Health, Education, and Welfare. His partner on the latter: a Massachusetts Senator and Presidential aspirant named John F. Kennedy. He also succeeded in obtaining grants for teachers of the developmentally disabled. The visibility McGovern enjoyed led Esquire to put McGovern on its list of "18 most promising" young Americans.

In 1958, McGovern was challenged for re-election by the state's Republican Governor, Joe Foss, who himself had a decorated war record. Fifty years later, McGovern told *The Daily Republic* he had it easy as Foss had hemmed and hawed over running before the state GOP prevailed upon him to do so. Colleagues didn't see it that way. Years later, he recalled many who had thought that his initial win had been such a fluke that they would come to bid him farewell, thinking he could not possibly hold. The result was an unambiguous 58%. Still, McGovern was enough of an anomaly in South Dakota that *The Almanac of American Politics* later credited him for having "really personified the Democratic Party in the state." But even that would end for a time. Mundt's election cycle was coming up again, and McGovern decided to take him on. Years later, he didn't sugarcoat his feelings about him. "I don't know how he felt about me but I knew I hated his guts." McGovern was considered such a strong get for national Democrats that Kennedy, Lyndon Johnson, and Hubert Humphrey all attended his campaign kickoff. He led for a good part of the night but, by morning, Mundt had edged him out 52-48%. In defeat, McGovern told supporters that "at least we won a moral victory." Bobby Kennedy, still not certain of his brother's election, called him at 4 a.m. to offer condolences - it was also a hint that the Kennedys wouldn't want him out of the limelight for long.

Kennedy had won the White House, and despite calls to name him Secretary of Agriculture (from Bobby Kennedy no less), he ended up with something that would prove equally as lucrative for his mission of eradicating hunger when Kennedy named him Director of the U.S. Food for Peace program. In that position, he played a central role building the United Nations' World Food Program, a humanitarian organization that has provided food assistance to hundreds of millions of victims of wars and natural disasters and provided foreign nations with credit to buy surplus U.S. crops.

Photo via the John F. Kennedy Presidential Library and Museum

It was after Kennedy sent McGovern to the Intergovernmental Advisory Committee meeting in Rome in early 1961 that McGovern asked his aides to draw up a plan for him to present to the delegates. The result was a nine-point plan. Jon Lauck, who authored a dissertation on McGovern's farm policy for the Universty of South Dakota wrote how "Almost singlehandedly, through a combination of courage, confidence and charm, he set in motion the process and the inspiration that would evolve into the world food program." Washington columnist Drew Pearson went farther: McGovern "has put three times as much life into the Food for Peace program in six months," he wrote, "as in eight years under Eisenhower."

McGovern's tenure was brief but this was his own doing. He resigned to challenge incumbent Republican Senator Case, an uncontroversial incumbent but one of obviously advanced age. His decision to return home was not universally embraced. One leading newspaper praised his work at Food for Peace, saying he had "made sense out of the usual Washington scramble." Case died that July, and South Dakota Republicans took 20 ballots before selecting Lieutenant Governor Joe Bottum as their standard bearer. The GOP tried to tie him to the Kennedy administration, but McGovern replied that no one has "dictated his vote or convictions and no one ever will except the citizens of my state."

McGovern's lead on Election Night was a mere 200 votes and the final margin was 597. But the seat was his, and he had six years to do as he pleased with it. He was assigned to the Agriculture and Interior Committees. For immediate purposes, that was rallying against the imminent Vietnam War.

McGovern was among the first senators on record who began publicly questioning American military involvement in Vietnam. What made this remarkable was that it was nearly a year before the Tonkin Gulf. In his maiden speech on the Senate floor, he called U.S. involvement "a 'trap' that had lured America into Southeast Asia." He also said Vietnam "will haunt us in every corner of this revolutionary world, if we do not properly appraise its lesson . . . the current dilemma in Vietnam is a clear demonstration of the limitations of military power. There in the jungles of Asia, our mighty nuclear arsenal - our $50 billion arms budget - even our costly new 'Special Forces'—have proved powerless to cope with a ragged band of illiterate guerrillas fighting with home-made weapons or with weapons they have captured from us."

McGovern assumed people would take notice: "I thought it was kind of a nugget that would catch some attention. But it didn't. People just thought I was talking about a rather obscure and insignificant little country and that it really didn't matter all that much." Worse yet, as Bob Mann would write, "Food For Peace was providing a valuable and flexible tool in the achievement of U.S. policy goals in Vietnam." Boy would that change. McGovern did support the Tonkin Gulf resolution the following year. But he couldn't have imagined that his prophecy would have been proven correct so quickly. By January 1965, he was backing up his own prophecy. "We are fighting a determined army of guerrillas that seems to enjoy the cooperation of the countryside and that grow[s] stronger in the face of foreign intervention," he said in a widely noticed Jan. 15, 1965, Senate speech that marked him as the leading Senate pacifist. "We are further away from victory over the guerrilla forces in Vietnam today than we were a decade ago."

Before it became clear that Bobby Kennedy would be running for President on an anti-war platform, prominent Vietnam War activists, including Al Lowenstein, tried to get McGovern to enter the race for the White House. He declined. Once

Kennedy was murdered, however, he began thinking about ways of continuing his murdered colleague's legacy. In one conversation with Lowenstein, he said, "You know, Al, if I had taken your advice [last] August, I don't think we'd be here today."

McGovern was genuinely devastated by Kennedy's death. The two had forged a close bond, which, according to the Anson biography, was not evident in their early days: "At first, McGovern had been put off by the younger Kennedy's abrasive brusqueness; in temperament and style, he was far closer to Jack. There was something about Bobby that made McGovern vaguely mistrustful; not so much his ruthlessness perhaps as the passion with which he pursued life and everything about it. As the two came to know one another, however, McGovern's suspicions disappeared." It was said that the tears McGovern shed on his assassination might have been a first in more than 30 years. He realized he had no choice but to go forward.

McGovern announced his candidacy in the Senate Caucus Room. He told supporters he "wear[s] no claim to the Kennedy mantle, but I believe deeply in the twin goals for which Robert Kennedy gave his life—an end to the war in Vietnam and a passionate commitment to heal the divisions in our own society." His goal was to mend divisions among members of the Democratic Party. According to a biography of Gene McCarthy, "McGovern knew Humphrey would win the nomination and wanted to try to heal the rift which only seemed to be widening. George was not only a gentleman from the start but actively tried to promote the Humphrey cause . . . give Humphrey all his support while seemingly pleading his own cause." These efforts were exemplified by his response to the mayhem on the streets of Chicago. McGovern struck back at those who favored law and order, calling it "pretty hollow unless it is coupled with justice. Hitler in his way enforced law and order. The cry I hear from sources about law and order has strong undertones of racism."

After the campaign ended with Humphrey as the nominee, McGovern joked that "at least I didn't peak too early." Meanwhile, he was up for re-election that fall and beat his opponent 57-43%. That was when he truly began putting his words into action on the Vietnam War. On September 1, 1970, the McGovern-Hatfield amendment, which would cut funds for any operations in Southeast Asia by December 31, 1971, was taken up. It failed 55-39 but not before McGovern issued a seething denunciation of continued involvement.

He spoke of "human wreckage at Walter Reed and Bethesda Naval and all across our land–young men without legs, or arms or genitals, or hopes . . . There are not many of those blasted and broken boys who think this war is a glorious venture. Do not talk to them about bugging out, or national honor, or courage. It does not take any courage at all for a Congressman or a Senator or a President to wrap himself in the flag and say we are staying in Vietnam, because it is not our blood that is being shed." In the kicker, he said, "Every Senator in this Chamber is partly responsible for sending 50,000 young Americans to an early grave. This chamber reeks of blood."

1972 featured a donnybrook of Democratic Presidential aspirants. McGovern was the first to enter the race, way back in January of 1971, a fact not lost on him following the devastating defeat when he told supporters on Election Night how, "All of the joy and satisfaction that we have found in the past 22 months are not going to be washed away with the tears and regrets over one night."

At that early date, McGovern was registering one percent in polls. It was not until primary season commenced more than a year later that McGovern was seen as a frontrunner. The first signal was the Iowa caucus where McGovern ran stronger than expected against Ed Muskie. But a more serious look came following the New Hampshire primary when Muskie, fresh off the "snowflake incident," limped to an unexpectedly weak win. It was then onto Wisconsin. With it came a never before kind of campaign. Eugene Pokorny, dubbed "the best young political organizer in the history of this country," managed the operation.

Photo courtesy of the Senator George McGovern Collection, Dakota Wesleyan University Archives, Dakota Wesleyan University, Mitchell, South Dakota

Tim Crouse summed up the typical McGovern volunteer in a profile years later on the legendary operation when he spoke of "beautiful, euphoric, slightly drunk, very young McGovern volunteers." Then came critical Massachusetts, a liberal bastion in which he could eliminate many of his rivals. Theodore White wrote of his dominance among students: "The college proletariat was all his. No bulletin board in any college or university, apparently, carried any other notices but those of McGovern volunteers or rallies." He won Massachusetts with a clear majority - 52% of the vote. So sweeping was his win that Tip O'Neill, a Muskie backer, was stunned when he called a Boston newspaper on primary night to find out how his slate had done—only to learn that McGovern had beaten him 2 to 1 in his own district, prompting him to say later, "we got beat by the cast of Hair. Oregon produced big dividends as well. Big crowds awaited. At one appearance at the University of Oregon, he drew 5,000 and generated huge applause when he called Vietnam a "moral outrage." The grassroots was unbelievable; it forced the media to acknowledge that McGovern had risen from the "phantom candidate status." *The Boston Globe* called it a "stunning-pollster confounding victory" and *The New York Times*, following his New York delegate-slate victory (voters didn't select an actual candidate), called it "the most astonishing climb out of political obscurity in recent political history."

Then came the all-important California primary. With its winner-take-all system, even a one-vote victory would send 312 delegates into the winner's column. McGovern seemed an underdog to Hubert Humphrey and needed to attract votes from liberals. That is when he established his "$1,000 plan." As *The Harvard Crimson* described it, the plan would "have provided a minimum income of $4000 to a family of four with no income and progressively diminishing amounts to families with incomes up to $12,000 a year." It was billed as a $1,000 income grant. Humphrey called it a "compounded mess." Next, McGovern called for a $31 billion defense reduction, which his rival said would "cut into the very muscle of our defense." It was a success. McGovern beat Humphrey by a closer-than-expected 44-39% but the consequences of the win were huge. Still, the proposal was widely mocked, and heading into the fall, it lent credence to the notion that McGovern was a "starry-eyed liberal." Years later, he acknowledged that he hadn't done nearly enough to combat that perception. "I am a liberal and always have been. Just not the wild-eyed character the Republicans made me out to be." That fact was attested to by such unlikely sources as Tower, who in his memoir conceded he was "no starry-eyed liberal." But there could be no compromise on Vietnam and the campaign's slogan would be "Bring America Home."

The victory in California put McGovern on a strong path to win the nomination and he succeeded, but only after a lot of not-so-private maneuvering. An "Anybody But McGovern" group (ABC) - led by an obscure Georgia Governor named Jimmy Carter - was organized as a last-ditch effort to stop their putative standard-bearer (partly as a result, four years later McGovern cast his vote for Republican Gerald Ford rather than Carter).

Even ahead of the game, McGovern knew he had fences to mend and began placing calls to Chicago Mayor Richard Daley and AFL-CIO President George Meaney (who conveniently was never around for the calls). And he made his plans crystal clear in his acceptance speech in Miami Beach. "In 1968," he said, "Americans voted to bring our sons home from Vietnam in peace—and since then, 20,000 have come home in coffins. I have no secret plan for peace. I have a public plan. As one whose heart has ached for 10 years over the agony of Vietnam, I will halt the senseless bombing of Indochina on Inauguration Day." However, a combination of dilatory tactics and legitimate parliamentary inquiries in part brought about by new rules put forth by reform-minded McGovernites prevented McGovern from taking the stage to deliver his acceptance speech until 2:48 a.m. EST when all but 3 million Americans had gone to sleep (as opposed to the 17 million viewers who had been tuning in during the primetime hours). That greatly hampered his ability to tell his story to voters who knew only what they had heard, including the still radical ideas of decriminalizing abortion and leaving drug laws to the states.

And then, the bottom fell out. First came selecting a running mate—which, having finally secured the nomination the night before he was due to accept, he had mere hours to find. His first, second, and third choice was unambiguously Ted Kennedy. McGovern had sought him out before but genuinely felt he could win him over at that time. "I thought that being a Kennedy and having an image of greatness like his brothers would eventually bring Teddy out. I was always after him to play that role. I was closest to Bobby. He was really the one who had my heart. But I had genuine affection and admiration for Teddy as well." It proved a Waiting for Godot scenario until the end. McGovern called Kennedy an hour after winning the nomination and was again turned down. It wasn't just Teddy who did. McGovern offered the spot to Abe Ribicoff, Gaylord Nelson (his best friend in the Senate), and several others. All turned him down. So it was in part with Kennedy's recommendation that McGovern turned to his colleague from Missouri, Thomas Eagleton. Despite having served in the Senate together for four years, the longest conversation between the two men had occurred in 1969 in the Senate steam room.

Eagleton assured McGovernites that he had no skeletons in his closet, but it was revealed that years before he had been hospitalized at the Mayo Clinic for depression and undergone electric shock treatments. "My father was a clergyman and he had to deal with people of emotional and all kinds of irregularities. So I grew up with compassion for people in some kind of psychological struggle." McGovern double-downed, saying, "there is no member of that Senate who is any sounder in mind, body and spirit than Tom Eagleton. If I had known every detail that he had discussed with me this morning . . . he would still have been my choice for the vice-presidency . . . I know enough about American history to know that some of our most honored Presidents have survived illnesses far more serious than anything that Senator Eagleton has touched on today."

Photo courtesy of the Senator George McGovern Collection, Dakota Wesleyan University Archives, Dakota Wesleyan University, Mitchell, South Dakota

And then, McGovern delivered what journalist Theodore H. White would later call "possibly the most single damaging faux pas ever made by a presidential candidate" as McGovern declared he was behind Eagleton "1,000 percent."

Steadily, though, McGovern's staff had been consulting psychiatrists who were almost unanimous in the opinion that Eagleton should be dropped. One even said, "he could do anything in America, except be President." Though the American public was overwhelmingly sympathetic to Eagleton, McGovernites were anticipating a razor-tight election and felt that even the slightest dropoff over the issue could tip the race. McGovern consequently did remove Eagleton though the two held a joint press conference to convey the sense of unity. McGovern said as much, blaming "the public debate over Senator Eagleton's past medical history [for continuing] to divert attention from the great national issues that need to be discussed." McGovern ultimately selected Sargent Shriver as his running mate, but the damage was done.

For the general, Nixon cultivated a Rose Garden strategy. Late in October, McGovern took issue with Secretary of State Kissinger's contention that "peace is at hand." The Senator's closing argument was reminding voters, "this is a choice which is probably the clearest choice between the candidates for President ever presented to the American people in this century."

McGovern thought carrying New York and California as well as a number of swing states would get him close to the magic 270 electoral votes. Instead, every conceivable scenario collapsed except for the most calamitous. Besides the District of Columbia, which was never in doubt, only the Commonwealth of Massachusetts came through (by a solid nine-point margin). His drubbing in New York was so bad (one million votes) that his margin in the city was mere 81,000 votes (Nixon even led there at 11 p.m. EST). At the Republican National Committee headquarters, the biggest cheer of the evening came when the Empire State's 41 electoral votes were awarded to Nixon just 45 minutes after the polls had closed. Theodore H. White in *The Making of the President, 1972* notes that McGovern surrendered 18 percent of the black vote to Nixon, 37 percent of the Jewish vote, and a majority of working-class and Catholics. Many historically Democratic cities voted what White calls "utterly out of political character" by backing Nixon, including many, such as Priovidence, Rhode Island with large Cathiolic populations. Even South Dakota stuck with the President, though by taking 46% - higher than many "swing" states - some voters were willing to show their loyalty to their Senator. One son of a Democratic family recalls his father coming home "white as a ghost" after having voted on Election Day." The lad asked if he was okay, to which the father replied, "I just voted for Nixon."

Despite his national stardom, South Dakota was McGovern's true pride and joy
Photo courtesy of Keith Wessel

In his concession speech, McGovern refused to surrender his beliefs, telling his supporters, "We do not rally to the support of policies we deplore. We love this country and we will continue to beckon it to a higher standard." Sensing the devastating loss before the election, he grieved more for his staff. And unlike Gene McCarthy - who never exhibited appreciation for his staff and devoted volunteers after the campaign ended - McGovern stated his unambiguous affection for their efforts, quoting the poet Yates, who said, "Count where man's glory most begins and ends, and say, my glory was I had such friends."

McGovern said the year after his loss that he "wanted to run for President in the worst way - and did." The Eagleton affair haunted him throughout. The interpretation of the "1,000 proposal" hurt as well. Most of all he acknowledged that he had allowed himself to be defined. The image of his supporters created an impression that he was the candidate of abortion, acid, and marijuana. His advisers pleaded with him to talk about his war experiences but he demurred.

With ex-Congresswoman Helen Gahagan Douglas (center),
whom Nixon beat for the U.S. Senate in 1950
Photo courtesy of Keith Wessel

Back in the Senate, McGovern was able to turn to his true cause: alleviating hunger. With Bob Dole, he pushed through The Dole-McGovern Food Stamp Reform Act of 1977. They expanded the domestic school lunch program and established the Special Supplemental Program for Women, Infants, and Children.

McGovern reflected years later that had the election occurred in 1974, he would have won. Yet despite the Democratic winds of that year, he did have a rougher than expected time even winning a third Senate term. He beat former

Vietnam POW Leo Thorsness 53-47% at a time when many Democrats were relying on Watergate to deliver them big margins. By 1980, he was in even worse shape, down 25 points at one point. Some allies pleaded with him to quit but McGovern said that the incessant and over-the-top conservative attacks made him want to run even more. The National Conservative Political Action Committee attacked McGovern early and often, to the point that at least some Republican-leaning voters were turned off and backed McGovern. However, the incumbent acknowledged it wasn't as many as he had hoped. But the impact was enough that Abdnor said, "I'd tell them to get the heck out" if they returned.

Meanwhile, McGovern tried to get Abdnor to debate, though the challenger, suspecting it was done to expose his speech impediment, declined. The Conservative PAC put McGovern on the defensive over abortion but he told voters he personally opposed it. McGovern hit the campaign trail and parade routes hard and outspent Abdnor nearly three to one. While not abandoning his liberalism, he tried to finesse it somewhat by backing a version of the B-1 bomber which liberals had derided as over-priced and antiquated. By Election Day, some thought his loyal followers might carry him. They were wrong - unambiguously. Abdnor prevailed 58-39%, carrying all but three counties.

To those close to him, McGovern's private persona was a man who was as loving and unpretentious as he seemed in public. Jeff Brocklesby, the Senator's assistant press secretary during the last two years of his Senate career and the top press person during his final, losing Senate race in 1980, describes McGovern as "a very kind, patient man. His staff adored him. He was incredibly even-tempered." So it was a shock when McGovern lost his temper with a member of his staff because as Brocklesby notes, he "virtually never did . . . Everyone was shocked because something like this virtually never happened." Brocklesby adds that McGovern yelled at him only once, in the closing days of that futile '80 election, which he describes as "quite understandable." His generosity with them was nevertheless second-to-none as he recalls the Senator and Eleanor McGovern hosting the entire staff in their home for what he describes as a Christmas/farewell party following the '80 election.

In retirement, McGovern opened a motel in Connecticut - a decision that gave him insight into the hurdles that ordinary small business owners face, a fact he acknowledged. By 1984, McGovern decided to go for the top prize one more time, but even Massachusetts, which had been so kind to him in campaigns past, would do so no more. A former vice-president, Walter Mondale, and Gary Hart, then a Senator who was also seeking the Democratic nod, eclipsed McGovern. He took just 17%. McGovern seriously toyed with throwing his hat into the ring again in 1992 before deciding against it, but he did say he couldn't possibly have stayed out if he were ten years younger.

Instead, he resumed his personal endeavors. He served as an ambassador to the U.N. Food and Agriculture Organization and founded the McGovern-Dole International Food for Education and Child Nutrition Program, which according to Dole "has provided meals to 22 million children in 41 countries."

McGovern suffered personal tragedy in 1994 when his daughter Terry, an on-again, off-again alcoholic, was found dead outside in the Wisconsin winter. Two years later, he wrote a book, *Terry*, the writing of which he described as "the most painful undertaking in my life."

Near the end of his life, he took up new adventures; driving a racecar and skydiving out of an airplane. Judy Harrington was a McGovern staffer for his last ten years in office and continued to serve him after he left office. When McGovern told his staff he was going to drive a racecar, they're reply was, "you're going to do what!" But he did it and left a voicemail for Harrington shortly after the endeavor telling her of the thrill. Harrington, who received a phone She called him "pretty tickled with himself that he didn't have a wreck," adding he liked "suiting up and being up there with the guys."

And with time came the forgiveness of old enemies. In 1993, he surprised some by appearing at the funeral for Pat Nixon. His response: "You can't keep on campaigning forever." That was the man McGovern was.

CHAPTER SEVENTEEN

Sex, Lies, Videotape and A Few Bad Men: Abscam Rocks Congress

Historic Tidbit: Seven members of Congress (six Congressmen and a Senator), were implicated in Abscam. The most colorful was John Jenrette, a Democratic Congressman from South Carolina; this stemmed not so much from his acceptance of $50,000, but from having sex with his wife Rita one night near a pillar on the Capitol steps. She eventually would pose for Playboy and the couple would divorce. Jenrette, meanwhile, lost his re-election bid in 1980, spent a year and a half in prison, andwas convicted in 1989 of stealing a tie and some shoes from a department store. Jenrette and his wife became the inspiration for the famous "Capital Steps."

John and Rita Jenrette entering federal court, 1980
Photo via Corbis Images

I t is impossible to talk about "statesmen and mischief makers"—or the 1970s for that matter—without including Abscam. The widespread scandal led to an undercover sting operation that ultimately destroyed the careers of seven lawmakers—some powerful and some not, some senior and some not. The sordid characters and transgressions of some of the members proved the old axiom that truth is stranger than fiction. At the same time, it created an atmosphere of amusement, befuddlement, and anger on the part of the American people.

According to *Political Corruption in America*, Abscam remains "the quintessential kickback scandal, one to which all others are compared." It was named for Abdul Sheik, the fictitious company that bribed the lawmakers. Little did they know the folks handing it over were undercover and wired FBI agents.

Image courtesy of Politics1.com

New Jersey's Harrison Williams was the only Senator involved—and the one whose deliberations were the most protracted. Williams was as close to a "golden boy" in New Jersey politics as can be. He won a special election to the House from a Republican area (Plainfield) in 1953 to succeed the man who would become his Senate colleague for 20 years, Republican Cliff Case. Williams sponsored his first bill with a Senator named John F. Kennedy. He held in 1954 but was narrowly unseated two years later amid the Eisenhower landslide. The difference was just 4,000 votes as Eisenhower was getting a big margin. After his term ended, Williams continued practicing law and became closely aligned with Governor Robert Meyner. He successfully enabled Williams to make a comeback, and the timing couldn't have been better. Meyner won his Senate seat in the Democratic landslide of 1958 by besting Congressman Robert Kean, the father of New Jersey's future Governor Tom Kean.

Photos courtesy of the Rutgers University Special Collections Archive

In the Senate, Williams compiled a voting record that was solidly pro-labor, and he rose to chair the Committee on Labor and Public Welfare. He was also a master at brokering compromises for landmark bills that often seemed, if not intractable, than certainly stalled. But he also had indelible legislation of his own. Among them: the Occupational Health and Safety Board (OSHA), the Employee Retirement Income Security Act, the Coal Mine and Health Safety Act, and the Urban Mass Transit Act. He was the first chair of the Senate Committee on Aging.

As various bills were being weaved together, Williams would always take care to make sure the people for whom the laws were intended to help were receiving maximum aid. In 1972, when Nebraska Republican Carl Curtis proposed an amendment to an OSHA reauthorization bill that would exempt firms with fewer than 15 people from regulations, Williams objecting, saying, "a great variety of high hazard activities...are very commonly performed by small firms." Also that year, as the Senate considered an extension of the Public Works Act, Williams proposed an amendment aiding workers hurt by the need to comply with environmental regulations.

Williams was a strong proponent of an increased minimum wage. As the Senate dealt with a flood of amendments in 1974, Williams said, "We want to promote the opportunity for people who work to be able to make enough money to support themselves and their families and not have a continuation of working people having to piece out a meager standard of living through resort to the welfare rolls."

Williams was so popular that his career persevered even as he revealed in the midst of his 1970 re-election campaign that he had a problem with alcohol (he was sanctioned by the NAACP when he showed up to a forum drunk). Then came the real problems.

Photos courtesy of the Rutgers University Special Collections Archive

Melvin Weinberg, as *The New York Times* told it, "posed as a fabulously wealthy sheik" who had "front men" who bribed Williams into, among other things, pressing immigration language and loaning $100 million to the mining company in which he had stock. The jury deliberated for 8 hours and 2 ½ days, ultimately convicting Williams on all nine counts. Williams addressed the press later that night and said, "In my heart, I know I did no wrong."

His Senate colleagues seemed to sway more toward the jury's view—and since Williams was the first Senator since 1905 to be convicted of a crime while in office, his fellow Senators faced a dilemma. Should they expel him or simply slap him on the wrist via censure? They debated it for five days. Daniel Inouye served as his lawyer. On August 24th, the Senate Ethics Committee called Williams' conduct "ethically repugnant" and unanimously recommended expulsion. But Williams refused to go quietly. In fact, his case did not go to the Senate floor until the following March. The chamber was not without splits. Inouye and Alan Cranston in particular were promoting censure, but many of Williams' friends, including Missouri's Tom Eagleton, refused. With expulsion inevitable, Williams bowed to reality and resigned.

In his 25-minute-long farewell speech, Williams said, "It is not only Pete Williams that stands accused or indicted. It is all of us. It is the entire Senate . . . I did not wish to see the Senate bring dishonor to himself by expelling me. I have fought the good fight. I have finished my course. I have kept the faith." Later, reporters asked why he hadn't apologized, to which he replied, "To be foolish is to be human. Should we apologize for that?"

Williams (fourth from left) and Thompson (far right) join President Kennedy as he signs the Delaware-New Jersey Compact

Williams was sentenced to three years in prison and, upon serving the bulk of it at a federal corrections center in Allenwood, Pennsylvania, finished at the Integrity House in Newark. Following his release, he was named to the board. Just before his death in 2001 at 81 years old, Williams sought a pardon from President Clinton. It was denied.

Two other longtime lawmakers who saw their careers end in the Abscam mess were intertwined via incident and indictment. Frank Thompson had represented a Trenton, NJ-anchored district for 26 years and had served as Assembly Minority Leader prior to that. He had chaired the House Administration Committee, which unofficially made him the "Mayor of Capitol Hill." That post did not come naturally, for in 1974, the race for the House Administration gavel became weaved in broader House politics.

One newspaper account described Thompson as "a wine connoisseur, a congressional junketeer, a chain- smoker, a liberal, a pal of labor, a scion of politicians, a fun-lover, a giver of nicknames. Everyone calls him 'Thompy' or 'Topper.'" He in turn coined the term, "Watergate Babies," for the 75 Democratic freshman who came to the House following President Nixon's resignation that August. For Thompson, the months that followed that election did not prove as auspicious as they were for his new colleagues.

After two decades of sitting alongside the autocratic and ruthless Wayne Hays, Thompson had not planned on challenging him for the chairmanship even though he viewed Hays as an "arrogant prick." But Missouri's Richard Bolling wanted to end any aspirations California Democrat Phil Burton had at leadership and Burton was backing Hays who had lost badly in the Steering Committee. But in an odd set of rules, Thompson had to be rejected by the full caucus on his own – even unopposed, in order to be voted on a week later. That did happen 176-109. Thompson was still unsure at whether to get into the race but after threats from Team Hays about losing his own subcommittee chairmanship if he followed through and lost, he continued. But Hays also chaired the DCCC and as much as he embodied everything that some newly elected reformers wanted to change, other, more conventional freshman were grateful for the help he provided. Hays held off Thompson 161-111. Two years later, when Burton was losing the Majority Leader's race to Jim Wright by a single vote, Thompson played a gleeful role in taking him down. "This guy worked me over and I want to teach him a lesson" was his rationale and Thompson converted three New Jersey colleagues alone.

"Thompy" was also a liberal in the truest sense of the word. He was a co-founder of the Democratic Study Group, which proved a forum for likeminded progressives to converge. It was his version of legislation creating the National Endowment for the Arts that made it into law (he referred to the United

States, "the last civilized nation on the earth to recognize that the arts and the humanities have a place in our national life." Ditto with the JFK Center for the Performing Arts.

Thompson fought for racial equality in the military. He said that since the Army became volunteer, half of its enlistees have been black, and "I can't imagine any black or Spanish speaking person wanting to take his basic training at Fort Benning," an installation he described as a Southern swamp in a cultural desert. Thompson was not adverse to letting foes have it he felt they were not doing right. When Nebraska Republican Congressman Dave Martin accused President Johnson of "giving in to a mob scene," by proposing the Voting Rights Act, Thompson accused Martin of "not only opposing giving the Negro the right to vote but fears that if they do, he will be defeated." He also pointedly accused House leaders of "concentrating so hard" on rounding up votes for the controversial House committee reorganization plan that "they were derelict in their responsibility to see that the rule was adopted." In 1975, after a shocking five vote fail by to pass a rule that would allow voter registration by postcard, Thompson criticized Speaker Carl Albert. If the Speaker, he said, had "spent the same amount of time and energy on voter registration as he has on committee reform, it would have passed."

Thompson (left and another member of Congress
Photo courtesy of the John F. Kennedy Presidential library and Museum

Since 1960, Thompson had been a passionate advocate of common-site picketing. In 1975, "It is my bill, with…more than 100 co-sponsors but at times in recent discussions I have found it…distorted and twisted virtually all out of recognition by its opponents and detractors." At one point, he was angry with his chairman, Adam Clayton Powell who wouldn't submit the bill to the Rules Committee until the House increased funding for the Equal Employment Commission, a strategy that put Powell at odds with many African-American leaders. With Democrats firmly in Congress and Democrat Jimmy Carter in the White House in 1977, Thompson thought the moment had arrived. He was correct – at least when it came to the House, as the bill passed 257-163 but the Senate never took up the matter. Thompson was floor manager of a bill that would give bargaining rights to non-profit hospital employees. He said enactment would, "bring stability to the hospital industry work force by reducing… recognition strikes and the incredible turnover in hospital employees."

Thompson was a politician whom *Congressional Quarterly* described as having "a witty raconteur with an affable nature," he was beloved by unions and staffers alike. As such, his involvement in the scandal was viewed as a genuine surprise.

Years after his conviction, a local newspaper called John Murphy "the lion of Staten Island's Democratic Party." By the time his troubles started, he had risen to the chairmanship of the Merchant Marine and Fisheries Committee. To serve his constituents, Murphy often had balancing acts. He was fairly conservative, while the lower Manhattan portion of his district was quite liberal. Murphy was also a champion of the unions, particularly in the maritime industry, and he tried assiduously to have cargo shipped in U.S. flags. He also vociferously opposed the return of the Panama Canal.

Thompson's role came via an introduction to the agents by Howard Criden, a Philadelphia attorney. Both took $50,000 for promised help on an "immigration matter." Thompson then proceeded to get Murphy involved, and he would subsequently have his own meetings with the agents at a hotel near JFK Airport. During the first few sting operations, Murphy played right into the FBI's hands, instructing his aide to "take care of it" as he accepted the $50,000. By their last session, though, he had clearly become suspicious. "You see, any time money's mentioned when a public official is mentioned, there's automatically an ability to link them to something illegal. No public official would do something like that. Particularly Thompson, [John] Murtha or myself. We'd never do anything like that, see." Murphy then claimed that the agent didn't give him any money, and the agent said, "Ok, I gave it to [Howard]." Murphy made clear that he "never received any money from anyone and would not accept anything - from you or Howard."

Murphy and President Johnson on Staten Island
Photo courtesy of the Staten Island Advance

Thompson and Murphy, in the middle of campaigns for new terms, were indicted on June 19, 1980. Thompson contended he had "committed no crime, violated no law, and broached none of my duties to the people of New Jersey." The voters saw it differently.

As Ronald Reagan was struggling to carry his district, Thompson lost to a 27-year-old Right to Life Director named Chris Smith—whom he had outspent by $169,000 to $79,000—57-41%. Murphy's 34.2% in the primary would be a harbinger of what to expect in the general election, and unlike Smith, the man Murphy faced was no novice. Guy Molinari was a well-respected New York State Senator, with big appeal for Staten Island's sizable Italian-American community, and a leader in the fight to contain the Borough's many land-fills. And Murphy was hurt by the presence of Staten Island Councilwoman Mary Codd, whom he had held off in the primary but was now running with the Liberal Party endorsement. Molinari won 48-35%.

For Thompson, the drop was steep. He first won his seat in 1954 and immediately became a leader and mentor of sorts to other members. In his second term, he was a member of the democratic Study Group and put forth an unabashedly progressive platform that backed civil rights, union protection and a strong defense.

The trials commenced a month later. Thompson was convicted and sentenced to two years in prison. When the jury rendered its verdict, Thompson shook his head "no." It was perhaps appropriate that as he prepared to depart Congress, Thompson told the New York Times he was "older and a little less flamboyant. Being a Congressman was a difficult job, but I loved it."

Upon his release, Thompson continued to advise labor unions until his death shortly before his 71st birthday in 1989.

Ray Lederer
Photo via the U.S. Government Printing Office

Oddly enough, Murphy was acquitted of the bribery charge one month later because he didn't appear to have promised anything. "He's too slick for that," one juror said after. But he was convicted of conspiracy. All the while, he had mounted a furious counter-punch, in particular going after NBC News. A request for a new trial was denied, and Murphy was sentenced to three years and served 20 months in prison, after which he remained a recluse until 2012 when his son John mounted an unsuccessful effort for a Congressional seat. Asked if he felt he got a raw deal, Murphy, then 86 years old, said, "I don't think about it. I never look back."

Murtha had agreed to use his influence to help the agents, but refused to accept money for doing so "at this time." He remained in the House until his death in 2010. Two fellow Pennsylvanians were not so lucky.

Michael "Ozzie" Myers was clearly the most indignant of the group, both on camera and in public and in terms of his level of resistance. For example, he got into a fistfight with a waiter at a Washington, D.C. restaurant because he felt, as described by *The Almanac of American Politics*, that he was "not showing proper deference to a member of Congress." He also "kicked and punched a security guard and cashier" at the rooftop lounge of a Pentagon City restaurant. When he accepted a bribe from a wired FBI agent, he uttered what has become among the most famous quotes in politics: "I'm gonna tell you somethin' real simple and short. In this business, money talks and bulls—t" walks And it works the same way down in Washington."

When indicted, Myers claimed he was simply "play-acting" and did not have any "criminal intent . . . I did not sell my office out. I did not do anything illegal. I did some ethical things . . . anything they wanted to hear." Instead, it was his colleagues who heard it. About 200 colleagues were said to have listened to the exchange.

Myers was an indicative of the Democratic machine pol. A longshoreman with a tenth grade education, Myers went to Congress in 1976 as a product of the Philly machine. Myers' indictment had come well before his 1980 primary, but he ran anyway and survived a "clown-car" 15-person field with under 30%. He almost held the general. But expulsion took its course. E. Barrett Prettyman said, "this man must not remain one day longer than necessary as a member of the House . . . it is impossible to find excuses for a man who broke so many laws and rules . . . who for personal gain, promised anything and made a mockery of his seat." Myers' attorney countered that the indictment was "a scheme that the FBI set up, a net to snare people." Myers was convicted and expelled by the House, the first member since 1861 to suffer such a fate, and as a result, local officeholders called on him to quit the race. He didn't. Longtime Philadelphia Councilman Tom Foglietta entered the race as an Independent but had support from much of the machine.

Unlike Myers, Ray Lederer actually held his seat through the 1980 elections, but his actions were nonetheless career-ending. When he accepted the $50,000 from the undercover agents at a New York motel, his words were, "I can give you me." Like Myers, he was on the verge of expulsion when he yielded to reality and resigned. He served 10 months in prison.

John Jenrette was the Congressmen with the most sensationalism, and that just involved his personal life. The South Carolina Democrat was part of the Watergate class of 1974 who was strongly supportive of Civil Rights at a time and in a place where doing so was not politically advantageous. Colleagues would soon learn, though, that Jenrette's eccentricities had to do his personal life. He and his wife, an aspiring singer, were once spotted having sex behind a pillar near the steps of the U.S. Capital. Their story encouraged the famous "Capital Steps." His wife got her singing career and also posed in *Playboy*. Jenrette went to jail but not before ending up in another court—divorce court.

Like most of the other lawmakers, Jenrette had a cohort. He was a fellow South Carolinian, a businessman. Together, the duo took $100,000, and Jenrette promised to intercede on getting the employer's immigration status relaxed. Jenrette was not caught on tape doing so but admitted doing so while being videotaped. The astonishing thing was that Jenrette very nearly kept his seat. Even while losing the Palmetta State, Jimmy Carter was winning Jenrette's district handily. With solid support from black voters, Jenrette lost to John Napier just 52-48%.

In a reminder that old habits die hard, Jenrette in 1989 was sentenced to 30 days for stealing a necktie from a store near Washington. At 77 years old, he still lives near the nation's capital.

Richard Kelly of Florida was the lone Republican mired in Abscam, but his past may have been of little surprise to anyone. He was a Circuit Court Judge who was impeached on charges that he "threatened and harassed public officials and disparaged the reputations of attorneys and elected officials," among other things. Somehow, Kelly made it to Congress in the Democratic year of 1974 and held his seat for three terms, the latter only barely. Kelly contended that he had accepted the money to launch his own investigation, and that, by having already been spending it down, he was in the process of doing so. Prosecutors didn't believe it. Neither did the voters. Kelly took just 18% as he stood for re-nomination in 1980. He was subsequently convicted and served 13 months in prison.

There were other influential political figures whose names surfaced in connection with Abscam but who had turned the money down. South Dakota's Larry Pressler flat-out rejected the cash on video tape. Upon being hailed as a hero, he questioned how low society has sunk to be hailed as a hero for rejecting a bribe.

CHAPTER EIGHTEEN

Despite Undoing, Wilbur Mills Possessed the Ways and the Means To Make Indelible Improvements For Generations

Historic Quote: "Why would you want to do that and give up your grip on the country?" - Sam Gibbons to Wilbur Mills when the Ways and Means Chair decided to throw his hat into the ring for President in 1972.

Courtesy of the Collections of the U.S. House of Representatives

Once upon a time, the House Ways and Means Committee had a legendary chair. Wilbur Mills was among the most respected men on Capitol Hill whom Tip O'Neill once called among the two most able men he'd served with (Rules Chair Richard Bolling was the other). He was capable, forward looking and, most importantly, knew how to close complex deals. In fact, during the period of LBJ, the ultimate compliment may have been that as the President applied his legendary "Johnson treatment" to the Chairman, Mills' response was often to stare him in the face – and win. A survey among Capitol Hill staff rating the leadership abilities of various members of Congress placed Mills a solid first with 104 votes (Carl Albert had 68 and Hale Boggs 11). While Mills' tenure did not end auspiciously, his professional record is one that would make many proud. And that was evident in his earliest days.

Kay Goss, the wife of Mills' administrative assistant and the author of Mills' biography, "Mr. Chairman," noted he had a dream unique to virtually any young boy from Arkansas, or anywhere. "He knew from the time he was 8 years old that he wanted to go on the Ways and Means committee," Goss said. "He played Speaker of the House in his backyard." His parents gave him a good head start. They had taught him book-keeping at age 11. But a more consequential decision may have been sending him to the prestigious Searcy High School where he "wore over-alls and long black stockings and the Searcy boys laughed at him and called him, 'country boy.'"

It wasn't unusual for Mills to exceed expectations and his mere existence was a symbol of what was possible for a young Arkansan. An observation of Mills in his high school yearbook may have captured a synopsis of his whole life. It read, "High above the common rabble Wilbur towers, undisturbed by life's ups and downs. Something fine within him prompts his gay outlook on life. His splendid grades are indicative of much 'gray matter.' Wilbur walks life's straight paths and is a boon companion for anyone who is 'down and out.'

Mills' grades were indeed splendid. He would graduate valedictorian, then go on to Hendrix College where, as a History major, worked his way up to class salutatorian. At the same time, debating became his trademark skill. Then it was on to Harvard Law School (his father was "the one that picked Harvard for me, really . . . If I was going to be a lawyer, I might as well go to Harvard"). Mills continued his sundry interests, becoming managing editor of the Bull Dog newspaper and president of both the Literacy Society and debating fraternity. His classmates elected him to the Hall of Fame.

Mills (second from left) as a young Judge
Photo courtesy of Rebecca Mills Yates

Mills left Harvard in his final semester and returned home to his native Kensett – and instantly found himself in big things. First came operating the Bank of Kensett (which his father saved during the Depression) as well as the family owned A.P. Mills general store, all while practicing law. At 25, he was White County Judge, the youngest in the state.

Acquiring that position took convincing, starting with his own father who startled young Wilbur by vowing to oppose him. But Mills campaigned as a fresh-face against incumbent Foster White's "courthouse gang," adopting the slogan, "Give a young man a chance." Voters obliged as Mills won by 357 votes out of roughly 4,500 cast. The year was 1934.

As a Judge, Mills' legacy was negotiating for affordable hospital stays and prescription drugs. But he also fulfilled his campaign pledge to rid the county of ¾ of its debt in his first year in office or forfeit his salary. Though he succeeded, he still lowered his pay by $1,600, to $2,000 a year.

The real prize would come in 1938 when a House seat came open in the second district. In the primary (in those days tantamount to election), Mills faced Roy Richardson who, like Mills, was capable of gifted oratory. But Mills had several things going for him. One was using a loudspeaker, a first for the district. Another was $17,000 that his father paid for the campaign. Perhaps most important, there was adaptation to modern campaigns. The White County Historical Society noted "it was not unusual for Mills to attract thousands even in rural areas, even though he put together his own speaking engagements rather than go to ready-made crowds at fairs and other public events." In the end, voters chose Mills by 5,000 votes out of 41,000 cast and made him the youngest Arkansan ever elected to Congress.

Mills was so young that a very senior colleague who happened to chair the all-important Flood Control Committee, mistook him for a page and asked him to run an errand. But Mills was so awed to be in Congress that he happily obliged. Even FDR was impressed. When Senator John Miller, whose place Mills had filled, introduced the new Congressman, the President replied, "Well, John, we are not only electing them younger but also better looking." Indeed, *Taxing America* notes Mills "combed back his thin brown hair with a smooth gel and wore thick-rimless, 'Benjamin Franklin' glasses; and he spoke with a thin, raspy voice."

**Mills' wife Polly was an asset to him during campaigns. Above, they proceed to enter their Washington D.C. apartment and attend a catfish fry on the White River carnival
Photo courtesy of Rebecca Mills Yates**

In office, Mills fought tooth and nail for his relatively poor constituency and they reciprocated. He would face opposition for re-election just three times in the 38 times his name appeared on the House ballot (primary and general). Mills provided many goods to his Delta district, including farm aid and dams. The Ozark Folk Center came through him. So did funding for the Rural Electric Cooperatives and the 1,704 foot wide, 243 foot tall Greers Ferry Lake and Dam, which President John F. Kennedy came to dedicate just seven weeks before his death in 1963.

Even major trade bills with international ramifications contained a touch of Arkansas as Mils would arduously champion his state's products. A write-up of Mills by the Arkansas Hall of Fame called him "a constant advocate of legislation to protect rice growers, and rice farmers prospered in his district to such as extent that Arkansas came to produce a large percentage of the rice eaten around the world." And his commitment to highways was so strong that not only did he secure funding for new and improved roads, but he shepherded the highway trust fund into law.

Mills didn't just pretend to be a regular guy, he was one. He drove a white Mercury which he would buy every other year from a dealer in Searcy, Arkansas. Even as a powerful chair, he would drive himself both in Washington and the district, although when he grew older he gave an old car to a man who would take him around. Back home, Mills' wife "Polly" was an asset as well. Her birthname was Clarine but few outside of her family called her that. "Polly," who loved crackers as a child, was a takeoff of the "Polly want a cracker," line. She loved meeting people while campaigning for her husband and as a secretary in the school system and later Postmistress in the town, knew everyone by name. She was considered a genuinely nice person loved by all. And that included Wilbur at a very early age. Polly's family lived in Kensett as a girl and he would drive her to high school.

Wilbur Mills' father owned three homes on the same block in Kensett, Arkansas. When Mills married his bride "Polly," he gave the new couple the home above. It was around the corner from where his brother Roger lived. Photo courtesy of Rebecca Mills Yates

On civil rights issues, Mills voted the way of the south but seemed to have little personal desire to stop advancement ("I couldn't stay in Congress unless I voted the way I do on these highly emotional issues"). For his part, Mills recalled he "was so close to my people that I thought as they did." And that enhanced Mills' presence as a stereotypical southern, cigar smoking pol who stayed close to home (he never traveled abroad) while cultivating special interests. He rarely missed votes and did much of his dealing on the floor.

Sam Rayburn became impressed with Mills' talents and made him one of "Rayburn's boys," in his "Board of Education meetings." Rayburn advised him not to "ever talk until you know what you're talking about." But Rayburn evidently reached the conclusion that Mills did know what he was talking about, for almost immediately after having him appointed to Ways and Means in 1942, he became Rayburn's go-to person on tax matters. In fact, according to Goss, Mills had long chaired Ways and Means in everything but name. "He was chairman of the committee from the day he went on. The guy who was chairman was 40 years older and he didn't really get along with Rayburn." That guy was Jere Cooper of Tennessee. When he died in 1957, Mills formally took the helm. And with it he'd be the youngest Chair of the Ways and Means Committee, and after 17 years of service by the time he stepped down, would hold the gavel longer than anyone else - before or since.

Mills' chairmanship defined him. He ruled Ways and Means with a tight hand. One of his successors, Dan Rostenkowski would be little different, but he had subcommittees. Mills was the subcommittee - he had none. The buck stopped with him - literally, as all tax matters went before him. Congressmen requesting the help of his top notch staff had to get permission from Mills. He usually got his way even on the House floor because the "Rules Committee" often adopted a "closed-rule" for tax consideration, meaning members couldn't amend it on the House floor. And with Mills, even Presidents knew they had limits. One high-ranking White House official once said, "If Wilbur wanted us to go down to Herber Springs and sing, 'Down by the Old Mills Stream,' we'd be glad to do it."

At the dedication of the Greer's Ferry Dam, 1963 (left) and with LBJ (right)
Left photo courtesy of the Encyclopedia of Arkansas; right
Photo via the Lyndon B. Johnson Presidential Library

The Encyclopedia of Arkansas said "when anyone in Washington DC spoke of 'Mr. Chairman,' everyone understood the reference was to Mills." Yet few had any qualms about Mills when it came to motives. Arkansas Biography: A Collection of Notable Lives said "Mills was regarded as an open and fair chairman who provided an atmosphere in which all members, freshman or ranking, could participate comfortably. He never had a rigid personal agenda but maintained the flexibility needed to draw passable bills." And the closed-rule wasn't necessarily for self-serving reasons. O'Neill recalls one day Mills presented a proposal to the Rules Committee to require life insurance companies to pay taxes. "But we can't have open hearings on this," he said. "If we do, there'll be ads in the newspapers all over the country with pictures of old people saying, 'Don't let Congress tax my savings. If we do, we'll never be able to get help.'" The bill was passed.

Above all, Mills' brilliance was recognized by all and it may have catapulted with the Kennedy administration.

Mills' relationship with Kennedy went back to both men's House days when he literally got an up-close image of Kennedy's war injury. "I had him take his shirt off one time and show other members. I never saw a back so lacerated in my life." Mills confided that of all the President's with whom he served, his opinion of JFK was the highest. The feeling was mutual. His name was mentioned as a potential Treasury Secretary in the administration and it was even rumored that Kennedy had offered him a Supreme Court appointment.

That Mills chose to remain on the Hill was probably to the benefit of both men. Mills guided the Trade Reform Act to passage, a major piece of legislation that Kennedy had major doubts about getting through. Mills, who told Kennedy he doesn't "know what the Senate will do, but I do know the House will support you," proved so instrumental in its passage that at the signing ceremony, Kennedy called it, "the Mills Act" (Mills shot back, "you never know unless you try").

Which brings us to Mills' most celebrated legacy and one that rightfully makes him a hero to many Americans whose quality of life has been enhanced by Social Security and Medicare. By 1965, Mills already had a hand in extending Social Security benefits to farmers and the disabled. In perhaps the ultimate compliment, Thomas Loker, in a piece years after Mills' death, said he "was considered, by many, to be the only person in Congress who truly understood the actuarial basis of Social Security, and was recognized as the Congress's primary tax expert." The Arkansas Biography: A Collection of Notable Lives" noted he "memorized the tax code and the Social Security laws." This was all the more improbable by the fact that, during Mills' time at Harvard, the curriculum didn't cover the federal code.

While Mills' position at the time made him a "Founding Father" of Medicare, he actually started out a critic. During the Kennedy administration, he had proposed a compromise with Oklahoma Senator Bob Kerr that was opposed by most Democrats but not because he opposed he concept, but because he worried about the sustainability of such a new entitlement. Robert Helms in a paper, "The Orgin of Medicare", noted a speech Mills gave in which he noted, "In practical terms, this meant that if the hospital insurance system which would be created by the bill was to remain sound, the taxable wage base would have to be increased by $150 each year. Clearly, this would be a case of the tail wagging the dog." Helms went on to say that "In 1964, the administration projected that Medicare, in 1990, would cost about $12 billion in 26 years (which included an allowance for inflation); the actual cost was $110 billion.

But by LBJ's time, he was fully on board. It was almost precision that brought Mills around – political precision. He had spent numerous time with Wilbur Cohen, Assistant Secretary for Legislation of Health, Education, and Welfare throughout much of 1964 in hopes of forging a compromise. It was unsuccessful. But the resounding re-election of LBJ so awed Mills that the next morning, he proclaimed himself "receptive to a Medicare proposal in the upcoming session." Mills said Johnson's stampede over Barry Goldwater, the major impact, made the major difference. He had espoused it in his campaign, you know, and here he was elected by a 2 to 1 vote, which was a pretty strong endorsement of it, I thought."

Johnson himself had appealed to Mills "If you can get something you can possibly live with and defend that these people will not kick over the bucket with, it'll mean more to posterity and to you and to me." But Johnson still pressed Mills on the timing. Audio tapes reveal him imploring Mills, "For God's sake, let's get it before Easter! . . . They make a poll every Easter . . . You know it. On what has Congress accomplished up till then. Then the rest of the year they use that record to write editorials about. So anything that we can grind through before Easter will be twice as important as after Easter."

The result was that Mills actually became more of a proponent than many of the original architects of the proposal. During a Ways and Means hearing to consider the Republican counter-proposal, Mills stunned Republicans by making a motion to accept the Democratic proposal, the American Medical Associations, and that of his Republican counterpart, Wisconsin Republican John Byrnes' (the latter's would include in the program payment for doctors bills, provided the patient paid the first $50). Many suspected Byrnes had put that language in with the specific intent of killing the bill. This became known as a "three-layer cake" and the "the villain of [Medicare]," in Johnson's words, was "now a hero to old folks." After the agreement was reached, Mills told Johnson "I think we've got something that we won't only run on in '66 but we'll run on from here after." Mills also had a task convincing the American Medical Association to support the proposal but recalls telling one doctor, "You ought to be for it. You're in the business of saving lives" (apparently, at least one physician was left unconvinced. Mills was challenged by one in 1966).

Years later, Mills' prophecy is proving correct as both parties are turning it into a political hot potato. As for his resistance about passing it earlier, Mills recalled years later, "I don't think we could have passed it in 1961. I told Kennedy that, and he agreed, I guess. He never did really press me about it."

Johnson and the Public Broadcasting Act was a different matter. Bill Moyers, then an aide to the President, recalls Mills being summoned to the White House for fierce lobbying for an excise tax. As he explained it, "they gossiped for an hour or so, shared rumors about friends and enemies . . . The President was sitting down again, leaning forward almost in the other man's face and these two crafty card-sharks, drinking buddies, shrewd and tough as nails, were looking right in each other's eyes. Then the Chairman said to the President (and Moyers said he was paraphrasing), "Well, that's all well and good, Lyndon. But you were up there long enough to know we ain't gonna give money to folks without some strings attached. We don't work that way."

Mills also proved a force to be reckoned with on Johnson's proposal to establish a Vietnam tax surcharge. Mills resisted the idea but told the LBJ Oral

History Project, "I was never opposed to it. What I wanted to do was to see if we couldn't balance the budget. I didn't want that additional money to be spent for new things, because he had a reputation of throwing dollars at any question and the question would disappear. I asked him if he wouldn't agree, and he wouldn't." Mills also knew that "after the war was over . . . it's always difficult for Congress to repeal a tax." But Mills genuinely wanted to simplify the tax code and was frustrated by his inability to do so. Still, even his aversion to deficits evaporated with societal reality. During one Chamber of Commerce speech, he told attendees, "My thought has been that over a number of years we should operate our fiscal in the black but that we should not necessarily try, year in and year out, to be in the black. We must recognize the need on occasion for tax reduction as a stimulus when our economy is turning down and we are losing the momentum and progress that we have had."

Despite Mills' ability to rule his committee, a prime attribute was his bi-partisan nature. "I never did just deal with Democrats," he said. "I always had the Republicans on my side, too, in a conference." That even extended to helping Republicans at election time. Over the objection of some Democrats, Mills didn't dissuade Arkansans from voting to re-elect Arkansas Republican Congressman John Paul Hammerschmidt which led his daughter Rebecca to recall that he credited her father with "total acceptance of A Republican at a time when Democrats were dominant in Arkansas." Nor did Mills seek to stall Hammerschmidt's advance in the House. Mills tried to secure a seat for his colleague on Ways and Means, though Hammerschmidt ultimately decided to stay where he was on Public works (culminating his tenure as the ranking Republican of that post). Mills was also able to navigate ideological differences in his own party. He really liked Bella Abzug whose outspoken feminism was second-to-none.

Image courtesy of the Museum of American History, Cabot Public Schools

By 1972, Mills was drafted to run for President. While he reluctantly acquiesced, he barely made a dent. Still, as evidence that his respect knew no regional boundaries, the effort was led by a liberal Massachusetts Congressman named Jimmy Burke with whom he worked closely on a number of initiatives. A $250,000 write-in effort was organized in New Hampshire and Mills did draw 5% of the vote but well behind the top contenders. It was an expedition that led his home-state newspaper, *The Arkansas Gazette* to opine that "what Mills is up to remains very much a mystery as ever." According to those close to him, what he turned out to be up to in running was simply trying to get his economic message across.

Eventually, Mills abandoned his bid though did earn 43 delegates. But Ted Kennedy was publicly floating his name about as a possible running-mate for McGovern. While the duo would clearly have been strange bedfellows, it was theorized later that Mills in an Executive position would help Kennedy attain his long sought goal of national health insurance. And the eventual Democratic nominee, George McGovern publicly stated his intention to name Mills Treasury Secretary. Mills' response was he'd wait to see if McGovern was elected before entertaining the offer.

Meanwhile, Mills was without question for the people. He pushed through tax hikes on the rich and he and Kennedy unveiled a major proposal modeled on the Nixon administration's CHIP bill in 1974. Much if not all of it may have been enacted had Watergate not intervened. Legislatively, Mills called his biggest failure not being able to obtain universal health care coverage.

A late-career pose of Mills
Photo via hench.net

Away from politics, Mills' first love was baseball. His daughter, Rebecca Yates called Mills, a fanatic. He played through college, and studied the game his whole life. He was a baseball encyclopedia, played catch with me and took us to Senators games. He grew up with Bill Dickey, met Baby Ruth in Boston with Bill Dickey, and befriended major leaguers from Arkansas." Mills' taste in music was consistent with him being a simple man; orchestras, Percy Faith and Henry Mancini. And he was obsessed with crossword puzzles, *The New York Times* puzzles in particular. Ralph Nader's report on members of Congress noted he "commences the working day with *The Times* crossword puzzle of which he is an avid fan." This appeared to be a Mills family tradition. His father was skilled at solving the puzzles as is his daughter.

Even before scandal struck, more than just chatter existed about Mills' future as Ways and Means head. By 1973, he was plagued by chronic back woes which was impacting his ability to shepherd legislation. The panel's number two member, Al Ullman at first shrugged concerns off, saying Mills, "does have some real bad days and has a lot of pain but the outlook is good." But he was forced to add, "Even if Wilbur decides to stay in Congress, he's going to have to revise his operations scheme because times have changed and the needs of the House have changed." Ultimately, Mills recovered and was firmly back in the game. Enter October 1974.

At 2AM, Mills was spotted by police in the driver seat of his car near West Potomac Park with the lights out, bloodied, trying to talk a woman from jumping out of his car and into the Tidal Basin. There were two others in the car. The Jefferson Memorial was in full view. The woman was Annabel Battistell, a stripper at the Silver Slipper whose show name was "Fannie Foxe." Some called her the "Argentine Firecracker." Mills called her "the Argentine Hillbilly."

Mills initially denied he was there even as a police officer said "we can assume it was Rep. Mills." *The Washington Post* reported Mills saying "his face was cut from his eyeglasses, which broke as he tried to stop an ill woman neighbor, Mrs. Eduardo Battistella, from leaving the vehicle . . ." Mills first said he was throwing a party for a family member of Ms. Battistella, a neighbor, while his wife was at home suffering from a broken foot. He even thanked the "Park Service for their alertness and to thank them for the courtesies extended to me and my friends." When it became obvious that Mills indeed was involved, he and his spokesman retracted it.

Mills' longtime Administrative Assistant, Gene Goss, had initially followed his boss's line in maintaining that he was not on scene. But when evidence was produced to the contrary, the *Washington Post* reported Mills statement. It read when Goss "related the report of the incident to me as it was quoted to him by members of the press, because of the manner in which it was phrased I told him that it was an inaccurate report. He mistook this to mean that I was not involved resulting in the previous statement issued in my name." Goss corroborated that.

At that point, Mills vowed to concentrate on his re-election. That wasn't a bad idea. That year, Mills had an opponent, Judy Petty, albeit not someone who would normally be taken particularly seriously. But Little Rock was newer to the district than most of the small rural counties for which Mills was renowned, and that required some cultivating. Petty managed to hold Mills to 59%. Luckily for Mills, however, the election had occurred a few weeks before what happened next.

Mills was at a burlesque club in Boston and Fannie called him to the stage. He got up on stage, accompanied by Foxe's husband, proclaiming his power and saying that "no one would bring him down." The club is where he'd conduct the press conference from Foxe's dressing room. Eventually, it became known that Mills had frequented Foxe at the Silver Slipper and the two would often argue. He was also forced to acknowledge a long problem with alcohol, including that he "mixed the drinks with some highly addictive drugs" that he had begun taking for a ruptured spinal disc.

Mills later acknowledged the effects of alcohol. "I don't even remember going up to Boston, or appearing on that stage - although at that point I guess anybody could get me to do anything. I was just plain drunk, mostly on vodka. They found four empty bottles in that theater - and quite a few in my hotel room." But O'Neill noted that despite Mills' problem, he "always kept his mind clean." Strangely enough, Foxe and her husband lived in the same building as Mills.

Mills stepped down as chair of Ways and Means. Indeed, in the first year that "Watergate era" Democrats pushed through a measure requiring committee heads be chosen by the full committee, it seemed nearly impossible that he could've hung on, much less served effectively.

In early 1975, Mills checked into the Palm Beach Facility. He quietly served the term that he had just won and retired in 1976 at 67. By all accounts, he recovered and resumed practicing tax law, returning to a happy life with his wife Polly, whom he had married in 1934 (and who herself had successfully nursed a problem with alcohol) and the two daughters he adored. Despite his posh position, Mills said wistfully, "Some things are more important that your job. Like staying sober."

In later years, he returned to Kensett and devoted quality time to solving the problems of others and touring his former Congressional district. In that time, he would never again touch alcohol and would continue working to help victims of the illness, initiatives that included seeking money for prevention programs and traveling across the country spoke to address various AA meetings, AMA conventions and state legislators in order to provide recovering alcoholics the proper resources. And that was classic Mills. He may have been in a different capacity but he didn't need a title to help his fellow citizen.

Mills died of a heart attack in May 1992 shortly before his 83rd birthday. A treatment center in Arkansas and many other facilities bears his name.

Mills had once said he decided early in life that "I wanted to be a Congressman. I've never regretted the decision." Did the voters? Probably not. 36 good years does not equal one or two bad judgements. His daughter Rebecca acknowledged her father "made mistakes but his whole life was about taking care of other people." And that is what ultimately defines a legacy and a man.

Mills and Polly on their 50ᵗʰ wedding anniversary in 1984
Photo courtesy of Rebecca Mills Yates

CHAPTER NINETEEN

Hats Off To Bella:
A Woman of Needed Chutzpah

Historic Tidbit: When Judiciary Committee Chair Emanuel Celler was bottling up the Equal Rights Amendment, his rationale was, among other things, that women were not at the last supper. Bella Abzug's response was that "we may not have been at the last one but we sure as hell will be at the next one."

Photo via the Library of Congress Prints and Photographs Division

Before Hillary Clinton became the first woman from New York to become a United States Senator, the state had a drought in female officials. Twice, and perhaps three times, the state arguably came within 1% of sending two women to the body two decades earlier. Liz Holtzman of course was one, likely being cost the Senate race by Jacob Javits's refusal to get out after his defeat by Al D'Amato. Even Geraldine Ferrarro's 1% loss to Bob Abrams in the primary may have doomed New York's odds of sending a female to Washington for eight years, as many feel she might have beaten D'Amato. Bella Abzug lost a 1976 primary to

Daniel Patrick Moynihan by fewer than 10,000 votes. Opinions are mixed as to whether she could've beaten Jim Buckley in the fall, but he was highly unpopular among an electorate that even 37 years ago still leaned left.

Abzug was one of the most enigmatic, eccentric, and ubiquitous members of Congress, assisted by her trademark hats and her loud voice, which she used to chew out allies and adversaries alike if she felt they were dragging their feet on progress. But her hats and views made her perhaps one of the most recognizable members during her tenure.

A tireless crusader for women's rights and against the Vietnam War, Abzug stopped at nothing to express her opinion. But it was never about Bella Abzug; it was about progress. And in an era when Hubert Humphrey was the "Happy Warrior," Abzug was the "Loud Crusader." But everyone, both allies and adversaries, always knew where she stood. Norman Mailer once said she could "boil the fat off a taxicab driver's neck."

Abzug's notoriety was undoubtedly helped by her status as one of fewer than 15 women in the House. After all, a man likely could not have generated that kind of exposure. But it wasn't always like that and that's where the hats came in. Why did she wear them? That was the only way she could get recognition.

Born to Russian immigrants, Abzug knew what she wanted early and went for it. She gave her first speech at a subway station at the age of 11. She tried to say Kadish (the prayer for the dead) in her synagogue, only to be frowned on by other congregants (Abzug pressed the issue and was allowed to participate). She couldn't go to Harvard because she was a woman. For Abzug, leadership came early. She was student body President in both high school and college.

Her most famed case was defending Jim McGee, a black Mississippian convicted of raping a white woman. Hotels refused to give Abzug a room so she slept on the park bench. The case dragged on for some time but eventually McGee was put to death.

By the mid-1960s, she started a group, "Women's Strike for Peace," which many believed influenced JFK's advocacy of the Nuclear Test Ban Treaty. She called women "America's oppressed majority."

In the 1970 primary, she began as an underdog to Congressman Leonard Farbstein, who had turned back challenges from his left from Congressman Ted Weiss, who ended up succeeding Abzug in 1976. *The New York Times* called him "a liberal but an unexciting legislator." One thing was for certain. The latter was one word that would never be uttered about Abzug, which Farbstein acknowledged: "it's true, I'm not as raucous as she is, but I'm effective." She set up free childcare for volunteers with children and had a fundraiser at Barbara Streisand's apartment. Gloria Steinem was an immediate early backer. This was Chelsea and the West Village, where out-liberalizing your foe is worn with a badge of honor.

Of Farbstein, Abzug said, "making speeches is no longer enough. We're in a crisis period and we've got to get out there and raise holy hell." She attacked his detachment from his constituents, pointing out that "once a year he sends out a pamphlet from the Department of Agriculture about how to make potatoes." Her slogan was, "A Woman's Place is in the House—the House of Representatives." That was enough.

Abzug put in 18 hour campaign days. Her supporters came up with a jingle

On June 23RD
Let Your VOICE be Heard,
Send someone knew to Washington.
Make Abzug Your Choice

And vote for the Voice
That knows how to get things done.

So Vote for Bella, Bella Abzug,
Bella's The One
She's Abzug-lutely Your Best Choice
For Our Congressman.
So help speak out for,
An end to the war,
A chance for a better USA
Don't Throw Your Vote Away,
On Primary Day,
Help Bella Abzug Win All The Way

Image via ronwadebuttons.com

Abzug was sworn in by her new colleague, Shirley Chisholm as onlookers yelled, "Give 'em hella, Bella!" Did she ever! Once in the House, Abzug did not hesitate to make her displeasure known and no figure was too high for her wrath. For Speaker Albert, it was putting off a caucus vote on ending the war (her first resolution was ending the war). For New York Congressional delegation head Hugh Carey, it was not getting her on choice committees (she wanted Armed services, nearly unheard of for a woman. Instead, she had to settle for Government Operations and Public works). And when Ford vetoed the aid package for New York City, she likened him to a sick patient with whom he was "pulling the plug."

But Abzug's mere presence could also catch the eye of the mighty and powerful in trivial ways. One day, the venerable Ways and Means baron Wilbur Mills approached her with a question pertaining to a newspaper crossroad puzzle. He quizzically asked, "What is Bella Abzug is one?"

**Abzug's letter to Speaker Carl Albert calling for censure of Nixon
Image via the Carl Albert Congressional Congressional
Archives, University of Oklahoma**

She had successes, one of which was fighting to make the Congressional swimming pool open to women. But her goal of gaining equality for women under the law proved elusive. When the chamber took up the ERA Amendment in 1970, Abzug offered stirring rationale for why it should be enacted: "The House has only 12 women among its 435 members, and women have been denied seats on some of the most important House committees. It is a "real outrange" that there are no women on the Armed Services and Foreign Affairs Committees

- those very committees which make the decisions that send our children and youths off to war in Asia." There are no women on the Rules Committee, which controls the House floor-action calendar, or the Judiciary Committee, which has juisdiction over equal rights for women."

All the while, Abzug's stature increased. She was booked for speaking tours all across the nation (she thought her staff was overbooking her) and was spotted wherever she went. Eventually, she was on a list of the 20 most admired women in the nation. She explained her philosophy thus: "I spend all day figuring out how to beat the machine and knock the crap out of the political power structure."

When it was revealed in early 1973 that the CIA had kept a 20-year file on Abzug, including letters she had written to clients, many of which they opened, she was not amused. "Let's get one thing clear right away," she told the CIA head. "Opening mail of a lawyer representing a client is clearly illegal. To find myself in your files is outrageous."

Abzug faced additional electoral peril when redistricting eliminated her seat. This was done by putting much of her liberal base in a conservative Staten Island district. When she found that out, she reacted in typical Bella fashion. Calling her chief political advisor, she said, "Do you know what those motherf—k—s in Albany want to do to me." Many Democrats, and even Republican Governor Rockefeller, advised her to challenge more conservative members of the delegation. Instead, she went after William Fitts Ryan, a widely respected liberal.

Photo courtesy of Liz Abzug

Again, Abzug made the campaign about style. "It's not enough to vote right and stand on the issues." Calling himself a "peacemaker." Ryan said he acted "ahead of the times." Abzug responded that she "ran for Congress because I elected guys like Ryan and they didn't change anything." She lost but fate intervened.

During the election, there were rumors about Ryan's health. He insisted he was fine but shortly after died of cancer. Abzug entered the race to succeed him, as did his wife. The Democratic Committee picked Abzug and she was able to extend her career—and influence.

When the Watergate scandal broke out, she was among the first members of Congress to tell Nixon to resign. But she also appeared to exhale. Albert said, "I would say she's mellowed. She realizes she doesn't have to get in front in every issue." Tip O'Neill, on the other hand, a Senate supporter, called her the "same old Bella."

In her campaign, she took on the role of a "new" Bella, as *The Times* described it. She vowed not to support Moynihan if he won the primary. But Moynihan was content to remind voters of the old Bella ("no one is good enough for her unless it is her"). He labeled her style "rule or ruin": "You can't be for Israel if you're for cutting the defense budget." Abzug attacked welfare proposal by Moynihan which she said bureaucratically would make things worse. She linked Moynihan to the Nixon White House (he was his director of urban and domestic affairs). And she fought for consumer agencies. Labor unions and bus drivers rallied her way and Abzug felt she had momentum as the primary neared. And being a woman was at the hallmark of it. Her philosophy was "we will never fulfill the American dream until images in the minds of women, as well as the minds of men, are allowed to share in the dream." Up to that point, she had been the only candidate to have been endorsed by NOW (the National Organization for Women).

Of 657,000 votes cast between the two, Moynihan edged Abzug by 10,000 votes. The presence of Ramsey Clark and Paul O'Dwyer, each of whom polled 9%, most likely hurt Abzug. Still, she carried areas well beyond her Manhattan turf, including Buffalo and Saratoga. On a flight to Washington the next morning, Abzug received an ovation from her fellow passengers. She did offer assistance to Moynihan days after the primary. Whether or not she would have beaten Buckley is an open question but the first-term Senator elected on the Conservative ticket was widely unpopular and in fact lost to Moynihan by 12%.

After her defeat, Abzug began letting non-supporters have it in classic Abzug style. She called Steve Solarz a "coward," and told Charlie Rangel he was "corrupt" (later she said she meant "corruption of values.)" After her death, Rangel expressed admiration.

Abzug tried several times for a comeback. She ran in the New York City Mayor's race the following year (her slogan was "Bella Means Business") but ran well behind Koch and Cuomo (Koch and Abzug were never best of friends. On primary night 1972, when Koch was asked at Ryan headquarters why Abzug was losing even her home area he retorted, "because her neighbors know her").

When Koch was elected Mayor, Abzug won the Democratic nomination but, in a low turnout special, lost to Republican Bill Green by 1,000 votes. And in 1986, she looked a little north, challenging very pro-life freshman Joe DioGuardi. She lost 53-47%. In 1991, her daughter Liz sought a New York City Council seat but lost the primary to Tom Duenne.

But Abzug didn't let her string of losses deter her from making her opinions known. *The New York Times* wrote in Abzug's obituary how George H.W. Bush was traveling to China and said he "felt somewhat sorry for the Chinese. Bella Abzug is one who has always represented the extremes of the woman's movement." Her reply: he was addressing a fertilizer group? That's appropriate.

Abzug cited her style plain and simple in her autobiography: "They call me Battling Bella, Mother Courage, and a Jewish mother with more complaints that Portnoy. There are those who say that I am rude, impatient, impetuous, uppity, rude, profane, brash, and overbearing. Whether I'm any of these things or all of them, you can decide for yourself. But whatever I am—and this ought to be made very clear at the outset—I am a very serious woman." After she left office, Margaret Chase Smith, who for most of her 24-year tenure in the Senate was the only female, paid a compliment to Abzug in bemoaning the fact that she lacked a restroom available to her male colleagues. "I presume had there been a more aggressive woman in the Senate, perhaps an Abzug, she would have barged into that area and declared her rights."

At a farewell luncheon on Capitol Hill, Abzug was given a hero's salute by everyone from colleagues to staff. Millicent Fenwick, the urbane New Jersey Republican, said she felt "as if I have lost a strong right arm. Perhaps in my position I should say left arm." Her husband Martin, who had served as her emotional rock throughout her career, said "she'll be around, unfortunately for me."

Left image courtesy of ronwadebuttons.com; right an official White House photo

When it came time for Abzug to speak, she was circumspect, looking forward. "As much as some of us enjoy farewells, we enjoy victories too. And that day will come. Keep your voices up, keep your faith up, keep your spirits up, and we'll all be heard. A woman's reach should exceed her grasp or what's struggle or a women's movement for. Like Jimmy Carter, I expect to be born again."

Abzug died in 1998 at age 77. Geraldine Ferraro, who would win a New York City House seat just after Abzug left acknowledged her abrasiveness. "Let's be honest about it," she said. "She did not knock politely on the door. She took the hinges off of it." But a former aide may have offered the best introspection Abzug, she said, was "first on almost everything, on anything that ever mattered." How proud she would have been to see Hillary win the seat she once sought.

CHAPTER TWENTY

To Distaste of Many, Capitol Hill Building Bears Name of Arch-Segregationist Senator

Historic Tidbit: 1958 was a very Democratic year nationwide. In fact, only one Democratic member of Congress lost her seat. It was Congresswoman Coya Knutson of Minnesota. Her husband had written a famous "Coya Come Home" letter to local newspapers asking her to make his breakfast again. Knutson, the first female Congressperson from Minnesota, did go home, but managed to get the house to herself soon after. The two divorced in 1961.

Photo courtesy of the Library of Congress Prints and Photographs Division

On Capitol Hill, there are six office buildings. Three are for the members of the House, and three for Senators. Each are named for members who, in their times, were viewed as larger than life on the Hill by members of both parties, and whose contributions were profound. But that often implies positive contributions and for one of these men, Senator Richard Russell, no such flattery is warranted. In fact, it's just the opposite. Russell was an ardent segregationist, and in his America, it would be law of the land today. And in Russell's day, they were detrimental to the dreams of many Americans of whole generations. Therefore, I have long felt that the name of the Russell Senate Office Building should be changed, and out of respect for those who fought to the death for Civil Rights, it can't happen soon enough.

251

The Senate office building that bears Russell's name was constructed in 1903 and was renamed for the long-serving Georgian in 1972, a year after his death. But, if the full scars of the Civil Rights movement were impervious to some at that time, it should not have been in the 40 years since. Some African-American politicians have raised the issue of stripping the building of Russell's name but no concerted effort has been made. That must change.

First, let's look at what Richard Russell was, shall we? Yes, he was an immensely venerable Georgian, Speaker of the Georgia House at 30, Governor at 34, and Senator two years later for the ensuing 38 years before his death in office in 1971, at which time he was President Pro-Tem of the body.

By all accounts, Russell was revered by his colleagues. The term "Senator's Senator" apparently came into existence because of him. Whether that was reverence was for his longservice and high position, who knows? He was a dogged advocate for Georgia. According to *The New Georgia Encyclopedia*, Russell "favored his role as advocate for the small farmer and for soil and water conservation."

Beyond that, Russell fought for hydroelectric energy and shepherded the opening of no less than 15 military installations in his state, undoubtedly contributing to the heft Georgia enjoys in the defense industry today. Russell's longtime Chairmanship of the Senate Armed Services Committee, and for a brief time before his death, Appropriations, meant anyone who wanted something done had to be on his good side.

And he knew his state like the back of his hand. JFK once called him in his Capitol office on Christmas Eve (the Capital receptionist questioned him as to whether he'd be there) to ask him where a Civil War battle that he and Teddy were discussing had been fought. Russell knew the answer.

Russell's style also rubbed off on his fellow Georgians. Many to this day proudly use his Russell Sweet Potato recipe.

Photo courtesy of the University of Georgia Libraries Special Collections

That's all well and good but it is only half the story. Russell was also a segregationist, a staunch one who, from the earliest days of the civil rights movement to the time his longtime friend, Lyndon Johnson, championed it into law, resisted. In fact, when President Kennedy was killed and many members of Congress went to greet the new President at Andrews Air Force upon his return from Dallas, Johnson knew he wasn't there. Russell was already expressing glumness about prospects for civil rights legislation, saying that Johnson would push it through. And Russell did not campaign for Johnson in 1964, a tact that many believe caused the President to lose Georgia 54-46% to Barry Goldwater, who opposed the Civil Rights Act. Lady Bird was reportedly furious.

Russell fought for "States' Rights," signed the Southern Manifesto, and was a founder of the infamous "Southern Bloc" of Senators who tried, unsuccessfully, to block progress in the long-term. Russell gleefully acknowledged that his dilatory tactics were designed to thwart enactment of civil rights legislation and as it became clear he was fighting a losing battle, the filibuster was the only tool. He once declared he'd "vote to gag the Senate when the shrimp start to whistling Dixie" (when the required 67th Senator – John Williams of Delaware, did vote to close debate in June of 1964, Russell was reported to have slumped in his chair).

Many believed that had it not been for the segregation issue, Russell would have won the Democratic Presidential nomination in 1952. Quite a few northern and western members of the party had asked him to renounce it but he refused.

Okay, so a few of the men the other Capitol Hill buildings are named for are also not my cups of tea, politically or procedurally speaking, but in one way or another, they shaped the Capitol. Russell's politics shaped a whole era. Or more appropriately, error. Next to slavery itself, "States' Rights" was one of the ugliest, most heinous chapters in humanity for which scars remain, literally and figuratively. One of the greatest heroes of the civil rights movement and Russell's fellow Georgian, John Lewis, was beaten savagely during this time. Countless others lost their lives. It's unclear whether Russell himself was racist (a few Senate colleagues, notably Mississippian James Eastland were), but it's not really relevant. His ardent defense of that way of life is.

Imagine what Lincoln would think. Jerry Ford had a malapropism on another matter— "If Lincoln were alive today he'd turn over in his grave"—but the sentiment fits. Senators Michael Cowan and Tim Scott, two native African-American sons of the Carolinas, occupy offices in the Russell Building (Cowan since moved to Massachusetts). How do they feel literally walking in the shadow (there is a bust of Russell) of a man who tried to hold their people back? And why should they be made to? The Sheriff of Birmingham apologized to Lewis recently for his beating. Were it not for men like Russell, that apology wouldn't have been necessary.

There is a biography of Thurgood Marshall, *Dream Makers, Dream Breakers.* For many people, Russell was the latter. And to reward him with a building! I don't think so!

And it's irrelevant to the issue at hand but ridding the building of Russell's name wouldn't even offend his family, because, as far as direct descendants, he's got none (Russell was a bachelor).

So who should bear the name of the hopefully former Russell Building? Well, since Civil Rights is at the heart of the matter, John Lewis would be a stirring choice, though I recognize he is a member of the House (not Senate) and one who is still serving.

What about Hiram Rhodes Revels, the first African-American Senator? He would've served longer had it not been for Reconstruction. Or perhaps "Scoop" Jackson, who served in Congress just as long as Russell, advocated for his state just as hard (he was called the "Senator from Boeing"), and advocated a muscular approach to defense and communism. Maybe even Hubert Humphrey—who, from his impassioned 1948 keynote speech ("get out of the shadow of states' rights and walk forthrightly into the bright sunshine of human rights") to becoming Vice-President was, next to LBJ himself, Russell's chief nemesis on the Civil Rights issue.

Whatever the case, to give healing and peace to future generations and the blood of the past, the name of this building must change.

CHAPTER TWENTY-ONE

Beyond Russell, the Capitol Hill Buildings
Are Named For Revered Men

Historic Tidbit: One of the most famous lines in American politics is Everett Dirksen's "A billion here, a billion there, and pretty soon we're talking about real money." No evidence exists of him having uttered the remark (though he did say something similar). Dirksen himself, asked about it later, said the "fellow misquoted me, but it sounded good so I didn't deny it."

The men for whom the other Capitol Hill office buildings are named are revered both as legislative masters and principled, warm human beings. Three of them—Speaker Sam Rayburn, Senator Minority Leader Everett Dirksen, and Michigan Senator Phillip Hart—encompass the era at hand. It's easy to see why their former colleagues would see fit to honor each of them with a building. One can only wonder whether such monuments are fitting.

**Photo courtesy of the Dolph Briscoe Center for American
History, the University of Texas at Austin**

Sam Rayburn fit the stereotype of an old-time politician in every way. He was a bald, cigar-chomping, back-slapping, irreverent man, but one whose honesty was unquestioned and his agenda forward-looking not as it related to future elections but rather, future generations. For Rayburn was not only among the most decent men in public life but a true embodiment of what a Speaker should be. Unlike Lyndon Johnson, whose initial motives for backing Civil Rights might not have entirely been altruistic, Rayburn appears to have been sympathetic to the cause from the start—and for all the right reasons (though he couldn't outright articulate that back home).

"Mr. Sam" was one of a long line of Texans who would lead their respective chambers in the 20th century. Rayburn was a protegé of John Nance Garner (who would outlive him by six years), and LBJ in turn was a protégé of Rayburn. Rayburn held either the Speakership or the Majority Leader's post for a quarter of a century (filling that role in the minority when the Democrats weren't in control).

One thing that is certain is his record longevity. He held the Speakership longer than any other person, beginning in 1940, though his tenure was interrupted twice when Democrats lost the majority. But Republican control could never suit Mister Sam and Democrats regained the majority each time two years later. Rayburn was fiercely committed to Democratic principles of all eras. A biography by Anthony Champagne notes that he "opposed Taft/Hartley and the Landrum/Griffin act even though they would have been popular in his district." At another point, the book notes that "Rayburn did not share Johnson's burning hatred of liberals nor was he hated by liberals as they hated Johnson" even though both regarded them as "extreme leftists."

Young Sam Rayburn
Photo courtesy of the United States Library of Congress Prints
and Photographs Division, Harris and Ewing Collection

Rayburn's proclivity for propriety was so strong that, as Champagne notes, he sold his law practice after going to Congress, accepted few gifts, and required his nephew to sell stocks he had owned before going to work for him. Rayburn himself had owned a stock until an oil company executive confronted him about preferential treatment. Rayburn "angrily dismissed the executive, sold the stock, and resolved never again to own stocks."

Rayburn had a stellar relationship with the press. One day he heard that the daughter of a reporter had died suddenly. Rayburn asked if the family had had their coffee. When they told him they hadn't, Rayburn said he could "at least make the coffee for them this morning." The reporter asked if Rayburn was supposed to be meeting the President, to which the Speaker replied, he was, 'but I called the President and told him that I had a friend who was in trouble and couldn't come."

Rayburn was a fierce partisan but that didn't impact his ability to reach out. He organized the Board of Education, where a group of bipartisan House members would meet. No one would dare bring an outsider to a meeting without checking with Mr. Sam. But the agenda didn't revolve around him in any way. One member of the group, neighboring Congressman Wright Patman recalled Rayburn "never did dominate the meetings. He was aggressive all right, when there was something up that he should speak on and be heard on, but he was not a dominating kind of a person."

Rayburn once said "in politics, you have to know how people feel and what they are thinking. You have to be fair. You have to have vision. You have to learn how to give and take." Rayburn took control of the Rules Committee. And he acknowledged that he was a footnote to history by offering - and taking - JFK's request for the vice-presidency to LBJ. Rayburn was a proud Democrat and presided with pride at all kinds of gatherings from caucus meetings to national conventions. But he was also known for working with the othe side.

In fact, the true testament of a man's reputation is how the opposition feels about you and when Rayburn was replaced as Speaker by his Massachusetts counterpart Joe Martin when the Republicans regained control of the House in 1952, Martin called him "a good friend and a square shooter" whose "word is as good as his bond" He reminded Rayburn that when the GOP was in the minority, "you treated us with respect and dignity, and we shall do the same."

Left photo courtesy of the Lyndon B. Johnson Presidential Library and right the Dolph Briscoe Center for American History, the University of Texas at Austin

Harry Truman was able to vouch for the fact that Rayburn could always keep his ego in check. One night while roasting him, he noted Rayburn's affection for hats and asked, "How many people do you know who have worn the same size hats as long as they've been in Washington." The duo litrally shared history together. One day, it was just the two men meeting in Raybrn's Board of Education room when the phone rang. It was for Truman and he was to report to the White House immediately. Unbeknownst to him until her arrived there, President Roosevelt had died and Truman was to assume the Presidency (Truman later summoned Rayburn without telling him what was ongoing).

Among the most prominent Rayburnisms: "Any jackass can tear down the barn but it takes a carpenter to build one" and "you have to go a long to get along" and the "but what have you done for me lately" question from supporters.

And a legendary tale of Rayburn involves newly elected House member Daniel Inouye. Hawaii had just become a state, and Inouye, a veteran, was elected to the House. Rayburn gave Inouye a hearty welcome and proceeded to tell Inouye that he was among the most recognized members. Inouye looked puzzled and Rayburn replied it was because "we don't have many one-armed Japs around here."

A man as legendary as "Mister Sam" had to have a personal quirk or two and in an oral history project, Florida Senator George Smathers recalls that "one of his little idiosyncracies" were raw onions. Smathers, who used to visit Rayburn with Johnson, recalls "Rayburn would always have a great big pail of onions, raw big round onions, and he would pull up the cuff of his coat and reach in there and pull one out, and ask, 'Would you like an onion?' Sam Rayburn would sit there and peel it off. Mostly they looked to me like Vidalia onions, and he would have those with his bourbon, and apparently do this every night." Smathers added that when restaurants knew the Speaker was on his way, "they had to have onions" and "they would have them in a pot right beside his chair, never up on the table. He would reach in and feel these onions, and pull them out and hand them around to anybody who might want one."

One rare moment of anger by Rayburn was the 1956 Democratic Convention. Adlai Stevenson had made the surprising, puzzling move of instructing delegates to choose his vice-presidential nominee. Rayburn was visibly flabbergasted, calling it "the damnedest fool thing I've ever heard of." He thought it would lend credence to the widely seen notion that Stevenson suffered from "congenital indecisiveness."

**Photo courtesy of the Dolph Briscoe Center for American
History, the University of Texas at Austin**

One state delegation chair, Hy Raskin, remarked, "Stay out of the old man's way—he's madder'n hell." Stopping Tennessee Senator Estes Kefauver was priority number one, and though Texas had awarded Al Gore, Sr. its delegates on the first ballot, Rayburn knew how to count. It would either come down to Kefauver or John F. Kennedy, and the former was not acceptable. Thus, the man Rayburn had referred to as "a wealthy dilettante" and a "piss-ant" was now poised to win his backing for VP. "Gentleman, you can vote as you please," he told delegates, "but Sam Rayburn is voting for Kennedy." But Rayburn, who controlled the gavel, was outmaneuvered twice. The first was when he recognized Tennessee, believing they were putting weight behind Kennedy. Instead, Gore, withdrew. The second was when John McCormack pleaded for him to recognize Missouri.

Rayburn, believing the delegation was for Kennedy, did just that only to watch the Congressman from the Show-me State cast his votes for Kefauver.

Because Rayburn was a bachelor, his sister often accompanied him. Rayburn's house in his beloved Bonham
Left photo via the Center for American History at the Dolph Briscoe Center and right photo courtesy of the Sam Rayburn House Museum

Four years later, when Kennedy was confronted with anti-Catholic sentiment, Rayburn was only too happy to bash opponents over the head. After JFK's Houston speech confronting the matter, Rayburn was impressed. "As we say in my part of Texas, he ate 'em blood raw." But Rayburn had been concerned enough about the impact of Kennedy's religion that early in the campaign season, he urged Lyndon Johnson to run "for the sake of the nation and the party, even if he did not want too." To Rayburn, Nixon in the White House would be a "cerebral horror."

Of his own experience, Rayburn remarked, "I am glad being a Baptist of the hard show that I have no religious prejudice. I have served in Congress with hundreds of Catholics. By no speech they ever made, no vote they ever cast did they indicate they were Catholic, protestant, or Jew . . . Please think again and vote for the man regardless of religion whom you think can best serve our country."

Rayburn was a founding father of Route 66 and shepherded many Democratic ideals into law. He was a what-you-see-is-what-you-get type of person whom Johnson said "ran his office from his ass back pocket." According to his biography, he "kept few notes, received few staff briefings, and handled much House and district business from the back of an envelope (his one attempt to gain a press secretary failed when he successfully recruited Johnson aide Booth Mooney. But neither man wanted to tell Johnson). "Within the district, Rayburn's speeches were hardly ever prepared and were given without notes." Just as future Speaker Tip O'Neill would become forever renowned for his "All Politics Is Local" adage, Mr. Sam's Rayburnisms (stories/quotes, etc.), could encompass entire books.

Photo courtesy of the Alabama Department of Archives and History

What's remarkable is that Rayburn was cut from the same cloth as Russell (actually born in Tennessee) but was committed to rights of all people, and the Kennedy agenda. Rayburn saw the Rules Committee as an impediment to both. He took particular aim at William Colmer, a Mississippi Democrat who had not backed Kennedy in the '60 election. He wanted to have Colmer removed. When he could not reach an agreement with the panel's chair, Virginia Democrat Howard W. Smith, Rayburn proposed enlarging the Committee and installing on the panel liberals who would be sympathetic to the "New Frontier." This also was met with resistance from Smith and the matter went to the House floor. In a rare display of reporting to personality, Rayburn would ask wavering members, "Are you for the Speaker or are you for that Old man from Virginia." By a vote of 217-212 (and relying on a few votes from GOP members), the House adopted Rayburn's proposal. But as Carl Albert wrote in his book, *Little Giant*, "Those 30 years seemed to take thirty years off of his tired old body and fifty off his spirit." It would soon be evident.

Rayburn was just a little over a year shy of his "Golden Anniversary" in the House when he died in 1961. His quick decline surprised those who knew him. When he began experiencing lower back pains near the end of summer, Rayburn was examined by President Kennedy's personal physician who suggested rest. Rayburn decided to take a break from his Congressional duties to return to his beloved Bonham for convalescence. But he vowed to return ("If I can just get home for some sunshine, I'll be all right"). But Rayburn had pancreatic cancer and it was inoperable and fast-moving. It would claim him within two months. Kennedy, ex-Presidents Eisenhower and Truman and of course Johnson, by then vice-president, were in attendance.

Newspaper courtesy of the Sam Rayburn House Museum; Funeral photo via the Center for American History at the Dolph Briscoe Center

Rayburn is the answer to those who say strong leaders and decent human beings are mutually exclusive.

Beyond the Russell Building, there are two on the Senate side.

One is named for Everett Dirksen, the longtime Minority Leader who delivered crucial votes to Majority leader Mike Mansfield on issues of Civil Rights and the "Great Society." In other words, Dirksen and many in his party provided crucial votes for Civil Rights because Democrats, despite controlling two-thirds of the chamber in the mid-60s, were hampered by the opposition of men like Russell.

Dirksen's ability to deliver GOP votes for a Democratic agenda was so wide-reaching that, in 1962, when he was facing re-election against Sidney Yates, a respected liberal Congressman from Chicago who would eventually become Illinois' longest serving Congressman, President Kennedy refused to campaign against him. It was said that Kennedy felt that if Dirksen lost, he wouldn't have such a congenial leader of the opposite party. And when Kennedy died, Dirksen reciprocated the affection. "We saw him come to this body at age 35, we saw him grow, we saw him rise, we saw him elevated," Dirksen wrote in the *Congressional Record*. "If at any moment he may have seemed overeager, it was but the reflection of a zealous crusader and missioner who knew where was going."

LBJ himself responded to NAACP head Roy Wilkins' request for help on Civil Rights legislation. LBJ said: "You're gonna have to persuade Dirksen why this is in the interests of the Republican party . . . I'm a Democrat, but if a fella will stand up and fight with you, you can cross party lines."

Photo courtesy of the collection of the U.S. House of Representatives

Dirksen unambiguously proved that to be correct. In an eloquent speech in the third month of the filibuster, Dirksen eloquently invoked Victor Hugo, who supposedly wrote in his diary the day he died, "Stronger than all the armies is an idea whose time has come." Dirksen added, "The time has come for equality of opportunity in sharing of government, in education, and it employment. It must not be stayed or denied." After the vote, Dirksen was asked why he came aboard the fight and he replied, "I am involved in mankind, and whatever the skin, we are all included in mankind."

Dirksen was born near Peoria in 1896 and dropped out of the University of Minnesota Law School to join the army. Dirksen was called "The Wizard of Ooze." He rarely gave a prepared speech instead relying on notes. And out loud, he was very contemplative. In his book *Consequences*, John Tower described Dirksen's voice as "throaty, mellifluous, baritone, which could soothe and cajole or range like thunder. His histrionic ability was superb, with a fine sense of timing, the essence of an actor's skill. He was a spellbinder in the 19th century tradition." He recalls a meeting where an aide offered him a drink and he replied, "brandy." After pausing, he added, "Yes, brandy. Winston Churchill foundered on it and that's good enough for me."

But despite a lackluster delivery, Dirksen could be biting with foes. When Tom Dewey wanted to endorse Eisenhower, Dirksen, presiding at the GOP convention and backing Taft said, "We followed you before, and you took us down the path to defeat!"

Dirksen's talents were evidenced by the fact that his first Congressional victory came countercyclical to the national climate. He won it in 1932 (having lost a race in 1930) and supported many New Deal programs. He was forced to retire in 1948 because of a bad eye but displayed his political acumen again by making a comeback in 1950. This time, it was for the Senate and he unseated a big fish: Senate Majority leader Scott Lucas. But his target wasn't so much Lucas as the Truman administration. The administration's foreign policy was a "failure . . . expensive, inconsistent, and ineffective." He dubbed the European Recovery "Operation Rathole."

Left photo courtesy of George Mason University, right photo courtesy of the Abraham Lincoln Birthplace

As his tenure advanced, Dirksen did become an ardent backer of Vietnam but also several Great Society programs. Conservatives liked him for an arduous promotion of prayer in the schools, which fell far short in 1966.

Wikipedia would say "Dirksen's canny political skill, rumpled appearance, and convincing, if sometimes flowery, overblown oratory (he was hence dubbed by his critics "the Wizard of Ooze") gave him a prominent national reputation." David Kyvig, author of Dirksen's Constitutional Crusades noted he "favored rumpled suits and an unruly crown of tousled hair that delighted cartoonists. A frustrated thespian, he enjoyed delivering long-winded, hyperbolic, and melodramatic speeches that rolled off his tongue in a rich bass voice."

These traits were evident even as a child. In his high-school yearbook, it was written that Dirksen suffered from "big-worditis." Byron Hulsey, Assistant Director of the Jefferson Scholars Foundation, wrote, "at the most superficial level, Everett Dirksen never escaped the caricature of a purposeless ham, well-meaning and good-natured but nevertheless a puppet like buffoon who used the nation's political stage more to entertain and amuse than to lead and inspire."

Joint press conferences with Charlie Halleck, the House Republican leader became known as the "Ev and Charlie Show (left); right with President Johnson Left photo courtesy of the Dirksen Center, Pekin, Illinois; right photo courtesy of the National Archives

Hulsey said "trust was at the center of Dirksen's treatment of his colleagues. His word was his bond." He said Dirksen possessed five traits (oratorical prowess, herculean work habits, knowledge of the rules, a deliberate flexibility, and an unparalleled command of human relationships) that helped him become a master legislator. He was noted for his "Twilight Lodge." Dirksen showed his heft with the rules over a labor bill, when his knowledge of the rules enabled him to take the floor until the clock ran out, thereby delaying action and getting concessions for Republicans on the bill.

And he would do it again on a more ever-lasting matter – civil rights.

Some were skeptical Dirksen could – or would rise to the moment but he proved them wrong. Early on, he said, "I trust that the time will never come in my political career when the waters of partisanship will flow so swift and so deep as to obscure my estimate of the national interest," he said on the Senate floor…I trust I can disenthrall myself from all bias, from all prejudice, from all irrelevancies, from all immaterial matters, and see clearly and cleanly what the issue is and then render an independent judgment."

In the run-up to the vote, Dirksen would participate in nightly strategy sessions with Mansfield and Democratic Whips. With unusual eloquence as the bill neared final passage, Dirksen noted that some "extremes" will "fuss," but said that should not inhibit the chips falling where they may. Calling civil rights "an idea whose time has come," He cited his mother who upon arriving at Ellis Island from Germany, noted the tag on her neck said "she be sent to Pekin, Illinois. Our family had opportunities in Illinois, and the essence of what we're trying to do in the civil rights bill is to see that others have opportunities in this country."

After the law was passed, Dirksen received a letter Wilkins who called himself "the first to admit that I was in error in estimating your preliminary announcements and moves… "there were certain realities which had to be taken into account in advancing this legislation to a vote. Out of your long experience you devised an approach which seemed to you to offer a chance for success."

On occasion, Dirksen's cageyness did not render him incapable of out-smarting himself. Toward the end of his career, he took aim at overturning decisions by the Warren Court by proposing Constitutional amendments overturning them. One was he decision codifying "one-man, one-vote." As it became clear that 2/3 of Senators required would be elusive, Dirksen thought he could use his mastery of parliamentary procedures to thwart it. As such, he proposed substituting that day's agenda with a proposal commemorating "National American Legion Baseball Week," which would require a simple majority vote. The move backfired and Dirksen's Illinois colleague and leader of the anti-amendment forces, Democrat Paul Douglas called it "the foul ball amendment." J. Douglas Smith in *On Democracy's Doorstep: The Inside Story of How the Supreme Court Brought "One-Person, One-Vote,"* to the United States, said the "unexpected play provided fodder for editorial cartoonists." But this didn't keep Dirksen from trying a similar tactic on school prayer. In this case, he moved to substitute the amendment with recognition of UNICEF (the United Nation's Children's Emergency Fund).

Dirksen was not immune to resorting to acrimonious language. Calling religious opponents of the prayer amendment a "godless mass," Dirksen said, "You cannot contemplate the gangs in our large cities, and the mass of atheistic Communism, and all of these other forces that are trying to destroy the religious traditions of this country, without coming to the conclusion that they have made a lot of progress in that direction."

Dirksen advocated the Marigold as the national flower
Image courtesy of DavesGarden.com

During the fight over Abe Fortas' ill-fated Supreme Court nomination, Dirksen had unusually harsh language for fellow Republican Bob Griffin who criticized Fortas for, among other things, his close proximity to Johnson. "You don't go out and look for an enemy to put on the high court! I find that term 'lame duck' as applied to the President of the United States as an entirely improper and offensive term" (Dirksen still voted against cloture for Fortas).

Dirksen won a fairly tough re-election bid in 1968, when his opponent, Attorney General William G. Clark, took aim at Dirksen's notable weakness—his frailty. Calling him "out of tune with the times," he called Dirksen a "loveable old celebrity whose most splendid rhetoric provides comic relief to the agonies that build upon this nation." He said, unfairly, that he "failed to make things any better." Referring to Dirksen's legendary love of the Marigold, Clark said, "the only thing he wants to change is the state flower . . . Well that's the one thing I don't want to change." And Dirksen was noticeably weak. Clark received the backing of both Chicago's newspapers but his funding was limited. Dirksen held on. But victory would be short-lived.

Photo courtesy of the U.S. Senate Historical Office

Dirksen was soon diagnosed with lung cancer. He died of complications in September of '69 at age 73. While President Nixon delivered the primary eulogy, his son-in-law, now Senator Howard Baker, followed him. While noting Dirksen's "terrible singing," Baker remembered him as a "man of imposing presence and bearing . . . eminent wit, humor, and perspective, who kept himself and others constantly on guard against taking themselves too seriously."

Michigan's Phil Hart was the one member who wasn't a leader or who didn't chair a major committee, but not a single person, colleague, or man on the street who encountered him could ever think of questioning the idea of naming a building after him. He was a wondrous representative of the people and would stand out in any era about what's right about Congress, even when little is.

Photo courtesy of Lake Superior State University, Hart Archives

Hart was referred to as "the Conscience of the Senate." Ronald Kessler, in his book, *Inside Congress*, quoted one colleague as saying that they'd vote a certain way, then gather around Hart to see "the right way to vote." And Ralph Nader in his Congressional ranking of all 535 members of Congress called him, "Unfailingly courteous, articulate but speaking at length on all sides of an issue, tolerant and tentative, fair and reasonable."

Hart was so strong an advocate of civil rights that he didn't hesitate to demonstrate it in a statement, literally and figuratively. He once asked George Wallace if he thought "that heaven is segregated?" and when Richard Russell died, he was the only Senator to oppose making Mississippi Senator Jim Eastland President Pro-Tem, as Eastland clearly had an animosity toward blacks. He also had a leading role in passage of the Voting Rights Act.

Ted Kennedy, to whom Hart was "like a brother," called him "a giant of the Senate. His voice never shook the rafters, but touched the conscience of every Senator who worked with him." But it wasn't just civil rights that loomed large in terms of Hart's reputation. He was also a dogged advocate for consumer protection and used his Chairmanship of the Judiciary Committee's Anti-Trust and Monopolies to promote this position. Hart took on special interests of all stripe, which, as Kessler writes, his own state wouldn't be immune to (he often summoned the auto industry). One of his missions included breaking up General Motors.

Hart with his wife Jane (left) and committee staff (right)
Photo courtesy of Lake Superior State University Hart Archives

At one point, his bill came within five votes of passing. He backed busing and gun control, the latter particularly courageous, as some parts of the state were vehemently opposed. "Recall cures Hart attacks."

Hart's for-the-people approach resonated with "Wolverines." Lucien Nedzi's tenure as a Congressman from suburban Detroit overlapped with Hart's Senate service for 16 years. He calls him, "an inspiration to me when I was a Young Democrat full of idealism which he brought to life" and recalls he and his wife traveling to Michigan's Upper Peninsula at their own expense to hang posters during Hart's successful 1958 campaign for Lieutenant Governor. Nedzi adds, "his mild manner and reasonableness made it always a pleasure to be in his company."

Hart was serving as Lieutenant Governor in 1958 alongside his close friend, G. Mennen Williams, and took advantage of the national winds to win the Senate seat. His 1964 re-election was won with 64%, and he took nearly two-thirds six years later against Lenore Romney, wife of the ex-Governor. In something of a déjàvu moment, *The Almanac of American Politics* said Romney's race was "a textbook example of how to not run a campaign," noting she alienated suburban women and blacks.

Hart's reputation was such that fellow Senators voted to name a new building after him while he was still in office. By that point, Hart knew he was dying and had already announced his retirement. As Hart was getting ready to leave the Senate, his colleague and friend, Tom Eagleton of Missouri, wrote him the following: "A human body has a brain, an ass, and a soul. In the Senate, we have a few brains, lots of asses, and one soul. You are that soul and with your retirement the Senate body is severely impaired." When Hart did succumb days before his term ended, President Gerald Ford called the family and asked what he could do. They asked him to issue amnesty to the people who had fled the draft during the Vietnam War. Ford made no commitments but said he'd see what he could do. He never acted.

Bob Dole met Hart along with another future colleague, Dan Inouye, when all were recovering from war injuries in Battle Creek, Michigan. Dole said: "It is not surprising that Phil Hart's name is not a household word. Phil never went out of his way to claim the spotlight. He saw his public service career as just that—an opportunity to serve the public—and sought no credit for it. He simply tried to do his best." That is the true nature of the man.

Photo courtesy of Lake Superior State University Hart Archives

The other two buildings on Capitol Hill are named for men of a far earlier period. Joe Cannon was an example of the phrase, "if at first you don't succeed, try, try again." He tried four times to win the Speakership before succeeding. That may be why his goal was to never to let it slip away. Cannon ruled with an iron fist, controlling the Rules Committee and committee appointments down to the member. Today, there would be backlash to such a style of a rule but in the days of limited communication, many voters were impervious. But not his colleagues. A few fellow Republicans tried to join with the Democrats to dislodge him but Cannon held on.

"Uncle Joe" Cannon (left) and Nick Longworth (right)
Left photo via the Collection of the U.S. House of Representatives; right
photo Photo via the Library of Congress Prints and Photographs Division

Cannon may well have been the modern-day Tom DeLay ("the Hammer"), not to mention Tom Craddick, a former Republican Speaker of the Texas House who employed similar tactics, particularly in the redistricting struggle. But his Illinois constituency loved him. They sent him to Washington for 46 of 50 years. Though he'd have the misfortune of losing his seats in 1890 and 1912 – when the climate worked against Republican, he'd be returned to Washington the following cycles.

If there is a book in existence on how to stay on your wife's good side, Nick Longworth surely did not write it, nor did his father-in-law. Longworth, then a sophomore Ohio Congressman, married Teddy Roosevelt's eldest daughter Alice at the White House in 1906 but veered away from him politically soon after. He also became disenchanted with Cannon, who was by that time Speaker.

In 1912, Longworth actually backed William Howard Taft over his father-in-law's Progressive candidacy, and Alice returned the favor by campaigning against her husband for re-election (and folks wonder how Bill and Hillary stay married). With a Progressive on the ballot, Longworth lost his seat (the same year as Cannon) but did manage to regain it two years later. He'd rise to Majority Leader and eventually, Speaker.

The ironic thing about Longworth's second stint is that he began employing many of Cannon's tactics, punishing Republicans who backed Bob LaFollette over Calvin Coolidge. But he also cultivated Democratic friendships and thus was well respected.

Okay, so a few of the men for whom the other buildings on Capitol Hill are named are not my cups of tea politically or procedurally speaking, but in one way or another, they shaped the Capitol. Russell's politics shaped a whole era. Or more appropriately, error. Next to slavery itself, "State's Rights" was the ugliest, most heinous chapters in humanity for which scars remain, literally and figuratively. One of the greatest heroes of the Civil Rights movement and Russell's fellow Georgian, John Lewis was beaten savagely. Countless others lost their lives. It's unclear whether Russell himself was racist (a few Senate colleagues, notably Mississippian James Eastland were), but it's not really relevant. His ardent defense of that way of life is.

Imagine what Lincoln would think. Jerry Ford had a malapropism on another matter, "if Lincoln were alive today he'd turn over in his grave," but the sentiment fits. Senators Michael Cowan and Tim Scott, two native African-American sons of the Carolina's occupy offices in the Russell Building (Cowan since moved to Massachusetts). How do they feel literally walking in the shadow (there is a bust of Russell) of a man who tried to hold their people back? And why should they be made too? The Sherriff of Birmingham apologized to Lewis recently for his beating. Were it not for men like Russell, that apology wouldn't have been necessary.

There was a biography of Thurgood Marshall, *Dream Makers, Dream Breakers*. For many people, Russell was the latter. And to reward him with a building! I don't think so!

And it's irrelevant to the issue at hand but ridding the building of Russell's name wouldn't even offend his family, because, as far as direct descendants, he's got none (Russell was a bachelor).

So who should bear the name of the hopefully former Russell Building. Well, since Civil Rights is at the heart of the matter, John Lewis would be a stirring choice, though I recognize he is a member of the House (not Senate) and one who is still serving.

What about Hiram Rhodes Revels, the first African-American Senator. He would've served longer had it not been for Reconstruction. Or perhaps, "Scoop" Jackson, who served in Congress just as long as Russell, who advocated for his state just as hard (was called the "Senator from Boeing"), and who advocated a muscular approach to defense and communism. Maybe even Hubert Humphrey, who from his impassioned 1948 keynote speech ("get out of the shadow of states' rights and walk forthrightly into the bright sunshine of human rights"), to becoming Vice-President was, next to LBJ himself, Russell's chief nemesis on the civil rights issue.

Whatever the case, to give healing and peace to future generations and the blood of the past, this must change.

Photo via the Library of Congress Prints and Photographs Division

Photo courtesy of the Collections of the U.S. House of Representatives

Longworth with his wife, Alice Roosevelt Longworth
Photo courtesy the Library of Congress Prints and Photographs Division

CHAPTER TWENTY-TWO

Russell Senate Building
Should Be Renamed For Clair Engle

Historic Quote: "I am a man of fixed and unbending principles, the first of which is to be flexible at all times." - Everett Dirksen

In a recent piece, I made my case that the Russell Senate Office Building on Capitol Hill should be stripped of its name. It is named after Richard Russell, a legendary Georgia Senator but one who was an avowed segregationist. Russell more than anyone else held up passage of civil rights laws. I won't reiterate my reasoning but I will make my case for the person for whom I think it should be named: Clair Engle.

The late California Democrat was not a Congressional leader. Five of the six buildings bear the names of people who were. But the sixth, the Hart Senate Office Building, was named for Phillip Hart, a Senator whose personal integrity garnered him the wide respect of both parties. Engle deserves to be ranked with Hart. His service was not as long, but he had a dramatic impact on passage of the civil rights in the face of his own personal adversity.

By June of 1964, Engle was dying of brain cancer, a revelation that had come only recently. He knew it, and so did everyone around him. But cutting off a filibuster was expected to be close. Engle had been hospitalized and by the time he was wheeled into the chamber and the clerk called his name, he couldn't speak. Therefore, uttering "aye" was impossible. So Engle simply affirmed his support for the bill by pointing to his eye. Three weeks later, he was dead.

Hailing from the town of Red Bluff, Engle, who, as one of Congress's few pilots, often campaigned by plane, won a Northern California Congressional seat in a 1943 special election. Democrats were buoyed by the result. The seat Engle won was that of Republican House Minority Whip Henry Englebright who had died, and Engle's victory was attributed to a split between his widow and a State Senator. Still, Democrats, who prior to the election held a slim 221-207 edge over the GOP, were happy. Indeed, in the heart of World War II, the head of the Democratic Campaign Committee eluded to having captured "an enemy stronghold."

The New York Times wrote that Engle had a reputation as the "Congressional Fireball" and "the only volcano in the House." But that didn't mean he wasn't effective. He chaired the Committee on War Claims and later, the Interior and Insular Affairs, which, in the days of California's rapid growth, was important. And his work on issues promoting the quality-of-life of his people (electricity, flood control, etc) was the hallmark of his agenda.

Engle sponsored the expansion of the California Central Valley Reclamation Project and pushed construction of what is now known as the Trinity Dam, now one of the largest in California. He sought a Senate seat in 1958 and faced outgoing Governor Goodwin Knight, who had switched to the race to avoid the likelihood of a brutal contest with Senator Bill Knowland. He won.

Engle had a "Marlboro Man" mentality. *The New York Times* reported him warning a witness that he had to leave the committee room but "when I come back in 10 minutes, I'm sure going to throw a skunk in your henhouse." Another time, he called himself "as happy as a fox with two tails." And he said that the way to get action from bureaucrats was to "harass 'em, burn 'em, sweat 'em, and give 'em hell."

In many ways, Engle epitomized the idea of comparing the making of laws to the making of sausages, as he preferred cloakroom/committee rooms to getting things done. But the cigar-chomping man was a "Senator's Senator."

By 1964, rumors of Engle's health were plaguing California politics. It was visible on the Senate floor. As he offered a resolution that April, he could not get a word out, and his Michigan colleague, Pat McNamara had to do it for him. *The Times* notes that he "was virtually carried out of the chamber by his aides." As such, he was forced to abandon his re-election campaign. Eventually, the true nature of Engle's condition was revealed and he underwent a craniotomy.

As the vote approached, all knew that the outcome on Civil Rights bill would be close. Engle's attendance might not have been expected but showing up in such a dramatic fashion was a true demonstration of courage.

I can think of nothing more appropriate than replacing the name of a man who shouldn't have a comforting place in history, much less be memorialized on a building, with someone who is clearly among the unheralded giants of the Civil Rights era. I urge it to be considered. For Clair Engle is a true American hero.

Photo courtesy of the University of California at Berkeley

CHAPTER TWENTY-THREE

History Can't Ignore Ervin
and Fulbright's Civil Rights Record

Did Sam Rayburn play a role in saving the world? In his book, Man of
the House, Tip O'Neill told a story passed on by another future Speaker,
John McCormack. In 1942, months after World War II had begun, the
Congressional leadership had been meeting at the White House with
President Roosevelt when the President asked everybody in the room to be
ready for a 5:30 AM meeting the next morning. Roosevelt told them a ride
would be waiting. But it had to be kept a secret. Sure enough, McCormack
was picked up at 5:30 and, upon being driven around, met at an undisclosed
location, saw the other leaders, Roosevelt and Albert Einstein. It was there
that they were informed of the atomic bomb and were told the Germans were
aiming toward building one as well. Roosevelt told the leaders that money
would be required to beat the Germans but wouldn't know how to do it
without giving away the secret. That was when Rayburn told the group to
"leave it to me." He immediately asked the committee chairs to earmark an
extra $100,000,000 in spending and they did so without a question.

Without question, Senators Sam Ervin and William Fulbright occupy
memorable places in American history. Ervin presided over the Senate
Watergate hearings, and Fulbright was the legendary Chairmanship of the Senate
Foreign Relations Committee during the Vietnam War. Their accomplishments
give esteem and veneration to both men and leave them somewhat revered by
history. But there is major blemish on the record of both men that should not
be ignored: civil rights.

Fulbright and Ervin voted against every civil rights bill that came forward
during their tenures, took part in the filibuster that Mike Mansfield and Everett
Dirksen needed every single last vote to overcome, and were part of the famous
"Southern Manifesto."

When Fulbright proceeded to run for Congress, he recalled hailing from
Washington County in northern Arkansas, which in his book, The Price of Empire,
he guestimated had a black population of fewer than 1%. While in the Arkansas
legislature, Fulbright had once voted in favor of a black man's compensation in
the Arkansas Legislature. His 1944 opponent for the Senate raised that issue, even
branding him "a nig–r lover."

How did Fulbright respond? By giving a speech declaring his opposition to
African-American participation in the Arkansas Democratic Party. Thus, he went

along with the poll tax. In his book, he explained his rationale. "Civil Rights was an issue I felt unable to confront." Understandable—to a point. It was the south in the 1940s. But he said, "I would go along with a majority view of my constituents on certain local issues within their personal experience, but that on national and foreign-policy issues that were beyond their experience, I would exercise my own personal judgement." In the abstract, few might quarrel with that either.

But personal judgement on equal rights wouldn't appear to be a complicated subject. It's a matter of right and wrong. His reasoning was that "in most cases the blacks do not vote at all (in primaries). If you oppose your constituents too directly on issues close to their hearts, you won't get elected." Of course, there was an incident in Fulbright's back yard: the Little Rock situation. He basically said he couldn't have "altered" Faubus's cause. He said his sister criticized him for not speaking out. Fulbright believed education was the best way to move black America forward, though he later conceded that the "gradualist" school he belonged to was "discredited."

Oh, but Fulbright did convince the backers of Southern Manifesto to "modify" its position. He was reluctant to sign, only doing so because they cited the need for "unanimity" and he said he would not go along with "extraordinary force," only expressing displeasure with the court's decision. He explained that Arkansas was in no way ready for civil rights. But his stance against a very basic issue cost him what may have been an unvblemished place in history, including a much-sought office. When Kennedy became President, Fulbright coveted the job of Secretary of State but the new President resisted ("colored people don't like him").

Photo courtesy of the University of Arkansas

For even when the civil rights struggle was ongoing, Fulbright loomed large on another matter: foreign affairs—particularly Vietnam, where his committee and his oratory gained international attentionand became known as a thorn in LBJ's Vietnam policy.

Fulbright also opposed much of the "Great Society," though that was when he voted. He was absent on several roll calls. He did back the Elementary and Secondary Education Act and the widely supported Immigration and Nationality Act, which created the "open door policy." When Fulbright got under a colleague's skin, an occurrence which over a 30-year career would prove to be plentiful, he derided him as "half-bright." But Fulbright's prescience on many matters extended to matters outside of Senate purview. He warned JFK not to make the trip to Dallas, calling it "dangerous."

Fulbright, who for years faced little or no electoral difficulty, saw signs of his base eroding in 1968. He won just 53% in the primary and 59% in the general. Still, his ability to win big was notable given that Arkansas was a hawkish state and Fulbright was so opposed to Vietnam. But his 30-year tenure came to an end when Governor Dale Bumpers, a true Civil Rights progressive in every sense of the word, beat him in the 1974 primary. The margin was 65-35%. Bumpers had said he wouldn't have run unless he was all but assured of ousting Fulbright.

**Clinton, who took advantage of "Fulbright Scholarships," presented his
mentor with the Presidential Medal of Freedom. But should he have?
Photo courtesy of the University of Arkansas**

Had Ervin retired a year earlier, his name would not have been known outside the "Tarheel" State. Ironically, not since his first year in office, when as a well-respected lawyer he was a natural pick to serve on the McCarthy Investigation Committee, had he garnered many headlines outside of North Carolina. But at 78 and in the last year of his Senate tenure, Ervin refreshed Watergate-weary audiences.

But a statement during the hearings that Ervin made displays without question the ironies of his opposition to civil rights. "If these allegations prove to be true," he said, "what they were seeking to steal was not the jewels, money or other precious property of American citizens, but something much more valuable—their most precious heritage: the right to vote in a free election."

How ironic it is that the man who blocked and opposed the Voting Rights Act and all civil rights laws, was talking about true democracy by virtue of the right to vote.

If that sounds paradoxical, that might totally encompass Ervin. A North Carolina reporter once observed that "if stereotypes are often misleading, they are downright laughable in the case of Sam Ervin. After 13 years in the Senate, Ervin still regularly enrages first the liberals and then the conservatives. He defies all the easy generalizations of journalism."

Ervin was a product of small-town, rural America - Morgantown, North Carolina - at the time Jim Crow was being enacted. As a lawyer (his father was among the most respected in the county), judicial matters were always logical to his pedigree and in Congress, his legal abilities usually made his name the first Senator to come to mind when confronted with a legally thorny area.

Radley Balko, in a piece for the ACLU, called Ervin, "a devoutly religious man who, while in the North Carolina legislature in the 1940s, single-handedly defeated a proposed law that would have banned teaching evolution in the state's public schools. Ervin was a brilliant man, who often slyly hid his intellect behind a veil of aw shucks country charm. But once he'd disarmed his opponents, he'd pounce with a devastating argument or flourish of rhetoric that would ultimately win the day."

On a personal level, Ervin was thought to personally harbor no animosity toward blacks. When Brown vs. Board of Ed was put out, Ervin joined the "Southern Manifesto" in opposing it, but eventually relaxed it because of the fact that he came to the conclusion that it would not adversely impact white people.

That's all well and good but in the end, he still joined with opponents in blocking any kind of progress for the remainder of his career. Even as late as 1969 as Senators were debating desegregating the schools, Ervin gave no ambiguities about where he stood. An amendment by Pennsylvania Republican Hugh Scott to break the logjam by adding the words "except as required by the Constitution "weasel-worded." But his views were far more indignant than that. "The Constitution of my country does not require, indeed, does not permit children to be herded around like cattle and shifted about like pawns on a chess board merely to mix the races in the schools."

For the record, civil rights was not the only socially progressive legislation Ervin opposed. He also voted against most of the Great Society, including

Medicare, and as the book Sam Ervin, the Last of the Founding Fathers points out, "consumer protection, the minimum wage, health and safety regulations, and the Equal Rights Amendment." On the latter, he used language that was especially antiquated. used reasoning that was quite antiquated. "Laws protecting women from heavy work or from the draft should be preserved," he said. "Some state laws continue to discriminate against women, but to enact an amendment to the U.S. Constitution to do away with them is about as wise as using an atom bomb to exterminate a few mice." As if to match his rhetoric, Ervin proposed a Constitutional Amendment that would spare women from the draft. Overall, he spoke of the damage the Warren Court "has done to the Constitution."

Late in his career, there is evidence that Ervin's views on aid to the disadvantaged appeared to change. He chaired the Judiciary Committee's Subcommittee on Constitutional Rights, and pursued new protections for the mentally ill, members of the armed forces, and Native Americans, as well as the 1966 Bail Reform Act and the Criminal Justice Act, which increased access to legal counsel for the poor. And when the Senate took up a controversial "no-knock" provision to a crime bill that was opposed by many in the African-American community, Ervin sided with liberals. Ervin explained his reasoning thus: "Since the last Presidential campaign was based on the law and order issue in part, I myself have been beset by temptation. But I shall not succumb. I sincerely pray that none of my colleagues will be beset, by the same temptation. The siren voice of that old devil, political expediency, has been whispering in my ear, "You had better vote for the District of Columbia crime bill because it is a law and order bill, and it is not politically sagacious or politically profitable for Senators to vote against a law and order bill such as the District of Columbia crime conference report, even to preserve the individual liberties of our people."

One issue on which Ervin, by virtue of his fidelity to the Constitution, joined with liberals was his opposition to Minority Leader Everett Dirksen's proposed Constitutional amendment allowing prayer in the school and in doing so, he displayed great passion. Calling the amendment, an "annihilation of the principle of the First Amendment" which as worded, would "give to every school board the power—now denied by the 1st Amendment to Congress, and by the decision of Cantwell v. Connecticut to the states—to make a law respecting the establishment of religion. For God's sake and for freedom's sake," he implored, "let us draw an amendment which will give equality of religious freedom to every human being in the United States, regardless of what his religion may be, and not vest arbitrary permission power in school boards like the proposed amendment does."

Yet it was Watergate that galvanized both Ervin's following and his legacy.

During the hearings, Ervin made clear that he was not amused by the administration's tactics. Responding to Nixon's refusal to let his aides testify, Ervin noted that Executive Privilege differed from "executive poppycock," and added that "divine Right went out with the American Revolution and doesn't belong to White House aides. What meat do they eat that makes them grow so great?" And the American people, who were growing weary of Nixon, were clearly in Ervin's camp. "Senator Sam" t-shirts popped up, and buttons were not far behind.

The Washington Post summed up Ervin's star status: "With his arching eyebrows and flapping jowls that signaled his moral indignation at much of the testimony before his committee, his half-country, half-courtly demeanor and his predilection for making points by quoting the Bible and Shakespeare and telling folksy stories, Ervin quickly became a hero to many."

Even as he was charming audiences with his Matlock-like demeanor ("I'm just an old country lawyer"), Tom Wicker of *The New York Times* was pointing out that he simply "put on new clothes," a clear reference to his civil rights record. And that is the fact of the matter.

Photo courtesy of the U.S. Senate Historical office

Most view Ervin's philosophy as more civil libertarian, and he routinely cited the Constitution. In response, one activist called Ervin some "overblown constitutional attorney." Years later, Ervin said of Nixon: he "certainly obeyed Mark Twain's injunction; truth is precious. Use it sparingly."

Voting records aside, did Ervin and Fulbright harbor personal animosities against African-Americans? No evidence supports that. Jim Eastland of Mississippi on the other hand was unquestionably bigoted. But their actions held back a whole generation of African-Americans, helped cause unfathomable violence (the beating of John Lewis, for example) and tragically, more than a few deaths.

History should take that into account.

CHAPTER TWENTY-FOUR

Wondrous Missouri Senator Symington, For One, Brief Shining Moment, Was JFK's Choice For VP

Historic Quote: "Especially when you can probably pick up these delegates when Jack fails to make it." – William Loeb, editor of *The Manchester Union Herald* explaining to Senator Symington why he shouldn't put his name on the ballot for the 1960 New Hampshire primary

Photo courtesy of the U.S. Senate Historical Office

I f Harry Truman had his way, there would have been another President from Missouri in his lifetime. It seemed impractical that the Show-Me State could have two White House occupants in eight years but Senator Stuart Symington made a credible, albeit losing bid for the Democratic nomination in 1960 and apparently was closer to the second spot than history ever imagined.

For Symington's career, however, that might as well have been a footnote. The distinguished and most-capable Senator would become, according to his colleagues, one of the most respected members in history to sit in the upper chamber whose guidance was widely sought. There was a reason for that. By the time he won his seat, Symington already had an abundance of private sector and high-level experience in government and his wide-range grasp on matters would continue throughout. One example: *The Almanac of American Politics* noted that during the Vietnam War,

Symington was the only Senator to sit on both the Armed Services and Foreign Relations Committee, thus became highly sought after for language, etc.

Dubbed, "a tall, sandy-haired, and strong shouldered" man, in his *New York Times* obituary Symington "looked like a President." But the fact of the matter was that when he went forward with his bid, he was less known than, well, everyone else. Aside from JFK and LBJ, Hubert Humphrey and Adlai Stevenson were in the mix, but Symington, who was well-liked and respected enough in Washington, had made a strong impression.

Unlike a number of politicians, Symington's desire to be President was not strong. That was demonstrated after the 1956 defeat of Adlai Stevenson. Jim Meredith, Symington's campaign manager, told the two Symington boys to saddle up, telling them "it's time to go on the road to get your dad elected President in 1960." The two boys embraced the prospect but Symington essentially told them not so fast. After his 1958 re-election, Presidential chatter again presented itself, which forced Symington to declare, "My political ambition is to be the best Senator possible for the people of Missouri."

Therein was a major reason for Symington's ambivalence was his obligation to Missouri. Son Stuart, Jr., (nicknamed Tim) said he felt the state "needed all the help it could get in the Senate," calling him, "extremely conscious of his obligation to the people of Missouri to hang in there and protect its interests." Eventually, however, he was in and the campaign decided to mount a strategy that, by virtue of timing and simply getting outfoxed, ultimately proved unsuccessful. It involved bypassing the states holding primaries and taking advantage of a brokered convention.

On its face, it wasn't a bad strategy. At the start of 1960, very few could envision a 43 year old Senator from Massachusetts would take the nod on ballot one. The Symington brothers cultivated a number of delegations. One was Wyoming. Tim recalls the Democratic chair, Teno Roncalio, telling him he wished "you had come last year. Teddy was here." But Roncalio vowed to divide the state's delegation into three parts. In other words, "if dad survived the first vote, it would've been open season." Ironically, it was Wyoming that put Kennedy over-the-top on the first ballot.

Still, advisors prevailed on Symington to formally launch a bid. He announced his candidacy in the Caucus room of Old Senate Office Building. And he criss-crossed the country like a true candidate. And for someone who seemed genuinely conflicted about whether to mount a bid, Symington's rhetoric was a mixture of confidence, gravitas and swagger.

At a West Virginia Democratic Women's event, Symington called peace the most important goal of the next President, asserting that it would require "all the intelligence, strength and brotherhood we have. Nothing is more important than that our children and grandchildren shall be able to 'beat their swords into plowshares and . . . shall not learn war anymore.'"

Symington also hammered away at America's place on the world stage. "American prestige," he said, "has suffered seriously because of the lack of firm American leadership and clear American policy. Moreover, our prestige has been seriously damaged by the failure of this country to put forth the necessary efforts to compete successfully with the Soviets in space accomplishments and to build up our ICBM strength."

Also in West Virginia, Symington mocked the failure on Eisenhower's watch to lure investment into rural areas, he charged that "This administration seems more interested in retrenchment than investment; more concerned with the value of today's dollar than with the value of tomorrow's world." He pledged "The next administration - a Democratic administration - will change this for the benefit of all people." Symington cited "poverty and disease" as "two of the foremost allies of communism" (occasionally adding "ignorance" to the list). And he rattled off a five-point plan to combat poverty many of which proved the model for much of the "Great Society."

At the end of the day, Symington was said to have been "everybody's second choice." Many of the high echelon Democrats had indicated that he was acceptable, since, like Truman, he had backing from a coalition of African-Americans and women. The "second choice" label was apparently the case with the vice-presidency as well, so much so that he almost landed a spot as JFK's running mate.

Symington did not see that happening ("I bet you a hundred dollars that no matter what he says, Jack will not make me his running mate. He will have to pick Lyndon"), and Symington bristled at talking to whites-only crowds and Kennedy needed a Southerner. According to James Olson's biography, *Stuart Symington: A Life*, RFK apparently was pushing hard for Symington at a time when many believed Minnesota's Orville Freeman had already been given the nod. "Scoop" Jackson was also on the short-short list.

Clark Clifford, Truman's most famed aide, said he was "carrying messages back and forth," even going so far as to say JFK himself had told him the day before the deadline that he was "now offering the nomination to Senator Symington. Take it to him and get back to me." It was being billed as the "second Missouri Compromise," which would actually have been the third, as Truman's selection in 1944 was considered number two.

However, other advisers prevailed on Kennedy to go with Johnson. One reason, as noted by Joe Alsop, was Johnson's 800-pound-gorilla status as Senate Majority Leader: "He's much too big a man to leave up in the Senate." Others theorized that Johnson went with Kennedy because he needed a Southerner, pure and simple. Whatever the reason, it didn't faze the Missouri Senator a bit. Clifford said upon giving Symington the news, "he seemed very relaxed about it. He didn't seem to be hungering for it anyway." This was confirmed by Symington's son James who told me that while his dad would have accepted, he was not "very anxious" about it. He had heard the rumblings about Johnson as well but was as surprised as anyone when the Texas Senator accepted. Still, Symington gave his all to help the ticket and his support was crucial. The ticket carried the "Show-Me State" by 10,000 votes out of 1.9 million cast.

Tim says his dad "liked Kennedy very much." He viewed him as all-American." In particular, he recalls his dad looking at a picture of Kennedy and exclaiming with awe, "Look at that swing!" (Symington was a good golfer). Above all, he appreciated Kennedy's "approach to life and upbeatness."

The Senator's other son, future Congressman Jim Symington told me his father's sole regret about not pushing harder for the second slot was that had he been selected, JFK "would never have gone to Dallas."

Truman, however, who said he had "no second choice" on Symington for President, probably was a different story.

Photo courtesy of the Harry Truman Presidential Library

Truman and Symington went way back, and it wasn't simply due to a Missouri connection. But it wasn't always sunshine and lollipops. Truman had sometimes irked Symington when the future President chaired the Senate Committee investigating national defense pricing. Truman thought the expenditures at Emerson Electric Manufacturing Co. were too high and hauled him before his committee to defend it. Symington creditably proved he was not a crook and earned Truman's everlasting respect. As a sign of the small degree of separation in the world of defense, Symington had been recommended for the Emerson post by future Pentagon Secretary James Forrestal, whom *Air Force Magazine's* Walter Boyne notes would "ironically" become his future boss as Defense Secretary. But first, Truman would make Symington head administrator of the Surplus Property Administration.

As a sign of how far Symington had come since the committee hearing, Truman by 1947 was offering Symington one of three positions. He chose to become the newly created Secretary of the Air Force. Boyne wrote his "business sense might be found in the small size of his staff: four officers and eleven civilians." Boyne said Truman and Symington did not always see eye to eye on matters of the Air Force. "Both had strong personalities, and they battled vigorously over the fundamental issue of the size of the independent United States Air Force and its share of the defense budget." Some of that clearly involved style. Boyne noted that Truman was "the son of a mule trader and farmer, was smaller, stockier, and had the common touch of a politician who had worked his way up from the ranks. Symington, the patrician son of an Amherst College professor, was tall, urbane, and sophisticated."

Symington eventually resigned but Boyne pointed out "the battles did not impair their friendship." Tim says he never heard his dad utter a cross word about Truman. In fact, years after his Presidency, he recalls going to the Truman Library and having the ex-President enter unannounced, take a seat at the piano, and play the "Missouri Waltz."

After his stint at the Air Force, Symington could have been the baseball commissioner but decided instead to convert his talents to elective office. It was a smart undertaking. A number of people pressed him to challenge first-term Senator Jim Kem in 1952. Symington hesitated but went forward. It was during that campaign that Lyndon Johnson came to Missouri to stump for him. Tim recalls driving Johnson back to the airport at which time the future-President called his dad "a racehorse. You should let him relax once in a while." Why did this stand out. Because the younger Symington, who would come to know LBJ fairly well, called him "the most intense guy I've ever met."

Symington ultimately unseated Kem with a solid 54%. It was an impressive win in a year Eisenhower and the Republicans were winning control of Congress. He became close with like-minded Senators including Florida Democrat George Smathers, Kentucky Republican John Sherman Cooper and his 1952 classmate, Henry "Scoop" Jackson of Washington. And whether it meant fighting local battles like advocating for his state's farmers or taking on Joseph McCarthy, Symington was anything but shy about showing up for the fight. It would give allies and critics alike a measure of his common-sense.

First came his fight against McCarthyism. Symington served on the infamous Senate Subcommittee on Investigations which McCarthy chaired and at one hearing, was futilely trying to get his attention. He reminded him that the "attention does not always have to be on you." McCarthy insinuated that the bright lights of the cameras were making "my friend from Missouri" confused and proceeded to refer to him as "Sanctimonious Stu." Symington took issue with McCarthy mocking his name and told him to "see a psychiatrist," a line that provoked applause from the audience.

Many commended Symington, telling him that was the first time anyone of stature had ever publicly gone after McCarthy. Still, Jim Symington said that his father didn't have anything against McCarthy on a personal level. Rather, by taking him on, he was "defending the honor of the people" to whom McCarthy had a "vendetta." Furthermore, it was characteristic of his dad being "straight-up, courteous and take no-nonsense from anybody demeanor." Tim said his father "bore no grudges." How was that proven? In a startling display of Symington's character, he went to console him. McCarthy reciprocated his affection years later by asking the Symington's to join him for dinner (they had already eaten). Tim also recalls running into McCarthy with his dad on the sidewalk one day after the hearings. "Dad introduced me to him cordially. McCarthy grinned up at me and said, 'What room have you got picked at the White House?'"

Symington also charged full-speed ahead at investigating agriculture inequities. In his first year in the Senate, he was assigned to the Public Works Committee as opposed to Agriculture and Forestry. But when he learned that the oversight of the Agriculture Stabilization and Conservation Programs (ASC) would be transferred from local to state control, he successfully petitioned the chairman of the special Senate committee, Hubert Humphrey, to let him sit on the panel. What followed was an arduous, two-day hearing in which it became evident that politics encompassed much of the process. Eventually, Symington won a seat on the full Agriculture and Forestry Committee.

On other issues, Symington had the foresight to recognize the Soviet Union's position as it prepared to launch Sputnik. In 1958, Symington condemned the Rand Corporation for studying how to "strategically surrender" to another nation. This, he said, was "defeatism."

Photos courtesy of the Harry S. Truman Presidential Library

William Poundstone wrote in his biography of Symington that critics charged he "had either not read or grossly misunderstood" the study, but it nonetheless became the impetus for a law barring funds for studies on surrender. Symington was also a solid supporter of his party on civil rights and labor issues. He refused to talk to segregated audiences, which many believed was another factor that hurt his chances of winning a place on the national ticket. But it was that openness may have won him the backing of famed African-American Congressman Adam Clayton Powell.

In 1960, Symington brought to light what soon became known as "missile-gap." It was the heart of the Cold War and he charged that Eisenhower administration's contentions, everything was not fine and dandy on the missile race. "The intelligence books," he said, "have been juggled (by the administration) so the budget books may be balanced." Specifically, he said the Soviets could soon have a 3-1 edge on the U.S and vowed to make his data public. Eisenhower called the charges "despicable" and Republicans issued a "Battle Lines" response which said he'd be committing "an act of total, reckless irresponsibility" if he followed through.

And there were his efforts for Missouri. When the National Baseball league gave the Kansas City Athletics the okay to move to Oakland, Symington threatened to take away their anti-trust exemption. They went but Kansas City ultimately got the Royals and the people knew who was behind it. Symington was given a standing ovation when he was invited to throw out the first ball. Symington also was a staunch backer of Israel. In 1968, he threatened to kill the Military Sale Bill if President Johnson refused to sell Israel F-4s. For constituent relations, this could be seen as killing two birds with one stone. Not only did Missouri have a decent- sized Jewish population, but the F4 was manufactured there.

Ask Tim his dad's proudest accomplishment and he points undoubtedly to the development of the Flat Water Recreation Area around Branson, Missouri. This turned a once sleepy area into a major tourist destination visited by hundreds of thousands of people from across the country each year. In pushing the project, Symington was seeking to emulate a Senate colleague he greatly admired - Oklahoma's Bob Kerr who once served as Governor of his state and whom he viewed as perhaps the smartest man in the chamber.

In the early 1970s, Symington and other Missouri legislators pressed the Army Corps of Engineers to construct a dam on the Meramec River just west of St. Louis. His reasoning, as his son told it, was that the city lacks "an ocean, beaches or slopes for skiing," so developing the area would be a sure-fire way to add jobs and stimulate the economy. But opponents, including some liberals on environmental grounds, maintained that only a few would benefit and Symington lost the fight - arguably his only major defeat in Congress.

Symington was born in Amherst, Massachusetts but that was because his father was a professor of Romance languages (French, Italian and Spanish) at Amherst College. The family's heart was in Baltimore which is where Symington was raised. As Harry Truman snuck into the Democratic Convention in 1900 when it was held in Kansas City, Symington got similar exposure when it was in Baltimore twelve years later. Admittance came easily and Symington sold drinks to delegates. One thing Symington did fib about was his age but it was for purely honorable reasons as he wanted to join the Army during World War 1. He received his commission as a Second Lieutenant in early 1919, just as the war was ending.

**Evelyn Wadsworth Symington (second from left) had
a storied background in her own right
Photo courtesy of the John F. Kennedy Presidential Library and Museum**

Symington then decided to attend Yale not because he had any burning desire to do so, but because his cousin Tom Symington, "whom I very much looked up to," was a big man on campus." But as Olson noted, Symington too would "become a big man on campus." He became involved with the *Yale Daily News* and the Dramatic Association. Tennis was a life-long passion of Symington's and despite an elbow-injury from a baseball injury that plagued him throughout his life, he managed to excel, even playing at the 1922 Nationals. Often, this would enable him to mix business with pleasure. Symington's journalism experience at Yale led him to a job at The *Baltimore Sun* covering tennis tournaments. He would often write and play at the same time. Then it was to Genseo, New York, a suburb of Rochester to stay with his uncle who owned Symington Co. The future Senator would mold iron (far removed from the patrician label).

In the ensuing years, Symington mostly specialized in saving companies that were on the verge of bankruptcy during the Depression. These included Colonial Radio Corp., and Rustless Iron and Steel Corp. In 1938, he took the helm of the Emerson.

Meanwhile, Symington married Evelyn Wadsworth, a woman who came from a family of political royalty. Her father, James Wadworth, was not only a U.S. Senator from New York but once upon a time, Speaker of the New York Assembly. Tim notes Wadworth "had a reputation for integrity which Dad sort of inherited, giving Dad easier acceptance when working with members of Congress." Her mother, Alice Evelyn Hay Boyd, was the daughter of an Ambassador and the granddaughter of President Lincoln's secretary. The couple would have two sons, Stu, Jr., (affectionately known as "Tim") and James, who would later become a U.S. Congressman. Stu, Jr., would author a book, *Tagging Along: Memories of My Grandfather James Wolcott Wadsworth, Jr.*

Symington (center) with his colleague, Jennings Randolph of West Virginia
Photo courtesy of the West Virginia Historical Society

Despite Symington's seemingly dominant electoral position in Missouri, he almost saw his career come to an end six years ahead of schedule. His 1970 opponent was John Danforth, a sincere 34-year-old Missouri Attorney General who became the future of the Missouri Republican Party. At 69, Symington was quite popular, and he may have assumed his victory was in the bag. It was, but only barely. Democrats sensed Danforth was gaining in the final month, and some Republicans accused Democrats of bribery, but Symington himself was never tied to it. Ex-Congressman William Hungate said on his death that he "exuded integrity. There was no question of any improprieties." No shadows ever fell on Stuart Symington.

On Election Day, Danforth came within 3% of Symington, with the veteran hanging on just 51-48% (at one point on election night, Danforth was doing so well that he asked Tim if "you think we are licked" (the younger Symington correctly responded "no"). Symington was also changing his tune on Vietnam, which he had initially backed wholeheartedly. He became one of Nixon's harshest critics. He was described as a "big-bomber" and "big-missile" man and as such was considered a strong supporter of the Vietnam War, but a visit to the region confronted him with the human cost, and he was also angered by a number of secret deals ("excessive secrecy") the Nixon administration had apparently made.

Symington did retire in 1976, though in late 1974 he had stated his intention to run again if his health was good. In his announcement, he took a parting shot at the way business in Washington was carried out. "I'm tired of having old men in Government passing laws that force young men to do battle in causes that are not essential to the United States." He had the honor of seeing his son win a Congressional seat and remained in Washington until his death in December of 1988 at age 87.

CHAPTER TWENTY-FIVE

Albert's Speakership Disappointed Hardcores, But The Man Was A Legend

Historic Tidbit: Carl Albert noted that he was the last person to whom JFK spoke in Washington. It was at a meeting of Congressional leaders on November 21ˢᵗ, just as Kennedy was preparing to leave for Texas. After the meeting concluded, Kennedy asked to have a few words with Albert alone. As the conversation concluded, JFK boarded the helicopter that would take him to Andrews Air Force Base, then proceed to Texas.

Carl Albert's official House portrait
Image courtesy of the United States House of Representatives

The Oklahoman to advance to the highest political office in America was Carl Albert. The gentleman who would make McAlester his home (he grew up in Bugtussle) represented the state's southeastern "Little Dixie" third Congressional district for 30 years. By the time he left office in 1977, he had been Speaker for six years and second in line for the Presidency on two separate occasions — far longer than what Albert was comfortable with.

Albert, who stood 5 foot 4, was called the "Little Giant from Little Dixie." One of his predecessors and a mentor was Sam Rayburn, who fueled his rise by appointing him Majority and Whip and who could intimidate members by "glaring" down at them from the Speaker's podium. His successor was Tip O'Neill, whose physical and national presence brought back gravitas to the job. And there was Albert, who acted more as the glue that kept the office together.

While O'Neill would write to House members warning them that going against him on rules could jeopardize their committee assignments, Albert could do no such thing. A fellow Oklahoma Democrat, Ed Edmondson told *The Oklahoman* he'd "never seen (Albert) twist a member's arm to get what he wanted. I've seen him say, 'We need you, we have to have you,' but I've never seen him say, 'you owe us this one.'"

An early Albert campaign poster
Image via the Carl Albert Congressional Archives, University of Oklahoma

Many think that was Albert's weakness. One colleague said, "He stayed with the soft sell and the tug on the sleeve but never resorted to the stick." After a shouting match with Bella Abzug, he ended by saying, "let's get a cup of coffee." This was not the first clash with the ubiquitous Abzug.

One reason may have been that in his heart, Albert was a moderate, something he seemed to admit. "I very much dislike doctrinaire liberals — they want to own your minds. And I don't like reactionary conservatives. I like to face issues of conditions, and not in terms of someone's inborn philosophy."

Albert was the son of a poor farmer and coal miner mother in Bugtussle, Oklahoma. He had wanted to become a member of Congress since he was six. Though he entered the University of Oklahoma with just $10, he gained notice as a gifted orator, a skill that would land him at Oxford on a Rhodes Scholarship.

When Albert sought his Congressional seat, Albert's Democratic opponent tried to make hay of Albert's Oxford adventure. He frequently mentioned Oxford. Every time he did, Albert would reply "Bugtussle." It was enough, though only barely. Albert won the primary by 391 votes.

His 1952 opponent, who was the last serious foe Albert ever had, noted that "for a while, I had Bugtussle's pride treed right on top of his well warn stump. But in the last two weeks of the campaign, he laid the lash of that biblical oratory on me . . . I don't know why they call that guy little. He's just wound up real tight. When he talks he commences to unwind, and before he shuts up, he's 10 feet tall." Albert won every county. He was a campaigner at heart and sometimes even bemoaned the fact that sometimes he wouldn't get an opponent.

But after Albert became Speaker, he was not considered to be ten feet tall. Many of the attributes that enabled him to command respect - his oratory and his ability to mediate, for example, were gone, or at least not exercised. He was not blindly ambitious. He had already achieved the Speakership and was content. In his autobiography, *Little Giant*, he said as much: "When I took the Speaker's chair, I took the prize by which had directed me my entire life. I knew what put me there. I was there because I worked hard, was loyal to my friends, because I tolerated differences, because I practiced conciliation, because I wanted the possible, not the ideal, because I sought the compromise, not headlines. For better or worse, what had made me Speaker would have to make my Speakership too."

It seemed different when Albert had taken the job. That was in January 1971, at the beginning of the new decade and seemed like he was set to pursue history. Upon taking his oath, Albert instructed his fellow members: "As I see it, it is by definition the duty of a legislative body to legislate. If we are to perform that duty and meet the responsibilities that we owe to those that sent us here, to our nation and to our generation, we must be about the job. We must not flounder. We must move cautiously, of course, but we must also move with dispatch in the disposition of the public business. There is too much to be done to delay in the performance of our duties . . . We cannot falter. We cannot fail. The biography of this Congress will shape the legislative destiny of the 1970's."

It seemed to start well. Ratification of the amendment giving 18-year-olds the right to vote, the prohibition of which Albert had likened to slavery, occurred. He called it a step toward "the removal of property, racial, and gender lines . . . It was akin to perfecting our democracy." On abortion, he said he'd "sooner lose my seat in Congress than vote for that Constitutional amendment (outlawing it)." And he shepherded through the Legislative Reorganization Act, an ad-hoc committee that would be chaired by Washington's Julia Butler Hansen to make internal recommendations. It would culminate in the creation of the Democratic House Steering and Policy Committee.

He would again tangle with, among others, Abzug. One day, when the freshman lawmaker introduced a resolution urging the censure of Nixon over Cambodia, a few in the gallery made their presence known. In a letter, Abzug expressed her displeasure with the Speaker. "You had these three women removed for signs and clapping," she wrote. "You should have been upset instead by these figures (citing Vietnam)."

Photo courtesy of the Collection of the U.S. House of Representatives

"Little Dixie" had Southern leanings and early on, Albert's philosophy reflected such. He bucked Truman on the override of Taft-Hartley but supported him on aid to education and farm price supports. This never got him into trouble with his district, as Albert's re-elections were effortless (even Dukakis nearly carried it in '88).

But he was an increasing loyalist, and by 1954, just eight years into his tenure, Sam Rayburn, whose Texas district was, as both men would take pride in pointing out, right across the river, made clear that he wanted Albert for Majority Whip. Rayburn's advice: "pay attention to constituents who write in longhand and pencil on Big Chief Tablets. They really mean business."

Albert got a rude taste of that early on when a voter wrote, "We Okies expect you to uphold our interests in the "ni—r' question." Albert had written that he "had been raised among people who held (the views)." Albert himself opposed the Civil Rights Act of 1957 but by '64 and thereafter, he had no reservations about supporting it.

Albert championed the first tax restructuring since 1954, and in doing so broke a logjam by outfoxing the House parliamentarian who, insisting tax bills needed to originate with the House, would not so much as walk to the other side of the building to meet with Senate conferees. Albert lured him there and Cannon found a conference committee waiting. "Damn you, Carl Albert,' Clarence Cannon said. "This is too important for little kids."

Albert advised JFK over how to get a Medicare package through Congress, which involved letting the Senate take the lead and attaching it to the conference report of a welfare bill. His own party, particularly House Ways and Means Chair Wilbur Mills, was the problem, as he told Albert: "he thinks he can beat me on this but I'm going to beat him." Indeed, the Senate rejected the measure 52-48. Incidentally, it was Albert's senior Senator, Bob Kerr, who was proving a thorn in the spine of Medicare in the other body.

Kennedy also enlisted Albert's help in ending a territorial standoff that literally threatened the operation of the federal government. Dubbed the "Battle of the Octogenarians," House Appropriations Chairman Clarence Cannon, 83, and his Senate counterpart, Carl Hayden, 85 had been engaged in a months-long dispute over which side of the Capitol to hold an Appropriations conference committee. The resolution of this dispute was nowhere in sight and Kennedy asked Albert to approach Cannon. He complied but Cannon would not. Finally, "I tried a different strategy." He told Cannon he needed to meet with him and invited Larry O'Brien to attend. "Damn you, Carl Albert. This is too important for a bunch of kids." Finally, Albert consulted the Capitol architect who 'found me the one place, Room 101 of the East front extension that could hold conferees in a place exactly half way between the Senate and the House wings." Cannon accepted the proposal.

Once Johnson became President, Albert had more luck. Of Johnson, Albert said he was "beside me, behind me, and seemingly all over me." Albert was loyal to Johnson, backing Vietnam. But he would write in his autobiography that "he had no great enthusiasm" for doing so and called it a "miserable war."

While Albert was viewed as unable to insert himself deep into Democratic causes, it may not be fair to call him impervious. But more likely is that he wanted to let the House work its way. Folks were given a preview of this at the 1968 Democratic Convention. Rumors of dispel were rampant, but Albert said the rules would govern the proceedings "and I can recite them in my sleep." But as *The Oklahoman* said, "the delegates knew nothing about the House rules and couldn't care less."

Television viewers saw Dan Rostenkowski, a relatively junior Congressman, come up to the podium to tell people to back off. Richard Cohen wrote in his book, *Rostenkowski: The Pursuit of Power and the End of Old Politics*, "The image of the hulking Rosty wresting the dwarfish Albert became fitted in DC."

Albert was not impressed, as it reflected, accurately, that Albert had lost control of the convention (it turned out that LBJ, watching the proceedings on television, had asked Rosty to step in). But it nevertheless hampered Rosty's rise, as Albert forces blocked him from becoming Caucus Chair.

Albert seemed ready to grant Spiro Agnew a trial via the Congress but other leaders, particularly Tip O'Neill, prevailed upon him to let the laws take their course. This put Albert in succession of the Presidency twice, and that made him quite uneasy. "One death or another resignation" would have done it." He spoke of the Secret Service parking "its van in the alley again, installed another hotline, and started drawing my drapes."

Albert had said that if he had become President, the only fair thing would have been to serve in that position in an acting capacity until Congress confirmed a GOP vice-president. And it was he who recommended Gerald Ford's name to Nixon, for he felt it was only a matter of time before Nixon would resign, and he believed that majority Democrats would ultimately be comfortable with Ford.

The impeachment proceedings began on Albert's watch, after he referred the matter to the Judiciary Committee. As resignation became inevitable, Albert reminded members of the committee of their duel role in screening whomever Ford would choose to replace himself. "You guys aren't on the Judiciary Committee. You're on the impeachment and confirmation committee."

Albert did have one brush with scandal. One night in September of '72, he struck two cars with his Thunderbird outside the Zebra Room, which the manager said Albert had patroned before. He settled with the owners of the vehicles (*The Washington Post* quoted "witnesses" as saying it was "for cash") and police drove Albert home and his son was called to drive the Thunderbird home. The manager of the Zebra Room told the *Post* he wouldn't comment because Albert "is a prominent man and if I said something I might get in trouble with the owner." Shortly thereafter, Albert said he was finished with alcohol, but few had ever seen it as problematic.

Albert had long indicated that he would not seek re-election to Congress after he turned 70. He actually left two years early - in 1976 at 68. Had he stayed, his pension would have reached the maximum level but he may have been concerned about either his ability to retain the Speaker's post or more likely, as he noted after the Agnew resignation, that he was tired. He retired to McAlister and died in 2000 at age 92.

As for his own critique of his tenure, "I never claimed to be much more than an average Speaker, either."

Albert with California Congressman "Bizz" Johnson, 1971
Photo courtesy of the Johnson Family

CHAPTER TWENTY-SIX

Great Scott!
For Legendary Pennsylvania Pol,
Not At Winning Votes

Historic Tidbit: Southern Ohio was once represented by a James G. Polk. A Democrat, he served 11 non-consecutive terms from 1931-59 before dying in office. There is no relation to the 11ᵗʰ President.

Photo courtesy of the U.S. Senate Historical Office

M y passion is elections. History, results, etc. So when I discovered a few things about Hugh Scott, it was stunning.

You think members of Congress today are constrained by re-election? The constant fundraising, worrying how votes will play back home? Campaigning is a never-ending cycle which, in the end, guarantees nothing. Indeed, in Hugh Scott's time, the non-stop game did not apply. Legislators legislated, then went home just before Election Day to campaign for new terms. Most were fine to let the chips fall where they may, and there was little second-guessing after the fact.

Hugh Scott was giant on the stage both in Pennsylvania and nationally. A Republican, he was the first Pennsylvanian to become a three-term Senator (only Arlen Specter would ultimately exceed that), and rise to Minority Leader. He served as more than a footnote in the passage of civil rights legislation and the Nixon resignation, personally telling the President that impeachment was inevitable. Folks called him "Great Scott." But when it came to getting votes, Scott was far from a giant.

While many members walk on eggshells when it comes to winning new terms, Hugh Scott walked on glass. His difficulties were such that even staying in office was hard, and, sometimes, he didn't.

Current members of Congress, take note. Scott won a House seat in 1940, lost it in1944 then reclaimed it in1946, a pattern not unlike some members of today's Congress who lost and came back. But that's when things got real hard.

Get this! Scott retained his seat by 403 votes in 1950, 52-48% in '52, by 1,751 votes in1954 and 51.5-48.5% in1956.

Things didn't get much easier for Scott in his Senate races. Twice, he ran in some of the most Democrat-friendly years in history, and twice, barely won. His 1958 win over outgoing Governor George Leader 51-49% was considered a major upset, and he was the sole Republican winner in a rout in which Democrats landed the Governorship and both Houses of the Legislature. His 1964 survival may have been even more remarkable as his 50.6-49.1% win came amid the LBJ landslide. 1970 was a more Republican-friendly year but Scott again struggled, ultimately winning what would be his last term 51.4-45.4%. He retired in 1976 when John Heinz, a fellow Republican from the other end of the state, won by a bigger vote margin than Scott ever had.

With his Senate counterpart, Mike Mansfield
Photo courtesy of the U.S. Senate Historical Office

Now Scott has not been the only member of Congress to find himself seriously pressed each election cycle. Arnold Olson and John Hiler, a Democrat and Republican from Montana and Indiana respectively, each served a decade in Congress staring defeat in the eye each time. Olsen never won more than 55% in his re-elections, while Hiler escaped defeat in 1986 by just 47 votes after a protracted recount. Both ultimately lost their bids for 6th terms by equally narrow margins.

Closer to home and our current era, Jim Gerlach, who like Scott also represented Pennsylvania's Sixth Congressional District prior to his 2014 retirement(albeit Gerlach has Berks and Chester counties, Scott was all Philly), may be a better model, as his early election battles were almost an exact mirror of Scott's. Gerlach won three successive elections 51-49% and a fourth 52-48%.

Yet Scott may have been the most high-profile and durable figure to be hunkered down for so long—in fact, for his entire career. I point that out because Hugh Scott was in a perilous situation electorally for literally his whole long career. Yet, that didn't stop him from carrying out his duties in the most effective manner.

If constant re-election worries proved a strain for Scott, the affable pipe-smoking Philadelphian who was born on a property previously owned by George Washington and whose mother was a descendant of Zachary Taylor, never let it show. In fact, it probably made him thrive. One day, during the heart of the civil rights debate, Alabama Democratic Senator and States Rights advocate John Sparkman remarked how he often wondered how Scott, hailing from the "Old Dominion, could be a Republican. Scot's reply was he "became a Republican as soon as I learned how to walk."

How did Scott go about this? Well, for starters, doing his job and not trying to please all of the people all of the time. *The New York Times* wrote in his 1994 obituary that Scott was at varying times "known as the Senate's most liberal conservative, its most conservative liberal, and its most extreme moderate." That's not to say Scott was above playing hardball. He proved otherwise his first year in the Senate during the fight to confirm Lewis Strauss, President Eisenhower's pick to become Secretary of Commerce. Scott said Strauss was a victim of anti-semitism. The nomination was ultimately defeated.

Now Scott may not have been everyone's cup of tea but that's just my point. William F. Hildenbrand, Scott's longtime assistant, said he was "a consummate politician." But that in no way inhibited his respect from the other side. Scott was close friends with Mike Mansfield, the Senate's Democratic leader who called him "one of the unsung heroes of our time. We worked together very closely and we were able to establish a bipartisan Senate insofar as that was possible."

Dick Murphy, a close assistant to Scott in the 1960s cited theories for his popularity. "He could laugh at himself and he had a marvelous sense of humor."

Murphy calls Scott "one of these guys who quickly grasped something, particularly in a committee session. He could really pick up on something and be right in the middle of it all in a committee." He also seemed to be a fatalist in the sense that his life would continue even if voters showed him the door politically. When Scott, enjoying himself with his Chinese art during a tough point in the campaign (the subject was a true passion throughout his life), one aide told him time was precious to which Scott replied, "Relax Bob. We're going to win this thing." And somehow he did. Years later, Murphy offered his theory. "Virtually everything that (Blatt) did turned out bad and almost everything he did turned out right and that was the difference."

Hugh Scott's ability to hold on in '64 against Genevieve Blatt was particularly noteworthy, as for some time it didn't seem likely. Johnson ended up carrying Pennsylvania by 1.5 million votes. Scott's margin was just 70,000—so close that, on Election Night, Johnson was heard in audio tapes saying a Blatt victory was likely. But her loss denied a rare opportunity for the Keystone State to put a third female in Senate (Blatt would've joined Margaret Chase Smith of Maine and Maureen Neuberger of Oregon). Voters have yet to change that, as Lynn Yeakel lost a race almost as close to Specter in another Democratic Presidential landslide year, 1992.

Blatt, a Pennsylvania Commonwealth Court Judge, adroitly employed a tactic that has also been proven effective by other candidates on tickets where landslides are pending, most recently Elizabeth Warren—tying the opponent to the ticket's leader regardless of how distant he was from it philosophically. Blatt indicated as much by saying she was "comfortable with my ticket. Mr. Scott is not."

Indeed, Scott had been an ardent supporter of his home-state Governor, Bill Scranton, for the nomination, and refused to endorse Goldwater for more than a month after he had won. He had called for a GOP platform condemning groups with extremist reputations, such as the John Birch Society. Ultimately, the necessity of attracting conservative votes persuaded him to hop on the Goldwater bandwagon. But Blatt had her own unity problems. She entered the race at the last minute when the Democratic organization was behind Supreme Court Justice Michael Musmanno. The results of the primary were so close that in the days after, each candidate would take the lead. Ultimately, Blatt's victory wasn't affirmed until October 6th when a 3-2 ruling by the State Supreme Court upheld a lower-court ruling. Years later, she told the *Philadelphia Daily News* that "Philadelphia never did get around to putting me on a sample ballot."

With close aide Richard Murphy
Photo via the U.S. Senate Historical Office

Scott's voting record made it easy to see why backing Goldwater would give him such agita. He backed cloture on the Fortas nomination, one of only 10 Republicans to do so; voted against amendments by GOP colleagues that would've weakened Medicare and federal Housing programs; and voted for the Gun Control Act (though not Ted Kennedy's banning mail-order sales). On civil rights matters, he sought out solutions. In late 1967, Scott flew back to Washington from London (Murphy ordered the Johnson White House to fetch a plane) to cast a deciding vote on a 1967 desegregation measure in committee that both sides knew was tied without him. It passed 8-7. On civil rights matters, he sought out solutions. During a stalemate over a school desegregation measure in 1969, Scott proposed an amendment to allow it "except as required by the Constitution." Southerners were not assuaged but the amendment was adopted 52-39. And Scott enjoyed substantial backing from the AFL-CIO, backing that had to have proven crucial in such tight re-elections.

Oddly, it was Scott's position as Minority Leader, a post he assumed when Everett Dirksen died in 1969, that forced him to do more politicking than in his campaigns. He had won the post 24-19 over the very junior Howard Baker both because of concerns about Baker's short tenure and because of long-standing friendships with the chamber's more conservative members (Norris Cotton and

John Williams). But he now had to carry water for Nixon, a task he performed with grace until he could do so no more. Years after leaving office, Scott said he told Nixon as early as December of 1973 that turning over the tapes was the only hope of saving his Presidency. More than half a year later, it was Scott who broke the news of impending impeachment, surrounded by his GOP colleagues. He informed him thus: "Mr. President, we are all very saddened, but we have to tell you the facts." Years later, Scott admitted that he waited too long before abandoning Nixon. Still, Scott was well-aware of the inevitable when before it became certain Nixon would depart, he told Vice-President Gerald Ford that "you're all we have, and I'm not talking about the party, I'm talking about the country."

The ironic thing about not having the demands of fundraising, legislating for favors, etc.—Scott's last year in office was plagued by his acceptance of $45,000 from the Gulf Oil Corporation. He said the contributions were legal and not for personal use. The Senate Ethics Committee concurred, voting not to take action. He retired in 1977 at age 76, having served his state in Congress for 34 of the previous 36 years.

Scott's ability to conduct his business even with a political bounty on his head was noteworthy. So for current members of Congress, the lesson of the day is doing the people's business and campaigning for votes should not be mutually exclusive. You can do both. Indeed, it is the number one requirement for the job.

**Genevieve Blatt came within an eyelash of ending
Scott's tenure in Congress in 1964
Photo courtesy of the Pennsylvania State History Project**

CHAPTER TWENTY-SEVEN

Smathers Proximity To Presidents
Gave A Front Row To History

**Historic Quote: "Now, you're going to have to speak for the groom. I want
you to be funny. I want you to be clever. I want you to say everything that you
can think of that's going to make Jack look good. I don't want the Bouviers
to be outshining us." – Joseph P. Kennedy when asking George Smathers
to give the toast at Jack's wedding reception. Smathers was the only current
Kennedy Congressional colleague in attendance.**

Photo courtesy of the U.S. Senate Historical Office

I f the mission statement of this book is to portray stories of officeholders who
were influential to Presidents, George Smathers would be front and center. The
Florida Senator was best friends and vacation companion of John F. Kennedy, was
with Lyndon Johnson when he suffered his 1955 heart attack and sold Richard
Nixon his vacation home on Key Biscayne, Florida which became the winter
White House. He also introduced the future President to the man who would
become one of his truest and most legendary friends, Charles "Bebe" Rebozo.
This was one reason Smathers was nick-named "The Collector."

Smathers was also called "Gorgeous George" for his good looks and movie
star demeanor but his career was somewhat paradoxical. His first Senate campaign

against fellow Democrat Claude Pepper was among the most venomous in ages, though Smathers said the statements attributed to him by a single reporter was never made and no evidence ever surfaced to the contrary. His voting record was anti-civil rights. He offered to bail Martin Luther King, Jr., out of jail if he agreed to leave Florida but was privately passage of the Civil Rights Act of 1964 and the following year, did actually depart from the company of all but four of his Southern colleagues by supporting the Voting Rights Act. And in proof that everything had to start somewhere, ever wonder why the Memorial Day and Labor Day holidays are observed on Mondays? It's parochial. Smathers proposed legislation making long weekends to entice potential tourists to Florida.

Legislatively, Smathers's mark can be seen on domestic and international front as he sponsored legislation creating Medicaid, the Small Business Administration and the Everglades National Park. His interest in Latin American affairs led many to label him, "the Senator from Latin America." But his place in history will likely be sealed by who he knew rather than what he did.

Like Kennedy, Smathers was born to privilege and family notoriety – his father was a Judge and uncle a U.S. Senator from New Jersey who lost his seat in the 1942 midterm (a great uncle was the President of the North Carolina Senate and a Republican). As Smathers explained years later, his father relocated to Atlantic City, New Jersey "because he was a Democrat, and there were no Democrats that he could find in Atlantic County. He figured this was the place to go to start the Democratic Party." The strategy was sound. Smathers caught the attention of Governor Woodrow Wilson who named him a county Judge.

Unlike Kennedy, the place Smathers would make his career was far, far away from his native state. Smathers was born in Atlantic City but moved to Miami with his family at age six. It was initially his goal to play football at the University of Illinois but his University of Florida biography notes that "his father refused, arguing that if George was to enter politics he needed to attend (UF) in order to meet boys from all over Florida." If that was a plan, it worked to perfection. Not only was Smathers named Outstanding Athlete of Dade County in 1931, but on campus, he became President of Sigma Alpha Epsilon, captain of the basketball and track teams, president of the student body and a member of Florida Blue Key. Smathers called those years, in which he also roomed with future *Washington Post* owner Phil Graham, the "happiest of his life." In 1963, after Graham committed suicide, Smathers drew wide criticism when he said "you would have killed yourself had you been married to Kay Graham."

Smathers would earn his Bachelors and law degree from the UF at which time he'd become an assistant U.S. Attorney, though World War II found him in the South Pacific as a member of the Marine Corp. Smathers first got to know Joe Kennedy when the Kennedy patriarch vacationed in Florida and Smathers was winning headlines for going after organized crime. Meanwhile, he purchased the first television station license in the state.

In 1946, Smathers was urged to seek a legislative seat. But his goal had long been Congress and, ignoring the advice of seasoned politicos, he decided to challenge a fellow Democrat, four-term Congressman Pat Cannon, who two years earlier had survived his primary just 54-46%. Yet when Smathers went to Cannon with the news, explaining that it wasn't anything personal, he just wanted to fulfill his Congressional aspirations, Cannon was smug, if not overconfident. "Well, George," he declared, "I've defeated fourteen fellows, and you'll be the fifteenth. I'm sorry you're going to do it, but you'll see what you got into. You'll learn." But Smathers received aid from high school friends – starting with --- who ran his campaign and they were referred to as the "Goon Squad." and a number of Veteran groups, anxious to send some of their own to Congress in the first post-war election, chipped in as well.

Smathers unseated him with an eyebrow raising 68%. In those days, winning a primary was tantamount to a general election victory and Smathers took 71%.

Smathers with his wife Rosemary and others at a ball
Photo courtesy of the State of Florida Archives

Smathers joined Kennedy and Nixon as both freshmen members of the House of Representatives that year and members of the House Education and Labor Committee. Writing in *The Kennedys*, Peter Collier and David Horowitz said "they established a friendly rivalry over who would do the least amount of time in the House before moving on to the Senate." It was said that when Nixon and Smathers landed there following the 1950 elections, Kennedy was truly motivated to move forward. But for the prodding of President Harry Truman, Smathers may not have run for the Senate. His inclination was to stay in the

House until Truman reportedly told him he "wanted you to run against that son-of-a-bitch Claude Pepper." Smathers had been a stalwart Truman supporter – his maiden speech in the Senate was to oppose Republican plans to cut the 33rd President's defense budget but in this instance, he resisted – House Speaker Sam Rayburn told him he'd "be making a mistake." But Smathers finally went forward.

The mind-boggling aspect about the vituperativeness of the Smather's Pepper campaign was that, as a student of UF, Smathers actually ran his campaign on campus and, when he won his seat with behind the scenes help from Pepper, viewed him as both a confidante and a mentor. But by 1949, it was becoming evident to nearly all Florida politicos that Smathers was seriously pondering taking the plunge. Pepper would write in his autobiography that Smathers brother approached Pepper about conditions for not making the race. One was that he be named U.S. Attorney for Florida and another that he give Smathers his backing for the Democratic nomination for Florida Governor in 1952. Pepper gave him a firm and unequivocal "no," and so emerged gradual degeneration into a campaign that literally appears in textbooks for its rancor.

"Are you aware that Claude Pepper is known all over Washington as a shameless extrovert? Not only that, but this man is reliably reported to practice nepotism with his sister-in-law and he has a sister who was once a thespian in wicked New York. Worst of all, it is an established fact that Mr. Pepper, before his marriage, habitually practiced celibacy.'" Smathers later called the line "apocryphal,'" and "offered $10,000 to anybody who could say that you would come up and testify and pass a lie detector test that they had ever heard me say anything like that." No one ever came forward. Pepper responded by calling Smathers a Northerner by birth but Pepper had his own, in some cases self-inflicted problems. Smathers hammered the theme that Pepper was a liberal who actually had kind word to say about Stalin (team Smathers labeled him "Red Pepper" and linked him to "Northern union bosses"). Pepper carried Miami-Dade County by a microscopic margin but Smathers overwhelmed him in much of the rest of the state except for a few areas in the Panhandle which neighbored Peppers' native Alabama. The final result was 55-45% and he defeated Republican John P. Booth with 76% in the general election Interestingly, a dozen years after the election, Pepper returned to Congress, winning a seat in the House where he stayed until he died at age 88. Near the end, Smathers made a contribution to his campaign to which Pepper joked had bounced.

Smathers on primary night, 1950 when it became clear that he had unseated incumbent U.S. Senator Claude Pepper following one of Florida's most acrimonious and personal races in perhaps the "Sunshine" State's history Photo courtesy of the State Archives of Florida

In the Senate, Smathers became close to Johnson. "For several years, he ran the United States government. He was the government, and it's hard for people to appreciate that and understand that, unless you were there and knew Lyndon Johnson and went through that experience that I went through. Johnson was the single most powerful person, even more so than Eisenhower."

Eventually, Johnson named Smathers to the number three post in the caucus, Secretary, and later, chair of the Democratic Congressional Campaign Committee which doled out money for candidates. But he made clear that Johnson was unambiguous when it came to calling the shots and which campaigns he should direct the money to. "I would have some input," he'd say, "but Johnson was damn sure that he approved, and most of the time he told me where he thought it ought to go. There was nobody else that made that decision but Johnson." Smathers said he "admired Johnson, although I couldn't stand (him) half the time."

It was Smathers' proximity to the Kennedy family that was truly notable. During their first years in the House, their offices were nearby and they travelled to Europe together and Cuba shortly after and engaged in Kennedy style social dalliances that included wine, women and song. The pair's Administrative Assistants were close as well (Grant Stockdale, Smathers' guy, would become Kennedy's Ambassador to Ireland).

In those days, a White House run for Kennedy was not even in the back of Smathers' mind. In the late 1980's, he told the oral history project how, "Of the fellows least likely to be president, you'd have to vote Jack number one. He only weighed about a hundred and twenty-five pounds, and he had this bad back, and he had another illness that we didn't know about at the time, but he didn't look well. He was not well, he was in pain most of the time." In fact, when headed for House votes, Kennedy would often lean on Smathers' arm.

But more triumphant times would loom. When Jack married Jackie, Joe Kennedy asked him to do the toast at the rehearsal dinner. "Ambassador Kennedy," as Smathers called him, also counseled him about getting past always having to pick up the tab on his frequent outings with JFK (Smathers once said "Jack always reached for the breast pocket when the check arrived: wallets are usually kept elsewhere"). The Ambassador acknowledged to an exasperated Smathers that money was not his son's strong suit but instructed him to continue paying the bills and keep his expenses "on chits like Jack does, then send them to my office." He promised to reimburse him for half the expenses, which he did.

When Jackie delivered a stillborn baby in 1956, it was Smathers who had to coax him back from Palm Beach. He exhorted, "If you want to run for President," he told him, "you'd better get your ass back to your wife's bedside or every wife in the country will be against you." When Kennedy was elected President, he wanted Smathers to become Majority Leader.

At that time, Smathers was becoming close to Johnson as well. In fact, in perhaps the ultimate compliment the hard-charging Texan could bestow on anyone came when Johnson delegated Smathers floor leader in his absence. As the United States Senate website notes, Smathers recalled that following Johnson's heart attack, "We never saw (him) again for some forty days, although he began to call us on the telephone in about a week. Just ran us crazy talking to him on the phone, getting things done." Smathers called Johnson, "the most hard-driving guy I ever saw in my life."

For Smathers, his proximity to both men meant dilemma's when it came to Presidential politics.

In 1956, he was hoping for a Johnson-Kennedy ticket. When that didn't materialize, he gave the nominating speech for Kennedy at the Democratic National Convention when he was mounting a bid to become Adlai Stevenson's running-mate, a cause that very nearly succeeded (commiserating with the Kennedy's after JFK fell 39 votes short, Smathers quipped, "now I know what an Irish wake is like"). Smathers arranged for a Mediterranean trip for his friend.

Meanwhile, Smathers was gaining mention for the Vice-Presidency as early as before the 1956 primary season got under way. Democratic National Committee Chair Paul Butler floated his name, calling him "one of the more articulate of the younger Senators." Reportedly, Hubert Humphrey actually did offer him the position in 1968 but he declined. Decades later, his son Bruce said his "father already had announced his retirement to enter private life at 55 and did not intend to change his mind."

Four years later, both Kennedy and Johnson (along with another friend and colleague, Stu Symington of Missouri), were running for the top slot. As the filing deadline approached, the field was a cacophony and Smathers himself confided that he had no desire "to make a choice between Jack and a couple of my other friends." The Florida powers temporarily remedied that.

Smathers was asked to mount a "favorite" son bid in order to keep Florida delegates in his fold until the field became a little less muddied. At first, he was very much resistant to the idea but as he said later, "Here I was caught between Johnson on the one side, who was my leader, I was his whip, and here was my dear friend, personal friend, Kennedy, and they're going to go into my state and ruin it. What am I going to do? Under prodding from party leaders, including some candidates themselves, he acquiesced and said "that would stop Johnson and Kennedy from dividing up the state." No one challenged him and he took 100%, though Kennedy was reportedly furious with the maneuver.

Smathers and Kennedy in Florida
Photo courtesy of the State Archives of Florida

At the Democratic National Convention, folks in the Florida delegation had placards that read, "If I had my rathers – Smathers." He again surmised a Johnson-Kennedy ticket would be the ultimate result. When Kennedy was contemplating tapping Johnson as his running-mate after having shocked nearly everyone by capturing the nod on the first ballot, it was Smathers who told the candidate to give a head's up to House Speaker Sam Rayburn because Johnson "is going to talk to him first."

For the fall campaign, Smathers was dispatched to aid the Kennedy campaign in Oklahoma and Texas. After Kennedy's election, Lyndon Johnson would soon be Vice-President, which meant that the position of Senate Majority Leader would be open. Smathers was said to be Kennedy's preference (Frank Ralph Valeo in *Mike Mansfield: A Different Kind of Senate* writes his "name was sent aloft like a Chinese fighting kite to puncture it"), though it's not certain how much interest the Floridian gave. When Johnson was Vice-President, Smathers suggested Kennedy send him on tours of other nations to free him from JFK's hair which he did. Smathers' proximity to Kennedy was said also gave him a front row seat when rumors circulated as the 1964 election approached that Kennedy would drop Johnson from the ticket.

Kenny O'Donnell, in his book, *Johnny We Hardly Knew Ye*, recalls a Kennedy visit to Palm Beach days before the assassination when Smathers asked if he planned to drop him. Kennedy was incredulous: "George, you must be the dumbest man in the world. If I drop Lyndon, it would make it look as if we have a really bad and serious scandal on our hands in the Bobby Baker case, which we haven't, and that will reflect on me It will look as though I made a mistake picking Lyndon in 1960 and can you imagine the mess of trying to select somebody to replace him. Lyndon stays on the ticket next year."

Kennedy's death rendered that speculation moot and Johnson moved the issue of civil rights to the forefront. Politically, Smathers couldn't come out in favor. In fact, as the Southern Democrats (dubbed the "Neanderthal Caucus") introduced a number of amendments to weaken the bill, Smathers put forth one that would exempt beauty salons from desegregation requirements. It was defeated. Yet few on either side doubted he wanted to see it happen.

Jerald Blizen, a reporter who later served as Smathers' press secretary, called him "a bridge between the South and North...Johnson used him to convince the Southerners to come around...But, behind the scenes, (Smathers) quietly supported federal voting rights bills, giving political cover to other Southerners to inch forward." He collaborated with proponents of the legislation. Smathers was always friendly with African-Americans. As a boy, one of his best friends was J.R. Williams. "He lived with us...He had a room just like I did, and he went to school, and we worked together, and we fought together, played together, and so on." Smathers initially opposed the first version of the Voting Rights Act but did back the conference committee report that President Johnson signed into law.

Smathers (far left) accompanies Kennedy to a visit to NASA headquarters
(left) and met with the three astronauts who orbited the moon (right)
Photos courtesy of the Florida State Archives

Other issues that gained Smathers notoriety: Cuba. With its proximity to
Florida, Smathers was profoundly interested in Cuba and claims to have been
the only member in either house of Congress to give a speech warning of what
was to come with Fidel Castro when he gained power in 1959. "I knew what he
was," Smathers recalled, "and I knew what he was going to be, but I couldn't get
anybody to believe me that this guy's a bad guy." When Kennedy was President,
Smathers actually raised the issue of having Fidel Castro assassinated several times,
though he'd he didn't know how beneficial doing so would be for the long-term
goal of stability in the region. But Kennedy's interest was limited to the point
that when the duo got together, he'd tell Smathers not to raise the issue of Cuba.
Still, Kennedy valued Smathers' expertise enough that he let him compose a good
portion of the speech he would deliver to the nation during the Soviet buildup
that became the missile crisis. Locally, as the population boomed, so did lawsuits
and Smathers pushed through a new judicial district for South Florida.

Smathers' rationale for Monday holidays was that "Florida would benefit
greatly if we cut out the holidays that occurred on Tuesday, Wednesday and
Thursday. If they were on Friday or Monday, all the federal employees would
come to Florida on vacation." The U.S. Chamber of Commerce agreed and
became a key ally. President's Day, Memorial Day, Columbus Day, and Veterans
Day (Labor Day already was mandated to be observed on a Monday) were
impacted. If Smathers had his way, Thanksgiving and the Independence Day
observation would have fallen on Monday's as well but that did not make its way
into the final version.

Smathers had a number of business interests, primarily in the area of real
estate, and he often found himself having to prove that they were not linked
to official business. At one point, he enlisted his close friend and frequent golf
partner, Stu Symington, considered ethically above reproach, to defend him.

Despite being Kennedy's polar opposite, his relationship with Nixon was strong as well. (Smathers once said "Nixon wore a suit and never seemed to unwind... "He didn't drink, he didn't play cards and he didn't chase women."). Bebe Rebozo found that to be the same when Smathers introduced them after the 1950 election. Nixon, Rebozo told Smathers is "a guy who doesn't know how to talk, doesn't drink, doesn't smoke, doesn't chase women, doesn't know how to play golf, doesn't know how to play tennis... he can't even fish....don't ever send a dull fellow like that here again." Most bizarre but fitting given Nixon's persona was that this first encounter place on a boat Nixon needed to rest and went to Palm Beach. The Nixons and Smathers had also vacationed together in Florida after the '52 election when Nixon was Vice-President-elect After Nixon won the Presidency, Smathers sold him his home next to Rebozo's – at the President-elect's request. Smathers, who had hoped Nixon was calling to offer him a cabinet appointment, had initially responded by saying, "hell no, where am I going to live?" But Smathers acquiesced and the home became known as the winter White House.

The same year Nixon won the presidency, Smathers decided against seeking fourth Senate term, even though it would have been in the bag. In fact, Democratic colleagues of all ideologies (Bill Fulbright, "Scoop" Jackson and Bobby Kennedy) begged him to stay on. But he demurred.

Later in life, Smathers donated $20 million to UF and $10 million to the University of Miami. He died at age 94 in 2007. Meanwhile, politics continued to be a family affair as Smathers' son Bruce served as Florida's Secretary of State.

CHAPTER TWENTY-EIGHT

Ralph Yarborough:
Far More Than A Historical Footnote

Historic Quote: "Do they hit Oxford, Mississippi?" – Attorney General Bobby Kennedy during the Cuban Missile crisis. He had been trying to get James Meredith admitted to Ole Miss.

T here are footnotes to history and there are major supporting players. Ralph Yarborough is definitely the latter.

The one-time Texas Democratic Senator was colleagues with one President, impacted the achievement of the Presidency for another, and was a major impetus on a trip to Dallas that ultimately may have led to the death of a third.

These happenstances enabled Yarborough to inadvertently leave a footprint on the shape of several Presidential tickets of both parties. Not to mention common legislation and acronyms that folks take for granted today, such as Presidential debates and OSHA (Occupational Health and Safety Act). He was also a solid liberal in a state trending away from it, which, in time, would ultimately serve as his downfall.

First for the man. *The Dallas Morning News* said Yarborough was considered the "patriarch of Texas liberals." Ordinary folks called him "The People's Senator." The reasons were many.

Civil Rights were a no-brainer. Yarborough sided with his colleague Johnson in backing laws in the 1950s, and in fact was the only was the only senator from a former Confederate state to support every Civil Rights law.

But it certainly didn't stop there and as *The Austin American-Statesman* pointed out, Yarborough was "a champion of progressive legislation." Much of that stands out today.

The National Defense Education Act was Yarborough's major pride and joy. Established in response to Sputnik, the act's proponents wanted to make sure Americans were competitive in math, science, and language, and Yarborough's bill established grants to make that happen. We know them today as student loans. But med school, fellowships, and vocational education were also part of it, as were grants for living expenses.

The Community Mental Health Center Act created the network of local mental health programs, and the Bilingual Education Act provided funding to districts with a large minority population. The National Aeronautics and Space Act championed the Lone Star State's growing reliance on the space industry.

OSHA addressed workplace safety. And Yarborough sponsored the legislation that provided for the televised debate between JFK and Nixon.

And there were environmental matters. Yarborough had called the "conservation and improvement of all natural and human resources" his most important accomplishment in his first decade in the Senate. He co-wrote the Endangered Species Act of 1969 and played a significant role in protecting the Padre Island National Seashore, Guadalupe Mountains National Park, the Big Thicket National Preserve, and the Alibates Flint Quarry in the Panhandle. Corpus Christie, one of the areas that would most benefit, had a Ralph Yarborough Day in 1962. Much of this was done without a chairmanship but in his last two years in the Senate, Yarborough attained the helm of the Labor and Public Welfare Committee.

Yarborough received publicity when he was wrestled to the ground outside the Commerce Committee hearing room door. The purpose was to prevent a quorum on a confirmation vote (Thurmond opposed ex-Florida Governor LeRoy Collins' nomination because he was pro-Civil Rights). Thurmond had proposed the match, with the wager, "If I can keep you out, you won't go in and if you can drag me in, I'll stay there." The scuffle continued for a few minutes and many feared for both men's health (Yarborough in particular was out of breath). Eventually, Chairman Warren Magnuson told the pair to "break this up," to which Yarborough replied, "I have to listen to my Chairman."

Left photo courtesy of The Dolph Briscoe Center for American History, the University of Texas; right photo via the Austin History Center

Yarborough received publicity when he was wrestled to the ground outside the Commerce Committee hearing room door. The purpose was to prevent a quorum on a confirmation vote (Thurmond opposed ex-Florida Governor LeRoy Collins' nomination because he was pro-Civil Rights). Thurmond had proposed the match, with the wager, "If I can keep you out, you won't go in and if you can drag me in, I'll stay there." The scuffle continued for a few minutes and many feared for both men's health (Yarborough in particular was out of breath). Eventually, Chairman Warren Magnuson told the pair to "break this up," to which Yarborough replied, "I have to listen to my Chairman."

All of this would seem enough to ensure Yarborough historic accolades through the ages. But here comes the direct correlation to figures.

**Photo via The Dolph Briscoe Center for American
History, the University of Texas at Austin**

The reason JFK even went to Texas was to "patch up" a feud between Yarborough and Governor John Connally. The feud did not happen overnight and much of it was ideologically driven. Connally had called Yarborough "a very despicable man." Yarborough in turn had called Connally, John Tower, and Attorney General Waggoner Carr "a biological miracle: political triplets." For much of their careers, Johnson and Yarborough had their differences, evident from were two Texas-sized different personalities. George Reddy, a close Johnson confidante said "Johnson was often trying to hold a middle course that was pretty difficult to do when you were around Ralph."

Yarborough, Connally, and Carr would share a ticket the following year and it was in the interest of the trio to have unity. LBJ supposedly wanted Connally to ride with him and Yarborough apparently wanted to be seen with JFK. No one, it seemed, wanted to ride with Yarborough and it appeared to be mutual.

On the morning of November 22, *The Dallas Morning News* ran a headline that read, "Yarborough snubs LBJ," a reference to him declining to ride with Johnson in the day's previous stops, San Antonio and Houston. Kennedy saw a copy of the paper and confronted Yarborough, "For Christ sake, cut it out, Ralph." Kennedy had confronted Johnson that morning as well, calling the feud petty. Even Connally was getting in on the action. He had no use for Yarborough either and was enjoying keeping him in suspense as to whether he'd sit at the head table at the dinner that was supposed to take place in Austin that evening. With the situation proving intractable, Kennedy finally took a stand. He told Yarborough, "You'll ride with Johnson or you'll walk." As it happened, the two did ride together with Lady Bird sandwiched between them.

JFK on the morning of his assassination with Johnson, Yarborough, and Connally (left) and updating reporters outside Parkland Memorial Hospital (right) Left photo courtesy of the Dallas Morning News; right photo courtesy of the Sixth Floor Museum at Dealey Plaza

When Johnson's speeding car ended up at Parkland Hospital, Yarborough walked past Kennedy's car. He would not describe the details of the dying President still inside. Yarborough would not, however, be on that Air Force One ride back to Washington. Johnson exercised control over who was permitted on board and Yarborough was excluded.

For much of their careers, Johnson and Yarborough had their differences, evident from were two Texas-sized different personalities. George Reddy, a close Johnson confidante said "Johnson was often trying to hold a middle course that was pretty difficult to do when you were around Ralph."

Yet Johnson recognized the necessity of electing Democrats, and he tactically helped his colleague in his tough election battles. The *Victoria Advocate* observed in '64 that "Johnson campaigned as heartily in Texas for Yarborough as he did for himself.

The President himself had sought to allay his audiences that Johnson and Yarborough were hunky-dory. "You have heard and you have read that Sen. Yarborough and I have had differences at times," Johnson said. "I have read a good deal more about them than I was ever aware of." But he added he didn't think "Texas has had a senator during my lifetime whose record I am more familiar with than Sen. Yarborough's. And I don't think Texas has had a senator that voted for the people more than Sen. Yarborough has voted for them. And no member of the U.S. Senate has stood up and fought for me or fought for the people more since I became President than Ralph Yarborough." Just after accepting re-nomination, the President told Texans "how proud I am, how grateful I am for (Yarborough's) steadfast, courageous support."

Which brings us to Yarborough's impact on another future President. Who was Yarborough's opponent in 1964? George H.W. Bush.

Photo courtesy of the Dolph Briscoe Center for American History, the University of Texas at Austin

Even with their favorite son, Johnson, dominating the ticket, Republicans were initially optimistic about this race. Texas had elected another Republican Senator, John Tower, against tremendous odds, and Yarborough was more liberal. One prominent Texas politico observed Bush had "two crosses to bear – running as a Republican and not a native Texan."

Yarborough and Thurmond after the latter wrestled him
to the ground to prevent him from a quorum
Photo courtesy of the U.S. Senate Historical Office

Yarborough gave up 43% to a primary foe and a number of Texas Democrats, including many in East Texas, throughout the state began organizing for Bush. One was Ed Drake, the former leader of the state's Democrats for Eisenhower in 1952. But for Republicans, the presence of LBJ, who took 65% in Texas, proved too much to bear and Yarborough won with 54%.

On Election Night, Yarborough acknowledged the role the President played in extending his Senate tenure saying the GOP realized they couldn't beat Johnson in Texas, so they "concentrated their fire on me." Yarborough called the race his most "vilest campaign of defamation and slander." And there was no love lost with Bush as a result. In a clear reference to Bush's New England upbringing, Yarborough said he "should pack up his baggage and go back where he came from."

Fast forward to 1970. Bush was back again, and this time, LBJ was not dominating the ballot. Richard Nixon was in the White House, and he was trying to win a working Senate majority and the road ran through Texas. In fact, it was his number one target. But Yarborough again had a primary. And this time, it was from a former Texas Congressman named *Lloyd Bentsen.*

Yarborough started out way ahead. But his votes against Nixon's Supreme Court nominees appear to have given Bentsen the ammunition he needed. Bentsen had saturated the airwaves for three months. Now he was labeling Yarborough an "ultra-liberal." Noting his opposition of the Vietnam War and his past support of Gene McCarthy, Bentsen ran an ad showed rioting in the streets.

Decades before the ad against Max Cleland showed Saddam Hussein and Osama bin Laden, Ho-Chi-Minh and Yarborough appeared on the same screen, apparently smiling at one another.

At first, Yarborough didn't show concern. A spokesman quipped "Mickey Mouse could run against" him in the primary "and get 40%." But as the primary approached, Yarborough began worrying about turnout. At one fundraiser he said, "I've never seen as much apathy two weeks before an election."

Eventually, he and Johnson made peace. He found him a Finance chair but was secretly have thought to prefer Bentsen. In the end, everything went against him. Bentsen won the primary, then, against the expectations of many, went on to surprise Bush in November, handing him his second prized Senate loss in six years. The Statesman said Yarborough was "bitter over the loss for years, unable to speak Bentsen's name without sputtering."

Had Bentsen lost to Yarborough, he may have resumed his career as a successful businessman and never made it to the Senate, in which case Michael Dukakis would not have tapped him as his running-mate in 1988. Had Bush beaten Yarborough, he still likely would have sought the Presidency but, absent the extensive experience he attained after the loss (CIA head, Ambassador to China), may not have been tapped as Reagan for the number two slot in '80.

For Yarborough, becoming a Senator in the first place required work. Lots of work. Yarborough sought statewide office in Texas four times, including three as Senator, though never made it out of the primary. He came close, losing the 1956 primary to Price Daniel by a razor-thin margin. ("they stole it from me," he said.). But that gave Daniel an opening for the Senate, and among 21 candidates, Yarborough emerged the pick.

Two years after his defeat, Yarborough sought a return to the Senate but again lost the primary, this time to "Barefoot" Sanders. He returned to practicing law, but continued to offer stinging critiques of Republicans. In particular, he saw Reagan as trying to undo much of his progress and commented that "it's incredible that a president of the U.S. would do that. Herbert Hoover and Richard Nixon were both far better presidents than Reagan."

With many conservadems having bolted the party, winning a primary today would not be Yarborough's problem. But he'd surely lose the general. And while Democrats would continue winning statewide in Texas for another two decades, Yarborough's loss may have been the beginning of the end. That certainly seems the case for liberals.

Yarborough lived to 92. Ex Texas Agriculture secretary Jim Hightower, himself the last true liberal to have held a statewide office in Texas called him "a hero, a guy willing to take on the powers that be, take 'em by the scruff of the neck and go right after them."

Charles Eagleburger spoke at a rally for him. "Ralph Yarborough would rather be right than be Senator." And while he didn't always come out on top his legacy and courage indicates that he was right. And it'll show for some time.

CHAPTER TWENTY-NINE

Culver, Ted Kennedy's Harvard Pal Was Iowa Senator Who Maintained Proud Liberalism Through Political Death

Historic Tidbit: It may shock folks to know but Jack Kennedy once made a political contribution to Richard Nixon. It was during his 1950 run for the U.S. Senate and Nixon was facing Helen Gahagan Douglas, a colleague of both men in the House. It's not clear why Kennedy made the contribution but the issue came back at Kennedy during his pursuit of the 1956 vice-presidential nomination.

Courtesy of the U.S. Senate Historical Office

John Culver, an Iowa Senator who in the 1970s encompassed a beloved mantra of liberalism, had very early exposure to one of America's most prominent families. He lived in the same house as Ted Kennedy at Harvard College and played with him on the football team. It was a lifelong friendship that would result in Culver giving one of the eulogies at Kennedy's memorial service in 2009. But his career took a path on its own and by all accounts, it was quite successful. Politically and personally, Culver was a man of great legislative acumen and tremendous intellect that resulted in solid achievements and respect and friendships across the aisle. More importantly, Culver was a man of deep convictions. He refused to back down from his liberal beliefs even when it proved a serious threat that ultimately proved fatal to his political career.

Culver was a Midwestern boy, born in Rochester, Minnesota and moving to Iowa with his family at a young age. That Culver could become a solid liberal would seem remarkable given his background. His family was so staunchly aligned with the Republican camp that the younger Culver was delegated the task of driving ex-President Herbert Hoover around Iowa on the ex-President's 80th birthday. Culver's father in fact was a delegate for conservative Ohio Senator Robert Taft at the 1952 Republican Convention. But by 1960, as Culver's dad was on his deathbed, his son asked his opinions on the upcoming Presidential campaign. His response: "John, you might be surprised, but I think if I have an opportunity I'll vote for John Kennedy" (he died that September before the election took place).

Culver, whose early goal was the foreign service, decided to attend Harvard after watching a Harvard-Yale football game. He almost didn't last at the school, not because of his grades by any means, but because he was homesick for Iowa. But he stayed and made the decision of a lifetime. Culver joined the football team and as a fullback for a time held the seasonal record for rushing (he later was inducted into the Harvard Football Hall of Fame). During that period, Culver was awarded the Lionel de Jersey Harvard Scholarship, a tribute then reserved for outstanding scholar/athletes. This enabled him to undertake a year of graduate studies at Emmanuel College at Cambridge University in England.

College vacations included stays at Hyannis Point where Culver would meet the large Kennedy clan, including the future President. It was 1951 and Culver, 18, was playing touch football (what else) on the lawn of the compound when Kennedy, then a third-term Congressman, arrived at the house. As Culver explained in an oral history project conducted by the John F. Kennedy Presidential Library and Museum, Kennedy, upon spotting the game from his bedroom, "rolled down the window and yelled 'Culver's a bum,' and slammed the window shut. I'd never met him, of course. He was, you know, having a lot of fun." Culver recalls Kennedy changing into recreational clothes but his back, injured in the war, precluded him from engaging in any rough-housing. "So he couldn't really run with us in touch football, but he played quarterback on both our teams that day and he threw the ball and so forth."

After college, Culver and Teddy stayed with JFK and Jackie at their Georgetown home during a trip to Washington D.C. The pair were newlyweds and Culver recalls Jackie asking Teddy to give her a political topic to discuss with Jack. During this time, Culver also became acquainted with Bobby Kennedy who was serving as a lawyer on the House Un-American Committee that Joe McCarthy had been chairing. In 1961 when both men were 29, Teddy was toying with seeking a statewide office from Massachusetts (though it wasn't yet certain that a Senate seat would be his pursuit). He asked Culver to assist him and he obliged. At this point, he was pursuing his law degree from Harvard after finishing up a 39 month stint as an officer in the U.S. Marine Corps.

Meanwhile, Kennedy won his Senate election and Culver worked in his office as both a press aide and legislative director. And he regularly traveled to Hyannis. He recalls going "down to the family house and watching Jack, President Kennedy then, and Robert Kennedy arrive in helicopters and Sarge Shriver and the kids, you've seen those films, run out to meet them." They'd go sailing on Joe's boat, the Honey Fitz." In the 1970s, at Ted's request, Culver traveled to Massachusetts to help pick out the land that eventually became the site for JFK Presidential Library and Museum (Culver told the cheering crowd during his Kennedy eulogy how "I think we all agree, Jack would really like this place").

In later years, Kennedy may have had an even more profound impact on Culver's life. In 1997, Culver needed emergency heart surgery and his wife immediately contacted Kennedy who, by virtue of his legislative work and family health issues, was something of an expert in health care, to ask about facilities, treatment options, etc.

Culver with his life-long friend
Photo courtesy of the U.S. Senate Historical Office

While Kennedy would remain one of Culver's best friends for life, Culver's pursuit of his own legacy came in September 1963 when he decided to run for Congress himself. If he captured the Democratic nomination for the seat, he'd be challenging two-term incumbent Republican James Bromwell the following year. But he had been away from Iowa for 13 years so that was a big "if." Culver wasn't sure who was who as far as the necessary political contacts in Iowa. So he sought out Ed McDermott who at that time was serving as director of the Office of Emergency Management. More importantly, he was a Dubuque native. He gladly provided Culver the names of the committee chairs in each of the districts counties and Culver, with "a pocket full of dimes" began calling each of them. It had an impact. Culver beat dentist James Feld to secure the Democratic nomination.

The fall battle might have marked the first test of Culver's commitment to liberalism and he made no mistake that he'd be embracing it. Bromwell made an issue of the growth of the government to which Culver replied, "Our government is bigger but so is the nation's population . . . Government should not infringe of the essential liberties of the individual but within that limitation government can, ad must be made an instrument of positive action." Helped by the strong coattail of President Johnson, Culver unseated Bromwell with 52% in the general election. Two years later, he became the only freshman in that class from Iowa seeking to hold his seat in a year Democrats lost 47 nationwide. Culver worked on issues local and international, proposing the Trade Adjustment Assistance Act and the Foreign Investment Study Act.

Culver also sat on a number of committees to promote efficiency, including the Bolling Commission on Committee Modernization and Reform. As Foreign Economic subcommittee chair, he he "presided over early hearings on the global energy situation." His bio cites the role in the panel in "call(ing) attention to the emerging energy crisis six months before the first OPEC oil embargo." During his final House term, he chaired the House Democratic Study Group.

By 1972, Culver had his eye on the Senate but he was lulled into accepting the prevailing thought that incumbent Republican Jack Miller could not be beaten, only to see his Senate assistant, Dick Clark, go on and do just that. If Culver had disappointments, though, they were short-lived. The state's senior Senator, Harold Hughes, called him one day and told him of his intention to retire at the end of his term in 1974. Culver recalls the news taking "me completely by surprise." Hughes told Culver he hoped he'd run for the opening but he needed no convincing ("psychologically, I was all ready to run"). And he immediately gathered support to secure the nomination.

Even in the year of Watergate, the general election against State Senator David Stanley was tougher as Stanley was well-known from previous bids for office. Culver struggled but Stanley's attacks appeared to have backfired, in part because Culver was adroit enough to know when to give it back to him. During one debate, Culver reminded his opponent how "there is always a fork in the campaign – the high and the low. It is you who have chosen this road"). Culver prevailed 52-48%. His victory gave Iowa two Democratic Senators for the first and only time in its history.

With a Capitol tour guide
Photos courtesy of the John Culver Papers, University
of Iowa Libraries, Iowa City, Iowa

In office, Culver developed a reputation as the quintessential liberal. When journalist Elizabeth Drew wanted a Senator who fit the typical profile to follow around the halls of Congress, she chose Culver. "Among the other Senators," she wrote, "Culver has a reputation for brains, tenacity, integrity, shrewdness at picking his issues and skill at pushing them, and an ability to work with colleagues . . . And what he accomplished he did in part through the sheer force of his personality and style." Culver was known to have a temper. When asked about it years later he replied, "Actually, I handle it on a case by case basis."

Drew noted Culver's reputation as "an unusually retentive mind, one that absorbs, generates questions, makes connections between things he knows." She wrote that he "doesn't mince words on whom he admires and who he does not." Ditto with Culver's voting record. It was solidly liberal, even if it meant taking on his own party. Culver was one of five Democrats to oppose an Armed Services proposal mandating registration of males between 18 and 26. The concern was that it could lead to a draft. He criticized the administration for sending radar planes to Iran.

The "Culver Commission" was one endeavor that made Culver stand out as among the best and the brightest among the abundance of age thirty and forty-something members of Congress.

**On the occasion of the bicentennial medal presentation
(left) and addressing Iowa Farm Bureau Delegates
Photos courtesy of the John Culver Papers, University
of Iowa Libraries, Iowa City, Iowa**

By his second year in the upper chamber, Culver was frustrated at the pace. He likened it to a "sick patent" in need of "a careful and probing study of the whole central nervous system of the Senate and its institutional well-being." In a body full of veteran lawmakers accustomed to ruling by committee and seniority, Culver undertook an initiative to examine change. He and a few other junior lawmakers convinced leaders of both parties to undertake a study and it became known as the "Culver Commission," or more officially, the "Commission on the Operation of the Senate."

The U.S. Senate website noted the 11 member commission "included university administrators, former state governors, and long-time Senate observers." Its members examined a number of facets of functions within the Senate (staff, space, technology, communications, etc,) and looked at ways to modernize its operation. They produced a number of recommendations.

A portion of the report read, "The survival of our democracy depends on the ability of our institutions to change in order to cope effectively with an increasingly complicated environment. In retrospect, one can more fully comprehend some of the changes in society to which the Senate adapted in the past. While many traditional activities continue, an array of new economic and social forces swell the volume and complexity of demands on the Senate's time and attention. The Senate website observed that to this day, "the Culver/Hughes Commission retains its status as the only outside body ever invited to review the Senate's internal operations."

His state and nation's future drew Culver's attention. He sponsored the historic Superfund law that in 1979 addressed clean-up of toxic waste dumps. He shepherded the Endangered Species Act before Congress after a spirited debate with then-Minority Leader Howard Baker. He fought for funding of Gasohol, a rural cleanup program and farmers concerned about soil erosion.

Modernization extended to Culver's legislative pedigree as well. By his last term, he had become chairman of the subcommittee on the Future of the Small Business where his main priority was eliminating unnecessary burdens of owners. This resulted in many "Iowa 2000" forums all across the state.

Culver says his proudest accomplishment was prevailing on President Carter to nix funding for the B-1 bomber. It was 1977 and the weapon was well into production but it was quickly being eclipsed by new and more and more modern military aircraft. Culver called the B-1, "way over budget, quite old . . . a complete waste of money." The defense industry was strongly in favor of the system. A year earlier, in the midst of the Presidential election, Culver had proposed postponing the decision to allow the winner of the election to make the decision. Carter, who had previously commissioned a study on the matter, called two separate White House meetings. One was with 8-10 proponents of the weapon while the other was with opponents, including Culver. Culver made the case for the opposition. After the meeting, Culver conceded that few attendees could credibly predict what Carter would do, contending, "I don't think there is any way to tell which way he is leaning and he gave us no indication." Ultimately, the President decided to scrap the program.

But that was only half the battle; Congress still had to approve the plan. Late one night, the Senate was debating the matter. John Glenn was making the case for killing the system but didn't seem to be striking the right notes. That's when staff summoned Culver to the floor. By this time, it was well past midnight and Culver lacked his notes and staff to assist him. Meanwhile, Texas Senator John Tower, a Republican arguing for continuation, was well prepared. Slowly, Senators bean taking their seats and Culver made the case. His presentation was considered to be so masterful that after the debate had ended, Senators on both sides of the issue approached him with congratulations with Bob Dole calling it the "finest extemporaneous speech he had ever heard on the Senate floor."

**Culver with Senator Mike Mansfield prior to the formation of
the "Culver Committee." Right: The committee at work
Photos courtesy of the John Culver Papers, University
of Iowa Libraries, Iowa City, Iowa**

By his own 1980 campaign, Culver had become one of the main targets of the "New Right." Clark had been beaten in a mild surprise two years earlier and both sides viewed that as a precursor of what could come. Culver recognized the odds he faced but felt it was more important than ever to step up and fight.

At that time, Kennedy was about to embark on his White House bid and Culver recalls the two taking a long walk around the Capitol to talk about the campaign. Kennedy had big leads over Carter in Iowa at that point and he asked Culver to forego re-election and take a senior position on his campaign (which presumably would have led to a big post had he won the White House). Culver called it "a tempting option" but ultimately decided to go forward with his campaign. Meanwhile, as the primary loomed, the electorate became focused on Kennedy's personal problems and his flubbed interview with Roger Mudd when he was unable to answer why he wanted to become President. Ultimately, Kennedy fell behind. The duo spoke about an 11th hour endorsement by Culver but ultimately concluded that it would further divide the party in ways that would be too detrimental to his own campaign ("I might as well hang it up") he said later. Carter ended up surging past Kennedy and winning re-nomination.

Meanwhile, Republicans recruited Congressman Charles Grassley, who was conservative on social issues but was perceived as not nearly as rigid as other conservatives seeking Senate seats around the nation. As a farmer, Grassley had good rapport with his constituency. The contest was the "Hawkeye State's" most expensive to date and it was dominated by outside groups trying to prop up their respective candidates (Culver had much Hollywood backing and Grassley religious groups).

The term liberal was certainly anathema that year. But rather than shy away from the term, Culver embraced it. At one appearance he noted that he had "searched the scriptures but I can't find anything saying that Jesus Christ opposed the Panama Canal Treaty or favored the Kemp-Roth tax cuts . . . They're trying to manipulate sincere people on religious grounds." The Equal Rights Amendment was another issue Culver unequivocally supported. When asked at a debate, Culver sdaid, "I'm for it at the state level. I'm for it at the federal level and I'm for it at the county level. With me, it's not a matter of geography. It's a matter of principle." Culver's wife, Mary Jane Checchi notes that many other Democrats hard pressed to win new terms were trying to distance themselves from their liberal histories but not Culver. His philosophy was, "I'm a liberal. I'm not going to pretend I'm something else." And it did not go unnoticed.

In mid-October, Columnist Jack Newfield contrasted Culver with his colleagues who were trying to "camouflage their colors." He wrote, "In a profession of cowards and opportunists, John Culver deserves a purple heart for political bravery under fire in enemy territory. He is not trying to get re-elected with false pretenses." Culver, he continued, "understands that losing a Senate seat is less important than losing his self-respect."

Left photo courtesy of the John Culver Papers, University of Iowa Libraries, Iowa City, Iowa: Right photo courtesy of the March of Dimes National Foundation

That approach may have been effective in a state like Massachusetts, but in Iowa in 1980, it was fatal. Still Culver was a masterful politician and by election eve, many were giving Culver at least a decent shot of surviving. Iowa (along with Idaho) were the only states for which Republicans had hopes of a serious pickup - which Senate Minority Leader Howard Baker did not cite when he named the states "we have to win and are going to win." For Culver had battled back from a

17 point deficit during the summer to a five percent edge over Grassley by mid-October. But in the end, it was not particularly close. Grassley won by 100,000 votes, 53-46%.

In the waning days of his Senate career, Culver received an outpouring of tributes from colleagues. Nebraska Democrat Jim Exon called him "the friendly giant of a man with the intellect to match . . . he is the kind of guy you would like to find yourself in a foxhole with, provided he was on your side. A unique combination of brain, brawn and effective fellow ship." Another Democrat, New Jersey's Harrison Williams echoed that sentiment but called him "one of our true futurists and one who has thought deeply about the country we ought to be able to live in during the next century." Ted Stevens, whose staple "Incredible Hulk" ties was noted by supporters and opponents alike said, "For the past six years, I have learned to listen John even though we have often looked at times from different viewpoints."

But it was Dole, once dubbed a "hatchet man" by rivals whose conservatism placed him squarely on the other side of the aisle who most summed up the man. He said, "Although John and I were many times, more often than not on opposite sides of the issues, his presence during consideration of these issues helped raise the quality of debate and improve the final outcome substantially. He is a man of exceptional principal and perhaps John will be most remembered for that. For at a time when liberalism seemed to be fading and a more conservative mood setting in, John stuck to what he believed in; he hung in there and hung tough."

**Culver testifying before the Senate Banking Committee and visiting Israel
Photos courtesy of the John Culver Papers, University
of Iowa Libraries, Iowa City, Iowa**

In retirement, Culver remained in the Washington D.C. area where he served on a number of boards and took a deep interest in arms control and NATO military standardization. He authored a book on Henry Wallace, a fellow Iowan. He joined the law firm of Arent Fox as a senior partner; when his portrait was unveiled in 2007, Kennedy and a number of other former Senate colleagues were present. One was ex-Arkansas Senator Dale Bumpers, a 1974 Senate classmate who was also active in the formation of the Culver Commission. He cited Culver as "one of the most cerebral people I know" and said his presence at the firm convinced him to join upon his own retirement from the Senate in 1998. Culver joked that the portrait was the "easiest way of dropping 15 pounds." He also served as a longtime member and chair of the Advisory Board of the Institute of Politics at Harvard's Kennedy School of Government and briefly was its interim Director.

Official White House photo
Courtesy of the John Culver Papers, University of Iowa Libraries

Three decades after his Senate service ended, in his laughter-filled eulogy for his friend, Culver recounted in hilarious detail his first sailing trip with Kennedy on a rough day at sea in 1953, when both were 21. "We only got about 200 miracle yards out and I lost the, um, sandwiches. I thought I was going to die and I've never been so miserable and I'm hanging over the side of the boat and he's screaming at me." The crowd was stitches.

Culver's son Chet was elected Governor of Iowa in 2006 but was unseated by Republican Terry Branstad four years later. The elder Culver resides in the Washington area with his wife Mary Jane, a fixture of the U.S. Senate in her own right as a prominent staffer for Senate Democratic Leader Rober Byrd.

Culver's "hanging" at the Arent Fox Law Firm. His two sons John and then-
Governor Chet Culver of Iowa (far right) helped with the unveiling
Photo courtesy of the Culver Family

CHAPTER THIRTY

Tydings Instrumental in JFK's Advancement In Maryland In 1960 And Had Many Indelible Accomplishments For America

Historic Tidbit: When it comes to political families, the Tydings and Beall's are two of the most durable in the state of Maryland. Both have had overlapping tenures on each side of the political spectrum as both fathers and sons served as U.S. Senators from the "Free" State. In fact, Joseph Tydings had the distinction of beating Beall's father, Glenn, Sr., and losing to his son, Glenn, Jr six years later. In another historical coincidence, the matriarch's of both families were prominent social heiresses who lived long. Very long. Millard Tydings' wife was Eleanor Davies Tydings whose father, Joseph E. Davies, was a major player in the election of Woodrow Wilson. He served as the first chairman of the Federal Train Commission in 1915 (FTC) and later, Ambassador to the Soviet Union, Belgium and Luxembourg. The family was close personal friends with General George Marshall and Eleanor in fact was swimming in the Adirondacks with him just as the invasion of South France was taking place (he asked her what time it was and when she replied, he casually told her what was happening overseas). Eleanor was part of official Washington long after Millard died (she and at age 93, published *My Golden Spoon: Memoirs of a Capital Lady*. She died in 2006 at the age of 102. Margaret Schwarzenbach Beall, 105, had passed a year earlier. She did not grow up in such opulence but her family was affluent enough to send her to private school. She was active with civic groups, and once her husband got to Washington, took a prominent role in the Senate Wives Club. Both ladies remained active in local affairs throughout their long lives.

Photo via the U.S. Government Printing Office

How's this for close proximity to late 20th century history? There was once a member of Congress who, before he was a member of Congress, had huge impact on John F. Kennedy's win in the Maryland Democratic primary. A man who as U.S. Senator, carried a torch to fulfilling the Kennedy legacy by advancing important gun control legislation just days after Bobby Kennedy's murder. And a person who, while lacking the name recognition, is actually a hero to many women as the author and principle sponsor of what today is known as family planning. The other sponsor of that legislation: future-President George H.W. Bush who, as a House member in the early years of his political career, was still pro-choice.

Tydings had become politically attracted to Kennedy well before it was certain that the junior Senator from Massachusetts would win the nomination and he encouraged him to compete in the state's primary. But that realization was not necessarily true of Kennedy's organization in Maryland. Why? Because there wasn't one. The state's Democratic Governor Millard Tawes, was urging Kennedy to stay out of the primary and this was one of many times he and Tydings would tangle. They argued on S&L regulation which Tydings was sponsoring and in 1964 Tawes, along with most of the rest of Maryland's Democratic establishment, supported Tydings' opponent for the Senate nomination to challenge Republican incumbent J. Glenn Beall, popular Comptroller Louis Goldstein.

Tydings says one reason for the failure to organize earlier was because "The Maryland primary was a week after West Virginia's," a state everyone thought he'd lose. Tydings thought otherwise. In fact, he and other Protestants were all urging Kennedy to campaign hard there. It was Catholics, still stung by Al Smith's devastating defeat in 1928, who were convinced a Catholic was not electable.

To get started, Tydings first contacted the Kennedy campaign in Washington D.C. with the hopes of organizing a strong campaign in Maryland. But their focus was on West Virginia. Tydings did however, have one key ear: the candidate himself. He would often visit Capitol Hill as Senators were voting and Kennedy was genuinely interested in Tydings' views (he recalls going for a short ride in Kennedy's convertible one day thinking, "I'll be glad when the drive is over").

Kennedy surprised everyone by winning heavily-Protestant West Virginia handsomely and as Tydings said years later, "he was now a viable presidential candidate. Everything changed all of a sudden, and Maryland was a hell of a lot more important." A profile for *Explore Harford* half a century later quoted Tydings as saying that with no organization, "it quickly evolved that delivering Maryland's primary votes fell directly on (Tydings') shoulders." With the help of other locals such as State Delegate Thomas Hatem, he delivered.

While Tydings booked Kennedy solid in Maryland (necessitated by breaks for the candidate to rest his bad back), arranging a visit to Harford County was a preeminent part of the strategy. He arranged for him to speak at Havre de Grace, because, as Tydings said, it was my home county (Kennedy even spent a night at his Oakington farm). The candidate's spouse and large family aided in the effort as well. Tydings recalls Bobby Kennedy speaking so long that he dropped him a note telling him to wind it up ("If you talk much longer, we're going to lose the election").

Kennedy won the Maryland primary with 70% and Tydings' hard work paid off as he was put in charge of representing the Massachusetts Senator at the state conventions in Delaware and Florida. Delaware was a challenge because the state's Senator, J. Allan Frear, was a Lyndon Johnson supporter. Kennedy had made one major visit to the state - a tea party (he drank punch). But Tydings made inroads, including working with a delegate who happened to be a classmate from law school. When the state convention adjourned, he believed he had a split delegation. Florida took a different path. Kennedy did not go down there personally but Bobby, along with other candidates (Missouri Senator Stuart Symington) addressed the Florida State Convention. In the end, Florida Democrats decided to back their junior Senator, George Smathers, as a "favorite son" candidate.

Photo courtesy of Senator Joe Tydings

With the nomination not assured as the Democratic National Convention gaveled to order in Los Angeles, Tydings' services with the Delaware and Florida delegations were still very much in demand and he'd serve as a coordinator responsible for maintaining ties with the delegates from Delaware and Florida. Tydings recalls Bobby running a tight-ship at strategy meetings. People were expected to arrive at 7 in the morning after a late-night of surveying the delegation landscape at post-session parties that ran as late as 2 a.m. This often proved difficult for at least one and Bobby publicly admonished him. Tydings himself was forced to confront Bobby when he realized that he would not be able to deliver Delaware for JFK. But Bobby was understanding, telling him he was gratified that "you told me right away so that we're not counting on them," adding "next time, you'll be a little bit wiser" (Tydings and Bobby were great friends and colleagues until the Senator's 1968 murder).

In August, as the general election took shape, Tydings was again dispatched to Delaware and Florida as a representative. His primary responsibilities were keeping team-Kennedy apprised of key people and developments in each state. Kennedy eked out a 3,000 vote win in Delaware and though he lost Florida by 47,000 votes, Tydings notes his showing was far closer than Adlai Stevenson's 165,000 vote drubbing four years earlier.

Having supported the future-President in a race-changing political campaign in 1960, now-President Kennedy would return the favor. When the President addressed graduates at Annapolis, Tydings hosted him for dinner at his Oakington home. Tydings was coming off a series of highs as U.S. Attorney (see later) and Kennedy urged him to make the race the following year against Beall. A week before Thanksgiving 1963, Tydings attended the White House for a dinner and President Kennedy reassured him about his prospects; "Don't worry," he told him. "You'll win, all you have to do is send your wife out to campaign and you'll be in great shape."

Two days later, Tydings announced his resignation as U.S. Attorney at an 11 a.m. news conference. It was November 22, 1963. Hours later, Tydings was having a farewell lunch with his assistant U.S. attorneys when he and the nation learned that Kennedy had been assassinated. Tydings said Kennedy was "always kind" to him and "didn't treat me like some political guy who was running his campaign."

**Kennedy was a magnet for attracting crowds and in Maryland,
Tydings was by his side every step of the way
Photos courtesy of Senator Joseph Tydings**

The Kennedy connections aside, Tyding's career and accomplishments have been storybook and it started with his own famous name.

Though born in Asheville, North Carolina, Tydings was a Marylander through and through. His adoptive father and "the only father I ever knew" was Millard Tydings, a longtime Senator who was denied a fifth term in part because he dared to take on Joseph McCarthy before it became possible. As a Foreign Relations Committee member, he conducted the hearings on the early accusations by McCarthy that General George Marshall was a traitor and that there were card-carrying Communists in the State department. While these were all blatantly untrue, this was the type of propaganda that was quickly degenerating into McCarthyism.

Millard Tydings was well ahead of his time on other issues. He was the only Senator warning Americans about the rise of Hitler as early as 1934 and unsuccessfully sponsored a resolution directing the President to protest the treatment of German Jewish citizens which, if adopted may have saved the lives of many Jews. He spoke of the "high privilege of being Americans" and urged his countrymen to pursue all avenues to minimizing or eliminating dictators throughout the world (Stalin, etc). He earned the ire of FDR by opposing his court backing plan, to the point that the President recruited a challenger to his '38 re-election bid. Tydings survived that race and later defended Roosevelt against Charles Lindbergh and isolationists who protested U.S. aid to Great Britain during World War II.

Tydings, who adopted Joe shortly after his marriage to Joe's mother, Eleanor Davies, in 1935, is memorialized in a way many motorists on I-95 can see with a picturesque bridge over the Susquehanna River that bears Tydings, Sr's name (the late Senator is also memorialized by a building on the campus of the University of Maryland).

**Tydings' father, Senator Millard Tydings, was a highly regarded Senator well ahead of his time
Photo via the U.S. Government Printing Offices**

Immediately following World War II, the younger Tydings was an Army Corporal in the European Theater of Operations which included the Sixth Cavalry Group of the Third Army. He was discharged as a corporal. Tydings attained his Bachelor's and his J.D. from the University of Maryland. Eventually, he became the President of the Young Democrats. He was elected to the House of Delegates at age 26, the top vote-getter for four positions in a seven candidate field. While Tydings credits his dad's goodwill for his strong showing ("I could have run my golden retriever and he would have won if his last name was Tydings"), he emphasized that he worked hard to secure his win.

Tydings entered the legislature determined to be a reformer – a self-described "straight arrow and independent," who "did not go along with what the majority wanted all the time." His biggest fight was getting the legislature to regulate the state's savings and loan association. With resistance from the leadership, nearly three years passed before it made its way to the desk of Democratic Governor Millard Tawes. He vetoed the measure. But all was not lost. Tawes did appoint a commission to study the issue and named Tydings a member. In time, the panel came up with a regulatory proposal that Tawes found acceptable enough to sign into law. Protecting the Chesapeake Bay also topped Tydings' legislative agenda.

Kennedy's election gave Tydings many avenues to further his career. He could have been an Ambassador or had a sub-cabinet post. But he wanted to be the United States Attorney for the District of Maryland. After solicited advice from Washington State Senator Henry "Scoop" Jackson, Tydings decided to go for the latter. His ability to pursue reform was now free of any impediments.

Tydings directed investigations into the Security Financial Insurance Corp. (SFIC), a phony company that was concocted on Preakness Day, 1959 by two powerful forces on the Maryland political scene: House Majority Leader A. Gordon Boone and House Banking Committee vice-chairman Charles F. Culver. Its purpose was to reward contributors. Instead, it drew the scrutiny of Tydings that culminated in jail sentences for its participants, including Boone. Another subcommittee resulted in the conviction of two U.S. Congressman, Thomas Johnson and Frank Boykin, Democrats from Maryland and Alabama respectively.

Next was his efforts against organized crime, which Bobby Kennedy, now U.S. Attorney General, asked him to oversee by appointing him director of (anti) organized crime. The FBI under J. Edgar Hoover had refused to target organized crime and Kennedy and the Criminal Division of the Justice Department identified the most dangerous leaders of the Mafia. While many were successful, Tydings proudly notes, "we got everyone from Maryland." This increased Tydings' name recognition as 1964 approached and that's when Kennedy importuned him to challenge Beall. Incidentally, when asked if he was ambivalent about running for the Senate, Tydings replied, "Are you kidding? Not when the President of the United States" asks you to do something. Tydings did have Senatorial aspirations but calculated that he would be roughly 55 before achieving that goal. Instead, he achieved his goal nearly 20 years ahead of his timetable). Had he lost the Senate race, he was prepared to seek the Maryland Governorship in 1966 and "clean up the state."

The Maryland Senate race was somewhat of a microcosm to the national environment. In the aftermath of Kennedy's assassination, the "Let Us Continue" mantra was a powerful enticement for voters and Tydings was able to boast of a closeness to the murdered President more than virtually any other candidate. But at 70, Beall had his weaknesses. Despite his longevity he barely held his seat in 1958 against Thomas D'Alesandro (the Baltimore Mayor and father of future House Speaker Nancy Pelosi).

To get to Beall, Tydings had to get past a challenge from Goldstein and with nearly the state's entire Democratic establishment and key labor organizations backing Goldstein, that posed a formidable challenge. Tydings readily admits that as the campaign got under way, even he was unsure he could beat Goldstein who had never previously lost an election. But Tydings did, by nearly 2-1 (incidentally, Tydings believed that had JFK lived, there probably would not have been a primary for the President would have cleared the field). He swamped Beall in the fall. In short, while Tydings' victory was not a surprise, his nearly 278,000 vote margin, 63-37% was eyebrow raising. Tydings particularly ran well in every area that had given Beall critical margins six years earlier. But for Maryland, the election would be more consequential than a six year Senate term. Tydings notes "a whole generation of new people either got involved in the race or was encouraged to become involved two years later and they would soon be impacting Maryland politics. One was a 26 year-old named Steny Hoyer who would rise to become Majority Leader of the U.S. House.

Tydings is certain that his father's career gave him an advantage over other freshmen Senators. Of the Senate, Tydings said, "I knew how it operated, I knew the customs. And my father was immensely popular with leading Democrats and Republicans." Many were the longtime Southern Senators he was fighting but Tydings said they "were personally on good terms even though I strongly disagreed with them on civil rights. They respected my father so much that it made it easier to work with them." Democratic leaders recognized his legislative acumen early on and named him one of four deputy Whips for the Voting Rights Act (Phil Hart, Ted Kennedy and Birch Bayh were the others and they'd hold regular strategy meetings with Majority Leader Mike Mansfield and Minority leader Everett Dirksen). Jackson and Symington became key role models.

Immediately, Tydings became an ally of another freshman who had made the transfer from law to the Senate. His name was Robert F. Kennedy of New York. The two made waves in early '65 by opposing attempts to overturn the Warren Court's great decisions on civil rights, criminal justice and one man-one vote which did away with "rotten-borough legislatures." One rare unsuccessful attempt was to stop efforts to gut the Mallory Rule, which codified the invalidation of confessions if a suspect was detained too long. An amendment the pair sponsored failed 26-67.

Defeating attempts to gut "one man-one vote" was not only the first major initiative Tydings undertook as a freshman, but also became the subject of his "maiden" speech on the Senate floor. Columnist Drew Pearson wrote that before the Court decision, "the vote of a Vermont farmer was worth 987 times more than the vote of his city cousin" but Senate Minority Leader Everett Dirksen and powerful special interests were fighting to overturn that decision.

Three Democratic Senators – Paul Douglas of Illinois, William Proxmire of Wisconsin and Tydings were leading the effort to save "one-man, one-vote," but because Tydings was the only one of the trio to sit on the Judiciary Committee, the bulk of the responsibility fell to him. He delivered. He delivered a speech dubbed "rotten borough" that related to Britain, which he circulated to Mayors of every major city. Tydings staff even wrote most of the speeches for the Senators who would speak against the Dirksen amendment and it was enough to beat it back. Two thirds of Senators voting were required, but it garnered only 57 votes. Tydings had won. He tangled with Dirksen again the following year over a measure to institute school prayer and again emerged on the winning end.

Dirksen's voluntary school prayer amendment to the Constitution was another matter on which the pair tangled and in the book, *The Fourth R; Conflicts Over Religion In America's Public Schools*, Joan DelFattore noted Tydings mocked the term "voluntary, by "tartly observ(ing) thatreading the King James Bible under the threat of being beaten or expelled was not what most people meant by "'voluntary.'"

The Millard Tydings Memorial Bridge is used by thousands of motorists per year

For the most part, Tydings was a solid liberal. He championed the "Great Society" and was among a bipartisan group of Senators proposing amendments to strengthen the Voting Rights Act as they were attempting to clear it from the Senate Judiciary Committee over a recalcitrant chairman, James Eastland of Mississippi. On the floor, he argued against an amendment by North Carolina Democrat Sam Ervin to move appeals of voting procedures declared in violation of the new law to the U.S. District court in that state, rather than federal. "To open the gates for litigation at this stage rather than in the areas covered by the sections of the bill which already provide for it would, in my judgement, bog down the entire registration process for which the bill provides and thus, in effect, by delaying litigation, cripple the magisterial effect of carrying out what the bill seeks to do, namely to enable persons to vote who have been previously denied that right on account of race or color."

In 1966, he persuaded the Judiciary Committee and the Senate to adopt another civil rights bill – jury selection reform. His legislation required federal jury selection to be a "fair, cross-section of communities." Later, he was a leading proponent of Open and Fair Housing legislation.

In 1967, Tydings became chair of the Judiciary Committee's Improvements in Judicial Machinery subcommittee. He was author of legislation creating the U.S. Magistrate System and reforming the D.C. court system.

That same year, Tydings had a major role in guiding Thurgood Marshall through his rigorous, five-week long confirmation and ensuring his place in history as the first African-American justice to sit on the Supreme Court. LBJ very much wanted to name Marshall to the court and was able to persuade Associate Justice Tom Clark to step down. The trade-off: LBJ would appoint his son Ramsey U.S. Attorney General.

But Marshall faced a cadre of aggressive Southerners on the Judiciary Committee – five "Old Bulls," eager to trip him up. Clark and Michigan Democrat Phil Hart picked Tydings to sit with Marshall during the hearings. While Marshall could not rely on anyone to answer the questions for him (and his tenure as Solicitor General and own smarts prepared him for not even flinching), Tydings, who as a fellow Marylander had a special affinity for Marshall, was able to interject when he thought a question was out of line or if he thought one was belittling the point.

On one occasion, an exasperated Tydings told North Carolina's Sam Ervin he didn't understand where he was headed with certain questions, to which Ervin replied, "All I can do is ask questions. I can't guarantee your understanding them." Tydings felt Marshall "was brilliant and rarely needed protection from me." Marshall, he adds, "never complained" about his treatment in private and was "master of the hearings'" as far as I was concerned."

On crime legislation, some Senators wanted to strip the Supreme Court of authority to review "voluntary" confessions if upheld by the state courts but Tydings pushed through an amendment to keep that in place. In 1970, Tydings was among just four Senators to vote against reporting the nomination of U.S. Supreme Court nominee Harrold Carswell out of Judiciary. In a minority report, the quartet cited "credentials too meager to justify confirmation" adding, "his decisions and his courtroom demeanor have been openly hostile to the black, the poor, and the unpopular." Tydings also called Carswell "simply unable or unwilling to divorce his judicial functions from his personal prejudices."

Initially, Tydings supported the Vietnam War but began having reservations shortly after returning from a trip to the region in 1965. Still, it took him time to come full circle and he often met with many young people who were staunch opponents of the conflict. He also spoke on the Senate floor in favor of a proposal by Pennsylvania Democrat Joe Clark extending the life of the Arms Control and Disarmament Agency.

Tydings had been seated near Bobby Kennedy on the Senate floor when he announced his candidacy for President and was one of the two Senators who announced his support. He campaigned in ten states for him and was devastated by his death. Kennedy had been scheduled to appear on NBC's "Meet the Press" the Sunday after his assassination and his staff asked him to appear in his stead. He used that forum to unveil plans to introduce a stringent anti-gun platform. Tydings, a life-long hunter, owned seven weapons. But he especially wanted to pursue the enactment of tougher laws "to say something meaningful so that (Kennedy's) death meant something." He later added, "It's something that (R.F.K.) would have wanted. Obviously he wasn't there to do anything. But he would have liked the fact that I did it. So would his brother, President Kennedy. And so would my father."

For his gun control proposals, Tydings had the support of President Johnson. But while Johnson was trying to operate in realism with the political hand he was dealt,

Tydings wanted something stronger, in particular licensing and gun registration. Instead, they got neither. The NRA circulated a letter labeling the measure a first step to confiscating all weapons which Tydings called "calculated hysteria." Johnson was able to sign minimal restrictions into law (owner licensing, firearms restrictions, importation of $10 specials and the ending of what he called "murder by mail order" and the "bar(ring) of the interstate sale of all guns and the bullets that load them)." But they were not nearly as stringent as Tydings had hoped prior to the gun supporters all-out lobbying campaign. Meanwhile, Tydings seconded the nomination of George McGovern for President at the 1968 Democratic National Convention.

Tydings, in 1969, was a champion of the Horse Protection Act of 1970
Photo via billygoboy.com

As 1969 began, Tydings initially expected approval and support for his leadership in the criminal justice arena. He was tapped to chair the 13 member Advisory Panel Against Violence and was now chair of the District of Columbia subcommittee. That gave him a major hand in the District of Columbia Court Reform and Criminal Procedure Act (the D.C. Crime bill), a 300 page document.

In committee and on the floor, Tydings was active in many amendments. In fact, he led the Senate conferees. But this proved to be a mixed blessing. He gained resentment from some minorities for backing "no-knock" legislation for Washington D.C., a cause that put him against liberals and surprisingly, conservatives whom Tydings said didn't understand the legislation. This would allow police to search homes unannounced, though Tydings said a warrant would be required. The other section opposed by liberals was Preventive Detention language Nixon insisted on.

Tydings amended the bill to protect the public from very dangerous arrestees. He said "High bail set in hundreds of cases is, in effect, preventive discrimination," explaining that Judges set bail at levels knowing it can't be met. Conservative North Carolina Democrat Sam Ervin and New York Republican Charlie Goodell, a fairly liberal Republican, opposed him in this regard.

One issue on which Tydings was proud to carry the torch for women of America was the Family Planning Services and Population Research Act of 1970. The bill, signed into law by President Nixon would prove indelible for advocates of family planning. This made available funding for private and public centers and created Office of Population Affairs, grants for research and counseling. Tydings had introduced similar legislation since his first days in Congress, at one point advocating earmarks to fund family planning. His rationale: planning advocates lack "necessary bureaucratic champions to safeguard its funds." This legislation is what conservatives in Congress have been trying to dismantle and are attacking today.

Another legislative success was the Horse Protection Act of 1970 which limited the practice of soring (applying irritants or blistering agents to horses to increase their volatility during races). To this day, many groups would like to outlaw soring completely and Tydings is active in assisting with those efforts.

As Tydings geared up for a second term in 1970, Republicans seemed underwhelmed at their chances. The name of his challenger - J. Glenn Beall, was familiar, as he was the son of the incumbent Tydings had dislodged six years earlier. But having served just a single term in the House of Representatives, even Republicans conceded he was something of a political lightweight.

That didn't stop Vice President Spiro Agnew, already barnstorming the nation in support of GOP Congressional candidates, from spending an inordinate amount of time in his home state. Tydings mocked him, saying he wanted "a docile and dismissive Senate, populated by little mechanical puppets who are called Republican Senators, Class of '71, programmed by the Republican National committee to march in lock step to the commands of the White House." He accused the White House of trying to "purge" him from the Senate.

But Tydings had his own problems and they emanated from both the right and left. Liberals were upset by his advocacy of "no-knock." Conservatives by contrast were angered by his zest for gun-control and formed a group, "Citizens Against Tydings." The incumbent was also hurt by a September 1970 *Life Magazine* piece which accused him of using his office to provide for special interests (ironically, a similar falsehood was instrumental in sinking the elder Tydings' career two decades earlier when the magazine had published a doctored photo of him with American Communist Party leader Earl Browder, despite the fact that the pair had never met). Tydings asked Bill Fulbright to ask the Office of the Inspector General to conduct an investigation and they determined two weeks before the election that the allegations were false. But the report was not released until after the election. But what he believes likely made the difference was that he was now a vocal opponent of the war. Tydings acknowledges few might have noticed had he simply opposed authorizations and went about his business. But, he said, that just wasn't his style.

The opening of an AP editorial shortly before the primary illustrated the political conundrum Tydings was facing. It began with the words "Cannon to the right of him, cannon to the left of him." Against multiple opponents, including perennial candidate George "A Man's Home Is His Castle - Keep It That Way" Mahoney, Tydings took just 53% in the primary, foreshadowing the difficulties that lie ahead. But as the campaign headed into November, most pundits still gave him even odds for hanging on. They were narrowly mistaken. Beall won 51-48%, a margin of just 25,000 votes out of 950,000 cast. Ryan Polk, in a paper, "Good Tydings," observed that he was "considered a martyr to control advocates, and still held as an example of what happens to politicians when you cross the NRA."

Tydings resumed practicing law after his defeat but did make an attempt to reclaim his Senate seat in 1976. He carried his home turf in Southern Maryland but lost to Baltimore Congressman Paul Sarbanes in the primary. He served on the University of Maryland Board of Regents in three different decades following appointments by three Governors. He also acted as an observer for elections in the Ukraine.

Tydings, 88, continues to practice law at Blank-Rome in Washington D.C. and is still a ferocious advocate on behalf of causes near and dear to his heart and his state.

Tydings as he received the "First Citizen Award" from Maryland Legislators
Photo courtesy of the Maryland State Archives

CHAPTER THIRTY-ONE

Tunney Son of Wrestler, Roomie of Teddy's, and Impetus for Movie "The Candidate"

Historic Tidbit: Shortly after he captured the Democratic nomination for President, *U.S. News and World Report* **noted John F. Kennedy was going to issue a challenge to his opponent, Vice-President Richard Nixon, to conduct joint television debates. But, the magazine noted, "The Vice-President is inclined to reject the Kennedy proposal on the ground that a personal debate would be unwise." Nixon was a paranoid guy but that hesitation turned out to be well founded.**

Ding! I had been searching for historical footnotes on ex-California Senator John Tunney and I found not one, not two, but three. One, Tunney was Ted Kennedy's law school roommate at the University of Virginia. Two, his father Gene was one half of one of the most famous boxing matches in history. And three, Tunney was the impetus for Robert Redford's hit movie *The Candidate*.

Throughout his career, Tunney's good looks and youth struck many as Kennedyesque, which he happily embraced. His association with Ted made it that much easier to do. Tunney was also glad to use his dad's fame as an asset. John Tunney, Sr. had twice beaten Jack Dempsey and retired as an undefeated heavyweight champion. And so it was only fitting that Tunney equated boxing with his campaign. "Put a fighter in your corner," he said. "John Tunney, the fighter." Of his opponent, he preached, "My father said, when the bell rings, the time has ended for talking. Well, that bell has rung for George Murphy and I'm coming out swinging."

Tunney, who had won a Riverside-Imperial-area Congressional seat in 1964, struggled somewhat to capture the 1970 Senate nod to face Murphy. He began with a wide lead over his House colleague from Riverside, George Brown, a true dove on Vietnam who was every bit as dignified and taciturn as Tunney was charismatic and ubiquitous. Nixon's decision to send troops to Cambodia helped Brown surge, and he took the lead. Tunney called Brown a "radical," to which Brown cited his Quaker upbringing. Legendary LA Supervisor Kenneth Hahn, the father of both a future Mayor and Congresswoman, was also in the race but his recognition was too meager to break out from his LA base. Tunney beat Brown 42-34%, with Hahn at just 16%.

Against Murphy, accusations flew. At one point, Murphy said, "either this young man has not been in Washington long enough to know the facts or he is so desperate he is disregarding the truth." Murphy attacked his attendance record, calling it 429ᵗʰ out of 435ᵗʰ. And that's where the Kennedy connection comes in. According to a rundown of the race by Bill Boyarsky, "his speaking style is reminiscent of the Kennedys and Murphy often makes fun of it. Tunney concedes that he makes some of the familiar John F. Kennedy gestures but says he learned it from . . . Ted Kennedy."

But when Tunney's hair-cut showed an uncanny resemblance to RFK, that was too much for Murphy. "What kind of nonsense is this," he asked. "We put up with a lot in this country but that is a little much."

John Tunney's resemblance to RFK was noticeable
Photo courtesy of Alfred Golub

Murphy also sought to link Tunney to the protesters, notably those "who try to downgrade our country." But Murphy was hurt by the $20,000 he received from the health care industry. Meanwhile, California was changing. "I want to serve our state in the Senate because I care about the tragedy in Vietnam," Tunney said.

Tunney attracted the crowds of a Kennedy rally
Photo courtesy of Alfred Golub

Ronald Reagan was Murphy's running-mate and he often had to aid his friend. Murphy joked that "neither one of us could go back to our old business. We're too old to take off our clothes."

Murphy led slightly in October, but Tunney won by 10%. Well into the 1976 campaign season, Tunney was hardly considered vulnerable. And the man who limped out of a contested primary, S.I. Hayakawa, 70, was not considered particularly imposing. The former President of San Francisco State College was aided greatly in the Republican primary by memories that conservative voters had of when, as President, he ripped the wires out of a sound truck during a demonstration. That made him the man of the hour to conservatives, and it was enough for him to beat two ex-Lieutenant Governors in the primary.

Against Tunney, a tougher fight seemed to loom. Hayakawa had a colorful background as a Hayakawa, a 70-year-old Canadian-born Japanese fellow. But he was 70 and had a reputation for dozing off at meetings.

Tunney, rare for the incumbent, wanted to frequently debate Hayakawa, who was more comfortable talking to conservative circles. But Tunney had a couple of problems, and it started with his own base. Liberals were angry that he opposed a national health insurance plan sponsored by Kennedy, and for backing gas deregulation. That helped him take an unexpectedly tepid win against Assemblyman Tom Hayden, Jane Fonda's husband who had a devoted following among the anti-war folks. In beating back Hayden, he used the same radical approach he had tried on Brown. And Hayakawa questioned his effectiveness, reviving Murphy's attendance bashing theme. He attacked Tunney as a legislative lightweight. Tunney claimed to be more of a behind the scenes player, particularly on Angola.

Hayakawa also portrayed Tunney as an elitist. *The Almanac of American Politics* noted that when photographs emerged of him vacationing with Kennedy, "it seemed to re-enforce the notion that he was a Playboy." Still, his 52-48% victory over the incumbent was something of a surprise. Tunney had actually run slightly behind Carter, who was losing the state, but only 51-49%. Of Hayakawa, Tunney later said, "To use a metaphor of my father's former profession, I found he was very difficult to lay a glove on."

Tunney eventually returned to practicing law in the Washington area. Later in life, an incident appeared to bear out his Playboy image out. In 1988, Tunney was arrested for DUI.

CHAPTER THIRTY-TWO

Salinger vs. Murphy:
The Press Secretary and the Movie Star

Historic Tidbit: JFK's press secretary, Pierre Salinger, was not the only one to seek a high office. RFK's gifted handler, Frank Mankiewicz, sought a Maryland Congressional seat in 1976. Mankiewicz had also gained fame running George McGovern's campaign in 1972. Thus, many viewed him as the man to beat in the primary for this Chevy Chase-Bethesda-based district. But 33-year-old attorney Lanny Davis, who had his own chitsfor his role in Gene McCarthy and Ed Muskie's campaigns, was also running and upset Mankiewicz by 5,000 votes in the primary (27-22% in a multi-candidate field). In the general, Davis ran an aggressive campaign that rubbed some Democrats the wrong way and lost to Republican Newton Steers 47-42%. He of course went on to become Bill Clinton's special counsel.

Returning en route to Tokyo after the assassination
Photo via fifties.web.com

1 964 was the "Let Us Continue" election. Americans, still shocked and numbed by the assassination of President John F. Kennedy a year before, solidified their tribute to the fallen President by electing like-minded Democrats left and right to succeed him. So who better to do that, it would seem, than his former press secretary for a U.S. Senate seat in California?

Pierre Salinger was already technically a Senator, having been appointed to fill the seat of Claire Engle who had died that July. And Johnson carried California by a big margin in the fall, though the state was not nearly as Democratic as it is today. So it may have surprised many that Salinger lost the seat for the full term. His opponent was George Murphy, a fairly well-known actor. But at the end of the day, his Kennedy connection may have hurt as much as helped.

Photo courtesy of the John F. Kennedy Presidential Library and Museum

Among Democrats, the "Let Us Continue" mantra appeared to be alive and well. Salinger's appointment came after the state's June primary, a month after he had beaten Alan Cranston, the California Controller who was a popular elected official in the "Golden State." Salinger's margin over Cranston was 140,000 votes so it's safe to assume the Kennedy connection helped.

Born to a French-Catholic mother and a Jewish father, journalism came early to Salinger; he began writing for the San Francisco Chronicle at age 17. He served on the Senate Select Committee to Investigate Improper Activities in Labor-Management Relations. But he then went to work for a Massachusetts Senator named John F. Kennedy which would change his world forever.

Salinger served as the "New Frontier" candidate's press secretary throughout the campaign and in that role he served as the emissary between the candidate and the press during the pre-dawn hours following the long, tense night that Kennedy's lead had been evaporating. He described Kennedy as "hopeful, extremely relaxed and when I last talked to him he was heading to his house to get some sleep." He told reporters that Kennedy would have nothing to say until "no earlier than 10 am Eastern." When pressed on the possibility that a winner might still not be known, he added "if it's later, then it'll be later." When asked if he believed Kennedy had won he replied, "I think we'll let the Senator make that statement."

Salinger also added that he did not view Richard Nixon's just-concluded remarks to his supporters as a concession.

The next day, however, Nixon unmistakably issued a concession in the form of a statement read by Nixon's own press secretary. The President-elect told Salinger that "he looks like more of a Frontiersman than you do."

Today, people take the role of a Presidential press secretary for granted. But in 1961, television was fairly new and Americans' access to Salinger was a novelty. Salinger changed that. He became the first press secretary to provide access to the press full-time, which involved JFK using the press more regularly than his predecessors. Salinger's rational was that "this would give the whole nation a chance to see the President as he actually answers the questions of reporters. We think it would be beneficial to the press. And, indeed, we think it would be beneficial to all concerned."

One way he provided that access was to have access himself, something he did not have during the first 100 days. The Bay of Pigs crisis changed that. "I went to the president and said I couldn't operate that way," he said. "My effectiveness would be destroyed unless I knew about even the most covert operations of government. He agreed and it never happened again."

Salinger was not with the President when he was assassinated. He was traveling to Tokyo with six other cabinet members, including Secretary of State Dean Rusk. But the plane promptly turned around and headed back to Washington.

In 1964, Democratic incumbent Senator Clair Engle was seeking re-election. But Salinger desperately wanted to carry the torch and when Engle was forced to withdraw his bid for a second term due to brain cancer, Salinger jumped into the race to succeed him. He beat Cranston for the nomination but Engle died a month later, weeks after he was wheeled into the Senate chamber to cast a vote for the Civil Rights Act (because he was unable to speak, Engle had to point to his eye to signal approval). Governor Pat Brown appointed Engle to the seat.

The Los Angeles Times said of Salinger: "The dark-haired, poker-playing Salinger was described in the press at the time as being sharp, brash and witty; a hard-driving, swarthy cherub who talked rapidly in short bursts; and a bon vivant who loved good wine, good food and good cigars."

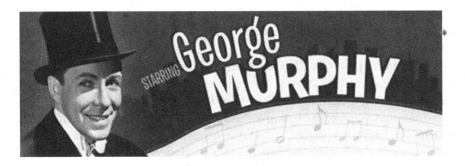

Photo via Turner Movie Classics

Murphy had his own media experience but in this case it was in cinematography. He played a role in at least 39 pictures, starring alongside such Hollywood big-shots as Shirley Temple in Little Miss Broadway, Judy Garland in Little Nellie Kelly, and with Garland and Gene Kelly in For Me and My Gal. He starred with a Ronald Reagan in This Is the Army and had a role in Tom, Dick, and Harry and Broadway Melody of 1938, among others.

Murphy was born to a coach in New Haven, Connecticut, and went to Broadway while he was in his 20s. After these films, he worked at MGM and Desilu Productions, the latter of which was operated by Lucille Ball and Desi Arnaz. He was known as Hollywood's "Ambassador of Goodwill" and was given an academy award for "his service in correctly interpreting the film industry to the country at large."

But the acting bug soon turned into the political bug as Murphy chaired the entertainment portion of the Eisenhower inaugural festivities and later, the California Republican Party's Central Committee. It was in 1964 that Murphy decided to aim for the Senate, though at the time, it was assumed he'd be taking on incumbent Engle.

Photo via notallwriteblogspot.com

For Me and My Gal

In accepting the appointment for Engle's seat, Salinger said he was responding to "a draft." Murphy contested Salinger's appointment on the grounds that he had not lived in California for the past year, as state law required. That went nowhere but ultimately may have been his downfall. Unlike Bobby in New York, Salinger was born in California. But he had not lived there for a while and Bobby's candidacy shed light on his east coast background. In addition, the candidates had major stylistic differences.

The Harvard Crimson summed up the candidates thus: "Murphy exemplifies the Midwestern ethic. Instead of addressing rallies, he discusses the campaign with small crowds in a subdued homey manner. In these little talks, the ex-song-and-dance man dispels the more frivolous connotations of his past by recounting his efforts to rid the entertainment industry of communist influences."

A campaign rally
Photo courtesy of the Nixon Foundation

As for Salinger, his "energetic campaign . . . exploits California's love of audacious good fun. Each day Plucky Pierre crisscrosses the state by helicopter, dropping dramatically out of the smog to embrace an ever-present bevy of giggling Salinger Girls. Waving an outrageously gnawed cigar to the crowd and patting his portly frame, Pierre turns every stop into a garnish tongue-cheek extravaganza."

Another article observed that Murphy "dresses fashionably, conservatively, and compatible to his old career – 'as if he just stepped out of a bandbox.'" It went on to note that "ironically, it is Salinger who has the showmanship approach." One event he did was called "a swinging with Pierre."

Salinger had been told by his advisers not to debate but he ignored this advice. While the debate fell predictably along liberal/conservative lines, a commentary afterward said that Salinger was agreed by both parties to have "emerged as the brash, almost arrogant young man while Murphy was the comfortable old shoe."

At one point in the campaign, Salinger made a complaint to the Fair Campaign Committee accusing Murphy's camp of distributing "anonymous hate sheets describing my mother as a Communist and casting doubts on my own loyalty." The Murphy campaign responded that they "found" the literature in their headquarters, "repudiated it, and denied vehemently that we had anything to do with it, had seen it, or much less authorized it."

As the election approached, Governor Pat Brown hypothesized that a number of Independent- and Republican-leaning voters who were voting for Johnson over Goldwater on ideological grounds would choose Murphy over Salinger for the purpose of not packing Washington with too many Democrats. So Salinger tried extra hard to link Murphy to Goldwater. The Presidential candidate visited the state and met briefly with Murphy. The press asked if they could photograph it and were told no. Murphy exited through a back door.

**Photo courtesy of the David M. Rubenstein Rare Book
and Photograph Library, Duke University**

Salinger was also hurt by Proposition 14 which would nullify the Rumford Fair Housing Act prohibiting racial discrimination in public housing and big apartments. Salinger opposed repeal while Murphy backed it. California voters approved it with 65%.

As Election Day approached, all knew that the race had tightened but most expected that Salinger would eke it out. Some were predicting the margin would be about 200,000 votes.

On Election Night, as early returns showed him trailing, Salinger didn't concede, but said he'd be "less than candid if he said it looked good." At 9 a.m. the next morning, Salinger did throw in the towel. The margin was 200,000 votes—the other way.

Murphy after his Senate win
Photo courtesy of the U.S. Senate Historical Office

One political analyst said he was "convinced that Bobby was the chief factor that beat Pierre. Bobby's entrance heightened Californian's sensitivity to a belief that this whole thing was a Kennedy power play. Too many Kennedys and close allies were trying to get into government. Californians decided they didn't want California to be a tail on the Kennedy dog." Meanwhile, Minority Leader Everett Dirksen, on a call with President Johnson, quipped that he "got a good exchange. I got a Hollywood actor for our friend from New York (speaking of Kenneth Keating, who had been unseated by Bobby Kennedy).

As for Murphy, not long after his election came the famous Tom Lehrer jingle: "Oh, gee, it's great, at last we've got a Senator who can really sing and dance."

Murphy served an uneventful six years. He voted mostly conservative, but there were exceptions. He backed the Voting Rights Act as well as portions of the "Great Society." But when Reagan won the Governorship two years later, Murphy faced endless comparisons to his fellow actor. While Murphy was calm, he lacked the future president's charm and reassuring demeanor.

As his 1970 re-election bid approached, Murphy was also tainted by a $20,000 lobbying gig by Technicolor Inc., a movie processing firm that continued to employ him even after he assumed office as a Senator. But throat surgery and his backing of the Vietnam War also hampered his ability to gain ground, and Murphy lost to Congressman John Tunney by 10%. He died of leukemia two months before his 90th birthday in Florida in 1992.

Salinger resigned his Senate seat on December 31, 1964, thereby allowing Murphy to gain seniority by being sworn in before the rest of his class. But he would not be removed from the Kennedy bug for long. When Bobby threw his hat into the ring, Salinger served as one of his campaign managers. And he was with him at the Ambassador Hotel when he won, and after he was shot.

Salinger was said to have been trying to stop him from entering the kitchen of the Ambassador Hotel where the shooting occurred, saying, "I've got to get the message to Los Angeles, under no circumstances should Bobby go through that (Ambassador Hotel) kitchen . . . there's usually grease on the floor. He's going to fall or something."

In the 1970s, Salinger became a correspondent for L'Express, a Paris publication. He went on to a variety of unique roles, such as appearing on ABC Sports and Batman.

In 2000, he bemoaned the thought of George H.W. Bush's possible White House win. "I don't want any more Bush Presidents," he said. "If Bush wins, I'm going to leave the country and spend the rest of my life in France." He followed through and died in Paris in 2005.

Photo via the National Archives

CHAPTER THIRTY-THREE

Kenneth Keating:
The Man RFK Ousted For NY Senate Seat

Historic Quote: "I see nothing wrong with giving Robert legal experience before he goes out to practice law." –President-elect John F. Kennedy defending his decision to name his brother Attorney General

Photo via Corbis Images

The name of Kenneth Keating will likely seldom be ever uttered outside of New York State political almanacs and Congressional monitors, but his footnote on history may tower as large as the Empire State Building. Bobby Kennedy ousted him for the Senate in 1964 and had he fallen short, hemight not have sought the Presidency in 1968.

Keating literally was a "Rockefeller Republican." He became a Senator in 1958, the same night Rocky was elected Governor. Keating's 1958 victory went against a severely anti-Republican trend that grasped the nation and enabled the Democrats to make major gains.

An attorney who had won a House seat in 1946, Keating was by no means a hardcore conservative, but neither was he an antagonist to his Congressional leadership. He voted for the override of Taft-Hartley and in 1949 he backed the party 74% of the time.

On civil rights, Keating talked the talk as well as walked the walk. It was he who integrated the Congressional Dining Room. How did he do that? By simply inviting Adam Clayton Powell and his wife to join him there. The dining room manager, also an African-American, gave Keating a hard time but Keating replied he'd take the blame. No one complained.

Keating's commitment to the cause continued into his last year in the Senate when the ideologically divided Republican Convention could not agree on a civil rights plank. Keating urged the platform to say "without qualification our belief in the constitutionality as well as the morality of the requirements of this legislation. Such a declaration will serve to isolate and deter those misguided elements seeking to mobilize support for a campaign of massive resistance. It will help assure that this legislation will mark the beginning of an era of reconciliation in race relations and not an era of heightened tensions, frustration and bitterness." But Keating was overruled by dominant conservatives.

Keating was mostly a quiet member but friendly and genuinely well-liked. He did cause somewhat of a stir when he said in 1960 that "scientists should only be on tap and not a politician because his training does not equip him for the job." He likewise asked scientists to make a "clear-cut division between science and politics."

On other issues, Keating was credited as being among the first members of Congress to recognize the threat of the Soviet Union, asking in mid-1961, "How long will it be before the Soviet Union establishes military bases and missile launching sites in Cuba?" He proposed the 23rd Amendment that, among other things, gave the District of Columbia voting rights at the Presidential level. As 1964 approached, he seemed assured of a spirited challenge but a sure win for a second term.

Then came Bobby.

When Kennedy was approached about taking on Keating, he was seen as the symbol of a nation's grief. His brother had been murdered less than a year before and delegates roused Kennedy by giving him a 23-minute ovation when he addressed the Democratic National Convention. The national Democratic theme was "Let Us Continue," and voters nationally and in New York took every opportunity to do so, even if it meant forgiving carpet-bagging. For Kennedy was still technically a resident of Massachusetts and he'd have to not only change that (New York had very liberal laws in that regard), but show New Yorkers he was well versed in their issues. For the latter, his staff presented him with a dossier of New York issues.

At first, Kennedy hesitated but after consultation with his inner circle, including his brother-in-law Steve Smith, he decided to go forward. At the time,

An Oliver Quayle poll showed him up 57-43% over Keating. More ominously for the Senator, 38% of New Yorkers didn't know who he was.

Tom Dewey gave the keynote at the state Republican Convention and previewed the Republican's theme against Kennedy. "A funny thing happened to the Massachusetts delegation on the way to the Democratic Convention last month," he began. "One of the elected members of the Massachusetts delegation who holds office in Washington stopped off here on his way to Atlantic City [the convention] from his home in Virginia. He stopped off to rent a house in Long Island and announced that he is to be the Democratic candidate for the U.S. Senate from—of all places, New York." Upon Kennedy's nomination, Keating naturally raised the carpetbagging issue. A statement said "we can all take pride in the fact that Franklin Roosevelt, Al Smith, and Herb Lehman had their roots in this state . . . but after years of boss rule, the leaders of the party now tell New Yorkers they have no homegrown candidate who is worthy of representing New York in the Senate."

Keating faced a mini-rebellion of his own. Knowing Barry Goldwater would be a drag, Keating openly addressed their differences. "I have said before . . . that I consider Senator Goldwater a sincere, patriotic American. But during our service in the Senate, Senator Goldwater and I have disagreed on many issues. Nothing either of us says at this point can alter our records on the issues." Congressman Paul Fino called Keating "a left-wing traitor" and flirted with challenging him but didn't.

Keating, aware of JFK's shadow, didn't go right for the jugular. He noted he served with the late president in the Senate and referred to him as "a man of courage and conviction."

Keating tried to make special overtures to demographics including African-Americans, Italians, and Jews who pointed out areas in Kennedy's record they may have had problems with. His outreach to African-Americans in particular was curious, as Keating said that by resigning his post in the midst of the Civil Rights movement, Kennedy was risking it all. Eventually, Kennedy's lead slipped and the polls were tied.

**The magic of Kennedy, in 1963, attracted crowds everywhere but Keating
was able to count on at least some Democratic backing. It wasn't enough.
Left photo courtesy of the Library of Congress Prints and
Photographs Division; right photo via Tsutpen.blogspt.com**

Kennedy began feeling the heat and enunciated positions, including to the
Jewish community, pledging more aid to Israel to "keep her from becoming
the victim of military imbalance." And he began attacking Keating's record,
launching mailings called, "Myth of Keating's Liberalism," particularly on
opposing legislation such as the creation of the National Youth Corps and votes
against public housing and aid to veterans.

Keating gained attention by filing a complaint with the Fair Campaign
Practices Committee taking up Kennedy's charge that he had opposed the
Nuclear Test Ban Treaty (he had actually supported its final passage). Kennedy
acknowledged he had erred and admitted it.

Sensing trouble and a big Democratic surge at the top of the ticket, Kennedy
began hitching himself to Johnson's fortunes, producing buttons that said, "Get
with the Johnson-Humphrey-Kennedy Team." Keating said: "I don't care how
much money my opponent may have, and I don't care about his grandiose
ambitions . . . I have worked too hard for the people of New York to allow this
kind of ruthless and unprincipled campaign to ride me out of office."

But Keating was hurt by a bad judgment on his own part. He had mocked
Kennedy for a failure to debate and booked a half hour at CBS where he would
show "the symbol of my opponent's ruthless contempt for the people of New
York." Keating vowed to debate an empty chair and "pin his ears back" while
Kennedy answered. However, Kennedy had a stunt planned.

Just as the debate would begin (but not before), Kennedy would show up at the studio and not be let in. When asked for a comment, Keating and his handlers fled the studio, throwing furniture so the reporters could not catch them. One reporter said, "I ran the Keating obstacle course" and newspapers, with photos of Keating debating an empty chair and Kennedy peering in the door, called it "The Great Non-Debate."

**Keating conceding to Bobby Kennedy (surrounded
by Nelson Rockefeller and Jack Javits)
Photo via ebay**

The election was not close and, next to LBJ's re-election, could easily have accounted for the biggest boast of Democrats that year. Kennedy's margin in the city was 710,000 votes—no surprise. But he carried upstate, where Democrats statewide had been accustomed to getting buried. And he only lost Long Island and the suburbs by 61,000 votes. But Keating expressed satisfaction that, having run miles ahead of Barry Goldwater, more New Yorkers split ballots in this race than any other.

Rockefeller called Keating's loss, "a tragedy." Asked whether the carpetbagger charge had hurt Kennedy, Keating replied "it had some effect. It was an issue in the campaign. I would not say the principle issue."

Photo courtesy of the U.S. Government Printing Office

After his defeat, Keating received redemption of sorts from voters. His victory the following year on the New York Court of Appeals was one of the biggest landslides in New York in decades. In 1969, he was appointed Ambassador to India, then was sent to the Middle East as the Israeli Ambassador. While he did suffer from heart problems, his death in 1975 at age 75 was still a surprise.

CHAPTER THIRTY-FOUR

Lonesome Doves:
Morse and Gruening Lone Senate
Tonkin Gulf Opponents

Historic Quote: "Well, Miss Bella. It's like one strawberry said the other strawberry. If we hadn't gone to bed together we wouldn't be in this jam." - Alabama Congressman George Andrews to Bella Abzug in 1971 following the release of the Pentagon Papers on his feelings about being misled on the Vietnam War. This may have been the pre-movie version of "Forrest Gump."

**Morse and Gruening near the end of their storied lives
Photo via Historic Images**

In 1964, only two Senators famously opposed the Tonkin Gulf Resolution that would shortly there after launch America firmly and unstoppably into the Vietnam War.

In terms of background, Oregon's Wayne Morse and Alaska's Ernest Gruening would seem like the last two men to be paired together by history in perpetuity, as both came from very different backgrounds. Morse was a Baptist who grew up in a rural farming family and found Robert LaFollette an inspiration. Gruening was a Jewish kid from Manhattan who studied medicine at Harvard before becoming a reporter.

But by the end of their careers, both were institutions in their respective states and both were surprise second fiddles in 1968 who didn't completely accept voters' verdicts without taking another look back. Most importantly, neither turned back and thus, both were able to see their once lonely positions vindicated well before they died a month apart in 1974, as the terms they would have won were about to end.

Morse was a durable figure in Oregon. He may be the only person in history to serve in the upper chamber as a Republican, Independent, and Democrat.

Morse actually grew up in Lafollette country in Wisconsin, one of ten siblings. The family was very much into Progressivism. Initially educated in a one-room school, he was sent to the Madison school system. By 1928, he had his law degree and moved west. And he would find success there. He became the dean of the University of Oregon Law School at the age of 31, the youngest of anyone at that time in the nation. During the war, he became a labor arbitrator. Benjamin Robert Dore in a piece about Morse noted that "deeply committed to fairness and justice, he was popular with both unions and employees."

Morse won his seat on the first try, in a 1944 Republican primary, by knocking off the incumbent Senator. In the Senate, Morse's gift for oratory became legendary early on. Morse's 22-hour-and-26-minute filibuster protesting the Tideland's Oil designation was the longest at that time and remains second only to Strom Thurmond's in 1957 and by 1962, he was doing it again with the satellite communications bill. Opponents tried to turn this into political hay at election time. His opponent that year, "Sig Unander," sought to make the case that "the taxpayers are paying for Morse's obstructionism" but Morse said that cemented his effectiveness. "Send me back to Washington," he argued, "and I'll do even more talking." The voters agreed and he took 54%, the same showing that he had received six years earlier as Eisenhower was sweeping the state.

Despite his intelligence, Morse's desire to express his strong views did not make him a particularly well-liked Senator. He got along with neither Richard nor Maureen Neuberger, his Democratic Senate colleagues from Oregon. On one occasion in 1955 as the Senate was aiming to adjourn for recess, Morse threatened to read a 27-page education proposal. He probably wasn't on media members' Christmas list as well. He began referring to them as the "American Republican Press" because they had not published a release he had sent out four days earlier.

So it might have struck some as odd that as New York Governor Thomas E. Dewey began faltering in the polls just prior to the crucial 1948 Oregon primary, he turned to Morse for advice. Morse told him to "overcome the impression that he was cold and impersonal and to get out to the crossroads where he could meet the people." Strange words from a man who was something of a loner, an enigma, and a profound annoyance to his colleagues. But for Dewey, it did work. He won the Oregon primary and the Republican nomination.

Morse occasionally found that his tactics could come back to hurt him. In late 1962, Morse opposed a request by a powerful Appropriations cardinal, Michael Kirwan of Ohio, for a zoo in Washington, DC (Morse referred to the project as "a fish hotel" and Morse said "we need it like I need a whale on my farm." Kirwan retaliated by cancelling five projects in Oregon. Morse, who was up for re-election, sought the intervention of Senate leaders and the White House and eventually, three of the five projects were restored.

While Morse was always a Republican, he was also a progressive. In fact, more progressive than many Democrats. Morse was said to have left the Republican Party over Nixon's selection as vice-president. He didn't become a Democrat. He was an Independent and firmly had his seat planted in the middle of the Senate chamber. In 1952, that didn't impact the make-up of the Senate and Morse lost his committee assignments. But in 1954, Republicans had a one-vote margin and it was Morse's call. LBJ, who became Majority Leader, dangled the prospect of a committee assignment (of Morse's choosing), and Morse, who had been stripped when he bolted the GOP, opted for Johnson. By the end of 1955, Morse had become a Democrat.

For a time, it seemed as though Morse could weave together his dream of a muscular Hell's Canyon Dam project with a civil rights bill. Morse had sponsored the Canyon bill but met strong resistance from Senators encompassing many geographic areas of the nation. Meanwhile, Southerners wanted the Civil Rights Act referred to the Judiciary Committee where Chairman James Eastland could weaken or bottle it up as opposed to sending it directly to the Senate floor. Ultimately, the Hells Canyon proposal cleared the Senate 45-38 with Morse being one of six Democrats (the sole non-Westerner being John F. Kennedy) to vote for it. Republicans charged the group with having traded the votes of Southern Democrats on a procedure for the civil rights bill. He called those rumors a "vicious and unwarranted falsehood."

Meanwhile, as 1957 dragged on and the prospect of civil rights legislation was still in a flux, Morse urged the Senate to resist recessing to pursue other matters. The Southern caucus, he reckoned, would use the extra time as a tool to kill the measure. But to Morse, nothing the chamber would consider was as important as civil rights, and putting other matters on the backburner "will not cause this nation to topple." Wen Senators were prepared to get rid of Part III, Morse threatened to oppose the measure altogether. "I cannot reconcile myself to voting for a civil rights bill so narrow and limited in its scope that I fear it will bear naught but a label so far as its practical effect on civil rights is concerned.... Part III of the bill breathes light, substance and liberty for the individual into the 14th and 15th Amendments. It is time that we implement those great Amendments granting equality of rights, in legal theory, to the Negro people of America."

Meanwhile, Morse became a master of civil liberties protection and signed the Declaration of Conscience against Joe McCarthy. In 1960, he briefly sought the Presidential nomination, and Kennedy forces, despite not believing that Morse was a "serious candidate," sent Rose and Ted Kennedy to stump for their son. Civil rights were also a hallmark of his creed. When Kennedy nominated Charles Meriwether to head the Export-Import Bank despite his ties to the KKK, Morse denounced it. The pick, he said, was "a horrendous and inexcusable mistake." He supported a strong United Nations and was solidly pro-Israel, arguing that the U.S. should send a message to the Arab countries that "we are not going to be blackmailed by them any longer."

For the most part, Morse was pro-labor. But that eroded somewhat with his 1966 legislation requiring airline strikers to return to work. The following year, he headed a Presidential Board that mediated a nationwide railroad strike. Not all were pleased by his appointment and *Congressional Quarterly* noted that subsequently, "The International Association of Machinists called for his defeat in 1968."

Fast-forward to the Vietnam authorization. Morse had been bemoaning military involvement in Vietnam as early as 1962, when American military involvement was in its infancy and only faintly conscious in the minds of most Americans. In a speech to the Senate chamber on September 9, 1963, he asserted that "as long as Diem is the head of the government of South Vietnam, we continue to support a tyrant; we continue to support a police-state dictator." He called for "sav(ing) the American people the hundreds upon hundreds of millions of dollars that our government is pouring down that rat hole . . . On the basis of the present policies that prevail there, South Vietnam is not worth the life of a single American boy."

On the Senate floor during the Tonkin debate, Morse asked for two hours of debate. Some think a longer filibuster may have changed more minds. Morse didn't think "the killing of a single American in South Vietnam is a justifiable killing." He said 'the place to settle the controversy is not on the battlefield but around the conference table." He closed with the words, "I am satisfied that history will render a final verdict in opposition to the joint resolution today. "The FBI apparently investigated Morse at the height of the opposition.

Photo courtesy of the U.S. Senate Historical Office

Shortly after the 1966 midterm elections in a speech at Duke University, Morse was asked about the impact immediate withdrawal would have on America's economy to which he replied, "There would be no negative effect. Our country does not have to operate under a war economy to be prosperous. For many years now we have been living under a defense economy anyway—not a free one." Next came a question about Johnson's motives with respect to the war to which he replied, "I think the President is sincere but I don't really see how he could go about achieving those ends in a worse fashion."

Morse had once said "Lyndon Johnson represents Lyndon Johnson." Yet when Johnson announced his surprise retirement in 1968, Morse was in the room with Humphrey and, nearly in tears, called it a "sad day." Merle Miller in the book *Lyndon* called Morse a "sorehead and a malcontent."

As Morse continued his crusade against the war, more and more Senators saw his side. But he wouldn't be there much longer to say I told you so. He was beaten by a State Representative named Bob Packwood. Though the two debated aggressively, Morse did not go hard after Packwood. The debate was telecast live in Portland, and those viewing it saw the 36-year-old Packwood clearly get the best of the four-term, 68-year-old incumbent. Perhaps that was a mistake. Packwood's 3,500-vote win was not affirmed for weeks.

In an election that close, anything could have made the difference. But it was said that loyalists of Democratic ex-Congressman Robert Duncan had either voted for Packwood or simply not voted at all. Duncan was the standard bearer against Mark Hatfield in 1966, but Morse backed the Republican over Vietnam.

Morse and Mark Hatfield had a tremendous relationship and, despite being separated by party (hardly at all by philosophy), displayed genuine public affection for one another. Hatfield as a State Senator had said Eisenhower should pick Morse as his running-mate in 1952. When Morse came up for re-election two years later, Hatfield clearly wanted to return the favor to his colleague, particularly since Packwood (whom Morse had once taught, similar to Morse's having taught his fellow Democratic colleague, Richard Neuberger) supported the war. But one article noted that Hatfield was dismissive of his fellow Republican's chances, so in the interest of party unity and not wanting to anger a base that already found him to be an anathema, Hatfield did unity events for Packwood.

Did that factor in to Morse's decision to challenge Hatfield? Maybe not. It's likely that he simply wanted back in the game. And ironically, Morse would beat Duncan in the primary, who this time vowed to assist him in the general.

At any rate, Morse saw a six-percent deficit in the polls climb back to 20% by the end of the summer. *The Eugene Register* wrote, "Morse constantly expresses his support for George McGovern in contrast to Hatfield, who downplays his support of Richard Nixon." Indeed, Oregon was changing and McGovern had feint hopes of taking the state. But Hatfield ultimately prevailed 54-46%.

But Morse needed one last hurrah, which came in 1974. Morse had managed to win the 1974 Senate nomination to take on Packwood in a spirited primary that focused on his age. But two months later, he was hospitalized. He was dead days later of kidney failure at age 73.

Bill Fulbright writes in his book *The Price of Empire* that Morse "was suspicious and he was willing as few individuals are, to be aggressive and abrasive to his colleagues on to President's when he believed the people's interests require it." Fulbright also called him "a great debater, a gifted practitioner of an art form now in decline—and he retained an old-fashioned faith in government and the place for that discussion was on the Senate floor."

Ernest Gruening (1887-1974)

Gruening's time in the Senate was foreordained to be short, not only because Alaska did not become a state until 1959, but also because he was 72 at the time he became a Senator. But he had actually been on his state's political scene even longer than Morse in Oregon, and was Alaska's patrician.

But he was only a natural as a Senator because he had already given a lifetime of service to Alaska as a territory. He was its territorial Governor for 14 years, from 1937 to 1951, and stayed there even when his term ended. His was a case of an Easterner migrating out to the Last Frontier. But he was intrigued with Alaska becoming a state and was determined to see it through, so much so that he became "Mr. Alaska." Gruening's background is colorful. Jewish, he was a medical student, editor of *The Boston American*, followed by copyeditor for *The Boston Evening Herald*. He later became editor of *The Nation*.

Indeed, Gruening had achieved some degree of fame as early as 1918 when *The New York Times* profiled him and he had a number of posts for the territory under FDR. He began lobbying for statehood in 1954 and created a flag with 50 stars.

Gruening easily won a Senate seat when Alaska entered the union. He drew straws with his Senate colleague Bob Bartlett and Gruening, ending with the long straw, won the four-year term. He immediately went to work for his infant state.

First came the Alaska Omnibus Act which authorized infrastructure for the state. He sponsored tax deductions for mineral expenses and money for the Rampart Dam Study Project. Gruening's 1962 opponent was Ted Stevens who at the time was winding down a stint as U.S. Attorney. Stevens made no secret of his apparent personal disdain for Gruening. He stressed Gruening's age (75) and his view that Gruening took different stands on issues of the day ("Which Gruening will you vote for," he asked)? But his rhetoric grew even more personal. Gruening, he said, was a "cantankerous old man" who had "back-biting techniques" and "insatiable appetite for personal publicity." Gruening shunned Stevens' call to debate because "there was nothing to debate with one who has so little experience in Alaska affairs." Gruening held off Stevens 58-41%.

Photo courtesy of the John F. Kennedy Presidential Library and Museum

Despite Gruening's deep minority status when it came to the Vietnam War, he nonetheless tried to push through creative techniques aimed at minimizing it. He constantly opposed Appropriations that would fund the operation and in 1967, sponsored legislation that would effectively render the draft moot by prohibiting draftees from being sent to the region.

By 1968, Gruening faced a challenge from within, not because of Vietnam but because of his age. Mike Gravel even said age was the only reason he took on Gruening. It didn't hurt that *The New York Times* referred to Gravel as a "dark, good-looking, 38-year-old challenger." Gravel had done a documentary about his life which may have cost as much as $1,000 a week before the primary. It aired all over Alaska (it was not called the "Undefeated"). He carried Juneau where Gruening lived and ran barely behind in Fairbanks, which the *Times* said was "considered to be a Gruening strong hold." Gruening at first said he was "not prepared to admit defeat" but conceded a few days later, 2,000 votes behind. Gravel called him "more in the American thought on Vietnam." Gruening remained in the race by launching a write-in bid for the seat and did garner an impressive 18%. But it was nowhere near enough.

Photo courtesy of the National Park Service

Gruening's grandson Clark returned the favor, ousting Gravel in the 1980 primary. In the fall, he seemed to be leading but lost the general election to Frank Murkowski.

But he continued his crusade. "The mess in Vietnam was inherited by President Johnson." That holds true for President Nixon today; he is under no more obligation than was President Johnson to perpetuate his predecessor's policies.

In 1970, about a year and a half after Morse and Gruening had left the Senate, they sat down separately for interviews, which were reproduced by Google as they appeared in *The Toledo Blade*. Both remained in Washington, Morse residing at the Watergate ironically enough. Despite their advancing ages, both maintained a vigorous speaking schedule and Gruening returned to the helm of *The Nation*. When asked why Congress gave LBJ the authorization, Morse said "because they were gutless wonders. That's why. They told me, 'Don't commit political suicide, Wayne. They were politically afraid. The doves cooed a good game but they didn't vote the way they thought." Gruening called "some of the so called doves sympathetic but a majority of the Congress were simply hawks who swallowed the idea that we must stop communism everywhere . . . The mood then was that papa knew best, that we didn't have information the President had."

Gruening, who spent most of his retirement working on his autobiography, was a little more charitable, calling one of "the glories of the Senate . . . that you can disagree with your colleagues without a loss of respect or cordiality. No one minds if you vote alone."

Overpopulation continued to be a top Gruening concern. In the Senate, he had sponsored the Presidential Commission on Population. His death in 1974 of cancer at age 87 was nonetheless unexpected. He had been on the lecture circuit five weeks before his death. At that time, Morse saluted his comrade as having "personified complete honesty and courage as a public official and private citizen." In little more than a month, he would be gone as well.

Ernest Gruening statue
Photo via Alaska Public

In 1964, only two Senators would famously oppose voted the Tonkin Gulf Resolution that would shortly thereafter, launch America firmly and unstoppably into the Vietnam War.

Background wise, Oregon's Wayne Morse and Alaska's Ernest Gruening would seem like the last two men to be paired together by history in perpetuity, as both came from very different backgrounds. Morse was a Baptist who grew up in a rural farming family and found Robert LaFollette an inspiration. Gruening was a Jewish kid from Manhattan who studied medicine at Harvard before becoming a reporter.

But by the end of their careers, both were institutions in their respective states and both were surprise second fiddles in 1968 who didn't completely accept the voter's verdicts without taking another look back. Most importantly, neither turned back and thus, were able to see their once lonely positions vindicated well before they died a month apart in 1974, as the terms they would have won were about to end.

CHAPTER THIRTY-FIVE

Gaylord Nelson:
Senator, Idealist, And Legend of Earth Day

Historic Tidbit: "Jesus, Christ, you're skinny!" "Jesus, Christ, you're not a General!" The first line was future Governor/Senator Gaylord Nelson upon being reunited with Carrie Lee Dotson at Okinawa. They had dated several times at Fort Indiantown Gap, Pennsylvania and Dotson was self-conscious about her weight. The second was Carrie's reaction when, contrary to what Gaylord had told her, he was a Captain in the Army and not a General. Old acquaintanes were soon forgot. Gaylord and Carrie Lee married after the war and enjoyed 58 years of bliss. Their war story was featured in Tom Brokaw's *The Gretest Generation.*

Photo via the Wisconsin State Historical Society

In April, millions of Americans observe "Earth Day," a commemoration of the natural beauty, the outdoors, and environmental treasures so often taken for granted. And with it, hopefully, introspection on how to do better. But how did "Earth Day" come to be? The idea itself actually came about on a plane but its inception was in the air (pun intended) long before. And the man of the hour in that regard was Gaylord Nelson, then a U.S. Senator and prior to that, Wisconsin's Governor, whose conservation mentality characterized his thinking from boyhood to death.

Nelson was a boy of the Wisconsin Wilderness: the little town of Clear Lake. He recalled with fondness the "magically mysterious" land and, according to his official biography on nelsonearthday.net, when the timber industry "wiped it out in an eyewink of history and left behind fifty years of heartbreak and economic ruin." For years, Nelson was frustrated by the intractability of gaining steam on environmental matters. Almost no pol - from President to colleague - would heed his thoughts for a national policy. That may explain in part why, at cocktail parties, he was known do one arm push-ups or rip apart a phone book.

Nelson's eureka moment came while flying back to Wisconsin following a tour of a devastating California oil spill. He was reading a magazine about "teach-ins" on the subject and before long began promoting the idea of an Earth Day during speeches to environmental and university groups alike. By the end of the year, planning was in the works for such an event. The date of April 22nd was chosen, according to his biography, "to fit best in college schedules between spring break and final exams." Nelsonearthday.net goes on to say that nearly every major news magazine (*Time, Life, Look*, etc.) produced an environmental-themed issue in anticipation of the event. The result was a bigger success than Nelson could have envisioned. Twenty-million people from coast to coast took part. People suggested an annual role in its planning but he demurred. He thought the idea could flourish more at the grass-roots level rather than in the hands of the federal bureaucracy.

Image via the Wisconsin State Historical Society

Who was Gaylord Nelson? For starters, he was one of the most principled public servants of the 20th century and one whose promotion of liberal causes was far from limited to the environmental movement. He advocated a five-cent tax increase to finance the "War on Poverty." And his story was such that the pre-marital romance of Nelson and his future bride, Carrie Lee Dotson, encompassed a chapter of Tom Brokaw's iconic book, *The Greatest Generation.*

Though Nelson was never anything but a reliable liberal, his background was fairly affluent. His father was a doctor who was well-known in Clear Lake. Nelson's first foray into politics was as a youth, when he organized a tree planting campaign on roads going into Clear Lake. But first, it was acquiring a law degree from the University of Wisconsin and joining the Army. It was then that he met Carrie Lee Dotson who, as Brokaw observes, "grew up in markedly different circumstances" (her widowed mother in poor Wise County, Virginia was forced to house she and her two brothers in a home). The scene was Fort Indiantown Gap, Pennsylvania.

Gaylord was in training as a soldier and Carrie Lee was in training to become a nurse when a friend convinced her to join a few couples on a date. Gaylord would be Carrie's partner. The date went well but not phenomenal (Carrie joked to Gaylord about his name). Still, the impression was strong enough that the next day, he called her and they continued to date until Nelson left for the war (Brokaw writes that because Nelson said he never even sent letters to his mother, Carrie never expected to see him again). That is when something akin to a Hollywood movie plot took place.

In time, Nelson was sent to Okinawa. Carrie eventually made it there as well, having attended Officer's Training School within the U.S. Army Nurse's Corp. Her mission in Japan was to help relieve the medical technicians in the hospital. She was one of only four women. But when arriving and getting off the boat, the Sergeant checking her in recognized her. "Weren't you at the Indiantown Gap," he asked. When she responded yes, he asked, "Didn't you go out with Nelson?" The Sergeant told her Nelson was on the boat. They reunited and started a courtship that was so successful that Gaylord extended his stay, not wanting to leave without her. They married stateside in 1947 and had two sons and a daughter.

After World War II, Nelson sought a seat in the legislature. He lost that race but won the next and was soon entrusted by his colleagues with the position of floor leader. He was ardently pro-civil rights, having led an all-black squadron in World War II and fought for abolishment of Jim Crow as well as for the integration of the Wisconsin National Guard. During that time, Nelson also co-chaired the state party which was badly in need of revitalization. It gave him many chips, which by 1958 he was ready to cash in as he embarked on a bid to become the first Governor from the northern part of Wisconsin.

In a state that revered LaFollette (and apparently still does - a descendant continues to serve as Secretary of State), Nelson made LaFollette a prominent part of his stump, saying he wanted to return to "the philosophy and the purpose of the

Wisconsin Idea as Old Bob LaFollette envisioned it." Nelson wound up beating incumbent Vernon Thompson. Why was LaFollette such a presence for Nelson? Because the iconic Wisconsin Senator and prototype for political reform had an impact on his boyhood. One day, Nelson's father took him to a LaFollette rally, afterwhich he asked his son if he'd one day like to be President. Nelson replied he'd love to but "I'm afraid that Bob La Follette will solve all of our problems before I get a chance to serve." The website wilderness.net noted how his father gave him a startling reminder of his earlier words when Gaylord was about to except the Democratic nomination for Governor in 1958. His father suffered a heart attack and Nelson recalled entering his hospital room. "He looked up and smiled and he said, 'Do you think Bob La Follette left enough problems behind for you to solve?' He had never mentioned it for 32 years."

To be sure, Nelson's impact as Wisconsin's Governor far exceeded conservation. He created a student-loan program and outlawed contracting by race/religion. But he was nevertheless known as the "Conservation Governor" which would far and away be his defining legacy. As Nelson's biographer writes, "Wisconsin favored the traditionally male sports of fishing and hunting, while doing little for parks used by whole families." He set out to change that real fast.

Nelson proposed $50 million for the "Outdoor Recreation Action Program" (ORAP), an ambitious plan that would transform the conservation movement in Wisconsin. To name a few of its lasting impacts, it cracked down on polluters and created new lakes in the southwestern part of the state as well as urban parks, youth conservation camps, local water treatment plants, and "green jobs for the unemployed." In addition, a penny-a-pack tax increase on cigarettes went toward the funding of open space. As Nelson biographer Bill Christofferson writes in *The Man from Clear Lake*, passing ORAP was not easy. The Republicans controlled the legislature and the proposal's popularity was so high that the GOP feared Nelson would get the credit. One Democrat's contention that "the only problem with this bill is that Governor Gaylord Nelson introduced it" was contradicted by neither Nelson nor the Republicans. At the end of the day, passage may have been accidental. The final tally showed ten Republicans joined in but it was the conversion of Leo O'Brien, whom GOP leaders had expected until the last moment (including in caucus) to vote with them, that sealed the deal.

Nelson did not get everything he wanted on the environmental front, however; his plea for a two-dollar sticker for state parks went nowhere. But the overall impact of his was unmistakable for generations to come.

Nelson had reinvigorated the party. He was only Wisconsin's second Democratic Governor in the 20th century, and in 1960 he had managed to become the first since 1891 to win a second term. But by 1962, he wanted to go higher: the U.S. Senate.

But trouble came just as he was preparing to challenge four-term GOP Senator Alexander Wiley, as Nelson and the GOP Senate President (later to become Governor himself) had negotiated the biggest restructuring of Wisconsin's tax system since 1911. Its anchor was a three-cent sales tax increase. All across the state, the slogan was "three cents for Gaylord." Many wanted it repealed but Nelson, even in the heat of an election, refused without saying how it'd be paid for. That's something you don't see every day, especially these days.

Wiley was respected but at age 78 his years were beginning to show. Wylie raised the issue of clout when he was summoned back following the Cuban Missile Crisis but Nelson tied himself to the Kennedy agenda. He unseated Wiley 52-47% and was eventually joined by other Governors (Mark Hatfield and Fritz Hollings) elected in 1958 from disparate states in the Senate.

Asked after the fact what the biggest issue was, Nelson replied "conservation" and continued his crusade, stressing early on the necessity for "a comprehensive and nationwide program to save the national resources of America. Our soil, our water and our air are becoming more polluted every day. Our most priceless natural resources - trees, lakes, rivers, wildlife habitats, scenic landscapes - are being destroyed."

**Smoking a peace pipe and in his Senate committee
Photos via the Wisconsin State Historical Society**

During his tenure, Nelson helped protect the St. Croix River, which was the first Wild and Scenic River in the country. He sponsored the Environmental Education Act and the Apostle Island National Lakeshore. The latter brought Kennedy to the area three months before his assassination. Nelson, along with his close allies, conservationsts Louis and Martin Hanson, were trying to protect the 21 islands and 12 lakeshore miles that are referred to as the "Jewels of Lake Superior" and he convinced Kennedy to take a helicopter tour while visiting the upper-Midwest for a series of speaking engagements. It did not come easily.

Former Nelson aide William Bechtel told a Lake Superior publication how Nelson was irate when Kennedy's itinerary initially excluded Wisconsin. Nelson asked Bechtel to drive him to the White House where he recalls sitting "outside the White House for a long, long time." When Nelson finally returned, Bechtel recalls "All the steam is gone, you see, and then he says, 'By the way, the President wants to come to Ashland.' The President wanted to disarm Nelson, and it had worked." Kennedy said the sailboats reminded him of Hyannis Point. That Kennedy saw it was no accident. Nelson and Hanson had instructed the pilot to fly low. It took seven years for protective status to become law but years later, it became known as the Gaylord Nelson Apostle Islands.

The infamously desultory condition of Lake Erie provided a strong example of Nelson's concerns. "If we want an example of where we are going," he said, "we need only to look at Lake Erie. Some people think it will eventually just fill up. But before it does, life will cease to exist in its waters."

To say Nelson's impact stopped with the environment would be false. It started with his independence and his ethics. In the tradition of a state that produced LaFollete, Nelson wanted to be a Senator from Wisconsin. His only form of income was his Senate salary. And as *The Almanac of American Politics* writes, "those who know him know that he acts solely out of conviction, without posturing." If nothing else, his national brethren were impressed.

Nelson was also the first Senator to join Ernest Gruening and Wayne Morse after the duo had cast their lone votes against the Tonkin Gulf resolution. It was on a 1965 war appropriations bill and in voting against it, Nelson said Johnson telephoned him at home asking for his vote but told him he "needed my vote less than I needed my conscience." Slowly, others followed his lead. But Jeff Nelson said his dad's relationship with Johnson was still strong. "They respected each other, Nelson was still given a tour of the LBJ Ranch and was always welcome to "stag" parties (White House gatherings of Senators and male staff – no women).

Nelson's devotion to liberal causes gave him a national constituency. He was among the people George McGovern offered the number-two slot in 1972 but he quickly declined ("I'm afraid you might win and then I'd be stuck with that damn job as vice president"). He then strenuously recommended the ultimate, albeit temporary choice, a Senate colleague of both men, Tom Eagleton. His "for the people" idealism was replicated by one of his successors, Russ Feingold, who refused to allow staff to attend functions being sponsored by special interests.

Nelson ardently backed civil rights and the "Great Society." But in Nelson's eyes, conservation was a common thread of the needle. "Environment is all of America and its problems. It is rats in the ghetto. It is a hungry child in a land of affluence. It is housing not worthy of the name: neighborhoods not fit to inhabit." Emulating what he tried in Wisconsin, he proposed a five-cent cigarette tax to contribute to his larger goal of conserving the environment.

However, he seemed to reserve much of his scorn for the pharmaceutical industry, and taking on the giants became a cause of Nelson's second in importance only to Earth Day. Indeed, one of his obituaries called him "one of the most astute and far-sighted critics that Big Pharma ever had." The height of the hearing was the "Nelson Pill hearings." Barbara Seaman had approached Nelson about unwelcome side-effects of contraception and he held hearings at once. Ultimately, warning labels were placed on the pill's packaging. Opponents claimed that informing women of the hazards might keep them from using it, thus coining the term "Nelson's Babies." But he persevered and ultimately, warning labels were required to be included with each prescription.

In the process of fighting for these changes, Nelson received criticism for not letting patients testify from some women's-lib activists, many of whom protested and were removed, but those working with Nelson on the issue believed he didn't want to set a precedent by letting those who weren't experts offer their positions.

Nelson (second from right) with Illinois Congressman Marty Russo, President Jimmy Carter, Iowa Senator John Culver and Iowa Congressman Neal Smith Photo courtesy of the John Culver Papers, University of Iowa Libraries, Iowa City, Iowa

But it didn't stop with contraception. The effectiveness of prescription drugs of all kinds was brought before his Monopoly Committee, and volumes as thick as 1,500 pages were printed in the Government Printing Volume, extending to areas such as "the seduction of doctors and medical students through lavish gifts." Tire manufacturers also came into play. He sponsored legislation to ban phosphates and DDT.

On other matters, Nelson's liberalism was almost universal. He was just one of three Senators to vote against Gerald Ford's confirmation and the $700 million

Appropriation that began the Vietnam War. In 1979, he authored language designed to address a Supreme Court decision (Zurcher vs. the Stanford Daily) which upheld the right of police to search newspapers with a subpoena rather than a search warrant. Nelson's language required a subpoena with a warrant to follow if there was reason to suspect illegalities. Searches would be allowed against those not suspected of a crime "within a reasonable time with reasonble effort" of trying to identify it.

In early 1977, Nelson found himself embroiled in a dispute over legislation that would limit the outside speaking fees that Senators can receive. A special Senate committee had been created to issue recommendations for dealing with the question of extra income for Senators. The body had recently voted itself a $12,900 pay increase and many, including Nelson, felt that was enough and wanted to codify the committee's recommendation to limit outside income to 15% of a Senator's $49,000 salary. He was met with angry resistance from, among others, Muskie who had voted against the salary increase. Nelson responded that "When the public loses confidence in public institutions, there is nothing left. That is a very fragile cloak that covers this institution, and we in government are obligated to take whatever actions we can to maintain it and restore it . . . The Senator from Maine voted against the pay raise and then comes here to the chamber with his lament about cutting into his opportunity to travel the country and speak as he pleases.

I do not shed tears for one who takes the posture that he is going to oppose the salary increase and then say, we do not have enough income. It falls on my deaf ear."

Senator Abe Ribicoff, whose Governorship of Connecticut coincided with Nelson's in Wisconsin, credited Nelson's gift for making points about legislation during committee hearings. routinely offered "amendments to improve an essentially good bill – or persuasively points out why another bill is hopelessly flawed and should go no further."

Nelson was an exceptionally well-liked member of the body. Though his closest friends were his fellow Midwesterners and ideological soulmates – McGovern, Eagleton, Hubert Humphrey and Walter Mondale, he was also quite friendly with Republican Congressman Mel Laird who would later become Richard Nixon's Defense Secretary. In fact, when one publication polled the Capitol Hill community asking who was among the best-liked Senator, Nelson topped the list. Carrie Lee was a major factor in that. She threw many parties at their home and was called "the hostess with the mostess." One reason for this: Nelson rarely liked to go out, instead preferring the quiet of his home.

While Nelson's re-election margins were not as high as his senior colleague (and fellow maverick) Bill Proxmire, he still topped 60% in both of his subsequent races. His 1974 opponent, Tom Petri, insinuated that Nelson was trapped in the

Beltway, referring to him on the trail as "the Senator from Maryland" (Petri won a House seat while Nelson was still a Senator, a position he continues to hold today). As Nelson's tenure advanced, he became Chair of the Small Business Committee and had a high-ranking slot on Finance. Going into 1980, Nelson seemed heavily favored for a fourth term but, like so many of his colleagues, he fell victim to the Reagan landslide. Nelson began the evening with a heavy lead but as more and more Republican areas reported, he saw it evaporate. Ex-Congressman Bob Kasten, who had previously lost a bid for Governor in the GOP primary, was not regarded as a serious threat at the beginning of the year. But drug manufacturers and chemical companies filled his coffers, and Nelson was edged out 50-48%.

Nelson was met by a plethora of praise in his final days as Hawaii Democrat Daniel Inouye invoked the "many times in these 18 years (that his) voice has risen above the thicket of special interests and concerbs to sound a clear and strong note of commonsense."

After his defeat, Nelson served as Director of the Wilderness Society and continued to vigorously promote environmental causes. In 1995, President Clinton bestowed on him the Presidential Medal of Honor, calling him "the grandfather of all that grew out of (Earth Day), the Environmental Protection Act, the Clean Air Act, the Safe Drinking Water Act." Nelson died of heart failure at age 89, perhaps appropriately on the day before Independence Day 2005. His legacy lives on with many parks that bear his name in Wisconsin and the nation.

And of course, every April 22nd.

Being awarded the Presidential Medal of Freedom
Photo via the Wisconsin State Historical Society

CHAPTER THIRTY-SIX

Golden Fleece's Dominated Career of a Golden Senator: Proxmire of Wisconsin

Historic Tidbit: After Adlai Stevenson delivered a speech while campaigning for the White House in 1956, a fan approached him. "Governor, your speech was magnificent. You'll get the vote of every thinking person." Stevenson replied, "It's not enough. I need a majority."

I t is not often a United States Senator earns the enmity of, well, everyone. There once was Senator from Wisconsin who was among the most idealistic, altruistic, and constituency-serving. But by taking on over-bloated special interests, sacred cows, and colleagues advancing them in the most public way, William Proxmire became that person. Some say he went overboard. Others say Congress could use 534 more like him. Whatever the opinion, no one disagrees that Proxmire was a force to be reckoned with - and the proof was everywhere.

To the rest of the country, Wisconsin has always had a reputation as a good, responsible-government kind of state, many policies of which were put in place by the LaFollettes. Herb Kohl's slogan was "nobody's Senator but yours." Russ Feingold's famous crusade of campaign-finance reform and his practice of it was to the annoyance of supporters and Democrats alike. Gaylord Nelson wouldn't take any money besides his Senate salary and was fanatical about voting his convictions, no matter how little company he had.

Ralph Nader's ranking of all 535 members of Congress called Proxmire "high voltage . . . enhanced by a strong academic background . . . fiercely independent and willing to criticize." But he was universally liked. He voted idealistically, and undertook lonely, often herculean crusades in the process. But his undertakings were, let's just say, irksome to the powers that be. And yes, many were real powers, in the Senate and beyond.

Proxmire was said to have made this impression on Lyndon Johnson almost as soon as he was sworn in, shortly after he had won a 1957 special to succeed Joe McCarthy when he argued with him on tax breaks for oil companies. If anyone suspected Proxmire would pussyfoot about taking on special interests, his confrontation with Johnson likely diminished that. Johnson had unrequited power and used it to reward allies with committee chairmanships. So when Proxmire not only crossed him in only his second full year in the Senate but did it publicly, members were amazed.

Proxmire had first made his views known in Wisconsin but when this got little recognition, he went national, as in the Senate floor. His criticism had to do with the way party caucus meetings ("What caucus") were carried out. "There has never," Proxmire said, "been a time when power has been so sharply concentrated as it is today in the Senate. The typical Democratic Senator has literally nothing to do with determining the legislative program and policies of the party. Without frequent caucuses, the individual Senator cannot exercise his responsibility to hold the leadership accountable . . . I see no reason why regular caucuses . . . with at least some guidance by the membership, should impede the drive and accomplishments of the leadership." Proxmire contended that "a number of other Senators have indicated to me that they feel the same way about Johnson's power but none of them are anxious to take him on."

Upon winning election to succeed Joe McCarthy
Photo via the Wisconsin State Historical Society

Proxmire's remarks had occurred just after the traditional reading of George Washington's farewell address and one commentator joked that "there had been two farewell addresses on February 23rd—Washington's and Proxmire's." Indeed, senior Senators who had long been close to Johnson came to the Majority Leader's defense with Bob Kerr saying Proxmire "talks too much" and Bill Fulbright taking part as well. Johnson responded by vowing to talk to Proxmire who recalled years later that it was "Lyndon doing all the talking. That was the beginning and end of the meeting."

Proxmire's thorn-in-the-side relationship emerged with Kennedy as President as well. He spoke against his choice of John Connally to become Secretary of the Navy. Ditto for Lawrence O'Connor, the new President's choice for the Federal Power Commission. O'Connor was an ex-President of a prominent Texas Utility company which made Proxmire view the choice as "ethical as brass knuckles." He compared it to "appointing Mickey Mantle to umpiring Yankee baseball games."

With Proxmire not shy about taking on Presidents and Majority Leaders, going after colleagues - even those with power - was pocket change. At least that's what Washington State's Senators would find out. In the early 1970s, Proxmire led a surprisingly successful long-term quest to cancel funding for Boeing's Supersonic Transport (SST) which would be based in the Seattle area. Proxmire brought Ernest Fitzgerald before the committee to defend Lockheed's costs. The matter culminated with Fitzgerald being forced to acknowledge cost overruns and getting fired.

It goes without saying that Proxmire was a different kind of Senator - sitting and standing. In fact, he stood for a lot but not at his desk. He often stood while working. He did 50 push-ups a day, jogged four miles in the morning, attended and addressed the Senate every day the body was in session, many times to promote the Genocide Treaty. He authored an exercise book: *You Can Do It: SenatorProxmire's Exercise, Diet and Relaxation Plan*. And he boasted of his hair transplant, the first member of Congress to have one. That would've been enough to provide Proxmire the kind of automatic publicity politicians dream of. But he got in another way: the hard way. The Wisconsin way, if you will.

Campaigning for re-election
Photo via the Wisconsin State Historical Society

Proxmire was a CPA and he thought the folks in charge of government should run it as accountants would. That said, efficiency was his major theme. Not a surprise for someone who was sworn in, according to his biographer, Jay Sykes, with "a borrowed tie and the shirt he had worn on Election Day." And so he took the efficiency idea to new levels. Every month beginning in 1975, Proxmire issued his "Golden Fleece" awards for what he branded as government waste. They became famous, feared, and anxiously awaited. And there were many—168 in 13 years.

The first recipient of "Golden Fleece" went to the National Science Foundation on why people fall in love. The Federal Aviation Administration felt Mr. Proxmire's wrath in perhaps the most famous fleece, for spending $57,800 on a study of the physical measurements of 432 airline stewardesses, paying special attention to the "length of the buttocks" and how their knees were arranged when they were seated.

Before Sarah Palin raised the issue of the "Bridge to Nowhere," Proxmire was doing the same. Another fleece singled out the Federal Highway administration for charging taxpayers $28 million to pay for "unused and unneeded" roads and bridges in Illinois, Iowa, Kansas, and Nebraska (you'll notice Wisconsin wasn't on that list).

Other famous "Golden Fleece Awards:" a $98,000 contract to study a volunteer army. One was to Congress for "living off the hog while much of the rest of the country is suffering from economic disaster." On another occasion, he went after the Office of Personnel Management and Budget for "sending out duplicate surveys asking top federal employees how they like their jobs" in the amount of $126,000.

It didn't stop with Washington. He singled out Mississippi River officials for taking advantage of a 1909 law that allowed fixing of existing locks by building new ones. He clipped Medicaid for "footing the bill for cutting toenails," which cost $45 million.

Some Fleeces, such as the $600,000 the Air Force spent "to operate a posh" public plane while transporting officials, may have been deserved but others, such as one for the Army "for letting former service members slip away with over $155 million in unpaid bills" may have been unfair given their service to the country.

Always Working
Photo courtesy of Tony Palmieri

But his aggressiveness did have its critics even among those who favored spending limits, and it went beyond Washington. Robert Irion wrote a piece, "What Proxmire's Golden Fleece did for—and to—Science," noting how the negative publicity caused "a slow death" of the research of a study of "why rats, monkeys, and humans clench their jaws." At one point, Proxmire subjected himself to a libel lawsuit that went all the way to the Supreme Court - and sought $8 million. The court ruled against Proxmire and the suit was settled.

One would think that Robert Byrd, the Democratic Leader throughout much of Proxmire's awards who likely was the author of some of these appropriations, would've been turned off, and he may have been. But he praised Proxmire, calling them "as much a part the Senate as quorum calls and filibusters."

Nelson often opposed Senators with a smile. Often, his votes weren't critical. But Proxmire was different. When he became Chairman of the Banking Committee in 1975, the financial community was scared. Colleagues were as well, particularly those from states where the times required dependency from the government, such as New York and Michigan. Proxmire did back the New York City aid package and Chrysler bailout, but with very strict conditions for payback. That was his mantra. The one place Proxmire drew the line with cuts was with dairy subsidies.

Photos via the Wisconsin State Historical Society

With Lockheed, it was different. Proxmire had already held up the aid package in committee, and then thrust Fitzgerald before the committee.

Proxmire's reputation was so established that he was seriously toying with a White House bid even before launching "Golden Fleece." Conceding that he'd be "about as dark a horse as you could find," he added, "we ought to have one candidate who's concerned with excessive and wasteful spending." There were even "Prox for Prez" buttons going around. Proxmire did test the waters and *The New York Times* reported that he had lined up $100,000 in pledges. But Proxmire pulled the plug, blaming in part the difficulty of "holding down government spending to a Democratic electorate" with unemployment so high. He likely would've become lost in a 15-person field that included many far-better known colleagues from the Mid-West alone. But Proxmire's failure to launch nationwide didn't deter his missions at home, often to the consternation of the officeholders in his own state.

Proxmire wasn't always an advocate of social spending, which, as *The Almanac of American Politics* pointed out, angered Milwaukee's Democratic Mayor. Proxmire's penchant for frugality extended to his own constituency. Congress was fully prepared to fund a river clean-up but Proxmire objected. Critics thereafter dubbed it "Lake Proxmire." Rarely do home-state Senators do this but New Mexico's Pete Domenici emulated Proxmire once by publicly speaking out against a widely supported project in New Mexico. But Proxmire spread the wrath evenly. He opposed the Reagan tax cuts and promoted tight budgeting. This often meant an "A" rating from the National Taxpayers Union. With two very different styles when it came to serving their constituency, one could imagine Proxmire and Nelson were at odds. In fact, it was not like that at all. They were not best friends but were far from competitors.

On social issues, Proxmire was fairly liberal but not universally so. He ardently backed Civil Rights but did support restrictions on abortion and a cap on food stamps. For Proxmire, winning the Senate seat was redemption. He had aimed for the Governorship three times in a row and was beaten. His victory was undoubtedly made sweeter by beating the man who twice denied him the Governorship, William Kohler.

For Wisconsin Democrats, it was a clear repudiation of McCarthyism. That Proxmire succeeded McCarthy in the Senate when he died in 1957 was felt as a revival of the Democratic Party in Wisconsin, completed a year later by Gaylord Nelson (his future colleague) capturing the Governorship. His margin was 56%.

They say that you can't please all of the people all of the time. But if that's true, Wisconsinites proved the expression wrong. After an initial scare in 1964, he made his love affair with Wisconsin well known. When Congress wasn't in session, he cultivated voters with intense retail politicking. He greeted voters with an outstretched arm at every opportunity. This occurred to such an extent that one tale began circulating around Washington that Proxmire once outstretched his arm to a man and performed the usual delivery. "Hi, I'm Bill Proxmire, I'm your United States Senator," to which the man replied, "Yes I know, I'm your brother-in-law."

Additionally, Proxmire never spent more than $200 on campaigns, and most of that was for postage. But it's not like he needed the money. Most of his re-elections were anti-climactic and he'd often exceed 70% and carry every county. In 1982, he beat Scott McCollum (who'd succeed to the Governorship when Tommy Thompson joined Bush's cabinet) 64-34%.

It would be interesting to see how Proxmire would feel about earmarks. On fiscal issues, he'd probably be an ideological soul-mate of Oklahoma's Tom Coburn, arguably the biggest spendthrift in Congress today, though Proxmire wouldn't likely take it to that extreme.

Proxmire opted against seeking a 6th full term in 1988 at age 73 (his age was a major reason he cited for his departure) but stayed in Washington. Some asked for permission to continue using the "Golden Fleece" logo but Proxmire said he might continue pursuing it in his retirement. He contracted Alzheimer's and died at age 90 in 2005.

PART III

Capitol Hill Figures With Legendary Reputations

CHAPTER THIRTY-SEVEN

After Thurmond, Green and Hayden
Oldest Serving Senators

Historic Quote: "No other man has had the distinction of serving this long in Congress, and I venture to say it will be a long time before another does." – Strom Thurmond on the retirement of Senator Carl Hayden. Thurmond of course would serve 48 years in the upper chamber and retire shortly after observing his 100th birthday.

**Life's Bill Walker captured the two most senior Senators with LBJ
Photo via Getty Images**

As everyone who is even remotely familiar with the Senate knows, the oldest ever serving Senator was Strom Thurmond who was in office until one month past his 100th birthday. As old as Senate standards are, it's highly unlikely that anyone will surpass this nor is it clear that anyone would want to. But there were two individuals who left office in the 1960s who served to the ripe old ages of 91 and 93—and Theodore Green of Rhode Island and Carl Hayden of Arizona had storied careers that deserve remembering.

Green's 1932 election as Governor had broken a Republican jinx, which Green himself had fallen victim to twice, in 1912 and 1930. The GOP had held the office for all but four of the past 28 years (strangely enough, the same is true today in a state that is far more Democratic than the days of yore). But Rhode Island (along with Massachusetts) was one of two northern states that had rejected Herbert Hoover in 1928, and at the height of the Depression, the state needed relief. Green gave it to them.

When he defeated incumbent Senator Jesse Metcalf in 1936, the Democratic bench in the Ocean State was deep, which would cause other ambitious figures to feel shut out in normal times. After all, their reasoning would be, how often do Senate seats open up in Rhode Island? But much of the competition demurred, figuring that with Green assuming office at age 69, another vacancy would arise in the not-too-distant future. Little could they have realized that Green would serve four six-year terms.

Green's margin over incumbent Metcalf was just 48.6-44.4% (7% went to an Independent). His next three elections prove remarkably stable (58% in 1942 and 59% in 1948 and 1954). His last opponent, Walter Sundlun, was the father of Bruce, who captured Rhode Island's Governorship as a Democrat in 1990.

In time, Green ascended to the chairmanship of the Senate Foreign Relations Committee. By the mid-1950s, his hearing and vision were issues, though his energy was not. In 1955, at age 88, he travelled to Israel. Yet as age took its toll, LBJ as Senate Majority Leader resisted calls to have him replaced, though Green did voluntarily yield his chairmanship to Bill Fulbright in 1959.

Green was close with Johnson and supported him for Minority Leader in 1953. But he was not an automatic vote. Green felt that a Southerner should hold the post and Green was friendly with Georgia's Dick Russell. Despite their obvious differences on Civil Rights and in their backgrounds (Green was a millionaire, Russell a Southern farmer), Green was prepared to support him. Indeed, but when Russell made clear that he didn't want the post he consulted carefully with him about who should get it.

With President Truman (left) and Senator Mike Mansfield in Burma (right)
Left photo courtesy of the Rhode Island Secretary of State; Right photo
courtesy of the Library of Congress Prints and Photographs Division

Green in fact was close with all of the Presidents, so much so that he was called "the President's Man." He was a staunch New Dealer and Rooseveltie, even backing his Supreme Court packing plan. But he was also an advocate of a strong defense.

Green was a bachelor who swam in the Senate pool daily. And he was a major fixture on the Washington social scene. Paul Boller in *Congressional Anecdotes* recounts a tale of a woman asking Green at one such event how many parties he was at that night. Green replied "four." Then, noticing a little black book, the woman asked Green if it was to tell Green where he was going next. He replied no. It's "to tell me where I am now."

Photo courtesy of Ray Hill's Personal Collection

Some actually felt that Green could have won another term in 1960 had he wanted one, and as it turns out, he would have served most of it. He lived 5 1/2 years after his retirement, passing away in 1966 at age 98. The airport in Providence bears his name.

Hayden (1877-1972)

A 40 year quest came to fruition
Photo courtesy of the University of Arizona Special Collections

If there was a "Grand Canyon" of Grand Canyon State politics, Carl Hayden was unquestionably it. Hayden, a local newspaper wrote, "more than any other man, created what America knows today as Arizona."

Until Robert Byrd, and more recently John Dingell who passed him in the past few years, Carl Hayden had served in the Congress longer than anyone else. When he left office following the completion of his seventh Senate term in 1969, he had been serving Arizona every day since it had achieved statehood nearly 57 years earlier. That meant his service began under Taft and ended just before Nixon took office. His longevity made him President Pro-Tem, which put him third in line for the Presidency when President Kennedy was assassinated.

Hayden was born in 1877, 35 years before Arizona became a state in what was then, appropriately enough, Hayden's Ferry. He served on the Tempe Town Council and eventually become Sheriff of Maricopa County, better known today as Phoenix (oh, would he have his hands full a century later). When Arizona became a state he won his House seat by beating a man from Tombstone near the southern border, which shows how few people inhabited Arizona at that time.

Photo courtesy of the Library of Congress Prints and Photographs Division

Throughout his long tenure in Congress, Hayden's crowning achievement was a career-long Central Arizona Project quest, a 21-year effort that culminated in a $1 billion 336-mile-long creation that brought water from the Colorado River through tunnels and dams to remote parts of Arizona. Other projects included the Coulee Mountain, Glen Canyon Dam, and the Kitt Peak National Observatory.

But while Hayden wielded a big stick, he spoke softly. He was known as the "Silent Senator." When he had to talk, his speeches were very brief (about five minutes). The cloakroom was more his style. His 14-year chairmanship of Appropriations was an automatic mechanism for making his voice boom, often without saying a word. His reasoning: "When you've got the votes, you don't have to talk." As such, LBJ called him the "third Senator from every State." A school kid once answered a question on an exam by noting three branches of government: "the Executive, the Judicial, and Carl Hayden."

For much of his long career, however, Hayden voted in the Arizona Pinto (conservative) tradition. He backed Prohibition and opposed bonuses for World War I veterans, which nearly cost him his first re-election to the Senate in 1932. He did sponsor Depression-era legislation (the Hayden-Cartwright Act) to provide matching funds to states for highway construction. And he was an early opponent, well before World War II broke out, of cuts to military budgets. Despite being around long enough to have voted for the Social Security Act in 1935, he did not initially back Medicare, though he ultimately supported its final passage in 1965.

For the longest time, Hayden was also very lukewarm on Civil Rights, refusing to repeal the poll tax in the 1940s. But when it came up in 1964, times had changed. LBJ persuaded Hayden to back the bill but Hayden was reticent to vote for closure, which he had never done since a filibuster was how Arizona had achieved statehood. However, Hayden promised LBJ that if his vote were necessary, he would provide it.

As it became clear that the bill had enough votes (Delaware's John Williams cast the 67th), Mike Mansfield walked over to Hayden and said, "It's okay Carl. We don't need you." But Hayden backed the bill itself as well as the Voting Rights Act the following year.

Hayden (top right) as Senate President Pro-Tem, 11/27/63
Photo courtesy of the Lyndon B. Johnson Presidential Library

Interestingly, it was Hayden who was the House sponsor of the 19th Amendment, which gave women the right to vote though he did have reservations about the Equal Rights Act. During the Depression, he sponsored the Hayden-Cartwright Act which would provide matching funds to states as a way to put people back to work.

Hayden was all about Arizona. Mo Udall wrote in the Congressional Record after Hayden's death that "he grew up with a nation, and particularly a West, that needed building and he set out to help build it." In his obituary, The New York Times wrote that FDR had questioned why Hayden always wanted to talk about roads in their meetings. Hayden replied "because Arizona has two things people will drive thousands of miles to see; The Grand Canyon and the Petrified Forest. They can't get there without roads." Hayden would know. He had after all sponsored the bill making the Grand Canyon a national park.

But it was the Central Arizona Project that defined Hayden. Water was literally an issue from the beginning of his tenure, and many times he was taking on the much mightier California delegation. A six-week filibuster he had taken part in as early as 1928 was about Western water rights, as Hayden resisted the building of the Boulder Canyon. When passage was inevitable, he tried to extract concessions.

During his final re-election campaign for a six-year term, Hayden's age was a minor issue but in the days when Arizona was still a small state, his pet issue was far bigger. He beat Evan Mecham (who would later become Arizona's Governor and get himself impeached) by 36,000 votes, a relatively modest 55-45%. He did not vote and delivered his victory speech from Bethesda Naval Hospital. He promptly went back to work on the bill, which passed on September 30, 1968, just months before Hayden was set to leave office—at which time LBJ proclaimed it "Carl Hayden Day." Upon its passage, Hayden said tgat his "efforts on behalf of the Central Arizona Project began while I was still a Congressman and I consider it . . . the most significant accomplishment of my career." And, one might add, the careers of others.

Roy Elson, Hayden's "right hand man" who himself came within an eyelash of winning a senate seat in 1964, told the Arizona Republic that he "spent half my life working on that damn thing," adding that "it turned out to be the biggest reclamation project, probably, in the history of the country."

Elson was also utilized on Appropriations. Ex-Senator Dennis DeConcini, the only Democrat from Arizona to make it to the Senate since Hayden, called Elson "sort of [Hayden's] arms and legs and muscleman" on Appropriations, noting that age had limited Hayden's abilities.

Many politicians have used the term "workhorses" as opposed to "show horses" but it appears that Hayden was the one who made it famous. He had given a long speech to the House in his first few weeks in office and another member had given him advice. He seemed to imply as much to JFK when, as a freshman in 1953, he asked Hayden what changes he'd seen. The then 40-year veteran replied, "In those days, freshmen didn't talk."

Hayden had another rule. To "make no personal attacks on any opponent, Republican or Democrat. To do so is a confession that your own position is weak. Many people resent it and call it mudslinging." He got along well with all sides and brought a team of rivals together. When he died, LBJ and Goldwater, one-time opponents, eulogized him. Upon his death, *The New York Times* continued its accolades, calling Hayden "the most inconspicuous of Senators, and one of the most powerful."

Like Green, Hayden was also urged by some to stay on when his seventh term ended in 1968, but he replied that "contemporary times demand contemporary men." He retired to his beloved Arizona and lived for three more years, to age 94.

Kennedy once said that "every Federal program which has contributed to the development of the West—irrigation, power, reclamation—bears his mark, and the great Federal highway program which binds this country, together, which permits this State to be competitive east and west, north and south, this in large measure is his creation."

CHAPTER THIRTY-EIGHT

Javits and Case, Senate's Last Rockefeller Republicans, Unseated In GOP Primaries

Historic Tidbit: The name of G. Gordon Liddy is synonymous with Watergate – it will forever go down in history as one of the Watergate burglars but, like everything, there is a story to how he began the path toward notoriety in Washington D.C. It dates back to the office of U.S. Senator Jacob Javits in 1969. Liddy had just come off an unsuccessful bid to win a Congressional seat from Westchester County – he lost the primary to Hamilton Fish, Jr. Frank Cummings was the top attorney on Javits's staff and he was tasked with interviewing and recommending clearance to individuals from New York seeking positions with the federal government (in Liddy's case, it was as an AFT agent in the Department of Treasury). Cummings asked Liddy about three investigative techniques —wiretapping, bugging, and breaking & entering. His answer was essentially that it never should be done without a court order. Looking back, Cummings said Liddy gave the correct answer and recommended him for the position, but expressed sadness that he didn't follow those principles for the duration of his career.

Jacob Javits (left), photo courtesy of the U.S. Senate Historical Office and Clifford Case, right, photo courtesy of Rutgers University

Richard Lugar's primary defeat in Indiana in 2012 marked another addition to the list of many moderate-to-liberal Republicans who have fallen victim over the years to the changing guard within the party.

George Norris, who as Nebraska's Governor and later Senator championed an abundance of reforms that made him a national hero to progressives, was ousted in the state as far back as a 1942 primary. Tom Kuchel's loss to Max Rafferty in California was overshadowed by Bobby Kennedy's assassination that same night. But two other Republican Mid-Atlanticites were also unseated in primaries in the years to come, and they were literally the last two men with direct ties to the once vibrant "Rockefeller Republicanism" in the upper chamber.

The term "Rockefeller Republicans" is now a cliché, but not too long ago, it flourished. The last two men of that era in the Senate were Jacob Javits of New York and Clifford Case of New Jersey - 70-something liberals who had served 24 years before falling to hard-charging conservatives almost no one took seriously at first. Both Case and Javits, whose 1980 defeat had been preceded by Case's two years earlier, were a distinct out-in-the-cold minority within their parties. And for most of their tenures, they were the pride and joy to almost all of their constituents: Democrats, Independents, labor, moderates, minorities, Jews. All except conservatives. For a time, that didn't matter. But as they began aging, it couldn't help but catch up to them.

Javits and Case often had higher scores than many Democratic Senators, and not always those from the South. Both set records as vote-getters for Republicans in their respective states.

Their backgrounds were night and day. Case's family was well known (his father a Dutch Reformed minister) while Javits was a Jewish city boy – the son of immigrants, with working class roots who shared a bed with his brother until age 13. If Case's family would go to all lengths to maintain their Republicanism (for example, his father cancelled a subscription to a newspaper for backing Woodrow Wilson), Javits backed FDR at least once (though also Fiorella LaGuardia). Case was well liked by his colleagues; Javits, while ranked among the highest in terms of influence, could get under the skin of at least some. Ditto with the wives – Case's was beloved among staffers, Javits's was tolerated. Finally, Case was immensely comfortable campaigning and an ebullient people-person; Javits not as much. But both were brilliant and used that gift in different ways. Having served together in the House before each took brief hiatuses to pursue other endeavors before becoming Senators, both were also friends.

By the time Jimmy Carter was in the White House, both men had backed the 39th president's policies frequently (Case 70% and Javits 82%), and in a time in which conservatives were overtaking moderates in the party, the newly realigned Republican base wanted one who was truly their own representing them. In the primary at least, they got it, a result that again showed a stylistic difference between the two men. Case accepted defeat gracefully, while Javits did not and in fact made futile attempts to overturn the verdict. Neither would have survived long enough to serve their 5th terms had they been re-elected. Yet their defeats were still shocking and illustrated the change sweeping the GOP.

Javits and Case both came to the House in the 1940s and served nearly a decade before going to the Senate. Things were different then. Their liberalism was a vestige of an abundant Republican party. Despite Taft-Hartley, Javits in particular stumped hard for his Presidential standard-bearer, Tom Dewey. In his 1980 campaign, Javits claimed to be the only one left of the original three: "Dewey, Rockefeller, and me." Being a moderate was something to be proud of and the Mid-Atlantic was at the forefront of progress. Early on, they showed colleagues taking aim at liberal ideals that they had little fear. They opposed the creation of the Un-American Activities Committee and were outspoken backers of civil rights (even faulting Senate Majority Lyndon Johnson in 1959 for not pursuing a stronger bill) and workplace discrimination legislation even at that unusually early time. Each had an interest in rules reform – particularly as it concerned the filibuster, and were both among the small group of legislators named by *Liberty Magazine* as "honest politicians."

Upon becoming Senators, Javits and Case continued to champion social progress. In addition to civil rights, there was the Great Society as well as judicial nominations, on which they wouldn't hesitate to cause agita even to Republicans in the White House. Javits and Case backed the Fortas nomination and opposed the nominations of Nixon Supreme Court nominees J. Harrold Carswell and Clement Haynesworth, as did many Senate Republicans. But they were also one of just three Republicans to oppose Bill Rehnquist's nomination as Associate Justice. The other member was Edward Brooke, who nearly lost his own primary in 1978.

The relatively liberal records of the pair were evident in their Presidential support scores. In 1961, Case backed JFK 76% and Javits 69%. In 1962, Case had a still high 73% and Javits 62%. In contrast, Roman Hruska of Nebraska backed the President just 21% and 30% respectively. A lack of disagreements with home-state Democratic colleagues was often notable. In 1965, Case disagreed with New Jersey Democrat Harrison Williams on only 16% of Senate roll calls, while Javits went against Bobby Kennedy a mere 19%. By contrast, Oregon's two Democratic Senators Wayne Morse and Maureen Neuberger, took contrary positions 27%.

Indeed, in many of his early elections, Javits was far from favored. His 1946 nomination for a Congressional seat was thought to be a worthless prize for having stuck with the losing candidate for Mayor the year before. He won, and two years later, defeated Paul O'Dwyer by a mere 3,000 votes. His ability to keep his seat as other Republicans were losing was accomplished in part by not hesitating to go against his party (such as in Taft-Hartley). In 1954, he took on

Franklin D. Roosevelt, Jr., for the New York Attorney General post. It was a lousy year for the GOP but he prevailed.

By 1956, Javits was ready to move up to the Senate, but that meant he'd have to beat popular New York City Mayor Robert Wagner. In the Eisenhower landslide, Javits won. In 1962, he became the first statewide GOP candidate to carry New York City since Calvin Coolidge, according to *The New York Times*. He again beat O'Dwyer in '68, this time by a punishing margin. And in 1974, ex-Attorney General Ramsey Clark was seeking to capitalize on the Watergate scandal (Javits did not condemn Nixon until the final days) but the incumbent still won by eight percent (46-38% in a three-way race, with conservatives expressing their distaste for Javits by going with Barbara Keating).

**Photo courtesy of Stony Brook University Libraries
Special Collections and Archives**

Civil Rights were a key interest of Javits. In 1960, he proposed legislation to force the U.S. Attorney General to, as the *Chicago Tribune* put it, "seek a civil injunction to enforce the rights of Southern Negroes on equal access and usage of parks, beaches and municipal waiting rooms and public transportation." In the ensuing years, as the tide for legislation became unmistakable, Minority Leader Ev Dirksen named Javits, Case and Tom Kuchel of California to a Steering Committee to drum up support for civil rights legislation among their GOP colleagues. When the landmark legislation was finally passed, Javits took note that "it is now clear that the mainstream of my party is in support of civil rights legislation and, particularly, support of this bill." As Goldwater prepared to vote against the 1964 Act, Javits told him he was making a mistake. Goldwater replied, "I'm sorry you feel that way, Jack" and walked away.

On another occasion, Goldwater suggested that Javits "go straight" and become a Democrat. Indeed, the two would continue tangling throughout 1964. During a meeting of the Republican platform committee, Javits spoke in favor of an amendment that would limit a President's ability to use nuclear weapons reserved for NATO commanders due to "the position taken by a leading candidate for President" (Goldwater was advocating more "leeway"). The amendment was defeated.

Javits addressing anti-war demonstrators
Photo courtesy of Norman Liss

Yet for all of the fire he aimed at his own party, Javits proved himself just as biting with the opposition. During his 1962 re-election campaign, he criticized the Kennedy administration for "a crisis of leadership in Washington as serious as any in this century. The President is still a 'Senator' and has not yet developed into a President"(he felt Kennedy was timid on civil rights). Javits was also critical of the president's brother Bobby, both as Attorney General and as he sought to become Javits' junior colleague in 1964 by moving to New York. Javits campaigned for his colleague, Kenneth Keating. But Javits Chief of Staff Rich Aurelio notes that once Kennedy won, "they had some understandable partisan tensions but because Kennedy treated Javits with deference and respect, they got along fairly well overall."

As a New York Senator, Javits could not abandon business, and throughout his career he always tried to balance his obligations. One person said, "He gets support from big business and labor. Jack Javits has no shame . . . He gives Chutzpah a big name." But Javits was unequivocally viewed as one of the smartest Senators with a top-notch staff. At an Oval Office visit, LBJ once told him, "With your brains, you should be sitting in that chair." Indeed, one thing unquestioned was his grasp. Aurelio said, "whenever we discussed an issue with him, he amazed me. He always seemed more informed than we thought he would be on the most minor issues." Aurelio said that ability also left Southern Senators reeling when they challenged him on the floor, particularly in the area of civil rights - he had more information than others and in some cases, he had more information about what went on in their home states than even they. "I don't like that man."

Of Javits, *The New York Times* wrote, "He was affable and ebullient, abrasive and brusque—qualities that made it difficult for him to win acceptance as an insider in the exclusive Senate club."

**Javits with nationally known Democratic colleagues
Hubert Humphrey and Ed Muskie
Photo courtesy of the U.S. Senate Historical Office**

Local Republicans were happy to have him in the Senate (and may not have found someone to replicate his vote-getting abilities) but resisted his higher aspirations. Javits wanted to be considered for vice-president in 1968 and New York City Mayor in 1973 but doesn't appear to have been seriously talked up. He acknowledged that he was not close to Rockefeller, often being forced to trail behind him when he visited Capitol Hill. The book *Bobby: The Years Alone* notes that more ebullient New York Republicans such as Rockefeller or Lindsay would often not make a serious effort to cultivate Javits until they needed to lean on his vote-getting abilities.

Javits did not like idle time. He was a serious individual, even to those who knew him best. His wife Marian said that not only would he put on a jacket and tie for breakfast, but on the train ride to their honeymoon destination, he brought newspapers to read. With unusual candor she noted, "there have always been papers between us." Aurelio spoke of, "a pompous and formal personality." – very full of himself." Yet he noted in a memoir of his time with the Senator that he could be exceedingly generous with staffers, even if he wasn't gushing. Aurelio noted that as Javits rode to Arlington National Cemetery in a limousine assigned to Senators following the assassination of President Kennedy, Javits ordered the driver to make room for Aurelio. Years later on a trip to Vietnam,

Javits refused to visit some of the destinations unless Defense secretary Bob McNamara cleared the way for Aurelio to accompany him (he did). And one-time press secretary Paul Lenenthal compared working in his office to being in the Army. "It's uncomfortable at the time, but some years later, you realized you learn an awful lot." Yet Javits had a top-notch staff, which was hard to ignore. Richard Murphy, a top aide to Pennsylvania Republican Senator Hugh Scott recalled "Javits often had as many as three people on the floor at once," comparing it to "a three-ring circus."

Frank Cummings was one such top-notch person. He had been working at a top notch law firm and was active on the case involving the collapse of the Studebaker automobile company. He said Javits went about choosing his staff way senior partners at a firm do – "strictly talent" (Javits became acquainted with Cummings by making inquiries with his old law firm). He called his boss, "not a jokester – very serious. Friendly but serious." But he was quick to add, "very, very honorable" and "loyal" to those around him." Aurelio echoes that. He spoke of, "a pompous and formal personality." – very full of himself." Yet he noted in a memoir how Javits, without prompting, arranged to get him into the limousine with him on the way to Arlington National Cemetery for the burial of President Kennedy, as well as how he refused to proceed on a mission to Vietnam unless Defense Secretary Bob McNamara approved his request to have Cummings accompany him (he did).

Cummings recalls that because Marian Javits spent most of her time in New York (she never developed Potomac Fever), the Senator would work late into the evening. Often, they would go to a local restaurant – Monocle, as it was getting ready to close. Cummings would have a special arrangement with the manager and, when he'd ask if the Senator was coming, he would make sure the steak was prepared well-done – just the way he enjoyed it (Javits also frequented a Jewish deli downtown). Javits didn't totally shun the D.C. social scene. He went to Kay Graham's parties a lot and was a terrific tennis player (much of his time was a the Senate gym).

When she did visit Washington, Marian wasn't exactly embraced by those in his office with open arms. One senior staffer called her, "a pain the neck to staff-nitpicky," adding that she often, "tried to inject New York fashion and celebrities into everything he did." Cummings recalls trying to rearrange the Senator's office wall every time he knew Marion was coming down – Javits liked pictures with constituents while Marion preferred a display of the city's culture.

Cummings called Javits "a very unusual guy – all ideas. He loved people who had good ideas."When he was hired by Javits, the Senator told him, "you write them (the bills), I'll pass them," and proceeded to ask Cummings if he had any legislative ideas. Cummings mentioned ERISA and Javits was intrigued. He ended up sponsoring the bill with his friend, New Jersey Democratic Senator

Harrison Williams, because it was more likely to advance with a member of the majority party.

Another idea Cummings had was what would ultimately become the War Powers Act – and it came about almost by accident. Cummings and several other lawyers from the Senator's office were at a restaurant when the idea came about. Cummings began scribbling notes on the back of the menu, then went back to the office to type it up and present to his boss. Javits looked at it and said he'd introduce it. "It won't go anywhere," he said, "but I'll introduce it." As he was presenting it on the Senate floor, he was distracted by a thick Southern accent from across the aisle asking him to yield. It was John Stennis, a powerful Senator from Mississippi who asked Javits if he could be the bill's principle co-sponsor. Javits immediately agreed and the longshot proposal that "wouldn't go anywhere," suddenly had legs. It took seven years to pass but in 1973, it became law over President Richard Nixon's veto.

Another big accomplishment: the creation of the National Endowment for the Arts and Humanities. On the latter, he invoked the Cold War in making a point that during a Congressional hearing that a strongly enriched arts program was needed saying, "the Russians have gotten more benefit from sending Oistrakh, their violinist, the Bolshoi Ballet and the Moiseyev Ballet to the United States than they have from Sputnik." He said he wanted to "first to assert the efficacy and the virtues of our free institutions, and second, to make human beings throughout the world feel that we are people who deserve to be followed."

Javits initially had been supportive of U.S. involvement of the Vietnam War but by 1967, decided, with the help of Aurelio, that circumstances made it right to begin shifting his views. The two had a long discussion at Monocle one night over how he would put forth his opposition and Aurelio found to his surprise that when he came to the office the next morning and saw what Javits had dictated to his secretary, "it went beyond my suggested rhetoric and essentially signaled the Senator's decision to openly oppose the Vietnam War." Javits did oppose Ted Kennedy's 1966 proposal for a draft via lottery, preferring instead to "defer to the wisdom and experience of General Hershey in his historic administration of our draft laws for the past 26 years." Later, he and junior colleague Charles Goodell beat back an amendment that would cut funding to schools unable to crack down on student demonstrations.

It is not an exaggeration to say that Javits put his imprint on nearly every controversial issue. When North Carolina Republican Senator Jesse Helms attempted to strike police and fire fighters from receiving overtime as part of 1974 minimum wage legislation, Javits declared that, "Policemen and firemen are workers, just like other workers. So there is no reason, in terms of compensation, why they should not get overtime pay for extra work outside of the normal hours."

Part of Javits' gift was knowing when to hold it and fold it. In 1962, New Mexico Democrat Clinton Anderson convinced him not to attach his Medicare proposal to a Social Security rider for fear that it would kill the whole thing. Instead, he convinced Javits to support his own proposal which failed that year but did set the stage for passage in '65. During a 1979 debate on revising the Criminal Code, many wanted to relax penalties for marijuana possession. Javits did not oppose the concept but recognized the dangers of doing so in that venue ("we liberals decided this bill was too important to get hung up"). And when the Senate passed legislation Jewish groups opposed Javits reducing the sale of Maverick missiles by more than half, Javits was among the backers. The agreement came after delicate negotiations on which Javits had played a major role and he admitted that going against his own was "with tears in my eyes."

By 1975, Javits was running for Minority Whip. Nebraskan Carl Curtis, another bald-headed four-termer, was his challenger. Curtis was not beloved either but conservative Senators were persuaded that Javits was not the ideological face the caucus wanted. Curtis won. His popularity in New York was still unparalleled. The year before, he had beaten Clark even as many veterans of the New York State GOP were losing due to Watergate. For a time, it seemed that 1980 would be a similar walk in the park.

When Al D'Amato told his father he'd be challenging Javits, he recommended his son "see a psychiatrist." He was a Hempstead Township Supervisor (Nassau County, Long Island) but had little name recognition beyond. Javits, on the other hand, was an institution. However, Case's upset would not allow Javits to take his eye off the ball.

Javits had developed a degenerative nerve disorder which had in no way impaired his mind. But his physical abilities were a different story, which ultimately became an issue - a big one. D'Amato ran three $500,000 ads that showed unflattering pictures of Javits and used the phrase, "and now, at age 76 and in failing health, he wants six more years." The D'Amato camp, in part to avoid being seen as insensitive, added the liberal label. Some noted his 82% backing of Carter. And Javits was forced to affirm his support for Reagan but could only do so in the most tepid language. He said he had been hoping Ford would seek a comeback, would "not walk away from" Reagan like he did Goldwater in 1964, claiming Goldwater "chased me away." Unmistakably, his heart seemed to be with John Anderson, another maverick, whom he called "an element that makes the Republican Party a national party." In the debate between the two, Javits claimed "crudeness and vulgarity" on the health issue. On the health issue, he said, 'that's about all his campaign is." But in fact, D'Amato was swinging at Javits on spending issues, which was hurting him as much as anything.

D'Amato won a shockingly large 57-43% victory. Bitter over his defeat, Javits declined to forfeit the Liberal Party line. Many think that the votes he received would have gone to Liz Holtzman, the Democratic nominee. Instead, D'Amato was able to eke out a 1% win over Holtzman with just 45%. Javits took just 13%, and his long career was over (friends said Javits more or less acknowledged that seeking a fifth term was a mistake). His departure was marked by tributes from members on both sides of the political spectrum. Rhode Island Democrat Claiborne Pell said he has "often marveled at his ability to break seemingly impossible deadlocks in committee meetings by coming up with ingenious compromises," adding, "His imprimatur is on practically every significant piece of legislation that has passed the Senate these past years."

Javits remained active in retirement, even testifying before Congress many times - often, true to the end, against positions his party was advocating. But his health worsened and he died suddenly in 1986 while vacationing in Florida. He was 81. The Jacob Javits Convention Center is a New York City hallmark, and two years before his death he was on hand for the groundbreaking.

Case, like Javits, was extremely bright and did much of his own research. He too was ardently pro-Israel (the pair - along with Hubert Humphrey in 1976 put together a compromise proposal when the Ford administration indicated its desire to sell six C-130 transport planes to Egypt but it was rejected by Secretary of State Henry Kissinger). But Case was more comfortable around people. In fact, he was incredibly gregarious. Still, *The New York Times* called him, "a quiet, scholarly man of erudite oratory who eschewed flamboyant campaigns." The Case's had moved to Poughkeepsie, New York when his father became pastor of a church. But the elder Case died when Cliff was just 16. His biography notes he, "supported his mother and siblings and then matriculated at Rutgers College in 1921. While there he was active in the Glee Club, played the tuba in the band, served as manager for the student musical clubs and was an attack man on the lacrosse team. He married Ruth Smith, a fellow student at the New Jersey College for Women in 1928. She would call him, "Buddy," and they would have three children.

Case, whose first political win was the Rahway Common Council in 1937, had served New Jersey in Congress since winning a House seat in 1944 (his only defeat prior to 1978 had been a race for the State Assembly three years before). His maiden speech was taking on Mississippi Congressman John Rankin, a rabid segregationist, for going after Supreme Court Justice Felix Frankfurter. Unlike Javits, Case did vote to override Truman's Taft-Hartley veto and he sponsored anti-lynching legislation in 1951. But the centerpiece of his career would be high marks with labor.

Case had resigned from Congress in 1953 to lead the group, "Fund for the Republic," a Ford Foundation Project with the goal of spreading democracy. But he soon decided he wanted back in and the following year, made a run for the Senate. That election came with much labor support. Some attacked his anti-McCarthy stance, calling him a "pro-communist Republicrat" and "Stalin's Choice for Senator." McCarthy actually came to New Jersey to campaign against him, a rare rebuke to a fellow Republican. But Eisenhower was popular and Nixon campaigned for him (Case had been an early backer of Ike). He defeated Congressman Charles Howell by 3,000 votes, the same margin he'd be unseated by in the primary 24 years later. No love was lost between he and McCarthy as Case testified before the Rules Committee that the Wisconsin Senator should be stripped of his chairmanship. Meanwhile, the state's senior Republican senator, Alexander Smith, became a mentor and cherished friend. Sam Zagoria became a chief aide and longtime Case confidante. He recalls that when he informed Case that he was a Democrat, he replied, "Fine. If it wasn't for the Democrats I wouldn't have been elected."

**Labor was a staunch ally of Case throughout his
career (left). He was also beloved by his staff
Photo courtesy of Rutgers University Special Collections**

Case proved extraordinarily popular. His voting record was so liberal that it was not uncommon for him to score a 100 from the Americans for Democratic Action and a zero from the conservative Americans for Constitutional Action. In 1962, he was the only Republican who backed Kennedy's Medicare plan (two years later, he'd be joined by Javits, Ken Keating of New York and Tom Kuchel of California). That same year, he backed Kennedy 76% of the time – nearly double that of a Northern Democrat from the president's own party, Frank Lausche of Ohio. And he backed a good government rules change advocated by Illinois Democrat Paul Douglas that would allow Senators to break a filibuster with a simple majority 15 days after 16 Senators filed a cloture motion. Case said "it never should be possible for the House to escape or avoid declaring its position on any important issue." But the amendment was opposed by both of the chamber's partisan leaders – Lyndon Johnson and Everett Dirksen, and it garnered just 28 votes.

Zagoria said Case faced "a lot of hoo-hah that he wasn't a real Republican." Some even suggested he resign. *The Star-Ledger* was particularly unfriendly. So vituperative was the relationship that the paper once labeled case's sister Adelaide a Communist sympathizer, which caused Case to issue a stern rebuke. *The Newark Evening News* was among the news outlets that was supportive. In fact, the paper's longtime cartoonist, Bill Canfield once made a drawing with the caption, "No money, no machine. All he's got is a great record."

But Case was clever and assiduous when it came to pursuing good relations with the press. Whenever he visited a town to give a speech, he'd make it a point to visit the office of the local paper and spend time with the editor. Zagoria said the editors felt, "they were respected," and as a result, Case "got respected." Why did he never change parties? Case said as early as 1964 that he, "started out a Republican. I came from a long line of Republicans. They gave me an office, and I have a very strong feeling that I should remain one of them."

Because Case was a champion of so many liberal ideas, it was only natural that he'd be friendly with was friendly with liberals across the aisle. Joe Clark of Pennsylvania and Paul Douglas of Illinois were two close friends. Case also forged a strong relationship with Ted Kennedy, with whom he worked on labor and public welfare legislation. Zagoria said Case and his Democratic colleague, Harrison Williams, had a harmonious relationship, noting their wives were particularly close. The pair successfully sponsored an amendment to a 1976 toxic substances bill that authorized $2 million for demonstration projects in three states to monitor the linkage between industrial chemicals and public health (*Congressional Quarterly* noted New Jersey "had the largest number of chemical plants and the highest death rate in the nation."

Neither would Case hesitate in holding the feet of those in his own party to the fire. Case was one of about a dozen true-liberal Republicans and while they were immensely loyal to President Dwight Eisenhower, Zagoria noted that, "Every once in a while, Ike would slip into a more conservative stance and they would keep the liberal lamp burning."

Nixon was another story and Zagoria said he "was not one of Case's idols, to put it mildly." In 1960, both men shared the ticket - Nixon of course was his party's standard-bearer for president, but Case didn't hold a single public appearance with him nor did Nixon's picture appear in Case's literature. Zagoria said that for starters, Case remembered what Nixon did with "the Hollywood folks," during his time on the House Committee on Un-American Activities. The senator's son, Cliff Case III, said this continued even when Nixon became president, noting Case saw his "Southern strategy" as "pandering to whites, thereby splitting the country and leading to the very unfortunate stalemates."

Conversely, Case's relationship with Johnson was strong. He appointed Zagoria to the National Labor Board which he said could not have happened had it not been for his high regard toward Case.

Case made clear he had zero tolerance for those who invoked sensitivity as a means for putting aside discussions on matters concerning civil rights. During a 1969 debate on desegregation Case said, "I am not being holier-than-thou about this matter at all. All I am saying is that I do not think that the way to attempt to deal with difficult problems is to disable ourselves from dealing with them." Late in his career, he backed the Panama Canal Treaty but implored all signs to ponder the "basic fact which has to be dealt with is the canal's vulnerability. If we vote to keep the canal 'ours,' in the 1903 sense, could we end up with a pyrrhic victory in the form of a useless ditch?"

**On the day of the 1963 March on Washington, Case
greets New Jerseyans at Washington's Union Station (left)
and testifying on the Bobby Baker matter (right)
Photo courtesy of Rutgers University Special Collections**

Zagoria said he first recalls Case's turn against the Vietnam War as having come shortly after a meeting with Defense Secretary Robert McNamara, who kept insisting, "there's light at the end of the tunnel" (a 1967 trip to the region was the first straw). Zagoria said when Case heard that, he said, "I'm getting off the wagon." In 1972, Case introduced an amendment with Idaho Democratic Senator Frank Church that ended U.S. military involvement in Southeast Asia unless Congress approved an extension. In a colloquy with Church on the Senate floor, Case said, "I believe that the American people instinctively recognize that we have been taking the wrong approach and that now the Congress should follow their lead." He then asked Church, "And is it not true, as it seems to me, that the only prospect for the success of the Vietnamization in its best sense - that is to say, of leaving the South Vietnamese in the position to defend themselves, is a course which our amendment has suggested?" The amendment was defeated 42-48 but did pass the following year with 64 votes.

In many ways, Case was ahead of his time. In 1959, he dropped a bill to provide for community college grants. It became part of the Education Facilities Act of 1959 and the Higher Education Act of 1965. As an ardent conservationist and defender of New Jersey's shores, Case proposed a cabinet-agency level position to address environmental issues and was a delegate to the U.S. Conference in Stockholm where he spoke about the significant amount of dumping taking place on the beaches. Reducing the dependence on fossil fuels was also high on his plate. And in the 1970s, Case was a supporter of strong work-safety requirements. During debate on OSHA, proposed an amendment removing language that prohibited funding for inspection of places with 15 or fewer employees. Conservatives opposed the amendment but Case, armed with a letter of support from Labor Secretary James Hodgson, pushed it through 47-33 (it was later amended to prohibit funding for the inspection of firms with three or fewer employees). He proposed a commission to monitor human rights abuses in compliance with the Helsinki Accord.

But ethics was an area where Case was way ahead of the curve. He released his finances annually and proposed disclosure laws throughout the course of his career (an early piece of legislation was sponsored with Oregon Democrat Richard Neuberger). President Carter signed it into law in October of 1978 and Case noted, "it's kind of nice to have it come to fruition before I leave."

The "Case Act," was another endeavor long on his plate. It would require a president to make public an agreement with a foreign nation within 60 days.

As an ardent defender of Israel, Case saw the nation as "the only real hope for stability in that part of the world." One prominent Israeli publication noted, how since the beginning of the recognition of the small nation, "only Clifford Case continued to stand alone as a solid rock in support of Israel." He was selected to represent the United States at the opening of the Knesset in 1966. In his final year in office, he spearheaded the opposition to the Carter administration's plan to sell warplanes to Egypt.

In 1972, Case was returned to the Senate by a record margin (Garden Staters incidentally have not chosen another Republican for the U.S. Senate since). Katherine Neuberger, an ex-Republican National Committeewoman, summed up his personal gifts by saying, "he may have been considered an ultra-liberal, but he was for his fellow man."

And as the Senator who got to recommend U.S. Attorneys, the men whom Case chose were proven corruption-busters who, once assuming the position, went after Democrats and Republicans alike.

Zagoria describes his boss as "a moderate man," saying, "when you made mistakes he would gloss over it," noting he himself made a few. He treated his staff exceptionally well. Zagoria recalls Case giving him his Senate parking space because he commuted to work via the streetcar. In a sharp departure from the practice of many Senators, Case was very generous when it came to crediting his staff. When educators visiting his office were lauding him for the community college legislation, Case turned to Zagoria and called him, "the fellow who made it happen." And Zagoria notes that one Case strategy for dealing with a controversial issue was to gather the top administrative staff with a tall yellow-pad and a running-line down the middle of the page where he'd indicate the pros and cons of the matter at hand.

By 1978, Case was expected to have a tough general against Bill Bradley. The real shock, however was not that Bradley won but that he didn't face Case to achieve it.

Case (center) during the Vietnam War - colleague
Harrison Williams is on the right.
On the right, Case attends a Bergen County GOP picnic
Photo courtesy of Rutgers University Library Special Collections

When Bell announced his candidacy, few took notice. In fact, there were always rumblings about distrust from conservatives but Case had always turned back their challengers handily (he had taken 70% in the primary six years earlier). In that primary, Bell spent $500,000, with *The New York Times* noting that 80% of his donors came from outside the New York City metropolitan area. He had hammered excessively the issue of a federal tax cut and of Case backing the Carter administration 70%. Case attacked Bell's tax cut platform, calling it "extraordinarily inflationary." Case, in conceding, called it "an interesting campaign," acknowledging "it fooled everybody." He blamed light "turnout," saying it may indicate "a deep unhappiness with the voters of the people in power." But among Republicans, his popularity was never universal. Case himself had summed up his philosophy thus: "If the needs of this country are not met by middle-of-the-road progressivism, the problems won't be met, and the time will come when only extremist solutions are possible." And on the night he lost, Case again expressed fear about extremists. Still, ever a loyal Republican, he vowed to remain so.

Some Republicans, including future Governor Tom Kean, Sr., attributed Case's loss to his "longtime reluctance to use modern campaign techniques." For instance, Kean said he should've "paid $15,000 for a credible poll" but instead spent less than $5,000 for a poll that, erroneously as it turned out, showed him far ahead. Nonetheless, Case, who after his term ended had begun teaching, told Rutgers students his loss was "not a matter of unhappiness. I think the miracle was that I lasted as long as I did."

Case had an eclectic array of hobbies: piano playing, fly fishing and tennis. His taste in music was mostly classical, particularly organ music. Cliff Case III said his parents "very much enjoyed reading to each other as they relaxed in the evening."

Case was diagnosed with lung cancer in 1981 and died the following March. He was 77 years old.

CHAPTER THIRTY-NINE

Kuchel's Loss Overshadowed By RFK's Assassination

Historic Tidbit: Actor Zach Galifianakis' uncle Nick was Jesse Helms' first Democratic challenger in the 1972 Senate race. Galifianakis started out favored but the Nixon White House really wanted Helms to take the seat of retiring Democratic Senator Everett Jordan. Nixon campaigned for Helms while ignoring pleas from endangered Republicans Caleb Boggs and Floyd Haskell, both of whom lost. Helms won the seat 54-46%.

There was once a rabidly moderate Republican Senator from California who is a footnote to history in a couple of very high-profile endeavors.

Thomas Kuchel was appointed by Earl Warren to fill Richard Nixon's seat when he became vice-president and he was ousted in a Republican primary on June 4, 1968. Few noticed, however, because it was overshadowed by the shooting of Robert F. Kennedy the same night and in the same state. In between, he was the GOP floor leader on the Civil and Voting Rights legislation. And it was Kuchel who first floated the rebuttal to Barry Goldwater's famous slogan, "In your heart you know he's right." Of Goldwater, Kuchel said, "in your gut you know he's nuts."

Photo courtesy of the U.S. Senate Historical Office

Unofficially, Kuchel considered himself the leader of the "baker's dozen" of Senate Republican moderates, backing Social Security, Medicare, LBJ's immigration measure, and numerous environmental measures for California. Early in his tenure, he and a handful of other Republicans joined Democrats in

416

backing legislation to thwart the filibuster. But it was his war against the John Birch Society, one of the earliest public officials to do so, that would earn the enmity of conservatives. He called the group "fright peddlers, from the simple simpletons to the wretched racists."

Kuchel's Republican stray did have limits. He did not favor spending simply for the sake of doing so and was a strong backer of the Vietnam War.

If Kuchel's expressive disagreements within his party hurt him, it wasn't with his colleagues. They made him their Whip in 1959, the number-two position in the Senate. He held that position for ten years. But conservatives in his home state were a different story.

Kuchel's progressivism was no surprise. As a boy, he crusaded against the KKK. Born in Anaheim, California to a family who had helped found the town, it took Kuchel little time to become a wunderkind of sorts in California Republican circles. He knew both Hiram Johnson and Earl Warren, both of whom played a major role in helping him to land in high places. Kuchel was a State Assemblyman at age 26, a Senator six years later, and State Controller by 1946, the latter post chosen by Warren. In that time, he was Chair of the Republican Party. When Nixon became vice-president, Warren was Governor, and his philosophical soulmate, Kuchel, seemed like a natural to take the Senate seat. Kuchel got the job, and Warren joked, "Now, you're on your own."

At first it was easy. Kuchel defeated future Los Angeles Mayor Sam Yorty for the remainder of Nixon's term 53-46%. But he took 54% for the full term two years later, and against the same foe, Richard Richards, he won 56% in 1962. Kuchel had been so well liked by liberals that at a 1962 rally promoting his own re-election, Brown actually expressed hope that voters would re-elect "Tommy Kuchel" before correcting himself to say the Democratic candidate. It was no wonder. Kuchel did not endorse Nixon in his bid to restart his career by seizing California's Governorship. And when it came to endorsing Kuchel, his ticket-mate at the time, Nixon said he was running "independently of candidates for national office."

Comparisons would be made to Nixon during much of Kuchel's time in the Senate and they would rarely be favorable to the 37th President. Legendary Johnson confidante and top Senate aide Bobby Baker shared recently that he "was always very fond of Kuchel. He was a fun guy." And in the ultimate compliment from the chief aide to the man referred to as the "master of the Senate," Baker said, "The difference between he and Senator Richard Nixon was that Senator Nixon could get 20 votes and Senator Tommy Kuchel could get 51."

Kuchel with Ike, a Republican he considered to be like-minded
Photo courtesy of the Bancroft Library, University of California, Berkeley

For a time, Kuchel was liked by all of his Senate Republicans as well. Despite being somewhat to the left of a fair amount of many of them, Kuchel's name met with little dissension when he sought the position of Senate Minority Whip in 1959 (he was less successful at getting Kentucky moderate John Sherman Cooper elected Minority leader). That was the case when Kuchel reluctantly had to oppose Eisenhower, such as after the president submitted his 1959 budget request. "The budget message suggests a 'breathing spell' in new starts for public works and water projects. I regret most respectfully that I cannot agree. The water problems of my own California grow more acute with each passing year…The federal government must discharge its responsibility in this field." But it wasn't long before things got really rough.

It might have begun in 1963 when Kuchel issued a strong denunciation of the far-right John Birch Society. The curious fact is that the freight peddlers from the simple simpletons to the wretched racists, all claim to be conservatives. They defile the honored philosophy of conservatives with that claim as thorough as the Communists defile the honored philosophy of liberalism. They are anything but patriotic. Indeed, a good case can be made that they are unpatriotic and downright un-American. For they are doing the devil's work far better than the Communists could."

Kuchel and Goldwater had tangled mightily and publicly in the lead-up to 1964. Kuchel was chairing Nelson Rockefeller's Presidential campaign and used every opportunity to accuse Goldwater of political grandstanding. Kuchel was a strong proponent of the Treaty while Goldwater was sternly opposed. Goldwater had said on the Senate floor that the treaty would "have a greater effect on the future of mankind than any event since the birth of Jesus Christ." Kuchel, who said Goldwater was reading from a prepared speech, accused him of posturing. Referring to "my friend from Arizona," he posed the question: "Is it not a fact that every member of the Joint Chiefs of Staff approved the treaty?" Goldwater acknowledged it was true but added, "It is also true that other members who have military responsibility have disapproved." Kuchel called Goldwater's nomination a "suicidal tragedy": "If the grand old Republican Party were to become a shriveled, shrunken, impotent political haven for an anachronistic few, then vast changes, and not for the good, would enter our way of life."

In the Senate race that same year, Kuchel refused to back Republican nominee George Murphy over Pierre Salinger because Murphy would not denounce the John Birch Society. Ronald Reagan received the anti-Kuchel treatment as well. There is some evidence it began after Goldwater's defeat. Reagan said, "We don't intend to turn the Republican Party over to the traitors in the battle just ended. We will have no more of those candidates who are pledged to the same goals of our opposition and who seek our support. Turning the party over to the so-called moderates wouldn't make any sense at all." Reagan suspected that some of it had to do with Reagan backing Kuchel's 1962 primary opponent, Lloyd. He later regretted it "because I realized I have been in a position where I could make a contribution to party unity and I endangered it in that campaign." There was also lingering suspicion over a rumor circulating that Kuchel in 1950 had been arrested for drunken-driving while engaging in homosexual acts. Kuchel sued a bar-owner for libel, won, and received a written apology (the arrest documents had been forged). Reagan denied knowledge and spoke of "the despicable acts to blacken his name."

**Kuchel assisted LBJ during his transition to the Presidency
(Photo courtesy of the Lyndon B. Johnson Presidential Library)**

When Reagan announced his campaign for Governor, Kuchel gave him similar treatment. In the primary, he backed moderate San Francisco Mayor George Christoher and said "within our California Republican Party is a fanatical, neo-facist, political cult, overcome with a strange mixture of corrosive hatred and sickening fear, recklessly determined to overcome our party or destroy it." This earned a strong letter of rebuke from California Republican Chairman Gaylord Parkinson who wrote his "refusal to support the Nixon ticket, the (George) Murphy ticket, and the Goldwater ticket" now left him with "a lot of fences to mend." Kuchel shot back that he was "glad to re-endorse Christopher" and, perhaps for personal kicks, asked a reporter, "Who in the hell is Parkinson?"

When Reagan won, Kuchel made clear he had no plans to back him. State Republican Chair Gaylord Parkinson took him to task in a letter. "In the Navy, when general quarters are sounded, every man is expected to go to his battle station, whether he likes the war or the direction the vessel is going." When he decided to respond, he said he "exercise(s) his rights as a free, independent American." Leon Panetta, an aide to Kuchel who was still a Republican in those days, called Reagan "Goldwater in a prettier package." Many Republicans predicted that Kuchel would "come on board." But the two never met and no endorsement was given.

Then came Kuchel's time to pay the piper - Republican primary voters.

Prior to 1968, Kuchel's penchant for outspoken moderation had not caused him many problems. He turned back a challenge from Howard Jarvis in the 1962 primary with 75%. And general elections were non-affairs. He carried all 58 counties in his 1962 re-election. But once Reagan was elected, he gave his blessing to a quest by allies to oust "that damn Tommy Kuchel."

Boomcalifornia.org describes five businessmen (Holmes Tuttle, Henry Salvatori, A.C. Rubel, Leonard Firestone, and Justin Dart) who met to choose a candidate to go against Kuchel. Eventually, they settled on Max Rafferty, the Superintendent of Public Instruction, a non-partisan post in California. But Reagan himself wouldn't take a public position. He vowed to watch from the sidelines and "lean back like the Tower of Pisa." *Congressional Quarterly* noted that Rafferty's fundraising was hurt slightly as a result. But he wouldn't need it. His $1 million dwarfed what Kuchel had.

Kuchel wrote that "there are certain elements of the Republican Party who have seen fit to denounce me but I have no intention of compromising the political principles I have followed for thirty years." Independent columnists called Rafferty's campaign "vicious" and "far below minimum standards of decent political behavior."

Rafferty called Kuchel "politically dishonest," claiming that his record was so liberal that he might as well be a "floor leader for the (Johnson) administration." Kuchel responded that he had backed the GOP on 76% of votes, but Rafferty said many of those were procedural, calling them "anything that doesn't mean anything."

Kuchel brandished statements in his literature from, among others, Majority Leader Everett Dirksen, who said, "California has an investment in your experience and devoted service and I am confident that the people of California will want to continue that kind of investment." Some Washington insiders thought Kuchel could succeed Dirksen when he retired (he ultimately died), but some in the caucus may have found him too far to the left.

Rafferty called Kuchel inadequate when it came to responding to "four deadly sins": violence, pornography, drugs, and lawlessness. "Until there is retribution— prompt, just, and drastic, we will continue to our friends murdered in the streets and our women ravaged by sneering packs of punks." And he called the Vietnam Peace talks, "a propaganda stunt," saying the U.S. "should take the handcuffs off our military people and let them do what's necessary to get that war over with as soon as possible. Let's stop fighting a phony war with one hand tied between us."

When Rafferty jumped into the primary to oppose Kuchel, few, including the incumbent, took much notice. He led by 15-18% a year before, a margin unchanged a month before the June primary. Kuchel didn't mount much of a defense.

On primary night, Kuchel enjoyed a slight lead but returns were extremely slow coming in, particularly from the Central Valley. Sometime around midnight, Rafferty pulled ahead, and it soon became evident that he had won. The difference was 69,000 votes, 50-47%. Rafferty's defeat of Kuchel was so shocking that it was reported that many were cheering even when they saw television reports of Kennedy's shooting. *The Almanac of American Politics* notes that Rafferty's big margins in the three GOP strongholds of California in those days, L.A. County, Orange, and San Diego, which he carried 60-40%, were enough to overcome Kuchel's lead in the rest of the state. Reagan tried to get Kuchel to back Rafferty, but it was for naught.

At Kennedy's funeral, Warren, by then Chief Justice of the U.S. Supreme Court, told him words couldn't express how "badly I feel" about his loss. Rafferty's win caused Republicans to basically forfeit a seat that, before Kuchel's loss, they had considered safely in their column. He ran a hard-hitting, but desultory campaign against State Controller Alan Cranston. Among other things, it was revealed that he had faked his disability during World War II and jumped out of his wheelchair as the peace treaties were signed. Cranston won by a wide margin.

In 1970, Rafferty lost his primary in his bid for a third term as Superintendent and become the Dean of Education at Troy University in Alabama. He died in a car accident in 1982.

Kuchel was true to his philosophy to the end. "Progressive Republicans," he said, "brought to politics the philosophy of governing for the many. What comes particularly to my mind is Medicare. If it weren't for Medicare today, there would be tens of thousands of Americans living in the poorhouse, with no care."

Kuchel died of lung cancer in 1994. He was 84.

CHAPTER FORTY

Margaret Chase-Smith
First Female Placed In Nomination For President

Historic Quote: In very risque humor for that time, Margaret Chase Smith was asked what she'd do if she woke up one morning in the White House. She replied, "I'd go straight to Mrs. Truman and apologize. Then I'd go home."

Photo courtesy of the U.S. Senate Historical Office

Perhaps the most famous woman ever to have served in Congress was Margaret Chase Smith. The Maine Republican's 32 years in Congress (including 24 in the upper body) went unrivaled by any other woman until Barbara Mikulski passed her in 2011. But she was the first woman whose name was put in nomination at a major party convention, and in her eyes, the unsuccessful but tireless campaign she waged to win the GOP nomination for the White House was far from futile.

Without question, one distinction will never be passed. Smith was the first woman to serve in both Houses of Congress. More importantly, the "Gentlelady from Maine," as she became known, was one of the most visionary, esteemed, and productive members whose determination to do the right thing made her stand out.

The proudest daughter of the town of Skowhegan, Maine, Chase Smith was born in 1897 and worked as a telephone operator, newspaper reporter, and wool mill manager before winning her seat in Congress following the death of her husband Clyde Smith in 1940. Clyde, 23 years her senior, had been ill for some time prior to his passing, and his wife had served as his chief assistant so he paved the way for her to succeed him. In a letter, he informed his constituents of the gravity of his health, noting his personal physician "informs me that I am a seriously ill man, that it is his opinion that even though I survive, I may physically be unable to take an active part in Congressional affairs for an indefinite time in the future." On his wife, he said, "I know of no one else," he said, "who has the full knowledge of my ideas and plans or is as well qualified as she is, to carry on these ideas and my unfinished work for my district." Clyde expired within 24 hours and Margaret undertook a campaign to succeed him. Life on the trail was hardly new. She had served as Clyde's secretary throughout their ten-year marriage, serving as his secretary, traveling with him, and maintain "a campaign diary" of folks she met along the way. Additionally, she had served as the head of a number of women's groups such as the BPW, Sorosis Club, Federation of Women's Club. She won and in her subsequent four re-elections never fell below 60%.

On a trip to the U.S. Capitol in 1916
Photo courtesy of the Margaret Chase Smith Library

In Congress, it was Smith's desire early on to serve on the House Naval Affairs Committee (now Armed Services) but seats on that panel were generally doled out by seniority. But by 1944, she secured a seat, which a piece by the Margaret Chase Smith Library notes came as "much to the surprise of many and to the delight of herself and the publisher of the Ganett Publications in Maine, headed by Guy P. Ganett, a highly civic and defense minded man."

Smith immediately turned her attention to addressing the problems of the U.S. Navy. Chairman Carl Vinson appointed a sub-committee that would tour 13 coastal facilities. Lt. William C. Lewis, Jr, the committee's chief aide "often slipped a timely and well-phrased question to Mrs. Smith, usually giving her publicity in the press and attention from the Navy." The result was a report that called for recommendations, starting with "a Presidential appointment of a committee to follow through on the committee action" when it came to improving the needs of Naval communities.

Margaret and Clyde Smith around 1936
Photo via the Margaret Chase Smith Library

By 1948, incumbent Wallace White was retiring and Chase Smith wanted to move to the upper body. To do so, she faced a sitting Governor, a former Governor, and a minister. Her slogan was "Don't trade a record for a promise." During the campaign, Smith faced questions about her gender, including from other women. Her answer was "women administer the home. They set the rules, enforce them, mete out justice for violations. Thus, like Congress, they legislate; like the Executive, they administer; like the courts, they interpret the rules. It is an ideal experience for politics." Smith handily won the primary with 52% and took 71% in the general, becoming the first Republican female to serve in the Senate.

Photo courtesy of the Margaret Chase Smith Library

As the only female Senator at the time, Smith might have expected a lot of ribbing from colleagues. But she would later confide to associates that the opposite would occur. During her retirement she told an aide, "there was no discrimination - she felt she was one of the 100 and not a "woman" senator but rather a senator just like the others. She expected no special privilege because of her gender and received none." But Congressional perks were another story.

Smith found that the gymnasium was not available to her. Did she mind? On the contrary. She was "proud to cost the taxpayers less money than any other member of Congress."

But after leaving office, Smith shed some light into what it was like to be a rare female Senator. One issue involved a women's restroom for Senator's. There wasn't one. In one column, Smith wrote that there did exist "toilet facilities for wives which was available to women of the Senate but I didn't have time to visit and it was difficult for me to go up there and find friends without taking time for a little conversation." She then remembers extracting a key from Rules Chair Carl Hayden who asked her if she'd mind sharing a facility with female Capitol employees. Smith responded "no, but of course this is not equal treatment - the men in the Senate don't share theirs." And that was only the half of it. Later that day, Smith encountered her senior colleague from Maine, Owen Brewster, who was quite mad. "The key fitted the lock on the washroom across from my private office near the Rotunda and the lock has been changed."

Photos courtesy of the Margaret Chase 6Smith Library

The 1960s seemed to bring more opportunity for Smith. The East Front of the Capitol was expanding and there was now another female Senator, Maureen Neuberger. Mike Mansfield gave her a room which would be private - with the exception of the toilet. Smith agreed but soon found this would cramp her style as well. "Senator Neuberger had many people coming and going. I had very few and sharing the toilet facilities meant that we ran into each other and each other's guests." It was only after Neuberger retired that Smith's request "that the door to her room from the small room between us be sealed off - thus finally giving me my own private washroom, flush and lavatory, plus the bar, refrigerator, etc). Smith said she at last "had my own washroom but it was a struggle."

Smith was an early defender of the United Nations. In a 1949 radio address, she said "the number one problem of the American people today is fear of insecurity . . . we have been, and are still, trying to meet this problem through the United Nations. The United Nations is a symbol of moral force. It is founded upon the fervent hope that men will ultimately be governed by moral force and that physical force can be eliminated or at least minimized, as a means of achievement and of settling differences." But it was Smith's "Declaration of Conscience" speech following Joe McCarthy's entrance that would forever enhance her stature.

**Hosting President Eisenhower at her home (left) and
with Maine GOP colleague Frederick Payne
Photos courtesy of the Margaret Chase Smith Library**

**Being administered the oath of office as a U.S. Senator by
Michigan's Arthur Vandenberg in 1949 (others included Lester
Hunt, Robert Hendrickson and Andrew Schoeppel)
Left photo courtesy of the Margaret Chase Smith Library; Right
photo courtesy of the U.S. senate Historical Office**

In a powerful speech, she said that "the greatest deliberative body in the world" had been "debased to the level of a forum of hate and character assassination sheltered by the shield of congressional immunity . . . I speak as a Republican. I speak as a woman. I speak as a United States Senator. I don't want to see the Republican Party ride to political victory on the Four Horsemen of Calumny - Fear, Ignorance, Bigotry and Smear." Five Republican colleagues joined her declaration which, without question, will go down as a study in political eloquence.

McCarthy called that group "Snow White and the Six Dwarfs." and stripped her of her seat on the Permanent Subcommittee on Investigations. Who did the seat go to? Richard Nixon. Smith backed censure of McCarthy. She said later, "Every human being is entitled to courtesy and consideration. Constructive criticism is not only to be expected but sought." Three months later, at a Republican rally in Fryeburg, Maine, Smith noted the importance of voting, telling the crowd, "bad candidates are elected but good people who don't vote."

In 1964, Smith tried to make history once more: throwing her hat into the ring for the GOP Presidential nomination. It was said that she had been prepared to announce her candidacy the previous November but held off because of JFK's assassination.

Smith, whose Maine residence made her a neighbor to New Hampshire from the north, finished fifth in New Hampshire to Henry Cabot Lodge, New Hampshire's neighbor to the south, who wasn't even a candidate (she watched the returns with George Aiken, her Senate colleague from Vermont, Maine's neighbor to the southwest). The high point of Smith's run was 26% in Illinois. When asked if she could pledge unconditional support to Goldwater should he capture the nomination, Smith replied, "I wouldn't put it that way. Let's say I'm a Republican and as such, I accept the decision of the Republican majority and will support the nominee." Still, entering San Francisco as the convention was about to kick off, Smith vowed to remain until "the last vote was cast."

**Smith campaigning at a grocery store and on a chilly
day in Pittsburgh, New Hampshire
Photos courtesy of the Margaret Chase Smith Library**

Arriving at 1964 GOP convention
Photo courtesy of the Margaret Chase Smith Library

She did not get many. Aiken placed her name in nomination and 27 delegates voted for her. But she made history, and when she returned to the Senate, she had to feel enormous pride in her accomplishment. But her Senate seat appeared to be hers for as long as she wanted it. In 1966, she congratulated her opponent, State Senator Elmer Violette, for "a responsible but virtually hopeless fight."

Smith continued to hold to the fire the feet of leaders of both parties. One day she fiercely questioned Defense Secretary Robert McNamara over what would happen to the women of the National Guard during a draft. She later said, "He looked at me as though it was foolish of me to ask such a question." And when he declared the military fully integrated, Smith said, "I could hardly believe my ears." But when she was confronted by college students demanding an end to the war, Smith called it "the most unpleasant experience of my entire public service career."

Another little known fact about Smith was that she knew no boundaries when it came to fear, yet with others, was deeply compassionate and empathetic. To hear New Jersey Congressman Gordon Canfield tell it, she confronted disease and foreign enemies head-on.

Canfield had been among the members who had traveled with Smith to Europe and the Middle East a few years after World War II. "Who was it the dead and the dying of cholera in Cairo? . . . It was the gentlewoman from Maine."

Canfield went on to say that, "Our colleague from Maine was undisturbed when we had engine trouble flying high over the Brenner Pass and she was distinctly a morale builder when on our return flight between the Azores and Bermuda, it looked as if we were to lose two engines and ditch." Canfield noted that upon the delegation's return, Smith was unanimously voted "the one who best withstood the rigors and dangers encountered." What prompted Canfield to detail these adventures. Because Smith had broken her arm, yet four hours later, was keeping a "speaking engagement at Rockland, 60 miles away." It may have paled in comparison to earlier endeavors but Canfield added, "I know she can take it."

Smith maintained her independence through her final term in the Senate. She opposed both of President Nixon's tempestuous choices for the Supreme Court – Clement Haynesworth and Harold Carswell. But the latter nomination showed allies and critics alike what Smith was all about. Smith was considered a crucial vote on the Haynesworth nomination but the day of the vote appeared publicly undecided. That was when a senior White House aide told Senator Birch Bayh, a leading opponent of Carswell, that she had told him she'd vote for confirmation. Bayh passed that along to Massachusetts Republican Ed Brooke who in his book, *Bridging The Divide*, recounts approaching Smith in the Senate Dining Room. He describes Smith as "outraged" and recalls her calling Nixon aide Bryce Harlow for an explanation (the theory was likely to create a false impression of Smith's vote to slow Carswell opponents' momentum). Smith and other key moderates voted no and Brooke wrote how Harlow, "an experienced political operative, should have known better than to give a waffling answer to Margaret Chase Smith."

In Maine, Smith was known as "our Maggie." She never missed Senate votes. The Senate became her life. "I have no family, no time-consuming hobbies," she said late in her Senate career. "I have only myself and my job as United States Senator." And she took her responsibilities quite seriously and no-where was that illustrated more than in her speeches.

In a piece for the library that bears her name, Smith said, "I worked very hard on my presentation, perhaps more on the appearance I would make rather than the substance of what I was saying.

In her days in the House, she would prepare many of her own remarks and put them on 5'8 cards (during campaigns, she would use color cards for "different issues"). After she became Senator, William C. Lewis joined he team who, upon hearing her thoughts about a speech of the day, would have the speech typed. Smith recants that on one such occasion, he inserted the line, "I might just as well stood in bed." Smith had never heard that and inserted the word "up" and paused for the applause Lewis had inserted. It didn't come until she resumed speaking.

On a light note, Smith would be seen every day with a fresh rose on her lapel. So string was her love of the flower that she sought to have it designated as the national flower. But her quest was thwarted by friendly rivalry from Senate Minority Leader Everett Dirksen who was infatuated with the marigold. It wasn't until 1987 that Congress did indeed give Smith her long-sought gift – proclaiming the rose. Incidentally, in a startling gesture to Dirksen – a symbol that the flower rivalry was in friendly in nature, Smith placed a marigold on his coffin when he died in 1969.

By 1972, Smith was almost as much a national institution as she was in Maine. Certainly, her reputation in her home state was such that it was perhaps understandable that she campaigned with her usual style of: let them come to me. She entered that campaign a heavy favorite. But she was also 75 years old. Rather than campaigning hard, her method was hosting receptions where voters could show up to shake her hand. And she did little to promote her "record" the details of which, with the passage of time, many were unsure of.

Meanwhile, Democratic Congressman Bill Hathaway was campaigning hard and tinkered around the edges about her age. Smith helped her cause little when her chief aide, William Chesley Lewis, answered tough questions for her (prompting one paper to ask, "Will the real Senator please stand up"). Still, Maine and the rest of the nation were shocked when she found herself on the losing end to Hathaway, 53-47%. So stunning was the loss that ABC News anchor Harry Reasener, while delivering election returns as Smith was trailing, opined that he "thought it was against the law in the state of Maine to vote against Smith."

Lewis read a concession the next day. And in a true sign of the veneration in which Smith was held by older Mainers, Hathaway noted his own mother's response following the defeat: "You should be ashamed of yourself," she said.

Smith accepted defeat in good grace, returning to Skowhegan, though she did temporarily lose her voting rights there (one newspaper said "the town felt she spent too much of her time in Washington"). In 1989, President George H.W. Bush, who famously vacationed in Kennebunkport and whose father Prescott served with Smith, presented her the Medal of Freedom. She died in 1995 at the ripe old age of 97.

Margaret Chase Smith may not have achieved every success she sought but she broke many barriers. And for that, she's a true trailblazer.

**Smith begins the groundbreaking for the dedication
of her library in Skowhegan, Maine
Photo courtesy of the Margaret Chase Smith Library**

CHAPTER FORTY-ONE

Two Senate Seats, Two Occupants In 70 Plus Years

Historic Tidbit: Edith Nourse Rogers was among the first women to serve in Congress (her 35 plus years have been surpassed only by Barbara Mikulski). And Rogers, who served Massachusetts from 1925 until her death, learned the disadvantages to being outnumbered in terms of gender. One day Rogers asked a male colleague to yield during debate and he replied, "Not now. It's not very often that we men are in a position where we can make the ladies sit down and be quiet."

It's remarkable to imagine but there are two U.S. Senators serving today who hold seats that have been held by only one other individual in more than seventy years. When I ask folks to wager a guess as to which Senators the pair might be, many are tempted to name someone from South Carolina. It's easy to imagine why. Strom Thurmond served in the upper chamber continuously from 1956 until literally just after his 100th birthday in 2002, meaning that he and his successor, Lindsey Graham, have had a monopoly on the seat for 57 years. But there are two whose predecessors go back even further. Pat Leahy of Vermont, elected in 1974, succeeded George Aiken, a Republican who first won his seat in

1940. And Thad Cochran became a Senator in 1978, succeeding James Eastland, a Democrat who won his seat in 1942.

Aiken and Eastland—individually, intellectually, and ideologically—could not be more different. Though Aiken was the Republican and Eastland the Democrat, guess who was more liberal? Aiken. And it's not even a close call. It's night and day.

Was realignment a key? No. In this case, both represented the majority of the views of their states and, for better or for worse, they did well. But as I'll explore, doing well does not mean doing good, and in examining the legacies of Aiken and Eastland, we'll find that one legacy is worth preserving as the embodiment of public service for all generations, while the other is an era of ugliness that we should hope to forget.

Let's have a look.

George Aiken

Aiken in later years
Photo via the U.S. Senate Historical Office

Vermont Today called Aiken a "man of integrity and simplicity whose voice of common sense was heard throughout the world." He was a simple man, one who thought of himself as a farmer and who was often seen feeding the many Capitol Hill pigeons. He was a Senator who, to the very last day of his 34-year Senate career, preferred to be called "Governor."

As a politician, Aiken had a citizen legislator perspective and practiced what he preached. In 1968, he spent, get this, $17.09 on his campaign (mostly for thank you notes for his volunteers), a figure that strains credulity today even for a small state, and he returned much of his office allotment to the federal treasury. Spending more wasn't necessary. Aiken's previous three re-elections were won with 78%, 66%, and 67%. Oh, and did I mention Aiken was unopposed when he won his sixth and final full term? But still.

Aiken had a long history of serving Vermont well before he went to the Senate in a 1940 special election, having been a two-term Governor, Lieutenant Governor, and Speaker of the General Assembly. A horticulturist by trade, he struck it big early in life.

Aiken was devoted to the outdoors
Photo via the Bennington Museum

If the term "Rockefeller Republican" was coined with the New York Governor in mind, Aiken could easily have paved the way. From his time as Governor through the twilight of his Senate career nearly four decades later, Aiken governed with a "for the people" approach. Elected Governor just as FDR was losing Vermont (one of just two states he failed to carry in 1936), Aiken nonetheless spoke favorably of the "New Deal" and advocated similar measures on a local scale. According to *Vermont Today*, "the banks, the railroads, the marble companies and the granite companies lost their monopoly on Vermont government when Aiken became governor. The forgotten farmer, Vermont's silent and suffering majority, was dealt a new hand as Aiken gave rural residents the will and the way to survive."

As Governor, Aiken signed legislation (left photo via Freedom and Unity) and
conducted Lincoln's Birthday address (photo via the Vermont Historical Society)

When Aiken made it to the Senate, his commitment to social justice
continued. Though his efforts didn't bear fruit right away, they yielded big
dividends later on.

For those who rely on food stamps, George Aiken is an unsung hero since it
was his bill that LBJ signed into law (Aiken briefly chaired the Senate Agriculture
Committee). For the many vacationers who flock to Vermont's bucolic atmosphere
of all seasons, Aiken may be their Senator, as his sponsorship of the Eastern
Wilderness Act opened the state's wilderness to recreation. Ditto for those who
use the St. Lawrence Seaway. Aiken was long a supporter of Civil Rights and
an amendment he authored was credited with helping to break the logjam and
secure crucial votes.

Left, Aiken being administered the oath of Senator as the state's senior
Senator, William Austin looked on; right, in his Senate pose
Left photo via Freedom and Unity; right photo
via the U.S. Senate Historical Office

Following the 1958 elections in which Republicans took a bloodbath nationally, Aiken blamed the rightward image of the Republican Party: "The very conservative element had access to the White House . . . the rest of us at the Hill have been expected to pull chestnuts out of the fire." He warned that unless liberals received adequate representation" in leadership positions, bad news would continue. For the position of Minority Leader, California colleague Tom Kuchel was one name that came to mind. Kuchel, he said, "would be excellent temperamentally and geographically." The position went to Hugh Scott.

Aiken did not always line up with liberals. On the tempestuous nomination of Lewis Strauss to be Dwight Eisenhower's Commerce Secretary, Aiken backed the administration even though he was outspoken in his annoyance over the coal industry's tactics. "When I see the coal and oil industry working as hard as possible to get the nomination confirmed," he said, "it is very disturbing to me." And Aiken opposed an early Kennedy administration initiative. The request was to authorize the Treasury to borrow $8,800,000,000 over five years for long-term development loans and his opposition pitted him against even some fellow liberal Republicans in the Senate, notably Jack Javits. Aiken acknowledged it had been done in the past but "only where it might reasonably be expected that the amount of money borrowed would be repaid in full as to principal and interest."

Aiken may be best known for a statement he made during the Vietnam War. In keeping with Vermont's dovish tradition, Aiken more or less called for U.S. withdrawal from Vietnam as early as 1966 when he said "the United States could well declare unilaterally . . . that we have 'won' in the sense that our armed forces are in control of most of the field and no potential enemy is in a position to establish its authority over South Vietnam." Aiken acknowledged that "it may be a far-fetched proposal, but nothing else has worked." LBJ declined to heed his former colleague's advice but when Nixon declared an end to active fighting in 1973, Aiken crowed, saying "what we got was essentially what I recommended six years ago - we said we had won, and we got out." His crusade earned Aiken the nickname "the wise old owl."

Aiken was also ahead of his time in terms of his party's ability to reach out. As early as 1938, he said Lincoln "would be ashamed of his party's leadership today," as the party's most recent standard bearer, Alf Landon, was bemoaning the "New Deal." He accepted a seat on Foreign Affairs because the person next in line was Joe McCarthy.

Aiken (and Maine Senator Margaret Chase Smith) would often have breakfast with the Senate's Democratic Leader, Mike Mansfield
Photo courtesy of Ray Dockstader

Colleagues Margaret Chase Smith of Maine and Leverett Saltonstall of Massachusetts (the latter served as Governor alongside Aiken) were similar Yankee soul-mates in age and temperament and points-of-view. To that end, he countered Barry Goldwater's capture of the 1964 Presidential nomination by placing Chase Smith's name in nomination ("if she were a man with her abilities she'd get the nomination on the first ballot"). But Aiken's real legacy was bemoaning partisanship, and he became a model for bringing the parties together. He once declared that "if a Democrat says we need better health, I am not going to come out for poorer health just to disagree with him." Breakfast with Democratic Majority Leader Mike Mansfield became routine. Mansfield in turn called Aiken "probably the most solid man in Congress. He has honesty, charm, humaneness and, above all, independence." Years earlier, he had said "any position Senator Aiken takes automatically becomes respectable simply because George Aiken has taken it." Even when the GOP had the minority, Aiken continued to chair a Foreign Affairs subcommittee on Canada - perhaps the ultimate tribute. Still, Aiken was a traditionalist to the end. When a number of younger colleagues began flirting with the idea of a summer break – now known as the "August recess," Aiken bemoaned it. In fact, following a test-run in 1969, Aiken returned to Washington that September to complain that the previous weeks were "no vacation."

Privately, Aiken was not incapable of taking shots at the other side. In his book *Aiken: Senate Diary*, he wrote that the George McGovern he saw on television was "not the George McGovern I used to know, nor has it been all week." Aiken went on to write that "unless I am mistaken, George McGovern will regret for as long as he lives some of his or his supporters' actions of today, and to try to atone by being more helpful at lower levels." Shortly after, he wrote that he did not believe Ted Kennedy "will ever be President of the United States of America."

Aiken's fellow native Vermonter, Calvin Coolidge, observed near the end of his life that "he no longer fit in with these times." Were he alive today, Aiken would have trouble adapting as well. He said "if we were to wake up some morning and find that everyone was the same race, creed and color, we would find some other cause for prejudice by noon." After his retirement, he also lambasted the political climate, opining that he had "never seen so many incompetent persons in high office. Politics and legislation have become more mixed and smellier than ever."

Ironically, Aiken should've been President Pro-Tem by virtue of having more seniority than Eastland but the Democrats had the majority. Aiken served until age 82, retiring in 1974. His reasoning: "I left much unfinished work at home and I now want to get back to it." But he wouldn't let go of civic affairs. He would become a presence at town meetings and freely lend his views on improving society. In short, he exemplified the term, "elder statesman." He died in 1984.

Incidentally, when Leahy, who was born the year Aiken became a Senator, succeeded Aiken in a 1974 upset, he became the first Democrat ever elected to the Senate from his state, a fact that still holds true today. Remember, Bernie Sanders is technically an Independent.

In addition to maintaining a close relationship with his constituents, Aiken was a devoted husband whose partnership with both of his wives was legendary. Beatrice Howard was his first-wife of 52 years whom by all accounts was the love of his life. He called her every Sunday and she never left the house until he did.

The fact that Bea was forced to drop out of school following eighth grade to work belied the fact that Bea had solid accomplishments for a woman of her day. She taught her children at home and was one of the first woman to register to vote after the 19th amendment was passed in 1920. His daughter Barbara Jones, who affectionately called him, "GDA" referred to her mother as "a very strong political ally," noting that "at every election, she got into her car to pick up people without cars" to take them to the polls. In order to allow him to fulfill his responsibilities to Vermonters, however, Bea stayed behind and ran the nursery in Putney.

In 1966, Bea was dying of cancer. Aiken was so bereft that for much of the time, he stayed outside with his apple trees as, "he could not bear to watch her die." When she did pass, he made the decision to have a granite stone for her burial site but instead gave the Town of Putney an 11-acre conservation site "in memory of my wife, Beatrice Howard Aiken. It is my hope that this land will be used for a wildflower and bird preserve in her memory" It is a trail treasured by many to this day.

A year later, Aiken married Lola Pierotti, his long-time office administrator (Aiken was among the few on Capitol Hill who in those days would have a woman running his office, leading one reporter to quip it was getting "a woman's touch."). Lola had started with him 27 years earlier while working for the Vermont Secretary of State and by the time of her promotion, had become an institution in her own right for her outspokenness and for doing much of the leg-work for Aiken (whom she referred to as "the Governor,"). Her advice was unsolicited and she loved to plunge into crowds. One day, she asked Nevada Senator Alan Bible whether Aiken would receive an appropriation. When Bible replied that he wasn't sure but "could be bribed," Aiken had him delivered Vermont maple syrup. However, by this point, she was no longer on Aiken's payroll. To avoid any improprieties, Lola would resign the official position but continue performing her duties. But, in true Aiken form, Lola recalled, "The Governor was taking me off on June 30 so it wouldn't disrupt the financial books."

Still, the marriage generated sensationalism on the Hill which Aiken rarely had seen. One headline read, "He Proposed 30 Years Later: Sen. Aiken and Lola are Capitol Hill's Love Story of the Year." Another profile said, "Lola Aiken Trades Payslips for Cowslips," referring to the fact that she resigned her position to avoid a conflict of interest but kept performing her duties.

Photo via the University of Vermont

Lola died as this book went to print at the age of 102. Before her death, she was treated to a bipartisan celebration led by a proclamation from current Vermont Governor Peter Shumlin. To her dying day, she referred to Aiken as "the Governor."

Stephen Terry, a former aide to Aiken called his former boss "so steeped in common sense, and its universal common sense. The quality of plain speaking is something that we really yearn for in public life or in the people in public life, and George Aiken certainly was that, personified."

Jim Eastland

Jim Eastland never achieved the recognition of Orval Faubus, Lester Mattox, Ross Barnett, or George Wallace but, for those let down by the cruelties of segregation, he had a similarly piercing impact. While Eastland didn't literally stand in the schoolhouse door blocking black students from entering, his actions over many years reinforced that old adage that in the Senate, it's sometimes not as important as where you stand, as where you sit. Indeed, as Chairman of the Senate Judiciary Committee for 20 years, Eastland boasted that he blocked more than 100 Civil Rights proposals. His attainment of that chairmanship led NAACP Clarence Mitchell to remark that "a mad dog is loose in the streets of justice."

If one doubts the accuracy of *Time Magazine* calling Eastland "the authentic representative of most of the South's 30 million white people, including the most respected and educated," the following ought to dispel those doubts.

After the Brown vs. Board of Education decision, Eastland said "you are not obliged to obey the decisions of any court which are plainly fraudulent sociological considerations." To Senate colleagues, he called the "Southern institution of racial segregation or racial separation . . . the correct, self-evident truth which arose from the chaos and confusion of the Reconstruction period. Separation promotes racial harmony. It permits each race to follow its own pursuits, and its own civilization. Segregation is not discrimination . . . Mr. President, it is the law of nature, it is the law of God, that every race has both the right and the duty to perpetuate itself. All free men have the right to associate exclusively with members of their own race, free from governmental interference, if they so desire."

But Eastland didn't stop there. He told LBJ that he believed the disappearance of three Civil Rights workers in Mississippi one night in 1964 to be "a publicity stunt" (they were later found murdered). He called the Warren Court "pro-communist" and wanted to subpoena *New York Times* reporters for communism. His staunch opposition was also a major factor in the failure to elevate Abe Fortas to the position of Chief Justice of the Supreme Court.

Accounts differ as to whether Eastland really believed what he preached but the general consensus was that Eastland was a racist. LBJ, knowing Eastland's penchant for agriculture subsidies, once said he "could be standing right in the middle of the worst Mississippi flood ever known and blame it on the nig—rs helped by the communists. But he'd say, we gotta have help from Washington." Still, LBJ courted Eastland, knowing of his influence and his advocacy for rural interests. In many ways, Eastland was the typical politician: a cigar-chomping figure who was more approachable behind-the-scenes than in public. But when it came to the "Great Society," not even LBJ's skills could sway his former colleague. He was one of just seven Democrats, all Southerners, to oppose the creation of Medicare; he also voted against Head-Start and the Appalachian Regional Development Act, which would've benefited Mississippians greatly. In his 1966 re-election campaign, he ran ads stating his opposition. Eastland also opposed Johnson-era legislation intended to ease immigration quotas/requirements. Aiken, by contrast, supported these proposals.

When Richard Nixon became President, Eastland maintained a working relationship to the point that in his last re-election campaign in 1972, Nixon quietly let it be known that he favored Eastland despite the presence of an active Republican candidate. It was enough but it was a last hurrah.

Arthur Schlesinger, in *Robert Kennedy and his Times*, called Eastland "devoid of any socially redeeming qualities" and said that he "lacked the courtliness" of Mississippi's other longtime Senator, John Stennis, who professed a similar philosophy. But Eastland got along well with the Kennedy brothers, and if his relationship wasn't harmonious, it was at least productive. In his last year in office, he invited Ted Kennedy to address a commencement ceremony at Old Miss, which prompted Kennedy to wonder out loud, "How can you invite a Kennedy to be graduation speaker at Ole Miss?" Eastland said, "Because I'm not running for re-election." Indeed, there is evidence that Eastland didn't entirely depart voluntarily, but that the changing of the times simply caught up to him.

By the mid-1970s, Eastland appeared to relax his hard-lined views on Civil Rights (even hiring African-American committee staffers, including Ed Cole) but his legacy defined him. As his seat came up in 1978, Eastland, 74, tested the waters about running again, asking Mississippi NAACP head Aaron Henry about possible African-American support for a 7th term. Henry told Eastland, whom Marten Zwiers in a thesis on Eastland once called the "Godfather" of Mississippi politics, that his "chances of getting support from the black community are poor at best. You have a master-servant philosophy when it comes to blacks." He then observed that "the old man just collapsed in tears."

One moment of levity in a career that is anything but: call it *Eastland's Sammy Davis, Jr. kisses Archie Bunker* moment. When Kennedy was at Ole Miss, Henry spotted Eastland and planted a kiss on his cheek. Seeing that, Kennedy quipped that there are two things that he would consider to be priceless. "A picture of Aaron Henry kissing Jim Eastland and a picture of Jim Eastland when he realizes someone has a picture of Henry kissing him."

Eastland's position as President-Pro-Tem actually elevated him to third in line for the Presidency twice: when Spiro Agnew resigned and when Gerald Ford took over the Presidency. One senator, Phillip Hart, opposed his ascension because of the Civil Rights issue, and it is likely many are grateful that the White House, which during Eastland's Senate tenure alone changed hands in the middle of a term, did not land in Eastland's lap.

Eastland was succeeded by Thad Cochran who was five years old when Eastland was sworn in for his first full term. Cochran had long had warm relations with his state's African-American community and, unlike his predecessor, is one of the most congenial, respected, and approachable Senators in the chamber.

Upon serving out the remainder of his term, Eastland went back to his plantation in Mississippi. He died at age 82 in 1986, somewhat broken by years of battles that he had at last lost.

Were he alive today, Eastland would without question be a Republican, probably among the staunchest of Constitutional conservatives. It would be interesting to hear his views of say, Clarence Thomas.

A modern Aiken is a little harder to predict. Vermont Republicans have changed little since his day but the national party has changed abundantly, which Aiken seemed to sense in his final days. He was not happy about it. That said, he might not be a Democrat, but even a man with his sincerity would likely have difficulty overcoming an association with his national brethren in a state that Democratic Presidential candidates routinely carry. An interesting footnote is that Aiken was one of the Vermonters Jim Jeffords cited as models in announcing why he could no longer remain a Republican.

And so it goes.

CHAPTER FORTY-TWO

Lev Satonstall, JFK's Massachusetts Senate Colleague: A Legend In Own Right

Historic Tidbit: As the motorcade prepared to enter the White House during the 1949 inaugural ceremonies, newly installed Vice-President Alben Barkley spotted Strom Thurmond who of course had tried to prevent the Truman/ Barkley ticket from winning the previous fall. Thurmond tipped his hat to Barkley who proceeded to do the same when an exasperated Truman stopped him. "Don't you dare tip your hat to that S.O.B.," Truman said.

With his esteemed colleague
Photo courtesy of the Massachusetts Historical Society Collection

There are many individuals who becomes footnotes in American history who, if they're lucky, might even get a moment in the sun by being an answer to a question in a game of *Trivial Pursuit*. Leverett Saltonstall could be one such figure. The longtime Massachusetts Senator was John F. Kennedy's senior colleague and served alongside the future President during his entire eight-year tenure in the upper body before he won the White House. By all accounts, the pair had great affection for each other. Saltonstall, a Republican, was actually a distinguished Senator in his own right, a 22-year member of the Senate who had been a rare Republican Governor before that and through his work made possible a great deal of social progress.

The prominence of the Saltonstall name in Massachusetts came before Leverett was born—way before. The Saltonstalls arrived in Massachusetts in 1630, when Sir Richard Saltonstall made Salem his home. *The Boston Globe* notes that they "helped found" Watertown, which folks may remember was in the news during the recent bombing of the Boston Marathon. *Inspirational Journeys* called him "the descendant of no fewer than eight governors of Massachusetts, including a leader of the Massachusetts Bay Colony, as well as one Lord Mayor of London from the reign of Elizabeth I."

Tending to his chores even as Governor-elect
Photo courtesy of the Trustees of the Boston Public Library, Leslie Jones Collection

The Saltonstall family's association with Presidents was also legendary. His great-great-grandfather was Mayor of Salem who served in Congress alongside John Quincy Adams as a Whig and his father was a classmate of Teddy Roosevelt's. He knew the family well. The younger Leverett's reputation came early, in Massachusetts and nationally. Indeed, Saltonstall's family was amongst the wealthiest in the state.

A first lieutenant in World War 1 and a tenth-generation Harvard grad, Saltonstall was a member of the Massachusetts House for 13 years, and in the days when Republicans were vibrant in the "Bay State," he was Speaker for seven. Colleagues called him "Lev" or "Salty." A defeat as Lieutenant Governor of Massachusetts coincided with FDR's sweep of the state but Saltonstall rebounded two years later with a successful bid for Governor.

Boston Mayor James Michael Curley, who was a surprise second fiddle to Curley in the 1938 Governor's race, called him a "Harvard accent with a South Boston face" and a later foe cited him as being born with "a diamond-studded spoon in his mouth." In Massachusetts, the "Brahmin" label has plagued many a pol across the generations, from John Kerry to William Weld. It didn't inhibit either from winning, however. One of Saltonstall's colleagues as Governor was a man he'd serve two decades with in the Senate—Vermont's George Aiken.

Riding in one parade and marching in Revolutionary War garb during another
Photos courtesy of the Trustees of the Boston
Public Library, Leslie Jones Collection

With his family
Photos courtesy of the Trustees of the Boston
Public Library, Leslie Jones Collection

Saltonstall had a pretty respectable tenure. He appeared on the cover of *Time Magazine* and was elected Chair of the National Governor's Association. Rivals had made an issue of his wealth but his early commitment to progress was evident. In addition to establishing an interfaith committee on equality, he created mechanisms for public safety. He cut taxes and eradicated the state debt by 90%. During his second term, a Teamsters strike got much of his attention, and an industrial defense committee was formed. He was re-elected twice and left office in 1944 with modest popularity.

When an opening for the Senate arose, Saltonstall took 64%. In 1948, he beat a guy by the name of John Fitzgerald by just 53-47%. His 1954 race was a true squeaker, as he held off the state's Treasurer (who would eventually become the first Italian-American Governor, Foster Furcolo) by 1%, a mere 29,000 votes as Democrats were regaining control of Congress.

It was said that Kennedy, who by that time was Saltonstall's junior colleague, had a rocky relationship with Furcolo and preferred Saltonstall. His 1960 re-election came with Kennedy at the top of the Democratic ticket 57-43%, a margin of 300,000 votes. Once again, in the midst of his own race for President, Kennedy again did not come to the aide of Saltonstall's foe. There was talk that JFK promised him the Ambassadorship to Canada should he lose re-election.

When he arrived in the Senate, Saltonstall's colleagues immediately recognized his skill. They selected him as their Whip, the second highest position, after the 1948 elections, a post that he'd hold for eight years before stepping down to take the ranking member's slot on Armed Services. He would also serve on Appropriations and Small Business. But political skills aside, his colleagues' personal admiration for him was also evident; they called him "the gentlemanly gentleman from Massachusetts." He spent hours prepping for hearings, almost unheard of in these times.

Often-times, Saltonstall was forced to walk a fine line. Shortly before standing for re-election, Saltonstall was forced to vote on the issue of the Watkins Report which recommended censure of his colleague. Saltonstall was deeply opposed to McCarthy's tactics but was fearful of offending Republicans whose votes he needed. He voted to delay it and narrowly won re-election. A month later, when the time came to censure McCarthy, Saltonstall was the only member of the GOP leadership to acquiesce.

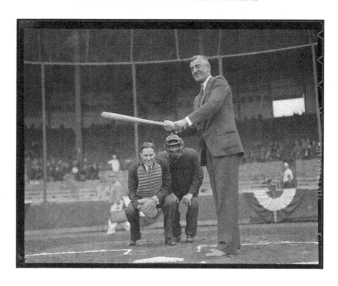

Opening day against the Dodgers
Photo courtesy of the Trustees of the Boston Public Library, Leslie Jones Collection

Saltonstall's skills were recognized by Presidents as well. For example, Truman appointed him Evaluation Commission for Operation Crossroads. When Wisconsin Republican Alexander Wiley asked Georgia Democrat Richard Russell to demand classified information from the Truman administration for the firing of Douglas MacArthur, Saltonstall objected.

Eisenhower, whose nomination he strongly backed in 1952, once told him in a letter "you are one of those I consider indispensable." For Saltonstall had stuck with the administration against an attempt by a more conservative Republican, Ohio's John Bricker, to limit President's treaty making powers. LBJ, upon Saltonstall's retirement announcement, said, "I have been privileged to know you well and to serve with you in the Senate. Your friendship is one of the treasures I shall always value most devotedly."

In his Senate days, Saltonstall, and ironically LBJ's 1960 vice-presidential rival Lodge, were among the Senators LBJ would take folks to the Senate floor to see, because as Johnson biographer Robert Caro wrote, they were "real New England statesmen, the kind you didn't find in Texas." But it was his relationship with his home-state colleague, the future President that is especially noteworthy.

Saltonstall held his Senate seat along JFK coattails
Photos via E-Bay and worthpoint.com; right photo
courtesy of the U.S. Government Printing Office

Though Saltonstall obviously preferred Richard Nixon for President in 1960 (Lodge was his running mate), his relationship with JFK was stellar. Saltonstall attended JFK's wedding and has an inscription by the future President in *Profiles in Courage* that reads, "To Senator Saltonstall—with the very highest regards of his colleague John Kennedy." One constituent once explained how he mistook Saltonstall for JFK's uncle; JFK was happy to oblige that perception ("If you are ready to admit it, I am"). As a sign of how bipartisanship and collegiality reigned even in an election season, Saltonstall hosted Kennedy on his television program, "Report To Massachusetts" which aired during 1959 and '60 (Lyndon Johnson, Richard Nixon and Admiral Hyman rickover were guests as well).

Even during his Presidency, Saltonstall did little to provide ammunition to critics. As Barry Goldwater's Presidential campaign was getting underway when Kennedy was still alve, Saltonstall gave the Arizona Senator a perfunctory introduction at a Boston fundraiser but it was so lukewarm that Kennedy quipped that he "used to get better introductions from Senator Saltonstall when I was in the Senate than that."

Their names appear together on Saltonstall/Kennedy, a 1954 act that would provide more money for fishing-related research grants, as well as on the Cape Cod National Seashores Bill, which included the creation of a national park. In office, Saltonstall didn't always support Kennedy (his Medicaid proposal for example) but did back the Nuclear Test Ban Treaty. For Saltonstall was supportive of a muscular defense. On a proposal by Wisconsin Democrat William Proxmire to cut funding for the long-range B-52 and B-58 missiles, Saltonstall made clear his opposition. "We simply must not choose to gamble," he said. "We must continue to provide the protection of a strong and modern-manned bomber force, while we push ahead with development of our missile systems capabilities."

Somewhat surprising in the land of the Adams was Saltonstall's stature on some matters that had the free-men orthodoxy. He was not among the signers of his fellow New Englander Margaret Chase Smith's "Declaration of Conscience" following Joe McCarthy's Communism crusade. As his tight 1954 re-election race approached, Saltonstall, not wanting to alienate conservatives whose votes he desparately needed, lobbied to delay release of the Watkns Report until after. However, he had no reservations about opposing McCarthyism early and often in other ways. Saltonstall also opposed Ted Kennedy (by then his new and much younger colleague) on his amendment to the Voting Rights Act to gut the poll tax.

And his early commitment to civil rights was unmistakable. He simply realized that getting it passed required carefully treading water. He told a visiting group of Harvard students early in 1964 that he hoped "a realistic civil rights bill goes through. I wouldn't be honest if I thought it would go through in its present form."

Saltonstall backed the Fair Employment anti-discrimination bill and worked to give children access to health care. He backed most of the "Great Society" measures. On labor issues, however, he was more conservative.

One of Saltonstall's sons was killed in World War II, which clearly impacted other parts of his agenda, including advocacy for veterans. Saltonstall also advocated for space exploration. His son William served as his administrative assistant for seven years and followed his dad into politics. He was a member of the Massachusetts Senator for ten years.

Saltonstall did not seek a fourth full term in the Senate in 1966. He was 74 years old, and a number of his fellow New Englanders (Aiken, Chase Smith) would stay longer. But he "wanted to quit when he was still doing the job rather than just fade away in the Senate."

After his retirement, Saltonstall returned to Massachusetts where he lived for a dozen years. He died in 1979 at age 86.

Edgar Druiscoll of the *Globe* said of Saltonstall, "reflecting in his bearing and character much of the thing that in bygone years won for Boston the title of the 'Athens of America': he is what men call a scholar and a gentleman, sort of survivor of the people who moved through the pages of the 'Flowering of New England.'"

That is definitely apt.

CHAPTER FORTY-THREE

Schoeppel and Carlson Gateway From Landon's Kansas GOP To Dole's

Historic Tidbit: The campaign of Martin Van Buren's use of the term "okay" (simply "O.K" in those days) made the word part of the everyday America lexicon. And Teddy Roosevelt's use of the phrase "good to the last drop" upon trying Maxwell House Coffee became an enduring term still used today? See. For everything, there is a story.

**Alf Landon's Governorship and 1936 Presidential campaign
created circles that endured for a generation
Photo courtesy of the Kansas Historical Society**

By the mid-1960s, rites of passage put the Kansas Republican Party firmly in the hands of Bob Dole and the state's senior Senator, Jim Pearson. Until that time, however, the party had been controlled by disciples of Alf Landon, the venerable Kansan and former Presidential candidate who lost to FDR by a record margin but who at home was, for all practical purposes, known as "Mr. Kansas."

Landon actually outlived many of the folks he mentored, including two Kansas Senators who succeeded him as Governor, Andrew Schoeppel and Frank Carlson. Though the duo served in the upper chamber together for more than a decade, Schoeppel and Carlson went their separate ways on issues such as McCarthy and even Presidential candidates. But theirs is a story of remarkable Kansas pride which can't be found in every state.

Schoeppel was a World War I vet who graduated law school before trying his hand at local politics, including a stint as Mayor of Ness City and chairman of the Kansas Corporation Commission. By 1942, he wanted to become Governor, a goal for which he had Landon's full backing despite the fact that he was little known. He won two terms but as the Kansas Historical Society reported, Schoeppel's relationship with the State Legislature was virtually non-existent, and Schoeppel also got into tussles with the federal government, which charged that he did not enforce the laws of Prohibition, even after raids on liquor stores. He often sided with business over labor, barring "sit-down" strikes.

Around the time Schoeppel's term ended, he and Landon had drifted. While Landon was viewed as the titular head of the Kansas GOP long after the 1936 debacle, Schoeppel tried to change that by challenging the state's longtime Senator, Arthur Capper. Landon loyalists stuck with Capper but Schoeppel's forces changed the rules. In the end, Capper retired and Schoeppel won the nomination, and Landon was relegated to a low-level status in the current affairs of his party.

Andrew Schoeppel (1894-1962)
Photo courtesy of the U.S. Senate Historical Office

Schoeppel won three terms as Senator with similar margins (between 54% and 56%). His record was somewhat right of center, which was evident in his championing of Robert Taft to be the party's standard bearer as opposed to Eisenhower. He opposed McCarthy's censure.

If Schoeppel strayed a bit, Carlson remained loyal. He was a legend. Upon his death, the AP called Carlson "a homespun farmer whose unassuming manner and close rapport with ordinary people carried him to 13 elections in 13 tries." And before Sam Brownback in 2010, he was the only Kansan to serve as Congressman, Governor, and Senator. Not that Carlson wanted it that way. Born to Swedish immigrants in 1893, Carlson was also a veteran of the first World War but also a Concordia, Kansas farmer. One day in 1928, Carlson was doing his chores when some friends approached him about running for the Legislature. He hesitated, not wanting to spend time away from the farm. "You won't win anyway," one said. And his supporters had stickers that said, "I'd rather be farming." But win he did.

Katherine O'Loughlin McCarthy, whom Carlson unseated for Congress
Photo courtesy of the Kansas Historic Society

Carlson then became Alf Landon's campaign chair for Governor of Kansas in 1932. It was a successful endeavor, even more remarkable considering FDR was sweeping the state and Kansas was electing a Democratic Senator for the last time. By 1934, it was Carlson's turn to go to Congress and he again went against the grain. Republicans were taking a bloodbath at all levels but Carlson unseated an incumbent, Katherine O'Loughlin McCarthy, by about 2,000 votes.

Shortly thereafter, Landon declared that he was running for President and Carlson served as his campaign chair. It was another historic Republican loss, as Landon was beaten soundly in his own state and in every state but Maine and Vermont ("as Maine goes, so goes Vermont"). But Carlson held onto his seat 52%-48%. His next three elections were non-affairs.

By 1946, Schoeppel had served two terms as Governor, and Carlson was ready to succeed him. With Landon's help, he secured the GOP nomination and took the job with 53%. If Schoeppel was considered a weak if pugnacious Governor, Carlson was quite forward-looking and well-liked (Dole said years later that he "didn't have an enemy in the world"). He championed improvements of mental health projects, highway construction, rural health programs, and workman's comp.

The Kansas Historical Foundation wrote in Carlson's bio that "prior to Carlson's administration, Kansas had been rated 40th place nationally in terms of the condition of its mental hospitals. By the summer of 1950 [it] jumped to 11th place." Carlson also took a hands-off approach when it came to Prohibition, which was removed when he was Governor. Calling himself "a teetotaler," Carlson said he didn't smoke or drink "but I have no quarrel with those who do. I'm a great believer in letting the people decide." It would have been interesting to see where he stood on the pressing social issues of the day.

As Governor and riding with his wife
Photos courtesy of the Kansas Historical Society

Carlson was elected to the Senate in 1950, just as his Governorship was ending. Immediately he became a major footnote to national politics. He was an early backer of Eisenhower, who grew up in Kansas, and was one of his confidantes

and strategists in the battle for the GOP nomination in 1952 against Ohio
Senator Bob Taft, whom Schoeppel was supporting. Eisenhower won of course,
and Carlson reaped the benefits with access, which led Carlson to becoming
an important footnote on another matter. One day early in his Presidency,
Eisenhower had confided in Carlson that "the White House is "the loneliest house
I have ever been in." He asked Carlson for advice. Carlson responded by inviting
Ike to the prayer breakfast. From then on, it became a tradition for the President
to attend the breakfast every year. This may qualify Carlson as a Founding Father
of the Presidential Prayer Breakfast.

On other matters as well, Carlson gained respect. In *Master of the Senate*
Robert Caro calls him "the administration's spokesman on postal matters." He
served on the Committee investigating Joe McCarthy and joined 21 other GOP
colleagues in voting to censure him (Schoeppel was among those who opposed
it). He also helped guide the income tax withholding system to passage. But Civil
Rights were a major concern for Carlson and he not only backed the legislation
but also Title IV, which barred gender discrimination. A year later, he became the
only member of the Kansas delegation to back the Medicare bill. He also backed
the Peace Corps. "Never have so many denounced so many without knowledge,"
he said.

Kansas historian Ross Dayer said Carlson could do "the right thing at the
right time so people thought a lot of him. But for us, the best thing about him
was that he never forgot where he came from. This was evident in a characteristic
Carlson statement: "there are no self-made men. It is your friends who make you
what you are." In the book *Unlimited Partners* which Dole wrote with his wife,
he referred to Carlson as "an authentic Kansas institution. He was also the rarest
breed of political animal, one who by, refusing power and popularity assures
him of both." Upon his death, he wrote that "another giant in Kansas politics is
gone." He called him "a friend, an adviser and a role model. He wrote the book
when it came to class."

Schoeppel died suddenly in 1962 at age 67 and was succeeded by Jim Pearson,
a loyal Republican who nevertheless would not hesitate to go his own way. At
times, conservatives openly spoke of a primary challenge to him, but never
followed through, and Pearson's electoral campaigns prior to his 1978 retirement
were uneventful.

Carlson declined to seek re-election in 1968 at age 75 but not before having
his name placed in nomination as a "Favorite Son" candidate at the 1968 GOP
convention. He was succeeded by Dole, who had to defeat yet another former
Governor, Bill Avery, to win the GOP nomination. Carlson died in May 1987,
at which time Landon was still living (he called Carlson "an outstanding Kansan,
a faithful, and dedicate public servant").

Nine years earlier, Landon had seen his daughter, Nancy Landon Kassebaum, win Pearson's Senate seat, and that September, he celebrated his 100th birthday. Other than Strom Thurmond, who did not carry the banner for a major political party, Landon lived longer than any Presidential nominee. When he had turned 95, Reagan asked him if he wanted to visit the White House on his 100th birthday. But as he began fading, the offer was scaled down to his 97th birthday. Landon replied, "I'll go both."

Carlson in later years
Photos courtesy of the Kansas Historical Society

CHAPTER FORTY-FOUR

Senator Douglas of Illinois: No, Not That Senator Douglas

Historic Quote: "Every speaker has three speeches. The one he intends to make. The one he actually makes, and the one he wishes he had made." – Paul Douglas of Illinois bemoaning the fact that the *Congressional Record* allows him to make the speech he wished he had made. "These considerations engender my belief that the Record is more a work of fiction that one of fact."

When one thinks of the most effective Senators of the 20th century, Lyndon Johnson and Everett Dirksen come to mind. That's certainly appropriate. Both were master strategists who contributed much to the generation-shaping legislation of the day. But there was another who may be the most underrated: Paul Douglas of Illinois. He may not have seen many bills over the finish line but he didn't have to because he was a major player from start to finish. And he was a rarity. One whose wife actually proceeded him in Congress.

While *Changes* describes Douglas as "a man of conscience and a stubborn defender of core principles," the book *Black Voting Rights* may be more apt: "Known for his keen mind, his intense preparation, and his quixotic forays against the windmills of economic privilege and racial injustice, the erudite Douglas was usually outside the Senate decision making. Many viewed him as a visionary." What is indisputable is that to friend and foe alike, Paul Douglas was the "Conscience of the Senate."

Photo courtesy of the U.S. Senate Historical Office

Douglas was a liberal's liberal. He was a passionate advocate for social justice, making perhaps his biggest contribution in the area of Civil Rights. When Senator

Jim Eastland, the crusty and rabidly racist senator from Mississippi, was bottling up the 1957 Civil Rights bill in the Judiciary Committee he chaired, Douglas confronted him. "This bill has been before the committee since January. Hearings were started in February. The hearings were concluded in March. It is now very nearly the end of May. If we do not get a bill on the floor very soon, we know exactly what will happen."

At the end of the day, Southern conservatives did not filibuster the bill because they felt it had been weakened to the point of being ineffective. Douglas agreed. He called the final bill "as effective as soup made from the shadow of a crow which had starved to death." His unhappiness was with many fellow liberals, particularly Westerners such as Wayne Morse whom he believed caved for higher demands when Lyndon Johnson dangled the Hells Canyon Dam project they long sought. Douglas reminded them the dam had virtually no likelihood of being enacted into law. To one of those Westerners, Frank Church, Douglas asserted, "you are gambling with fake money."

The jury trial amendment was another gamble. There was no jury in most civil contempt cases. Criminal contempt cases were different. Many, including John F. Kennedy, had sided with the South. Douglas also played a significant role in the creation of public housing. In *Democracy Can't Live In These Houses*, which he wrote for *Colliers Magazine*, Douglas described the projects as "one of our moral, political, and economic responsibilities to do something to lift more homes at least to the minimum level for satisfactory living. The 15,000,000 or more Americans who live in the blighted areas are not inferior to the rest of us. They are only less fortunate."

Douglas advocated many pieces of legislation that languished for years before enactment. Medicare was one. Douglas viewed these delays as part of the process. "Long periods of public education are needed before these issues are accepted," he explained. "I see my own role . . . primarily as one of introducing and trying to develop these much-needed but controversial issues so that they eventually gain success." Another piece of legislation, which American.edu reports was "drafted by a Legislative Reference Service economist," was intended to promote "social capital" in depressed communities. It would give them "preferential treatment in government contracts, technical assistance, vocational retraining, and loans and grants to help lure industry."

Douglas learned about opponents' tactics of obfuscation when it came to his own causes. The Indiana Lake Shore bill is one example. Douglas introduced it in 1958 and it languished for eight years. So did the Truth-In-Lending Act which passed in 1967. Douglas had just begun his involuntary retirement, having been unseated a year earlier. But the Senator who ultimately did get it through, Wisconsin's Bill Proxmire, hailed Douglas' efforts and contributions.

In the 1960s, Douglas and other liberals found themselves playing defense, in many cases against his fellow Illinoisan, Minority Leader Everett Dirksen, who had been proposing a series of Constitutional amendments to roll back sweeping Supreme Court decisions, including "one-man, one-vote." 67 votes were needed for passage. When Dirksen proposed substituting the measure with a call for "National American Legion Baseball Week," which would instead require majority passage, Douglas labeled it, "the foul ball amendment."

That Douglas ended up in the Senate was almost totally accidental. He was nominated under regular order but somewhat as a sacrificial lamb. Douglas initially wanted to run for Governor but powerful Cook County machine boss Jacob Avery promoted him for the Senate instead—not out of any great love for Douglas but because few thought the Republican incumbent, Wayland Brooks, could be beaten. But in the year of "Dewey Defeats Truman" (a headline that emanated from Illinois), Douglas won perhaps an even bigger upset. He unseated Brooks 55-45% as Truman won by 33,000 votes. Had Brooks been seen as remotely vulnerable, it's unlikely Douglas would have been anywhere near the top of the list of candidates.

There were no Brooks-Douglas debates because Brooks had refused, so Douglas resorted to putting an empty chair in the studio, and he maintained a vigorous travel schedule throughout Illinois. Douglas was such a hit that some wanted to draft him for President as early as 1952. A fellow Illinoisan named Adlai Stevenson wanted the prize that year but Douglas heartily backed Estes Kefauver. Years later, he defended Kennedy in relation to charges concerning his supposed Senate absenteeism during the campaign. "There is no more responsibility than campaigning for the office of President of the United States."

Photo courtesy of the Institute of Government and Public Affairs

Nor did Douglas' background suggest he'd be in the Senate. He was born in Massachusetts and grew up in rural Maine after his stepmother fled his abusive father with Paul and his brother in hand. He attended Columbia University and was anti-Tammany Hall. But his crusade for social justice began as a defender. Douglas eventually made his way to Chicago as an Organizer for the International

Ladies Garment Workers Union. He began teaching economics at a number of schools but was firmly settled in Chicago.

Douglas could credibly claim to be part of the "New Deal." He knew both Harold Ickes and Labor Secretary Francis Perkins, both of whom were instrumental in making him part of the Consumer Advisory Board of the National Recovery Administration. Douglas was urged to seek the Chicago Mayoralty in 1935.

One publication wrote, "To the consternation of his advisers, Douglas seemed to take a perverse pleasure in proclaiming that position in front of the most antagonistic audiences. When speaking before notoriously conservative business groups and white homeowners associations, he insisted on confronting the issue straightforwardly and, in many cases, making it the centerpiece of his remarks."

That may also have extended to his Senate colleagues and often, Douglas proved himself capable of displaying scholarly linguistic impatience for those who strayed from the reservation. When Douglas took the floor following remarks by Dirksen, he told the chamber that he had "listened for 55 minutes to a speech by my colleague full of charming irrelevancies, which covered virtually every subject under the sun except the amendment in question to which he referred only incidentally and at random."

In some cases, Douglas found the result of his style could be penetrating. One day, powerful Senate Appropriations chair Kenneth McKellar of Tennessee thought a package he was pushing would be routine. But Douglas, arguing the package contained too much pork, questioned it. A stunned McKellar responded by asserting his leverage. He proposed that all appropriations reserved for the state of Illinois be stricken from the bill. Fellow Senators, fearful of crossing an octogenarian baron, voted with McKellar. It took pleading by Illinois' other Senator, Dirksen, to reinsert the money but not before forcing Douglas to make an apology.

Douglas knew that much of his ability to make sweeping change would come from changing the rules that often allowed both the old guard and the status quo to prevail. His proposal in 1959 to end a filibuster by a simple majority in the Senate within 116 days following the signing of a petition by 16 Senators could be seen as a precursor to civil rights, but it was opposed by both Dirksen and Senate Majority Leader Lyndon Johnson. The alternative they put forward would require two-thirds of those voting rather than Senate membership. But Douglas called them out. "It is clear that on measures of importance on which a filibuster would be conducted, virtually the entire membership of the Senate would be present on the floor for the final vote. Therefore, there is no real difference between two-thirds of the total membership and two-thirds of those present and voting under the Johnson resolution." Douglas's proposal garnered just 28 votes and he called the win by Southerners, 'a great victory. They have reversed the drive for civil rights."

In 1966, Douglas was 74 years old and up for re-election; he decided to go one last time. He kept a rigorous schedule but his age was noticeable (even Democrats could tell he was worn out after a full day). The stature of his opponent, Charles Percy, a 47 year old already being hailed as the future savior of the Republican Party, did not help. In his memoirs, Paul Simon said the "appearance of the youthful Bobby Kennedy and the aging giant unfortunately reinforced the issue." Simon recalls receiving a call from one woman who suggested a paternity suit against Douglas. Doing so, she said, would "limit the age issue overnight."

**Douglas's wife, Emily Taft Douglas, served a term in the U.S. House
Photo courtesy of the U.S. House of Representatives**

Photo courtesy of the Institute of Government and Public Affairs

The national climate was a bigger problem. Martin Luther King, Jr., had spent the summer of 1966 marching in Chicago demanding "open-housing" laws, which caused a "white backlash," but Douglas hoped to benefit from Adlai Stevenson III, who was seeking the job of Illinois Treasury. Both Douglas and Percy suspended their campaigns when Percy's daughter was mysteriously murdered in September and didn't get back into full gear until just before Election Day. But by Election Day, Douglas' loss was a foregone conclusion. He managed just 57% in Chicago and was swept out downstate. The result was a 12% loss. He lived ten more years, passing at age 84 in 1976.

Douglas had the rare distinction of having his wife proceed him in Congress. Emily Taft Douglas served one term in the House, having won an election in 1944. She lost in the anti-Truman landslide in 1946 but continued her work for justice internationally and stateside, in particular marching with Dr. Martin Luther King, Jr., in Selma in 1965.

As an appropriate postscript, Douglas taught economics to future Senator Paul Simon whose fashion bears an uncanny resemblance to Douglas' (both men wore bowties frequently). More importantly, the two men were also cut from the same cloth when it came to far more important virtues: decency and commitment to social justice.

CHAPTER FORTY-FIVE

Emanuel Celler's 50-Year House Tenure
Ended With Loss To Holtzman

Historic Quote: "The Lord Giveth, the Lord taketh away. You'll do fine around here as long as you remember I'm the Lord." – Armed Services Chair Ed Hebert to newly elected Congresswoman Pat Schroeder. She was assigned to his committee.

Photo courtesy of the Library of Congress Prints and Photographs Division

At the beginning of 2013, the territory that was for so long New York's 8th Congressional district ceased to exist. A casualty of redistricting, the Brooklyn-Queens district encompassed much of the Borough's Jewish neighborhoods. What is remarkable is that for nearly nine decades prior to Bob Turner's 2011 election win, the seat was held by just four individuals. These people were not just anybody, but in their respective tenures, their beliefs, voices, and mere presence made them four of the most colorful and distinct figure both on Capitol Hill and nationally. I'm talking of course about Emanuel Celler, Elizabeth Holtzman, Charles Schumer, and Anthony Weiner.

Holtzman gained fame from the Watergate Committee and for her 1980 Senate run, which she lost to Al D'Amato by 1%. Schumer's fame is a result of, well, Schumer. And Weiner? Well, there's that whole weiner thing. After he resigned, Turner won a special election to succeed him, then watched as the district was decimated. But Celler held the seat for the majority of those 89 years. And his story encompasses the changes of the district and the nation itself.

Celler was in office 50 years, leaving him at the time just short of being the longest-serving Congressman ever (only Georgia's Carl Vinson, who left office in 1965, served two months longer, and Jamie Whitten and John Dingell subsequently passed him). In the end, it was Celler's longevity that was turned against him, as he was shocked in a 1972 primary by a young lawyer 56 years his junior named Elizabeth Holtzman.

It's not often that someone who's been in office 50 years loses but that's exactly what happened in 1972. Holtzman was just 28, and her defeat of the 84-year-old Celler would alter at least one important footnote in history. Celler, known as "Manny," had chaired the House Judiciary Committee for years and, had he held his seat, he would have likely presided over the Watergate hearings. Instead, that honor went to Peter Rodino, his colleague from across the river who would endlessly "thank Holtzman for what she did."

Celler with NAACP President Clarence Mitchell, Senator Hubert Humphrey and Congressman William McCulloch of Ohio following passage of the Civil Rights Act
Left photo via the papers of Clarence Mitchell; Right photo via crooksandliars.com
Courtesy of the U.S. Senate Historical Office

In his autobiography *Man of the House*, Tip O'Neill aptly summed up how many people viewed Celler by the end of his tenure. He was "a distinguished-looking old man and an eloquent speaker with the greatest vocabulary of any politician I've ever known. [He was] very difficult to deal with. He was brilliant but also arrogant and stubborn. Nobody could get him to move—not Sam Rayburn, not John McCormack, and certainly not Carl Albert." For Celler was a man who could be biting with his style. During the Eisenhower administration, when members were debating how to handle allegations of impropriety involving White House Chief of Staff Sherman Adams (acceptance of favors, etc), Celler said it was time to make "Sherm squirm."

Celler was first elected when Warren G. Harding was President. His defeat came as Richard Nixon was preparing to win a second term. When he lost, the district was numbered New York-16, and had once been NY-10. In a *New York Times* article, Richard Madden said NY-16 "resembles a child's sock, stuffed with candy and nuts and tacked to the mantle on Christmas morning." But Republicans in Albany had designed it for Celler. It took in Crown Heights, Flatbush, Sheepshead Bay, and the Eastern Parkway. It was overwhelmingly Jewish, and for years was suited to Celler's politics. But it may have changed a little too fast for him to keep up.

Celler was born in 1888 to a Brooklyn "whiskey rectifier." He wrote in his biography *Never Away from Brooklyn* that "my grandfather, in 1848, had fled from Germany to find political freedom in the United States. My grandfather was Catholic; my grandmother was Jewish." Jewish was how he was reared. Celler attended Columbia Law School. His 1922 House election came in a district that had never sent a Democrat to Congress. His campaign was anti-Prohibition and pro-League of Nations. He won by a hair and became a solid liberal, which meant being pro-Civil Rights and and condemning restrictive immigration laws such as the one Calvin Coolidge signed into law in 1924. He left the door to his home open on Saturdays so that observant Jewish constituents wouldn't have to knock if they wanted to share their views. As the years went on, Celler backed the "New Deal," and strongly oppose McCarthyism. During World War II, a local rabbi asked Celler why more wasn't being done to rescue the Jews: "If six million cattle had been slaughtered, it would have attracted greater interest." Celler began to speak out forcefully, though to little avail with the powers that be.

Celler himself got a mild exposure to anti-Semitism in Congress as John Rankin, a rabidly anti-semitic Senator from Mississippi, addressed Celler on the floor as "the Jewish gentleman from New York." Celler objected which made Rankin question whether it was because he referred to Celler as "a Jew or as a gentleman."

He had better luck in later years. By 1954, he was Judiciary Chair, a position in which he was able to shepherd civil rights and anti-trust legislation through the ranks with pride. When Virginian Howard Smith, the Rules Committee Chair, made signals about not wanting to advance the 1957 act, Celler threatened to use the discharge petition. "Patience is finite," he said. "It is small wonder the Negro's patience and forbearing is at an end." He added the "die is cast," and the "movement for civil rights cannot be strayed." Nor was Celler shy about faulting President Dwight Eisenhower for not taking a more hands-on approach in fighting for a strong bill. Eisenhower, he said, "need(s) elbow grease to get such legislation passed." Instead, he was simply making, "some pontifical declarations."

Another major initiative was the Hart-Celler Act, which barred quota via ethnicity. As consideration of the Voting Rights Act got underway, LBJ ordered Celler to begin the hearings that evening. When Celler replied that it was not practical (he'd schedule them for the following week), Johnson turned stern. "Manny, begin the hearings this week."

But Celler was best known for displaying the powers that accompanied his chairmanship. "It's not where I stand, it's where I sit," Celler said when asked by a junior Congressman about posting a bill. "It rests four-square under my fanny and will never see the light of day." The cigar that hung from his mouth may have made him seem like an old-style politician. But there was more to Celler than that. He loved the opera, played the piano, and had a knack for telling stories.

As for his district, eventually Republicans would no longer factor in, which made Celler's wins foregone conclusions. But his opposition to the Equal Rights Amendment and his support of the Vietnam War angered many younger voters. Enter Holtzman, who got the idea to challenge Celler two years before when, visiting her parents, a neighbor said, "I can't believe that man is still on the ballot. He's been there far too long and he's way too old."

When Holtzman ran, Celler was beyond dismissive. She was "a toothpick trying to topple the Washington Monument." On her chances, he said, "they are about as good as they have been in any year ending in two, four, six, eight, or zero." He called her a "non-entity." Brooklyn Democratic organization head Meade Esposito's views weren't much better. He called her "a young broad." As Holtzman recalled in her book, "she's got all kinds of young girls running around for her. Indians. Freaking squaws." Actually, she had been an aide to Mayor John Lindsay, a lawyer, and was currently a state committeewoman from Flatbush. Holtzman's campaign was boundless. She visited subways and supermarkets. Celler was slow to pick up his pace but eventually, as *The Times* noted, he was "commuting much more frequently than has been his custom between Washington and Brooklyn."

Celler cited the 400 bills he had authored, as well as four Constitutional amendments, quipping that it was "a record only exceeded by Thomas Jefferson." He noted every civil rights bill enacted bore his name. But Holtzman countered by linking him to special interests. In his book, *The Jews of Capitol Hill*, Kurt Sone says Holtzman "brought up his consistent approval of the anti-ballistic missile defense system which would benefit Fishbach and Moore, a New York City based engineering firm which he owned stock." She also brought up "double-dooring," which appeared to be Celler's way of getting around a Congressional rule barring sitting members from having law clients.

Holtzman also hit him for not having an office, saying the only Celler listed in the phone book belonged to his late wife. He says he never had it changed to his name. But age was an issue. Daniel Felder, author of *Tales from the Sausage Factory*, recounts panic when a canvasser relayed that a voter answered the phone saying, "I'm 84 years old!" The canvasser felt much better when the voter continued, "And if Celler feels like I do, he shouldn't be in Congress." Another thing that was pivotal to Holtzman was running on McGovern's delegate slate, rather than Muskie's (New York was choosing its delegates the same day). And she noted noted that "a televised debate was held on "a rainy Sunday" which meant a larger than-would-be-expected audience.

In 1968, Celler had referred to his primary opponent, a colleague named Edna Kelly, as "a lovely lady." He didn't share the same sentiment for Holtzman. To him, she was "as irritating as a hangnail, which I am going to cut off on June 20 (primary day)." He called her "fulminations as useless, as we say, as a wine celler without a corkscrew."

On primary night, the first returns showed Holtzman leading 856 to 798 votes. In the end, her margin was a mere 562 votes. Issues had plagued the York City Board of Elections all day, leading Controller Bob Abrams to say he couldn't ever recall so much disorganization. Much of it was chaos. The organization made that an issue, though Holtzman did have the machines secured in the wee hours of primary night. Celler could have continued his quest for re-election, and possibly won, by keeping the Liberal Party line, which had already re-nominated him. He declined.

Holtzman campaign poster
Image via Diana Mara

After his defeat, Celler returned to practicing law and showed up to the office nearly every day until his death at age 92 in 1981. He opened up about many, including Nixon, who he said "should have gone to jail." And in a sign that time heals all wounds, he even had kind words for Holtzman, whom he called, "a very able young lady. She must be able to have beaten me."

Celler in early years
Photo via the Library of Congress Prints and Photographs Division

CHAPTER FORTY-SIX

The End of Wayne Hays: Not A Paperback Novel

Historic Quote: "He would threaten me during intimate moments telling me to do this or that or 'I'll kick your teeth in. But you know, I'd much rather be having fun in the bedroom instead of doing all this talking in the living room." - Elizabeth Ray to a *People Magazine* reporter referring to her sexual relationship with Wayne Hays.

Elizabeth Ray (Sandiegoreader.com)

1976 was a year of change in America. Jimmy Carter won the Presidency, centering a good part of his campaign on not being from Washington, DC. But it seems to have been out with the old and in with the new on a variety of fronts.

A longtime figure on Capitol Hill, a pillar of wheeling and dealing and corrupttion who prioritized taking care of the home folks, concluded his long tenure in office that year amid a revelation of embarrassing, lewd, and tawdry incidents that left official Washington stunned, but, in hindsight, not entirely surprised. His departure had given Washington and the nation stories that sounded like an *As the World Turns* episode.

The events surrounding Hays' disintegration were stunning. At the time the scandals broke, he was 65, married, and a powerful committee chair. The affair, which was conducted very surreptitiously, culminated with a bizarre rant during the Congressional business day on the House floor.

I'm not kidding! The tale Ohio Democrat Hays, who chaired House Administration is a sordid, X- rated tales turned into Capitol Hill reality. Under 17 not admitted.

Capitol Hill had already been reeling from the scandal involving ex-House Ways and Means Chair Wilbur Mills. But if Mills was happy in the national spotlight, Hays was just fine behind the scene - because outside of Capital Hill, the House Administration gavel meant nothing, but in the halls of Congress, it was everything. Literally. The Chairman is called the "Mayor of Capitol Hill," and Hays signed every employee's paycheck. And he never let them forget it. He made elevator operators stand, and, to quote the *Almanac*, "terrorized" restaurant staff.

From the early days of his 24-year career, which followed a stint on the Belmont County Commission, Hays could be called the quintessential hack: writing congratulatory letters, attending fairs, knowing everyone by name. He was a hero of sorts for promoting the interests of this poor, coal-dependent Appalachian district on the Ohio/West Virginia border which *The Almanac of American Politics* referred to as a "rural, industrial slum." His popularity was reflected by one woman who told *People Magazine* that she'd be voting for Hays even after the scandal "because he got the water out of my basement. It stood there for six years before I wrote to Wayne Hays." And he was entrusted enough by his colleagues to be given some serious assignments.

Hays was not shy about what he thought. "I figured if I'm going to do all these things, I might as well hold an office," he said on the many personal requests for favors he received between his resignation from Congress and his return to the Ohio Legislature. He added, "I've dealt with bureaucrats in Washington and I've dealt with bureaucrats in Columbus, and, believe me, there's not a damn bit of difference between them."

Some called Hays "the Archie Bunker of Capitol Hill" but that nickname would probably be too flattering for the character Carroll O'Connor portrayed (Bunker's rhetoric was stinging, but few can argue he'd cause harm to anyone).

Photo via the Marshall Levin Collection

UPI's obituary labeled Hays, "one of the most hated and feared men in Congress," and California Democrat Phil Burton, himself no shrinking violet, called him "the meanest man in Congress." *The New York Times* wrote that "Hays was often accused of using his power to bully fellow members of the House." Author James Michener, who had numerous encounters with on the Hill once summed up his power by saying, "You oppose Wayne Hays and you find yourself parking your car one mile from downtown Baltimore." Vulnerable members in particular had some reason to fear him. He was also chair of the Democratic Campaign Committee, which allotted money to specific races, a position he was not shy about reminding fellow Democrats of on the rare occasions he'd face a challenge. He'd greet the potential detractors with the pitch, "I'm Wayne Hays. You might remember my name. It was on the bottom of those campaign checks."

One day, Hays got a taste of his own medicine. He had requested a chance to speak but was denied by octogenarian Rules Committee Chair Bill Colmer. When Hays finally got the floor, he referred to "this very arrogant, drastic usurpation of the power of the leadership," and continued by stating how he awaited the day when we "get some chairmen who are responsive to the leadership and not a power unto themselves at eighty or ninety years of age." Members were stunned. Here was among the most prominent members of the "Old Guard" who was railing against the very thing that he, more than perhaps anyone else, had epitomized.

In 1957, Hays had taken aim at his Democratic colleague, Adam Clayton Powell, when the New Yorker singled out elected officials from Pennsylvania and Ohio for taking "their orders from the middle men who serve the White Citizens Councils in Mississippi and Alabama?" Hays called Powell's words, "scurrilous" and cited him as "doing more to divide Negro citizens from other citizens" than anyone else.

But Hays' pugnacious streak didn't stop with members. He was nasty to officials whom he suspected might give him a hard time. He said the U.S. Immigration Commissioner "will not be able to physically hold the job" if he denied citizenship to his step-daughter, and later asked a congressman defending the Commissioner to step outside. *The Dictionary of the Downfall* reported that he engaged in a high speed chase with a police officer who had pulled him over. So his situation might be a case of what goes around comes around.

1974 had seen the election of a massive group of reform-minded "Watergate Babies" to the House and they took aim at ousting a number of Chairmen. Hays was one of them. His own Ohio colleague, James Stanton, took up his cause, conceding that "Wayne Hays is a son-of-a-bitch." But, he added, "he is our son-of-a-bitch." With the reformers divided, Hays kept his post 161 to 111 and conceded, "From everything that has been said in the newspapers and quite a few things that have been said in the corridors, and a few things said publicly, I am a miserable SOB. But I will try to be a nicer SOB."

Elliot Spitzer had the $4,000 hooker. Hays had a $14,000-a-year virtual ghost employee.

It started when Hays placed Elizabeth Ray, a 33-year-old former Miss West Virginia, on his payroll for one purpose: to have sex. Hays contended that she did have official duties, but Ray said "work" is not her strong point. Some-time after the revelations, she admitted, "I can't type. I can't file. I can't even answer the phone." "Supposedly," she added, "I'm on the oversight committee. But I call it the Out-of-Sight Committee." Ray even had her own rationale of the affair: "He would threaten me during intimate moments telling me to do this or that or 'I'll kick your teeth in,'" she said. "But you know, I'd much rather be having fun in the bedroom instead of doing all this talking in the living room."

Elizabeth Ray
Images via congressionalbadboys.com

Hays said in the scandal's early days that "I hope that when the time comes to leave this House, which I love, Wayne Hays may be remembered as mean, arrogant, cantankerous and tough, but I hope Wayne Hays will never be thought of as dishonest." Few would quarrel with the first four adjectives. Hays was one of those Congressman who believed the role of a Congressman was showing up, casting votes, and taking care of the home folks.

This all came out five weeks after Hays' second marriage to a 34-year-old, which occurred just after he divorced his wife of 38 years—they had married when Ray wasn't even born and he had used his marriage to deny the affair ("Hell's fire. I'm a happily married man"). Which means Hays didn't even try to be creative when it came to covering his tracks.

How did the affair come out? According to *The Dictionary of Downfall*, Ray had asked about whether their relationship would continue after his wedding. He replied, "I'm getting married. I should be good for about a week." As to whether she should continue working, Hays replied, "if you behave yourself, we'll see." She then asked if she had to keep "screwing him," to which he replied, "That never mattered." Ray took issue with that.

Hays told Ray of his fears that Bob Woodward would be snooping around so he advised her to come to work a "day or two a week." He did in fact accuse the *Washington Post* of "blowing it out of proportion." But he invited criticism by giving her the phone number 555-5555.

On the day he was to get re-married (with the reception to be in the House Administration committee room), Hays invited his entire staff to the ceremony—except Ray. She complained, and the result was a loud altercation, with Hays calling the police. Ray then went to a phone booth and placed a call to a reporter, whom she had met years ago on a delayed train. She had told the reporter that she knew of many escapades and was anxious to dish. And dish she did.

Hays denied the allegations. He seemed to be aided, if inadvertently, by *Time Magazine*, which quoted Ray's former boyfriends as calling her "nutty, spacey, neurotic, or dim." In his speech, Hays said, "I'm not guilty of anything except a little damn foolishness. And if they sent everybody to jail who made a mistake—and I made one and I apologize for it—well, you know there wouldn't be enough to go around . . . jails, that is."

As the scandal was in its early days, Hays was facing a primary. He stepped down as DCCC head and took 62%. But throughout the summer, it became obvious that Hays had problems, punctuated by an overdose of Dalamin sleeping pills that nearly killed him. The Ethics Committee investigated and the Black Caucus demanded that hefty action be taken against Hays because Adam Clayton Powell had been forced out for breaking rules (Hays had issues with Powell stemming from his backing of Eisenhower).

Hays resigned on September 1, 1976, three months after the saga began, which may have saved Hays from censure (House Speaker Carl Albert said he felt he "did it to save his family"). The Justice Department declined to prosecute. Ray for her part took the whole naive girl approach: "It was exciting. I thought politicians were gods. They did no wrong. You have to understand—me, a little girl from the South talking to a Congressman."

Hays did get a second act in politics, but only briefly. He won a seat in the Ohio House but was unseated after a single term. And it went lower and lower. He chaired the Belmont County Democratic Party and served on the school board. In a sign that old habits die hard, Hays threatened to punch out a reporter during a hearing. He lived another eight years, to age 77, at which time he was breeding horses and cattle and still married to his second wife.

In a sign of how things change, the person who beat Hays for re-election to the State House and who would later hold his House seat was Bob Ney, who was jailed for his role with lobbyist Jack Abramoff. According to Wikipedia, Ray, after "making unsuccessful attempts at being an actress and stand-up comedienne . . . faded back into obscurity." She is now 71.

Finally, there was a much-reported yarn in Washington D.C. about LBJ calling Hays at 2 a.m. and asking if he was sleeping. Hays replied, "No Mr. President, I was actually sitting here hoping you'd call." But after the incident, one has to wonder if Hays was indeed up to something at that hour.

CHAPTER FORTY-SEVEN

Gore, Sr.'s Election-Year Connundrum On Civil Rights Act Belied Real Record On Issue

Historic Tidbit: One day, a young boy asked JFK how he became a war hero. The President replied, "It was involuntary. They sank my boat."

Photo courtesy of the U.S. Senate Historical Collections

Over the past several years, an astounding 13 Senators have made public their support for marriage equality. The tally includes moderates, Senators preparing for tough re-election bids next year, and even a Republican, Mark Kirk. The sole liberal among this group is West Virginia's Jay Rockefeller, who hails from a culturally conservative state but who has announced his retirement. The conversions leave four Democratic Senators remaining on the fence, the most noteworthy being Mary Landrieu, the three-term Louisianan who also faces voters next year. Landrieu's primary conundrum is that in 2004 the Pelican State approved the amendment prohibiting same-sex marriage with 78%. This invites a comparison with Al Gore, Sr., the former vice-president's father and a prominent Tennessee Senator, and the Civil Rights Act of 1964.

Gore was not exactly a conservative on civil rights. The Tennessee Democrat had been one of three southern Senators who refused to sign the "Southern Manifesto" (he told Strom Thurmond "hell no") and had opposed the poll tax as a member of the House as far back as 1942 (his Tennessee colleague, Estes Kefauver, who had been his party's standard bearer for vice-president just before, was another, with Lyndon Johnson the third). During his own Presidential campaign, Al Gore, Jr. cited his father's courage on the civil rights issue, which while certainly debatable, is not totally without merit.

The Civil Rights Act of 1964 came to the floor just as Gore was facing re-election. He had no Democratic opposition in the primary but faced a tenacious Republican in his bid for a third term. Tennessee hadn't sent a Republican to the chamber since 1868 (one briefly filled a vacancy in 1912) but Gore was facing an erstwhile foe. And much of the deep South was rebelling against LBJ on the Civil Rights issue.

Gore voted against it and survived his re-election bid by just 53%-46%, as Johnson's 55% in Tennessee was far below Democratic norms. Whether Gore would've backed the landmark legislation had the election already been held will never be known. But his actions before and after the vote indicate that he was sympathetic to the movement.

Enter 1965, a different ballgame. The Voting Rights Act came before the chamber, and Gore, safely back in the Senate for another six years, had no qualms about voting for it. He backed the Fair Housing Act three years later. Meanwhile, on other issues, Gore was a solid liberal. *Tennessee4Me* called Gore "the forerunner for Medicare" and noted his legislation for minimum wage increases and the construction of the Interstate Highway System. And he had no qualms about opposing Everett Dirksen's legislation to allow prayer in the schools, gun control, or an anti-busing amendment. Yet Gore would prove his commitment again and again.

Maryland Democratic Senator Joseph Tydings served with Gore for six years (they both lost their re-election bids the same day). He calls Gore "one of the finest and most courageous Senators of my time. He was absolutely fearless and took very, very difficult political positions and votes which were vital to the nation but very politically unpopular Tennessee."

Tydings recalls that in 1969, he, along with Birch Bayh of Indiana, were leading the opposition to President Nixon's nominee to the U.S. Supreme Court, Harrold Carswell. As the vote neared, Tydings informed Gore that a sufficient number of Senators were prepared to vote against Carswell and that, in order to have a chance to save his seat, he could do the politically expedient thing and either abstain or not skipping the vote altogether. Gore replied, "No, Joe. I am staying here and casting my vote against that incompetent, miserable excuse for a nominee."

When it came to politics, Gore was a natural and his zest for campaigning was evident before even throwing his hat into the ring for office. Gore graduated from Middle Tennessee State Teachers College and earned his law degree from the

Nashville Y.M.C.A Night Law School. But it was his teaching stint that he had hoped would catapult him forward in the political arena. His friend and roommate, Rollie Holden, asked Gore if he wanted to hit the town one night. Kyle Longley noted in *Al Gore, Sr: Tennessee Maverick*, Gore was in the midst of writing letters, many of whom were from former students. Holden was bewildered as to why answering them couldn't wait. Gore replied that he was planning on running for county superintendent next year and "I expect all of those kids to get their mothers and fathers to vote for me." Gore was just 23 and lost that election but did get the post the following year when the incumbent died.

Gore had first won his Senate seat by doing the unthinkable: challenging Senator Kenneth McKellar in the Democratic primary. To Tennessee, McKellar was a 1950s version of what, more recently, Robert Byrd was to West Virginia: the chairman of the Appropriations Committee. But at age 83, his step had slowed considerably (he proceeded to take a drink at rallies but was shaking so hard the glass never reached his mouth). Gore refused to attack McKellar, however. In fact, he praised his rival for his many accomplishments, including the Tennessee Valley Authority. But other avenues made the point. *Time Magazine* ran the headline "44 vs. 83" and as Ray Hill observed in "Tennessee's Old Gray Fox," "McKellar's own appearances were carefully planned and highly choreographed." His supporters crowned a slogan, "Thinking Fellow Votes McKeller." Gore and his wife Pauline sat at their kitchen table attempting to craft another slogan. She came up with "Think Some More And Vote For Gore."

Meanwhile, Gore had stopped at nothing to build the party traveling to east Tennessee, the one region of the state where it was weak, by stumping for a Congressional candidate who was mounting a tough challenge in an open seat (he lost). He gave as many as a dozen speeches a day and impressed audiences by playing checkers with them and playing a fiddle. He won with 58%.

After the 1954 elections, Gore asked Minority Leader Lyndon Johnson for a seat on the Atomic Energy Committee. The more senior Kefauver wanted the seat as well. But he recalls in an oral history project that there "was not a good equation between Senator Kefauver and Senator Lyndon Johnson at the time. There was a very good equation between Senator Johnson and me at the time." So Gore got the seat.

Six years later, Gore faced a surprise primary from ex-Governor Prentice Cooper who was widely anticipated to try to regain the statehouse. In not-so-veiled language, he vowed to "preserve the southern way of life" and to be "a Senator FOR Tennessee, Not From Tennessee." The results were nearly a re-run of six years earlier. Gore did poorly in west Tennessee but again took nearly 60% of the whole.

Going into that campaign, Gore had been fresh off national fame. In 1956, he had emerged as one of the three most serious candidates for the vice-presidency.

The party's standard bearer, Adlai Stevenson, had shocked big-time players by instructing delegates to choose his running-mate. In the end, this would do little than expose the schisms within the party but the drama that played out at the time became a spectator sport. At first, Gore was not inclined to enter the competition but Oklahoma Senator Mike Monroney, angered that JFK had opposed high farm support prices, urged him in. His primary competition was his Tennessee colleague, Estes Kefauver, and a young Massachusetts Senator named John F. Kennedy (a third Tennessean, Governor Frank Clement, as well as Senator Hubert Humphrey and New York Mayor Robert Wagner, were also in the mix). For many, stopping Kefauver was the name of the game but Gore emerged with some key delegations on his own: Arkansas, Oklahoma, and the mighty Texas. Eventually, Texas and Arkansas decided to support Kennedy while Oklahoma was going for Kefauver.

In his eight-part series "Tennessee's Old Gray Fox, Albert Gore" in the *Knoxville Focus*, Ray Hill tells what happened next. Gore's initial strategy was to benefit from a Kefauver-Kennedy feud but that was clearly not panning out. Still, Gore refused to withdraw. Instead, he wandered off to a convention bar where *Nashville Tennessean* publisher Silliman Evans, scion of a prominent family that had actually backed Gore in his 1952 primary against McKellar, discovered him - and he kicked the dejected Senator when he was down. "You son of a bitch," he screamed, "my father helped make you and I can help break you! If you don't get out of this race, you'll never get the Tennesseans support for anything again, not even dogcatcher. The Tennessean will beat you if it takes a million years." At that point, Gore strode to the microphone and told delegates: "With gratitude for the consideration and support of this great Democratic National Convention, I respectfully withdraw my name and support my distinguished colleague, Estes Kefauver." His senior colleague went on to capture the nomination.

Ironically, Gore and Kennedy had another, more profound link. The Gore's were among the few present at a small gathering when Kennedy met Jacqueline Lee Bouvier, who would later become his bride. Ray Hill calls Gore "a hell of a good campaigner but a very aloof man." He "could be convivial when he wished. Could greet you with a grin and warm handshake but wasn't someone you felt close too." He wasn't a "senatorial barren."

1960 was another Presidential campaign year, and Gore once again tried maneuvering for the second spot. There was drama but this time Gore was hardly part of it. But when Kennedy did win the White House, many put Gore's name forward as a potential Treasury Secretary. He would have none of it but he was nonetheless dismayed when Kennedy picked Douglas Dillon. He was, in Gore's words, "an affable easy-goer." He speculated that the choice was due to Dillon's "awesome regard or a kind of mythical respect for the financier and big businessman." The reason, as Gore later explained, was because of Joe Kennedy's power.

The aftermath of that election also found Gore tangling with Kennedy's vice-president and outgoing Senate Majority Leader, Lyndon Johnson., Gore was outspoken against Mike Mansfield's plan to allow Johnson to continue attending Senate lunches. *Francis Valeo in Mike Mansfield: Majority Leader: A Different Kind of Senator* called Gore's "face (was) flushed with indignation beneath the neat and orderly waves of gray hair, and his speech was slow and deliberate as he released his words in a profound drawl, intensifying the agony that they seemed intended to inflict on Lyndon Johnson." Valadeo continued Gore "ran off a checklist of grievances, both real and imagined, that Senators had suffered for eight years under the towering Texan."

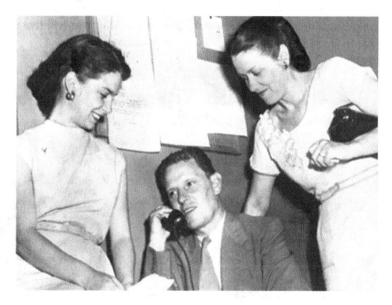

On winning the election
Photo courtesy of the Ray Hill Collection

Gore lost his Senate seat in 1970 to Bill Brock, later President Reagan's Secretary of Education.

The younger Gore credited his father's vote for Civil Rights as a decisive element in his loss and, minus the 1964 law, he was partially right. But it was Gore's vocally dovish position on the Vietnam War that also played a major role in his loss. At the 1968 Democratic Convention, Gore had made a heartfelt plea for a peace plank, and many in his own delegation had sat on their hands.

Gore's anti-Vietnam stance had earned him the enmity of the Nixon White House; so had his votes against Nixon's Supreme Court picks, Clement and Haynesworth. At the time he voted against the latter, Gore readily conceded it would cost him. Ray Hill noted that Gore began emulating the name-advancing techniques of McKellar and Kefauver, such as sending out birthday and congratulatory letters, but because Gore had not done this previously, it was greeted with some degree of cynicism. Worse, his campaign organization, so energized in 1952, was at this time, according to biographer Bob Zelnick, "skeletal."

Nixon's team went all-out to beat Gore. Spiro Agnew said Gore's voting record "was located somewhere between the *New York Times* and the *Greenwich Village Voice*." In Brock's campaign, Gore and many Democrats spotted veiled racial overturns in Brock's messages. He confronted him about it at a debate. "Mr. Brock," he said, "yours is an honorable name. You come from an honorable family. If you don't repudiate this low road your campaign managers have taken in your name and denounce these smears, and innuendos, you will live the rest of your life in shame and regret."

On the stump in that final election
Photo courtesy of the Ray Hill collection

To hear Gore tell it, the new movement was one of his prime reasons for running again. "If just my seat were at issue, I wouldn't run. I have had an honorable career and could retire with dignity. But a national party and ideology are at stake. If the right wing wins here and shows that the Southern Strategy works, no liberal or moderate in a border or southern state will dare raise his head again. That will be the death of the Democratic Party."

But, to everyone's surprise, the anti-Gore watchers were only narrowly successful.

For Gore, the seeds had been planted during the primary season. Gore faced a primary from Hudley Crockett, who had the support of Tennessee Governor

Buford Ellington. He prevailed just 51%-45%, losing west Tennessee. At that point, the dye was pretty much cast for November. As one observer noted, "Hudley Crockett roughed him up pretty badly and Buford Ellington and the Democrats didn't lift a finger to help Albert in the general election. Many of the things that were said in Brock's campaign repeated themes that emerged in Hudley's campaign."

In his concession, Gore spoke eloquently. "First, I should like to express my faith in our system. We do not have a perfect system of government but it is the best devised. It has been a very hard, very hard fight. We knew from the beginning that the odds were terrifically against us, but we had to make the fight . . . I told the truth as I saw it. The causes for which we fought are not dead. The truth shall rise again."

It was during that campaign that Tex Ritter gave Gore the "Old Gray Fox" name. Ray Hill explained the reason. Gore was "a shrewd politician, crafty and hard to pin down."

Gore took 48%, indicating he successfully touted his long work on behalf of the state. Landrieu's problem is that she must also deal with a White House, only this is one of her own party she'd rather not be reminded of, which indicates that, like Gore, other issues will also come into play. And it starts with marriage equality.

Landrieu has tinkered around the edges of the same-sex marriage issue and like Gore, has already taken stands that may get her into trouble. While Gore opposed the Civil Rights Act, he did back a previous version years before. And as early as 1957, he nominated two African-Americans from Memphis to the Air Force Academy, which was not without controversy.

Election Night, 1970
Photo courtesy of the Ray Hill Collection

CHAPTER FORTY-EIGHT

Brooke First African-American Senator Since Reconstruction

Historic Tidbit: Ronald Reagan once sent a note that read, "Nancy and I were saddened to hear of your illness. Get well soon. God bless you." The recipient was a fictional character from the soap opera "Santa Barbara."

Photo courtesy of the Collections of the U.S. Senate Historical Office

Edward Brooke was the first African-American to be elected to the Senate since Reconstruction, when, 85 years earlier, Mississippi's Blanche Bruce would not be reappointed to his Senate seat. The year was 1966 and the place was Massachusetts and Brooke captured the seat of retiring Senator Leverett Saltonstall in an electorate that was just 3% black. That wasn't the remarkable thing. What was remarkable was that race encompassed little, if any role at a time when civil rights was a dominant issue.

While the Senate race lacked any kind of racial acrimony, Brooke's early life did not. He grew up in Washington D.C. but eventually moved to a primarily white neighborhood. His relations with the white community were harmonious, and Brooke graduated from Howard University. But he served in the Army during

World War II in a unit - the 366th Combat Infantry Regiment, stationed in Fort Benning, Georgia that was one of three all-black units in the nation. Eventually, the troops, who were initially going to serve as bodyguards, petitioned their way into battle but that would fall under the command of a racist General, Edward Almond of the 92nd Airborne to which Brooke's unit was attached. Brooke would later say that he "felt racial discrimination more keenly than ever before. I could not ignore that our government's policy endorsed blatant inequalities." In particular, he learned about segregation and discrimination (designated movie times, not being able to go to the Officers Club, etc).

It was just as the war was ending, while stationed in Italy that Brooke met Remigia Ferrari-Scacca on a beach in Pisa. He was immediately taken with her and, though she told him she was married though in actuality, she was simply engaged. But it didn't take long for Ed to win her heart and before he left Italy, she was talking about coming to America with him. That worked out as planned and they married in 1947. At least once during his early political campaigns, voters would ask Brooke why he married a "white" woman. His response would be "Because I loved her."

When he returned home, he found himself unable to get a job by any of Boston's big law firms. So he sought to turn lemons into lemonade. First, he convinced the owner of an old theater in Roxbury to let him rent as a law office. But challenges still awaited. In his memoirs, *Bridging The Divide*, Brooke wrote of the slowness of his law practice. "I was only twenty-nine and looked younger. Some clients came into my office, looked right at me, and asked to speak with the lawyer" (he tried to rectify his youthful appearance by buying a pipe and dangling it from his mouth). Eventaully, he gained a clientele, mostly in the area of divorce, wills, and real estate.

The Black Individualist of the Republican Party quoted "Black Biography" as saying two of Brooke's Army buddies wanted him "to run for office to improve living conditions for the great masses of blacks who lived in Roxbury, Massachusetts." As to why he joined the GOP: "My parents were Republicans, and I had always admired the party of Lincoln and the Republican virtues of duty and self-help."

Brooke sought a State Senate seat in 1950 using "cross filing," where a candidate for office can submit his name in both party primaries. Brooke did win on the Republican line, but as expected, not the Democratic. He narrowly lost the election. But, he would write in Bridging the Divide that "My surprisingly high vote in the Twelfth Ward, in a solidly Democratic city and year, caused a buzz." More importantly, "In political circles, I was the man to watch." Still, it did not come easily.

He lost again in a bid for Secretary of State in 1960 (Massachusetts' favorite son JFK was on the ticket), but only by 112,000 votes. His opponent was future

Boston Mayor Kevin White whose slogan "Vote White," led some, including Brooke, to wonder whether it was meant to inject race into the campaign. Whatever the case, by becoming the first African-American in Massachusetts to win a nomination for a statewide office, his stock was soaring. And the people who counted took note. He rebounded by being tapped by the Governor for a major banking post.

Eventually, though, Brooke could not resist the office bug and this time, he was successful. It was for Massachusetts Attorney General. Brooke stared down Elliot Richardson in the primary, who entered the convention a heavy favorite. But Brooke outmaneuvered him and captured the nod. His win in the fall was so huge that JFK called it, "the biggest news in the country," which meant it apparently exceeded his brother Teddy winning a Senate seat that same day.

Photo courtesy of stanleyforman.com

Brooke's tenure coincided with a number of events that are legendary in the history books today and his capability was unquestioned. One was the killing spree by the person who came to be known as the Boston Strangler and Brooke created a Boston Strangler Task Force (even using a room down the hall from his office as the "Strangler Bureau). On the recommendation of a friend, he hired known psychic Peter Hurkos to help with the investigation which he notes led to derision in the form of newspaper cartoons painting him as a witch doctor.

Brooke championed desegregation, though he differed with the state NAACP in their call for boycotts of schools. Another issue was bible reading in the schools. After the U.S. Supreme Court ruled that the daily practice could not continue in

Pennsulvania, Brooke issued an opinion that the ruling had similar implications for the Commonwealth. But it was Brooke's crusade against local corruption that thrust him into the spotlight, and his capabilities were acknowledged as being far-reaching. Brooke was also Acting Governor of Massachusetts when President Kennedy was gunned down and other state officials left the state to attend the funeral.

In 1964, Brooke shunned Barry Goldwater. "To me," he explained, "theirs was a pseudo-conservatism, sharply at odds with our party's honored past. Their racial views would have appalled Abraham Lincoln. Their contempt for our environment would have disgusted Theodore Roosevelt. Their blind hatred of every federal program was a slap at every veteran who had used the GI Bill to go to college or buy a house." But the drubbing of the national ticket in Massachusetts – Goldwater took just 24%, had no impact on Brooke. He won re-election by nearly 800,000 votes.

Then came the Senate race. Brooke's first task was to secure the Republican nomination which he did by calling every other potential candidate – including the one man he was prepared to defer to, Governor John Volpe, to inform them of his intentions. They questioned why he had to declare so early but, one by one, they decided against a bid. Brooke was viewed as a sure-loser to outgoing Governor Endicott Peabody. But he used his forceful speaking ability and strong personal skills to his advantage, and that meant a win. But his 61% margin (exceeding 400,000 votes) was eyebrow raising. His slogan was "Ed Brooke of Massachusetts–Integrity and Independence in the U.S. Senate."

During the campaign, Brooke had made it clear he wasn't "running as a Negro. I never have. I'm trying to show that people can be elected on the basis of their qualifications and not their race." But predictably, he became an overnight sensation and race was a major reason. Al Gore Sr., said, "I don't think he was elected because of that. He was elected because of his abilities as a citizen and I believe he retains the same view." When he approached the well of the Senate for his swearing-in, he was given a standing ovation.

On some issues, Brooke was unmistakably liberal. He backed federal funding for abortions, and the "Brooke Amendment" to the federal publicly assisted housing program limited the tenants' out-of-pocket rent expenditure to 25 percent of his or her income. He was the Senate sponsor of a national holiday for Martin Luther King, Jr., more than a decade before the birthday of the civil rights leader actually became law. On other issues, such as the Kemp/Roth tax cuts, he stuck with his party. His biggest accomplishment may have been the Equal Credit Act, which authorized credit for women separate from their spouses.

The national party complicated Brooke's disposition, particularly the Nixon White House. Brooke liked Nixon personally but hadn't supported him in the 1968 primaries. First, his backing went to George Romney (how ironic that his son would serve as a future Governor of his state). Then, he backed Nelson Rockefeller. But he did give a zealous seconding speech at the Republican Convention in 1972 when Nixon was re-nominated. "One thing about Richard Nixon's administration stands out above all others," he declared. "Through his diplomacy, the president has actually done more to establish a lasting world peace than any President or any national leader in our lifetime. It may be true that the time for leadership has been right. But it is also true that the president's leadership has been right for the times." A year later, Brooke's name was at least bandied about as a replacement for Spiro Agnew.

Photo courtesy of stanleyforman.com

But some areas troubled him. As recently as 1966, he authored a book, *The Challenge of Change: Crisis in Our Two-Party System"* and asked "Where are our plans for a New Deal or a Great Society." Particular grievances were on nominations. Brooke not only opposed Carswell and Haynesworth for the Supreme Court, but also Bill Rehnquist, one of just three Republicans to do so (fellow Northeasterners Jack Javits and Cliff Case were the others). He chided Nixon for proposed funding cuts for, among other things, the Job Corps and the Equal Opportunity Commission. He faulted Nixon for not pushing for renewal of the Voting Rights Act. And he became the first GOP Senator to call for the President's resignation, telling him in an October meeting that "voluntary giving up the most powerful office in the land would not be taking the easy way out." Later that night, he faced an expletive-filled confrontation from Rosemarie Woods, Nixon's loyal secretary who lived on his floor at the Watergate. The nxt morning, Brooke found a scratch on his Mercedes. He couldn't trace it to Woods but did write of it being "a reminder of the weird, ugly legacy of Watergate." On foreign affairs, he opposed the expansion of nuclear arsenals.

An example of Brooke's liberalism occurred on the issue of housing in 1978. Brooke wanted to increase funding for Section 8 above the President's request and his amendment to do so prevailed in Banking, Housing and Urban Affairs 9-8. Opponents felt that inflation should be dealt with but Brooke responded, "Although I recognize our responsibilities to hold down federal spending and sense the 'Proposition 13' fever which has taken hold in both Houses of Congress, I strongly believe that housing for low-income families and the elderly is one national priority which should not be lightly disregarded in our rush to slice the federal budget."

Brooke played a role in the renewal of the Voting Rights Act, countering on the Senate floor devious measures meant to weaken it. One was by Mississippi Democrat John Stennis which Brooke in his autobiography wrote was written "so deceptively fair on the surface that he fooled some people." Stennis wanted every municipality in the nation to submit the changes to the Attorney General. Brooke wrote the provision "not only would have created an immense backlog in the Justice Department." The amendment was tabled 58-38.

When it came to personal characteristics, Brooke was extremely well-liked by staff and colleagues. In his autobiography, *Bridging The Divide*, he writes he and his "mostly" young staff "worked hard, but we also found time for fun." That included taking the staff on a tour of the Potomac by boat and taking a nighttime bus-ride of Washington and its monuments. Stanley Forman, who worked primarily on Brooke's campaign, said "he had a great personality," noting "everyone who worked with him seemed to love him." As a Senator, Brooke counted many of his fellow moderates as among his close friends but cites a number of very liberal Democrats, including Birch Bayh, Phil Hart and Hubert Humphrey as among his closest friends. He said conservative Republicans and Southern Democrats did little to reach out to him.

Brooke was also a master of calling out impropriety, even when it came to the White House. In his autobiography, he wrote of being "appalled by the chaos and disarray," early in the Carter administration. "The blue jeans, piles of trash and debris, and general poor housekeeping." He said that to a reporter shortly after which a number of well-known newspapers ran a cartoon of Brooke with the caption, "Guess who won't be coming to dinner."

By the time Brooke was running for a third term in 1978, he faced additional problems. One was that Ted Kennedy, with whom he had always got along, campaigned for the Democratic nominee, Paul Tsongas. Another was not strongly enough attending to the "Bay State's" needs.

But Brooke also had serious personal woes, the most damaging being that his mother in-law had improperly received $27,000. Who was leaking these stories? His daughter.

Tsongas did not raise the issue of Brook's alleged improprieties, but may have been helped by his clever ads (poking fun at his name helped him win his tight primary). Plus, Tsongas may have been helped by a shift to the right, even among the strongly Democratic Massachusetts electorate. Remember, Michael Dukakis was being unseated in the Gubernatorial primary by Ed King, who ran well to his right. Tsongas had actually run to Brooke's right. True to form, Tsongas beat Brooke 55-45%.

In a concession speech, he said "now that the campaign has concluded, I trust that there will be people in the United States Senate who will fight for our senior citizens, for our minorities, for our blacks, for our Hispanics, for the handicapped and the poor and the middle class who are becoming the poor and who will fight for peace on earth, things in which you and I believe, will fight for full equality for all women, for equal justice for all people . . . As obviously you have given me . . . the greatest opportunities of my life . . . I leave the job only with a feeling that there is so much more to be done and a strong belief that I could do it."

Brooke stayed in the nation's capital and resumed practicing law. On Brooke's death at age 95 in January of 2015, he was the nation's oldest living former Senator. Margaret Pearson, whose husband, Senator James Pearson and Brooke were close friends called him "a wonderful human being."

CHAPTER FORTY-NINE

Adam Clayton Powell A Member Like No Other

Historic Quote: "Rosa Parks integrated buses, James Meredith integrated the University of Mississippi, Martin Luther King, Jr. integrated churches and lunch counters. But it was left to Adam Clayton Powell to integrate corruption." – Then Congressman Andrew Young, publicly proclaiming support for his embattled colleague but privately bemoaning his transgressions.

Photo courtesy of Black Past

As early as 1960, there was an African-American Congressman who had a surprising amount of power in the halls of Washington for that time period. He was almost certainly the most influential African-American on the state or federal scene at least through the 1980s when Gus Hawkins took control of the same panel and Doug Wilder became Virginia's Governor. His name was Adam Clayton Powell and the New York Congressman was sought out by Presidents and colleagues alike during his Chairmanship of the House Education and Labor Committee.

Powell's was a story of elegance, eloquence, panache, and good looks, all of which helped to give his Harlem constituency a much-needed voice. Bernie Goldberg, noting his "mixed race, his skin color coffee with cream," may have been "too handsome for his own good." In the end, behavior that led to an expulsion by his colleagues, a case before the U.S. Supreme Court, and major, self-destructive judgement flaws detracted from all of his contributions to American society.

In his early years, politics and Powell seemed worlds apart. His father was a prominent minister at the iconic Abyssinian Baptist Church and the pulpit seemed to be Powell's niche. In fact, after graduating from Colgate University, Powell secured his Masters from Columbia in Divinity and succeeded him on the pulpit. But by this time, Powell's fight for social justice was ingrained. He organized picket lines and established methods to promote the hiring of more minorities at major events, including the New York World's Fair of 1939. He led a boycott of shops along 125ᵗʰ Street that wouldn't hire minorities, adopting as the slogan, "Don't Shop Where You Can't Work."

By 1941, Powell, despite protests from his wife, sought a seat on the New York City Council and won, taking the third highest number of votes among six winners. He served in the New York Office on Price Commissions. That was also around the time he took up a publication, "The People's Voice," which allowed him to showcase issues of concern to the black community. Three years later, he ran for a newly created Harlem-anchored Congressional seat and immediately won the backing of Tammany Hall. His church was a powerful asset on the trail as well.

Powell won the nomination of both Democrats and Republicans and had no opposition in the general. He caused a stir by pledging to "represent the Negro people first and after that, all the other American people," but then backtracked. It was a first for an African-American in New York in both positions.

Taking the oath as New York City's first African-American Councilman
Photo via Harlem World Magazine

Well before rising to power in the House, Powell was a major force to be reckoned with. He desegregated the House Dining Room by bringing in many constituents, saying, "These are the days for strong men to courageously expose wrong." He fought segregationists tooth-and-nail, often engaging them in debates on the House floor. And he held Congress to task for not taking bolder action on civil rights. In a speech to the chamber in 1955, Powell told colleagues "the United States Congress is a 19ᵗʰ century body in a 20ᵗʰ century world. In the field of civil rights, we are still conducting ourselves along the pattern of yesterday's world." When the body did take up civil rights legislation in 1957, Powell bemoaned attempts by Southern lawmakers to keep criminal jury provisions in the bill. He said, "There can be no (effective) civil rights bill if the amendment – trial by jury – is in it and no one knows this better than the gentlemen of the South."

Though Powell's politics were solidly progressive, outside factors made some suspect his loyalty to the Democratic Party. In 1952, angered that Adlai Stevenson had picked a segregationist as his running-mate (John Sparkman of Alabama), he actively backed Eisenhower for the Presidency. He did the same in 1956.

1960 was more complex. During the primary season, Lyndon Johnson was his candidate, and he argued that he could not support John F. Kennedy under any circumstances. But by the time the Massachusetts Senator had captured the nomination, Powell was all for him. In fact, when a KKK leader in Florida endorsed Richard Nixon, Powell accused him of "exploiting the worst fears of bigotry in America." Locally, he refused to back Mario Procaccini, the Democratic nominee for Mayor of New York City.

Another Powell gift was that he knew how to deal. Iowa Democratic Congressman Neal Smith said Powell "was intelligent and also had street smart, which is not the same thing. He knew what was going on all over the country as well as Congress. He knew how the system worked." And he knew what couldn't be accomplished. Once, upon being asked if he'd ever run for President, Powell replied that "America was not ready for a President who is a Baptist minister." At no time perhaps were Powell's instincts more evident than in the 1960 campaign.

Powell officiated at the wedding of singer Nat King Cole and his bride Maria
Photo via Harlem World

Initially, Powell backed Lyndon Johnson for President which, according to *The Making of the President 1960*, was "in return for validation of his claim on the Committee Chairmanship for which he yearned." But when Johnson's candidacy faltered, he quickly pivoted to Kennedy. Powell reportedly made a deal with Kennedy that he would help him cultivate votes in the black community in exchange for more jurisdictional power when he assumed the Chairmanship of the Education and Labor Committee.

By 1961, Powell had attained his chairmanship and backed funding for the deaf and a minimum wage increase." He expressed frustration that school aid, another chief Kennedy priority could not advance (Catholic Democrats Jim Delaney and Tip O'Neill had opposed it because it didn't contain aid to parochial schools). Powell said, "If the 319 Congressman who get that aid want to keep it, they'll have to take it in a package of federal aid to the rest of this nation. Someone's got to blow the whistle . . . someone beyond the Committee and the Congress." Eventually, Kennedy penned a letter to Powell which read "the contribution of your Committee . . . has enhanced substantially the legislative accomplishments of the past two years."

By 1965, it was time to move the Elementary and Secondary Education Act. Powell initially pledged quick action to the Johnson administration, but Lyndon Johnson in his memoir *The Vantage Point* wrote that Powell "held the bill hostage to free the funds he had requested for staffers. Then he left for Puerto Rico." He missed the February 17 markup but conducted it a week later. Less than a year later, Johnson was effusive in his praise of Powell. In a letter to Powell, he noted "49 pieces of bedrock legislation" Powell had helped pass and told him of his "brilliant record of accomplishment . . . an ability to get things done."

Mo Udall, in his book *Too Funny To Be President*, noted Powell's ability to "always put on a lively show. When another member proposed a vaguely worded amendment to one of his bills, Powell was dubious. 'I'm not sure what this means,' he said. I suspect there may be a Caucasian in the woodpile." And it would be downhill from there."

But in addition to his elegance, Powell also had eloquence. An Example was about three weeks after the education legislation when Powell was moving the anti-poverty legislation. "I think all of us will be pleasantly surprised at the splendid accomplishments of this more glorious war. During the hearings, these accomplishments will be presented and outlined in detail. The overblown myth of so-called scandals saturating the program will be laid to rest once and for all." He spoke of oversight, noting some programs were "mired in the swamp of mediocrity" while some administrators had "subtle contempt for the poor."

For Powell, missing votes was far from unusual. His absenteeism grew each year. His response was, "You don't have to be there if you know which calls to make, which buttons to push, which favors to call in."

The Legal Dictionary wrote that Powell, "despite being a minister, liked the high life." He called a constituent, Esther James, a "Mafia bag woman." Because he made the charges on the House floor, he was protected, but he later repeated it on a Saturday television show. James sued and won a judgement of $46,000. Powell refused to pay and was issued two arrest warrants which eventually resulted in a thirty-day jail sentence. Powell pleaded Congressional immunity which the New York State Court dismissed.

Powell did continue returning to New York but only on Sundays, as the process server could not legally deliver Powell. He'd give his usual sermon.

There were other matters. Powell engaged in extensive travel abroad, mostly to his resort in Bimini, and used massive amounts of government funds to do so. Funds from the Education Committee were also suspicious. The House Administrative Committee investigated this but Powell refused to show up to plead his case. For the most part, Powell's constituents didn't care. One summed up the obviously predominant view by saying, "That cat sure knows how to live." But his Congressional colleagues were another story.

At the beginning of the Congressional session, the House Democratic Caucus established a Select Committee to investigate the situation while voting to strip him of his committee chairmanship. It was chaired by Rules Committee Chair and fellow New Yorker Emanuel Celler. Missouri Republican Thomas Curtis proposed a resolution declaring Powell "excluded from membership in the 90th Congress."

On March 1st, the House voted 307-116 to accept the motion which stripped Powell of his seat. Powell's reaction: "On this day, the day of March in my opinion, the end of the United States of America as the land of the free and the home of the brave." He called it "a second Dred Scott decision when Justices ruled a black citizen "be sold as slaves." Powell made the comments from Bimini, which led one colleague to quip he had "a glass in one hand and a woman in the other." Still, Powell did not want members – at least some, to jeopardize his career by appearing to be giving him sympathy. David Pryor, a future Arkansas Senator who was taking the oath as a freshman Congressman that day, wrote in *A Pryor Commitment* of Powell approaching him on the floor the day of the vote. Pryor said he "felt as if every House member plus a packed spectator gallery was watching us." Powell gave it to him straight. "Let me tell you something," he said. "I know your district and when your name is called, I don't think you should vote to seat me. Maybe in another couple of years if this thing drags on but not today. Don't do it.'

Pryor acquiesced. So did many others. But the verdict was not unanimous. The entire Congressional leadership of both parties (including Speaker McCormack and Gerald Ford) had initially voted for a resolution that would allow for Powell to be sworn in, issue a fine, and strip him of his seat only if he didn't show up.

That measure failed 202-222. Michigan Democrat John Conyers, one of few blacks in the House in those days, called the removal "violative of our system of government."

Images courtesy of the U.S. House of Representatives

Days later, a Harlem rally of 4,500 featured backers shouted, "no, no, no." The resolution also prohibited the House Clerk from issuing payment to Powell. Because the provision of the resolution had called for the Governor of New York to be notified of a vacancy, Nelson Rockefeller was able to declare a special election. Powell ran and won with 86%. But rather than fight for the oath, he fled to Bimini, and yet he returned to California to raise money. Celler acknowledged "if I were representing Adam Clayton Powell, I'd urge him to take the matter to court right away. I think he's got a good case."

Powell and several constituents subsequently filed another suit against the Congressional leadership but because Powell was suing the House, the case was ironically called Powell vs. McCormack. A number of lower courts dismissed Powell's suit, claiming they lacked jurisdiction to hear it. When the matter ultimately reached the U.S. Supreme Court, the 90th Congress had expired. Meanwhile, Powell was held in such regard by his constituents that despite not having been allowed to cast a vote, he was re-elected in 1968. The court ruled in Powell's favor. Though expulsion of members is permitted, that member had to be initially sworn in before it could be carried out. That Powell was prevented from doing so made that impossible. They said that his "obvious and continuing interest in his withheld salary" disproved the notion that the case was moot. That year, he settled with James.

Powell won the battles but ultimately lost the war. As 1970 approached, Powell's troubles and ever more frequent absences had taken a toll on even his most indestructible backers. There was a 40-year-old State Senator named Charles Rangel who was waiting in the wings to take on Powell in the primary, urged on by Manhattan Borough President Percy Sutton. If anyone was aware of Powell's lionesque status in Harlem, it was Rangel.

As Rangel wrote in his memoir *And I Haven't Had a Bad Day Since*, "Kicking Adam out of Congress brought him more support than he had had in decades." He wanted to give him the dignity to bow out gracefully. He noted that a former Powell aide who had challenged him in the 1968 primary received 40%. He flew down to Bimini and presented Powell the data. "These were real numbers representing real people . . . Had Adam come home it would have fit in nicely with me practicing law and legislating in Albany." During the campaign, Powell said, "My people would elect me even if I had to be propped up in a casket." He was almost correct. In a multi-candidate field, the first count showed him trailing Rangel by 206 votes. After the recount, the margin was 150 votes. Though Rangel's plurality was just 32%, Powell's absence clearly proved fatal. Turnout was poor and young African-Americans in particular were turned off. One 30-year-old perhaps best summed it up. Powell, he said, "was good in the 40s and 50s but things are changing now and they're changing in a different way. Now we need someone who will feel the pulse of the people." Powell continued to pursue a re-election campaign on an Independent line but he was ultimately ruled ineligible by the Supreme Court.

In 1969, Powell learned he had cancer and initially used that as a reason that he might not stand for re-election in 1970. Ultimately, he reversed course and ran. But the cancer was back with a vengeance and it silenced Powell in age 63 in April 1972. A Harlem office building Powell once fought against erecting bears his name, and one of the most recognizable streets anywhere is called Adam Clayton Powell Boulevard.

Image courtesy of Newyorkcitystatues.com

CHAPTER FIFTY

Ford Unseated Halleck As Republican Leader In 1965

Historic Tidbit: Ever hear the phrase, "Good to the last drop?" It is commonly associated with Maxwell House coffee but is used today in many respects. But Teddy Roosevelt brought that into being when he took a sip of the new coffee and, in the presence of its manufacturers, exclaimed, "Good to the last drop!"

O nce in a while, a House leadership election changes history. 1989 may have been a rare example, as Newt Gingrich defeated Ed Madigan for the position of House Minority Whip by two votes. That election would propel Gingrich's rise to the Speakership, but not the Presidency. Gerald Ford's defeat of Charlie Halleck would do the opposite.

Photo courtesy of the U.S. House of Representatives Collection

Ford's defeat of Halleck for the position of House Minority Leader in 1965 was most remarkable because Halleck was the incumbent. The Indiana Congressman had held that position for six years, encompassing three Congresses. But that was precisely Ford's ammunition. The Goldwater debacle had reduced to GOP House conference to mere rubble — 140 seats of 435. It was one factor that would relegate the party to seemingly permanent minority status. Ford had just won his ninth term as a congressman from Michigan and was urged by many junior members – some of whom were among his closest friends, to tale the leap.

Halleck was born in Jasper County, Indiana at the turn of the century, 1900, to Abraham Lincoln Halleck. His rise would be quick. A World War I vet, Halleck would go to law school and by age 24, was Prosecuting Attorney for the thirteenth district court. He'd hold that position for ten years. He won his House seat in a 1935 special election following the death of incumbent Frederick Landis, as Republicans were again licking their wounds from a national landslide and record low seats. He'd just barely hold off a Democratic challenger in '36.

In those days, Halleck was a hard-core conservative, an isolationist who opposed the Lend Lease Act. He called himself "100 percent Republican," and made clear his opposition to the government "snooping into our ice boxes" (rationing was an issue). Halleck said that Americans should "live again as God meant us to live and not as some bureaucrat in Washington . . . would like us to live." But he did back the Marshall Plan as well as aid to Greece and Turkey.

Halleck became chair of the Republican Conference Committee after just seven years in 1942, the same year his friend Leslie Arends of Illinois, who had won his own House seat a year before Halleck in the regular cycle, would become Whip. Ironically, as Halleck took the top leadership slot, it would be Arends who played the part of the Sancho Panza to Halleck's Don Quixote).

Halleck tasted national prominence as early as 1940 when he nominated fellow Hoosier Wendell Wilkie for President. "I got more brickbats and more bouquets over that speech than any other I've ever made." In 1948, when he put Indiana in Tom Dewey's column at the national convention. Reliable sources told him that could mean the vice-presidency. But the nod went to Earl Warren instead "My trouble was, I believed what people told me." Dewey did promise Halleck a prominent post in the administration but bad feelings may have lingered. Dewey managed a bare 1% win in Indiana, which didn't help. Again in 1952, Halleck was one of five men deemed to be "acceptable" by Eisenhower forces but Richard Nixon got the nod.

Ford's challenge to Halleck was ironic because six years earlier, after the in 1958 elections, it was he who had convinced Halleck to challenge incumbent Joseph Martin of Massachusetts for the position of Minority Leader. Republicans had been decimated and while Eisenhower was still popular, Ford felt no one was in charge of promoting the GOP message. Furthermore, many Republicans believed Martin was too close to Speaker Sam Rayburn. So Halleck's challenge was to "democratize" the House. Halleck agreed to make the challenge and, won a crucial caucus rule change that allowed secret ballots.

It was needed. The vote was 74-70.

Halleck may have been a prime reason the "New Frontier" was forced to transform into the "Great Society", as he colluded with southern Democrats to kill various social legislation (the minimum wage, etc). But Halleck would moderate, and the first sign of that was when he agreed to support a Civil Rights bill promoted by Kennedy. In fact, just prior to his assassination, Halleck and Kennedy had agreed to a debate mechanism that would attract Republican votes. But the Johnson presidency changed the direction of the bill. Some questioned his motives, to which he would say, "They couldn't understand that once in a while, a guy does something because it's right." One tape had Halleck saying to Johnson, "you know, if you scratch me pretty deep Mr. President," before Johnson cut him off and said, "I don't want to scratch you because I want to pat you."

LBJ had been trying to get Halleck to agree to a vote on anti-poverty legislation before they adjourned for their convention. He said, "You ought not hold up my poverty bill. That's a good bill and there's no reason you ought to keep a majority from voting on it. If you can beat it, go on and beat it but go on and give me a fair shake." Halleck ultimately had no choice but to acquiesce.

Much of Halleck's mechanism for promoting the Republican message involved colluding with his Senate counterpart, Everett Dirksen. The "Ev and Charlie Show" consisted of joint television appearances, and statements. One example. When Kennedy introduced his school aid package, the duo argued that it would "not only become permanent but also, by natural progression, it would also result in federal control of education."

Charlie Halleck Day was attended by ex-President Eisenhower in 1962
Photo courtesy of the Rensellaer Republican

Ford's path to unseating Halleck began in 1962. The "Young Turks," which primarily featured Mel Laird, Don Rumsfeld, Charlie Goodell, and Bob Griffin, asked Ford to challenge Charlie Hoeven of Iowa, the current Conference Chair. It apparently did not take Hoeven by surprise when he told reporters after a conference meeting that "something's brewing in there." Ford readily obliged and unseated Hoeven 86-78, after which the dethroned Iowan admonished Halleck to "watch out; he's just taken my job and the next thing you'll know, he'll be after yours."

That would indeed prove to be the case, but it might not have been obvious at first. Missouri Republican Congressman Tom Curtis said, 'we have a saying in Missouri that when a mule is stubborn, you get his attention by hitting him across the head with a two-by-four.' Ford's dethroning of Hoeven was the two-by-four.

But after the debacle of 1964, the "Young Turks" wanted more which meant that now, Halleck was a direct target. But for Ford, challenging Halleck would not come without careful weighing. As Ford cited in his memoir, *A Time To Heal*, Ford was about to assume the top Republican position on Appropriations, and also had the matter of his young family.

Meanwhile, Halleck would broach the subject to Ford at a leadership lunch in his office. He posed the question with the words, "now I assume everyone is going to run for the same office again." Ford responded: "Charlie, I'm not going to make any commitments here. You know, there's a group that's talking about finding somebody else for your job. They haven't selected a candidate but the possibility does exist that I might run." But he'd write in his book, that the deal was sealed when his son said, "go for it dad."

Given the proximity of Indiana and Michigan, the battle for whip could easily have been one of friends and neighbors. Among the Midwest, it was. Ford's good friend Elford Cederberg put his name forward, while Halleck's Indiana colleague, Ross Adair, would do the same. In launching his campaign, Ford said "citizens of all political faiths . . . are gravely concerned about the very survival of the two party system . . . I feel we must begin a new chapter with new ideas, a new spirit, and new leadership."

Photo courtesy of the Jasper County Library

Ford hadn't planned to formally launch his campaign until after the new year but he got an urgent phone call from Rumsfeld begging him to return to Washington. Prior to that, Ford believed a handy win was at hand. He vowed to "expand the effort to present positive alternatives," and in clear outreach to the more junior members said, "We're going to use everybody's talents. Every Republican will be a first-team player, a 60-minute ball player."

The first ballot was 72 for Ford and 69 for Halleck, with 1 present. The second was 73-67, at which time Halleck asked that the election for Ford be made unanimous. The vote was a little closer than expected. Ford said he had expected John Lindsay to vote with him, but didn't (likely taking a few other New Yorkers with him). But he credits Bob Dole for securing Kansas' five members to putting him over. More than a decade later, Ford would repay Dole in a big way, awarding him the vice-presidential slot when seeking a full term.

Griffin, announcing the vote said, "a new chapter in the Republican Party has begun." He also credited Ford as the most "electable" candidate saying, "Jerry gets along with all segments of the party." Halleck accepted the verdict with grace saying, "that's the way the ball bounces. I wish him well." In his memoirs, Ford credited Halleck with being a gracious loser, noting that he "displayed no personal animosity."

The same, Ford wrote, could not have been said of Joe Martin who, upon his defeat by Halleck in 1959, "had sulked for weeks and refused to speak to Halleck." And Ford was gracious back. He offered Halleck any committee assignment he desired. Halleck in turn would provide Ford key advice.

Halleck's own electoral security was strong but hardly invincible, particularly in those bad Republican years that knocked so many of his colleagues out. In 1964, he finished 10,000 votes ahead of his rival, garnering 53%. In 1958, he was down to 52%. On average, his elections would finish between 57 and 63%.

After his loss to Ford, Halleck sought one more term in the House and won 56-44%. He chose not to seek re-election in 1968. "I knew my race had been run," Halleck said of that loss of leadership. "The chance to be Speaker of the House would not come in my effective time."

As he was leaving, a colleague said, "Charlie has had his hours of greatness, glory and triumph. Charlie has had his hours of disappointment. In both he has always been a gentleman."

Halleck would return to Indiana and, with his law practice and "hunting and fishing," generally live happily. But his wife's death in a boating accident in 1973 left him despondent. He died in Lafayette 1986. The federal building in that city today bears his name.

CHAPTER FIFTY-ONE

Five Congressman Were Shot By Puerto Rican Nationalists on House Floor In 1954

Historic Quote: "I've had all the shooting I can take for one day." – Iowa Congressman Ben Jensen to his Tennessee colleague Clifford Davis. The two had been sharing a hospital room after being wounded in the U.S. Capitol shooting and were arguing over whether they should listen to "Raw Hide" on the radio (as Davis wanted) or music. Jensen got his way.

The five wounded members of Congress stricken by gunfire in the House chamber posed for a photo on the Capitol steps. From left to right: Alvin Bentley (R-Michigan), George Fallon (D-Maryland), Ben Jensen (R-Iowa), Cliff Davis (D-Tennessee), and Ken Roberts (D-Alabama)
Photo courtesy of the Collection of the U.S. House of Representatives

On March 1, 1954, four Puerto Rican nationalists gunned down five members of Congress. Astonishingly, all survived. The House had been voting on whether to advance a Mexican labor bill and in those days, a teller called the names of each of the 435 members prior to their recording their votes. The vote was at the midpoint and 254 members were on the floor. Had more been present, the chamber would have been more densely populated which almost certainly would have meant more casualties or deaths.

The assailants - Lolita Lebron, Rafael Miranda, Irving Flores Rodriguez and Andres Figueroa Cordero were Puerto Rican nationalists, part of the same group that tried to assassinate President Harry S. Truman four years earlier. Their cause was anger over the new Constitution that gave the U.S. latitude over Puerto Rico's affairs. The four wanted complete independence for the island.

Lebron as the lone woman was the most infamous of the quartet. *The New York Times* observed that she was dressed "stylishly with high heels and bright red lipstick." She also apparently expected that she would be killed on the spot and when arrested, was found with a note that read, "My life I give for the freedom of my country. The United States of America are betraying the sacred principles of mankind in their continuous subjugation of my country." They claimed their actions were no different than the actions Americans had taken against the British during the Revolutionary War.

In the lead-up to the shooting, the four acted casually and methodically. They took a bus to Washington from New York, lunched at Union Station and walked to the Capitol where they were seated in the Ladies Gallery. A *Washington Post* recap noted that "a security guard asked whether they were carrying cameras; they were not" But they were carrying Luger and Walther semi-automatic pistols which, after getting situated and watching the House proceedings for a time, they emptied on an unsuspecting chamber. Lebron was "holding (the Luger) in her two hands, and waving it wildly." She then attempted to wrap a Puerto Rican flag around her before being subdued by onlookers, Capitol police and a few brave House members. Another assailant yelled, "Viva Puerto Rico Libre"

On the floor, *The New York Times* noted that at the sound of the gunfire, "House members at first thought the sounds were those of firecrackers. But as their colleagues fell or took cover as they heard the slugs hit around them, all realized what was happening." One, an Alabama Democrat named Frank Boykin, 69, joined many in running toward the exits. That would be hardly unusual except for the fact that most of his other colleagues were hiding behind desks. At that point, somebody yelled out, "Where are you going Boykin?" He replied, "I'm going to get my gun." The man replied, "Where is your gun, to which Boykin said, "It's in Alabama."

Many on the floor, including House Majority Leader Leslie Arends, felt splinters from the gunfire. Republican Congressman James Van Zandt of Pennsylvania ran from the floor to the gallery, tackled Lebron and another gunman and grabbed her flag (she bellowed "It's the flag of my country. Give it to me!"). Down below, two members/physicians Walter Judd of Minnesota and William Neal of West Virginia tended to the wounded, as did a number of pages, including two future Congressmen, Paul Kanjorski of Pennsylvania (who "felt the spray of marble") and his 16 year old colleague, Bill Emerson of Missouri.

The five wounded members encompassed a broad array of the House membership: junior, senior, Democrat and Republican. They were the following:

House interns and future members Paul Kanjorski (holding the gurney on left) and Bill Emerson (holding the gurney on the far right) assist critically wounded Michigan Republican Alvin Bentley
Photo courtesy of the Collection of the U.S. House of Representatives

Ben Jensen (R-Iowa)

Jensen was the senior member of the five. Describing the shooting, *The Des Moines Register* said, "Jensen pitched through a door of a cloakroom after a bullet had struck him in the right shoulder." He had been standing near his Iowa colleagues who helped stretch him out. One fellow Iowan, Karl LeCompte, worried that it "might have been Ben's heart," before realizing it was only his shoulder.

Jensen was born one of 13 children to Danish immigrants in the rural town of Marion. His birth name was Benton Franklin Jensen and he used the name because his love of history gave him an affinity to the Founding Father. Jensen worked as a yardman and assistant auditor, then served as a First Lieutenant in the First World War before becoming manager of the Green Bay Lumber Company,

SCOTT CRASS

a company that built brooder houses for baby chicks which were then sold to hatcheries. He was elected to Congress in 1938.

No one would dare mistake Jensen for anything other than a staunch conservative. He boasted about being called, "the watchdog of the Treasury," and said, "I am proud of that title." When the House took up the Reclamation Law revision in 1948 and would pay the subsidies, he opposed an amendment measure favored by Speaker Rayburn that would give hydro-electrical power from Arkansas, Oklahoma and Texas preference and he derided the proposed transmission program a move toward "government control of all utilities." At one point, he offered an amendment prohibiting Americans from receiving services if they conducted strikes against the government or advocated a forcible overthrow. It was adopted 166-163. In his last year in office, Jensen opposed the Civil Rights Act of 1964.

Jensen was legendary for his temper – in fact he once took a swing at his chairman on Appropriations, Democrat Clarence Cannon, himself no shrinking violet. But those who knew him generally found him amenable professionally. Iowa Democrat Neal Smith, elected in 1958, called him "conscientious about his work and desires to do what he believes is right." Smith called him very cooperative with his own Appropriations requests.

Jensen had won re-election with ease for two decades until 1958, when the farm revolt that took down many of his fellow prairie Republicans allowed him to escape defeat by just 2,500 votes, 51.5-48.9%. Jensen rebounded somewhat and became top Republican of the House Appropriations Committee after the 1960 election when New Yorker John Tabor retired. But by 1964, his luck had run out and as Lyndon Johnson was pummeling Barry Goldwater at the national level, he lost to John Hansen by more than 10,000 votes. In a post-election mortem, Jensen said he "could not overcome those big landslides both at the White House and Statehouse levels." He said Goldwater, "a man defeated to the degree that he was, cannot claim" a mandate to lead the party. Instead, he spoke glowingly of Richard Nixon as a future face. He visited Nixon in the White house at least once and died in 1971 at age 79.

Clifford Davis (D-Tennessee)

When talking about personal background and politics, Tennessee Democrat Clifford Davis was not a member of Congress whose story should be preserved. When he sought elective office for the first time at the age of 26 - for City Judge, Davis could not win the backing of either his boss, Memphis Mayor Rowlett Paine, or the legendary machine organization headed by Ed Crump. Davis calculated that the only way chance for him to win the election was to court the Ku Klux Klan. Support was granted and Davis won the post (all of the other Klan endorsed candidates lost). *The Tennessee Encyclopedia of History and Culture* noted the win made Davis "the only avowed Klan member to ever win elective office in Memphis."

It does not appear as though Davis was personally hostile to African-Americans, as his bid for vice-Mayor with Watkins Overon garnered support from both blacks and whites. But near the end of his Congressional career - which began in a 1940 special election when he won a race to succeed Walter Chandler, he was still vocal about thwarting progress for African-Americans. Davis could boast of some major accomplishments throughout his long tenure. The Tennessee Valley Authority Self-Financing Bill and he co-sponsored the Federal-Aid Highway Act.

When the 1964 Civil Rights Act was passed, Davis called it "untimely," adding, "the events (rioting) in Harlem prove it." Davis vowed to "would vote the same way tomorrow and the South needs a congressman who knows how to represent the views of the South." At that time, Davis was in the race of his political life against George Grider, a pipe-smoking, World War II naval officer and well-respected attorney who had much support among the black community. Davis had fallen below 80% only once - in the 1956 general election but that changed in 1962. In that primary, Davis fell under 50% against Ross Pritchard which turned out to be foreboding of a general election that he survived by a mere whisker against Robert James, his Republican opponent. Against Glider in '64, his luck ran out.

Wayne Dowdy, in his book, *Crusades for Freedom: Memphis and the Political Transformation of the...*, notes that in predominantly black ward 39, Davis Grider received 358 votes while a mere 55 were cast for Davis." That was not the only issue Glider used against Davis. The incumbent, he said, had "grown lazy in the job." Davis attempted to counter by stumping hard for support in rural areas. Grider unseated him by a healthy 9%, 50-41%.

Davis returned to Tennessee where he died in 1970 at age 72.

Kenneth Roberts (D-Alabama)

Images courtesy of Allison Sinrod

If Davis's past suggests racial animosity, nothing of the kind was prevalent in the thinking of Kenneth Roberts of Alabama. His family had a long history with African-Americans and Jews, the latter of whom he believed were "the noblest people in the world." That's not to say he backed civil rights – he voted with his Southern colleagues to defeat every measure that came up. But he had limits. Behind the scenes, he was believed to have told folks that times were changing and he viewed George Wallace's standing in the schoolhouse to door to prevent integration childish. But on other issues, he was not only a staunch supporter of an activist federal government but was a champion of causes identified with the liberal wing of the Democratic party at an unusually early time.

Among those causes: backing migrant workers, product liability and Native American Healthcare. His most important legacy may have by pushing through legislation allowing working mothers to deduct expenses for child care, a cause he worked on with Alvin Bentley, his Michigan colleague who was also shot.

Among the five members shot, Roberts was the least seriously wounded – the bullet tore through his leg, but that was by sheer happenstance. The colleague sitting near him, Percy Priest of Tennessee, gave Roberts his neck tie and fountain pen to stop the bleeding and allowing him to crawl to the next room (Roberts' grateful wife bought Priest a new necktie and fountain pen).

Roberts grew up in rural Alabama, the son of a dry good store clerk. He attended Howard College, then earned his law degree from the University of Alabama. He established a practice in Anniston and Talladega. In 1941, Roberts was elected to the Alabama State Senate but his tenure wouldn't last long. The reason: World War II. Roberts resigned and served in the Naval Reserves in both the Atlantic and Pacific Theaters. He continued his service as a lieutenant in the reserves. Returning home, he was the Piedmont city attorney and sat on the State Board of Veterans Affairs. He won his Congressional seat in 1950 and, like virtually all of his Southern colleagues in a region where the GOP was dormant if not non-existent, Davis would routinely run unopposed or exceed 80% of the vote. In 1962, he placed third for eight seats as Alabama's Representative-At-Large.

Testing out an electric automobile in the U.S. Capitol
Photo via Historic Images

Roberts' sponsorship of a deduction for female providers came in response to a conference sponsored by the Children's Bureau and Women's Bureau of the Department of Labor. "The conference concluded that these women, many the sole support of their children, required government aid for their children's care." In promoting his bill that would allow deductions for mothers earning less than $6,000 a year, Roberts called it "a little hard to reconcile the present insensitive attitude on the part of the government which allows a lawyer to deduct entertainment fees lavished upon a prospective client, a professional golfer to deduct his equipment for tournaments…which will not grant this privilege to the working mother who toils all day in the factory and works for her family in the evening in the hope that her children have a better life."

Beyond that, Roberts used his chairmanship of the House Health and Safety subcommittee to promote refrigerator safety, The Bounds Law Library of the University of Alabama points out that Roberts "was credited by Ralph Nader as one of the people directly responsible for the national interest in automobile safety." Finally, Roberts decided that any chances of getting the law enacted would have to be done piecemeal. His first proposal, as Michael Lemov noted in *Car Safety Wars: One Hundred Years of Technology, Politics and Death* that Roberts introduced a bill that called for the "36,000 automobiles purchased by the General Services Administration for the federal government to be required to meet mandatory safety standards…" Though the House cleared the legislation, the Senate would not until Roberts worked out a compromise with Washington Senator Warren Magnuson in 1964. Educational television also consumed much of his time. But he was thwarted in what was perhaps his most ambitious goal – federal safety standards for automobiles and incurred the enmity of the automobile industry. Roberts was also chair of and the Interstate and Foreign Commerce subcommittee on safety and he used that to fight for legislation on substance labeling and child health.

Roberts demonstrating refrigerator safety
Photo via the University of Alabama Law School

Initially, 1964 was shaping up to be another routine rout over his Republican opposition, if he would even attract any. Legislatively, he was coming off the biggest success of his legislative career. But while the year proved one of the most for voter approval of an activist federal government, except in Alabama. The Civil Rights Act had just been enacted and voters were revolting by voting for Barry Goldwater over President Lyndon Johnson. Voters made no distinction between the top of the ticket and bottom and ousted five Democratic members of Congress. Roberts was one of them. Defeated by Arthur Andrews, he lost every county by wide margins – Andrews amassed 70% in two and could do no better than the 44% he received in St. Clair County. His daughter Allison Roberts was quoted in the Lemov book as saying, "I remember my mom broke down and cried. My dad just shrugged it off."

But he felt the unpledged system that Wallace had used to keep President Lyndon Johnson from appearing on the ballot had cost him, though the Goldwater sweep because of the backlash over civil rights also undoubtedly played a role.

Roberts was close with President John F. Kennedy and after his assassination, Lyndon Johnson, knowing of his fondness for his predecessor, gave Roberts one of the first Kennedy Silver Dollars.

Roberts led a very active retirement, focusing on the areas he addressed in Congress. Counsel for the Vehicle Equipment Safety Commission. Johnson appointed him to the National Highway Safety Advisory Committee from 1966 to 1970. Allstate Foundation, Physicians for Automotive Safety and American Nurses Association all bestowed on him awards.

By 1989, Roberts was dying but was transported to Maryland. When he was dying, his daughter said she knew he wanted to see the U.S. Capitol again," and had the ambulance drive past it. Death came days later at age 76, after which he was interred at Arlington National Cemetery. Incidentally, after Wallace was shot while campaigning for president in Maryland, Roberts paid him a visit, telling him he could commiserate with how he was feeling.

George Fallon (D-Maryland)

Fallon, who took a bullet in the leg, would ultimately achieve the highest standing of the five lawmakers, which some would see as appropriate given his height. At 6'2, Fallon was called "The Big Man from Baltimore," and when he rose to chair the Public Works Committee in Congress, he clearly became a pretty big fish in Washington. Yet he didn't need a title to become one of the most important lawmakers of his time. Fallon was referred to as a "mild-mannered legislator who rarely ventured onto the floor of the House to speak for any other cause in his 13 terms" and was said by Congress watchers to never hold a grudge when it came to earmarking road related projects for the Congressional districts of other members. As Tom Lewis wrote in *Divided Highways: Building the Interstate Highways, Transforming American Life,* "Fallon's blandness endowed him with a capacity to endure tedium and enabled him to have a successful career." And Duane Cronk, who wrote transportation language, called him, "surprisingly modest. He is courteous, but not suave. He is no orator, and couldn't make a soapbox speech if he had to. But he is relaxed and congenial, and makes friends easily."

So committed was Fallon to improving roads that many joked that the "H" in his middle initial stood for "highways" (it was actually "Hyde"). The Baltimore-Washington Express was one such road endeavor but establishing an interstate highway system was his major source of energy (Fallon himself disliked driving on highways strangely enough and would often make the 45 minute commute to Washington by train).

With Al Gore, Sr., Fallon sponsored the Federal-Aid Highway Act. President Eisenhower signed it into law in 1956 and American means of travel would change forever. But the journey took a wild ride and the beginning was not auspicious.

**Fallon (second from right), watches as President Kennedy
signs the Federal Highway Act into law in June 1961
Photo courtesy of the John F. Kennedy Presidential Library and Museum**

The first version – introduced in 1955, was called the National System of Interstate and Defense Highways. Fallon's means of paying for the bill involved the creation of a highway trust fund, but also a tax on fuel and anything else that made vehicles move (Lewis mentioned trucks, trailers, buses, tires, inner-tubes and recapped tires). But the fuel industry had a fit and launched an angry campaign that Fallon said resulted in 10,000 telegrams arriving on Capitol Hill. Lawmakers defeated the bill 292-123. It was July of 1955 and Speaker Sam Rayburn pronounced the measure dead. But in his 1956 State of the Union, Eisenhower implored lawmakers of the necessity of a highway system and time eased the anger of many of the highway interests. Fallon made the bill palatable by making it "pay-as-you-go." The bill passed with just 19 dissentions and Fallon made the statement that "not only will every person in the United States benefit from it, but the favorable impact on our economy already is felt."

As the 1950s turned into the 60s, other projects awaited. Fallon worked on the Port of Baltimore. He sponsored the Clean Waters Restoration Act with Senator Ed Muskie of Maine.

A graduate of the Calvert Business School and John Hopkins University, Fallon's rise in Democratic Party politics was helped by the recognition of the advertising sign company that his father had founded in 1904 – the Fallon Sign Co. When it started, it grew at a meteoric pace. In 1938, he was on the Democratic state Central Committee of Baltimore and a year after that, he was on the city council. In 1944, he sought a seat in the House and won with 59%. His re-election margins for the rest of the decade were healthy but he struggled somewhat through the 1950s. In '54, his first vote after the shooting, he mustered just 55% and two years later, in the midst of the Eisenhower landslide, he took just 53.4%. But by 1958, through 1968, his tallies were uneventful – in the general. As early as 1960, Fallon began facing primary challengers that he dispatched comfortably, but not the earth-shattering margins accustomed to entrenched incumbents (the low 60s).

By 1968, the culture was changing and Fallon at 66 might have been detached. He was not a fan of environmental regulation and that garnered him the ire of many in the growing movement. He supported the Vietnam War which certainly did little to endear him with youths. His primary opponent was Joseph Curran, Jr., Fallon squeaked by with 976 votes to spare.

Many think Fallon should have heeded his close scrape and retired in 1970. Meanwhile, a freshman State Representative named Paul Sarbanes was also rejecting advice – leading politicos were urging him to be patient and not risk a promising career by challenging Fallon. But he spotted vulnerabilities and The League of Conservation Voters established its list of "Dirty Dozen," legislators.

Fallon was on it. Sarbanes had cash and hit him for supporting the Vietnam War. In the end, he defeated the incumbent 51-45%.

Fallon returned to Baltimore where he lived another decade. He died in 1980 at age 78.

Alvin Bentley (R-Michigan)

Bentley with his fellow colleague from the Wolverine State, Gerald Ford
Photo via Historic Images

While the injuries of Jensen, Davis, Martin and Fallon were all relatively minor, Alvin Bentley's was far from it. As a freshman, the Michigan Republican was also the most junior member of the five and the two bullets that struck lodged in his lung and liver, Doctors, after performing surgery that had lasted several hours, rated his chances of survival at only "50-50." But Bentley had been lucid enough to ask his fellow Michigander, Elford Cederberg, to call his wife. She was pregnant and he didn't want her to get wind of the incident on the news. Ultimately, Bentley's bright political future ended not by an assassin's bullet but by two close statewide losses in the 1960s.

While Bentley did come through and resume his Congressional career after a two month recovery, Kanjorski noted he "was never really the same." Meanwhile, citizens of Puerto Rico were horrified at what their countrymen had done and *The Battle Creek Enquirer* noted on his death that he "received about 4,000 letters of sympathy" from residents "and when he recovered he vacationed on the island at the invitation of the island governor."

Bentley's early years were governed by both fortune and misfortune. Born in Maine, Bentley's father was killed in France in World War 1 when Bentley was just three but money wouldn't be a problem; his grandfather owned the Owosso Manufacturing Company in Michigan. He earned his degree from the University of Michigan and served in the Foreign Service during World War II. During the war, he served in Columbia and Mexico but was in Italy and Hungary post-war. He resigned in 1950 after finding himself, in "finding himself at odds with the foreign policy of the Truman administration." Two years later, he challenged a Republican incumbent for re-nomination and won by a surprisingly large margin. Though Fred Crawford, had served in the House since 1934, voters nearly ditched him in the 1950 primary, just as he was about to become chair of the Interior and Insular Affairs Committee. His international pedigree experience was a prime reason House leaders placed Bentley on the Foreign Affairs Committee, the only freshman to do so.

Bentley was a loyal Republican vote but it would be a mistake to call him a down-the-line conservative (he had actually worked with Ken Roberts on the tax deductions for child care). But he was virulently anti-communist and he urged support for "any nation trying to overthrow a communist government" which included Hungary in 1956. He was against recognition of Communist China by the U.S. government and Russian denomination of the Baltic States. He advocated severing relations with Cuba.

Joe McCarthy had stumped for Bentley before a gathering of Saginaw Young Republicans in 1952 and Bentley reciprocated by supporting the Un-American Activities Committee. But he was embarrassed somewhat by revelations that his new wife, Arvilla Bently, had exceeded the legal limit by giving him $7,000– then skipping the country to the Bahama's under the name Mary Peters before the Senate Ethics Committee was to serve her with a warrant (McCarthy had used the money for commodity speculation).

An Enduring Gift: The Bentley Historical Library, Keeper of Michigan's History, noted that he was "one of the earliest users of the Congressional questionnaire. Every January, just prior to the opening of a new Congressional session, he polled the people of his district on issues likely to come before the House." Bentley also made use of the radio – and at a very early time the television, to get his views out to constituents. As a result, his re-elections were a cinch.

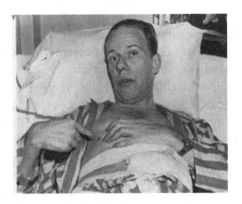

Recovering in the hospital
Photo via the Collection of the U.S. House of Representatives

Bentley faced no imminent electoral danger but in 1960, decided to challenge Democratic Senator Pat McNamara who was seeking a second term. Though Bentley spent $1.3 million, he could not oust McNamara. Two years later, he tried to return to the House by way of an At-Large House seat that would be chosen by the entire Michigan electorate.

Post Congress, Bentley served as a delegate to the Michigan Constitutional Convention. He chaired the Education Committee which for Michigan, his ultimate legacy may be creation of the State Department of Education. In 1966, Governor George Romney appointed him to a vacant seat on Michigan's Board of Regents. But a disease impacting the central nervous system afflicted him that year and ultimately confined him to a wheelchair. He died on a vacation in 1969 at age 50.

James Van Zandt (R-Pennsylvania)

Photo via the U.S. Government Printing Office

If any member of Congress was the hero of the day, it was Pennsylvania Republican Jimmy Van Zandt who played a major role in subduing the assailants.

Van Zandt had served in both World Wars – he had enlisted in the Navy during his senior year of high school to serve in the First and actually resigned his seat in Congress to continue to serve in the second (he had been stationed in the Pacific and North Atlantic before-hand). In between, he was commander of both the Altoona post and the Pennsylvania chapter of the Veterans of Foreign Wars where he traveled the nation in search of new recruits. This result in his being awarded the Distinguished Service Medal by that organization. In World War II, Van Zandt's primary role was to command a ship and he eventually received the Bronze Star and the Legion of Merit. He continued in Korea – at which time he had returned to Congress and retired rear-Admiral at age 71.

Van Zandt knew the sound of gun shots from the service so, upon hearing them, he crawled to the cloakroom and ran up the stairs to the gallery and, along with a bystander and tourist, wrestled at least one of the gunmen to the floor.

Van Zandt was a lifelong resident of Altoona. After World War 1, he became a district passenger agent for the Pennsylvania Railroad. He won his House seat in 1938 over a two-term incumbent, Don Gingerly, by a solid 57-43% margin. Van Zandt proved enormously popular and, when he sought to reclaim his seat a year after a three-year absence following the war's conclusion, voters returned him with 66%. Van Zandt never again sweated re-election but gave up his seat to challenge freshman Democratic Senator Joe Clark. He attacked Clark for his alliance with the organization, Americans for Democratic Organization. Clark responded by calling his opponent "trigger happy," and said that if he had his way, the U.S. would constantly be going to war "unilaterally." He noted that ADA had been founded by none other than Eleanor Roosevelt. Van Zandt took nearly 49% but could not oust the incumbent.

Van Zandt tried to unseat U.S. Senator Joe Clark in 1962 but came up short
Photo via ronwade.com

After his loss, Van Zandt continued his ties to his two chief passions: issues concerning veterans and Congress. The protests that took place during the Vietnam War disenchanted Van Zandt enough that he called them really anti-American…when Americans are in a fight we are there to win and right or wrong it's our country we stand for." Governor William Scranton had named him secretary to the Congressional delegation, which Democratic Congressman Joe Gaydos recalls he served, "without pay for years; he loved Pennsylvania. There was no political affiliation when it came to serving Pennsylvania. We looked up to him and had a profound respect for him. He was always active no matter how old he was."

The veterans facility in Altoona, Pennsylvania bears Van Zandt's name.

Meanwhile, the four assailants received 70 year prison sentences. While Cordero had died in 1975, the sentences of the other three were ultimately converted by President Carter in 1979 as part as a prisoner swap, after which *The Washington Post* noted Lebron, "embarked on a tour of Puerto Rican population centers in the United States. She was also received in Havana as a guest of President Fidel Castro." She died in 2010 at age 90.

CHAPTER FIFTY-TWO

House Members Forced To Go Along To Get Along With Autocratic Southern Committee Chairs That Dominated The House

Historic Quote: "You just have." – Armed Services Chairman Carl Vinson to a very junior Congressman named Lyndon B. Johnson, who during a Congressional hearing politely asked Vinson, "When can I ask a question?"

A profile of political figures of influence in the 1960s wouldn't be complete without a look at the proverbial "powerful Chairman" who dominated the House. Mostly Southern, autocratic, segregationists, and king of malapropisms, these chairmen rose to their posts by seniority then proceeded to wield the House with an iron-fist to the point that, until most were deposed (which ultimately happened by removal by the House Democratic caucus or by the voters in primaries), neither their priorities nor authority would be questioned. They were also, as John Darrell Sherwood noted, "famous for pork-barrel politics and arbitrary management of committees." They were inclined to, as a *New York Times* piece described Rules Committee Chair Howard W. Smith, "rock(s) gently back and forth in his swivel chair, puffing quietly on his cigar and radiating antebellum courtesy and beatific calm." While a majority of the House Committees were run by Southerners in the 1960s, the House Armed Services Committee and the Committee on Rules were most evocative of promoting this culture. As a result, a handful of successive chairmen, proved adroit at effectively running their fiefdoms.

Armed services Committee heads Mendel Rivers and Ed Hebert
Photo courtesy of the Collection of the U.S. House of Representatives

At the time he became Chairman, *Congressional Quarterly* described Rivers thus: "In appearance and manner, he looks like the stereotyped image of the Southern Congressman. He wears his silver-white hair long on the back of his neck, as did his idol, Senator John Calhoun of South Carolina." *CQ* also called Rivers "a florid speaker of the old school (who) can quote poetry at length." He was also gung-ho for America flexing her military might, no matter its realism.

In the early 1950s, Rivers had urged President Harry Truman to drop the Atomic Bomb on North Korea. During the Cuban Missile Crisis, he said, "If blockading Cuba brings on war, let our boys die for America." During Vietnam, it was, "They are not interested in Laos, they are not interested in Indonesia, they are not interested in Berlin. But they are damned interested in America." Cambodia was "a first-class logistic operation." Indeed, so legendary was Rivers' advocacy of force provoked or not that a Republican colleague once asserted that "if Mendel was running things, we'd be in World War III."

For a man with such lofty ideals, Rivers' background was quite contraire. Rivers was born in the small, rural town of Gumville, South Carolina, the son of a farmer. When his dad died, his mother and the family moved to a farm just outside Charleston but, for the remainder of his life, Rivers referred to himself as "just a country boy from Gumville in Hell Hole Swamp." The story is told that while in high school he got up at 4 a.m. and delivered papers and milked the cows before catching the trolley for school. He continued his habit of early rising throughout his life and routinely arrived at his office before 7 a.m., earning a reputation as a hard worker." Rivers worked as a sheet-metal worker but attended the College of Charleston followed by the University of South Carolina Law School. But he was not considered particularly scholarly and throughout his life, he was evidently cognizant (and not too sensitive) about his lack of intellectualism, as he would often say Rivers would also say "the lightening of intellect" hadn't struck, "the taproot of my family tree."

Rivers' political career got underway when he won a seat in the South Carolina State House in 1932 and served four years. In 1940, he pursued the Democratic nomination for the First Congressional District of South Carolina and won the all-important primary with 55% and thus the seat (Republicans rarely fielded candidates in those days). Other than the 1966 primary which he won with 76%, Rivers again would never face electoral opposition. In office, his early cause was repealing the tax on oleomargarine and his persistence garnered him the name "Oleo" Rivers.

Armed Services was called the House Naval Affairs Committee when Rivers first took office. *Congressional Quarterly* noted on his assuming the Chairmanship that "he had chaired at one time or another every subcommittee of that group and of the present Armed Services Committee."

For much of Rivers' time in the House, Armed Services was not simply chaired but run roughshod by Carl Vinson of Georgia. Known as the "Father of the Two Ocean Navy," Vinson might have himself set the stage for the powerful chair. His chairmanship dated back to 1937, more than 22 years after the man from rural Baldwin County and the Georgia Military Graduate had captured his House seat at age 31 in a 1914 special election (he was in his House seat when America authorized World War 1). While Republican control of the House on two separate occasions forced him to temporarily hand over his gavel, his tenure as top Democrat would not end until his retirement at age 81 in 1965 (with Dick Russell Vinson's Senate counterpart, Georgia was well taken care of militarily).

Tip O'Neill once quoted a Republican friend as saying that when Vinson convened Armed Services meetings, he would often give an opening statement that dragged on for two-three hours before even recognizing the ranking Republican. He limited the questions that junior members could ask to one per year. It became known as the "Vinson Rule."

Carl Vinson
Photo courtesy of the Collection of the U.S. House of Representatives

There was no question that Vinson's power came from the committee rostrum. One time, Vinson was asked about a rumor that he would be appointed Secretary of Defense to which he replied, "I'd rather run the Pentagon from up here." And he did. He referred to the fleet as, "My Navy," and was called the "Admiral," the "Swamp Fox," and "Uncle Carl." Robert Caro in, *Lyndon; The Path to Power*, explained how Vinson addressed junior members as, "Ensign" but those who had been around a while reassured them by saying, "when he starts calling you Captain, you know you've arrived." It was said that members would dare cross Vinson – in either committee or the floor, for fear of alienating him should their districts ever need help from a big fish on military matters. Caro wrote how one Capitol Hill aide summed up Vinson's power by referring to him as, "a blank check to operate as a one man committee." But reporters were less charitable, with one describing his demeanor as, "Like the country lawyer he is and at once removed from the cracker barrel."

Rivers made clear that he worshipped the ground on which Vinson walked. "As Saint Paul sat at the feel of our master," he once said, "it has been my privilege to sit at the feet of Mr. Vinson." He became chair in 1965 when Vinson retired as the dean of the House and the longest serving member of Congress to that point (Jamie Whitten of Mississippi surpassed him in 1992).

Rivers made no ambiguity in trying to show that he had authority. "I don't know why we should always wait for proposals to emanate from the Executive. I am not implying that I don't plan to cooperate fully with the president and Secretary of Defense, but there should be a mutuality." Rivers made clear that he was not going to roll over for anyone. "I take this to mean that...there is vested in this Congress the exclusive right to deal with the military...I don't mean a quasi-right. I mean the exclusive right." Showing he meant business, Rivers inserted into a bill a mandate that the Armed Services Committees in both chambers of Congress approve a President's proposed base closing

The president was not always amused by his antics. On one 1965 tape, Johnson was angered by Rivers being quoted by the *Charleston News and Review* in which he took credit for Johnson signing a military pay raise he had earlier been resistant as exorbitant. Referring to Rivers as "the admiral of the Charleston Navy Yard," Johnson instructed McCormack to "just tell him this. He's gettin' too big for his britches, and I'm gonna ...The damn fool is out here advocating bombing Peking." He mocked Rivers having said "I will accept nothing but total and complete victory in Vietnam." Johnson wondered to McCormack, "Now who the hell is I? What meat does this Caesar feed on, John?"

Johnson and Rivers
Photo courtesy of the Lyndon B. Johnson Presidential Library and Museum

Rivers ran the committee by relying on a six member group called, "The Junta." It consisted mostly of philosophical allies who shared his priorities, which meant what he wanted he mostly got. But by 1969, that was changing. *Congress and the Cold War* by Robert Johnson noted that the "Junta" would be challenged by the "Fearless Five," a bipartisan group of Congressmen who challenged Pentagon spending priorities. They included Democrats Robert Leggett of California, Lucien Nedzi of Michigan, Otis Pike of New York and Republicans Bob Stafford of Vermont and Charles Whalen of Ohio. Leggett himself had made clear the oversight the group was conducting wasn't particularly personal. Of Rivers, he said, "He's not underhanded. But because of his geography, and because he's the man he is, our chairman tends to run the committee like a private club." But that didn't prevent Rivers from mocking their priorities. To him, they were "Johnny-come-lately military experts...(who put) their own political ambitions ahead of the country's international status." Still, the "Fearless Five," produced the lower chamber's first dissension of the Pentagon Authorization bill since before the Korean War."

Rivers had once predicted, "I don't believe the Yankees will ever pick a fight with us again because, when we get through, there'll be precious few installments North of the Mason-Dixon Line." Still, in an extraordinary tribute to a political figure living – much less still in office, Johnson dedicated the Mendel Rivers Federal Building in Charleston as early as 1964.

In the fall of 1970, Rivers underwent surgery to repair a leaky mitral valve with a plastic valve. Recovery was expected until he died suddenly. President Richard Nixon's statement read: "The death of Mendel Rivers will be mourned by a great many people. They include servicemen and their families who benefited greatly from his work. They include that great majority of American citizens who understand the essentiality of a strong defense and who know he was one of the foremost champions of a strong defense for our country."

But he was also hailed by ideological adversaries. Leggett noted how "there are only a few people with the charismatic power or mind that could put together the coalition he did. There is a question of whether any new chairman could do it."

That new chairman would turn out to be Eddie Hebert, a Louisianan five years older than Rivers who had been elected to the House with him in 1940. He played the part of the dominant Southern chair in every sense of the Word. He called himself a "Grand Titan," and had a rare five suite office which as Pat Schroeder wrote in her memoir, *Twenty-Four Years of House Cleaning and the Place Is Still A Mess* of pornography on the walls, a bar and a myriad of paintings.

Hebert (pronounced a-bare) was close to Richard Nixon, with whom he first became acquainted when they served on the infamous House Un-American Activities Committee. The two men – along with a Pennsylvania Republican named John McDowell, interrogated Alger Hiss and Hebert flat out told Hiss that, "either you or Mr. Chambers is lying. And whichever one of you is lying is the greatest actor that America has ever produced."

Hebert grew up in New Orleans, the son of a streetcar motor operator and teacher. Though he took his law degree from Tulane University, Hebert's strong suit was journalism. At the same time he had been editor of the Tulane newspaper, Hebert was sports editor for *The New Orleans Times Picayune*. He became a political columnist for the New Orleans States and became city editor in 1937. He used that role to investigate alleged corruption into confidantes of the late Governor and Senator, Huey Long, which the *Washington Post* noted, "helped his paper win an award for 'courage in journalism' given by the Sigma Delta Chi journalism fraternity, and propelled him into politics." So into the press was his heart that even after decades in Congress, he'd refer to himself as "an old reporter on a long sabbatical."

Hebert's record was solidly conservative. During the protests of the Vietnam War, Hebert said "let's forget the first amendment." In 1965, his Johnson support score was just 21% (Rivers' was 40%) and in '69, his ADA score was zero (this was still better than that of Rivers, who had zero (though it went to 25% and 17% in '68). He explained his opposition to the Civil Rights Act as "not believ(ing) it is equitable. I do not believe it is valid on the grounds of a life-long abhorrence to Big Brotherism." But it wasn't just cultural issues on which he was a solid "no." When opponents of the Vietnam War said the draft was unnecessary, Hebert replied that, "the only way to get an all-volunteer army is to draft it."

One positive trait about Hebert is he didn't make the different ideological lines personal. Michigan Congressman Lucien Nedzi was a junior member of Armed Services and, despite the age gap, had become friendly with both Vinson and Ed Hebert, the chairman of the subcommittee on Military Personnel on which he served. When Vinson retired, Nedzi liked serving under Hebert and made clear that he wanted to remain on the subcommittee. He asked him to intercede with Rivers. A few days later, Hebert approached Nedzi and said, I've got good news for you. Mendel appointed you to my subcommittee." Nedzi said he, "thanked him and then inquired who else was appointed. It turned out to be Eliot Hagen of Georgia, Porter Hardy of Virginia, Alton Lennon of North Carolina and Speedy Long of Louisiana," all hard-line conservatives. Nedzi then then said to him, "Mr. Chairman, you didn't have to bring up all that heavy artillery to take care of poor little ole me." His response was, "Don't give me that poor little ole me shit, but I love man who's perceptive."

For Southerners chairs such as Hebert, any thinking that they would be able to rule their committees as business as usual was evaporated in early '71, and it was other Southerners no less who helped do so. Two Massachusetts freshman, Louise Hicks and Michael Harrington, were competing for a single seat on Armed Services. It was already foregone that Les Aspin, a newly elected liberal from Wisconsin, would be getting a seat on the panel and Hebert wanted to minimize his impact and keep the conservatives who dominated it in control. Therefore, Hebert favored the more conservative Hicks, who had actually been promised the slot by Rivers prior to his death.

The liberal Harrington, ignoring the admonishments of his elders in the Massachusetts delegation, first took his fight to the New England delegation. Meanwhile, Hicks was escorted to that same meeting by Hebert. Harrington prevailed 9-6. Hebert then approached Arkansas Democrat Wilbur Mills who, not only chaired the powerful Ways and Means Committee, but also the Committee on Committees which doles out panel assignments. Mills said he was incline to give chairmen the prerogative of who they wanted on their committees but, as *The New York Times* noted, "when the Committee on Committees met on Wednesday, however, Mr. Mills did not speak out on the Armed Services vacancies," and Harrington got the position. One Congressional Democrat surmised that, "I think Albert, Boggs and Mills were determined to prove that theirs was not going to be a conservative administration, partial to the South. So they took their first opportunity to make this point and that was on committee assignments."

Incidentally, powerful Appropriations Chair George Mahon (see volume two) was also rebuffed that year when Albert increased the size of the panel to make room for four new liberals. Interesting, the most ubiquitous liberal of all, New York's Bella Abzug had written in an early memoir that she found Hebert "charming," if somewhat underhanded, and that when she approached him about sitting on the committee, he replied that he didn't have a problem with it, though he also made clear it wasn't up to him but the Committee on Committees. That panel rebuffed Abzug.

When Congresswoman Pat Schroeder, a liberal Democratic Congresswoman from Colorado and Ron Dellums, a liberal African-American from California, won Armed Services seats two years later, Hebert only provided one additional chair. Hebert had derided them as "the white-woman liberal bomb thrower from Denver" and the "black male bomb-thrower from Berkeley," but the two shared the chair, joking they were "sitting cheek-to-cheek" (chairs were provided for both members at the next meeting but Dellums later wrote "our lack of welcome at the committee had been made abundantly clear"). That was made clear when Schroeder tried to make peace with him. His response: "The Lord giveth and the Lord taketh. You'll do fine around here as long as you remember that I am the Lord." Army. Navy, Air Force and Coast Guard academies when Schroeder, who was prepared to support the amendment, arrived with a Missouri Congressman, William Randall who was not. Hebert let Randall vote but not Schroeder.

Following the 1974 elections in which Democrats gained 42 seats (many of the newcomers were liberals), they decided to pursue the rule that mandated committee chairs be voted on by the full Democratic caucus. The Steering Committee re-nominated Hebert by a vote of 14-10 but he now had to face the full caucus. Hebert had not helped his cause by referring to the freshmen as "boys and girls." Tip O'Neill, in his book, Man of the House, recounted that Hebert gave "a Rayburn like speech about how freshmen should be content to sit quietly and learn the ropes for a few years. The new members were furious that Eddie, in their view, was taking down to them."

Republicans, among them John Anderson of Illinois, argued that because the committees impacted every House district in the nation, the entire House, rather than simply the majority party, should have a say in who became chair. That did not happen and Hebert lost his chair by a vote of 133 to 151. He blamed, "the propaganda show led by Common Cause," which he called "an insidious organization," and "a lobby organization trying to run Congress." He called their allegations "inaccurate, misleading, distorted, irresponsible and hardly worthy of comment."

Common Cause, meanwhile, which also succeeded in ousting Texans Wright Patman and Bill Poage from their respective chairmanships at Banking and Agriculture (see volume two), called the vote, "the final healthy act of demolition that brings the seniority system crashing down." Unlike Patman and Poage, Hebert, angered at seeing his chairmanship come to an end, threatened to take the matter to the full House ("Let the full House ... let the American people see what is going on") but didn't.

From there, insult became injury. Hebert had already been impacted by eye issues but the 73 year old took a fall on ice later in the year at a party given in his honor by the Navy. It was shortly thereafter that he decided not to seek re-election in 1976. His reasoning: "I want to be able to take the last curtain call while still sound in mind and body. He died three years later. A year earlier, a $22 million 250 bed F. Edward Hebert Naval Hospital in New Orleans had been closed because of its limited use (the entire military facility had been set to expand before Hebert's defeat).

In closing, despite what folks thought about these Southern autocrats, the military loved them. The U.S.S. Carl Vinson and the U.S.S. Mendel Rivers are among the many fleets that at one time or another have graced the military.

The Rules Committee had as its chair the man who may have become the most historically infamous of them all, Virginia's Howard W. Smith. Elected in 1930, Smith was known for pulling magical tricks and simply disappearing. Susan Dudley Gold in *The Civil Rights Act of 1964* noted that, when he encountered a bill he did not like, Smith left his post and retreated to his 200 half-cow dairy-farm in Fauquier County - a ploy he used to stall the Civil Rights Act of 1957. Without its chairman present, the Rules Committee could take no action on the bill in question." The most infamous of examples came in 1959 – when he said a barn had caught fire. On another, occasion, he said he had to tend to a "sick cow." Smith made no bones about his strategy. "As long as I'm chairman," he said in 1960, "I'll continue to exercise my judgment as to what goes to the floor of the House of Representatives."

Throughout his long career, Smith made it a habit of thwarting liberal priorities. Though he started out a "New Deal," backer, he gradually became a thorn in the spine of presidents and liberal colleagues alike. In 1940, he guided to passage the Alien Registration Act (better known as the "Smith Act,") which required aliens to register. By the time the 1964 civil rights legislation was about ready to be taken up, *The New York Times* noted, "he helped bottle up in the Rules Committee F.D.R.'s historic Wage-and Hour Bill in 1937. He battled Harry Truman's abortive legislative program. He helped throttle education and welfare measures during both the Eisenhower and Kennedy Administrations. He blocked statehood for Alaska for almost a full year."

Smith's career began as a commonwealth attorney for Alexandria. He then became a corporation judge. As a result, he was often referred to as "the Judge." He was born in a 1797 farmhouse in Broad Run (Fauquier County) and *The New York Times* noted "his mother would entertain him as a boy with true tales of the Yankees marching through." Throughout Smith's entire tenure in Congress, the farm was operational and Smith, despite residing in Alexandria, he played a substantial role. This made him a hero to the Virginia Farm Bureau, which honored him in 1960. "Farmers have got more problems today than a dog has fleas—and one of those is Washington. We've got a lot of people in Washington who want to help the farmer—especially about election time. The trouble is most of them have never had a hand on the plow nor put a milking stool under a cow and they have a lot of impractical suggestions." It also set the stage for his legendary out decades later with taking up bills he opposed.

Eventually, Rayburn grew tired of Smith's tactics and had the rare success of doing an end-run around him. It was after the 1960 presidential election and Rayburn knew that Smith – along with most Southerners, would be heavily resistant to John F. Kennedy's agenda. So Rayburn put forth legislation that would pack the Rules Committee – giving those sympathetic to the administration the extra slots (one additional Republican would join two extra Democrats which would theoretically mean an 8-7 majority). In unusually personal terms, Rayburn did little to hide his personal animosity toward Smith, asking undecided members, "Are you for the Speaker or are you for that old man from Virginia?" With help from a few House Republicans, the change narrowly passed (217-212).

This did not mean that all would be well. Smith still had the power to refuse to – as he did in 1963 with the Youth Conservation Corps and most of Kennedy's other legislative priorities. *The New York Times* said "his best talents, however, are hidden in quiet little conferences in the cloakrooms or the splendid privacy of a closed-door session of his committee."

It wasn't clear that every Southern chair who opposed civil rights held personal animosity toward African-Americans but Smith made it clear that he was as close to a racist as possible. "The Southern people," he said, "have never accepted the colored race as a race of people who had equal intelligence... as the white people of the South." Smith had referred to Smith had referred to the pending '64 legislation "as full of booby traps as a dog is of fleas" so it was no surprise that even when it reached the floor, that he would try to kill it even after he was forced to advance it in Rules. But the course he settled on was somewhat curious, at least to those who didn't know him.

Surmising that the House might vote down a civil rights amendment if the prohibition of gender discrimination were part of the bill, Smith proposed an amendment that would do just that. In fact, snickers could be heard in the chamber as he explained his amendment. Yet there are also reasons to believe Smith was acting altruistically - at least where gender was concerned. He had been friends with Alice Paul. Members debated whether this was the right time to include an amendment of this nature but ultimately passed it, along with the bill. The irony is that Smith might have inadvertently helped make a bill he opposed stronger.

Into 1965, Smith opposed much of the "Great Society," and the National Endowment of the Arts was one example. "What are the arts," he asked mockingly? "And here is where I display my ignorance. I do not know. . . I suppose fiddle players would be in the arts and the painting of pictures would be in the arts. It was suggested that poker playing would be an artful occupation. Is this going to subsidize poker players that get in trouble?"

Howard W. Smith and Bill Colmer ran the Rules Committee
Photo courtesy of the Collection of the U.S. House of Representatives

Ultimately, the voters, as opposed to the Congressional leadership, put an end to Smith's antics but even that required a stroke of luck – and good cartography. The Commonwealth's lines were redrawn that year and mapmakers joined parts of more liberal trending Fairfax County with Smith's rural district. It seemed highly unlikely that the goal was to unseat Smith but whatever the case, an outspokenly progressive State Delegate named George Rawlings, Jr. (who was nine when Smith first came to Congress 36 years earlier), yielded to the entreaties of his colleague in the legislature, Henry Howell and decided to challenge him. He focused on younger voters and African-Americans, some of whom were exercising their rights to vote for the first time. Smith noticed and was forced to campaign.

The result was a bitterly divided primary with Rawlings topping Smith by 645 votes. *The Fredericksburg Free Lance-Star* termed Smith's defeat, "the upset of the century." Rawlings took 64% in Fairfax and even carrying counties at the Southern end such as King and Queen, Charles, New Kent that had long been accustomed to backing Smith, who meanwhile took 2/3 of the vote in just one County – Louisa (even being held to just 61% in Fauquier).

After leaving Washington, Smith resumed his law practice and died at age 93.

The man who was at the impetus of Rayburn's desire to enlarge the Rules Committee was a fellow named Bill Colmer of Mississippi. Colmer came to the House two years after Smith, also as a "New Deal" Democrat but also had drifted away quite quickly, so much so that when he lost his seat on Rules after the

Democrats lost the House in '46, Rayburn scoffed at putting him back on when they regained it in '48, particularly because Colmer had backed State's Rights candidate Strom Thurmond over Harry S. Truman in that year's presidential election. But Colmer was a "poker-pal," of Majority Leader John McCormack and he reinstalled Colmer. By 1960, Colmer had committed a far worse offense in Rayburn's eyes. He had backed Virginia Senator Harry Byrd (the candidate of "unpledged electors" in Mississippi) over the Democratic nominee, John F. Kennedy. Rayburn vowed revenge and once again tried to get Colmer kicked off Rules (by this time, he called him, "a very inferior man").

Only when it became clear that he would lose (he rejected an offer from Smith to send five Kennedy priorities to the House floor) did Rayburn decide to fight to enlarge the committee (he wanted all of Kennedy's proposals to advance to the floor while Smith replied that they "have made every offer we properly could to settle the matter amicably").

The vote had a surprising savior – Carl Vinson. He promised Rayburn the Southern votes necessary to enlarge the committee – and delivered, even voting "aye" himself.

Colmer became chair following Smith's surprise defeat and many expected it would be more of the same. But he surprised some. *The New York Times* wrote in a 1972 profile, "To most of his colleagues, including liberals, however, the courtly Mr. Colmer is a gracious, honorable man who seldom if ever has wielded his power as chairman of the Rules Committee to block legislation from reaching the House floor." The paper noted he even went out of his way to ensure that Abzug had an opportunity to speak. But it would be inaccurate to say that Colmer had abandoned the old Southern way. As late as his final year in office, he exasperated more liberal Democrats by refusing to move minimum wage legislation out of Rules.

Colmer, who, growing up in "a one-teacher school house" once said was "crazy enough to think that I might be President one day," retired at age 82 in 1972. The man he asked to run in his place was his Administrative Assistant, Trent Lott who captured the seat as a Republican. Colmer died in 1980 at age 90.

There was at least one other member of Congress who governed like a titan. John McMillan of South Carolina was one of them. It may be hard to imagine McMillan's entire tenure having overlapped that of Rivers- in fact he actually went to Washington a term before in 1938, because while Rivers chaired the prestigious Armed Services panel, McMillan's perch was the District Committee. And for residents of the nation's capitol, this was as high and mighty as other panels. But under McMillan's stewardship, he gave them little to like.

McMillan's chairmanship began in 1948 and lasted 24 years. To hear the *Washington Post* tell it in his obituary, McMillan's initial stewardship was the same as his other Southern brethren. *The Post* noted in his death that, "Liberal congressmen and other supporters of self-government here depicted him as a tyrant, who they claimed ran his committee with a dictatorial hand. Many leaders of the black community accused him of racism." That's not particularly difficult when he sends the African-American Mayor of Washington D.C. a truckload of watermelons (Washington had submitted McMillan his budget request). But Congressional leaders, under the auspice of President Johnson, acted sooner than with other chairs.

McMillan had been bottling up a home-rule bill for the District for ten years but in 1965, Congressional leaders decided to let the House have its say. Lawmakers voted 213-183 to bring it to the floor. McMillan was vocally against it. The District, he claimed, was a "federal city...the only city created for a federal purpose." Home rule, he contended would "give it away."

Back home, McMillan's hold on his district was almost as firm as his grasp on his committee. That changed around the same time as home-rule. In 1970, he was forced into a runoff for the first time in his career, though won it with 70%. By 1972, the times had caught up with him. A State Representative named John Jenrette advanced to the runoff and dislodged the longtime incumbent by 845 votes.

McMillan would find, as his colleagues had, that change had come.

The U.S.S. Carl Vinson

CHAPTER FIFTY-THREE

Surprise '62 Upsets Marked End of Capehart and Wiley: Produced Bayh Wonder and Glorious Gaylord

Historic Tidbit: After receiving a nasty letter from a constituent, Wisconsin Senator Alexander Wylie wrote the man back. "Sir," he said, "my stenographer, being a lady, cannot type what I think of you, I, being a gentleman, cannot do so either. You being neither, will understand what I mean."

November of 1962. "He's a Rebel," "Big Girls Don't Cry," and "The Monster Mash" were topping the radio charts; *The Longest Day, Whatever Happened to Baby Jane,* and *Mutiny on the Bounty* were popular at the box office, and Gunsmoke and *The Beverly Hillbillies* dominated the ratings game. Across the Midwest, young Democrats were validating the two-year-old "New Frontier" by replacing long-time, elderly Senators with youthful activists. While George McGovern narrowly captured a South Dakota Senate seat that had been in GOP hands for a generation, it was the respective defeats of Homer Capehart in Indiana and Alexander Wiley in Wisconsin are what turned heads - and also allowed the victors, Birch Bayh and Gaylord Nelson, to prove that "Camelot Fever" was here to stay.

The results were surprising, since they were unexpected even at the beginning of the fall and occurred in several states that were thought to be favorable to Republicans. However, Capehart's and Wylie's defeats, along with the Democrats' ability to peel off long-time Senate seats in South Dakota and New Hampshire, not only sent major Capitol Hill institutions packing, but also gave Democrats and the Kennedy administration some unexpected crowing rights with their midterms. These elections also gave us a new generation of sorts. Birch Bayh may very well have been the most important Senator who wasn't part of leadership, and Gaylord Nelson, who I focused on in earlier pieces, as well as McGovern and Tom McIntyre, also had more impact on today's world and everyday life than anyone realizes. Indiana and Wisconsin were the most fascinating races, though, insofar as they ended in the defeat of long-time Republican Senators.

Indiana

Capehart, who had only a high school education, first achieved success as a maker of coin-operated record players, jukeboxes, and popcorn machines for Packard in rural Indiana. His respect among GOP elders grew after he hosted a "Cornfield Conference" on his farm in 1938 to lend a moral reinvigoration to

Republicans heading into the mid-term elections. *Fortune* described Capehart's attire as a "floppy canvas sun hat, white long sleeved shirt, long checked tie, tan cotton trousers, and cigar in the corner of his mouth." The convention was a spectacular success but Capehart was still a political novice when he was picked to run for the Senate in 1944.

Capehart hosted the great cornfield conference on his farm in 1938
Photo courtesy of William B. Pickett

Capehart defeated Democratic Governor Henry Schicker, starting the streak of Indiana Senators who would narrowly defeat popular statesmen. He had the good fortune of appearing on the ballot at the same time as Thomas E. Dewey carried Indiana. He backed additional housing for veterans. After calling a Capehart rider in the Defense Production Act renewal, Truman included "the terrible Capehart Amendment" in his version of the bill.

Capehart was not a hard-line conservative but rhetorically, he established a pugnacity that could pass for a modern-day Jim Inhofe or Jim Bunning. *The Toledo Blade* called him "one of the hottest tempered of Republicans." He sparred with everyone from fellow members of Congress, sons of Presidents, and Chief Executives themselves. He attempted to censure Wayne Morse over questioning Claire Booth Luce's mental fitness, House Banking Chair Wright Patman over pricing, and James Roosevelt, the son of FDR, over why he was hired by a firm to testify against a savings-and-loan bill after it had been introduced. He was also a man prone to a verbal slip-up or two. He once called himself "the senior

Senator from Junior," and during a debate promoted himself as "the distinguished Senator from Indiana."

Capehart once had a legendary run-in with LBJ on the Senate floor. Just before a vote on landmark public housing legislation, Capehart told LBJ "I'm going to rub your nose in s–t" to which Johnson acknowledged it looks "like you got me." Johnson deftly maneuvered to beat it back by wooing the southern Democratic coalition, which Capehart thought he had in the bag. George E. Reedy, in his book *The U.S. Senate*, notes that when Harry Byrd, the venerable Virginia Dixiecrat, voted nay," Capehart's "head jerked around so rapidly I was afraid it was going to fall off. For once, it was a literal truth to say that a man's jaw dropped as southerner after southerner voted against the Capehart amendment." On another occasion, the Banking and Currency Committee called a witness whom Capehart had accused of writing favorably of communism.

Capehart spoke out in early 1960 when a parade of Southern Senators galvanized the floor with their opposition to pending civil rights legislation. "This exhibition is hurting the United States. We are advertising to the world, not the benefits enjoyed by our minorities but our mistreatment of them."

Capehart won his second and third terms easily, and by 1962, there seemed little reason to believe he wouldn't run a fourth. However, an international happenstance and an erstwhile 34-year-old challenger named Birch Bayh combined to create a perfect storm, and with it came the end of Homer Capehart.

During the summer of 1962, Capehart saw the threat and urged an immediate blockade to Cuba, urging JFK to "send in the Marines." The President in turn offered an angry rebuttal in a campaign appearance for Bayh, calling Capehart one of "those self-appointed generals and admirals who want to send someone else's son to war." Unlike the "acceptable" Wiley, Capehart was known as an "Indiana neanderthal." When Ted Sorenson, who had categorically denied that missiles existed, was reported to have said in private, "Would you believe it? Homer Capehart is the Winston Churchill of our time," that may have changed, however. The crisis would consume Americans—perhaps sooner than even Capehart had thought possible. But it was too early for him to reap the benefit? Or as Kennedy biographer Joseph Siracusa suggests, did he even try? Sircusa writes, "Capehart all but withdrew from the campaign in the final week." John Tower, then a freshman Senator, wrote in his autobiography that he saw what Capehart was up against on a campaign visit to Indiana. He recalled calling admonishing Everett Dirksen in a phone call, saying, "Homer's supposed to win easily out here. Take it from me. He's in trouble. The missile thing isn't helping."

Photo via antiquesnavigator.com

Chris Sautter wrote that Bayh, meanwhile, ran the quintessential underdog retail politics campaign. He had heavy labor backing, and "his fresh faced appeal and non-stop courthouse campaign appearances in a Mercury" proved a welcome touch. There was a jingle to accompany it: "Hey, look him over/He's your kind of guy/His first name is Birch/His last name is Bayh/Candidate for Senator/for the Hoosier State."

Two future Senator Bayhs just after Birch's improbable victory
Photo via knicklas.blogspot

In the end, Bayh pulled off an 11,000-vote win in what was by far the biggest Senate upset of the year. As the returns were coming in and Bayh stretched out an early lead, the Capehart camp was still confidant (wait for the rural areas, he implored supporters). However, Bayh's courtship of small towns, many of which were Republican, paid off, and he came close to matching the incumbent in many of them.

Bayh had among the keenest minds in the United States Senate and that was reflected by his enactment of heavy-duty legislation to fruition and enactment. In office, it was Bayh who sponsored the Constitutional Amendment giving 18 year olds the right to vote. It was Bayh who sponsored the ERA and Title IX.

In many ways, the two went hand in hand. In a 2005 interview with ESPN reporter Melissa Isackson, Bayh credits his wife Marvella for pushing Title IX in part because, a s Isackson writes, she was denied admission to "her dream college," the University of Virginia because she was a woman. Bayh would later recall her saying "we can't afford to ignore the development of 53 percent of the brainpower in this country. I had no idea how far that basic idea would go." On ERA, Bayh fought against what he viewed as "poison" amendments by opponents, including one by Utah Republican Jake Garn to allow states that have already ratified the measure to opt out. Bayh, in arguing the need to give proponents of the measure seven additional years for ratification, argued that there should be "no time limit on the pursuit of equality and justice in America." But that proved little more than brief respite. No further approval for the measure took place in legislative chambers and by 1982, advocates were forced to concede defeat. For Bayh, that marked a rare one Bayh, a deputy Whip on the Voting Rights Act, successfully fought to expand the measure to include Latinos, championed bilingualism and led opposition to Nixon Supreme Court nominees Carswell and Haynesworth. He outfoxed Everett Dirksen's on the Minority Leader's voluntary school prayer amendment by holding a hearing in his sub-committee. But on the floor, Bayh introduced a measure stating that nothing in past Supreme Court rulings that had invalidated school prayer could "prevent voluntary prayer or meditation." Senators defeated that amendment. But the same went for Dirksen's proposal.

By 1973, however, Dirksen had passed away and Bayh was in no mood to hold a hearing. In fact, he resisted until pressure forced him to do so. But there was no ambiguity about his passion against it. "What we are dealing with here," he said, "is an effort to change the Bill of Rights. We are here to discuss the wisdom of altering the First Amendment to the Constitution – the amendment from which we derive our four freedoms – freedom of religion, freedom of speech, freedom of the press and freedom to peaceably assemble." He then continued that "being for or against prayer; for God or against God. It is a question involving the propriety of the state, through its schools, mingled in an intimate area generally reserved to the family, the home and the church." Bayh backed U.S. action in Vietnam longer than most liberals would have preferred, but he later said that the conflict "ranks among this country's greatest and most tragic mistakes."

Bayh has so many legacies it's hard to choose a most significant. But for many Americans, FEMA may come close. Today the agency is known nationally, but that was far from always the case. Bayh's interest had stemmed from a Palm Sunday hurricane in his home-state that killed 138 people and had already chaired hearings on the matter and the full chairman of the Public Works Committee, Jennings Randolph of West Virginia, asked him to chair the newly created Special Subcommittee on Disaster Relief from the Senate Public Works Committee which Randolph had proposed. He soon introduced the Disaster Relief Act of 1969 which became law the following year. *Acts of God: The Unnatural History of Natural Disaster in America* by Ted Steinberg wrote "the act allowed the federal bureaucracy, once the President had declared a disaster area, to extend all kinds of relief to John Q. Public."

New Jersey Senator Harrison Williams, issuing panegyric praise of his defeated colleague on the Senate floor as he prepared to leave office, said "the oft-forgotten residents of our nursing homes, hospitals, and other institutions can be assured that their rights will not be compromised because Birch Bayh made sure that the Justice Department could intervene on their behalf."

**Speaking at a college campus and jogging with students
during the battle for gender equality in sports
Photos via the Senatorial Papers of Birch Bayh, Indiana University**

Bayh's visibility on national issues compelled him to undertake a national campaign. He sought the White House in 1976, and as a three-term Senator from a Republican-leaning area, his campaign was about as credible as they come. Bayh had flirted with running four years earlier and was aided at that time by Robert Friebert, the President of the Wisconsin chapter of the American Civil Liberties Union. He demurred, however, because of his wife's ill health and the fact that he found unappealing the thought of going from airport to airport.

A chief aide outlined a key strategy: making strong showings in a series of early states before capturing the key prize - New York - whose residents voted in April. His publicist, Bill Wise, outlined the strategy as follows: "By the time we reach the

New York primary, the field should be narrowed to one liberal candidate. The others aren't going to disappear, but in terms of real effect, only one will be important." Wise predicted Bayh would "face Jackson and Wallace for the nomination."

Bayh felt that the Republican administration had feet of clay when it came to economic conditions, and he went out of his way to exploit it with a hammer. "We need a President," he said, "who is less concerned that too many jobs will cause inflation, and more concerned that too few jobs will cause human suffering." Two Republican administrations, following a deliberate policy of planned unemployment, have led us through two recessions and record inflation. Only a genius for ineptitude could have produced recession and inflation together. Only a totally insensitive Republican Administration could have tolerated both.

Against other liberals and, in particular, a charismatic peanut farmer from Georgia who was honing his outsider message, Bayh didn't perform particularly well (Jackson and Wallace had been long gone from the race at this point as well—so much for proper prognostications).

Image via ronwadebuttons.org

There was no denying that Bayh was a liberal in a conservative state and electorally, he would never have it easy. For quite some time on Election Night 1968, William Ruckelshaus, who later became EPA director and a Nixon official, led him. Bayh finally won 52-48%. 1974 was the Watergate election in which Democrats were supposed to be running strong, but Bayh had a formidable opponent in Indianapolis Mayor Richard Lugar and won just 50-45% (Lugar won the seat two years later and Bayh calls him a wonderful person).

By 1980, his luck had run out. Against Dan Quayle, he had a true ideological battle; for Democrats, that was the worst year to have it. Bayh led big early in the year but lost his seat 54-46%. Days after the election, he told The Kokomo Tribune, "We've gone through the post-mortem: If only? What if?" he said after his loss. "I don't know what we could have done to withstand a Reagan tide of 400,000 votes." Also, with Indiana's unemployment second in the nation only to neighboring Michigan, Bayh said, "The people of Indiana were deeply concerned about economic problems that President Carter had not handled well. I really think we were hurt more by people who had jobs and were afraid of losing them than by the people who were out of work."

Bayh would have a footnote to history in another, lifesaving way. It was he who, in 1964, pulled Ted Kennedy from the wreckage of a small plane that crashed, badly wounding Kennedy and killing two others.

Bayh during the 1976 Presidential campaign
Left photo courtesy of The Monticello Herald; Right photo via Jo Freeman

After his defeat from the Senate, he remained in Washington where, though semi-retired, he still practices law.

In paying his tribute to his defeated colleague, Maryland Republican Senator "Mac" Mathias said "Birch Bayh's conscience gave new direction to social justice in America." There can be no finer legacy than that."

Wisconsin

Wiley was 78 years old, more than a decade older than Capehart. He seemed a typical Midwesterner, calling himself "just a small town banker, businessman, lawyer, and operator of a dairy-farm who became a typical American success." He had a major hand in the creation of The St. Lawrence Seaway; one of its canals, the Wylie-Dondero, is named for him. He backed the Marshall Plan and NATO.

Though the Kennedy administration backed Nelson, it privately made claims that it was "satisfied" with Wiley. Wisconsin wasn't the only state in which the administration was inserting that claim. Next door in Illinois, JFK wasn't keen on helping Sid Yates, the Democratic nominee for the Senate there, believing Ev Dirksen would be the friendliest opposition leader he'd get. Dirksen won. Wiley did not.

By the 1962 race, Wiley was ranking Republican on the Foreign Affairs Committee and had previously ascended to the same post on Judiciary. Wylie backed Kennedy on school funding but not on Medicare. He was at odds with Estes Kefauver over the Tennesseans desire to rein in price fixing by the utility industry, which he labeled a "publicity venture." *The Milwaukee Journal Sentinel* reported that "the party still had its Eisenhower and Taft wings and Tafties were in command of a strong Wisconsin majority." In an election that was of landslide proportions such as 1956, the desertion by a few folks may not have mattered, but in 1962, any lost votes could've hurt.

Alexander Wiley
Left photo courtesy of the U.S. Senate Historical Office, right
photo courtesy of the Harry S. Truman Presidential Library

Wiley's 1956 campaign may have lulled him into a false sense of security. He lost the party endorsement to another Republican but managed to eke out a 10,000-vote win. The general election was a non-event: he beat Henry Maier, later Mayor of Milwaukee 60-36%. However, Eisenhower was winning big that year and Maier was a novice. Nelson was a dynamic man with ideas a-plenty, who traveled the state up and down.

It was Nelson's election as Governor, along with Bill Proxmire's seizing of Joe McCarthy's Senate seat that revitalized the Democratic Party in Wisconsin. Nelson was put on the defensive of a carefully negotiated tax package, including a sales tax increase that sparked the slogan "three cents for Gaylord' around the state.

Wiley also may have believed his statesmanship would allow him to skate, but opponents used that against him as well. In *The Man from Clear Lake,* Bill Cristhofferson writes that some called it "questionable whether Wiley is fully aware of what is going on in Washington, even though he has been there for 24 years." He was called "a glad-handler type and no orator" and "an overstuffed armchair in a modern living room." *Time* noted after the election that "if Nelson's strategy was to campaign energetically around the state, irk the old gentleman, let him lose his temper, and then shrug it all off as though it were pitiful proof of senility. The Nelson strategy worked." Indeed, Wylie called Nelson "stupid" and "nitwit."

Photo via nelson.blogspot.net

Then the Cuba Missile Crisis erupted. Wiley was summoned back to Washington, one of 16 members of Congress chosen to discuss the situation with President Kennedy. The matter seemed to stall Nelson's momentum, reminding voters of Wiley's influential role at a crucial time, but Wylie was refusing Nelson's call to debate by showing an empty chair. Wylie responded by mimicking "an empty chair in Madison." Nelson won 52-47%. Wiley would not have lived to serve a full fifth term. He died in 1967 when he was 83 years old.

If Bayh and Nelson's victories stemmed from facing incumbents who had lost some of their seasoning, McGovern was truly put over the top by the "New Frontier."

Republican Senators Francis Case and Joe Bottum of South Dakota
Courtesy of the U.S. Governmental Printing Office

Still, McGovern's win was not a total shock. Francis Case had passed away, and Joe Bottum, the state's Lieutenant Governor, had been appointed to take his place. But that appointment did not come easy. Bottum faced five other candidates at the special Republican Convention and only on the Seventeenth ballot did his chief rival drop out (at which time the state's Governor appointed him to fill the remainder of the term left open by Case's death).

McGovern had challenged two-term Senator Karl Mundt in 1960 and held him to 55%. Prior to that, he had served the state in the U.S. House and was well known. Bottum labeled McGovern Kennedy's "yes" man while McGovern replied that his allegiance was only to South Dakotans. The interim Senator seemed to start out with an advantage but was hurt by his vote against the Kennedy's Medicare proposal. Bottum also linked McGovern to Henry Wallace whom he supported for President in 1948 but McGovern responded that "we all mature and season with age and my life since the end of World War II has been crowded with hard, practical experience."

McGovern meanwhile was aided by the administration's handling of the Cuban Missile Crisis. Going into Election Day, the race was viewed as a genuine tossup but Bottum wasn't helped the day before during a family television broadcast when his wife seemed confused during the taping opf a pre-election message.

The margin was just 597 votes. In New Hampshire, Tom McIntyre took advantage of a previous split to win a seat long held by the Republicans (which I covered in a previous chapter). Other traditionally Republican states had close races as well. In Utah, Republican Wallace Bennett eked by with 52-48% (a *Desseret News* poll the Sunday before actually showed him trailing), and in Idaho, Democrat Gracie Pfost nearly upset Len Jordan, a former Governor, for an unexpired term. After serving three terms, Bayh, Nelson, and McGovern all met the same fate as Capehart and Wiley, as McIntyre had done two years before (his 1962 special election meant that his cycle was in a different year).

All in all, the Democrats picked up two Senate seats. They would lose Colorado and Wyoming but gain the four above. For a young President who just cleared the biggest test of his administration, that may have been the biggest compliment of all.

Yes, 1962 was some race - and the lessons of Capehart and Wiley ought to be: don't take your eye off the ball.

CHAPTER FIFTY-FOUR

Nebraska's Senate Duo Hruska and Curtis Spelled Mediocre and Lackluster

Historic Quote: "Elected officials are not sent back here to be great legislators. There's too much legislating going on." – Kansas Republican Congressman Larry Wynn, under fire for being too low-profile despite being a senior member. Is this a House member's version of Roman Hruska's mediocrity defense?

Photo courtesy of the Nebraska Library Commission History

Ah, how to classify Roman Hruska and Carl Curtis? Of Nebraska's two long-ago U.S. Senators, one was famously associated with the term mediocre and the other epitomized the term lackluster. Both were unsung—one as a person who made one of the most famous statements ever uttered in Congress, the other as co-author of one of the most meaningful pieces of legislation for the American people. Together, the duo could unquestionably be considered hacks, yet thrived in wonkish undertakings of the minutia of policy. Each had intelligence that could be torpedoed by tempestuous if not bewildering defenses of figures whom few others saw justification in defending. As such, their last elections, even with considerable seniority in friendly constituencies, demonstrated that voters felt the same way, as they awarded each a final six-year term with 53%.

Hruska and Curtis were both quite true to Republicanism, following Reagan's commandment to a tee about not speaking ill of another, regardless of how they might actually feel. Both were generally hardline conservatives, but their rhetoric belied the fact that both knew how to stop—at least temporarily—when Nebraska and the nation demanded it.

For more than two decades, Hruska and Curtis were a team in Washington. With a difference in age of less than one year (both also died at the same age—94), they began service a mere 20 days apart and started a new guard following the death of both of the state's Senators. Except for the two years Curtis remained in Washington to complete his own term following Hruska's retirement, their service was simultaneous. They made up the crucial Senate block that sided with Ev Dirksen and against Barry Goldwater in passing the Civil Rights Act and the Voting Rights Act. Beyond that, their records gave liberals little to crow about. They opposed most of the "Great Society" and instead focused their interests on a strong defense and on championing Nebraska's interests, even as they preached limited government.

Despite their respective defenses of shady characters, neither had a whiff of scandal and were hailed by friend and foe alike as masters of integrity. They complimented each other: Hruska worked on detailed Judiciary matters and Curtis on Finance—roles in which, by the time of their retirements, both had achieved top Republican spots. But a reputation is a hard thing to waste, and when Jack Anderson called them "dolts," and as Michael Malone writes in *The American West*, "the two worst members of the Senate," many found it hard to disagree.

Roman Hruska (1904-1999)

If the name Roman Hruska pops up in history books, one word will define him: mediocrity. It wouldn't be so much about him—he was actually bright, a "Senator's Senator"—but rather about his defense of Judge Harrold Carswell.

The year was 1970, and President Nixon had nominated Carswell to a seat on the U.S. Supreme Court. Many Democrats and a number of Republicans were questioning Carswell's qualifications, to which Hruska issued a declaration for the ages. "So what if he is mediocre? There are a lot of mediocre judges and people and lawyers. They are entitled to a little representation, aren't they? We can't have all Brandeises, Cardozos, and Frankfurters and stuff like that there." Officials in Washington, the Nixon White House, and Carswell supporters guffawed, and Carswell's opponents were given more ammunition. The Democrats mounted their anti-Carswell campaign with, "What's wrong with a little mediocrity?"

Hruska acknowledged that the comment was poorly worded, and Curtis himself later said that "Senator Hruska at no time defended mediocrity. It was taken out of context when he was referring to judges who did not come from academia." But the damage was done, and the Carswell nomination was defeated 58-42. Hruska also advocated for Nixon's FBI nominee who was defeated.

Photo via eBay

Nor did the comment do much to help Hruska in his backyard. The conservative Nebraska was still open to electing Democrats and, toward the end of the decade, elected a prominent string of them. Hruska was also facing a challenge from a popular former Governor, Frank Morrison.

In a strange twist for a law-and-order incumbent, Morrison went after Hruska for showing violent movies at the five drive-ins he owned—movies with sexual content such as *The Blood Drinker* and *Easy Rider*—and talked about it in Washington (he posed the question, "can Roman Hruska sermonize against loose sex and low morals while displaying filthy situations upon the public screen for money?"). Hruska said he showed many commercial films, including Disney productions, calling Morrison "desperate," and filed a complaint.

After trailing on Election Night until midnight, Hruska prevailed just 53-47%, running behind in Omaha by 2,200 votes.

Hruska's defense of Carswell may have stemmed from the fact that Hruska himself did not view the Constitution as living and breathing, and may have felt that in a laissez-faire atmosphere, sterling credentials were not required.

Indeed, Hruska may have been as much of a law-and-order Republican as one could possibly have found in the 1960s. He opposed gun control, fought for penalties for marijuana, and sponsored legislation ridding television of pornography and violence. One Senator quipped that was Hruska was "holding up more legislation than anyone else I've ever seen. He's the most effective damn roadblock around here." That no doubt limited his effectiveness with colleagues. Following Everett Dirksen's 1969 passing, Hruska mounted a bid to succeed him only to quickly realize he didn't have the votes. He promptly withdrew.

But as one editorial remarked after his death, Hruska did have a reputation for "honesty and integrity. There was never a question about that, even from his political adversaries." He looked after Nebraska's interests, such as import controls on beef—and his legal mind was well respected. The Judiciary Committee was his pride and joy.

The *Omaha World Herald* cites among his accomplishments the "Omnibus Crime and Safe Streets Act of 1968, the Criminal Justice Act of 1965, the Prisoners Rehabilitation Act of 1965 and the Bail Reform Act." One of his continuing interests was the reorganization and improvement of the federal court system, with Hruska immersing himself in complicated and mundane matters. One laborious undertaking was a mission to rewrite the criminal code.

Hruska had long been a prominent lawyer and debater who was good on the stump but the *Herald* observed in his death that "curiously, Hruska was regarded as an uninspired speaker on the floors of the House and Senate."

Filling a void on the Douglas County Commissioners Board (where he boasted that taxes never went up during his tenure) was something Hruska was proud of. It was meant to be a temporary assignment for a friend who was called into World War II; the neighbor was killed in action and Hruska kept the post.

If mediocrity would prove an example of Hruska not properly using his skills, his shrewdness was evident in another way. Upon arriving in Washington as a freshman House member, he sought a seat on the Appropriations Committee—almost unheard of for freshman. Hruska brandished letters from everyone from his soon-to-be Nebraska delegation mates to ex-President Herbert Hoover and somehow obtained the seat. Perhaps appropriately, Hruska seemed to have an anti-government mindset similar to Hoover's.

Because Hruska by his very nature was so judicious, his sense of operating by the book was generally unquestioned. When Eisenhower's White House Chief of Staff Sherman Adams was implicated for taking gifts (a vicuna coat, an Oriental rug and hotel rooms), Hruska called the allegations, "more serious in nature and degree than in several instances where persons in this administration were required to submit their resignations."

Hruska retired in 1976 and sought to anoint Second District Congressman John McCollister, who held the same seat as Hruska in 1954. The Mayor of Lincoln, Ed Zorinsky, a Democrat, kept the seat. Hruska had the honor of seeing Omaha's federal courthouse named after him in 1996. He died at 94 years old after a fall in May of 1999.

Carl Curtis (1905-2000)

Photo courtesy of the U.S. Senate Historical Office

Curtis had served Nebraska in the House for 16 years prior to going to the Senate and, by the time of his retirement, he was the longest-serving Nebraskan in Congress and ranking member on the Senate Finance Committee. His proudest accomplishment was bringing flood irrigation to his Central Nebraska district.

By rights, it was Curtis who should have been the senior Senator. While Curtis had been serving in the House since 1938, Hruska had been elected to an Omaha seat only the term before. However, incumbent Senator Hugh Butler had died in July of 1954, when Curtis was a candidate for the state's other seat, necessitated by the death of the state's other Senator, Dwight Griswold. Hruska was chosen for the vacancy, which made him the senior Senator by about six weeks. Curtis had actually announced his retirement altogether but was persuaded to make a comeback after Griswold's death

Curtis's background was not all that different from Hruska's. Both were lawyers, though Hruska put himself through school while Curtis taught himself with books, with each coming from middle-class families in rural Nebraska (Hruska in Abbie in Butler county and Curtis in Minden). Hruska was one of 11 from a Czech immigrant family and Curtis belonged to a family of farmers; each was forced to take odd jobs to put his way through school. Hruska learned debating early in his life. Curtis practiced on barn animals at his family's farm.

Image courtesy of politics1.com

Curtis' opposition to social spending, including on school lunches, came despite his hailing from agriculturally-dependent Nebraska. "It didn't hurt me to walk to school carrying a lunch pail," he said. He sought to limit Social Security increases because he was concerned about its solvency for future generations. And in 1972, Curtis was against proposed revisions to the Occupational Health Safety Administration (OSHA) so soon after its enactment. He called it detrimental, "to force the little people to comply with a law that is largely regulation, that has not even been published in the *Federal Registar,* and (that) takes a stack of books 17 feet high to find out about." At another point, he said, "do not think that your federal government is generous, kind, understanding and affectionate in its enforcement procedures. They are applying this law with the heel."

The consistency Curtis displayed was such throughout his long career. After the election of 1948, Curtis urged the re-elected President Harry Truman and the newly installed Democratic Congress to crack down on government waste prior to increasing taxes. "Before saddling additional taxes upon our people," he said, "I expect to find out how many millions of dollars in revenue we are losing by faulty or loose administration."

After Kennedy's assassination, Curtis was among those who were most vociferously urging Barry Goldwater to remain in the race for President. They had differences of opinion on the Civil Rights legislation, but this was one of only a few. He served as a floor manager for Goldwater at the convention. He also staunchly defended Richard Nixon until the end, including after the release of the famous 18-minute gap—he even uncharacteristically hit the talk circuit to declare him "totally innocent of any wrongdoing," a stance that was not only mocked but would surely have finished him had his final election not occurred two years before. "I believe Watergate was played all out of proportion," he said.

Later, Curtis said he "believed a different yardstick was used in dealing with Mr. Nixon than was used on other presidents and officials" and that if he didn't defend Nixon, "he would've gone undefended." Nixon declared that it was not for naught. At his retirement dinner, the ex-President declared, "Carl Curtis has guts galore."

Curtis was called the "Little Giant" by Barry Goldwater, but that could not be said of the way he was viewed by his colleagues. *The McCook Daily Gazette,* in an editorial published after his death, wrote that Curtis "was not an imposing figure, short in stature, stocky and balding throughout his later life." But he was good with people: "I didn't miss a pool hall, barbershop or hardware store," he said, and he had what ex-Congressman and later Governor Charles Thone called "the best constituent service operation around."

He pursued Republican causes and investigations such as Bobby Baker, an LBJ confidant, asking such probing questions, *The McCook Daily Gazette* wrote, that they "made the people appearing before his committee squirm." He said, "I've always lived by luck. It's so much better than brains." It showed. In his last two years in the Senate, Curtis did win the position of Senate GOP Policy Chair over Jacob Javits, but only because he mobilized like-minded conservatives.

While Hruska always knew he was going to have a tough go in 1970, Curtis was expecting no such thing in 1972. His opponent was Terry Carpenter, 72, who, amazingly, had been swept into Congress on FDR's "New Deal" coattails but had little other political involvement. In fact, *The Almanac of American Politics* wrote that he was one of the "zaniest" brands in politics. He operated gas stations and became, for a time, a Republican so that he could nominate "Joe Smith" as Vice-President at the 1956 Republican convention in order to protest Nixon. He eventually returned to the Democratic fold.

Curtis, like Hruska, took just 53% of the vote - an unexpectedly anemic showing but one that Curtis must have been grateful for, since neighboring Senators Jack Miller of Iowa and Gordon Allott of Colorado (not to mention Caleb Boggs of Delaware, who lost to a 29-year-old named Joe Biden) were being upset. And he was the only Nebraskan Senator to win without carrying Omaha or Lincoln. Despite their differences, he and Morrison would be friends for life.

After his first wife died in 1969, Curtis remarried. His wife was credited with, as the *Herald* wrote, giving him a more "modern look with a loosely flapped necktie."

Given his views, it may be stunning to learn that Curtis actually entered politics as a Democrat, even winning his first elective office as such (in the role of the Kearney County Attorney). But he was unseated by a foe who questioned his loyalty to the party. He switched by 1936 and was elected to the House two years later as FDR Democrats lost 77 House seats. Curtis won by running on an anti-Roosevelt platform.

For the ensuing 20 years before his death, Curtis remained active in the party, mentoring a new generation of Republican wannabees.

It would not be fair to say that Curtis lacked significant contributions. He showed great skill at amending legislation in committee. He co-authored the small-watershed program, prompting Morrison to say, "I used to like to kid him about the fact that … his greatest claim to fame in my opinion was his sponsorship of the Pick-Sloan plan for the development of the water resources of the Missouri basin, which was a tremendous government program, and an immense expenditure." But it was Curtis who authored the Individual Retirement Accounts (IRA), a 12-year struggle. Until his dying day, Curtis bemoaned the fact that so few were taking advantage of the program. His memoir was entitled *Forty Years against the Tide.*

Hruska died in May of 1999; Curtis followed in January of 2000. Both were 94 years old. A who's who of Nebraska's Democratic and Republican establishments came together to salute them.

If Hruska and Curtis were alive today, they'd likely fit in very well with the Ted Cruz's and Mike Lee's of the Senate. Strict constructionists when it came to the Constitution, they also looked after their home folks, Nebraskans, for whom they had to have been grateful.

CHAPTER FIFTY-FIVE

Senators Fannin and Montoya: Mediocre, Hacks, Or Both – With A Tint of A UFO

Historic Quote: "The brave men who died in Vietnam, more than 100% of which were black, made the ultimate sacrifice." - Washington DC Mayor Marion Barry.

Fannin and Montoya
Photos courtesy of the U.S. Senate Historical Office

W hen it comes to members of the United States Senate, the word mediocrity is a word that is most often associated with Roman Hruska, the senior Senator from Nebraska—not because he was, but because he used that term to describe Supreme Court nominee Harrold Carswell. However, there were a few members of the Senate during that era who may have ably reflected the views of their constituents but were little more than backbenchers somewhat mocked by colleagues. Their presence created distractions that made it impossible for them to be seen as statesmen.

Joseph Montoya, a Democrat from New Mexico, and Paul Fannin, a Republican from Arizona, were two such individuals. Both were elected in 1964, and both left office in 1976, having been harmed by newspaper investigations. While one was shown the door by voters and the other can claim to have left on his own terms, the latter may well have seen the door shutting in his face.

Image via ronwadebuttons.com

Tom Daschle famously said of his senior colleague, Larry Pressler that "A Senate seat is a terrible thing to waste." Fortunately, most of Fannin's tenure would overlap with his friend Barry Goldwater, and Montoya's with Pete Domenici, and few would call those two hacks of any kind. In fact their intellectual capabilities, personal integrity of the highest nature, and strong national exposure (both sought the Presidency) probably accentuated their state's standing.

Paul Fannin

Fannin was a former three-term Governor of Arizona which, one would think, would have given him heft when it came to playing a more active role, but he was a backbencher. In fact, his biggest notoriety may have followed a drunken driving arrest in 1972, which, as columnist Jack Anderson noted, the prosecution would later blow, likely to get Fannin off. The result at the time was that the charge he pled guilty to was changing lanes, which carried with it a charge of $12. As publicity mounted, Fannin agreed to pay a fine if the case were to be refiled, and he would plead guilty. The Maricopa County Republican prosecutor did just that. Fannin said "the controversy has inflicted suffering on my family and dedicated doctors and lawyers and their families. It has been a preoccupation with me at a time when state and national problems demand my fullest attention."

For a man who never seriously considered a career in public service until he was 50 years old, Fannin rose to amazing heights in state and national politics. He and his brother Ernest launched a butane gas business in the depths of the Depression and survived some difficult early years to build one of Arizona's most successful companies in that field. He became affiliated with car dealers statewide, and that's what helped him make such strong contacts statewide.

At this time, many outsiders were moving in. Hailing from Ashland, Kentucky, Fannin was among them. Though Fannin would rank unambiguously among the most conservative Senators, Fannin's record as Governor was arguably fairly progressive. Elected in a 1958 upset, he pushed through a sales increase in order to both aid the public schools and build a medical school. But he also worked on the Colorado River Project, and created the Arizona-Mexico Commission to promote tourism and trade across the border.

In 1964, Fannin sought the seat Barry Goldwater was vacating for his Presidential bid. He departed from candidate Goldwater's platform ever-so—slightly by coming out in favor of civil rights legislation (which Senate Minority Leader Everett Dirksen noted during closing debate - a not so veiled attempt to win Goldwater's backing). His opponent was Roy Ellson, Chief of Staff to the venerable other Senator, Carl Hayden. Goldwater was barely carrying his home state, and Fannin's victory was almost a carbon-copy. He won 51-49%, by 14,000 votes.

Fannin campaign button
Left image via loriferber.com; Right image via ronwadebuttons.com

When he was office, the Americans for Democratic Action and organized labor gave Fannin a zero, according to *The New York Times*. He was opposed to the Equal Rights Amendment. In his first year, he successfully cobbled together Democrats and Republicans to beat back a bill that would repeal right-to-work laws. "Fannin was the only one paying attention to the issue," said Reed Larson, president of the National Right to Work Committee, who was active during the Senate fight. "For a time, it looked like he was going to have to go it alone." Closer to home, he worked on the enactment of the Central Arizona Project, which his very senior colleague, Carl Hayden, had championed. It was signed into law in 1968.

On Fannin's Senate victory and with constituents
Photos courtesy of the University of Arizona Library, Special Collections

By the time Fannin came up for a second term in 1970, he should have been a heavy favorite. It was a Republican year, and Fannin seemed to be as inoffensive a staunch conservative as one could be. But the state had begun experiencing heavy growth, which put Fannin's low-key style at a disadvantage. Sam Grossman was a television game show host from LA. He moved to Arizona and won a hotly contested primary. Within weeks, a series of hundred-thousand-dollar commercials saw him leap to a 12% lead over Fannin. The Senator's own supporters admitted that his manner was not one of his strong points. Rather, it was his "credibility." But then he began hitting hard. *The Arizona Republic* ran a series of stories questioning Grossman's residency. He had no choice but to say he was a resident of Arizona. Grossman attacked the paper. Meanwhile, Grossman linked himself to Nixon on the issues of busing and Vietnam and spoke of "reordering national priorities"; he was forced to concede overkill in the ads. In the end, a large Mexican-American turnout for gubernatorial candidate Raul Castro kept the race tight, but Fannin prevailed 54-46%.

In October 1973, as impeachment was becoming a very integral part of the political lexicon, Fannin spoke on the Senate floor and called, "the impeachment hysteria...sadly reminiscent of the lynch law of the frontier days. In those days," he continued, "it was not too difficult to stir up a mob of vigilantes to hang a man for alleged improprieties, real or imagined. In yet earlier days we had the witch trials at Salem."

Fannin wisely chose not to seek a third term in 1976, at which time he was ranking Republican on the Interior Committee. He lived another quarter of a century, dying at 94 years old in 2002.

Joseph Montoya

Montoya's Senate loss in 1976 made him one of three Rocky Mountain Democrats to fall (in the attack on the "M" Senators, his colleagues Frank Moss of Utah and Gale McGee of Wyoming were unseated as well). But Montoya gave voters plenty of ammunition.

In a big "oops" moment, Montoya got the IRS to block an audit of his tax returns. He was chairman of the committee that gives to the IRS. He was half-owner of a building—against the law. He was also worth $4 million, and no one could connect the dots as to how. He fell asleep at the Watergate hearings and was often called, "Little Joe."

His downfall was all the more stunning given that Montoya had held public office in New Mexico since 1936, when he was just 21, before he even graduated law school. He was Majority Leader by the end of his second term and later became Judiciary Chair. At 32, he was Lieutenant Governor, a position he held for ten years before filling a vacant Congressional seat. The Vocational Education Act and the Wilderness Protection Act were among his accomplishments. He earned his Senate seat through the self-appointment of Republican Senator Edwin Mecham following the death of Democrat Dennis Chavez, which Montoya won in concurrence with the general election. Montoya spent much time working on agricultural issues.

At the beginning of his statewide career, there was another episode in Montoya's past that was, shall we say, out of this world. In 1947, the then-Lieutenant Governor was visiting Roswell, New Mexico, when an "unknown object" crashed in the desert. Some residents claim it was a UFO (I'm not making this up). Montoya was in Roswell at the time to dedicate an Air Force base; he called his brother and said, "I'm at the big hangar. Get your car, and pick me up. Get me the hell out of here. Hurry!" As a cook, he was able to get in and off the base, and along with the Anaya brothers (Tony eventually became Governor), they were sworn to secrecy.

A crash and objects being removed from the site have been validated. What has never been validated was what the objects were.

Montoya's actions sometimes gave fuel to the fire. He was very intelligent but was not regarded as one of the Senate's heavyweights. One day, at the start of a speech, he said, "Ladies and gentleman, it is a great pleasure to be here with you tonight. For immediate release only"—Montoya had been late to the event, and his staff had handed him the press release with the text to read.

Electorally, Montoya was able to show his skills but not overwhelmingly so. He initially garnered 54% in 1964 but took just 52% in 1970. However, his problems by 1976 were such that survival would have taken an act from space.

Image via roundhouseroundup.blogspot.com

Montoya, who chaired the Senate Appropriations subcommittee that funds the IRS, had planned to hold hearings on IRS abuses. One week later, the IRS "added his name to the list of tax protesters who were capable of violence against IRS agents." It was then that the New Mexico IRS Director sought to find info on Montoya, but David Alexander "called off the dogs in the summer of 1973" just as Watergate got underway. Fast-forward another two years, and the matter became public. Who uncovered it? Bob Woodward. It was a year after Watergate, and he perhaps was looking to set his sights lower. But the question of the day is why the IRS dropped the ball on the Montoya case. For his part, Montoya was defiant. "I never talked to him about my returns. I never asked him for a favor and I never received one." Indeed, Woodward never established that Montoya had committed wrongdoing, only that Alexander likely cleared him because of his oversight role on the IRS. He attributed the release to "some bastards in New Mexico."

But there were other concerns that Montoya did not address. One was how he got so rich. "I started working in the drugstore when I was nine. I had to feed them (the chickens), water them, and clean the coop," noting that after that time, he was "unable to eat eggs for ten years." Evidently, voters didn't believe that could add up to $4 million—that would be a lot of chickens. Word also came that Montoya had received $5,000 in campaign contributions and gifts from Korean rice dealer Tongsun Park. "I tell them the IRS has been zeroing in on me but I'm not afraid, because I'm indestructible," he said. "And the reason I'm indestructible is because I'm clean." A year later he was out of a job. Harrison Schmidt had recently gained fame as an astronaut, and his slogan "Honesty for a Change" apparently resonated with the voters. It's no wonder that he beat Montoya by 14%, 57-43%. Montoya's showing was five percentage points behind Jimmy Carter's, who only barely lost the state to Ford.

Being of different parties, from neighboring states and with similar, sometimes off-putting traits, it was only inevitable that Fannin and Montoya would spar. They might have done so many times but one highly public event was during consideration of the Public Works Act of 1972. Montoya was advocating the creation of an Indian Developmental Commission while Fannin thought existing agencies were "doing an excellent job of aiding Indian economic development." He accused Montoya of "perverting a concept which, although still in infancy, has had some remarkable success and shows great promise. We are being asked to superimpose another Bureau of Indian Affairs on the country." As *Congressional Quarterly* noted, he said it would "create an administrative nightmare," would "tend to further divide rather than integrate Indians into the mainstream of American economic life. "Fannin added that despite Montoya's contention, he could "not recall one Indian leader contacting me personally to urge creation of a separate Indian development commission." That drew a sharp rebuke from Montoya who said, "We have 110,000 Indians in New Mexico. I think I am as qualified to speak for the Indians as the Senator from Arizona." With Fannin threatening to, in Montoya's words, "speak at length," against the new agency, he reluctantly pulled the proposal.

Montoya was not as fortunate in years as Fannin. He died of liver failure in June 1978, a little more than a year after leaving office.

CHAPTER FIFTY-SIX

Cokie Roberts' Father Hale Boggs
Was A Giant In The House

Historic Tidbit: Politics is a world of small connections but this one may take the cake. House Majority Leader Hale Boggs boarded his initial flight to Alaska from Texas. Boggs of course would perish on his return home the following day along with Alaska Congressman Nick Begich. Who drove Boggs to the airport to catch his Northwestern bound flight? A 26 year old George McGovern field coordinator named Bill Clinton.

Hale Boggs was a legend in Louisiana and in Washington. Not only was he Majority Leader of the House who tragically disappeared in a plane crash while campaigning for a colleague, but he was also among the most respected members of the House, epitomizing courage on key issues well ahead of his time.

Boggs' 1972 death was untimely both in terms of his own life and in terms of what he was poised to accomplish in the years to come. Appropriately, his name lives on. Not only did his wife Corrine ("Lindy") succeed him and become one of the most beloved members in her own right, but their daughter is none other than journalist Cokie Roberts. Yet another daughter, the late Barbara Boggs Sigmond, served as mayor of Princeton, New Jersey and unsuccessfully sought her party's nomination for Governor in 1989. She died of cancer at age 51 in 1990. Finally, a son, Thomas Hale Boggs, Jr., who as a teenager operated Speaker Sam Rayburn's private elevator, once ran for Congress. Though he didn't succeed, he ultimately became a highly successful lawyer and one of Washington's best known lobbyists in his role as one of two founding partners of the firm Patton/Boggs.

By 1960, Boggs had represented a New-Orleans-anchored Congressional district for most of the previous 20 years, breaking only to go off to war. Before that, he had been a lawyer who gained fame by attempting to break Huey Long's stranglehold on government, an endeavor that wasn't entirely unsuccessful.

A Tale of Two Seasons by Bert Bartlett calls Boggs "an imposing and gruff but amiable character." One example came when summing up his feelings toward what House members typically refer to as "the other body," which Boggs made clear rated below even Republicans. "House Republicans are not the enemy," he'd say. "They are our opposition. The Senate is our enemy."

Boggs was Majority Leader John McCormack's choice to be Majority Whip after the election of 1960 (the Whips were selected by the leader in those days). But Sam Rayburn preferred Carl Albert of Oklahoma, a protégé ("his district is right next to mine," Rayburn said). Albert got the job, and Boggs became deputy whip. However, Rayburn died later that year, and Albert and Boggs both moved up a notch. Years after Boggs' death, then House Speaker Tip O'Neill recalled Boggs as "a true bridge among the disparate members of the House. When he first ran for the leadership they said he never could win because he was too liberal for the South and too conservative for the North. And that was his great strength—he could move between both groups, between all groups." These qualities became evident very early on when it came to some of the most divisive issues of his time—and his region.

With his handsome young family
Photo via the Collection of the U.S. House of Representatives

Boggs was a tireless promoter of LBJ's agenda, but it was civil rights that proved to be his defining moment.

In 1965, Louisiana's 2nd district was almost as conservative as the rest of the state and Boggs' opposition on the Civil Rights Act of 1964 reflected that. However, he had previously voted to suspend literacy tests and to federally criminalize illegal voter disqualification and by the time the Voting Rights Act was brought up, things were different. Selma had taken place and the Civil Rights movement was unstoppable. Boggs rose to the moment, not only backing the Voting Rights Act but speaking in favor of it on the House floor. In language of true eloquence, Boggs said, "I wish I could stand here as a man who loves my State, born and reared in the South, who has spent every year of his life in

Louisiana since he was 5 years old, and say there has not been discrimination. But unfortunately it is not so." The chamber was hushed. After, Boggs was applauded and Judiciary Chair Emanuel Celler said his words would "go ringing through the ages." As such, the reaction back home was not all positive. His lawn was the sight of a cross-burning.

At the time, Boggs' popularity did nosedive because of the vote, and he knew it, but before long, he just might have prescribed his career-saving own medicine. It came in the form of the New Orleans Saints. Dave Dixon had been a fraternity brother of Boggs' at Tulane University and was now a prominent entrepreneur in New Orleans who had long dreamed of bringing a football team to the city. Meanwhile, he and NFL Commissioner Pete Rozelle had been lobbying for a limited immunity amendment for teams forced to merge, which Judiciary Chair Emanuel Celler opposed. But Boggs and the state's junior Senator, Russell Long, who also happened to be the Senate Majority Leader, both sat on the conference committee that would iron out the differences between the two chambers. Dixon sent a former Boggs aide "with a full set of instructions" on the language to use with his old boss and it was successful—with a huge caveat.

The New York Times recalls Rozelle telling Boggs he didn't know how to thank him to which a bemused Boggs replied, "What do you mean you don't know how to thank me? New Orleans gets an immediate franchise in the N.F.L." *The Times* said Rozelle "waffled a little," to which Boggs countered, "Well, we can always call off the vote while you—." Rouzelle cut him off. "It's a deal, Congressman," he replied. "You'll get your franchise." And Boggs held his head to the fire until moments before the vote actually occurred. Thomas Boggs told *The Times,* "My old man was out in the hall with Rozelle who asked, "Have you done anything with our amendment?' and my father said, "Have you done anything with my team?'"

Announcing the merger of the New Orleans Saints, 1966
Photo via utsandiego.com

Later, Boggs sat on the Warren Commission, but before his death he disputed the harmoniousness of the committee's ultimate findings. "It is a myth," he said, "that the Warren Commission was united in its conclusion that a lone assassin killed President John F. Kennedy." He accused J. Edgar Hoover of "lying his eyes out" and an aide quoted him as saying that the FBI Director greatly fabricated "on Oswald, on Ruby, on their friends, the bullets, the gun, you name it." Lindy told folks later, "Hale felt very, very torn during his work [on the Commission] . . . he wished he had never been on it and wished he'd never signed it."

Boggs was a firm proponent of space funding and in 1972, he passionately urged lawmakers to reject an effort by Wisconsin Democrat Les Aspin to cut the entire proposed appropriation for the shuttle. With typical passion, Boogs said he, "hope(s) the House will reject this amendment. I say that with all the conviction I can command because in my judgement, to delay and cut back this program at this time would really kill the space program."

When McCormack retired as Speaker in 1970, Boggs ran for Majority Leader and faced Mo Udall. Boggs wasn't entirely trusted by anyone (Doutherners, liberals, etc) but he did win and devoted boundless energy to helping his colleagues. Ultimately and tragically, that would prove fatal.

Boggs had been elected to the House in 1940 but was unseated in the following primary, after which point he went off to the Navy during World War II. Following his return, Boggs waited for the calendar to move by practicing law, but only until the next opportunity to return to the arena came up—in 1946, when he reclaimed his old House seat. In 1951, Boggs attempted a run at the Governorship only to have an opponent question his membership in the American Student Union. That was enough to finish him. He placed third. Beyond that setback, however, his House elections were uneventful, at least until late in his career.

Photo courtesy of the LBJ Library

In 1968, George Wallace's coattails very nearly cost Boggs his seat (his opponent was future Governor David Treen), but he hung on 52-48%. Ironically, both sides suspected that Wallace voters had backed Boggs. The 1972 remap made his district safer. Nixon won 60% there in 1972, but Humphrey would actually have edged out Wallace in the new district, even as Wallace was winning statewide.

In 1972, Boggs was traveling to Alaska to campaign for Nick Begich, a freshman colleague, who, as a former Alaska Senate Whip, was a force in his own right in his state. He didn't have much of a race but Tip O'Neill suspected in his book *Man of the House* that Begich was trying to raise his own profile for a statewide race. Boggs in fact had asked O'Neill to make the trip instead, but he turned him down. The plane went down somewhere, igniting a search of more than 100 planes. No sign of the wreckage was ever found. Meanwhile, both Boggs and Begich were re-elected, and the House, upon each being declared legally dead, ultimately declared their seats vacant.

Boggs' widow Corrine won the special election to succeed him and became a major force in her own right. She once said, "There are some days in the House I feel like turning around as if he were there and saying, 'Why in the world don't you go down in the well and straighten this thing out?'" She served as an Appropriations cardinal, and her retirement in 1990 made it the first time since 1947 that a Boggs would not represent the New-Orleans-centered district. But her service was not over by any means. President Clinton appointed her Ambassador to the Vatican. She died at age 97 in 2013.

St. Charles Parish in Louisiana houses the Hale Boggs Memorial Bridge. And the twin peaks of the mountain where the plane supposedly went down was renamed Mount Boggs and Mount Begich.

CHAPTER FIFTY-SEVEN

Alaska's Begich, Other House Member To Have Perished With Boggs, Made Tremendous Impact In Short Tenure

Historic Quote: "Just think what my margin might have been if I had never left home at all." - John F. Kennedy reacting to losing the state of Alaska, which he had visited but winning Hawaii, which he did not.

Photo via the U.S. Government Printing Office

Much is known about Hale Boggs, the legendary, deal-making House Majority Whip who perished in Alaska on a campaign swing in 1972. But his larger than life presence and family (his wife Lindy succeeded him and daughter Cokie Roberts became a well-known journalist) often obscures the memory of the other member of Congress who presumably died that day. While Nick Begich of Alaska did not have nearly the seniority or the notoriety of the gentleman from Louisiana, he was not without accomplishments. His gift was consensus-building which helped yield dividends on legislation of progress for his barely decade-old state. And he produced a family legacy of his own that continued in the mold of his dad nearly four decades later.

Like so many Alaskans, including his two delegation-mates during his single term in the House (Senators Ted Stevens and Mike Gravel), Begich came to Alaska from somewhere else. But he was no stranger to cold climates nor was his family. He was born in Eveleth, Minnesota to parents of Croatian descent (ironically

Eveleth was the same place another member of Congress, Paul Wellstone), would die in a plane crash three decades later almost to the day. Begich received both his Bachelor's and Master's in Minnesota (Saint Cloud State and the University of Minnesota respectively) before pursing his doctorate at the University of Colorado and the University of North Dakota.

Begich moved to Alaska shortly after and made education his pride and joy. He began as a high school guidance counselor and worked up to becoming Director of Student Personnel Services for the Anchorage School System. Meanwhile, Begich would marry Peggy and have six children.

In Alaska's first Presidential campaign for since achieving statehood, Begich was an energetic volunteer for John F. Kennedy who lost the state by a hair. Two years later at the age of 30, he decided to try his hand at elective office. He sought a State Senate seat and won. By 1968, Begich was ready to go east, to Congress. That meant challenging Republican Congressman Howard Pollack for the At-Large Congressional seat. Pollack was a freshman but as *Congressional Quarterly* noted, the only legislator from the Anchorage area to survive the GOP sweep of 1966. Begich gave him a spirited run but could not oust the incumbent as Pollack prevailed 54-46%.

At that point, Begich had been serving as Superintendent of the Alaska School System (and had also been building houses) but was forced to abandon that when the state Supreme Court ruled that teachers could not serve in the legislature simultaneously. It's easy to see why Begich would be loath to give up politics for he was now Minority Leader of the Alaska Senate. But change in his national luck would be on the horizon.

Photo courtesy of the University of Alaska Fairbanks

In 1970, Pollack left his Congressional seat behind to make an unsuccessful run for Governor and Begich had earned enough respect among Democrats to win the nomination unopposed. In the general, he faced the state's Commissioner of Economic Development Frank Murkowski, considered a moderate who had beaten a hard-line conservative, Clyde Lewis to capture the GOP nomination. Begich won 55-45% (nearly four decades later, Begich's son Mark and Murkowski's daughter Lisa would represent Alaska in the U.S. Senate).

In the early 1970s, Alaska was a swing state. Yet Begich would generally prove a party loyalist. In 1972, his party unity score was 93%. He opposed a school prayer resolution, backed the foundation for the Consumer Protection Agency and the Nedzi/Whalen Southeast Asia withdrawal deadline. He was in the majority on a contentious higher education vote that authorized money for desegregation programs (busing). And in an acknowledgement of his state's firm labor base, he opposed a bill that would limit mandatory raises that had been adopted before the wage freeze.

Begich succeeded by developing an Alaska-centric record. Part of that was guarding against an overzealous federal government. He once explained his rationale: "We're tired of always having Easterners say, 'Because we made a mess of our backyard, we want to make sure your backyard isn't messed up.'"

"The Atomic Energy Commission concluded today three days of environmental impact hearings in which almost every witness not employed by it testified in opposition to a projected underground nuclear test. One issue was the Alaska pipeline. "In the past three years since the filing of the pipeline application, there have been many technical breakthroughs, including new automatic welding techniques, pipeline refrigeration and elevator techniques in response to permafrost conditions, new oil tanker designs, block valve, monitoring and earthquake reaction systems which are capable of insuring pipeline leak security better than any before."

Begich's most lasting contribution throughout his brief tenure was his work on the Alaska Native Claims Settlement Act. This was landmark legislation signed by President Nixon in 1971 that ultimately extended the ownership of federal land owned by Alaskans to 44 million from the current 1 million. Large sums of money were also paid out. Former Begich aide Guy Martin summed up the enormity of the bill when he said it was "felt by many to be the most important Indian legislation ever to be enacted in the United States . . . the Alaska natives actually 'won.'"

Begich watches Alaska Governor William Egan sign a bill into law
Photo courtesy of the University of Alaska Fairbanks

While the legislation had been pushed by the powerful Alaska Federation of Natives (AFN), enactment proved as rugged as the Alaska terrain. It had been before Congress during at least three previous sessions (Washington's "Scoop" Jackson had steered it to passage in the previous Congress but the House never acted) and the measure was opposed by various business interests, including the state Chamber of Commerce and the Greater Anchorage Chamber. Begich himself found himself under attack from powerful voices, including the Fairbanks Miner, for allegedly shoving aside the views of a majority of Alaskans by supporting the proposal. But in fact, as Martin noted, Begich "always refused to take sides (on the issue) and generally stayed in the middle to help compromises." Even when introducing the bill in the House interior Committee, he was doing so to move it along.

Robert Zelnick of *The Anchorage Daily News* reported a succinct demonstration of that. Writing in 1971, he described Begich as having "chided the board for confusing its role of advocacy with his own role of reconciliation and compromise. He warned that an extremist, obdurate position on his part now would offend senior Interior Committee members and ultimately jeopardize his chances for appointment to the crucial House-Senate conference committee on the legislation. And he requested that he be judged on his final accomplishments with respect to the bill rather than on the basis of preliminary oaths of adherence to the AFN cause. Begich thus escaped from the session with his flexibility intact."

Ultimately, Martin said the bill's 334-63 vote belied the long struggle that had entailed. Guy noted that Begich in particular emerged a winner "because first-term Congressman are rarely appointed (to the conference committee) by the House)."

By the fall of 1972, Begich faced a colorful opponent in a State Senator named Don Young. But the impression he made was stellar enough that he seemed a near shoe-in for a second term. Still, not wanting to take any chances, Begich asked for and secured a campaign visit from Boggs, the House's number two Democrat to speak at an event. For a time, it looked as though Boggs might be detained in Washington and Begich extracted a promise from Jim Wright to go, but only if Boggs couldn't (he asked Tip O'Neill to join them as well but his interest was non-existent). At the last minute, Boggs' conflict cleared and the two traveled together. Boggs gave a great speech that wowed the crowd. On October 17, Boggs, Begich and an aide, Russel Brown, boarded a twin-engine Cessna 310 that was to take the trio to Juneau from Anchorage. Flying them was Don Jonz, an experienced pilot. But there were low clouds, fog and drizzle. The plane was believed to have disappeared in the Chugach mountain range. Meanwhile, much of the campaigning for the seat was suspended and Begich did go on to win re-election (presumably posthumously 56-44%).

After Begich's death, his widow Peggy surprised observers and politicos by throwing her hat into the ring to succeed her husband. But the state Democratic Committee was leery of her true qualifications (having had kept a low profile raising her kids during her husband's tenure) and rejected her, instead nominating a Bethel Native leader named Emil Notti. Young won the seat by fewer than 2,000 votes and holds it to this day. The Begichs' son Mark, having been serving as Mayor of Anchorage, ousted Ted Stevens in 2008 and took his seat as Alaska's junior Senator. He narrowly lost his bid for a second term in 2014. Another son, Nick, Jr., has become known to Alaskans as an author and two-time President of the Alaska Federation of Teachers and the Anchorage Council of Education.

In short, the Begich legacy is one that is truly something to bring pride to all Alaskans and for that matter, to all Americans.

CHAPTER FIFTY-EIGHT

Iconic Host John McLaughlin
Once Sought U.S. Senate But Longtime Incumbent
John Pastore Was True Gift From Heaven

Historic Tidbit: "First of all, I want to say how delighted I am to be representing the great state of ah, ah." Bobby Kennedy at a dinner the day he was sworn in as Senator from New York. He joked that he had no Presidential ambitions "and neither does my wife. Just ask Ethel Bird."

Some things about *McLaughlin Group* host John McLaughlin might surprise folks. He is 89-years-old. He used to be a priest. And he was once a candidate for a U.S. Senate seat from the state of Rhode Island. The year was 1970 and McLaughlin had a futile - kamikaze is even appropriate—quest to unseat the venerable John Pastore, a devoted son of the "Ocean State" who was so kind-hearted, mild-mannered and well-liked even by the deepest of political adversaries that he himself could have been considered saintly.

In the words of McLaughlin, "Issue One."

Pastore was no rookie in Rhode Island politics. He was seeking his fourth full term, having been elected in a 1950 special. He had been Governor before that and hence was the first Italian-American to win both the Governorship and Senate seat in the state.

Pastore and his wife Elena with President Kennedy and
witnessing the signing of the Nuclear Test Ban Treaty
Photo courtesy of the John F. Kennedy Presidential Library and Museum

Pastore was legendary in many ways. At 5'4, Pastore was a small man but his vote-getting abilities were huge, which "Short Person Support" attributed to his "honesty, oratory, good relations with the press, and his ability to keep his finger on the political pulse of the voter." "Rhode Island is the smallest state in the union," he once said, "and I am the smallest governor in the United States." He was also eloquent. Pastore gave the 1964 keynote address and delegates were so enthralled that his name was briefly mentioned for Vice-President. It's easy to see why. For in the Senate, Pastore's record was extensive.

Pastore may have been one of the unsung heroes on civil rights, for he authored much of the complicated languages and served as a senior captain on the Senate floor. He wasn't shy about using his rhetorical gift to mock opponents. When Southerners continued to reject compromise legislation, Pastore said "of course…because it is now more likely to pass." As Al Gore, Sr., made an 11th hour motion to recommit the bill to the Judiciary Committee, Pastore called it similar to "what we have already voted down." When passage was finally secured, he said, "We have acted neither in haste nor in hate. We have acted only in hope. It is our hope that once this measure is signed into law it will be accepted without hate. We have surrounded it with safeguards so it will not be administered with haste."

The Nuclear Test Ban Treaty was likely Pastore's other most ever-lasting achievement. He was chairing the Joint Committee on Atomic Energy at the time but also had been haunted by the threat of nuclear war. President Kennedy said enactment "could never have been possible without Pastore." He provided crucial assistance to Kennedy on the space initiative as well.

Pastore played a major role in the creation of public television but also, allowing the landmark television series *Mister Rogers* to touch generations of children. It was 1969 and host Fred Rogers appeared before the Subcommittee of Communications that Pastore was chairing with a request that the committee not decrease funding for public television. Pastore was so moved by Rogers' testimony that he agreed to maintain funding at current levels. And in the process, he nearly lost it. "I'm supposed to be a pretty tough guy and this is the first time I've had goosebumps for the last two days," he told Rogers. "I think it's wonderful. Looks like you earned the 20 million dollars." It turns out Rogers had an even more powerful advocate; Pastore's young grandson, whom the Senator's son told him was a fan of the series.

In late-1968, as it became clear that Abe Fortas' nomination was going to die, Johnson toyed with names that might make it through. Pastore's name was raised (on the Oval Office tapes, Johnson said "they'd say that's cute," but also said that as a fellow Senator, "I think Pastore would put 'em in a helluva shape. He's a damned able lawyer who was attorney general of his state. He's a governor. He's a helluva speaker. He's a well-informed fella." But nothing came of it.

Issue two.

Pastore had a long fidelity with the people of Rhode Island and was deeply representative of the state. Ted Kennedy served with Pastore in the Senate for 14 years and delivered a eulogy at his funeral. He called it "safe to say that no one has ever served any state better than John Pastore served the people of Rhode Island." Calling him, "one of the greatest orators in the history of the Senate," Kennedy noted "his voice would shake the rafters in the Senate. He always commanded an undivided attention or respect whenever he rose to speak."

In person, Pastore was "the mildest of individuals." A White House audio recording exists of LBJ offering him the keynote address and Pastore stoically replied, "I'd be honored." (Johnson referred him to Bill Moyers for help drafting the speech). Kennedy recalls taking his son to see Pastore long after he had retired. As they prepared to return to Providence, Patrick went back to ask the senior statesman for directions and he could be seen waving his hands. When Kennedy asked what Pastore had said, Patrick replied, "Go back the way you came! Go back the way you came!"

Dr. John Pastore, Jr., says his father "lived so simply" that one day during his Governorship, *The Providence Journal* published a picture of the two-story house in which they resided. They lived on the bottom floor and the newspaper referred to it as "the Governor's Mansion." But Pastore was a good singer to nearly his last days and at his 90th birthday party surprised guests with Italian songs. He loved dancing but, Pastore, Jr., says, "not a social butterfly." He was, however, an impeccable dresser. *The New York Times* on his death said "he changed his shirts in the middle of the day if they bore the slightest signs of wear." He was also deeply patriotic man who would raise and take the American flag down every day and end many of his speeches with, "May God bless the United States of America."

More importantly, Pastore took a deep devotion to people big and small.

Joe Biden cites him as instrumental in convincing him to take his Senate oath after his wife and daughter were killed in a car accident shortly after his first election. But Pastore, Jr. recounted a story from a visitor at his father's wake. As a boy, he suffered from a speech impediment but, upon hearing Pastore's convention speech, he told his mother he wanted to learn to speak like "that man." He did and Pastore helped him overcome the deficiency (the man is now a speech therapist).

Martin Donovan was Pastore's Legislative Assistant during the last four years of his Senate tenure. He called his boss "extremely easy to deal with because he had a steel-strapped mind. I'd just feed him information and he processed it and retained it forever." Donovan adds that he had a tremendous ability to "say the right thing at the right time. We never had to worry about him putting his foot in his mouth." Pastore was also a wonderful man to work for. Donovan recalls that when his daughter was born, Pastore would routinely send him home at a regular hour (as opposed to sending him to receptions) so that he could spend time with her before going to sleep.

It's easy to see where that came from. Pastore was himself devoted to his family. He was legendary for his "7:00 rule," which meant "no good speech should be made after 7:00 P.M." For Pastore was a family man. His eldest son recalls he would always return from Washington in time for dinner on Friday night, then take him across town to a high school dance. As the dance would conclude, Pastore would drive back to pick up his son, then proceed to drop them off at a diner and wait in his car as they got to know each other (John, Jr., says the only thing that worried his dad was someone recognizing his Senate plate and wondering what he was doing at a diner at 11 P.M.

Pastore was literally using his charm when he met his wife, Elena Caito, the youngest of ten children. She was walking past his office and heard him preparing for an oral argument. Upon inquiring about whom he was, the pair was introduced and married shortly after. They were 13 years apart in age (Elena was 21) but would share 59 blissful years together. He called her "mama" and legend had it that he had a buzzer on his desk to alert him whenever she called and he would stop what he was doing – however important, to talk with her. Though Elena was not particularly political, he counseled her on every major decision.

Besides his friendships with like-minded individuals – Hubert Humphrey, Mike Mansfield, Warren Magnuson, "Scoop Jackson," and his home-state colleague Claiborne Pell, Pastore got along with ideological opposites. He was friends with Norris Cotton, a conservative New Hampshire Republican who once inscribed a photo, "Johnny, I miss you" after both men had retired from the Senate. He tangled ferociously with Mississippi's Jim Eastland on civil rights but they got along. And two decades after his fiery speech against Barry Goldwater in 1964, the two warmly embraced on a visit to Capitol Hill. Strom Thurmond, when he learned Pastore was in town, came to chat as well. Much of this had to do with a quintessential Pastore characteristic. Pastore, Jr., recalled his anger being confined to a French phrase he'd utter which meant, "I think I might get angry." But Donovan said if one crossed Pastore, watch out - for his adversary was likely no match for him politically.

Pastore had an up-by-the-bootstraps upbringing. He was born in the "Little Italy" section of Federal Hill to an immigrant father from Potenza, Italy, Michele Pastore, who died suddenly when Pastore was nine, forcing his mom to work as a seamstress. He recalls "the ghetto,"... We had no running water, no hot water. I used to get up in the mornings and have to crank the stove, to go out in the back yard and sift out the ashes and come back with the coal that I could recoup. I had to chisel with the ice pick the ice in the sink so that I could wash up in the mornings. And that was everybody in the family. That wasn't me alone. That was my wife's family, that was everybody's family."

Pastore initially wanted to become a physician but economic realities inhibited that. So he put himself through law school while working as a claims adjuster for $15 a week, then set up a practice. But he wanted to go higher and eventually approached a political leader outside church about starting a career. The result was a Rhode Island House seat in 1934. By 1940, he was an assistant Attorney General. His rise to the top centered around J. Howard McGrath. He asked Pastore to be his running-mate in 1944. The ticket won but McGrath was appointed Solicitor General the following year, making Pastore Governor. He was the people's Governor – The New York Times notes he often had lunch with state workers. He was progressive (implementing a sales tax measure) but also worked well with the business community. Pastore was re-elected twice. By 1950, McGrath was in the Senate but would then earn another appointment: U.S. Attorney General. Who succeeded him? Pastore.

The always approachable Pastore wowed delegates with his
1964 Democratic National Convention keynote address
Photos courtesy of the Rhode Island Secretary of State

The relationship between Pastore and the Kennedys was strong. He and JFK sponsored the Azorean Relief Act of 1958. And after the 1964 plane crash that nearly killed Teddy, Pastore "did a lot of campaigning for him because he couldn't get around much" (Pastore was also facing re-election that fall).

Another unlikely alliance was with Richard Nixon. The two came to the Senate together in 1950 and were friendly throughout their time in Washington. That changed after the 1972 elections when Pastore got wind that Nixon was considering moving the North Atlantic Fleet out of Narragansett Bay. Pastore met with Nixon who assured him that he'd do no such thing. But he reneged on his word and Donovan said "that was the end of that friendship."

Enter 1970. In one of the most solidly Democratic states in the union, and one in which reverence is a guide, McLaughlin seemed to face a tough enough hurdle against Pastore without other issues. But he faced another resistance: the church.

John McLaughlin challenged Pastore in 1970
Photo via Media Matters

McLaughlin's superiors told him not to run. He didn't listen. The Reverend Russel J. McVinney told *The Providence Visitor* that "Father McLaughlin announced his candidacy and is now conducting his campaign for public office without permission from me and without endorsement of any kind from the Diocese of Providence." McLaughlin told *The New York Times* that the diocese doesn't have the authority to restrict him - only to deny him the ability to "preach and hear confessions." McLaughlin also noted that Canon Law was being revised and that he took advantage of the fact that the changes were not yet made.

Pastore reacted with incredulity that he was being challenged by a priest. "How can I debate with a man my religion teaches me to call Father." McLaughlin replied that his collar is a "one-inch piece of plastic."

Some might say the dynamics of the race made the issue moot. Pastore was immensely popular and took 68%, slightly lower than previous races but still impressive even in a Democratic state. After the election, Nixon hired McLaughlin as a speechwriter.

Pastore, meanwhile, decided to retire following the completion of the term he beat McLaughlin to win. Following his announcement, he turned to his wife and with his distinct Rhode Island dialect said, "I think the time has come that

John Pastore had a little fun; don't you think lo, Mummy?" Friends pleaded with him to stay but he hated raising money and felt it best to go out on top. In his farewell speech on the Senate floor, he said, "Whatever you do, keep that torch of opportunity lighted. Protect that flag. Maintain our institutions. Debate your differences if you have them. But always realize what that insignia says, 'E pluribus unum' - from the many there are one." Pastore, Jr., says that, to the family at least, his father's proudest accomplishment in four decades of public life may have been that he "never had his integrity questioned."

Pastore continued to lecture on the nuclear freeze movement and died in 2000 at the age of 93.

McLaughlin, meanwhile, got his own Sunday morning show, with four panelists typically trying to provide a liberal/conservative balance and debate the issues. Jack Germond and Bob Novak participated in the early days. Thirty-three years later, the panelists have changed but John McLaughlin is as feisty as ever. And John Pastore is as respected as they come.

And now, as McLaughlin's trademark has come to be known, "Bye-bye." Cue music please.

CHAPTER FIFTY-NINE

Montana's Murray An Early Crusader For Universal Health Care And Other Post "New Deal" Causes

Historic Quote: "I was going to try to get a ride with Jack on his plane but he thought I ought to catch the next bus. Why don't you fellows come along? We're selling popcorn concessions." - Hubert Humphrey following his loss of the 1960 Wisconsin Democratic primary to John F. Kennedy. It was now on to a similarly futile effort in West Virginia.

One of the most celebrated, longest serving, and oldest Senators from Montana was James Murray. A literal and figurative FDR Democrat, Murray left office – and died just as John F. Kennedy was preparing to assume the presidency. He championed liberal causes from the "New Deal" to education and health care. Some were enacted during his time. But others fell by the political wayside and only now, fifty years after he left the national stage, are they bearing fruit.

Murray was actually a Canadian by birth. He was born in St. Thomas (Ontario) in 1876 and graduated from St. Jerome's College before attending NYU. He would earn three degrees, including his J.D. before returning to Butte to set up his practice. But it was during his education that Murray gained exposure to another life. He would come home during vacations and his uncle would find him work in a mine.

Photo via the U.S. Government Printing Office

Politically, Murray rose with FDR. He had campaigned for Roosevelt in 1932 and he reciprocated by naming him to the board of the Public Works Administration. By this time, he was also a millionaire. A year later, the state's Senator, Thomas Walsh died and Governor John Erickson had himself appointed to the seat. Murray challenged him in the primary and vowed to give FDR "one hundred percent support." Murray won the election and immediately followed through.

Murray backed Roosevelt's court backing plan as well as his efforts on foreign affairs all the way through World War II. This often put him on a collision course with Montana's senior Democratic Senator, the isolationist Burton K. Wheeler (who in 1924 had been the running-mate of Bob LaFollette, seeking the White House as an Independent).

Murray's liberal pedigree was solid and the *Great Falls Tribune* noted he "supported legislation to aid labor, education, health care, small business, full employment and public power over the next 26 years in the Senate." In fact, a 1945 AP publication noted Murray was the number one sponsor of "reform" (pro-New-Deal) legislation than any other member of Congress. He sponsored the Full Hearings Bill, and the Missouri Valley Authority. The latter called for naming a three person commission to control dams and federal projects in the Missouri River area (in response to a series of major floods that had swept the area) but little came out of it, He was successful with hospital construction but little else in that area.

For Murray would join with future New York Mayor Robert Wagner's father and future Michigan Congressman John Dingell's father by the same names in introducing legislation to provide national health insurance at the start of every Congress. As one hearing got under way, Majority Leader Bob Taft called it "the most socialist measure that this Congress has ever had before it." Murray responded, "You have so much gall and so much nerve. If you don't shut up, I'll have ... you thrown out." Taft responded that he had another meeting to attend and kept talking. Murray told him to "shut to your mouth up and get out of here!" At that point, Taft urged adjournment of the meeting until "you have recovered your temper." Murray shot back, "You are so self-opinionated and think you are so important that you can come into any committee and disrupt it." Taft left but vowed to fight the proposal if it ever made it to the Senate floor.

But at the end of the day, it wasn't Taft that killed the bills chances of enactment but the American Medical Association a group that actually were very organized in their attempts to stop it. In fact, after Harry Truman's surprise re-election, Princeton University professor Paul Starr would later observe "the AMA thought Armageddon had come."

Murray also had a major impact on education, the panel of which he chaired in the Congress prior to the Democrats losing control in 1946. In 1957, with his Montana colleague Lee Metcalf the sponsor in the House, Murray proposed a $4,500,000,000 Senate legislation that would provide aid to schools by the pupil, teacher raises, and a significant amount going toward school construction. A less costly Education Act was enacted. But by 1960, the bill was back and Murray was engaged in a furious tit-for-tat with President Eisenhower himself.

The President contended the bill would see a "very serious weakening of state and local responsibility," to which Murray responded he had already authorized a sizable amount of money for these projects.

Murray did have success with the post-World War II measure, the Full Employment Act of 1946, another piece of legislation he sponsored with Wagner. It called for the federal government "to provide such volume of federal investment and expenditure as may be needed to assure continuing full employment." It read, "All Americans able to work and seeking work have the right to a useful and remunerative job in the industries, or shops, or offices, or farms, or mines of the nation." The bill required the president to submit production and employment budgets with his annual fiscal plan. Farm groups were quite supportive of the measure. Because the conference committee decided that promoting "maximum employment" rather than full was their preferred method, the bill ultimately signed was called the Employment Act of 1946.

Murray found himself briefly in the national spotlight when a group of liberal Senators, led by Hubert Humphrey, were looking for an alternative to face Lyndon Johnson for Minority Leader after the 1952 elections. Murray was not their first choice but with other perspective names either for Johnson or lacking interest, Murray emerged as the choice. But at 76, age had caught up with him and come ballot day, he received no-more than mid-single digit votes.

After the '34 win, Murray asked Montanans to return him back to Washington four times. They obliged each time but twice by similar, and the narrowest of margins. In 1942, FDR's third mid-term, he hung on by 1,212 votes. The race featured Wellington Rankin, brother of the state's current Congresswoman who in 1916 had been the first female to win a seat in Congress. She had also been the only member to have opposed entry into either war. The isolationist charge hurt Rankin, whose election, Murray said, "Nazi newspapers in Berlin would hail." Murray squeaked by with fewer than 1,500 votes to spare.

1948 produced a more comfortable win. But shortly after, age began creeping up. Robert Caro, in his much acclaimed biography on Lyndon Johnson notes how evident this was becoming even to newer members. "Once a broad-chested man bursting with vitality, his stride was now slower, even at times uncertain… Lyndon Johnson, who had been close to Roosevelt (and other "New deal" players) would…in talking to Murray, turn the conversation to those days-and keep it there. It was noticeable how Murray, once he realized it was to be kept there, would become his old charming self."

But by 1954, age was a major factor and though the Democrats nationally were regaining strength from their drubbing two years earlier, So Republicans tried a new tactic against both Murray and his colleague to the south, Joe O'Mahoney of Wyoming: The "Red Issue."

The Montana Republican State Senate Committee circulated a pamphlet attributed to Senator James E. Murray entitled, "A Tribute To Lenin," from a 1945 publication of "Soviet Russia Today." The D'Ewart campaign distributed 50,000 copies of a brochure entitled, "Senator Murray and the Red Network over Congress." And Joe McCarthy, quickly becoming an albatross even in his own party but not yet totally discredited, authored a letter opposing Murray. Murray called these attacks "reprehensible."

D'Ewart also targeted the "highline" counties that ran near the Canadian border with farm issues.

To blunt the attacks, Murray enlisted the support of Mike Mansfield, his now junior colleague. Meanwhile, Lyndon Johnson, who would be Senate Majority Leader if Democrats reclaimed the majority, took control of the Democratic Senatorial Committee and invested a sizable amount of time in the Mountain West. The counting would not be complete for nearly three days but Murray won his fourth and final term by under 2,000 votes.

By this time, Murray had become chair of the Senate Interior Committee but age made full exertion of his responsibilities and his agenda difficult. He introduced a wilderness bill but little meaningful was enacted until the 1960s. And he continued taking on industry, contending they will "object to any preservation of wilderness they think might interfere, even at some uncertain future time, with their own interests in exploiting such preserves for profit."

One success, however was shepherding Alaska into statehood. When Murray opened debate on the Senate floor, he noted Congress previously had admitted 35 states and "had never made a mistake."

Murray actually flirted with seeking one more term in 1960 but with help from his son, wisely abandoned that thought. And for good reason. Retirement lasted but two months. Murray died in March 1961 at age 84.

CHAPTER SIXTY

McNamara Roots Were Geared Toward The Working Class As Were His Ideals: Legacy Was Fairness In Service Contracts

Historic Quote: "It's better to be silent and pretend dumb than to speak and remove all doubt." – Sam Rayburn.

Photo courtesy of the U.S. Senate Historical Office

I n the 1950s, there was an Irish Senator from Massachusetts making a name for himself nationally as he prepared to run for re-election. At that time, there was an Irish Senator from Michigan born in Massachusetts who represented the state in the U.S. Senate.

Ethnicity aside, the comparison between Jack Kennedy and Patrick McNamara were thin. The future Senator was young, athletic, charismatic and from a well-to-do family whose presence in Congress was just a matter of time. McNamara was a 60 year-old blue collar guy with a raspy voice whose ticket to Congress gave after a confluence of unexpected circumstances. But the duo shared a major trait: a willingness to fight for issues that would improve the American dream.

One reason McNamara wasn't shy about doing battle for the working-class was that for his entire career, he was literally part of the trenches. For 34 years, McNamara had high ranking union positions which culminated with his Presidency of Pipefitters Local 636. In the 1920s, he had been foreman of a construction crew at the Grinell Company, a general Superintendent for several companies and during the Depression, a maintenance foreman for a Chrysler plant. In that time, he was vice-president of the American Federation of Labor. But it was even evident during his boyhood as McNamara transferred to an apprentice school during high school and learned pipe-fitting. It was in 1946 that McNamara decided to try his hand at politics, first winning a seat on the Detroit Council, then going to the city's Board of Education.

One similarity Kennedy and McNamara did share was a large family. McNamara was the oldest of eight children (Kennedy by contrast was the second of nine). He was schooled there, played semi-professional football, then moved to Michigan at age 27.

As the 1954 campaign season got under way, McNamara filed to take on two-term incumbent Republican U.S. Senator Homer Ferguson. He was not the favorite of leading Democrats and it was no wonder why. Three years earlier, following the death of Republican U.S. Senator Arthur Vandenberg, Governor G. Mennen Williams had appointed Blair Moody to the seat. Moody lost the election for a full term in the Eisenhower sweep of '52 but was trying again this year. Naturally, he enjoyed the full backing of Williams and his youthful allies. Additionally, McNamara was part of the "old" guard that seemed in many ways out of place from the "new" up and coming politicos that Williams had put forward (the man who would become Lieutenant Governor that year and future Senator Phillip Hart was one such protégé). But Moody died suddenly two weeks before the primary and local democrats, though they flirted with the option, had no way to place another Democrat on the ballot. Reluctantly, they rallied around McNamara who was nominated for the seat, though Moody still drew a notable 40%.

The Democratic ticket united fully for November and it proved critical. One would think unions would be enamored with the prospect of electing one of their own but they were reticent. Ferguson was not without union support, having amassed the backing of the United Federation of Teachers. In fact, as one representative said, "about all you can say is they didn't campaign against him." But McNamara's own skills could not be discounted. He hit Ferguson --. Eisenhower made a late campaign visit to Detroit to rally Ferguson but in the end, Williams' statewide sweep proved too much for his to overcome. Every statewide Democratic officeholder seeking election in Michigan got it and though Ferguson had compiled a 200,000 vote edge outside of Wayne County, the Detroit vote enabled McNamara to sneak past him by 39,000 votes, 51-49%.

McNamara wasn't shy about sharing his opinions on the 1957 Civil Rights Act. After Georgia Senator Richard Russell noted on the Senate floor that Michigan is not subject to the outside intervention civil rights supporters were advocating, McNamara replied, "You've had 90 years…and you haven't done anything about it." As the Senate further deliberated, McNamara felt a strong bill should take precedent over assuaging Southern concerns. "The die-hard opponents of this legislation will vote against it" he said, regardless of how many olive branches are offered. "Their ultimate weapon, the filibuster...is the weapon that the Senate must bury forever."

McNamara was one of the earliest proponents of an expansion of Social Security that would offer increased care for the aged. As chair of the Labor and Public welfare committee's Problems of the Aged and Aging subcommittee, McNamara immediately displayed his advocacy for aging related issues. That program became known as Medicare and McNamara was able to vote on its passage in 1965, less than a year before his death.

The attempt to create Medicare was not without bumps in the road. Indeed, the chamber's more conservative members blocked a stronger version in 1962. However, McNamara was successful in pressing for the creation of a Special Committee on Aging. After a White House Conference on Aging, McNamara circulated a letter to colleagues. It praised the federal government by acknowledging "the knowledge... as demonstrated by the calling of this conference is keenly aware of the problems affecting the elderly and the need to do something about them." But he continued that "we must not believe that the federal government simply by conducting this conference has discharged its obligations or responsibilities in this vital area." His efforts were rewarded when in 1961, colleagues named him its first chair.

McNamara, who once said his "vocation finds me in the capacity of management, while my avocation has been the labor movement," continued his focus on the working people. As the economy made only meager recovery, McNamara in 1960 introduced a measure that would have extended the 1958 Unemployment Act but the Senate didn't pass it. When the Senate Select Committee on Improper Activities in the Labor and Management field issued its report on labor corruption, McNamara, calling the report, "anti-labor" was the only member who didn't sign it.

Photo courtesy of the U.S. Government Printing Office

As the 1950s became the 60s, McNamara had better luck. He sponsored the Public Elementary and School Construction act as well as efforts repealing the Right-to-Work section of Taft/Hartley. He also was the sponsor of President Johnson's proposal to extend double time to 735,000 workers (restauranteurs, hotel employees and those in laundromats). Another piece of landmark legislation was the McNamara-O'Hara Act Service Contract Act required federal service contractors subject to the same payment of "rates and fringes prevailing in that locality."

While McNamara's political leanings were clearly toward the left, he was hesitant to embrace the "liberal label." Instead, he called himself "pro-people." "You have these parts of the country where this business of being a liberal means to a lot of people that you are just a wide-eyed, bug-eyed radical."

In 1960, McNamara geared up for a second term. He faced Alvin Bentley, one of five Congressmen who had been shot during the 1954 rampage by Puerto Rican nationalists on the House floor. Of the five, his wounds were the most severe (the carnage injured his lung and liver) and his survival was in doubt. *The Traverse City Record* called the backgrounds of McNamara and Bentley "as different as wine and water." McNamara union background contrasted with Bentley's wealth – his grandfather started a carriage business.

The differences between the two may have caused bad feelings as captured by *The Ironwood Daily Globe* succinctly captured a synopsis of the campaign as it neared its conclusion. "Paradoxically, bluntly outspoken McNamara has followed a relatively leisurely pace, while the normally reserved and shy Bentley kept up a grueling grind of 16 hour days of handshaking, speeches and coffee klatches. McNamara has largely ignored his opponent. He seldom mentions Bentley's name and has ignored most of his challenges."

Photo courtesy of the Walter Reuther Library

In his second term, McNamara took aim at inefficiency and it started with the military. He called it "grossly inefficient because the three armed services divisions were working at cross purposes, duplicating efforts that cost the taxpayers billions of dollars." He refused to sign off on the RS-70 or nuclear power plants. He tried to merge that National Guard and Army Reserves but was thwarted.

At the start of 1966, McNamara was 71 and plagued by retirement rumors. By mid-year, he had still not declared his intentions but the betting was he was going to stick around. Whatever his plans, McNamara did not live to fulfill them. He was felled by a stroke that April.

Former Michigan Congressman John Dingell, who came to the House a year after McNamara won his Senate seat called his Wolverine colleague, "a great guy... unsurprisingly, what he was because of his background in labor." Dingell went on to say McNamara was "a man of extraordinary good-will which he received from his colleagues in the Senate." He had "tremendous integrity. I don't know anyone who didn't admire him."

CHAPTER SIXTY-ONE

Lausche and Young, Ohio's Two Senators In the 1960s Both Dems: End Of Similarities

Historic Quote: "Members of Congress are often elected by accident but are seldom re-elected by accident." – House Speaker John McCormack

O nce upon a time, Ohio had two Senators who served side-by-side for ten years. Both were Democrats over age 60 when elected and each lived into their mid-90s—but that's where the similarities end.

Frank Lausche was quiet and religious, not known for taking initiatives on many issues but one whose honesty and frugality became his legacy. Stephen Young was about as outspoken as can be and could easily have been mistaken for inventing the phrase "he suffers fools gladly." Lausche was an electoral powerhouse, winning most of his races by huge margins. Young was considered a fluke who twice had the fortune of beating candidates with stellar names by running in especially Democratic-favored years. Lausche had a long career in Ohio politics, becoming Governor before he was 50; Young did not win statewide office until he was nearly 70. Finally, Young was the most loyal Democrat around, sometimes even to the left of the rank and file—for example, he was adamantly against Vietnam. In contrast, Lausche supported the war and openly flirted with the other party (which flirted back).

Neither men were bad speakers but while Young could throw in a malapropism or two, Lausche's abilities were gifted. Predictably, there was tension between the two, stemming from one not supporting the other and vice-versa. Yes, elections make strange bedfellows and Lausche and Young are an interesting study in colleagues of the same party and state not exactly being enamored with one another.

Lausche (1895-1990)

Lausche, the son of Slovenian immigrants, could be spotted a mile away with what *The Toledo Blade*'s Josh Boak refers to as his "unkempt steel wool hair." Lausche was the second of ten children and his dad was a steel mill worker. He lost his father at age 12 and, after serving in the Army during World War I, he could have become a professional baseball player but decided to go to law school instead. Lausche was deeply religious and a regular at his church, Cleveland's St.

Vitus, his entire life. He made a couple of unsuccessful runs for the Legislature but in defeat he gained notice of party leaders, and eventually, his rise took another route: the bench. Lausche became a Cleveland Municipal Court Judge followed by common plea. Albert Woldman writes that in that role, Lausche was thought to have "committed political suicide" by going after gambling clubs and their owners, many of whom were Democrats, but this enhanced his popularity and he easily won the Cleveland Mayoralty in 1941.

Scan provided by Cleveland SGS (www.clevelandsgs.com)

Lausche's first brush with fame came shortly after that election. Democrats and unions wanted him to fire the famed crime-fighter, Elliot Ness, which he did not. And his mobilization of war relief efforts in Cuyahoga gained him a reputation as "an inspired war leader for the people of Cleveland." George Voinovich, a Lausche successor as Governor and the Mayor of Cleveland and a master of frugality, was asked his party affiliation, to which he replied, "I'm a Lausche Republican." Boak said that at the time of his election as Governor that Lausche owned two suits. It would not be far-fetched to think he couldn't afford another. How much did he spend on his 1944 race for Governor? $27,132 (and he reimbursed Cleveland for time on the trail). Conversely, the GOP spent just under $1 million.

By the time he left office, Lausche had served a record number of terms as Ohio Governor. In 1956, he decided to try for the Senate and beat incumbent George Bender; his status as a weathervane became known proceeded his arrival in Washington. When he won his seat, the Democrats had a single-vote margin. Lausche had said publicly that he might vote for California's Bill Knowland as Minority Leader, and Merle Miller, in his book *Lyndon*, called Lausche "more conservative than most conservatives." Lausche did keep everyone hanging until the last minute, a roll call in those days but in the end, he stuck with Johnson.

Lausche was initially very lukewarm to JFK and it wasn't until well into the fall campaign that he came on board—when he was in, he was in with both feet. When people wanted to know how the Kennedy/Nixon debate went, it was reported that Lausche's banging on Kennedy's hotel door meant he'd won. Lausche was among the advocates pushing for the strongest possible Civil Rights bill and he proved a solid backer of the "Great Society," but he always had problems with the unions. Until 1968, though, he was never threatened.

Lausche and his wife with Averill Harriman
Photo via Historic Images

Until his last race, Lausche did pretty well in Ohio. His five terms as Governor is a record. Surely he would have won re-election to the Senate had he not lost the primary. Dissatisfaction among Democrats did not stop

Lausche from capturing the Democratic nomination for Governor in 1944, and he beat ex-Cincinnati Mayor James Garfield Stewart 52-48%. Some, including Bob Taft, surmised that his Catholicism and the fact that he looked foreign might hurt him in rural Ohio, but he appealed to the Southern part of the state by opposing strip mining and the many Cleveland minorities via his background. He was seen as a man of the working class, which propelled him to a 52-48% win.

Photo via the U.S. Senate Historical Office

Lausche was turned out of office 51-49% in Republican-favored 1946 (a Governor's term was two years at that time), mostly over his refusal to call a special session of the Legislature to deal with World War II bonuses.

Lausche made a comeback in 1948 and served eight more years. In 1952, he beat Charles Taft, son of the former President and brother of the famed Majority Leader, by 450,000 votes and was the first Ohio Chief Executive to poll two million votes. This time he learned from past mistakes: he authorized money for Korean War vets, spearheaded a "Plant Ohio" conservation program, expanded welfare rolls, and modernized state buildings (which led to the construction of new schools and hospitals), all of which made him popular among his constituents. He also put through the Ohio Turnpike which, for the state, was considered a giant step forward, though he did face grumbling over a gas tax used to pay for it. Still, voters approved a $500,000,000 bond referendum.

With General MacArthur, 1952
Photo via WXIL

In early 1956, Eisenhower was urged to dump Richard Nixon as VP and put Lausche in his place. Ike was heard to have said he'd "love to put a Catholic on the ticket, if only to test it out." Ike's interest in Lausche came despite his flirtation with seeking the 1956 Democratic nomination. He said he "dreaded the thought of occupying the nation's highest office [but] would be available." As such, he was put forth as a "Favorite Son" candidate and did say that "everything else being equal [i.e. Ike's health]" he would back the Democratic nominee. He did the same in 1960 but was so incensed by Governor Mike DiSalle's early endorsement of Kennedy that he threatened to run as a "Favorite Son." Lack of time for organization kept him from following through.

In the Senate, Lausche became known as "Frank the Fence." Some of his foes derided his style as "Lauschesh-t." He opposed JFK's Medicare plan and other Democratic initiatives in the Senate, but voters didn't seem to mind. When his seat came up in 1962, he beat John Marshall Briley 62-38% after Briley called him "a little old and tottery." One of Lausche's gifts was that he said what he was and was what he said. Boak pointed out that Lausche "spoke to a group of hostile Cincinnati Democrats for about an hour in 1944. Before he came out, it was dead sure that 90 percent of the people would vote against him. When he left, 90 percent of the people were on his side." During Prohibition, he had received applause after addressing the Chagrin's Fall's Women's Temperance Union when he was asked how he felt about wine and beer. Lausche said he "could use a cold glass of beer right now."

Photo via the Akron Beacon

That forthrightness was ultimately his undoing: Lausche became very hawkish on the Vietnam War and his relations with labor did not get any better, leading ex-Ohio Congressman John Gilligan to challenge him in the 1968 primary. Lausche hardly took him seriously. Why should he have? After all, Gilligan had been bounced from the House after one term two years earlier. In 1968, though, the nation was changing and when the votes were counted, Gilligan had beaten Lausche by over 100,000 votes (he lost the general election).

In *Ohio Politics*, Alexander Lammis and Maryanne Sharkey write that Lausche's explanation was that, "For 25 years, labor unions fought me. They flooded Ohio with money from the unions throughout the country. I wasn't conscious of what was going on. I was late recognizing it and the turn against me occurred very late in the campaign. By then it was too late." Lausche said that he'd vote for the GOP nominee for President, who ended up being Richard Nixon. He died in April 1990. Appropriately, his bio by James Odenkirk was titled *Frank Lausche: Ohio's Great Political Maverick*.

Young (1889-1984)

Young was the last Senator to have an 1880s birthdate which, since he was 69 years old in 1958, was a factor which many thought would hinder him in his challenge to John Bricker. Certainly the issue plagued him even more in 1964 when he was 75. Ex-Ohio Governor John Gilligan recalled, "There were lots of people counseling him against making those two races. But he went right out there and did his thing and won both races. He beat the two best names in Ohio." Those names were Bricker and Taft. Bricker had been Governor of Ohio (and Lausche's predecessor) but still had national fame from having been Tom Dewey's running mate in 1944.

At the beginning of 1958, Young was as entrenched as entrenched could get. How did he win? There was an anti-union initiative on the ballot that would allow employees to refuse to join. Ironically, Lausche supported the initiative, which was widely unpopular among Democrats, but it brought them to the polls. Even without the initiative, 1958 was shaping up to be a huge Democratic year, and Young attacked Bricker for being outside the mainstream. "My opponent is John W. Bricker, the darling of the reactionaries." He attacked Bricker for his "phony campaign oratory" by opposing air strength and backing a cut to the Marines.

John Bricker (1893-1986)
Photo courtesy of Ohio History Central

The Blade reported that Young attacked Bricker for voting for "the special interest of the Pennsylvania Railroad, which he had represented as a lawyer." Bricker had also seen his influence diminish by the one-vote loss of the Bricker Amendment. In a year of many upsets, Young's was perhaps the biggest. He sent Bricker packing 52-48% and called his win "a victory for the people over the conservative 'Old Guard' interests." Who ran Young's campaign? Future Senator

Howard Metzenbaum, who would tell the story of "a 69 year old man [coming to] me asking me to run his campaign. We were not real close but I thought John Bricker the antithesis of everything I believed in." They spent just $45,000 - and Lausche had given him nary support.

As a result, Young refused to allow Lausche to stand next to him when he took his oath.

Young's dearth of statewide wins prior to his Senate race was not for lack of trying. He had won his first elected office when he was 23 years old—46 years before he became a Senator, winning a seat in the Ohio House in 1912. His first statewide run came in 1922, when he ran for Ohio Attorney General. He lost. Ditto for a 1930 primary for Governor. He made two more runs for Attorney General again and one for Governor, and lost both. In between, there were three separate stints in the U.S. House (one of which ended in defeat) and service as counsel to the Ohio Attorney General. Despite being well into his 50s, Young also served in World War II.

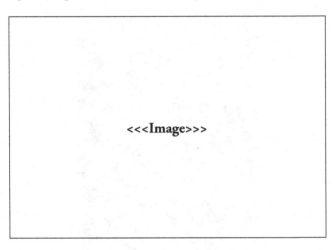

Young after his 1958 Senate election and entertaining visitors
Photos via the Western Reserve Historical Society

By the time Young came up for a second term in 1964, it seemed unlikely that he could repeat his luck. He faced Robert Taft, Jr., a political golden boy whose namesake was his famous late father, "Mr. Republican," and his grandfather, the former President. Early on, there was no guarantee that Young would make it to the primary. Bobby Kennedy was encouraging John Glenn to challenge Young in the primary, and he was prepared to do so until he sustained serious injuries in a bathtub accident; Glenn withdrew from the race. Taft didn't bring up the age issue but it was nevertheless on the minds of many voters. Young responded thus: "I'm not as young as I used to be. But I'm not as old as I expect to get."

The race was close—very close. The returns see-sawed the entire night and when the counting was done, Young was just 17,000 votes ahead of Taft. Not until he was driving to Washington the next day was he fully assured that his lead was irreversible. It was another improbable win for which, as Young acknowledged, Johnson's coattails were pivotal. "Without it," he said, "I doubt I could have won." But Washington was just beginning to get to know the real Stephen Young. Asked whether the Civil Rights issue played a role, Young said probably not, "as Taft campaigned vigorously for the Negro votes," but he added that he enjoyed widespread support.

In 1964, Young backed the Tonkin Gulf resolution but within one year was one of three Senators joining the original "No's"—Morse and Gruening—in voting against the Vietnam Appropriation. By early 1966, he was calling for a complete pullout. "I would sleep better at night," he said, "if someone other than Dean Rusk were Secretary of State."

Adversity often presented Young with an opportunity to showcase his humor further; not even home-state colleagues of the same party were spared. On one occasion, Ohio Congressman Wayne Hays appeared to question Young's patriotism because of his dovish views on the Vietnam War. Young made a parliamentary inquiry on the Senate floor. "Would it be a violation of the rules of the Senate were I to assert in this chamber at this time that Representative Hays of Ohio and one-term Representative Sweeney of Ohio are guilty of falsely, viciously, and maliciously making stupid, lying statement, assailing the loyalty and patriotism of Senators ... and that they are liars in alleging that 'we have aided our enemies.'"

With Washington Post Sunday editor Robert Jordan
Photo via the Western Reserve Historical Society

Ironically, the presiding officer was Alaska's Ernest Gruening, one of the two Senators who had opposed the Tonkin Gulf Resolution, but Gruening had no choice to remind Young that it has "been held out of order" to refer to members of the other body "in opprobrious terms, or to impute to him unworthy motives." Young replied that "if, however, on some future occasion a similar contemptible attack I made on me with insect-like buzzing of lying allegations by either or both of these publicity seekers, I shall surely embalm and embed them in the liquid ambers of my remarks."

Staffer Al Baldwin called Young "a colorful guy," adding that the Senate "was less colorful" after he left. Baldwin called him "very outspoken and courageous. He was a real fighter … he wouldn't say things to be popular. He'd said what he believed, whether it was popular or not. That kind of outspokenness tends to be rare in politics."

Classic examples were his responses to hostile letters. On one occasion, he wrote back, "Dear Sir: It appears to me that you have been grossly misinformed, or are exceedingly stupid. Which is it?" Another time, he wrote, "Some lunatic keeps sending me crazy letters. He's signing your name to them and I thought you should know about it." He called Vietnam, "an Asiatic Eden of Eden converted into a hell on earth by man's inhumanity to man." At Harvard, he referred to Chinese laborers as "junks full of Chinks," apparently unaware that the term "chinks" was derogatory.

Legend had it on Capitol Hill that at one time, he responded to a constituent by calling him "lower than a snake's belly and a wheel-rut." Young went on to tell him that if he was in his presence, he'd punch you in the nose. The constituent apparently got in his car and proceeded to drive from Ohio to Washington. When he dropped into Young's office, an exasperated staff warned him to remain in his office. But he would have none of it. Young emerged, took one look at the man and popped him in the nose.

As expected, Young did not run for re-election in 1970, retiring at age 81, but he briefly considered running if Glenn were to run. Young said that he didn't "regard Glenn as a problem" and stressed his support for "open primaries." Young said he doubted Glenn's qualification to hold a Senate seat, though even some Young supporters saw his threats as hostility toward Glenn, calling Young "vindictive." In the end, Young retired when Metzenbaum agreed to challenge Glenn, beating him in the primary but losing the general election (both won Senate seats later in the decade).

Young resumed practicing law and managed tennis games at the Congressional Country Club (he was a "novice"). He lived 15 more years, passing away in December of 1984 at age 95.

Young's 1964 re-election seemed at times improbable. Here he
is meeting reporters the evening after with his wife
Photo via the Western Reserve Historical Society

CHAPTER SIXTY-TWO

Delaware's Williams Vote Put
Civil Rights Act Over Top

Historic Tidbit: Senate Minority Leader Everett Dirksen was a fan of the Marigold flower. He loved it so much that toward the end of his life, he sought to make the Marigold the official United States flower. That idea didn't blossom. But when Dirksen died, he was so beloved that his colleague, Margaret Chase Smith, a devoted fan of red roses, placed Marigolds on his casket.

John Williams had many nicknames. He was the "Sherlock Holmes of the Senate," the "Lonewolf Investigator," the "Watchdog of the Treasury," "Honest John," and "Mr. Integrity." Forty years after the four-term Delaware Republican Senator bade farewell to Capitol, he'll likely stand out little beyond Delaware, but he cast one vote that proved a giant leap for history and forever earned him a place in the history books; the 67th vote for cloture on the Civil Rights Act of 1964.

The timing did not appear orchestrated, and ultimately, four more Senators would vote in favor of limiting debate. But once Williams whispered "aye," supporters and opponents alike knew they had reached their milestone. Mike Mansfield said, "it's over." According to Senate.gov, "Richard Russell slumped and Hubert Humphrey beamed." Others cried. And for an African-American community that had been subjected to discrimination and even death as a result of bigotry, Williams' vote granted them their most important milestone thus far.

That Williams cast the decisive vote for the civil rights bill might have been hard to reconcile a decade earlier. After the Supreme Court handed down Brown vs. Board of Education, he made clear he was against it, But he helped quell unrest by saying that the law must be adhered to. In the days leading up to a vote that all sides knew would be close, Williams seemed genuinely ambiguous. He believed "in the principal of public accommodations and I believe that every citizen, regardless of color, has the right to be served by places of accommodation on public highways," yet he added he was "against civil disobedience. No man has the right to take the law into his own hands." But after the vote, his commitment continued. When the Voting Rights Act came up, Williams strengthened the bill by making it more difficult to kick people off voter rolls.

In the Senate, Williams was known as a master of investigations. A 15-year period saw 200 investigations and 150 indictments. The Bobby Baker investigation, launched by Williams, exposed the Johnson confidante's link to organized crime. As a result, Williams introduced legislation allowing the

Rules Committee to investigate Senators' "own financial or business interests or activities involving the giving or receiving of campaign funds under questionable circumstances." *Fortune* magazine called Williams the "Lone-Wolf Guardian of Federal Morality." His successor, Bill Roth, believed they could've taken down the President.

Williams with colleague Cale Boggs
Photo courtesy of the University of Delaware Special Collections

When Williams decided to seek a Senate seat, he was a political unknown not expecting to have much chance. He and his brother had founded the Millsboro Feed Company, which specialized in poultry feed. The incumbent, Jim Turnell, was popular but Williams thought federal spending was out of control. 1946 turned out to be the year to be making that argument. It was a heavily Republican year and he beat Turnell with 45%.

For the most part, Williams held his seat with ease. The expectation was that 1958 would be no different. His opponent, ex-Governor Elbert Carvel, had lost his bid for re-election six years earlier. Carvel campaigned under the slogan "Delaware First" and hit Williams for not bringing back funds. Williams began the race with a huge lead but in the end he beat Carvel by just 10,000 votes, 53-46%.

1964 was slightly more difficult and almost proved that all politics was national. Carvel was back and tweaked his slogan somewhat. "What Delaware wants in the Senate is not a policeman but a statesman." Though Johnson was not implicated in Williams' investigation, he may have been fearful of what future scrutiny might bring. He had reason to be. Beyond investigations, Williams opposed the President on virtually every "Great Society" initiative, backing only funding for highway beautification. Election Night transcripts reveal several conversations the newly re-elected President was having with Bill Moyers, who was discussing the possibility of a net gain in the Senate, which Johnson surmised may not happen. "Now, unless we can pick up Carvel - and GOD, I pray on that one," LBJ said. Moyers informed the President that Carvel was leading Williams. That was at 10:00 p.m., but Williams ended up pulling ahead by 7,000 votes.

The next morning, Johnson told Moyers, "I guess this son-of-a-bitch Williams was re-elected." He joked to Dirksen saying, "Yeah, yeah. John's been a little rough on us. And he and his secretary are going to have to quiet down some. They oughtn't be so mean to us now."

Whether being pugnacious was a characteristic or whether he simply thought He was Uncovering mischief, Williams used his feisty rhetoric on other political figures. When New York Congressman Adam Clayton Powell's overseas indiscretions were reported, Williams commented how "on the front page of every newspaper were accounts of Mr. Powell's European vacation with his lady friends, where he attended all the night spots of the European capitals on a tax-paid junket that was financed through the State Department" (Powell responded by calling Williams' statement, "motivated by racial prejudice because I am a Negro."

It was no secret that unlike many Washington lawmakers, Williams was not drawn to the nightlife/social circuit. A deeply religious man who neither drank nor danced, Williams clarified why to his inquisitors: "For one thing, you can't go out every night and do your work. For another, we just don't plain care for it. Neither my wife nor I drink and you can't hear what anybody is saying." His biographer, Carol Hoffecker, writes that he "did not appear to his constituents as an especially warm personality. To them, he seemed cool but observant." However, no one questioned that Williams was anything but beyond reproach: sincere, intelligent, and dedicated. Hoffecker spoke of his "gift for arithmetical calculation, which became the basis for his success both in business and government ... among his greatest assets were patience and perseverance ... He held every proposed program, every proposed tax break, every budget, every government agency to the highest standards for purpose and accountability ... perhaps most important, he believed that in fulfilling the watchdog role that he assumed, fairness should begin with careful attention to fact gathering, honest assessment, and a scrupulous effort to protect the reputations of the innocent."

Williams did not seek re-election in 1970 and retired to Delaware where he died in 1988 at age 84.

CHAPTER SIXTY-THREE

Despite Lacking Name Recognition, Vermont's Prouty Had Solid Contributions In Senate

Historic Quote: It was Senator Winston Prouty who was speaking on the floor of the United States Senate that Friday in 1963 when President Kennedy was shot. Upon hearing the news, Oregon Senator Wayne Morse dashed onto the floor and asked his colleague if "he would yield for an emergency." A few moments later, Majority Leader Mike Mansfield led the 69 Senators who were present in a prayer. It was not known that the President had already passed away.

Senator Winston Prouty (VT)
Credit: U.S. Senate Historical Office

Photo courtesy of the U.S. Senate Historical Office

Over the years, Vermont has had a number of Senators who would often make national headlines: men like George Aiken, Pat Leahy, and Jim Jeffords. Winston Prouty may never have been a household name outside of Vermont, but he enjoyed a career of distinction in the Senate, one that ultimately meant many accomplishments for his state and nation.

The most tangible of Prouty's achievements may be Amtrak—of which Prouty can claim to be a founder through his having shepherded the National Rail Passenger Corporation Act to passage. He sponsored the Older Americans

Assurance Assistance Act, designed to lift up to 30% of seniors out of poverty; the Handicapped Children's Early Education Assistance Act of 1968 was also his. Prouty wanted to also assure senior citizens a minimum income. During Senate consideration of the Tax Adjustment Act of 1966, Prouty proposed minimum monthly Social Security payments of $44 to unmarried seniors and an additional $22 to their spouses. Senators approved the measure 45-40 (a conference committee reduced the payments to $35 for a single person and $17.50 for a spouse).

Prouty also made a big mark on civil rights. In introducing his own desegregation bill in 1963, a year before passage of the bill that ultimately would become law, Prouty made a creative argument for outlawing segregation. He based it on the 13th Amendment, saying it "does not simply abolish involuntary servitude. It also gives Congress to enforce this article by appropriate legislation."

On most issues, Prouty was fairly centrist. He backed nearly all of the "Great Society," and in 1968, he even supported the Gun Control Act, which was not always the right side of the issue in the minds of Vermont's many hunters. His support score of President Lyndon Johnson in 1968 – the last year he served under a Democratic president, was 51%. But he took on the Johnson administration in early 1965 when a proposal was made to closing a number of VA hospitals in order to consolidate resources.

Prouty wasn't universally liberal, however. He supported Vietnam to some extent, though was one of 13 Senators to urge peace in through negotiations. He was not among the Republican Senators to vote for cloture on Abe Fortas' stalled nomination to the Supreme Court. And when Nixon assumed office, Prouty lent him backing in surprising ways. While opposing Carswell for the Supreme Court, he did support Haynsworth; he also gave credence to both the bombing of Cambodia, which he called "bold and courageous," and, against expectations, the anti-ballistic missile system. Nixon reciprocated. The President's first visit of the 1970 campaign season was in Vermont. For a time, Prouty needed it.

Prouty's first two Senate elections were uneventful and as 1970 approached, it seemed that a state that had never before sent a Democrat to the upper chamber would not start at Prouty's expense. In fact, The New York Times wrote that a Democratic Senator from Vermont was as unlikely as "a Protestant Pope," but Phil Hoff was running, and by becoming the first Democrat in 108 years to win the statehouse, he had already defied the odds once before.

Hoff had an ebullient, energetic style, and his campaign was one of "constant motion." There are signs Prouty recognized the tough hurdle that confronted him early on. According to The New York Times, as 1970 began, he "has begun to travel Vermont regularly for the first time in years," but business in Washington hampered his ability to return to Vermont, while Hoff, no longer having the responsibilities of being Governor, was free to devote all of his time to campaigning.

Hoff used Prouty's backing of Nixon policies against him, painting him as "a man with no discernible philosophy." However, he had problems with his own base, particularly those upset with his opposition to Vietnam and subsequently, his support of Gene McCarthy. Polls in early autumn showed the race a dead heat but, by October, Prouty declared that he was "well ahead." As an aide said, "He never made a raving enthusiast of anyone but he never made anyone angry either." Voters evidently had the same view. Prouty was re-elected 59-41%

Prouty was as much a Vermonter as anyone. An AP report upon his death described the "stereotyped Vermonter" as "a thin, quiet man with a flat accent and strong Republican bent. That person was Winston Prouty." He was called "Mr. Vermont."

Prouty's political career began as Mayor of Newport, Vermont, in 1937. In 1940, he was elected to the Vermont House and went on to serve as Speaker of the body. While he failed in his attempt to become Lieutenant Governor in 1948, voters compensated two years later when he won his first of four terms in the U.S. House of Representatives in 1950. He backed the Tidelands legislation, school construction, and opposed efforts to develop hydroelectricity on the Niagara River. His opportunity to move to the Senate came with the retirement of Republican Ralph Flanders in 1958.

After his 1970 win, Prouty seemed set for another six years in the Senate. However, in September 1971, he was hospitalized for severe stomach pain, which had briefly forced him off the campaign trail a year earlier. The diagnosis was advanced gastric cancer and within 16 days, he was dead. He was 64 years old.

CHAPTER SIXTY-FOUR

Bartlett Played Most Pivotal Role Of Any Alaskan In Securing Statehood

Historic Quote: "He wasn't paranoid – he was busy." – A prominent Nixon White House staffer.

**Photo courtesy of the Edward Lewis Bartlett Papers,
Archives, University of Alaska Fairbanks**

When Alaska became a state, it elected two U.S. Senators. The first was Ernest Gruening, whom I wrote about extensively in another volume; Bob Bartlett took his seat the same day, and he had just as much impact as Gruening on seeing that the "Land of the Last Frontier" achieved statehood. But while Gruening promoted statehood from the inside (he was Governor), Bartlett was able to focus on making it a reality from inside Congress, where personal relations may have been equally critical.

Beyond Alaskan statehood, Bartlett's impact nationally was significant. According to The Library of Congress, he passed more bills than any other member of Congress, and his sponsorship of legislation concerning the accessibility of federal buildings can easily make him a hero to the disabled community decades before the enactment of ADA. Aside from these accomplishments, colleagues viewed Bartlett as a genuinely nice person.

Like so many Alaskans, Bartlett was born in the Lower 48. Hailing from Seattle, a fellow Northwestern city that was also developing, he nevertheless had a great deal more in common with the Alaska express than other stalwarts (Ted Stevens, for example, who often tangled with Bartlett, hailed from Indianapolis). For practical purposes, Alaska was Bartlett's home for life.

His parents moved to Fairbanks when he was one and, after zig-zagging between Washington and Alaska for college, he became a reporter for the *Fairbanks News Miner*, and married a childhood friend whose daughter was also a miner. But politics soon took him to the other Washington—the nation's capital. Bartlett had become acquainted with Anthony Dimond, who in 1932 became Alaska's non-voting delegate. By 1938, he was Secretary of Alaska, which often made him Acting Governor. In 1944, after initially hesitating, he became Alaska's delegate in his own right.

At a ribbon-cutting as Secretary of Alaska and explaining
the option of statehood to Alaskans
Photo courtesy of the Edward Lewis Bartlett Papers,
Archives, University of Alaska Fairbanks

Bartlett first introduced the statehood bill in 1947 and had the Committee on Public Lands hold hearings in many cities throughout the state. As Eric Gislason writes in *The Architect of Alaska Statehood*, "Congressional opposition usually fretted about Alaska's non-contiguity with the continental states, dwelt on the difficulty of defending Alaska, and expressed insecurity about the racial diversity of the region's population." The bill finally passed the House in 1949, but it would be years before it would even come to a vote in the Senate. Meanwhile, Bartlett proved adroit at securing federal funding for the state.

In a show of major legislative skill for a non-voting member, Bartlett secured more money for Alaska than any other member of Congress had for the territory they served. One was the Alaskan Public Works Act, which provided $70 million to the state. The Alaska Mental Health Act and the Radiation Act were also his, as was a bill that forbade foreign fishing in territorial waters.

As the years passed and statehood lagged, Alaskans, starting with a Constitutional Convention, put on a full-court press for statehood. As the convention took shape, Bartlett urged delegates to pass a measure that would protect Alaska's resources from outside control. He summed his concerns up thus: "A failure to write into fundamental law basic barriers to minimize fraud, corruption, non-development, and exploitation may well be viewed fifty years from now as this Convention's greatest omission."

Archives, University of Alaska, Fairbanks

**Photos courtesy of the Edward Lewis Bartlett Papers,
Archives, University of Alaska Fairbanks**

Bartlett warned that "Two very real dangers are present. The first and most obvious danger is that of exploitation under the thin disguise of development. The taking of Alaska's mineral resources without leaving some reasonable return for the support of Alaska governmental services and the use of all the people of Alaska will mean a betrayal in the administration of the people's wealth. Outside interests, determined to stifle any development in Alaska which might compete with their activities elsewhere, will [also] attempt to acquire great areas of Alaska's public lands in order not to develop them until such time as, in their omnipotence and the pursuance of their own interests, they see fit. If large areas of Alaska's patrimony are turned over to such corporations the people of Alaska may be even more the losers than if the lands had been exploited."

Basking in the glow if victory following the long slog to statehood
Right photo courtesy of the Alaska Dispatch, left photo courtesy of the
Edward Lewis Bartlett Papers, Archives, University of Alaska Fairbanks

Bartlett's long hard slog came to fruition in April 1958 when both Houses passed the resolution. His daughter later said it was he who "reeled in Sam Rayburn and Lyndon Johnson." Once the resolution was signed, he won the election to become the state's first voting Senator with 83% of the vote. Gruening won his seat the same day but Bartlett, prevailing in a coin-toss, gave him the seniority. Forced to stand for re-election in 1960, Bartlett racked up 63% over Lee McKinney, a dentist who had served a single term in the Alaska Legislature. Facing McKinney again six years later, Bartlett exceeded 75%.

By 1968, Bartlett knew he needed heart surgery. "He was carrying a heavy responsibility in hacking away at me ... because if I die on the table I have ... a strong feeling, although not the definite knowledge, that the governor of Alaska would not appoint a successor of my political faith." His prescience proved all too prophetic as Bartlett died during the surgery. He was only 64 years old. Gruening, who had been beaten for re-nomination by Mike Gravel, left office that year, leaving Alaska last in seniority. Governor Wally Hickel, who ironically that day had been named Interior Secretary by Richard Nixon but had not yet resigned, indeed named Stevens to the seat.

Gislason cites two obituaries that summed up the affection many felt for Bartlett. One said, "The people of this state who loved him are known for their individualism, divisiveness, sectionalism, arrogance, and clannishness. Yet [Bartlett] held them united behind him for 24 years—a longevity in public office that is unequalled in Alaska" (Stevens would ultimately surpass that). Another called him "a humble man, but one who was terribly proud—of his state, his friends, of the loyalty he felt to those who had earned his respect." A statue of Bartlett stands in Statutory Hall in the nation's capital, donated by his beloved Alaska.

The Bartlett statue stands in Statuary Hall
Photo via xroads.org

CHAPTER SIXTY-FIVE

Hiram Fong
First Asian-American Senator, A Republican From Hawaii

Historic Quote: "When a House member goes to the Senate, it raises the IQ of both chambers." - Everett Dirksen who was a member of both chambers.

Photo via the U.S. Government Printing Office

I t seems unimaginable that Hawaii could elect a Republican to the United States Senate today but once upon a time, literally, for one moment in time, there was such a person. His name was Hiram Fong, and he served the 50th state for the first 18 years of its 54 years in the union. He would also be the first Asian-American Senator in history.

Daniel Inouye's monopoly on one Senate seat from Hawaii pretty much deprived any one of either political persuasion from even attempting a run at his job. But after Fong's retirement, the other seat was Democratic as well. The ultimate test came in 1990, when Congresswoman Pat Saiki lost a bid to her colleague, Daniel Akaka, who had been appointed to the chamber when Spark Matsnuga had died. Akaka took 54%.

At the House level, the GOP's luck has been slightly better, but only by a fraction. Saiki held her seat for two terms before her Senate run, and Honolulu Councilman Charlie Djou was able to take advantage of a Democratic split in a special election to win the seat of the state's new Governor, Neil Abercrombie. He was unseated that November. So that leaves Fong. What was his recipe for success?

Why, he was a centrist.

Fong was born to poverty in China. His name meant "ah," for master, but Hiram came about when he joined the military. He would be elected to the Hawaii territorial House and become Speaker. In 1945, his "Wagner Act" gave rights of workers to unionize. But even before statehood and at the local level, the Democrats reigned supreme and Fong was unseated in 1954.

After, *The Honolulu Advertiser* said Fong "founded more than a half-dozen Honolulu firms, many with the word 'Finance' in their titles, including Finance Factors, Finance Realty, Finance Home Builders, Finance Investment and Finance Factors Foundation." His return came in 1959 upon Hawaii achieving statehood, as he one a seat in the upper chamber that year.

Fong's first Senate poster, 1959
Image courtesy of the University of Hawaii, Hiram Fong Papers

Fong would fly back to Hawaii nine times a year, which he'd say would leave him "drained." "Being the first Asian in there, I was very, very careful. I knew that if I did anything that was in the line of dereliction of duty, why it would shame me and my family. It would also shame those of my ethnic background and it would shame the people of Hawaii."

Image courtesy of the University of Hawaii, Hiram Fong Papers

But Fong did use his symbol to make a questionable move or two. In both 1964 and 1968, Fong mounted a "Favorite Son" bid for President. There was little activity outside Hawaii but, it was still eyebrow-raising. Nevertheless, his name was put into nomination at the Republican Convention, which made him the first person of Asian-ancestry to have that distinction.

In office, Fong was distinctly moderate, in favor of civil rights. That led to much ticket splitting which enabled Fong to hold his seat 53-46%, even as LBJ was winning the state with a staggering 79%.

Photo and image courtesy of the University of Hawaii, Hiram Fong Papers

In Hawaii, the respect Fong enjoyed was as deep as ever. But by 1970, the state's Democratic trend was almost impossible to beat. Fong won, but just barely. He held off Cecil Heftel by just 8,000 votes, 52-48%. That would prove to be his last hurrah. That year, as in all of his campaigns, his support from the International Longshoremen's and Warehousemen's Union were key to his victories. But as time progressed, he became increasingly loyal to Nixon.

Fong was the top Republican on the Post Office and Civil Service Committee.
Above, he is discussing postal issues with President Nixon, Postmaster
General Blount and his Chairman, Wyoming Senator Gale McGee
Photo courtesy of Robert McGee

Fong in retirement
Photo courtesy of the Honolulu Advertiser

Retirement was not prosperous for Fong. He tried to open a shopping
complex, "Senator Hiram Fong's Plantation and Gardens," but that failed. This
plantation left him a debt of $700,000. Fong would live to the ripe old age of 97.
He was said to have been working until a week before his death.

CHAPTER SIXTY-SIX

Nina Totenberg's Late Husband Haskell Beat George Will's Employer Allott For Colorado Senate Seat

Historic Quote: "Politics is supposed to be the second oldest profession. I have come to realize that it bears a very close resemblance to the first." – Ronald Reagan

It's not unusual for a wealthy State Senator to upset a three-term United States Senate incumbent, but it is unusual when the incumbent is a Republican in a Republican year and the challenger, until two years earlier, was a member of the same party. The man who did the ousting was Floyd Haskell, and the Senator on the receiving end was Gordon Allott of Colorado. But everything has a twist or three, and in this case, one of Allott's employees was a guy by the name of George Will. Haskell's future wife would be famed National Public Radio correspondent Nina Totenberg, and his senior colleague in the Senate would be his high school roommate, Peter Dominick.

Gordon Allott (1907-1989)
Photo courtesy of the U.S. Senate Historical Office

In politics, the term "upset" may be considered art imitating life but Allott's loss is a rare example of life imitating art. After three terms, Allott was a reliable conservative but, with a low-key style, not at all out of line with his state's electorate. He backed all of the civil rights measures and at least some having to do with the "Great Society" and gun control, but also Nixon's judicial nominees.

He reluctantly backed the test ban treaty and nominated William E. Miller for vice-president. But when it came to water issues, particularly Colorado water rights, he was assertive and effective. At one point, he proposed mandating that Congress approve any wilderness proposal. Advocates saw this language as an attempt to gut the bill and momentarily panicked when the amendment passed. Ultimately, Chairman Clinton Anderson beat it back later in the day.

Allott also hand a hand in uncovering at least a few substantive—as opposed to partisan—problems that played a major role in the defeat of Abe Fortas' nomination for Chief Justice of the Supreme Court. Allott needed information on an Appropriations Committee measure and believed only President Johnson himself knew the answer. Johnson was not at the White House when Allott phoned but was told, "Fortas is here and he is handling the bill." For Fortas and Johnson, that became a sticking point which, in an election year, proved too deep to get out of. The nomination was defeated. Allott's crusades didn't necessarily make him popular with his colleagues. After Everett Dirksen's passing in 1969, Allott sought support to succeed him but soon bowed to reality and ended his bid.

Senator Gordon Allott with constituents (left) and President Eisenhower (right) Left photo via the Colorado State University Library; right photo courtesy of the Arthur Scott Photography Collection

By 1972, the environment was changing. The state was growing and many of the new residents were liberal and had never seen Allott's name on the ballot. Plus, a referendum to host the winter Olympics in Denver was being soundly rejected by voters.

And Haskell wasn't your typical Democrat. Why? Because until 1970, he hadn't been a Democrat at all. In fact, he had served in the Colorado Legislature - including as Judiciary Chair and assistant Majority Leader - as a Republican. But he was not particularly conservative, and Nixon's Vietnam policy convinced him to make the switch.

Even then, Haskell was introducing a resolution in the chamber to disapprove of Nixon's Vietnam policy, one of which failed just 29-32. He had sponsored a truth in lending bill which, as Kopel observes, was never allowed to receive a vote. As Haskell recalled, "I never planned to run for office again. I had become more and more opposed to the war in Vietnam, and when Nixon invaded Cambodia, that was it. I just felt I couldn't stay in the Republican Party any longer." He called it a private act of conscience."

Floyd Haskell
Image via ronwadebuttons.com; Photo courtesy
of the U.S. Senate Historical Office

Haskell had more than enough money to make his case, which he did by running a major television ad just before the election, focusing on clips Allott had made that could discredit him with liberals. Will wrote after the election that "Gordon Allott is not the sort of malleable man who finds it easy to pull himself into new molds." He added, Allott "did his job so well that he changed his constituency and brought about his defeat."

On Election Night, Haskell's lead was just 5,000 votes, but final totals doubled that number, and his margin over Allott ended up being one percentage point, 49-48%. When the dust had settled, Will took no prisoners when it came to lack of help from the Nixon administration.

Will said the campaign had made an urgent appeal to Nixon to do a campaign visit but that the President's advisers, insisting their surveys showed Allott well over 50%, decided against it. The White House also felt snow might keep people away and that their "secret" information showed Allot poised to win by 15%. But in actuality, there had been a large number of undecided voters that the Allot campaign was worried about. And for good reason. "[When] it came time for Nixon to do a favor, all he got was an evasive, dishonest, and in the end contemptuous refusal … Today Nixon has all the friends he has earned and deserves (he won't have Allott's vote to save him)."

In short, Allott's loss shouldn't have been viewed as a sneak attack. Democrats sought to make an issue of Allott's low visibility as early as his 1966 race against Roy Romer, who went on to win the Governorship 20 years later. They called him an "invisible man," which Romer himself took a shot at in his concession ("I went to the Cosmopolitan Hotel to congratulate my opponent Tuesday night but even in defeat I couldn't find this man"). Allot had won 58-42%, but 1966 was a Republican year and by 1972, Nixon's 64% notwithstanding, things were different.

Jerry Kopel, a 22-year Democratic Colorado State Representative, called Allott "a silver-haired, one-time track star, conducted a subdued campaign marked by handshaking tours. He substituted paid political advertising—a luxury his opponent said he couldn't afford—for the joint television appearances used by other candidates."

Photo via the Colorado State University Library

Haskell grew up in Morristown, New Jersey and earned a law degree from Harvard. In the Senate, Haskell served on the Senate Finance Committee, but he wasn't a press-the-flesh kind of guy. *The Washington Post* wrote that he "tended to be shy in the presence of people he didn't know." One person he did know was Dominick, who after Allott's defeat became his senior colleague. Dominick was also from the East Coast – Connecticut - and the two were sent to private school. As fate would have it, they were roommates.

The Senate partnership didn't last that long. Dominick was walloped in his bid for a third term in 1974 by Gary Hart, in part because of health issues, in part because of visibility, and in part because he called Watergate "insignificant." Haskell lost by 18% to Bill Armstrong, a three-term Congressman who was part of the New Right. While he ran as a staunch conservative, among the major issues on which he took aim at Haskell were tax cuts, particularly his opposition to Kemp-Roth. Meanwhile, Haskell divorced his longtime wife and married Totenberg a year after his Senate term ended.

Jimmy Carter campaigned for Haskell and called him a "national treasure." But conservatives were making a major push and Bill Armstrong won the seat by 16%. After his defeat, Haskell worked for Common Cause. In 1994, he slipped on ice in Washington DC and died four years later at age 82. Allott died of leukemia in 1989, also at age 82. Dominick died in 1981.

CHAPTER SIXTY-SEVEN

Hathaway of Maine Had Compelling War Story – And Paved Way For Women To Enter Military Academies

Historic Quote: "You know, it's hard enough around here to figure out what the right thing to do is. When you add the politics on top of it, it becomes practically impossible." - U.S. Senator William Hathaway of Maine

Photo via the Collection of the U.S. House of Representatives

William Hathaway no doubt will go down in history as a principled and highly effective Senator from Maine but, some may see his story as a politician as secondary to his story in defending America. In short, Hathaway's experiences – his mission, his courage and the betrayal he faced, epitomizes what has come to be known as the "greatest generation."

Like many young men of that era, Hathaway enlisted in the Army Air Corps shortly after his high school graduation in 1942. He flew in a B24 and his position on the crew was navigator but was forced to parachute to the ground after he was struck by enemy fire on the 13th mission over German-occupied Ploesti, Romania (a number of his crewmates were killed). Hathaway landed on a family farm and gave his gold watch to the family but they turned him over to the Germans anyway. He was held as a P.O.W. for three months and upon release, was sent to a hospital in Texas to recover. It was there that he met his wife, an Army nurse, Mary Lee Bird. He was awarded the Distinguished Flying Cross, the Purple

Heart and the Air Medal. When the war ended, Hathaway, who had grown up in Allston, Massachusetts near the city of Cambridge, enrolled at Harvard College where he earned his degree in Philosophy. He remained at Harvard to attend its Law School and set up a practice. Soon he was Androscoggin County assistant attorney (he also served as a hearing examiner for the State Liquor Commission). It was employment from Democratic Party stalwart Frank Coffin that brought Hathaway to Maine.

Hathaway's first political foray came in 1962 when he just missed upsetting freshmen Republican Clifford McIntire (the result was 51-49%). The addition of Lewiston, necessitated by Maine's loss of a House seat, had made the district more competitive and his home-town appeal mitigated Republican voters. Hathaway benefited from an economic slump among potato farmers. Hathaway criticized McIntire for "consistently opposing every broad gauged measure aimed at improved economic prosperity in Maine." He called McIntire, "stubborn, backward looking opposition."

Hathaway (far right) as President Johnson and Lady Bird visited Lewiston, Maine. LBJ's trip was the first by a sitting president to the state Photo via the Edmund S. Muskie Archives and Special Collections Library

Hathaway's subsequent appointment as Maine's Democratic Party Chair gave him a number of chits to fall back on when the time for a second run would come. And come it did in 1964. McIntire took the audacious step of challenging

Democratic Senator Edmund Muskie for a second term and predictably lost. But his decision opened the seat which Hathaway promptly entered. This time, the result was not close and he waltzed in with 62%. He won re-election twice with 56% and found himself up to 64% in 1970. The district's Republican lean did not stop Hathaway from compiling a liberal voting record. Assigned to the Education and Labor and Merchant Marine and Fisheries Committees, Hathaway devotedly backed the "Great Society" but did come to oppose the Vietnam War.

In 1968, Hathaway took the lead on President Johnson's proposal to advance the Occupational Safety and Health Act of 1968 (OSHA). The president's goal was to, "protect the worker on the job." Hathaway tweaked the bill to make it palatable to lawmakers who had concerns about the bill's reach. In particular, members were concerned that the Labor Secretary could become "an absolute czar" in implementing OSHA. Throughout his career, Hathaway in no way supported weakening safety protection. In fact, when Senators voted 90-1 to exempt those with fewer than five people, the sole "no" belonged to Hathaway. By proposing a weakening of the '68 version, Hathaway was simply trying to improve chances for its enactment. But as Stephen Minter noted that "with an abundance of more pressing issues to consider, it died." The following year, Hathaway and California Democrat Phil Burton proposed an Occupational Safety and Health Court but it was defeated. Hathaway was active in another version enacted in 1970. Two years later, he successfully authored an amendment to the Farmers Home Administration to provide loan authority to farmers and ranchers to aid them with OSHA compliance.

In 1972, Hathaway decided to seek a U.S. Senate seat in Maine, challenging the "Grand Lady" of Maine politics, Margaret Chase Smith. Though he entered the contest anything but a favorite against the state's most durable politician (she had served in Congress since 1940), a contrast in styles was evident almost from the get-go. Hathaway's personality epitomized the term glad-handler and gift for gab. Smith attended events at her leisure. Years later, one journalist from Maine, M.D. Harmon, summed it up by saying she was trying to "nonchalant her way to a fifth term." And nearing her 75th birthday, many Mainers, including those who gave her the benefit in recognition of her past service, felt she was seeking one term too many. Hathaway refused to speak ill of his rival but did contrast her energy by visiting every town in the state twice.

Smith carried populous York County by a microscopic margin along with a few others along the southern tip but Hathaway won everywhere above that for a 53-47% margin. His mother evidently was not among his supporters. Her reaction, as Hathaway dryly told it years later was, "You ought to be ashamed of yourself" (though family members say he was only joking – that she was immensely proud).

Hathaway's crusade on behalf of allowing women in U.S. Military Facilities came from a constituent who in 1973 wrote him dismayed that she could not be accepted to West Point because there were no facilities for women. An "infuriated"

Hathaway proposed an amendment that would require the admittance to women. His reasoning: "My feeling is that if we are going to have women in the services, they should get the best training possible. While the legislation failed twice, Hathaway decided to introduce it as an amendment to a Budget bill in 1975.

In explaining his amendment on the Senate floor, Hathaway told his colleagues he was doing so "in order to enable women to obtain the same superior educational opportunities presently available only to men at our service academies." He asked them to "consider for a moment what our military forces need the most, now and in the future. What abilities and strengths are required in our military officers in order to maintain our defense in the complex setting of détente?" He went on to say that "as women have conclusively demonstrated that their abilities to perform in school and at work are equal to the abilities of men, and as there is no question that women will continue to make a valuable contribution to our armed forces, it behooves us now to eliminate the groundless and inconsistent prohibition against their admission to the service academy." Hathaway made clear that in order to minimize disruptions for an academic year about to get underway, the amendment would not take affect until the following year. It was a surprisingly short struggle for a fairly controversial issue but President Ford signed the entire measure (which contained the provision) into law.

Photo courtesy of Fred Hathaway

Ford evidently was holding no grudges when it came to Hathaway. Two years earlier, he had been one of just three members of the Senate to oppose his nomination for vice-president. It wasn't personal – Hathaway just felt Watergate needed to be fully disposed of before Ford could assume the post (he had also opposed the appointment of his colleague, Ohio Republican William Saxbe as Attorney General) citing the, "emoluments clause." In 1975, Hathaway did speak against Ford's swift response to Cambodia's seizure of the U.S. freighter, Mayaguez. "You'd think the Cambodians had landed in San Diego the way the president reacted to this."

Hathaway was also an ardent proponent of the War Powers Act, legislation sponsored by his senior colleague, Ed Muskie. Stating that, "even Hamilton, the great proponent of a strong executive branch, felt bound to say that the war power belongs to Congress." Hathaway told Senators, "the war powers legislation which we consider here today does not seek to alter the constitutional balance of power between Congress and the President; it simply seeks to restore it. It seeks to restore it to a balance achieved by the framers of the Constitution, but a balance since tipped, not by the conscious abuse of a wanton Executive, but by the encroachment of a series of well-meaning Executives onto an area of power ill-defined and, indeed, ill-recognized by most Members of past Congresses."

Whether in the marble corridor halls of Capitol Hill or away, Hathaway was known as a garrulous man with a roaring sense of humor with a human nature second-to-none. Clarence "Chub" Clark was an Aroostook County staffer for Hathaway and a longtime friend and he told the *Portland Press Herald* on the Senator's death that when accompanying him, it was not uncommon for the two to always run behind schedule due to the fact that Hathaway just couldn't resist talking to people.

Campaigning in Palermo, Maine
Photo courtesy of Fred Hathaway

Angus King, a future Governor and Maine Senator himself was among his employees who in 1972, was diagnosed with melanoma. King was awestruck. "One of the most vivid memories of my life was waking up in the hospital after my surgery in the recovery room and looking up, and I saw my wife on one side of the bed, and standing at the end of the bed in hospital green scrubs was U.S. Senator Bill Hathaway...I was 28 years old, and yet he left the Senate (to visit him). I will never, ever forget that." And in a panegyric tribute on the Senate floor after Hathaway died, King said, "that was the kind of guy he was...One of the things that I noticed about him, which was a tremendous influence on my life, was he was exactly same person in private as he was in public." King recalled that when he delivered a memo to Hathaway arguing of the political ramifications on the issue at hand, Hathaway scribbled outside the margins, "I pay you for policy, not political advice. He really and truly didn't pay much attention to politics. He always wanted to do what is right."

It showed. Throughout his career, Hathaway had been advocating for the Dickey-Lincoln public power proposal for Aroostook County. The proposed hydro-electric dam project on the St. John River had long been controversial among Mainers (the surprising adoption of an amendment by Connecticut Democrat Bob Giaimo had put it on hold as early as 1965) but unions liked it because of the construction jobs that would be required. Hathaway was also on the wrong side of public opinion when it came to compensating Indians for land they had long claimed was seized illegally. Both were prominent in the news at the time Hathaway was seeking a second term. His vote for the Panama Canal Treaty hurt as well.

The race had already been guaranteed to be difficult. Bill Cohen had taken Hathaway's House seat when he had moved to the Senate and now was trying to take his Senate seat as well – involuntarily. Cohen had gained fame as a Judiciary Committee Republican who had abandoned Nixon and backed impeachment during Watergate and was immensely popular in his Congressional district. Maine Democratic Chair Harold Pachios admitted as much in early October. While he did boast that, "We Democrats say it's a race between a workhorse -and a show horse, so far there haven't been any issues, they have not slugged at each other. It's a contest between two decent candidates that everyone likes." The not slugging didn't exactly last. Hathaway called Cohen a "pretty boy," while Cohen attacked the incumbent for bringing in celebrity politicians such as Ted Kennedy.

Hathaway relied on his personal touch which, as *Congressional Quarterly* noted, often brought him to the "small hamlets that dot the potato and timber lands on the North." But there were other candidates on the ballot and when the votes were counted, Cohen had won a decisive 57-34% win.

In 1990, President George H.W. Bush appointed him to the Federal Maritime Commission, who of course has a family compound in Kennebunkport, though the pair had gotten to know each other while both were in the House and Hathaway being on the Senate Intelligence Committee when Bush headed the CIA (Hathaway was friendly with Vice-President Dan Quayle as well). He also served on the state's Blue Ribbon Commission to examine the state's worker's compensation system.

To Bill – With High Personal Regard And Friendship, too – Geo B

Photo courtesy of Fred Hathaway

Near the end of his life, Hathaway would bet folks at the country club he attended that he'd live to be 100. While he did have a full life, he passed at age 89 in 2013. A former constituent, Rod Scribner of Pittston, Maine, expressed the sentiment of so many others when he said "his willingness to do the right thing even if unpopular is an example to all."

CHAPTER SIXTY-EIGHT

Michigan's Griffin Led Fight To
Block Fortas Confirmation

Historic Tidbit: It was no secret that, personally and politically, Richard Nixon was a paranoid man. In 1971, he put a great deal of political capital into Senate ratification of the ABM Treaty. Just before his vote, he told his aide Bryce Harkey to "make sure that all our guys are there. Don't let anyone get sick. Don't let anyone go to the bathroom until it's over." In this instance, Nixon's paranoia was warranted. Vice-President Agnew cast the deciding vote.

Photo courtesy of the U.S. Senate Historical Office

Aside from 1994, Michigan has elected a Republican Senator in just two elections since 1952. That man was Robert Griffin of Traverse City who, prior to his mild upset win in 1966, was a protégé of future President Gerald Ford. However, Griffin's Senate run, while like a chess game in the sense that it was cut short from bad luck and bad moves, was fairly hefty as far as influencing national issues was concerned.

Griffin's rise resulted from timing, shrewd moves, and knowing key players he ultimately wouldn't need. Ironically, his end would result from a major miscalculation.

A son of Detroit, Griffin served in the 71st infantry division and returned to receive a degree from Central Michigan College. It was off to the University of Michigan Law School from there, and as one classmate, future U.S. Circuit Judge

Albert Engel, observed, "it was a class which was ultimately to include, as of today, no fewer than twenty-two members of the state and federal judiciary in Michigan and elsewhere in the United States." Upon graduation, Griffin began a law practice in Traverse City. In 1956 Griffin was persuaded to run for Congress, but that meant ousting an incumbent Republican, Ruth Thompson. His literature included his picture and one word: integrity. He won by an impressive 52-36% and took the general election with 55%. It was his 33rd birthday.

Griffin took a seat on the Education and Labor Committee where he co-sponsored the National Student Loan program. It was in his second term that he gained fame. Hearings chaired by Arkansas Democratic Senator John McClellan had exposed corruption in unions, and the Senate passed legislation, backed by the AFL-CIO, that would mandate reforms. Its sponsor was one John F. Kennedy, and its 88-1 passage (Barry Goldwater was the sole "no") seemed to assure its easy sledding in the House. Enter Griffin. Working with Georgia Democrat Phil Landrum, a bill was proposed that Chester Bowles said "went beyond the scope of the McClellan Committee's findings to affect the economic balance at the bargaining table by honest and legitimate unions and employers." It passed the House, and Kennedy lobbied for key changes in the conference committee that labor could live with. What Griffin accomplished was passing major legislation in a Democratic house and taking on the Kennedy brothers and winning.

In 1965, Congress again took up the issue. Specifically, the House was debating eliminating the Right to Work requirement. Griffin called "a vote for this bill...a vote against the rank and file union members; it will be a vote against the protection they have now under the 1959 Act." He downplayed the advocacy from some unions., "Most of the pressure for this bill has come from the Teamsters Union. There may be lip service support coming from some of the other unions, but they do not seem to be so interested in it. I have not received any particular pressures from companies." The repeal cleared the House but failed to advance in the Senate. He then proposed an amendment to, as *the Chicago Tribune* reported, "prohibit discrimination by unions on the basis of race and color, using dues for politics or non-union business, and firing or disciplining a member for exercising his legal or civil rights." Griffin argued that proponents were, "voting to force a man to choose between bread for his family and his religious convictions. You are blocking Negroes from apprenticeship jobs." That amendment was rejected. Later that year, Griffin proposed an amendment to recommit legislation establishing the National Endowment for the Arts (a GOP report called the measure "frivolous," "hasty," and "a mockery of the legislative process"), but it was killed 128-151 and the program was enacted.

Photo via eBay

Meanwhile, Griffin was becoming a major confidante of a fellow Wolverine by the name of Gerald Ford. After a disappointing 1962 election cycle, Griffin was among the group of "Young Turks" who convinced Ford to challenge Charles Hoeven for the position of Secretary of the House Republican Conference; much of the conversations were conducted in the Griffins' living room. Two years later, he was there to persuade Ford to take on Charlie Halleck for the position of Minority Leader. "Halleck is too old, a bad image," Griffin said. Ford narrowly won, but shortly thereafter, he had bigger fish to fry. A Senate race was coming up in 1966, and John McNamara was not running. Griffin geared up to replace him. That April, however, McNamara died, and Michigan's Republican Governor, George Romney, appointed him to the seat.

In the general, Griffin faced ex-Governor "Soapy" Williams and was not the favored candidate. Proponents composed a song, "Give Bob The Ball," that was designed to remind voters of his youth. It was, ironically, a similar maneuver that had worked so well for Williams in his 1948 run for Governor. Williams hit Griffin's absenteeism, labeling his voting record "disgraceful." Griffin acknowledged trying to combine a Senate record with campaigning but said the votes were "routine" and noted John F. Kennedy did the same thing while running for President. Griffin took a solid 56-44% margin.

As in the House, Griffin attained much recognition. It started in 1968. Abe Fortas had been nominated Chief Justice of the Supreme Court, and Griffin led the charge against Fortas' confirmation. He attacked his receipt of a $15,000 lecture fee and his proximity to Johnson, noting his work on the President's State of the Union, and asked the Judiciary Committee to reopen hearings. When Fortas refused to reappear, Griffin called it "inconceivable." At the Judiciary hearing, Griffin added, "Never before has there been such obvious political maneuvering to create a vacancy so that a 'lame duck' President could fill it and thereby deny the opportunity to a new President about to be elected by the people."

Griffin contended his opposition to Fortas "sprang from the fact that it had all the earmarks of a political maneuver." He said Fortas had "a reputation as a fixer" and that he was "prepared to talk at great length." Asked if that was different from a filibuster, he replied, "No difference." And he did talk—for three hours. Ultimately, the nomination was defeated when supporters couldn't muster more than the 45 votes required to invoke cloture.

Griffin's colleagues soon recognized his skill. Later that year, Everett Dirksen died, and Hugh Scott took over the position of Minority Leader, leaving open the position of Minority Whip, which Griffin won, defeating Howard Baker on a 24-19 vote. He opposed Nixon's nomination of Haynesworth and the SST and supported the ERA, but he was in the pits with labor. His scores with the ADA rarely topped more than a third. His 15% in 1972 was well below his 33% the year before. In 1972, Griggin opposed the Church-Case amendment that would put a timetable on military operations in Vietnam, quipping, "It looks as though a counter-offer is already being made here in the Senate...It seems to me that the bargaining with the enemy is being done here in the Senate."

Photo courtesy of the Gerald R. Ford Presidential Library and Museum

By 1972, Griffin was up for re-election. His challenger was a well-known name in the Wolverine State. Frank Kelly was Attorney General and generally popular but he had one hurdle: busing. He actually had backed it. As the election drew closer, however, he reversed his position. Griffin meanwhile billed himself as, "Michigan's muscle," while Democrarts dereided him as "Bobby zero." Griffin was aided by Nixon's coattails - not as high in Michigan as elsewherebut emerged victorious 53-47%.

Griffin was in no mood to reciprocate the President for his assistance during the waning days of Watergate. In late July, upon seeing the final transcripts, admonished Ford. "Jerry," he said, "you might think about toning down your public statements supporting Nixon." Those closest to Nixon, however, now knew that it was a lost cause. Specifically, Al Haig asked Griffin to encourage him to resign. Griffin began drafting his letter on a flight back home to Michigan, and upon landing, he drafted it word for word over the phone to his secretary, with instructions that it be hand-delivered to the White House. First, though, he read the draft to Ford who was at a campaign rally in Jackson, Mississippi. Ford's reply: "Bob, do what you think is right."

By the mid-1970s, Griffin seemed to have it made. Ford had made it to the White House; he was in Senate leadership; and he seemed to have found a balance between liberal and conservative Michigan. At the end of 1976, though, things quickly went downhill. Ford lost the Presidency to Jimmy Carter, and Griffin thought he had the votes to become the new Senate Minority Leader, but in something of an upset, he lost to Baker on a vote of 19 to 18. Griffin had begun the race a clear favorite as Baker hadn't even declared himself to be a candidate. Baker overcame a clear hurdle, however, when the newly-elected Republican Senators vowed to remain neutral until just before voting. The day of the vote, supporters of both men were out of town; Baker actually told Griffin he didn't know whether to proceed. Griffin replied, "Good luck if you win," but the fact is, Baker could see from Griffin's face that he did not have the votes either. When the tally was announced, a gracious Griffin shook Baker's hand and popped open the champagne he had brought for his own win.

What ultimately hurt Griffin was his style. While capable and a master of parliamentary procedure, he was not as camera-ready as his rival. In fact, the term folksy wasn't even the word for Griffin. Jack Germond captured it better when he said that Republicans chose the "cheerleader with the dimples" over the "diligent secretary of the glee club."

A few months later, sensing no place to go, Griffin announced his retirement from the Senate. Nine months went by, Republican candidates jumped in (particularly UP Congressman Phil Ruppe), and Griffin began missing votes. Many votes. Republicans, led by Griffin's good friend Governor Bill Milliken, grew fearful about losing the seat and prevailed on Griffin to run again, but the damage of wanting out and then in again had been done.

Griffin earned a primary opponent but put that down with 77%. With Detroit Council President Carl Levin, though, he could do no such thing. Levin had forged trust from blacks and whites and had support where Griffin lacked it: Detroit. However, Griffin was also abandoned by Republican friends of Ruppe when he changed his mind. He called for "new blood." And he raised the issue of his absenteeism. Levin said that "if any of us missed 216 days of work in a year, we'd be fired."

Meanwhile, Griffin did dive back into his legislative duties. After the Panama Canal Treaty was approved, Griffin remarked, "I hope history will prove President Carter right. I have been very concerned that history is going to prove advocates of this treaty wrong." Ford took part in an Election eve rally for Griffin but it wasn't enough. Levin won 52-48%. The day after the vote, Griffin said after he had "no instant analysis" but admitted his change "must have been quite a factor ... more than I ever had anticipated." He added, "I did change my mind. I really did." Michigan Republican Party Executive Director Jerry Rowe said, "Griffin had a very difficult time convincing people he could do the job after saying he wanted out." For his part, Levin called the day "the time to thank Robert Griffin for his service in Washington."

Griffin returned to Travis City and became senior counsel to the law firm Miller, Canfield, Paddock & Stone in Detroit; eight years after his defeat, however, he got a new lease on political life. He was elected to the Michigan Supreme Court and upon his swearing-in said, "If instant wisdom does not come automatically with the donning of this robe, at least I want you to know that I shall be doing my very best to grow into those measurements. In so doing, I shall keep in mind the guidance of Benjamin Cardozo, who wrote, 'The judge ... is not a knight-errant, roaming at will in pursuit of his own ideal of beauty or of goodness. [Rather] he is to draw his inspiration from consecrated principles. He is not to yield to spasmodic sentiment, to vague and unregulated benevolence. He is to exercise a discretion informed by tradition, methodized by analogy, disciplined by system, and subordinated to the...necessity of order in the social life." Williams was on hand for the occasion, quipping, "I also am particularly grateful to you Bob, that you waited long enough to let the constitution retire me, rather than take more direct means."

Griffin is now 91 years old and still lives in Traverse City.

Photo courtesy of Central Michigan University

Republican Mathias' Liberalism Caused Him Problems With Own Party But Affection Second To None

Historic Tidbit: In his book *Too Funny To Be President*, Mo Udall recalls receiving a letter that stated the following: "I read where Congress is staying up late at night trying to find something else to regulate or tax. Have they thought about sex? It is a luxury; would not produce undue hardship; could be spread over a large segment of the population: would let the teenagers contribute; would give the oldsters a tax break; and is not discriminatory to race, religion, or national orgin."

Normally, when a Senator appears on Nixon's "enemies list," opposes a Balanced Budget amendment and conservative judicial nominees, enjoys strong backing from labor, and attacks the "New Right," that person would be a Democrat. Not Charles McC.Mathias. The three-term Senator from Maryland was called "one of the last unabashed Senate liberals in the GOP" by *The Washington Post* and was among the most popular politicians in the state—so much so that in his last re-election in 1980, he carried every county in the state.

Photo courtesy of the U.S. Senate Historical Collections

For Mathias, if it sometimes felt as though the only thing he had was his Senate seat itself, that was sometimes the case. In a state like Maryland, outreach and partnership with Democrats were a must, and his popularity suggests he was quite successful. In Washington, though, it would prevent his career from going at maximum speed.

The Almanac of American Politics called Mathias a "model of probity and integrity . . . one of those Senators whose balance is considered sound and whose judgement on difficult issues is respected and sought."

With his middle name - McCurdy - Mathias was known as "Mac." He long had a career in western Maryland, serving as the Frederick Attorney and being sent to Annapolis as a State Senator. He won a seat in Congress in 1960 partially by attacking his opponent for voting too much with the ADA, perhaps not realizing that he would soon become an ally. He became the only Republican from Maryland to win a federal office that fall.

Mathias played a key role in the Civil Rights Act of 1964. He attempted to do the same with open-housing provisions in 1966 but was not successful. Mathias met Martin Luther King, Jr. in Selma, and at the start of the new Congress in 1965, he was among 22 members (17 Democrats, 5 Republicans) who advocated for not seating the Mississippi delegation due to the exclusion of African-Americans at polling places during the previous election. When the Voting Rights Act became law that year, Mathias was equally pleased. The Act, he said, was "really the whole core of the civil rights movement. It made a tremendous improvement . . . There was a new recognition of black citizenship." And on another subject entirely, Mathias authored a paper: "How to End the Draft: The Case for an All Volunteer Army."

For the Presidential election that fall, Mathias was clearly uncomfortable with GOP nominee Barry Goldwater. He took three weeks before making a public decision but finally declared his support for "Republican nominees at every level . . . I am for Goldwater, Beall, and all others on the ticket."

When Mathias decided to challenge U.S. Senator Daniel Brewster in 1968, his odds were not great, but neither were Spiro Agnew's when he had sought the Governorship and he had been elected just two years before. In a strange twist, Brewster had been Mathias' roommate at the University of Maryland—but he was also an alcoholic, which by then was no secret in Washington, and Mathias attacked him as a "messenger boy" for labor.

Agnew's place on the national ticket gave Mathias an additional boost. The Nixon/Agnew ticket narrowly lost Maryland, but it's probable that Mathias was able to swim on his own. George Mahoney, a conservative Democrat ("A man's home is his castle") who often waged quixotic but nevertheless losing bids for office, was running for the seat as an Independent. Mathias himself used his opposition to the war and his support for busing and D.C. home rule to cut into Brewster's support among liberals, who were upset with Brewster for backing the war. This allowed Mathias to beat Brewster with 48%. The incumbent took just 39%.

Mathias immediately showed that his independence was genuine. He marched with liberals, including Gloria Steinem, in support of the Equal Rights Amendment. He championed campaign finance and undertook a 450-mile tour of the Chesapeake Bay, which he made it a major undertaking to preserve. Keeping intact Maryland's battlefields, such as Antietam, was also high on his list.

Mathias opposed Nixon's two controversial Supreme Court nominees, Carswell and Haynesworth. Of the latter, he said "The only conclusion to which I can bring myself, is that his confirmation would lower all judicial standards at a time when the public is anxious to see them raised." This earned him a place on Nixon's "enemies list." *The Post* wrote that he "supported his Republican colleagues only 31 percent of the time during his first term and compiled a voting record more liberal than those of most Democrats." He also favored reigning in certain Presidential powers which the Nixon Administration might not have appreciated.

A Mathias button and a meeting via Supreme Court nominee Lewis Powell
Photo via NPR

Joe Tydings, Mathias's Democratic colleague for two years prior to his 1970 defeat, called him a "great guy" and eventually, Mathias became known as the "Conscience of the Senate." This reputation undoubtedly helped him in the Watergate year against a brash, determined social worker named Barbara Mikulski, against whom he carried every county except for Baltimore - where he came close - only to retain his seat with 57%.

Mathias bemoaned those who sought to pigeonhole his ideology. "I'm not all that liberal. In fact, in some respects I'm conservative. A while ago I introduced a bill preserving the guarantees of the Bill of Rights by prohibiting warrantless wiretaps. I suppose they'll say it's another liberal effort, but it's as conservative as you can get. It's conserving the Constitution." Campaign finance was another passion. "Watergate is the turning point in our nation's history," he said in 1973. "If we turn our backs to the grievous attacks that have been made on the Constitution and the laws of the land under the vague incantations of one man's view of national security, we will have lost our right to hold the precious gift of freedom won for us almost 200 years ago by men of courage, integrity and intelligence."

Mathias' disenchantment with the system enabled him to seriously flirt with making a Presidential bid in 1976, but he withdrew without serious support.

After the 1976 elections, Mathias rightfully should have assumed a place as ranking member of the Senate Judiciary Committee, but more rank-and-file Republicans opposed his ascension and reluctantly persuaded Strom Thurmond, far more senior to Mathias, to abandon his own cushy ranking-member position at Armed Services to bump Mathias. Thurmond continued at Judiciary when Republicans took control of the Senate in 1980. Mathias, who at first wasn't even awarded a consolation sub-committee Chairmanship, was eventually given the helm of the unglamorous Patents, Copyrights, and Trademark Chairmanship. Eventually, Howard Baker gave him a full committee chairmanship – Rules - but that was more internal. Mathias had complained that "New Right" candidates backed by Jerry Falwell were "cannibalizing" the party.

Baker's wife, Kansas Senator Nancy Kassebaum, another thoughtful moderate who served with Mathias, said he had a "good, quiet sense of humor, sense of balance and was knowledgeable about what was valuable." In particularly, she cited his perspective of history. When Baker was Ambassador to Japan, Mathias stayed with them in Tokyo while visiting on business.

On economic and defense matters, Mathias was no less independent. He opposed an amendment retaining funds for the "Star Wars" defense research program, school prayer, and the Balanced Budget Amendment; on the latter, his vote was pivotal. He joined just three other Republican Senators in opposing President Reagan's plan to stop COLA increases for Social Security. Even in routine election matters, Mathias often proved a thorn in the spine of his party. He refused to serve on the steering committee for Ronald Reagan in 1980, the same year he was facing the voters or a third time.

Maryland colleagues Mathias and Sarbanes on Judiciary.
Photo courtesy of the U.S. Senate Historical Collection

This jarred Mathias somewhat as he faced re-nomination that same year, as Republicans called him a "communist' and "baby killer." Conservative GOP Congressman Robert Bauman toyed with the idea of taking on Mathias, who considered standing for a third term as an Independent, but ultimately didn't (having been implicated in a sex scandal a year later, Maryland's Democratic Governor would have chosen his successor had he won). Five opponents held Mathias to 55%, but the general was no contest, as he dispatched his Democratic opponent with 66%, this time carrying Baltimore.

In 1985, Mathias announced his retirement: "the season has arrived to shift to a new field of activity." While he predicted the age of the Republican moderate would rise again, he must've known that it would not come in his lifetime—in 2008, he endorsed Barack Obama for President, writing, "my great-grandfather ran for the Maryland Senate from Frederick on the anti-slavery Republican ticket. At the top of that ticket was Abraham Lincoln." He died of Parkinson's in 2010.

In 1980, Mathias payed tribute to Birch Bayh, a recently defeated Democratic colleague from Indiana. He spoke of how "politics of conscience is high risk politics. It's practitioners are few; it's rewards uncertain" and added Bayh "did not shrink from doing what he thought was right." It was a touching tribute and Mathias could just as well have been speaking about himself.

CHAPTER SEVENTY

Lincoln Expert Schwengel Founded
the Capitol Hill Society

Historic Quote: "Fred won't be happy until he's shot at Ford's Theater." – A friend of Iowa Congressman Fred Schwengel, a Republican whose passion for knowledge about the 16th president and the Civil War was legendary.

Photo via the U.S. Capitol Historical Society

Fred Schwengel represented farm country in Iowa so it was unusual that he could be such a profound champion of the interests of Washington D.C. But Schwengel was a student of history and as a result, he deeply cared about the capitol city – as well as the Capitol building itself, realizing its potential and achieving recognition as the crown jewel that it was. The same went for preserving the memory of his here, Abraham Lincoln

For many, including Donald Kaul, Schwengel was "a Midwestern cornball idealist who never forgot where he came from or lost sight of where he was going." Schwengel's parents were German immigrants - Baptist he notes in a country that was heavily Roman Catholic or Lutheran. Describing Germans as, "kind of clanish," Schwengel credits the area as "good for farming and easy to get to by train in that period. He recalls his father putting a sign on the door of their home which read, "Children, here we speak German." This gave him a limited grasp on English which he said made it difficult when he began school.

The Des Moines Register, in its obituary of the lawmaker, noted that Schwengel's "father believed an education was sufficient that taught a boy reading, writing and some math skills. Schwengel wanted to go on to high school, however, so he left home and lived with another family while working his way through Sheffield High School." He didn't stop at high school. He attended college – Northeast State Teacher's College where he earned a Bachelor of Science in Education. He was active in track and field, football, the drama club and of course, the school's Historical Society. It was in college that he met Clara Ethel Cassity. They married shortly after graduation and had two children. Schwengel then earned a Master's degree at the University of Iowa. But he returned to Missouri to both teach and coach. When low pay forced Schwengel out and he turned to insurance. He eventually served as president of the Iowa Chamber of Commerce.

Schwengel (top row, third from left) with his family
Photo via the U.S. Capitol Historical Society

Schwengel's political career began when he won a seat in the Iowa State House in 1944. Simultaneously, he would serve as a member of the Iowa Development Commission. In 1954, Schwengel won the House seat being vacated by Republican Thomas Martin with 57%, a solid margin given that Democrats were recapturing control of both houses of Congress. Assigned to the Public Works Committee, he was among the leaders of legislation creating an Interstate System of Highways.

He also requested assignment to the District of Columbia Committee because he felt strongly in the need for the city to have home-rule.

So devoted to Lincoln was Schwengel that it was not unusual for him to lead several commemorative events related to important events in Lincoln's life. As the 150th anniversary of his birth approached, his hard work set the stage for Lincoln poet and author Carl Sandberg to address a joint session of Congress on the 150th anniversary of his birth. And he introduced legislation to restore Ford's Theater to its appearance at the time of Lincoln's murder. He also co-chaired the Civil War Centennial Commission. But Schwengel went well beyond Lincoln when it came to preserving ideals. By 1962, he realized that there was no mechanism for the Capitol to preserve its rich history whether it be its construction or the colorful men (and at that time a handful of women), who served there. When Schwengel approached House Speaker Sam Rayburn, he delegated him the honor of rectifying the matter. The result was a Capitol Historical Society of which Schwengel served as president for 30 years. The organization's first publication - a Capitol guidebook, was being printed on the afternoon President Kennedy was assassinated. WhenSchwengel got the word, he ordered the presses stopped and the insertion of the late president's photo along with the words, "We the people mourn."

Pride in his capital wasn't Schwengel's only aspiration. He also wanted Americans to have pride in their flag and every Flag Day, he would deliver a speech entitled, "I am the flag." It delineated America's early history and how its government came to be.

**Schwengel (left) accompanies President Eisenhower
at the Lincoln Sesquicentennial
Photo via the National Park Service**

When it came to issues, though the district Schwengel represented was fairly conservative, it did have a sizable university presence andSchwengel's voting record was that of a quintessential moderate. He himself summed it up his philosophy thus: "I believe that moderation is a virtue--especially in a democracy of contending interests--and that extremism is a divisive vice ... I have come to the conclusion that moderation is to be recommended above all political philosophies because it alone recognizes the common fate and aspiration of all human beings; it alone understands the influence that drive people to extremes; and finally, moderation alone respects the sacredness of humanity."

As well expected from an idol of Lincoln, Schwengel was a passionate supporter of civil rights legislation. At the Lincoln Memorial, Schwengel credited the 16th president with Lincoln. "The authoritative position of the government of the United States is the position this nation left us from the restatement you left us of the meaning of free government; that is government of the people, for the people, and by the people - as originally stated by the Founding Fathers. Not some people - all people. It began from the hour you issued the Proclamation of Emancipation." Schwengelinitially was cool to the 1968 civil rights legislation - in part because he viewed the open-housing portion of the legislation was weaker than Iowa's law, but that changed with the riots that accompanied the assassination of Dr. Martin Luther King, Jr.

Calling it, "the time for us in the white community to go the extra mile and to have patience." Schwengel was also disturbed by the fact that House members would not be permitted to offer amendments upon receiving the legislation from the Senate and was hoping that spending required to address poverty would be paid for by cuts in other areas. "We need new approaches that harness the talents of business and more closely involve state and local government." He steadfastly favored home rule for Washington D.C. and with California Democrat Ron Dellums, introduced legislation to make it the 51st state. But Schwengel was also fiscal conservative and took heat from Democrats for backing the GOP alternative for renewal of the Education and Secondary Education Act in 1967. "A number of educators are wondering why he has asked for their advice after the House has already acted and after he himself has cast four consecutive votes to either weaken or destroy the bill." Boyle continued "Schwengel supported a motion to recommit the entire bill for further study which is the classic and traditional method of killing a piece of legislation."

Schwengel was against school prayer and was among five Representatives - and the only Republican, to gather in the office of Congressman Jim Corman for a meeting with Jim Hamilton of the National Council of Churches. He took issue with the bill's sponsor, Ohio Congressman Chalmers Wylie, who contended that local governments should be able to structure prayer. Schwengel responded, "I think we'd lower the quality of prayer if we let the state write it." On other matters, Schwengel led the crusade against legislation to allow wider buses on highways. In a 1971 debate, he said we are "woefully lacking in solid information with respect to the effect of this legislation on highway safety."

During Schwengel's first ten year stint in Congress, his firm electoral hold on his district never wavered. As late as October of 1964, he was considered a safe for a sixth term. But '64 was LBJ'S year and his opponent, John Schmidhauser, hit him for spending too much time on affairs of Washington D.C. He ousted the incumbent by a slim 51-49% margin. By 1966, Democrats were on the defense and Schwengel wanted back. Ex-Vice-President Richard Nixon, seeking support for his forthcoming political comeback, stumped the district for Schwengel. Vietman was an issue and Schwengel took middle ground between Schmidhauser, who opposed the conflict, and President Johnson. "We ought not to escalate the ground war in any manner", and should try harder to solve "the political, economic and social problems of Viet Nam." However, he also has said, "we should. . . blockade North Viet Nam's ports and deny them any help from nations we're helping and who should be our friends."

Schwengel also tried to lay the blame of inflation at the Democrats feet. They name the farmer, they've tried to blame the banker, they've tried to name the wage earner who wants increased pay, but when it comes right down to it, they have no one to blame but themselves." He narrowly won back the seat. The two men met a third time in 1968 but this time, Schwengel's margin was less ambiguous. That was anything but the case two years later. First came the primary. David Stanley had just come off a shocking near upset of Iowa Governor Harold Hughes for the open Senate seat and he used his name recognition to challenge Schwengel from the right. He held him to 56%. Ed Mezvinsky. In one of the closest contests in the nation, Schwengel escaped defeat by just 765 votes. Mezvinsky sought to finish the job in '72 and attacked Schwengel for often "being uncommitted on issues." Schwengel carried seven of the district's 13 counties but Mezvinsky took handsome margins in the most populated (save Muscatine which Schwengel carried) for a 53-46^ win. Schwengel stayed in Washington, not as a lobbyist but as a congressional tour guide.

Jim Leach, who in 1976 won Schwengel's district back for the GOP by beating Mezvinsky said on his death, "There is literally no member that has ever served here who loved this Congress and history more than Fred Schwengel. He was guided, he noted, as a member, by three principles: One was to respond to his conscience. One was to represent his constituents. And the third was never to do anything that reflected unfavorably on this body." Neal Smith called him "an absolute model of integrity."

A Fred Schwengel Memorial Bridge over the Mississippi in the Quad Cities is a monument to the man who gave so much to the region. A U.S.

Capitol Historical Society Chairman's Fred Schwengel award is presented to "individuals and organizations that have promoted freedom, democracy and representative government." Ethel outlived Fred by 18 years, passing away in 2011 at age 102.

The Fred Schwengel Memorial Bridge

Chapter Seventy-One

Stewart Udall: The Quieter Brother of the Two—But No Less Influential

Historic Tidbit: Barry Goldwater and Hubert Humphrey were friends. Even in their fiercest legislative disagreements, they never let politics come between them. One day, Humphrey joked that Goldwater was handsome enough that he should consider a movie career. He said Goldwater should be part of "19th Century Fox."

Stu Udall in 1961 and during Mo's 1976 Presidential Campaign
Left photo courtesy of the Office of the U.S. Department of the Interior and right Photo courtesy of the University of Arizona

When one thinks of the Udall brothers, Mo is the one who naturally comes to mind. After all, he was a major Presidential candidate, had one of the most legendary senses of humor of nearly anyone in public life, and is a hero to many generations of environmentalists for his contribution to the movement. Some may not even be aware that another Udall exists. Stewart was more than content to play second fiddle to Mo, but as far as contributions to society go, he was anything but. In fact, Stewart actually paved the way for Mo to assume a role in public life, and his accomplishments as Secretary of Interior in the Kennedy and Johnson administrations made some of Mo Udall's early dreams a reality. In terms of history at large, he was the last surviving member of JFK's cabinet. On a lighter note, it was he who arranged for Robert Frost to read poetry at Kennedy's inauguration.

Stewart was a Congressman from Arizona from 1954 to 1961. When newly-elected President John F. Kennedy named Udall Secretary of Interior, it was one of only a few appointments that were a surprise to no one. Upon confirmation by the Senate, Stewart resigned his House seat, and Mo won it. For the older Udall, just 40 years old, his career was already one of many distinctions.

First there was basketball. Following service as a Mormon missionary and a World War II gunner, Stewart was a member of the first Arizona team to play at the National Invitational Tournament at Madison Square Garden. However, Udall also had politics in his blood. Born to a large Mormon family in tiny St. Johns near the New Mexico border, Udall's father Levi served on the Arizona Supreme Court. According to Udall.gov, Levi's philosophy was for young folks to seek political office: "If good folks don't run for office and try to make things go, the bad folks will." Stewart said he "never called it politics. He called it public service." That opportunity came in 1954 when incumbent Harold Patten retired. At that time, Arizona had just two Congressional seats, and the seat Udall would win contained every part of the state but Phoenix. He took 62%.

Ardently pro-labor (opposing Right-To-Work laws) and civil rights, Udall became an influential part of the 100-member Democratic Study Group. Success came in his first year when Speaker Rayburn made him the only freshman to serve on the House delegation for the NATO committee and when minimum wage legislation he co-sponsored (to $1.00 an hour) was signed into law. He also championed local needs, such as dams. His legislation led to the Glen Canyon Dam, and he was successful in getting the town of "Page" on Arizona's side.

Udall's influence intensified when he helped organize "organizational seminars" for the heavily Democratic freshman Congressional class of 1958; he also became close with Kennedy, at the time the junior Senator from Massachusetts, and worked with him a labor issues. At a convention where every vote counted, he became pivotal. Arizona was thought to be firmly in the hands of Johnson, and ex-Senator Ernest McFarland was thought to be a force sure to preserve it. However, Udall almost singularly promoted Kennedy among the delegation, and when the roll call came, all 17 went to the man who would become the 35th President.

That fall, Udall won his fourth House term with 56%—by far his lowest percentage—but it mattered little. Everyone expected Kennedy to reward him with a position, and it was no surprise that what he got was Secretary of the Interior. In making the announcement, Kennedy said Udall "will bring vision and imagination" to preserving "America's vast and abundant natural resources." Sure enough, at his first press conference after winning confirmation, Udall told reporters, "We are looking to the horizon. We are not afraid of big ideas . . . big programs if they are in the national interest."

Udall, who joked that he was born with "a shovel in his hand," had a mission: for Americans to have a "land conscience." He operated under the belief that "nature will take precedence over the needs of the modern man," but privately, and to some extent publicly, he worried that it wouldn't. In a 1963 book, *The*

Quiet Crisis, he expressed fear that pollution and drilling could cause a "quiet conservation crisis." Udall's overriding goal, though, was preservation.

For those who travel to Ellis Island to celebrate their ancestry, Stewart Udall is the man to thank—it was designated a national monument on his watch. For those who love to vacation at Cape Cod or the Outer Banks of the Carolinas, Stu Udall's protection made that possible. And for those who enjoy the Appalachian National Scenic Trail, the North Cascades National Park, Canyonlands National Park, to name only a few, Stewart Udall played a significant role in their development as well.

Udall was instrumental in getting Robert Frost to read poetry at JFK's inaugural
Photo courtesy of the National Park Service

The latter was particularly burdensome to enact. According to NPS.gov, during a flyover, "Bureau of Reclamation Chief Floyd Dominy showed Udall where he wanted the 'next big dam.' But where Dominy saw a reservoir, Udall saw a national park."

Udall didn't necessarily see eye-to-eye with President Johnson, but aside from Dean Rusk, he was the only Kennedy cabinet Secretary to remain for the entirety of both administrations. Insofar as the "Great Society" focused on environmental matters, Udall was very much at the helm when it came to passage. The Wilderness Act of 1964 protected 440 acres of wilderness in 44 states. There was also the Solid Waste Disposal Act, the Environmental Species Protection Act, the National Historic Preservation Act, and, for Arizona, the long sought Central Arizona Project. California's delegation was mighty—38 members. "To save Arizona's project, Udall had to offer incentives for California's support, but his attempt almost cost him a rebellion in Arizona."

Photo via Treehugger.org

Culture was not left out of the mix, either. His department had a hand in the preservation of Ford's Theater, the Kennedy Center, the National Endowment of the Humanities, and Wolf Trap Farm Park.

How was he able to achieve and sustain his success? For starters, "I never lost an argument with the budget people under either Kennedy or Johnson. If you had a new national park or a new policy on wilderness or something on wild rivers . . . they'd say, 'Go ahead. It's a good idea.'" Udall's zeal had limits, however, as evidenced by the fact that he was often hard at work on his agenda until the last possible moments. As he prepared to leave office, Johnson's final act was to review a Udall plan that would preserve 7.5 million acres by Executive Order. Johnson favored conservation but was concerned about the level Udall was proposing. "A President shouldn't take this much land without approval from Congress," LBJ told an aide. He settled for four parks, among them Marble Canyon.

**Udall (jacketless) with Congressman "Bizz" Johnson
and other northern California officials, 1968
Photo courtesy of the Johnson Family**

While Udall's expertise was environmental policy, he couldn't help but create a stir or two on other matters. For instance, he said after the Bay of Pigs that "the fascinating thing about this business is here was a plan conceived by one administration—this from all I can find out began over a year ago and President Eisenhower directed it. And here the actual plan was carried out under a successor administration." The administration dismissed the assertion, defining a part of the Kennedy legacy of accepting the blame. A statement read, "He bears sole responsibility for the events of the past few days and is strongly opposed to anyone within or without the administration attempting to shift the responsibility."

Udall (center) at the Canyonlands
Photo courtesy of the National Parks Service

Stu Udall's contribution to helping others did not end with his cabinet service. For example, he helped Navajo workers sue the federal government after they acquired cancer as a result of working with uranium. Through it all, he continued his personal love of nature. He hiked the Grand Canyon well into his 80s. When he died at 90 years old in 2010, he had the thrill of seeing the torch passed to a new generation of Udalls. His son Tom was elected U.S. Senator from New Mexico, and on the same day, Mo's son Mark became a Senator from Colorado. Both have served as Congressmen during the last ten years.

In closing, Udall had a saying, "Cherish sunset, wild creatures and wild papers. Have a love affair with the wonders of the earth." Under his long career, he made all of that possible. And the nation will be forever grateful.

Photo and image courtesy of the Stewart L. Udall
Collection, The University of Arizona Library

The Morton Brothers –Thruston and Rogers Enjoyed Capitol Hill Respect: Realistic And Able Pols With Close Proximity To Nixon and Ford

Historic Tidbit: "The primaries are really narrowing down the candidates. The Democrats are down to 28 – and the Republicans are down to one and a half. Governor Reagan did stop in at the White House not too long ago. He wanted to take a look around. He said he couldn't stay long. I said, 'You better believe it." He went to the bathroom to wash up and I told him to be sure he used the guest towels. Let me congratulate Governor Carter on his fine speech. There's the Governor over there. It's easy to see where he sits. Now if we could only figure out where he stands." - Gerald Ford at a 1976 Gridiron dinner. At the time, he was in the midst of a furious primary battle with Ronald Reagan. Multiple Democrats, led by Carter, were waiting to take him on.

Before the Bush brothers, there were the Mortons: Thruston Ballard Morton of Kentucky and Rogers Clark Ballard Morton of Maryland. Throughout his time in Congress and the White House, Gerald Ford was befriended by both. Rogers and Thruston, the latter of whom later moved onto the Senate, each were well-versed in Presidential advising as well as vice-presidential selection (Ford felt Thruston should have had the post in 1960 while eight years later, a very reluctant Roger sold his fellow Marylander Spiro Agnew to Nixon against his judgement but at his candidate's prodding). Each served as Republican National Committee Chair but were ultimately recognized for always putting their best feet forward when it came to comity and the interests of the nation. As such, they were considered to be among the most realistic, able, and respected politicians of their era, serving their nation and Presidents with tremendous honor.

"Thrust" had befriended Ford when both served in the House together. "Rog" also served with Ford in Congress in addition to having been a member of the Nixon cabinet; however, he probably reached the pinnacle of power as a member of Ford's transition team and as his trusted advisor. Politically, the brothers had similar inclinations with a single exception—in 1968, Thruston was a hearty supporter of Nelson Rockefeller, while Roger was a floor manager for Nixon at the Republican Convention.

With the brothers coming in at 6'2 and 6'6 respectively, a running joke in the Morton family when Thurston was in office was that he could not be overshadowed—little did they know. Even Thurston couldn't help stirring the pot. "My kid brother Rog—why he's the biggest man in Congress," he said. "He's a hog farmer and he weighs anywhere from 235 to 275 pounds. When the price of hogs goes up, he sells them. When the price of hogs go down, he eats them."

The Mortons were born in Louisville, descendants of Kentucky settlers who owned a flour business called Ballard and Ballard. The pride of the family business was reflected in both names, as each contained "Ballard." And both ended up with storied Washington careers.

Both were Yale men. Upon graduation, Thruston returned to take a hand in the business, eventually becoming chairman of the board. First, though, war interrupted his plans, and during the war Morton achieved quite a record. As he recalled in an oral history project, he "spent 51 months in the Navy, most of it at sea." He returned to find that "the business had gotten in pretty bad shape during the war . . . I couldn't get interested in it." By 1946, Thruston was persuaded to go for a seat in Congress. As he recalled, "anybody that had run on the Republican ticket without a jail record would have been elected—and I was, very, very easily." In fact, he stunned incumbent Emmett O'Neil by winning with a solid margin of 58-42%. John F. Kennedy and Richard Nixon were in that class, and Ford joined them a term later when Thruston had a little more difficulty in his own race—Kentuckian Alben Barkley was atop the ticket but won with 53%.

Nixon appeared in Kentucky with Thruston for a hotel dedication
Photo courtesy of the Ray Hill Collection

Morton remembered his first major advocacy as a Congressman for his district—who was there to help him? Lyndon Baines Johnson. Private companies were being given incentives to take over government plants but one Louisville area plant was having some difficulty. Enter Johnson. Democrats were in the minority but Johnson had a commanding presence, and he was ranking member of a critical subcommittee. Johnson promised to help him. As Morton recalls, "I couldn't get the same cooperationfrom my Republican friends. And he did, and went to conference, and finally we got the amendment in the final bill. So my first contact, or association, with President Johnson was one that helped me, and for which I've always been grateful."

Rogers did not run for re-election in 1952 and instead accepted a State Department post in the Eisenhower administration. Ike had reason to be grateful. The Kentucky delegation was solidly behind Bob Taft but Morton led a group of you Republicans for Eisenhower. In the end, every Kentucky delegate but one voted for Taft. The sole exception: Thruston Morton. Morton's job included sifting through intelligence for the higher-ups at 5 a.m. He recalls having been the first person to see LBJ after the Majority Leader's 1955 heart attack. But by 1956, he was persuaded to resign and seek a return to electoral politics.

It seemed that Kentucky Governor Earle Clements would glide into the seat but Morton gave an early boost to Republican fortunes that night by beating him by 7,000 votes, 50.3-49.7%. The party surely savored that one as Republicans could not regain control of the Senate. He won a more comfortable-than-expected win in 1962 against Lieutenant Governor Wilson Wyatt. In that race, Kennedy made a personal visit to Louisville to stump for Wyatt; he asked to "say a word . . . in defense of Wilson Wyatt's opponent. He has been criticized, unfairly, I think, because he has refused to put the word 'Republican' on his signs, even though he was once chairman of the Republican Party. But I ask you: If you were a candidate for office in 1962, would you put the word 'Republican' on your literature? What does it mean to elect the man?"

Courtesy of the U.S. Senate Historical Office

Ford thought so highly of Thruston Morton that in 1960, he was his first and only choice for a running mate for Richard Nixon. In his book *A Time To Heal*, he wrote that Morton's had many diverse strengths. He "was a moderate, he'd served in both Houses of Congress, and in the state Department as an Assistant Secretary under Ike and he would, I felt, give the ticket a nice balance geographically." Nixon had apparently already decided on Lodge but was still inviting Ford to a meeting to discuss the selection. Ford wondered why the meeting was necessary if he had already decided but he attended nevertheless and still made the case for Morton. That may have been his first exposure to the true Nixon. "Making up his mind and then pretending that his options were still open—that was a Nixon trait I'd have occasion to witness again."

Ike appointed Thruston chair of the Republican National Committee after the 1958 elections in which the party had taken a bloodbath. Almost immediately, he recognized the importance of attracting minorities. It was just after the razor-tight election of John F. Kennedy; Morton, noting Kennedy's margin of 2,700,000 votes in twelve cities, vowed that it "won't happen again." He also said, though, that the party needed to appoint more minorities to high-ranking GOP positions. Despite his role, Morton sided with the administration on an early initiative: an administration request to borrow $8,800,000,000 for long-term development loans overseas.

Often, Thruston found himself in the position of simply trying to stabilize disputes. During the 1964 platform discussion, Nelson Rockefeller was repeatedly shot down by backers of Barry Goldwater. It fell on Morton to tell them to mind their manners ("now look, the Governor has been up here for ten minutes and he's only talked about four"). Then, Morton tried to steer attention toward the Democrats. Delegates, he said, should "fasten your seat belts." He called the other party a "bumbling bunch of party hacks" with "one of the biggest bundles" in history. When Everett Dirksen criticized Ford –who was by then his House counterpart in terms of strategic moves—Morton often tried to broker understandings and unity.

Monitoring the 1966 election results
Photo courtesy of the Gerald Ford Presidential Library and Museum

Morton was ashamed when Kennedy was killed because he had just finished delivering a "partisan" speech in St. Louis when informed of the news but, headed into 1964, an election year, he recognized the futility of trying to overcome the "Let Us continue" popularity that the Johnson administration was enjoying. The party, he said, would just have to "ride out" Johnson's popularity. Even during election time, Morton stuck by that philosophy. The 1966 midterms were a time in which the Vietnam War was raging; Morton viewed as critical the opinion of the watching world. Appearing on one talk show, Morton said, "The point that I make is that we as a (Republican) party going to attack him (Pres. Johnson) on matters of this kind (Vietnam). We're going to basically support him in the strong policy there. We're going to point out, as the Loyal Opposition and a responsible, I hope, opposition suggestions we think we can help bring this thing to an honorable close quickly, regardless of the political situation. I think the political situation would die. I think it would at least calm down if the people realized that there is in fact a pacification of the country."

Socially, Morton was solidly in favor of civil rights legislation, even urging many in his own party not to remove federal protections as they debated the 1968 act. During the contentious debate over the jury amendment a decade earlier, he had tried to offer a "perfecting" amendment but it was voted down. Like his Kentucky colleague John Sherman Cooper, Morton became a critic of the Vietnam War. When the Kennedys gave speeches opposing it, Morton inserted them into the Congressional Record. However, he did oppose Medicare and a few other aspects of the "Great Society." Morton, along with George McGovern, introduced the resolution that would ultimately reduce the cloture requirement to 60 from 67.

The New York Times noted that Morton "suggested that President Johnson not seek re-election" in 1968 yet he also said, "I do not expect a man so mesmerized by power to relinquish it voluntarily." Thruston himself was ready to not seek re-election that year ("To use an old Kentucky expression, I suppose I am just plain track sore") and left office with his dignity intact.

At the San Francisco Bridge (left) and during the Ford years (right)
Left photo courtesy of the Oliver Atkins Collection of the George Mason
University Libraries; right photo courtesy of the Gerald Ford Library and Museum)

Around the same time, Rogers was rising to high levels of prominence in the nation's capital. Like his brother, he had attended Yale and briefly pursued a medical degree at Columbia University College of Physicians and Surgeons. Rogers served in the war as well, in the field artillery. His return found him at the helm of Ballard and Ballard before Pillsbury acquired it. His love of the environment had been evident even since his boyhood days. "My brother was a hell of a good boatman at the age of eight," Thruston recalled. "When we were kids . . . he was always missing at lunch and our mother would send me out to find him. I never had to look very far because he would always be down at the pond fishing, and if I didn't get him, he'd fish right through lunch."

Rogers had been his brother's campaign manager, which taught him the tricks of the trade, but he wound up pursuing campaigns outside of Kentucky. For Rogers, it was off to Maryland where he purchased a 1,000-acre, 14-room house named Presqu'Ile that overlooked the Wye River. As operator of a cattle fishing business, Morton was literally living high on a hog, but the political bug is hard to shake and Morton again found himself managing a Congressional campaign. In a heavily Democratic district, the candidate lost but Rogers was persuaded to run himself two years later and took a 53% win. He hung on by the same margin in 1964, a year that was much less favorable to Republicans. Rogers agonized somewhat but did back the Civil Rights Act (many in his district opposed it). Despite his wealth, his mindset was one of compassion for the poor. "How can we expect people who live with rats and filth and squalor to embrace the American dream," he asked. In fact, Rogers traveled the country following Barry Goldwater's defeat in an effort to rebuild the party and spoke of attracting minorities and the poor. Ford described him as "a hulking bear of a man . . . but he was also one of the gentlest people I have ever known. No one got mad at him."

In a Democratic House with a Democratic President, Morton's Congressional career was going nowhere though he did have some success protecting the Eastern Shore and Cheseapeake Bay. His nature was always a great gift, however. His aide Jay French recalls a drive in D.C. during the tensions over Vietnam. "We were in a place where kids were clearly going to disrupt the event we were attending. They were radicals, and loud, and he walked right into the middle of the group, and of course towered over them with that 6'7 foot frame. By the end, everyone was laughing. It was just the way he had with people when there were disagreements. He seemed so darned reasonable to people."

That may have been one reason that Morton submitted his name to the Maryland General Assembly for the Governorship when Spiro Agnew became vice-president but, with a heavily Democratic majority, he never had a chance. 1969 saw a change in fortune. First he won a seat on the powerful Ways and Means committee, but then, Republican National Committeeman Ray Bliss resigned and Nixon offered Morton the post. He accepted the position minus the salary. Soon, there were bigger fish to fry. As it came time to name a running mate, Nixon huddled with six advisors, including Morton. "Rog, what's your take on Agnew," Nixon asked. Morton replied that he "has a tendency to be lazy." When Nixon told Morton, "you might be a better choice for me," Morton quickly shot back, "If it's between me and Ted Agnew, Ted would be the better choice." Nixon immediately turned to John Mitchell and ordered him to "call Agnew." The rest is history.

Rogers was tapped to be Richard Nixon's Secretary of the Interior in 1970, having been passed over for his dream job when Nixon first took office and promised Alaska Governor Wally Hickel the post during the campaign. No Easterner had ever held it. That would change. Hickel was dismissed in 1970 and Morton got the job. As he was sworn in, Nixon lauded his environmental credentials. He told the audience "Rogers Morton has this feeling in his heart, because he loves the outdoors, because he spoke to me about the environment very feelingly long before I became a candidate for president in 1968 . . . And I think Theodore Roosevelt in this historic room, if he were here today, would say, 'This is a great time.' And I believe it requires a big man for a big job." Obviously referring to Morton's size, Nixon added, "We have a big man, big in every way."

Morton's most lasting legacy was approving the Alaskan pipeline, but his relationship with Ford was such that when it became clear he would be taking over the Presidency, he wanted Morton on his transition team. The first decision Ford faced was filling his old role as Vice-President. Advisors drew up score sheets of five perspective candidates. Morton ranked number two behind George H.W. Bush (interestingly, the ultimate choice, Nelson Rockefeller, placed fifth). But Ford was sensitive to the fact that Morton's health might become an issue and it's not clear he seriously desired the job. Instead, he tapped Morton to serve as Commerce Secretary.

Ford felt the Nixon administration was lax when it came to promoting the interests of United States commerce abroad. Rogers, by contrast, didn't have that problem because he was a person "who could talk to business leaders in their own language." Morton resisted calls to reveal the companies that were taking part in the Arab boycott of Israel. While he explained that he was "in no way, shape or form in sympathy with the boycott . . . I can't take the law into my own hands. If I did that every time an emotional issue came up, we'd have chaos in this country." Ford was soon preparing for the race of his life against Ronald Reagan and whichever Democrat would emerge from primary season, and Ford needed Morton in the role he performed best: offering advice. So Morton left Commerce and became one of Ford's top advisors, and eventually campaign chair.

When asked if he was going to change strategy, Morton replied, "that would be like rearranging the chairs on the deck of the Titanic." Morton immediately knew he screwed up and when Ford told him the next day his "comments didn't help one bit," he replied, "Mr. President, I know it. Please don't make me feel worse than I do." The battle went on and on but ultimately Ford was able to narrowly hold off Reagan at the Republican Convention. But shortly after, Morton got his boss into even more trouble when, facing Southerner Jimmy Carter, Morton insinuated to reporters that Ford was conceding the south. That led to a newspaper headline that read, "Ford Would Write Off Cotton South."

Morton recognized the distraction that he was becoming and thought about resigning. But ultimately, Ford was gearing up to face the race of his life and needed him as an adviser in some respect. So he asked him to stay on as an advisor. Morton would tell the press he was stepping down as chair because he could no longer bear "the responsibility and accountability of the chairmanship"

Ford lost the election narrowly and Morton remained in Maryland, but the prostate cancer that he had contracted in 1973 began spreading and he died at age 64 in 1979. Ford said "he gave so much and expected nothing but friendship. The nation has lost a big man." Thurston died three years later at age 75.

CHAPTER SEVENTY-THREE

Laird, A Capitol Hill Giant, Was Nixon's Secretary of Defense And Close Ford Confidante Whose Advice About Pardon Proved Critical

Historic Quote: "I would have made a good Pope." - Richard Nixon.

Photo courtesy of the U.S. Department of Defense

Mel Laird may be best known as Secretary of Defense during the Nixon administration but the Wisconsin Republican may have been heir to a number of important footnotes that shaped the 1970s. Laird was close friends with Gerald Ford before either went to Congress and continued to correspond with him regularly and socially until just before the former President's death in 2006. Yet the man who convinced Nixon to make Henry Kissinger an advisor may have been part of a far more powerful footnote to history had Ford listened to his friend's wisdom when it came to the Nixon pardon (read on).

Laird had other footnotes that I'll touch on later in this chapter but he also had legislative accomplishments that have impacted the lives of many future generations. As a Congressman, it was his legislation that gave free milk to school kids, created health advances and codified the terms "Under God" in the Pledge of Allegiance and "In God We Trust" as the national motto. But it's his connection to national figures that defines his legacy and that's where we begin.

In an uncanny occurrence, Laird's birth place was Omaha, Nebraska, the same as the future President's. But while Ford would move straight to Michigan almost as an infant (nine years before Laird was born), Laird would float around the upper Midwest, attending high school in Mansfield, Wisconsin and the Lake Forest Academy in Illinois. For college, it was back to Minnesota where Carlton would serve as his alma mater. But World War II soon called him and he readily enlisted. Laird served aboard the USS Maddox in the Navy and was wounded by shrapnel. By the time his enlistment had ended in 1946, he was the recipient of the Purple Heart and several other awards. His brother was not so lucky. He died in the line of duty and Laird was affected greatly.

As coincidence would have it, he and Ford were in the "same task force" and Laird would first exchange pleasantries with him there, before politics would encompass either of their lives. Laird recalls "we met on a little island in Magaw where we had a couple of beers."

As a soldier
Photo via ussmaddox.org

Laird's routes were always in Wisconsin. His maternal grandfather, William Connor, had been Governor of the state from 1907 to 1909. Returning home, it's not often that a son gets to succeed his father in public office, particularly at the age of 23, but fate gave that honor to Laird. His father, a Wisconsin State Senator, died suddenly in early 1946 and Laird was tapped to succeed him. There, his enthusiasm was so noticeable that one colleague called him a "cloud rider." Six years later, a Congressional seat opened and Laird won a four candidate Republican primary with a near majority – 49%. The general election was a breeze. He took 72% and, though he was reduced to 59% two years later, never saw his showing fall below 61% after that.

By that time, Laird's old Navy buddy Ford was already comfortably ensconced in the House, having won a Grand Rapids based House seat four years earlier. But the two had renewed their acquaintanship well before. Laird later recalled,

"I'd known him through (Wisconsin Congressmen) Glenn Davis and Johnny Burns. I'd been out to visit them in Washington and I'd met him at that time." In those days, he said Ford's "ambition was on the U.S. Senate but that really never developed. (Arthur) Vandenberg had been his idol in the Senate from Michigan and it just never developed."

Laird's election occurred during the first Eisenhower landslide which also gave control of the House to the GOP. That allowed freshmen to land seats on the prestigious Appropriations panel. Laird was one. El Cederberg of Michigan was the other. Both were among Ford's closest friends. Laird was assigned to an astounding four subcommittees creating a tremendous workload. When asked why, John Taber, another committee member replied, "Mel likes hard work."

Laird would acquire a seat on the Defense subcommittee. But he would also rise to the top Republican position on the panel's Health, Education, Welfare, and Labor committee where he'd work on many issues relating to health. This included the establishment of the Communicable Disease Center and, according to his bio, "enlargements of the National Institutes of Health, the Library of Medicine and eight national cancer research centers." He took tremendous pride when he heard of a woman being inserted with a "man-made" heart pump, for his bill had made the funding possible. Mental health was also high on his agenda and the National Mental Health Association recognized this by naming him, "Man of the Year." The Mel Laird Center Research in Marshfield, Wisconsin opened in 1997.

And, perhaps obligatory for a Wisconsin pol, Laird looked for a solution to excess milk. He soon figured that a perfect use would be to give it to school-kids for free. Thus, it was Laird's bill that created the School-Lunch program.

Being from Wisconsin also forced Laird to dive head first into the McCarthy issue. Later, he said, "I understood what a phony he was, and a lot of people didn't. A lot of people in Wisconsin didn't. A lot of conservatives didn't." At one point, Laird had to chair a convention event which was almost totally pro-McCarthy. When one single delegate rose to speak against McCarthy, Laird eagerly recognized him. But he was booed by nearly everyone else in the room. After the McCarthy saga had ended, Ford recognized Laird's deftness in keeping his distance, noting, "they (Wisconsin Rs) had a very narrow path to follow because McCarthy was quite popular in Wisconsin. I think Mel handled the McCarthy problem very skillfully. He stayed outside of the McCarthy envelope, so to speak."

At the start of Laird's tenure, Joe Martin was Speaker and "Mister Sam" Rayburn, Minority Leader. Rayburn did little to pump up Republicans but one day, became so impressed with seeing Laird shepherd an Appropriations subcommittee bill to the floor that he approached him and informed him that he was going to give him nicer digs in the capital building. Laird later said he didn't think "Mister Sam" extended that privilege to any other Republican.

Many others, from colleagues to the President, recognized Laird's capabilities. Eisenhower cited him as among "ten men in America best qualified to serve as President of the United States," a major testimonial given that Laird had barely exceeded the Constitutional age of 35 by the time Eisenhower left office. Well-versed Republicans named him to the party's platform committee in '56. And as Ford moved up, so did Laird. He became Secretary of the House Republican Conference in 1965 just as Ford ousted Charlie Halleck to become GOP leader. Some insinuated the promotions sparked a rivalry.

In his book, *Gerald Ford and the Future of the Presidency*, J.F.ter Horst wrote "Ford found himself constantly looking over his shoulder at the ambitious Melvin Laird, who frequently behaved as if he, not Ford, were calling the signals for the Republican minority," noting Laird in fact took to the floor with "a major speech setting forth his version of House Republican goals." Though people around the two men talked, it seemed unlikely any tension resulted between the two men as Ford himself was acknowledged to have had initial trouble adjusting to the high profile nature of his new role.

Nevertheless, the sentiment was ironic because a decade later, Laird would advise Ford not to worry about sharing the limelight with Nelson Rockefeller should he tap the former New York Governor to serve as his VP, which he did. Laird's reasoning: "I have an idea that Nixon picked Agnew because he was insecure and didn't want anyone who would overshadow him. Don't you worry about that. When you're President, you don't have to worry about being overshadowed by anyone."

Together, Ford and Laird forged a productive relationship. One issue they tackled was the open housing legislation. Ford had opposed it in 1966 but had taken a different tack by the time the bill came up again two years later. He would support it but wanted it sent back to committee. Failure of the leadership to do so led the two to oppose the bill on the first round but back it for final passage. They also worked on revenue sharing for states.

Meanwhile, Laird continued to be given high profile roles. He was disappointed in 1960 when Charles Percy, yet to be elected Senator from Illinois, was chosen to chair the Republican Platform committee. But by '64, the job was his. But it may have been a case of be careful what you wish for. The Republican Party was in turmoil. The Goldwater/Rockefeller factions of the party were at odds and Laird had to navigate it so that every word that ended up in the platform would receive the utmost scrutiny. His biographer cited four rules: "don't tarnish the reputation of America or its people; don't dodge the tough issues; don't equivocate; and don't make promises that the party can't keep."

Laird was successful, over Goldwater's objections, of getting support fror civil rights in the platform. But at the end, he was confronted with how to deal with the term "extremism." Liberal elements, notably Pennsylvania Governor

Bill Scranton, wanted to single out groups by name, particularly the John Birch Society. Laird opposed the amendment. At the end of the day, the final product of the Republican plank did not please everyone. But Laird was commended for his fairness. And he won applause for another deft maneuver. Not wanting the public to witness the fractiousness of the proceedings, Laird demanded that the platform be read in its entirety before entertaining the divisive amendments. By the time members got around to debating the provisions, it was well after prime time when most Americans had gone to bed.

The result in '64 was among the most disastrous debacles for any party and Ford and Laird used those wilderness years to rebuild. But bigger things would be on the horizon for both men.

Nixon tapped Laird to serve as Secretary of Defense in 1969. Upon announcing the pick, he called Laird "a strong man and a shrewd politician" with respect in Congress.

His confirmation hearing lasted 20 minutes. When some suggested the United States should clear the way for Russia's near arms parity with the U.S. to ease the tensions between the two nations, Laird dismissed it, saying, "I disagree with that theory. It is absolutely important that the US maintain a superior position." Instead, he spoke of superiority which would lead to negotiating through strength.

Laird's resignation from the House triggered a special election that led to a Democrat – Dave Obey, capturing the seat for the first time in the 20th century (Obey had volunteered for Laird's first campaign as a 13 year old and confessed to voting for him at least once since he became a Democrat post-McCarthy).

Laird's influence with Nixon would prove limited, if not non-existent. Stephen Ambrose's biography of Nixon notes "(Secretary of State Bill) Rogers and Laird hardly ever saw the President and certainly were not taken into his confidence." But he made a strong mark at the Defense Department. He was rated by employees and defense advocates "the most effective, likeable, trustworthy, strong and forthcoming Secretary of Defense."

By this time, Americans had grown weary of the situation in Vietnam. Laird himself had been critical of the Johnson administration's handling of operations, saying later he "felt they had not prepared themselves for the long haul in Vietnam. They kept committing more and more and more." They had "Americanized" the war. They had taken it over and said: "No, you Vietnamese stay away, this is going to be our operation." And he believed LBJ kept the cost of the war and escalation to himself, not wanting to exceed "the much publicized $100 million ceiling" prior to the 1966 midterm elections. As a result, he said the GOP "will not refrain from telling the American people of their extreme displeasure at the way in which this administration sees fit to inject political consideration into its proposals."

Photo courtesy of the U.S. Government Archives

The way the operation was handled was a key reason Laird and two other GOP colleagues invoked a rarely used procedure to the 1966 Defense markup to point out "grave reservations" and "phony math." They called it "more of a policy of seeking to achieve a balanced deterrent rather than ensuring a decisive superiority." Ultimately, they voted to approve the bill.

Laird prescribed a strategy for withdrawal. In keeping with the strategy, he took steps to implement "zero draft calls" and an all-volunteer Army by 1972. As such, he was called "the Architect of Vietnamization," which essentially ended the operations and turned them over to the South Vietnamese. And he was genuinely engaged in the effort to bring POW's home.

Consistent with Nixon's record of ignoring certain people in key positions, Laird privately had qualms about the Cambodian bombing. When he took office, it began as a monthly turnover. He pressed for an increase in Polaris submarines, advocated for the ABM, the B-1, Trident, and other cruise missiles and created the Japanese Military Council. And with Nixon's blessing, he instituted a Blue Ribbon Defense panel designed to make 100 recommendations for how the Department could better operate.

Laird's respect in the military and his relations with Congress were considered excellent. This was a major departure with other Secretaries of Defense during war-time before and after his tenure, and was further evidence of Laird's strengths. After the 1972 elections, in keeping with the vow he had made to only serve as Secretary for four years, Laird stepped down. The Vietnam Peace Treaty was signed two days before Laird left office and in a final report, the departing Secretary wrote, "Vietnamization . . . today is virtually completed. As a consequence of the success of the military aspects of Vietnamization, the South Vietnamese people today, in my view, are fully capable of providing for their own in-country security against the North Vietnamese."

At that time, it was thought that Laird's goal was to seek the Presidency in 1976. But Nixon wasn't done with him yet. Five months after he stepped down, he was asked by the President to rejoin the administration as councilor on domestic affairs. Because Laird had often publicly stated a contraire view of the administration's defense policies, this again said wonders about his abilities. But hesoon recognized that Watergate was growing out of control and resigned his post in February of 1974.

During a visit to Vietnam as Defense Secretary
Photo courtesy of the U.S. Department of Defense

Which brings us to more footnotes. Laird had already been the person who had urged Nixon to make Henry Kissinger his national security advisor following his first election, a move that would lead to Kissinger's historic tenure at the State Department later on (Laird first called on Kissinger's assistance while drafting the '64 policy convention). He would now do the same with a pick that, for history's sake would bear even more enormity.

Vice-President Spiro Agnew had resigned the previous October and it was Laird who would not only place the call to Ford to gauge his interest, but it was the former sailor who steadfastly steered Nixon in his direction to begin with. Nixon's choice to replace Agnew was John Connally – there was no plan B. Laird knew it would be very difficult for Connally to win confirmation and told Nixon so. The President was still insistent. So Laird took a gradual tact and asked Nixon to at least consider members of the House and Senate leadership. In truth, he only had a single name in mind.

Ford with Laird and his wife Betty shortly after assuming the Presidency
Photo courtesy of the Gerald R. Ford Presidential Library

Next, Laird would call the Ford's at home around 10PM one night and in typical fashion, begin with a few minutes of small-talk. Ford would later say that's when he knew the discussion would soon turn serious. Indeed it was. Laird would pose the question: "if asked," would you accept the job as vice-president. Ford would write in his memoirs that he "knew Mel too well to know the question hadn't come just like that. Someone had told him to call." Ford told Laird he'd talk it over with Betty but, before long, the job would be his.

More importantly, Laird had a hand in the lawyers surrounding the whole Watergate investigation. His intricate knowledge of the cast of characters coupled with his access to Ford could have meant that history might have turned out dramatically different if Ford had taken Laird's advice.

John Doar, a native of River Falls, Wisconsin, was the person recommended by Laird to be the lead council for the impeachment committee. Laird had also had a hand in naming Leon Jaworski special Watergate prosecutor. Texas Congressman Bill Archer, who lived next door to Jaworski had recommended him to Laird. Little did Archer know that Laird was thinking the same thing. Jaworski, both agreed, was exquisitely fair and as a Democrat, yet one who had backed Nixon in '68, was someone who could fill all angles. The two plotted ways to get the Nixon White House to accept Jaworski. Laird's first step was to convince the President, fresh off the firings from the "Saturday Evening Massacre," not to abolish the special prosecutor's office as he had threatened to do.

In the days after Nixon resigned, it was known in the inner-circle of Washington that Jaworski was not likely to indict Nixon. And without an indictment, there was no need for a pardon. Ford knew that but as Laird said, he "went the other way." Where did this come to a head? On the golf course, naturally. Laird recount's Ford asking, "What do you think about that pardon?" I said, "Jerry, you know what I think about the way that was handled. If you don't, you're blind, deaf, and dumb, because I've talked to you about that." And I said, "Now, listen, we've got a chance to win this tournament, we're only two shots behind. I'll talk to you about the pardon, what happened today, after this golf game."

The pardon aside, Ford relied on Laird heavily throughout his administration. He became part of Ford's "kitchen cabinet" that would meet with him in the cabinet room for face to face critiquing. And when Ford surprised his wife Betty with an intimate party attended by 100 of their closest friends as they prepared to leave office, the Lairds were among them.

In retirement, Laird began writing for *Readers Digest* and continued commenting on national and defense related affairs. He watched Chuck Hagel's confirmation on television and said Hagel "wasn't as prepared as well as he should have been," though he didn't oppose his nomination."

At 92, Laird is now one of the oldest former members of Congress. Not a single individual who served in the House before Laird survives today. He resides in Washington D.C.

By December 19, 2006, Ford was in poor health and obviously knew the end was near. Laird called him. "Mel," he said, "I have to hang on for Christmas. The whole family is coming." Exactly one week later, Ford was dead.

Of Ford, Laird says, "He should be remembered as the man that saved the country at a very important time after a great disappointment. As far as Nixon is concerned we could have completely lost faith in our system. We didn't because of Jerry Ford."

CHAPTER SEVENTY-FOUR

Berkley of Iowa Among the Most Honorable Iowans To Serve In House

Historic Quote: "I personally don't know what could be better than for neither side to have confidence in the operational capabilities of their nuclear arsenals. It sure would discourage a first strike." – Iowa Congressman Berkley Bedell

B erkley Bedell never let the hammer down on anyone. During his dozen years in Congress he had a reputation as among the most gentle souls. So to gain fame from a hammer was somewhat ironic. That said, Bedell had gained fame through numerous other endeavors that started at boyhood and followed him into prosperity. He continues amazing folks with his talents and at age 96, retains an impressive sense of vigor and outreach ability that he uses to promote his causes.

So devoted was Berkley to fishing that at the age of 15, he took $50 from his savings as a newspaper delivery boy to make fishing flies and the sky became the limit. Well, in his case, the streams. An advertisement was run in a local sports magazine and He ran an advertisement in a sports magazine and before-long had a nationwide clientele, employing seven people while still in high school. By the early 1960s, Bedell received loans from the Small Business Administration for a major expansion. That soon resulted in a business that grew to 700 employees. It was an endeavor that would be recognized by President Lyndon B. Johnson at a 1964 White House ceremony long before Berkley became politically active (in fact he was still a Republican) at which Johnson bestowed upon him the Small Businessman of "best exemplifying the imagination, initiative, independence and integrity characteristic of America's millions of small businessmen."

Bedell attended Iowa State University. While he didn't finish, he met Elinor Healy and in 1943, they married. He called his "decision…the most important and best decision of my life."

It was now the middle of World War II and he would be graduating as a pilot shortly thereafter. He became a training instructor and was sent to Macon, Georgia. But he recalls that he was "always trying to get into battle and was always trying to find an opening." Finally, he got word that fliers of B29s were needed and was headed to San Francisco when he got word that the war was over. Returning home, he started Berkley and Company. As his bio pointed out, "one evening, while reading Popular Science, Berk learned about a Connecticut company that was producing nylon-covered cable for sailboat rigging. After visiting their plant, he began to work on nylon-coated wires for use in fishing leaders." While fishing lines was a major component, it also expanded to nylon monofilament fishing lines. By 1959, it was "Berkley Trilene," his answer to DuPont's new Stren (Du Pont had earlier granted him a license for the monofilament lines). Bedell promoted this by asking store owners to "have their best fisherman try it on a spinning reel. Fisherman loved the line."

Bedell during World War II (back row, far left)
Photo courtesy of Berkley Bedell

One reason for Bedell's strong appeal among Republicans may have been that he used to be one. "It was so organized that all the slots were filled." Declaring, "I've been up against stiff things all of my life," Berkley was not under illusions about the difficulties he faced in unseating Mayne. He attacked the incumbent's support of a deal that sent wheat to the Soviet Union. Early returns from Sioux City gave Bedell a lead but as the rural counties began pouring in, Mayne pulled ahead and won. But his 52-48% margin in the midst of Richard Nixon's sweep was uninspiring and Bedell, acknowledging years later that his loss was '"probably was due to the fact that I did not get well enough known to all the people of the district." He immediately set eyes on 1974. It would be a far different atmosphere.

Mayne was hurt by his dogged defense of Nixon as a member of the House Judiciary Committee. Shortly before the president resigned, he labeled Mayne his "yes-man," and said "our Congressman has acted more like a defense lawyer for Nixon than like a representative of the people." But Mayne's problems went beyond Watergate. During his four terms, he had earned the enmity of unions. Mayne said Bedell's campaign was controlled by unions but Bedell countered by calling him a lackey for the Nixon/Ford agenda. Among the evidence he cited: Mayne had voted for eight pieces of legislation that were ultimately vetoed, then "switched his vote on six of those eight bills (refusing to override).We could only find one other congressman who switched his vote more than six times to support presidential vetoes. My belief is that we have to have strong, independent people in Congress who will support the president when they think he's right and will stand up to him when they think he's wrong." Mayne cited his seat on the Agriculture Committee as being valuable to serve the district but inflation also weighed heavily on the minds of voters.

Still a Republican, Bedell was presented an award by President Johnson
in recognition of his achievements as a small businessman
Photo courtesy of Berkley Bedell

Bedell, riding the national Democratic headwinds, ousted Mayne 55-45% and said in victory, "I pledge to all of you tonight that, as your congressman, I will be listening to you, I will be back with you as often as possible and I will be working hard in Washington to make the changes we talked about in this campaign."

One area in which he listened to constituents was what they came to view as exorbitant usage fees by the barge industry, As a result, he introduced legislation requiring the industry to pay for usage of government funded waterways.

In his first term, Bedell voiced strong support for an amendment that would require members to publish their overseas travel in the *Congressional Record*. Not doing so, he said, "gave the impression that Congress was trying to keep information about its foreign travel from the public. What is of great concern to me is that the comment reporting procedure still gives the appearance that Congress wants to burn information on its foreign travel activities. In 1977, he proposed a resolution expressing the sense of the Congress that the Secretary of Health, Education and Welfare should consider the impact on rural America prior to issuing guidelines dealing with excess hospital beds.

During the 1982 farm crisis, Bedell spoke passionately for his people. "I know members of Congress have heard time after time about the problems of our farmers. Let me tell them, this time, our farmers really have problems." In 1985, he proposed an amendment allowing self-employed farmers to deduct losses from operations in order to qualify for food stamps.

By the middle of 1984, Bedell was chair of the Small Business Oversight Subcommittee and he was presented with a chance for publicity most members dreamed of. As a quiet servant of Western Iowa, Bedell was not one of them. But the "hammer" changed that. He had been questioning a Pentagon official on overcharges, including a hammer that had been purchased that had allegedly cost $400. The man promised Berkley future details and when they arrived, he said, "I almost fell off my chair." But when they defended it as "exorbitant but legal," Berkley said he, "about tore my hair out." As the *New York Times* explained it, it was revealed a purchase of "21 small hardware items, including the infamous hammer that cost a total of $10,168.56. Mr. Bedell went to two local hardware stores and purchased the identical items. His bill for the 21 tools came to $92.44. A crusader was born." That became the focus of legislation that would require a more competitive bidding for supplies, expanding the "qualified sellers list" and purchasing them at commercial, "customer friendly" prices. Some contended this would compromise the quality of future Pentagon purchases but the House cleared the bill 324-75. It became known as the military spare parts bill.

Another initiative Bedell was most proud of was "House Res 3" which he sponsored with a fellow Iowan, Republican Congressman Jim Leach. It called on the president to resume negotiations with Russia on a test ban treaty. Despite having 205 co-sponsors, House leaders acceded to Reagan administration threats that including the amendment would jeopardize the entire bill Thus, they declined to bring it to a vote.

For Bedell, being at odds with the Reagan administration was not unusual. His policy toward Central America was "sheer lunacy," and he felt as early as 1983 – after a trip to the region, that the administration was illegally aiding the contras.

One reason for Bedell's popularity in a heavily GOP district was his accessibility in many forums, among them the above town meeting
Photo courtesy of Berkley Bedell

Bedell had no problems practicing what he preached. One aide recalled how when folks entered Bedell's office, "they saw a guy who tried to root out waste, fraud and abuse in government brought a cheese sandwich for lunch. In a re-use paper bag when he was one of the wealthiest men in Congress...He stayed very grounded. He didn't spend the people's money any more than he spent his own." And when it came to promoting good government, he actually practiced what he preached. Berkley opposed ratification of the Equal Rights Amendment (ERA) for the sole reason that he didn't think the measure had gone through regular order to reach the House floor.

Elinor meanwhile thrived in Washington, often granting tours to constituents. Back home, she founded the Voluntary Action Center and Peace Links. Later and life, she and Berkley donated 80 acres of land on East Okoboji Lake to the Iowa Department of Natural Resources. It is now the Elinor Bedell State Park.

Bedell and his wife Elinor on Capitol Hill
Photo courtesy of Berkley Bedell

Bedell had hoped to seek a seventh-term in 1986 but soon 'I am forced to admit that I plainly do not have the energy to do this job for three more years the way I know it must be done. I do not believe it would be fair to anyone for me to continue in a job unless I can give it 100 percent." Bedell had been suffering from Lyme Disease (coincidentally, that year he sponsored the Federal Insecticide, Fungicide, and Rodenticide Act Amendments). After he retired, he was diagnosed with prostate cancer. The experience with prostate cancer put him on a path to a new crusade. As a result, he and Elinor sponsored the Office of Alternative Medicine at the prestigious National Institutes of Health (NIHOAM) in Bethesda, Maryland. He has remained politically active. In 2004, he endorsed Howard Dean for president and in fact was standing behind him during his now infamous scream.

As the 2016 presidential election cycle neared, Bedell sought to galvanize students with three issues: climate change, student loan debt and money in politics.

Elinor died in early 2017. Bedell credited her as "a major reason for my political success, both at the ballot box and during our service." And in an extraordinary statement by anyone who had been in marriage, he added that "In our 73 years of marriage, we have never had a major argument and I know of no one who did not love Elinor."

A book, *Tackling Giants: The Life Story of Berkley Bedell* was published by Larry Ramey and Daniel Haley in 2005.

Photo courtesy of Congressman Berkley Bedell

CHAPTER SEVENTY-FIVE

Deadlock: Durkin, Wyman and Closest Senate Race in Nation

Historic Quote: "There comes a time when one must take a position that is neither safe, nor politic, nor popular, but he must take it because conscience tells him it is right." – Martin Luther King, Jr.

W hen it comes to final results, the election of Howard Cannon was the closest Senate race since the public began electing Senators by popular vote in 1914, but there was actually one race that was closer—in fact, nearly tied. It is not recorded because ultimately, after see-saw winners and single digit leads by both candidates, a new election was ordered. It was in New Hampshire in 1974.

Republican Congressman Louis Wyman was a heavy favorite going in. The Democratic nomination had gone to ex-State Insurance Commissioner John Durkin. On Election Night, Wyman's lead was just under 1,000 votes, which dwindled to 355 when the final tabulations had come in. In a bizarre post-election rant, Wyman said he had expected a 20,000-vote victory and seemed to attack the voters of Portsmouth for voting against their interests by opting for Durkin.

When Wyman had appeared to have emerged the winner, Republicans exhaled. They had won North Dakota by 177 votes and Nevada by 645 (not to mention Oklahoma by 3,500), so New Hampshire would be the fourth seat they had managed to hold by a hair. The good thing for the Republicans was that they appeared to have done so, but as Durkin said, "it's still a horse race." Then, things got tricky and for a while seemed to go Durkin's way.

A re-count produced a 10-vote win for Durkin, which Republican Governor Meldrin Thompson, a Republican, refused to certify, but he was ultimately forced to do so by the courts.

**Durkin (left) and Wyman during the protracted deliberations
to determine who won the Senate election of 1974
Photo courtesy of the Manchester Union Leader**

Wyman appealed to the state Ballot Law Commission, which was charged with making decisions on "write-ins, strangely marked ballots and voter intentions." One point of contention was whether "crooks" should have their votes included. Ultimately, the Commission's rulings on various ballots put Wyman up by two votes, and Thompson rescinded Durkin's certificate (he said he had acted prematurely) and issued one to Wyman. With a dispute still looming, he also filed for an interim appointment for Wyman to be seated.

Durkin tried an injunction to put the matter in the hands of the Senate. A Judge denied that but he still appealed. Meanwhile, Wyman was trying to gain his own temporary appointment. When the full Senate began hearing the matter in January, Wyman and Durkin were present, each sitting on opposite sides of the chamber.

Not only did the Senate deadlock on the 35 counts, but also on whether to seat Wyman temporarily. This went on for 32 roll call votes and, as his obituary said, "a record-setting six cloture votes to cut off debate." Wyman proposed a re-run. Durkin was originally leaning against it but said his eight-year-old daughter convinced him to go forward. "She said, 'Dad, don't you realize they can't make their mind up about anything?' When the kids realize it, I thought I had to do something." The Senate declared the seat vacant on July 30, 1975. Norris Cotton, now comfortably in retirement, returned to the body as an interim Senator until the special. It was now August 1975, nine months after the initial election. This time, a recount wasn't needed.

Photo courtesy of NPR

Wyman was again haunted by an issue that probably cost him the election outright in 1974. He had introduced Ruth Farkas to the Committee to Re-elect the President and, following a $250,000 contribution, she was named Ambassador to Luxembourg. That factored in and as such, there was no need for a recount this time. Durkin won a solid 55%, a margin of 27,000 votes. Reflecting on the contest later, he said, "I'd much rather have read about it than have lived it."

Durkin was so late getting into office that, once in, he had only five years. He was strongly pro-life but backed his party on most issues, including the Panama Canal Treaty and opposing Kemp-Roth. He fought to keep price controls on New Hampshire's utility industry, important for a state with such cold winters.

Ironically but perhaps unknowingly, he may have sealed his own 1980 defeat. President Ford had nominated popular Attorney General Warren Rudman to the Interstate Commerce Commission but Durkin, remembering that Rudman had served on the elections board that temporarily reversed his victor, blocked it.

By 1980, Rudman was ready to challenge Durkin and he captured the GOP nomination to take him on. His margin was small, just 20% in a field that included John Sununu and ex-Governor Wesley Powell. Rudman called him beholden to unions, but with his sky-high approvals, Rudman was probably the one candidate Durkin did not want to face.

Indeed, as Reagan was seizing New Hampshire and once venerable Democratic incumbent after incumbent saw their careers end, the remarkable thing was not that Durkin lost, but that he did so well. Rudman beat him 52-48%, a margin of just 16,000 votes.

Years later, Rudman would write in his memoir that had he been confirmed, he likely would not have run for the Senate; Durkin's strong showing suggests he may have been able to hold off Sununu, and most certainly the tempestuous Powell.

In 1990, Durkin won the Democratic nomination for the open seat of retiring Senator Gordon Humphrey. His opponent was Congressman Bob Smith. But New Hampshire was still a Republican bastion, not yet the moderate land it would soon become. Durkin mustered just 31%. Wyman became a Judge. He died in 2012 when he was 76 years old.

Photo courtesy of the Manchester Union Leader

CHAPTER SEVENTY-SIX

1980 Saw Unlimited Big-Name Democrats Fall

Historic Tidbit: In May of 1987, Ronald Reagan was told of the alleged affair of Gary Hart, who at the time was hoping to succeed him, by an aide who stopped him as the elevator doors were closing. Reagan's reaction: "Men will be boys. But boys will never be President."

1980 was a year that many remember for **Ronald Reagan** coming in like a tractor-trailer, denying **Jimmy Carter** a second term. But that was only part of the story. Reagan's landslide victory also had ramifications nationwide. For not only did Republicans regain control of the Senate for the first time since 1954, but voters turned out big name after big name Democrat, some of whom were top vote getters in their state with decades upon decades of experience.

The Democratic loss that started the evening, and the one with the most historical ramifications was **Birch Bayh**, who of course lost to future Vice-President Dan Quayle. Bayh had led by as much as 20 points over the summer but was targeted by the New Right.

George McGovern's loss was no surprise. He had struggled in 1974, a strong Democratic year, holding just 53-47%. But the size of his margin was. Jim Abdnor had represented half of South Dakota in the House, but he himself had problems in his last House race, solidly Republican territory no less. So his 58-39% defeat of the 1980 standard bearer was a surprise.

Frank Church, the Chair of the Senate Foreign Relations committee, who hailed from a state that gave Ronald Reagan 66% should have been automatic toast, but in fact, the day before the election, Howard Baker, when running down a list of states the GOP would pick up, left Idaho off. Steve Symms wasn't universally liked even among Republicans, and Church lost just 50-49%. Remarking on his fellow casualties he quipped it's "nice to go out in good company."

Gaylord Nelson, whom I covered extensively as the founder of Earth Day, was considered safe as can be. But he lost 50-48% to Bob Kasten, a former Congressman who had lost his party's nomination for Governor in 1978.

Warren Magnuson's defeat was the most stunning. By Election Day, it wasn't a surprise at all but the fact that Magnuson was not only Appropriations Chair but

President Pro-Tem made it improbable. Age and poor health very much hampered Magnuson's ability to stave off longtime Attorney General Slade Gorton, who contrasted Magnuson's age. Magnuson responded with his clout. "So I can walk as fast as I used too," he said in one ad. "The meeting can't start until I get there."

John Culver of Iowa was only a freshman from what was in 1980 a Republican leaning state, but his campaign style was indefatigable. Despite efforts to portray Chuck Grassley as too far to the right, he was among the main targets of NPAC and lost 53-46%.

As a four term Senator and former Governor, **Herman Talmadge** was considered so secure at home that he was actually projected the winner on Election Night, when he led by 100,000 votes with a good ¾ counted. Talmadge's position as Senate Agriculture Chair, coupled with the fact that he had served as Governor of his state before going to the Senate in '56, made a defeat far more improbable. The fact that Jimmy Carter was dominating his home state with 59%. seemed poised to thwart even any of the smallest Republican strides. But Mack Mattingly reeled in the suburban Atlanta newcomers, and edged him 51-49%.

Other first term Senators who lost: **John Durkin** of New Hampshire unseated by Warren Rudman, and **Bob Morgan** of North Carolina, in an upset literally out of no where. Jim East was the beneficiary. The latter's race was on few radar screens, as his ideology seemed to perfectly align with the state. But his vote against the Panama Canal Treaty and East's assistance from Jesse Helms' political action committee did him in. The margin was a mere 10,000 votes, 50-49%.

Democrats also lost a series of open seats where incumbents had fallen in primaries (Alabama, Alaska, and Florida), and failed to take New York, where **Jacob Javitz** had been unseated by **Al D'Amato** in a primary. The result was that this class would boast of 16 freshman Republican Senators, and just two for the Democrats (**Alan Dixon** of Illinois and **Chris Dodd** of Connecticut). Both won the open seats of **Adlai Stevenson III** and **Abe Ribicoff** respectively.

There were a few unlikely survivors. **Pat Leahy**, who in 1974 had become the first Democrat to represent Vermont in the Senate ever, proved that his win was no fluke. He narrowly fended off a challenge from Richard Ledbetter. **Gary Hart** beat Mary Estill Buchanan by the same margin, despite the fact that Reagan was sweeping Colorado and Hart's early campaign was laisseth faireth.

And while Bayh, Church, Culver, and McGovern all fell victim to the conservative PACs, **Tom Eagleton** survived, albeit 52-48%, and **Alan Cranston** won a clear victory (57%).

Ironically, while liberal after liberal was going down, the one who may have emulated the anti-government that was carrying the day, it's original champion, **Barry Goldwater**, was very nearly among the casualties. He was slow to recognize that he was in trouble and his campaign team was not prepared for a tight as a tick race. He trailed during the entire election night count, only keeping his seat 50-49% when all of the absentees were tabulated.

Three Democratic Governors lost. Missouri's **Jim Teasdale** and North Dakota's **Art Link's** surprised few. But a young southerner named **Bill Clinton** was considered a shoe-in even as late as Election Night when a number of networks declared him the winner, and called him as results tightened to tell him they were sticking with the projection. His opponent, **Frank White**, when asked if voters were trying to send him a message, replied, "I think they're sending him a message that they want me to be Governor."

House Democrats lost 35 seats, more than enough to keep Tip O'Neill as Speaker, but now just 25 seats above a majority. And the many "Boll Weevils" in the caucus would essentially mean a working majority for Reagan. But it's not just the numbers that were notable. Like the Senate, a caliber of big-name talent and vote-getters, junior and senior, were lost. Eight members with service of 18 years or more were shown the door, including a number I profiled in previous pieces. Another, **John Brademas** of Indiana, was the House Majority Whip, the number three position in the House leadership. The Chairs of Ways and means, Public Works, and House Administration were unseated, although the latter, *Frank Thompson*, was among the many members caught up in Abscam.

And like their Senate counterparts, a few of the casualties were on zero radar screens. **Richardson Preyer** was one of them. The North Carolinian was no longer a major power, having lost his coveted Health sub-committee Chairmanship to Henry Waxman after the '78 elections. But, having garnered 68% two years before, his loss still came out of nowhere. Ditto for Missouri's **Bill Burlison,** though there was some discontent among Missouri farmers. And folks who had proven survival skills in very politically perilous districts (Washington's **Mike McCormack** and Utah's **Gunn MacKay**, were second fiddles).

And the GOP was finally successful in knocking off several junior members, such as California's **Jim Lloyd**, New Jersey's **Andy McGuire**, and Virginians

Joe Fischer, and **Herb Harris**, who had all won their seats in the 1974 GOP Watergate tsunami. The first three lost to David Dreier and Marge Roukema and Frank Wolf, all of whom had fallen short of the trio in '78. Harris fell at the hands of Stan Parris, whom he had unseated in '74. Another "Watergate Baby," Wisconsin's **Alvin Baldus**, who had taken 63% in 1978, lost a squeaker to Steve Gunderson.

Even the survivors had close calls. **Tom Foley**, a future House Speaker who at the time chaired the House Agriculture Committee, held off just 52-48%. **Paul Simon**, who would later become a beloved Senator from Illinois, came within 2,000 seats of being blindsided by a novice. So did **Jim Howard**, who would, with Johnson's defeat, take over the chairmanship of Public Works.

Yes, 1980 was a year of reckoning for Democrats all across the country, one that, until 1994, forced many to contend with a whole new world of minority status for the first time in their careers.

PART IV

The Kennedy/Johnson Connection

CHAPTER SEVENTY-SEVEN

Vibrant Wyoming Democrats Put Kennedy Over Top In '60

Historic Tidbit: In early 1957, future Wyoming Congressman Teno Roncalio walked into the Washington D.C. office of then-Senator John F. Kennedy and presented a staffer his card." When the Senator runs for President," he said, "give me a call." Sure enough, Roncalio was instrumental in securing Wyoming for Kennedy, which ultimately put him over the top at the convention. But Roncalio wasn't finished. He told Kennedy he had to carry Wyoming in the fall. "If you don't," he said, "my name will be mud." Kennedy lost the state by ten points. The next time he saw Kennedy, the President said, "Hello, mud."

JFK with Wyoming Governor John Hickey, his successor Jack Gage, and Wyoming Eagle editor Tracy McCracken
Photo courtesy of the Wyoming Almanac

Throughout the Bush Presidency, Dick Cheney joked several times that he had "delivered" the state of Wyoming's three electoral votes to the ticket. That remark was not made in total levity. While Wyoming was among the most safely Republican states in the nation, every state proved critical in allowing Bush/Cheney to clear the 270 electoral vote mark. But at one time, Wyoming was a crucial state for helping to pick the next President — at the Democratic Convention. It was 1960 and John K. Kennedy was four votes shy of going over the top to receive his party's nomination in Los Angeles. Wyoming had 15 delegates. And Ted Kennedy was at the forefront.

For in 1960, Wyoming's Democratic Party was vibrant. It had a Democratic Governor, John "J.J" Hickey, and two Democratic Senators, Joe O'Mahoney and Gale McGee. The state's Democratic chair was a Kennedy loyalist named Teno Roncalio, who would go on to represent the State in Congress. McGee is covered extensively in a previous chapter involving Frank Church and Frank Moss, but his role in putting Kennedy over the top cannot be understated.

McGee initially backed Lyndon Johnson in '60 and it was not difficult to understand why. He had won his Senate seat barely a year before and LBJ was his Majority Leader, and a powerful one at that. But as it became clear that the nomination would be more and more up for grabs, McGee became neutral. Never in his wildest dreams could he have realized the enormity that would mean to a single moment as the convention roll call approached Wyoming on the first ballot.

Like his younger brother, Bobby Kennedy apparently came to the conclusion that Wyoming would put his brother over the top as well. This came as Vermont began casting its votes. He and his forces hurried toward the portion of the convention hall where Wyoming was situated.

At that point, JFK was 11 votes shy of clinching the nomination. Eight and 1/2 were committed to him, while Johnson controlled six and Stevenson had half a vote (convention lingo). By this point, Ted Kennedy was there as well and he planted himself firmly in the middle of the Wyoming delegation at the convention hall. When Wyoming was called, a voice was heard from the top of the chair yelling, "Give me four votes! We can put him over the top! Please give me four votes!" Tracy McCracken was the delegation chair, a position McGee had hoped would be his. But McCracken was a well-known publisher of a number of Wyoming newspapers and so, the who's who of state Democrats acceded to his request to have the title.

Johnson forces, who had been hoping to force Kennedy into a second ballot, tried to grab the microphone, but the delegates exceeded to their man's request. Wyoming's Democratic Chair said the words, As a CNN profile later exclaimed, McCracken, "his white hair glistening in the spotlight" loudly proclaimed, "Wyoming casts all 15 of its votes for the next President of the United States . . ." Kennedy was the pick. He was over the top. Now it was on to November, and on to history.

**Kennedy began wooing Wyoming backers as early as 1958 when he flew
on the Caroline to stump for longshot Senate candidate Gale McGee
Photo courtesy of Robert McGee**

The man who had stood up on the chair was Senator Gale McGee. He would not become a household name. He wouldn't even become recognizable in the convention hall. But by asking for those votes, his place in history is undisputed.

Robert McGee, the Senator's son said his dad's loyalties with Johnson were obligatory because of the heights to which he helped McGee soar. Johnson had stumped for McGee during the 1958 election and made the promise, "If you send me Gale McGee "he'll be placed on the Appropriations Committee in his first year in office. McGee did win and Johnson delivered. Bob McGee called that "unprecedented," but also a key reason "Dad thought he had to go for Johnson." But Kennedy had campaigned in Wyoming in '58 as well and McGee spotted his potential even then. Robert recalls his dad asking him to "come to the airport to meet this man. He's likely to be the next President of the United States." The spotting of one another's talents was mutual. When McGee had delivered his "maiden speech" on the Senate floor as a freshman, Kennedy called it the best he had ever seen. As colleagues, McGee and Kennedy were friendly but not close though Robert recalls his parents having dinner at least once at Kennedy's "N" Street home in Washington D.C.

That Wyoming Democratic chair was Teno Roncalio, who would go on to win a House seat and would ultimately become the last Democrat to hold federal office from Wyoming. He recalls "In the roar greeting the announcement, I kept my eyes on the man who had begged for four votes. He was jumping up and down, slapping a beaming Ted Kennedy on the back, apparently beside himself with joy. I recognized him as our old friend Senator Gale McGee."

The convention roared. The young Senator from Massachusetts, younger than McGee and Roncalio, would now carry the torch for their party in November. And they had Wyoming to thank, which is why McGee and Roncalio are true footnotes to history. And the characters I will cover also show the small degrees of separation in such a small state.

Kennedy had campaigned for the Democratic ticket in 1958, when their odds for success had seemed uphill. McGee was challenging incumbent Frank Barrett for the Senate and Hickey was taking on MilwardSimpson for Governor. Simpson was the father of the future Senator Alan Simpson.

Hickey hailed from Carbon County and was forced to take odd jobs to put his way through school (his father had died when Hickey was three). His first brush with fame came when he was plucked by Harry Truman in 1949 to serve as a United States District Attorney.

His win against Simpson was unexpected, and narrow. Hickey was not someone who was forceful, and often was described as "quiet and unassuming who talks in a low voice. At gatherings, he'll stand along the sidelines talking with small groups."

In many ways, the election blurred party lines, certainly by today's standards. *A New History of Wyoming* notes Simpson was against capital punishment, an issue that resonated due to a series of murders that had occurred throughout the state. Conversely, Hickey supported it. But Wyoming observers credit Simpson's codification of a "non-partisan" highway commission's recommendation that the Interstate highway intersection would go through Buffalo. T.A. Larson's *New History of Wyoming* says "he angered Sheridan County voters who sat out the fall election." Simpson, who according to Larson had taken Sheridan by 741 votes in his '54 election, this time lost to Hickey by 1,708 votes. Simpson also was unpopular for wanting the state to purchase the concessions from Yellowstone, which he felt Wyoming was not getting its fair share, causing him to lose ground in Teton County as well.

McGee, O'Mahoney, and Carl Hayden of Arizona, 1958
Photo courtesy of the University of Wyoming

Meanwhile, Hickey campaigned against the "interference" by the federal government and won the election by 2,582 votes. He was said to be so surprised by his win that he "apologized" to Simpson on their congratulatory call.

Hickey's Governorship was a mixed bag. Larson notes he tried to reduce the budget proposal to $30 million, about $5 million less than what the Legislature wanted, but they restored about $3 million of it. Because legislators would not give him a severance tax, he could "not deliver" on a pledge to restore Homestead exemptions. He worked out a plan to allow the state to accept federal aid for the Board of Education. He advocated the creation of a "little cabinet" to centralize state government. And Larson notes that he and legislators "became very much excited about state's rights with regard to choice of color used in painting stripes on federal aid highways." But he was not a favorite of his own party. State officials were quoted as saying they "can't believe he's a Democrat. He's more conservative than most Republicans."

Meanwhile, O'Mahoney was the elder statesman of the bunch and in many ways may have been the last national politician from the state to be a true national Democrat. O'Mahoney had been appointed Assistant Postmaster by James Farley early in the Roosevelt administration, but he would soon go on to something better. Late in 1933, Democratic Senator Kendrick died and O'Mahoney was appointed to fill the seat.

In the first FDR midterm, he had no trouble securing a full term. And he was a true champion of Roosevelt. About the only issue he opposed him on was his "court-packing" plan. O'Mahoney helped push through the Temporary Economic Committee, which he chaired. But he also played close attention to

Wyoming issues, chairing the Committee on Indian Affairs and eventually, the committee on Interior Affairs. He was a dogged advocate of Wyoming industry.

Image courtesy of Politics1.com

O'Mahoney won two re-elections since '34, including one over Simpson, and by '52, seemed poised to do so again. But the Eisenhower landslide, which delivered Congress to the Republicans, was enough to knock him out 52-48%. However, O'Mahoney, nearing 70, did manage to get a rare second act a little over a year later. In 1954, the state's other Senator, Democrat Lester Hunt, committed suicide and O'Mahoney was appointed to take his place. A number of Republicans tried the "Red" theme on O'Mahoney calling him a "left-winger" but the Senator countered by citing his Catholicism.

O'Mahoney
Photo courtesy of the Library of Congress Prints and Photographs Division

In the end, 1954 proved to be a much more favorable Democratic year than past cycles and at 70, he won a six year term to serve in the Senate where he became instrumental in passage of the 1957 Civil Rights Act. It was O'Mahoney who, according to Bethine Church, the wife of his very junior colleague from Idaho, "refined the language" on Church's idea to have mixed juries ("He was a wonderful lawyer", Bethine recalled). He also took on the corporations, wanting "concentrated industries" to provide notice and explanations for rate increases.

In 1959, O'Mahoney, 75, suffered a stroke, which basically set in stone a decision not to seek re-election in 1960. Wayne Morse, who wheeled him onto the floor for his farewell, called him among the most "able and effective" at fairness issues. He died two years later at 78.

Republican Congressman Keith Thomson, 41, won the election to succeed O'Mahoney and seemed headed for a long career. But he dropped dead of a heart attack at his Cody ranch just two weeks later. Hickey had the power to appoint the new Senator. And he decided that he knew just who he wanted that to be: himself. Hickey resigned the Governorship in January of 1961, just a day before the new Senator would have to take office in order to be on parity seniority wise with other Senator's from that class.

Hickey said it had been his intention to appoint Tracy McCraken, a well-known entrepreneur and owner of the *Wyoming Eagle* in the state to fill the seat, but he himself had died of a heart attack that December. So upon resigning the Governorship, Hickey made an arrangement for his successor, JackGage, to appoint him to the seat. That immediately brought howls from Wyomingites of many stripes. Hickey, noting that the appointment would be short term, noted that voters would have the ultimate say in whether he kept the seat. "If I do the job I want to do," he said, "I will certainly be a candidate."

Roncalio with William Henry Harrison, Simpson, Hansen, and FDR JR
Photo via Wikipedia

Ultimately, the voters did decide and it was not the verdict that Hickey had hoped for. By the time November of 1962 rolled around, Wyoming was the one Senate seat Democrats held that knew they would not salvage. And he'd lose the election to fill the remaining four years of his term by a lopsided 58-42%. Who unseated him? Milward Simpson, returning the favor of four years earlier. Hickey became a Circuit Judge but would himself die young in 1970, at just 59. Hickey's son would seek the Governorship in 2002, but would lose the Democratic primary to Dave Freudenthal.

McGee continued in the Senate, becoming among the most distinguished and recognizable members of the body among his colleagues, until his loss to Malcolm Wallop in 1976, one of the first signs of the forthcoming rise of the "New Right"

Meanwhile, Roncalio, the eighth of nine children of Italian immigrants, won a House seat in the Johnson year of 1964, defeating William Henry Harrison, grandson of the 23'rd President and great-grandson of the 9th. Born Domenico Roncalio, he'd say, "I went from bootblack to banker."

Roncalio had a tightrope to walk representing a state that was only getting more conservative as time went on, but did so without signs of bother – or backlash. Why? Because it was never about him. It was Wyoming that was foremost among his priorities. Actually, it was always about his nation.

Roncalio epitomizes the "Greatest Generation." During World War II, he took part in seven combat campaigns across the globe, including D-Day. That won him a Silver Star for gallantry. Earlier at the University of Wyoming, he had been student body president.

Teno Roncalio
Photo from the collection of the U.S. House of Representatives

On his death, *The Trib* said "Roncalio's unusual coalitions could include such diverse groups as Italian-Americans, African-Americans and anti-Vietnam war activists. Roncalio backed civil rights and Medicare but locally, fought for the Washakie wilderness area and the Trans-Alaska Pipeline. He also stopped "Project Wagonwheel" (also known as "Project Plowshare,") a plan conceived by the old Atomic Energy Commission to build five nuclear devices to release gas from the rocks. He offered language to a 1972 Atomic Energy authorization to delete the $10.5 million for the project. He urged members to, "Please consider the following two questions: First, is natural gas the proper fuel of the future and, second, what effect will gas stimulation have on the populations located near proposed gasfields? Natural gas is an expendable resource that is wasted as an energy fuel; and the people directly affected are not certain that they want this development until some pending questions are answered." That amendment was defeated. But Roncalio was just getting started.

As Kathy Karpan, a long-time Roncalio staffer who eventually became Secretary of State would say, this "would have detonated underground nuclear devices sequentially to free natural gas trapped in tight rock formations. It came to our attention when the AEC, after three tests, planned a test for the Green River Basin 'Project Wagon Wheel.' Teno, on his second year of attacking the funding for the program, evidently led AEC to come to its senses.

Project Plowshare wasn't heard from again."

Roncalio thought he could parlay his success into a U.S. Senate seat in '66 and came surprisingly close. But Republican Governor Cliff Hansen, himself considered among the most genuine individuals in politics, edged him 52-48%. Roncalio won the seat back by 608 votes in 1970 and, while he had inched up to 56% in '76, McGee's defeat that year perhaps scared him, and he chose to retire in '78 (he announced it at a football game). A guy by the name of Dick Cheney succeeded him. Though several have come close, no Democrat has won a federal office since.

Image courtesy ronwadebuttons.com

A one-time employee, Kathy Karpan, a former Secretary of State who had herself run for Governor and the Senate, seemed to note that by calling Roncalio, the last Wyoming representative to Congress who "was able to advocate for the environmental and energy agendas." She attests to Roncalio's integrity and also, for his gift of public service. Karpan called him "great on constituent services (who) took phone calls at home at all hours of the night."

Roncalio with colleague David King of Utah
Photo courtesy the University of Utah, Department of Special Collections

Karpan remembers collective groans among the staff when he would return to Washington from Wyoming, he summed us into the office and began pulling out from his pant and shirt pockets his scribbled notes about people he met in Wyoming who asked for his help." But there was nothing Roncalio asked his staff to do that he wasn't willing to do himself. Often, he would try to solve an intractable constituent problem by calling an agency himself, and he would gladly inform his fellow Wyomingite when he was able to succeed.

Roncalio died at 87 in 2003. On his death, State Senator Jayne Mockler called him, "one of the most genuine people I have ever met. He was one of the most genuinely sincere political figures in the state, and he did it for all the right reasons. Even the state Republican chair added he "loved Wyoming," adding, "The true measure of the man is that 25 years after he retired from an active political life, we still remember what he did." "He did it for the people, he did it to help move the state forward, and there didn't seem to be a lot of personal self-motivation."

As for Kennedy, he of course narrowly won the Presidency in November but Wyoming had nothing to do with it. Nixon carried the state 55-45%. That was not for lack of trying on Roncalio's part. He told Kennedy that winning the state was a must, for if not, "my name will be mud." Shortly after the election, Kennedy shook hands with Roncalio and greeted him with, "Hello Mud."

Still, grateful for the state's role in putting him over the top, he would visit Wyoming once again in September of 1963, this time as President. (McGee was instrumental in arranging the visit). The 10,000 folk crowd that greeted him at the Cheyenne Municipal Airport was said to have been the largest ever assembled for a gathering in the state. And *Wyoming Eagle* Editor Bernard Horton wrote, "More than 30,000 persons, one-tenth of Wyoming's total population, turned out yesterday to see, hear and cheer" the President who, in addition to Cheyenne, would also be stopping in Jackson and Laramie.

**JFK made a much ballyhooed visit to Wyoming nearly two
months to the day before he was assassinated
Photo courtesy of Kathy Karpan**

One person who was able to join the dignitaries in greeting the President was Karpan, editor of the Branding Iron, the student newspaper at the University of Wyoming. Phillip White, Jr. in a piece observing the visit, noted "the president initially departed from his prepared remarks to speak to the students directly." Kennedy said, "What we are attempting to do is develop talents in a nation which requires education . . . knowledge is power" and that it "can be brought to bear to improve our lives." But Kennedy also had a message for his young audience. "I hope that all of you who are students here will recognize the great opportunity that lies before you in this decade, and in the decades to come, to be of service to our country. White notes that among the students in the crowd that day: future Vice-President Dick Cheney. And Kennedy, speaking to a crowd of largely native Wyomingites, noted that O'Mahoney, who had died a year earlier, was actually a native of Massachusetts.

Less than two months after his Wyoming visit, an assassin's bullet felled Kennedy. But Wyoming's legacy lives on in his, and in America's history.

**Gale McGee and his family joined the rest of the
nation in mourning the slain President
Photo courtesy of Robert McGee**

CHAPTER SEVENTY-EIGHT

Smith Appointed To JFK's Senate Seat In 1961

Historic Quote: "I think, Jack, we Protestants proved in West Virginia that we'll vote for a Catholic. What we want is some of the Catholic states to prove that they'll vote for a Protestant." Lyndon Johnson at a joint appearance to the Texas delegation during the 1960 Democratic National Convention before the dup ended up as running-mates. Before an abviously hostile audience, Kennedy's knees were reportedly shaking and Johnson's line elicited cheers from the crowd.

**Benjamin A. Smith, Whom Furcolo would grudgingly
appoint to fill JFK's Senate seat
Photo courtesy of the U.S. Senate Historical Office**

When President-elect John F. Kennedy resigned his Senate seat in 1960, his seat went to a true loyalist. He was JFK's roommate at Harvard And most importantly, he had no ambitions of holding the job beyond the fall of 1962 when the President's youngest brother Teddy would achieve his eligibility to continue the family dynasty by reaching the Constitutionally mandated age of 30. His name was Benjamin Smith and his only political experience was serving as Mayor of Gloucester, Massachusetts. But that was a largely ceremonial position that would be dwarfed by his ultra-close Kennedy connection.

Smith was so close to the family that he was among the elite group of people known as an "honorary Kennedy." In 1960, he hit the hustings for JFK as hard as virtually anyone. He served as the 10th Congressional district coordinator for

Wisconsin (a portion of the state where JFK was not successful), then it was on to West Virginia.

The Smith family had established a legacy in Gloucester long before Benjamin was born. The Smith's prominence was such that when he became engaged to Barbara Mechem, newspapers as far away as Chicago published the announcement. It was while attending Harvard that he met the future President. After college, Smith served his country in the Navy during World War II and attained the rank of Commander. He was based in the Pacific and was on an anti-submarine, anti-torpedo vessel. Returning home, he took the helm of the family business, the Merchants Box Company. He and JFK would both be ushers at one anothers wedding.

When Kennedy confidants were debating who should be given the interim appointment, it was JFK who made his preference known for Smith. The only remaining hurdle was persuading outgoing Governor Foster Furcolo.

Like JFK, Furcolo was a Democrat but that's about where the similarities ended. There was no love between the two men. And Furcolo himself had coveted the seat, making it no secret that he might consider appointing himself. But JFK had an ace in his sleeve. Furcolo was actually a lame-duck and had been succeeded as Governor by John Volpe, a Republican. If Furcolo were to follow through on naming himself, Kennedy would simply hold off resigning his seat until Furcolo's term ended which, conveniently for him, was before he was to assume office as the 35th President. The Governor acquiesced.

In a two-sentence statement to reporters that stressed the interest of "promoting unity in the Democratic party." Furcolo agreed to accept Kennedy's "suggestion" to appoint Smith. A particularly important addendum, he said was that he had been "informed that he will serve two years and not seek re-election in 1962."

Kennedy was not certain Teddy would be ready to assume the mantle in 1962 so he encouraged him to pound the pavement, telling his brother, "I'll hear whether you are really making a mark-up there I will tell you whether this is something that you ought to seriously consider."

In Washington, Smith's impact as a junior member of the Senate was obviously limited though his ties with Kennedy made him a big fish. He was assigned to the labor, public works, and District of Columbia Committees.

In 1963, with Smith once again a private citizen, Kennedy made him a U.S. ambassador to an international fisheries conference where the Soviet Union, Canada and Japan would be taking part. His association with the family would not end with JFK's death. He served on both brothers Presidential campaign.

CHAPTER SEVENTY-NINE

Homer Thornberry A Johnson Confidante Since Boyhood

Historic Tidbit: Jackie Kennedy was said to have wanted to witness LBJ's swearing-in as President. That may or may not have been true. But the book *Sam Johnson's Boy* reveals Johnson growing so impatient waiting for her to arrive that he was about to get her. He didn't want her wearing her blood soaked clothes. And when she arrived on Air Force One with the murdered President's body, she was stunned to walk into the Presidential bedroom to find Johnson lying on the bed barking out orders.

Leaving Parkland Hospital with his confidante, the new President
Photo via Corbis Images

The word confidante is sometimes overused but Homer Thornberry may have been among the biggest of Lyndon Baines Johnson. His history, from boyhood, to the future President's Senate run, heart attack, selection as Vice-President, and assumption of the Presidency very much overlaps with the 36th President's. Through Johnson, Thornberry had a respectable House tenure that resulted in bigger things. And unlike many who tolerated Johnson, Thornberry actually seems to have liked him.

Homer Thornberry first met Johnson in the early 1920s when young Lyndon would accompany his father, State Senator Sam Johnson to Austin for the Legislative sessions. When Johnson gave up his House seat, Thornberry ran to succeed him. Johnson was on pins and needles over a protracted 87 vote win. But Thornberry won comfortably and went on to serve 15 years in the lower chamber. When Thornberry arrived in Washington, who would be on hand to give him a tour of the Capitol? None other than Lyndon, whose victory in his own race was now finally in hand.

Thornberry as D.A.
Photo courtesy of the Austin Public Library

The challenges Thornberry faced during boyhood were enormous. His parents were both deaf and were unable to speak. In its obituary of Thornberry, *The New York Times* said "his parents were so poor they could not afford the windowpanes for several yearsafter his carpenter fatherbuilt their house." *The Times* continued that Homer "did not speak until he was three and spent the rest of the time making up for it." But Thornberry advanced to high places, putting himself through the University of Texas Law School.

In 1955, when Johnson suffered his heart attack, Thornberry was a regular at the hospital. He would entertain the patient with dominoes which the nurses would make sure stayed short. Meanwhile, his friendship with Johnson persevered. The day after he became President, he actually called the boyfriend of Thornberry's daughter, admonishing him to treat her well.

When Johnson suspected Kennedy was going to dangle the vice-presidency in front of him, the usually self-confident Johnson asked Thornberry what he should do. His response: "Don't touch it with a ten-foot pole." He added, "Tell Jack anything you want but don't take it." After the convention, Johnson enjoyed a brief respite in Acapulco, and Thornberry and his wife accompanied him.

Kennedy, partly through Johnson's insistence, had nominated Thornberry to be a Texas District Judge in 1963. But Thornberry was also an administration supporter and Kennedy feared an early departure from the House would put his Rules Committee seat in the hands of a less sympathetic lawmaker. So Thornberry delayed his resignation until December 20. By that time, an assassin's bullet made his friend the President.

As it happened, Thornberry was riding in the motorcade with Johnson when the shots rang out. After Kennedy expired, he rode with Johnson from Parkland to Air Force One and actually moved in to Johnson's home, The Elms, in order to facilitate his friend's first couple of days as president.

Thornberry was part of the Suite 8F Group (Shown with Sam Rayburn)

A few days after being sworn in, Johnson invited Thornberry, whom he had referred to as "my Congressman,' to "come on down and have a drink with me.' The pair discussed many matters, including attending parties at the home of Bobby Baker, the aide who would soon become notorious in a non-flattering way.

Johnson promoted Thornberry, naming him an Appellate Judge. And then came the big reward for years of friendship. Chief Justice Earl Warren had stated his intention to retire and Johnson decided to go for a one-two. Abe Fortas would be elevated to Chief Justice while Johnson would nominate Thornberry to take Fortas' seat. That brought a rebuke from an aide, Larry Temple, who felt some might see the position for his longtime friend as cronyism. At that point, Johnson unleashed.

"What political office did you get elected to? . . . don't come to me as any knowledgeable political expert until you've run and gotten elected to public office." But Lady Bird, who was in the room, agreed ("Lyndon, he might be right about that and that's the one thing that worries me about Homer, as much as I'd like to see him on the Supreme Court"). Johnson's mind was made up. Others had concerns about Thornberry, which left Johnson bemused. In a phone conversation with Senate Minority Leader Everett Dirksen, Johnson rattled off his experience. "Thornberry practiced 18 years, tried cases every day. And the Bar says they want somebody that has judicial experience. He acted a prosecutor, elected by the people, for many years. Then he belonged to the best law firm in the state for many years." Johnson added, "I think I'm in a hell of a lot better shape nominating somebody like you or Homer than I would be, by God, with somebody I didn't know." Dirksen agreed, calling it "easily defended." But as it happened, Fortas fell victim to a filibuster, so the spot for Thornberry never opened.

Thornberry continued on the 5th Circuit and stayed on as a Judge under part-time status until his death. It came in 1995 at 86.

CHAPTER EIGHTY

Albert Thomas Rode From Parkland To Lovefield With LBJ Before Oath Administered

Historic Tidbit: When President Kennedy called Congressman Albert Thomas, he told the powerful Appropriator that he needed his help on three bills. Thomas told Kennedy he couldn't help him. Kennedy courtly said, "Now you know, Jim Webb is thinking about putting this (space) center down in Houston?" Thomas replied, "In that case Mr. President."

Thomas gave a wink to LBJ after the swearing-in
Photo courtesy of the Lyndon B. Johnson Presidential Library

Next to the Johnsons and Jackie Kennedy, the most recognized person in perhaps the most recognizable photo in American history is hardly known to anyone at all. Albert Thomas is the man in the bowtie standing directly behind Lady Bird Johnson when LBJ was administered the Presidential oath hours after President Kennedy had been assassinated. But his footnote was more than just happening to be standing in the right place for perpetual posterity. For Thomas' career by itself was one to be reckoned with.

When President Kennedy traveled to Texas for his fateful trip, his itinerary took him to more places than just Dallas. There was San Antonio, Fort Worth, and Houston. The latter city is where Kennedy spoke at a testimonial dinner on the evening of November 21st for Congressman Al Thomas, the longtime Texas Democrat and ally of Lyndon Johnson who was contemplating retiring from Congress. JFK and LBJ had major differences but both men agreed on the need to keep Thomas in office. And after Kennedy's death, Thomas was one of two Congressmen who rode with LBJ back to Lovefield before the oath as the 36th President would be administered. Thus, he shared a front seat to history.

It was Thomas who broached the idea to Connally of Yarborough introducing Johnson at the dinner before Connally would present Kennedy. The Governor thought that ridiculous and Thomas dropped it. Still, the dinner took place and appeared to convey to the public its main objective: the impression of one big happy family.

The event, at the Sam Houston Coliseum, was pure JFK. Telling the tale of "wondering how other Congressman got there (to Washington)," Kennedy said he never questioned that about Thomas. "It's always been clear to me." He told Thomas he hoped he'd, "Stay as long as I stayed, I didn't know how long that would be . . . When he rises to speak, they listen, some of us at the other end of Pennsylvania Avenue."

Photo courtesy of the Collection of the U.S. House of Representatives

Kennedy went on to tell the crowd how Thomas "helped steer this country to its eminence in space." "Next month, when the United States fires the largest booster in the history of the world into space for the first time, giving us the lead, fires the largest payroll – payload into space giving us the lead." Realizing his error, Kennedy quickly added, "It will be the largest payroll too." Kennedy recounted that "there were those in 1936, as there are today, those who are opposed to growth and change, who prefer to defy them, who look back instead of forward. But Albert Thomas and those who work with him did not heed that view in the mid-30s and this country, this state, and this country are glad they did not."

When Thomas took the microphone, he made clear that Houston's renaissance was well in sight. "Our city,' he said, "will continue to grow and grow and grow because you will make it grow."

The next afternoon, it was Thomas who provided the first reports to the media about Kennedy's condition. On his accounts, the media reported that both

Kennedy and Connally were "still alive." But he also added that the President "is in very critical condition." That may have been technically true but any hope the American people may have felt about recovery would be quickly dissipated.

After Kennedy expired, Thomas got his biggest brush with history. While Thomas shares the distinction of riding with Johnson to Air Force One, it was virtually an accident. Johnson had already exited the hospital and, unsure of the safety, wanted to proceed to Air Force One immediately. He had asked Thornberry to wait for him. But in his memoirs, "The Vantage Point," Johnson wrote that he looked out the window and saw Thomas wandering about and "when I saw who it was, I told them to let him in."

Much has been made of the wink Thomas had given to LBJ after Judge Sarah Hughes administered the oath. Johnson turned toward Thomas to smile and it's probable that Thomas wanted to politely acknowledge it while maintaining a subdued composure in light of the day's events. Some might have nodded. Others would give a half-smile. Thomas simply winked.

Thomas came to Congress less than a year before Johnson, having defeated the Mayor of Houston in a 1936 primary. Born in Nacogdoches, he worked in his father's store before serving in the Army during World War 1. He graduated from Rice Institute, now Rice University, and eventually, UT Law School. But it was at Rice that his love affair, and the seeds for much of Houston began.

Thomas' roommate at Rice had been George Brown, who would later lead the world renowned Brown and Root Construction Firm. Both men were part of the 8F Study Group, named for the suite in the hotel at which they met. Though Johnson and Connally were also members, Johnson's influence was limited. "Johnson was linked to Kennedy. Much of the group were conservative Democrats." Eventually, the Humble Oil Company donated about 1,000 acres of the West Ranchland to Rice which in turn, offered it as the site of the upcoming Manned spacecraft Kennedy had spoken of. As one opined, it was scrubland that "wasn't particularly valuable sitting empty."

By this time, Thomas had risen to chair of the House Appropriation Defense Committee which gave Thomas wide latitude on where to place the center. Thomas had already been miffed about Maryland having scooped up the Goddard Space Center in 1958 and he wasn't about to let it happen again. That came to fruition one night when Kennedy had called Thomas asking him for help on three projects he had been seeking. Thomas balked but when Kennedy brought up the space center, Thomas did a u-turn. "In that case, Mr. President," was all he needed to say. Thomas took Kennedy's word as a verbal commitment and though some employees in Maryland expressed displeasure at having to move to Texas, the deal was done.

Thomas was a valuable ally to Johnson on other issues. He was one of just three white Texas Democrats (Jack Brooks and Jake Pickle were the others) to back the Civil Rights Act. But Thomas also got on the wrong side of Johnson.

Audio-tapes released show Johnson berating Thomas for a House passed provision "put on by this damned fool Humphrey," to make the President report to Congress on wheat sales to the Soviet Union. "Why should I report to everyone that I screwed the girl? You screwed one last night but you don't want to report it." Thomas said "I wish I did." Johnson, getting back on track, continues that the amendment "is just publicizing that I'm pro-Russian just when Nixon runs against me." Thomas tells him that won't happen.

Thomas was at a loss for words which gave Johnson ammunition to continue. "Don't try to s—t" me because I know better." Thomas said he's worked with that language before but Johnson reminded him it was "under Republican Presidents." On other matters, Johnson cooperated whole-heartedly with Johnson. Thomas was a driving force behind the President's proposal to build the Corpus Christie Naval Air Station.

The lavish attention on Thomas by Kennedy on the final night of his life did indeed persuade him to seek another term. And it was one in which his colleagues rewarded him with the Chairmanship of the House Democratic Caucus. But he wouldn't live to serve all of it. Thomas battled cancer for much of the last year of his life but continued to go about his duties until close to the end. He died in April 1966 and his wife Lera won the election to serve the remaining half year of his term.

A year later, the Houston Convention and Exhibit Center was named for Thomas.

Thomas was succeeded by his wife
Photo via the Collection of the U.S. House of Representatives

CHAPTER EIGHTY-ONE

John Tower:
From Succeeding LBJ In Senate to Bush
Defense Secretary Nominee

Historic Tidbit: Ronald Kessler, in his book *In the President's Secret Service*, details Reagan's fondness for mailing personal checks to people with needs, even without his wife approving – or even knowing. But his genuine warmth was a hallmark of his personality. One day, his motorcade was proceeding along M Street in Washington D.C. when Reagan noticed a man giving him the finger. Still "smiling and waving," he rolled down the window and said, "Hi there, you son-of-a-bitch." Agent Dennis Chomicki imitated the President's "buttery smooth delivery."

It has been a quarter of a century since the Senate refused to confirm John Tower as Secretary of Defense. The rejection came along fairly partisan lines that focused on unsubstantiated – and according to those who knew Tower best, untrue accusations about his personal life. While Tower's professional qualifications for the Defense-post were unanimously viewed as Texas-sized, at the end of the day he was abandoned by many of the colleagues he had befriended during his nearly quarter-of-a-century in a chamber where his service had ceased just four years earlier.

Tower was a tireless, humble man whose love for public service was exceeded only by his devotion to his three daughters.

Tower had a firm place in history even before the nomination. When Lyndon Baines Johnson became vice-president, it was Tower, a 35-year-old Republican, who won the special election to succeed him. That made him, along with George H.W. Bush, among the founding fathers of the modern Republican Party in Texas, though of course Bush lost his Senate races twice when Tower had already made it to the body.

The seed for Tower's win in the special was planted in November of 1960 when the Witchita Falls political science professor had taken 41% against LBJ. At the state level, most Democrats (and Republicans for that matter) would have considered that number a ceiling in a state that had a Congressional delegation that was almost unanimously Democratic. Some were liberals, some conservative, and others in between, but nearly all were Democrats. As it was, Tower was treated more as a sacrificial lamb. But he only viewed that more as an incentive to fight harder.

Now there is evidence that some voters opposed LBJ because they begrudged him for continuing to seek re-election to the Senate as he was running for Vice-President (his ability to do so would famously be called the "LBJ law"). However, the fact that Tower was able to do so well against LBJ is, in my view, emblematic of the ways in which the South was beginning to signal its change, however small, from the Democratic reign that is now beyond complete. Kennedy being helped over the finish line by Johnson in Texas was all the more evidence that this was the case.

When LBJ resigned, Governor Price Daniel appointed Congressman William Blakely, a "Tory Democrat," to fill the seat. Tower immediately began campaigning, though few expected him to perform much better than the past November, much less win. Sam Rayburn called him a "pipsqueak." The field of candidates vying for the seat was colorful and long: 71 in all. But only a handful were serious. One of them was Jim Wright, still an obscure Congressman from Fort Worth. Another was Henry Gonzalas, who that spring would capture his San Antonio Congressional seat.

Left image via flickr.com; right image courtesy of the Tower Family

Blakely emerged from the primary in second place. Tower actually placed first but, as the lone serious Republican candidate, had only 31%, and he was still not seen as the person to beat. Blakely was a conservative Democrat who had not only backed Eisenhower in both of his campaigns, but had also challenged incumbent Senator Ralph Yarborough in the 1958 Democratic primary. Though he didn't come close to toppling him, Yarborough didn't do a thing to help his former nemesis. In fact, he remarked that both candidates seemed to be engaged "in a competition as to determine who could denounce the Kennedy administration the hardest."

Meanwhile, Tower's energy was boundless. Often with his wife Lou in the front and their three young daughters in the back seat, he hit 18 Texas towns in a three day period. Tower received help from Barry Goldwater and Prescott Bush, which began his life-long friendship with the future President, Prescott's son. Tower won by 11,000 votes, becoming the "Lone-Star" State's first GOP Senator since Reconstruction. He was 5'5 but forever earned the nickname the "little giant." As a sign of the improbability of his win, virtually all of Tower's family were Democrats. At the time of his win, his dad told him how proud he was and added, "most of us voted for you."

As President of the Senate, Johnson swore Tower in; as he recounts in his autobiography *Consequences*, he stepped down from the Senate rostrum and "stood on the lower step. LBJ, who [at 6'4] loomed over me when we were both on equal footing, remained on the top step, forcing me to crane my neck back to look him in the eye . . . It didn't bother me a bit."

Taking the oath following his improbable 1961 win
Photo courtesy of the Tower Family

Tower's voting record was solidly conservative. During debate on the Nuclear Test Ban Treaty, he proposed amendments requiring Soviet reimbursement for peace and security operations and another postponing the treaty's implementation until "an adequate system" was in place to detect violations. Both were defeated by large margins. He opposed civil rights legislation but made clear he deplored the condition of blacks. "As a native southerner," he said before the vote, "I am deeply ashamed of the way that we have treated our Negro citizens in the South. I cannot justify that. We have held them down." But he continued that "we cannot overturn the mores of society overnight and that is what we are trying to do with this bill." Still, as a close Tower confidante said, "his actions spoke louder than anything," going on to note that he "hired people of all colors in high ranking positions that no other people were doing." As the years went on, he appears to have regretted his "no" vote. And he still got along fine with Democrats. "Scoop" Jackson of Washington was a close friend.

Tower was also a staunch advocate of increased military spending. He favored the war in Vietnam and had a map of Vietnam on the wall of his office. He would often invite colleagues who wanted an up-close view of the battleground. The war caused so many divisions among Democrats that, near the end of his Presidency, LBJ invited Tower for a drink at the White House and told him, "John, I get more loyalty from you than my own party." Around that time, Tower was instrumental in urging Nixon to pick Spiro Agnew, the unknown Governor of Maryland, as his running mate.

In his early years, Tower was not perceived as a workhorse (though his family is quick to point out he was very much in demand), but as he gained seniority and proved his durability by continuing to win re-election, that changed, leading *The Almanac of American Politics* to conclude that "he does not use his charm to ingratiate himself to others but he does have influence by virtue of his hard work and brain power." That was on display early on when he and Ted Kennedy, who along with Birch Bayh were the youngest members of the body, conducted a debate at American University. It was so universally agreed that Tower had won that even Bobby Kennedy approached him after asking how he did it.

Tower served on the Intelligence Committee where he worked surprisingly well with the panel's Democratic Chairman, Frank Church. When Tower became chairman of the Armed Services Committee after the Republicans took the Senate in 1980, however, he hired a partisan staff.

Against early odds, Tower won re-election fairly easily in 1966 when the Democrats again put up a Torycrat, and a number of people crossed party lines to back Tower. In 1972, he beat Harold "Barefoot" Sanders 55-44%. Sanders was accepted by liberals and conservatives alike, but Tower received substantial aid from Nixon's massive win.

1978 proved tougher. His opponent was two-term Congressman Bob Krueger, whose base was in Bexar County (San Antonio), but he also served some of the adjacent GOP counties. He gained a following among usually GOP-friendly oil and gas industries as the main proponent of a deregulation bill that failed. But Krueger, an attorney, was unlike any opponent Tower had previously faced. He was erudite, often quoting Shakespeare. And he didn't hesitate to go for the jugular.

Krueger had often told audiences that Tower was a "womanizer" and attacked him for not releasing the financial records of his ex-wife Lou, who was still prominent in his campaign (even in divorce, John and Lou Tower maintained a warm relationship). Tower backers said the then-single Krueger knew "little about marriage, and knows nothing about the sensitivity involved in a marriage between two people with children from previous marriages and longstanding career."

Tower said, "When a woman marries a man, she doesn't give up her privacy even if she marries a U.S. Senator."

The most high-profile moment came when Krueger approached Tower to shake hands during a luncheon in mid-October. Tower pointedly turned away. Some newspapers criticized him, and Tower, who had been tied in the polls at that point, dropped slightly. But he then undertook a serious offensive. He taped an ad in which he said, "I was brought up to believe that a handshake was and is a symbol of friendship and respect. I was not brought up to believe that a handshake is a meaningless and hypocritical act done for public display." *The Almanac* observed that "for once, the Senator's sour personality seemed to have worked to his benefit."

Meanwhile, Tower called Krueger a man of "inherited wealth" and campaigned in Hispanic areas, which he credited with helping him at the finish line. Money was also pivotal, as Tower had nearly twice as much of it as Krueger. The race was decided by just 12,000 votes, but it was enough to give him a 4th, which would also be his last. He did not stand for re-election in 1984 and family members attributed one reason to fatigue of the process.

Some conservatives may have resisted Tower because of his support for Ford over Reagan in 1976. Tower believed that he had a duty to back Ford as the incumbent President, but Reagan beat Ford in Texas and controlled the delegate selection. It was something that would haunt him for the remainder of his Senate career. Tower recalls in his memoirs that he suggested the name of a friend for an Ambassadorship only to be told by a White House secretary that the man had backed Ford. Tower replied that he had done so as well, to which the secretary replied, "We're well aware of that, Senator." Yet when Tower shared his plans with the President to not seek another term in 1984, Reagan urged him to reconsider.

Years later, many found the line about Tower having a sour personality peculiar. Though he was not a rah-rah kind of guy (one family member says Tower "was not great at small talk and was more comfortable with a small group") but nonetheless was "a great story and joke teller" who had an ability to "talk about things most people didn't understand."

On one occasion, Tower dressed up as Superman for a National Press Club Roast. He joked that even being 5'4, he'd "Tower" over others. And each year for Texas Independence Day, he'd read William Barratt Travis' last letter to the Alamo. He was a die-hard Dallas Cowboy's fan who would scream at the television set when they were not doing well. He was an avid reader who really did not have any hobbies. The family says "work was his hobby." And he was humble.

Periodically, Tower would go on official Congressional delegations but, rather than attending prestigious parties, instead preferred to spend time with military servicemen and women.

Tower was known to have among the most outstanding staffs on Capitol Hill, most of whom were, in the words of the family, "devoted to him and each other." Phil Charles was one such person. During the 1989 confirmation hearings, he labeled himself "an individual who had a longer and closer relationship with him than of any of the staff, both as a legislative assistant and principal traveling aide." He recalled once how he and another staffer, Charles Fahey were at lunch. When they returned, Tower gave them a stern look and when Fahey responded that he was at lunch, Tower responded, "for 20 years?"

As a boss, Tower had a wry sense of humor which Phil Charles and Charles Fahey recalled when he called a surprise staff meeting at a time when two of his staffers were at lunch. When they returned, Tower gave them a stern look and when Fahey responded that he was at lunch, Tower responded, "for 20 years?"

About the only time Tower ever became stern with his staff was when they mocked his car. That was a 1972 Dodge Charger which, next to his daughters, may have been his first love. He called it, "The Green Bullet" (his personal secretary, Mattie Mae McKee, upon referring to it as "The Green Bomb," learned never to make that mistake again).

McKee, in her book, *In the Shadow of the Greats*, recalled a time a muffler fell off the car when a staffer, Vic Sherlock, was driving him back to work. When he exited, Sherlock retrieved it and presented it to Tower at his birthday party to which the delighted Senator exclaimed, "Hello Baby." Tower and the car were inseparable "he would drive 'The Green Bullet' rather than walk the one block to the Monicle restaurant" on Capitol Hill and would do the same if he had to make a vote. A young Capitol Policeman once recalled his first interaction with "The Green Bullet." As the car was approaching the Capitol, a startled new police officer initially "thought it had no driver. The car sported an oversized engine, and the driver's eyes barely cleared the steering wheel."

It was only after that he became aware of the legend that was Tower's height and his car.

All in all, when the family asked McKee how the staff felt about Tower, her response was a poignant, "we loved him."

**Tower in front of the Russell Senate Office Building with his and his beloved
"Green Bullet"
Photo courtesy of The Tower Collection**

When his term ended, Tower stayed on the national stage. Immediately, he chaired the American delegation to the Geneva Arms talks, a 15 month endeavor where talks with the Russians centered on the dismantling of nuclear arms. He didn't hesitate to use straight-talk. When a prime minister was stating facts, Tower said, "bulls—t."

His performance was thought so laudable that in 1993, two years after Tower's death, his two living daughters received an unsolicited letter from President Bill Clinton, whom neither had ever met, praising his service. The Tower Commission was even more high-profile. It was the Iran-Contra investigation and Tower and the panel's lead Democrat, Ed Muskie worked well, interviewing 80 witnesses and producing a comprehensive report. While it absolved Reagan's knowledge, it faulted him for a "hands-off" management style and said he needed to listen more to the National Security Council.

Fast forward to 1989. When Bush won the Presidency, Tower was only a natural for the position of Defense Secretary. As he wrote in his memoirs, one Senator, Democrat Alan Dixon of Illinois, had even told Tower he didn't even have to bother making the customary courtesy call to his office. But Tower had been known to pick up a drink and while few if any ever could say it had ever affected his abilities (that he never missed a day of work was beyond dispute) Democrats expressed concern. Whether they were genuine or out to tar the new President is unclear but well past Bush's announcement, very few expressed Democrats or Republicans expressed hesitancy to confirm him or even publicly mentioned rumors of alcoholism. As it happened, only one person of prominence, conservative activist Paul Weyrich, brought to light accusations of excessive alcoholism and he was already opposing the nomination from Tower's right (others refused to testify under oath for fear of losing their jobs).

In fact, close Tower confidantes believed many of the rumors emanated from Tower's second wife whose stability many questioned (his relationship with his first wife was one of genuine respect until the day he died). Some suspected a personal vendetta. Still, the Senate Armed Services Committee, led by Sam Nunn of Georgia, vowed to conduct hearings on the matter. Tower also had a cancerous polyp removed shortly before the announcement but a recovery was fully expected.

What was clear, as Tower admitted, was that he had drank on occasions (mostly social) to excess. What was not proven even on tertiary grounds was that he was an alcoholic, inebriated or that it even affected his judgement. The FBI reported revealed no substantiation of the charges. Aides and people who worked closely with Tower thought he was the most well-qualified nominee for Defense perhaps ever. No former colleague or staffer could say he drank to impairment and the world of the Senate is close-knit enough that what happens on Capitol Hill never stays on Capitol Hill, particularly when it involves a four-term Senator. Even Nunn was forced to acknowledge mid-way through the proceedings "all sorts of allegations. Some of them have been discounted; some of them there are differing views on; some of them you have hearsay evidence; some of them you have direct personal observation."

That was backed up by Phil Charles who offered personally poignant testimony on his former boss's behalf. "As an individual who had a longer and closer relationship with him than of any of the staff, both as a legislative assistant and principal traveling aide, I feel competent in addressing the notion of alcohol abuse which has figured so prominent in the debate over Senator Tower's fitness to serve. Without belaboring the point, I state simply that I am unaware of any instance when Senator Tower's judgement or ability to render reasonable and cogent decisions on matters of import was impaired owing to alcohol abuse or dependency. My observations in that regard are from the perspective of a recovering alcoholic who sought treatment for my alcoholism in 1979 at the insistence of Senator tower . . . in my view, Senator Tower does not now, nor did he in the past, manifest those characteristics of dependency which typify the alcoholic."

The hearings went on five weeks and culminated in Tower pledging to abstain from alcohol or else resign. Democrats were still not convinced. Nunn said he couldn't "in good-conscience" approve the nomination and the Armed Services Committee moved the nomination to the Senate floor unfavorably.

The ambivalence about Tower was by no means limited to Democrats. John Warner, the ranking Republican on Armed Services, expressed skepticism; so did Chuck Grassley of Iowa and Larry Pressler of South Dakota. Warner had gone so far as to stun all in the room at one hearing by challenging backers to "tell me why I should vote for this man." John McCain replied, "Tell me why you shouldn't vote for this man."

Goldwater again came to Tower's defense, saying that if all sins disqualified folks, "we wouldn't have a government." That ultimately was Tower's defense as well. In the end, all of the wayward Republicans came home, with the exception of Kansan Nancy Kassebaum. However, she reportedly said she would have voted "aye" had her vote made the difference.

Three Democrats backed Tower. Howell Heflin of Alabama implored his colleagues to "give him a chance." His longtime Texas colleague Lloyd Bentsen backed him, noting many Texas projects the duo had worked together, as did Chris Dodd, perhaps remembering that he voted against censuring his own father. Had Dodd's vote been pivotal, it's hard to know what he would have done. The vote was 53-47.

Despite many admonitions, Tower resisted fighting back saying, "it doesn't work that way." He emerged from the vote restrained saying, "I will be recorded as the first Cabinet nominee in the history of the Republic to be rejected in the first 90 days of a Presidency and perhaps be harshly judged. But I depart from this place at peace with myself, knowing that I have given a full measure of devotion to my country. No public figure in my memory has been subjected to such a far-reaching and thorough investigation, nor had his human foibles bared to such intensive and demeaning public scrutiny." It pained at least one person quite close to Tower that Ted Kennedy opposed the nomination on grounds of excessive drinking.

The Tower episode left so many bitter tastes that two decades later, McCain referred to the episode as "the worst thing I have ever seen in my life . . . the crucifixion of John Tower where they delayed for three months and destroyed a good and decent man."

About a year later, Tower did address the allegations head-on, telling *The New York Times*, "Have I ever drunk to excess? Yes. Am I alcohol-dependent? No. Have I always been a good boy? Of course not. But I've never done anything disqualifying. That's the point."

Tower's rejection also presented us with one of those classic *what ifs*. If Tower had been confirmed, he may have served for the full four years George H. W. Bush was in office. Had he done so, Dick Cheney, whose pick for Defense Secretary after Tower was rejected, allowing him to preside over many briefings during the Persian Gulf War, may never have been vice-president. Cheney—at least for the moment—would have remained in the House, thereby preventing, at least temporarily, Gingrich's rise to Minority Whip and eventually, the Speakership.

After the vote, Tower formed a consulting firm and guest-lectured at Southern Methodist University. In April of 1991, Tower boarded a plane along with 20 other people, including his daughter Marian; the plane crashed as it prepared for landing in Brunswick, Georgia. He and every other passenger on board were killed. The crash occurred only one day after Republican Senator John Heinz died in another crash of a private plane. Bush called it a "sad day."

That close Tower confidante said Tower was "so proud of Texas." And a historical marker on his grave details many of his accomplishments for the state he loved. Typically, getting a marker takes years after a person's death but Tower's prominence and great love by his countrymen enabled that to be moved along.

Tower and his daughter Marion who died in the plane crash in 1991
Photo courtesy of the Tower Collection

CHAPTER EIGHTY-TWO

Allard Lowenstein A Microcosm of 1968 And Beyond

Historic Tidbit: One day early in his Congressional term, Lowenstein encountered Mendel Rivers, the hawkish, segregationist old-time South Carolinian who chaired the House Armed Services Committee. Lowenstein approached him and said, "Mr. Chairman, I have relatives who are constituents of yours," pointing out that some are named Rivers. "Well," Rivers replied, "there's been a lot of intermarriage down there." The two laughed and began referring to each other as "cousin."

For those familiar with the events of 1960s and the direction of the nation immediately after, Allard Lowenstein could easily have been a microcosm. Though he served a single term in Congress, it pales in comparison to his impact on civil rights, candidate recruitment, student marches and his inspiration of young people in the cause for peace. Even his burial place is in the shadow of history.

Lowenstein grew weary of the Vietnam War quite early, and as such, was among the first figures to begin looking at an alternative to President Johnson. Late in 1967, he began seeking out Bobby Kennedy. As Arthur Schlesinger, Jr., tells it in *RFK And His Times*, one night over dinner, a group around the table wondered what the chances were of denying an incumbent President renomination. Lowenthal surmised Johnson would quit if he lost early primaries, to which Kennedy replied, "I think Al may be right. I think Johnson may quit the night before the convention opens."

But Kennedy wouldn't be the man to do it, at least not at the moment. He decided the nation would be divided even more by his candidacy. Lowenstein's stormed out of his office, saying, "We're going to do this with or without you . . . you could've been President but you don't have the balls." Kennedy put his hand on Lowenstein's shoulders and said he hoped he understood. He suggested he seek out George McGovern, who would also decline. He then approached Gene McCarthy who, to the surprise of many, took up the offer.

Lowenstein was fully aboard the McCarthy bandwagon and would remain there even after RFK ultimately reconsidered and entered. But Lowenstein kept in contact with Kennedy officials as late as the night of the California primary, when Kennedy sought Lowenstein and others influential in the peace movement out, recognizing the necessity of rallying behind a single peace candidate if they were to beat Hubert Humphrey (McCarthy had won Oregon, thereby splintering the field). Lowenstein agreed, but only if other luminaries such as John Kenneth Galbraith would do the same.

That night, an assassin's bullet intervened and changed it all. While Humphrey was poised to ultimately capture the nomination, Lowenstein, like many other liberals were at first hesitant to get behind him. At convention time, he had wanted young people to go to Chicago and protest the Humphrey "coronation." He wanted it to be peaceful. Television cameras obviously captured different images and Lowenstein was among the people trying to stand down Daley inside the convention hall.

Lowenstein wouldn't back Humphrey until he vowed to stop the bombing, which didn't happen until late in the campaign when LBJ let him do so. In fact, he was prepared to place Ted Kennedy's name in nomination despite a complete lack of interest on the Massachusetts Senator's part. Lowenstein's change of heart may have stemmed from an encounter with Charles Evers, whose brother Medgar had been murdered himself. He startled Lowenstein by asking, "You're not going to do that to that family a third time, are you?"

Ultimately, the holdout of Lowenstein and others proved to be one of the factors of Humphrey's inability to gain momentum until the last days, which meant a razor thin loss.

Well before his interaction with the Kennedy's, Lowenstein's career was storied, and Humphrey had been a part of it. Lowenstein had served on Humphrey's staff in 1959, when the future vice-president was about to make his first Presidential bid (and be defeated by John F. Kennedy).

Having attended Yale Law School, Lowenstein taught at Stanford and UNC. He would work under Eleanor Roosevelt at the American Association for the United Nations. In the late 1950's, he traveled to South Africa and, years before Mandela was jailed (Lowenstein would narrowly escape arrest himself), would author a book, *A Brutal Mandate*. Mrs. Roosevelt wrote the prologue.

It was Lowenthal who had a large hand in "Freedom Summer," organizing bus rides of people from Yale and Stanford to travel to the south and register African-Americans to vote.

Photo via maryferrell.org

But for Lowenstein, 1968 would close on a high note, perhaps the highest of his life. To the surprise of many, he won a Long Island Congressional seat. The margin was narrow, about 4,500 votes (51-49%). Lowenstein's opponent was the founder of New York's Conservative Party, Mason Hampton. The district had strong Democratic pockets, but candidates who won there would often struggle. But it's possible that Hampton, who had a reputation as "the George Wallace of Nassau County," was a little too far to the right for Long Island.

Lowenstein started the night down slightly, but when County Executive Eugene Nickerson announced that, "I don't have the figures but it's my understanding that we've won," the crowd went wild. Lowenstein told his supporters his "victory is not a victory for an individual. It is a victory for a point of view. This only means we've been given the opportunity to do things, not that we've done them." The band played *Man of La Mancha's*, "The Impossible Dream."

The New York Times reported that while Lowenstein, like his fellow freshman Shirley Chisholm, was assigned to the Agriculture Committee, he didn't mind it, figuring that while New York may not have farms, it did have residents that required food stamps. He aimed for a seat on the Armed Services Committee, and apparently had the support of Chairman Mendel Rivers. But the Steering Committee, controlled by old style Democrats, rejected his bid. Among one of the 50 bills Lowenstein dropped early was taking aim at the selection process.

Lowenstein and his wife
Photo via Diana Mara Henry

When Lowenstein arrived, colleagues didn't know what to expect and were pleasantly surprised. One from New York told *The Times*, "Like any child prodigy, Al was looked upon by some members with concern. But they have found that he is not the wild-eyed maverick most people thought him to be. He's quietly doing his homework, and as a result he's gaining much respect in the House."

Staff was a different matter. Lowenstein would often remain at his office until 2AM, so his aides would organize their shifts to stay with the Congressman. He had high turnover. But his trademark didn't stop. An abundance of students continued to call upon him, so many that the Capitol Hill police would simply begin directing them to Lowenstein's office.

Lowenstein's improbable 1968 win would be reversed two years later. Redistricting would remove the "Five Towns," known as a fairly liberal block, from the district and add heavily Republican Massapequa. He would face State Senator Norman Lent, who would attack Lowenstein for being ultra-liberal.

Among the charges: that he wanted American boys to "use their bodies for confrontation," and attacking his attendance at a rally where "the Vietcong flag was prominently displayed while the United States flag was desecrated." Even some Republicans admonished Lent to tone it down, and some observers actually gave Lowenstein a chance to hold his seat. But the changes would ultimately prove enough for Lent to oust him with 54%.

Image courtesy of Politics1.com

For many, that would have been a career-ender, but in the words of Chicago, coming to prominence at that time, it would be "Only the Beginning" for Lowenstein. He would run an "ex-Congressional office" and continue addressing college and anti-war groups (an ex-aide who was roughly the same size would speak of lending Lowenstein his jacket because his was always rumpled). One of the men he inspired was a young Mayoral aide named Barney Frank, who would pick Lowenstein up at the airport for a speaking engagement (and it was said in Frank's bio, emulate his rumpled suits).

Eventually, he would become President of Americans for Democratic Action. His prominence in the "Dump Nixon" movement made him number seven on Nixon's enemies list. And he kept aiming for Congress. In a battle that was marred by accusations of anti-semitism and improprieties, Lowenstein opposed conservative Democrat John Rooney and lost by about 800 votes. But he cried foul and the election was re-run. But this time Rooney prevailed by more than

2,000. In 1974 and '76, Lowenstein challenged GOP Congressman John Wydler, only to fall short both times.

Finally, Lowenstein in 1978 sought to unseat Republican Bill Green, who had upset Bella Abzug for Ed Koch's seat when he was elected Mayor. But he was edged out in the primary by Councilman Carter Burden.

Lowenstein was not convinced that Sirhan Sirhan had acted alone in murdering Kennedy and for years, publicly sought unsuccessfully to have the case reopened.

Meanwhile, President Carter would appoint him United States Representative to the United States Commission on Human Relations, and as Harriet Eisman would say, he "continued his usual routine of fifty other projects at the same time." Talking to students would be among them. And he'd use the most unconventional ways to reach them, even doing an interview for *Penthouse* Magazine.

Tragically, Lowenstein would meet the same fate as his beloved Kennedy's. In 1980, as he was working in his Rockefeller Center office, Dennis Sweeney, walked into the office in jeans, had a brief conversation with Lowenstein and opened fire, seven times. Five bullets hit him and, despite a blood transfusion and surgery, he could not be saved. He was 51.

Greg Craig, who would later go on to be Bill Clinton's top lawyer, would say that as far back as six months before, Lowenstein had been fearful of Dennis's mental state. He was found not guilty by reason of being a paranoid schizophrenic.

Indeed, at that time, Lowenstein had been supporting Ted Kennedy against Carter and, when he heard the news of Lowenstein's murder, he was ashen. Kennedy interrupted his campaign and proclaimed, "with his endless energy, with his papers, his clothes, his books, and seemingly his whole life jammed into briefcases, envelopes, and satchels — all of it carried with him everywhere, he was a portable and powerful lobby for progressive principles." Kennedy continued: "all by himself, he was more effective than an organization by the thousands. He was a one-man demonstration for civil rights; even when he walked alone. He was a multitude marching for peace. He had a gentle passion for the truth." William Buckley, his sometimes rival, eulogized him.

Don Riegel, elected to the House two years before Lowenstein as a Republican, said he "had some considerable bearing on my decision to change parties." Pat Schroeder said "he had a knack for focusing in on issues that no one else was paying attention to and getting people to understand that these were vital struggles. That just shows you the energy and the passion of the man."

And David Broder called it "beyond dispute that he brought more young people into American politics than any individual of our time."

Lowenstein's biography at Yale Law School's Orville Schell's Jr., Center For International Human Rights notes "his passionate leadership played a crucial role in the civil rights, anti-apartheid, anti-war, and human rights movements of the 1960s and 1970s."

So many figures who inspired the young with messages of peace and non-violence were taken by tragedy. Bobby Kennedy and Martin Luther King Jr were taken in 1968 alone. Paul Wellstone would perish more than a generation later. And in between thee was Lowenstein, who may well have made the rise of all possible.

Lowenstein was an Army veteran, and thus earned the right to be buried at Arlington. Appropriately, his plot is just near the graves of both Kennedy's. The words on his stone contain a verse by Emerson, which Bobby Kennedy had given to Emerson in a note on a bus during the campaign. It read, "If a single man plants himself on his convictions and there abide, the huge world will come around to him."

A book, *Never Stop Running: Allard Lowenstein and the Struggle To Save American Liberalism* was published by William Chafe.

Lowenstein's grave lies just near JFK and Bobby's

CHAPTER EIGHTY-THREE

Goodell, RFK's GOP Senate Successor, Carried His Torch On Vietnam

Historic Tidbit: Frank Boykin, an Alabama Democrat, was one of many House members in the packed chamber in 1954 when a group of Puerto Rican Nationalists opened fire. Five members were wounded. As the bullets were still being fired, Boykin, 69, ran toward the exit. That would be hardly unusual except for the fact that most of his other colleagues were hiding behind desks. At that point, somebody yelled out, "Where are you going Boykin?" He replied, "I'm going to get my gun." The man replied, "Where is your gun, to which Boykin said, "It's in Alabama." See, some find humor in the most unexpected of circumstances.

Photo courtesy of the U.S. Senate Historical Office

Charles Goodell's name is even more obscure than Kenneth Keating's. But after Kennedy's assassination, Governor Nelson Rockefeller appointed him to fill Kennedy's seat.

Tragically, Kennedy's assassination changed the political dynamics not only nationally but in New York State. For starters, Governor Rockefeller was a Republican, which meant that the Senate seat would shift back to a GOP occupant. But ironically, Goodell, who before his appointment had been a fairly conventional Republican, may have given a whole generation of Americans the hope and idealism they had expected of Bobby.

Rockefeller's pick of Goodell came in 1968, three months after Kennedy had been assassinated. Under New York's quixotic election laws, a seat is not technically vacant until the Governor declares it so, which was drawn out to prevent a special election from occurring in the general election that November. Due to the timing, he did not have to stand for election to the seat until 1970, at which time the term that Kennedy had won in '64 would have expired. That may have ultimately eluded his chances.

A lawsuit that sought to force an earlier election failed.

For nine years (he had won a 1959 special election), Goodell, a Yale Law graduate and a father of five, had represented a western New York district in Congress. With Democrats controlling two-thirds of the chamber, any Republicans influence was pre-ordained to be vastly limited. But not to Goodell. He and a young colleague named Donald Rumsfeld organized a coup to make Gerald Ford the Minority Leader. They helped Ford round up the votes and he dislodged incumbent Charlie Halleck of Indiana by six votes.

Goodell's voting record was hard to classify but it did lean toward the conservative end of the spectrum. According to Grantland.com, Richard Reeves of The New York Times called Goodell "kind of the Paul Ryan of the time," which Rumsfeld validated by saying they "put forth what were called constructive Republican alternative proposals." *The New Yorker* explained that on many of the bills that make up the "Great Society," Goodell offered or supported amendments to change and sometimes to curtail the various programs. When the amendments failed as they usually did, he then voted against the entire bill." One of these alternatives came when the House took up labor backed legislation to revise the Davis/Bacon Act to subject federal contractors earning $2,000 or more to the same rates as private contractors in that area. Goodell took the lead on proposing "judicial review" to allow a court to set aside a proposed rate. The House rejected it.

Goodell did back Medicare and the Appalachian Aid package (he did oppose the Elementary and Secondary Aid plan) and sponsored open housing legislation. In 1968, when it looked like the presence of George Wallace might prevent either Hubert Humphrey or Richard Nixon from getting a majority of the Electoral College, Goodell sponsored a bill with Morris K. "Mo" Udall that would allow the winner of the popular vote to become President. The bill went nowhere but Nixon taking a majority of the Electoral College rendered it unnecessary.

But civil rights were a different matter. Goodell was unambiguously in favor. And once he got to the Senate, he began moving gradually left. He told The New Yorker he "expect(ed) to have a record that will be independent. It won't please the 'ultras' at either end." It was not so much a philosophical metamorphosis. Rather, it was a reflection that Goodell's constituency was no longer a rural, primary monolithic, Republican-leaning Congressional district in the western part of the state. He now represented an entire, diverse, liberal-leaning state.

Vietnam was the exception to a a gradual shift left. Up until that point, he had been a steadfast supporter of U.S. involvement. But he'd soon begin citing the administration's "failure to face the immorality of this war." Much had to do with his staff, whom *Grantland* says he polled on what should be done. Legislative aide Michael Edwards said, "this wasn't, where do you want to stand on aid to Turkey? We had people in the office every day who were making decisions on whether they were going to Canada or not."

And boy, did Goodell respond. He didn't just advocate withdrawal; he sponsored it. Under his measure, funding for the operation would cease entirely by a certain date -

December 1, 1970 - and the bill number would be S3000.

Goodell took part in many anti-war marches, including one with Coretta Scott King. At one he asked incredulously, "We are told that a United States pullout would result in a bloodbath in South Vietnam. What in the world has been going on for the last six and a half years if not a bloodbath?" That enabled Spiro Agnew to call Goodell, who had since become friendly with Jane Fonda, a "radical liberal" and the "Christine Jorgensen of the Republican Party" (she had a sex change).

This made him popular—among Democrats.

Grantland says Mo Udall invented a special play at Congressional Baseball games. It was called the Goodell Shift. Historian Tom Sullivan said, "the congressmen gathered on the right side of the court. Then someone would yell, 'Senate!' And just like Charlie Goodell, a player ran to the left."

Goodell's conversion was not confined to Vietnam. He backed Johnson's nomination of Abe Fortas but opposed Nixon's picks of Carswell and Haynesworth and sponsored legislation improving the sewage system for upstate communities. When Nixon's nomination of Warren Berger and Abe Fortas were made, Goodell, who by that time was out of office, said "it says something about this administration that we have to have seventh and eight choices before we got people of competence. Maybe if he had to settle for his 25th choice, he'd have gotten someone really great."

Republicans were not amused. Conservatives felt so much disdain for Goodell that they nominated James Buckley on their line. The Nixon White House clearly wanted him to win.

Goodell learned that to live by the sword is to die by the sword. And in the election of 1970, Rockefeller was the sword. Concerned about his own prospects that fall, he "stopped mentioning Goodell's name." But he also started holding back crucial funds, which Goodell's people purposely leaked to *The New York*

Times. That basically sunk his chances and he had to run a spot pre-election stating that he was not bowing out.

In addition, *Grantland* mentions a secret taping system, not from Nixon's office but from Kissinger's. Kissinger was furious over Goodell's attempts to stop the war and made it clear he'd maneuver behind the scenes.

Ottinger meanwhile called Goodell a "Johnny-Come-Lately" on the war.

Goodell attacked Ottinger's effectiveness in the House and said Buckley's economic plan was "for the 19th century."

Buckley nipped Ottinger 39-37%, with Goodell getting just 23%. In his concession, he said, "sometimes, for great causes, there have to be sacrifices. And I'm very proud to stand with you as a sacrifice." Had it been Ottinger vs. Goodell, he may have prevailed. But conservatives had a place to go. And Buckley was that place.

In his later years, it became clear that Goodell's conversion was not just for political expediency. His prognostication was not great. According to a Google article, a year after his defeat Goodell said Democrats would "unite and defeat Nixon" and called the chances of his retaining Agnew "very slim." McGovern was one "who could unite" them. At this point, I still feel I can embarrass the administration by acting as a voice for those Republicans who do not agree with Spiro Agnew, John Mitchell, or Martha (Mitchell), the latter of whom he called "a bond lawyer who has no sensitivity to the issue of criminal or civil rights."

Goodell represented Daniel Ellsberg in the Pentagon Papers case but was said by Elizabeth Kaye in *A Case to Remember* to be "more a phantom than a presence." His main contribution to the case seemed to be the donation of his name to the letterhead of the Committee for the Defense.

Incidentally, while Charlie Goodell was the politician in the family, his son Roger has clearly exceeded his father's stardom as Commissioner of Baseball. He has fond memories of his father's political days.

PART V

Key Watergate Figures

CHAPTER EIGHTY-FOUR

Saxbe, Nixon's Attorney General, As Independent As "A Hog on Ice"

Historic Tidbit: Vietnam put Ohio Senator William Saxbe in a tough spot. During his 1968 Senate campaign, he said withdrawal could've occurred a year earlier and quipped Nixon "lost his mind" by bombing North Vietnam. Back home, after attending a dinner where Agnew spewed invectives at opponents of the war, Saxbe told a reporter, "What can I say? I've got to fly back to Washington with the man. It's too far to walk."

Photo courtesy of the Richard M. Nixon Presidential Library and Museum

So what does a Republican President do with a Republican Senator who often opposes his key priorities, who publicly called his administration, "the most inept in history" and who called his chief aides "Nazis?" Why, he makes him his Attorney General of course. That was indeed the case with William Bart Saxbe, a Republican Senator from Ohio. It's not that Nixon gave much consideration to Saxbe's views. It's more likely that, in the aftermath of the "Saturday Evening Massacre," Nixon wanted a steady, tell it like it is person whose penchant for integrity was second to none. And in Saxbe, he'd be getting just that.

One eyebrow raising factor in Saxbe's selection is that his appointment meant Ohio's Democratic Governor would choose Saxbe's successor and he did (the man was Howard Metzenbaum). But Saxbe had already announced his retirement from the Senate and at that point in Nixon's Presidency, image was everything and Saxbe, as Nixon told it, was as "independent as a hog on ice." Which is why, given Nixon's doom and his own ethics, it may've been odd for Saxbe to even accept. But, he viewed doing so as a duty to his country. "I have been around here for five years, bitching about what I would do if I had the opportunity. All at once, they give me the ball. Should I throw it away? It's not something you just walk away from?" He said he didn't "feel inhibited about taking the job," and expressed his proclivity to get the President "back to routine affairs."

Photo courtesy of William Saxbe, Jr.

No more was Saxbe's bluntness in display that on August 6, 1974. The resignation announcement was just two days away and everyone except Nixon itself had accepted would be happening. That was evident by Nixon, at a cabinet meeting, instructing his team to talk about upcoming "policies." For Saxbe, that was a crock. The Attorney General raised his hand and said, "Mr. President, don't you think we should be talking about next week, not next year. I don't think we ought to be having a summit conference. We ought to be sure you have the ability to govern." With that, Nixon stood up and left the room.

Few who knew Saxbe would be surprised. The career of the man *The Cleveland Plain Dealer* labeled a "tobacco chewing country boy" was made by socking it to the entrenched. His first run for the Senate was in 1954, when he challenged Congressman George Bender in the GOP Senate primary. Bender had the party establishment support but Saxbe gave him a run, and ended up with an impressive 42%.

Photo courtesy of William Saxbe, Jr.

During his 1968 Senate run, he portrayed himself as a "Republican liberal," likely to the consternation of the more centrist-to-conservative Ohio GOP. Nowhere was that more evident than Vietnam, where called for "an honorable withdrawal. We can march out with flags flying." He said during the campaign "we missed an opportunity a year ago to announce we won. Who's going to know the difference in this kind of war?" And with major prescience, Saxbe said South Vietnam would have the same government "as if we pulled out in 1975." The irony of Saxbe's statement was that was exactly the year the withdrawal occurred.

Another major issue on which Saxbe demonstrated his independence was healthcare. He was the only Republican to co-sponsor Ted Kennedy's legislation for a single-payer system.

On other issues, Saxbe handled his straddle carefully. While touting law and order, he also made it clear that "firm but fair" is the way to go. "We have to move fast, protect the firemen, but use no more force than absolutely necessary. Shoot a looter and what do you get – a 12 year old boy with a $5 pair of shoes." He favored continued investment in vocational and technological schools.

Saxbe's centrist image converged with Nixon's win in Ohio may have put Saxbe over the top. He beat ex-Congressman (and future Governor) John Gilligan 52-48%, with much support from Democrats. Years later, Gilligan, stunned by his former opponent's independence said, 'If I had known he was going to be like this, I would've voted for him myself." Other Democrats, notably Cleveland Democrat Louis Stokes called him "someone I respected and admired tremendously" and called their "personal relationship . . . excellent."

Saxbe's potential for leadership was spotted early on. Born in Mechanicsburg to a cattle buyer, "Billy Bart," as his friends called him, loved the outdoors. He received his Bachelor's from Ohio State in 1940 but education would take a break. World War II was calling and, though an injury spared Saxbe from being deployed abroad, he was faithful to the U.S. Army Air Corps. Among the places he was stationed: Kansas, Louisiana, and Texas.

At 30 in 1946, he won a seat in the Ohio House ("I needed the money and I thought I was going to reform the world"). It was an auspicious year. He got married and was now pursuing his law degree at Ohio State. The degree would come two years later. After just four years, Saxbe was Majority Leader and one term after that, Speaker of the House. All the while, his service to his country continued as the Korean War was calling. Saxbe would serve in the Ohio National Guard.

Saxbe's son Charles, who would go on to serve in the chamber himself, said that of all the professional titles Saxbe would hold, this was the one he enjoyed most. But he gave up the post quickly to make his losing Senate bid. He was down but not out for long as he rebounded by becoming Attorney General two years later.

That was brief as well, for Saxbe was unseated two years later in what for Ohio Republicans would be their most devastating night for perhaps 50 years. It rivaled 2006 when they lost a U.S. Senate seat, the Governorship, and most statewide offices. The cause was a Right-To-Work ballot initiative. Saxbe opposed it but couldn't avoid being tarred by the same brush of GOP leaders who backed it.

But again, Saxbe's political hiatus would be brief. During his first stint as Attorney General, he compared the office to "killing snakes." Nevertheless, he soon decided to regain the post. He did in 1962 and this time, would enjoy at least one fifteen minutes of fame. Dr. Sam Sheppard, the believed inspiration for the television series, "The Fugitive" was trying to reverse his conviction for murdering his wife a dozen years earlier. After a string of see-saw results, Saxbe argued against reversal before the U.S. Supreme Court for Ohio. Defending Sheppard: famed-criminal defense lawyer F. Lee Bailey. The court, finding evidence of "virulent publicity," reversed the conviction. Meanwhile, Saxbe had no trouble holding the job in '66.

To be sure, Saxbe's rocky relationship with Nixon during his time as Attorney General was not the first time he had earned his ire. When Saxbe came to the Senate, Nixon learned of his independence on a major fight. He desperately wanted the ABM and Saxbe was leaning toward voting "no." An advisor sent Nixon a memo saying the premise of getting Saxbe to flip was rectifying his $250,000 campaign debt. The Ohio GOP would pay the debt, but remind Saxbe that loyalty was important. Nixon wrote, "I disagree. Make the deal tougher. He doesn't understand anything else." Saxbe still voted no.

On Supreme Court Justice matters, Saxbe started by opposing Clement Haynesworth. When Nixon tapped J. HarroldCarswell, Saxbe wrote a private letter to Nixon that got an unusual amount of publicity. He complained about

Carswell's "weakness on Civil Rights" and noted Nixon's enthusiasm toward Carswell "appears on the surface to be less than wholehearted." Nixon replied it was a President's prerogative to have his Constitutional nominees confirmed. Saxbe was swayed.

But Saxbe's willingness to leave the administration behind was not limited to domestic affairs. Working with Idaho Senator Frank Church, Saxbe successfully led the effort to cut off U.S. aid to Pakistan. It was in the midst of a genocidal war with Bangladesh in which the administration was supporting Pakistan in its genocidal war against Bangladesh in 1971 and by the time it ended, it had left three million dead, 300,000 women raped and 10 million refugees. Nixon and Secretary of State Henry Kissinger were furious for according to his son, they "had planned to use Pakistan as the intermediary for Nixon's overtures to China."

On other issues, he was a solid conservative, opposing the Lockheed Loans. By mid-1973, Saxbe had already announced his retirement. His son, William Saxbe, Jr., said that aside from asking people for money (he bemoaned the fact shortly after he got out that that "60 percent of the effort down there is spent on getting re-elected"), he felt that his effectiveness was limited as a member of the minority party.

Part of Saxbe's legend was his mouth. He had a number of Saxbeisms," many of which he'd share with casual gatherings of the press in his office – complete with refreshments. Among them: "That's a ticket on the Titanic," or "he couldn't carry cold guts to a bear." He told a White House official upset about his prosecution of an official to "go piss up a rope." When a number of "Old Bulls" in the chamber opposed changing rules so that a Senator could not chair more than one committee, he torted, "All the old rams have put their tales together and their horns against the world." And following Nixon's resuming of the bombing of Hanoi just after claiming peace was "at hand," Saxbe said Nixon had "taken leave of his senses."

And he came under fire for his 9 to 5 work habits, which were typically followed by a round of golf. "When I see a guy working all night," he explained, "I see a guy who can't get his work done." He was so blunt that, legend has it, he asked his future wife in college if she "liked necking." When she replied yes, the pair proceeded to do so in a nearby oval. The first impression evidently went over well. The pair wed in 1946 and had an enduring marriage that lasted 64 years. Dolly was an artist taught high school for several years. William called her, "outgoing and nice. She enjoyed people, and was a lot of fun." But, he adds, "she wasn't political."

Dolly was the love of Saxbe's wife for 69 years, including 64 in marriage
Photo courtesy of William Saxbe, Jr.

Once in a while, he'd land in hot water (he once called Patricia Hearst "a common criminal"). But by and large, his opinions with a common touch were gold to friends and critics alike. But as Thomas Suddes of the *Plain Dealer* opined after his death, "He was plain as dirt, clear as top water – someone who believed a hedge was something you planted, not a means of ducking a question."

When the Attorney General appointment came around, *The New York Times* recounted, Saxbe "drove up to the front of the White House in his Cadillac convertible – a pack of chewing tobacco on the passenger seat and his waterfowl shot gun in the trunk." He wrote years later that he had genuinely believed Nixon when he told him, at that meeting, that he wasn't involved in the cover-up. But when he found out otherwise, he wrote of Nixon, "he had lied to me as he had lied to everyone else and he tried to involve me in his lies. And for that I cannot forgive him."

When it looked as though impeachment might go forward, Saxbe prepared his own report and opined that the President is required to pay his own legal fees. Haig once told him "We can always get a new Attorney General." Saxbe replied he'd have to be fired. "I'm not going to flounce out of here like Richardson did."

Beyond Watergate, Saxbe's chief accomplishment was breaking up AT&T's monopoly. Saxbe stayed on briefly in the Ford administration but Ford wanted his own people. But India was a bigger incentive. The current U.S. Ambassador, Daniel Patrick Moynihan, wanted badly to come home and when Saxbe was offered the job, he readily accepted. But he was frustrated by the deteriorating U.S.-India relationship

Saxbe's retirement was a mixture of law and raising cattle. He nicknamed his house, "Jubarock," after his children Juli, Bart (William) and Rocky (Charles). *The Plain Dealer* noted that when he "returned to Mechanicsburg, Saxbe brought with him the usual Indian tiger-rug souvenirs, plus a new-found fondness for mixing betal nut with his chewing tobacco." He became the "Squire of Mechanicsburg" and *The Plain Dealer* said he became a regular at the neighborhood Pub, Toops.

Saxbe died in 2010 at 94 after which Suddes authored a column that was titled, "Saxbe's Greatness was his Honesty." Charles', whose tenure in the Ohio Legislature lasted eight years, said his dad was "always thankful that he swam with the sharks and didn't get bit."

The government of Bangladesh honored Saxbe in 2011, William, Jr., and his son traveled to Dhaka to receive his award.

**After his stint as Attorney General, Saxbe had the
time of his life as Ambassador to India
Photos courtesy of Charles Saxbe**

CHAPTER EIGHTY-FIVE

Ex-Iowa Congressman Greigg's Signature On Watergate Break-in Complaint Gave History Changing Event Legs

Historic Quote: "Did you catch the kids?" - Democratic National Committee Deputy Chair Stanley Greigg upon being informed of a break-in by the Washington D.C. police chief at the party's headquarters at the Watergate apartment complex. The police chief replied, "No, sir, these men we arrested were in business suits."

I t's one of the most talked about scandals but one big detail rarely comes up? How did the break-in of the Democratic National Committee headquarters become a crime? The answer: Stanley Greigg, the deputy national chair of the party, was contacted by the Washington D.C. Metropolitan Police in the middle of the night and was asked to report to the station. The burglars had been caught in his outer-office where his receptionist sat and it fell on Greigg to sign the complaint, thus opening the most public political investigation in history and giving Greigg a link to history far more colorful than his single, albeit very productive term as a representative from Iowa.

When Greigg witnessed the police line-up, he recognized one man: he was the director of national security at CREEP (the Committee to Re-elect the President). Greigg then proceeded to prepare a memo to his boss, the DNC Committee's chair, Larry O'Brien, in which he told him "all hell had broken loose. In the ensuing months, Washington Post reporter Carl Bernstein spent a great deal of time in Greigg's office.

When he embarked on his bid for Congress in 1964, Greigg could hardly have expected that his name would become a footnote to a major historical occurrence. He had been serving as Mayor of Sioux City but had been pursuing what seemed to be a longshot bid for a Congressional seat in a district that had, for the most part, been fertile territory for Republicans.

Greigg was born in Ireton, Iowa and grew up in Sioux City. He received his Bachelor's from Morningside College and a Master's in public policy from Syracuse University. After serving in the Navy, he returned to Morningside as its dean of men where he also operated a restaurant. His political career began when he won a seat on the Sioux City Council in 1960. At 29, he was the youngest person to sit on council in the city's history, a distinction only surpassed by two people since. The Council selected Griegga s Mayor in early 1964, again setting a record. Not long after, he began running for Congress.

The race was to succeed Charles Hoeven, the one-time Minority Whip of the House before he was dispossessed of that post by a more junior Representative from Michigan, Gerald Ford. Hoeven was retiring after ten terms and at the outset, the GOP appeared to be in decent shape to hold the seat.

State Representative Howard Sokol was the Republican candidate. Sokol had faced a cacophonous primary in which he had actually placed third (he and two others each garnered 18%). Because no one had received the required 35%, the field headed to a convention where Sokol was selected and, calling Greigg "a tough opponent," vowed to "carry a big stick" to the fight. He spoke of "cutting expenses first and taxes second" and was critical of Democrats for unemployment. *Congressional Quarterly* noted that Griegg responded by saying that while "everyone should be concerned with the national debt," the gross product was increasing "faster."

Greigg, on the other hand, spoke of unity. "We cannot afford the luxury of pitting one group against another: the farmer against the laborer; the laborer against the businessman; the businessman against the farmer. We must realize that our problems will only be solved by unity of purpose." To that end, he hit Sokol for opposing a Medicare proposal and a beef import program.

The race was considered to have no clear favorite headed into Election Day but Lyndon Johnson's landslide over Barry Goldwater propelled him into the seat with 53% (he carried eleven of the eighteen counties, including 62% in populous Woodbury). The 58% Johnson received in the district was actually his lowest in the state and the only one in which he received below 60%. He was assigned to the all-important Agriculture Committee.

As a freshman, Greigg passed two pieces of legislation. One was the Emergency Feed Grain Bill while the second called for surplus buildings to be given to "area communities, organizations, and non-profit industrial development corporations." *The Algona Upper Des Moines* newspaper quoted a Congressional leader as calling it "indeed unique in the history of the house." For Greigg, that time would be immensely auspicious. During his first summer in Washington, he would marry Cathryn Thomson and would eventually have three daughters. But 1966 would be a year of revolt against the Johnson administration and the members of Congress most impacted were the freshmen in marginal districts. That impacted Greigg.

Greigg would be facing Wiley Mayne, a prominent attorney. During the campaign, Democrats expressed optimism that Greigg could hang on. *The Mason City Globe* surveyed the various Democratic county chairs in the district in early October who cited "his numerous appearances in the district" and "youth and vitality" as reasons they thought he'd prevail. One said, "Greigg has met his constituents and has done his job. It's easy to get our workers enthused where he is involved."

The result was not close. Mayne took a 20,000 vote plurality and more than 57%. In 1968, after the Democratic nominee against Mayne dropped out, Greigg was courted by local Democrats to run but declined. He had been put in charge of the United States Post Office Department's Office of Regional Administration and that fall, would be coordinating the Humphrey-Muskie field operation in Northern California, an area where Humphrey outperformed expectations even while losing the state. That attracted much attention as he soon was tapped to join the Democratic National Committee as director of the Office of Campaigns and Party Organizations, a role in which he served as liaison to members of Congress. Before long, he was a deputy. Greigg was immensely loyal to the DNC's chair, Lawrence "Larry O. Brien," Upon being notified of the DNC break-in, Greigg contacted O'Brien twice. The first was to inform him of its occurrence and the second was the "all hell had broken loose" call. When O'Brien was challenged, O'Brien defended him and whipped up support. But the uncertainty over whether he would keep his role caused Greigg to ponder his own future, and he decided to resign that July. Shortly after, he was named director of the Lawrence F. O'Brien Center at Dag Hammarskjold College.

Greigg thought about making another run for Congress in 1974 but he opted against challenging Berkley Bedell, who had very nearly sent Mayne packing in '72 (and would unseat him by a solid margin in the fall). Instead, he joined the Congressional Budget Office. By the time he retired 23 years later, he was Director of International Government Relations under the agency's director Alice Rivlin.

Rivlin became acquainted with Greigg in early 1975 when Senate Budget Committee leaders prevailed over their House candidates in hiring Rivlin as Director of the new Congressional Budget Office. Someone had recommended him and she immediately hired him. It was a decision she'd never regret. She called him, "incredible," and a "nice, engaging man."

Rivlin particularly needed help navigating the House side of the Capitol, quelling the suspicion among members because their candidate had been defeated. She calls Greigg, invaluable to, "helping me learn the names on the Hill." She also credits him with serving as her liaison on the Hill, taking her to Capitol receptions, and hiring "some terrific people." On top of that, Greigg had to deal with the early responsibilities of acquiring furniture and hooking up telephones. What most impressed was that he had only served in the chamber for two years and that had been nearly a decade earlier but he still had "kept up his contacts, and not just among Democrats" (he knew the Senate also). Rivlin described him as both "hard-working and cheerful" and took pride in getting to know his family.

On a lighter note, *The Sioux City Journal* said Greigg was" a civil war buff and collected antiques with a soda fountain motif." Later in life, he loved to visit history classes and talk about his experiences during Watergate. He also was a trustee at the Grace Evangelical Lutheran Church.

Greigg died suddenly in 2002 in Roanoke while at a church convention. He was 71. Those around him remembered him lauded him endlessly. A fellow Sioux City Mayor, Earle Grueskin, who served with Greigg on council, called him, "100 percent honest in his approach. He never backed down, he had a great sense of humor, a boisterous sense of humor." Grueskin also cited Greigg's loyalty.

Meanwhile, the Watergate affair would give the Greigg family one last moment in the spotlight following his death. In 2005, when Mark Felt was identified as "Deep Throat," the *Washington Post* had republished an excerpt of coverage in which Greigg's phone number had been printed. Cathryn Greigg still resided at that home and the number was still in use. That prompted the curious to begin calling. Family members said they took it in stride. After all, Greigg would have done the same.

CHAPTER EIGHTY-SIX

MacGregor Headed Committee To Re-Elect The President But It's Not What You Think

Historic Quote: "If Hubert were a girl he'd be pregnant all the time; he just can't say no." - Clark MacGregor, Hubert Humphrey's challenger in the 1970 Senate race.

Photo courtesy of the MacGregor Family

C REEP—The Committee to Re-elect the President—is quite possibly the most famous acronym out there. It symbolizes an era of law-breaking, cover-up, and abuse. Ironically, though, the man who headed CREEP was anything but. The reason: he had actually somewhat begrudgingly replaced Attorney General John Mitchell as its head two weeks after the break-in at the Watergate Hotel. Thus, Clark MacGregor, who had served Minnesota in Congress for ten years prior to going to the Nixon White House, left Washington with his reputation fully intact. In fact, there were even rumors that he was Deep Throat.

Clark MacGregor was the kind of Congressman who was beloved by all. He was articulate, energetic, and enthusiastic. He often served as a go-to person with the press. Those qualities enabled him to take a marginal House seat and make it safely Republican. Early in his tenure, he also possessed another means of affability: poking fun at himself. It was all part of a skit at Dudley Riggs, a Minneapolis coffee shop, and MacGregor so amused himself and his audience that he took part several times a year. A classic line: "I stand for everything that is good. And you can't hardly beat that." Another line: "There are many things I've done in office that I'd rather not talk about." The script was composed by the Minnesota Press Corps.

On a more serious note, during the 1968 campaign, MacGregor served as Midwest coordinator of Nixon's campaign. He therefore could bask in the glory of Nixon's narrow—and decisive—wins in the key states of Illinois and Missouri.

In 1970, Nixon, hoping to win control of the Senate, persuaded MacGregor to challenge the state's senior Senator, Eugene McCarthy, whose 1968 run for the Presidency had suddenly made him quite unpopular. McCarthy evidently sensed that as well, however, and decided not to stand for re-election; the most beloved Minnesotan of the 20th century, Vice-President Hubert Humphrey, eagerly ran in his stead. MacGregor slipped up a few times. His most memorable gaffe may have been when he said, "If Hubert were a girl he'd be pregnant all the time; he just can't say no."

MacGregor's deficit was 17-20 percent in the polls but the Nixon White House gave him "at least a fighting chance." H.R. Haldeman wrote, "the key here is that MacGregor should be working hard to drive [Humphrey] to the left and he should be pushing Humphrey hard." MacGregor vowed to be "a problem solver for the '70s" and called Humphrey a "political chameleon." MacGregor touted the progress by the Nixon administration and said, "It's time we proclaimed the truth that only in an ordered society can you maximize freedom of a basis of equal opportunity."

With his family during the 1970 Senate campaign.
Photo courtesy of the MacGregor Family

But for all of his support from Nixon, MacGregor hesitated on Agnew acknowledging what most knew to be fact, that, "The vice president evokes strong reactions, on both sides," When Agnew called Charles Goodell part of the "radical-liberal element of the GOP," MacGregor called the party "broad enough to embrace Charles Goodell and others containing views different from those of the President of the United States." Humphrey replied that MacGregor "would like to have me held accountable for every mistake that's been made over the last 10 years . . . and on the other hand he disavows that he has any real relationships with President Nixon or Vice President Agnew." In response, MacGregor said, "My record on each should put me in the Senate very easily, but people don't know my record." He said he was slowing the pace of "Hubert Humphrey's inflation."

In the end, MacGregor's most futile task was trying to compete with the Humphrey name. Ultimately, Humphrey won 58-42%. "I got clobbered," he said the day after. Years later, he admitted, "If I had known it was Hubert I had to run against, nothing could have dragged me into that race." There would be a consolation prize in a high place, however. Nixon's relations with Congress, even members of his own party, were rocky, and in 1971, the President asked MacGregor to become his counsel for Congressional Relations.

Upon his death, MacGregor's daughter Laurie said that Nixon "pretty much created the position for Dad because there were problems between [him)] and Congress." Not only was MacGregor's friendship with Nixon strong but he was also close with Attorney General John Mitchell, who as the 1972 campaign got underway was also in charge of CREEP.

If MacGregor's main objective was mending fences between the White House and Congress, he succeeded with flying colors. Even communication was improved. MacGregor set that path in motion shortly after the President lambasted Congress for not acting on his agenda without notifying him. MacGregor immediately told Nixon of the difficulties that caused and it never happened again. For MacGregor's part, his responsibilities as a liaison were carried out so dutifully that not only was he a frequent presence on Capitol Hill but he often had members of Congress to his home for dinner.

MacGregor said, "when he asked me to succeed John Mitchell as campaign manager, he assured me that no senior person in his administration had anything to do with Watergate. That was some ten days after he had already begun to orchestrate the cover-up." A few months later, the White House taping system picked up Nixon advising MacGregor: "just don't let this keep you or your colleagues from concentrating on the big game . . . this thing is just uh, you know, one of those side issues and a month later, everybody looks back and wonders what the hell the shouting was about" (Nixon closed the conversation by exhorting MacGregor to "get a good night sleep").

When he took the helm of CREEP, MacGregor said, "I am comfortable enough in my 12 years of association with Richard Nixon. I don't have to check." For that, MacGregor likely considered himself blessed. If there are disagreements, "I'll hear from him." He had least heard from the White House. At one point, MacGregor wanted to write a report on campaign finance irregularities only to be rebuffed by the White House. His first order was guarding the troops against overconfidence.

Some tied to impugn MacGregor but no evidence ever existed of his involvement in the cover-up. If anything, his reaction was of revolt. In the early days, though, his defense of the White House, mitigated by his sincere belief that no top official was involved, was strong. In response to *The Washington Post*'s investigation, MacGregor said, "Using innuendo, third-person heresay, unsubstantiated charges, anonymous headlines and huge scare headlines, the Post has maliciously sought to give the appearance of a direct connection between the White House and the Watergate—a charge that the Post knows—and half a dozen investigations have found to be false." At one point, he even demanded an apology from Democrats who sought to impugn top-level White House officials—to which Haldeman, in a taped conversation with Nixon, was heard to exclaim, "Fat chance!"

Based on what is now known about how Nixonians operated, it would not be hard to envision that MacGregor was indeed out of the loop. Bob Dole, who chaired the National party alongside MacGregor's stint at CREEP, called him "sort of the chairman," adding, "I was sort of chairman of the party too. We had a budget of $4 million. They had a budget of $44 million.

The New York Times credited MacGregor with having "steadied the committee even as the Watergate affair grew into a national scandal. He took charge of major elements like strategy and fund-raising, was never tainted by the swirling accusations and revelations, and led his team to resounding victory over the Democratic challenger, Senator George McGovern of South Dakota." Then he decided to go out on top. MacGregor resigned the day after the election.

MacGregor's rise made it easy to envision his likability. Born in Minneapolis, he graduated Cum Laude from Dartmouth College and the University of Minnesota Law School. During World War II, his Army service saw him become Office of Strategic Services, the forerunner of the Central Intelligence Agency. He was a second lieutenant in Burma and received a Bronze Star and the Legion of Merit. Upon returning home, he began practicing law. In 1960, he was given the GOP nomination to take on Democratic Congresman Roy Wier, who had held his seat since 1946 but had never hit 55%, and his previous two wins were true squeakers. That year, his luck finally ran out. Despite wins at the top of the ticket by Kennedy and Humphrey, MacGregor won a solid 53%.

In Congress, Albert Eisele, a now legendary national commentator who covered MacGregor as a Minnesota reporter, called him "a very decent, progressive Republican, and he was a good legislator and respected in the party." His role in a major satirical skit in 1963 cemented that reputation. So did his legislative portfolio. He was significantly involved with the crafting of the Civil Rights Act and the Voting Rights Act. However, the Omnibus Crime Control and Safe Streets Act was his baby; "his happiest legislative day," he said, came when the House passed his bill that gave the states certain control of the program's administration.

In retirement, MacGregor became President of the United Technologies Corp. There was little, if any, personal interaction between him and Nixon. On Nixon, MacGregor said, "He'll go down in history as perhaps one of the most farsighted presidents in terms of foreign policy but tragically, he had almost a paranoia about those he deemed to be his enemies in politics." In response to rumors that he was Deep Throat, MacGregor's daughter said upon his death in 2003, "I think we used to hope so."

CHAPTER EIGHTY-SEVEN

Peter Rodino Set
A Model For Congressional Investigations

Historic Quote: "Politics would be a helluva good business if it weren't for all the damn people." - Richard Nixon

Without question, Peter Rodino rose to the moment. Or you might say the moment rose to him.

In the 26 years that Rodino served in Congress prior to the Watergate Committee hearings, he wasn't exactly a rank and file member. He was heavily involved in passage of Civil Rights and Fair Housing Laws in the 1960's, somewhat courageous given that his very ethnically-mixed district was not universally in favor. And with the 1972 defeat of Emanuel Celler, Rodino had finally succeeded to the Chairmanship of the Judiciary Committee the previous year. But never in his wildest dreams did Pellegrino Wallace Rodino Jr, the son of an Italian carpenter from Grafton Street in Newark, believe that he would be undertaking the role of a lifetime, and one for the history books.

Shortly after assuming the role, Rodino thought as much. "Why me," went through his head. Why Peter Rodino?" Shortly before the hearings began, he exclaimed, "My God! I haven't questioned anyone on cross examination in 30 years."

Courtesy of the Peter W. Rodino Jr. Papers, Seton Hall University School of Law

Courtesy of the Peter W. Rodino Jr. Papers, Seton Hall University School of Law

Rodino was already distinguished even before Congress. Stationed in North Africa and Italy in the Army during World War II, Rodino became a captain and won the Bronze Star. Woodward and Bernstein's, "The Final Days" notes he included the Cavaliere di Gran Croce of the Ordfer of Al Merito della Republica in one of the Congressional directories. Rodino recalls that when he returned to work, his boss, "took one look at those ribbons and he said, 'You're running for Congress." He lost that race, in 1946, but won in a more favorable Democratic climate two years later.

Courtesy of the Peter W. Rodino Jr. Papers, Seton Hall University School of Law

In his own mind, Rodino may have had time to think. Only months before, he had been trying to convince the House Democratic Leadership to let the Judiciary Committee take the lead in determining the guilt or innocence of Spiro

Agnew. The vice-president faced tax evasion charges, but was seeking to have the matter heard by the full House. Speaker Carl Albert seemed poised to grant him the request, but was persuaded that it was more of a legal matter. Had he stayed, there may very well have been a hearing for Rodino to conduct, but he resigned soon after. Not so with Nixon. This was the real thing.

From the beginning, Rodino would be guided by principles: fairness and bipartisanship. In the end, few would say that he achieved anything less. And in an extremely tough and fluid situation, Rodino had a style that would put many at ease. *The New York Times* described him as having "a voice like Gene Kelly's" and The *Philadelphia Inquirer* called him "a small and unassuming man with a high, raspy voice" (Rodino had taken lessons as a youth to rid that).

According to James Farrell's *Tip O'Neill: A Democratic Century*, O'Neill was upset that Rodino was taking his time hiring counsel and told him one needed to be on board by the time Congress adjourned for its winter break. When he confronted his colleague, Rodino said, "Get off my back." O'Neill replied, "Get off my back! I've got 240 people on my back" (he once told O'Neill to "go f-himself" and his second wife Joy said he almost never cursed).

Ultimately, Rodino selected James Doar. This may have had credibility with Republicans, as Doar was one, though he had served in the Kennedy and Johnson administrations.

Joy said her husband was "so determined to conduct the hearings fairly and impartially. He went out of his way to see that secrecy was totally enforced. If he heard that any staff, including Doar was talking to the press, he'd be fired. Nobody was to come to a conclusion until all the facts were in. Only at that point (when the evidence was in) could Doar voice an opinion." This also meant including Republicans, whose support would be necessary, in on everything. The prior chair of Judiciary, Emanuel Celler, who would have conducted the hearings had a 28-year-old upstart named Elizabeth Holtzman, was "autocratic." Rodino, conversely, was able to use his "conciliatory and gentle manner to get results." And it worked. Tom Railsback was among the Republicans Rodino needed to give credibility to the investigation– and got. Railsback said, "Rodino was propelled into a very difficult role as the presiding officer of the impeachment. I thought he did a very good job in trying to be fair. We had some differences but he would usually defer knowing that he needed bipartisan support."

The one negative stain on Rodino's role had little to do with what he said. It was, as *The Final Days* portrayed it, the way a reporter had interpreted it. Rodino's secretary had been briefing reporters when Rodino walked in and said that he was fairly sure all 21 Democratic committee members would vote to impeach, but that he wanted five Republicans. Jack Nelson of the *Los Angeles* Times wrote that Rodino "expected" the 21 Democrats to vote with him. But as "The Final Days" told it, "his offhand comments could destroy his carefully constructed image of impartiality and with it all hope of bringing Republican votes over."

The White House called for dismissal. Rodino was forced to take to the House floor and stress "unequivocally and categorically that this statement is not true. There is no basis in fact for it, none whatsoever." Had the Nixon White House had credibility, that comment may have hampered bi-partisan attempts going forward. But whatever credibility the White House did have was so quickly eroding that the story ended there.

Conducting his role of a lifetime – the Watergate hearings
Courtesy of the Peter W. Rodino Jr. Papers, Seton Hall University School of Law

Another thing that may have stung Rodino's credibility was his vote against confirming Ford to the vice-presidency. Ford was a colleague, having come into the Congress the same year as Rodino. But he said it had more to do with "misgivings about the Ford voting record," particularly on matters that could harm his poor constituency." Ford, he would say later in the year, was "a man of character, decency and integrity." But when the new President issued his pardon of Nixon, Rodino, "questioned, very, very seriously his judgement" about it.

Rodino next sparred with the White House over getting copies of the White House tapes, where the President was talking to John Dean. The tapes were matched against the sound equipment of the Judiciary Committee, and it was determined that there were inconsistencies. Meanwhile, Rodino was working so many 20 hour days that at one point, he had to be hospitalized at Bethesda Hospital for six days.

Courtesy of the Peter W. Rodino Jr. Papers, Seton Hall University School of Law

When he opened the final round of hearings that would culminate with the committee's impeachment vote, Rodino directed an impromptu to the committee, and the American people. "Before we begin, I hope you will allow me a personal reference. Throughout all of the painstaking proceedings of this committee, I as Chairman have been guided by a simple principle, the principle that the law must deal fairly with every man." He noted that "it is now almost 15 centuries since the Emperor Justinian, from whose name the word 'justice' is derived, established this principle for the free citizens of Rome." That eventually led to the vote. The first article passed 27 to 11 and the second 28 to 10. Six and seven Republicans voted to impeach, respectively.

Photo courtesy of Keith Wessel

That evening, Rodino was in tears as he spoke to his wife. "I pray that we did the right thing," he told her. "I'd hoped it didn't have to be this way." Less than three weeks later, Nixon would resign, to which Rodino said, "It has been an ordeal for President Nixon and for all our people. I know it was necessary. I believe our laws and our system will be stronger for it. I hope we will all be better for it," adding "these past few months have been the most solemn of our lives." Meanwhile, the formal committee report was compiled, which the full House passed 412 to 3. Tip O'Neill, who had been among those pushing for Rodino to chair the hearings, called him, "a symbol of purity in Congress."

After the ordeal of Watergate, Rodino could have decided that his career had hit its peak and moved on to other ventures. But ego and the limelight was never his strong suit and he stayed in Congress another 14 years. His reputation nationwide had soared, and O'Neill even suggested Rodino (along with colleague Mo Udall) to Carter aides for consideration for the vice-presidency. Toward the end of his tenure, Iran Contra came on the radar but Rodino decided one was enough: he wanted no part in that investigation.

Perhaps Rodino sensed the upcoming partisan nature of investigations in the wind. Indeed, Joy would recall the Clinton impeachment hearings "made Peter crazy." He believed it was "biased and the anti-thesis" of the way he had tried to conduct the Watergate hearings. "There was no way," she added, that members were "following the Rodino Rule."

Interestingly, both Nixon and Rodino spent their final days in Northern New Jersey (Nixon moved to Saddle River, New Jersey in the 1980s). But only on one occasion did they come close to bumping into each other and that was as both men prepared to board the Eastern shuttle at Newark Airport. It was a route Rodino took often and he always had the same seat but on that particular day, he was informed that he would be put in a different seat. The reason: Nixon was on board and he was assigned to that seat. It's not clear whether Nixon knew Rodino was on that flight but the two did not exchange words. Rodino did however call a Newark reporter upon landing and told him of the experience. "It's only fitting," he said. "I took Nixon's seat and he took mine."

Rodino's passion was always Judiciary but more policy. He pursued immigration and anti-trust matters and in 1976, Hart/Scott/Rodino was signed into law.

But in his early days, civil rights consumed much of his energy. The night of passage, he returned to his office to receive a call from President Johnson. The staffer assigned to Rodino that evening believed the man was an imposter and replied, "And I'm Marilyn Monroe." Eventually, Johnson convinced her that he was indeed the President and the two men spoke. Later, it was Rodino, who along with a few others, insisted on adding Title 9 (anti-gender discrimination provisions) to the books.

Not only did Rodino have many friends in Congress but he also had a trait not easy to come by: he was beloved by the press. Why? He was so accessible to reporters, to a tee. Kojo Nnamdi of the Capital Hill newspaper *Roll Call* always cites Rodino as a man who could always be counted when a reporter was in desperate need of a last-minute comment. That was the case for length as well. Nnamdi would recall Rodino asking, "Whaddya want, 20, 40 or 60 (minutes)?" He continued, "You'd respond, depending on the length of the audio story you soon had to file, Um . . . 40. And he'd proceed to speak for exactly 40 seconds, as if he'd prepared a statement."

Rodino was also very well-thought of by the staff. Joy, who worked for him for six years decades before they were married, described him as "wonderful. Very kind and even and fair. He never raised his voice and pretty much left the running of the office to his staff." She jokes that the only "objection" was that after the House finished its business, he often play paddleball (future President George H.W. Bush was one of his partners) and he often wouldn't return to the office until late at night. One staffer would usually be assigned to him per evening to assist him with him to go through the day's mail or other important events. Those talks would often turn to art, music and opera. Joy calls that "the most special part of the day." Many times the committees would go on fact-finding trips to Europe and he'd return with presents for the staff. He was an opera fan who liked music of all kinds - easy listening, Sinatra and classical. He memorized many classics including fairly large works by Shakespeare that he'd recall well into his advanced age.

All the while, Newark had been transforming into a majority-minority area, and occasionally, Rodino would face a challenge in a primary (in 1986, he faced his future successor, Donald Payne, who said nothing negative against him). But Rodino, solidly pro-labor and, except for his support of the Vietnam War, a true liberal, always won hands down.

Rodino at portrait unveiling
(photo from the Msgr. Collections of the Seton Hall Library)

When he did retire at 79, Rodino returned to New Jersey and resumed teaching at Seton Hall University. He was known to friends and neighbors as a wonderful person. A woman who lived down the street from him recalls that in 2004, her daughter had to do a school report on Watergate. She had never met Rodino but urged her to give him a call. He was in the midst of his 95th birthday party, but talked with her for more than 45 minutes. Rodino died the following May.

In his obituary, *The New York Times* opined that "to his colleagues on Capitol Hill, Mr. Rodino was a symbol of possibility — a reminder that events can conspire to choose one United States Representative out of 435 and lift him to glory."

The Peter Rodino Federal Building in Newark, NJ

CHAPTER EIGHTY-EIGHT

Barbara Jordan:
Small In Height, But A Tall, Eloquent Trailblazer

Historic Quote: "One thing is clear to me: We, as human beings, must be willing to accept people who are different from ourselves." - Barbara Jordan

Photo courtesy of the Collection of the U.S. House of Representatives

She was mythodical, a short woman but high among the giants as far as stature. Her speaking style was powerful and eloquent, a combination of a somewhat preacheresque boom with a can-and-must do command. Her name was Barbara Charline Jordan, and had she come onto the scene a few years later, lived longer, or professed more ambition, she may well have been the first African-American to appear on a national ticket.

It's not that Jordan was ahead of her time. All who were in proximity to her said her skills and diligence were second-to-none. It's that our nation was dreadfully behind its time. By the time a man named Barack Obama entered the scene, that had changed.

Jordan's similarity to Obama, at least as far as being a national figure, is noteworthy. Unlike Obama, Jordan had already served in Congress for four years and won accolades for her performance on the Judiciary Committee, when during Watergate she expressed enormous concern for the Constitution. But the two were really catapulted to stardom by electrifying the Democratic Convention as a keynoter.

Jordan's rise in itself was an American success story, against steep odds. She grew up in poverty in Houston but graduated high school with honors. Segregation prevented her from attending UT, so she chose Texas Southern.

There, her reputation for spellbinding oratory and fierce debating skills gained her a following. The opponents took notice as well. "When an all- black-team ties Harvard," she said, "we win." Eventually, Jordan found herself at Boston Law, and upon getting her law degree, returned to Texas and operated a practice out of her parents' home.

The rise of Barbara Jordan
Photo via chocolaterose.biz

At 30, Jordan in 1966 became the first black woman elected to the Texas Senate and in a rare display of respect for a black woman in Texas in those days, was named President Pro-Tem, a largely ceremonial post, by her colleagues, one of whom had once referred to her with a slur. Her own experiences helped guide her legislative agenda. Among other things, she helped steer Texas' first minimum wage law to passage.

Jordan's political rise continued. In 1972, she became the first southern black woman to be elected to the House of Representatives. Her hard work ethic was absolutely unquestioned.

The Watergate hearings encapsulated Jordan's national exposure. "I felt somehow for many years that George Washington and Alexander Hamilton just left me out by mistake," she told a hushed audience. But through the process of amendment, interpretation and court decision I have finally been included in 'We, the people.'"

Photo via the Dolph Briscoe Center For American History, University of Texas

That phrase had not been a natural inclusion. As late as an hour before the start of the hearing that would vote on the Articles of impeachment, Jordan's staff was not certain which way she would vote. A Jordan biography notes she herself had asked her secretary, due to leave at 6:30, to stay a little later and type out remarks which Jordan recalls dictating from the "little disjointed notes that I read from all of my reading on impeachment." Referring to previous speeches, Jordan said "it occurred to me that not one of them had mentioned that, back then, the Preamble was not talking about all the people." Yet distraught about having been put in a position to impeach a President, Jordan was in no mood for publicity, saying, "I don't want to talk to anybody." This auhor recently talked to a patron in a bar when Jordan's speech came on television. The bar was populatd with a number of truck drivers, yet fell silent when Jordan delivered her remarks.

Still, her conscience and mechanism for dealing with it impressed all. Caldwell Butler, who like Jordan was a freshman but on the other side of the aisle, would later call her "respected by the Committee beyond her experience in the House of representatives. She was just naturally a person to whom you looked for guidance."

Jordan's preaching continued into the next Congress. When President Gerald Ford and Congressional Democrats seemed locked in numerous impasses, Jordan faulted Ford. "It is the President who must set the moral character of the government. Congress is the voice of the people reacting." She could be acerbic. When Congress was debating the Hyde Amendment that would prohibit federal funding of abortions, Jordan referred to "clowns on the floor talking."

Mostly, Jordan's style was to tell it like it is and perhaps naively, she expected it in return. "I admire and respect people who will level with you and tell the truth about things, not fuzz the issues. I've found only a few people in Congress who are forthcoming about what is political talk and what is real talk. It's more difficult for a politician to put aside that other thing and level with you."

The fact is, Jordan's stature and disposition was so remarkable that even the most powerful and pugnacious would seek her counsel. George Mahon, the cantankerous and sometimes autocratic Appropriations Chair readily told Texas Monthly that, "Since she sits near the aisle, I'll come in and ask her what the pros and cons are (on a bill before the House". She'll say something like, 'George, coming from your district and with your conservative views, I think you want to vote no.'" The magazine also noted noted how after his first speech to the House defending his relationship with Elizabeth Ray, (House Administration Chair Wayne) Hays immediately came over and sat next to Jordan."

**In typical speeching mode (left) and addressing the 1976
Democratic National Convention (right)
Courtesy of the Bernard Rapoport Papers, The Dolph Briscoe Center
for American History, The University of Texas at Austin**

As Watergate faded more and more into the past, Jordan's fame showed no sign of dissipating. In 1976, Jimmy Carter selected Jordan to give the keynote address at the Democratic National Convention, a speech that proved so mesmerizing that it is ranked as among the "Top 100 Speeches of the 20th Century" by *American Rhetoric*. The keynote was also a first for a black woman which led some to offer her name for the vice-presidency.

Among the highlights: "My presence here . . . is one additional bit of evidence that the American dream need not forever be deferred . . . Now, I began this speech by commenting to you on the uniqueness of a Barbara Jordan making the keynote address. Well, I am going to close my speech by quoting a Republican President.

And I ask you that as you listen to these words of Abraham Lincoln, relate them to the concept of a national community in which every last one of us participates. As I would not be a slave, so I would not be a master. This expresses my idea of democracy. Whatever differs from this to the extent of the difference is no democracy."

Yvonne Burke, a California Congresswoman and one of just four African-American women in the House at the time, thinks Jordan "had a great sense of pride in her impact." Burke notes that on a personal level, Jordan had only a small group of friends. Instead, "she had a close relationship with the people from Texas and her sorority." But Burke notes "she could be very personable. I don't think she really let her hair down but she was fun and entertaining," particularly impressing those around her with her guitar skills.

After Carter was elected, many urged her to seek a post in his administration. Jordan did meet with the President and when he asked what post she'd like, she replied, Attorney General. That's when Hamilton Jordan chimed in, "Oh, no. Not that. That's Griffin Bell (it hadn't yet been made public). After that, Jordan lost interest.

Sixteen years later, at another convention in New York, she would again give a keynote, noting "the last time I gave the keynote at the convention, the Democrats won, and we can do it again." In that speech, Jordan took notice as being a rare Democrat to stress the need to reform the entitlement system.

In 1988, she had placed fellow Texan Lloyd Bentsen's name in nomination for VP. Indeed, the two had a long history. When Bentsen beat liberal icon Ralph Yarborough in the 1970 Senate primary, Jordan came under fire for backing him, as he had run as a conservative.

Just as her national stock was soaring, Jordan decided she had had enough. Late in 1977, she announced that she wouldn't stand for re-election the following year. "The longer you stay in Congress, the harder it is to leave. I didn't want to wake up one sunny morning and say there is nothing else that Barbara Jordan can do." She dismissed reports about her health, saying, "I've got a bum knee which assures I won't join the cast of "A Chorus Line" or join the Houston Oilers." But in just a few short years, she'd be in the early stages of MS which would eventually confine her to a wheelchair.

In later years, Jordan would become Texas Governor Ann Richards' special counsel on ethics (later the two were seen at the Convention on the podium, Richards pushing Jordan in her wheelchair). President Clinton named her to the Commission on Immigration Reform and also gave her the Presidential Medal of Freedom. Jordan died of leukemia in 1996. She was only 59. Richards remarked "there was simply something about her that made you proud to be a part of the country that produced her."

Remarkably, Jordan's impact was obvious on students a full three decades after she left the national scene. In 2004, "She stood watch over the Constitution of the United States, and now she's about to stand watch over the University of Texas."

Courtesy of the Bernard Rapoport Papers, The Dolph Briscoe Center for American History, The University of Texas at Austin

Years after Jordan's death, Molly Ivens told Jim Lehrer that Jordan was "a woman of magisterial dignity, and she wore that dignity like armor because she needed to. We always said that if Hollywood ever needed somebody to play the role of God Almighty, they ought to get Barbara Jordan."

Image courtesy of Bruce Wolfe who designed the Jordan statue that stands today at UT

Baker's "What Did The President Know" Defined Place In History, But He Had Many Slots Regardless

Historic Tidbit: Missouri Senator Tom Eagleton was among the Democrats who were close with Tennessee Senator Howard Baker. When the Majority Leader was preparing to exit the Senate in 1984, he wrote to him the following: "Since you have all of the skills, talents, and abilities to be President of the United States, you can never be nominated by the Republican Party." He added, "Your smile ain't like Reagan's, your one-liners reek of logic and God knows, logic isn't what this country wants or needs." As James Giglio writes in *Call Me Tom*, his biography of Eagleton, he suggested Baker return to law and start with suing Eagleton's neighbor, whose dog repeatedly did his business on his lawn and whose other habits were apparently not very neighborly: "If it's too big a deal for you, I'll call Clark Clifford."

Throughout all of American history, one of the most famous statements uttered is: "What did the President know and when did he know it?" Certainly, with the possible exception of Richard Nixon's "I am not a crook," that statement took the cake during the Watergate saga. It was a line from Howard Baker, the genial, folksy, honest as the day is long Tennessee Senator who made a national name for himself during the Watergate hearings - one of many high-profile accomplishments in his long career. Howard Baker was Senate leader, Presidential candidate, White House Chief of Staff, Ambassador to Japan, and perhaps most importantly, a mentor to so many both in and outside of his home state of Tennessee. His greatest strengths were his sense of fairness, his sense of humor, and his congeniality, which together helped to earn him the nickname "The Great Conciliator." His reputation is one that all should strive to emulate.

Despite his national and worldwide travels, Baker's hometown of Huntsville was not merely a P.O. Box - it was a place for which he felt lifelong pride, one he'd dub "the center of the universe." In Huntsville save for his war years, some schooling, and while he was working on political endeavors, he was born there, practiced law there (in the same building as his father and grandpa), and returned there nearly every weekend (even while helping to run the country), and he died there.

Baker's father, Howard Baker, Sr. (profiled in volume two), was a Congressman who had actually mounted a bid for Governor of Tennessee in 1938; Baker's mother had died when he was eight. But the state was monolithically Democratic in those days, and Baker predictably lost to an ally of the famous "Boss Crump" machine of Memphis. Still, in an op-ed piece for the *Washington Post* near the end of his life, Baker, Jr., wrote how, "even at 13, I remember being offended by the idea that Republicans could not be elected to a major office in Tennessee." He'd spend the rest of his life using his talent to make competition a reality, not a luxury.

Photos courtesy of the Baker Family

His first opportunity to showcase that talent was already upon him, as Baker was a champion debater. Baker first served his nation in the Navy on a PT boat in the South Pacific. After his formal education at the McCallie School in Chattanooga, he attended the University of the South and Tulane in Louisiana where he flirted with electrical engineering. However, he ultimately realized law was his calling and took his degree from the University of Tennessee. He began practicing law and also manned the store while his dad was in Washington.

Baker, Sr., was elected to the U.S. House of Representatives in 1950. Everett Dirksen had been elected Senator from Illinois that same day. But a similar Baker/Dirksen Alliance was beginning with the daughters in the family. Baker's sister Mary was named 1951 Tennessee Cherry Blossom Princess, and Dirksen's daughter Joy held the same title from Illinois. Mary introduced Howard and Joy at the Ball, and they married later that year. It was a union that endured 42 years and, given the cancer that afflicted Joy later in life, it proved the axiom "in sickness and in health."

Meanwhile, the new couple didn't live in Washington. They made their home—where else - Huntsville, Tennessee. One reason was that Joy had been exposed to the nation's capitol long enough as a result of Dirksen's public service career and simply preferred to stay elsewhere.

Howard Baker and Joy Dirksen on their wedding day
Photo courtesy of the Baker Family

Baker, Sr., died suddenly in 1964, and his widow Irene was elected to succeed him. But she was merely completing the term. Baker could have taken the seat for the asking but stunned some by making a more brazen move: seeking a U.S. Senate seat instead. This was 1964, and Baker was taking on Ross Bass in the special election to replace Senator Estes Kefauver, who had died a year earlier. Baker stressed inclusion: "We can't simply react to the Democrats proposals … but we must offer … positive proposals. We must see that the Republican Party is so broadly based that it can support widely divergent viewpoints and express the majority view." Many gave Baker an even chance. He never once exploited the civil rights issue—which could easily have created backlash for Democrats. But Barry Goldwater was the GOP Presidential nominee and poisoned his own already slim chances in Tennessee by stating support for privatization of the Tennessee Valley Authority. That trickled down to the rest of the ticket as well, and Baker lost. But by taking 47%, he received more votes than any statewide Republican in the Volunteer State in history. More importantly, he had set the stage to run in what would be a much more favorable election, when the seat was up for a six-year term in 1966.

Baker easily won the nomination but, rather than face Bass, found himself up against a far more durable figure: Governor Frank Clement, who had unseated Bass in the primary. But he appeared on both sides of the segregation issue and faced a lukewarm reception from labor. He campaigned aboard the "Baker Special." He not only courted African-Americans but also opened a field office in a black Nashville neighborhood. Many still thought Tennessee had yet to ripen for a Republican, but Baker was a believer. Future Governor/U.S. Senator Lamar Alexander, one of Baker's protégés, recalls being with Baker during a campaign swing in Knoxville and "being embarrassed by his prediction to the media that he would win by 100,000 votes (he called it 'gall gone crazy') and then, a few days later, he did just that." He took nearly 70% of union households and 20% of the African-American vote.

Baker had described himself as "a moderate to moderate conservative"; Irene Baker even compared him to the Tennessee River: "He flows right down the middle." And Baker gave everyone a bone to chew on. According to *The New York Times*, he called busing "a grievous piece of mischief" and added that "he supported fair-housing and voting-rights legislation." He generally opposed gun restrictions. Parochially, he was fierce in his backing of Appalachian aid. His biggest accomplishment in his first term, however, was working with Ed Muskie on landmark anti-pollutant legislation as a member of the Public Works Committee. From his earliest time on the committee, Baker spoke of the necessity of Congress imposing "barriers between the public and causative agents producing stress." He pushed through the Big Southfork River and National Recreation Area and surmised pre-Watergate that this might be what he'd be remembered for. That would be a rare example of his being slightly off.

Howard and Joy Baker and family (left) and campaigning for the Senate (right)
Photo courtesy of the Baker Family

At this time, Dirksen was still in the Senate. This gave Baker a boast unable to be matched by any colleague: having his father-in-law not just as a colleague, but also as the powerful Minority Leader. Still, though, as Jr. J. Lee Annis writes in *Howard Baker: Conciliator in an Age of Crisis*, many in the press referred to him as "a junior-grade Everett Dirksen." Baker shuddered at the possibility of having to oppose him, but Dirksen told him not to worry. Later, Baker surmised that Dirksen "told everyone except me how to vote at one time." It was more important that Dirksen was on hand to provide advice. A starting point was at the conclusion of Baker's maiden speech on the Senate floor. When he asked Dirksen how he did, he replied, "Howard, perhaps you should occasionally enjoy the luxury of unexpressed thought."

To colleagues, however he expressed himself was of secondary importance. For his style made him beloved by Democrats and Republicans alike. Baker's daughter Cissy can recall she and her brother swimming in Senate Majority Leader Mike Mansfield's pool as children.

Father-in-law Everett Dirksen (far right) looks on as Baker is administered the oath of office by Vice-President Hubert Humphrey
Photo courtesy of the Baker Family

Less than three years into his term, Dirksen was dead. Baker ran to succeed him, but despite the significant respect and reputation for effectiveness he enjoyed, colleagues chafed at the idea of giving such a high-ranking position to a person so junior. Still, the vote was close, 24-19. In 1970, Baker tried again but lost 24-20 (Delaware Senator John Williams was at least one who had switched from Scott to Baker). In 1975, when Scott prevailed on Baker to take a position on the Church Committee investigating the CIA, colleagues joked that he was "getting revenge by handing him two back-to-back dirty jobs." One position for which Baker was not viewed as too junior was a seat on the U.S. Supreme Court. President Nixon offered him the post in 1971, but Baker was genuinely unsure whether to accept it. When he finally telephoned the President to inform him of his intention to accept, Nixon had offered it to William Rehnquist.

Baker's name had been semi-prominent on the national stage. Though very much a junior in the Senate in 1968, he was respected enough in political circles to have been considered by Richard Nixon as a running mate (Baker had supported Nixon early in the '68 nominating season). But he still toiled in relative anonymity, which, for a man from Huntsville, suited him just fine. Then came Watergate.

According to *The Christian Science Monitor*, the President, in an Oval Office meeting with Nixon as the process got underway, "suggested a deal whereby the highest-ranking witnesses would give private testimony. Baker demurred. He could not have approved such an arrangement on his own in any case." *The Monitor* also noted how political scientist Jonathan Bernstein wrote nearly four decades later, "At least Baker is smart enough to get through the meeting without being drawn into obstruction of justice himself.

First, Baker took issue with Nixon's refusal to release his papers. Vowing that "some other means be worked out," Baker drafted a letter signed by the panel's chairman, North Carolina Senator Sam Ervin, which said, "The committee feels that your position, as stated in the letter, measured against ... committee's responsibility to ascertain the facts ... present the very grave possibility of a fundamental constitutional confrontation between the Congress and the Presidency. We wish to avoid that, if possible." The letter added that members were "ready to discuss the matter with you at your convenience," but that time is of the essence.

Even before the age of hyper-partisanship, it was an extraordinary display of both parties working together to attain the facts. Nixon subsequently agreed to release the papers though ruled out testifying.

Photo courtesy of the Baker Family

The "what did the President know and when did he know it" line came during an appearance before the committee by John Dean, a top Nixon attorney who had been fired alongside John Ehrlichman and H.R. Haldeman on April 30, 1973. In an example of the behind the scenes of history, Baker almost didn't use the line because he felt it wasn't "snappy" enough as far as making his point. A television sound-bite the farthest thing from his mind. Just prior to his questioning of Dean, Baker had been trying to come up with a line that would get at the facts. When, in the back-room of the Watergate Committee, he approached his press secretary with the line. He liked it but Baker still thought it was too dull. Nevertheless, Cissy said he decided to ask it because he genuinely wanted to know what Nixon knew and when he knew it. He had "no idea that it would become such a monumental quote."

Dean had actually begun his testimony days earlier, but Baker accompanied his question by noting how, "Yesterday, I asked you to respond in terms of the quality of your knowledge that is to say whether it was direct, firsthand information, circumstantial or heresy." Griscom responded, "What you saw was an East Tennessee lawyer figuring out how he would approach these things in a courtroom."

What was Baker's relationship with the former President post-Watergate? For starters, Nixon appeared in his Capitol office, which was being used as a holding room with other dignitaries prior to the funeral of former Vice-President Hubert Humphrey (whom Nixon had beaten a decade earlier). Beyond that, associates say they didn't cross paths much but were cordial. In fact, Cissy recalls finding a letter from the President to Baker after he left office. But the two would have a lengthy meeting in 1987. Baker was Ronald Reagan's Chief of Staff at the time and the current President set up a meeting with the former President and Baker prior to the INF Treaty (Reagan viewed Nixon's knowledge on Russian affairs as first-rate).

1976 was a mixed year for Baker. He tried to position himself as Gerald Ford's Vice-Presidential nominee and felt he might be able to appeal to the President by using his keynote address at the Republican National Convention to take shots at his opponent, Jimmy Carter. But Ford had just survived an ideological battle against Ronald Reagan and desperately needed to regain footing with the Reagan conservatives for the general election. Baker couldn't overcome the conciliatory factor, and Ford tapped Baker's Senate colleague, Robert Dole of Kansas. But later in the year, Baker rebounded by finally achieving the Leader's position: he beat Robert Griffin of Michigan by a single vote. *The Almanac of American Politics* called it "typical of Baker that the coalition he assembled [in winning] was so diverse."

Baker's first test was approval of the Panama Canal Treaty. Conservatives - and early on some Democrats—were steadfast in their opposition. Baker himself began the process uncommitted, a fact not lost on Senate Majority Leader Robert Byrd, who told the press, "If Baker comes out against the Treaty, it's dead." But early in the process, he made clear to Panamanian Brig. General Omar Torrijos Herrera that a blank check would not be given with the sale. In particular, Baker mentioned that the U.S. must continue to be permitted to defend itself militarily and that its ships be given priority for passage. According to *The New York Times*, Baker traveled to Panama and met with his colleagues "at length to almost every Senator who had strong views on the Treaty, pro or con." Once Baker decided to support the Treaty, however, he plowed full speed ahead. A biography of Idaho Democratic Senator Frank Church noted that Baker was "risking his 1980 presidential hopes by supporting the agreement' and even acted as "a back-channel of information" to the Carter White House on Senate developments regarding the Treaty.

The Treaty cleared the required two-thirds vote by a single vote. Conservatives were infuriated enough about Baker that some suggested he cede his post as Leader. That came to pass after that November's election. Baker, meanwhile, was winning his third term by a reduced 56-42% margin against Jane Eskind, a community leader and wife of a prominent businessman. Using "she hasn't lost touch with the people of Tennessee" as her slogan, she hit Baker on his support of the Treaty. But she also opposed ERA, which likely kept her from making inroads with more Democrats. Meanwhile, Baker confidantes worried that the anger on the right might be tested two years later when Republicans marched to power. This was the night Reagan was winning the Presidency and Republicans were picking off a surprising number of Democratic incumbents to attain a majority for the first time in 100 years. Many of the newly elected Republicans were hardline conservative. But Griscom knew a challenge wouldn't materialize when Nevada Senator Paul Laxalt, Reagan's closest friend on Capitol Hill, telephoned him that night to inform Baker that he was indeed the man the President-elect wanted as their leader.

It was a smart move. Griscom later recalled that the first priority of the young administration was enacting Reagan's tax proposals. This required coalition building among Democrats and Republicans, including perhaps initially from Baker himself (the Leader had called the initial proposal "a riverboat gamble"). Forty-eight votes were held on varying parts of the proposal, and each time, the coalition held together as Baker never suffered a defeat on the floor on that issue.

That's not to say he agreed with the President on everything, for it was said later that he had second-guessed the size of the tax cut and program cuts. In 1983, with the Democrats in firmer control of the House, Baker negotiated a five-cent increase in the gasoline tax with Tip O'Neill. He rarely put pressure on undecided colleagues but his colleague, Nancy Kassebaum Baker of Kansas (who would later become his wife), recalls he did offer them mints from a table on the Senate floor "if you were mulling over a vote." His philosophy: "Just take one of these mints and you'll feel better." It worked.

Baker himself decided he wanted to be President in 1980 and mounted a bid in the Senate caucus room where he gained fame by the "what did he know" question. His pitch: "Judge me now as you judged me in Watergate in this very room." That didn't work. Among his opponents: Reagan (as well as George H.W. Bush). Griscom believes his bid was hindered by two strengths that actually were pulled from under him by the Carter White House. The first was his commentary on the SALT 11 Treaty in the context of his belief that his position as Minority Leader and on the Foreign Relations Committee would "put him in everyone's homes" via television. Baker opposed the Treaty and said in his announcement that "if we defeat the Treaty, we will be saying, 'we intend to be the masters of our own fate again.'" He added that while Carter and Massachusetts Senator Ted Kennedy may be "on the right political side, they are short-sighted and they are wrong about the Treaty." But Carter deprived Baker of that chance by pulling back on the Treaty.

The second, more devastating blow came as Baker and Griscom were en route to Iowa to campaign when Carter made public his plans to implement the grain embargo. NBC News crews were waiting at the airport seeking his reaction. Baker's answer might have surprised many. He said he "needed to talk with the President." It was diplomacy at its best—a leader of the opposition seeking that person's job willing to withhold judgment until he learned Carter's reasoning. Griscom acknowledged it was not smart politics. "If you're running for President, you don't" be accommodating. "But that was the respect he had for the

Presidency." Though some polls showed Baker the second choice of Republican voters to Reagan (albeit a distant second), Baker finished third in the Iowa and withdrew shortly after. But his professional career would soon rise to the top.

Photo courtesy of the Baker Family

If anyone doubted that Baker would prove the accommodationist he had appeared throughout his career, he laid those doubts to rest with his olive branch to Byrd. The West Virginia Democrat could not have been happy about seeing his rule over the Senate come to an end following the 1980 elections, but Baker allowed Byrd to keep his office. He then vowed to "not surprise you if you won't surprise me." Byrd took a day to consider the offer and ultimately agreed. Nancy Kassebaum Baker later said the two men certainly had their disagreements, "but they were able to express it in a way that wasn't trying to dam one side or another."

With his outreach, Baker certainly wasn't doing himself any favors. Byrd, as a master of the Senate rules, was able to rule the Senate with tremendous dexterity. That led *The New York Times* to opine on Baker's retirement that "rough persuasion has had to yield to gentle and good-humored goading. He has had to ride herd on a flock ranging from the uncontrollable Jesse Helms to the unpredictable Lowell Weicker, and to steer a course between a Democratic House and a conservative White House." He often had to deal with numerous amendments to major legislation. In many cases, this would be little more than an attempt by the sponsor to make a point; Baker called these amendments "like mushrooms. They glow in the dark." Pennsylvania Republican Arlen Specter once called Baker "like a political neutron bomb. He destroys his opponents and leaves their egos standing."

As for Baker the person, Griscom says that unlike some Senators whose public and private images are paradoxical, with Baker, "what you saw publicly, there were not two different Howard Baker's." Griscom adds he was also "a very private person. He valued his own time." His relationship with Huntsville confirmed that. Nearly every weekend as Senate business concluded, he would fly back to Huntsville. He would drive to his law office himself and chat with people he had known for ages. Much of that time was spent with Joy, who had been undergoing off-and-on cancer treatment. According to Griscom, Baker would be at her side whenever required, even if it meant flying home from Iowa in the middle of the night.

In Huntsville, there was also a local passion: a love of Krystal hamburgers, an East Tennessee staple. Griscom said the staff "takes credit [as the first people to figure out how to freeze Krystal Burgers]." He recalled buying 100 burgers and a large orange soda to take back to Washington and that later he and Baker wrapped the burgers in bundles of threes (here I am with the Senate Majority Leader). He said the buns were a little hard but that the aroma left everyone on the plane in envy.

Photograph courtesy of the Baker Family

Photography was a Baker love as well, to the point that Griscom refers to him as a "full-time photographer, part-time politician." At one point as Chief of Staff, he talked White House officials into letting him fly in restrictive air space to photograph the White House from aerial view. Griscom recalls accompanying Baker to an Indy 500 race late in his life for the sole purpose of getting photographs. In the middle of the race, Baker turned to Griscom and said, "Let's go." An exasperated Griscom said the best part of the race was yet to come; Baker replied, "I'm done." He later said, "When I leave this mortal coil, I may have no money, I may have no reputation, but I'll have a lot of good pictures."

Years after leaving office, Baker addressed the importance of humor in politics. "Politics by its very nature almost by description is an adversarial proceeding. Adversarial proceedings can turn very tough, very bitter and very ... But at some place along the line you've got to find a way to get things done. And the best way to get things done is occasionally to realize, don't take yourself so seriously. Put yourself in perspective. Politics is tough enough without making it tough on each other. Humor ... is the lubricant of government and politics."

Another Baker legacy - albeit one that enjoyed far less national attention - was having succeeded with his quest to have cameras televising Senate proceedings. But he soon regretted it. For starters, he found that many Senators politicized their remarks. But he also found that common-folks not understanding the arcane lifestyle of members of Congress were perplexed that he wasn't making speeches. He recalls one person acquaintance approaching him in Tennessee and saying, "Howard, you're not doing your job. I watched and watched and never saw you up there."

Baker decided not to run for a fourth term in 1984. As his tenure wound down, he spoke one last time on the Senate floor. "We have not only survived, we have prevailed. We have shown in the clamorous, cumbersome, chaotic way we do business ... we do it in the peoples' name and with the peoples' consent and in a manner that reflects...the passion...and common-sense of the American people themselves."

It had been Baker's steadfast intention to seek the Presidency in 1988. Instead, there was another calling. Baker had been working at a Washington law firm for $1.5 million a year when a number of Republicans began complaining that Reagan's Chief of Staff Donald Regan was impotent and in some ways responsible for getting the administration knee-deep into the Iran-Contra deal (which Ted Kennedy predicted would have taken Baker "about one second to veto"). Consequently, his approvals were mired in the low 30s. They finally prevailed upon Reagan to let him go. Nancy Reagan and Laxalt hatched a plan to bring Baker aboard. He asked Baker to fill the job. It proved a grand way to save face. As he had begun laying the groundwork for his White House run, Baker felt he had to raise $12 million. As liked as Baker was, though, many were hedging their bets and staff finally had to tell Baker they could not raise the money. He accepted, though only under the condition that he would be allowed to bring in his own people (Reagan agreed). Ken Duberstein was one such appointee. He wanted to "give Reagan reality."

Ironically, Baker was able to employ his "what did the President know and when did he know it" mantra again. As the Baker team was taking the White House reins, Reagan was in the middle of Iran-Contra. Baker believed the best strategy was to "not let it fester," noting that if Nixon had done the same, his Presidency might have survived. So Baker and his staff's first goal was to determine Reagan's involvement. Griscom calls it "almost like turning the page back. [He] had been there years before. It was really kind of valuable to have his experience." Griscom said they quickly reached the conclusion that Reagan had no knowledge and the mood could shift to "get[ting] done what needed to get done."

As far as eliminating problems at their outset, Baker in 2005 cited the example of Nancy Reagan consulting an astrologist. He had been handed a copy of Don Regan's memoirs. He knew that once it came out, there would be a media firestorm and so approached the President about it. He directed him to "talk to Nancy." She confirmed that it had indeed been true which Baker promptly acknowledged to the public. He explained that "If we tried to explain it, deny it, or do anything with it," it would have created more of a firestorm than simply admitting it.

Six months into his job, Baker called his new position "an exhilarating job and I enjoy it," adding, "It's a nice, hard, tough job at the focal point of Government policy."

John Tuck served in many high-level government positions, including for Baker during the later years of his Senate run and Assistant to President Ronald Reagan, as Deputy Assistant for Legislative affairs. He noted that Baker always had a story, a trait that went hand in hand with the President. Reagan and Baker would often swap stories to the point that Baker's major worry as Chief of Staff was that he'd run out of stories. Baker really liked Reagan. Conversely, he wasn't best of friends with George H.W. Bush; as Tuck notes, both had been "competitors" eyeing the Presidency since the 1970s. That said, Bush held him in high enough regard to send him to the Soviet Union to meet with Gorbachev in 1991.

Just after Baker assumed his new post, Republicans lost control of the Senate. The first bills the new Democratic majority sent to Reagan were two that he had vetoed in the previous session—a highway bill and clean water legislation. Reagan vetoed them again. In order to stave off overrides, Baker encouraged Reagan to travel to Capitol Hill to meet with Senators to lobby against the override. Reagan asked Senators who had voted for the package the first time to stick with him but the vetoes were overridden. Shortly after, Baker asked Tuck to put together a reception in the White House Blue room as a show of appreciation for the members of Congress who stuck with Reagan; as Tuck recalls, "it couldn't be filled up" (he guestimates that only roughly 40 people attended).

The capstone came when the Senate approved the INF Treaty. Baker had helped Republicans—including Reagan and Dole—overcome their reservations regarding the treaty.

Even in the winter of his career, Baker sought solutions and pragmatism in an unsuccessful attempt to head off an ideological battle. For example, Supreme Court Justice Lewis Powell was retiring and a number of Reaganites—including Attorney General Ed Meese—wanted Reagan to nominate Robert Bork. Baker preferred Anthony Kennedy. Baker lost the battle but won the war. Reagan nominated Bork whose nomination was ultimately voted down. Kennedy (following a brief nomination of Douglas Ginsburg) got the nod and won swift confirmation.

Baker taking the oath as Ambassador to Japan by Secretary of State Colin Powell
Photo courtesy of the Baker family

Baker could not finish out Reagan's term. Joy's health was steadily worsening (as was his step-mother Irene's) and he stated his intention to resign in mid-1988. But Reagan convinced him to postpone leaving until July 1 and Baker made sure he left Reagan in good hands: Duberstein succeeded him. His legacy was undoubtedly turning the ship around. Tuck said the camaraderie of White House staff improved post-Regan, of whom he said the everyday pressure was such that his eyes "sunk back into his head like dark cave holes." Tuck would continue to handle legislation but noted that high ranking Congressional staff "didn't call us anymore. They contacted Baker." Eventually, he said Baker asked Tuck to take over because he was tired of fielding so many calls. At the end of the day, with

Iran-Contra behind them and Reagan's popularity nearing a high point, Tuck believes Baker "saved Reagan's presidency."

Joy succumbed to her long battle with cancer in 1993. A few years later, Baker began courting Kassebaum. When he arrived at her home to pick her up for their first date, he told her he felt as though she was 12 years old. She replied, "You don't look like you're twelve." The two married in late 1996; their mutual colleague from Missouri, John Danforth, who was an ordained minister, conducted the ceremony.

But public service was not finished with Baker yet. In 2001, President George H.W. Bush appointed him Ambassador to Japan. Baker faced a very pressing diplomatic challenge over which nation should have custody of U.S. Staff Sgt. Timothy Woodland, who was charged with raping a 20-year-old Okinawan woman. The standstill went on for a week—a protest was mounted outside the large military base of Kadena, which threatened to derail cooperation within the two nations. Many felt the U.S. should have custody, but Baker countered that expatriating a soldier still on Japanese soil would be as if the U.S. was still occupying Japan. Woodland remained in Japan and Baker expressed confidence that "we have satisfied ourselves that our U.S. service member will receive fair and humane treatment throughout his custody." Months later, the Japanese showed there were no hard feelings in a big way. The 9/11 attack on American soil took place and Tuck—who also went with Baker to Japan—said the government "did a number of things on their own to cement their alliances with the U.S" (conversely, they had been slow to extend support following the 1991 Persian Gulf War). This included, among other things, allowing ships to refuel and use their bases.

After his four-year stint in Japan ended in 2005, Baker devoted more time to the Baker Center. In 2008, he backed Fred Thompson for President while Kassebaum supported John McCain ("There was no place in the wedding ceremony that we had to support the same person for President," he said). He died of complications following a stroke in 2014 at age 88.

Meanwhile, Baker's daughter Cissy attempted to create a third generation of Baker politicians but lost a Congressional race to Democrat Jim Cooper. In 2003, The Howard H. Baker Jr. Center for Public Policy was established on the campus of the University of Tennessee.

CHAPTER NINETY

Bill Hungate Perhaps Most Underrated
Judiciary Member During Watergate

Historic Quote: "Suppose you were an idiot, and suppose you were a member of Congress; but I repeat myself." - Mark Twain, a native of the area in Missouri about to be covered.

**Hungate (seated) conducted the post-pardon hearing which
featured testimony by President Gerald Ford
Photo courtesy of the Chicago Sun-Times**

The Ninth Congressional District of Missouri has a long history of electing Democrats who rose to national prominence, and not just in public service (Mark Twain's home-town of Hannibal is located here).

Champ Clark may have been the most famous. As Speaker of the House, he gave Woodrow Wilson a run for his money for the 1912 Presidential nomination, and also with enacting his policies. He'd lose his seat in the anti-Wilson climate of 1920 and, when asked for a reason, simply uttered the President's name.

And for four decades beginning in 1922, Clarence Cannon, a Clark staffer and former House Parliamentarian who would rise to chair the Appropriations Committee, held the seat. He once punched the ranking Republican in the nose and engaged in a tit-for-tat with his Senate counterpart Carl Hayden over which side of the capitol a conference committee should meet for so long that it held up an Appropriations bill for months.

William Hungate also had a role of historic enormity but, save for a brief period in 1973-74 as Watergate progressed, never became a household name, even as he continued to play a lead role in the House Judiciary Committee's final action against Nixon. But his combination of a trial lawyer's skill, impeccable honesty, and most of all, a sense of humor, made him perhaps the most underrated member of the House Judiciary Committee during every aspect of Watergate, including even after Nixon's resignation.

Hungate's impact was such that, when he died, a colleague on the bench (his true passion which would later become a reality) called him "one of the giants of northeastern Missouri."

Hungate was a native of Illinois whose family would move to Missouri when he was in grade-school. He would attend the University of Missouri and Harvard Law School, and as a member of the Army during World War II, compile a war record that gave him tremendous distinction (a Bronze Star, and a Combat Infantry badge). He would marry his high school sweetheart and establish a respected legal career which would eventually entail his becoming an Assistant Missouri Attorney General.

When Cannon died in early 1964, Hungate was hardly the best known candidate to succeed him. Ten Democrats had filed, including a few State Representatives, and while Hungate was known in his home county of Lincoln as its prosecuting attorney, his name was nearly an asterick in polls in other parts of the 21-county district.

Hungate's education was used against him, particularly his Harvard Law degree. When folks tried to use the "Harhh-vad" thing against him, he'd acknowledge he was "a Harvard lawyer. But, it just so happens that I'm not a very good Harvard lawyer!" He made up ground by traversing the sprawling district in his red and white Ford. It was enough to propel him past his nearest rival, but with less than 18% of the vote.

General elections were non-affairs in those days, and Hungate's only close general election would come against a 29-year-old Princeton educated lawyer named "Kit" Bond. In 1968, Hungate edged Bond by just over 9,000 votes (52-48%) to hold his seat.

In Congress, Hungate had anticipated a career of taking care of the home folks and letting others have the national spotlight. For a time, he was able to do just that, starting with his two famous predecessors. He helped restore the Champ Clark Honey Shuck Home and a Clarence Cannon bridge. There were numerous projects devoted to Mark Twain.

Voting-wise, Hungate often cast his lot with his national Democratic brethren, particularly with civil rights. Then came Watergate. Even as the scandal ballooned, Hungate made clear that the limelight was hardly ideal for him. But by its end, his folksy manner, ability to mimic critics, and overall talents, enabled him to reconcile disputes, which only brought him closer to the public eye.

It started with a song. Hungate was a gifted musician, playing clarinet, saxophone, piano and accordion, and put himself through college by performing in bands. By the middle of 1973, before Watergate had truly taken hold, Hungate had composed a song, "Down at the Old Watergate." Its lyrics were, "Come, come, come and play spy with me, down by the old Watergate. Come, come, come love and lie with me, down by the old Watergate. See the little band, Ehrlichman and Haldeman, doesn't Martha Mitchell look great." The Democratic National Committee arranged to have a number for folks to call (202-333-0017) but the diddy became so popular that the phone lines would often jam and callers would often come away with a busy signal.

Hungate's humor was often stepped in sarcasm, pointing out the sharp, partisan differences on the committee in light of what he saw as the obvious. "There were some Democrats who would vote to impeach the President today," he said. "And there are some Republicans who wouldn't vote to impeach Nixon if he were caught in a bank vault at midnight." To highlight that point, Hungate offered one of the most famous quips during the hearings. "There are some members of the room who, if an elephant walked into a room, might say, 'wait. It might be a mouse with a glandular condition.'" On another occasion, when a Nixon supporter made the case for more "specificity," Hungate replied, "If they don't understand what we're talking about now, they wouldn't know a hawk from a handsaw anyhow."

Hungate explained his philosophy thus: "Your own sense of responsibility need not destroy your sense of humor. In my own case, I have always felt that it is better to have a sense of humor than no sense at all."

But as the final days approached, Hungate was all business, and unbeknownst to him, about to take his place straight in the annals of history.

Hungate fulfilling his Congressional duties
Photo courtesy of the Champ Clark House

Operating under the core philosophy that, "the issue here is broader than criminality," Article II would become his creation, a substitute for Massachusetts Democrat Harold Donahue's proposal, which was considered too strongly worded for those on the fence. It removed the language "abuse of power" and "making false and deceptive statements to the American people."

Instead, it said that Nixon, "in disregard of his constitutional duty to take care that the laws be faithfully executed, has repeatedly engaged in conduct violating the constitutional rights of citizens, impairing the due and proper administration of justice and the conduct of lawful inquiries, or contravening the laws governing agencies of the executive branch and the purpose of these agencies."

Shortly before the vote, Hungate invoked Normandy Beach, and the monument above the military cemetery at Omaha Beach, and said, "They endured all and suffered all that mankind might know freedom and inherit justice." He called himself a "catalyst" of the resolution. It passed 28-10.

As for his views on Nixon himself, Hungate would take a local view. "Perhaps an old Missouri saying is appropriate. If the Lord loved a liar, he'd hug him today."

Nixon would resign and Ford would pardon Nixon, but that didn't end Hungate's 15 minutes of fame. In fact, it catapulted even higher. Many were obviously livid about Ford's pardon and the President offered to come to Capitol Hill to explain it and Democrats extended him an invitation. And as Chairman of the Judiciary Committee's Criminal Justice subcommittee, it would fall on Hungate to chair the hearing. Of special significance is that this would be the only occasion that a sitting President would testify before a U.S. House Committee. Hungate began the hearing promising not to keep the President past noon. Ultimately, it voted 6-3 to cease further investigation into the pardon.

In later years, Hungate's grandson would understand Ford's point of view with respect to the pardon, and received a handwritten letter of thanks from the former President.

Shortly after that, Hungate won re-election but it would be his last. Early in 1975, he announced his retirement. "The duties have increased dramatically," he said, "exceeded only by public dissatisfaction with this Congress . . . in the last Congress, politics has gone from the edge of 'Camelot' when all things are possible, to the age of Watergate, where all things are suspect." He likened his early years in Congress as "a very junior partner in a large law firm," but said his feeling now was one of "invisible restraints."

With characteristic levity, Hungate in his farewell to the Congress told his colleagues he hoped the future would "bring all the best to you, your family, and friends, and may your mother never find out where you work."

In 1979, President Carter named Hungate a U.S. District Judge. Four years later, he oversaw a school desegregation plan. Some, including a friend, John Briscoe, said he could have "ducked it," but instead "had the courage to say 'I'll go ahead and handle those cases.'" There was certainly no reward for him, as Hungate received death threats. But he performed masterfully while not neglecting his other judicial duties. Another colleague said Hungate "was very aggressive in moving his dockets."

Hungate died in 2007 at 84, at which time he'd be lauded by his colleagues in every walk. Judge James Reinhardt said, "He was never big-headed, and he never forgot Northeast Missouri." And Harold Volkmer who succeeded him in Congress and would go on to serve for 20 years, paid the ultimate compliment to a fellow politician, saying "I don't think he had an enemy in the world.

CHAPTER NINETY-ONE

Tom Railsback First Republican To Back Nixon Impeachment

Historic Tidbit: As the 1980 Republican Presidential primary season took shape, Illinois Congressman Tom Railsback had a decision to make. John Anderson was a home-state colleague whom Railsback deeply respected. George H.W. Bush and Railsback came to Congress in 1966 and though Bush had left office a decade earlier, remained a close friend. And Ronald Reagan was born in Tampico, which was in Railsback's district. Ultimately, Railsback went with Bush but it was a decision he could not have made with ease.

Photo courtesy of the Collection of the U.S. House of Representatives

Tom Railsback, who before and following the summer of 1974, was a total unknown quantity outside of his rural district in Illinois. But as a lead negotiator in the drafting of the articles of impeachment and ultimately, the first Republican to vote for it on Judiciary, he deserves accolades as a footnote in history.

Railsback, was an attorney who was selling Christmas trees for the Jaycees when a friend encouraged him to seek a House seat. First, he wanted to check with his dad who also happened to be his law partner. The elder Railsback gave him his blessing. His prospects were uncertain. The Democratic incumbent, Gale Schisler, was serving his first term, having won his seat largely on LBJ's coattails. But by 1966, much of Johnson's mandate had evaporated and Railsback, at 34, won the election to represent this working class, yet very Republican, Congressional district from the land of Lincoln. And in his 16 years in the House, he would appropriately established himself as a very moderate Republican.

It was not unusual for him to grab significant union support (United Auto Workers, who appreciated his support of the Chrysler bailout), and he advocated for the Legal Services Corp. as well as media copyright protections. He sponsored Common Cause backed legislation with Wisconsin Democrat Dave Obey that would limit the influence of PACs and voted against most of his party for the Justice Department's fair housing enforcement. But that was nothing compared to the role that awaited him when Watergate arose, and few if any have said that Railsback did nothing but rise to the moment.

Railsback would prove so influential that Woodward and Bernstein in *The Final Days* would write that when Judiciary Chair Peter Rodino made an inadvertent slip up with the press, Railsback, the "barometer of impeachment," was the one he worried about losing. They wrote "he could take two to four Republicans with him."

When Nixon asked his aides how the vote was looking, he was told that there were a few undecideds. Railsback was one of them. Nixon's reply: "well, that should be easy."

In fact, Woodward and Bernstein's described Railsback as "genuinely conscience stricken." Railsback felt an affinity for Nixon going back well before Watergate. He campaigned for Railsback, and they belong to the Congressional Chowder and Marching Society. And when his daughter disappeared (she ran away from school), Nixon phoned Railsback to reassure him. "Tom, I want you to know I just talked to FBI Director Pat Gray. He's gonna help find Maggie." Railsback acknowledged, "Richard Nixon was kind to me. That made my job a rough deal." But Railsback wasn't a down-the-line supporter of the administration. He had voted for a House resolution to disapprove of the administration's decision to delay pay raises to federal employees (his district was home to many).

Photo courtesy of Tom Railsback

Some Republicans couldn't bring themselves to vote against Nixon. Railsback eventually realized that the climate was against him. Yet in all likelihood, his personal integrity guided him so that Nixon could not continue.

It started with the publicity which left Railsback utterly stunned. He recalls that, "when I went home to Moline, Illinois in the winter of 1973, I was followed by Sam Donaldson of ABC and Ike Pappas of CBS." When NBC followed he replied, "the other two are already here." At that time, Railsback was "wondering what in the world is going on." Members of Congress, he said "were not used to this publicity." He noted, "Everywhere I went, I was followed by Sam and Ike. To my daughter's sixth grade class, a Moline-Rock Island basketball game." His return to Washington would prove even more intense. "All of a sudden, I was getting requests for interviews from all kinds of people – *The New York Times, The LA Times,* the international press."

That was not always welcome. Railsback would receive death threats which forced the FBI to guard his home. He was compared to Pontious Pilate and the normally GOP friendly *Peoria Journal-Star* ran an editorial with the headline, "Tom Railsback Dead Duck." It urged GOP voters to stay home that November rather than vote Railsback.

Still, there was work to be done. The *Idaho Statesman* reports that as spring turned to summer and impeachment was moving forward, Railsback didn't seem likely to back impeachment. Woodward would treat him to dinner three times. But Railsback would never tip his hat. Yet Woodward and Bernstein would later write that "it was hard (for Railsback) to escape the conclusion that directly or through Haldeman, Nixon had given the orders (for the cover-up)." Actually, Railsback said he was "very private about how I was going to vote right up until the end." He believes that epiphany came around June after listening to the White House tapes. Recalling that, Railsback said he 'came to the conclusion that a case had been made to impeach him and he would be given a trial (in the Senate)."

**Railsback plays the starter in a race between colleague
Bob Mathias and another member
Photo courtesy of Tom Railsback**

Around that time, Railsback was becoming part of a "fragile coalition," a group of three Democrats and four Republicans all considered swing votes that didn't like the draft of the impeachment articles. He was also said to be angry with the Republican staff. Railsback had said he felt "that certain events occurred to which Mr. Nixon didn't respond or responded to in an improper way." And there were personal issues. "He has not been contrite. He has not been remorseful . . . he has never admitted he made a mistake."

One of the committee's swing Democrats, Walter Flowers of Alabama, suggested each side "get some guys." The fact that all the players were friendly did not hurt. Railsback and Flowers were close friends. Flowers had arranged for Railsback to speak at the University of Alabama and Railsback would ultimately serve as a pallbearer at Flowers' funeral. Meanwhile, they had a job to do. The members met in Railsback's office and drafted the language. As for the consequences, Railsback said, "Everybody seemed ready to forsake that worry. And at this particular point everybody was really ready to get down to business to decide what to do, I think, for the most part without consideration."

In the hearings, he became the only Republican to speak (a Democrat yielded him two minutes when his time expired), and he did so without notes. "He declared himself an anguished friend of Richard Nixon." But he added that "if we are not going to get to the truth. So I hope that we just keep our eye on the ball and keep trying to get to the truth." He implored Nixon to find a way to spare himself and his colleagues any further agony, adding, "I hope the President — I wish the President could do something to absolve himself. I wish he would come forward with information that we have subpoenaed. I am just, very, very concerned."

Railsback told the *Idaho News* that in the aftermath of his statements, he "couldn't go anywhere without people recognizing me. And I wasn't used to that. I didn't particularly like that." He even turned down the barrage of media requests for interviews, calling himself "emotionally drained." The whole thing," he said, "was the most difficult legislative experience by far of my life." And he made clear that serving on Judiciary was "not all roses." He said it could be "very antagonistic, disputatious and impassionate." While Railsback had now found common ground on impeachment, it could not be said that he agreed with them on everything. At one point, convinced Rodino and the Democrats were going too far he admonished the chair, "You watch what happens to your fragile coalition."

Railsback disputes a portion of Woodward and Bernstein. Railsback calls disputes between he and Judiciary colleague and fellow Illinoisian Bob McClory "not true. Bob was a good friend." And he notes the book excluded the admonishment of his good friend, Bill Hewitt who chaired Deere and Company, the biggest job creator in his district. While Hewitt, at the administration's request, did meet Raisback for dinner at the administration's request, he refused to pressure his friend, instead telling them, "I trust your judgement. You do what you think is right."

Railsback also had words for Mark Felt, the FBI agent who 31 years after Nixon resigned, was revealed to have been "Deep Throat." "The honorable thing," Railsback said, was that Felt "should have to go to [FBI Director] Pat Gray and convey his concerns, and then if Gray refused to do anything, he [should have resigned . . . He would have been given plenty of protection by the Democratic-controlled Congress at the time. It's hard to second-guess, but that may have saved the country from that ordeal."

Beyond Watergate, 1974 was a watershed year for Watergate in other regards. *Time Magazine* recognized him as among America's 200 future leaders. And for good reason. Railsback had an impressive array of legislative accomplishments. Addressing flooding issues with the Army Corp of Engineers was a necessity for a district situated near the Mississippi. Campaign reform was a priority. And his authorship of "the first comprehensive juvenile justice legislation" won him the first-ever Flandrau Award from the National Council on Crime and Delinquency. He would also be recognized by ex-Attorney General Elliot Richardson.

Railsback also sought a legislative remedy to address a Supreme Court decision to a Citizens Privacy Protection matter. In Zurcher vs. The Stanford Daily, the Justices ruled that searches of newspapers without warning by police officers was permissible (the Stanford police had done so to the newspaper office). Railsback and his Senate counterpart, "Mac" Mathias of Maryland, authored language that prohibited a state, federal, or government official from "obtaining a warrant to search for and seize any matter in the possession of a person not suspected of a crime." If officials still hoped to conduct a search, a hearing would be held. And when the House passed a bill giving the U.S. Attorney General the authority to sue states with inadequate protections for the institutionalized, Railsback resisted an amendment by Pennsylvania Democrat Democrat Allen Ertel to exempt prisons. Railsback responded that he visited many prisons and the conditions "would have shocked the most callous prosecutor."

In the years after Nixon, Railsback saw little or no repercussions from Republicans in his district, and in this heavily Republican territory, general elections were an after-thought (Ford took 53% and Railsback 57%). But in 1982, a conservative State senator named Kenneth McMillan filed to challenge him in the primary, and he upset Railsback by 1,047 votes In his concession, he said, "maybe the majority of Republicans wanted someone more conservative than I," saying of impeachment, "finally came back to haunt me a bit."

Democrat Lane Evans, who had filed for the seat as a sacrificial lamb, went on to capture it that November, and held it for 24 years. Railsback meanwhile resumed practicing law and briefly served as Executive Vice President of the Motion Picture Association of America, Inc. He has since relocated to Idaho but has not stopped speaking out on Congressional comity when it comes to investigations against a president. Railsback is very disenchanted with the tenor of investigations against the Executive Branch.

Photo courtesy of Tom Railsback

CHAPTER NINETY-TWO

Bob McClory Authored Article III of Impeachment

Historic Quote: "I realize that there is no nice way to impeach a President of the United States." - Robert McClory to his colleagues on the House Judiciary Committee as they debated impeachment.

Ever wonder why Memorial Day and Labor Day fall on a Monday? Robert McClory had a lot to do with it. He sponsored legislation to make the observed holiday on that day. But McClory's claim to fame goes well beyond that. During Watergate, he became one of the most influential members of the House impeachment committee, and the Illinois Republican proposed thoughtful measures aimed to make the trains move. One such amendment ultimately resulted in Article III.

McClory
Photo courtesy of the Collection of the U.S. House of Representatives

McClory was often a quiet presence, but one who seemed concerned with acquiring the facts. At the time of Watergate, he was not the top Republican on the committee. That distinction belonged to Edward Hutchinson, his Michigan colleague who equaled McClory in seniority, but who had won the top spot by a coin flip. But many on both sides, including Hutchinson, viewed him as one of the intellectual powers on the GOP side. *The Wars of Watergate: The Last Crisis of Richard Nixon* by Stan Kutler noted that "for Hutchison, "intelligent but not very energetic, leadership essentially consisted of a passive and feckless faith that no Republican would vote to impeach the President. He often deferred to the greater activism of his colleague." That would be McClory.

Ironically, McCrory's fellow Illinoisan, Tom Railsback, with whom McClory would often be at odds, was likely the other most influential Republican player during the ordeal. "The Wars of Watergate" noted that "McClory and Railsback had feuded for many years. They competed throughout the inquiry for leadership within the minority, and particularly among Republicans who would consider impeachment."

Hailing from the "Land of Lincoln," McClory undertook his responsibilities on Judiciary with true Lincolnesqe statesmanship. Carefully deliberating, he hesitated on impeachment for the sole reason that he wasn't sure the evidence indicated Nixon was involved in the cover-up. But pursuit of the facts remained his prime concern. "I have heard it said by some that they cannot understand how a Republican can vote to impeach a Republican president. Let me hasten to assert that that argument demeans my role here. It would make a mockery of our entire inquiry."

At first, McClory resisted the impeachment brigade. But he was among the first to say that enough Republicans would likely vote in favor as to make passage inevitable.

Photo courtesy of the Chicago Sun-Times

By late June, with evidence mounting, he told his caucus that his conclusion was that Nixon had "technically" violated the Constitution. He would not support Article 1. The evidence, he believed, was "weak and fuzzy." However, he was angered by the administration's tactics with regard to the tapes, prompting him to say, "Now if you ever see an example of stone-walling the prime example is right there." But he would support Article II. "While I bear no malice and no hostility toward the President, it seems to me that I have an obligation of myself as a member of this committee when I see the constitutional obligation in default to support an article of impeachment."

When McClory told colleagues he would offer an Article of impeachment, one colleague said it might be "an elephant" in the room. Actually, McClory said, it would be "more like a mouse with a glandular condition." That became known as Article III.

Article III, which said "without lawful cause or excuse" of not turning over the subpoenaed material, "in derogation of the power of impeachment." Railsback among others believed the language might "alienate" attempts to attract other Republicans. Indeed, Railsback and all but one other member of the "fragile coalition" (Ray Thornton of Arkansas), would oppose the measure, which nonetheless was adopted 21-17.

Before the articles were voted on, McClory proposed an amendment on July 26 that would postpone further impeachment proceedings for ten days if the Nixon administration would indicate willingness within 24 hours to turn over the tapes. McClory never actually believed the administration would follow through on delivering the tapes. He simply wanted it noted that the committee gave them every opportunity to do so. But the majority felt they had been stonewalled long enough, and it was defeated 11-27, with six Republicans joining the Democrats.

Photo courtesy of the Chicago Sun-Times

In that vein, McClory addressed the dwindling but still present theory that partisanship was behind impeachment. "I've heard it said by some that they cannot understand how a Republican could vote to impeach a Republican President. Let me hasten to assert that that argument demeans my role here." But that fall, enough backlash was present — perhaps from some Republicans angered that he'd sponsor an amendment. He was held to just 55% in the general election. But by '76, he was back to 61%.

That year, he was in no mood to compromise on another high-profile committee matter. McClory was ranking member of a Select Intelligence Committee chaired by Otis Pike. The full House had ultimately voted against releasing its own report. Pike, citing an agreement with the Ford White House, threatened to release it anyway. McClory responded that he didn't "interpret the mandate given to our select committee to permit it to undertake unilaterally to declassify secret information." The issue became moot when CBS News published the findings.

McClory won his House seat at a relatively old age for a member of the House (54), at which time he described himself as a "Herbert Hoover liberal." This meant, McClory explained, that he was "a liberal as far as individual freedoms are concerned and a conservative as far as the extension of government authority is concerned." Yet his voting record actually grew more moderate as his tenure went along. There may have been a reason for that. McClory's district was among the few in Illinois that Barry Goldwater carried, so he may have wanted to guard his right flank. But he could only assuage them so much, and by 1978, he was mustering just 59% in the primary.

Eventually, McClory became a "knee-jerk" moderate. McClory opposed abortion but backed busing and the Alaska Wilderness Protection Act. He was a prime sponsor of the Equal Rights Amendment and the Fair Housing Act and opposed attempts to cut food stamps benefits. But on other issues, McClory would align with his party, opposing the creation, for example, of the Consumer Protection Agency. He sponsored highway legislation and bills mandating drivers be 16 to drive. But he was known for his expertise on Judiciary matters, and it was a perch from which few could doubt his intelligence, even if they were sometimes irritated by his techniques.

After Hutchinson retired, McClory became top Republican on Judiciary. But his problem became redistricting. A plan enacted in 1982 paired the bulk of McCrory's territory with fellow Republican moderate John Porter, which he called "blatantly political." McClory was far more senior, in both age and position (he was 74, Porter was the reversed 47). McClory was not ready for his career to end, but ultimately yielded to political reality. He'd be the 4th senior Illinois Republican who would not be returning to Congress following year's end. Railsback lost his primary, as did Ed Derwinski, elected in 1958. Downstate colleague Paul Findlay lost the general to Dick Durbin. And a fifth, House Minority Leader Bob Michel, narrowly avoided joining them.

McClory returned to Illinois where he died in 1988 at 80.

CHAPTER NINETY-THREE

The Gentleman From Roanoke: Butler Asked Fragile Coalition For Consensus On Impeachment

Historic Tidbit: During the height of Watergate, Dan Rather asked a rather pointed question of Nixon, prompting the President to ask Rather if "he was running for something." Rather then replied, "No sir, Mr. President. Are you?"

As Watergate dragged on and it became clear President Nixon was in on the shenanigans, a number of disparate factions slowly came to the conclusion that he could no longer serve. One such faction was the "fragile coalition," a seven member group composed of southern Democrats and on-the-fence Republicans. Caldwell Butler was not the leader. That fell to Tom Railsback of Illinois. But it was Butler who after hours of deliberations raised the question to the other participants: "Knowing what we all know now, does it justify the extreme action of removal from office?" Everyone in the group nodded yes. Thus, it was all over but the shouting. Or in this case the quiet deliberations.

It was July 23 and the "fragile coalition" had been gathered in Railsback's office. In the process, Butler revealed himself to be what was evident to all around him: that he was an honorable man, an exceptional judge of character, and most importantly, a true statesman.

Butler was just the type of Congressman Nixon could not afford to lose. A freshman Republican from a southern Virginia district that had given the President his largest margin in the state (73%), Nixon had helped Butler into a seat that had been open due to the retirement of Richard Poff, himself on Nixon's friends list (he was considered for a Supreme Court appointment).

Plus, Butler's record pointed to a pretty strong Nixon loyalist which is why in privately announcing his intention to support impeachment he added "there will be no joy in it for me." But Butler was no Nixon lackey. He viewed Nixon as "cold-blooded" and a *People Magazine* profile notes Butler, being a descendant of Chief Justice John Marshall, "is no less independent of mind."

Butler was a true middle-of-the-roader, a member of the centrist Wednesday Group of other like-minded Republican lawmakers in the House. A Roanoke son, Butler served in the Navy and received his law degree from the University of Virginia. His law partner was former Virginia Governor Linwood Holton who himself famously angered conservatives when he escorted his children to an integrated school.

By the time he had come to Congress, Butler had spent a decade in the Virginia House of Delegates and had risen to the position of Minority Leader where he would use his Virginia twang to respond to the all-Democratic rule. On a funding request by Governor Mills Godwin (then a Democrat – he would switch parties in 1973), Butler viewed it as asking for "a pig in a poke as they say . . . all he wants is a rubber stamp legislature" of "docile Democrats" whom he would label, "a courthouse gang." The *People* profile indicated he "was never one to suffer fools gladly."

**Photo courtesy of the WSLS-TV News Film Collection,
Rector and Visitors of the University of Virginia**

Butler was also known for enjoying a good laugh. A year after Nixon's resignation, a reporter dropped by Butler's office to discuss the anniversary. Butler greeted him with, "Robert E. Lee, I presume?" He was actually referencing the bill he had recently filed to restore the former Confederate General's citizenship posthumously.

When Butler made it to Congress (winning the special election to succeed Poff concurrent with the general), he was told that the Judiciary Committee "was a quiet, non-controversial place to learn the job."

It sure started out that way. Early in his tenure, he would call his Judiciary colleagues "a bunch of crazies." But as he got to know them, Butler said he "wouldn't mind being stuck on an island with them for a day or two." One person who stood out was Barbara Jordan, a fellow freshman whom Butler said, "was respected by the committee beyond her experience in the House of Representatives."

Even as Watergate reared its ugly head, Butler's low profile seemed likely to change little. But by mid-1973, it soon became clear that business as usual could not continue. Initially, it appears Butler was genuinely torn. But those around him were not. His wife would read him *All The President's Men* at night and his four sons and staff were urging a pro-impeachment vote. But like any good lawyer, Butler had to weigh the facts. Indeed, when people asked him how he was going to vote, he'd tell them he was weighing the evidence.

The tapes were, if not a start, a clear turning point. On April 27, Butler became the first Judiciary Committee Republican to vote to subpoena the tapes. When he heard them, the gravity of the moment was evident. Usually, Butler said, Nixon "knew the right directions." Yet now, "he missed the boat. Quite obviously, he missed the boat."

**Photo courtesy of the WSLS-TV News Film Collection,
Rector and Visitors of the University of Virginia**

Butler knew there would be hell to pay in his backyard. In the meeting in Railsback's office, fellow "Fragile Coalition" member Walter Flowers, an Alabaman joked, "Caldwell, do you realize that every pickup truck in Roanoke is going to be up here after you by nightfall."

The fact is Butler had tried to hold out for as long as he could. Of additional evidence he said, "It is not too late. I am starving for it but I will do the best I can with what I have." In late July, he had even called the presentation of Nixon attorney James St. Clair "masterful," acknowledging that, "If the Judiciary Committee were a jury that had to retire and deliberate and conclude its deliberations immediately . . . St. Clair would have carried his day." Similarly, all members of the "Fragile Coalition" agreed that John Doar had dropped the ball in his own presentation (Butler called it "incompetent").

Regarding the politics, however, Butler recalled years later that he "didn't have any problem separating the Republican problem." He said. "It was my first term in Congress, and I wasn't all that crazy about the job anyway (he had confided to a friend that 'the job's not that good,') . . . I think it would have been a terrible thing if we had decided to vote strictly along party lines in the committee."

Salon Magazine in a later profile observed Butler the day of the impeachment vote. "Behind his large, Coke-bottle glasses, Butler gave a rousing and emphatic speech to the committee." It read, "If we fail to impeach, we have condoned and left unpunished a course of conduct totally inconsistent with the reasonable expectations of the American people. We will have condoned a presidential course of conduct designed to interfere with and obstruct the very process he has sworn to uphold. We will have condoned and left unpunished an abuse of power totally without justification. In short, a power appears to have corrupted. It is a sad period in American history, but I cannot condone what I have heard, I cannot excuse it and I cannot and will not stand still for it." Calling Watergate, "our shame," he directed his ire toward his own party, saying "We cannot indulge ourselves in the luxury of patronizing or excusing the misconduct of our own people." Republicans in particular, he said, bore "special responsibility" to transcend party loyalty in their "sacred" impeachment duty . . . "I mean, the institution is more on trial at this moment than even the president." He would say later that impeachment "should be used only as a last resort and about once every 200 years is enough."

Butler may have suffered minor political repercussions from Watergate but it went countercyclical to the national mood. He held his seat that year with just 46%, but much of his margin came not from his Democratic opponent, the Roanoke Sheriff, who took 27%, but from an Independent candidate who took nearly as much from his right. It would be the last time he would even have to semi-sweat. In 1978 and '80, he had no major party opponent.

On nearly every issue, including defense and economic, Butler was solidly aligned with his party. The exceptions were social issues, which meant support for abortion rights, (including federal funding), and the backing of fair enforcement by Department of Justice officials. He opposed repeal of the Hatch Act for federal employees (Roanoke was far enough away from Washington DC so that he likely didn't represent many). But he would soon find that, for party loyalists, an almost perfect record wasn't enough.

**Butler was a member of the Wednesday Group along with,
among others, Joel Pritchard of Washington
Photo courtesy of the Washington Secretary of State**

Butler decided to step down in 1982 and resumed his law practice. But he soon decided he still had an appetite for the political arena. That was in the form of the Governorship. But his on again off again feud with Godwin would prove consequential again when the former Governor, who at first said Butler would make a formidable candidate, endorsed Wyatt Durette in mid- 1984. That forced Butler to take a hard look and conclude that, "the campaign for the nomination will deteriorate and jeopardize our chances for whoever holds the banner and I would prefer not to be a part of that." Once again, Butler was showing his true statesmanship. But he was not averse to taking a parting shot on the way out.

Butler claimed Godwin had "misled people as to my strength and had firmed up Durette's people." But he also found the repercussions from Watergate were not in the sunset. "I thought I had been vindicated on that."

Butler returned to Roanoke and died this past July 28, one month after his wife and almost 40 years to the day after he cast that famous vote for impeachment. Jack Betts, the retired associate editor of the *Charlotte Observer*, lauded Butler for rising to the moment, calling his passing, "more than a sad moment in Virginia politics; it was a reminder that the model of the elected politician who chooses to do the right thing rather than bow to pressure of party or electorate has virtually disappeared from American politics." Indeed, Butler can truly be proud of the contribution he made by rising to the moment at a most difficult chapter in history.

CHAPTER NINETY-FOUR

Flowers' Watergate Service Completed Trip
From Wallace Confidante To Statesman

Historic Tidbit: "In the obstruction of justice there is a dead skunk. You can smell it. But you have to find it." - Alabama Congressman and Judiciary Committee member Walter Flowers, essentially agreeing with committee Republicans seeking specificity to the articles.

Photo courtesy of the Collection of the U.S. House of Representatives

The House Judiciary Committee produced a number of talented members on the Democratic side that enjoyed 15 minutes of fame. Whether it resulted from eloquence, strong legal minds, or simply having the ability to express themselves, these abilities provided Americans exposure to the process. And if the machinations of the Nixon White House gave Americans reason to lose faith in government, the abilities of Walter Flowers reversed that tide.

The eloquence of Flowers, more than nearly any member of the Judiciary Committee save Barbara Jordan (a portion of whose words she echoed in her remarks) truly rose to the moment. What made that stand out was that Flowers, until the final days, was genuinely conflicted about how he would vote.

Flowers' 15 minutes of fame was so remarkable because at first glimpse, it seemed anything but likely. Why? Because Flowers was just the type of member that Nixon needed – or thought he had, in order to stave off impeachment. Nixon knew it. Judiciary Chair Peter Rodino knew it and so did virtually everyone who knew Congress.

It was not difficult to understand why. Nixon had taken 66% in Flowers' district and the incumbent stayed popular by voting a conservative line on nearly everything (his ADA score in 1972 was 6%). Flowers opposed the creation of the Office of Economic Opportunity, a 1970 appropriations funding bill of health, education, and welfare, as well as the Elementary and Secondary Education Act. Flowers was close to Alabama Governor George Wallace (whose picture he had hanging in his office) and supported many of the policies championed by the Governor of Alabama, including, for a time, segregation. And an anti-Wallace candidate, with major support from black voters, had drawn 38% against Flowers in the 1972 primary.

But a couple of tactics from the Nixon White House began to irk Flowers as early as October of 1973. For starters, he was "thoroughly turned off" by moves of the President himself, including his attempts to influence a respected elder statesman of the south, John Stennis, whom he referred to as "Judge Stennis." The failure of key Watergate players in the White House to be contrite also drew Flowers' ire. "The March 21st tape was devastating . . . the general lack of morality by people in the Oval Office, when the President talked about paying off – a crime of obstruction of justice, in every day chit-chat terms."

As the hour became late, Flowers was engaged in informal negotiations with a handful of equally undecided Democratic and Republicans who would become known as, "The Fragile Coalition." The group had not yet sat down. Sensing his opportunity, Nixon reached out to George Wallace. Nixon's biography by Stephen Ambrose noted that Nixon had tacticly aided Wallace in his 1970 comeback attempt and that he had help the Governor's brother with "IRS problems." So he assumed Wallace owed him one and he would cash in his chips by asking the Governor to call Flowers to put pressure on him. When Wallace offered no commitments, Nixon, upon hanging up apparently recognized the gravity of the situation and turned to told Al Haig and said, "Well Al, there goes the Presidency."

Well, almost, but not yet.

Peter Rodino apparently knew that Flowers was a key vote as well and approached him one night. It was at that point that Rodino pressed Flowers to convene a meeting of the "Fragile Coalition," which was truly living up to his words. For so fragile was the coalition that no formal meeting had even been held. That, Flowers assured Rodino, would change. It was now two days before the televised hearings were set to begin.

Flowers' first step was to approach the Republican leader of the "Fragile Coalition," Tom Railsback of Illinois. He asked him to "get some guys together." Railsback recalls, "Walter Flowers and I were buddies and we knew each other and trusted each other. We were the ones that gathered the troops. All of the people in the coalition contributed. It was truly a joint effort." It was at that meeting that Flowers posed a statement and a question to the group, in Railsback's office that would probably not change history, but nudge it along more quickly. The statement was about forging ahead. "We were all amazed at how close we were as to the . . . gravity of the evidence . . . and I said, 'It's nice to discuss these legislative details. But we ought to discuss whether we are willing to discuss to impeach the president of the United States.'"

That led to the inevitable question. "Knowing what we know now," he asked, "does it justify the extreme action of removal from office." Each signified yes. The dye was now cast firmly in favor of impeachment.

The only condition was specificity of the charges and the group carefully, albeit informally, worked out language among themselves for the various Articles. Flowers, fully aware of the enormity of his predicament, told colleagues, "Let's face it. It is more difficult for some than the others." But the decision had to signify at least minor relief as the stress of the indecision had led to an ulcer.

But first Flowers had unfinished business. Republicans, led by New Jersey's Charles Sandman, were proposing amendments, nine to be exact, aimed at weakening the Articles. Because there was unanimity among Democrats, the 27 votes needed for passage were guaranteed. But Flowers insisted the debate take place, if not for posterity.

Flowers had to stave off critics, including Sandman and California's Charles Wiggins who were still bemoaning the lack of specificity surrounding the allegations. Flowers would call them "the specificators" and he and Sandman were frequent sparring partners. At one point, Sandman chastised Flowers for voting "present" on one such amendment. Flowers' response was that "the caliber of debate (is) so outstanding on both sides . . . that it leaves me undecided." Sandman retorted by accusing Flowers of cynicism: "200 million Americans can see what you're doing. You're not kidding anyone." But when it came time for Flowers to take the microphone and deliver his statement, it was pure eloquence.

"What if we fail to impeach," he said. "Do we ingrain forever in the very fabric of our Constitution a standard of conduct in our highest office that in the least is deplorable and at worst is impeachable. Make no mistake, my friends, one of the effects of our action here will be to reduce the influence and the power of the Office of the President. To what extent will be determined only by future action in the House or the Senate . . . That is what we are doing here. But we will and should be judged by our willingness to share in the many hard choices that must be made for our nation . . . In the weeks and months ahead I want my friends to know that I will be around to remind them when some of these hard choices are up and we will be able to judge then how responsible we can be with our newly found Congressional power."

"We do not have a choice that, to me, represents anything desirable. "I wake up nights - at least on those nights I've been able to go to sleep lately - wondering if this could not be some sordid dream. But unfortunately this is no bad dream," he said. "It is the terrible truth that will be upon us here in this committee in the next few days."

At that point, Flowers' eloquence was more than proven but he would proceed to speak the words that would complete his journey from junior Congressman to a true statesmen. "We the People of the United States – and surely, there is no more inspiring phrase than this – "We the People of the United States' not we the public officials of the United States, not we the experts or we the educators, or we the educated, or we the grownups over twenty one or twenty five, not we the privileged classes or whatever but quite simply, 'We The People."

Jordan was so mesmerized by her colleagues "We the People" line that she herself used it as a preamble to her remarks. The amazing thing is that had both lived in different times, the African-American lawyer from Texas could have been addressing her remarks to the white lawyer from Alabama.

Flowers was certainly not enjoying his new found fame but seemed to realize his siding for impeachment was noticed. Iowa's Ed Mezvinsky, among the most vocal of Nixon opponents, recalls during one vote on the House floor Flowers sat with him and California's Jerome Waldie. "You know, I think I'll sit with you hard-liners," he joked. "The others don't seem to want me anymore."

Post impeachment, Flowers expected to pay the piper in his very pro-Nixon Congressional district. He faced no opponent in his bid for a fourth term but was prepared for tremendous backlash. Little materialized and Flowers would quietly serve his next two terms.

Meanwhile, Flowers would put together another fragile coalition. He was the chair of Judiciary's Administrative Law Subcommittee and took on the arduous battle of steering to House passage of major lobbying reform legislation. Getting there was not easy and the debate was sometimes acrimonious. At one point, Flowers denounced dilatory tactics and accused opponents of "playing games with this bill" (his words were later stricken from the *Congressional Record*). Once such amendment Flowers was blasting was one by Ohio Republican Tom Kindness that would call for 12 contracts for lobbying. Flowers mocked that idea, charging it would impact "local Boy Scout troops that write 12 letters in a six-month period. If any such bill passed Congress, the smoke would go up."

Ultimately, the legislation passed after House leaders kept the chamber in session for 17 hours. But it was late in the session and members were facing re-election. The Senate could not move the bill in time, forcing Flowers to declare, "We're at a stymie. We're unable to move because of a logjam." Ultimately, the body adjourned.

In 1978, Flowers mounted a bid for the U.S. Senate seat that was going to be vacated by John Sparkman. Wallace would be his only obstacle and he declared himself uninterested.

Flowers faced Howell Heflin, Chief Justice of the Alabama Supreme Court. Heflin labeled Flowers "part and parcel of that Washington crowd" and hit him for a connection to Tongsun Park and revelations that he'd take expensive flights back to Alabama on the government dole. Flowers did manage to force Flowers into the runoff but only barely. Heflin took 48% in the primary then proceeded to romp him 65-35% in the runoff. The loss marked an unceremonious end of a ten year career.

Flowers had won his seat in 1968 emerging second in a field of two to secure a seat in the runoff. There, with support from Wallace, he edged out attorney Rick Manley 51-49%. His early background was impressive. He grew up in Tuscaloosa and graduated from the University of Alabama, after which he studied international law as a fellow at the University of London. When his House term ended, Flowers remained in Washington and became an executive with Signal CO.

Flowers collapsed and died in 1983 while playing tennis on his 51st birthday.

CHAPTER NINETY-FIVE

Mann, A South Carolinian To The Core, An Integral Part of the "Fragile Coalition"

Historic Tidbit: The day before Richard Nixon resigned, one of his staunchest defenders in Congress, Indiana Republican Earl Landgrebe, made his views known. "Don't confuse me with the facts,' he said. "I've got a closed mind. I will not vote for impeachment. I'm going to stick with my President even if he and I have to be taken out of this building and shot." Voters respectfully passed on the firing squad but did opt for death by the ballot. Landgrebe lost his 1974 re-election bid to Democrat Floyd Fithian

South Carolina Democratic Congressman James Mann may be the one member of the impeachment committee whose very name was overshadowed – because a Washington Post reporter by the same name was very instrumental in cracking the case. For before and after Watergate, James Mann the Congressman was obscure as obscure could be. Despite his obvious intelligence and capability, his very junior status and member of the southern Democrats marginalized him in a chamber where liberals held sway. And Mann liked it that way. He was not a rabble-rouser by any means, rarely sought headlines and was simply content to serve his very conservative South Carolina constituency. That is where his district and the impeachment of Richard Nixon converged. And boy, did he rise to the moment in rhetoric and in deed.

Mann was part of the "Fragile Coalition," the group of Democrats and Republicans who would meet regularly in the final stages of Watergate to plot the road ahead (which would presumably lead to impeachment) that all could support. Flowers sought out Mann. BUT Mann was already under watch by Judiciary Chairman Peter Rodino. In fact, as the time for impeachment drew near, Judiciary Committee Chair Peter Rodino, as *The Wars of Watergate: The Last Crisis* of Richard Nixon worded it, "rework the articles in consultation with his allies and present them to the committee," to give members "something." Mann delivered, producing offenses that focused on Nixon's reliance of investigatory agencies – the CIA, FBI and IRS to quash opponents

Mann represented a district that had given Nixon nearly 80% in 1972 and arguably had a legislative philosophy to the right of the President's. His Conservative Coalition rating was quite high – 82% in 1976 and 69% in '77. He opposed union priorities such as common situs picketing legislation and voted against the establishment of a Consumer Protection Agency. But he also opposed the Hyde Amendment which prohibited federal funding for abortion. On another occasion, he opposed an amendment that would make it easier to reveal the identities of rape victims. Doing so, he said, "serves no real purpose and probably results in embarrassment to the rape victim and unwarranted public intrusion into her private life."

All that aside, from day one of the proceedings, he made clear that ideology was completely without bearing – the only factor was country and the Constitution. With tremendous eloquence, Mann reminded colleagues that, "We have built our country on the Constitution," he said on the first day of debate. "That system has been defended on battlefields and statesmen have ended their careers on behalf of the system and either passed into oblivion or immortality." That was good enough. *The New York Times* noted committee members had been deeply impressed by Mr. Mann's oratory in the early days of the hearing, and his quietly moving appeals to duty and principle circulated widely in the news media. And as the "Fragile Coalition" took shape, both parties acknowledged the gift of Mann's legal mind. A Republican staffer credited Mann with giving "the (Fragile Coalition) its integrity." A Democratic aide said that was exactly what Mann was all about. "He could cross the aisle. Few members of the committee could."

Mann was necessary to establish credibility: "He has a kind of entree into the Republicans and the conservative Democrats that Waldie or Drinan could never establish in a lifetime. "He can go to them and say, 'I have the same problem as you in my district. I can support this. So can you.'" And that's exactly what occurred. On August 4, 1974, *The News and Courier* of Charleston noted how "such respected people as our Sunday columnist James Jackson Kirkpatrick and U.S. congressman James Mann . . . have added depth and respectability."

And once Mann was in, he was in. When California Republican Charles Wiggins complained that the President was not given adequate notice, Mann responded that, "In my judgement, the charges that are included in Article 1 notify him of what he is charged with. And they set out something extra . . .

the means by which he is alleged to have committed the offense . . . Let us be reasonable." Besides, Mann added that Nixon's Attorneys were part of the proceedings all the while.

As the time came to wind down and vote, Mann issued his closing argument with utmost eloquence. "We should strive to strengthen and preserve the presidency. But if there be no accountability, another president will feel free to do as he chooses. The next time there may be no watchman in the night."

In voting, Mann voted with the majority to back the first two Articles. But with his Alabama colleague Walter Flowers, they opposed Article Three, which focused on Nixon's refusal to comply with the subpoena of 147 page documents. They were the only Democrats on the committee to do so which Don Edwards, his very liberal Judiciary colleague from California

Mann was a South Carolinian to the core. After graduating from the Citadel, he joined the Army. Then it was on to the University of South Carolina Law School where he edited the South Carolina Law Review. From there, his political and professional career took off. He began practicing law in Greenville and at 28, he won a seat in the South Carolina House of Representatives. At 34, he was a Solicitor for the 13th Judicial Circuit of South Carolina. When Democratic Representative Robert Ashmore stepped down in 1968, Mann took first place in the primary. However, his 32% mandated a runoff with Spartanburg Municipal Judge E.C. Burnett, Jr., who had taken 27%. Mann prevailed 57-43%.

After Watergate, Mann continued to immerse himself in the Judiciary Committee where as chair of the Subcommittee on Criminal Justice, he played an active role in the revision of the Criminal Code.

CHAPTER NINETY-SIX

Conable Came Up With Phrase "Smoking Gun," and Put The "K" In 401K

Historic Tidbit: Sherman Adams was a Dwight Eisenhower's legendary Chief of Staff. So hands on was he that he that a joke around Washington was "What if Adams should die and Eisenhower becomes President of the United States?" Sherman also decided who got to see the President, and often said "no." This created very low-standing for Adams among members of Congress which earned him the nickname "the abomidable no-man." Sherman's downfall came when it was revealed that he had accepted expensive gifts (a Vicuna coat, an oriental rug and hotel stays) from a close friend, Bernard Goldfine who was also seeking his help with government agencies. When this was made public, Adams realized just how few friends he had in Washington. Democrats demanded he resign and most Republicans, long alienated by Adams, saw little political benefit in defending him.

Conable in 1991
Photo courtesy of the World Bank Organization

E ver wonder how the phrase, "Smoking Gun" came to be a part of the political, and in turn American lexicon? It was brought out by Barber Conable, a Congressman from upstate New York who was among the most respected in his conference. His esteem was such that many viewed his ultimate decision to vote for Richard Nixon's impeachment as their own turning point. But Barber also made a number of contributions as ranking Republican on the House Ways and Means Committee and later, as head of the World Bank. And he put the "K" in 401K.

Conable was a moderate but one would never know it from the causes he espoused. He promoted the lowering of capital gains and believed in tax cuts and the lowering of personal income tax rates to stimulate the economy. He shepherded Reagan's 25% tax cut. The interesting thing about Conable ascending to the top spot on Ways and Means was that, like many of the panel's leaders, he was not skilled in economics. His major in college was medieval studies.

Yanek Mieczkowski said Conable "embodied the virtues of small town America." To wit, he also embodied the Greatest Generation. James Fleming writes that in Conable's words, his father, "convinced that Roosevelt was going to ruin this country," wanted to move his family to small town territory. "So during my school period, I grew up in the country."

Though Conable fought at Iwo Jima, he very nearly didn't get there. Applying in the Army, Conable found himself waiting, and waiting to hear back. Finally, he penned a terse letter telling recruiters he's "been wasting my time in a damn canning factory while you fuss around with my paperwork." The Army turned him down. But the Marines accepted him. Conable returned home but was one of the lucky ones. He said he "lost a lot of friends. My unit had a 57% casualty rate." He returned to get his law degree from Columbia but re-enlisted to fight in Korea. Conable's talents were recognized early.

Conable's election to the House came just two years after he won a New York State Senate seat. It was 1964 and Conable had to withstand LBJ's sweep at the top of the ticket. But this may have been one of the few districts that Goldwater may have aided Republicans. His running-mate, Bill Miller, represented a district just next door, and given the seat already Republican lean, Conable took 55%. It would be the lowest margin he'd ever take.

Conable would keep in close contact with his constituents by holding Saturday meetings at a local hardware store. He refused to accept contributions of more than $50. He needed those talents to pass the State and Local Assistance Act of 1972. But it was his amendment that was designed to save the pensions of Eastman-Kodak in his district. On economics, his record gave conservatives a lot to like as time after time, he proved himself one of them. He supported a cap on food stamps, voted against the Chrysler bailout, creation of a Department of Education, and backed only a limited version of an Alaskan Land bill. But on other social issues, he was moderate. He backed abortion rights and resisted attempts to rescind the ratification of the Equal Rights Amendment. For Conable's wife Charlotte was a major force in her own right when it came to women's advancement. She authored, "Women at Cornell: The Myth of Equal Education."

As Watergate emerged, Conable became far more than a casual player. At first, mindful of the overwhelmingly liberal bent on the House Judiciary Committee, Conable advocated a Select Committee to investigate Watergate. The day Democratic leaders went in another direction, Conable said he was "upset and concerned" because "every time we go down this chute it has tended to weaken the system and the process and add to the paralysis of government."

In *All the President's Men,* Bob Woodward and Carl Bernstein wrote "Conable's influence in the House was enormous. Nervous, vocal, intellectual, he was regarded by his colleagues as almost puritanical in his standards of personal and political conduct, a man of unquestioned integrity." It may be why after the transcripts were released that Conable became convinced Nixon's role was not accidental. He was among the final Republicans of any consequence to make up his mind, a fact not lost on House Minority Leader Jay Rhodes who told Conable, "You are the only member of the leadership that I care about." Thus, he vowed to vote for impeachment. ("I don't approve of leaders who mislead."). But it went further. Feeling personally betrayed by Nixon, Conable never again had correspondence with him, not even returning his letters.

One reason Conable may have felt so betrayed by Nixon was because he had tried so hard to see his innocence. At a meeting called by Alexander Haig and the President's lawyer, Mark St. Clair, Conable remarked, "Now that the President has been forced to take off his clothes in public, the question of additional tapes can be handled like a game of Russian Roulette." Conable proposed the White House turn over random tapes, thus "making it clear that the President has nothing to hide." As the election approached, Conable sensed the dangerous winds for Republicans of all stripes, noting, "The suburban middle-class people who are humiliated by their support of Richard Nixon are either going Democratic or going underground."

When Spiro Agnew resigned as Vice-President, Conable, along with Wisconsin Republican John Byrnes had circulated a petition among House members urging Nixon to replace him with Ford and now that Ford had assumed the Presidency, Conable was asked for advice many times. The first was whom he should tap for Vice-President (Ford was stunned that Conable had never been in the Oval Office and he had to explain to him that "Nixon wasn't interested in me"). While Conable's list involved two men, his home state Governor Nelson Rockefeller and George H.W. Bush, Conable didn't want to give Ford the impression he favored either one. He presented his case thus: "If you want to legitimize your administration, you should appoint someone who has been elected to high office many times and who is an accepted public figure like Nelson Rockefeller. On the other hand, if you want to start rebuilding the Republican Party, you should get somebody who is part of the future and George is that." Later, Conable noted he "appeared to have offended both sides and convinced them that I was for the other, the worst of all possible worlds."

Photo courtesy of the World Bank Organization

Barber himself felt a slight wrath of Watergate. His routine re-elections by 2/3 of the vote was won with 57%. But there was evidence he was in a no-win situation with conservatives as well. That September, he was beaten for the Conservative line, receiving just 43% in the primary. He would serve another decade and could have held the seat as long as he wanted. But in 1984, he called it quits explaining, "the vitality of the system depends on new people and new ideas."

Conable took one parting shot at the system on his way out the door. In an interview with *Congressional Quarterly*, he said, "I personally believe that representative government is alive and is well and is functioning the way it was intended to function - not very well." On another occasion, he said, "exhaustion and exasperation are frequently the handmaidens of legislative decision." But Conable himself embodied the best of the institution. His collegiality was unquestioned and his friendships on both sides of the aisle ran deep – he would often visit Mo Udall's office whenever the Arizona Democrat got acquired a new piece of Coconino art.

Conable's name was not on the radar screen when President Reagan named him to head the World Bank. But *The New York Times* called it "his legislative skill on the domestic front that made him a formidable choice for the job." Fairness for women was a major initiative. "Women do two thirds of the world's work," he said. "Yet they earn only one tenth of the world' income and own less than one percent of the world's property. They are among the poorest of the world's poor."

Upon his retirement from the World Bank, Conable returned to upstate New York and gave his service to a number of boards. He died of a staph infection at 81 in 2003.

Photo courtesy of the World Bank Organization

CHAPTER NINETY-SEVEN

Maryland's Hogan First Judiciary Republican To Back Impeachment

Historic Quote: "Now we can do what our wives have wanted us to do all along." - A Republican Congressman on House Minority Leader John Rhodes' decision to back the impeachment of Richard Nixon, apparently implying it was now safe to follow the leader.

Photo courtesy of the U.S. Government Printing Office

L awrence "Larry" Hogan was an obscure Congressman from southern Maryland whose quest for higher office failed. But his place as a footnote in history has been well secured. He was the first Republican member of the House Judiciary Committee to reveal that he would vote to impeach Richard Nixon.

Hogan's announcement, three days before the scheduled Judiciary Committee vote and in the midst of a primary campaign for Governor, came as a surprise to many, including even his wife. But it served to remove any existing ambiguity that despite the attempts by Nixon supporters to portray it as otherwise, Watergate was now a bipartisan affair.

Consider this. Hogan was so solidly anti-abortion and anti-busing that he proposed Constitutional amendments to outlaw both. In fact, the day the Supreme Court issued Roe vs. Wade, Hogan took to the House floor and admitted being so shaken that he could hardly deliver his speech. An FBI agent, he sponsored a resolution saying it "should be the sense of Congress that no pardon, reprieve, or amnesty be given to deserters or draft evaders." So it was only natural that Nixon would have considered him in his corner, right? Wrong?

At his announcement, Hogan told the crush of reporters that he backed impeachment because Nixon "lied repeatedly" to the American people. He suggested "my President" was in on the hush money. "The thing that's so appalling to me," he said, "is that the President, when this whole idea was suggested to him, didn't, in righteous indignation, rise up and say, 'Get out of here, you're in the office of the President of the United States. How can you talk about blackmail and bribery and keeping witnesses silent? This is the presidency of the United States.' But my President didn't do that. He sat there and he worked and worked to try to cover this thing up so it wouldn't come to light." Ultimately, he said, "I have come to the conclusion that Richard Nixon, beyond a reasonable doubt, committed impeachable offenses which, in my judgement, are of sufficient magnitude that he should be removed from office."

It was partly because Hogan was on so few – if any radar screens that the tide toward impeachment, which prior to had been humming along, suddenly catapulted at lightening speed. One Congressman said it "had a profound psychological impact. Many Republicans who were not on anybody's list for impeachment were talking for the first time about their votes for it being possible or probable."

John Anderson, the number three House Republican who had already indicated his support for impeachment called it "quite obvious that the committee is disposed to vote one or more articles and I would gather that the House would follow suit, from what I hear in the corridors."

Hogan had once said, "I've always needed challenges in life." After his statement, he surely wasn't disappointed. Timing was the first order of criticism. Some questioned his decision to announce his decision just before the vote. Others criticized the statewide television tour that followed. A leading Baltimore politician said "people here felt his jumping the gun on Nixon was done for political purposes . . . that he made a political publicity show out of the nation's trauma." Among Democrats, one quipped, "That is what happens when a guy has a pollster," adding a lot of them will be getting one in the next few weeks." It inspired a joke from a liberal Democrat, Jim Corman, who said, "I wish more of you guys were running for Governor."

Predictably, Hogan was attacked by the Nixon White House for making the move solely for political expediency. They mentioned his "faltering campaign." Nixon would write in his memoirs that, "In San Clemente we tried to minimize the damage Hogan caused by concentrating on the many people who criticized him and his motives. But the fact was that he had dealt us a very bad blow." Dean Burch said Hogan's "ambition to be Governor of Maryland weighed heavily" and he acted "from what he viewed as his political interest."

Actually, to hear Hogan tell it, his epiphany was reached very mythodically. He had been returning home from a veteran's event in Washington. "All the way I began sifting the thing through, then I dictated some thoughts in my own head." The drive home took about an hour and Hogan said the entire way, "I debated with myself . . . And when I got home I said to my wife, 'I'm going to vote for impeachment.' She said 'good,' that's all I remember her saying. It was a relief in a way. Because it was agonizing."

Of his colleagues, Hogan would say years later that, "We had to do all of the work that everybody else had to do. And yet had this burden, every single day closeted in this room. Not only the time burden but the psychological burden. Knowing what we were about was of such enormous importance." The White House put in two calls to Hogan but they proved futile: he took neither. After Hogan's announcement, people from both parties argued that while he might suffer somewhat from his vote, his platform gave him no choice. Hogan had been centering his campaign around ethical improprieties of the Mandel administration and as one "If he voted against impeachment, Marvin was going to hang the thing around his neck."

Steny Hoyer, then a State Senator, summed up Hogan's predicament. "With a candidate for Governor trying to project the image that Hogan is, it seems to me that he was always precluded from not voting for impeachment. He's had too." Others faulted his timing. Republican State Senator Jervis Finney "It will be hard for him to get the credit for not having made a political decision. People are very suspicious of politicians' statements . . ."

The obscure politician even in his own state was suddenly a media darling. His television bookings went through the roof, including national shows such as "Today." When Charles Sandman tried to delete the portion of the Article charging Nixon made false and misleading statements, Hogan told his colleague he had "subjected all of us yesterday to belabored arguments of the need for specificity. We're trying to be responsible and specifically support the articles of impeachment."

Hogan said later, "After Nixon resigned, I thought my vote might be an asset [among Republican voters], but it wasn't. At first, the calls running to his office were fairly positive. But the opposition mail he received labeled him, "Benedict Arnold," and "Judas Hogan." One pro-Nixon Judiciary Republican colleague, Roger Zion of Indiana, boasted that he had raised $1,600 for Hogan's opponent within 24 hours of the announcement. That may have been a mistake on Zion's part. He would lose his re-election bid.

If Hogan had hoped to win votes by his call for Nixon to step down, it backfired. It was said that Hogan didn't focus enough on Louise Gore, his Republican opponent. Gore a Republican National Committeewoman, a socialite, and the first female Republican elected to the State Senate from Maryland and had a footnote in history of her own; she introduced Nixon to Agnew. Instead, he trained fire on the man he would have faced, incumbent Democratic Governor

Marvin Mandel. That proved costly. In his concession, Hogan knew he had won Democrats but noted "unfortunately, there were not enough Republicans who could forgive me for that rate."

To that point, Hogan's rise in Maryland politics was pretty solid. A Gonzaga graduate, he had first sought a Congressional seat in 1966 but lost to Democratic incumbent Harvey Machen, 54-46%. But 1968 had more favorable winds. Agnew was a top the ticket and Nixon just missed carrying Maryland (he was actually declared the winner at one point in the evening). But it was enough to aid Hogan past Machen.

Hogan said in the years after his defeat, his vote inhibited his ability to get a job in Republican circles. But by 1978, much of the stain within his party had worn off.

After leaving office, Hogan did make a comeback of sorts. Not in his district. The then fast growing Prince Georges County was then solidly Republican turf. Now, it gives Democratic candidates 70%. But In 1978, he was elected Prince Georges County Executive.

Interestingly, for all of Hogan' law and order background, he was involved in a skirmish over his own ability to practice law. Hogan, now 86, continues to reside in Maryland. His son, Larry Hogan, Jr., was elected Governor of the state of Maryland in November 2014.

CHAPTER NINETY-EIGHT

Chelsea Clinton's Father-in-Law An Ex Iowa Congressman Who Went To Jail

Historic Quote: "We got beat by the cast of Hair." Tip O'Neill on the 1972 Democratic primary victory of George McGovern whose slate against O'Neill backed Ed Muskie came by 2-1 in his own Congressional district.

Photo courtesy of the Collection of the U.S. House of Representatives

Everyone knows Chelsea Clinton's mother-in-law is former – and if she has her way, future Pennsylvania Congressman Marjorie Margolies Mezvinsky. But did you know that her father-in-law was also a member of Congress? He certainly was, and he was from the state of Iowa if you can believe that. And now, he's an ex jailbird (for everything, there is a story).

Ed Mezvinsky's Congressional tenure dates back to the 1970's when he overcame the Nixon landslide to win a Congressional seat. Actually, he had been a staffer long before that, to Congressman Neal Smith, on ethic bills no less. But 1972 was not a bad year to be a Democrat in Iowa. McGovern, while losing the state, didn't do any worse than Humphrey, and Dick Clark was shocking everyone by sending Senator Jack Miller packing.

Mezvinsky's win was not a shock. What was a shock was that he had come within 765 votes of longtime Republican Fred Schwengel two years earlier. Schwengel's party label had helped him hold the seat (though he had lost it once before), but he was not particularly attentive to his district, which was borne out in a primary that saw him lose 40%.

Mezvinsky was a lawyer and consumer affairs activist who ran ads of voters mispronouncing his name, and by attacking the Nixon administration. He ran a true grass roots campaign that centered on modern techniques such as voter id's, etc.

For 1972, Mezvinsky was back. This time, he beat Schwengel 54-46% as Nixon was taking 56%. Mezvinsky did well in Iowa City, where many of the UI students were likely coming out to back McGovern. But the numbers suggest Mezvinsky would have won anyway. What was his name among the Congressional press corps? "Fast Talking Ed."

Mezvinsky, Senator John Culver and Congressman Neal
Smith meet Iowans on the steps of the Capitol
Photo courtesy of the John Culver Papers, University of Iowa Libraries, Iowa City

Mezvinsky immediately snagged a seat on the House Judiciary Committee, just in time for the big Watergate show. Mezvinsky actually proposed that among the things Nixon should be impeached for is his misuse of funds but that motion struggled to garner serious support (Judiciary Chair Peter Rodino had even asked him not to offer it). Nonetheless, Mezvinsky could not stopped from making his statement prior to the votes on the Articles and while junior status pushed him back to virtually the end of the line but like many of the previous speakers, he cited the Constitution.

"I know that I am one of the last speakers but I shall not have the last word because we all know that the last word belongs to the Constitution. My colleagues and I who have anguished over this task know this all too well. You can tell it from the words they have spoken, whichever side of the aisle they were on. I just hope that I am able to make a contribution to a further understanding of our grave responsibility." He described the Presidency as "a rare trust. It is truly a culmination of a national trust and confidence."

**Photo courtesy of the Special Collections Department
of the Iowa State University Library**

Mezvinsky then spoke of his parents who were immigrants and his Iowa upbringing. There, he spoke of "a great admiration for our Presidents, whether they be Republican or Democrat. And I found it personally very unsettling to be faced with the harsh evidence that Richard Nixon has abused the Presidency; but the committee must face the evidence – and that's what it is – it is the evidence."

Mezvinsky's first re-election challenge had come from Jim Leach, a foreign service officer who resigned his post amid the Saturday Night massacre. So the election was in a sense about who could out-Watergate who. He attacked Mezvinsky for accepting money from outside Iowa and vowed not to (it was a practice that he'd adhere to throughout his 30 years in Congress).

With '74 being such a Democratic year, Mezvinsky kept his seat, but not by a super-imposing margin, 54-46%.

By 1976, Mezvinsky's fortunes had changed dramatically. Mezvinsky, who had separated from his wife early in his first term, had remarried to, as *The Almanac of*

American Politics noted "a woman who is a reporter on one of Washington's local newscasts." That would be MMM. Mezvinsky was not returning to the district as much as he used to, and in a swing seat, doing so was a must. Leach was able to reverse the margin, 54-46%.

Soon after his loss, Mezvinsky moved to Pennsylvania where his ambitions of returning to public life were obvious. For a time, he was the United States Ambassador to the United Nations Commission on Human Rights. But he yearned for elective office and sought the Democratic nomination for the U.S. Senate in 1980 but lost, though he did score enough chits to Chair the Pennsylvania Democratic Party.

In 1988, Mezvinsky won the nomination to challenge Ed Preate for Attorney General and centered a large part of his campaign on ethics. "I'm sick and tired," he said, "of public officials abusing the public trust. We're going to have to restore the integrity of our government that was envisioned when they decided to make this office independent." Ironically, Preate himself would be imprisoned for embezzlement.

In 1992, Marjorie shocked many when she won a Montgomery County Congressional seat. The margin was fewer than 2,000 votes and it was the first sign that the rock-ribbed Republican county was changing. But Mezvinsky was famously booted out when she cast the deciding vote for Clinton's tax package after having promised voters during the campaign that she wouldn't (House Republicans broke into a chant of "Goodbye Marjie." Mezvinsky sought a comeback in 2000, but her bid for the Democratic U.S. Senate nomination ended amid her husband's legal troubles.

Meanwhile, Chelsea and Marc had dated throughout the 90's, but had several on and off periods.

Mezvinsky was sentenced to 80 months in prison for a massive investment scheme, dubbed the "Nigerian advanced payment ponzi scheme that ultimately robbed victims of $10 million. He was convicted of 31 of 69 charges, including mail and bank fraud and would serve seven years in federal prison near Elgin Air Force Base in Florida, which would be followed later by probation. That's where he was by the time of the wedding.

Ed Mezvinsky was supposedly permitted to attend Marc and Chelsea's wedding ceremony, but not the reception. Around the time of the wedding, he said he was "remorseful for what happened, it was a terrible time, and I was punished for that. And I respect that and accept responsibility for what happened, and now I'm trying to move on and am grateful I have the opportunity for that."

Ed and Marjorie divorced in 2007. Ed, 78, has finished probation.

CHAPTER NINETY-NINE

Danielson Served On The House Judiciary Committee With Distinction

Historic Tidbit: The post-Watergate class of 1974 was famous for voting out three aging committee chairs in their full caucus meetings following the election. But little known was that Bob Poage of Agriculture, Ed Hebert of Armed Services, and Wright Patman of Texas were first up by virtue of their committees place in the alphabet. It was suspected that most of the "Watergate Babies" simply wanted to flex their muscles to show more senior colleagues what they were capable of. As the remainder of the roll was called, no other chairs were ousted.

Another Democrat who served on the House Judiciary Committee during Watergate who would play an intricate part in the deliberations and crafting of amendments was George Danielson.

The Californian, a former U.S. Attorney and FBI agent, combined humor and brains to home his points, traits that were evident through his entire life. Danielson would use these attributes to play an active role in the impeachment hearings, including offering an amendment that passed. But the question he posed at the start of his remarks, "Just what is an impeachable offense" may have been his contribution.

Upon graduating from the University of Nebraska, Danielson became an FBI agent where he was stationed, among other places, in Latin America. He served in the Navy during World War II, then moved to California where he became an assistant U.S. Attorney. In the years ahead, he would open a law firm.

Danielson was elected to the Assembly in 1962 and the Senate in 1966, the same year Ronald Reagan became Governor. It was not a glorious time for Democrats but Danielson was still able to push through a bill establishing a governing board for the Los Angeles Community College District. His tenure seemed threatened when redistricting merged it with the much more senior Chet Holifield but at 71 and potentially facing a challenge to his committee chairmanship, Holifield decided to retire.

Danielson still did not have a free ride. The district was becoming increasingly Hispanic and he faced a determined effort in the primary from East Los Angeles Community Action founder Esteban Torres. He won the primary 53%-37%, then cruised through the general. Danielson was a major proponent of campaign finance disclosure and in particular wanted the public to see where members received their campaign contributions. His voting record was solidly, though not unanimously liberal.

Fast forward to Watergate. One Danielson article of impeachment said Nixon had intended to interfere with the various Congressional committees that were carrying out their own investigations, specifically the Banking and Currency committee, the Senate Watergate Committee, and the House Judiciary Committee. Charles Wiggins said one of the committee's Danielson was citing, Banking and Currency, had never even conducted an investigation for Nixon to impede and that he was simply making a "good faith claim" to Executive Privilege.

Danielson said the offense set forth was "truly a high crime and misdemeanor within the purest meaning of the words" because it was "uniquely Presidential. Only the President can abuse the powers of the office of the President" and the "crimes or offenses were against the very structure of state, against the system of government."

In his formal remarks prior to the impeachment vote, Danielson addressed colleagues who were demanding more specificity. "I want to point out that circumstantial evidence is just as valid evidence in the life of the law and that of logic as is direct evidence. In fact, sometimes I think it is much stronger. And the best example I can give you is the fact that there are 38 members of this committee – they are all well trained, skilled, competent people—who sat here day after day, listening to tapes, listening to witnesses, and yet they walked out of these doors into the arms of the press and you had 38 different versions of what expletive the President used when he talked to Dean on March 21, 1973 when he said, 'Get it.' So you can see that even direct evidence has its imperfections."

Most of all, Danielson was known for his prolific humor in making points. "We use good judgement and common sense and we bear in mind that people probably intend to do what they do in the serious matters of this life." John Mitchell was "like trying to nail a drop of water to the wall." After Gerald Ford was sworn in as President, Danielson wondered whether "a 4-0 watt bulb was in a 100 watt socket."

In 1982, Danielson became a federal judge and was involved in, among other things, the Rodney King trial. His death in 1998 came as the House was taking up another impeachment battle."

Wolverine Brown Quashed Watergate Investigation Before '72 Election

Historic Quote: "I have friends who live there. They tell me it's very nice." - Richard Nixon of the Watergate apartment complex years after his resignation.

Image courtesy of the Collection of the U.S. House of Representatives

G arry Brown is an interesting footnote to history. The Republican who served six terms as a House member from Michigan was a lead organizer of the effort to stop the House Banking Committee's attempt to investigate the break-in at the Democratic National Committee's headquarters.

At that time, the term Watergate was in its infancy and a number of fearful Republicans had hoped to keep it that way, at least until after the election. House Banking Committee Chair Wright Patman had other ideas and he sought to spearhead an investigation through his committee. Specifically, he wanted to subpoena Attorney General John Mitchell and Nixon's Finance Chair, Maurice Stans. But publicly and privately, Brown mobilized support against it.

It was later revealed that he had done so not only under the auspices of the Justice Department, but of the administration as well.

The goal was to convince committee members that a Banking Committee investigation would impede a regular investigation. They produced phone calls and documents to that affect and stated their reluctance to testify. Many were orchestrated by the Committee to Re-elect the President (CREEP). Nixon had suggested Brown, along with his fellow Michigander and Republican leader Gerald Ford, take the initiative for the White House saying, "they ought to get off their asses and push it . . . there's no point giving (Patman) a free ride." On Brown, the White House tapes picked up him saying, "tell him that, tell, tell tell Ehrlichman to get Brown in . . ."

On cue, Brown accused Patman's staff of conducting conducted an ad hoc hearing . . . and calling Stans as a witness without any authority." He suspected it was done for "political ramifications" and urged members to ask themselves if "the political benefit which we hope to derive" from the committee investigation is worth the cost of potentially botching the investigation. Patman replied that he acted within the rules of the House.

With the aid of six Democrats, Brown succeeded in defeating the motion to hold hearings 20-15. Dean testified that "another sigh of relief was made at the White House that we had leaped one more hurdle in the continuing cover-up." Indeed, the matter would basically be laid to rest until after Richard Nixon would romp George McGovern.

But Brown's name would not be laid to rest in the matter. John Dean had testified that Brown's involvement was even deeper, a charge Brown angrily denied. Instead, Brown said he was opposing the investigation before Dean even initiated his meeting with the President. His message, he said, was to warn CREEP to "stay away." He said the committee "probably should have gone ahead with the investigating," adding "it would have to be different but you must realize all Patman had at that time was a very sketchy Mexican money deal worked out by a contributor.

Later on, Brown would be at the center of another controversy. 18 executives of major corporations had received Congressional questionnaires about their lobbying but Brown went to bat for them. He said he was "advising those who contact my office . . . that the mailing of this questionnaire is not pursuant to action taken by this subcommittee." That led columnist Jack Anderson to call Brown a "fast talking, chain-smoking" Congressman "whose heart belongs to the titans of Commerce."

During his time in Congress, Brown did typify the Republican Party in Congress. His voting record was more right-leaning than not. But the likelihood is that Brown more than anything was ardently parochial. When Upjohn, a drug manufacture howled about the FDA not funding a major drug, Brown took their cause. Ditto with Checker Cab Service, based in his district, when they wanted to be exempt from safety standards.

Though Brown's record was more conservative he did display more independent streaks on cultural issues. He voted to allow federal funding of abortion. And he was at the forefront of housing legislation that would provide block grants to states for low income housing. During a debate on food stamps, Brown proposed denying benefits to those who were on strike (they would still be eligible through local means). It was defeated by a lopsided margin.

The fact is, the district did give Hubert Humphrey and George McGovern 37 and 38% respectively). But his philosophy did hew to that of a Republican.

A resident of Schoolcraft, Michigan his entire life, Brown earned his degree from Kalamazoo College and secured a law degree from George Washington University. In the interim, Brown came to Congress after a distinguished career in criminal justice. He was an FBI agent, then a United States District Court for Michigan's western district and was a member of the state's Constitutional Convention. The following year, Brown won a seat in the State Senate and in 1966, took on incumbent Democratic Congressman Paul Todd. Brown was an underdog in both races but at the end of the day, emerged victorious.

Demographically, Brown's district was diverse. It contained a large student population with western Michigan but also large corporations such as Upjohn and Kellogs. But it was heavily Republican throughout. So it was somewhat amazing that his grasp began to slip. 1974 was explainable. It was the post-Watergate election and a number of more senior members in more secure districts were swept away. As it is, Brown hung on just 52-48%. But it was against Todd who refused to make an issue of Brown's role in quashing the investigation and the Ford's pardon of Nixon. Todd was not the campaigner that he had been ten years earlier and Brown may have gone on the offensive in the most expedient ways. He didn't criticize the pardon but said it had come too soon.

In 1976, Brown faced an energetic, albeit underfinanced challenge from Howard Wolpe, a State Senator who had become the first Democrat to represent Kalamazoo in the state legislature in 100 years. Wolpe, a former political science professor, had held hearings on high utility rates and boasted of sponsoring legislation that allowed motorists to turn right at red lights. Meanwhile, he attacked Brown for his contributions from the Banking industry. It did not go unnoticed that Brown did not spend as much time in the district as in the past and by mid-October, the general feeling was that Wolpe was ahead. But on Election Day, Michigan Republicans were aided by the presence of Gerald Ford at the top of the ticket and that may have been critical to Brown hanging on. But the margin was close. 4,000 votes out of 195,000 cast, 51-49%. Brown lost Kalamazoo and Battle Creek but was saved by Eaton County near Lansing.

In 1978, Wolpe was back and by now, he had even more connections by virtue of being a staffer to new Senator Don Riegel. It was said Brown considered foregoing a certain hard fight. But *Congressional Quarterly* reported "his personal animosity toward Wolpe persuaded him to run for another term."

In fact, Brown geared up even sooner than before, tying Wolpe to the Carter administration and labeling him a liberal. But Wolpe learned from his past mistakes as well. He bought a house in Eaton County and developed a high-tech campaign operation, aided by labor, teachers, and environmental interests. Brown meanwhile, had won a dubious place on the League of Conser-vation's Dirty Dozen. This result was a complete reversal of '76. The margin was again 51-49%, a 4,000 vote difference. But this time, Brown was on the losing end. Yet for all of their past problems, Wolpe would later credit Brown for being gracious, offering him the advice that "there is life after Congress, and at the end of the day, you still have to look at yourself in the mirror."

Brown returned to Schoolcraft where he would spend the next 30 years. He died in 2008 at 75. Todd, who would pass only months later, was also effusive in his praise of the rival who vanquished him. In an extraordinary statement, Todd said "While we sparred in our campaigns, and I, perhaps more than he, said things which were overstretched, we retained our friendship, our belief in honest politics and the ability to conduct reasonable discourse on the issues which divided us.

Watergate Catastrophic For House Rs In '74

Historic Tidbit: Chuck Grassley and Jim Jeffords were rarities in the gigantic post-Watergate class of 1974— Republicans. In fact, two of just seventeen. But their elections did not come easy. In fact, Grassley was expected to lose to Iowa State Senate colleague Steve Rapp, 25, but his age counted against him. Grassley won 51-49%. Jeffords wasn't as hard pressed but Vermont was still fairly Republican, as Pat Leahy's upset Senate win that year made it the first time a Democrat had won a seat in that chamber from that state. Jeffords won 53-40%. Before their swearings-in, Jeffords broke a leg and Grassley his wrist. As they were about to take their oaths, a Democratic colleague looked at them and said, "There are two more we almost got."

Charles Sandman (New Jersey) and Wiley Mayne (Iowa) were two of Nixon's staunchest Judiciary Committee defenders during Watergate. Both lost their seats
Left photo courtesy of the Government Printing Office;
Right photo courtesy of the Mayne Family

1974 was a bloodbath for House Republicans. The Watergate scandal, coupled with Gerald Ford's pardon of Nixon, cost Republicans dearly. And the new President, who had proclaimed "our long national nightmare over" would suffer mightily. He may have best captured the impending doom just after signing the pardon, when he prepared to play around of golf. "Today," Ford said, "I will try to get into a hole in one. Tomorrow, I'll need to get out of one." Indeed, Election

Night was heinous. As one of his aides said, "many of his close friends lost." But beyond that, many of the losers were people he had led as Minority Leader, and in some cases, had mentored.

No region of the country was spared the Watergate wrath. Five of seven members Republican from Indiana alone were shown the door, including a twelve-term Congressman who was the senior member of the Armed Services Committee. New Jersey Republicans lost four seats, including one of Ford's 1948 classmates. The New York GOP was relegated to its fewest number of representatives since 1912. Iowa's Congressional Republicans went from three to one. A former Governor of Wisconsin who had been ensconced in the House for 13 years went down. And several members thought safe in North Carolina, Tennessee, and Virginia saw their careers end as well.

Ford on Election Eve Trying To Get the Vote out
Photo via NBC News

Many of the casualties were the President's staunchest defenders, from on the Judiciary Committee or off. Committee Republicans who opposed impeachment until literally the 11th hour (or in the case of many, 72 hours), were crucified.

Four Judiciary Republicans fell into this category. Charles Sandman of New Jersey, Joe Maraziti of New Jersey, David Dennis of Indiana, and Wiley Mayne of Iowa voted against the articles of impeachment in committee and were prepared to do so on the floor, until August 5, 1974, when the evidence pointing to Nixon's role in the cover-up would be irrefutable. That day, all four, along with their remaining seven Judiciary colleagues who had opposed impeachment, said they were now prepared to do so. And all faced rematches with foes they had faced in a recent election.

Among the foursome, Sandman, 53, fell the hardest. In the span of just one year, he would literally lose it all.

Sandman had taken 66% of the vote in his re-election bid in 1972 and had wrested the GOP Gubernatorial nomination from incumbent William Cahill a year earlier, who was in trouble with his own party for raising taxes. But the political detriment of Watergate really encapsulated between the primary and the November general election and Sandman lost to Brendan Byrne by over 700,000 votes. He lost 20 of the state's 21 counties, only managing to win his home, Cape May, in the southern tip of the state.

That alone should have signified the perilousness of his electoral position in '74. Indeed, Sandman did get the jolt the rest of the party faced. He would write to George H.W. Bush, then serving as RNC Chair that, Every Republican in NJ was severely punished. We lost 13 incumbent State Senators . . .15 Assemblymen. Not one of these was due to any state or local issue. To the contrary. Our candidates were far better than their conquerors."

But the four-termer kept defending Nixon. Apple spoke of Sandman's "glasses perched on the end of his nose, a pencil grasped between his hands, looks toward the majority and heaps scorn on their arguments."

Reagan tried to fuel Sandman's campaign for Governor but it proved little help
Left photo courtesy of politics1.com; Right photo courtesy of Bill Sandman

Wiggins said Sandman's outreach was geared toward the Republican hard-core out there in televisionland, trying to turn them on." His shtick was bemoaning the lack of specificity in advocates arguments and he sought to remedy that by introducing amendment after amendment to the imp Sandman asked, "Do you not believe that under the due process clause of the Constitution that every individual, including the President, is entitled to due notice of what he is charged for?" "Maybe I overlooked something. Maybe there is a tie-in with the President. All-right. There are 37 of you. Give me that information. Give it to 200 million Americans because up to this point you have not."

Referring to inconsistencies, he'd say, "Isn't it amazing? Isn't it surprising? Isn't it astonishing?" At another point, he insisted "my role is not one of defending the President – that's for sure." He said his philosophy was "a strict construction of the Constitution. If somebody, for the first time in seven months, gives me something that is direct, I will vote to impeach."

In a debate, Sandman could go for the jugular. R.W. Apple of *The New York Times* called Sandman "a master of sarcasm who sounds like W.C. Fields." Following a vote on one amendment to an impeachment article in July, he questioned why Alabama Democrat Walter Flowers had voted "present." When Flowers responded that both sides were compelling, Sandman retorted, "Two hundred million people know what you are up to. You aren't kidding anybody." And just before the July impeachment vote, Sandman angrily addressed his fellow New Jerseyan, Judiciary Chair Peter Rodino. "Please, he said," let us not bore the American public with a rehashing of what we have heard. You've got 27 votes. Let's go on with our business." That business, Sandman felt, was being impeded what he felt were overly drastic articles. At one point he said advocates "now want to strip (Nixon) of every asset he has left, possibly send him to jail."

With his re-election approaching, Sandman faced one of the best campaigners in the entire country. Bill Hughes had come within 5,000 votes of denying Hughes re-election in 1970 and now was running again. And this time, the result would be unambiguous. Hughes would take 59% and this time, Cape May would not support Sandman, who returned to New Jersey and would eventually be appointed a Superior Court Judge by Tom Kean. He died in 1983.

Maraziti, 62, was a freshman who had been so instrumental in the drawing of his district that it was called the "Maraziti district." But his performance on the committee was considered a spectacle. He would hunt down reporters and mounted defenses that even his supporters would call ridiculous. After the impeachment vote, he had said, "we have weakened the hand of the President and the 220 million people he represents," But it wasn't just Watergate that tied him down. He was already under scrutiny for office irregularities. Helen Meyner, the wife of the former Governor that he had walloped in 1972, returned the favor 57-43%.

Mayne, 57, in his fourth term, not only refused to distance himself from Nixon, but Ford as well. He had appeared with the President at a September fundraiser in Iowa. Actually, Mayne's troubles had begun well before Watergate. In a district that had given Nixon 62% in '72, Mayne had almost been dragged under by Berkley Bedell, a millionaire. Now, Bedell was back for a rematch, and he was labeling Mayne, Nixon's "yes man." He said Mayne opposing impeachment "was a vote to cover-up by killing the matter in committee. Our Congressman has acted more like a defense lawyer for Nixon than like a representative of the people." Indeed, Mayne gave the other side plenty of ammunition. As the impeachment committee debated an Article pertaining to Nixon's tax problems, Mayne asked, "Is it a high crime and misdemeanor to be less than perfect in the performance of one's office."

At a 2003 forum, Mayne was very mythical. He said he "felt it took a very, very strong body of evidence to justify the drastic remedy to impeach him. But at the time our committee voted, I did not think that it was there. Of course, just a few days later on August 5, the President released those transcripts . . . in which it was clear that he was instructing the FBI to discontinue its investigation . . ." Asked if he felt betrayed by Nixon, Mayne would say, "no," adding that he "accomplished a lot of great things for the country. And I stood with him because I did because I did not think . . . there was sufficient evidence to justify this very, very extreme remedy, which had been attempted only once." In another interview, he said he "felt a very strong case had to be made before I would be willing to vote for impeachment. I felt many of the things that the Democrats on the committee were complaining about had been committed to an even greater degree by other presidents." However altruistic, the voters did not stand with Mayne. Bedell ousted him 55-45%.

Mayne died at 90 in 2007. His son John hoped he be remembered for his personal skills above all else. "He really liked meeting people and enjoyed working for them as individuals."

Dennis, 62, in his third term, had lacked a secure hold on his seat even before Watergate, though evidence suggests that he was slowly building strength. Nixon had won an astounding 69% in 1972, yet Dennis was only able to hold off he held off a 28 year old named Phil Sharp by just 2,500 votes in 1970, 51-49%. He beat Sharp more decisively (57-43%) in '72. But he raised a lot of technical objections during the proceedings One obvious fault was that he did not always phrase his sentences in the most artful form. At one point, he compared arguments put forth by impeachment backers to the "Nazi Penal code." But when he cast a vote against Nixon's impeachment, that was enough for his voters. Still, Dennis prepared to dig in for the long haul. "It's only Round One," he said. "There'll be a good scramble in the House." And as it turned out, for his House seat, as well.

Wiley Mayne (R-Iowa) with his wife Betty (left) and on Judiciary (right)
Photos courtesy of the Mayne Family

Sharp had said "he talked for a while about open-mindedness, but on all the procedural votes, he took the Nixon line." But when Dennis came out for impeachment, hard-line conservatives were enraged as well. The third time would prove the charm for Sharp, who this time beat Dennis 54-46%.

On the cover-up, he said, "I've never understood why it was done. That's still a great puzzle."

Others

The other Judiciary Committee Republican who lost was a Wisconsin freshman named Harold Froehlich, a freshman Republican from Wisconsin. He came around very late, but backed two articles, which angered Republicans. His slogan was "Putting It together for people."

Beyond the Judiciary Committee, there were other characters who fell, and some were people who would exceed eccentricity.

Indiana's Earl Landgrebe, 58, sat in a district where Nixon had taken 74%. But Landgrebe almost lost in 1970 and took an unimpressive 55% in '72. He held off his '74 primary with under 60%, without the support of many Republicans who feared he wouldn't be able to hold the seat in November. It's easy to see why. Even a district this Republican likes some deviations, and Landgrebe didn't give it to them.

Landegrebe was the only member to oppose the District of Columbia's request for home rule. He considered certain public education curriculum as "akin to witchcraft." And he called for his senior Senator, Vance Hartke, to be shot for questioning the American economy, though he later would relax that. But the day before Nixon resigned, Landgrebe, made his views known, issuing his "don't confuse me with the facts,'" line. "I've got a closed mind. I will not vote for impeachment. I'm going to stick with my President even if he and I have to be taken out of this building and shot." Voters respectfully passed on the firing squad but did opt for death by the ballot. Landgrebe lost his 1974 re-election bid to Democrat Floyd Fithian by 22%, 61-39%.

Landgrebe would continue his rants out of office. As the operator of a furniture business, he literally confronted picketers twice with a tractor trailer. Legal struggles with the unions ensued and Landgrebe was prohibited by the court from entering the building. He died at 70.

Landgrebe's fellow Hoosier, Roger Zion, 53, had also made some tempestuous remarks, but was not nearly as flaky. He had actually been known for assiduous constituent service. He called Vietnam era protesters "traitors" and said "any of them involved in illegal acts be treated comparably with Frenchmen whose heads were shaved if they were caught collaborating with the Germans in World War II." And he defended Nixon until fairly late in the game as well. Nixon won 65%, but Zion had struggled, winning just 53% in 1970. And this year, he had another problem. He was named one of the environmental groups "dirty dozen." Congressional Quarterly described his opponent, State senator Phillip Hayes as "an urbane lawyer . . . and a glib and effective campaigner."

But Zion had become known for assiduous constituent service and in early October, his race was still considered a tossup. That was downgraded to "Democrat Favored" the first week in November, and Zion fell to Hayes, whom he had outspent, 53-47%. At 92, he lives in Washington and remains active.

Wisconsin's Vernon Thompson was a former Governor of his state. That was a single two year stint but his House tenure had spanned 13 years. Furthermore, Democrat Alvin Baldus was not the favored Democrat to emerge from the primary. But Thompson not only had backed Nixon, but also the pardon, and labor came in big for Baldus. It paid off. Thompson lost.

Iowa's Bill Scherle, 51, had thought to have weathered his toughest race in 1972. He had been held to just 55% by a little-known lawyer named Tom Harkin, as Nixon was grabbing 63%. Scherle's legislative agenda hit the liberal-conservative divide on the head. In 1968, he proposed two amendments. One would deny federal funding to anti-war protesters while the other would nix funding for the proposed Office of Economic Opportunity.

Harkin was running again but Scherle was thought to have received a wake-up call. His reaction on the resignations of John Ehrlichman and H.R. Haldeman

was, "Good riddance." He traversed the district like never before and began
criticizing the Nixon administration on a number of stances that were detrimental
to his farm-based constituency. Many Democrats even were predicting Harkin
would fall short. But Scherle proved to be a canary in the coal mine, denting
Scherle a fifth term 51-49%. After the election, Scherle insisted he "didn't lose, my
district lost due to a multitude of issues, mainly Watergate." Given the closeness of
the margin, his theory had credibility. When the Ford White House was quizzing
defeated members on what post-Congress position they might like, Scherle simply
responded with, "a job." As for Harkin, ousting Scherle would begin a 40 year
career that is set to culminate when he retires later this year.

Vernon Thompson was a former Governor of Wisconsin
Photo via the Wisconsin State Historical Society

Many other, less high profile members were also shown the door.

John Hunt was Sandman's southern New Jersey neighbor. But he was junior
and, having taken just 53% two years before, was naturally endangered. He may
also have had a misfortune in his name, as Hunt was of course the last name of a
major Watergate conspirator. He was demolished by Jim Florio, who would later
become Governor.

The bloodbath was so widespread that it swept away even the most senior,
and seemingly secure incumbents. William Bray of Indiana, 71, was first been
elected in 1950 and had won his '72 re-election with 65%, as Nixon had taken
74%. He had backed civil rights legislation. Appropriately, his race was rated as
safe Republican by *Congressional Quarterly* as recently as mid-October. He lost

52-48% to a 28 year old assistant principal named David Evans. Ford made his friend Commissioner to the American Battle Commissions the following year.

Virginia's Joel Broyhill had served 11 terms. He was another member who had excelled at constituent service. But he opposed home-rule for the District of Columbia and his area was changing. He seemed to recognize that and was prepared to retire, only to be talked into running again by Ford, then vice-president. He was stunned by Herb Harris.

And New Jersey's William Widnall, elected to the House alongside Gerald Ford in 1948, would have been the most senior Republican had he returned (Leslie Arends was retiring, and his seat would also fall to the Democrats). Windall was not all that conservative, but at 68, he had become relaxed in his campaign techniques, while Andy McGuire, 35, was doing everything to match it. McGuire won 53-47%.

Indiana also turned out William Hudnut, a fairly respected moderate who, by holding off colleague Andy Jacobs in a redistricting matchup, appeared to have cleared his toughest hurdle. But Indianapolis, though relatively conservative for a large city (Nixon got 66% district wide), had turned sour and Jacobs regained his seat. But his city would later assure Hudnut that it wasn't personal. They'd reward him with the Mayoralty. And Sam Young found his fortune reversed from a rematch win over Abner Mikva two years earlier.

Others remarkable upsets. Seven-term New Yorker Jim Grover, sitting in a district that had given Nixon 72%, was beaten by a 25 year old New Yorker named Tom Downey. Grover was well respected and Downey's initial decision to enter the race had come a year earlier, before he had reached the Constitutionally required age of 25, over frustration with gas prices. But Downey saw the tide turning when a liquor store owner told him "there was more champagne sold that August than New Year's Eve." The pardon reopened the wounds. But Downey wasn't naive enough to know the Republicans "did not vote for me. They just didn't vote."

Robert Hanrahan, of Illinois, was nipped by Marty Russo after being labeled "Safe R" and Colorado's Donald Brotzman lost to Tim Wirth, in a race which *Watergate in America: How We Remember, Forget, and Reconstruct the Past* by Michael Schudson says Brotzman had led by 30 points in late summer. With said "Brotz never heard the footsteps, never heard a sound, didn't know what had happened, stayed in Washington." He never debated With, who won 52-48%.

Downey, Russo, and Wirth would come to epitomize the youth and reform-mindedness of the "Watergate Babies."

Nor were southerners where Nixon was backed immune. Oklahoma's John Happy Camp had taken 73% in his last election as Nixon had won 79%. But he lost to Glenn English. Georgia's Ben Blackburn faced similar circumstances.

In short, issues — particularly inflation, played a role in many of these GOP losses.

Another genuinely surprising second fiddle was Wilmer "Vinegar Bend" Mizell, a North Carolinian and former Met, Cardinal, and Pirate who lost to Stephen Neal 52-48% in a race that *Congressional Quarterly* had rated "safe Republican" a week before the vote. Oklahoma's John Happy Camp had taken 73% in his last election as Nixon had won 79%. But he lost to Glenn English. Georgia's Ben Blackburn and South Carolina's Ed Young faced similar circumstances. And in Tennessee, Lamar Baker, whose smooth ride to re-election appeared to get smoother when his challenger, Mort Lloyd, was killed in a plane crash on primary night, was upset by his widow Marilyn, whom Democrats had selected in his place. His western Tennessee colleague, Dan Kuykendall lost to Harold Ford Sr by a mere 744 votes, but enough to give Tennessee its first African-American Congressman.

Ford suffered a setback by failing to rescue four-termer Bob Mathias in California, for whom he had campaigned. He would lose 52-48% to John Krebs. Freshman Republican Victor Veysey in southern California suffered the same fate. His conqueror, Jim Lloyd, did not campaign on Watergate but, as Veysey would recall later, "he did not need to do so. Our analysis revealed that over ten thousand registered Republicans in the area declined to vote, which was a devastating margin. We could not get them to the polls." Veysey lost by fewer than 800 votes.

When the dust settled, Republicans had lost 43 House seats, enough to, by the numbers at least, give the Democrats a veto-proof majority of 292 (three more than required). Republicans would pick off four Democratic incumbents and two open Democratic seats. But the Democrats unseated 36 Republican incumbents and grabbed 13 open GOP seats.

Ford's home state would prove rare comfort. Three Republican Congressman, Marvin Esch, Phil Ruppe, and Garry Brown would struggle, but win new terms (only Bob Huber was unseated), but their races weren't expected to be close. Against the odds, Ron Sarasin of Connecticut and Burt Talcott of California also held on, as did Virginia's William Wampler, who was in a tossup. Iowa elected a State Senator named Charles Grassley, in a race that was expected to go to his Democratic rival. But that was small comfort for so many colleagues lost.

One North Carolina lady summed up the soon-to-be carnage by saying, "If we vote Republican in November we'll be eating rabbit by August." And few did. Voted Republican that is.

PART VI

Candidates Who Sought Their Party's
Nomination and Runningmates

Deep Down, Sparkman and Hill Not Anti
Civil Rights, Just Political Cowards

Historic Tidbit: A longtime southern lawmaker was once reminded that he had been around a while. "You must have seen a lot of changes," the person said. "I have," replied the lawmaker. "And I was against every damn one of them."

Image via lakecountyhistory.blogspot.com

As civil rights legislation was clearing Congress in the 1960s, the Southern caucus would prove stubborn holdouts. Members who signed the "Southern Manifesto" fought tooth and nail against any and all legislation designed to advance racial progress. But evidence exists that at least a couple of those Senators didn't really believe what they were preaching, that they were simply going along because they feared the consequences of even hinting they might be in favor of racial harmony.

Footnotes show that at least one even made secret deals, promises, etc with African-Americans in exchange for a promise to back Civil Rights if the stars aligned. Two such Senators were John Sparkman, the longtime Alabama Senator who made the national ticket as Adlai Stevenson's running mate in 1952. Another was his senior colleague, the venerable Lister Hill who nominated FDR for a third term in 1940 and who, unbeknownst to nearly everyone, had Jewish blood. Both were populists; economic liberals beloved by labor who apparently favored progress for all — and who apparently only voted on civil rights issues because they had to.

To be clear, the majority of the Senators who signed the "Southern Manifesto" were not just doing it for political convenience. Most were hard core racists. South Carolina's Olin Johnston once declined an invitation to a dinner party because his wife would have to sit next to a black man. Harry Byrd, Jim Eastland, and Allen Ellender in particular were singled out by Robert Caro in "Master of the Senate" for being anti-black. Even John Stennis and Herman Talmadge weren't particularly inclusive even their heart. But others, including Fulbright and Louisiana's Russell Long, simply refused to stand up to the times. But Alabama's two Senators offered the most interesting case study.

The New York Times referred to Sparkman as "a burly, 6-foot, ruddy-faced man with white hair and a jolly disposition." He was called "the Senate's only Cherub." Sparkman could not have had racial animosity. Paul Douglas, among the most prominent backers of Civil Rights was prepared to nominate Sparkman for the position of Majority Whip in 1950. Sparkman promptly disavowed interest and the post went to a freshman Texas Senator named Lyndon Johnson. And Truman had suggested to Stevenson that he pick Sparkman as his running mate.

Sparkman's selection was a marriage that Stevenson, himself not vocal on the issue of rights at that point, had made because he needed the deep south in his already uphill battle with Ike. And it provoked backlash with northern African-Americans.

Adam Clayton Powell, the New York Congressman said "we may have but they can't make us vote for him." Powell apparently made good on his threat. He reportedly backed Eisenhower.

On matters other than civil rights, Sparkman and Hill were national Democrats. Even in the midst of the Civil Rights era, Sparkman would stick with his party. He backed nearly piece of the "Great Society." It was Sparkman who sponsored legislation that would extend low-income housing in the 1950's. Hill sponsored the Fair Labor Standards Act of 1938.

John Sparkman (Images)

One day, Lyman Johnson, in his book, *The Race of the Dream* details a meeting he had with Sparkman. Johnson had been taking heat for actively backing the Stevenson ticket with Sparkman on it. Friends had told him that the vice-presidential candidate was going to be in town and told him to join them and meet him. Johnson had little interest. But his friends persuaded him to go and, one by one, the five white folks that were with him ditched the room, leaving Johnson alone with Sparkman. It didn't take long for Johnson to realize that this was a set-up so "I could tell him the problems blacks were having in supporting him."

lakecountyhistory.blogspot.com

Johnson addressed Sparkman as "Mr. Senator," at which point Sparkman told him to "Call me John." Johnson obliged and proceeded to tell him of the problems his friends had reconciling his decision to support Sparkman, even saying the perception was "he's a racist." Sparkman said, 'I've got to do what the white voters in Alabama say for me to do. As long as I'm at the mercy of the present votes in Alabama, I've got to run on a white supremacy platform." But Sparkman also said, "Help me get out of Alabama, and I'll be another Hugo Black. Leave me in Alabama, and I can't do any good. I'll have to do what will get me back in the Senate." That's hardly a profile in courage. In fact, it's political cowardice, pure and simple. And for the "Freedom Riders" who were beaten, it eases the pain they endured little.

As expected, the ticket lost big but Sparkman continued in the Senate.

Photo courtesy of the United States Military

When the Nixon presidency took shape, Sparkman used the "Southern Strategy" for political advantage as well. He opposed busing. Still, Ralph Nader in his rankings was satisfied enough that he graded Sparkman as "cautious, inconspicuous, very effective in marshaling support for legislation in which he is interested, and conservative in terms of his personal power as a senior Senator and committee chairman." Sparkman faced a serious challenge for re-election in the primary. State Auditor Melba Til Allen. Three candidates combined came within 1,000 votes of forcing Sparkman into a runoff, but he did take the 50% necessary.

The general was expected to be close but Sparkman would remind voters at each campaign stop what he had done for the respective county he was in. took an unexpectedly robust 61%. In 1974, many bankers funneled money to Bill Fulbright's campaign, petrified that a loss in the primary would make Bill Proxmire Chairman of Banking. Fulbright lost and Sparkman did go to Foreign Relations. In comparison to Bill Fulbright, many viewed Sparkman as lacking the energy or desire to take on the Executive Branch. And many viewed his age as an impediment.

For Sparkman, the rose to the top was long and hard. He grew up dirt poor. He'd study by a kerosene light, walk four miles to school and ultimately put himself through college by a $75 loan on a cotton crop. *The Times* said he, "then got a job tending furnaces that paid $4.20 a week."

Sparkman with Alabama Secretary of State
Photo courtesy of the Alabama Department of Archives
and History, Mongomery, Alabama

Sparkman's longtime Alabama colleague was another member who may have been pro-Civil Rights in his heart. If Sparkman struggled through his early life, Hill was born fortunate. His father was a prominent physician in Montgomery, who would become renowned for various experiments on the human heart and discovered antiseptic. It fueled his son's lifelong advocacy for advances in the medical field, which he'd pursue legislatively. Hill would attend the University of Michigan and Columbia Law School, then return home to Alabama.

Hill went to a Methodist church but was raised Catholic and his mother was part Jewish (Hill wouldn't let that be known).

**Vice-President Garner swearing-in Lister Hill as Senator (left)
and Hill addressing as he placed FDR's name in nomination
at the 1940 Democratic Convention (right)
Photo courtesy of the Alabama Department of Archives
and History, Mongomery, Alabama**

Background aside, Sparkman and Hill were two peas in a pod. *The Encyclopedia of Alabama* notes the Hill machine convinced Alabama's overwhelmingly white electorate to vote based on their economic needs; as a result, Alabama was often described as the most liberal state in the Deep South" and notes a study ranked the duo as the "fourth most effective" in the Senate.

Hill was a legend of his time. He won a House seat in 1922 and by the 30's, was a loyal "New Dealer." It was Hill who sponsored the legislation establishing the Tennessee Valley Authority. He went to the Senate in 1938, when Hugo Black's appointment to the Supreme Court created an opening. Despite the difference on the rights issue, Black and Hill would become lifelong friends.

The Encyclopedia says that despite early talk of a Presidential bid, "Hill became a national laughingstock when a huge radio audience, as widely reported in the anti-Roosevelt press, jeered at his southern accent and florid oratory." Still, his Senate career went far. He'd become Majority Whip and Chair the Labor and Public Welfare Committee. But his contribution in the medical field defines him. He was called a "statesman for health." He sponsored the Hospital and Health Center Construction Act of 1946 the Hill-Burton Act 9,200 which created new hospitals, and legislation dealing with the mentally ill. His interest for rural progress, including electricity, telephone assistance, agriculture, and vocational assistance was also strong.

Hill was trusted enough to win the support of a number of Senate liberals for the position of Minority Leader. After Ernest MacFarland lost his bid for re-election, a number of stalwart Democrats led by Hubert Humphrey, were unhappy about the prospect of two Texans leading their party (Sam Rayburn in the House and Johnson in the Senate). Hill emerged their consensus. Hill was reached at home but told them he was already committed to Johnson.

Hill would stay in the Senate 30 years, including five terms, the latter of which he almost didn't get.

Hill's opponent, Republican James Martin, pressed him unusually hard for a Republican in Alabama. He called him a "Kennedycrat." Hill tried to use the administrations order of federal troops to the University of Mississippi to his advantage, issuing a fierce condemnation. The vote was so close that Hill at one point trailed slightly on Election Night, but ultimately secured his fifth and final term by 9,000 votes.

It was by far the closest a Republican would come to seizing a Senate seat in the south since Reconstruction. Hill served that term and retired in 1968 at 74.

The New York Times described Hill as a politician "trapped by the racial history of [his] region . . . who [nevertheless] dared to be progressive on every issue except civil rights." But he strongly backed other colleagues' interests of all regions. Robert Kennedy asked Hill for a sub-committee Chairmanship on Indian Affairs and Hill obliged.

Sparkman retired in 1978 at 79 and died in 1985. He was proceeded in death by less than a year by Hill, whose death in December 1984 came eight days before his 90th birthday.

In closing, Patrick Henry said "Give me liberty or give me death." He did not say, "If the right circumstances arise, I'll be with you." The voting records of Sparkman and Hill on Civil Rights were inexcusable. History may not be kind to them in that regard, nor should it be. But it's comforting to know that talk is cheap and that, all things considered, they were cherubs in their heart.

Photo via the Encyclopedia of Alabama
Photo courtesy of the Alabama Department of Archives
and History, Mongomery, Alabama

Bob Kerr:
The Single Most important
Oklahoman Since Statehood

**Historic Quote: "Moby Dick Nixon and his whale of a pet Checkers."-
Oklahoma Senator Robert Kerr on the Vice-President and 1960 Republican
Presidential nominee, Richard Nixon.**

Photo via the Carl Albert Congressional Archives, University of Oklahoma

R obert Kerr, an Oklahoma Governor turned Senator, once explaining that
he votes his beliefs first, his state second, and his party third. Often, he had
Oklahoma in mind and he is widely credited to have been the "Sooner State's"
most effective Governor in its 106 years of statehood. He would continue to be
a force to reckon with in his later years, as a member of the Senate.

When one thinks of the term "Boy Wonder" of Democratic politics in the
mid-20th century, Robert Kerr is the man (his Republican counterpart was fellow
Minnesota Governor Harold Stassen, which ultimately didn't end to well). More
important, every state has a Governor that provided a boost which led to an indelible
transformation. And in Oklahoma's case, Kerr again stepped up to the plate.

When you think of the Broadway show, "Oklahoma," Bob Kerr may resemble
that. The first Native-American Governor (also Log-Cabin born), he took office
in 1942 as the state was still crippling from the Depression and the "Dust Bowl"
and, as Arrell Gibson in his book "*Oklahoma: A History of Five Centuries*" points
out, Kerr helped bring about "a resurgence of state pride and spirit and a broad
determination the Sooner States image." In his inaugural address, he called for

ending the "smearing (of) the reputations of persons who did not agree with the administration." Gibson called him "firm but not arrogant." But his legacy to stand by principal enhanced his reputation.

But he was also one who mastered the art of sophistication. That proved a valuable trait for fighting for his people in Washington, as George Reedy, in his book, *The U.S. Senate* called Kerr "something of a pirate – a man who could demolish a political opponent with a single cutting speech."

Gibson notes that he provided an "earthy and subtle humor" that resonated with fellow Okies. And forward he did. Kerr's net worth was $10 billion but he made improvement of the "Sooner States" image. Kerr took numerous tours of the nation to promote Oklahoma's potential, which paid handsome dividends as his land became a focal point for military training, industry, and bases. He continued his efforts on behalf of industry after the war.

Kerr wowed delegates to national conventions with his oratorical ability (left) and with Adlai Stevenson (right) Left photo via distinctlyoklahoma.com; Right photo via the Carl Albert Congressional Archives, University of Oklahoma

A loyal "New Dealer" Kerr gave the Keynote address at the 1944 Democratic convention and played a vigorous role in Harry Truman's selection as vice-president, a pick credited with allowing Oklahoma Democrats to soar. Kerr made his way to the Senate in 1948 in a campaign that Kerr biographer Ann Hodges Morgan notes he "talked nothing but land and water and his opponents never had a chance." He mounted a bid for the Democratic nomination for President in 1952.

Kerr came away with the assumption that he would have Truman's backing were he to retire and won backing from crucial state delegations at a Midwest convention in the event that happened. He even entered the Nebraska primary as a stand-in for the President. Truman bowed out days before the primary but

Kerr was trounced by Tennessee Senator Estes Kefauver. He visited nearly every western state. Come convention time, he tried to woo delegates with a replica of a log-cabin to display his modest roots. The speaker would be playing Frank Sinatra tunes and music from the recent Broadway hit "Oklahoma." It would sit in his hotel room. One problem was it cost $225 a night. Ultimately, Illinois Governor Adlai Stevenson captured the nomination and Kerr wholeheartedy backed him.

Kerr's Presidential ambitions may not have advanced very far but that sure wasn't the case in the Senate.

Kennedy cultivating Kerr (the president spent the night at the powerful chairman's ranch) and discussing space priorities with Johnson, then Vice-President Left photo via the Oklahoma State University; Right photo via the Carl Albert Congressional Archives, University of Oklahoma

It's a matter of debate as to whether Kerr had more impact as a Governor or in the U.S. Senate. In the former, his accomplishments are felt today. In the Senate, it is more his presence and master of debate that drew notice, and, where he sat, it was impossible for it to have not. He chaired the Finance Committee, and the Senate Commerce Committee on Space and Aeronautics. There was a reason he was called the "Uncrowned King of the Senate." And beyond. One day he hosted an event for "1,000 of my closest and dearest friends." Fellow Okie, freshman Congressman Tom Steed Congressman Tom Steed once called Steed either "a genius or madman.'

Kerr tried to remain true to his party. Paul Boller's book, *Congressional Anecdotes* recites a tale of Kerr on the campaign trail at a forum, when his opponent credited the Lord with "telling me that it was my duty to run." with getting him to run. Kerr conceded the possibility that the "Almighty might urge an individual to run for the Senate. It's inconceivable, however, that the Almighty would tell anyone to run on the Republican ticket."

Nor did Kerr go without wheeling and dealing. Kerr became an unapologetic defender of the natural gas industry, paramount to his state's economy. He remained true to his region by promoting development of the Arkansas River throughout his entire Senate career. He traded support for the Interstate Highway System for funding of three reservoirs on the water. Many, including for a time, his junior colleague from Oklahoma, Mike Monroney, were cool to the idea. Kerr did not live to see the project completed but his efforts have made the 18 lock river accessible to barges, and commercial traffic, and a center for hydro-electricity. It bears his name.

Kerr's rise as a Senate baron was in many ways linked to Lyndon Johnson's. They took the oath as Senators together and Kerr advised the future-President on ranching, cattle, etc. Kerr was Johnson's chief backer for Majority Whip in the Senate and the pair were close allies when he was Majority Leader. It was perhaps because of that reason that Kerr initially was cool to Johnson accepting the vice-presidency with Kennedy – and leaving the Senate in the hands of someone who would not be as friendly to Oklahoma's interest (Kerr heartily had backed Johnson for the nomination).

Kerr was actually in the hotel room with Sam Rayburn (another close friend) at 6AM when the matter was being discussed. He was up for re-election that fall and what should have been a waltz to a third term ended up a little more difficult than expected. Anti-Catholic sentiment in the state was high yet when Kennedy came to Oklahoma City, Kerr introduced him, explaining, "Why my Baptist father and my Baptist mother would turn over in their Democratic grave if they thought I would not speak up for my nominee for President." That proved costly as Kerr defeated his Kennedy called Kerr the following day and told him he knew his backing proved costly he'd "never forget it." Kerr was stung and angry about "what my Baptist friends did to me in the campaign" but vowed to "continue to do all in my power to better serve them (the people) and our great state and nation."

Once the new President took office, *The Saturday Evening Post* summed up the relationship between the pair. "Kennedy asked. Kerr decided."

A classic example, cited in Boller's book, is a zinc bill, which Kennedy told him he'd be vetoing. He told Kerr that "Ted (Sorensen) and Mike (Mansfield) explained it to me." That provoked Kerr to raise the matter of JFK's tax bill "If I'm away in Oklahoma, your tax bill, which lies in the Finance Committee that I chair, will never come to the floor," JFK did an "about face" saying, "Bob, this is the first time anybody really explained the zinc bill to me."

But it wasn't quite as one sided. In fact, the Kennedy-Kerr cultivation of one another went both ways. In 1961, Kerr asked Kennedy to come to the state to dedicate Oklahoma 103, which as the *Tulsa World* later pointed out says, "ran through the Ouachita Mountains between Heavener and Broken Bow." It would be an overnight visit and Kennedy would stay overnight at Kerr's ranch in Big Cedar, a sprawling town but one with fewer than 50 residents (a Secret

Service agent joked Kennedy "could have his own political district." Kennedy had declined many invitations outside Hyannis Point to that point but felt he owed something to Kerr. In fact, the state's Democratic Governor, Howard Edmundson, had no clue why Kennedy was visiting the state and traveled to Hyannis Port to ask him personally. Kennedy's response: "to kiss Bob Kerr's ass." During the visit, Kennedy joked about the bulls "not gelling along," to which Kerr quipped "somebody might have let a Republican bull in." Even so, the visit was no bull for Oklahoma. In the years ahead, the state was awarded many major projects. *The Tulsa World* said Kerr "scored a home-run" for the state.

But that didn't mean they'd see eye-to-eye. Kerr used his Finance post to become a major player on entitlements. To say that he had his reservations about Medicare is an understatement. He was among the Democrats who successfully blocked Kennedy's proposal in 1962, which lost 52-48. But Kerr's own bill, with Wilbur Mills, which ultimately became known as the Medicare Assistance for the Aged, was enacted into law, and Sue Nevins in her book, *Medicare's Mid-Life Crisis* noted the programs coverage of dental and prescription drugs would ultimately be much more "generous" than Medicare (though it did require means testing"). Kerr was against mandates but he had done much to help the disadvantaged. He favored mechanisms to "enable low income groups to secure the necessary health services" and in the 1950s pushed for additional Social Security benefits for women.

Kerr died of heart failure of New Year's Day, 1963, just as he had appeared to be on the mend. Kennedy, Johnson, and scores of colleagues were present at the funeral.

Photo via the Oklahoma State Historical Society

Compared To Other Runningmates, William E. Miller Obscure After Loss – And Liked It That Way

Historic Quote; "I've often said if I hadn't known Barry Goldwater in 1964 and had to depend on the press and cartoons, I'd have voted against the son-of-a-bitch." - Barry Goldwater on the image he was given during his Presidential campaign.

Most individuals who are their party's standard bearer for the office of Vice-President stay in the national limelight long after the ticket has gone down to defeat. But for William E. Miller, the New York Congressman who was the beleaguered Barry Goldwater's running-mate in 1964, he was only too happy to have that as his peak. Miller never became Vice-President but, as the joke goes about men who do attain the office, he was never heard from again. In fact, when people spotted Miller on the street, he'd joke, "They remind me more of the American Express card commercial" than his spot on the ticket. But that was the way he preferred it.

When Goldwater selected Miller to be his running-mate, he didn't exactly have a wide bench to choose from. Most of the rank and file in the Republican Party were either too moderate, or didn't want to be near the tractor-trailer named Lyndon Johnson for fear of diminishing their own future electoral prospects. So Goldwater turned to Miller, an upstate New York Congressman who shared his views, and who was thought to have done a capable job as Republican National Committee Chair.

Goldwater would tell it years later. "He was an outstanding member of Congress; he was one of the best national chairmen of the Republican Party we have ever had; he was a hell of a gin rummy player and a good poker player. He was the kind of a man other men like to be with. I think that's the best way to put it."

Button courtesy of ronwadebuttons.com

Upon graduating from Albany Law School, Miller was a U.S. Commissioner for western New York. Then it was off to the army. But serving as a prosecutor for some of the Nazi criminals gave him national prominence which eventually led him to become Niagara County Assistant District Attorney. Eventually, Governor Thomas Dewey gave him the position but he soon won it on his own. In 1950, Miller won a Buffalo area Congressional seat, defeating Mary Louise Nice. His record was staunchly conservative and in 1960, colleagues chose him over an outspoken moderate, Ohio Congressman William McCulloch to head the Republican Congressional Campaign Committee. Two years later, he was chairing the National Republican Committee. The party had just come off a razor-close loss at the presidential level and was deep in debt and so Miller's service gave him positive notoriety.

To hear him tell it, "We came in here owing $750,000." By 1962, that had been erased, and the committee raised $750,000 and by the next year, $1.2 million. In 1964, it was over $2 million. The only discontent Miller faced was that he hadn't used the position to delegate much but he addressed those critics: "I know of no policy decision (that) has been made without my consent . . . In other words, I can't be here if I am at a fund raising dinner in Michigan . . . but if the committee wishes to have a full time chairman, I told them I would not be interested in the job."

Miller mentioned his family but the truth is, his one-time safe hold on his New York Congressional district was becoming threatened as well. He won re-election with just 53% in 1960 and squeaked by with 5,000 votes to spare (52-48%) in 1962, a year he began by saying the GOP theme should be "private enterprise ad private ingenuity."

As 1964 approached, Goldwater was clearly his heart. However, it was also said Miller "played fair with Rockefeller who comes from his own home state of New York." during primary season. If Goldwater noticed, he didn't seem to mind. In supposedly offering Miller the number two slot by phone, might have been referring to his long odds against Johnson. He said, "Bill, it looks like I'm going to take a long walk and I want some company? You want to come along?"

Democrats derided Miller's obscurity with the line, "Here's a riddle, it's a killer. Who the hell is William Miller?" *The Saturday Evening Post* called him, "an obscure and totally undistinguished Congressman who had resigned himself to retirement until Goldwater pushed him forward for two discreditable reasons: reward for using the position of RNC Chairman whose ethics required him to be impartial as a hidden base for Goldwater." The second was "to use Miller's religion as an effort to force the Democrats to choose Robert Kennedy and alienate the South."

Miller did have a reputation as an attack dog that would fulfill the needs as a number two quite well. He once called Kennedy "the foundering father of the New Frontier," and advised him to learn the difference "between a sense of history and a sense of histrionics." Miller wasn't particularly known when he was selected but Goldwater wanted someone "who would go out and break his back campaigning for 90 days. He knew Miller fit this requirement." And he told advisors, "Miller drives Johnson nuts," a charge not totally substantiated.

Another factor in Miller's favor: he brought balance to the ticket. Goldwater surely did not expect Miller to help him carry New York State, but he was from the North and he was Catholic. Plus, an informal survey of delegates showed him to be a top choice. Still, many, including for a time Goldwater himself, had expected the nod to go to Bill Scranton, but the Pennsylvania Governor erased this possibility by running hard against Goldwater.

In his acceptance speech, Miller said "I vastly admire and respect the courage, the integrity, the surplus commitment to principal of one of the most dynamic and forceful leaders in the nation's history."

For Goldwater, Miller was an ideological soul-mate if ever there was one, which Miller confirmed on the important issue of civil rights, calling them "almost the same as mine." He had voted for aid to certain education facilities (vocational schools, etc.) but otherwise was solidly conservative. He blamed the farm crisis on "ill-conceived" schemes of "confused and inept" bureaucrats. And while Miller backed the few civil rights laws that had passed thus far (after initially being against them), he made his position unambiguously clear on the stump. "We believe in states responsibilities. We believe in state's rights."

Miller fulfilled his role in firing up the GOP base. At one appearance he said, 'I know something about the Liberal Party of New York. If we ever adopted for the U.S. the program adopted by the Liberal Party of New York, overnight, we would have socialism throughout America." On the threat of some centrist Republicans to break away, Miller responded, "I don't approve of splinter parties. I saw what splinter parties made possible in Germany."

If the typical responsibility of a running-mate is to deliver blows allowing the actual nominee to stay above the fray, Miller fulfilled his role with gusto. He caused a stir when, in denouncing support by the KKK, called Goldwater "half-Jewish" (also adding he himself was Catholic). The American Council on Rabbi's denounced it. He attacked Humphrey for his connection to the Americans for Democratic Action, accusing the group of favoring, "foreign, socialistic, totalitarianism," to the United States." Miller even went after Johnson's war record, stating that because President Roosevelt declared, "You could not be a Congressman and in the service." Johnson "elected to be a congressman instead of a soldier" and "was back home again before the shooting had ever started.

The election of course was history. Goldwater-Miller lost 44 states. Miller appeared to happily accept it. Unlike many of his brethren who lost national elections, he left the political spotlight, going out of sight out of mind. When asked if he missed it his response was "no. I think probably because I had such a saturation of it in my life . . . For 10 solid weeks, you're up in the morning for breakfast in Alabama and lunch in Los Angeles. Believe me, when that was over I had had enough." He also noted the traveling he undertook for other officials and said "for a family man that took its toll." He offered to help Rockefeller in 1966 but was told he wouldn't be needed.

Miller suffered a stroke in 1983 and died four days later. He was just 69 and remembered fondly by Goldwater who said, "He was the one of the greatest men I have ever known and I feel his loss very deeply."

White House Proved Elusive To Rockefeller But Impact On New York As "Rich As Rockefeller"

"Ever since I was a kid. After all, when you think of what I had, what else was there to aspire to?" - Nelson Rockefeller in response to a question about how long he wanted to be President. He did achieve the number two office but acknowledged he "never wanted to be vice-president of anything."

Photo courtesy of the Library of Congress Prints and Photographs Division

A song by Louie Armstrong, "On the Sunny Side of the Street," contains the lyrics, "If I never have a cent/I'll be rich as Rockefeller/With gold dust at my feet/On the sunny side of the street."   .

Nelson Rockefeller was an example of if at first you don't succeed. Keep trying. The four-term New York Governor and heir to the famed oil magnate family never captured the one attainment that eluded him – the White House despite three tries. But less than a year of having resigned himself to the fact that his public office career had maxed out, he was handed a consolation prize as close to spot number one: spot number two.

At times bellicose, at times charming, at times showcasing the characteristics of true a New Yorker ("Hi ya, fella," or "you're terrific," he'd say to strangers) but at all times pragmatic and rich, Rockefeller epitomized the term moderate. In fact, so reliable was that classification that four decades after leaving the political spectrum, his name still remains and his contribution to history may be a vanishing breed but being known for a term for the ages in the political lexicon: a "Rockefeller Republican." But his contribution to the state he loved was that for all his wealth, Rockefeller, through his infrastructure, environmental, social and economic advancements made New York almost as rich.

That Rockefeller would one day seek the Presidency became evident almost from the moment he won perhaps the second most high-profile office in the nation: Governor of the "Empire" State. This would have been bragging rights in any case but for Republicans in 1958, it was a trophy prize. Why? Because Republicans in nearly every region of the country were getting slaughtered amid a national recession and an unpopular Eisenhower administration. But Rockefeller kept his distance from the players and in doing so, actually picked up a job for his party. He unseated incumbent Governor Averill Harriman. This was a big get, for not only was it a major prize but Harriman himself was a major Democratic luminary who had his eye on the White House not too far back. So it was only natural that "Rocky" would follow.

Rockefeller's literature in 1968 read that "Nelson Rockefeller is one of the great political campaigners of our time. He is warm. He is tireless. He genuinely loves to meet people. And he wins elections." So what happened? Why, in three campaigns, was he never able to capture the prize?

Rockefeller knew he would be highly sought after for the 1960 Republican Presidential nomination but sought to put that to rest fairly early. In December 1959, he declared, "I am not, and shall not be, a candidate for the Presidency. This decision is definite and final." It is probable Rockefeller was genuine. His Governorship was a year old and plagued by problems and unpopularity that stemmed from a sales tax increase. But a few high-profile incidents on the domestic and international front throughout the early months of 1960 might have convinced him to change his mind. There was the "U-2" incident and what he viewed as an inadequate civil rights pursuit from the Eisenhower administration. So he briefly challenged Vice-President Richard Nixon for the Republican nomination.

Nixon and Rockefeller met at the latter's Fifth Avenue apartment, after which Rockefeller issued a statement saying he "and Nixon reached an agreement on… specific and basic positions on foreign policy and national defense," then spoke of the same on domestic affairs. Civil rights was one area but it was near the bottom. Nonetheless, Rockefeller said "our program must assure aggressive action to remove the remaining vestiges of segregation or discrimination in all areas of national life – voting and housing, schools and jobs." He also addressed support for "sit-in demonstrators." Health insurance by way of a "contributory system" for the aged was also prominently included. Conservative Arizona Senator Barry Goldwater dubbed the meeting the "Munich of the Republican Party" and as a result, mounted a last-ditch yet unsuccessful effort to win the nod.

Many assumed 1964 would be Rockefeller's year. A *U.S. News and World Report* headline just after the '62 midterms pointed that America was poised for a Kennedy-Rockefeller match at the national level and the Kennedy world – led by Kenny O'Donnell knew it and were hoping to wound him during primary season. But as the book. *Presidential Campaigns in America* opined, "The attempt to cut down Rockefeller's commanding lead proved unnecessary because Rockefeller did it himself." Earlier that year, he divorced his wife of 32 years, the daughter of a prominent Philadelphia family. Little more than a year later, he married Margaretta Filter Murphy – known since childhood as "Happy" because of her always "up" demeanor. "Happy" was a mother of four but had forfeited custody of the kids to her husband who had refused to grant her a divorce otherwise. The public frowned on this.

Rockefeller had led Goldwater among Republicans 43-26% but the month of his nuptials, the Arizona Senator actually pulled ahead 35%-30% and it was reflected in New Hampshire where ex-Senator Henry Cabot Lodge of neighboring Massachusetts took 35% - without even appearing on the ballot. Goldwater meanwhile racked up wins – albeit by margins below expectations, in other states throughout the fall.

Rockefeller did score one semi-important win in Oregon, beating Goldwater 33% to 17% (Lodge took 27%). But up-and-coming was the California contest, a winner-take-all delegate rich (86) state. Rockefeller put on a brave-face, even making hey of the Goldwaterisms that would so define him in his fall campaign against President Johnson ("Who do you want in the room with the "H" bomb)?" But he fell short 51-49% (he wasn't helped when Happy gave birth to Nelson, Jr. three days before) and promptly dropped out. Rockefeller made a half-hearted attempt to recruit another moderate but Pennsylvania's Bill Scranton faltered and Michigan's George Romney was uninterested. California aside, the party was changing. When one person advised him to get the "Eastern Establishment" on board, Rockefeller told him, "You're looking at it, buddy. I'm all that's left."

Nelson and his new bride Happy (center) honeymooning in St.
John in 1963. Rockefeller's son Laurence is at the far left
Photo courtesy of the Library of Congress Prints and Photographs Division

Goldwater did become the nominee and was predictably trounced by Lyndon Johnson that November. Still, Rockefeller had one more act. At the GOP Convention, Rockefeller told delegates, "During this year I have crisscrossed this nation, fighting … to keep the Republican Party the party of all the people … and warning of the extremist threat, its danger to the party, and danger to the nation. These extremists feed on fear, hate and terror, [they have] no program for America and the Republican Party…operate from dark shadows of secrecy. It is essential that this convention repudiate here and now any doctrinaire, militant minority whether Communist, Ku Klux Klan or Birchers." Many booed him and held up Goldwater placards.

1968 was a totally different avenue. Goldwater was out of the picture and Nixon rarely wavered from his front-runner status. It was later revealed that President Johnson, not convinced any Democrat, including his own Vice-President, Hubert Humphrey, could beat Nixon, actually tried to recruit Rocky into the race as a Democrat. Aware of Happy's aversion to politics, the President informed him that "I talked her into letting you run." For much of the cycle, Rockefeller was not interested and was at least tactically aiding Romney. But Romney's "brain-washing" comment regarding Vietnam killed his chances and once he withdrew, Rockefeller said he was "ready and willing" to run if other Republicans wanted him, only to issue the furthest thing from a Shermanesque statement days later. That was, "I am not a candidate campaigning directly or indirectly for the Presidency of the United States."

There was the matter of a draft but Rockefeller would simply "expect no call and will do nothing to encourage such a call." He wasn't making the calls either – to even bow out. *Presidential Campaigns in America* wrote, "The Governor's closest allies and supporters –Governors, Senators, and finance men who had staked their own political reputations on his expected candidacy – learned of his decision not to run in the same way the rest of his country did – by watching his televised press conference" and that angered some and did no favors among others.

During the 1968 Presidential campaign
Left image via politicalbuttons.com; right image, with fellow
Governors Romney and Reagan, via Corbis Images

But on April 30, he reversed course and decided to run. His rationale: said "the gravity of the crisis we face as a people and the new circumstances that confront the nation, I frankly find that to comment from the sidelines is not an effective way to present the alternatives." He would say, "What our country needs now, and needs desperately, is a healer -- a man who can pull together the disparate elements, who can find solutions that are within our system and our traditions. I think I can do that." Perhaps hoping to blunt memories of his personal problems, he gave his wife a kiss on stage. Others agreed. Illinois Senator Charles Percy called him "the best-equipped man to be President." Romney said, "No other candidate in either party can match his executive experience in national and state government." But the fact is, primary season was over and Rockefeller was too late.

Years after that third loss, Rockefeller offered a theory for his failure. "I had a very interesting misconception which was if you did a good job, really had strength and compassion and people felt it…that was what it took. But there is a little thing called a nomination. I spent my time preparing for the presidency and not for a nomination."

In late-1973, Rockefeller stunned New York by announcing that he'd leave the Governorship a year early. Happy wanted to spend more time at their farm in Pocantico Hills but Rockefeller wanted to devote time to two Commissions he chaired: Critical Choices for America and the National Commission on Water Quality. He thwarted future ambitions relating to the Presidency but admitted he'd keep his "options open."

To say Rockefeller was born to wealth would be a big understatement for his family was among the wealthiest scions anywhere. His grandfather was John D. Rockefeller, Sr., the founder of Standard Oil and in his time the richest man in the world. His maternal grandfather was a powerful Republican Senator from Rhode Island, Nelson Aldrich.

Nelson was the third of six children, all but the oldest of whom were boys. One, Winthrop, would serve as Governor of Arkansas concurrent with Nelson's tenure as chief of New York. The U.S. Senate website noted, "He and his brothers grew up in the family home on West 54th Street in New York, which was so filled with art that his parents bought the town house next door just to house their collection." But they were raised, according to *The New York Times*, "with the strong belief that money should not be squandered or spent ostentatiously."

As a boy, Nelson attended the Lincoln School of Teacher's College, a progressive-oriented prep school at Columbia University that his dad put $3 million into. He then achieved his B.A. from Dartmouth College where he served as vice-president, as well as a member of the New Hampshire volunteer fire squad (he had aspired to join his brother at Princeton but was denied admittance due to dyslexia).

Whether Nelson was a boy scout in his days at Dartmouth may be never known, but because he elected to not smoke or drink, his father gave him $2,500 upon his graduation. But what cannot be disputed is that Rockefeller was willing to work hard. His first post-college job was a clerk at the Chase Bank but he also served Westchester County Board of Health. After, he was a rental agent for Rockefeller Center, which his grandfather had created decades earlier. He founded the American International Assistance for Economic and Social Development with his brothers and headed Creole Petroleum, which was designed to create the same empire for Venezuela as Standard Oil had for America. This took him a great deal to that country and its where he'd spend a great deal of time.

John D. Rockefeller, Jr (far left) stands with his sons (Nelson is third from left) to receive the body of his father, John, Sr., founder of Standard Oil in 1937
Photo via Corbis Images

Rockefeller was on President Franklin Roosevelt's radar screen as early as 1940 when he made him Coordinator of Inter-American Affairs. It was no accident. Roosevelt had undoubtedly known the Rockefeller's during his own stint as Governor of New York and when Roosevelt came to dedicate the New Museum of Modern Art in Manhattan in 1940, Rockefeller told him about Naziism in South America. The President listened, then told him to put it in writing. He did and it became part of the administration's "good neighbor" policy. In that role, Rockefeller found portions of the 1940 movie, "Down Argentine Way" with Don Ameche and Betty Grable potentially offensive to the Argentinians and asked for changes. His respect continued under Harry Truman as Rockefeller chaired the International Development Advisory Board which looked at the "Four Points" program. Both men suggested Rockefeller become a Democrat but he demurred.

Rockefeller's chance to become well-versed on the domestic scene came shortly after Eisenhower assumed power. For starters, he chaired the President's Advisory Committee on Government Organization. Among the suggestions: creating a Department of Health, Education, and Welfare. He wanted to be the first Secretary of the new department but had to settle for being the number two man. As *Congressional Quarterly* noted he "helped develop broader Social Security coverage and vocational rehabilitation programs."

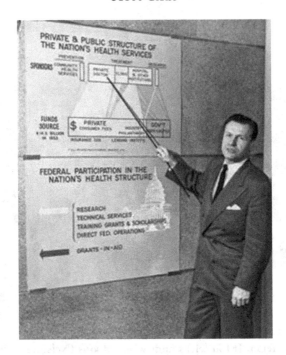

Photo via the U.S. Department of Health, Education and Welfare

In 1958, Rockefeller tossed his hat into the ring for Governor. Republicans were not initially high on their chances of beating Harriman but felt Rockefeller's wealth would give them – and the rest of the ticket, credibility. Indeed, with Harriman worth $100 million, the campaign was a campaign dubbed, "The Battle of the Millionaires." A profile in *The New Yorker* years later noted, "Rockefeller outspent Harriman, but his real advantage turned out to be a natural buoyancy, a talent for appealing to voters far from the world of the Rockefeller brothers." He liked people so much that as he spoke to gas station attendants near the end of the campaign, his son said, "Let's get out of here before he starts shaking hands with the gas pumps."

It didn't hurt that Harriman was publicly at odds with powerful Tammany Hall head Carmine DeSapio who succeeded in handing Harriman a running-mate he didn't want or that African-American Congressman Adam Clayton Powell, while not straying from the party, did little to hide his regard for Rockefeller. He won by nearly 600,000 votes. After the election, he headed to his farm in Venezuela "to get some rest and be in shape, ready to go after the job." But he was truly a man of the people. He walked to his office and attended even the smallest event when possible at even the most remote corners of New York State.

If progress defines the word "progressive," Rockefeller was without question New York's most forward looking Governor, a desire he made no attempt to conceal in his first State of the State address, when he said, "There lies before us a joint mission of the highest calling. That mission is to achieve a resurgence of human progress in New York State based on accelerated economic growth. The ultimate purpose of our effort is to ensure the opportunity of each individual to attain his fullest potential and achieve the maximum development of his own capacity."

So many monumental accomplishments occurred on Rockefeller's watch that picking out the most important would be a job in itself. Worth noting is that Rockefeller faced a $700 million budget deficit upon taking office. He instituted pay-as-you-go rather than borrowing, but also proposed $277 million in tax increases which *The New York Times* notes was greeted with "howls of protests in the Legislature, but Mr. Rockefeller prevailed." Ditto with the first state sales tax increase.

Image courtesy of politics1.com

The expansion of the State University of New York SUNY system would have to be near the top. The administration extended the number of campuses from 29 to 72. A strenuous Department of Environmental Conservation and anti-water pollution measure often predated or set the stage for federal programs, as did the first-ever State Council on the Arts in the nation. The Pure Waters program led to 200 new water-treatment plants. The Hudson River Valley Commission and the Adirondack Park Agency became law, leading Rockefeller to boast "The Adirondacks are preserved forever." During his first term, new parks were abundant. Rockefeller had fired the venerable Robert Moses as Chairman of the State Council of Parks and appointed his brother Laurence to head the effort. He wrote a book, *Our Environment Can Be Saved.*

Less successful were the approvals of bonds for transportation and low income housing (voters twice rejected proposals for each). But both initiatives ultimately took shape through the legislature approving the ability of public authorities, including the Urban Development Corporation and the Housing Finance Agencies. The Long Island Express and the Verrazano-Narrows Bridge came to fruition (in having signed legislation for the latter, Rockefeller yielded to pleas from the Italian-American community who wanted it named for Giovanni da Verrazano rather than Henry Hudson). And in 1961, he signed legislation to build the World Trade Center. Ironically, the report calling for such a structure was issued by his brother David, along with the Downtown-Lower Manhattan Association (D.L.M.A.) a month after Nelson was elected Governor and was dedicated the year he left office. But near the end of his term, he was using the borrowing gimmicks he had once scorned. And as Joanne Reitano noted in *New York State: Peoples, Places, and Priorities: A Concise History with Sources*, "Rockefeller's tendency to create public benefit authorities to implement his proposals was often controversial...(they were) really designed to avoid legislative oversight."

Rockefeller reflected on the progress that had been achieved in his State of the State Address as he began his second term. He made clear that cultivation of markets abroad was necessary for stimulating future growth. "This administration," he said, "has set as its goal the simulation of the greatest economic expansion in the state's history. Five hundred thousand new jobs in the next four years. To advance this effort, I opened a Commerce Department office in Montreal last September. The first outside the country. A similar office will be opened this year in Europe."

Rockefeller was at the forefront of stronger civil rights laws and in his own administration, walked the walk with his hiring of women and minorities. He signed legislation removing the prohibition on abortion in New York State. To combat drugs, the State Narcotics Addiction Control Commission was created. But when voluntary rehabilitation didn't work, he pushed through mandatory sentences for violent offenders (in some cases life that many felt too harsh. He was in favor of capital punishment and allowed 14 executions while Governor. The Attica Prison uprising tested him immensely. He refused to visit the site and ordered it raided, resulting in the deaths of a number of inmates.

For Albany, he put plans in motion for an architectural design on the South Mall. It was dubbed, "Rocky's Folly," and the ultimately $1.5 billion project included high-rise buildings, hotels, a shopping area and a bus terminal (along with paintings Rockefeller picked out). His hands-on approach led his utility commissioner, John Egan to lament that, "Conceptually, every bit of the project was his idea. . . . When our fellows came back from New York, we held our breath, because we knew there was going to be something new. . . . Something was going to change." Indeed, as Jeffrey Resnick wrote in *The New Yorker* piece, his insistence on Vermont and Georgia marble for the building held it up for almost a full year.

As enduring as the term "Rockefeller Republican" was, he rejected labels. His reasoning was, "When I make a decision, I think, 'it's human, it's right, it's neither liberal, nor conservative but it's the right thing to do.' I have as much to conserve as anyone."

With civil rights leaders at the NAACP Convention (left) and with New York Cardinal Joseph Francis Spellman and reverend Dr. Martin Luther King, Jr. (right) Photo courtesy of the Library of Congress Prints and Photographs Division

Rockefeller's congeniality had limits his entire life. An internal White House memo said Eisenhower "was extremely disappointed at the way Nelson, for all his external sweetness, had managed to antagonize everybody—'literally everybody.'" As his involvement with the mall project showed, he could be a little too hands-on. He once had a shoving match with the Republican Assembly Speaker and as vice-president, was seen tearing up a Reagan poster from a delegate. And not everyone was turned on by Rockefeller's personality. Democratic Congressman Lester Wolff called him, "a Brahmin an elitist as his greeting, 'Hi, fella,' not ever using your name."

Finally, some of his governing principals changed as well. Where he once scorned debt and borrowing, by the end of his tenure, it had become a hallmark of his governance so that, as *The New York Times* noted "the state debt increased from $92 million in 1959 to $3.4 million in 1973."

By the time Rockefeller came up for a second term, he was so highly regarded that Democrats struggled to field a challenger. They eventually settled on U.S. Attorney for Southern New York Robert Morgenthau, whose father Henry had been U.S. Treasury Secretary. But *Congressional Quarterly* noted Morgenthau "appeared to lack the crowd-pleasing techniques which have made Rockefeller a strong vote-getter." Morgenthau tied Rockefeller to rent-control scandals and charged that he was planning on raising taxes after the election. Rockefeller countered by pointing to $7 billion investments in businesses, raising state aid to schools and instituting a "pay as you go" type budget as opposed to the "deficit financing" of the Democrats. He earned the endorsement of *The New York Times*. A Conservative Party candidate, labeling Rockefeller as being "wholly devoted to tax, tax, spend, spend," did take votes from his right but not by nearly enough to swing the election. Rocky won 53-44%, a 529,000 vote plurality that was just 44,000 fewer than his '58 margin.

In 1966, Rockefeller had a tougher time. The tax issue had finally caught up with him and again, he was hampered by a conservative rival, Paul Adams. But New York City Council President Paul O'Dwyer had a liberal rival with the most magical name in America – Roosevelt, as in the former President's son. Roosevelt and Adams literally polled the same percentage of votes and Rockefeller held his post 45-38%. 1970 was tough as well. Retired Supreme Court Justice Arthur Goldberg challenged Rockefeller and tapped Basil Patterson as his running-mate. It was a spirited campaign and Goldberg hoped for voter malaise after twelve years of Rockefeller's governance. But Rockefeller won 52-40%.

Ford nominated Rockefeller to replace himself as vice-president within weeks after he assumed the Presidency. A year earlier, after Spiro Agnew resigned the post, Rockefeller made overtures to Nixon that he was available but Happy knew it wouldn't happen saying, "weakness never turns to strength." But Ford resisted the warnings of some who were afraid that Rockefeller might overshadow him (he recall his close friend, ex-Defense Secretary Mel Laird telling him no one overshadows a President).

An Official White House Photo

The person Ford most considered besides Rockefeller was Ambassador to China George H.W. Bush. At his Senate confirmation hearing, Rockefeller tussled with Senators over his wealth. New York's senior Senator, Jacob Javits told colleagues, "If you gave a civil service examination for President, the head of the class would be Nelson Rockefeller." But he faced serious questioning about his wealth – which he placed at $62.5 million and referred to his holdings in the family owned Standard Oil and Chase "minimal percentages." He was grilled about the Nixon pardon which he called "an act of conscience, compassion and courage." At one point, West Virginia Senator Robert Byrd called Rockefeller "about the hardest man to pin down," to which Rocky replied, "You, sir, certainly no how to put a man on the spot."

Rockefeller was confirmed in December but the delay seemed to hurt his ability to hit the ground running in the administration. One aide later called the, "first four month shakedown (of the Ford administration) critical and he wasn't involved. That was when the relationship evolved and we were on Capitol Hill fighting for confirmation." He declined to live in the newly constructed vice-presidential mansion. Rockefeller wanted to create many committees. Two people who may have hampered Rocky jumping in fill steam were two Ford aides named Don Rumsfeld and Dick Cheney. In his autobiography, *A Time to Heal*, Ford wrote Rumsfeld, "didn't think there was enough time in the day for Rockefeller to do all the things he had signed on to do." Accustomed to being an executive, Rockefeller often used his role as presiding officer of the Senate to make rulings that while, procedurally sound, were rarely enforced, thereby exasperating Senators.

Photo courtesy of the Gerald R. Ford Presidential Library and Museum

By 1976, things had changed. Ford was facing an ideological struggle for the Republican Presidential nomination from Ronald Reagan. As Spring turned into Summer, Ford's ability to hold off Reagan were growing less certain. When Ford was told that replacing Rockefeller with a conservative could stop the hemorrhaging, Ford resisted. Eventually but painstakingly, he came to the conclusion that it was a must. Rockefeller accepted it with good grace but Ford had self-doubts. He confided to New York Republican Chair Richard Rosenbaum, a Rockefeller confidant that "I hope Nelson doesn't hold this against me." He later called it "It was the biggest political mistake of my life. And it was one of the few cowardly things I did in my life" (Ford lost New York State and the election narrowly).

One of the things Rockefeller took heat for as Vice-President was employing young aides many might have felt were not up to par for such an important job. One was Megan Marshack, who served as his assistant. He began spending an increasing amount of time in her company. It was in her apartment that Rockefeller died in January 1979 at age 70. Despite the fact that Nelson had told some close to him that he suspected the end might be near, his death shocked many. His grandfather lived to nearly 98, his father 86 and Nelson had always kept in shape. He took vitamins, rode horseback, played golf and walked to his office as Governor.

Goldwater eulogized him on the Senate floor. "While we had great political differences they were never of any great nature. But I came to know this man and I can say, too, without hesitancy, that I do not think I have known another man who lived in America who so strongly supported American ideals and who always put America and the American people at the forefront of everything that he was thinking."

Meanwhile, controversy lingered over the circumstances of his death, particularly given that Mary telephoned a friend, who then called paramedics. But the Rockefeller family was satisfied with the explanations regarding the circumstances.

Still, a running joke thereafter became, "How did Nelson Rockefeller die? Low blood pressure: 70 over 25."

Romney's Dad Was Among the 1960s' Most Innovative and Progressive Political Figures

Historic Quote: "If Lincoln were alive today he'd be turning over in his grave." – Gerald Ford

Photo courtesy of Scott Romney

It's very rare that a man becomes a footnote in history more than 40 years after he left office particularly when, throughout his life of service, this person was among the most innovative and noted Governors in his own right. But with Mitt Romney's undertaking of a Presidential run in 2012, the record of his dad, George Romney, received more scrutiny than perhaps at any time since his Governorship. For historians, aspiring politicians, and serial do-gooders, the life of George Romney deserves a close look: his undertakings and ideals in public life may be something very close to the way things ought to be today.

George Romney was a Presidential candidate in his own right. Though he didn't get very far in that endeavor, his success as a businessman and accomplishments as Michigan's Governor have left him in high esteem long after his death.

To understand Romney is to understand his background. His parents were American citizens but as Mormons, they had moved south of the border to escape the United States' ban of polygamy, a practice they themselves took no part in. It was Colonial Dublan, Chihuahua, Mexico that George Romney was born in 1907. His parents moved back to the states when George was a boy, mostly residing in Idaho and Utah. The family was not wealthy and George did missionary work in England and Scotland. Eventually, he married Lenore, who had given up the prospects of a movie contract at MGM. The couple raised four boys (Mitt was the youngest) and George worked for Alcoa. The Romneys were devout Mormons but urged the church to recognize civil rights.

Romney and his family in Idaho in 1921
Photo courtesy of the K. Willard Marriot Library, Special
Collections, The Miles Pratt Romney Papers

Romney had a number of careers. After a stint at speechwriting for a Massachusetts Senator (a Democrat), he became a lobbyist for Alcoa and was often found championing the aluminum industry, which frequently required him to testify before Congress. By 1939, he made his way to Detroit and joined the American Automobile Manufacturers Association. When Nash-Kelvinator merged with American Motors, Romney became the President, and the success he achieved by bringing the company back from bankruptcy was monumental. How did he do it? By promoting the "compact" Rambler as the car of the future and labeling the "Big Three" as "gas-guzzling dinosaurs."

In that time, Romney helped rewrite the state's Constitution and served on boards seeking to improve the Detroit school system; he made such an the impression that he was asked to seek the Governorship in 1962. After a 24-hour prayerful fast, Romney was ready to announce his candidacy, a contest in which he'd square off against incumbent Democrat John Swainson.

Romney and his revolutionary Rambler
Photo via Rovalocity.com

Swainson had lost both his legs in the war. Early polls gave him the lead but by September, Romney was a fraction ahead, but Democrats had controlled the "Wolverine Statehouse" for 14 years and many thought it was time for a change. Romney tried to woo some of those people: he showed up at union rallies, though he would not be invited to speak. Romney drew 40% in Wayne County (Detroit), hampering Democrats' goals of holding him to 34%. The margin was so close (79,000 votes) that Swainson did not concede until 4 a.m.—but he won, and his success started instant chatter about a possible Presidential bid.

Unlike past Michigan Governors, Romney had a legislature of his own party which ultimately made for a convivial relationship. But it didn't start out that way. One of his first acts was to push for a flat-rate income tax, lower corporate taxes, and nixing food and drug taxes, but a combination of urban Democrats and rural Republicans rejected them. He fought to revise the state Constitution, which passed by a mere 7,000 votes, but his quest for a minimum wage went nowhere. Frustration was inevitable. He once compared the Governorship to "being the quarterback of a team chosen by your opponents." Polls suggested that Swainson would beat him and talk of a presidential run had subsided so much that when the question arose, Romney replied, "I was afraid you weren't going to ask me that."

But JFK was asking many people that. He had posed the question of Romney's candidacy to General Douglas MacArthur as early as the summer of 1962, before Romney had even won the Governorship; JFK even confided to Jack Fay that "the one fellow I don't want to run against is Romney." Citing his "no vices whatsoever, no smoking, no drinking," Kennedy said, "that guy could be tough ... imagine someone we know going off for 24 hours to fast and mediate, awaiting a message from the Lord whether or not he should run." Bobby added, "He spoke well, looked well." It turns out Kennedy wasn't the only one scoping him out. Richard Nixon, pondering a second run after his razor sharp loss a few years earlier, told Rockefeller, "Romney wants to run, but the regular Republicans don't like his independent attitude toward the party. His greatest weakness is that he knows too little of the word and is too sure of what he doesn't know."

Indeed, it was on social issues that Romney made his mark, both locally and nationally, starting with Civil Rights. Geoffrey Kabaservice wrote in a *New York Times* Sunday Reader that it "was Romney's lifelong, passionate cause, undertaken in defiance of his church as well as the conservative wing of his party." He had declared in his first State of the State that "Michigan's most urgent human rights problem is discrimination - in housing, public accommodations, education, administration of justice, and employment." In early 1963, two months prior to the "March on Washington," Martin Luther King, Jr., came to Detroit for a march that ultimately saw 120,000 protesters. Romney designated it "Freedom March Day in Michigan" and took to the streets with him on another occasion.

Eventually, Romney did get his minimum wage increase. Same with increased unemployment benefits. He fought for an open housing law. He fought for pollution controls, the latter extraordinary in industry-friendly Michigan. And he had a lot to show for it. An $85 million deficit became a $38 million surplus. In his next State of the State, Romney proclaimed, "During 1963, Michigan did more to put its house in order and prepare for the future than in any single year this century."

As 1964 approached, Romney was viewed as a heavy favorite against Congressman At-Large Neil Staebler, but something happened on the road to a second term: Barry Goldwater. Romney had let it be known from the start that Goldwater was anathema not only to his own views but to the direction of the country. "If Goldwater's views deviate as indicated from the heritage of our party, I will do everything within my power to keep him from becoming the party's presidential nominee." Many in Michigan and nationally began urging Romney to seek the office but he dismissed it. "I'm more likely to die before November than I am to be drafted for the office," he said. He ultimately demurred, however, because he wanted to honor the pledge he made to Michigan voters to seek re-election. Still, he honored his pledge to bring the Republican Party to the center.

As the Republican National Convention opened, Romney fought to add two resolutions to the platform - both supported by Dwight Eisenhower - that would fight racial discrimination and end "extremism" in both parties. He called the latter taking a stand against "purveyors of hate." Both were defeated. Still, Gerald

Ford, then a Congressman from Michigan, placed Romney's name in nomination as a Favorite Son candidate.

On Goldwater's nomination, Romney "accepted" it but would not "endorse" him. Asked whether he was backing Goldwater, Romney replied, "You know darn well I'm not." Goldwater in turn accused Romney of caring only about his own re-election (perhaps punctuated by Romney quickly leaving a Michigan rally at which Goldwater appeared) to which Romney replied that "would play into the hands of Democratic State candidates to involve myself in the national campaign." Some Republicans wondered whether an exceedingly strong win by Johnson could do in even a heavily favored Romney. Michigan Republicans had passed a bill prohibiting straight-ticket voting but Democrats successfully suspended it prior to a referendum. That fall, Romney bucked the LBJ landslide to win a second term by 350,000 votes and immediately engaged in an angry tit-for-tat over recriminations with Goldwater.

It started with a letter Goldwater penned attempting to correct points from Romney's appearance on *Face the Nation*, in which the Governor spoke of becoming "inclusive" rather than "exclusive." Goldwater's reply was, "Let's get to 1964 and ask ourselves who it was in the party who said, in effect, if I can't have it my way, I'm not going to play. One of those men happens to be you." Romney's reply came 13 days later in a 12-page reply that appeared to mock Goldwater's importance by offering "my apologies for not having answered it sooner." Romney started by responding to Goldwater's assertion that the Democrats and Republicans realign into "liberal" and "conservative" parties: "I disagree. Experiences of some ideologically oriented parties in Europe realize chaos can result." On Goldwater's drubbing, he said, "A party which drops from 35,000,000 votes in 1960 to 27,000,000 votes in 1964 has certainly narrowed its orientation and support. The party's need to become more broadly inclusive and attractive should be obvious to anyone."

Romney glided through his own 1966 re-election. His 550,000 vote margin (61%) included 30 percent of the black vote. The next day, he called a newly elected Republican Governor of California named Ronald Reagan and suggested using his model to "put together throughout the country what you have put together in California" (when reporters asked about a Romney/Reagan ticket his response was, "that's so hypothetical I don't even want to count on it"). Whether he wanted to or not, the presidential chatter could be ignored no longer, which Romney did nothing to discount ("The people have lost confidence in Washington"). Lest there be any doubt, Romney continued to press the inclusion theme, often in hard-hitting and unmistakable terms. In Charlotte, he said, "At the state level, there are too many who still preach the dusty dogma of states' rights … states have no rights. Only people have rights. States have responsibilities." He stated himself "unable to follow the gobbledy gook about conservatives, liberals, and moderates. I'm a Republican. Let's begin to talk about the things that unite us."

As 1966 drew to a close, he led Nixon in Gallup by 8%. While that wouldn't continue into the following year, his numbers consistently hovered near 30%, and the reasons seemed clear. *The Harvard Crimson* said Romney "bore a good deal of resemblance to the Eisenhower of 1952. He has the same a-political and up-with-purity image … his support does not stem from his policies and statements." They also credited his "engaging smile, solid handshake, confident tone, and eye-to-eye delivery … his broad shoulders, handsome face, and square jaw give him an athletic look. His dark hair, blending into white at the hairline, adds dignity to his rugged appearance … George Wilcken Romney has the look of an ideal salesman." Driving the deal home would be the hard part.

Photo via Fortune Archives

Romney became the consensus choice of many moderate Republicans, including Nelson Rockefeller, his New York counterpart who twice previously had sought the White House under the guise of stopping the party's drift to the right. He asked to debate Nixon, to which the former President replied, "The great debate of 1968 should be between the Republican nominee and Lyndon Johnson. The only winner of a debate between Republicans—as we learned in 1964, would be Lyndon Johnson." But 1967 would mark the beginning of his problems.

First came the riots, which began when a predominantly black nightclub, Economy Printing, on Detroit's famous 12th Street was raided at 3:30 a.m. one Saturday night. It took an hour for mass arrests to be made but, as the law enforcement vehicles were speeding away, someone through a bottle, which soon erupted into riots. Before long, the chaos had enveloped the other part of the city. Romney called state police which did little to ease the situation.

After 24 hours, Romney asked Johnson for the National Guard; the President refused. When similar events had broken out in California and New Jersey, President Johnson offered to send the National Guard, but the Governors of those states were Democrats who lacked designs on the White House. Michigan was a different matter, so Johnson instead sent Cyrus Vance to Detroit as his envoy. After touring the city with Mayor Jerome Cavanaugh, Vance said it didn't look too bad. Cavanaugh replied, "Usually, the city isn't burning."

Johnson ultimately sent out the Guard but not before going on television citing "the clear, unmistakable, and undisputed evidence that governor Romney of Michigan and other local officials have been unable to bring the situation under control." Romney felt that by not acting sooner, Johnson was playing Presidential politics by trying to make Romney look unable to control his turf. The event did lead to the creation of the Kerner Commission, which examined issues governing racism. But Romney's problems continued. Darcy Richardson in *A Nation Divided* wrote of David Broder mentioning Romney's "fuzziness" and notes that "some party leaders began complaining that his speeches were dull and unexciting." *The Harvard Crimson* noted that Romney "cannot shrug off a question. Instead, he fondles with it for a while, then tosses it back to the questioner." One supporter said, "George's only sin is his syntax."

Photo courtesy of the Reuther Library

Romney also faced a deficit in his knowledge of foreign affairs, burdening him with the task of trying to burnish his credentials which he decided to do by taking a trip to Vietnam. While he re-affirmed his support for LBJ, he later said he had been 'brainwashed" by the generals and "they do a very good job." That single word—brainwashing—sent Romney's support spiraling. Nixon lept in front of him, but Romney went full speed ahead to win the nation's highest office. He undertook a 17-city tour of ghettos (his advisors warned against it).

By the time the New Hampshire primary approached, Rockefeller said that while he still backed Romney, he would be available for a draft, which seemed to persuade many potential Romney backers that Rockefeller was interested. Romney soldiered on. *US News and World Report* noted that "one snowy night, he rode his campaign bus 40 miles to meet 25 grocery shoppers and to speak to an audience at a school cafeteria." Finally, he withdrew just before the primary explaining with considerable class, "My candidacy has not won wide acceptance ... I will support wholeheartedly the candidate for President to whom the Republican Governors give their support." Rockefeller did jump in but, like 1964, his bid went nowhere.

Many Romneyites hoped for a consolation prize for Romney in the form of the vice-presidency. They were publicly dismayed when Nixon chose Spiro Agnew and vowed to press forward. John Lindsay placed Romney's name in nomination. Nixon was not amused and called on John Mitchell to quash it. Mitchell's reply was, "Ah, screw 'em Dick. It'll blow over." Nixon's reply was, "I'm not going to stand for that kind of revolt. If the sore losers get away with something like this now, they'll do the same thing during my Presidency." In the end, Romney did win 186 delegates but they were far below the 1,082 that Agnew received. In a sign of where the hearts of the delegates may have been, loud cheers were elicited during the roll call every time a state delegation announced votes for Romney. But Romney still got a decent prize; Nixon made him Secretary of Housing and Urban Development. He made his impact quickly—so quickly that *The New York Times* opined that he "left the impression that he could not wait until January 20 to shake up the government." Indeed, two of his early appointments as HUD aides went to African-Americans. At that point, the administration had only appointed three. Romney, ever the maverick, took a shot at parochial schools on the way out, urging Michigan not to fund them.

Images courtesy of ronwadebuttons.org

The relationship between Nixon and Romney was always complicated. *The Boston Globe* said it "played out like a Shakesperean drama." The reason was simple. Romney wanted to advance progress in the cities. The administration had other priorities. First Romney promoted a plan to desegregate housing in the cities. Attorney General John Mitchell nixed that one. During the 1970 mid-term campaign, Nixon was trying to attract hard-core conservatives to support Republican candidates, and when he heard that Romney was touting the administration's outreach to minorities, Nixon ordered aides to "stop him" but they were unsuccessful. When suburbanites resisted integration, Romney cut their funds. The administration worried it would hurt their base. More than once, Nixon told aides to "keep me away from Romney." H.R. Haldeman wrote in his diary that "George won't leave quickly, will have to be fired." He tried to get Romney to challenge venerable Democratic Senator Phil Hart but Romney came up with a ploy to have his wife run instead.

The relationship between Nixon and Romney was complex
Official White House photo

One by one, Nixon overrode Romney's decisions. In turn, Romney struggled to figure out what Nixon believed in, saying, "Perhaps he doesn't believe in anything." After Romney wasn't told that he would be overseeing the response to Hurricane Agnes, a heated confrontation ensued. One official said, "You don't care whether we live or die." Romney made it clear he wanted out. He held back until after the election but submitted his resignation four days later.

In retirement, Romney was still for the common man. In 1994, he spent a sizable amount of time in Massachusetts helping Mitt's race against Ted Kennedy. It was said that when he landed at Logan Airport, he hopped on a bus and then the subway. Four days before his death, Romney drafted a proposal to encourage volunteerism. The day before, he drove to a meeting promoting volunteerism. He collapsed on his treadmill in the summer of 1995, only to be discovered by his wife. She knew something was wrong when the red roses he gave her every day during their marriage had not appeared that morning. He was 88 years old.

Of Romney, Theodore White said "the first quality that surfaced, as one met and talked with George Romney over a number of years was sincerity so profound that in conversation, one was almost embarrassed."

With ex-President Ford on a panel
Photo courtesy of the Gerald R. Ford Presidential Library and Museum

Until Recently, Bill Scranton Was Oldest Living Presidential Candidate

Historic Quote: "Ladies and gentlemen, I'm pleased to tell you today that I've signed legislation outlawing Russia forever. We begin bombing in five minutes." – President Ronald Reagan prior to his Saturday weekly radio address, not realizing the microphone was on. The Russian military was on high alert for 30 minutes.

Images via ronwadebuttons.com

Until Bill Scranton died in 2013 at the age of 96, he was the oldest living individual to have made a run for his/her party's presidential nomination. The former Pennsylvania Governor made an energetic run for the GOP nod in 1964, at which time he was in his second year of leading the Commonwealth. Scranton had not entered the primaries but at that time, the convention was the dominant factor in securing the nomination. He would be challenging Barry Goldwater, who at that point was all but assured of getting the nomination, but Scranton was briefly Goldwater's candidate. Sound convoluted? I'll explain.

The California primary, which was 86 delegates and winner take all, was crucial to the nomination, but Goldwater wasn't sure he could win. If Nelson Rockefeller, whose policies he abhorred, defeated him, Richard Nixon might be waiting in the wings. But with Nixon, it was more than policies. The loathing was personal. Thus, Goldwater mused that if forced to choose, he'd go with Scranton. "He was not a conservative and it would have washed away years of work,' Goldwater wrote in his memoirs. "But the Pennsylvania Governor had one thing going for him—he had not assailed the conservative movement. We could

865

live with him and fight another day. It was an extremely painful consideration but politics is often an agonizing process."

However, Goldwater's win in the California primary, albeit with just 51.4%, meant that it was moderates who would be searching for an alternative. Later, *Occasional Planet* summed up the GOP conundrum: "Nixon was about as conservative as moderate members of the GOP could tolerate; Goldwater was considered beyond the pale." Which meant it would soon fall to Scranton.

Scranton had captured the Governorship in 1962, defeating Richardson Dilworth, the Mayor of Philadelphia who had been heavily favored from the get-go. Scranton argued that Pennsylvania was being left behind "while Democrat Administrations in Harrisburg and Philadelphia have peddled influence, protected corruption, sold license, and built a fantastic pyramid of graft and civic dishonor."

Scranton was not a forceful orator but his message could be stirring, particularly when he spoke of the economy. One speech went: "A gray army of 400,000 strong stands victimized by Pennsylvania's failure to cope with the greatest industrial revolution in the history of the human race ... They are living, breathing, feeling human beings. Their children cry at night. They have wives and they have mothers and fathers. And they suffer." He pledged a "mighty all-out-people-to-people crusade" to attract jobs and called the transportation system "inefficient mish-mash."

Photo reproduced with the permission of the Special Collections Library, the Pennsylvania State University Libraries

Dilworth could not attack Scranton's wealth since he was a blue-blood himself, but he charged that his family did not put their fortune on the side of the common folk and called him an "accidental one-term Congressman." The bottom line was that Dilworth's rough-and-tumble style did not go over well with voters outside of Philly, and Scranton carried 62 of the state's 67 counties and won 55-44%.

Scranton as Governor
Photo courtesy of the Pennsylvania State Archives

Descending into a coal mine
Photo reproduced with the permission of the Special Collections
Library, the Pennsylvania State University Libraries

Almost as soon as that occurred, a "Draft Scranton" movement began for the Presidency, which was not unusual for Governors of large states. His colleague next door, Ohio's Jim Rhodes, was already being floated, but given Scranton's background, many viewed him as a "Republican John Kennedy." Scranton at first resisted. With Goldwater the leading candidate among conservatives, the party had only room for one moderate, and that was Rockefeller, his senior and much better known colleague to the north. Rockefeller also had it all riding on California but fell 59,000 votes short, at which time his candidacy was over.

That still didn't clear the way for Scranton. George Romney of Michigan was interested and many of his fellow Republicans were prepared to back him. Scranton, on the other hand, was sending mixed signals. The first may have resulted in a misinterpretation from a conversation with Ike. The ex-President, now a full-time resident of Gettysburg, wasn't thrilled with Goldwater and all knew it. Newspapers erroneously said that Eisenhower was prepared to back Scranton, but amid these reports, Ike phoned Scranton to say that he was neutral, that he couldn't be party to a "cabal." This led to a press conference which *American Presidential Elections* called "a miserable performance. He failed to declare his candidacy or even speak out against Goldwater." This in turn led Rockefeller to ask, "Did you see his press conference?" Romney seemed like the man of the hour, but he ultimately concluded that he could not break his pledge to Michigan voters to not seek re-election.

For a time, Gettysburg resident Eisenhower was a prime
booster of Scranton's Presidential ambitions
Photo reproduced with the permission of the Special Collections
Library, the Pennsylvania State University Libraries

Scranton was not charismatic. *Newsweek* described him as "a lanky, languid man," and comedian Dick Gregory called him "the guy who runs to John Wayne for help." But he was not Goldwater and many Republicans desperately wanted an alternative.

A few days later, Scranton was in and Rocky lent him his backing. Henry Cabot Lodge, then in Saigon, came back to assist him. New Jersey Senator Cliff Case said that "of the two, Scranton is the one who represents the thinking of the Republican Party and of the people of New Jersey generally." His candidacy announcement was essentially a descendant of what the GOP of today grapples with: issues of tolerance. Scranton said, "the nation and indeed the world waits to see if another proud political banner which is our own will falter or limp and collapse in the dust. Can we pretend even to ourselves," he continued, "that it is possible to stand with one foot in the 20th century and the other in the 19th?" As many supporters chanted, "no." Scranton replied, "you and I know we cannot. Lincoln would cry out in pain if we sold out our principles." He called Goldwater "ignorant."

At first, there seemed to be a forum for Scranton's candidacy. A Harris poll showed that he was the choice of 62 percent of Republicans, but delegates ruled the day; and as Lodge, who had very nearly been elected vice-president with Nixon just four years earlier, met with them, he wondered, "what in God's name has happened to the Republican Party! I hardly know any of these people." Scranton took part in the traditional motorcade and handshaking but as *American Presidential Elections* observed, "to call the struggle uphill would be bad geography. It was up-cliffside, straight up, with nothing to latch onto." Scranton could count on at least 84 delegates, many from the Keystone State, but that wasn't even a fifth of what Goldwater had and so Scranton cultivated backing the old-fashioned way: by crisscrossing the country.

Scranton captured the backing of ten delegations but not the ones that mattered. He made his case before the Illinois delegation, only to receive zero delegates. He had a promise from Jim Rhodes to "hold" his delegates for Scranton, only to eventually have Rhodes release them.

**Photo reproduced with the permission of the Special Collections
Library, the Pennsylvania State University Libraries**

Over the weekend before the convention was set to open, Scranton continued his eforts, hoping to influence the plank, particularly on the issue of strong stands on Civil Rights and nuclear disarmament. On the former, Scranton suffered the indignity of seeing the rejection of his proposal put over the top by Pennsylvania. During the roll, opponents were two votes shy of preventing the language from going into the platform, but then Pennsylvania came forward. While 62 of the "Keystone State" delegates did vote with Scranton, two did not, and that's all it took for the measure to fall.

On the latter, Scranton's forces once again believed they had Eisenhower's support, only to be told that he couldn't acquiesce. One of his supporters forged a letter stating that "Goldwaterism has come to stand for nuclear irresponsibility" and a "whole crazy-quilt collection of absurd and dangerous positions." The letter challenged the front-runner to a debate but he would do no such thing.

**Photo reproduced with the permission of the Special Collections
Library, the Pennsylvania State University Libraries**

In time, Goldwater received a second letter from Scranton, and this one
was authentic. "Will the convention choose a candidate or will it choose you
... you are a minority candidate," he said. Previously, Scranton made it known
that he would be willing to accept the vice-presidential slot, but the tone of that
letter eliminated that. Also a contributing factor was Scranton's vehement push
to include a condemnation in the platform committee of extremist groups such
as the John Birch Society, a proposal that was rejected. As expected, Goldwater
won the nomination on the first ballot, capturing 883 votes. Scranton did end
up with 214 delegates, fewer than he had hoped for but enough to make his
presence known. More importantly, his having taken on the cause, coupled with
the booing Rockefeller received when he emphasized Civil Rights, meant further
erosion for unhappy moderates, which contributed to Goldwater's lopsided loss
in the fall.

Scranton resumed the Governorship, a role in which he continued to promote
his Pennsylvania quest. Education was a focal point of his concerns as the state
community college system and the Pennsylvania Higher Education Assistance
Agency all came about during his tenure. Unemployment also loomed large; at
that time, Pennsylvania had the second largest rate in the nation.

**Photo reproduced with the permission of the Special Collections
Library, the Pennsylvania State University Libraries**

Scranton was born into politics and wealth in a city that bore his name
(though his birthplace was actually in Connecticut where his parents vacationed).
His great-grandfather was one of the owners of the Lackawanna Steel Company, a
major force in the area. His fame led to the city, then known as Slocum Hollow,
being named Scranton in 1866. His mother, sometimes referred to as "The
Dutchess," had hoped for a political career for one of her sons but was skeptical
of Bill due to his asthma. Scranton was both a Yale and an Air Force man, serving
in World War II. After that, he worked at a prominent law firm before launching
a political career at age 43.

Scranton had been elected to Congress in 1960 from a Lackawanna district
with a Democratic registration advantage of 50,000 that had last elected a
Republican in 1938. He was dubbed a Kennedy Republican for his support of
Civil Rights, social security, children's aid programs, and the Peace Corps. Shortly
thereafter, Scranton was persuaded to run for Governor. In this case, the "draft"
proved successful but Scranton had strong conditions. He said he'd run only if
all 67 GOP county chairs endorsed him. Sixty-six did, but this was apparently
enough. In the general, Dilworth's rough and tumble style did not go over well
with voters outside of Philly, and Scranton carried 62 of the state's 67 counties.

After his single term as Governor ended (Scranton was the last Governor the
Constitution limited to one term), Scranton accepted a number of prominent
Presidential appointments, but he declined a big one. Nixon had approached

Scranton about serving as Secretary of State and he turned it down; however, he did serve as an envoy to the Middle East, and in the wake of the Kent State shooting he chaired the President's Commission on Campus Unrest. The "Scranton Report" indicated that the shooting was "unjustified." When Gerald Ford assumed the Presidency, he made it known that he wanted Scranton to be one of a handful to serve on his transition team. Later, Ford named him Ambassador to the UN.

Scranton's son very nearly became Governor in 1986, but lost 51-48% to Bob Casey, Sr. (Scranton was hurt by an ad that showed him with long hair and "smoking dope" in the 1960s). Scranton, Jr. again briefly sought the GOP nomination for Governor in 2006.

Photo reproduced with the permission of the Special Collections Library, the Pennsylvania State University Libraries

The Minnesota Twins: Once-Serious Contenders Stassen and McCarthy Notorious For Never-Ending Presidential Bids

"He chased all of those communists out of the State department so I think we can give him a chance." - A voter to Jack Germond on why he was voting for Eugene McCarthy for President. The voter was mistaking him for ex and long deceased Wisconsin Senator Joseph McCarthy.

They rose to the top so fast and so young that in their heydays, Harold Stassen and Eugene McCarthy impressed many. Both became serious candidates for the nation's highest office and, in at least one campaign, came to be known as "the other candidate" who early in their careers each pulled off accomplishments many had dismissed as impossible not long before.

Stassen surprised front-runner Thomas E. Dewey in at least one primary contest for the 1948 Republican Presidential nomination before losing critical Oregon. Two decades later, McCarthy famously jarred LBJ in New Hampshire and until Ted Kennedy's unsuccessful primary bid in 1980, he remained the only candidate ever to defeat a Kennedy (in the Indiana primary).

When multiple bids failed, neither wanted to exit the stage and become the butt of laughter for continuing and continuing; but these were two very different personalities. Stassen's endeavors, however eccentric, were carried through by his sunny disposition and "Minnesota-Nice" attributes that allowed him to enjoy a holy status of true greatness and admiration in the minds of those who knew him. McCarthy by contrast was socially awkward and never one to sport a garrulous demeanor to begin with; he became defined in later life by grudges and self-righteousness and in many ways died a lonely and bitter man.

Harold Stassen:

The terms "boy-wonder" and "perennial candidate" may have been created with Harold Stassen in mind. He left office before 1960 but continued to undertake bids for political office. He did it again and again to the point that, more than 40 years after his term as Minnesota's Governor had concluded, he was still the energizer bunny of quixotic runs in two states for local offices and nine times nationally.

The New York Times wrote that "almost from the start, Mr. Stassen showed signs of being a live wire." Born on a farm in St. Paul to parents of Czech and Norwegian ancestry, Stassen graduated high school at 15 but could not enter the University for another year, so he delivered newspapers. When enrollment finally came, he put himself through as a Pullman car conductor who worked the Minneapolis to Milwaukee route. He was also a baker and a grocer. At 6'2 and 220 pounds, Stassen measured up to the size of the fight in the dog and a dog in the fight. A master debater, he started the first club of college Republicans in Minnesota. He excelled on the rifle team as well.

After getting his law degree, Stassen opened a practice in St. Paul with a classmate, Elmer Ryan, a Democrat. They paid $25 a month for the space. The practice was so successful that it saw the hiring of five additional lawyers which *The New York Times* noted "made headlines with some dramatic horseback arrests of criminal suspects and prosecution of gangsters."

The following year, Stassen sought the office of Dakota County Attorney and won, even though he was sidelined for much of the campaign by tuberculosis (Ryan would also go on to bigger and better things, winning a seat in Congress).

As Dakota County Attorney
Photo courtesy of the Minnesota Historical Society

Eight years later at age 31, he was elected to lead the Gopher State. Folks called him the "boy" Governor. A boy he may have been. With a Lieutenant Governor who was 26 years old and a youthful staff, Stassen's team was even called "the diaper brigade"— but he governed like a man. Minnesota has a reputation as having a particularly clean government and Stassen may have set the stage for helping to make that so.

Stassen's obituary credits him with having implemented "civil service and anti-corruption reform." He named a Democrat as his Chief of Staff. His theme was "Enlightened capitalism," which, as the *Star Tribune* observed, offered the doctrine of "combining respect for labor rights along with demands for real democracy within its ranks." One was the creation of a 30-day cooling off period before a strike could begin. The New York Times noted that Stassen, " brought the first black officer into his state's National Guard, and he did so before World War II, when such a move was truly daring."

Al Quie was a teenager when Stassen became Governor and would assume the office himself 40 years later. He had a picture of Stassen on his wall and his parents were backers of Stassen in both of his major presidential runs and said one reason they liked him was "because he was young, articulate and had ideas on government that appealed to them." He also "had a personality that radiated."

Roscoe Drummond later described his subsequent tenure as governor as providing a "progressive, solvent and humane Republican administration which ultimately won even the support of labor leaders." The national party noticed: in 1940, Stassen was tapped to give the keynote address at the GOP Convention.

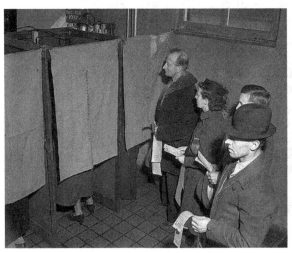 

Minneapolis residents preparing to vote and a Stassen button
Photo via the Minnesota Historical Society and button courtesy of Matt Paul

Stassen and young family
Photo via the Minnesota Historical Society

By 1942, war was raging and there were questions as to whether Stassen would seek re-election. He did but vowed to resign after the conclusion of the legislative session. In a sign of how his policies may have rubbed conservatives the wrong way even then, Stassen had to fend off a Republican challenger that year. He did but his 51% was just 14% ahead of a State Senator. Still, Stassen made good on that vow and was off to the Pacific as a member of the Navy. As a rarity but a sign of respect, he was called "Harold" by his superior, Admiral William Halsey. Stassen witnessed the Japanese surrender. Meanwhile the impression he had already created was such that Stassen was asked to consider a White House bid in 1944.

Stassen did not campaign because of his military duty but took exactly the opposite of a Shermanesque pledge. He announced himself willing to accept the nomination if offered, which was to the consternation of Republicans in Wisconsin—at that time the most pivotal contest, particularly Wendell Wilkie who was counting on a big win there. According to Stassen's biography, Wilkie "exploded in unprintable words." At one point, questions as to whether Stassen was actually a candidate were so numerous that his surrogates often had to issue assurances that, indeed, he was.

Meanwhile, Stassen had been pushing the creation of a United Nations, and in April of 1945, Roosevelt appointed him as a delegate to the United Nations charter conference. Stassen signed the charter and at the time of his death he was the last living member. Stassen signed the United Nations Charter.

**With Herbert Hoover during a rally for the relief of Finland and getting his stripes
Left photo via the Minnesota Historical Society;
right photo an official U.S. Navy photo**

But 1948 was another election year and it was well before this time that Stassen decided he wanted the job—and he hit the stump hard. Stassen made his bid known in December of 1946, and by the time primary season was underway he had visited 37 states and made "more than 300 major speeches."

The New York Times credited Stassen with having "yanked the stretched gray beards of the GOP Old Guard on every appropriate occasion." Stassen was back in the states and was ready to campaign hard. As the cycle began, he was favored over New York Governor Thomas E. Dewey, despite the fact that Dewey had seemed to have laid the groundwork by leading the charge against Franklin D. Roosevelt four years earlier.

Stassen struck an interesting chord. New York Times reporter Abell Phillips, who traveled with Stassen just before the Wisconsin primary, said Stassen, while not "whip(ping) up spontaneous outbursts of stomping and handclapping in his listeners . . . does get across a compelling sense of earnestness and of moral and intellectual integrity." His energy was evident. When his press secretary Larsen explained that a grueling schedule that was forthcoming, Phillips quipped, "And on the seventh day he resteth," to which he replied, "On the seventh day he dictateth."

Still, his energy paid off - for Wisconsin anyway. Stassen's backing of Taft-Hartley limited his backing from labor though he was always careful to qualify that he opposed the anti-striker provisions. After his aides pondered what kind of impact the presence of Douglas MacArthur would have, Stassen won a 39-34% win over the General as Dewey was relegated to less than a quarter of the vote; this would prove to be his heyday. In those days, contests were few and most were decided within single digits. But while Stassen did defeat Dewey in Nebraska and manage a 31-30% win in Pennsylvania, Dewey not surprisingly took New Jersey.

The last contest was Oregon, which as *The Almanac of American Politics* reports was "much ballyhooed." Its selection was pivotal.

The Dewey-Stassen radio debate (left) was heard by 40 million Americans; right, Stassen arriving at the Republican National Convention
Left photo via Crooks and liars; right photo via forum.paradoxplaza.com

Momentum appeared to be on Stassen's side, but a debate was proposed and Dewey got to choose the topic: "Shall the Communist Party be outlawed?" Stassen, despite his worldview, actually took the position that it should while Dewey argued against it. His contention was that it would play into the hands of a future Hitler or Stalin. An audience of well over 40 million gathered around their radios and listened to the debate; at its conclusion, it was generally assumed that Dewey had won (Stassen had considered withdrawing from the debate but believed doing so would hurt him more). Dewey's win may not have entirely been on substance. He realized he suffered from a certain aloofness and sought advice on how to change that. Among the people he called was U.S. Senator Wayne Morse, still a Republican. As a result, *U.S. News* observed that "it was a new Dewey who appeared before the country in his radio debate with Stassen. The voice was mellow. The personality was warmer. His attitude was calm and poised." His changed demeanor may have caught Stassen off guard. Regardless, it changed the dynamic of the election.

For Stassen, an ominous precursor may have come when the Midwest Council of Negro Republican Clubs announced its backing of Dewey, though they did indicate Stassen was their second choice. Dewey prevailed by a 52-48% margin. Stassen congratulated his rival but vowed to "redouble our efforts to gain support for a sound liberal program in the Republican Party and for victory in November." He vowed to fight for delegates in Illinois, Missouri, Massachusetts, and the South at the convention.

One of Stassen's backers was a future Chief Justice and Minnesotan to the core named Warren Berger who said of his candidate, "We've got the nucleus, at least of a Stassen organization, in every state in the union, except one. That's Michigan. It's Harold's special orders that we not go into Michigan at all. He's very fond, you know, of Senator Vandenberg." There were thoughts that if Vandenberg were drafted, Stassen would be his vice-presidential pick.

Come convention time, Stassen joined other leaders who wanted to take part in a Stop Dewey movement, but they couldn't agree on a consensus. Therefore, Stassen resisted calls to withdraw. He said he owed his supporters two roll calls (he won 157 and 149 votes respectively). Meanwhile, with no signal from Vandenberg, Michigan flipped to Dewey and the New York Governor was over the top. He huddled throughout the night with advisors to choose a VP and Stassen's name was seriously entertained but met many objections. California's Earl Warren got the post.

Like a good soldier, Stassen embraced Dewey's cause and stumped for him throughout the country. Yet his experience with the New York Governor might have been indicative of why the once indomitable campaign turned into the biggest upset in history. Stassen recalled 40 years later for the television series, "Our World" that, "by holding back on the issues, (Dewey) gave an impression that he was talking above the people and not being decisive." He visited Dewey in early-October and told him, "I don't like what I'm hearing around the country. You've got to take stronger stands." Stassen then described that Dewey, without saying a word, reached into his desk and handed me a Roper poll that showed an incredible lead." The problem was, Roper had stopped conducting polls by that point because they saw a Dewey win as a foregone conclusion.

Could Stassen have beaten Truman? Perhaps. He certainly had more of a way with people than Dewey, but Truman's attacks on the "Do Nothing 80th Congress" hurt Dewey, and he wasn't a member of Congress. It seems likely Stassen would've had at least some fallout as well.

Stassen embarked on one more serious try for the White House in 1952 but this time, Republicans had moved on. Convention delegates were choosing between Dwight Eisenhower and Robert Taft (and to a lesser extent, Douglas MacArthur). It was said that Stassen was in that race simply to help Eisenhower and prevent a more conservative Taft surge, but in a contest where every state delegation mattered, Stassen earned the gratitude of Eisenhower when he put Minnesota's delegation behind the General. At that time fellow Republicans began calling him, "the Grand Old Party's grand old loser."

Photo courtesy of the Dwight D. Eisenhower Presidential Library

After the 1948 campaign, Stassen was President of Penn but in his heart he was always trying to secure 1600 Pennsylvania Avenue. Eisenhower named him Director of the Mutual Security Agency. He said "working for peace" was the most important thing he ever did. For much of 1956, Stassen's goal was to have Richard Nixon replaced as the GOP Vice-Presidential nominee. That failed, but he tried to get back in the ring himself. Then a resident of Pennsylvania, Stassen sought the Pennsylvania Governorship in 1958 and lost the nomination. Republicans did award him the nod for the Philadelphia Mayoralty the following year but he won just 34%.

Stassen jumped back into national politics the following year, aiming for the Republican presidential nomination in every cycle from 1960 through 1992 (save 1972 and 1976) and doing little better than an asterick. Between 1978 and 1994, Stassen took a run at the GOP nomination for a Minnesota Senate seat twice and the Governorship three times but failed to garner more than 13%. A general election run for a St. Paul based Congressional seat saw Stassen take 27%. Stassen could not have expected to be successful but his philosophy was, "If you just speak out on a major issue and you're only a professor or a teacher or even an editor, it doesn't carry as . . . it would if you're in office or a candidate for office," he was quoted as saying in one news report. "To be effective," he said on another occasion, "you have to lay it on the line. It's my life."

David Durenberger served as a U.S. Senator from Minnesota and got to know Stassen in 1977. He called him "a brilliant guy," and that, "what you see is what you get." His impression was that Stassen, "never really changed." Durenberger acknowledged that Stassen, "made some political misjudgments as everyone does once in a while." To that effect, Durenberger said he, "understood better why he continued running for president even though people might have thought of him as a buffoon." That reason was because he wanted to pursue ideas. Republican Governor Elmer Andersen echoed that. "It was unfortunate that he became a victim of scorn because he kept running for President," he said. "He felt that was the only way to get his ideas in front of people." Stassen himself admitted as much, saying his mantra would have been, "I tried." And Durenberger recalls Stassen saying that eventually, his ideas "bore fruit," with one presidency or another.

Though Stassen declined to offer his name as a Republican candidate yet one more time in 1996, he did offer to serve as vice-president for Bob Dole in order to deflect questions about Dole's age. Stassen died in 2001 at age 93.

Eugene McCarthy

Photo courtesy of Susanna Quinn

McCarthy's Presidential pursuit began when anti-war Senators were looking for a candidate to oppose Johnson. A number of Senators were approached, including Bobby Kennedy, George McGovern, Gaylord Nelson and Lee Metcalf. All laughed it off. But when McCarthy was approached he flabbergasted many by offering an instant yes. "There is only one thing to do—take it to the country!"

Journalist Albert Eisele interviewed McCarthy in 1967 and surmised later, "I think I was the first person to write he was seriously thinking of that, which was hard to believe but was true. And I asked him, 'What makes you think you can take on a sitting president in your own party, someone as powerful as Lyndon Johnson?' And he said, 'This war. When the coffins start coming home to the small towns of Minnesota, people are going to turn against this war.' And he was right." McCarthy's theme would be "Vietnam did the United States no real harm. It is no threat to our country . . . In the name of GOD and man and in the name of America, let the fighting stop."

In his announcement, McCarthy said, "I don't think it's a qualitative difference. It's just been kind of a quantitative escalation. And at some point you make a prudential judgment that whatever good you can get out of the war, or what good is going to come from it, is not proportionate to the destruction of life and property and the draining away of moral energy, which goes along with the pursuit of the war in a way in which we are now pursuing it." Johnson, McCarthy said, "seems to have set no limit to the price which he is willing to pay for a military victory" to which McCarthy offered up, "I am hopeful that this challenge may alleviate this sense of political helplessness and restore to many people a belief in the processes of American politics and of American government."

McCarthy's first test was the New Hampshire primary. New Hampshire's Democratic Governor John King called McCarthy "spokesman for the forces of appeasement," predicting Johnson would "murder" McCarthy, who might be lucky to get 12%. Some in the administration called him "a footnote to history."

Images via ronwadebuttons.com

McCarthy didn't disagree with those sentiments which is why he considered bypassing New Hampshire for what he viewed as a much more winnable Wisconsin. But aides prevailed on him to run. McCarthy immediately attracted a "children's crusade" of students; *The New York Times* observed that "upwards of 500 students were canvassing for McCarthy." He so inspired the student population that many of them, including those with long hair, shaved. They called themselves "Clean for Gene," and money came in at an unbelievable pace for a man challenging an incumbent President. John Kenneth Galbraith said "money was never raised so easily as for McCarthy" and it was guestimated that more than $2 million came from Wall Street alone."

McCarthy's biggest problem was that he lacked a "passion gap." Columnist Henry Fairlie called him "the nearest there is to Calvin Coolidge." Many bemoaned his saying that he would be "willing" to serve as President, but his message was all that was required. Tip O'Neill, in his book *Man of the House*, wrote, "For a guy who wanted to be President, he never really worked the streets by asking for help from organizational types like me. Instead, he made his move outside the regular party structure."

McCarthy's slogan was, "Vote for a man you believe in. Eugene McCarthy for President." As McCarthy's bio noted, though, his strong showing was not so much a sign of war malaise but rather unhappiness with the way it was being carried out; in like manner, McCarthy was not an overwhelming fan of the student contingent. He asked his campaign manager Blair Clark, "Why don't you get rid of all those people and just you and I have a couple of people to hold our coats and go round and talk to people." By primary day, most put McCarthy's ceiling at an optimistic 30%. McCarthy won 42.2%, 4,000 votes shy of Johnson's 49%. McCarthy attracted 5,000 Republican votes (mainly believed to have favored George Romney had he entered the race) and swept 20 of the state's 24 delegates which *The Times* attributed to bad planning by the state committee. "On Wisconsin. I think the 12th of March is the day." A student pasted "Victory" over the television and McCarthy said, "I said earlier that I thought I could bridge the generational divide. Your turn will come and we are going to advance it— more or less, in the next administration. We'll see you in Wisconsin."

Though McCarthy had technically lost New Hampshire, his strong showing may have set up a new phenomenon in the election lexicon, for it might have been the first time a "loss" may have been referred to as a "win."

Timing is everything in elections and McCarthy had a number of things in his favor. One was the Tet offensive. Another was General Westmoreland's plea for 206,000 more troops. And there was McCarthy's opposition to the ten-percent income tax surcharge Johnson requested. But reality soon caught up to euphoria as three days after New Hampshire, Bobby Kennedy jumped into the race. "In no state will my efforts be directed against Sen. McCarthy." He would not even run if Johnson agreed to set up a peace commission, or so he hinted. If that was an offer, it was rejected by McCarty who said he wondered if he "intended to fatten me up for the kill." Even when Kennedy entered, McCarthy appeared to publicly laugh off his rival's strength. Murray Kempton wrote Kennedy had "rage at Eugene McCarthy for having survived on the lonely road he dared not walk himself" and had "in one day . . . confirmed the worst things his enemies have ever said about him." Kennedy's feeling toward McCarthy was mutual. He once said "Gene is a mean guy." McCarthy's bio said that he resented them as "a political phenomenon . . . the rich, highly motivated kids who were going to make it because that's what Daddy wanted them to do." In response to Kennedy's initial refusal to enter the race, McCarthy said he was "willing to stay up on the mountain and light signal fires and bonfires, and dance in the light of the moon. But none of them came down, and I tell you, it was a little lonely in New Hampshire."

From there it was unmistakably, game on. It started with style. O'Neill, in his book, recalled the days he and a couple of other colleagues with offices on the same floor walked together when the bells rang for votes and later had drinks. McCarthy, O'Neill wrote, "would join us if he wasn't in the middle of writing poetry or reading a book. He was a whimsical fellow who would come over if he happened to feel like it." He was "lazy and a bit of a dreamer. He was also a loner." That's quite a difference from simply having a rich dad.

McCarthy was the son of a postmaster and cattle buyer, his mother a deeply religious Irish Catholic. He recalls there being "sort of three cultural threads that ran through the town. One was baseball. We worried a great deal about baseball. You started worrying about whether you'd make the team when you were about 11, and stayed on through it [McCarthy did in fact make a minor league team]. The church was quite central for a number of reasons, but in any case it was there, religion. But it wasn't as a religious force but rather as a cultural reality. And the third was the railroad track. It sort of punctuated the day. There were two flyers at that time, one called the Mountaineer and the other the Winnipeg Flyer, which went through about 8:00 at night. And it was part of the great excitement of every day."

Poetry also played a role in McCarthy's life and while he bemused and sometimes put to sleep audiences with his references, they accompanied him throughout.

Young Gene attended prep school and flirted with the idea of becoming a monk; he spent nine months at a monastery before leaving to attend the University of Minnesota. He taught in public schools, then returned to St. Johns to teach economics. Meanwhile, McCarthy became chair of the Ramsey County (St. Paul) Democratic-Farmer-Labor Party which created an opening for a Congressional bid in 1948. He won the primary by a single percentage point, then cruised in the general election.

McCarthy won his Senate seat ten years later by beating incumbent Republican Edward Thye. McCarthy was not the favorite of Democratic leaders to face Thye. Governor Orville Freeman and Humphrey's team wanted Eugenie Anderson, a former Ambassador to Denmark who had been an early member of the "Cold War Liberal" circle that was seeking to rebuild the Minnesota DFL. She enjoyed strong backing in Minneapolis, but McCarthy benefited from labor support which helped him in the critical "Iron Range" region and won the convention's backing.

Even then, McCarthy was criticized for a lackadaisical approach to campaigning (aides had to persuade him to hit the trail more than five days a week) and for not helping fellow members of the party. The farm crisis hurt Thye but so did his initial vote for a proposal by Agriculture Secretary Ezra Benson. Thye's change of heart on the proposal sparked a mini-feud among Republicans and McCarthy was able to make hay of it. "Only a few months ago Mr. Thye voted for the Benson farm program," McCarthy said. "He now says that same program is hurting the farmers, in a last, desperate effort to save his own skin." McCarthy enjoyed a slight lead in the month prior to Election Day but was confronted with the question of how his Catholicism in a Protestant state would impact him. Apparently, the Democratic nature of the year had more of an impact and he won 53-47%.

In the open 1960 campaign, he was an unabashed promoter of Adlai Stevenson to carry his party's banner for the Presidency. He had the honor of placing Stevenson's name in nomination at the convention that ultimately nominated JFK. Reflecting on Stevenson's two previous losses for the White House, McCarthy argued, "Do not reject this man who made us all proud to be called Democrats!" After the speech, O'Neill wrote in his memoirs that McCarthy walked over to the Massachusetts delegation and said of himself: "Any way you measure it, I'm a better man than Kennedy. I'm smarter, I'm a better orator and a better Catholic. Of course, I don't have a rich father."

McCarthy campaigning in Wisconsin during the 1968 primary season
Photo via Jo Freeman

When Walter Cronkite asked him whether the effect of the two candidates would be to split the anti-Johnson balloting, McCarthy replied, "I don't suppose that together we could muster much more than I could muster alone." But he conceded his goal was to stop a first ballot nomination. "Well, Walter, I suppose if it was a case of really carrying through in this course that his support of me would have been the strongest way to proceed. But since the issue is most important, I think in this campaign, rather than in identification with delegates, I think we can continue to make the case really on the issues and then work out some kind of settlement at the convention itself."

First, there was Indiana. An Oliver Quayle poll weeks before the primary showed Kennedy leading McCarthy 41-19% in Indiana, which buoyed hopes that by primary day he could hit 50%, perhaps knocking McCarthy out of the race. Instead, he took just 42%. So what happened? While Kennedy merged an income of low-income and African American voters, McCarthy held his own among the middle class. Nowhere was that more evident than in Gary. Kennedy took 80% of the black vote but McCarthy won the 70 white wards 49-34% (Governor Roger Branigan was also on the ballot but was merely serving as a stand-in for President Johnson, who of course was no longer in the race). McCarthy for his part called the results "inconclusive," adding, "I think I made a good showing; I don't see this as a very serious setback." McCarthy and Branigan benefited from 15% of GOP crossovers which Kenned discouraged, knowing it would likely help his rivals. He thought it cost him 2%.

Ray Boomhower in *Robert F. Kennedy and the 1968 Indiana Primary* wrote, "McCarthy staffers never seemed to hit their stride in Indiana." What also hurt was, as one supporter put it, his "hidden iceberg qualities. Often detached, he gave the impression that campaigning was undignified and beneath him. As one supporter said later, McCarthy decided early that the Indiana people just weren't his kind."

Meanwhile, Kennedy won Nebraska. Next came Oregon. *RFK: The Years Alone* notes that at the end of April, Kennedy's Oregon campaign consisted of "two desks and three people" (a telephone strike added to the woes). By contrast, McCarthy's campaign had been fully staffed in December. Bloomhower also said "personal organization in Multnomah County (Portland) was insufficient." Kennedy, who seemed to be inching ever so slightly ahead, may have been hurt by his dismissal of McCarthy's calls to debate, which enabled McCarthy to draw the distinction with Kennedy's earlier reluctance to get into the race when Johnson was still a candidate. "He wouldn't stand up to Johnson in New Hampshire and now he won't stand up to McCarthy in Oregon." Instead, McCarthy, who had actually reserved the time for the debate, had the floor to himself.

Kennedy's tactical error may have come to a head when McCarthy's forces learned their rival would be campaigning at the Portland Zoo. Their plan was to meet him there and confront Kennedy about skipping the challenge. By that time, Kennedy had been alerted and dashed toward his campaign bus. McCarthy got within feet Kennedy but it was enough for rolling cameras to capture images of McCarthy's forces calling their rival a "chicken"; those images were captured on the evening news. In the end, McCarthy's margin was 44-38%—but it was the first of 27 elections that a Kennedy had lost.

In victory, McCarthy was ecstatic. "I said in Nebraska election night the record of the westward movement shows that almost every wagon train got as far as the Missouri river. But the real test began once you crossed the Missouri and started up the Oregon Trail. We proved who had the best horses and the best wagons and the best men and women. We proved that, here today in Oregon. Here we had the right issues and the right candidate, and here it's just a question of finding our constituency . . . The campaign here not only bridged the generation gap; there wasn't any generation gap; it was solid all the way . . . It will be solid all the way to Chicago and on beyond Chicago. I said early if I were the candidate, we wouldn't have riots, we'd have singing and dancing in the streets. We'll have a short inauguration speech; take down the fence around the White House; and have picnics on the lawn." The band played "California, Here I Come."

Kennedy had that in mind as well. The duo barnstormed the state in an effort to show voters they were the champions of the cause.

A single debate was held on June 1, three days before the primary. Besides taking aim at Johnson, McCarthy trained his fire at Secretary of State Dean Rusk and FBI Director J. Edgar Hoover, likening them to "a no-decision bout with three referees and 16-ounce gloves." While both men said they favored troop withdrawal, Kennedy took a different tack. "I would make it clear that we are going to the negotiation table not with the idea of surrender and that we expect the National Liberation Front and the Vietcong to play some role in the future political process of South Vietnam." McCarthy responded by saying he "didn't say I was going to force a coalition government on South Vietnam. I said we should make sure we are welcome."

On civil rights, Kennedy said McCarthy wanted "take 10,000 black people and move them into (primarily white) Orange County, which McCarthy called "a crude distortion of my proposals." Overall, McCarthy spoke of his work on many issues as a Senator while Kennedy asserted that he took them on firsthand as Attorney General.

For practical purposes, stylistic characteristics may have exceeded those of policy. Robert Donovan delineated the differences between the two men in a Los Angeles Times write-up. Donovan wrote that, "McCarthy spoke quietly and easily, looking professional and benevolent to his fingertips. Kennedy's – was modest, studiously eradicating the notion that he is arrogant. He was careful not to appear any more ruthless say, than Lawrence Welk, whose show preceded the debate on ABC." Donovan added how "Kennedy's hair had a distinctly gray tone on a colored television, which made him look somewhat more mature than pictures often portray him."

In losing the state 46-41%, McCarthy actually took more counties (38 to RFK's 20) but Kennedy's win came through a coalition of African-Americans and low-income voters. While the victory was not conclusive, Kennedy had won the key prize. He of course would not live to savor it. There was the small matter of the Democratic Convention in Chicago. "I said before the vote we were not going to win, and there was no point in having the student delegations in the streets thinking we could."

In speech after speech, McCarthy had told followers to "be intensely and deeply political, more fully citizens than you have ever been in the past." Yet after Chicago, McCarthy's backing of Humphrey was nearly non-existent. After the convention, he embarked on a ten-day vacation on the Mediterranean coast of France, then covered the World Series for *Life* magazine. However, he still wasn't ready to come forward. He said he owed it to the youths who backed him to extract more concessions but Humphrey biographer Edgar Berman said he never interacted with them. He was alone.

In the last week of the campaign, McCarthy issued a begrudging endorsement of his former Senate colleague saying he has "a better understanding of our domestic needs and a stronger will to act." He mentioned "scaling down the arms race and reducing military tensions." Humphrey lost by a hair. Many of his supporters, including Tip O'Neill, a McCarthy friend, called the tepid and late endorsement costly. Clark, his own campaign manager said "Somehow in 1968, McCarthy was unable to do what had to be done to get the results he sought. He wasted weeks campaigning in the primaries against Bobby Kennedy, the interloper, not Johnson/Humphrey and the war. He made no effort to reassemble the anti-war coalition after Kennedy died." The day after Nixon's win, a cold and damp day in the nation's capital, McCarthy perhaps realized his mistake in prolonging getting aboard the Humphrey bandwagon. He told a *New York Times* reporter that it was "a day for visiting the sick and burying the dead. It's grey everywhere—all over the land." By early 1969, it became clear that McCarthy's image would cause his influence to evaporate. He surrendered his seat on Foreign Relations to the more hawkish Gale McGee and announced that he would give up his Senate seat in 1970. He obviously sensed that the DFL was frustrated by him.

McCarthy was not ready to let go of the Presidential bug in 1972 but the magic was gone. He didn't bother entering New Hampshire and Wisconsin was a huge disappointment. So he soon withdrew.

In 1976, McCarthy mounted another run for the White House. This time, however, he ran in the general election as an Independent. His presence likely deprived Jimmy Carter of a loss in Iowa, Maine, and Oregon (the latter of which the Georgia Governor fell short by 1,700 votes). The tipping point was probably New York. McCarthy was ruled off the ballot in the Empire State late in the campaign but had his name stayed on, most pundits believed the state—and the election—would have tipped in favor of Ford. Four years later, he shocked many by endorsing Ronald Reagan. "Mr. Carter quite simply abdicated the whole responsibility of the presidency while in office. He left the nation at the mercy of its enemies at home and abroad. He was the worst president we ever had." After failures to win the Presidency, McCarthy decided to aim lower. He returned to Minnesota and sought the DFL nomination to challenge incumbent Republican Dave Durenberger, but he lost to Mark Dayton. In 1992, McCarthy once again sought the Democratic nomination for President but, due to his poor standing, he was prohibited from debates (he did appear with other candidates on the *Donahue* show where he bizarrely spent much time quoting the Bible).

In his spare time, McCarthy was a master of poetry and a book he published near the end of his life, *Parting Shots from My Brittle Bow: Reflections on American Politics and Life*, put his work into print. He died in 2005 at age 89.

The Last Liberal in Oklahoma:
Senator Fred Harris

Historic Tidbit: At the traditional coffee with the incoming and departing Presidential administrations, Nixon turned to Hubert Humphrey and deadpanned sarcastically, "Why don't you make it for me, Hubert." Nixon had edged Humphrey in an extraordinarily close race and Humphrey may not have seen the humor in that remark. But he had a ready-made response: "I planned to Dick but you kind of got in my way."

Today, the thought of a liberal Senator from Oklahoma is highly laughable. The state gave President Obama his lowest margin in the nation, 33% in 2008, and his vote dropped in every county in the state compared to Kerry's in 2004. In 2012, only Utah and Wyoming gave Romney higher showings, and the state gave George W. Bush 66% in 2004. Further, Oklahoma has an all-Republican House delegation and two of the most tempestuously conservative members of the Senate who regularly get returned to office by sizable margins.

Photo courtesy of the U.S. Senate Historical Office

Suffice it to say, the "Sooner" State would sooner elect a dead bird than a live Democrat, let alone a liberal, but before Howard Dean's net roots, enthusiasm, and deeply committed followers, there was Fred Harris. For eight years beginning in 1964, Oklahoma was represented in the Senate by Fred Harris, a liberal Democrat turned Presidential candidate who provide a populist approach in a conservative state not seen since William Jennings Bryan.

To be sure, Harris was not elected as a liberal. He had become "well-acquainted" with highly esteemed Bob Kerr, a Democrat who had a national following and often became a thorn in the side of JFK, particularly in relation to his Medicare package. Harris himself opposed the bill in the Senate though as I'll explain later, that was only to keep a campaign promise and after waiting to see that passage was assured. Harris also initially backed the Vietnam War (which he later called "awful") and advocated for the closing of the Interstate Commerce Commission.

But that didn't mean Harris lacked idealism. His biographer, Richard Lowett, in the book *Fred Harris: His Journey From Liberalism to Populism*, noted how he won an Oklahoma State Senate seat at age 26 and became a powerful force for good government in Oklahoma. As Chair of the Economic and Industrial Development Committee, he pushed through expansion of financing of industrial plants and the Oklahoma Human Rights Committee.

Harris could clearly have been labeled a young man in a hurry, reflected by his bid for the Governorship in 1962 at age 32. He finished fifth in the primary. Perhaps he wanted to emulate Kerr, a Governor turned Senator who is recognized nationally as the panorama of what the "Sooner" State has become.

In his early years, Harris himself was a prototype of Oklahoma. Both of his parents were undereducated - his father had a third-grade education and his mother's stopped at grade eight. Harris said his dad started out as a farmer-laborer but "by the time I was in high school, made us a fair living as small-scale cattle trader, buying cattle locally and selling them at the stockyards in Oklahoma City." His mother was a house cleaner who ran the family home and clerked at auction sales. But work came naturally to young Fred who earned a dime a day starting at age five by "riding a horse or mule around and around to power a haybaler." This was an operation undertaken with his paternal grandfather and uncles and it earned them the name, the "Haybaling Harrises." The Senator notes he "continued working in the hay fields at more advanced jobs every summer until I was twelve." That was when he began wheat harvesting with his dad, a task that began in Oklahoma in May and ended in North Dakota in August.

Harris would undertake that ritual for nine summers. Other jobs in school: mowing lawns, paper routes, a janitor in a dry-goods store and finally a printer, Harris calls the latter "a trade I learned that paid my way through undergraduate school and law school at the University of Oklahoma." When he earned his degree, Harris formed his own firm, "Harris, Newcombe, Redman, and Doolin."

Photo via the Oklahoma State Digital Library

Kerr died suddenly in 1963 and ex-Governor J. Howard Edmondson was appointed to the seat, at which time another former Governor who also happened to be an Edmondson enemy, Raymond Gary, jumped into the race. Harris had no desire to seek the seat. He was looking at another bid for the Governorship and said he "had reason to believe that (Kerr) would have supported me for governor in 1964, had he still lived and I had then run." Meanwhile, Kerr's son initially decided to seek the Senate seat but soon realized that he was not cut out for politics and abandoned the race. It was at that point that Harris was pressed into running and because, "Kerr had said good things about me to his family and associates (and) that carried over and caused them to support me for the Senate." He would be facing Edmondson in the 1964 primary for the remaining two years of Kerr's seat and predictably trailed him in the runoff, but the anti-Edmondson forces came together and Harris won by an amazing 100,000 votes.

The general election was tougher. His opponent was Bud Wilkinson, the legendary football coach at UNO, and he was the favorite to win the seat. Amazingly, he had once been a JFK guy, and the President wanted him to lead his physical fitness initiative (Wilkinson did not want to give up coaching). He would be solidly for Nixon four years later. But Harris recalls that Harris' All-American background provided Oklahomans a lift following "the Dust-Bowl and tornadoes." That lift was expected to land him in the U.S. Senate. It did not.

Harris campaigned on LBJ's coattails with the slogan "Harris-LBJ All the Way" (which may have been the only time LBJ was second to anyone). The President responded: "Send me Fred Harris and we'll bring home the bacon and tack the coons to the wall." It was also where Johnson famously declared, "There are people who want us to go North in Vietnam but I don't think American boys should do what the Vietnamese won't." Johnson was applauded but Harris recalled that less than a year later, Johnson indeed decided to go North.

Wilkinson attacked Harris' attendance record in the Senate, vowing to put Oklahoma "first, not forty-first," but Dick Pryor, in a piece for the Oklahoma Education Television Authority, observed years later that Strom Thurmond backing Williamson had "helped turn black voters against him." Thurmond had campaigned in Oklahoma and though it was in areas that were receptive to George Wallace, "not only did that turn off black voters but it scared the daylight out of a lot of other people." Harris eked out a 21,000-vote victory. Still, the tenor was so clean that Oklahoma's senior Senator, Mike Monroney, commented to Johnson on audio tapes just after the election that the race had seen "no kinds of smear" and that *The Daily Oklahoman* said they ran the cleanest race in the history of the state." Still, Monroney acknowledged to Johnson that "we would have lost the damn thing" had he not run so strongly.

Harris got to work in the Senate, employing his then-wife LaDonna (to this day a force in women's advancement and Indian Rights) as an aide. Medicare put him in an early and unexpected conundrum. He years later recalled he wanted "more than ever to provide medical care for old people." The problem was that during the campaign, two main bills had been pending on that issue: a version of Kerr-Mills and King-Anderson. Few knew which bill would emerge from the conference committee ad Harris told voters that while he supported Kerr-Mills, he'd oppose King-Anderson. By 1965, Kerr's passing dramatically reduced leverage from his supporters and King-Anderson emerged from committee. A despondent Harris said he "was presented with a choice between the King Anderson bill or nothing" and studiously began pouring over the bill. But at the end of the day, he "felt that I could not in good conscience vote just the opposite of what I had promised during my campaign." Still, he "waited to the end of the Senate roll call to be sure that the King-Anderson bill was going to pass overwhelmingly, then voted no." He adds he "always regretted that I had no choice but to vote that way."

Medicare aside, Harris backed the entire "Great Society." He sponsored the National Foundation for Social Sciences with Walter Mondale and the Rural Job Development Act. A main accomplishment was shepherding through a bi-partisan bill that would give the Carlson National Forest to the native people of the Taos Pueblo. This was during the Nixon administration and at the bill signing, Nixon said, "I can't believe I'm signing a bill sponsored by Fred Harris." He also advocated for the elimination of the Interstate Commerce Commission, a position that put him at odds with most fellow Democrats.

In 1966, Democrats were losing seats nationally and many thought Harris might be among the casualties. He hung on 53-47%. He was attacked for opposing Dirksen on school prayer. Harris responded that no issue in recent years has so divided persons of "sincere religious faith." He vowed to make it clear that "voluntary prayer is permitted . . . consistent with the separation of church and state."

Harris was very close to his 1964 classmate Bobby Kennedy as well as to Hubert Humphrey. In a town known for its cliques, Harris once recalled *Time* citing him as the "only person in Washington DC who could have breakfast with Lyndon Johnson, lunch with Hubert Humphrey, and dinner with Bobby Kennedy."

In 1968, Humphrey toyed seriously with offering Harris the vice-presidential slot. Had he picked him, Humphrey may have been able to galvanize disillusioned liberals, many of whom did not get aboard until the last minute. In explaining his decision to tap Harris' colleague, Ed Muskie of Maine (whom Harris nominated at the convention), Humphrey explained, "I went for the quiet man. I know I talk too much, and I wanted someone who makes for contrast in style. Two Hubert Humphreys may be one too many." Harris did get a consolation prize, however. As the Democratic Party standard bearer, Humphrey got to choose the Democratic National Chair, and he picked Harris. In a sense, he got to practice what he preached with the Kerner Commission.

Left photo courtesy of News 9; Right photo via the Carl Albert Congressional Center, University of Oklahoma

Harris appointed a Reform Commission, naming Senator George McGovern as it's chair, made up its membership in such a way as to assure the reforms which they would eventually come up with - full democratization of the Party in all its processes and elections and requiring full representation of women and minorities, neither of which had been the case earlier" It was the greatest satisfaction of his career.

However, the Kerner Commission (better known as the National Advisory Commission on Civil Disorders) was what really catapulted Harris to national prominence. Appointed by Johnson, the report produced findings citing "white racism," which Harris called "the greatest dispute since the Civil War." It led to a bill that Harris would back that called for independent screening of social science projects and the image they would create abroad.

Harris knew that his future in Oklahoma was non-existent after his senior colleague Mike Monroney lost his seat in 1968. In stumping for him, he noted the benefits of government programs even for a state that bemoaned liberalism. It was clear that he was not ready to follow his state's lead on the road to conservatism.

Harris backed Ted Kennedy for Senate Majority Whip, despite pressure from "southwestern oil magnates," as his biographer Lowett wrote. A *Congressional Quarterly* survey showed him as having a "zero" rating from conservative groups. He opposed Richard Kleindienst's nomination as Attorney General in the Nixon administration, contending the Justice Department had already caused an "inordinant concentration of economic power" for failing to adequately enforce anti-trust protection laws.; he was the only Senator to vote against Lewis Powell's confirmation to the Supreme Court; he was one of just four to oppose Nixon's Economic Stabilization Act (pre-conference report); and he was a "nay" on Lockheed Emergency Loans. Not only was he a faithful warrior of Cesar Chavez but he traveled to Southhampton, New York to talk "to the rich and the superrich" to persuade them to get behind the mission. And a "sense of the Congress" resolution that Harris proposed stating the need for "student representation on the governing boards of colleges and universities" was approved 66–28.

Harris' support of the little people enabled him to focus on the rights of the Native-Americans in Alaska. In 1971, he and Ted Kennedy, introduced the Alaska Native Claims Settlement Act. Backed by the AFN, it would turn over more than 60 million acres of federal land to the Alaskan Indian, Aleut and Eskimp population and provide monetary restitution. Attempts in past Congresses to reach a settlement had proven fruitless and while changes were enacted on the way to passage (the final version awarded 40 million acres of land), the bill became law later that year. Another measure Harris introduced was the Ocean Mammal Protection Act.

Harris wisely chose not to seek re-election, which he likely would have lost. He had initially planned to seek the 1972 Presidential nomination and announced his candidacy in September of 1971 ("the issue is privilege"). Early on he asked, "What is more important to the American people than decent rates and sanitary housing and a good quality of education for the young people of this nation." Eventually, he began to gain a reputation. *The New York Times* featured a piece that read, "All he talks about are human issues" and a write-up by local press following a speech to the Pennsylvania State Democratic Committee called him the most "impassioned," but Tom Wicker may have most succinctly captured it: "it is the populist style that gives Fred Harris his chance - if any."

Image via politicalmemorabilia.com

Initially, it appeared Harris might find great appeal. Sam Brown, coordinator of the "Dump Johnson" movement and Vietnam Moratorium Committee, signed on as a campaign coordinator in six states. He wanted his appearances to feature "normal" people, but soon realized that McGovern had "pre-empted our progressive side of the Democratic field." That also made fundraising difficult and Harris withdrew from the election 2 1/2 months later.

Harris again sought the Democratic nod in 1976 and had Jim Hightower, the future-Texas Agriculture Secretary serve as his campaign manager (Hightower, a humorist and author would be the last genuine populist elected in his own state). Harris went around the country in a camper because he wanted it to be a depiction of the way "people lived." His campaign was largely grassroots. Much of his staff was unpaid. His hosts threw barbecues on his behalf and he stayed in supporters' homes, giving his hosts an IOU, a card that was to be "redeemable for one night's stay in the White House upon his election."

By then, there was no ambiguity as to his liberalism. He spoke of an "institutionalize idealism," and a "New Populism" which would be his slogan. He said, "the two groups who respond most enthusiastically to what I say are wage-earning workers and blacks." He told Maureen McDonald that the biggest problem plaguing his campaign was the "viability crisis." He championed a massive jobs program, breaking up oil companies and "taking the rich off welfare." He elaborated that "by that I mean stopping these tax subsidies to the Lockheeds, the Penn Central, the timber industry, the oil and gas crowds, we can get this country back to work." He advocated a graduated tax loopholes and credited the "primary problem of inflation" to monopolies.

Initially, Harris had little reason to be discouraged. The field was wide open and Harris actually finished first with nearly 40% at the Presidential caucus of Citizens for Participation in Political Action. But he had assets that could have helped him with those barriers.

Martin Schram, author of *Running for President: A Journal of the Carter Campaign* reveals that crowd applause was loudest for Harris. *Newsweek* portrayed him as "coming across as the best stump speaker in the field and the candidate (along with Wallace), who has the most deeply committed supporters." They cited 100 Boston cab drivers who signed up to pitch Harris to their passengers. Harris may well have been the most liberal candidate, but in a field that included fellow liberals Birch Bayh, Morris Udall, and Sarge Shriver to name a few, there was little room for him to break out.

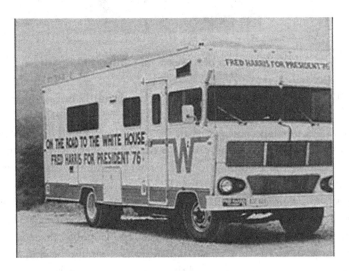

Photo courtesy of News 9

Harris did take 10% in Iowa and 11% in New Hampshire, edging out Shriver in the latter, but that was good enough only for 4th place. He got just 7% in Massachusetts a week later. Down South, there was little ground to be had, for much of it belonged to Carter or Wallace. And there was Lloyd Bentsen.

The Texas Senator had barely an asterisk in polls nationally but was challenging Harris in his own backyard. And that proved embarrassing. Carter edged Harris in Oklahoma; Harris still dismissed the idea that he couldn't win but, by Pennsylvania, he was scaling back his hopes to winning "some" delegates. After New Hampshire, he quipped, "I guess the little people weren't tall enough to reach the voting levers. Maybe next time we should provide stools." He would've needed many.

After that folded, Harris packed up his camper and moved to New Mexico, a state somewhat more conducive to his views. At 84, he teaches at the University of New Mexico. He remains active in local affairs and never hesitates to speak out on what he believes in.

A typical campaign stop
Photo courtesy of T.S. Eggleston

There were a few other liberals in Oklahoma during that era. Carl Albert remained Speaker and Congressman Mike Synar famously defied his "Little Dixie" constituents on everything from guns to grazing fees, but eventually his luck ran out as well and he lost the 1994 primary to a conservative. But they did not hold statewide posts. As a sign of how the state changed, even Michael Dukakis had carried a few Congressional districts.

Harris published a memoir, with the title derived from a favorite saying: *Does People Do It?* As for the Presidential run, Harris would say, "I'm glad I did. Just as I'd thought, even a good, though unsuccessful, campaign for president can have important influence toward progressive policies." His sentiment for his Senate record was similar. "We made real progress on the twin problems of poverty and racism, but not as much as I would have liked."

For Iowa Senator Hughes, A Field of Dreams Story

Historic Tidbit: One evening, Milton Eisenhower, brother of the President, was at a cocktail party when a blue-blooded woman approached him. Thinking the Eisenhowers were Jewish, she told him, "what a pity it is that you think the Eisenhowers are Jewish," to which Milton replied, "Ah, Madam. What a pity it is that we are not."

Photo Courtesy of the U.S. Senate Historical Office

When George W. Bush was campaigning for the Presidency, much was made of his past struggle with alcohol. In fact, Bush was not the first Presidential candidate to make that revelation. Harold Hughes, a Governor turned Senator from Iowa, had waged a similar battle, and while he never came close to attaining the office (he withdrew after four months), his story was perhaps a "Field of Dreams" of sort, for he nonetheless became among the most successful politicians in Iowa. His personal story, physical bent, and struggles made him a character few could match.

For starters, much was made of the fact that that Hughes had a very intimidating public frame. He was 6 foot 2, 235 pounds, a truck driver, and, as *U.S. News and World Report* observed, "a barrel-chested man." He was nicknamed "Pack" for pachyderm. *The Cedar Rapids Gazette* called him "an orator with a booming voice and keenly honed rhetoric." Donald Kaul of the *Des Moines Register* opined that only Martin Luther King, Jr., was a better speaker. Hughes used this gift to raise the pride of his state to soaring levels.

While Herschel Loveless had served the state as a successful Democratic Governor just two years prior to Hughes' election, it was Hughes who was thought to have built up the party. Author and Professor Joseph Frazier Wall said Hughes "gave the state its most exciting and progressive administration" in some time. The fact that Hughes had once been a Republican made that even more remarkable. One reason may have been that, as ABOUT.com (a site devoted to alcoholism), described, his speaking style was "eloquent and forceful," and he had a personal, genuine approach with voters few others could match. One person said, "When he walked into the room, he doesn't make you feel comfortable like, 'Here's a pal' - he makes you feel there is a very special presence in the room."

Iowa Congressman Mike Blouin went even further, saying upon his death that "in five minutes, he could bring tears to the strongest person in an audience." And Bonnie Campbell, a future Iowa Attorney General who worked for Hughes in his Senate days called his gift "an uncommon ability to figure people out" She called him, "extremely candid," noting that characteristic is "shocking thinking about him as a politician."

Hughes' daughter recalls the family driving to Miami for a Governor's Conference without any security. Kyle Munson, in a piece for the *Des Moines Register* wrote how "Hughes on a weekend loved to slip on a ratty hat and sunglasses and sneak down to the Des Moines River to fish anonymously among the locals."

Image courtesy of politics1.com

A piece by Myra McPherson described Hughes as "complex, moody, quick-tempered, stubborn, dad honest, and bright." He was the first Democratic Governor to tell Johnson - to his face no less - that the Vietnam War was a mistake

(Hughes ironically had seconded the nomination of LBJ in 1964 and had called his Vietnam policy in 1965 the only one "for those who despise totalitarianism and love freedom." But his change of herart led Hughes to place in nomination Gene McCarthy at the Democratic Convention. McCarthy, he said, had "caused a clean wind of hope to blow across this land . . . The People found Gene McCarthy for us. They found him; they followed him; they have urged him on us. He is more accurately the people's candidate than any other man in recent history."

Hughes' past is noteworthy. Having grown up without electricity until the age of 13, he served in World War II as an infantryman, where he was thought to be the largest man in his unit. He would call himself a "college dropout and a drunk with a jail record" (he once beat up the town sheriff while consumed by alcohol). Or as Hughes put it, "a drinking but functioning alcoholic."

Hughes supported his family by pumping gas and doing construction work, but his profession was mostly driving trucks for the Iowa Motor Truck Association. But in 1955, he founded the Iowa Better Trucking Bureau which, in the words of *Congressional Quarterly*, would "serve small truckers and compete with the large trucking association." Recreational shooting was also a part of his life as Hughes' daughter, Phyllis Hughes Ewing, recalled "the only room in our house where you could stand and not see guns was the bathroom." But even with his fondness for guns, Hughes urged Iowans not to resist minimal laws regulating their use. "People who hunt should lead the way," he said. "Registration is a minor inconvenience to pay for saving human lives."

But Hughes' battle with alcohol would define his early life. It started when he drank "some bathtub juice called Cream of Kentucky" at age 16 and raged on. A bout with malaria and nightmares was said to have exacerbated it. It wasn't until 1952 that a "deep spiritual experience" caused him to quit. Bonnie Campbell "forged through obstacles that would've stopped other people" and it took shape pretty quickly. A few years later, he was as Iowa Senator Tim Harkin would observe years later, "a rough-hewn, young Iowa truck-driver . . . a disgruntled fellow." Park Rinard changed that.

Rinard was a master of Democratic causes who was listening to Hughes gripe about issues involving truck regulation, particularly the monopolies he felt the big companies held. Rinard told Hughes to do something about it. So in 1958, he ran for the Iowa Commerce Commission. It was a splendid year for Democrats nationwide, including Iowa, where opportunities for the party had been less than prosperous (they were also winning three Congressional seats). Two years later, he sought the Democratic nomination for Governor but failed to get the nomination. However, in 1962, he tried again and unseated first-term Republican incumbent Norman Erbe. Erbe accused Hughes of "filling the air with fiscal buzz" and conducting his campaign "on a platform of political wisecracks." But voters liked his style by a solid 53-47% margin.

Two young, charismatic and gifted politicians
Photo via the Harold Hughes Papers, University of Iowa Libraries, Iowa City, Iowa

Bob Saigon, a trusted aide who worked on Hughes' Presidential campaign, said he "simply scooped the state government up in his huge hands and dropped it into the middle of the twentieth century." He signed the liquor-by-the-drink law which said that while beer could be sold over the counter, anything else had to be sold in licensed places. He fought to consolidate 140 state agencies to one-fifth of that number and give home-rule to localities. He increased school aid, established vocational education and junior schools and, perhaps mindful of his past, used his skills to persuade businesses to give tax credits to ghetto youths.

In other areas, Hughes worked on the legal code and presided over the abolishment of the death penalty. And he was able to win enactment of a Human Rights Commission and anti-discrimination measures in housing and employment. *Congressional Quarterly* notes that though Hughes refunded tax relief to the elderly, he "refused to grant taxpayers a rebate when a surplus accrued in the state treasury. Instead, he channeled the surplus funds into health, education and welfare programs."

The remarkable thing was that Democrats did not control the legislature at that time which accounts for one reason Hughes was unsuccessful at enacting his entire agenda, including an attempt to lower the voting age to 18. Hughes also endeared himself to the common Iowan by setting up office hours for any citizen to meet with him and discuss any topic/problem, etc. Campbell adds that today, "it would almost be unthinkable."

Hughes did not reveal his past struggles until he was seeking his second term as Governor. In his 1964 re-election campaign, Hughes' GOP opponent raised the issue of his alcoholism in a debate. Hughes acknowledged he is "an alcoholic and will be until the day I die . . . But with God's help I'll never touch a drop of alcohol again. Now, can we talk about the issues of this campaign?"

Hughes was immensely popular, perhaps due to his bluntness. One example was to a group of Methodist ministers: "I'm tired of you people preaching Love on Sunday, and Hate on Monday, Tuesday, Wednesday."

Cooking in front of the Iowa Statehouse and inspecting his beloved 1965 Mustang
Photos courtesy of the Harold Hughes Papers,
University of Iowa Libraries, Iowa City, Iowa

He probably would have thrived more in this era, for he openly boasted of favoring the legalization of marijuana. Bob Novak asked him if it would impair judgment but Hughes replied "he had smoked it during the war, but got more of a kick from looking at the bottom of an empty whisky bottle." Hughes smoked three packs of cigarettes a day, which so exasperated his staff that Saigon said they once taped a couple of cigarettes to the mouth of a mounted animal that he had hunted.

After three terms and a popularity that was sky high, Bobby Kennedy encouraged Hughes to run for the Senate in 1968 (Bourke Hickenlooper was retiring and the seat was open). He did and spoke of the need for national health insurance. Hughes entered the cycle with a 20 point lead but, after a nip'n'tuck battle on Election Night, found himself squeaking past State Senator David Stanley by a mere 6,000 votes out of nearly 1 million cast (he was said to have taken the weekend before the election off for badly needed recreation). But Hughes may have also been hurt by the drubbing Hubert Humphrey was taking at the hands of Richard Nixon in Iowa, and for Stanley's efforts to link him to the radical peaceniks, accusing Hughes of favoring "peace at any price." In particular,

Stanley used the McCarthy endorsement against Hughes, presenting it at evidence that the Governor "moved to the left" when he "could have moved to the center." He attacked Hughes for his gun stance, the crime rate and spending, making the accusation on the latter that "Harold Hughes' unnecessary spending is leading Iowa into bankruptcy." The unexpectedly close margin detailed the difficulties of Iowa sending a Democrat to the Senate in those days.

Hughes (with his cigarette) loved fishing
Photo courtesy of the Harold Hughes Papers, University
of Iowa Libraries, Iowa City, Iowa

Unlike Bush, Hughes centered his Senate career on his battle with alcoholism (curiously, both became "Born Again"). Bemoaning the fact that "treatment is virtually nonexistent because addiction is not recognized as an illness," Hughes established Alcoholics Anonymous in his hometown of Ida Grove, Iowa.

However, his personal story led him to see the paradox upon taking office. "I had been elected to the Senate only 17 years after admitting that I was an alcoholic and reaching out for help. As my plane landed, I thought of the hundreds of thousands of men, women, and children who had never found help, many of whom lived as derelicts or had died tragically. I asked myself if one of the reasons I had been brought to Washington as a U.S. Senator was to represent those still suffering from addiction to alcohol and other drugs." Hughes bemoaned the fact that "treatment is virtually nonexistent because addiction is not recognized as an illness." It became a hallmark of his legislative portfolio. The Comprehensive Alcohol Abuse and Alcoholism Prevention, Treatment and Rehabilitation Act of 1970, which established the National Institute on Alcohol Abuse and Alcoholism were his bills. On a personal note, he and aides often "swapped drunk stories."

Saigon also said Hughes, who had many Jewish colleagues, had a deep interest in the religions of others. He asked one staffer, "What does Judaism mean to you?" The reply was, "Lox and bagels on Sunday."

Hughes had been mulling over the possibility of a Presidential bid with a kitchen cabinet of six but, when he ultimately decided to go forward, he brought on some seasoned folks. He began attending Senate prayer breakfasts to cultivate some of the more conservative Democrats, and as Means said, he avoided the "l" words (liberal), saying he wished to be viewed more as a populist like "William Jennings Bryan."

Myra McPherson wrote in a piece that Hughes could "preach peace to the hard hats and the Bible to kids and get away with it." He raised about $250,000 but he was hampered by low name recognition outside Iowa (perhaps a win in his home state could have propelled him to fame, though as Tom Harkin would show two decades later, it failed to amount to much after). Hughes was out by July of 1971, well before primary season began

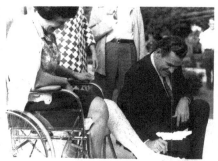

Signing a woman's cast and visiting Japan
Photo courtesy of the Harold Hughes Papers, University
of Iowa Libraries, Iowa City, Iowa

After he abandoned his White House run, Hughes said he did so largely because he could not focus on his legislative agenda. "My legislative efforts have been hampered and my public statements have been discounted by the imputation of presidential motives." But he also was quite uncomfortable asking for money and with low name recognition, he was also thought to be at a disadvantage because, though his Democratic and anti-war credentials were solid, the field was dominated by many such men. The fact that he was a spiritualist also seemed to have hampered his bid. He did say, though, that if the vice-presidency were offered, "he would be forced to give it serious consideration." Eventually, Hughes endorsed Ed Muskie over his far more dovish colleague, George McGovern, a reminder that an ideological soulmate doesn't necessarily circumvent personal friendships.

Hughes easily could have held his Senate seat in 1974 but chose not to seek re-election, instead choosing to focus on the Harold Hughes Religious Center and becoming a Disciple of Christ. He said the nation needed a "spiritual revival." Saigon tried to talk him out of it, saying "there are people in this country who don't even know who you are, that really need you." And with that, the rest of the nation was exposed to Harold Hughes more than they likely ever would have been had he stayed in the White House race. A post by *AA History Lovers* said *Parade* had him on the cover, *The Washington Post* did a big story, and *The Saturday Evening Post* devoted nearly five thousand words to the decision.

**Hughes visited Vietnam (left) and backed Eugene
McCarthy in part over the issue in 1968
Photo courtesy of the Harold Hughes Papers, University
of Iowa Libraries, Iowa City, Iowa**

Beyond his struggle with alcohol, Hughes' personal life had more than a few tribulations. He lost one daughter to cancer during his Senate term and another in the 1980s. And in 1996, he had been ordered to pay alimony to the wife of 45 years he had divorced (he married his secretary). Hughes died of emphysema that year at the age of 74. And his life and was as productive as multiple number of pols in one career. His Senate successor, Democrat John Culver called him "an extraordinary man in terms of his humble orgins, in terms of his family and education." He adds that Hughes was "a man of enormous integrity."

It would be 30 years before another Democrat would serve as Governor of Iowa.

**Hughes with fellow Senators Humphrey, Muskie, Bayh and McGovern
– all viewed as possible Presidential candidates for 1972**

Chisholm First Black Woman In Congress And To Be Placed In Nomination For President

Historic Quote: "LBJ now means, Let's Back Jack." – A congratulatory telegram from Lyndon Johnson to JFK after the latter secured the Democratic nomination for President. It was on the basis of that telegram that the Massachusetts Senator decided to meet with Johnson about the vice-presidency.

Chisholm's official House portrait
Image courtesy of the Collection of the U.S. House of Representatives

For African-Americans and for women, Shirley Chisholm was a true trail blazer. Not only was she the first African-American woman to serve in the House of Representatives, but in 1972, she'd become the first black Presidential candidate to have her name placed in nomination for the Presidency. Many would call it the nomination. She stood no chance of gaining the nomination and she readily admitted as much. But she waged as credible and dogged a run as any of her 12 other mail rivals and made a tremendous contribution. Not to mention, she won some delegates.

Chisholm's Presidential nomination may get overlooked in the history books, but her election to Congress broke a major barrier. She was the first African-American woman to be elected to Congress and she hired an all-female staff, half of whom were black.

Chisholm, who went to school in Barbados, received her Master's in Education from Columbia and worked in a nursery school before going on to direct a child care center, before serving in the New York State Assembly for four years. When she opted to seek a newly created Brooklyn Congressional seat in 1968, her slogan was "Unbought and Unbossed." When she won, she said, "Just wait, there may be some fireworks." She didn't disappoint.

Many of us Congressional scholars have heard the famous story of Chisholm's assignment to the Forestry Committee of the House Agriculture Committee. Agriculture was about as important to Brooklyn as pizza was to Texas, and Chisholm was not amused. "Apparently all they know here in Washington about Brooklyn is that a tree grew there. Only nine black people have been elected to Congress, and those nine should be used as effectively as possible." She slammed Wilbur Mills, who led the steering committee (ironically, he threw his hat into the ring in '72 as well). Chisholm was eventually able to add Education and Labor to her other assignment, Veterans Affairs was her other assignment.

In the House, Chisholm's advocacy was on behalf of poor mothers and a bill she sponsored would have provided day care to mothers. The bill passed the House but was vetoed by President Nixon. Chisholm's eloquence was reserved for issues that affected her constituency and it was on full display during a House vote to ban busing in late 1971. "Racism," she said, "is so inherent in the bloodstream of this country that you cannot see beyond a particular limit. You are only concerned when whites are affected. I say to the members: Where were you when the black children were being bused right past the white schools in the community? Come out from behind your mask. Forget they are white children. Just remember one thing. They are America's children."

Chisholm also had stern feelings on when Congress was debating student disruptions on college campuses. Congress, she said, "cannot solve the problem of campus unrest. We should not, if we could. Instead, we should listen to what our children—the students—are saying." She advocated aid to students to remedy the situation.

But it was busing that truly stoked her anger. When Republicans were debating an emergency funding measure to aid schools, Chisholm looked square in the eye of the chamber's Minority Leader, Gerald Ford and gave him a verbal lashing. She called racism "so inherent in the bloodstream of this country that you cannot see beyond a particular limit. You are only concerned when whites are affected. Where were you when the black children were being bused right past the white schools in the community? Come out from behind your mask. Forget they are white children. Forget they are black children. Just remember one thing. They are America's children."

In 1972, Congress was debating the Equal Opportunity Education Act. The proposal was unique in that a portion would prohibit busing except to perhaps the next term. Chisholm called the name of the bill a "subterfuge" and, "an anti-busing measure designed to fit an election year bandwagon." What more is necessary? The victim – the American child has been knocked down. Must he be kicked also?

It was in late 1971 that Chisholm decided to go for the big prize. The fact that she was in the midst of her second House term took a back seat to the criticism, that unlike Barbara Jordan who had yet to be elected, Chisholm wasn't a major player on her committees. And she seemed to be under no illusion that she might actually win the nomination. But her candidacy was meant to "to give a voice to the people the major candidates were ignoring." Furthermore, it was designed to guarantee that the ultimate winner of the nomination "will not be a white, inside decision." In that vein, she hoped to excite the young voters and the ratification of the Amendment giving 18 year olds the right to vote would mean that there were plenty more to go around.

Still, Chisholm took part in the Presidential debates. On Vietnam, she wouldn't negotiate for the release of POW's because she felt it could delay the end of the war. She withheld a promise to support the eventual Presidential nominee because she said she wanted to "try to keep them honest at the convention."

On the trail, Chisholm derided the "tired and glib cliches." While acknowledging her odds were "hopeless," she hoped to "demonstrate the sheer will and refusal to accept the status quo." But she made clear she could do the job. "I could serve as President of this country, believe it or not."

Florida was a major focus of her attention. But she had little money for professional staff and she finished with just three percent. But there was a little reward. Only Chisholm and ex-North Carolina governor (and later Senator) Terry Sanford had entered the New Jersey primary. Chisholm won, making her the first female to win any primary.

Images via ronwadebuttons.com

John Nichols of *The Nation* would write Chisholm's run was dismissed from the start as a vanity campaign that would do nothing more than siphon votes off from better-known anti-war candidates such as South Dakota Senator George McGovern and New York City Mayor John Lindsay. They were not ready for a candidate who promised to "reshape our society," and they accorded her few opportunities to prove herself in a campaign where all of the other contenders were white men."

When George Wallace was shot, Chisholm went to visit him. She recounts him asking, "What are your people going to say." She replied, "I know what they're going to say. But I wouldn't want what happened to you to happen to anyone.' He cried and cried and cried."

Despite the fact that everyone knew Chisholm would not be the nominee (many openly hoped she could get the vice-presidential nod), she stayed in the race to the convention. She was hoping to play power broker of sorts. Eventually, Humphrey released his black delegates to Chisholm. And she got 151 delegates and had her name placed in nomination.

After her Presidential bid, Chisholm returned to the House with greater respect, and dove head first into her legislative responsibilities. There would be no more overlooking her with bad assignments. Now, she would have a seat on the coveted Rules committee. And she successfully passed a bill that extended the minimum wage to domestic workers. Chisholm was one of four founders of the Women's Political Caucus (her New York colleague BellaAbzugwas another). She noted she "had met far more discrimination because I am a woman than because I am black."

Left photo courtesy of austinmccoy.wordpress.com; right photo courtesy of brooklyn rail.org

Chisholm continued serving in Congress until 1982, when she decided to retire. "I had been so consumed by my life in politics," she said. I had no time for privacy, no time for my husband, no time to play my beautiful grand piano. After he recovered, I decided to make some changes in my life. I truly believe God had a message for me."

Chisholm would eventually move to Florida and die on New Year's Day 2005 at 80. Robert Williams, president of the Flagler County NAACP called her "our Moses that opened the Red Sea for us."

And as for Chisholm on her own legacy: "I want history to remember me not just as the first black woman to be elected to Congress, not as the first black woman to have made a bid for the presidency of the United States, but as a black woman who lived in the 20th century and dared to be herself." Most importantly, "I'd like them to say that Shirley Chisholm had guts."

Vance Hartke:
Unknown and With Questionable
Donation, Run for President

Historic Tidbit: J. Harrold Carswell, Richard Nixon's rejected Supreme Court nominee, sought to do an in your face to his colleagues. The year he was rejected – 1970, Carrswell began seeking a U.S. Senate seat from Florida. This caused a number of schisms within the Republican Party. Carswell won several high profile endorsements, including from the state's Republican Senator Edward Gurney but he garnered just 34% on primary day, losing to Congressman Bill Cramer. But Republican disunity was one factor credited with helping "Walkin Lawton" Chiles take the seat.

S o what's a Senator to do who has been criticized for taking unquestionable loans and who holds on to his Senate seat by the hair on his chinny-vhin-chin? Run for President of course. That's what Vance Hartke did in 1972, just after his '70 re-election that was so close that it required voting machines to be impounded.

Photo courtesy of the John F. Kennedy Presidential Library and Museum

In announcing his candidacy, Hartke believed he would be the only candidate "to successfully handle the issues on an intellectual basis as well as a basis which people could still understand." His intellectualism didn't help him when it came to avoiding a bad deal or two, but Hartke could still make a reasonable claim to having a good handle on the issues. For he was very much a part of it.

Hartke was a liberal Senator's dream. A solid supporter of civil rights and the Great Society, he sponsored the Railway Safety Act and the Highway Safety Act, the latter which mandated the installation of seatbelts in cars. And as chair of the Surface subcommittee on Commerce, he can credibly claim to have helped get Amtrak rolling. Ditto with Head Start. And the expansion of student loan programs. A bill signed into law created the Executive Service Corps, which would assist Peace Corps affiliated businesses overseas. And he played a large role in the promotion of kidney dialysis.

Other endeavors went nowhere. Hartke wanted to increase Social Security benefits by 10% and, as a solid opponent of Vietnam, filed a bill creating the Department of Peace (fellow anti-war Midwesterner Dennis Kucinich introduced that bill four decades later), which even in a Vietnam mired environment seemed to attract little interest.

Additionally, he sponsored the Burke-Hartke act that would put quotas on items that foreign companies can make more cheaply in other nations. *The Almanac of American Politics 1974* notes that "Nader's Raiders" criticized Hartke's proposal for giving aid to railroad companies while maintaining subsidies for the trucking industry.

Hartke's first brush with bad publicity came from his 1964 acceptance of a $30,000 contribution from Spiegel Inc, a Chicago mail order house that was against rate increases for third class "junk" mail. In the next term, Hartke was given a seat on the Senate Postal Committee — at his request. He subsequently sponsored a proposal that would raise air mail rates and reduce the third class rate. His argument was that raising the third class rate could cause as many as 4.5 million people to lose their jobs. The Justice Department launched an investigation. Hartke called it "insulting" that any inference of a link was made.

Vance Hartke with the Mayor of Monticello, Indiana following a deadly tornado
Photo courtesy of the Monticello Herald Journal

Hartke was a lawyer who had served as Mayor of Evansville and gained notoriety for integrating the city's pool. But he arguably got lucky in his first two Senate runs. In 1958, he had the good fortune to be running in a heavily Democratic year and it didn't hurt that his opponent, Harold Handley, though the sitting Governor, was branded as "High Tax" Harold" for putting through tax increases. Hartke's had already impressed delegates to the state convention that spring by personally contacting most of the 2,122 delegates who would select the nominee. But his 56.5%, more than 14% above Handley, signified that Hartke succeeded in establishing credibility.

Hartke's second election, 1964, was an even better year for Democrats, as LBJ was sweeping Indiana and most of the nation. Hartke won 54%. 1970 was a little bit more difficult. In facts, weeks before voters went to the polls, Indiana Republicans were counting Hartke's seat as a likely pickup. His opponent was Congressman Richard Roudebush.

Hartke refused to go down without a fight. He cited Roudebush's four marriages and attacked him on Vietnam. He called Roudebush the Nixon White House's candidate, and Roudebush conceded that intervention to get his primary rival to withdraw came from "high places." That seemed to be backed up by a complaint to the FEC by the Hartke campaign demanding equal time to combat a televised Spiro Agnew appearance, which they claim Agnew made "inflammatory and untrue remarks." The second complaint was over an ad Roudebush ran that claimed Hartke had voted for a bill that would allow America to trade with "communist countries" that provided the Vietcong weapons they used to kill "American servicemen." He also called Hartke a "big spender."

On Election Night, despite being 4,000 votes behind at the end of counting, Roudebush appeared to claim the seat, saying "we have indicators that we have won. We are sitting here in anticipation of victory." But the margin held and Hartke claimed his third term by the skin of his teeth. Perhaps he viewed that as a mandate to go higher.

With Governor Reuben Askew of Florida during
his brief foray into Presidential politics
Courtesy of the State Archives of Florida, Florida Memory

Hartke's presidential bid, though denied by all parties, was thought to be something of a stalking horse for Hubert Humphrey, whose campaign Hartke would end up co-chairing. The theory was his presence was designed to take votes away from other liberal contenders to aid Humphrey. But Humphrey had long been a model for probity and the move would seem beneath him.

In 1976, Hartke attempted to override the odds again but didn't come close. In fact, his own party very nearly dumped him in favor of a freshman Congressman named Phillip Hayes, who, like Hartke, had the good fortune of winning office in a solid Democratic year (Hartke took 52%). But Richard Lugar, who had almost wrested Birch Bayh's seat from him two years earlier, beat Hartke by 19%, 59-40%. Hartke carried only Lake County (Gary). Only Rick Santorum's 18% loss in 2006 approached the level of a defeat for an incumbent Senator.

Image via ronwadebuttons.com

Trouble found Hartke later in life. In 1993, he had been lobbying for a casino company that supported a river-boat casino referendum. The day of the vote, he bought poll workers lunch and gave out souvenirs to voters. Hartke was indicted on a misdemeanor.

Hartke died in 1998 at 78. Other family members have tried to break into politics. In 2002, his grandson challenged GOP Congressman John Hostettler and came reasonably close to unseating him.

Lindsay, Yorty Very Different Mayors Who Sought '72 Democratic Presidential Nomination

Historic Tidbit: For nearly a decade, Frank Cummings was a chief aide to New York Senator Jacob Javits. One of his duties was to appoint Senate pages from New York State and at one point, he decided to do the virtually unprecedented by making one female a page. The Senator's wife Marion heard about this and asked Cummings how the girl would dress. Cummings replied in a dress. Mrs. Javits noted that because pages sit on a low floor by the desk, that would not be possible. But have no fear, she said. "Ralph and I will be flying down." The "Ralph" she was referring to was famed designer Ralph Lauren, with whom she was friends.

In the 1960s, two one-time Congressmen became mayors of America's two largest cities. One, John Lindsay of New York, was a Republican, albeit among the most liberal in the nation while the other, Sam Yorty of Los Angeles, was a Democrat, though only nominally. Both presided throughout a time of rapid demographic change in their cities and while Lindsay took radical means to improve race relations, Yorty resorted to divide-and-conquer rhetoric that created a major wedge between various groups. Because one switched parties well before the other, both were briefly Democratic Presidential candidates in 1972, but by the end of their careers, both had were firmly situated within their new identities. But their legacies in the cities they loved were decidedly mixed.

Lindsay (1921-2000)

Lindsay was every bit the patrician as his father was a wealthy investment banker who sent the future mayor to prep school. He was also a Yale man – having attained both his undergraduate and law degree there, and interrupted his studies to join the Navy where he took part in the invasion of Sicily and the Pacific theater. He won five battle stars.

Lindsay's first job out of law school was at the firm, Webster, Sheffield, Fleischmann, Hitchcock & Chrystie. In 1947, he was an usher at the wedding of George H.W. Bush's sister Nancy and it's where he'd meet his wife, Mary Lawrence, a teacher whose father was a prominent bank vice-president. It was not love at first site. Mary later revealed John didn't pay any attention to her but did say that, "when we knew each other a lot better, he said he had been assigned to be very nice to the groom's younger sister." But they grew closer and the rest was history. The young couple resided in Stuyvesant Town.

The future Mayor's political involvement began when he organized "Youth for Eisenhower." In 1958, when liberal Republicans were still capable of winning as many elections in Manhattan as Democrats, Lindsay captured a Congressional seat on the Upper West Side's "silk stocking" district (Mary hosted a number of coffees for him with voters). He initially sought a seat on the Foreign Affairs Committee but his fellow New York Republican, Katherine St. George, the delegation's leader, refused to entertain his request. She asked him, "You know what you'd be if you go on Foreign Affairs? You'd just be a cookie–pusher around Washington cocktail parties. You're a lawyer. Now go on a good committee where you can do something."

Throughout his career, Lindsay told folks, "I happen to be a Republican. I hope you won't hold it against me." But he was among the most liberal members of his caucus in the House, voting with Democrats on most of the pet issues. It was Lindsay who proposed the Department of Urban Affairs and it was he who, along with Maine Republican Stan Tupper, introduced a measure considered crucial to the enactment of the 1965 Medicare legislation that made the program voluntary. Lindsay provided the lone GOP vote against a measure that would allow the postal service to intercept obscene material and later, became one of two Republicans to oppose intercepting mail to communist countries. When a fellow Republican questioned him about his opposition, Lindsay replied: "The 17th district would be a depressed area."

Voting correctly by his constituents on nearly every issue made Lindsay enormously popular. He won re-election with 71% in 1964 as Barry Goldwater was getting bludgeoned in the district, though Kenneth Keating was beating Bobby Kennedy by twelve points even while losing statewide. Lindsay had refused to back Goldwater.

Congressman John Lindsay
Photo via the Library of Congress Prints and Photographs Division

In 1965, Lindsay threw his hat into the ring for the New York City Mayoralty. The Democratic nominee was New York City Controller Abe Beame (the race also included Bill Buckley as the Conservative nominee." Lindsay struck hard at the loss of 90,000 jobs in the city and in one ad, angrily blamed "harassment, bureaucracy, and red tape from City Hall," which he said Beame as Controller bore responsibility. He put out "white papers" on his solutions to dealing with major issues of the day and edged out Beame 45-42%. President Lyndon Johnson, in an effort to repay Lindsay for shunning Goldwater, offered only tepid backing for Beame. But it was s last-minute endorsement by Ed Koch that was considered a major factor in putting him over the top (the two would part ways when Lindsay wouldn't do the same for Koch in his 1968 bid for a Congressional seat). However, Lindsay had other major assets.

At 6'4, he looked like he was straight out of central casting which *The New York Times* lent credence to in calling him an "urbane, matinee-idol mayor, who hobnobbed with movie stars and battled the bureaucracy." Journalist Murray Kempton said he was "fresh and everyone else is tired." He was also called the "urban messiah." Mary was a major asset as well. Once described as, "smarter than 16 Yale men," one time campaign manager Robert Price called her, "a political force more powerful than patronage.'"

Hours into Lindsay's term, his star qualities were put to the test when a transit strike took place, one of many that would dog his administration (others would involve Broadway, sanitation workers, etc.) This one would drag on 13 days. When it was over, many felt the head of the Transport Workers of America, Mike Quill, had gotten the better of Lindsay, even from jail (he had been cited for contempt and other members of the union had to conduct the negotiating). The settlement was the first part of a spending image; so were increases in welfare spending. The city's budget went from $3.6 billion to $6.1 billion. Eventually, taxes rose heavily as well, but Lindsay tried to encourage efficiency by separating the city's 50 major departments into "super agencies."

Photo via wax-wane.com

During that strike, when Lindsay was forced to walk the four miles from his hotel room to City Hall, he proclaimed that, in spite of it, New York was still "a fun city." That comment was mimicked and so the concept for Lindsay's next endeavor became making clear that New York was under-utilized by ordinary citizens.

Many of the parks, concerts and festivities that make New York "the city that never sleeps" are because of Lindsay's efforts. For example, he opened a bicycle path on the Brooklyn Bridge, established the Mayor's Office of Film, Theater and Broadcasting, and campaigned to bring filmmaking back to the city. Mary, who would regularly be seen bicycling through Central Park, was also pivotal in that regard.

Lindsay had less success when it came to the "Ocean Hill-Brownsville" plan. This pilot resulted from a board Lindsay created that was designed to give more power to allocate more school resources evenly in wealthy and poor communities, in part by giving parents more control over hiring. It was called the "community control system." The result was a domino effect that led to the firing of 20 teachers, a strike by others as a protest, and ultimately a Supreme Court ruling that said there was no authority to remove these teachers. Because many of the teachers were Jewish, some saw the episode as a major factor in straining relations between Jews and blacks. Lindsay called this period, "the low point of my career."

Lindsay carrying his 1966 budget
Photo via the Library of Congress Prints and Photographs Division

Another Lindsay initiative that didn't go as planned was his attempt to create a Civilian Complaint Review Board, which he did by Executive Order. This allowed citizens to comment on their local police and Lindsay pushed his proposal at a campaign-style rally that was attended by U.S. Senators Jacob Javits and Bobby Kennedy (the latter somewhat reluctantly according to Deputy Mayor Richard Aurelio). The union sued and voters soundly rejected it. Given these setbacks, Lindsay's mantra that being mayor of the city of New York is "the second toughest job in America" was likely appropriate – and it is a description still in use today.

Despite Lindsay's privilege, he tried to come off as a man of the people and often, he'd walk the streets of ghettos. Mayoral Assistant Sid Davidoff would say that on a typical day, "my phone would ring and Lindsay would ask, 'Where are we walking tonight'" (Davidoff had often expected to have a night to himself). In order to maximize the authenticity of these visits, neither the police nor the press would be informed. One such visit came during the days following the assassination of Martin Luther King, Jr. Where other cities saw riots, Lindsay was credited with keeping things under control and was able to boast in his re-election campaign that, "we didn't have a Detroit or Watts or Newark." On top of that, Lindsay was often personally seen picking up city trash. He returned $5,000 of his salary.

Aside from serving as Deputy Mayor, Aurelio managed both Lindsay's re-election campaign and the '72 presidential race. He said his boss had "a terrific sense of humor," who in the office was "very calm, very loose, very relaxed." He also had "a lot of confidence in staff," and "trusted people to execute his ideas. Meanwhile, his national prominence very nearly propelled him to a spot on the national ticket. Ex-Pennsylvania Governor Bill Scranton started a "draft Lindsay for VP" movement, and many believe it would have gone to Lindsay had the pick been made 24 hours earlier. Whatever the case, Lindsay seconded the nomination of Maryland Governor Spiro Agnew – in those days still regarded as a moderate, with good grace.

A New York City sanitation strike impacted the city
Photo courtesy of Dennis Harper

Other problems Lindsay faced included the fact that people and businesses were leaving the city, forcing him to make up the revenue base with increased immigration and tax increases. And then there was the snowstorm. A blizzard in February of 1969 had dumped more than 15 inches of snow in the city but, more than a week later, portions of Queens had yet to be plowed. When Lindsay showed up, angry residents heckled him. But Aurelio called the criticism, "largely exaggerated by the media," and noted that much of the slow response had later been attributed to faulty equipment. That may have been validated by the fact that Lindsay actually carried that particular Queens precinct in his bid for re-election that year.

That campaign was anything but conventional. The primary outcomes of both parties were ideologically counter-intuitive. Lindsay faced a challenge from Staten Island State Senator John Marchi (pronounced MAR-key) who was far to his right. As if to demonstrate which demographic he was trying to appeal to, Marchi associated himself with figures nationally, both religious and political, who would never be mistaken as liberals. Marchi used the same ad agency – Foley&Wheeler, that had helped both Nixon and Goldwater and offered support to the Rev. Billy Graham in his effort to rein in pornography.

According to Aurelio, the Lindsay team had been planning to use the Liberal Party endorsement they had earlier received as a mechanism to winning a second term. "We knew we were the underdog in that primary because the Republican Party had very few registrants. Most of them were people who were not his base (blacks, Latinos and Jews)." Rather, the GOP of New York encompassed mostly ethnic Europeans. As it happened, Aurelio said the ultimate result was far closer than they had expected with Lindsay coming within a mere two percentage points of winning re-nomination on the Republican line.

The Democratic side meanwhile was a donnybrook that featured a split between two men from the liberal faction – ex-Mayor Robert Wagner and Manhattan Borough President Herman Badillo on the left, and City Controller Mario Procaccino on the right. Procaccino emerged from the fractious primary 33% to 29% for Wagner with Badillo an ounce behind with 28%

Still, Lindsay used the Liberal Party endorsement to proceed to November as planned and also managed to secure an Independent line. While some of his old coalition went to the other two contenders, Aurelio's realization of strong support from minorities proved prescient. Jewish groups were among them. Israeli Prime Minister Golda Meir was among Lindsay's many admirers and she vowed to assist him in any possible way. Chief of Staff Jay Kriegel, said they decided to use "a carefully calibrated visit" to New York to take her up on the offer and two such appearances were a rally in front of City Hall and a visit to a Sukkah in the parking lot of the Brooklyn Museum.

Lindsay's media campaign was first-rate, invoking a variety of powerfully memorable taglines. One featured a man saying, "Mayor Lindsay knew what the Navy Yard meant. He fought for three years to bring it back? Who knows," the man said, "maybe he'll bring back the Dodgers" as a number of former teammates in their uniforms cheered.

Another spot zeroed in on the issue of Sulfur dioxide and portrayed Lindsay as, "the first Mayor to fight for clean air - and he's starting to win." A beneficiary of Phoenix House taped a spot for the Mayor as well, with the narrator saying, "three years ago, there was no place for a kid like this to go - except to jail." Lindsay hit the issue of a commuter tax, telling New Yorkers, if they (out-of-towners) paid their share, you wouldn't have to pay it for them." And yet another spot focused another spot on parents of veterans. Estimating that city residents were paying three billion from city residents for the Vietnam War, Lindsay looked into the camera and said, "We're not only sending them our money, we're sending them our sons." Every ad ended with, "the second toughest job in America line," but Lindsay said, "The things that go right are what make me want it."

Equally effective may have been the fact that Lindsay did not shy away from issuing mea culpas- and the improbable victory of the '69 Mets gave him an even more fortuitous platform from which to do so. In one ad, he said, "I guessed wrong on the weather and that was a mistake…the strike went on too long and we all made mistakes." But he proceeded to lay out many of his accomplishments, pausing for emphasis after each and adding, "those were no mistakes." Then in an act of brilliance, he said, "For one afternoon this fall, a baseball team brought this city together. New Yorkers forgot all about their differences….It showed me how close our city can be. If anyone tries to tell you it can't be done, remember the Mets. If they can do it, we can do it."

Knowing that he and Procaccini were courting many of the same voters, Marchi referred to the Democrat as Lindsay's "silent, acquiescent partner until recently." Lindsay rebutted by noting the "reactionary elements" in the Republican Party "that seek to destroy the progressive traditions of Republicanism in New York." Neither was Marchi helped by a penchant for malapropisms. He said Lindsay symbolized, "delusions of adequacy." Appealed to "the basest instincts of our society," and were "verbal muggers."

On Election Day, Manhattan again came through for Lindsay in a career saving way as the borough gave him 67% (Queens favored him by a hair while he lost the Bronx by a similar margin) and Lindsay prevailed 42-35%. Procaccino won Brooklyn and took 35% overall while Marchi received just 22% though he did manage to carry Staten Island with 62%. At his inauguration on New Year's Eve, Lindsay lamented the tumult of the 1960s: "This is the last day of the decade and we have, all of us, been through much hope and much sorrow. And if we have learned anything from these 10 turbulent, unsettling years, we have learned not to assume too much, because assumptions have a way of falling before the merciless assault of facts. So it is best not to plan on promises and dreams."

Lindsay had prevailed but his relations with his old team, including Nelson Rockefeller, deteriorated (Aurelio said that "during his first term, they had their battles (but) like all Mayor-Governor relationships, it was generally under control." While the Governor had been present for Lindsay's re-election announcement (even adding to Lindsay's incredulity that he encouraged it), he refused to offer his support after the primary. Lindsay confidantes actually thought he had recruited Marchi to challenge Lindsay. The following year, Lindsay essentially returned the favor by backing Rockefeller's opponent, Democrat Arthur Goldberg for Governor. By the end of the following year, Lindsay – disillusioned with Nixon's stance on social issues and the Vietnam War, had become a Democrat himself (just a few years earlier, Mary had said to a friend, "Can you imagine anyone being a Democrat?"). But shortly thereafter, he was running for the White House.

Upon announcing his candidacy, Lindsay chided the other candidates in the race, most of whom were members of the U.S. Senate. "It's time that the people had a chance to send somebody to Washington to be the President," he said, "someone who has at least lived where the people's problems are instead of waiting for the tight, closed, and unchanging community of Washington to send somebody out to the country ... there are too many politicians speaking from Washington and there are too few speaking to Washington from America." He spoke fervently in support of busing and favored an unmanned space station, since one that was manned would be too expensive.

US News and World Report called Lindsay "every advance man's dream candidate - sensitive to the shifts in place and mood. He knows when to roll up his shirtsleeves and loosen his tie and button up again." While glamour, they said, was "no problem here," they cautioned that it might be "Lindsay's hope." And he had talent. Famed consultant David Garth was his, as was RFK's Ronnie Eldridge.

**Lindsay earned the city's wrath for his slow response
to a snowstorm in the winter of '69**
Photo courtesy of the U.S. National Oceanic and Atmospheric Administration

Indeed, Lindsay's star power had its drawbacks. An AP paper observed, "The political idiom of a blue blood, Manhattan sophisticate trying to educate blue collar blacks and rural whites on the crisis of the cities fell flat, leaving most of his audiences restive and slightly embarrassed." When then-Congressman Ed Koch was asked how Lindsay could be such a rock star in Arizona but at rock-bottom in New York, Koch replied, "Too know him is not to love him." That apparently was true Florida as well, as Theodore White noting in *The Making of the President 1972* that "some awful miscarriage of judgment by Manhattan advance men" marred his reception there. His musical introduction was from the cast of *Hair*, and while his speech was "one of the finest ... of his political career," his direct challenges to George Wallace where the former Alabama Governor would dominate didn't go over well. Still, Lindsay was buoyed by an unexpectedly strong second-place showing in Arizona's delegate selection in early January and vowed to enter primaries in states with like-minded electorates (Kansas, New Mexico, etc).

Lindsay took just 7% in Florida in late February and insisted that "his campaign is far from over," but it was having impact back home. Meade Espisito said, "I think the handwriting is on the wall; Little Sheba better come home." That was the feeling among Lindsay advisors as well but Mary convinced him to compete in Wisconsin as a favor to the influential LaFollette family who had lined up as supporters. But after a disappointing 7% in the Badger State, Lindsay withdrew.

Lindsay returned to New York to deal with the many issues on his plate but was in essence a man without a party. He opted against seeking a third term the following year. "My love for this city and the work still to be done have tempted me to carry on," he said. "Eight years is too short a time, but long enough for one man." Mary said the Mayoralty was, "beginning with chaos, ending with chaos and with a slight climactic middle."

After his disappointing Wisconsin primary
Photo via the Library of Congress Prints and Photographs Division

Lindsay made one more try for public office - the U.S. Senate seat in 1980. He had hoped to face his one-time ally, Jacob Javits, but managed just 16% in the Democratic primary and failed to carry a single county in New York State. He died in 2000 at age 79.

Lindsay once invoked John Kennedy, who "once said, 'Life isn't fair.' And he was right. But that has never stopped men from trying to make it fair." This quote sums up Lindsay's approach to politics. Few doubt his accomplishments, which were many, but economically and racially, he led the city into a period of aimlessness from which it would take years to recover.

Sam Yorty (1909-1998):

California State Librarian Kevin Starr noted that in terms of racial composition, "L.A. had become a new city" during Yorty's Mayoralty. In movie terms, he began his career in something like *Chinatown*, came to political strength during L.A. *Confidential*, and was mayor during *Dragnet*.

Yorty's background was different from Lindsay's. Born in Lincoln, Nebraska, he moved west at a time in which L.A. had an abundance of Midwesterners (it was called "Iowa by the sea"). His family consisted of "Democrats in a Republican state" and Yorty's heroes were William Jennings Bryan and Woodrow Wilson. The political bug bit him early. He challenged legendary U.S. Senator Hiram Johnson when he was 31 and predictably lost (his slogan was "Elect Sam Yorty—Stop Hitler Now"). He was an attorney for labor unions. He challenged Tom Kuchel for the right to finish Nixon's remaining two years as a Senator.

Museum of the San Fernando Valley

During his early days in politics, Yorty was as liberal as any (ex-California Governor) Hiram Johnson progressive. Elected to the California Assembly at age 27, he advanced bills outlawing strike-breaking and anti-union injunction, as well as a bill to create a Labor Board modeled after its national one. But when political foes labeled Yorty a communist, he never again gave them ammunition.

By the time he won an LA Congressional seat in 1950, he was quite conservative and on the outs with many Democrats, but the party's disenchantment with Yorty reached a fever pitch when he abandoned Kennedy for Nixon. In making the surprise announcement, Yorty put out a pamphlet, "Why I can't take Kennedy." While it's hard to say that this endorsement swung California to Nixon (Yorty was not mayor at the time), the difference was only 18,000 votes, which suggests that it certainly was possible.

Photo via the San Fernando Valley Museum

A year after this occurred, Yorty was able to win the LA Mayoral election. It was a surprise, but could be attributed to the fact that they were non-partisan affairs. His middle-class, African-American coalition came with promises to make the city more accountable and, as *Urban Development* writes, to "reform the police department."

As Mayor, few could say that Yorty was anything but forward-looking. He paved the way for the convention center, zoo, and music center. He was the first mayor to have women and African-Americans on his staff, and he appointed them to key positions. He became a regular on Carson. He was called the "Maverick Mayor." For Yorty, this would be flattering compared to what was to come. The many trips abroad he took, to Israel and to the far East, coupled with his hawkish views on Vietnam, earned him nicknames such as "Travelin Sam" and "Saigon Sam" and led *The Nation* to call L.A. "the only city with its own foreign policy." His absence even inspired a weight-related joke: "Did you hear about the Sam Yorty diet? You eat only when he's in town."

Mayorsam.blogspot.org

Yorty overcame a challenge from James Roosevelt, FDR's son, in 1965. The following year, he challenged incumbent Pat Brown in the Democratic Gubernatorial primary and captured 36%. He did little to aid Brown in the fall, which was seen as a factor in Reagan's defeat. Brown himself called Yorty "the cleverest concotor of phony issues I ever knew." Two years later, Yorty again backed Nixon and had hoped to get a cabinet post (he angled for Secretary of Defense) but it did not come his way.

Yorty's relations with African-American defined his legacy. Though he did have blacks on his staff, he did not remove Sheriff Parker for calling federal troops to Watts during the 1965 riot (he called them "the kind of force we ought to have"), which caused permanent distrust. Hwoever, his race against African-American Councilman Tom Bradley may have been the low point of his career. Bradley was inheriting many of the folks Yorty had alienated and his 42% in the runoff was 100,000 votes ahead of Yorty. He opened a lead of as much as 16%, but Yorty wouldn't roll over and play dead. In ads that made the indignant race-based campaigns of Jesse Helms pale in comparison, he played the card on his rival. Bradley, he said, wanted to turn L.A. into "a black city" and said that "to elect him would be an invitation to violence in this city." He ran an ad with Bradley's face that said "will your family be safe" and questioned what Bradley's response would be to campus unrest in the city. He also questioned law enforcement's view of Bradley, even though he had served on the LAPD. It was enough for a 53-47% win.

Newsweek said Bradley won "mainly by placing him somewhere in the middle of Eldridge Cleaver and H. Rap Brown in the American spectrum." 1973 offered an opportunity for a re-do, which again went to a runoff. Yorty sent fliers to white neighborhoods that noted that turnout in Watts was higher than the city. Bradley won 56-44% and called the campaign "the most scurrilous racist appeal I have ever seen in the city of Los Angeles."

In between, Yorty launched a bid for the Democratic Presidential nomination. He made clear that he was running to the right of virtually all of his rivals. "My position on issues will be that of a moderate Democrat," he said, "a position I hope will appeal not only to a majority of Democrats but also to many Republicans who are disillusioned with the current resort to sheer political expediency by the Nixon administration in its effort to win re-election at all costs or by any means in 1972." Yorty took particular aim at "Scoop" Jackson, contending that the Washington State Senator is "a lot more liberal than he wants people to know."

Photo via historyforsale.com

With the backing of William Loeb of the *Manchester Union Leader*, Yorty did take third place in New Hampshire, but that was good enough for just 6%—this would be his high point. Yorty tried to have his name removed from the Florida ballot, where his campaign had virtually collapsed, but the state Supreme Court denied his attempt. Shortly thereafter, he announced that aside from California, he would do no further campaigning.

Following his term, Yorty hosted a television show and in 1981, he tried to regain the Mayoralty, this time as a Republican. By that time, the racial gloves had fully come off. "Black people," he said "are really racist. They vote for black people because they are black." Yorty died in 1998 at age 88. Bradley died a few months later.

Nixon Faced Two Republican Congressman For Re-Nomination In '72

Historic Quote: "For those who believe in omens, the photocopying machine in the Nixon headquarters kept breaking down and, last week, burst into flames." – Columnnist David Broder in a Washington Post column just prior to the 1972 primary season.

McCloskey (left) and Ashbrook (right)
Photos via the U.S. Government Printing Office

I n the 1972 Presidential primaries, much of the attention was on the cacophonous Democratic field. But Richard Nixon was facing two challengers within his own party, one from the left, and one from the right. Paul McCloskey and John Ashbrook were both members of the House. Both would suffer electoral ramifications as a result of their quixotic bids but neither fatal, as both managed to serve an additional decade in the House prior to undertaking Senate candidacies in 1982. Nixon himself would say later that though McCloskey or Ashbrook never had a chance, "those a—holes caused me some problems."

Ideologically, the pair had nothing in common. While McCloskey's 1971 rating from the liberal Americans for Democratic Action was a very high 65% (for a Republican), Ashbrook's rating was just eight percent. Conversely, while the conservative Americans for Constitutional Action awarded Ashbrook a 93% score, his counterpart McCloskey took just 23%.

McCloskey and Ashbrook's high point of their challenge to Nixon was the New Hampshire primary, as Nixon surrendered a third of the vote to the two. McCloskey won 20%, and Ashbrook 10%. In fact, on primary night, McCloskey and his then-Republican House colleague and supporter, Congressman Don Riegel, went to visit Ashbrook in his hotel room and, after congratulating one another, agreed that 30% of GOP voters opposing Nixon couldn't send anything but bad news to him for the fall. But that was the limit. Nixon would exceed 80% in nearly every other primary and of course glide to re-election over George McGovern in the fall.

McCloskey's opposition to Nixon stemmed from the Vietnam War. He was a Korean vet but research had made him very much opposed to the Vietnam, calling it "one of the most tragic mistakes that we ever made" (McCloskey was actually the first member of Congress to call for repeal of the Tonkin Gulf resolution). He cited, "the two men I fought under in Korea, General MacArthur and General Ridgeway" who espoused the view, "never again fight a land war on the Asian continent; it is not a place for Americans."

McCloskey, whom people would call "Pete," had an interesting electoral history. When a Congressional seat opened up in 1967, his main rival was Shirley Temple Black, and she ran to his right on Vietnam. Actually, it's not hard to see how she'd be to his right on virtually everything. In his early tenure, McCloskey backed busing, corporate campaign limits, co-chaired Earth Day, and opposed strip mining, school prayer and the Cambodia bombings.

On some issues, McCloskey's record could place him to the left of even some Northern Democrats. Water pollution control was one such issue. During a 1971 markup, McCloskey proposed giving citizens who resided away from an area where pollution was occuring the right to sue. The proposal before the committee, he claimed, "adds a new definition of 'citizen' for the first time in history . . . In my judgement, I believe the distinction made between citizens who can sue under the bill and citizens who cannot to be an improper, if not an unconstitutional distinction." His proposal was rejected. A year later, he argued that legislation that would grant licensing of certain nuclear power plants was "not only bad law and bad precedent but also might not even be necessary."

Consequently, from the beginning to the end of his Congressional career, he'd be walking on eggshells in his primaries. In 1968, McCloskey was re-nominated with just 53% and 60% in 1970.

McCloskey mounted his challenge against Nixon because he wanted to give "truth a chance."

But he also made the friends in high places argument, condemning the administration for opposing dairy subsidies until a few well connected people began contributing to the RNC. McCloskey called "restoration of faith the most important goal of the campaign."

As primary day neared in New Hampshire, McCloskey made clear his goal was to garner 20%. "Nineteen-point-nine percent and I drop out," he said. "Twenty percent and we continue to make the fight." Early returns on primary night left McCloskey euphoric as a scattering from precincts around New Hampshire showed him getting an astounding 34%. By the time the dust had settled, McCloskey was hovering at the 20% figure and ended up with 19.8% (Ashbrook took 9.7%). He attempted to continue but after mustering just 4% in Florida a week later, he realized he could no lnger raise the funding required and dropped out.

After the loss, McCloskey continued to struggle. Redistricting had carved up much of his district, but he found a nearby, more Republican one to make his race. But he may have alienated voters by changing his registration to "decline to state." Still, he beat two primary foes with 55%, and the general election with the same margin against an attorney named James Stewart. But he'd show no signs of abandoning his maverick ways, backing federal funding of abortion, the creation of the Consumer Protection Agency, and limiting the production of the B-1 bomber. In the 1974 primary, he came within 2% of defeat (50-48%). But he recovered after that. And set his sights on the Senate. The primary was heavy with GOP heavyweights (Pete Wilson, Barry Goldwater Sr, Maureen Reagan, etc), and McCloskey garnered just 8%.

In 2006, McCloskey at 78 attempted a comeback, challenging conservative Republican Richard Pombo in the primary. Pombo chaired the House Resources Committee, and had a bullet on his back from environmental groups. He also was a staunch social conservative. McCloskey called himself, "a Republican since 1948, before Pombo was born. But I'm ashamed of what my party has become, and to me, Pombo represents the very worst of it." His campaign was launched from a motor home, which he called the Real Republican Voters Express. When he lost, McCloskey endorsed Democrat Jerry McNerney who went on to beat Pombo. The following year, he announced he was leaving the Republican Party.

Ashbrook's modus operendi for challenging Nixon was anger over his position on two fronts. The "Wage and Price" controls and his opening up relations with the Soviet Union and the People's Republic of China, both on which he thought Nixon was straying too far from the right. But he also hit him for backing the EPA and welfare and blasted the President on other issues, specifically citing his "presentation of liberal policies in the verbal trappings of conservatism." When an anti-busing amendment in the Senate failed by a single vote during the campaign season, Ashbrook chided the President for lack of leadership saying, "Never has the gap between Mr. Nixon's rhetoric and actions been more clear than this last week in the Senate." It was perhaps appropriate that his slogan was "No left turn," and he called his New Hampshire journey "a small Paul Revere ride."

Ashbrook's devotion to conservative causes was nothing new. Since his initial election to Congress, he had been the yin to the liberals yang on nearly every high-profile and substantive proposal made. In almost every endeavor did he fail. *The Almanac of American Politics, 1982* called his career "almost a catalogue of lost causes." But few could say he lacked zealousness and drive. Charles Moser, writing for the Ashbrook Foundation, underscored that point. The Congressman, he said, "had little influence on the Committee because he found so few allies there even on the Republican side, but on the House floor many ameliorating amendments bearing his name were adopted because he was in a position to follow some of the most radical legislation to move through the House of Representatives."

A classic example of Ashbrook plowing full steam ahead was during Congressional debate on a federal education bill in 1965. Calling the bill, "full of loopholes," he said it presents "a virtual bulldozer for federal bureaucracy to overrun our lng-established policy regarding local control over our schools."

A web-site devoted to Ashbrook's life calls him" big blond with a ready grin and friendly manner–was a natural-born politician." A native of Johnstown, Ohio, Ashbrook was a Navy man who would return home to attain his degree from Harvard University and his law degree from Ohio State. But politics did not appear to be his first calling. At 25, he became editor of the Johnstown Independent, a newspaper that had been founded by his father in 1884.

Ashbrook's tilt at the political windmill came in 1956 when he won a seat in the Ohio Assembly. Four years later, it was off to Congress, winning a heavily Republican Congressional seat, succeeding his father who had retired. During that race, he spoke of "unbridled national power with a resultant loss of individual freedom and local autonomy."

In office, his pursuit of conservatism led him to take leadership in a what's what of conservative organizations, including a chairmanship of the Young Republican National Federation. He became one of the founders of the Conservative Victory Fund. He would had been ranking member of the House Internal Security Committee (a descendant of the Committee on Un-American Activities) when it was abolished. In his final term, he was the top Republican on Education and Labor.

While Ashbrook's view toward even moderate Republicans was unambiguous ("the only things that you find in the middle of the road are yellow lines and dead skunks"), he was not disliked. Paul Simon, the Illinois Democrat who was almost as liberal as Ashbrook conservative, said in his book that he enjoyed working with him. But his opinion of Nixon did not improve. He said as Watergate mounted "we kept waiting for the other shoe to drop but then we realized he was a centipede."

After folding his Presidential bid, Ashbrook couldn't quite glide to re-election the way he had done so previously. His 57% in 1972 was down, but not necessarily in the danger zone. But his 53% against an underfunded foe two years later was. By '76, Ashbrook was back to 57% but, adding insult to injury, saw his committee abolished. He then became ranking Republican on the Education Committee. He was the only Ohioan to oppose the Civil Rights Act of 1964 and in later years, spoke against the holiday observing Martin Luther King's birthday.

But Ashbrook would go after Nixon one last time – on Watergate, as he became the first House Republican to call for Nixon to step down.

In the spring of 1982, Ashbrook had filed to challenge Howard Metzenbaum for his Senate seat that fall and seemed likely to capture the GOP nomination. In March, he collapsed, as a result of what aides said was exhaustion. But a month later, he suddenly died. A hemorrhage was listed as the cause.

An Unusual Democratic Split Gave Maryland – And The Nation Spiro Agnew In 1966

Historic Tidbit: Did you know that Edgar Allen Poe served as Attorney General of Maryland? Well, not that Edgar Allen Poe but pretty close. Poe the Attorney General was second cousins twice removed of the author. He served as Maryland's Chief law enforcement officer from 1911 to 1915. Both the author and AG shared a love for Baltimore. But unlike the author, who had a frail disposition, Poe the AG was known for his physical stature as he was a star quarterback for Princeton University's football team during the 1889 season. Health would not be a trait the two men would share either. While Poe the author died shortly after being found on a Baltimore street, the AG lived 90 years, surviving his Attorney General tenure by nearly half a century.

The surprise nomination of George Mahoney (left) for the Democratic nomination for Maryland Governor led to Spiro T. Agnew (right) winning the office

Left image via politics1.com; right image courtesy of the U.S. Senate Historical Office

When he entered the 1966 Maryland Governor's race, Spiro Agnew was regarded as anything but the favorite. The Baltimore County Executive was fairly well-known but Maryland was insulated with Democratic officeholders and registered Democrats outnumbered Republicans in Maryland 3-1. But parts of Maryland – particularly along the Eastern shore, always had an element of resistance to the civil rights movement (George Wallace had taken an unusually large 43% in the 1964 presidential primary against Johnson stand-in, U.S. Senator Daniel Brewster) so it shouldn't have been a complete shock when building contractor George Mahoney upset two seasoned politicians to secure the Democratic nomination.

Mahoney's slogan was, "Your home is your castle - protect it,'" and prior to 1966, he had sought the nomination for either U.S. Senator or Governor on six separate occasions as far back as 1950. That year, Mahoney very nearly wrested the nomination from progressive Governor William Lane (Mahoney had taken advantage of Lane's backing of tax increases to fund road projects). Two years later, he came within five points of denying J. Glenn Beall, Sr., re-election to the Senate in the very Republican year of 1952 and in '54, yet again nearly won the Democratic nomination for Governor over Harry Clifton "Curley" Byrd. After that near-miss, Mahoney's star began falling and he lost three more races by unambiguous margins. But '66 was different.

LBJ's "Great Society" had been fully enacted and Mahoney in particular felt he could tap a nerve among voters on open housing legislation, which he staunchly opposed. That helped him garner the support – veiled or overt, of blue-collar workers. That might not have been without reason. Mahoney started out as one of them. *The Washington Post* detailed how in Mahoney's obituary. "Self-described as 'the kid from the wrong side of the tracks who made good,' he was born the 11th child of a Baltimore police officer and went to work at 13 on a New York City subway construction gang. Starting with a secondhand truck that he used to haul gravel, he built an asphalt contracting firm that made possible the sartorial elegance he exhibited on the campaign trail as well as the 312-acre Baltimore County estate he owned." In the meantime, Democratic Governor Herb O'Connor had appointed him to the State Racing Commission.

Still, when he announced his intention to seek the Governorship, few took notice. Two other men who had been elected statewide in Maryland – Congressman At-Large Carlton Sickles (known as the "father" of Washington D.C's metro) and Attorney General Thomas Finan, were seeking the party's nomination and it was expected that whichever man emerged from the primary would have no trouble dispatching Agnew in the fall. That may well have happened but, neither man ended up prevailing.

Instead, both politicians tore each other to shred over the current administration which caused them to split the vote and allow Mahoney to pull out a 1,839 vote win over Sickles, 30.2%-29.8% (at one point, Sickles' deficit was just 154 votes before the absentees were counted). Finan was not far behind with 27%. The presence of a prominent attorney, Clarence Miles, the one-time president of the Baltimore Orioles, likely deprived Finan of victory.

The irreparably nasty tone had to do with everything from outgoing and future politics. Finan had the backing of the departing Democratic Governor,

Millard Tawes (*The Harvard Crimson* called him "machine through and through, (who) based his entire campaign on defending the administration"). As such, Sickles made references to the "Tawes-Finan administration." Tawes shot back that Sickles was conducting "the dirtiest campaign in recent memory," to which Sickles responded that if that is the case, "it is simply because this is the first time in memory that anyone in a Democratic gubernatorial primary has lifted up the rug."

The two also bickered over open housing. Sickles supported the legislation that Mahoney s so virulently opposed. Finan took the middle ground which called for exempting private homeowners but Sickles at one point accused Finan of being in "bed with bigots" for not denouncing a group of Prince George's County supporters that were against that legislation. But late in the campaign, Sickles adopted a similar stance.

Sickles was not considered the most inspiring speaker but he nonetheless enjoyed the backing of Brewster and the state's junior Senator, Joe Tydings. Brewster called Sickles, "the best qualified to provide the new leadership necessary for modern state government,"

Quite possibly, a plurality of Democratic voters intended to vote for Sickles. But through incompetence, many in Sickles' home base were not able to. Prince Georges County had a ballot of about 250 names which caused voters to spend an average of six minute inside the voting booths. Consequently, long lines resulted and many walked out in disgust without voting and Sickles only won it by the skin of his teeth – depriving him of a big margin to offset Mahoney's surprising strength elsewhere. Mahoney carried 12 counties, including Baltimore by a wide margin.

The win immediately changed the trajectory of the general election, as holding their nose and voting for Mahoney was not even an option for many Democrats. That was enough to draw more than a few disaffected members of the party to Agnew.

Though Agnew would go down in history as a hard-charging conservative, in 1966 he was still perceived as a moderate - or at least he was posturing as such as it became clear that he would be facing Mahoney. For example, he became a supporter of the same federal anti-poverty program that he had earlier called "a dangerous invasion of our Constitutional rights." He focused on what, as Theodore Sheckels said in his book, *Maryland Politics and Political Communication, 1950-2005*, were the "key issues: transportation, tax reform, education and water pollution." His platform included state aid for kindergarten, vocational schools and clean-up of sewage plants. He had an exceptionally strong relationship with the state's Tydings and the two worked exceptionally well together and worked side-by-side on the attempt to pass revisions to Maryland's Constitution.

Agnew also favored helping property tax payers by shifting funds to the income tax. And on the issue of open housing, the Maryland Secretary of State noted he "opposed legislation which would apply to the individual home owner, but instead, he stated that he would only support state measures if they applied to new apartments and sub-divisions." His slogan was, "your kind of man."

In his book, *Veil of Voodoo: George P. Mahoney, Open Housing, and the Coming of the Southern Strategy*, Richard Hardesty cited a letter by voter R.W. Duncan that summed up the conundrum of a typical Democratic voter. "For the first time," Duncan wrote, "I shall vote Republican not because I am for Mr. Agnew – I am not, but because I am against a political appeal to racist hatred and there is nothing negative about being counted as one against hatred." The Americans for Democratic Action and a number of prominent religious leaders openly backed Agnew as well.

Finan stuck with Mahoney ("the Democratic party is bigger than any one man"), as did Tawes and much of his organization. But Miles threw his weight to Agnew, Sickles sat out altogether but stated his thought that "I have not seen it fit to support the nominee ought to speak rather loudly." Brewster and Tydings took no public position but behind the scenes sent word to Democratic interest groups (unions, etc.), that they should back Agnew. President Johnson, in an appearance in Maryland, did not mention Mahoney by name. A number of Republicans, meanwhile, led by the man Agnew had vanquished in the primary, got behind Mahoney. Meanwhile, Mahoney refused to debate and received a number of phoned in death threats. Still, victory for Agnew was not inevitable. In fact, he trailed Mahoney in at least one poll ten days prior to Election Day.

There was an attempt by some regular-Democrats to carry on in spite of the results. Baltimore City Comptroller Hyman Pressman mounted an Independent campaign who denounced Mahoney's "hate-mongering campaign" but many assumed he was simply posturing for a Mayoral bid the following year. Both the Mahoney and Agnew camps saw him as a spoiler and urged him to withdraw but he resisted those calls.

On Election Day, Agnew took just shy of 50%, garnering 49.5% to Mahoney's 40.6% with Pressman pulling 10%. The span of his win was awesome. Agnew won Baltimore City by 10 though Mahoney did hold on to the county. He won normally Democratic Prince George's County with 54% and Montgomery with a whopping 71% (Mahoney had been met with blank stares as he pleaded with Democratic Party leaders for their support). Mahoney did hold on to Anne Arundel as well as counties along the Eastern Shore (Wicomico proved an exception). He carried Howard (at the time fairly tiny) by a single percentage point. The 90,000 votes Pressman received slightly exceeded Agnew's winning margin though it was widely believed that he took votes from both candidates.

Whether the Democratic establishment would have come around to Sickles had he won the primary is an open question as well given that his relationship with Tawes was acrimonious. But immediate – and very nearly long-term history was impacted, as Agnew became vice-president and would have become president upon Nixon's resignation had his tax evasion charges not forced him to resign.

What prompted Agnew's rapid metamorphosis from respected moderate to a hard-lined conservative? Those around him say two things in particular.

One was his service as the temporary chair of the "National Rockefeller '68 Committee," which came to an abrupt end when Rockefeller pulled out of the race – without informing Agnew. He learned about it with the rest of the press as he had arranged for a television set to be brought in so all gathered for his press conference could watch what they thought was a candidacy announcement. Agnew kept cool but many think that left a sour taste in his mouth as Justin Coffey noted in *Spiro Agnew and the Rise of the Republican Right* that he told his secretary, "I feel like I have been hit in the stomach by a sledgehammer." When Rockefeller reversed course and did decide to enter the race, Agnew wanted little to do with him.

Another was the Baltimore riots that followed the assassination of Dr. Martin Luther King, Jr. Agnew had summoned a number of black leaders to the Governor's mansion for what had been billed as a press conference. Instead, Agnew lambasted them publicly, calling them "circuit riding, Hanoi visiting, caterwauling, riot inciting, burn America down type of leaders."

Mahoney meanwhile, would take two more runs at elective office – as an Independent against Brewster and challenging Tydings in the 1970 Democratic primary, partly due to Tydings having incurred the NRA's wrath for his strong support of gun control (he took 37% to the incumbent's 52%) but did end back in some good graces of Maryland Democrats. In 1973, Governor Marvin Mandel appointed him Director of the State Lottery. He had little reason not to. After all, it Agnew hadn't beaten him, he likely never would have become vice-president and Mandel might not have become Governor. He died in 1989 at age 87. Asked if he had ever regretted undertaking so many quixotic runs, his son, George Mahoney, Jr., replied, "No, he was just a man with great determination . . . . He was a great man and a great father."

Milton Shapp for President in '76:
What the Hell?

Historic Quote: "Think of the House and Senate as a couple. They have almost two years of foreplay and it's not until the last two weeks that they get down to the real thing." - Bob Neumann, an assistant to Mo Udall, to a *Washington Post* reporter. Udall recounted that in his book, "Too funny to be President." Looking at Congress today, it can be said that some things never change.

Milton Shapp (1912-1994)
Photo via One Vote Counts

Campaigning
Photo via Historic Images

W hen Pennsylvania Governor Milton Shapp decided to run for President in 1976, he compared himself to "the people who were talking about becoming candidates. In knowledge of the economy, in ability to develop programs and get them implemented, I couldn't see anybody comparable. I saw the caliber of these people and I said, 'What the hell.'"

As Governor of one of the largest states, Shapp had as much credibility as anyone seeking the Democratic nomination that year. His experience and accomplishments certainly exceeded that of a peanut farmer from Georgia who ultimately took the prize. He could claim to be just as much of an outsider as Carter. But Shapp got off to a late start and never exceeded 2% anywhere, which made his campaign over virtually before it began. But a colorful life, entrepreneurial abilities, and pretty darned-successful Governorship make's Shapp's story one to tell.

Milton Shapp doesn't seem the perfect part for Governor of Pennsylvania; a true liberal who marched with McCarthy. But timing is everything in politics and Shapp truly came along at the right time. On the 25th anniversary of the state lottery which was one of Shapp's many babies, State Senator Vince Fumo said Shapp "did more for Pennsylvania than any other chief executive in modern times to put this state on a sound financial footing, while at the same time helping the people of our State who needed the help most." That, in a nutshell, sums up his record. But there's far more to his life than that.

Milton Shapp was born Milton Shapiro in Cleveland, but would change his name out of fear of anti-semitism. He molded Jerrold Electronic Systems from a company of two to 2,100. It became a major heavyweight in the cable industry, which was then in its infancy. And it created a fortune for Shapp. He sold it, but said he "surely have become a billionaire" had he not. He used this to parlay his political endeavor. A supporter of Kennedy in 1960, Shapp may be a Founding Father of the Peace Corps. He had written a letter to Bobby Kennedy during the campaign urging him to create some sort of abroad service program. The Kennedy's heeded his advice.

Image via Westorange.com

Shapp had sought the Governorship in 1966 and surprised nearly everyone by beating Bob Casey in the primary. Shapp lost to Ray Schaefer but it hardly deterred him. Four years later, he mounted a television campaign unaccustomed to most "Keystoners," and beat Schaefer, who was stubbornly resisting a tax increase that, in the face of a $500 million deficit, few were against. He was the state's first Jewish Governor.

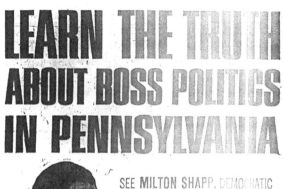

Photo via Lulac Political letter.blogspot

Shapp got the prize but his style did not go hand in hand with a state that had long been used to schmoozing between its Governor and legislators regardless of party. One statehouse reporter called him "a loner who runs state government close to his vest" with another lamenting that he "has almost no record at all in the passage of major bills. He has put in very little." Shapp learned that was to his detriment very quickly, like the first four hours of his tenure. The legislature rejected his ten cabinet appointments mostly due to lack of consultation.

Shapp got his tax increase (an income tax) but also, a legacy of sorts. That was making government work for the people: taxpayers, consumers, seniors, handicapped, and schools. "In the name of economy, genuine human needs are being neglected," he had told legislators in one State of the State.

Photo via philadelphiareflections.com

Shapp proposed property tax measures and made the state a partner in school districts. He enacted what at the time was called the most comprehensive Sunshine Law. There were welfare reforms, day-care for working mothers, and help for folks who required special ed. The National Governor's Association website says Shapp also pushed through "divorce law reforms, prison reforms, improvements to Pennsylvania's portion of the Appalachian Trail, and $300 million in tax breaks to small and medium-sized businesses." He pleased environmentalists by opposing a tourist tower at Gettysburg.

The Bilerico Project noted Shapp's efforts in the area of gay rights were a novelty. "At a time when no one higher in government than a mayor would meet with gay activists, Gov. Shapp in 1973 became the first governor in the nation to do so. He issued an order barring discrimination against homosexuals in the workplace which was a novelty. He found the term "illegitimate children" degrading and had it abolished from the state's lexicon.

A bad experience on the Pennsylvania Turnpike as Governor (bad food, high prices, and pay toilets) made him undertake a quest to improve rest stops (Shapp joked that his legacy would be "getting rid of pay toilets on the Pennsylvania Turnpike").

The Pennsylvania lottery was initially designed to pay for needs of the underprivileged (senior prescriptions, etc), and the State Department of Aging ("my greatest success"). Without outside assistance, Shapp was forced to mediate a strike with the Pennsylvania independent trucking industry and he was praised by all sides. And he opened the Pennsylvania Governor's mansion for disadvantaged senior citizens as well as a school for handicapped children. But he did argue with the Democratic controlled legislature (Fumo said it was because he "was so far ahead of his time in many ways") and that inhibited what he was trying to do.

Shapp's 54-46% win in 1974 was below his 57% in 1970, but still signaled approval from the voters. And that was important as he set his sights higher.

Shapp tried to parlay his talents into a 1976 Presidential big and, with his background from such a big industrial state, had to be taken seriously. He would be the first Jew to seek a major party Presidential nomination. He claimed early on to have "broken it open," but *Newsweek* observed "exactly how is unclear to most voters." His strategy seemed to be going after several states in the northeast and targeting Florida, where he cited at one point a poll showing him second to Carter. "I want to come into that convention showing I can get votes...(from) a cross section of the electorate."

In his announcement, Shapp claimed it was the economy, saying, "I'm very much concerned about the major issue of the economy, which no one else is addressing." He said "no other issues will really be solved unless we have a healthy economic base." He wanted a national rail trust fund. And he called President Ford's fee on imported oil a "blueprint for economic disaster" that would "create a shock wave of inflation through the country greater than the one we had when the Arabs lifted their embargo."

His efforts landed him the endorsement of a very junior but increasingly influential Senator. Future Vice-President Joe Biden became the first to back Shapp's Presidential bid, saying, "I consider Milton Shapp, as one of the most qualified men to be President of the United States...the nation needs a man who will act, who can respond to the challenge of economic adversity. Milton Shapp is willing to do something."

On the trail, Shapp displayed some level of red-meat that, had he entered earlier, might have enabled him to stand out to liberals ("It's Richard Nixon who should have been deprived of his citizenship, not war protesters"). But there were at least 4 other serious liberals in the race and unlike Shapp, they did not appear to have entered the race on a whim. That hampered his ability to gain traction. *The Pittsburgh-Press* said that while Shapp was sometimes recognized in Florida, they were by "tourists from Pennsylvania." Age may have also been a factor. At 64, Shapp was the same age as "Scoop" Jackson, and both were far older than any other Democrat running.

Doing a radio shoe (Newsworks.com)

In Florida, Shapp would garner just 2% (no preference out-polled him) and he withdrew before the Pennsylvania primary, where he released the delegates that had been bracketed to back him. The campaign had lasted 89 days.

Newsweek reported Shapp spent $700,000 (including $100,000 from a personal loan), was ruled eligible for matching funds before that was reversed a year later, meaning Shapp had to pay it back.

Shapp may never have attained the Presidency but Fumo predicted that like Truman, he'd "be appreciated more decades later." He called Shapp "a humble, down-to-earth man who did not mind a laugh at his own expense" (joking he'd be remembered as the Governor who abolished pay toilets).

Was Shapp's campaign for the Presidency a model for others? No. But was his life and his Governorship? Indubitably.

Photo via the University of Pittsburgh at Bradford

Eagleton Changed Attitudes Of Mental Health, and Helped Return Rams To St. Louis

**Historic Tidbit: "This time, I'm going to think about it very carefully." -
George McGovern on whom he might choose as a running-mate in 1984, his
second try for the Democratic nomination.**

Image via ebay.com

Tom Eagleton is a household name. His removal from the national ticket in
1972 following revelations that he had undergone electric shock treatments
years earlier was likely a giant step forward in creating awareness of mental health
issues. As such, he became a hero and mentor for the millions of Americans who
suffer from mental illness, and for fans who wanted St. Louis to get back a major
league football team, Eagleton may be a hero as well.

In terms of picture-perfect politicians, Eagleton had it all. He inarguably
had politics in his blood. His father Mark had sought the St. Louis Mayoralty
and made it his mission to make young Tom an over-achiever. According to *The
Missouri Biographical Edition*, he sent both Tom and his brother to school at age
four, "sent them to summer school, and hired tutors in national and international
affairs as well as public speaking." His father's prestige provided them with seats
at history-making events. He accompanied his father to the 1940 Republican
Convention at age 11 and heard Winston Churchill's "Iron Curtain" speech in
person six years later. Indeed, James Giglio, author of *Call Me Tom*, wrote that he
"got the distinct impression the dad wanted him to become President." Eagleton
himself said he wanted to be a Senator since high school.

St. Louis was not Boston, but Eagleton's decision to pursue his education back east wouldn't have been culture shock. Following a stint in the Navy, he went to school at Amherst and Harvard—and the rise came fast. Eagleton became the circuit attorney for St. Louis at age 27 and in 1960, at age 31, he was Missouri's Attorney General.

Eagleton became Lieutenant Governor in 1964 (winning with 58%) but Joshua Glasser observes in the book *The Eighteen-Day Running Mate*, "he always intended (the office) to be a transitional position." When Eagleton saw his chance for stardom, he took it, barely a year later. Missouri already had a Democratic Senator but Edward Long was tainted by, among other things, a *Life Magazine* story in which it was claimed that he accepted aid from Jimmy Hoffa's chief attorney, Morris Shanker. The Senate Select Committee on Standards and Conduct dismissed the charges, but new allegations had surfaced as primary day neared. It wasn't just Long's woes that boosted Eagleton, however. He launched himself as "a fresh new face with fresh new ideas." Eagleton's strength, like so many other youthful Senators who won their seats in the 1960s, was that he dazzled with his charisma. Jim Reeves, one of his county campaign managers, observed that "by the sheer force of personality and magnetism [Tom] overcame what I call the conservative attitude [against] social and political issues that he espoused. It worked." Eagleton beat Long 37%-33%, with wealthy businessman and Assistant U.S. Treasury Secretary True Davis getting 29%. It was now onto the general, where Eagleton faced Congressman Thomas Curtis.

Photo courtesy of the U.S. Senate Historical Office

Curtis was among the colleagues who had urged Jerry Ford to take on Charlie Halleck for House Minority Leader. He also had a reputation for opposing many popular initiatives, such as the Peace Corps, model cities, and repealing the poll tax. *Congressional Quarterly* noted that during a debate, Eagleton said, "now we've heard an Alice-in-Wonderland story on why I'm for everything but have to be recorded as voting against everything at the same time." Curtis said he preferred to be thought of as a "yes, but" man, which led *Time* reporter Jonathan Larsen to peg the contest as "the yin and yang of Missouri politics."

Many analysts said Curtis had to run 50,000 votes ahead of Nixon to win, which was on the money. Nixon carried Missouri by 20,000 votes. Eagleton won by 35,000 votes, 51-49%. In the Senate, Eagleton became a member of the Appropriations Committee where he advocated Home Rule for Washington, DC. He opposed abortion and the death penalty but was otherwise a solid liberal. He called himself a "constructive" and "practical progressive."

For the most part, this philosophy meant Eagleton would oppose much of the Nixon administration's priorities. This included the anti-ballistic system, tax breaks and controversial Supreme Court nominations. But he did depart from other liberals by backing William Rehnquist.

In 1970, Eagleton and several other Senators decided to take the Nixon administration to task on what they viewed as an unnecessarily expensive military spending bill. Each Senator focused on a different weapon and Eagleton covered the MBT70 tank. In doing so, he took on fellow Democrat and defense hawk John Stennis of Mississippi for four hours on the Senate floor and in future meetings, Stennis would routinely greet Eagleton by saying, "Hi tank."

As a boss, Eagleton had a reputation as a stand-up guy. Biographer James Giglio said, "Not only was he close and accessible to the lowest staffers but he also exhibited tremendous loyalty to him, and they in turn did so to him."

When it became evident that George McGovern had secured the Democratic nomination, he found himself in a conundrum over whom to choose as a running-mate. Perhaps it was because so few saw that McGovern had a chance, but he was unable to persuade any officeholder who may have provided a tangible boost to join his team. Eagleton was hardly McGovern's first choice. In fact, astonishingly, in the nearly four years the duo had served together in the Senate, the pair had only shared two substantive meetings (once at a cocktail party, the other in the Senate steam room), and McGovern was further pressed by time constraints. The convention was literally opening, which meant that the ultimate pick had to be ratified in a matter of days, and eventually, mere hours.

McGovern held strategy sessions with a core cabinet. Theodore White in *The Making of the President 1972* notes that "of the six or seven names that emerged . . . the name of Kevin White, mayor of Boston, led the list. There followed Sargent Shriver [Pierre Salinger's choice], Abraham Ribicoff [who had already turned down an offer of the slot from McGovern], Governor Patrick J. Lucey and Senator Gaylord Nelson of Wisconsin, and Eagleton." The person McGovern really wanted was Ted Kennedy, but the Massachusetts Senator flat-out refused.

African-American groups liked Shriver but White seemed to be the choice. Eagleton received little consideration, but when McGovern phoned Kennedy to tell him, the Senator's reply was to give him "time to think it over." Kennedy was cool to the idea, which signified his opposition. White was dropped and McGovern offered the spot to Florida Governor Reuben Askew, who turned it down. Then he approached Nelson, his 1962 classmate who as a Governor prior to going to the Senate also had executive experience. Nelson said no but recommended Eagleton.

The McGovern camp had heard rumors of Eagleton's drinking but they spoke to Missourians who were close with Eagleton who assured him that not only had they been unaware of alcoholism abuse but that previous hospitalizations were due to stomach ailments. Frank Manciewicz asked Eagleton if he had any health issues, and Eagleton responded that he didn't. That seemed to do it for McGovern, who telephoned Eagleton to offer him the job. His response: "George, before you change your mind, I accept."

As anonymous reports about Eagleton began trickling in, Mankiewicz and McGovern's campaign manager, Gary Hart, approached Eagleton, who admitted everything over a breakfast meeting (they had initially spoken briefly on an open line but in the age of Watergate they decided to put a moratorium on that). His hospitalizations had not been frequent. They only came after a 1960 campaign for Missouri Attorney General, in 1964 and 1966. During those stays, two electric shock treatments were performed. The idea that he had problems with alcoholism, which had been brought to light by columnist Jack Anderson, was deemed false, after Anderson acknowledged he lacked evidence. Eagleton responded that "the reason he doesn't have the documents is that they do not exist." He added he never had a problem "in any iota."

Plunging into crowds before the fall ("Call Me Tom" Bio)

After meetings and assurances, McGovern and Eagleton held a joint press conference in which the Presidential nominee called his colleague "fully qualified in mind, body, and spirit to . . . if necessary, to take over the Presidency on a moment's notice." The next day was his famous "1000 percent" line of being behind Eagleton and that he had "no intention of dropping him from the ticket." Eagleton insisted there had been no attempt to mislead McGovern. "My health just wasn't on my mind," he said. "It was like a broken leg that had healed." In an in-depth interview with *Newsweek*, he said, "It may look otherwise, but I haven't been beset by fear and guilt these past twelve years. There are 365 days in a year and I didn't get up every morning, look in the mirror and say to myself: 'Well, Good Morning Tom Eagleton. Today, somebody is going to mention that you were in Barnes Hospital back in 1960 and that while there, you had electroshock therapy.'"

But the American people took a slightly different views. A Newsweek poll found that the public, by a 2-1 margin, thought he should remain on the ticket. But 4 out of 5 voters felt he should have told McGovern before his selection and many Democrats felt even minor bleeding could tip the scales in what they believed would be a close election.

Rallies indicated strong support for Eagleton but they belied newspaper editorials from a liberal media that called for Eagleton to be dropped, and fundraising was drying up. McGovern, according to Theodore White, told Eagleton he knew "he had gone through hell this week but so have I." He told Eagleton that their mutual friend, Walter Mondale, facing re-election that year in Minnesota, had, among others, worried about Eagleton's presence on the ticket.

Eventually, he, Nelson, and Eagleton met, and Eagleton told McGovern that "if my presence on the ticket causes you any embarrassment, or hindrance, or impediment, I'll step aside." McGovern simply said "Yes." Publicly, he put on a brave face. He acknowledged that "thousands and thousands of people have phoned, have telegrammed, or written to me or Senator McGovern urging me to press on." In the end, he withdrew because "I will not divide the Democratic Party, which already has too many divisions . . . my personal feelings are secondary to the necessity to unify the Democratic Party and elect George McGovern the next President of the United States." Eagleton was privately bitter. "Why in hell, did he have to table hop. Why couldn't he pick up the phone, call me collect if necessary, and tell me there were concerns." He was far from alone. Others included Harry Truman, who was in the last year of his life in Independence, Missouri. Eagleton had support from Republicans as well. Senate Minority Leader Hugh Scott issued a call to the Democrats: "You have made statements that become you. Go on with your campaign."

McGovern ended up picking Shriver, who checked with his brother-in-law, Teddy Kennedy, about inhibiting his future ambitions before he accepted. Eagleton dutifully campaigned for the ticket but they would go on to lose 49 of the 50 states. Eagleton called himself, "one rock in a landslide." More than three decades later, McGovern expressed regret, saying that if he "had to do it over again, I'd have kept him. I didn't know anything about mental illness. Nobody did."

During their deliberations following the revelations, Eagleton had told McGovern "You can't win without me." There's evidence he strongly believed that. He had privately told columnist Bob Novak that during the nomination process "the people don't know that McGovern is for amnesty, acid, and abortion. Once middle America, Catholic middle America, find out about that, he's dead." Eagleton considered himself a stalwart of that wing and Novak reported the quote as one by an anonymous Senator.

Indeed, during the campaign, McGovern became known as "the candidate of amnesty, abortion and acid." That image contributed to his epic loss. After Eagleton's death, Novak identified him as the source (he had refused Novak's request after the 1972 vote because he didn't want to jeopardize McGovern's Senate re-election).

Eagleton returned to the Senate, disappointment hardly showing, but he'd earn solid legislative accomplishments, including fostering compromises for clean water/air legislation. He would become one of three sponsors of the War Powers Act. Eagleton contended that without it, "Congress surrenders its Constitutional prerogatives to gain a Phyrric victory." His biographer Joshua Glasser wrote that he "handwrote" the amendment that ultimately ended the bombing of Cambodia, and with it, the Vietnam War.

Eagleton also made clear he had little confidence in the foreign policy inclinations of Secretary of State Henry Kissinger. During a debate on a fiscal year 1975 foreign aid bill, Eagleton Eagleton called "our Secretary of State (is) famous for his tilts. He tilts toward the junta in Chile. He tilts toward Thieu in Vietnam.

His most famous tilt was his pro-Pakistan tilit. His current tilt, his Turkish tilt, is no wiser than his other tilts." Eagleton had been arguing for a complete aid cutoff to Turkey following its invasion of Cypruss. President Ford declared that the Unirted States "will have lost its negotiating flexibility and influence."

As his seat came up in '74, he was again challenged by Curtis. He questioned whether Eagleton still harbored national ambitions, to which Eagleton responded that he had none. "And you can put a triple exclamation point after that . . . running for President or Vice-President, either one, involve almost cruel and inhumane punishment." The result was a near-landslide, as Eagleton took 60%.

1980 was tougher. Challenging Eagleton was St. Louis County Executive Gene McNary. He was lacking in dynamism and name recognition (he had drawn just 16% against "Kit" Bond in a bid for the GOP Gubernatorial nod in 1972) and Eagleton led him 2-1 in polls. However, he did have two major factors on his side. One was the pending Republican storm. The other was that he and the Senator shared the same geographic base, which would neutralize Eagleton's advantage in fairly Democratic turf.

McNary argued that his county experience would be a plus, but Eagleton argued he left poor people out of his program development. Eagleton was one of six Senators challenged by the National Right Political Action Committee. By Election Day, their challenge to California's Alan Cranston had fizzled. Of the remaining five, including McGovern, Eagleton was teh only one to survive, but it did not come easy. The margin was 52-48%. McNary did cut heavily into St. Louis but Kansas City pulled him through.

Eagleton's final term was served in the minority, and he announced his plans to step down after the conclusion of his third term in 1986 ("public office should not be held in perpetuity.") He called his career "full and complete" but bemoaned the fundraising demands and the growing ideological purity increasingly demanded by both sides. Indeed, his decency was a hallmark of his qualities. His penchant for moral rectitude was so strong that when Senators were debating whether Harrison Williams, a Democratic colleague and friend, should face censure or expulsion, Eagleton made clear he favored the latter. "I ask 98 of my colleagues, would any of you have engaged in this tawdry, greedy enterprise. If your silent answer of inner conscience is in the affirmative, then do your soul a favor by serving out your term and fading into deserved oblivion."

Fellow Missouri Senator John Danforth, a Republican, said, "There is nothing devious about Tom . . . What has set Tom Eagleton apart from the rest of us is not his intellect and energy, as impressive as they are. It is his moral passion, his capacity for outrage, his insistence that justice be done, that wrongs are made right." Eagleton was equally complimentary. When fellow Missourian John Ashcroft was tapped for Attorney General in 2001, Eagleton noted, "John Danforth would have been my first choice. John Ashcroft is my last choice."

But he had another act in public service.

Eagleton was appointed to a seat on the Chicago Mercantile Exchange but left two years later, saying "It was run by insiders for insiders." It was at that time that he began teaching at Washington University, practicing law and becoming involve in civic causes. It was partly Eagleton's efforts that returned the St. Louis Rams to the city (the team had gone to Los Angeles in 1984). Just two years after leaving office, Eagleton was one of two ex-Senators asked to speak to his former colleagues for the 200th anniversary of George Washington's inauguration. In his speech, he said "The Government's life force—what makes it work and endure—is our capacity to accommodate differences and to find a way beyond parochial, partisan, and ideological concerns to live together as a free nation."

In 2006, Eagleton, still pro-life, campaigned for the Missouri ballot initiative that legalized stem-cell research. Voters approved it. Eagleton died of complications of heart and respiratory problems in 2007. He was 77 years old.

Well before that, the wounds with McGovern had healed. In 1996, as McGovern appeared in St. Louis to discuss his book on his late daughter's bout with alcoholism, Eagleton introduced him. McGovern himself joked that, "Tom and I ran into a little snag back in 1972 that in the light of my much advanced wisdom today, I think was vastly exaggerated."

Photo via Thompson Coburn

Reagan Picked Schweiker As VP In Last Ditch Attempt To Head Off Ford in '76

Historic Quote: Ronald Reagan's Secret Service code name was "Rawhide." Ronald Keesler, in his book, *In the Presidents Secret Service*, he told an agent that during his 1988 visit to the Soviet Union, he had a gun in his briefcase. One day during his 1980 race, Reagan left his home wearing a pistol. When one of his agents questioned the need, he replied, "Well, just in case you guys can't do the job, I can help out."

Left image vialulacpoliticalletter.blogspot.org; right Photo via Corbis Images

The 1976 primary contest between Gerald Ford and Ronald Reagan was nip'n'tuck almost until the close of the Republican Convention. Both sides did everything and anything to get an edge with the various delegations that could be pivotal. Reaganwas under fire from moderates and knew he needed to win some over. So he took the unusual step of announcing before the convention his choice for Vice-President: Senator Richard Schweiker of Pennsylvania. Let's say that didn't go as planned.

It's not that anyone discounted Schweiker's qualifications for the office. He had been a member of Congress for 16 years, and had won two hard fought races for a statewide office in one of the nation's most populous states. It was simply that his views were so radically different from the man he was now sharing a ticket with.

Schweiker's record as a Senator from Pennsylvania was so centrist that he may have felt more comfortable with Democrats than his own party. And he nearly acknowledged as much. Indeed, it was. Schweiker called "independence . . . my life. I'm not a Republican steretype. And I'm not the kind of guy who can get the word from the party and vote for something that I don't belive in."

Schweiker had a 100% rating from labor which made him the first GOP Senator from the state to be endorsed by the AFL-CIO. Schweiker had an 89% from the ADA, a lifetime score of 57% from the League of Conservation Voters and opposed Nixon Supreme Court nominees Haynesworth and Carswell. He opposed Ford's tax breaks to oil companies and, well before many others in his party, the war as well. And he didn't like the draft, instead opting for a volunteer army. He sponsored the National Diabetes Mellitous Research and Education Act.

His life was a typical American success story. A son of Norristown, Pennsylvania, he served in the Navy and entered the family business; tiles, eventually becoming President of the American Tile Company, which was at the time the leading producer of ceramics. He won a Congressional seat in 1960 by ousting an incumbent, when even the GOP Chair said "he doesn't stand a chance." Then he took on three-term Democratic Senator and popular former Philadelphia Mayor Joe Clark in 1968 and, against similar dismissals, won that as well. And his wife was known as well. She had hosted the longtime children's show, "Romper Room."

Still, when he opted to take on Clark, many questioned what he was thinking. In February of 1968, Clark was so far ahead in the polls (62-38%) that some Republicans thought he'd win by one million votes. Instead, the national mood disintegrated for Democrats, with Clark being as much a visible prototype of any other member of his party. In the Democratic primary, Clark was held to a shockingly low 53% against Congressman John Dent, upset that Clark had questioned whether he could support LBJ in the wake of the Vietnam War.

Clark's vocal backing of gun control (Schweiker's was more subdued) made him the target of sportsmen. That may have helped him lose Allegheny County (Pittsburgh), as Schweiker took a 6,500 vote plurality out of 643,000 cast. With huge margins in the states's rural areas, Schweiker was easily able to overcome a deficit in Philly, and beat Clark by 282,000 votes. He said "personal contact and hard work did it for me." Even more remarkable was that Humphrey was winning Pennsylvania. But Schweiker said that not only was "Joe overconfident," but that "one reason he underestimated me was that he had never run against a liberal Republican . . . he didn't quite know how to campaign against someone who wasn't a typical right wing Republican."

In his concession, Clark said he thought Schweiker might make a good Senator but added, "I think I might have made a better one." Fast forward eight years and Clark was saying he "could not have lost to a better person." That may have added fuel to the fire of Republican delegates.

How did we get to this point? As the convention opened, Ford and Reagan had been in a furious, near-dead heat struggle for delegates. As primary season went on, Ford had squeaked out pivotal New Hampshire and seemed to have made it through the rain against Reagan when, out of nowhere, the ex-Governor won North Carolina. The state's conservative Senator Jesse Helms had endorsed him, and Reagan and Ford each traded wins in the primary contests that remained. Through July, it was genuinely unclear which man would emerge as the Republican standard bearer and Reagan needed something to give. So in picking Schweitzer, he said, "since I now feel that the people and the delegates have the right to know in advance of the convention who a nominees vice-presidential choice would be, I am departing from my tradition and announcing my selection."

Ford said when his two aides walked in and told him the news about Schweiker, he thought they were pulling his leg. Schweiker had been a committed to delegate to Ford, and had a moderate voting record to boot. Furthermore, it made little sense for Reagan, running as the conservative alternative to Ford, would risk alienating the true believers who were so squarely behind Reagan. But it was no joke.

Ford's campaign manager, Rogers Morton said the choice "appears to be an effort to trade the second highest office in the land for a handful of delegates." Reagan's press secretary, Jim Lake essentially validated that. Schweiker "has lots of friends in New York, in New Jersey, in Delaware, in Pennsylvania." He thought there were "soft" Ford delegates in each of those states and that Schweiker could help him over the top. Reagan also had another strategic ploy: getting Ford to reveal his own trump card and make his own pick for VP.

Schweiker (second from left) with Surgeon General C. Everett Koop
Public Domain Photo

Many branded Schweiker an opportunist, but he said Reagan's willingness to pick him "shares my deep desire for an open and broad based party." He called his move "bold."

Instead, it proved a gamble that failed. Conservatives were furious. Ford would write in his memoirs that conservative Congressman John Ashbrook called Schweiker's pick, "the dumbest thing I've ever heard of," and Henry Hyde compared it to a farmer who sold his last cow in order to buy a milk machine. And John Connolly called Ford and told him he'd be endorsing him the next day.

New Hampshire Governor Meldrin Thompson threatened to withdraw his support of Reagan, though didn't. But the Mississippi delegation, which Ford did not expect to win due to its conservative proclivities, was not amused. Congressman Thad Cochran called him "the most liber kook on Capitol Hill and it scares me that he would be a heartbeat away from being President." Three decades later, Cochran would say the same about John McCain. And one prominent in the Mississippi GOP told Reagan, "You have just given me the worst dose of castor oil I have ever had in my life. You got every part of my hollow insides. I am a hollow shell." Though their pick when down to the wire, its block selection went to Ford.

And Helms' anger was so strong that he actually went about promoting his Senate colleague, New York's Jim Buckley for the nomination. This may have helped Ford hold off Reagan, though by just more than 100 delegates.

After Reagan's loss, Schweiker returned to the Senate where he served the final four years of his term. He did not seek re-election in 1980. And to prove that Reagan's feelings about Schweiker were genuine. When he finally did win the Presidency in 1981, he made Schweiker his Health and Human Services Secretary.

Jackie Kennedy Backed John Anderson For President In '80

Historic Tidbit: "I saw a poll recently showing beer is more popular than Billy Carter. The American people much prefer something with a head on it." - Vice-Presidential candidate George H.W. Bush on a campaign swing in 1980.

Photo used with permission from the Rockford Register Star and rrstar.com

Jackie Kennedy was married to the most famous Democratic family in American history. It may be a surprise that she'd back anyone other than Democratic candidates. But she did just that in 1980. She didn't support a Republican, at least one who appeared on the ballot as such.

That candidate was an Independent, John Anderson, whose third party run in the 1980 general election against Reagan and Carter gave a voice to many disenchanted voters, particularly moderates. When it was over, Anderson had not only gained fame as a Doonesbury character, but he also won the heart and affection of folks for articulating a platform that was not what people wanted to hear, but what they didn't want to hear. In short, advocating for the next generation rather than the next election.

When folks think of Anderson, they may think Ross Perot without the accent flamboyance. But few think he was anything other than realistic. Today, he would certainly be an Independent in the mold of Angus King.

One remarkable fact about campaign '80, as pointed out by the *Almanac of American Politics* was that his Congressional district was home, at least at some point in their lives, to two of the three Presidential candidates. Anderson represented the area in Congress and Reagan's boyhood home was in Dixon.

A World War II veteran who had served as Winnebego County (Rockford) states attorney, Anderson won a Congressional seat in 1960 in a district that was so Republican that general elections would never be a problem. Due-diligence was another reason.. Anderson hadn't lifted a golf club since his election to Congress until a 1968 fundraiser and it showed, leading him to joke that, "After this, voters should know I'm not wasting my time on the golf course."

The first few terms of Anderson's tenure did not indicate that Anderson would be anything but a stalwart conservative. For one, he proposed a Constitutional amendment that "recognized the law and authority of Jesus Christ." That went nowhere but colleagues recognized his skills as a leader and in 1969, they awarded him the post of Republican Conference Committee. The margin was only 89-81 over the rigidly conservative Samuel DeVine. The margin revealed that conservatives either backed Anderson because they didn't like DeVine, or that they reluctantly voted for DeVine because they viewed Anderson as becoming more of a centrist (see below).. After the '74 elections, Anderson was mentioned as a possible candidate for Republican Whip but decided against it in part for that reason. "The position under (fellow Illinois Republican Leslie) Arends," he said, "has become that of a mere functionary. I'm not interested in it. I've come to the conclusion that I can best use the maneuverability I have" in my present position.

Anderson's ideological metamorphosis came in the late 1960s. In 1968, shortly after the assassination of Dr. Martin Luther King, Jr., he cast the decisive vote on moving a Fair Housing Bill out of the Rules Committee, saying, "We are not simply knuckling under to pressure or listening to the voices of unreasoning fear and hysteria if we seek to do that which we believe in our hearts is right and just. I legislate today not out of fear, but out of a deep concern for the America I love. We do stand at a crossroad. We can continue the ... slide into an endless cycle of riot and disorder or we can begin the slow and painful ascent toward that yet-distant goal of equality of opportunity for all Americans, regardless of race or color." On other social issues, Anderson was solidly pro-choice, opposing attempts to weaken access. He favored affirmative action and the Equal Rights Amendment. He was against Nixon early and came around to opposing the Cambodia bombings. He was also lukewarm on the Alaska pipeline, wanting it to go through Canada instead. But he was a steadfast supporter of the Alaska Wilderness Act and served as Arizona colleague Mo Udall's second prime sponsor on the bill that cleared Congress in 1980. Anderson and Udall also worked together on a campaign finance rewrite, which provided for matching funds.

Anderson also hoped to draw a line of accountability for Congress to voters, and he felt that could be done by giving Americans exposure to Congress via television. The endeavor that got off the ground is C-Span. Gerald Ford once called Anderson "the smartest guy in Congress, but he insists on voting his conscience instead of party." And Ralph Nader, in an extraordinary compliment, called him "a thoughtful man who has . . . moved toward the political center during his twelve years in Congress . . . In debate, he appears unruffled but forceful, his style marked by flashes of humor."

When it came to the party, Anderson was not shy about keeping it in the middle. At one retreat in late 1977 organized by Michigan Governor Bill Milliken, Anderson claimed "extremist fringe elements who claim to be in our party seek to expel the rest of us from the GOP, using their own, arbitrary philosophical purgative." He claimed to be on the rights "hit list whose apparent goal is to rob the party rather than revivify it, whose devotion to doctrine outstrips their dedication to party." He warned that "if the purists stage their ideological coup d'etat, our party will be consigned to the historical junk heap."

By 1978, there was no doubt that Anderson's forewarned "hit-list" was coming full throttle ahead for him. His ideology was hurting him back home, and he was becoming a constant target for re-nomination. In that year's primary, he was held to 58% and at that point, the nation wasn't getting any less conservative. That's when he decided it was up or out and he announced his bid for the Republican Presidential nomination (he also considered a Senate run). When asked why he was doing so, he called "the process of running for President is debilitating and demeaning, but the job would be exciting—charting a course for the nation." When asked why he was doing so, he called "the process of running for President is debilitating and demeaning, but the job would be exciting—charting a course for the nation."

Walter Shapiro had done an article that seemed to capture all of the qualities of Anderson that people from the ordinary and the frustrated typically find so appealing. "Before a large crowd, Anderson can be a fiery speaker, with perfect timing and a voice that rises and falls for emphasis, even though in ordinary conversation he sounds more like Jason Robards than William Jennings Bryan." It noted Anderson driving by themselves in a rental car with reporters in the back seat, speaking frankly. One such example was when he asked his wife why he was running. Her answer: His wife said, "It's easy, John. You know why you decided you should run. Someone must address our pressing national problems."

Anderson also acknowledged that he was in it for his country. "I know I'm going to lose," he said. "And, in the immortal words of Rhett Butler, "Frankly,

I don't give damn." The article was entitled, "John Anderson: The Nice Guy Syndrome."

Anderson casts his vote in the Illinois primary
Photos used with permission from the Rockford Register Star and rrstar.com

Incidentally, Shapiro noted that Anderson was friends with Mo Udall, who, like Anderson, finished second in a number of close primaries.

Anderson actually tied Bush percentage-wise in Massachusetts, losing by fewer than 2,000 votes among 167,000 cast. In Vermont, He finished fewer than 700 votes to Reagan in Vermont. But even if he had won, his strength was still confined to New England. And a strong but losing bid in his home state of Illinois (Reagan beat him 48-37%) would clearly mean curtains.

But there would be a second act.

Anderson decided to mount an independent campaign. The first task was making the ballot on all 50 states, a task that proved to be a little more herculean than he had expected, as it took the entire summer, and forced him to overcome ten lawsuits. The next was participating in the Presidential debates.

In mid-summer, there were signs that Anderson's candidacy, if taken seriously, could catch fire. To do that, Anderson needed to be bold and he was. One of his proposals was a 50-50 plan, which "Crazy Dreaming: The Anderson Campaign, 1980," described as a 50 cent tax on a gallon of gasoline to increase conservation while using the newly generated revenue to offset a 50 percent reduction in Social Security payroll taxes." Michigan Republican Congressman Carl Purcell said, "John's the best of the three. He's a good man and a Great American." But as the author of "Crazy Dreaming,' explained, Anderson's skill was not presenting his ideas in a manner that average Americans could comprehend.

**Image via ronwadebuttons.com; Photo used with permission
from the Rockford Register Star and rrstar.com**

President Carter was refusing to participate in any debates that included Anderson, but Reagan was willing. So the two debated together and, as Anderson said, "I was very proud of the fact that in the post-debate reporting that when they took a poll among debate coaches, college and high school debate coaches, they felt that if you judged the debating on points, clearly I had the advantage."

Anderson's platform was a national sales tax, and pro-choice on abortion. As his running mate, he selected former Wisconsin Governor Patrick Lucey, who, having been UN Ambassador, also brought foreign policy heft to the ticket. But the major issue was the economy, particularly inflation, which an Anderson campaign brochure called, "the cruelest tax of all and that is the tax I intend to cut." Although anti-inflationary measures will require sacrifice on the part of all citizens, no sector of the society will be asked to bear a disproportionate share of the burden.

He called for, a "50-cent-per-gallon energy conservation tax on all motor vehicles to cut consumption and reduce our dependence on foreign supplies." Anderson said his quest was "not designed to win votes. It is designed to address itself to what I think is a problem of crisis proportions. I believe that when you are facing that kind of emergency, you have to be willing to prescribe some pretty tough action. I think the American people are ready for some straight answers . . . When you are confronted with a genuine emergency, then I think you have to look at the interest of the country first."

Often, when Independent candidates are running for office — any office, voters are hesitant to back them not because they find them unappealing, but because of the perception that they can't win, and that a vote for that person could throw the election to the candidate that person does not want. Such may have been the case with Anderson. At one point, he had 16% in some polls.

He attracted support from liberals such as Norman Lear and on Election Day, drew 7%.

Out of office, Anderson continued his quest for good government. He became chairman of Common Cause. At 93, he lives in Illinois. Asked whether he felt bruised by his loss, Anderson replied, "Disappointed, yes. Bruised, no." And whether in office or out, he continues to be the gift the American people could use today.

Wisconsin's Lucey Capped Off Colorful Career As Anderson's Runningmate

Historic Tidbit: One day as a junior member of the House, Gerald Ford gave a somewhat elongated speech. After, a colleague from Texas approached him and said, "Jerry, that was the best Longhorne speech I ever heard." Ford stared quizzically. The man explained that a Longhorne speech is one that has "two points, far, far apart with plenty of bull in between."

I n the summer of 1980, Wisconsin Governor Patrick Lucey had fulfilled a true career of public service: legislator, party chair, Lieutenant Governor, Governor, and finally, Ambassador to Mexico. That seemed to encompass all an aspiring pol could ask for. But Lucey would find the call of duty knocking one more time. John Anderson selected him to be his running-mate during his Independent run for the Presidency in 1980 partly because of these attributes.

A LaCrosse native, Lucey's great-grandfather came to America from Ireland and added a "y" after his name. His success surprised nobody – except maybe himself. He enrolled in college for a year but instead opted to run the business, Lucey's Cash & Carry." He also ran the butcher shop which his family lived over. It was then that politics began calling – not a total surprise given that his father and grandfather were members of the Crawford County Board. The first was a stint as Justice of the Peace for Ferryville, Wisconsin. After, he served on the school board.

His election to the Wisconsin Assembly in 1948 made him the only Democrat from the western part of the state to win a seat this year. Campaign resources were sparse so Lucey resorted to creative tactics such as placing ads in the classifieds which read: "HANDY MAN FOR HIRE: Just place an (X) after my name next Tuesday and you've hired a handy man for Crawford County to have in Madison." Even more improbable; he beat the sitting Assembly Speaker. That may have been the first test of Lucey as an organizer. At that time, Lucey was one of just 26 Democrats in the 100 member Assembly and shortly after his term began, he decided the time was ripe for rebuilding.

He attempted to win a Congressional seat two years later but was defeated.

Eventually, Lucey became Chair of the Wisconsin Democratic Party and was one of the key players in convincing JFK to enter the Wisconsin Presidential primary. Little known was that the Massachusetts Senator was ambivalent about entering. Hubert Humphrey grew up right next door and seemed to have backing from farmers and labor. But Kennedy had money and a solid organization. Conversely, Humphrey's campaign was hampered from disunity. But he recognized that his backing from labor was not unanimous so he courted labor by personally speaking with every one of the "Badger State's" leaders.

As JFK was preparing to depart Wisconsin shortly after deciding to give it a go, he posed a question to Lucey at the airport. "Now that you've conned me into this thing, how do you feel? "As of today, my chances of getting the nomination are slightly less than 50-50. If I win the Wisconsin primary, they'll be slightly better than 50-50. So if you look at it that way, I'm not gambling very much."

But Lucey spotted JFK's talents a mile away. "He just seemed totally disinterested in what was going on and assessed the various elements of the campaign and make studious judgements of what they should do next." It was said that at a local function, JFK spent little time eating but a fair amount chatting with Lucey.

And it paid. Kennedy won a 110,000 victory out of 850,000 cast.

Left photo via the Wisconsin State Historical Society; Right photo courtesy of the John F. Kennedy Presidential Library and Museum

The following year, Lucey faced a test for a third term as Chair, particularly from the schism that had backed Humphrey. But Lucey had the strong backing of Wisconsin Attorney General John Reynolds, who credited his ability to "get along with all factions of the party and practically all of the elected officials." He held his post.

As the 1962 elections approached, division still reigned within the party but as another major election approached, Lucey adroitly pulled a rabbit out of his hat. He succeeded in getting then Attorney General Robert Kennedy to a fundraiser for the party's entire slate. At first, low sales worried Lucey and he thought he might only sell about 650 tickets. Instead, 835 went, prompting

Lucey to joke that "he'd never so badly misjudged a crowd in my life." More importantly, the event rallied those ambivalent, particularly labor, around the party's Gubernatorial nominee, Reynolds. Upon taking the microphone, Kennedy joked that when Lucey "called and said I had to come to the dinner, he said it would be non-partisan."

It paid off. Gaylord Nelson won the Senate seat, Reynolds eked out a narrow victory which was rewarded the following January when Reynolds made Lucey his only allowed guest for a dinner with President Kennedy in Washington (Reynolds first had given the ticket to his wife but she couldn't attend). But as events unfolded, Lucey would only have Reynolds by his side for so long.

Reynolds lost his 1964 bid for re-election to Warren Knowles. But Lucey, running for Lieutenant Governor on his own line (the two were elected separately at the time), prevailed by 40,000 votes, defeating Jack Olson 51-49%. In its endorsement, *the Milwauklee Sentinel* said "Lucey means business – for Wisconsin." That all but assured Lucey the right of first refusal for the next statewide office which came in 1966 when he decided to challenge Knowles, though he did have to fend off a determined primary foe.

Basking in the glow of re-election with Senators Nelson and Proxmire Image courstey of Politics1.com and photo via the Wisconsin State Historical Society

Lucey lost to Knowles 54-46%, held his powder by declining to challenge him in '68, instead, preferring to help Bobby Kennedy. Lucey recalls meeting with Bobby "the Sunday before he was killed," and being asked "to come to L.A. because we're going to win this primary (California) and the next morning, we're going to have a strategy meeting on what we do from now until the convention." Lucey recalls checking into the Ambassador Hotel and, upon hearing a "commotion in the big ballroom…two women came out with their mascara running."

Returning to Wisconsin, Lucey leapt at the next opportunity in 1970. In that election, he'd face Jack Olson, his predecessor and successor as Lieutenant Governor. Olson tried to tie Lucey to campus unrest that had occurred that summer at UW as well as tax increases. But Olson was hurt when Knowles acknowledged that additional revenue would be needed for the coming year. Democrats made sure their slate – including Lucey's primary foe. He won 54-44%.

In office, Lucey's chief initiative was one that had eluded Governors of both parties since the 1890's; a merger of the WSU system with UW Madison. The plan was not universally embraced, particularly by the faculty at UW, as they feared that its influence would be diminished. But Lucey argued that not only would it would be the best way to deal with cost containment but it would put the system even further on the map. Ultimately, it was approved by a one vote margin in the Senate.

Lucey also focused on taxpayer relief, as Wisconsin had among the nation's highest property taxes in the nation. He worked on ethics and campaign reform and promoted tourism. "Our Campaigns" notes that since 1974, Mt. Telemark in Cable, Wisconsin has hosted "the American Birkebeiner each year, the largest cross-country ski race in North America."

Photo courtesy via the Wisconsin State Historical Society

In 1974, Lucey won re-election by a 53-42% margin, not particularly impressive given the strong Democratic nature of the year, and that he had outspent his opponent by $200,000. His opponent, while a skilled speaker, was not ideologically in sync (two years later, he'd be the Vice-Presidential nominee on the American Independence party).

But when he delivered the state to Jimmy Carter by a 36,000 vote margin two years later, the new President rewarded him with the position of Ambassador to Mexico. Lucey pondering the move and his ultimate acceptance was a surprise to many (he said he'd remain as Governor for 90 days until the budget was approved). But Lucey may have been motivated by the future. Though he had been building huge campaign coffers in anticipation of a tough race for a third term. There had been rumblings of Lucey's own Lieutenant Governor Martin Schreiber, 38, challenging Lucey in the primary. Instead, he assumed the post upon Lucey's unanimous confirmation by the Senate.

By 1980, things had soured between Lucey and Carter. He left his post in 1979 and backed Ted Kennedy for the Democratic Presidential nomination the following year and had unsuccessfully lobbied for an "open convention." When Carter was re-nominated, Lucey's career seemed to fade, but Anderson's offer both rekindled it, and fulfilled the Republican turned Independent candidates quest for "National Unity."

Anderson said Lucey's "intellect, character, and experience." passes all of these tests magnificently" and shot down calls that Lucey was a geographical mismatch for Anderson, who hailed just south of the border in Illinois. "It is old politics to think that because the candidates are separated geographically this adds some balance to the ticket." As for the Democratic Party, Lucey said he is entitled to a "sabbatical leave."

Lucey called his decision to bolt the Democrats "difficult and painful" but said "Jimmy Carter can't win," Ronald Reagan is "irrelevant," and that his bolting after years of faithful service was merely "a sabbatical." But he hit the trail with fire. "Only John Anderson," he said "stands between us and a Reagan administration that would turn this country over to Jesse Helms, Phyllis Schafly, and the Taiwan lobby."

Photo via ronwadebuttons.com

Lucey fulfilled his many obligatory stump speeches. "I was taken to task for being negative. And so we decided to continuously explain our platform wherever we go. What gets publicity is our attacks." And he kept the morale going in the face of discouraging polls. "I think John Anderson is going to be the next president," he said in one interview. I think things are moving very well in his favor." That wasn't exactly the case but through no fault of Lucey.

As for Lucey the man, he would call himself, "charismatically challenged," once saying, "I don't really have any hobbies. I mean, I don't play golf. I guess my hobby has been politics."

Lucey was 96 when he died in 2014. A few years earlier, he joked that he had his driver's license until he was 100.

Stumping during the 1980 campaign
Photo via the Wisconsin State Historical Society

Mondale's Twelve Years In The Senate As Accomplished As Many Of The Body's Longest Serving Members

Historic Quote: "Grits and Fritz in '76." – A commonly used slogan that emerged for the Carter/Mondale ticket after the Georgia Governor picked Minnesota Senator Walter "Fritz" Mondale as his running-mate in 1976.

**Mondale was perhaps most content serving in the U.S. Senate
Photo courtesy of the University of Minnesota Law Library Archives**

I n 2002, former Vice-President Walter Mondale delivered an address to his old colleagues in the Old Senate Chamber. In his remarks, he noted that, "Since the start of our nation, the Vice Presidency has been an awkward office. Its occupants are notoriously unhappy. The Constitution, as you know, only assigns the duty, if wanted, to preside and to break ties if you so desire. Here is a public officer, the only one in our government system, who belongs to both the executive branch and the legislative branch. But for most of our history, since the Vice Presidents were in both branches, they have been treated as if they were in neither."

Mondale just as well might have told the tale that was made by legend of one of his predecessors, Thomas Marshall of Indiana, who as vice-president under Woodrow Wilson joked about a woman with two sons – one went off to sea and the other became vice-president. "Neither was heard from again." Or he could have invoked the colorful and irascible John Nance Garner who once called the vice-presidency "not worth a bucket of warm spit" (that quote was said to have been cleaned up). At any rate, Mondale changed that.

The nation's 42nd vice-president was known as the first strong occupant of the office - the first person with that title to hold an office in the West Wing and was an unmitigated presence in the sausage-making on both the domestic and foreign front. He was the nominee of his party for president of the United States in 1984 and further ensured his place in history by picking the first woman running-mate, Geraldine Ferraro. The ticket lost but Mondale's contribution to his nation was not finished – in 1993 he was appointed Ambassador to Japan by President Bill Clinton.

Mondale and his father
Photo courtesy of the University of Minnesota Law Library Archives

Yet before taking the office of vice-president, Mondale was a Senator from Minnesota. In fact, it's not an inaccurate to call him forever a Senator at heart. first He called his years in that body, "the happiest of my public career," adding, "I found my sweet spot here. I loved working with friends and colleagues, and I loved learning new things." And Mondale was enormously effective. From open housing to preserving the St. Croix River to filibuster reform, Mondale took on the serious and complex and often got results that had long proven elusive to colleagues.

Mondale was born in Ceylon, Minnesota, one of three children. His mother was a music teacher and his father a farmer before becoming a Methodist minister, the latter which might have instilled Mondale's unflappable commitment to social justice. Though the Mondale's had a long put down roots in Minnesota by the time young Walter was born, his family's heritage is colorful. As his bio from the University of Minnesota Law Library states, his great-grandparents hailed from the Mundal Valley in Norway. "Upon arriving in the United States, they changed their name to 'Mundale' following the advice of an immigration official that the extra vowel would make the name 'more American.' The spelling again changed, this time to Mondale, when Mr. Mondale's grandfather, Ole, filed papers for land in southern Minnesota. When the papers came back from Washington, the name had been recorded as Mondale. Not wishing to take any chance of losing the land, he adopted the new name." And the rest was history.

"Fritz" was a nick-name Mondale acquired through friends as a child but it stuck and would became a name of affection among colleagues and friends. His political interest began as a freshman at Macalester College. *The New York Times* noted Mondale, "helped organize fellow students to move into the DFL and force out the ultra-left wingers and Communist sympathizers." Two years later, he earned his degree from the University of Minnesota. At that point, Mondale's goal was to attend law school but because money was an issue, he joined the service. But the Korean War was booming and Mondale enlisted in the U.S. Army, attaining the rank of Corporal. Meanwhile, he met his future wife, Joan – on a "semi-blind date" and was engaged within 53 days (he said the one condition was that he'd learn to ski and the *New York Times* reported in 1964 that he, "now is a better skier than she").

Mondale had the fortune of becoming prodigies of two of the most respected and durable names in Democratic Farmer-Labor (DFL) politics: Hubert Humphrey and Orville Freeman. When Humphrey sought a Senate seat in 1948, Mondale was assigned to organize the state's Second Congressional District. It was Republican territory and Mondale's mission was to produce a number for Humphrey that would simply keep him competitive statewide. Instead, Humphrey carried the district. In 1960, Freeman, then Governor, appointed Mondale Attorney General and he won the position in his own right that November with 58%. He was up to nearly 60% in 1962 – running far ahead of the top of the ticket (Democrat Karl Rolvaag famously became Governor after a protracted recount that dragged into March).

The Mondale Family
Photo courtesy of the University of Minnesota Law Library Archives

In that role, Mondale often took on causes that went well beyond the Minnesota border. One was an amicus brief urging the U.S. Supreme Court to direct states to spend some money on free counseling. Another was the Supreme Court case of Gideon vs. Wainwright. Clarence Gideon had unsuccessfully petitioned the courts for an attorney as he awaited charges for stealing from a vending machine at a Florida pool hall and the matter had made its way to the U.S. Supreme Court. Florida's Attorney General had urged Mondale to support his anti-Gideon view but he on principle favored Gideon's right to an attorney and instead filed an amicus brief urging justices to rule in Gideon's favor. Along with his Massachusetts colleague, Eddie McCormack (the House Speaker's nephew), he recruited other attorneys general to the cause and got 22 to join him. His reasoning: "I believe in federalism and states' rights too," Mondale said. "But I also believe in the Bill of Rights.... Nobody knows better than an Attorney General or a prosecuting attorney that in this day and age furnishing an attorney to those felony defendants who can't afford one is fair and feasible." *The Minnesota Post* observed the fact that Mondale had little to gain by inserting himself into these matters. "He had political ambition and siding with a four-time convicted felon simply made no political sense." But he believed they were right and as such, were an important part of his convictions.

Another initiative included investigating the Sister Elizabeth Kenny Foundation and the Minnesota Boys Town, the latter that focused on the fact that the organization, "had raised $250,000 in private donations but had never spent a penny on troubled teens. "Mondale tried to broker a compromise on the Mississippi seating during the 1964 Democratic Convention and while both sides were close, an agreement proved elusive. But that year, Humphrey had been tapped to be Lyndon Johnson's running-mate and when the ticket was elected, Mondale put his name in the mix. Rolvaag would make the selection and Mondale prevailed over several well-known politicos that included longtime Congressman John Blatnik of the Iron Range.

The letter Mondale's mother wrote to Governor Rolvaag after he named her son to fill Hubert Humphrey's Senate seat
Image courtesy of the University of Minnesota Law Library Archives

Much of Mondale's early effort was spent on local issues. He was a strong supporter of the "Great Society" and championed meat inspections. His committee assignments reflected a sundry potpourri of his many interests. The Aeronautical and Space Sciences Committee, Finance, Budget, Banking, Housing and Urban Affairs and Labor and Public Welfare, the latter which he was awarded in 1968 following Bobby Kennedy's assassination. He would use his positions – in fact, nearly every endeavor he undertook, to forge compromises. One of Mondale's colleagues, Missouri Democrat Tom Eagleton explained the method to his effectiveness. "Some Senators would rather stake out a position – and lose, just to have staked out that position. Mondale would rather stake out that position and see how much of that position he could change into a finite result."

Improving the conditions of migrant workers was one cause Mondale assiduously pursued and, having worked with them as a teenager, seeing to it that safety rules applied was one aspect. "We've got to realize how difficult it is to make progress in helping a powerless group which is politically, economically and socially unable to help itself." He summed up his philosophy thus: "Liberals can pass a law and go back to sleep but a migrant has to live that life every day."

But Mondale also wanted to make sure the progress of migrant workers was not to the detriment of American workers. In 1969, he chaired the Senate Labor and Public Welfare Subcommittee on Migratory Labor and held a seven-part hearing on problems pertaining to migrants and seasonal labor. That year, Mondale, along with his colleagues, Ted Kennedy and Ralph Yarborough, marched a portion of 100 miles from a town in the California desert to a town just shy of the Mexico border.

Mondale with his parents and the Humphreys
following his becoming a U.S. Senator
Photo courtesy of the University of Minnesota Law Library Archives

The Wilderness Act was likely the crown jewel of Mondale's legislative career and he called it, "one of the most satisfying things I've done." Plus, he noted, "we got there just in time." In *The St. Croix: Midwest Border River*, James Taylor Dunn wrote how, "in 1964, "federal study teams were traveling the river's upper region, renewing the hope that in spite of previous setbacks, the St. Croix and the Namekagon Rivers might be placed among America's protected wild rivers."

This led to passage of the Wild and Scenic Rivers Act and Mondale was able to get the Upper St. Croix River included. The Lower St. Croix did not make the final cut but Mondale rectified that in 1972 with the signing of the Lower St. Croix National Scenic Riverway. Mondale called the river, "sort of a spiritual center for me. My wife and I got married because we went down the river together, and a few years later we bought a house on the St. Croix in Scandia. I still sit there and watch the river go by and think of her ... It's a beautiful thing that can't be matched."

Civil rights was also a defining part of Mondale's Senate legacy. He and Massachusetts Republican Senator Ed Brooke sponsored the Johnson administration's bill which would move open housing into three parts. He said it was clear "this will be our only opportunity for Senate consideration of civil rights legislation in this session," and argued, "We are fighting for the minds and hearts of the vast middle ground of responsible Negroes who have persevered in their commitment to progress through the courts and through the legislative process." When a motion to end a filibuster to the legislation failed 55-37, the duo was forced to settle for compromise language which he labeled, "a miracle." Johnson signed it into law six days after the assassination of Dr. Martin Luther King, Jr., at which time Michigan Senator Phil Hart, a major civil rights proponent, penned a letter to Mondale that read, "You were magnificent—your energy, your counsel, your courage, and your leadership combined to move the Senate 'to do right.'"

Mondale had chaired the Senate Select Committee on Equal Education Opportunity which was investigating a way to combat segregation. A report recommended more federal money. But as a hearing showed, the bureaucracy would balk at making that a reality.

When Internal Revenue Service Commissioner Randolph Thrower testified before the committee in 1970, Senators accused the Nixon administration of granting tax exempt status to primarily white schools who simply promise the hiring of minority teachers and admittance of minority students. Mondale called the policy a "fraud and a hoax," and "palpably ridiculous," and before adjourning the hearing said, "We have in this country a dramatic, unquestionably new movement in education--all-white, tax supported segregation academies have flowered throughout the area where courts have ordered desegregation. The tax exempt status is essential to their operation. I am personally persuaded this (IRS tax exemption policy) will continue. I hope I'm wrong. This leads me to believe these academies are going to continue enjoying a success; that will take us back to where we were 16 years ago (prior to the U.S. Supreme Court decision Brown vs. Board of Education). That would be one of the most tragic things ever to happen in this country and I deeply regret it."

Two years later, when Senators debated the Higher Education Act, Mondale opposed anti-busing language sponsored by Michigan Republican Robert Griffin. The House had passed a bill that barred force busing for desegregation purposes and Mondale noted the challenge ahead of amalgamating that and the Senate version into a compromise. He said, "This bill that comes over to us cannot be called a desegregation bill," he said. "It does nothing to encourage or assist desegregation."

The Griffin measure would have prohibited busing "on the basis of their race, color, religion or national orgin." Mondale retorted that the measure "provides all the excuses as is needed for the Justice Department to stop trying any school desegregation cases at all." It cleared the chamber 43-40. But the following week, the amendment was brought up again and this time, Senators who were presidential candidates returned from the trail to cast a vote. Mondale again led the charge against it, labeling it, "a blatantly unconstitutional attempt to prevent enforcement of the U S. Constitution by U.S. courts." It failed 50-47.

At the end of the day, neither side completely got its way. A carefully drafted compromise by the Senate's two leaders, Majority Leader Mike Mansfield of Montana and his Republican counterpart, Hugh Scott of Pennsylvania that prohibited federal funds for busing unless they had been specifically requested by localities. It cleared by a big margin.

That fall, Mondale won re-election by a bigger than expected 57-43% over Phil Hansen, the director of a drug alcohol treatment center Hansen had attacked Mondale's stance on busing and branded him "destructive" to Nixon's agenda. He also labeled him a "McGovern liberal," even linking him to the legalization of marijuana (Mondale in fact had been sought out as a possible running-mate for his South Dakota colleague but shunned interest).

Another key component of Mondale's accomplishments was filibuster reform. In 1975, the threshold for invoking cloture on legislation and nominations was 67 out of 100 Senators, which Mondale said if left in place, "every one of the crucial issues we face, including tax reform, energy priorities and broad economic policies will be delayed." So Mondale and his Kansas Republican colleague, Jim Pearson, proposed lowering it to 60. The change was enacted but not before a few false starts. A rules change requires a simple majority vote and by voting 51-42 to implement the change. That was when Alabama Democrat James Allen won a ruling by the chair – Republican Vice-President Nelson Rockefeller, that the motion was "divisible," and could be debated (Mondale said Rockefeller correctly interpreted the rules). But at the end of the day, Allen's jubilation was short lived. A number of motions to reconsider were made and Louisiana Senator Russell Long proposed the 3/5 rule – so long as it only applied to the current Congress. as two weeks later, Senators voted 73-21 to adopt the compromise. And in a true compliment of Mondale being the consummate legislator, Allen later said "we have opposing views but we joke back and forth quite a bit. I see him as a friendly opponent on the Senate floor."

In 1968, Mondale associated himself with Ted Kennedy's proposal to establish a "sane" draft system. Mondale delineated five reasons, one of which "eliminates the uncertainty among young people that is inherent in the present draft system." The ability of a student to attend college was another reason. On the War Powers Act, Mondale noted the Herculean effort it took to forge a final product. He called it "appropriate that the war powers bill has such consensus for earmarking decisions involve both political parties in the most profound kind of bipartisanship.... Presidents have usurped Congressional power but only because Congress has placed too much confidence in the Executive. Congress has acquiesced and accepted various presidential rationalizations and therefore, must share part of the blame for our involvement in the Dominican Republic, Vietnam, Cambodia and Laos."

Visiting Norway
Photo courtesy of the University of Minnesota Law Library Archives

Another issue high on Mondale's plate in the 1970s was consumer legislation. In 1973, he pushed through $85 million to combat child abuse. Money was also earmarked for demonstration projects. A year earlier, legislation Mondale passed would authorize the National Institute of Child Health and Human Development to use everything within their powers to study the causes of sudden infant death syndrome. When Congress cleared a 20% increase in Social Security benefits, Mondale vowed to protect beneficiaries by including language that prohibited public housing authorities from raising rent due to the increase. In 1975, Mondale introduced legislation that would outlaw "pyramid schemes." Penalties of up to $10,000 and jail time would result. "Literally thousands of Americans have been defrauded of millions of dollars by pyramiders," he said. The pyramid sales scheme is America's number one consumer fraud problem." Also that year, when President Ford wanted to lower oil import fees, Mondale, noting the high price of oil, called that "very dangerous economically."

Also in 1975, when President Ford announced plans to limit Social Security increases to five percent, Mondale called it, "indefensible, heartless, and cruel to the millions of elderly persons who depend upon Social Security benefits." He took the bipartisan lead – along with Ted Kennedy and Frank Church in authoring a resolution condemning the proposal.

Mondale had no problem trying to stop things he felt weren't in the national interest and 1972 was an example of that when, along with Birch Bayh of Indiana, he tried to stop construction of the proposed Alaska pipeline until a study on a trans-Canadian pipeline was complete. He said the Alaskan pipeline would thwart oil from getting "east of the Rockies," whereas the trans-Canada route would involve Alberta, Canada and the east coast. "That is why so much oil will be sold to Japan," he said. The measure was rejected 29-61.

Mondale also made an early contribution to raising the issue of driving while under the influence. An amendment he proposed to a 1966 highway bill that would study the link of alcoholism and accident fatalities was adopted. He proposed a bill banning the sale of simulated police badges. And he advocated cutting off aid to countries that refuse to limit the production of opium.

In 1971, Mondale and New Jersey Republican Clifford Case essentially got the Nixon administration to back off funding for a new $700 million nuclear carrier. The two Senators were especially disturbed that the project would not warrant Congressional approval. They called it "back-door financing," which, "bypasses the normal legislative process, avoiding consideration and a vote by the full membership of both houses." The Pentagon decided to not proceed with the project. A year earlier, Mondale and Case had lost an attempt to delete $377 million in funding for a new carrier (fellow Senators tabled it 51-34) but did manage to earmark money for a study on the feasibility of its future use.

In 1972, Mondale proposed zeroing out the $227.9 million requested for the space shuttle, calling it the, "tip of a multi-billion dollar iceberg." He said, "We continue to hear the $5 billion figure. In fact, the total program cost over a 12 year period of operations is $35 billion. It should be emphasized moreover that this $35 billion figure still does not include the multi-billion cost of developing a permanent manned station to be placed in earth orbit. Because the shuttle is inevitably linked to the eventual development of such a space station, the complete cost of this program, assuming no cost-overruns, will approach $40 billion." His amendment was defeated 21-61.

Mondale served on the "Church Committee" which was created in the wake of revelations of illegal domestic abuses on the part of the Nixon White House. He spoke of the necessity of "scrupulous adherence to the law and the Constitution by the agencies of Government." It was said that Mondale played a major role in the committee's function following the presidential bid of the panel's chairman, Idaho Democrat Frank Church.

During his tenure, Mondale authored numerous op/eds for *The New York Times*. He proposed an amendment creating a council of social advisors to measure the impacts of social programs.

Were there any legislative endeavors that Mondale pursued that were not successful? His few setbacks were generally confined to the area of child care. With Indiana Congressman John Brademas, he took the lead in crafting legislation - the Comprehensive Child Development Act, that would have created federally funded day care centers. To the surprise of Mondale, Nixon vetoed it even though his administration helped craft it. Mondale would later quip, "Even for Nixon, it was surprising." During debate on the unsuccessful override, he said, "We all know there are hundreds, thousands, and millions of children who never have a chance, who are mangled and destroyed the first 5 years of life. This bill is the best that the House and Senate could think of to undo the monstrous and immoral wrong that we now visit upon the lives of those tragic children." In the next two Congresses, Mondale recalls he, "really worked hard on shaping the bill we called the Family and Child Services Act which we passed and Nixon vetoed. That was a great disappointment because if we had these laws this many years later, there would be millions of kids in better shape." Later, he told Elizabeth Drew in an interview that, "this country must do a far better job than it's done, and spend more than it has and spend it more wisely and with more spirit and compassion, and with a fuller commitment than we ever have had, to give every child a chance, and I think that's so central that I am sickened by some who would abandon that effort."

Mondale also noted that he "failed to get the Summer Camp Safety bill." That left him befuddled. "There was lots of evidence that kids were in dangerous situations in camps and we couldn't get it done. I think the Senate thought we were going one step too far. I didn't get it."

Mondale's deep legislative portfolio and his capable disposition led many to talk about a higher calling; the presidency. James Reston in the *New York Times* wrote, "Mondale has a kind of moral authority and determination that might just change the question in Democratic politics. There is plenty of evidence the country is tired of the old faces, and would welcome a new cast of characters. He's not very fancy but he's straight." Mondale considered it but ultimately decided against it because - perhaps proving Reston's point, declared, "I don't think there's enough show biz in me." Plus, he said, "I don't want to spend the next two years at Holiday Inn's" (later, he clarified that, "I've checked and they've all been redecorated. They're marvelous places to stay and I've thought it over and that's where I'd like to be").

But Mondale would still have an engagement with the national stage. A peanut farmer from Georgia named Jimmy Carter captured the Democratic nomination for president in 1976 and as an outsider, needed someone with gravitas. While the initial parlor talk had Church favored to get the nod (followed by Ohio Senator John Glenn), Mondale emerged as the choice just as the Democratic National

Convention was gaveling to order. The ticket was elected, thus setting the stage for a top-notch vice-presidency and future head of his own party.

Years later, Carter paid tribute to the wisdom of his running-mate. "He was a perfect partner, and I don't believe we ever had a serious argument during the four years -- which was better than my relationship with my wife."

Photo courtesy of the U.S. Senate Historical Office

A Few Good Men:
Coincidences and Anomalies of the (Obscure)
Men Who Shaped 13ᵗʰ Amendment

Writer's Note: Okay, so this book is obviously about the men and women who were unsung heroes of the 1960's. But the movie "Lincoln," which took place in the 1860's obviously gave me an opportunity to explore characters of that age. I was even able to incorporate them with more modern political figures. Read on. You'll enjoy it. And see the movie.

16. Abraham Lincoln 1861-1865

I recently saw Steven Spielberg's much acclaimed "Lincoln." It was an unbelievable film that deserves every accolade it will receive. And there'll be many. And for the many Lincoln experts who believe they know all of the intricacies and enigma relating to Lincoln the man, the movie will open many new windows about our 16ᵗʰ President. My respect for his leadership, abilities, and compassion have only grown.

Naturally, as a Presidential buff, "Lincoln" fascinated me. But as one who specializes in political figures and election anomalies, the film gives me an opportunity to point out some coincidences and anomalies between the cast's central figures and some of their more modern successors. In other words, for me, "Lincoln" was a junkies gold mine.

The focus of "Lincoln" was trying to secure passage of the 13th Amendment, which would of course outlaw slavery. As the movie portrays, the amendment's fate was far from assured. The Senate had passed it by a wide margin but the House had actually failed to do so earlier in the session. Passing it in "Lame-Duck" would require securing votes of at least some of the members who had been unseated in the previous election. That made winning over these lawmakers partly with, shall we call it, er, favors.

Chief among those Lincoln was cultivating: Alexander Coffroth, the Pennsylvania Congressman with a forever mangled name ("cough drop, etc), whose vote was crucial. Just as Spielberg portrayed it, Coffroth was contesting his election, trailed William Koontz by 68 votes. But his vote for the 13th amendment sealed the deal for his return, as the Governor gave the House the authority to decide who to seat.

Coffroth resided in Somerset County, and his turf today encompasses the bulk of the old Murtha district, though Cambria County (Murtha's beloved Johnstown) wasn't a part of it in those days. It would've been interesting to see how Coffroth would've adapted to matters such as earmarks, which the late Murtha was so adept at providing.

Coffroth's electoral challenge today? Not overcoming the local antipathy over the 13th amendment, but surviving redistricting. Always a struggle, though the fact that he became a Republican (keeping his word to Stevens), may've seen him through.

Kentucky Congressman George Yeaman was another outgoing Congressman whose vote Lincoln needed. He had a special and rare affinity to the 16th President. Both were born in Hardin County, Kentucky. Lincoln's nurturing of Yeaman with his stories of his father made that bond a reality.

After initially resisting Lincoln's entreaties, Yeaman elicited guffaws in the chamber by voting for the amendment. One of Yeaman's successors in Owensboro area district was Bill Natcher, whose legacy was having never missed a vote in his nearly 41 years in office (until just before his death). But he surely didn't inherit that diligence from Yeaman Between December 1862 and March of '65, Yeaman had missed 45% of his votes, perhaps a prime reason he had already lost his seat (54-45%) by the time the 13th amendment came along.

The amendment's author, James Ashley, was a remarkable man, but it would defy imagination to call him a remarkable vote getter. In his five races for the House of Representatives, Ashley never garnered more than 53.4%. In one case, he escaped defeat by just 51-49%., and in his 1862 re-election, he mustered just 38.6% in a three way race. His Lucas County (Toledo) based district exists in similar form today and is heavily Democratic, so much so that a great-grandson Thomas "Lud" Ashley served the same area in Congress from 1955-'81 and was friends with George H.W. Bush at Yale. Marcy Kaptur holds the seat today.

While eradicating slavery was lifelong cause for Ashley, it was not only area of prominence. He became active in impeachment proceedings against Andrew Johnson and in later years, went west, serving as territorial Governor of Montana. He died in 1896.

House Ways and Means Chair Thaddeus Stevens was James Buchanan's Congressman, though as a Republican who opposed slavery, was likely not Buchanan's candidate.

Unlike Ashley, Stevens' hold on his district was firm (he ran unopposed in 1860). Indeed, his worry-free elections likely gave him more time to investigate Mary Todd Lincoln's finances, which means the portrayal of her awkward confrontation at the White House New Year's party that intrigued guests and left her husband in a shamefaced daze must have been accurate.

Stevens had a non-consecutive House tenure. He did not serve between 1853&'59. He was also instrumental in Andrew Johnson's impeachment episode and died a year later, with his African-American housekeeper/mistress by his side. Little has changed politically for Stevens' Lancaster based district. It is as Republican as it was in his day.

One of those men at that New Year's party was Ben Wade. His minor role in the movie belies the fact that he had a major historical footnote. Had the impeachment of Johnson succeeded (as even the President believed it would), it was the Ohioan who would've assumed the Presidency.

Also a part of Stevens' political world, in politics and in life was Edward McPherson, who read the names of each Congressman. McPherson was an associate at Stevens' law firm, then became a colleague in Congress. They clearly saw eye to eye. The irony is that McPherson lost his bid for re-election to a Democrat, Archibald McCallister, who ended up voting for the 13th. Stevens then helped McPherson become clerk of the House, a position that he held on three separate occasions before his 1895 death.

George Pendleton was a thorn in the spine, but it may've been sour grapes. The Congressman from Ohio had been the running mate of General George McClellan just a few months before and Lincoln/Johnson had beaten them soundly. Pendleton wanted to block passage but that was as successful as his running mate's execution of the early war. It was said that had McClellan pursued Lee, the war may've ended sooner. But and so Lincoln relieved him.

The ironies of history may also extend to Lincoln's family. His eldest son and the only one to live to maturity, Robert Todd, was a political force in his own right, serving as Minister to Great Britain and War Secretary in the Garfield and Arthur administrations. He witnessed James Garfield's assassination and was at the Pan American Exposition when the same fate felled a third President, William McKinley. If that weren't enough, he is buried at Arlington National Cemetery, where John F. Kennedy lies. Robert was supposed to be at Ford's Theater on the night of April 14, and was said to feel guilty long after about not.

Schuyler Colfax was the Speaker of the House of Representatives who presided over the debate. He insisted on casting a vote for the 13th amendment even though he acknowledged that it was "highly unusual" for the Speaker to do so. Colfax later became Vice-President under Ulysses Grant, inviting a similarity with another future Vice-President who had a highly prominent role in a major Civil Rights issue 100 years later. Hubert Humphrey helped shepherd the Civil Rights Act to passage, staring down giants of the Senate (Richard Russell and the entire Southern bloc) determined to block it.

By the end of the year, he was Vice-President. But one key difference. While Humphrey was unquestionably honest, Colfax, while never charged with wrong doing, was involved in what today would be called a campaign finance scandal. It was enough to get him dumped from the ticket in 1872.

My sole problem with "Lincoln." For a movie that so elaborately researched and choreographed, you'd think they could've used the actual names of the Congressman in the roll call.

The Connecticut delegation that was first to answer the call, Benjamin, Bentleigh and Ellis, never existed. Neither did Missourian's Appleton and Josiah "Beanpole" Burton.

Even Clay Hawkins, who cast a stunning "aye" before he bellowed out "shoot me" and Ed LeClerk, who said "shoot me too" (before ultimately abstaining) were composite characters

Harold Hollister, the virulent gun-wielding Indiana Congressman who refused to back 13th, was also fictional, though I'm sure he accurately displayed the feelings of many back then.

Finally, there's always a lesson of how past history relates to current events. I'm not in any way comparing this election to 1864 (though in many ways, our nation remains sharply divided) but I did find one similarity to Lincoln's 2nd win.

Through September of 1864, national Democrats were sensing that Lincoln might be beaten. But Sherman's capture of Atlanta turned opinion of war. This year, a late brightening of the unemployment picture and Sandy definitely aided Obama. And so it goes.

Books On/By My Subjects

One of the most fascinating things I uncovered in my research was the number of books that have been written on my subjects, including the most obscure. I have provided a list of the books that I have been able to find of the fascinating characters that appear in all three volumes volumes of *Statesmen and Mischief Makers.*

Bella Abzug
Bella: By Bella Abzug
Bella Abzug (By Doris Faber)
Bella Abzug: How One Tough Broad from the Bronx Fought Jim Crow and Joe McCarthy, Pissed Off Jimmy Carter, Battled for the Rights of Women and Workers, Rallied Against War and for the Planet, and Shook Up Politics Along the Way (By Doris Faber)

George Aiken
Pioneering With Wildflowers (By George Aiken)
Aiken: Senate Diary (By George Aiken)

Carl Albert
Little Giant: The Life and Times of Speaker Carl Albert (By Danney Goble)

Clinton Anderson
Outsider in the Senate (By Clinton Anderson)

Elmer L. Andersen
A Man's Reach: (By Elmer Andersen)
Honorable Al Quie

Leslie Arends
Leslie C. Arends: (By Delmar Thomas C. Stawart)

Reuben Askew
Reuben Askew and the Golden Age of Florida Politics (By Martin Dyckman, David R. Colburn, and Susan MacManus)

Howard Baker
Howard Baker: Conciliator in an Age of Crisis (By Jr. J. Lee Annis)

Bob Bartlett
Bob Bartlett of Alaska: A Life in Politics (By Clause M. Naske)

Birch Bayh
One Heartbeat Away: Presidential Disability and Succession Hardcover (By Birch Bayh)

Berkley Bedell
Tackling Giants: By Larry Handy and Daniel Haley)

Alphonzo Bell
The Bel Air Kid: An Autobiography (By Alphonzo Bell with Marc L. Weber)

Henry Bellmon
The Life and Times of Henry Bellmon (By Henry Bellmon and Pat Bellmon)

Alan Bible
Senator Alan Bible and the Politics of the New West (By Gary Elliot)

Ray Blanton
Ray Blanton and I (By Sherry Friedland)
Coup (By Keel Hunt)

Hale Boggs
The Big Lie: Hale Boggs, Lucille May Grace and Leander Perez (By Garry Boulard)

Richard Bolling
America's Competitive Edge (By Richard Bolling and John Bowles)

Otis Bowen
Doc: Memories from A Life in Public Service (By Otis Bowen)

Dolph Briscoe
Dolph Briscoe: My Life in Ranching and Politics

Edward Brooke
Bridging The Divide: My Life (Ed Brooke)

Pat Brown
California State of Mind: The Legacy of Pat Brown (Film)
California Rising: The Life and Times of Pat Brown (By Ethan Rarick)

Phil Burton
A Rage For Justice: The Passion and Politics of Phil Burton (By John Jacob)

Homer Capehart
Homer E. Capehart: A Senator's Life (By William Pickett)

Raul Castro
Adversity is my Angel: The Life and Career of Raul H. Castro
(By Raul Castro and Jack August)

Howard Cannon
Senator Howard Cannon of Nevada (By Michael Lernetti)

Hugh Carey
The Man Who Saved New York: Hugh Carey (By Seymour P. Lachman and
Robert Polner)

Emanuel Celler
You Never Leave Brooklyn: The Autobiography of Emanuel Celler

Frank Clement
Lead Me On: Frank Goad Clement and Tennessee Politics (By Lee Greene)

Shirley Chisholm
Shirley Chisholm: Unbought and Unbossed (By Shirley Chisholm)
Shirley Chisholm: Catalyst for Change (By Barbara Winslow)

Bert Combs
Bert Combs: An Oral History (By George W. Robinson)

John Sherman Cooper
The Global Kentuckian (By Robert Schulman)
Senator John Sherman Cooper: Consumate Statesman (By Clarice James
Mitchiner)

Frank Church
Fighting The Odds: The Life of Frank Church (By LeRoy Ashby and Rod Gramer)

LeRoy Collins
Floridian of the Century: The Courage of Governor LeRoy Collins (By Martin
Dyckman)

John Culver
Senator (By Elizabeth Drew)

Carl Curtis
40 Years Against The Tide: Congress and the Welfare State
(By Carl Curtis and Regis Courtemanche)

Mike DiSalle
Call Me Mike: A Political Biography of Michael DiSalle (By Richard Zimmerman)

Everett Dirksen
Everett Dirksen and His Presidents: How a Senate Giant Shaped American
Politics (By Byron Hulsey)
Dirksen of Illinois: Senatorial Statesman (By Edward L. Schapsmeier and
Frederick H. Schapsmeier)

Paul Douglas
Crusading Liberal: Paul H. Douglas of Illinois (By Roger Biles)

Robert Drinan
Robert Drinan: The Controversial life of the First Priest Elected To Congress (By
Raymond Throsh)

Winfield Dunn
From A Standing Start: My Tennessee Political Odyssey

Tom Eagleton
Call Me Tom: The Life of Tom Eagleton (By James Giglio)
The 18 Day Running Mate: Eagleton, McGovern and A Campaign in Crisis (By
Joshua M. Glasser)
War and Presidential Power: A Chronicle of Congressional Surrender (By Thomas
Eagleton)

Bill Egan
Alaska's Homegrown Governor: A Biography of William A. Egan Paperback (By
Dr. Elizabeth A. Tower)

Sam Ervin
Sam Ervin: Just A Country Lawyer (By Paul Clancy)

Bill Fulbright
The Price of Empire (By William Fulbright)
Fulbright (By Randall Bennett Woods)
The Arrogance of Power (By William Fulbright)

Daniel Flood
Dapper Dan Flood: The Controversial Life of a Congressional Power Broker (By William Kashatus)
Daniel J. Flood: A Biography The Congressional Career of an Economic Savior and Cold War Nationalist (By Sheldon Spear)

Nick Galifianakis
Pick Nick: The Political Odyssey of Nick Galifianakis (By John E. Semonche)

Cornelius Gallagher
The Privacy War - One Congressman, J. Edgar Hoover and the Fight for the Fourth Amendment

John Gilligan
Ohio's Fighting Liberal: A Political Biography of John J. Gilligan (By David Richard Larson)

Barry Goldwater
Goldwater-An Autobiography
Barry Goldwater (By Robert Alan Goldberg)

Al Gore, Sr
Senator Albert Gore, Sr: Tennessee Maverick

Charles Goodell
Political Prisoners in America (By Charles Goodell)

Kenneth Gray
Pass The Plate (By Maxine Pyle and Marleis Trover)

Ernest Gruening
Ernest Gruening: Alaska's Greatest Governor (By Claus Naske)
The Autobiography Of Ernest Gruening (By Mary Battles)

William Guy
"Where Seldom Was Heard a Discouraging Word . . . Bill Guy Remembers" (By Bill Guy)

David Hall
The Fall of David Hall (By James Edwin Alexander and William Burkett)
Twisted Justice (By David Hall)

Jay Hammond
Tales of Alaska's Bush Rat Governor: The Extraordinary Autobiography of Jay Hammond, Wilderness Guide and Reluctant Politician (By Jay Hammond)

Fred Harris
Does People Do It: A Memoir (By Fred Harris)

William Hartsfield
Hartsfield: Atlanta Mayor (By Harold H. Martin)

Charlie Halleck
Charlie Halleck: A Political Biography (By Henry Scheele)

Phil Hart
The Prince of the Senate: A Biography of Senator Philip A. Hart, Jr. (By John F. Willertz)

William Hartsfield
Hartsfield (By Harold Martin)

Phillip Hoff
Phillip Hoff: How Red Turned Blue in the Green Mountain State (By Samuel B. Hand, Anthony Maro, and Stephen Terry)

Chet Holifield
Mr. Atomic Energy Congressman Chet Holifield and Atomic Energy Affairs, 1945-1974
(By Richard Wayne Dyke)

Linwood Holton
Opportunity Time: A Memoir (By Governor Linwood Holton)

Harold Hughes
The Man From Ida Grove: A Senator's Personal Story (By Harold E. Hughes-with Dick Schneider)
The Honorable Alcoholic (By Harold Hughes with Dick Schneider)

Richard Hughes
Richard Hughes and the Era of Civility (By John Wefing)

Hubert Humphrey
Hubert: (By Dr. Edgar Berman)
Hubert Humphrey: A Biography (By Carl Solberg)

Henry Jackson
Henry Jackson: A Life in Politics (By Robert G. Kaufman)
Scoop: The Life and Politics of Henry M. Jackson (By Peter J. Ognibene)

Jacob Javits
Senator Jacob Javits Autobiography: Who Makes War

Barbara Jordan
Barbara Jordan: Politician (By Rose J. Blue, Nathan Higgins, Corinne J. Naden)
Barbara Jordan (By Mary Beth Rogers)

Len Jordan
Home Below Hell's Canyon (By Grace Jordan)
The Unintentional Senator (By Grace Jordan)

Walter Judd
Missionary for Freedom: The Life and Times of Walter Judd (By Lee Edwards)

Kenneth Keating
Government of the People: (By Kenneth B. Keating)

Estes Kefauver
Estes Kefauver: A Biography (By Charles Fonteney)
Crime in America (By Estes Kefauver)
In a Few Hands: Monopoly Power in America (By Estes Kefauver)

Otto Kerner
Otto Kerner: The Conflict of Intangible Rights (By Bill Barnhart)

Robert Kerr
Robert Samuel Kerr: Oklahoma's Pioneer King (1896-1963) (By Paul William Bass)
Robert Kerr: (By Ann Hodges Morgan)

John Krebs
From Berlin To Capitol Hill (By John Krebs)

Frank Lausche
Frank Lausche: Ohio's Great Political Maverick By Oden Kirk

David Lawrence
Don't Call Me Boss (By Michael Weber)

Paul Laxalt
Nevada's Paul Laxalt: A Memoir (By Paul Laxalt)

Arthur Link
When the Landscape is Quiet Again (By Clay Jenkinson and David Jensen)

Jerry Litton
Jerry Litton: A Biography (By Bonnie Mitchell)

Andy Maguire
Toward 'Uhuru' in Tanzania: The Politics of Participation (By Andy Maguire and Janet Welsh Brown)
Bordering on Trouble: Resources and Politics in Latin America (By Andy Maguire)

Warren G. Magnuson
Warren Magnuson and the Shaping of 20th Century America (By Shelby Scates)
Politics of Urbanism: Seeing Like a City By Warren Magnusson

Marvin Mandel
I'll Never Forget It (An autobiography)

Mike Mansfield
Mike Mansfield, Majority Leader A Different Kind of Senate, 1961-1976 (By Francis Valeo)
Hon. Politician: Mike Mansfield (By Louis Baldwin)
Senator Mansfield: The Extraordinary Life of a Great American Statesman and Diplomat (By Don Oberdorfer)

Clem McSpadden
The Cowboys Prayer (By Clem McSpadden)

William Milliken
William Milliken: Michigan's Passionate Moderate (By Dave Dempsey)

Wilbur Mills
Mr Chairman: The Life and Legacy of Wilbur D. Mills (By Kay Goss)
Taxing America: Wilbur D. Mills, Congress, and the State, 1945-1975 (By Julian E. Zelizer)

Walter Mondale
The Good Fight: A Life in Liberal Politics (By Walter Mondale)

Frank Morrison
My Journey Through The 20th Century: (By Governor Frank B. Morison)

Wayne Morse
Wayne Morse: A Political Biography (By Mason Druckman)
Wayne Morse: A Bio-bibliography (By Lee Wilkins)

James Murray
New Dealer from Montana: The Senate Career of James Murray (By Donald E. Spritzer)

Ed Muskie
Ed Muskie-Biography-Maine Politician
Muskie (By Theo Lippman and Daniel Hansen)

Gaylord Nelson
The Man From Clear Lake: By Bill Christofferson

William Proxmire
Senator William Proxmire: The Fleecing of America
You Can Do It (By Senator William Proxmire)

Al Quie
Riding Into The Sunrise: Al Quie, A Life of Faith, Service &Civility (By Mitchell Pearlstein)

Richard Ogilvie
Richard Ogilvie: In The Interest of the State (By Taylor Penseneau)

Tip O'Neill
Tip O'Neill: Man of the House (By Tip O'Neill)
Tip O'Neill and the Democratic Century (By John Farrell)

Jerry Pettis
Congressman Jerry L. Pettis: His Story (By Miriam Wood)

William Poage
My First Eighty-Five Years (By William Poage)
McLennon County Before 1980 (By William Poage)
Politis Texas Style (By William Poage)
The Wat We Lived (By William Poage)

Adam Clayton Powell
Adam by Adam: The Autobiography of Adam Clayton Powell
Adam Clayton Powell Jr – The Political Biography of an American Dilemma (By Charles Hamilton)

Robert Ray
Robert Ray: The Treasures of Iowa (By Robert Ray)

Sam Rayburn
Rayburn: A Biography (By Albert Steinberg)
Rayburn: A Biography (By D.B. Hardeman and Donald C. Bacon)

Tom Railsback
Tom Railsback: (By Jesse Russell and Ronald Cohn)

Mendel Rivers
Rivers Delivers: The Story of Mendel Rivers (By Marion Rivers Ravenel)
Mendel and Me: Life with Congressman L. Mendel Rivers (By Margaret Middleton Rivers)

Henry Reuss
When Government Was Good (By Henry Reuss)
On The Trail of the Ice Age: A Guide for Wisconsin's Hikers, Bikers, and Motorists (By Henry Reuss)

The Critical Decades: An Economic Policy for America and the Free World (By Henry Reuss)
To Save A City (By Henry Reuss)
The Unknown: The South of France (By Henry Reuss)

John Rhodes
Man of the House (By Ben Smith)

Peter Rodino:
52 Words My Husband Taught Me: Love, Inspiration, and the Constitution

Nelson Rockefeller
On His Own Terms: A Life of Nelson Rockefeller (By Richard Norton Smith)

Alberto Rosellini
Rosellini: Immigrants Son and Progressive Governor (By Payton Smith)
Leverett Saltonstall
Saltonstall: Salty: Reflections of a Yankee

Grant Sawyer
Hang Tough: An Activist In The Governor's Mansion (By R.T. King, Gary T. Elliot, and Grant Sawyer)

William Saxbe
I Saw The Elephant (By William Saxbe)

John Seiberling
A Passion for the Land: John Seiberling and the Environmental Movement (By Daniel Nelson)
A Tree Grows in Washington: The John Seiberling Story (By Paul R. Jacoway)-**Movie**

Margaret Chase Smith
Politics of Conscience: A Biography of Margaret Chase Smith (By Patricia Ward Wallace)
An America Stand: Margaret Chase Smith and the Communist Menace (1948-1972)
(By Eric R. Crouse)
Margaret Chase Smith: A Woman For President (By Lynn Plourde)
No Place For a Woman: A Life of Senator Margaret Chase Smith (By Jannan Sherman)

Preston Smith
Preston Smith: The People's Governor (By Wanda Evans)

Robert Smylie
Robert E. Smylie (By Lambert M. Surhone, Miriam T. Timpledon, and Susan
F. Maresken
Robert Smylie Remembers (By Robert E. Smylie and Howard Berger)

Robert Stafford
Robert Stafford (By Lambert M. Surhone, Miriam T. Timpledon, and Susan F.
Markesen)

William Stratton
A Political Passage: The Career of Stratton of Illinois (By Dave Kenney)

Carl Stokes
Carl B. Stokes and The Rise of Black Political Power (By Leonard B. Moore)
Promises of Power: An Autobiography of Carl Stokes (By Carl Stokes)

John Swainson
Wounded Warrior: The Rise and Fall of Michigan Governor John Swainson (By
Lawrence Glazer)

Stuart Symington
Stuart Symington: A life (By James C. Olson)
Stuart Symington: Portrait of a Man with a Mission (By Paul Wellman)

John Tower
Consequences (By John Tower)

Joseph Tydings
Born To Starve (By Joseph Tydings)

Morris K. Udall
Mo: the Life and Times of Morris K. Udall (By Donald W. Carson)
Too Funny To Be President (By Morris K. Udall)

Jesse Unruh
Big Daddy: Jess Unruh and the Art of Power Politics (By Bill Boyarsky)

Richard Vander Veen
Words and Actions: The Writings of Dick Vander Veen (By Richard Vander Veen)

John Volpe
The Life of an Immigrant's Son (By Kathleen Kilgore)

Dan Walker
The Maverick and the Machine (By Dan Walker)

G. Mennen Williams
Soapy: A Biography of G. Mennen Williams (By Thomas Noer)

William Winter
William Winter and the New Mississippi (By Charles Bolton)

Milton Young
Mr. Wheat: A Biography of Senator Milton R. Young (By Andrea Winkjer Collin)

ACKNOWLEDGEMENTS

Editor
Lauren Choplin

With Appreciation
Liz Abzug
Carl Albert Congressional Archives, University of Oklahoma
Albertson's Library at Boise State University
The Ames Historical Society
The Austin History Center
Cissy Baker
The Boston Public Library
William Breer
The Dolph Briscoe Center For American History at the University of Texas
Jeff Brockelsby
Ruth Bryan, The Margaret I. King Library, The University of Kentucky
Honorable Walter F. Mondale
Honorable Al Quie
Honorable Bonnie Campbell
Casper College Western History Center
Mary Ann Checchi
Forrest Church
The Champ Clark House
The Clemens Library, University of Virginia
The Concord Monitor
Senator John Culver
Dakota Wesleyan University Special Collections
The Dallas Morning News
Thomas and Katherine Detre Library and Archives, Senator John Heinz History
Center
Kerri DiBrienza
Nancy DiGiovanni
Peggy Dillard
Honorable John Dingell
Martin Donovan
The Dirksen Center, Pekin, Illinois
Honorable David Durenberger
Bob Feldman

Chris Feldman
Gerald R. Ford Presidential Library
Stanley Forman
Congressman Rodney Frelinghuysen
Al Golub
Heather Greigg
Tom Griscom
Val Halamandaris
Dennis Harper
Diana Mara Henry
William Hilgers
Ray Hill
Jim Hooker
Mercer County Executive Brian Hughes
Helen Hughes
Honorable Skip Humphrey
Andrew Isidoro
The Henry M. Jackson Foundation
Peter Jackson
Matt James
The Jasper County Library
Jane Jiang
Gerry Johnson
Lyndon B. Johnson Presidential library
Barbara Jones
The Kansas Historical Society
Honorable Kathy Karpan
Honorable Nancy Kassebaum
Tom Keefe
Diane and Lindsay Kefauver
John F. Kennedy Presidential Library and Museum
Margaret I. King Library, University of Kentucky
Lake Superior State University Archives
Guy Lancaster, Encyclopedia of Arkansas History and Culture
The Las Vegas Mob Museum
The Abraham Lincoln Birthplace
Lubbock Avalanche-Journal
Elizabeth Malyon Safran
The Mike and Maureen Mansfield Foundation
The Mike and Maureen Mansfield Library, University of Montana
Chris Matthews

Wiley Mayne, Jr
John Melcher
Kirk McGee
Robert McGee
The Minnesota Historical Society
The Monticello Herald
Brian Moss
The Karl Mundt Library, Dakota State University
The Edmund S. Muskie Archives and Special Collections Library
Stephen Muskie
Carrie Nelson
Gaylord "Happy" Nelson Jr
Jeff Nelson
Congressman David Obey
Ocean Township Public Library Reference Staff
John Pastore, Jr.
Pennsylvania Historic Archives
Pennsylvania State University Special Collections Archives
Congressman John Porter
Rosemary O'Neill
Dianne Oster, Seton Hall Law Library
Congressman Tom Railsback
The Sam Rayburn Museum
The Rensselaer Republican
Alice Rivlin
Norman Sherman
Jane Ribicoff Silk
The Rockford Register Star
Scott Romney
William Sandman
Joe Scranton
Norman Sherman
Jane Silk
Allison Sinrod
Skillman Library, Lafayette College
Rebecca Spencer
Angie Stockwell, The Margaret Chase Smith Library
Brian Stratton and Family
United States House of Representatives Historical Office
United States Senate Historical office
The State Archives of Florida

Congressman James Symington
Stuart Symington, Jr.
Paul Szep
The Texas Portal
John Tuck
Honorable Joseph Tydings
Honorable Mark Udall
University of Arkansas Library, Special Collections
University of Delaware Library, Special Collections
University of Washington Libraries, Special Collections
U.PS. Store, Spotswood, New Jersey
Washington State Legacy Project, Office of the Secretary of State
Ron Wade (ronwadebuttons.com)
Garry Wenske
Ernie Wentrcek (affordablepoliticalbuttons.com)
Keith Wessell
Congressman John Wold
University of Wyoming
The Wilson Library of the University of North Carolina at Chapel Hill
Jane Winton
The Wisconsin State Historical Society
Bruce Wolfe
Bruce Wright
The Wyoming State Historical Society
Rebecca Yates

SOURCES

Abscam

AP (June 19, 1980, December 4, 1980); Congressional Quarterly (June 19, 1980); The Almanac of American Politics, 1982; Congressional Bad Boys. com; Political Corruption in America: An Encyclopedia of Scandals, Power and Greed (By Mark Grossman); The LA Times (November 20, 2001); The New York Times-Ex Sen. Harrison Williams, 81, Dies. Went to Prison Over Abscam Scandal (By Douglas Martin, November 20, 2001); The New York Times-Frank Thompson, 70: Career Ended With Conviction in Abscam (By Joseph Fried, July 24, 1989); Staten Island Live (June 11, 1989); History.com

Bella Abzug

Bella (By Bella Abzug); The New York Times (By Grace Lichenstein, June 9, 1970); (By Thomas Ronano) August 21, 1976; (By Frank Lynn, August 21, 1976); (By Martin Tolchin, December 11, 1976); The New York Times 4/1/98); Bella By Bella Abzug; The New York Times, June 15, 1970 – New Jersey pages;The New York Times (June 9, 1970); (By Grace Lichenstein, April 29, 1972); The New York Times (By Steven R. Weisman, November 3, 1972); New York Magazine (By Michael Kramer, June 19, 1972); The Week In Review; The New York Times, March 6, 1975 (By John M. Crewsdom August 10, 1976); The New York Times (By Ronald Smothers - New Jersey Pages); The New York Times By Frank Linn (August 31, 1976) ;The New York Times August 21, 1976 By Thomas P. Ronan; The New York Times (By Maurice Carroll, September 16, 1976); The New York Times (By Martin Tolchim, December 11, 1976); The New York Times; August 29, 1976 - The Week In Review; The United States House of Representatives

George Aiken and James Eastland

The Barre Montpelier Times Argus –George Aiken In His Own Words (By Fred Stetson February 13, 2005); Vermont Today.com-Vermont's Great Moments of the 20th Century; No Place For a Woman: A Life of Senator Margaret Chase Smith (By Jannann Sherman);Outsider In The Senate (By Clinton Anderson); The New York Times (By Albin Krebs, November 20, 1984); Robert Kennedy and His Times-By Arthur Schlessinger; The Almanac of American Politics 1974 and 1978; James Eastland-The Mike Wallace Interview (Harry Ransom Center- the University of Texas, at Austin) Interview July 28, 1957; The Paradox of Power: James Eastland and the Democratic Party (By Maarten Zwiers); Great Compromisers: Edward Kennedy and James Eastland in the U.S. Senate (By Maarten Zwiers-Fall 2009); Aiken: Senate Diary (By George Aiken)

Carl Albert
Bella (By Bella Abzug); Tip O'Neill and the Democratic Century (By James Farrell); The Daily Oklahoman (February 6, 2000); Lawton Constitution (February 6, 2000); LA Times-(February 6,2000 from a Times Staff Writer)

John Anderson
The Atlantic (By Walter Shapiro, February 2, 1980); The New York Times (By Adam Clymer, September 19, 1977); PBS: The 1980 Presidential Debate (Reagan/Anderson); The Almanac of American Politics 1974, 1978, 1980, and 1982; Crazy Dreaming: The Anderson Campaign of 1980 (By Georgs M. Golubovskis)

Howard Baker
Howard Baker: Conciliator in an Age of Crisis (By ; Conversation with Tom Griscom: Conversation with John Tuck; Congressional Quarterly (September 1979); The New York Times (By Adam Clymer, April 19, 1978); The Almanac of American Politics, 1982; The Washington Post (By Helen Dewar, February 16, 1982); The New York Times, Opinion (October 13, 1982); The New York Times (By David Eisenhower, September 6, 1987); The New York Times By James Gerstenzang June 26, 2014); The Washington Post (By James Gerstenzang June 26, 2014); cjonline (By Tim Carpenter, April 23, 2007);

Birch Bayh
Acts of God: The Unnatural History of Natural Disaster in America (By Ted Steinberg); The Kokomo Tribune (11/3, 6 and 10, 1980); Juvenile Justice and Delinquency Prevention Act (A Handbook of Child Welfare: Context, Knowledge, and Practice (By Joan Laird, Ann Hartman); Congressional Quarterly, 1966; ESPN (By Melissa Isackson, May 3, 2012); AP (October 1978)

Hale Boggs
Congressional Quarterly, 1965; Talking Points Memo-Flashback: 1972 Alaska Plane Crash Killed Dem Congressman; The New York Times (By Francis X. Clines, May 20, 1981); The New York Times (By Richard Sandomir, January 26, 2010)

Boland, Conte, Burke, Donohue, Philbin (Tip O'Neill Crowd)
Man of the House (By Tip O'Neill); Tip O'Neill and the Democratic Century (By James Farrell); The New York Times (October 2001); Eddie Boland papers (provided by Mary Boland); Worcester Telegram (November 5, 1984)

Garry Brown
The Milwaukee Journal (7/22/66); ourcandidates.com; The Almanac of American Politics 1974, 1976, and 1978; Congressional Quarterly, 1974, 1976, and 1978; AP (6/22/73); AP (4/30/77); The Washington Post (By Lawrence Meyer and Peter Osnos); Abuse of Power (By Stanley Kutler); Kalamazoo Gazette (8/28/1998)

Frank Carlson and Andrew Schoeppel
Kansaspedia-Frank Carlson-Biography; Frank Carlson: Cloud County Tourism; Master of the Senate: (By Robert Caro); Kansas Historic Society: Frank Carlson's 1946 Campaign Papers; Lawrence Journal Herald (May 30, 2012); ourcandidates. com; Kansas Republican Party-Wikipedia; The Blade Empire (November 6, 2009); Superior, Nebraska: The Common Sense Values of America's Heartland (By Denis Boyles); The New York Times (By Marvine Howe, May 31 1987)

Emanuel Celler
Congressional Quarterly, 1957; The New York Times (March 19, 1960); The New York Times (By Linda Charlton, June 13, 1972); The New York Times (By Francis X. Clines, June 22, 1972); The New York Times (By Richard Madden, October 5, 1972); The Presidents and the Jews; Emanuel Celler (By Frank Linn, March 29, 1978)

Frank Church
The Almanac of American Politics 1974, 1978 and 1980; Congressional Quarterly: Candidates' 76; The New York Times-The Cast, By Joseph Kraft, 1974); The New York Times November 4 and 5, 1980; CQ (1974); Spartacus Educational; Master of the Senate (By Robert Caro); The New York Times (By Judith Miller, November 6, 1980); US News & World Report-Round Two Begins (April 12, 1976); Esquire (By Charles Pierce, October 2, 2013); Fighting The Odds (By LeRoy Ashby and Rod Gramer); Smithsonian Magazine (June 2002); Congressional Quarterly (March 20, 1976)

Congressional Anecdotes By Paul Kessler
Frank Church, Dirksen/Chase Smith, Gerald Ford/Lincon, Ford Longhorne speech, Ford/Humphrey Christmas, H.R. Gross/Barbara Jordan bull/ "Scoop" Jackson, Edith Nourse Rogers, Sam Rayburn, Mo Udall

Barber Conable
The Final Days: By Bon Woodward and Carl Bernstein; The New York Times (December 2003); Congressional Quarterly, 1974

John Sherman Cooper

The New York Times (By Albin Krebs, February23, 1991); Spartacus. schools.net; Kentucky Senator John Sherman Cooper Remembered (WUKY-OralHistoryProject); John Sherman Cooper: The Global Kentuckian (By Robert Schulman); osi-speaks.blogspot; northumbriacountdown; Bridging The Divide (By Edward Brooke)

John Culver

The Almanac of American Politics 1974, 1978, 1980, and 1982; The New York Times-November 4, 5, and 6, 1980; Congressional Quarterly-October, 1974 and 1980; The New York Times (By Robert Sherrill, May 13, 1979); Rowland Evans and Robert Novak, August 31, 1979); A Conversation with John Culver; A Conversation with Mary Ann Checchi;Terminating Public Programs: An American Political Paradox (By Mark R. Daniels); Washington Post (By Harold Walsh and Edward Logan, July 11, 1977); CBS Radio-Spectrum (By Jack Newfield, October 1980); A Conversation with Senator John Culver; A Conversation with Mary Ann Checchi: The Congressional Record (December 1980)

Everett Dirksen

The Dirksen Congressional Center: A Billion Here, A Billion there; The Dirksen Congressional Center: Dirksen-Master Legislator: By Bryan Hulsey; The New York Times (By E.W. Kenworthy September 8, 1969); PBS-The Evolving Role of National Party Conventions (January 26, 2004); 5NBCChicago-WardRoom: (By Edward McClelland, May 30, 2012); Everett Dirksen's Finest Hour (CongressLink. org); Everett Dirksen-Brainy Quotes; Allthewaywithlbj.com; The New York Times (By Fred Graham, September 10, 1968); Congressional Quarterly (1966 Roundup); Congressional Quarterly (October 29, 1968); Congressional Record; Everett Dirksen's Constitutional Crusades (By David Kyvig)

Paul Douglas

Institute of Government and Public Affairs (University of Illinois); Congressional Quarterly, 1966; Master of the Senate: By Robert Caro; Historymatters.gdu.edu; Illinoisissues (By Peggy Boyer Long); P.S-The Autobiography of Paul Simon

Tom Eagleton

Congressional Quarterly (October 25, 1968, August 5, 1972, and October 11, 1980); The Making of the President, 1972 (By Theodore H. White); The Almanac of American Politics 1974, 1980, and 1982; AP (August 7, 1974); Newsweek (July 18 andAugust4, 1980) The Southeast Missourian (November 2, 1972); The 18 Day Running Mate: Eagleton, McGovern and A Campaign in

Crisis (By Joshua M. Glasser); The New York Times (By Adam Clymer, March 7, 2007); NPR (By Debbie Elliot, March 5, 2007)

Sam Ervin
The Washington Post (By James R. Dickerson, April 24, 1985); Sam Ervin and the Last of the Founding Fathers; ACLU.org (By Radley Balko); Rise of the Warrior Cop: The Militarization of America's Police Force (By Radley Balko); Congressional Quarterly, 1966

Walter Flowers
Congressional Quarterly, 1976 Commemorative; The Almanac of American Politics, 1978 and 1980: Conversation with Tom Railsback:

Bill Fulbright
Fulbright: The Price of Empire (By Bill Fulbright)

Al Gore, Sr.
Senator Albert Gore Sr: Tennessee's Political Maverick (By Kyle Longley); Tennessee's Old Gray Fox (By Ray Hill); Senator Al Gore: Tennessee Maverick (By Kyle Longley); JFK: The Man and The Myth: A Critical Portrait (By Victor Lasky); Master of the Senate (By Robert A. Caro); Gore: A Political Life (By Bob Zelnick); Mike Mansfield, Majority Leader: A Different Kind of Senate, 1961-1976 (By Francis R. Valeo); Al Gore, Sr: Tennessee Maverick (By Kyle Longley); The Almanac of American Politics, 1974

Barry Goldwater
Goldwater: By Barry Goldwater; Barry Goldwater (By Robert Alan Goldberg); Conversation with Barry Goldwater Jr; The New York Times (By Adam Clymer, May 30, 1998); Consequences: By John Tower; The Washington Post (By Bart Barnes, May 30, 1998); The Almanac of American Politics, 1982

Charles Goodell
The New York Times (By Frank Lynn, January 22, 1987); Grantland (By Bryan Curtis, February 4, 2013)

Theodore Green
Congressional Anecdotes (By Paul Boller); Master of the Senate (By Robert Caro)

Stanley Griegg
Carroll Daily Times Herald (July 3, 1964); Congressional Quarterly (October 1964); The Sioux City Journal (June 15, 1972); The Washington Post (June 15,

2002); The Mason City Globe Gazette (January 3, 1964); The Mason City Globe Gazette (October 5, 1966); A Conversation with Alice Rivlin

Charlie Halleck
A Time To Heal: (By Gerald Ford); Ford (By Jerald Terhorst); Jasper County, Library, (September 13, 1962); US News and World Report (July 16, 1948); Tip O'Neill and the Democratic Century; Congressional Quarterly, Week of December 25, 1964, Week of January 2, 1965, and week of January 9, 1965; Our Candidates.com; The New York Times (By Ben E. Franklin, March 4, 1986)

Fred Harris
Oklahoma Historic Society's Encyclopedia of Oklahoma's History and Culture (Richard Lowitt)
The Almanac of American Politics 1974; Newsweek (January 21, 1976); OEATV. COM-A Conversation with Fred Harris (April 13, 2010); Fred Harris (By Richard Lowitt); Almost To The Top (By Albert Eisele); Alaskool.org; Congressional Quarterly, 1972 Chronology)

Carl Hayden
The New York Times (November 18, 1961); The New York Times-(January 26, 1972); Carl Hayden Retires: Senate.gov; Carl Hayden-Wikiquote

Wayne Hays
Washington Post (By Marion Clark and Rudy Maxa, May 23, 1976); The New York Times (AP, February 11, 1989); Wayne Hays-Congressional Bad Boys; Elizabeth Ray-Wikipedia; The Downfall Dictionary-July 5, 2009; Zimbio-Wayne Hays' Girlfriend Goes To The Press (May 29, 2011); O Congress (By Donald Riegel)

Vance Hartke
The Indiana Museum of History (January 21, 2013); AP News, via Google (January 3, 1972);
The Almanac of American Politics, 1974 and 1978; The New York Times (By Wolfgang Saxon, July 29, 2003)

Hubert Humphrey
Hubert: By Dr. Edgar Bergen; Hubert Humphrey: A Biography (Carl Solberg); Hubert Humphrey and the Politics of Joy (By Charles L. Garrettson III); Almost To The Top (By Albert Eisele); Hubert Humphrey-You Tube (Election Night, 1968); C-Span, 1997; Man of the House (By Tip O'Neill); A Time To Heal (By Gerald Ford); The Making of the President, 1960; Hubert Humphrey:

The Man and His Dream (By Robert Wagman); Hubert Humphrey (By Carl Solberg) Conversation with Congressman David Obey; LBJ Library.UTexas. edu; The Washington Post (By Brian Mooar, September 21, 1998); Senate.gov; Congressional Quarterly, 1971; Conversation with Norman Sherman

Harold Hughes
The New York Times (By Eric Pace, October 25, 1996); About.com-In Tribute To Harold Everett Hughes; Congressional Quarterly, October 1968; Chicago Tribune (By Chesly Manley, October 24, 1968); The Des Moines Register (October 20, 1968); Conversation with Bonnie Campbell; Conversation with John Culver; The Des Moines Register (By Kyle Munson, November 3, 2015)

William Hungate
Too Funny To Be President: By Morris K. Udall; Hannibal Journal News (2010); Congressional Quarterly (July 29 and August 5, 1974); The New York Times

Henry Jackson and Warren Magnuson
The Almanac of American Politics, 1980; The New York Times (September 1983); The Twin Towers of Power-The Seattle Times Sept. 29, 1996 (Sharon Boswell and Lorraine McConaghy); Crooscut.com (By Abe Bergman); Radioactive Ranch: How Hanford's History Reflect's the West (By Knute Berger); Atomic Frontier Days – Hanford and the American West (By John Findlay and Bruce William Hevley); historylink.org; tdn.com (January 1, 2006); Seattle PI (By Fred Fellman, June 27, 2006); The Herald of Everett, Washington (By Julie Muhlstein, June 3, 2012); Warren Magnuson and the Shaping of the 20th Century (By Shelby Scates); Henry M. Jackson: A Life in Politics (By Robert Kaufman); The Seattle Times (By Dick Larsen, September 7, 1983); The Congressional Record (May 2012); A Conversation with Peter Jackson; A Conversation with Anna Marie Laurence: A Conversation with John Hempleman
In The President's Secret Service (By Ronald Kessler)

Jacob Javits and Cliff Case
Congressional Quarterly (September 14, 1962); The Almanac of American Politics 1978, 1980, and 1982; The New York Times (By Tom Wicker, July 16, 1964); The New York Times (By Martin Tolchin, May 25, 1980); The New York Times (By Irwin Molotsky, April 19, 1980); The New York Times (By Frank Lynn; May 17, 1980); The New York Times (By Robin Herman, September 7, 1980); The New York Times (By Frank Lynn, September 10, 1980); The New York Times-(By Joseph F. Sullivan, June 7, 1978); The New York Times (March 8, 1986); Congressional Quarterly (1974); The New York Times (By Joseph Sullivan June 7, 1978); The New York Times (By Martin Waldron, June 8, 1978); The

New York Times (By Joseph F. Sullivan, June 11, 1978); The New York Times-(By Robert D. Madden March 7, 1982); Congressional Quarterly, 1957 and 1972)

Kenneth Keating
RFK: William Vander Heavel and Milton Guetzman; Robert Kennedy and His Times: (By Arthur Schlessinger); Congressional Quarterly (September 3, 1964); U.S. News and World Report (November 14, 1964); The Harvard Crimson (By Robert J. Samuelson-Reprinted November 6, 2009); Ambassador to Israel Kenneth Keating Dies

Estes Kefauver
Remembering Estes Kefauver-Progressive Populist (By Theodore Brown Jr., and Robert B. Allen); The Evening Independent (August 10, 1963); Pophistorydig. com-U.S. Senator Estes Kefauver; Master of the Senate: By Robert Caro; JFK: The Man and The Myth: A Critical Portrait (By Victor Lasky); The Knoxville Focus: The Greatest Campaigner By Ray Hill); Talmadge (By Herman Talmadge); Master of the Senate (By Robert Caro): Robert Kerr (By Ann Hodges Morgan)

Robert Kerr
Master of the Senate (By Robert Caro); Robert Kerr (The Tulsa World, January 2, 1963); Robert Kerr-Oklahoma State University Library; 100 years of Oklahoma Governors (state.ok.us); The Political Life of Medicare By Jonathan Oberlander; Tracing the History of CMS Programs: From President Theodore Roosevelt to President George W. Bush (cms.gov);): Robert Kerr (By Ann Hodges Morgan)

Tom Kuchel
AP-June 27,1964; Congressional Quarterly (June 10, 1966); The New York Times (August 2, 1966); The New York Times-(June 6, 1968); The Los Angeles Times (November 23, 1994); Boom: A Journal of California Demise and Accent (by Todd Homes, Winter 2011); The New York Times (By Geoffrey Kabaservice March 11, 2012); The RSS Ronald Reagan (Posted by Justin) Blogspot.org February 17, 2012; FOFWEB.CON; Congressional Quarterly (May 23 and June 12, 1968)

Allard Lowenstein
RFK: The Man and His Times; The Harvard Crimson; Allard Lowenstein-Biography, Yale Law School; The New York Times (By Richard L. Madden, October 16, 1969);The New York Times (March 15, 1980); The New York Times (By Paul Montgomery) March 16, 1980; The New York Times (By David Harris August 17, 1980)

Pat Lucey
Our Candidates; The Milwaukee Journal Sentinel (By Ira Kaperstein, October 8, 1962); The Milwaukee Journal Sentinel (November 3, 1964); The New York Times (By Stephen Weisnar) JFK-A Biography (By Michael O'Brien), AP (By Frank Kane, August 26, 1980) ; Wisconsinopinion.com (April 3, 2009)

Torbert Macdonald
Torbert MacDonald Biography: Spartacus Educational; Daily JFK.com; www. baseball-reference.com; The New York Times; The Boston Globe (May 22, 1976); The Boston Herald Advertiser (May 23, 1976); The New York Times (By Robert Hanley, May 23, 1976); The Congressional Record (May 6-24, 1976); A Conversation with Laurie Macdonald

Mike Mansfield
The Almanac of American Politics 1974 and 1978; www.Senate.gov-Mike Mansfield: Quiet Leadership in Troubled Times"; Mike Mansfield, Majority Leader: A Different Kind of Senate, 1961-1976 (By Francis R. Valeo)The Great Falls Tribune.com-125 Montana Newsmakers; Gun Control (The Mike and Maureen Mansfield Library); Congressional Quarterly (1966 and 1974); The New York Times (By Fred Graham, September 10, 1968); AP (7/28/64); The New York Times (By David E. Rosenbaum, The Mike and Maureen Mansfield Foundation; October 6, 2001); Seattle Post Intelligencer (By Joel Connelly, October 6, 2001); Bloombergview (By Albert Hunt, August 12, 2015); The Chicago Tribune (November 16, 1988)

Eugene McCarthy
Eugene McCarthy (By Dominick Sanbrook); Hubert (By Edgar Bergman); The Huffington Post (By Joseph Palerno); The New York Times (By E. W. Kentworth, March 13, 1968); The New York Times (March 17, 1968); The Harvard Crimson (By Robert Krim.May 8, 1968); PBS
crosscut.com (By Bob Royer); Published on H-Indiana (November, 2008); Robert F. Kennedy and the 1968 Indiana Primary (By Ray E. Boomhower); Robert Kennedy and His Times (By Arthur Schlessinger); RFK: The Years Alone; The New York Times; The Washington Post

Robert McClory
The Almanac of American Politics, 1974, 1980, and 1982; Congressional Quarterly; Newsweek (August, 1974); The New York Times, July 26, 1988; Chicago Sun Times (By Mark Brown, July 26, 1988); Chicago Tribune (By Kenan Heise)

Gale McGee
US News and World Report (November 9, 1958); The New York Times (April 10, 1992); The Almanac of American Politics, 1978; Conversation with Bob McGee; Congressional Quarterly, 1959 and 1974; The Wyoming News (By Rodger McDaniel, (March 13, 2015)

George McGovern
Bobmannblog.com; The New York Times: The Washington Post; Congressional Quarterly, 1968; George S. McGovern and the Farmer: South Dakota Politics, 1953-'62 (By Jon Lauck); The Making of the President, 1972 (By Theodore H. White); Newsweek (July 24 and August 7, 1972); ABC/CBS Election Night Coverage, 1972; Rolling Stone (By Timothy Crouse, April 27, 1972); The Washington Post (By David Broder, November 9, 1972); The Washington Post (By Helen Dever, October 26, 1980); Running For President: History of American Presidential Elections

Wilbur Mills
LBJ Library Oral History Project; The New York Times (By Dennis Hevesi, May 3,1992); Washington Post (By Stephen Green and Margot Hornblower, Oct. 11, 1974); Encyclopedia of Arkansas and Culture; The Almanac of American Politics, 1974; Campaign '72: Press Opinion From New Hampshire To November (Edited by Edward Knappman, Evan Drossman, and Robert Newman); The Heart of Power: By David Blumenthal and James Morone); The Washington Post; Conversation with Rebecca Mills Yates

Walter Mondale
University of Minnesota Law Library; CQ (1968, 1972, 1973 and 1975); Wilson Daily Times (April 29, 1971); St. Cloud Times (October 31, 1972); The New York Times (By Paul Delaney, August 13, 1970); The New York Times (March 22, 1971); The New York Times (April 18, 1971); The New York Times (By David Rosenbaum, November 6, 1972); The New York Times (August 11, 1974); The New York Times (November 24, 1974)
The New York Times (February 11, 1975); The New York Times (By David Rosenbaum, February 21, 1975); The New York Times (January 22, 1975); The New York Times (February 9, 1975); Newsweek (July 18, 1976); The St. Croix Valley Area Lowdown (By Jackie Bussgaeger, July 7, 2017)

Thruston and Rogers Morton
The American Presidency Project; A Time To Heal (By Gerald Ford); Gerald Ford: An Honorable life (By James Cannon); The New York Times (March 18, 1961); The New York Times (By E.W. Kenworthy, August 8, 1961); The New

York Times (By Richard D. Lyons, November 20, 1970); The New York Times (By Joan Cook, April 20, 1979) The New York Times, 1982; The Politics of Reason: The Life of Rogers Morton (Crooks and Liars); The National Party: Chairmen and Committees: Factionalism at the Top (By Ralph Morris Goldman) Divide and Dissent: Kentucky Politics (1930-1963)

Frank Moss

Conversation with Brian Moss; Conversation with Val Halamandarisl Profiles in Caring: Advocates for the Elderly (By Val Halamandaris); Congressional Quarterly, October 9, 1976; The Almanac of American Politics, 1978; US News and World Report (November 9, 1958); The New York Times (January 31, 2003); Deseret News (January 2003); A Quote from Chris Matthews

Wayne Morse and Ernest Gruening

www.senate.gov; Congressional Quarterly 1945-1964; Gladstone/University of Oregon Wayne L. Morse: A Political Maverick (By William Prince); The New York Times (July 23, 1974);
Eugene Register (December 9, 1962); Congressional Quarterly, 1962 and 1968; Ernest Gruening-Jewish Virtual Library; The New York Times (By John T. McQuiston, June 27, 1974)
JFK: The Man, The Myth; Juneau Empire-Ceremony scheduled for Ernest Gruening Day
Posted:February5,2013); Alaska Dispatch (By Donald Craig Mitchell, August 10, 2010); Bobmannblog.com;

Ed Mezvinsky

AP (January 26, 1988); The Almanac of American Politics 1974 and 1978; Congressional Quarterly-October 12, 1974); Congressional Quarterly-October 9, 1976); A Term To Remember: By Ed Mezvinsky

William E. Miller

The New York Times; Congressional Quarterly-August 14, 1964 and September 25, 1964

Ed Muskie

Muskie of Maine (By David Nevin); You Tube-Ed Muskie Cries Before NH Primary – Or Did He (Uploaded by Jack Coleman, January 6, 2011); The Making of the President, 1972 (By Theodore H. White); Too Funny To Be President (By Morris K. Udall); The New York Times-March 27, 1996; Answers. com-Gale Encyclopedia of Biography: Edmund Sixtus Muskie; Congressional Quarterly (1977 Chronology); Stan Tupper Oral History Project

Gaylord Nelson
The Man From Clear Lake (By Bill Christofferson); NelsonEarthDay.net (Gaylord Nelson and Earth Day); Gaylord Nelson: Wilderness.org; The New York Times (By Keith Schneider, July 4, 2005); The Greatest Generation (By Tom Brokaw); The Almanac of American Politics 1978, 1980, and 1982; Congressional Quarterly (1977 Chronology); The Congressional Record (December 1980); The AP (By Ryan Foley, April 25, 2008); A Conversation with Jeff Nelson; Lake Superior Magazine (By Julie Buckles, October 25, 2013); The New York Times (op/ed By George McGovern, August 25, 2008)

Tip O'Neill
Man of the House: By Tip O'Neill; Tip O'Neill and the Democratic Century (By John Farrell); American Experience: Biography, Tip O'Neill; The New York Times (By Martin Tolchin, January 6, 1994); Baltimore Sun (By Sandy Grady (January 10, 1994); A Compassionate Conservative: A Political Biography of Joseph W. Martin, Jr., Speaker of the House (By James J. Kenneally); Boston Globe (By Jessica Teich, October 20, 2012); NPR (October 21, 2013); People Magazine (By Garry Clifford, August 18, 1980); Newsweek (January 12, 1994); The Harvard Crimson (By Evan Grossman, November 4, 1985); The Congressional Record (January 10, 1971); A Conversation with Rosemary O'Neill; Twenty-Four Years of House Cleaning and the Place is Still A Mess (By Pat Schroeder); P.S (By Paul Simon); And I Haven't Had A Bad Day Since (By Charlie Rangel)

Political Babble:The 1,000 Dumbest things Said By Politicians (By David Olive)
Ronald Reagan-Santa Barbara/Russia, Chic Hecht-overt, John East-Sandinistas, Dan Quayle/Phoenix, Lyndon Johnson/Pearson, Joe Biden/Clarence Thomas, Al Simpson/guns/

John Pastore
The New York Times (By Richard Goldstein, July 17, 2000): C-Span: The Congressional Record (July 21, 2000); A Conversation with John Pastore, Jr. A Conversation with Martin Donovan;

Adam Clayton Powell
Biography.com; Bernardgoldberg.com (By Arthur Louis); Blackpast.org Congressional Quarterly (March 3, 1967 and July 2, 1970; Inside the appel.net; The Downfall Dictionary: Bad Boys in Congress; The Urban Dictionary; Adam Clayton Powell -The American Experience; The Legal Dictionary; And I Haven't

Had A Bad Day Since (By Charlie Rangel); Scholastic.com; Mr. Smith Went to Washington (By Neal Smith); A Pryor Commitment (By David Pryor)

William Proxmire

The Almanac of American Politics 1978, 1980, and 1982; Master of the Senate (By Tobert Caro); The New York Times (By Richard Severo, December 16, 2005); The Almanac of American Politics 1978, 1980, and 1982; Golden Fleece Awards; Science.com-What Proxmire's Golden Fleece Did For--And To--Science (By Robert Irion, December 12, 1988); Proxmire (By Jay Sykes)

Tom Railsback

Idaho Statesman (By Dan Popkey July 1, 2012); The Final Days (By Woodward and Bernstein); The Almanac of American Politics 1974; AP (March 17, 1982); Congressional Quarterly, 1976, 1978 and 1979 Commemorative

Sam Rayburn

Rayburn: A Biography (By Albert Steinberg); The New York Tmes (By Unted Press International, November 17, 1961); The U.S. House of Representatives; A Compassionate Conservative: A Political Biography of Joseph W. Martin, Jr., Speaker of the House (By James J. Kenneally); Robert Kerr (By Ann Hodges Morgan); George Smathers Oral History project with Don Ritchie (August 1989); Kennedy (By Jack Parrett)

Abe Ribicoff

Congressional Quarterly (September 14, 1962, July 20, 1974 and 1972 Chronology); The Almanac of American Politics 1974, 1978, and 1980; The New York Times-February 23,1998; The New York Times (By Richard Parke, November 24, 1956); The Hartford Courant-February 23, 1998; The Spokesman (By Victor Lask, February 23, 1998); The New York Times (By Peggy McCarthy, August 25, 1966); The New York Times (op/ed By George McGovern, August 25, 2008)

Nelson Rockefeller

The Daily News (By William McFadden, January 27, 1979); Presidential Campaigns in America; 4president.org; pbs.org: The New York Times (By Sam Howe Verhovek, September 24, 1990); AP (October 19, 1958); AP (November 5, 1958); The New York Times (By Sam Roberts, December 31, 2006); The New Yorker (By Jeffrey Frank, October 13, 2014); senate.gov; The Hartford Courant (November 21, 2014): rockinst.org (By Henry Diamond); WRVO Public Media (By Sidsel Overgaard & Garrick Utley); New York State Archives

Peter Rodino
The New York Times (By Michael Kaufman (May 8, 2005); Tip O'Neill and the Democratic Century (By John Farrell); The Final Days (By Woodward and Bernstein); Congressional Quarterly, 1976 Commemorative; A Conversation with Joy Rodino

Pierre Salinger and George Murphy
The New York Times (By Thomas J. Luceck, October 17, 2004); NBC News (Election Night 1960); Salinger, Murphy Stage Close and Bitter Fight for the Senate (AP By Rob Wood

Leverett Saltonstall
Masshist.org; Facts on File History Database Center; Congressional Quarterly (September 1961); JFK: The Man and The Myth: A Critical Portrait (By Victor Lasky); The Fisherman's News (March 14, 2012); Boston Globe (By Matt Collette, January 25, 2009);

Fred Schwengel
German Americans in Congress; The Des Moines Register (April 8, 1968); Abraham Lincoln and the Forge of National Memory (By Barry Schwartz); Congressional Quarterly, 1971; The New York Times (April 4, 1993); Carroll County Times (Octber 29, 1966); The Muscatine Journal (September 21, 1966); Iowa City Press (June 15, 1967); Des Moines Register (April 1993); The Truman Library -Lincoln Collection

Hugh Scott
The New York Times: Congressional Quarterly (July 1964); Oral History Interview with Richard Murphy (November 5, 2010 and November 16, 2011)
Margaret Chase Smith
Maine History On-Line: Margaret Chase Smith for President; Margaret Chase Smith Library-Declaration of Conscience; Margaret Chase Smith Library-Rest Room for Women; Margaret Chase Smith Library-House Naval Affairs; No Place For a Woman: A Life of Senator Margaret Chase Smith (By Jannan Sherman); Roosevelt, Smith First Women to Appear on You Tube (You Tube); The Almanac of American Politics, 1974; Congressional Quarterly-1949, 1964, 1965, and 1968; The New York Times (By Richard Severo, May 30,1995); Bridging The Divide (By Edward Brooke)

Southern Chairs
Charleston Post and Courier (By Frank Woodell, May 25, 2013)

Covenant Betrayed: Revelations of the Sixties, the Best of Time; the Worst ...(By Mark Dahl)
Congressional Quarterly (January 28, 1961)
Congressional Quarterly, February 5, 1965
Congressional Quarterly (1974)
June 14, 1965 (California Digital Collection)
Congress and the Cold War (By Robert David Johnson)
John William McCormack: A Political Biography (By Garrison Nelson)
The New York Times (David Rosentbaum, February 1, 1971)
The New York Times (By Richard Lyons, January 17, 1975)
Fort Myers Press (January 17, 1975)
The Washington Post (By John Pope, August 25, 1978)
The Washington Post (September 4, 1979)
The Washington Post (December 30, 1979)
The Chicago Tribune (December 30, 1979)
Black Sailor, White Navy: Racial Unrest in the Fleet During the Vietnam War Era (By John Darrell Sherwood)
Man of the House (By Tip O'Neill)
Little Giant (By Carl Albert)
Bella (By Bella Abzug)
Twenty-Four Years of House Cleaning and the Place is Still A Mess (By Pat Schroeder)
The Harrisonburg Daily News and Record (July 13, 1966)
Virginia Chronicle (November 1, 1960)
The New York Times (By Don Oberdorfer, January 12, 1964)
The New York Times (November 17, 1960)
The New York Times (By John W. Finney, March 7, 1972)
Lyndon: The Path to Power (By Robert Caro); The New York Times (By John Finney, March 7, 1972); Encyclopedic Virginia

John Sparkman and Lister Hill
The Almanac of American Politics, 1974 and 1978; Congressional Quarterly; The Encyclopedia of Alabama; The Rest of the Dream: The Black Odyssey of Lyman Johnson
The New York Times-Lister Hill Dies-Senator 30 Years

Harold Stassen
The Economist (March 8, 2001); The New York Times (January 25, 1948); US News and World Report (July 1948 and 1952); NPR (January 8, 2004)

Stuart Symington
The New York Times (By Eric Pace December 15, 1988); A History of Missouri: 1953 to 2003 (By Lawrence H. Larsen); Dictionary of Missouri Biography (Lawrence Christiansen); Stuart Symington-Air Force Magazine (February 1999); US News and World Report (November 14, 1953); American Policy Alliance in the Middle East -1945-1992 (By John Miglietta); A Conversation with Congressman James Symington

Albert Thomas
JFKLibrary.com; Millercenter.org; Houston Chronicle (By Eric Berger, September 15, 1963); Electoral Realignment and The outlook For American Democracy (By Arthur C. Paulson); Lone Star Rising: John Connally; Congressional Quarterly (November 29, 2013)

Homer Thornberry
Sam Johnson's Boy (By Alfred Steinberg); Our Campaigns.com; The New York Times (1995); Indomitable Will: LBJ in the Presidency (By Mark Updegrove)

John Tunney
The Almanac of American Politics 1974 and 1978; Congressional Quarterly (October 9, 1976)

Joseph Tydings
Conversation with Joe Tydings; Judicial Politics in the D.C. Circuit Court (By Christopher P. Banks); AP (May 24, 1965); AP (2/28/1970); AP (August 5, 1970); Congressional Record (1965); The New York Review of Books (By Herbert Packer, October 22, 1970); Capital News Service (By Jeremy Barr, April 10, 2013); Explore Hartford (By Allan Vought, May 14 2010); On Democracy's Doorstep: The Inside Story of How the Supreme Court Brought ...By J. Douglas Smith; Various Editions of Congressional Quarterly; Career Notes and Time Line: Senator Joseph Tydings (Ryan Polk, Research Archivist, Archives of Maryland On-Line); The Fourth R: Conflicts Over Religion in America's Public Schools (By Joan DelFattore)

Mo Udall
The Lowell Sun (May 9, 1979); The Washington Post (By Margot Hornblower, May 17, 1979)
Congressional Anecdotes (By Paul Boller); Conversation with David Obey; Running For President-1976: The Carter Campaign (By Martin Schram); The Almanac of American politics 1974, 1978, 1980, and 1982; Congressional Quarterly: Candidates' 76; The New York Times-The Cast; Newsweek (January

31, 1976); Too Funny To Be President (By Morris K. Udall); The New York Times (By Richard Severo, December 14, 1998); The Washington Post (By Nicholas Lemann, September 30, 1979); The Washington Post (By Richard Pearson December 14, 1998); This Fella From Alaska (By James Perry); AK History Course; Arizona Republic (December 3, 1980); Goldwater (By Barry Goldwater); Conversation with Steve James; Conversation with Bruce Wright; Congressional Record (September 6, 2001)

Watergate
Congressional Quarterly (October 12, 1974, November 1974); The New York Times (By Peter Kerr August 27, 1985); The Almanac of American Politics; The Final Days: By Bob Woodward and Bernstein; The New York Times (By Dennis Hevesi, October 19, 2012); On Capitol Hill: The Struggle to Reform Congress and Its Consequences, 1948-2000 (By Julian E. Zelizer)

Charles Wiggins
Nixon: By Stephen Ambrose; The Final Days (By Bob Woodward and Carl Bernstein); The New York Times: Congressional Quarterly (1971 Chronology, August 3, 1974 and 1978 Chronology)

Wyoming
New History of Wyoming; Chapter 18: The 1960s: Economic Change, Severance Tax, Vietnam War and the "Black14"

Ralph Yarborough
The New York Times (By Stephen Labaton);The Victoria Advocate (October 27, 1964); Congressional Quarterly (1964 and 1970)